Solaris Systems Programming

Solaris Systems Programming

Rich Teer

✦✦Addison-Wesley

Boston • San Francisco • New York • Toronto • Montreal
London • Munich • Paris • Madrid
Capetown • Sydney • Tokyo • Singapore • Mexico City

For Jenny, Judge, and Nan.

Table of Contents

Part 4   Processes and Process Control   601

Chapter 14   The Environment of a UNIX Process 603

Chapter 15   Process Control 629

List of Programs

List of Figures

Preface

Introduction

This book describes the systems programming interface to the Solaris operating system. Despite the word "Solaris" in the title, this book is suitable for programmers of any UNIX or UNIX-like operating system (that being said, some of the features we describe *are* specific to Solaris).

Like most operating systems, Solaris provides a huge number of services to programs. Examples include: opening a file, reading that file, allocating memory, getting the current time, starting a new program, and so on. We describe many public interfaces, but unfortunately, despite our best intentions, we can't cover *everything*. (A book that tried to cover everything would be so big as to be unwieldy, and would likely never be finished!)

Because the use of undocumented interfaces is hindersome to writing portable programs, we do not describe them. Also, the use of private, undocumented interfaces voids Sun's Application Certification, since these interfaces can change without notice from release to release.

The functions we describe in this text (nearly 540 of them) are documented in Sections 2 and 3 of the Solaris *Reference Manual Collection*. However, those manual pages do not provide background material and full examples: that is what this book provides.

Audience

This book can be used both as a tutorial for novice and intermediate programmers, and as a reference for experienced programmers. It is also suitable for use as a text for undergraduate or graduate level programming courses.

The book assumes that the reader has some experience with C programming (although not necessarily on the UNIX platform), and has at least a passing familiarity of UNIX concepts like interacting with the shell, editing programs with a text editor, and pipelines.

Although it isn't mandatory, access to a Solaris system on which the examples can be tried is highly recommended.

Organization of the Book

This book is divided into six parts:

- Part 1, *Introduction*. This part contains introductory and historical background information. It consists of two chapters:

  - Chapter 1, *Introduction*, is an overview and introduction to many basic UNIX programming concepts and terminology.

  - Chapter 2, *A Brief History of Solaris*, contains a description of how Solaris has evolved over the years, and it also describes the various standards to which Solaris complies.

- Part 2, *Fundamental Topics*. This part describes the interfaces and topics essential to UNIX programming, and consists of seven chapters:

  - Chapter 3, *Utility Functions*, describes most of the utility functions provided for manipulating character classes, character strings, and byte arrays. It also talks about dynamic memory, temporary files, parsing command line arguments, error reporting, and suspending a process. Many readers will be familiar with most of this material, but it provides a common starting point from which we can build.

  - Chapter 4, *Basic File I/O*, describes low-level file I/O—how to open and close files, how to read and write them, and how to change the current file offset. It discusses file sharing, and the buffering that programs using these functions must perform for themselves.

  - Chapter 5, *The Standard I/O Library*, describes the high-level I/O functions that are provided by the standard I/O library.

  - Chapter 6, *Date and Time Operations*, describes how to get and set the system clock, and the various functions for converting time to and from various formats.

  - Chapter 7, *Users and Groups*, describes the format of the user, group, and password files and how to obtain information from them. It also explains how to determine who is currently logged into the system, and when a user last logged in or out.

  - Chapter 8, *System Information and Resource Limits*, describes how to get and set various system and user resource limits, such as the amount of

CPU time a process may consume, the maximum number of open files per process, and information such as the system's hostname, how much memory is installed, and so on.

- Chapter 9, *Secure C Programming*, describes several common security flaws in programs (e.g., buffer overflows) and presents some tips for writing programs that are secure by design.

- Part 3, *Input/Output*. This part describes the I/O facilities offered by Solaris and consists of four chapters:

  - Chapter 10, *Files and Directories*, describes the features of files and directories, and the function available to manipulate them. It describes concepts such as the various file types; file permissions; resolving symbolic links; creating, reading, and removing directories; as well as set-user-ID and set-group-ID programs.

  - Chapter 11, *Working With File Systems*, explains how to read the on-disk data structures for file systems, how to mount and unmount them, and how to read the mounted file system table.

  - Chapter 12, *Terminal I/O*, talks about terminal I/O, including special input characters, and about examining and modifying terminal attributes. It also describes the functions used to manipulate serial lines (e.g., changing the baud rate or number of bits per character).

  - Chapter 13, *Advanced I/O*, covers more advanced I/O topics, such as record locking, nonblocking, multiplexed, and asynchronous I/O. It also discusses memory mapped files, access control lists, and extended file attributes.

- Part 4, *Processes and Process Control*. This part is about processes and how to control them. It consists of five chapters:

  - Chapter 14, *The Environment of a UNIX Process*, describes the environment in which a UNIX process runs. It also describes process start-up and termination.

  - Chapter 15, *Process Control*, describes how to create new processes and how to start another program running. It also discusses how to wait for the termination status of a process, how to avoid race conditions, and process accounting.

  - Chapter 16, *Process Relationships*, explains the concepts of sessions, process groups, and controlling terminals.

  - Chapter 17, *Signals*, describes the concepts of reliable and unreliable signals, including how to send them, catch them, block them, and ignore them.

  - Chapter 18, *Daemon Processes*, describes the characteristics of a daemon and shows how a process can become a daemon. It also describes the facilities for logging messages and how to start only one copy of a daemon.

- Part 5, *Interprocess Communication*. This part describes the facilities by which processes may communicate with each other. It consists of four chapters:

  - Chapter 19, *Interprocess Communication Using Pipes and FIFOs*, describes the oldest, and possibly most oft used, methods of interprocess communication: pipes and FIFOs. It also describes the differences between iterative and concurrent servers.
  - Chapter 20, *The System V Interprocess Communication Facility*, describes System V message queues, semaphore sets, and shared memory segments.
  - Chapter 21, *Advanced Interprocess Communication*, describes the concepts of passing file descriptors to other processes, both related and unrelated. It also describes how to attach a detach a pipe to or from a pathname in the file system.
  - Chapter 22, *Doors*, describes Solaris doors, which facilitate fast remote procedure calls between processes on the same host.

- Part 6, *Pseudo Terminals*. This part describes pseudo terminals and consists of just one chapter:

  - Chapter 23, *Pseudo Terminals*, describes what pseudo terminals are and shows how to create them. From that, it shows how to execute other programs via a pseudo terminal, which is useful for scripting programs that would otherwise have to be run interactively.

There are also five appendices:

- Appendix A, *An Internationalization and Localization Primer*, provides a brief introduction to the subjects of internationalization and localization. That is, it describes the concepts of locales and how to write programs that are portable to different languages and regions.
- Appendix B, *The BSD Source Compatibility Package*, very briefly describes the BSD Source Compatibility Package, which is a transitionary tool designed to enable programs written to the BSD-based SunOS 4.x APIs to be compiled.
- Appendix C, *Function Summary*, presents a summary of all the functions we describe in this text. As well as showing a function prototype for each function (including any return values), the availability of each function—by Solaris version and standard—is also tabulated.
- Appendix D, *Miscellaneous Source Code*, shows the source code for the header file we include in most of the example programs. It also presents the source code of the library functions we developed for use in the example programs.

- Appendix E, *Solutions to Selected Exercises*, shows possible solutions to many of the numerous end of chapter exercises.

To aid in use as a reference, a thorough index is provided, along with a comprehensive bibliography. To help those reading the book in a random order, numerous cross references to related topics are provided throughout the text.

Source Code and Errata Availability

The source code for all the examples presented in the text is available from the author's home page (the URL is shown at the end of this preface). The best way to learn the interfaces and techniques described in this book is to take these programs and modify them. Actually writing code, perhaps using these examples as a starting point, is the only way to fully understand these concepts and techniques.

All of the examples in this text have been tested on several systems (including a SPARCstation 20, a SPARCstation Voyager, a couple of Ultra 1s, a Sun Blade 100, and an Ultra 60), running various versions of Solaris. They were compiled using version 5.4 of Sun's C compiler, and version 2.95.2 of gcc. The examples have also been tested on a number of systems running Solaris x86.

A current errata for this book is available from the author's home page.

Acknowledgements

I am indebted to my family for their love and support over the last three years. Thank you Jenny and Judge (our canine child) for putting up with the long and weird hours that go into writing a book. Now that it is finally finished, they can have their husband and daddy back. I am also indebted to other members of my family and friends for their support and encouragement while writing this book: thank you everyone!

My thanks to the following technical reviewers, who provided invaluable feedback catching lots of errors, pointing out areas that needed more detailed explanation, and suggesting different wording, presentation, and code: Philip Brown, Alan Coopersmith, Casper Dik, Stefaan Eeckels, Peter Baer Galvin, Alexander Gelfenbain, Anthony Mandic, Chris Morgan, David Robinson, and especially Dragan Cvetković, who reviewed the entire manuscript.

The following people took time from their busy schedules to answer my (sometimes *many*) email questions, all of which helped improve the accuracy and presentation of the text: Dave Butenhof, Dennis Clarke, Alan Coopersmith, Casper Dik, Darren Dunham, Bill Fenner, Markus Gyger, Zhishun Alex Liu, Darren Moffat, Jim Moore, Alec Muffet, Greg Onufer, David Robinson, Karl Schendel, Andy Tanenbaum, and Tony Walton.

Special thanks to W. Richard Stevens for his inspiration and encouragement when this book was just a twinkle in the author's eyes. Thanks too to Michael Slaughter from Addison-Wesley for making the first contact and for being the catalyst that made all this happen.

My thanks to Bill Moffitt and Karen Hill for arranging for me to join the Solaris 9 Beta program. Thanks also to Sun Microsystems for supplying a license for the SunONE Studio 7 Compiler Collection.

Last, but by no means least, many thanks to the wonderful staff at Prentice Hall: Kathleen Caren, Raquel Kaplan, and especially my editor, Greg Doench; their seemingly infinite patience with my increases in page count, and many slips of the due date (not to mention, letting me do things "my way") is very much appreciated. (The author, being originally from England and currently living in Canada, uses British spelling and punctuation.)

Colophon

This book continues the time-honoured tradition of writing *real* UNIX books using vi and troff. I produced camera-ready PostScript using James Clark's excellent groff package on a Sun Ultra 60 running build 60 of Solaris 10. I typed in all 417,259 words using the vi editor, created the 84 illustrations using the gpic program, produced the 91 tables using the gtbl program, performed all the indexing (using a set of awk scripts written by Jon Bentley and Brian Kernighan), and did the final page layout. My own script, c2ms, the expand program, the nl utility, and one of my sed scripts were used to include the 12,619 lines (in 281 programs) of C source code in the book.

I welcome email from any readers with comments, suggestions, or bug fixes.

Kelowna, British Columbia   Rich Teer
July 2004   rich.teer@rite-group.com
                                                 http://www.rite-group.com/rich

Part 1

Introduction

1

Introduction

1.1 Introduction

In this chapter we provide a basic introduction to much of the terminology and features used in Solaris systems programming. This is because describing how to program a system as large as Solaris is nearly impossible without mentioning features that haven't been introduced yet. Topics glossed over in this overview are dealt with in much greater detail in the rest of this book.

Solaris is the version of the UNIX operating system that is developed by Sun Microsystems. It initially only ran on Sun's SPARC (Scalable Processor ARChitecture) processors, but has since been ported to Intel's x86 processors (and their clones). One release of Solaris (Solaris 2.5.1, to be precise) was even ported to the PowerPC processor from Apple, IBM, and Motorola. The UNIX operating system itself was developed in the late 1960s and early 1970s at AT&T's Bell Labs.

Although this book focuses on Solaris 2.5 to Solaris 9, most of the material is relevant to other versions of Solaris and other implementations of UNIX, including Linux.

> Strictly speaking, the operating system colloquially referred to as Solaris is more properly called the Solaris operating environment. The Solaris operating environment is made up from several components, for example, the kernel, which is called SunOS, and the windowing system. The latter is currently based on the X Window System, using either the Common Desktop Environment (CDE) or the GNU Network Object Model Environment (GNOME) user interface (previous versions of Solaris used the OpenWindows user interface, and there is nothing preventing system administrators from installing alternative user interfaces, like the K Desktop Environment (KDE)). In this book we'll just say "Solaris" unless we need to be more specific.

> Throughout the text we will use parenthetical notes like this to add detail or to make historical references. Sometimes it is easier to understand *how* something works if we understand *why* it works the way it does.

Solaris is a descendent of UNIX System V Release 4 (SVR4), and most of the material in this book applies to both. Solaris-specific details are flagged as such, as are any differences between SVR4 and Solaris. A history of Solaris appears in Chapter 2.

Solaris provides a set of Application Programming Interfaces (APIs) and Application Binary Interfaces (ABIs) that are defined in the C programming language. Hence, we use C throughout this book, although developers may use other languages such as C++ or Java. However, if that is the case, some of the details may differ.

Compiling C Programs on Solaris

There are many example programs in this text. Before we can run them, they must be compiled by a C compiler. Solaris ships with everything needed to compile C programs (i.e., header files, libraries, and tools) except the actual C compiler. The following packages must be installed (not all of these packages may be present, depending on which release of Solaris we are using):

- For tools (e.g., as, ld, make, sccs, and truss): SUNWbtool, SUNWsprot, and SUNWtoo.
- For libraries and header files: SUNWhea, SUNWarc, SUNWlibm, SUNWlibms, SUNWxwinc, SUNWolinc, and SUNWxglh.
- For 64-bit development: SUNWarcx, SUNWbtoox, SUNWdplx, SUNWscpux, SUNWsprox, SUNWtoox, SUNWlmsx, SUNWlmx, and SUNWlibCx.

(The easiest way of ensuring that all the necessary packages are installed is to select at least the "Developer System Support" software group when installing the OS.)

The two most popular compilers available for Solaris are Sun's C compiler, cc, and the GNU C compiler, gcc. Sun's compiler is a commercial product, so a licence must be purchased to use it. On the other hand, gcc is free, but the code it produces is not as good as that generated by Sun's compiler. It can be downloaded from the Internet, or starting with Solaris 8, it can be installed from the Solaris Software Companion CD. (A copy of Sun's compiler is also included in Solaris media kits, and a free 30-day or 60-day evaluation licence can be obtained from Sun.)

The directory /usr/ccs/bin must be in our PATH before /usr/ucb (even better is to remove /usr/ucb from our PATH altogether), and the directories in which the compilers are installed should also be in our PATH.

Sometimes applications need to be linked against libraries that are not in the default Solaris directories. When this happens, we need to specify the following compiler command line flags: -L/path/to/lib and -R/path/to/lib. Our programs will successfully compile if we omit the second flag, but we will then have to set LD_LIBRARY_PATH to point to the appropriate directory. This is undesirable, so we should make sure that -R is always specified when -L is used. (With precompiled binaries, this may not be possible, so using a small wrapper script that sets LD_LIBRARY_PATH for the duration of the program being run is the best workaround.)

Relying on LD_LIBRARY_PATH when compiling code is undesirable because it often leads to developers using it for the wrong reasons (an example of a good reason for using LD_LIBRARY_PATH is when we are developing a new version of a library that we haven't installed in the system library directory yet).

The real danger is when applications are installed that don't have a run-time path configured, forcing users to set LD_LIBRARY_PATH. Once it gets set globally for a user, the user starts relying on it, which causes grief when LD_LIBRARY_PATH has to be changed or removed.

We can make three recommendations of how to handle shared libraries with applications:

1. Wherever possible, use the shared libraries supplied with the system.
2. If our applications do make use of private shared libraries, make sure that LD_LIBRARY_PATH is unset (at least when performing the final build), and that a proper run time library path is specified.
3. Starting with Solaris 7, the job of creating relocatable software that doesn't depend on LD_LIBRARY_PATH was made easier, by using $ORIGIN (not to be confused with a shell environment variable) in the library path, which is evaluated at run time. Assuming we put all our libraries in the lib subdirectory, linking with -R$ORIGIN/../lib will allow us to move the installation directory without breaking anything.

These recommendations are especially important if we are developing commercial applications, as users will usually not have the luxury of being able to fix our mistakes.

1.2   Logging In

The very first thing we must do when we want to use a Solaris system is log in. Logging in identifies us to the system, which sets up our environment and permissions. To log in, we must type in our user name and password either at the traditional login: prompt or, more recently, by using some sort of graphical login manager. (On the console, at least. Remote logins using telnet or ssh still present the traditional interface unless steps are taken to override the default behaviour.)

Our user name and password are verified, and if they match with the ones stored in /etc/passwd and /etc/shadow, we are allowed access to the system. As well as the traditional /etc/passwd method of authenticating a user, Solaris supports the Network Information Service (NIS, formerly known as Yellow Pages), NIS+, and starting with Solaris 8, Lightweight Directory Access Protocol (LDAP). Which databases to search, and what order to search them in, is defined in /etc/nsswitch.conf.

Once we have been authenticated, our user ID and group ID are set, and we are placed into our home directory running our designated shell. The password file, which contains a list of all the accounts local to the machine (one per line) or one of the other name services supplies the necessary information. In Chapter 7 we'll look at the functions that enable us to interrogate and update these files.

1.3   Shells

The way we interact with Solaris at the command line level is through a shell. Other methods of interaction include using a local GUI, or remotely (e.g., using a browser). A *shell* is a command line interpreter that reads commands and attempts to run them, either as a separate process or as a built-in command. Shells are also programming languages, with control constructs, variables, arithmetic facilities, and support for regular expressions. Programs written in a shell's programming language are called *shell scripts*, the writing of which is beyond the scope of this book. If the shell is an interactive session, the commands are supplied by the user. Commands can also be read in from files which contain shell scripts.

Three shells are supplied as standard with Solaris. These are:

- Bourne shell (sh)
- C shell (csh)
- Korn shell (ksh)

Starting with Solaris 8, the open source bash, tcsh, and zsh shells are also supplied, but are not installed with the core OS. These shells, and others, can also be downloaded from the Internet.

The Bourne shell, /bin/sh, is named after its author, Steve Bourne, who developed it at Bell Labs. It has been distributed with just about every release of UNIX since Version 7, which was the last public release of UNIX from Bell Labs before System III.

> The early releases of UNIX were named after the version of the manuals that were distributed with them.

A statically linked version of the Bourne shell can be found in /sbin/sh. By default, this is the shell for the superuser, root. Resist the urge to change this to a more featureful shell (for example, /bin/ksh), because if any of the libraries that the new shell relies on get deleted or corrupted, root will not be able to log in: this is the last thing we want when our systems need emergency maintenance. A better way to get a more featureful root shell is to run the shell of our choice from within root's .profile: if there are any problems running it, /sbin/sh can still be used.

> Some people argue that changing root's shell is OK, stating that most disasters would require booting from an alternative source (e.g., the CD-ROM, or a network bootserver) in order to recover. This is true, but a statically linked shell is still safer. This is because it is self-contained rather than being reliant on several dynamic libraries, any or all of which could become unavailable for some reason. Statically compiling the shell of our choice and placing it on the root file system (the only acceptable substitute for /sbin/sh in the author's opinion) is an option, but seems to be a lot of work for very little gain.
>
> Starting with Solaris 9, Solaris is more resilient when it comes to root's shell: if the shell listed in /etc/passwd cannot be executed, /sbin/sh is tried as a failsafe measure. On balance, however, keeping root's shell as /sbin/sh is probably the safest option.
>
> Support for 32-bit programs statically linked with the system libraries (including /sbin/sh) is not provided from Solaris 10 (Solaris has never supported statically linked 64-bit executables). Therefore, the technical reasons for not changing root's shell have been rendered moot.

One of Sun's cofounders, Bill Joy, wrote the C shell, /bin/csh, while at the University of California, Berkeley. Based on the 6th Edition shell (not the Bourne shell), the C shell has a control flow similar to the C programming language (hence its name) and provides features that weren't supported by the Bourne shell—like job control, a history mechanism, and command line editing. While fine for interactive use, some of the C shell's features make it undesirable for writing shell scripts (see [Christiansen 1995] for more about this).

The Korn shell, /bin/ksh, is considered the successor to the Bourne shell, and was written by David Korn at Bell Labs. It has all the desirable features the C shell has (job control, history mechanism, and command line editing), but its syntax is a superset of the Bourne shell, so scripts written in the latter will work with the former.

1.4 Files, Directories, and File Systems

One of the UNIX programming paradigms is that everything is a file. Ordinary files are files, directories are files, and all devices are files (the latter are known as special files). A *file* is an unordered stream of bytes. This byte stream is not structured in any way; any interpretation is left to application software (contrast this with some other operating systems that impose a record-orientated view of files, or make a distinction between binary and nonbinary files).

A *directory* is a collection of files, and possibly other directories, that have been grouped together (creating a hierarchical structure) by one or more users. Directories are implemented by the kernel marking a file as a directory; this file contains a list of files and their attributes. More accurately, a directory file consists of a list of entries (the names of each file in the directory) and their corresponding inode number.

An *inode* is a fixed-length data structure (128 bytes) where most of the information about a file (e.g., the owner, the permissions, access times, the list of data blocks, and the file type and size) are stored. (We'll have a lot to say about these file attributes in Chapter 10, when we talk about the stat, fstat, and lstat functions.)

The reason why a file's attributes aren't stored in the directory entry is flexibility: by making the two separate, it is possible to have multiple filenames refer to the same inode. This arrangement also allows a file to exist without having a name in the file system. This is useful for creating temporary files that are automatically disposed of when our process exits. The disk blocks for a file are freed only when the last reference to the file's inode is removed, unless a process has opened the file. In this case, the file is deleted only when the last process that has the file open closes it. So by creating a file, opening it, and then deleting it, we create a temporary file that graciously disappears when our process exits.

Each directory contains at least two filenames (which get created automatically whenever a new directory is created): "." (called *dot*) and ".." (called *dot-dot*). The former refers to the current directory, and the latter refers to the current directory's parent (the one exception to this is the root directory, where *dot-dot* also points to itself).

Files and directories that reside on the same logical device are collected together in a *file system*. Before the files and directories on a file system can be accessed, it must be attached to the hierarchical file tree by mounting it. A typical Solaris system will have several file systems mounted at any one time.

Solaris supports three types of file system: storage based (or regular), network, and pseudo. A regular file system is one that provides persistent storage for files and directories. A network file system makes files that are stored on a remote server appear to be local, and a pseudo file system is one that uses virtual files to represent various abstractions. Figure 1.1 summarizes the different file system types.

Type of file system	Type of files	Examples
Regular	Files are stored on a persistent medium	`ufs, hsfs, tmpfs`
Network	Files are stored remotely	`nfs`
Pseudo	Files are an abstraction of something	`procfs, doorfs, fdfs`

Figure 1.1 Summary of the different file system types.

Filenames and Pathnames

A lot of functions require a filename or pathname as one of their arguments. A *filename* is a name that consists of one or more characters that are used to name a file. These characters may be anything, with the exception of the slash character (/) and the NUL character. A filename is sometimes referred to as a pathname component. A *pathname* is a character string that consists of one or more characters that is used to identify a file. It has an optional beginning slash, followed by zero or more filenames separated by slashes (multiple successive slashes are considered the same as just one slash). To compare these two terms, let's consider the password file. The pathname of the password file is /etc/passwd, but its filename is just `passwd`. For most of our discussion the difference between the two terms is academic, and we will use them interchangeably.

> Some systems allow pathnames to end in / but others do not; portable programs should therefore not rely on trailing slashes being allowed. Indeed, from Solaris 10 references to pathnames ending in a slash that do *not* refer to a directory will return an error.

There are two types of pathnames: absolute and relative. If a pathname starts with a /, it is called an *absolute pathname* because the name of the file is specified from the root directory; a pathname without the leading / is called a *relative pathname*.

When dealing with filenames and pathnames, there are two constants we need to be aware of. These are MAXPATHLEN (which is defined in <sys/param.h>) and MAXNAMELEN (which is also defined in <sys/param.h>). MAXPATHLEN is the maximum length of an absolute pathname, and MAXNAMELEN is the maximum length of each component of a pathname. Each of these constants includes space for the terminating NUL character.

Example: Simple directory listing

Listing all the entries of a given directory is quite straightforward. Program 1.1 shows our implementation of a program that does this.

> The format of the source code we show in Program 1.1 is used throughout the text. We number each nonblank line, and the text describing portions of the code has the starting and ending line numbers in the left margin. We sometimes precede the descriptive paragraphs with a bold heading, which provides a summary of the code being explained.
>
> The horizontal lines at the beginning and end of each code fragment specify the name of the directory and file in which the code can be found (for this example, the file ssp_ls.c in the directory intro is what we're referring to). Because the source code for all of our examples is freely available (see the preface for details), locating the appropriate file is easy. Compiling, running, and modifying these examples while reading the text is an excellent way of learning the concepts we discuss.

——————————————————————————————————————— *intro/ssp_ls.c*

```
1 #include <stdio.h>
2 #include <sys/types.h>
3 #include <dirent.h>
4 #include "ssp.h"

5 int main (int argc, char **argv)
6 {
7     DIR *dir;
8     struct dirent *dirent;

9     if (argc != 2)
10        err_quit ("Usage: ssp_ls file");

11    if ((dir = opendir (argv [1])) == NULL)
12        err_msg ("%s: opendir failed", argv [1]);

13    while ((dirent = readdir (dir)) != NULL)
14        printf ("%s\n", dirent -> d_name);

15    closedir (dir);

16    return (0);
17 }
```
——————————————————————————————————————— *intro/ssp_ls.c*

Program 1.1 List all the files in a directory.

Let's look a bit closer at this 17-line program.

Include header files

1–4 We include some standard header files, and our own, ssp.h. The latter contains definitions for the many constants and functions we develop for use in the examples in this text. The difference between #include <file.h> and #include "file.h" is that the former only searches for the file in the system include directory (and those specified on the command line), whereas the latter searches for the file in the current directory first. In this text, we'll adopt the convention of using <file.h> to refer to a header file supplied with Solaris, and "file.h" to refer to our own header files.

Check the number of command line arguments and open a directory stream

9–12 After checking that the program was invoked with the right number of arguments, we use one of the command line arguments, `argv [1]`, as the name of the directory to list. In Chapter 14 we shall see how the `main` function gets called, and how to retrieve command line arguments. Notice that in line 10 we call our own error function, `err_quit`, which prints out the supplied error message before terminating. On line 12 we call another of our error functions: `err_msg`. This function prints the message we pass it, followed by the error message associated with the value of `errno`. We have more to say about error handling in Section 1.7, and we show the source code for our error functions in Appendix D.

Print each directory entry

13–14 We call `readdir` in a loop, printing out the name of the current directory entry. The loop terminates when `readdir` returns a NULL pointer, which indicates that there are no more directory entries. The `readdir` function returns a pointer to a `DIR` structure; the contents of the structure don't matter to us, because the only member we're interested in is d_name, which contains the name of the current directory entry.

Close the directory stream

15 When finished with the directory stream, we close it by calling `closedir`.

Indicate successful completion to our caller

16 We return the value of zero to our caller (usually the invoking shell), which conventionally means all is OK. A non-zero return value from `main` (between 1 and 255) indicates an abnormal termination, but any more specific definitions are program dependent. Negative return values from `main` are not allowed, and we show how processes can interrogate this exit value in Chapter 15.

If we compile and run Program 1.1 a few times, we get the following:

```
$ ./ssp_ls /
.
..
lost+found
var
usr
etc
bin
[...]                                        Several lines deleted to save space
share
$ ./ssp_ls ssp_ls
ssp_ls: opendir failed: Not a directory
$ ./ssp_ls /dev/rdsk/c0t0d0s0
/dev/rdsk/c0t0d0s0: opendir failed: Permission denied
```

When we show interactive sessions like the previous example, we show the text that we type in a **Bold Courier** font. We show program output and command prompts in the Courier font, and if we add any comments, they will be displayed in an *italic* font. The $ sign before our commands is the default command prompt from the shell that we use in all the examples, ksh. Occasionally, we must become the `root` user to run some of our examples. In this case, the prompt will be shown as a # character.

Notice that although the output of our program resembles that of the ls(1) command, the output isn't sorted. This is because ls performs the sorting itself.

> The notation ls(1) is the standard way of referring to an entry in a specific section of the UNIX manual. Section 1 is for user commands, section 1M is for maintenance commands, section 2 is for system calls, and so on. Every function in the standard libraries has a *manual page* (or just *man page*), and most of them include information about which headers and libraries must be included, examples, attributes, and cross references.
>
> To read the manual page for an entry in a specific section of the manual, we use the -s command line option. For example,
>
>   man -s 1m newfs
>
> will show the manual page for the newfs command. If we don't specify a section, then each section is searched, and the first matching manual page is displayed. So in this particular example, we could simply type
>
>   man newfs
>
> If we do not know which section of the manual we need to look in, we can use the apropos or man -k commands (each of these commands displays the synopsis for each man page that contains the specified keyword). We can only do this, however, if the system administrator has previously run the catman command, which creates the keyword database.
>
> Sun's documentation web site, http://docs.sun.com, also contains extensive information.

Current Directory

Every process has a *current directory* (or *working directory* or even *current working directory*) associated with it, which it can change by calling the chdir function (which we discuss in Section 10.24). The current directory is the directory from which relative pathnames are searched, and is the default for commands that operate on files (e.g., ls). For example, assuming the current directory is /home/rich, then a reference (when calling the open function, for example) to the file doc/ssp/intro.ms will look for the file /home/rich/doc/ssp/intro.ms.

Root Directory

We said that pathnames that start with a "/" are absolute pathnames, and that they start from the root directory. In UNIX, the term "root directory" is an overloaded one. As well as its usual meaning of the top directory in the file system hierarchy, it also refers to the "top" directory of a file system. The root directory of a file system contains a directory called lost+found, which is created by the newfs(1M) command.

When we mount a file system, we actually mount its root directory on the specified mount point. For example, if we keep users' home directories on a separate file system, we might want to mount it as /export/home. In this case, /export/home is the root directory of the home directory slice. The usual meaning of root directory satisfies both descriptions: it is the top directory in the root slice, and it is the top of the directory hierarchy.

A process whose effective user ID (see Section 7.7) is zero may change its notion of the root directory by calling either of the `chroot` or `fchroot` functions we discuss in Section 10.25. After a successful call to one of these functions, all pathnames that start with "/" will start their searches from the new root directory.

Home Directory

When we log in to a UNIX system, we are placed into the directory specified in the sixth field of our entry in `/etc/passwd`. (Other name services like NIS and NIS+ store the home directory differently, but the end result is the same: once we have authenticated, we are placed in our home directory.) This directory is conventionally a directory in `/home` that is the same as our user name, e.g., `/home/rich`. The directory in which we are placed when we first log in is called our *home directory*. The automounter helps us enforce the `/home/username` policy, even when home directories are physically located on different file systems.

> The automounter is facility that automatically mounts directories under its control when attempts to access them are made. If the mounted directory is not accessed for a certain period of time (10 minutes by default), the automounter daemon, `automountd`, will unmount it. The directory `/home` is by default under the control of the automounter.

If the home directory specified does not exist, an error is printed and we will be unable to log in. On the other hand, if no home directory is specified, a warning is printed and we are allowed to log in—although the root directory "/" will be used as our home directory.

1.5   Input and Output

Given the "everything is a file" philosophy of UNIX programming, we shouldn't be too surprised that all input and output (I/O) involves files in some manner. All open files have at least one file descriptor associated with them. The file descriptor is used for all file I/O, either directly or indirectly. When we perform unbuffered file I/O, we use the file descriptor directly, but when we use the standard I/O library, file descriptors are only used behind the scenes.

File Descriptors

A *file descriptor* is a non-negative integer used by a process to refer to an open file. The usual method of acquiring one is by opening a file: a successful open returns the file descriptor that the kernel allocates for that file. It is possible for a process to open the same file more than once. Each successful open results in a different file descriptor being allocated by the kernel; the file descriptor that gets allocated is guaranteed to be the lowest numbered one that is free.

Standard Input, Standard Output, and Standard Error

Conventionally, the first three file descriptors (i.e., 0, 1, and 2) are reserved for standard input, standard output, and standard error. By default these I/O streams are connected to our terminal, but most shells provide a method to redirect them. For example, we can redirect standard output to a file like this:

```
ls > file_listing
```

Similarly, we can use the "<" operator to redirect standard input, and the "|" (pipe) operator to connect the output of one process to the input of another, creating pipelines. The idea of connecting several programs together in a pipeline to accomplish a task, rather than building a single monolithic program to do the same thing, is a fundamental UNIX programming paradigm. UNIX provides many of these tools out of the box, which can be combined together in pipelines. For example,

```
du -sk * | sort -nr | head -10
```

will display the top ten largest files in the current directory (in descending order), and

```
ps -ef | grep rich | cut -c 10-14
```

will display the process IDs for all processes being run by the user rich.

Unbuffered I/O

The file I/O provided by the open, close, read, and write functions is called *unbuffered I/O*. This is because these functions don't provide any buffering of data beyond any the kernel does. All data I/O gets passed immediately to the underlying device driver. All the unbuffered I/O functions use file descriptors, either as an argument, or a return value.

Example: Copy a file using unbuffered I/O functions

Program 1.2 copies a file from its standard input to its standard output, using the unbuffered I/O functions read and write.

After we've compiled it, we would use the program like this:

```
$ ./copy1 > output_file
some stuff to copy
```
After pressing Return, we type Control-D to quit
```
$ cat output_file
some stuff to copy
```

Data is read from the terminal and copied to the file output_file. The shell will automatically create the file for us if it doesn't already exist. Control-<letter> or ^<letter> conventionally means that the Control and <letter> keys should be pressed at the same time. (We'll use Control-<letter> in the running text, and ^<letter> when required in examples to save space.) Control-D is the standard end of file (EOF) character. We should note that unlike some other environments (e.g., MS-DOS), the EOF character is

intro/copy1.c

```
 1 #include <unistd.h>
 2 #include "ssp.h"

 3 int main (void)
 4 {
 5     ssize_t n;
 6     ssize_t res;
 7     char buf [BUF_SIZE];
 8     char *ptr;

 9     while ((n = read (STDIN_FILENO, buf, BUF_SIZE)) > 0) {
10         ptr = buf;
11         while ((n > 0) && ((res = write (STDOUT_FILENO, ptr, n)) > 0)) {
12             ptr += res;
13             n -= res;
14         }

15         if (res == -1)
16             err_msg ("write failed");
17     }

18     if (n == -1)
19         err_msg ("read failed");

20     return (0);
21 }
```

intro/copy1.c

Program 1.2 Copy standard input to standard output using unbuffered I/O functions.

not stored in the file itself. Typing Control-D sets the EOF indicator for the file descriptor, which causes read to return 0.

The program reads data in from the file descriptor STDIN_FILENO in BUF_SIZE chunks. STDIN_FILENO is defined in <unistd.h> to be zero. We could just specify 0 in place of STDIN_FILENO, but using this constant makes our code more portable.

We'll see the effect of different values of BUF_SIZE in Section 4.11, when we take a closer look at unbuffered I/O. It doesn't matter what value BUF_SIZE has; the entire file will be copied.

The read function returns the number of bytes read, or 0 if there is no further input ("no further input" is considered to be normal behaviour, rather than an error). Like most system calls, read returns −1 if an error occurs. We have more to say about handling errors in Section 1.7.

The reason why the code to write out the data we've just read (i.e., lines 10 to 16) seems to be relatively complicated is because we have to handle the possibility of write not writing the entire buffer in the first invocation. So we write as much of the buffer as we can, looping back to write the remainder if necessary. This is not likely to happen if we are writing to a regular file, but writing a large buffer to a pipe might require several iterations through our loop.

The Standard I/O Library

The standard I/O library (which includes functions like fopen, fclose, fread, and fwrite) is a set of functions that provides a framework for file I/O. The I/O provided by the standard I/O library is internally buffered, which means that reads and writes are not necessarily passed immediately to the underlying device driver. Instead, the library collects the data into chunks (usually lines), which can make the I/O more efficient.

Rather than directly using file descriptors, the functions in the standard I/O library use pointers to FILE structures, called file pointers. The FILE structure is defined in <stdio.h>, but our programs should never access the contents directly: FILE structures should be regarded as opaque objects. One of the advantages of using the standard I/O library is that it frees us from the burden of having to worry about buffer sizes (BUF_SIZE in our previous example) because the implementors of the library have done this for us.

Example: Copy a file using standard I/O functions

Program 1.3 is a reimplementation of Program 1.2, but uses the standard I/O library functions getchar and putchar instead of read and write.

intro/copy2.c

```
 1 #include <stdio.h>
 2 #include "ssp.h"

 3 int main (void)
 4 {
 5     int c;

 6     while ((c = getchar ()) != EOF) {
 7         if (putchar (c) == EOF)
 8             err_msg ("putchar failed");
 9     }
10     if (ferror (stdin))
11         err_msg ("getchar failed");

12     return (0);
13 }
```

intro/copy2.c

Program 1.3 Copy standard input to standard output using standard I/O functions.

Strictly speaking, getchar is a macro that expands to

```
getc (stdin)
```

Similarly, putchar (c) is a macro that expands to

```
putc ((c), stdout)
```

The identifiers stdin and stdout are similar to their unbuffered I/O counterparts STDIN_FILENO and STDOUT_FILENO, and are defined in <stdio.h>.

Program 1.3 reads standard input one character at a time until an end of file condition is detected; each character read is written to its (i.e., the program's) standard output.

We'll be taking a more detailed look at the standard I/O library in Chapter 5.

1.6   Programs, Processes, and Threads

The terms program and process are often used interchangeably. This may be fine for everyday conversation, but we need to provide more specific definitions. A *program* is an executable file that contains instructions and static (initialized) data. A successful call to one of the six variants of the `exec` function we describe in Section 15.11 results in a program being read into memory and executed. A *process* is an instantiation of a program that is being run, and includes all the executable instructions, shared and private data segments, disposition of signals, and hardware state (e.g., CPU registers). With one or two exceptions, all processes are created as a result of a call to one of the variants of `fork`. (The exceptions are various system processes that are hand-built as part of the system boot process.)

Most modern UNIX variants, including Solaris, offer a facility to have more than one thread of execution in a process (in fact, all processes in Solaris are threaded; processes that aren't explicitly written to be multithreaded run in a single thread). A *thread* holds the state of a single flow of execution through a process, which includes at least a stack and the CPU's registers. A thread operates within the context of its bounding process (i.e., all the threads share the address space of the process), and most data is shared between all threads in a process (the exception to which is the thread-specific data). For detailed a treatise on threads programming, see [Butenhof 1997].

A common misapprehension about threads and multiprocessor systems is that they are inherently faster than a single threaded application or uniprocessor machine. This is not necessarily the case, as the following (deliberately simplified) analogy hopefully illustrates.

Suppose we have a road with a certain speed limit and a given number of lanes. Getting a number of people from one end of the road to the other represents the task our program must complete, the speed limit represents the CPU clock speed, the number of lanes represents the number of CPUs, and the number of cars is the number of runnable threads.

If we want to increase the system's throughput (i.e., how many people can traverse the road in a given period of time), we have three options:

1. Raise the speed limit. This is the same as installing a faster CPU.
2. Add more lanes and cars. This is the same as adding more CPUs and threads.
3. Both of the above.

Adding more lanes to our road but using the same number of cars will have no effect on how fast we complete our task (this is like adding a CPU to speed up a single threaded task). Adding more cars without adding lanes will help somewhat, but the best improvement would be to add more lanes and more cars. Even though each car takes the same length of time to make the journey, more cars can make the journey in a given time period, thus increasing the throughput.

Raising the speed limit won't necessarily help: if the speed limit is 200 km/h, but the cars can only go 150 km/h, 150 km/h is our effective maximum speed. Similarly, increasing the CPU clock speed isn't always as useful as the vendors' marketing departments would have us believe, especially if our tasks are not CPU-bound.

> There are limits to how many lanes or cars we can efficiently use, and this is where a system's scalability becomes a factor: the better a system scales, the more efficiently it can use more CPUs and threads.

A detailed discussion of the Solaris kernel's scheduling algorithms is beyond the scope of this text, but we should be aware that the kernel schedules individual threads onto a CPU, not a whole process. Basically, the highest priority thread that is in a runnable state gets to use one of the CPUs. The distinction between scheduling a process and scheduling a thread becomes important when we are talking about a multithreaded processes on a machine with more than one processor (a multithreaded process on a uniprocessor machine, or a single threaded process on a multiprocessor (MP) machine has the same net effect: only one part of the process will be executing at any given time). If the threads that make up a multithreaded process are independent of each other, and the process is run on an MP machine, two or more of those threads have the potential to be running at the same time. An example of this would be a typical GUI application: one thread could handle the GUI updates while another could be performing some other task. If a computationally intensive process can be broken down into several independent threads, the potential performance increase is substantial: a CPU-bound process might run in half the time on a dual-CPU machine, and even less if the problem scales well to more CPUs. Conversely, having more threads than CPUs might be detrimental to performance because of the cost of switching from thread to thread.

Most of the material in this text is relevant regardless of whether or not a process is multithreaded (the exceptions will be highlighted when necessary). Therefore, from now on we shall only talk about processes, which implicitly includes all threads running within the process.

Process IDs and Parent Process IDs

A *process ID* (PID) is a positive integer that uniquely identifies a process. Every process has a process ID, and a parent process ID (PPID). The *parent process ID* of a process is the process ID of the process that called one of the `fork` functions to create it. Note that although each process has a unique process ID, many processes may share a common parent process ID.

Example: Printing the process ID and parent process ID

Program 1.4 prints out its process ID and parent process ID.

The reason why we cast the value returned by `getpid` and `getppid` in our `printf` statements is because we want to make sure our code is both 32-bit and 64-bit clean. In a 64-bit environment, certain types like `pid_t` and `uid_t` are defined as an `int`, whereas in a 32-bit environment, they are defined as a `long`. As we shall see, `int`s and `long`s are the same size in a 32-bit environment, so we can get away with just using `"%d"` or `"%ld"` as the `printf` format string. This size equality is not true in a 64-bit environment, however, so we must cast the value in `printf` statements if we want to avoid compiler warnings and keep our code portable.

intro/getpid.c

```
1 #include <stdio.h>
2 #include <unistd.h>

3 int main (void)
4 {
5      printf ("PID = %ld, PPID = %ld\n", (long) getpid (), (long) getppid ());

6      return (0);
7 }
```

intro/getpid.c

Program 1.4 Print our process ID and parent process ID.

If we compile and run Program 1.4, we get the following:

```
$ ./getpid
PID = 17787, PPID = 6502
$ ./getpid
PID = 17790, PPID = 6502
```

Notice that the process ID changes between invocations, but the parent process ID stays the same. This is because we ran getpid twice from the same shell.

Process Control

There are three functions to consider when we talk about process control: fork, exec, and wait. Although each of these functions has several variants, for now we'll just refer to these functions by their generic names. In Chapter 15, when we look more closely at process control, we'll examine each variant in detail.

The fork system call is the only way to create a process in UNIX. New processes are created by copying the virtual memory of the processes calling fork. The process that called fork is the *parent* of the newly created process, which is called the *child*.

The exec function is used to overlay the image of the current process with a new one. When a program wants to invoke another, it usually calls fork to create a new process, which then calls exec to run the new program (i.e., it is usual for the child to call exec). The parent process then waits for the child to exit, by calling one of the wait functions.

Example: A simple shell

To illustrate better the relationship between the fork, exec, and wait system calls, Program 1.5 implements a very simple shell.

The program reads a line from standard input, then calls fork to create a new process in which to exec the command we entered.

Print prompt and read a command line

12–19 After printing out a prompt ("-> "), a line of input is read from standard input using fgets. We overwrite the new line character at the end of the line read with the NUL character. This is because we will be passing the line to the execlp function, which

—————————————————————————— intro/sspsh1.c

```
 1 #include <stdio.h>
 2 #include <unistd.h>
 3 #include <sys/types.h>
 4 #include <sys/wait.h>
 5 #include <string.h>
 6 #include "ssp.h"

 7 int main (void)
 8 {
 9     char buf [LINE_LEN];
10     pid_t pid;
11     int status;

12     printf ("-> ");
13     while (fgets (buf, LINE_LEN, stdin) != NULL) {
14         if (*buf != '\0')
15             buf [strlen (buf) - 1] = '\0';
16         if (strlen (buf) == 0) {
17             printf ("-> ");
18             continue;
19         }

20         switch (pid = fork ()) {
21             case -1:
22                 err_msg ("Can't fork");
23                 break;

24             case 0:
25                 /*
26                  * Child process
27                  */
28                 execlp (buf, buf, NULL);
29                 err_msg ("Can't exec %s", buf);
30                 break;

31             default:
32                 /*
33                  * Parent process
34                  */
35                 if (waitpid (pid, &status, 0) == -1)
36                     err_ret ("waitpid");
37                 break;
38         }

39         printf ("-> ");
40     }

41     return (0);
42 }
```

—————————————————————————— intro/sspsh1.c

Program 1.5 A very simple shell program.

expects its arguments to be terminated by a NUL, not a new line. If a blank line is entered, we simply print out another prompt and loop around again.

Call `fork` to create a new process

20–23 We call `fork` to create another process. We call `fork` within a switch statement because `fork` returns one of three types of value:

- −1, which means that an error occurred
- 0, which is returned to the child process
- The process ID of the newly created child, which is returned to the parent process

The astute reader will notice that a successful `fork` actually returns twice (even though it is called only once): once in the parent and once in the child.

If the call to `fork` fails, we inform the user and exit.

Child process

24–30 Call the `execlp` function in an attempt to run the command we just entered. The first argument passed to `execlp` is the name of the program we want to run, and the subsequent arguments are the ones that get passed to the invoked program's `main` function, terminated by a NULL pointer. The first argument passed to a program is its name, hence we pass *buf* to `execlp` twice. A successful call to `execlp` does not return, so line 28 prints out an error message before exiting.

Parent process

31–38 The parent process just waits for its child to exit, by calling `waitpid`. Note that although we collect the exit status of the child, in this example we ignore it. However, we could use the status value to determine the exit reason. (We'll see how in Chapter 15.)

Read another command from the user

39 This line just prints out the prompt before looping around again to read another command.

Although this program has several limitations (not least of which is the inability to pass arguments to the programs it calls), it serves as a useful introduction to process control.

Let's see our program in action.

```
$ ./sspsh1
-> date
Wed Jul 25 16:46:12 PDT 2001
->
-> ps
   PID TTY        TIME CMD
 29346 pts/3     0:00 ksh
 29942 pts/3     0:00 sspsh1
 29948 pts/3     0:00 ps
-> pwd
/home/rich/doc/books/ssp/src/intro
-> ls -l
Can't exec ls -l: No such file or directory
->                              Type Control-D to quit
$
```

The last command we try illustrates the fact that our shell is incapable of passing arguments to the programs it runs. To fix this, our shell would have to parse the line typed by the user by breaking it into tokens at white spaces (i.e., the space and tab characters). It would then have to pass each token to execlp.

In Chapter 15 we'll be taking a more detailed look at process control.

1.7 Error Handling

Conventionally, a function that returns a numeric result that wants to flag to its caller that an error has occurred returns −1; a function that returns a pointer usually returns NULL to flag an error. In both cases, the global variable errno (which is declared in <errno.h>) is set to a number that indicates the nature of the error (the error codes and their meanings are listed in <sys/errno.h>). Note that errno is not usually set to zero by a successful function call.

It is essential to check the return value from functions we call, so that errors can be caught and brought to the attention of the program's user. To this end, there are two idioms we often see in source code. The first, which uses the perror function we discuss in Section 3.9, has two variations. The first is the simplest case, which just prints a simple error message.

```
if ((fd = open (file, flags)) == -1) {
    perror ("example: Can't open file");
    exit (1);
}
```

The second variation prints out more information (in this example, the name of the file that we unsuccessfully tried to open).

```
if ((fd = open (file, flags)) == -1) {
    snprintf (buf, sizeof (buf), "example: Can't open file %s",
        file);
    perror (buf);
    exit (1);
}
```

Notice that we use the snprintf function rather than the more common sprintf. The former allows us to specify the maximum number of characters to copy to the buffer, and allows our code to avoid buffer overflow problems. Solaris 2.6 was the first release to support the snprintf function (the undocumented __snprintf function was available in Solaris 2.5 and 2.5.1, but because of its nonportability, we do not recommend its use).

The second idiom uses the strerror function we discuss in Section 3.9 to supply the text of the error message. The method has the advantage of freeing us from the necessity of declaring the buffer, *buf*.

```
if ((fd = open (file, flags)) == -1) {
    fprintf (stderr, "example: Can't open %s: %s\n", file,
        strerror (errno));
    exit (1);
}
```

The preceding examples print out an error message and then exit, but exiting is not the only option we have. Depending on the circumstances of the error, our programs could just continue, or we might want to call the `abort` function (see Section 17.24) to produce a core dump.

To avoid unnecessary verbosity in our examples, we will use several convenience functions for our error handling. The functions we use are:

`err_dump`	This prints out our error message, plus the text from `strerror`, then calls `abort` to produce a core dump.
`err_msg`	This prints out our error message, plus the text from `strerror`, then calls `exit` to terminate the process.
`err_quit`	This prints out our error message (without the text from `strerror`), then calls `exit` to terminate the process.
`err_ret`	This prints out our error message, plus the text from `strerror`, then returns to the calling function.
`log_msg`	If the calling process is a daemon, this function logs the message using the `syslog` facility we describe in Chapter 18. Otherwise, the message is printed to standard error.

We show the source code for these functions in Appendix D.

1.8   User Identification

When we log into a UNIX system, we are assigned a user ID and a group ID from our entry in `/etc/passwd` (or some other name system like NIS or LDAP if that's being used).

User ID

A *user ID* (UID) is a number associated with our user name that identifies us to the operating system. This number is usually unique for each user, but is sometimes overloaded so that the same user ID is associated with several user names. Our user ID and user name are usually assigned to us by the system administrator. Several user names and user IDs are reserved by Solaris (they are already in `/etc/passwd` when we install the OS); the most important of these is the user `root`, which has a user ID of 0. Processes running with a user ID of 0 bypass most file system permissions checks, and a number of privileged operations are restricted to these processes. Because of its elevated privilege status, the `root` user is also known as the *superuser*.

From the perspective of a process, there are two types of user ID: the real user ID and the effective user ID. The *real user ID* is the user that we log in as, and the *effective user ID* is the one a process is currently running as. Most of the time the real and effective user IDs are the same, but as we shall see later, Solaris provides a mechanism by which a program that is run one user may run with another user's credentials.

Group ID and Supplementary Group IDs

Each user belongs to between one and sixteen groups, although this limit can be raised to a maximum of 32 by setting `ngroups_max` to the desired value in `/etc/system` and rebooting. However, doing this is not recommended, because it may give rise to NFS interoperability problems.

> The `/etc/system` file is used to customize the operation of the kernel and set various kernel tunable constants. It can be modified only by the `root` user, and it's a good idea to make a backup copy of it before making any modifications. See the `system`(4) man page for all the details.

The group specified in `/etc/passwd` is the user's *primary group ID* (GID); the first `ngroups_max` groups listed in `/etc/group` that contain the user's user name are the user's *supplementary groups*. The id(1M) command shows us our user- and group IDs.

```
$ id -a
uid=1001(rich) gid=10(staff) groups=10(staff),3(sys)
```

The `-a` flag tells `id` to show us all the groups we belong to (interestingly, `id -a` will list up to 32 groups regardless of the setting of `ngroups_max`).

There are two types of group ID: the real group ID and the effective group ID. Like user IDs, the *real group ID* is the same as our primary group ID when we log in, and the *effective group ID* is the current group ID of a process. Most of the time, the real and effective group IDs are the same.

User and group IDs form the basis of the protection mechanism of the UNIX operating system. Every file and system resource (e.g., shared memory segments, semaphores, etc.) belongs to a particular user and group; there is no such thing as an anonymous file or resource. The owner of a resource and members of the group to which the resource belongs have special privileges compared to other users on the system. Hence, there are three sets of permissions maintained by the kernel for each resource: the permissions of the owner of the resource, the permissions of those belonging to the same group as the resource, and those of everyone else (others). Note that when we refer to a group in this context, we refer to the group that the resource is a member of, which is not necessarily one of the groups that the owner of the resource is a member of. For example, a file could be owned by the user "rich" and be in the group "bin"; however, the user rich does not need to be a member of the group bin for this to be valid.

Solaris offers a finer-grained version of file permissions, called Access Control Lists (ACLs). Very briefly, an ACL allows us to specify file permissions on a per-user basis. ACLs are used to supplement (rather than replace) the standard UNIX file permissions. We discuss ACLs in much more detail in Chapter 13.

Example: Printing our user ID and group ID

Program 1.6 prints out the caller's user ID and group ID. It does this by printing out the values returned by the `getuid` and `getgid` functions, respectively.

intro/getuid.c

```
1 #include <stdio.h>
2 #include <sys/types.h>
3 #include <unistd.h>

4 int main (void)
5 {
6     printf ("User ID = %ld, group ID = %ld\n", (long) getuid (),
7         (long) getgid ());

8     return (0);
9 }
```

intro/getuid.c

Program 1.6 Print our user and group IDs.

The output of Program 1.6 looks like this:

```
$ ./getuid
User ID = 1001, group ID = 10
```

We'll have more to say about user and group IDs in Chapter 7.

1.9   Signals

Signals are a method of notifying a process that a particular event has occurred. For example, an attempt to access a location in virtual memory that hasn't been mapped into the address space of the process, or the user typed Control-C to interrupt a program.

Once a signal has been sent to a process, it has one of four dispositions:

1. The signal may be ignored. An ignored signal is silently discarded; the process is unaware that the signal was ever sent to it.
2. The signal may be blocked. A blocked signal is also not delivered to the process, but unlike an ignored signal, a blocked signal is placed on the queue of pending signals. If the process ever unblocks the blocked signal, it will be delivered at that time.
3. The signal may be caught. When a signal is caught, a user-supplied function, which is known as a *signal handler*, gets called.
4. The default action may happen. Exactly what the default action is depends on the signal, but usually results in the process being aborted and a core dump being produced. Some signals are by default ignored.

With one or two exceptions, we may change the disposition of most signals by calling the sigset function, which takes two arguments. The first argument is the name of the signal we want to change the disposition of, and the second takes one of three values: SIG_IGN to ignore the signal, SIG_DFL to set the disposition to its default action, or the name of the function to call if we want to install a signal handler.

As we shall see in Chapter 17, we can also use the `signal` or `sigaction` functions to change a signal's disposition. The problem with `signal` is that it handles signals unreliably, so new applications should avoid it and use `sigset` or `sigaction` instead. We'll explain what we mean by "unreliable signals" in Chapter 17.

The two signals that can't be caught or ignored are `SIGKILL` and `SIGSTOP`. The former causes a process to terminate immediately, and the latter suspends a process until it receives a `SIGCONT` signal.

Example: Installing a new signal handler

The default disposition of the signal sent to a process when we type our interrupt character (usually Control-C), `SIGINT`, is to terminate the process. For most programs this behaviour is acceptable, but programs like shells usually benefit from having a more deliberate exit mechanism. The shell program we showed in Program 1.5 suffers from this limitation: typing Control-C will cause the process to exit.

We'll add some code to catch `SIGINT`; the new handler will just print out a message and continue.

Program 1.7 shows the modified version of our shell. The lines in bold are the ones we added to provide the signal catching functionality.

When we run this new version of our shell, we see that Control-C is caught.

```
$ ./sspsh2
-> date
Sun Jul 29 12:59:55 PDT 2001
-> ^CCaught SIGINT                        Type Control-C to generate SIGINT
->
-> ps
   PID TTY      TIME CMD
 10874 pts/15   0:00 a.out
 28830 pts/15   0:00 ksh
->                                        Type Control-D to quit
$
```

Let's take a closer look at the modifications we had to make to our shell so that we could catch interrupts. Notice that we use an infinite `for` loop (lines 18 to 50) to ensure that the program keeps running until we type Control-D.

Include extra header files and declare interrupt handler

6–7 Include the extra header files we'll need.

9 Declare our signal handler function, `sigint`.

Change `SIGINT`'s disposition

15–16 This is where we actually change `SIGINT`'s disposition to call our signal handler.

47–49 These lines allow our program to continue after we type Control-C, by clearing `errno` and returning to the top of our `while` loop. When we type Control-C, `fgets` returns NULL with `errno` set to `EINTR`. System calls interrupted by a signal are not restarted in Solaris when their disposition is changed using `sigset`; we'll see in Section 17.9 how to restart interrupted system calls.

-- *intro/sspsh2.c*

```
 1 #include <stdio.h>
 2 #include <unistd.h>
 3 #include <sys/types.h>
 4 #include <sys/wait.h>
 5 #include <string.h>
 6 #include <signal.h>
 7 #include <errno.h>
 8 #include "ssp.h"

 9 static void sigint (int sig);

10 int main (void)
11 {
12     char buf [LINE_LEN];
13     pid_t pid;
14     int status;

15     if (sigset (SIGINT, sigint) == SIG_ERR)
16         err_msg ("sigset");

17     printf ("-> ");

18     for (;;) {
19         while (fgets (buf, LINE_LEN, stdin) != NULL) {
20             if (*buf != '\0')
21                 buf [strlen (buf) - 1] = '\0';
22             if (strlen (buf) == 0) {
23                 printf ("-> ");
24                 continue;
25             }

26             switch (pid = fork ()) {
27                 case -1:
28                     err_msg ("Can't fork");
29                     break;

30                 case 0:
31                     /*
32                      * Child process
33                      */
34                     execlp (buf, buf, NULL);
35                     err_msg ("Can't exec %s", buf);
36                     break;

37                 default:
38                     /*
39                      * Parent process
40                      */
41                     if (waitpid (pid, &status, 0) == -1)
42                         err_ret ("waitpid");
43                     break;
44             }

45             printf ("-> ");
46         }
```

```
47          if (errno != EINTR)
48              break;

49          errno = 0;
50      }

51      return (0);
52  }

53  static void sigint (int sig)
54  {
55      printf ("Caught SIGINT\n");
56      printf ("-> ");
57  }
```
—— *intro/sspsh2.c*

Program 1.7 Our shell, modified to catch SIGINT.

Signal handler

53–57 Our signal handler just prints out a message and a prompt before returning. We should point out that calling printf from a signal handler is usually ill-advised. However, we can get away with it in a simple example like Program 1.7.

In Chapter 17 we'll be taking a detailed look at all the signals and the functions available to manipulate them.

1.10 UNIX Time Values

Solaris keeps track of three types of time:

1. The current, or calendar, time. In UNIX, the calendar time is defined as the number of seconds since the *epoch*, which was at midnight on Thursday, January 1st, 1970 UTC (Coordinated Universal Time). This number is stored in a variable of type time_t, which is usually a signed long. On 32-bit systems, the maximum value a signed long number can have is 2,147,483,647. This means that at 03:14:07 on Tuesday, January 19th, 2038, 32-bit time_ts will wraparound. On 64-bit systems that use a 64-bit time_t, the wraparound problem will be delayed for about 292,271,023,017 years! (Note that a 32-bit process running on a 64-bit kernel also suffers from the 2038 wraparound problem.)

   The calendar time is used, among other things, to keep track of file access and modification times.

2. Process execution times. The kernel keeps track of two types of CPU usage for each active process: the *User time*, and the *System time* (these are sometimes collectively referred to as the *CPU time*). System time is the time the kernel spends executing code on behalf of the process, and the User time is the remainder. Both the User and System times are measured in clock ticks (which are of type clock_t); there are HZ clock ticks per second (POSIX—which is a set of standards defining a portable operating system interface—uses the symbol CLK_TCK); Solaris uses a HZ value of 100. Solaris 2.6 introduced the ability to

enable a higher-resolution clock tick. The HZ value can be set to 1000 by adding the following entry to /etc/system:

```
set hires_tick = 1
```

(Like all changes to /etc/system, a reboot is required for this to take effect.) Be wary of doing this on old hardware because of the order of magnitude increase in the number of clock interrupts.

We can use the time(1) command to show us these values. The output of the time(1) command includes one more value: the *Real time*. This value, sometimes called the *wall time*, is the amount of time the process took to run. The difference between the sum of the CPU times and the wall time is the amount of time the CPU was busy doing something else, like running other processes, waiting for I/O, or idling.

```
$ time ls -1R > /dev/null

real    0m17.45s
user    0m4.13s
sys     0m2.48s
```

Here we see that the ls command took 17.45 seconds to run, although the CPU only spent 6.61 seconds of this time executing code (the rest was no doubt spent waiting for I/O, because the directory listing in this example was for an NFS mounted file system).

3. The time since the most recent reboot, measured in clock ticks. This is stored in the kernel variable, lbolt, which is of type clock_t. As this value is not easily accessible from user space processes, and is of little interest anyway, we won't discuss it further.

In Chapter 6 we'll examine the date and time functions in more detail.

1.11 System Calls and Library Functions

Apart from the type of their return values, the C programming language makes no distinction between different types of functions: a function is a function. In the context of UNIX programming, there are two types of function we need to differentiate: *library functions* and *system calls*. Library functions are essentially the same as normal C functions. They are part of the address space for each process that uses them and don't have any context switching overhead.

System calls, on the other hand, are implemented in the kernel. To execute a system call, a context switch into the privileged kernel mode must be made. In Solaris, the majority of system calls are implemented by wrapper library functions that cause one of two software traps to occur. The first of these traps is used for 32-bit system calls, and the second is used for 64-bit system calls. Using different software traps for the 32-bit and 64-bit system calls enables 64-bit kernels to run 32-bit applications without any changes or recompiling.

A very small number of system calls don't use the generic interface we just described. These fast system calls (for example, `gethrtime`, `gethrvtime`, and `gettimeofday`), each have their own software trap, which makes them much faster (about five times faster in some cases) than normal system calls. This is because the overhead incurred by saving state and determining which system call to actually execute is removed. Even these fast system calls have a large latency compared to a normal C function call.

Example: Comparing system call and function latencies

Program 1.8 calculates the average latency of a system call, a fast system call, and a normal C function call.

intro/times.c

```
 1 #include <stdio.h>
 2 #include <unistd.h>
 3 #include <sys/time.h>

 4 #define ITERATIONS 100

 5 static void nop (void);

 6 int main (void)
 7 {
 8     hrtime_t start;
 9     hrtime_t stop;
10     int i;

11     start = gethrtime ();
12     for (i = 0; i < ITERATIONS; i++)
13         getpid ();
14     stop = gethrtime ();
15     printf ("getpid = %lld\n", (stop - start) / ITERATIONS);

16     start = gethrtime ();
17     for (i = 0; i < ITERATIONS; i++)
18         gethrtime ();
19     stop = gethrtime ();
20     printf ("gethrtime = %lld\n", (stop - start) / ITERATIONS);

21     start = gethrtime ();
22     for (i = 0; i < ITERATIONS; i++)
23         nop ();
24     stop = gethrtime ();
25     printf ("nop = %lld\n", (stop - start) / ITERATIONS);

26     return (0);
27 }

28 static void nop (void)
29 {
30     /* Do nothing */
31 }
```

intro/times.c

Program 1.8 Calculate the average system call latency.

Program 1.8 uses the `gethrtime` function (which uses a timer that has nanosecond granularity) to ascertain the latency of the various functions, averaged over a number of iterations. Figure 1.2 shows the results when we run Program 1.8 on four different machines.

Function	Latency (ns)			
	SS 20	Ultra 1	SB 100	Ultra 60
`getpid`	1952	3288	1184	1215
`gethrtime`	1520	565	944	204
`nop`	140	45	23	16

Figure 1.2 System call latency on four architectures.

The first column in Figure 1.2 shows the name of the system call we are measuring the latency for. We chose `getpid` and `gethrtime` because they are both relatively simple system calls, so most of the time we show can be attributed to the latency of the system call trap rather than the work the system call is actually doing. The last four columns show the average latency in nanoseconds for each of the four machine types we tested. Column two shows the results for a SPARCstation 20 with two 75 MHz SuperSPARC II processors, the third column shows the results for an Ultra 1 170E (with a 170 MHz UltraSPARC I processor), the fourth column shows the results for a Sun Blade 100 with a 500 MHz UltraSPARC IIe processor, and the last column shows the results for an Ultra 60 with a pair of 450 MHz UltraSPARC II processors. The SPARCstation 20 was running Solaris 8, and the other machines were running Solaris 9.

The last row shows the overhead for a simple "do nothing" function. We can see that the overhead (latency) for a system call can be as much as two orders of magnitude greater than that of an ordinary function call.

Figure 1.3 shows the relationship of an application, library functions, and system calls (for the sake of brevity, we have omitted the wrapper functions for system calls). Also, although Figure 1.3 might imply it, not every library function makes use of system calls.

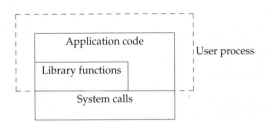

Figure 1.3 Relationship of applications, library functions, and system calls.

What we are trying to show here is that system calls may be made directly by an application, or by a library function that the application calls. For example, `open` and `close` are examples of system calls our applications might call directly, whereas `getdents` and `sbrk` are examples of system calls usually called from a library function (although there's nothing preventing us from calling them directly).

Another feature that distinguishes library functions from system calls is that that former usually have more functionality than the latter. For example, the various date and time handling functions provide facilities for converting dates between human-friendly and machine-friendly formats. The underlying system call, `time`, merely returns the number of seconds since the epoch; it is up to the library functions to format this value.

In this text, we'll just use the term *function* to refer to system calls and library functions, except when the distinction is necessary.

1.12 Introduction to 64-Bit Programming

Since the release of Solaris 7 in 1998, Solaris has been a fully 64-bit capable operating system. (Solaris 2.6 started introducing 64-bit functionality in the form of the large file feature set, which allows a 32-bit process to manipulate large files. From a Solaris programming perspective, a *large file* is one whose size is equal to or exceeds 2 GB.) This 64-bit capability does not come at the expense of backward compatibility: a 64-bit kernel is capable of running 32-bit processes, without recompiling or relinking, as well as 64-bit processes. The converse is not true, however: a 64-bit process requires a 64-bit kernel.

The 64-bit kernel only runs on 64-bit hardware. This means that only the UltraSPARC family of processors from Sun and Fujitsu's SPARC64 processors currently support 64-bit operation; previous generations of the SPARC architecture (e.g., sun4c, sun4d, and sun4m) and all x86 processors, are 32-bit only. (At the time of writing, this is true. However, starting with Solaris 10, 64-bit computing will be supported on those x86 processors that are 64-bit capable.) Although running 64-bit applications is supported only on 64-bit hardware, 32-bit systems can be used to develop 64-bit applications, provided that the 64-bit tools and libraries are installed. To determine whether the kernel we are using is 32-bit or 64-bit, we can use the `isainfo`(1) command:

```
$ isainfo -k                          We first run the command using a 64-bit kernel
sparcv9

$ isainfo -k                          Now we're using a 32-bit kernel
sparc
```

Similarly, we can use `isainfo` to determine what sort of applications we can run:

```
$ isainfo -v
64-bit sparcv9 applications
32-bit sparc applications

$ isainfo -v
32-bit sparc applications
```

Sun's latest processors (the UltraSPARC IV and derivatives, and the UltraSPARC IIe) only support a 64-bit kernel, although full backward compatibility with 32-bit processes is maintained. Future UltraSPARC processors will also require a 64-bit kernel.

As well as having a vastly increased theoretical virtual address space (about 18 exabytes, which is four billion times as large as the 4 GB limit imposed on 32-bit processes), a 64-bit process overcomes many of the limitations imposed on 32-bit applications:

- The 256 file descriptor limit for the standard I/O functions has been raised to MAXINT, which is defined in <values.h>. That is, the value has been raised from the maximum value a char (i.e., one byte) can store to the maximum value an int (i.e., four bytes) can store.

- The use of a 64-bit time_t derived type avoids the year 2038 problem.

- The use of 64-bit registers and instructions means that 64-bit arithmetic operations are faster (64-bit operations have always been available with Solaris, but 32-bit registers and instructions were used to implement them).

- A 64-bit process can perform certain operations faster and in a more straightforward manner. For example, it can map a whole large file into its address space, rather than explicitly handling smaller chunks.

Other advantages of using a 64-bit kernel include the ability of having swap devices greater than 2 GB in size, and the ability to have files larger than 2 GB in tmpfs file systems.

> The temporary file system, tmpfs, is a Solaris feature that allows the virtual memory of a machine (i.e., its RAM and swap space) to be used for temporary file storage. Given sufficient RAM, this has substantial performance advantages over traditional disk-based temporary file storage, because /tmp effectively becomes a RAM disk. Another benefit is that we can guarantee that files in /tmp will be removed when the system is rebooted, even those in subdirectories.

The disadvantages of a 64-bit environment include larger memory requirements, and the chance of a slight performance degradation. This results from the increase in size of every pointer and address (variables of type long also double in size). Applications embed many addresses and pointers in their code and data. When they all double in size, the application grows, reducing cache hit rates and increasing memory demands. All other things being equal, we can expect a small decrease in performance for everyday applications when moving from a 32-bit to a 64-bit environment. That said, the performance decrease is likely to be negligible, given the performance of contemporary CPUs.

1.12.1 Writing 64-Bit Clean Programs

Before we describe how to compile a 64-bit program, we should first look at the issues raised by writing 64-bit programs (and porting existing 32-bit programs to 64 bits). Addressing these issues will also help us write single-source programs that support both 32-bit and 64-bit compilation.

The problems associated with writing programs that are 64-bit clean (and especially with porting 32-bit programs) derive from the fact that 64-bit programs use a different data type model than 32-bit programs. The data type model used by 32-bit C programs is called ILP32. This is because all ints, longs, and pointers are 32-bit. However, 64-bit programs use a data type model called LP64. In this model, ints are still a 32-bit quantity, but longs and pointers are 64-bit quantities (shorts and chars are the same as in the ILP32 model). Despite the different data type model, the standard relationship between integral data types remains the same, i.e.:

```
sizeof (char) <= sizeof (short) <= sizeof (int) <= sizeof (long)
```

Figure 1.4 lists the basic C types, and their sizes in bits for both the ILP32 and LP64 data type models.

C Data Type	ILP32	LP64
char	8	8
short	16	16
int	32	32
long	32	64
long long	64	64
Pointer	32	64
enum	32	32
float	32	32
double	64	64
long double	128	128

Figure 1.4 C data type sizes in bits for the ILP32 and LP64 data type models.

Many of the problems we encounter when trying to write 64-bit clean code come from the assumption that `int`s, `long`s, and pointers are the same size. But as we have just discussed, this is not the case for 64-bit programs. Solaris provides several resources to help us write single-source code that is both 32-bit and 64-bit clean. These include:

- Derived data types
- Fixed-width integer types
- Limits
- Format string macros

Let's take a closer look at these resources.

Derived Data Types

Derived types allow us to abstract away an object's underlying type, thus freeing us from worrying about implementation-specific details. For example, we can refer to the derived type `time_t` without knowing (or caring) whether the underlying type is an `int`, a `long`, or something else. Using derived types is good programming practice, as it makes porting our code to new platforms, as well as adopting new data models, easier. Using derived types helps make our code 32-bit and 64-bit safe, because the derived types themselves must be safe in either model.

Derived types are defined in two header files: `<sys/types.h>` and (starting with Solaris 2.6) `<inttypes.h>`. The latter contains constants, macros, and derived types that help us make our programs suitable for compilation in 32-bit and 64-bit environments, and allows us to use explicitly sized objects independent of the compilation environment.

Fixed-Width Integer Types

The fixed-width integer types provided by <inttypes.h> allow us to define objects that are fixed in size, independent of the compilation environment. Both signed and unsigned types are defined: int8_t, int16_t, int32_t, int64_t, uint8_t, uint16_t, uint32_t, and uint64_t.

> The names of these fixed-width data types are from [ISO/IEC 1999].

Although they should not be used indiscriminately, the fixed-width types can be used in the explicit binary representation of the following:

- On-disk data
- Over-the-wire data (i.e., data coming across a network connection)
- Hardware registers
- Binary interface specifications
- Binary data structures

For things like loop counters, file descriptors, and array indexes, ints and longs should be used as usual.

The <inttypes.h> header file defines other useful types. For example, intptr_t and uintptr_t define an integral object large enough to hold a pointer. Using these types for performing integral operations on pointers is better than using a fundamental type like unsigned long, because even though an unsigned long is the same size as a pointer in both the ILP32 and LP64 data type models, there is no guarantee that this will never change. In the event that the data model does change, all we need do is change the definition of intptr_t or uintptr_t.

Limits

The limits defined in <inttypes.h> are constants that specify the minimum and maximum values of the various integer types. This includes the minimum and maximum values of each fixed-width type (i.e, INT8_MIN to INT64_MIN and INT8_MAX to INT64_MAX), and their unsigned counterparts.

Also defined in <inttypes.h> are the minimum and maximum values of the largest supported integer types. These are defined by INTMAX_MIN and INTMAX_MAX, and their corresponding unsigned counterparts.

Format String Macros

Another area that could cause problems when we are developing code that can be compiled in a 32-bit or 64-bit environment is the format specifiers we pass to printf(3S) and scanf(3S). These macros (defined in <sys/int_fmtio.h>, which is included by

`<inttypes.h>`) prepend the format specifier with an `l` or `ll` to specify the argument as a `long` or a `long long`. The number of bits in the argument is built into the macro name. For example,

```
int64_t num;

printf ("num = %" PRId64 "\n", num);
```

will print the variable `num` as a 64-bit quantity regardless of the compilation environment.

Similarly, a set of macros are provided for `scanf` to read in integers. For example,

```
int32_t num;

scanf ("%" SCNx32 "\n", &num);
```

will read a 32-bit hexadecimal number and store it in the variable `num`, regardless of the compilation environment.

We take a closer look at `printf` and `scanf` in Chapter 5, when we discuss the standard I/O library.

Sun's version of the `lint` utility has been enhanced to detect potential 64-bit problems. Also, the `-v` command line flag for Sun's C compiler can be very helpful.

Rules For Writing 64-Bit Clean Code

The following rules should be observed to ensure the 64-bit cleanliness of our code. Following these rules will also make it easier to port 32-bit code to the 64-bit model.

- Do not assume a pointer and an `int` are the same size. Unfortunately, a lot of code relies on this assumption, because it is true in the ILP32 model. Pointers are sometimes cast to `ints` or `unsigned ints` to perform address arithmetic. Instead, they should be cast to `long` (or `unsigned long`) because pointers and `longs` are the same size in both the ILP32 and LP64 data type models. Even better is to cast pointers to `uintptr_ts`, because it expresses the intent more clearly, and makes the code more portable.

- Do not make assumptions about the relative sizes of variable types. A classic example of this is to assume that the size of an `int` is the same as the size of a `long` and use them indiscriminately while implicitly or explicitly assuming they are interchangeable. Although this is typically true for 32-bit processes, it is not true for 64-bit ones.

- Be wary of sign extension problems. This is quite a common problem when converting code to 64-bits, and is hard to detect before it actually occurs because `lint` doesn't warn us about it. Also, the type conversion and promotion rules are quite obscure. Hence, we should use explicit casting to fix sign extension problems. Program 1.9 illustrates this problem.

- Use pointer arithmetic rather than address arithmetic. As well as leading to cleaner code, pointer arithmetic is independent of the data model. In other words, if `start` and `end` are defined as pointers to `ints`, then

```
start = malloc (sizeof (*start) * NUM_ELEMENTS);
end = start + NUM_ELEMENTS;
```

is preferable to

```
start = malloc (4 * NUM_ELEMENTS);
end = (int *) ((unsigned int) p + 4 * NUM_ELEMENTS);
```

- *Never* cast the value returned by `malloc` (or its related functions): doing so will mask compiler warnings resulting from the missing function prototypes.

- By default, external variables and functions are assumed to be (or return) an `int` by the compiler unless we declare them otherwise. Because of this, we should always put appropriate declarations for our functions and variable, and include all necessary header files for functions included with Solaris. For example, suppose we use the `malloc` function to allocate some memory. Without including the appropriate header files, the compiler will assume that `malloc` returns an `int`. In the ILP32 data model, this would not present a problem (as pointers and `int`s are the same size), but the top four bytes of information will be lost in the LP64 data model, probably causing our program to crash because of an illegal memory reference.

- The `sizeof` operator returns an integer of type `size_t`, which has an effective type of `unsigned long`. We should be careful not to pass the returned value to a function that expects an `int`, nor should we attempt to assign the value to a variable whose type is `int` or smaller. In either case, the truncation might cause data loss.

- Check internal data structures for holes. On SPARC platforms, each member of a structure is aligned to at least the size of that member's type. To ensure that structures are packed as tightly as possible, make sure that `long`s and pointers are grouped together at the beginning their structures. For example, in a 64-bit environment, the following structure occupies 32 bytes:

```
struct foo {
    int i;
    long j;
    int k;
    char *p;
};
```

By rearranging its members, we can shrink the structure's size to only 24 bytes:

```
struct foo {
    char *p;
    long j;
    int i;
    int k;
};
```

- On a related note, make sure that the members of unions don't change their sizes when changing data type models. For example,

```
typedef union {
    double u_d;
    long u_l [2];
} ll_t;
```

will work as intended when compiled in the ILP32 model, but will fail when compiled in the LP64 model. Changing the type of the u_l member to an `int` will solve this type of problem.

- Be careful to avoid data loss in a constant expression resulting from lack of precision. These kinds of problems can be very hard to find, so we should be explicit about specifying types in our constant expressions. We do this by adding some combination of u, U, l, or L at the end of each integer constant. The following is an example that illustrates this kind of problem:

```
int i;
long j;

j = 1 << i;
```

The above expression evaluates to 0 because the right-hand side is an integer expression. The following code avoids this problem:

```
int i;
long j;

j = 1L << i;
```

- Take care when using the `printf` family of functions. We should always use the %p conversion specifier to print a pointer, and always add the `long` size specifier, l, for `long` arguments. Check that enough room is allowed for in buffers and character strings: at least 16 digits may be required.

- A number of derived types have grown to represent 64-bit quantities in the LP64 data model. While this shouldn't present a problem to programs that adhere to these rules, programs that import or export data described by these types may need to be reevaluated for correctness. An example of this would be programs that directly manipulate the `utmp` or `utmpx` files. Rather than directly manipulate them, any documented functions should be used instead (e.g., the `getutxent` family).

- There are times when we can't avoid using explicit 32-bit and 64-bit interfaces. Code intended for use only in the LP64 data model should be conditionally compiled using the _LP64 feature test:

```
#ifdef _LP64
    /*
     * 64-bit specific code here
     */
#endif
```

A similar construct using the _ILP32 feature test can be used to conditionally compile 32-bit only code.

Once our code has been made 64-bit clean, we should review it to make sure that the algorithms and data structures still make sense. Because some data types are larger, data structures might use more space. It's also possible that the performance of our code will change too.

Example: Avoiding sign extension problems in 64-bit code

Program 1.9 illustrates how sign extension problems can manifest themselves. Even though `addr` and `foo.x` are unsigned types, `addr` becomes sign extended when Program 1.9 is compiled as a 64-bit program (we'll show how to do this in the next section).

intro/sign_ext.c

```
 1 #include <stdio.h>

 2 struct a {
 3     unsigned int x:19;
 4 };

 5 int main (void)
 6 {
 7     struct a foo;
 8     unsigned long addr;

 9     foo.x = 0x40000;

10     addr = foo.x << 13;
11     printf ("addr = 0x%lx\n", addr);

12     addr = (unsigned int) (foo.x << 13);
13     printf ("addr = 0x%lx\n", addr);

14     return (0);
15 }
```

intro/sign_ext.c

Program 1.9 Sign extension problems in 64-bit code.

Running Program 1.9 gives us these results:

```
$ ./sign_ext
addr = 0xffffffff80000000        This has been sign extended
addr = 0x80000000                This has not been sign extended
```

Compiling Program 1.9 as a 32-bit program does not cause this behaviour.

Now that we know how to write a program that will compile in 32-bit and 64-bit environments, let's look at how we compile and install a 64-bit program.

1.12.2 Compiling and Installing 64-Bit Programs

Sun's Forté C compiler version 5.0 or later is required to compile 64-bit code (the SunONE Studio products, as they were called at the time of writing, were previously known as Forté and Sun Workshop). At the time of writing (mid 2004), the 64-bit code produced by `gcc` was not as good as that generated by Sun's compiler, so we recommend the use of the latter for 64-bit development. (It is arguable that the use of Sun's compilers is mandatory for commercial 64-bit applications.) All the 64-bit examples in this text were compiled using Sun's compiler.

By default, Sun's compiler generates 32-bit code; passing the `-xarch=v9` command line flag to `cc` will cause it to generate 64-bit code. In other words,

```
cc foo.c
```

will generate 32-bit code, whereas

```
cc -xarch=v9 foo.c
```

will generate 64-bit code.

> If we use `gcc` for 64-bit development, the earliest version we can use is version 3.1. We must also use the `-m64` command line argument, like this:
>
> ```
> gcc -m64 foo.c
> ```
>
> But again we recommend that commercial applications—and especially 64-bit commercial applications—be compiled using Sun's compilers.

A 64-bit program must be linked with 64-bit libraries; attempts to link with 32-bit libraries are reported as an error by the compiler. Similarly, 32-bit programs must be linked with only 32-bit libraries.

It is sometimes desirable to have both a 32-bit version and a 64-bit version of our programs. Rather than calling them by two different names, Solaris provides a program called `isaexec`, which automatically selects the right version of a program to run. The different versions of the program are placed in appropriately named subdirectories of the original, and a copy of (or hard link to—a symbolic link will not work) `/usr/lib/isaexec`, is put in place of the real name of the program. The names of the subdirectories can be selected from the output of `isalist`, but are usually `sparcv7` (or `sparc`) for 32-bit programs and `sparcv9` for 64-bit programs.

> Very briefly, a *hard link* (or just *link*) is another name for a directory entry that refers to a file in the file system. UNIX file systems support the concept of a file being known by many names; each of these file names is a link. A symbolic link is a file whose contents are the pathname of the file being linked to. We'll describe links and symbolic links in more detail in Chapter 10.

The `isaexec` program, which is not designed to be executed by that name, determines its fully resolved, symbolic link free pathname, and gets the list of suitable architectures using `sysinfo (SI_ISALIST)`. The first executable file in the resulting list of subdirectories that has the same name as the original is then executed, with the command arguments (including `argv [0]`) and environment variables intact. For example, if we have a program called `foo` that will reside in `/usr/bin`, then we would place the 32-bit version in `/usr/bin/sparcv7/foo` and the 64-bit version in `/usr/bin/sparcv9/foo`. The file `/usr/bin/foo` would be a hard link to `/usr/lib/isaexec`, which would arrange for the correct version to be run.

1.12.3 The Large File Compilation Environment

We mentioned earlier that Solaris 2.6 introduced the large file feature set, which allows a 32-bit process to access files that exceed 2 GB in size. By definition, 64-bit processes can manipulate large files. However, a 32-bit process must be compiled in a way that enables large file access. This can be achieved by using one of two command line options with the compiler: `-D_FILE_OFFSET_BITS=64` or `-D_LARGEFILE_SOURCE` (the latter is used in the transitional large file compilation environment, which we talk about in the next section).

A program that can manipulate large files in the same manner that it manipulates small files (i.e., files less than 2 GB in size) is said to be *large file aware*. A program that is large file aware must be able to read, write, and create large files. A program is *large file safe* if it causes no data loss or corruption when it encounters a large file. A program that is large file safe is not able to process a large file properly, but returns an appropriate error.

> There is another reason to make our programs large file aware or safe, even if they never need to access files that exceed 2 GB in size: some of the derived types in the `stat` structure (see Chapter 10) can also be extended. This can cause problems when programs that are not large file safe try to `stat` files on NFS mounts from other systems that use 64-bit inode values.

Making a program large file safe requires no changes to our Makefiles, but we must ensure that our source code correctly handles errors that occur when we call a function that cannot manipulate or represent an attribute of a large file, such as size or offset information that exceeds the 32-bit limitation. When this happens, the function that returns the error sets `errno` to either `EOVERFLOW` or `EFBIG`.

Making our programs large file aware requires a little more work, however. We should write new programs to be 64-bit clean, but existing source code may require some changes. As well as modifying our Makefiles to pass the `-D_FILE_OFFSET_BITS=64` flag to the compiler, we should make sure that there are no type clashes. This can occur when we use a fundamental type rather than the derived type defined by POSIX and other standards (for example, using `long` where an `off_t` is specified). The following derived types have been extended to include a 64-bit version: `ino_t`, `off_t`, `fpos_t`, `rlim_t`, `blkcnt_t`, `fsblkcnt_t`, and `fsfilcnt_t`.

Example: Compiling a large file aware program

Program 1.10 attempts to open a file that we create using `mkfile(1M)`.

We first create a 1 GB file, and then run Program 1.10. A file only 1 GB in size is not a large file, so Program 1.10 should run successfully, which it does. We then replace it with a 3 GB file, and rerun Program 1.10; this time an error is printed. Because an error is printed and no data corruption occurs, we can say that Program 1.10 is large file safe, but not large file aware.

```
$ make large_file
$ mkfile -n 1g /space/big_file
$ ls -l /space/big_file
-rw-------   1 rich     staff    1073741824 Oct 19 15:37 /space/big_file
$ ./large_file
Open successful
$ mkfile -n 3g /space/big_file
$ ls -l /space/big_file
-rw-------   1 rich     staff    3221225472 Oct 19 15:37 /space/big_file
$ ./large_file
Can't open /space/big_file: Value too large for defined data type
```

—— *intro/large_file.c*

```
 1 #include <stdio.h>
 2 #include <unistd.h>
 3 #include <sys/types.h>
 4 #include <sys/stat.h>
 5 #include <fcntl.h>
 6 #include "ssp.h"

 7 #define BIG_FILE "/space/big_file"

 8 int main (void)
 9 {
10     int fd;

11     if ((fd = open (BIG_FILE, O_RDONLY)) == -1)
12         err_msg ("Can't open %s", BIG_FILE);

13     printf ("Open successful\n");
14     close (fd);

15     return (0);
16 }
```

—— *intro/large_file.c*

Program 1.10   Large file demonstration.

We now recompile Program 1.10 to make it large file aware, and run it using the same large file.

```
$ cc -D_FILE_OFFSET_BITS=64 -I../lib large_file.c ../lib/ssp.a
$ ls -l /space/big_file
-rw-------   1 rich     staff    3221225472 Oct 19 15:37 /space/big_file
$ ./a.out
Open successful
```

As we would expect, the large file aware version of Program 1.10 has no problems opening a large file.

> Newcomers to UNIX programming may be a little confused by our introduction of a program called a.out. This is the default filename of programs created by a compiler on UNIX, and is derived from "assembler output". (Strictly speaking, a.out is the name of the file produced by the linker rather than the compiler.) Most of our examples were compiled using the make facility of UNIX, which allows us to build programs based on various dependencies. The rules used to build a program are stored in files called Makefiles; the Makefiles we use contain directives to the C compiler to produce an executable with a name other than a.out.

1.12.4 The Transitional Large File Compilation Environment

Solaris also provides a number of transitional interfaces. The transitional interfaces have the same name as their 32-bit counterparts, with the number 64 appended to them. Hence, open becomes open64, lseek becomes lseek64, and so on.

To make use of the transitional large file compilation environment, we must pass the -D_LARGEFILE_SOURCE flag to the compiler. This allows us to use the regular 32-bit functions and data types, as well as the 64-bit ones.

One reason to use the transitional large file compilation environment is that it enables us to mix code that is large file aware and code that isn't large file aware in the same program. Even so, the transitional large file compilation environment should be used only to allow existing 32-bit programs to access large files safely. New programs should be designed to be 64-bit clean, using the large file compilation environment if they are to be 32-bit programs.

Figure 1.5 shows how the different compilation environments affect our programs.

Compilation environment	Compilation flags	Source symbol	Maps to
Default	None	`func`	`func`
Large file	`-D_FILE_OFFSET_BITS=64`	`func`	`func64`
Transitional	`-D_LARGEFILE_SOURCE`	`func` `func64`	`func` `func64`
Hybrid; don't do this	`-D_FILE_OFFSET_BITS=64` and `-D_LARGEFILE_SOURCE`	`func` `func64`	`func64` `func64`

Figure 1.5 The effect of the various compilation environments.

The transitional interfaces do not comply with POSIX or the Single UNIX Specification, so they should be avoided: the large file environment we described in the previous section should be used instead.

Like the large file compilation environment, the transitional interfaces are only intended to be used by 32-bit processes that must be large file aware; they are not intended to be used by 64-bit processes, which are by definition large file aware.

1.13 Summary

This chapter has been a brief introduction to some of the concepts we need to understand if we are to be proficient Solaris systems programmers. We first talked about logging into a Solaris system and looked at the some of the shells provided. Then we looked at files, directories, and file systems, and described the differences between a filename and a pathname. We presented a short program that lists all the files in a given directory, and then spoke about current, root, and home directories.

Next we turned our attention to input and output. We described file descriptors, the standard I/O streams (standard input, standard output, and standard error), unbuffered I/O, and the standard I/O library. To illustrate the differences between these two methods of I/O, we presented two versions of a program that copies from standard input to standard output.

We looked at programs and processes next, where we introduced the concept of process IDs and parent process IDs, before looking at the `fork` and `exec` process control functions. We used these functions to write a bare-bones shell.

After looking at error handling, we talked about users and groups. This was followed by a discussion about signals, where we added the ability to catch the `SIGINT` signal to our shell program.

Then we looked at the different types of time Solaris keeps track of, and described the differences between system calls and library functions. Finally, we presented an introduction to 64-bit programming. We discussed some of the pros and cons of 64-bit processes, showed how to build a 64-bit program, and demonstrated the recommended method of installing a 32-bit and a 64-bit version of the same program on a system. We also showed how to access large files from a 32-bit process by using the large file compilation environment and the transitional large file compilation environment.

In the next chapter we'll take a look at the history of Solaris and how it complies with various standards.

Exercises

1.1   Verify that the *dot* and *dot-dot* directory entries refer to different directories, except when in the root directory.

1.2   When we ran Program 1.4, the process IDs assigned to us by the kernel were 17787 and 17790; what happened to process IDs 17788 and 17789?

1.3   Add the ability to pass arguments to the programs that the shell we developed in Programs 1.5 and 1.7 executes. (Hint: the `strtok` function we discuss in Chapter 3 could be useful.)

1.4   Rewrite Program 1.10 to use the transitional large file interfaces, and compare the run times by using the `time` utility (we might have to open and close the file several times to have a noticeable effect). What effect does compiling Program 1.10 as a 64-bit program have on the execution time and the size of the executable program? Explain your findings.

1.5   Modify Program 1.10 to seek to the end of the file and report its size. (Hint: the `lseek` function we discuss in Chapter 4 could be useful.)

2

A Brief History of Solaris

2.1   Introduction

In this chapter we take a brief look at the history of Solaris, starting with the early releases of SunOS. Although an in-depth study of the history of UNIX is beyond the scope of this book (interested readers are directed to [Salus 1994], which contains all the details), it is instructive to look at the history of Solaris to see how it has evolved and improved over time.

We also discuss the various standards that Solaris complies with. Standards are important, because adhering to them allows us to port our applications to (or from) another platform more easily.

2.2   The Early Days: SunOS

In the early 1980s, long before Solaris was a twinkle in anyone's eye, Sun Microsystems was shipping workstations and servers based on Motorola's 68000 family of processors. (Sun also produced a workstation based on Intel's 80386, the Sun 386i, but this product was very short-lived.) These machines came bundled with the Sun UNIX operating system (OS), whose name changed to SunOS in 1986 with the release of SunOS 3.2. The early releases of the OS were based on Unisoft V7 UNIX, and the Berkeley Software Distributions (BSD). The BSD relases were produced by the Computer Systems Research Group (CSRG) of the University of California at Berkeley.

One of Sun's cofounders, Bill Joy, was very involved with the BSD releases, so it was natural that Sun's computers would use an OS based on BSD—specifically, 4.1BSD and 4.2BSD. Subsequent releases of SunOS saw the addition of Remote Procedure Calls (RPC), Network Information System (NIS), and the Network File System (NFS). In 1987,

SunOS 3.5 PSR was released, which was the first version of SunOS to support Sun's SPARC processor. (PSR is an acronym for Platform Specific Release, which is essentially the same as the regular release, with whatever is necessary for the new hardware to boot.)

In 1988, SunOS 4 was introduced, which came with a completely new virtual memory system. The new virtual memory system allowed various devices and objects to be abstracted as virtual memory, and facilitated the sharing of memory, and mapping files and hardware devices into the memory space of a process.

> It is interesting to observe that even the very early releases of SunOS came with a GUI: first (in 1982) was SunTools. This was later followed by SunWindows, which was renamed SunView when SunOS 3.0 shipped in 1985. OpenWindows started shipping with SunOS 4.0 in 1990. OpenWindows consisted of the OpenLook Desktop Environment running on top of a hybrid X11/NeWS server. This server was replaced in Solaris 2.3 with a pure X11 server based on the X Consortium release. Although they were originally considered as part of OpenWindows, the X Window System (X11) components were split out when OpenLook was replaced by newer desktop environments.
>
> Later releases of Solaris used the Common Desktop Environment (CDE), followed by the GNU Network Object Model Environment (GNOME); both of these environments run on top of the X Window System.
>
> CDE was copackaged with Solaris 2.5 and 2.5.1, and was integrated with Solaris 2.6. GNOME was copackaged with Solaris 8 and Solaris 9, and was integrated in Solaris 9 8/03.
>
> GUI programming is beyond the scope of this text. Readers interested in C or C++ GUI programming on UNIX systems are referred to O'Reilly & Associates' multivolume series on the subject, or any book that describes the Motif (CDE) or GTK+ (GNOME) toolkits.

Quite separate from the work being done by Sun and the CSRG was the UNIX development being performed by AT&T's Bell Labs, the original home of UNIX. AT&T had released several versions of UNIX, culminating with System V Release 3 (SVR3).

In 1987, Sun and AT&T announced an alliance that meant that future versions of SunOS would be based on the forthcoming SVR4 rather than BSD. SVR4 was an attempt to take the best technologies from SVR3.2, Microsoft's XENIX, SunOS 4.x, and 4.3BSD and put them into one OS. The resulting version of SunOS would be SunOS 5.0.

> Rather ironically, it was a British company, International Computers Limited (ICL), not Sun, that was responsible for the reference port of SVR4 for SPARC. Also, SunOS 5.0 was not just a port of SVR4, but a forking of the code. Significant parts, such as the multithreaded kernel and user space applications and libraries, as well as the networking code, were specific to Sun.
>
> XENIX was based on UNIX Version 7, but later added features from System V.

2.3   Beyond SunOS: Solaris

It was around this time that Sun's marketing nomenclature changed. The name of the new Sun operating system was not going to be SunOS; SunOS was now merely the kernel component of the Solaris 2.x operating environment. Other components of the Solaris operating environment include the windowing system (X), the GUI (initially OpenWindows, which was replaced in 1997 when Solaris 2.6 included CDE), and various other libraries. The previous versions of SunOS 4.x were renamed to Solaris 1.x; the last release of SunOS 4.x, SunOS 4.1.4, was called Solaris 1.1.2. These days, when they say "Solaris", most people mean Solaris 2.x and later; similarly, the name SunOS is usually reserved for the earlier, BSD-derived versions of the OS.

In 1998, Sun's marketing changed the naming scheme again: the version of Solaris that was to be Solaris 2.7 was released as Solaris 7, with Solaris 8 and Solaris 9 following suit. (The implication of dropping the major number "2" was that Sun will not be releasing another incompatible major release.) For the sake of simplicity, we'll just refer to Solaris in this book from now on unless we need to be specific about the version.

2.4   Standards

Before we take a closer look at the specific versions of Solaris this text covers, we need to examine the various standards that Solaris adheres to. In this chapter, we will concern ourselves only with the official standards most important to Solaris programmers. But we should also mention that Solaris complies with many other de facto and de jure standards we don't specifically mention here (e.g., Internet Engineering Task Force (IETF) Request For Comments (RFCs), various ISO standards, Java, etc.).

To paraphrase Andrew Tanenbaum [Tanenbaum 1981], the nice thing about standards is that there are so many to choose from. Fortunately for the modern Solaris programmer, several standards have converged.

2.4.1 ANSI/ISO/IEC C

The C programming language and the UNIX operating system have long been associated with each other. Even after 30 years, most major programs for UNIX are written in C.

This is not surprising, given that one of the people who wrote the language, Dennis Ritchie, was also involved with the implementation of UNIX. C was originally designed for and implemented on the UNIX operating system. Once the language was written, most of the tools and compilers for UNIX were rewritten in C. The UNIX kernel itself (apart from a few very low-level assembler routines) was rewritten in C, something that was almost unheard of at the time.

The original version of the C specification, described in [Kernighan and Ritchie 1978], became known as "K&R C". As the C programming language became more popular, it changed and evolved beyond that described in [Kernighan and Ritchie 1978]. In 1983, the American National Standards Institute (ANSI) established the X3J11 Committee, whose goal was "to develop a clear, consistent, and unambiguous Standard for the C programming language which codifies the common, existing definition of C and which promotes the portability of user programs across C language environments" [ANSI 1989]. This work culminated in 1989, with the release of ANSI Standard X3.159–1989. Later, the International Standards Organization (ISO) formed the technical committee JTC1/SC22/WG14 to review and augment the work of X3J11; the resulting standard, ISO/IEC 9899:1990 [ISO/IEC 1990], was essentially the same as X3.159.

The ANSI and ISO standards later converged, and the current version at the time of writing is [ISO/IEC 1999]. However, the versions of Solaris we cover in this text only conform to the 1990 edition of that specification. In this text, we'll use the term *ISO C* to mean the version of the C language specified by ISO/IEC 9899.

The intent of the ISO C standard is to specify the syntax and constraints of the C programming language, the semantic rules for interpreting C programs, and the representation for I/O to be processed and produced by C programs. It also specifies the restrictions and limits imposed by a conforming C implementation. As well as the preceding, the specification also specifies a set of functions and header files that must be provided. The details, and an example implementation of, the Standard C library can be found in [Plauger 1992].

ISO C specifies a portable, platform-independent version of C. Many of the facilities provided by UNIX are outside of its scope and are covered by other standards.

2.4.2 System V Interface Definition

Issue three of the System V Interface Definition (SVID) [AT&T 1989] was published by AT&T, and it specified the commands and functions that had to be provided by a compliant implementation of SVR4. First available to end users in 1990, SVR4 conformed to both POSIX.1 and XPG4 (see the following two sections). The SVID is an interface specification, not an implementation specification, so it makes no distinction between library functions and system calls (those details are implementation-specific).

As we mentioned in Section 2.2, SVR4 incorporates functionality from SVR3.2, XENIX, and 4.3BSD. Some of the functions provided by 4.3BSD have the same name, but different functionality, as those provided by SVR3.2 or XENIX (for example, the `signal` function). To make these different interfaces available, SVR4 includes a BSD Source Compatibility Package (SCP). Using this package allows us to recompile legacy code for newer systems. Having said that, new applications should not use the BSD Compatibility library. (In Appendix B we take a closer look at the SCP.)

Although the SVID is important from a historical perspective, most UNIX standardization these days is being done by POSIX and The Open Group.

> The SCO Group are the current owners of UNIX. The fourth edition of the SVID is available from SCO's web site: `http://www.thescogroup.com/developers/devspecs`. However, Solaris and various other standards are based on issue three of the SVID, so we'll say no more about the fourth edition.

2.4.3 IEEE POSIX

The Portable Operating System Interface (POSIX) is a set of standards developed by the Institute of Electrical and Electronic Engineers (IEEE). They have also been adopted as standards by ISO and the International Electrotechnical Commission (IEC), called ISO/IEC.

> In 1986 a trial version of the first POSIX standard was known as IEEEIX. Richard Stallman (of the Free Software Foundation) coined the name POSIX.

There have been several versions of the POSIX standards. The first, IEEE Std. 1003.1–1988, specified the C language interface to a UNIX-like kernel, and covered areas such as process primitives (e.g., `fork`, `exec`, and signals), the process environment (user and group IDs), files and directories, terminal I/O, the system databases (the password and group files), and the archive formats of the `tar` and `cpio` commands.

Two years later, the slightly updated version, IEEE Std. 1003.1–1990 (which was also known as International Standard ISO/IEC 9945–1:1990) was published. The changes between this and the 1988 version were minimal, although "Part 1: System Application Program Interface (API) [C Language]" was appended to the title. The title change was to indicate that this standard was for the C programming language; other standards specify the API for other languages.

IEEE Std. 1003.2–1992, "Part 2: Shell and Utilities" defined the shell (based on the Korn shell, `ksh`), and about 100 utilities. The utilities are the commands mostly described in section one of the manual pages and include commands such as `awk`, `bc`, and `vi`.

IEEE Std. 1003.1b–1993 was an update to the 1003.1–1990 standard and was originally known as IEEE P1003.4. It was developed by the P1003.4 working group to include realtime extensions: file synchronization, asynchronous I/O, semaphores, memory management (`mmap` and shared memory), process scheduling, clocks and timers, and message queues.

IEEE Std. 1003.1c–1995 was also an update to the 1003.1–1990 standard, and was originally known as 1003.4a. It was developed to define a platform-independent threads interface. The threads implementation described by 1003.1c–1995 is known as POSIX threads, or Pthreads.

IEEE Std. 1003.1, 1996 Edition incorporated 1003.1–1990 (the base API), 1003.1b–1993 (realtime extensions), 1003.1c–1995 (Pthreads), and 1003.1i–1995 (technical corrections to 1003.1b). This standard (which was also known as ISO/IEC 9945–1:1996) added three chapters on threads, including sections on thread synchronization (mutexes and condition variables), thread scheduling, and synchronization scheduling.

IEEE Std. 1003.1, 2001 Edition [IEEE 2001] was a major revision, and incorporated 1003.1–1990 and its subsequent amendments, 1003.2–1992 and its subsequent amendments, and the core volumes of the Single UNIX Specification, Version 2. It is technically identical to The Open Group Base Specification, Issue 6; they are one and the same documents, the front cover having both designations.

Unless context otherwise dictates (or we specifically state otherwise), when we use the term *POSIX* in this text, we are referring to POSIX 1003.1-1996.

FIPS 151–2

The U.S. government publishes the Federal Information Processing Standards (FIPS), which it uses for the procurement of computer systems. FIPS 151–2 (published in 1993) was based on the 1990 edition of IEEE Std. 1003.1 (its predecessor, FIPS 151–1 was based on 1003.1:1988 and a draft of the ANSI C standard), and is essentially a tightening of the POSIX specification, in that it requires some features that POSIX lists as optional. Because of this, we won't consider FIPS 151–2 as another standard.

2.4.4 The Open Group's XPG4

In 1992, The Open Group (a consolidation of the X/Open Company and the Open Software Foundation (OSF)) published a five volume portability guide called XPG4 [X/Open 1995], which superseded the seven volume XPG3 published in 1992 [X/Open 1992]. Volume 2 of XPG4, called *System Interfaces and Headers*, specified a UNIX-like OS based on IEEE 1003.1–1990.

Version 2 of XPG4, published in 1994, was the direct ancestor of the Single UNIX Specification. It was also known as Spec 1170, 1170 being the sum of the different interfaces it specified: 926 programming interfaces (functions), 174 commands and utilities, and 70 header files.

2.4.5 The Single UNIX Specification

In December 1993, Spec 1170 was delivered to X/Open for processing into a proper industry-supported specification. In October 1994, this work culminated in the publication of version one of the Single UNIX Specification (SUS).

The Single UNIX Specification, Version 1 (UNIX 95)

Version 1 of the Single UNIX Specification (SUSv1) was made up from five X/Open Common Applications Environment (CAE) documents. They were:

- System Interface Definitions, Issue 4, Version 2 (XBD). This document outlined the common definitions used by the XSH and XCU documents. It included items such as regular expression grammars, locales, and a glossary defining common terms and concepts.

- System Interfaces and Headers, Issue 4, Version 2 (XSH). This document described all the programming interfaces and headers except the networking and terminal interfaces, which had their own documents. It addressed issues such as the compilation environment, usage guidelines, error numbers, and types. It also contained a reference page for each interface and each header file.

- Commands and Utilities, Issue 4, Version 2 (XCU). The XCU document described all the available commands and utilities. It covered the syntax and functionality of the shell, and had a reference page for each command and utility.

- Network Services, Issue 4 (XNS). This document described the three sets of networking interfaces defined in the Single UNIX Specification: the X/Open Transport Interface (XTI), XPG4 Sockets, and IP Address Resolution interfaces.

- X/Open Curses, Issue 4 (XCURSES). This document described the terminal interfaces. They were upwardly compatible to those defined by X/Open Curses, Version 3, but were extended to support enhanced character sets, internationalization, and different writing directions.

Operating systems conforming to SUSv1 may be branded "UNIX 95".

The Single UNIX Specification, Version 2 (UNIX 98)

In February 1997, Version 2 of the Single UNIX Specification (SUSv2) was published. This was an evolution of Version 1, and consisted of the following CAE documents:

- System Interface Definitions, Issue 5 (XBD)
- Commands and Utilities, Issue 5 (XCU)
- System Interfaces and Headers, Issue 5 (XSH)
- Networking Services Issue 5 (XNS)
- X/Open Curses, Issue 4, Version 2 (XCURSES)

SUSv2 incorporated and aligned with the following:

- ISO/IEC 9945–1:1996, which is the same as IEEE Std. 1003.1, 1996 Edition
- ISO/IEC 9899:1990/Amendment 1:1995 (E), which added multibyte character support
- The Large File Summit extensions, which enables UNIX systems to support 64-bit file offsets, i.e., files up to 2^{64} bytes in size
- Extended threads functions beyond those provided by Pthreads
- Dynamic linking extensions, to permit applications to share common code
- Changes to remove any architectural dependencies, also known as the N-bit cleanup (64-bit and beyond)
- Year 2000 alignment to minimize the impact of the year 2000 roll-over

The number of interfaces was increased to 1434 for the base version, although for a workstation, this number jumped to 3030. This is because the workstation version included CDE, which relies on the Motif user interface and the X Window System.

Systems that conform to SUSv2 may be branded "UNIX 98".

The Single UNIX Specification, Version 3 (UNIX 03)

In January 2002, Version 3 of the Single UNIX Specification (SUSv3) was published. Version 3 incorporates the 1999 version of the ISO C standard, and is a combination of the core volumes of Version 2 of the Single UNIX Specification and IEEE Std. 1003.1–1990 and its subsequent amendments, and IEEE Std. 1003.2–1992 and its subsequent amendments. SUSv3 has been adopted by ISO/IEC, and is known as ISO/IEC 9945:2002.

The following documents make up SUSv3:

- Base Definitions, Issue 6 (XBD)
- System Interfaces, Issue 6 (XSH)
- Shell and Utilities, Issue 6 (XCU)
- Rationale (XRAT)
- X/Open Curses, Issue 4, Version 2 (XCURSES)

The number of interfaces defined by SUSv3 increased to 1741—over 300 more than the previous version.

> SUSv3 can be read online, from `http://www.unix.org/version3/online.html`.

Systems that conform to SUSv3 may be branded "UNIX 03".

2.5   Solaris 2.5

Let's take a look at some of the features of the versions of Solaris we cover in this text.

In 1995, Sun released Solaris 2.5, which was the first release to support the UltraSPARC processor (although UltraSPARC support was limited to uniprocessor systems). Doors, a mechanism for fast local interprocess communications, was also added, although they were not a public interface until Solaris 2.6.

Solaris 2.5 also saw the introduction of support for large kernel memory pages (a large page is typically 4 MB, compared to the normal 8 KB for UltraSPARC and sun4, or 4 KB for sun4m and sun4c).

Some of the other features introduced or improved with Solaris 2.5 include the Name Service Cache Daemon, UNIX File System (UFS) Access Control Lists (ACLs) for finer grained file permissions, and the process tools available in `/usr/proc/bin`.

Solaris 2.5 conforms with the XCU4 (Commands and Utilities) portion of XPG4, and the 10th draft of POSIX.1c. It is also compliant with much of Spec 1170.

2.5.1   Solaris 2.5.1

Solaris 2.5.1 was released the year after Solaris 2.5, in 1996. As well as being the only release to support the PowerPC processor, Solaris 2.5.1 added support for multiprocessor UltraSPARC systems, and large user and group IDs (they were raised to 2,147,483,647, the maximum value of a signed 32-bit integer).

Solaris 2.5.1 conforms to the same standards as Solaris 2.5.

2.6   Solaris 2.6

Released in 1997, the UNIX 95-compliant Solaris 2.6 introduced support for large files: the old 2 GB UFS file size limit was replaced by a 1 TB one (NFS and some other file systems supported full 64-bit file offsets). Solaris 2.6 was also the first release to ship with a Java Virtual Machine (JVM), and was also the first release where CDE was the default desktop environment.

Other notable features were the provision of kernel-based sockets, UFS Direct I/O, processor sets (the ability to bind processes to a specific set of processors), the `isalist` utility (allows users to determine which instructions sets are supported on their machines), and the bundling of the Solaris Software Developer Kit (SDK).

Solaris 2.6 is UNIX 95 branded and conforms to POSIX 1003.1b.

2.7   Solaris 7

The UNIX 98-branded Solaris 7 was the first 64-bit version of Solaris; it shipped in 1998. The 64-bit kernel will run both 32-bit and 64-bit applications, the latter overcoming many of the limitations of the former by supporting a 64-bit virtual address space and removing other 32-bit limitations. The 64-bit functionality was implemented in a manner that allowed 32-bit applications to run unmodified.

> On October 30th, 1998, Sun registered Solaris 7 and subsequent versions as conforming to both the CDE and UNIX 98 Workstation product standards; this was the first ever UNIX 98 Workstation registration.

Two of the features added with Solaris 7 were UFS logging (which allows `fsck` to be avoided in the event of a system crash), and the `noatime` mount option, which ignores access time updates for UFS file systems. Solaris 7 also added the `pgrep` and `pkill` commands, which make it easier to search for or kill a process by using its name rather than its process ID. Also of interest to the software developer was the enhanced `truss` command, which was updated to trace the entry and exit of user functions in addition to the system calls. Finally, Solaris 7 introduced the priority paging algorithm (which was subsequently made available as far back as Solaris 2.5.1 with the addition of a kernel patch).

2.8   Solaris 8

Solaris 8 was released in 2000. The features introduced and updated for this release included the next generation Internet Protocol, IPv6 (although IP Security (IPSec) was only available for IPv4), and the Java 2 SDK, Standard Edition. Solaris 8 also introduced another virtual memory management algorithm, superseding the priority paging algorithm in Solaris 7.

The modular debugger, `mdb`, allows the low-level editing and debugging of user processes and crash dumps, as well as the running kernel and kernel crash dumps. A supplement to the `poll` functions is `/dev/poll`, which provides much higher performance when a large number of events must be polled for on file descriptors that remain open for a long time.

Solaris 8 is UNIX 98 branded.

2.9   Solaris 9

Solaris 9 was released in 2002 and is UNIX 98 branded. Some of its new features included the integration of Solaris Secure Shell (which is based on OpenSSH) and TCP wrappers, a pseudo random number generator which is available as the `/dev/random` and `/dev/urandom` devices (the entropic data is gathered from kernel memory pages and maintains a high level of randomness at all times), IPSec for IPv6, and extended file attributes.

Solaris 9 also added an improved threading library, support for multiple user page sizes, the Remote Shared Memory API (RSMAPI), and integrated the Solaris Volume Manager (previously known as DiskSuite) and the iPlanet LDAP server.

Subsequent update releases of Solaris 9 added features such as support for multiterabyte UFS file systems, Solaris Flash Archives, UFS logging enhancements, and an improved password encryption infrastructure.

2.10   Solaris Standards Compliance

The standards compliance of the various releases of Solaris we cover in this text (plus Solaris 10) are shown in Figure 2.1.

Standard	Solaris version						
	2.5	2.5.1	2.6	7	8	9	10
ISO C	•	•	•	•	•	•	•
SVID	•	•	•	•	•	•	•
POSIX.1–1990	•	•	•	•	•	•	•
POSIX.1b	•	•	•	•	•	•	•
POSIX.1c			•	•	•	•	•
POSIX.1–1996			•	•	•	•	•
SUSv1			•	•	•	•	•
SUSv2				•	•	•	•
SUSv3							•

Figure 2.1   Standards compliance of Solaris.

Solaris complies with many more de facto and de jure standards than we show here; Figure 2.1 shows just the most important standards, that is, those that we describe in Section 2.4.

More details about the standards various releases of Solaris comply with can be found in the `standards`(5) man page.

2.11   Compiling Standards Conforming Applications

On their own, the standard compilers (i.e., cc and gcc) will compile code that does not necessarily comply with any of the standards we just described. If we want to compile our applications so that they do conform to the various standards Solaris supports, we must use the utilities and command line options we show in Figure 2.2.

Specification	Compiler and flags	Feature test macros
ISO C	c89	None
SVID	cc -Xt	None
POSIX.1-1990	c89	_POSIX_SOURCE
POSIX.2-1992	c89	_POSIX_SOURCE and POSIX_C_SOURCE=2
POSIX.1b	c89	_POSIX_C_SOURCE=199309L
POSIX.1c	c89	_POSIX_C_SOURCE=199506L
XPG3	cc -Xa	_XOPEN_SOURCE
XPG4	c89	_XOPEN_SOURCE and _XOPEN_VERSION=4
SUSv1	c89	_XOPEN_SOURCE and _XOPEN_SOURCE_EXTENDED=1
SUSv2	c89	_XOPEN_SOURCE=500
SUSv3	c99	_XOPEN_SOURCE=600

Figure 2.2   Commands and flags required to build standards conforming applications.

Users of gcc can achieve similar results by specifying the -std=*standard* command line option, where *standard* is the desired conformance standard. The gcc documentation details which standards it supports.

There's one further thing we should be cognizant of when we specify compliance with a given standard for our programs: only those interfaces defined by that standard can be used; other programming interfaces are off limits.

2.12   Summary

In this chapter we gave a whirlwind tour of the history of Solaris, from the early versions of SunOS derived from BSD to the latest generation of SVR4-derived Solaris. Included in our tour was a summary of the different windowing systems the various releases included.

We then described the major standards that Solaris complies with: ISO C, SVID, POSIX 1003.1, and the Single UNIX Specification. We also showed how to build applications that conform to these standards.

We concluded the chapter with a brief summary of the versions of Solaris we cover in this book: Solaris 2.5 to Solaris 9 inclusive.

Exercises

2.1   Make a list of all the architectures in your environment (e.g., sun4m, sun4u, and x86). Which ones support 64-bit operation?

2.2   Make a list of all the versions of Solaris in your environment.

Part 2

Fundamental Topics

3

Utility Functions

3.1 Introduction

Solaris provides a large number of utility functions that we can use in our programs, many of which will be familiar to experienced C programmers (even those who don't have a UNIX programming background). We discuss them now because of their ubiquity and because most of the functions are quite straightforward.

The utility functions can be grouped into several categories, including manipulating character strings and byte arrays, dynamic memory allocation and freeing, parsing command line arguments, and error reporting.

Almost half of this chapter describes the functions we can use to perform various operations on characters and character strings. This is because strings and ASCII files are a fundamental part of the UNIX philosophy: local accounts are stored as text in `/etc/passwd` and `/etc/shadow`, network settings are stored in text files (e.g., `/etc/hosts` and `/etc/hostname.hme0`), and most configuration files are also stored as plain text. This allows them to be human readable, portable, editable with a wide range of editors, and parsable with simple ad hoc tools. The binary files employed by other operating systems enjoy none of these benefits; they need dedicated tools to display and manipulate their contents.

Many examples in this chapter use the `printf` function. Very briefly, `printf` allows us to print formatted messages to the standard output stream. Two related functions we use in this chapter have similar functionality: `fprintf` allows us to specify which file stream the formatted message is to be printed to, and `sprintf` enables us to place a formatted message into a buffer. We'll have a lot more to say about these and the other functions provided by the standard I/O library in Chapter 5.

3.2   Manipulating Character Classes

There are two sub-classes of character class manipulation; we can ascertain which of several types a character is (a letter, a digit, etc.), and we can change some characters to another. Note that in this section we don't consider multibyte Unicode characters. (Unicode is a standard that provides a unique number for every character, no matter what the platform, no matter what the program, no matter what the language. All the details about Unicode can be found at the Unicode web site, www.unicode.org.) More specifically, the functions we describe in this section work correctly only on integers in the range 0 to 255 inclusive. Note that because a char is a signed type by default, it is typically wrong to use any of the functions we describe in this section with variables of this type. Values from –128 to –2 are valid for signed chars, but are not in these functions' domain.

3.2.1   Testing Character Class Membership

We can use a dozen functions to determine which class a character belongs to. A character belongs to one or more of the following classes:

- An upper- or lower case letter
- A decimal or hexadecimal digit
- One of the white space characters
- One of the punctuation characters
- A control character

Each of these functions is a predicate that returns false (i.e., 0) if the character being tested is not a member of the class being checked for, or true (i.e., non-zero) if it is.

Some of these functions come in two versions: the default version, and a version that is strictly standards compliant (i.e., is locale aware). Applications wanting to use the standards compliant version of these functions must define __XPG4_CHAR_CLASS__ before including <ctype.h>.

The isalpha, isupper, and islower Functions

These functions are used to determine if a character is an upper- or lower case letter.

```
#include <ctype.h>

int isalpha (int c);

int isupper (int c);

int islower (int c);
```
All three return: see text

The default version of the `isalpha` function returns true if *c* is a character for which `isupper` or `islower` is true.

The standards conforming version of `isalpha` returns true if *c* is a character for which `isupper` or `islower` is true, or any character that is one of the current locale-defined set of characters for which none of `iscntrl`, `isdigit`, `ispunct`, or `isspace` is true. For the C locale, the standards conforming version of `isalpha` is the same as the default one.

The `isupper` function returns true if *c* is a character that is an upper case letter, or is one of the current locale-defined set of characters for which none of `iscntrl`, `isdigit`, `ispunct`, `isspace`, or `islower` is true. In the C locale, `isupper` returns true only for those characters defined as upper case ASCII characters.

The `islower` function returns true if *c* is a character that is a lower case letter, or is one of the current locale-defined set of characters for which none of `iscntrl`, `isdigit`, `ispunct`, `isspace`, or `isupper` is true. In the C locale, `islower` returns true only for those characters defined as lower case ASCII characters.

The `isdigit` and `isxdigit` Functions

These two functions test if a character is a decimal or hexadecimal digit.

```
#include <ctype.h>

int isdigit (int c);

int isxdigit (int c);
```
Both return: see text

The `isdigit` function returns true if *c* is a decimal digit character, i.e., the characters 0 to 9 inclusive.

The default version of the `isxdigit` function is similar to `isdigit`, except it returns true if *c* is a hexadecimal digit, i.e., the characters 0 to 9 inclusive, plus the letters A to F (or a to f).

The standards conforming version of `isxdigit` tests for the same characters as the default one, plus the current locale-defined sets of characters representing the hexadecimal digits 10 to 15 inclusive. In the C locale, the standards conforming version of `isxdigit` is the same as the default one.

The `isalnum` Function

This function returns true if a character is a decimal digit or a letter.

```
#include <ctype.h>

int isalnum (int c);
```
Returns: see text

The `isalnum` function returns true if *c* is an alphanumeric character, i.e., it tests for the set of characters for which `isalpha` or `isdigit` is true.

The `isspace`, `ispunct`, and `iscntrl` Functions

These three functions test for characters that are not alphanumeric.

```
#include <ctype.h>

int isspace (int c);

int ispunct (int c);

int iscntrl (int c);
```
All three return: see text

The `isspace` function returns true if *c* is a white space character: in the C locale, a white space character is either space, tab, carriage return, newline, vertical tab, or form feed. Other locales may define other characters for which `isspace` is false.

The `ispunct` function returns true if *c* is a punctuation character. A punctuation character in the context of `ispunct` is any printable character which is neither a space nor a character for which `isalnum` or `iscntrl` is true.

The `iscntrl` function returns true if *c* is a "control character", as defined by the character set. For ASCII, this any character whose value is less than 32 (the space character).

The `isprint`, `isgraph`, and `isascii` Functions

These last three functions test for a wider, more general range of characters.

```
#include <ctype.h>

int isprint (int c);

int isgraph (int c);

int isascii (int c);
```
All three return: see text

The default version of the `isprint` function returns true if *c* is a printable character. In the context of `isprint`, a printable character is one for which `isupper`, `islower`, `isdigit`, or `ispunct` is true, or the space character.

The standard conforming version of `isprint` returns true if *c* is a character for which `iscntrl` is false, and `isalnum`, `isgraph`, `ispunct`, the space character, and any current locale-defined "print" class are true.

The default version of the `isgraph` function returns true if *c* is a character for which `isupper`, `islower`, `isdigit`, or `ispunct` is true.

The standards conforming version of isgraph returns true if *c* is a character for which isalnum and ispunct is true, or any character in the current locale-defined "graph" class which is neither a space character nor a character for which iscntrl is true.

The isascii function returns true for any ASCII character whose value is from 0 to 127 inclusive.

3.2.2 Changing Character Class Membership

There are times when we need to change, or enforce, the class of a character. Solaris provides two functions to convert a character to lower case, two to convert a character to upper case, and one to convert a character to 7-bit ASCII.

The toupper and _toupper Functions

These two functions are used to ensure that a letter is upper case.

```
#include <ctype.h>

int toupper (int c);

int _toupper (int c);
```
                                                                   Both return: see text

If the character *c* represents a lower case letter, and there exists a corresponding upper case letter (as defined by the LC_CTYPE category of the current locale), the toupper function will return that upper case letter. Otherwise, *c* is returned unchanged.

The _toupper function is the same as toupper except that *c* must be a lower case letter.

The tolower and _tolower Functions

These two functions are used to ensure that a letter is lower case.

```
#include <ctype.h>

int tolower (int c);

int _tolower (int c);
```
                                                                   Both return: see text

If the character *c* represents an upper case letter, and there exists a corresponding lower case letter (as defined by the LC_CTYPE category of the current locale), the tolower function will return that lower case letter. Otherwise, *c* is returned unchanged.

The _tolower function is the same as tolower except that *c* must be an upper case letter.

The `toascii` Function

This function is used to ensure that a character is a member of the 7-bit ASCII character set.

```
#include <ctype.h>

int toascii (int c);
```
Returns: see text

The `toascii` function converts c into a 7-bit ASCII character and returns the result. The character is converted by performing a bitwise-AND of c with 0x7F.

3.2.3 Summary of Character Classes

Program 3.1 demonstrates the character class functions we talked about in this section. The program asks for a character to be tested, and then prints the result of each of the character class member test functions, followed by the effect of calling each of the character class changing functions.

The `scanf` function on line 7 reads a character from standard input and stores it in the variable c. We discuss the `scanf` function in Section 5.8.2.

Let's see what happens when we compile and run Program 3.1.

```
$ ./char_class
Enter the character to test: f
isalpha ('f') is True
isalnum ('f') is True
isascii ('f') is True
iscntrl ('f') is False
isdigit ('f') is False
isgraph ('f') is True
islower ('f') is True
isprint ('f') is True
ispunct ('f') is False
isspace ('f') is False
isupper ('f') is False
isxdigit ('f') is True

tolower ('f') gives f
_tolower ('f') gives F        This is not what we would expect...
toupper ('f') gives F
_toupper ('f') gives F
toascii ('f') gives f
```

Notice that calling `_tolower` with an argument of a lower case letter converts that letter to upper case (in this example, at least). This illustrates why we should call the character class conversion functions only if we know that the character to be converted is within the domain of the function we are calling. To avoid this problem, we could write some code like this:

utils/char_class.c

```
 1 #include <stdio.h>
 2 #include <ctype.h>

 3 int main (void)
 4 {
 5     char c;

 6     printf ("Enter the character to test: ");
 7     scanf ("%c", &c);

 8     printf ("isalpha ('%c') is %s\n", c, isalpha ((int) c) ? "True" : "False");
 9     printf ("isalnum ('%c') is %s\n", c, isalnum ((int) c) ? "True" : "False");
10     printf ("isascii ('%c') is %s\n", c, isascii ((int) c) ? "True" : "False");
11     printf ("iscntrl ('%c') is %s\n", c, iscntrl ((int) c) ? "True" : "False");
12     printf ("isdigit ('%c') is %s\n", c, isdigit ((int) c) ? "True" : "False");
13     printf ("isgraph ('%c') is %s\n", c, isgraph ((int) c) ? "True" : "False");
14     printf ("islower ('%c') is %s\n", c, islower ((int) c) ? "True" : "False");
15     printf ("isprint ('%c') is %s\n", c, isprint ((int) c) ? "True" : "False");
16     printf ("ispunct ('%c') is %s\n", c, ispunct ((int) c) ? "True" : "False");
17     printf ("isspace ('%c') is %s\n", c, isspace ((int) c) ? "True" : "False");
18     printf ("isupper ('%c') is %s\n", c, isupper ((int) c) ? "True" : "False");
19     printf ("isxdigit ('%c') is %s\n\n", c,
20         isxdigit ((int) c) ? "True" : "False");

21     printf ("tolower ('%c') gives %c\n", c, tolower ((int) c));
22     printf ("_tolower ('%c') gives %c\n", c, _tolower ((int) c));
23     printf ("toupper ('%c') gives %c\n", c, toupper ((int) c));
24     printf ("_toupper ('%c') gives %c\n", c, _toupper ((int) c));
25     printf ("toascii ('%c') gives %c\n", c, toascii ((int) c));

26     return (0);
27 }
```

utils/char_class.c

Program 3.1 Showing the character class of a character.

```
if (isupper (c))
    return (_tolower (c));
```

A better approach would be to use `tolower` and `toupper` instead of `_tolower` and `_toupper`.

3.3 Manipulating Character Strings

In the C programming language (which doesn't include strings as one of its basic data types), a string is a contiguous array of non-NUL bytes; a NUL character (a byte whose bits are all zero) marks the end of the string. (Some programming languages, e.g., Pascal, store the length of a string as part of it.)

> Some texts refer to a string's terminating character as NULL or null. We will use the ASCII term "NUL" to mean a character whose bits are all 0, and the term "NULL" to mean a pointer that doesn't point anywhere. These two terms are not interchangeable in meaning, even though they both have a value of 0 (NUL is an 8-bit quantity, whereas NULL is a 32-bit or 64-bit quantity).

Interestingly enough, the ISO C Standard itself uses the word "null" to define a string's terminating character.

A quoted string is actually just a convenient method of constructing a character array. That is,

```
char *string = "string";
```

is a shorthand way of writing

```
char string [7] = {'s', 't', 'r', 'i', 'n', 'g', '\0'};
```

Manipulating strings is something that programs do quite frequently. The C programming language, together with some of the libraries provided with Solaris, provides a wealth of functions for string manipulation. Among the operations we can perform on strings are: getting the length of a string, comparing two strings, and copying strings.

The functions we look at in this section work correctly only on NUL terminated strings; the functions we discuss in Section 3.4 should be used to operate on arbitrary binary data.

3.3.1 Finding the Length of a String

We can use three functions to determine the length of a string, two of which are used to calculate the length of the initial part of a string.

The `strlen` Function

We use the `strlen` function to determine the length of a string.

```
#include <string.h>

size_t strlen (const char *s);
```
Returns: the number of bytes in s

The `strlen` function returns the number of bytes in the string pointed to by s, excluding the terminating NUL character.

The `strspn` and `strcspn` Functions

The `strspn` and `strcspn` functions are used to ascertain the length of initial string segments.

```
#include <string.h>

size_t strspn (const char *s1, const char *s2);

size_t strcspn (const char *s1, const char *s2);
```
Both return: see text

The `strspn` function returns the number of characters in the initial segment of the string pointed to by *s1* that consists entirely of characters from the string pointed to by *s2*. Conversely, `strcspn` returns the number of characters in the initial segment of *s1* that consists entirely of characters that are not in *s2*.

Example: Using `strlen`, `strspn`, and `strcspn`

Program 3.2 demonstrates the use of these functions.

—————————————————————————————————————— *utils/strlen.c*
```
 1 #include <stdio.h>
 2 #include <string.h>

 3 int main (void)
 4 {
 5     char *s1 = "aabbccdd12345678";
 6     char *s2 = "abc123";
 7     char *s3 = "123";

 8     printf ("strlen (\"%s\") = %d\n", s1, strlen (s1));
 9     printf ("strspn (\"%s\", \"%s\") = %d\n", s1, s2, strspn (s1, s2));
10     printf ("strcspn (\"%s\", \"%s\") = %d\n", s1, s3, strcspn (s1, s3));

11     return (0);
12 }
```
—————————————————————————————————————— *utils/strlen.c*

Program 3.2 Using `strlen`, `strspn`, and `strcspn`.

When we compile and run this short program, we get the following output.
```
$ ./strlen
strlen ("aabbccdd12345678") = 16
strspn ("aabbccdd12345678", "abc123") = 6
strcspn ("aabbccdd12345678", "123") = 8
```
A total of 16 characters are in the first string. The first six of these consist entirely of characters from the string "abc123" (the counting stops with the first "d", which isn't in the second string), and the first eight characters are those that are not in the string "123".

3.3.2 Comparing Strings

We can compare two strings for equivalence, or find out which is lexicographically greater or lesser. On most systems that use an ASCII character set, lexicographical order is the same as alphabetical order. On systems that use a different character encoding (e.g., EBCDIC), this may not be true.

> One thing we must be wary of is that the C locale sorts mixed case characters differently than other locales. This is most apparent when we use `ls` to list the files in a directory. In the C locale, files starting with an upper case letter will be listed before those starting with a lower case one. In other locales, the files starting with an upper case letter are likely to be mixed in with the files that start with a lower case one.

All the string comparison functions assume the default locale, "C". For some locales (i.e., those that use Unicode multibyte strings), the strings should be transformed using the `strxfrm` function we discuss in Appendix A before passing them to these functions. We'll talk more about locales in Appendix A.

We have four string comparison functions at our disposal. Two are case sensitive, the others are not. A case-sensitive comparison would determine that "ABC" is not the same as "abc", whereas a case-insensitive comparison would find them the same.

The `strcmp` and `strncmp` Functions

The `strcmp` and `strncmp` functions perform case-sensitive string comparisons.

```
#include <string.h>

int strcmp (const char *s1, const char *s2);

int strncmp (const char *s1, const char *s2, size_t n);
```
                                                                              Both return: see text

The `strcmp` function compares *s1* with *s2*. If the strings are the same, 0 is returned. If *s1* is lexicographically greater than *s2*, then a positive integer is returned; similarly, if *s1* is less than *s2*, a negative integer is returned. The sign of a non-zero result is determined by the sign of the difference between the values of the first pair of bytes that differ in the strings being compared.

The `strncmp` function performs the same comparison as `strcmp`, but only looks at the first *n* bytes (rather than the whole string).

In both functions, bytes following a NUL byte are not compared.

Example: Sorting strings using `strcmp`

Program 3.3 illustrates the use of `strcmp` in a sorting program. The sort we use in this example is called a *bubble sort* because the sorted values "bubble" up the list until they get to their correct location. We use a bubble sort for this example because the algorithm is very simple. (It's also not very efficient: real programs should use the `qsort` function—the Solaris implementation of which uses the Quicksort algorithm—instead.) Readers interested in knowing the full details of this and many other sorting algorithms will find [Knuth 1998] especially useful.

Read strings to be sorted from standard input

12–17 We use a `for` loop to read up to NUM_STR lines from standard input, using the `fgets` function we describe in Section 5.6.3. Each string is stored in an array, and a pointer to each string is stored in another array. The latter gets passed to our `bubble_sort` function.

————————————————————————————————— utils/bubble_sort1.c

```
1 #include <stdio.h>
2 #include <string.h>

3 #define STR_LEN 80
4 #define NUM_STR 1024

5 static void bubble_sort (char **string_ptrs, int num_strings);

6 int main (void)
7 {
8     char strings [NUM_STR] [STR_LEN];
9     char *string_ptrs [NUM_STR];
10    int num_strings;
11    int i;

12    for (num_strings = 0; num_strings < NUM_STR; num_strings++) {
13        if (fgets (strings [num_strings], STR_LEN, stdin) == NULL)
14            break;
15        strings [num_strings] [strlen (strings [num_strings]) - 1] = '\0';
16        string_ptrs [num_strings] = strings [num_strings];
17    }

18    bubble_sort (string_ptrs, num_strings);

19    for (i = 0; i < num_strings; i++) {
20        printf ("String %d = '%s'\n", i, string_ptrs [i]);
21    }

22    return (0);
23 }

24 static void bubble_sort (char **string_ptrs, int num_strings)
25 {
26    char *tmp_string;
27    int i;
28    int done;

29    done = 0;

30    while (!done) {
31        done = 1;
32        num_strings--;
33        for (i = 0; i < num_strings; i++) {
34            if (strcmp (string_ptrs [i], string_ptrs [i + 1]) > 0) {
35                tmp_string = string_ptrs [i];
36                string_ptrs [i] = string_ptrs [i + 1];
37                string_ptrs [i + 1] = tmp_string;
38                done = 0;
39            }
40        }
41    }
42 }
```

————————————————————————————————— utils/bubble_sort1.c

Program 3.3 Bubble sort using strcmp.

Sort the strings

18   Call our `bubble_sort` function to sort the strings.

Print out sorted strings

19–21   After the strings are sorted, we print them out.

Bubble sort

24–42   This function sorts the strings using a bubble sort. We iterate through the input, comparing adjacent strings. If the first string we compare is lexicographically greater the next, the two strings are exchanged. If no exchanges are performed, then we are finished.

When we run Program 3.3, this is what we see.

```
$ cat /tmp/test_file
This
is
a
TEST
file.
$ ./bubble_sort1 < /tmp/test_file
String 0 = 'TEST'
String 1 = 'This'
String 2 = 'a'
String 3 = 'file.'
String 4 = 'is'
```

Notice that the word "TEST" in all upper case has been sorted to the top of the list. This is because the upper case characters precede the lower case ones in the ASCII character set (the `ascii(5)` man page shows the collation sequence for all 128 characters of the ASCII character set).

The `strcasecmp` and `strncasecmp` Functions

The `strcasecmp` and `strncasecmp` functions compare strings in a case-insensitive manner.

```
#include <strings.h>

int strcasecmp (const char *s1, const char *s2);

int strncasecmp (const char *s1, const char *s2, size_t n);
```
                                                            Both return: see text

These functions perform the same comparisons as the `strcmp` and `strncmp` functions we described in the previous section, but disregard differences in case when comparing upper- and lower case letters (they assume the use of the ASCII character set).

Example: Sorting strings using `strcasecmp`

We can use the `strcasecmp` function as the basis for the comparisons in our bubble sort from Program 3.3 by including `<strings.h>` after `<string.h>`, and by changing `strcmp` in line 34 to `strcasecmp`.

Let's see what happens when we run our new program:

```
$ cat /tmp/test_file
This
is
a
TEST
file.
$ ./bubble_sort2 < /tmp/test_file
String 0 = 'a'
String 1 = 'file.'
String 2 = 'is'
String 3 = 'TEST'
String 4 = 'This'
```

This time we see that the word list has been sorted with disregard for letter case: the upper case word "TEST" appears in the list, rather than at the top, and similarly for the word "This".

3.3.3 String Concatenation

String concatenation is the process of adding one string to the end of another. Solaris provides us with three functions to accomplish this.

The `strcat`, `strncat`, and `strlcat` Functions

We use the `strcat`, `strncat`, and `strlcat` functions to join strings.

```
#include <string.h>

char *strcat (char *dst, const char *src);

char *strncat (char *dst, const char *src, size_t n);

                                                        Both return: dst

size_t strlcat (char *dst, const char *src, size_t dstsize);

                                                        Returns: see text
```

The `strcat` function appends a copy of *src*, including the terminating NUL character, to the end of *dst*. The first character of *src* overwrites the NUL at the end of the string pointed to by *dst*; *dst* is returned.

> The etymology of these function names, as well as the `cat`(1) command, is fairly well known: they derive from the word "catenate", which means "to connect like the links of a chain".

Care must be taken to ensure that the buffer pointed to by *dst* is big enough to hold the concatenated string. If it isn't, potentially disastrous buffer overflow bugs will occur. One way to avoid buffer overflows is to use the `strncat` function, which does the same as `strcat`, but only appends at most *n* characters to *dst*.

The `strlcat` function is similar to `strncat`, but provides an easier method of checking for buffer overflows. At most, (*dstsize* - `strlen` (*dst*) - 1) characters from *src* are appended to *dst*, where *dstsize* is the size of the buffer pointed to by *dst*. Like `strcat` and `strncat`, the first character of *src* overwrites the NUL character at the end of *dst*. The `strlcat` function was introduced with Solaris 8.

The return value from `strlcat` is the sum of the lengths of the two strings, that is, `strlen` (*src*) + `strlen` (*dst*). This allows us to check for attempted buffer overflows as follows:

```
if (strlcat (dst, src, dstsize) >= dstsize)
    printf ("Buffer overflow attempted.\n");
```

Example: Concatenating strings

Program 3.4 uses `strlcat` to concatenate several strings safely.

———————————————————————————————— utils/strlcat.c

```
 1  #include <stdio.h>
 2  #include <string.h>
 3  #include "ssp.h"

 4  #define BUFFER_LEN 80
 5  #define STR_LEN 80
 6  #define NUM_STR 1024

 7  int main (void)
 8  {
 9      char strings [NUM_STR] [STR_LEN];
10      char buf [BUFFER_LEN];
11      int num_strings;
12      int i;

13      for (num_strings = 0; num_strings < NUM_STR; num_strings++) {
14          if (fgets (strings [num_strings], STR_LEN, stdin) == NULL)
15              break;
16          strings [num_strings] [strlen (strings [num_strings]) - 1] = '\0';
17      }

18      buf [0] = '\0';

19      for (i = 0; i < num_strings; i++) {
20          if (strlcat (buf, strings [i], BUFFER_LEN) >= BUFFER_LEN)
21              err_quit ("Buffer overflow on string %d: '%s'", i + 1, buf);
22          if (strlcat (buf, ", ", BUFFER_LEN) >= BUFFER_LEN)
23              err_quit ("Buffer overflow on string %d: '%s'", i + 1, buf);
24      }

25      printf ("Buffer = '%s'\n", buf);

26      return (0);
27  }
```

———————————————————————————————— utils/strlcat.c

Program 3.4 Safe string concatenation.

Read in strings from standard input

13–17 Like Program 3.3, we use `fgets` to read in an array of strings from standard input.

Ensure our buffer starts with a length of 0

18 We make sure the first element of `buf` is NUL. We do this because we are concatenating strings, and we have no idea what `buf` contains (being allocated from the stack, it's quite likely that `buf` will contain garbage). By setting the first byte to the NUL character, we ensure that the first string we concatenate will start at the first character of `buf`.

Safely concatenate the strings

19–24 Using `strlcat`, each string in the array we read in is attempted to be concatenated to `buf`. We follow each array element by a comma so that we can see the component strings when we print out the result. Note that we check for buffer overflows and print out an appropriate error message.

Let's see what happens when we run Program 3.4 a couple of times. The second time we run it, we'll change the value of BUFFER_LEN on line 4 to cause a buffer overflow attempt.

```
$ ./strlcat < /tmp/test_file
Buffer = 'This, is, a, TEST, file., '
```
                              Change BUFFER_LEN *to 15 and recompile.*
```
$ ./strlcat < /tmp/test_file
Buffer overflow on string 4: 'This, is, a, T'
```

On the second test, `strlcat` stops after the first character of the string "TEST".

3.3.4 Copying Strings

There are times when we want to copy a string from one buffer to another. The three members of the `strcpy` family enable us to accomplish this.

The `strcpy`, `strncpy`, and `strlcpy` Functions

These functions allow us to copy strings.

```
#include <string.h>

char *strcpy (char *dst, const char *src);

char *strncpy (char *dst, const char *src, size_t n);
```
                                                              Both return: *dst*
```
size_t strlcpy (char *dst, const char *src, size_t dstsize);
```
                                                              Returns: see text

The `strcpy` function copies the string pointed to by *src*, up to and including the terminating NUL character, into the buffer pointed to by *dst*, overwriting its previous contents; *dst* is returned. No check is made to ensure that the buffer pointed to by *dst* is large enough to hold the string, so we must take care to avoid buffer overflows when using `strcpy`.

The `strncpy` function also copies *src* to *dst*. However, `strncpy` will copy exactly *n* characters, truncating *src* or adding NUL characters to *dst* as necessary. If the length of *src* is the same as or exceeds *n*, the resulting string will not be NUL terminated, so again, care must be take to avoid buffer overflows (compare this with `strncat`, which does ensure that the resulting string is NUL terminated). One way to prevent buffer overflows when using `strncpy` is to use something like the following code sequence:

```
char dst [BUF_LEN];

strncpy (dst, src, BUF_LEN - 1);
dst [BUF_LEN - 1] = '\0';
```

Solaris 8 introduced the `strlcpy` function, which is similar to `strncpy`, but provides an easier method of checking for buffer overflows. At most, (*dstsize* − 1) characters from *src* are copied to *dst*, where *dstsize* is the size of the buffer pointed to by *dst*. The resulting string is always NUL terminated.

The return value from `strlcpy` is the length of *src*, i.e., `strlen` (*src*). Attempted buffer overflows can be checked for as follows:

```
if (strlcpy (dst, src, dstsize) >= dstsize)
    printf ("Buffer overflow attempted.\n");
```

Example: Copying strings safely

Program 3.5 safely copies strings while avoiding buffer overflows.

Program 3.5 reads in a line from standard input, and then copies it to the buffer `buf` using `strlcpy`. It prints out the resulting buffer, with a suitable message if a buffer overflow was detected.

```
$ ./strlcpy
This should be OK.
Buffer = 'This should be OK.'
$ ./strlcpy
This will cause a buffer overflow.
Buffer overflow on detected, buffer = 'This will cause a b'
```

3.3.5 String Searching Functions

There are times when we need to find the location of a character or characters within a string. We can search for a specific character, any character from a given set, or a substring within a string.

The `strchr` and `strrchr` Functions

The `strchr` and `strrchr` functions are used to find a specific character in a string.

-- *utils/strlcpy.c*

```
 1 #include <stdio.h>
 2 #include <string.h>
 3 #include "ssp.h"

 4 #define BUFFER_LEN 20
 5 #define STR_LEN 80

 6 int main (void)
 7 {
 8     char string [STR_LEN];
 9     char buf [BUFFER_LEN];

10     fgets (string, STR_LEN, stdin);
11     string [strlen (string) - 1] = '\0';

12     if (strlcpy (buf, string, BUFFER_LEN) >= BUFFER_LEN)
13         err_quit ("Buffer overflow on detected, buffer = '%s'", buf);

14     printf ("Buffer = '%s'\n", buf);

15     return (0);
16 }
```
-- *utils/strlcpy.c*

Program 3.5 Safe string copying.

```
#include <string.h>

char *strchr (const char *s, int c);

char *strrchr (const char *s, int c);
```
                                                          Both return: see text

The `strchr` function is used to find the first occurrence of the character *c* in the string *s*. If *c* is not in *s*, then a NULL pointer is returned.

Conversely, `strrchr` is used to find the last occurrence of *c* in the string *s*. As with `strchr`, if *c* is not in *s*, then a NULL pointer is returned.

Example: Finding a character in a string

The next few examples highlight the character or characters we are looking for in a string by using the `highlight` function we show in Program 3.6.

The `highlight` function highlights one or more characters in the string `line` by replacing them with a carat (^); the characters not to be highlighted are replaced by spaces. The first character to be replaced is pointed to by `start`; `finish` points to the last character to replace.

To get the highlighting effect seen in the examples, we first print the line that contains the characters to highlight, call the `highlight` function to change the string as just described, and then reprint the same line. The reprinted line will contain just spaces and carats in the appropriate places.

———————————————————————————— utils/highlight.c

```
1 void highlight (char *line, char *start, char *finish)
2 {
3     char *c;

4     for (c = line; c < start; c++)
5         *c = ' ';

6     for (; c <= finish; c++)
7         *c = '^';

8     for (c = finish + 1; *c != '\0'; c++)
9         *c = ' ';
10 }
```

———————————————————————————— utils/highlight.c

Program 3.6 Our highlight function.

Program 3.7 illustrates the use of the strchr function to find the first occurrence of a character in a string.

———————————————————————————— utils/strchr.c

```
1 #include <stdio.h>
2 #include <string.h>
3 #include "ssp.h"

4 extern void highlight (char *line, char *start, char *finish);

5 int main (int argc, char **argv)
6 {
7     char buf [LINE_LEN];
8     char *c;
9     char look_for;

10    if (argc != 2)
11        err_quit ("Usage: strchr character");

12    look_for = *argv [1];

13    while (fgets (buf, LINE_LEN, stdin) != NULL) {
14        buf [strlen (buf) - 1] = '\0';
15        if ((c = strchr (buf, look_for)) != NULL) {
16            printf ("%s\n", buf);
17            highlight (buf, c, c);
18            printf ("%s\n", buf);
19        }
20    }

21    return (0);
22 }
```

———————————————————————————— utils/strchr.c

Program 3.7 Searching for the first occurrence of a character.

Initialize the character to look for

12 This line sets the variable look_for to be the same as the first character of the second command line argument (the first argument is the name of the command itself). We'll have more to say about command line arguments in Section 3.8.

Search each line for the requested character

13–20 For every line that we can read from standard input, look for the first occurrence of the requested character. If the character we're looking for is in the current line, highlight this fact by using our `highlight` function.

When we compile and run Program 3.7, these are the results we get:

```
$ cat /tmp/test_file
The quick brown fox jumps over the lazy dog.
There's no letter A in this line.
She sells sea shells on the sea shore.
A man, a plan, a canal-Panama!
$ ./strchr a < /tmp/test_file
The quick brown fox jumps over the lazy dog.
                               ^

She sells sea shells on the sea shore.
        ^

A man, a plan, a canal-Panama!
   ^
```

The last line of our test file is a palindrome—in fact, it is probably the best known example of a palindrome—i.e., a word or phrase that reads the same backward as forward. In October 1983, Jim Saxe, a computer science graduate student at Carnegie-Mellon University, added "a cat" to the list. A few weeks later, Guy Jacobson extended the Panama palindrome to 17 words: "A man, a plan, a cat, a ham, a yak, a yam, a hat, a canal—Panama!". Also in 1983, Guy Steele produced a 49 word variation: "A man, a plan, a canoe, pasta, heros, rajahs, a coloratura, maps, snipe, percale, macaroni, a gag, a banana bag, a tan, a tag, a banana bag again (or a camel), a crepe, pins, Spam, a rut, a Rolo, cash, a jar, sore hats, a peon, a canal—Panama!".

The next year, Dan Hoey wrote a program in C that used the UNIX dictionary for the `spell` program to generate the following 540 word Panama palindrome: A man, a plan, a caret, a ban, a myriad, a sum, a lac, a liar, a hoop, a pint, a catalpa, a gas, an oil, a bird, a yell, a vat, a caw, a pax, a wag, a tax, a nay, a ram, a cap, a yam, a gay, a tsar, a wall, a car, a luger, a ward, a bin, a woman, a vassal, a wolf, a tuna, a nit, a pall, a fret, a watt, a bay, a daub, a tan, a cab, a datum, a gall, a hat, a fag, a zap, a say, a jaw, a lay, a wet, a gallop, a tug, a trot, a trap, a tram, a torr, a caper, a top, a tonk, a toll, a ball, a fair, a sax, a minim, a tenor, a bass, a passer, a capital, a rut, an amen, a ted, a cabal, a tang, a sun, an ass, a maw, a sag, a jam, a dam, a sub, a salt, an axon, a sail, an ad, a wadi, a radian, a room, a rood, a rip, a tad, a pariah, a revel, a reel, a reed, a pool, a plug, a pin, a peek, a parabola, a dog, a pat, a cud, a nu, a fan, a pal, a rum, a nod, an eta, a lag, an eel, a batik, a mug, a mot, a nap, a maxim, a mood, a leek, a grub, a gob, a gel, a drab, a citadel, a total, a cedar, a tap, a gag, a rat, a manor, a bar, a gal, a cola, a pap, a yaw, a tab, a raj, a gab, a nag, a pagan, a bag, a jar, a bat, a way, a papa, a local, a gar, a baron, a mat, a rag, a gap, a tar, a decal, a tot, a led, a tic, a bard, a leg, a bog, a burg, a keel, a doom, a mix, a map, an atom, a gum, a kit, a baleen, a gala, a ten, a don, a mural, a pan, a faun, a ducat, a pagoda, a lob, a rap, a keep, a nip, a gulp, a loop, a deer, a leer, a lever, a hair, a pad, a tapir, a door, a moor, an aid, a raid, a wad, an alias, an ox, an atlas, a bus, a madam, a jag, a saw, a mass, an anus, a gnat, a lab, a cadet, an em, a natural, a tip, a caress, a pass, a baronet, a minimax, a sari, a fall, a ballot, a knot, a pot, a rep, a carrot, a mart, a part, a tort, a gut, a poll, a gateway, a law, a jay, a sap, a zag, a fat, a hall, a gamut, a dab, a can, a tabu, a day, a batt, a waterfall, a patina, a nut, a flow, a lass, a van, a mow, a nib, a draw, a regular, a call, a war, a stay, a gam, a yap, a cam, a ray, an ax, a tag, a wax, a paw, a cat, a valley, a drib, a lion, a saga, a plat, a catnip, a pooh, a rail, a calamus, a dairyman, a bater, a canal—Panama!".

There are numerous other examples of palindromes, many *much* longer than this one.

We can search for the last occurrence of a character by changing the `strchr` on line 16 to `strrchr`, which would give these results on the same data:

```
$ ./strrchr a < /tmp/test_file
The quick brown fox jumps over the lazy dog.
                                ^
She sells sea shells on the sea shore.
                          ^
A man, a plan, a canal-Panama!
                      ^
```

The `strpbrk` and `strrspn` Functions

These functions are used to find the location of one of several characters in a string.

```
#include <string.h>

char *strpbrk (const char *s1, const char *s2);

cc [ flag ... ] file ... -lgen [ library ... ]
#include <libgen.h>

char *strrspn (const char *string, const char *tc);
```
Both return: see text

We can use the `strpbrk` function to find the first occurrence of any of the characters from the string *s2* in *s1*. If there are no matches, a NULL pointer is returned.

The `strrspn` function does the opposite: it is used to trim characters from a string. It searches from the end of *string* for the first character that is not in the string pointed to by *tc*. If one of the characters in *tc* is found, `strrspn` returns a pointer to the next character. If not, a pointer to *string* is returned.

We can use `strrspn` to strip trailing white space from a line; for example, we just call `strrspn` with our line of input, and set *tc* to the white space characters. We then set the character we get a pointer to to NUL, thus terminating the string at the first trailing white space character.

Example: Finding one of a group of characters

Program 3.8 searches for the first occurrence of any of the supplied characters by using the `strpbrk` function.

When we run Program 3.8 using the same data file as before, we get these results:

```
$ ./strpbrk osn < /tmp/test_file
The quick brown fox jumps over the lazy dog.
          ^
There's no letter A in this line.
     ^
She sells sea shells on the sea shore.
     ^
A man, a plan, a canal-Panama!
     ^
```

―― *utils/strpbrk.c*

```
1  #include <stdio.h>
2  #include <string.h>
3  #include "ssp.h"

4  extern void highlight (char *line, char *start, char *finish);

5  int main (int argc, char **argv)
6  {
7      char buf [LINE_LEN];
8      char *c;

9      if (argc != 2)
10         err_quit ("Usage: %s character", argv [0]);

11     while (fgets (buf, LINE_LEN, stdin) != NULL) {
12         buf [strlen (buf) - 1] = '\0';
13         if ((c = strpbrk (buf, argv [1])) != NULL) {
14             printf ("%s\n", buf);
15             highlight (buf, c, c);
16             printf ("%s\n", buf);
17         }
18     }

19     return (0);
20 }
```
―― *utils/strpbrk.c*

Program 3.8 Find the first of several characters.

The `strstr` and `strfind` Functions

If we need to location of a substring within a string, one of these two functions will be useful.

```
#include <string.h>

char *strstr (const char *s1, const char *s2);

cc [ flag ... ] file ... -lgen [ library ... ]
#include <libgen.h>

int strfind (const char *as1, const char *as2);
```
                                                      Both return: see text

The `strstr` returns the location of the first occurrence of the string *s2* within *s1*. If *s2* is not found in *s1*, a NULL pointer is returned, and if *s2* is a zero length string (i.e., ""), *s1* is returned.

The `strfind` function is similar, except that it returns the offset of the first occurrence of *as2* in *as1*. If *as2* is not a substring of *as1*, −1 is returned.

Example: Finding a substring

We can use Program 3.9 to locate a substring within a string.

utils/strstr.c

```
 1 #include <stdio.h>
 2 #include <string.h>
 3 #include "ssp.h"

 4 extern void highlight (char *line, char *start, char *finish);

 5 int main (int argc, char **argv)
 6 {
 7     char buf [LINE_LEN];
 8     char *c;

 9     if (argc != 2)
10         err_quit ("Usage: strstrs character");

11     while (fgets (buf, LINE_LEN, stdin) != NULL) {
12         buf [strlen (buf) - 1] = '\0';
13         if ((c = strstr (buf, argv [1])) != NULL) {
14             printf ("%s\n", buf);
15             highlight (buf, c, c + (strlen (argv [1]) - 1));
16             printf ("%s\n", buf);
17         }
18     }

19     return (0);
20 }
```

utils/strstr.c

Program 3.9 Searching for a substring.

When we run Program 3.9 on a new test file, this is what we get:

```
$ cat /tmp/test_file
This is the first line.
No pain, no gain.
Are you for or against?
This is the last line.
$ ./strstr ain < /tmp/test_file
No pain, no gain.
    ^^^
Are you for or against?
            ^^^
```

3.3.6 Duplicating Strings

There are times when we want to duplicate a string while dynamically allocating memory for the new copy. The strdup function is used to duplicate a string, placing the copy in a region of dynamically allocated memory.

```
#include <string.h>

char *strdup (const char *s1);
```
Returns: see text

We use the `strdup` function to duplicate the string *s1*, storing the duplicate in memory dynamically allocated using the `malloc` function we describe in Section 3.5.2. If there is insufficient memory for the new string, a NULL pointer is returned; otherwise, a pointer to the new string is returned.

The `strdup` function is particularly useful when we want to save strings of arbitrary length having to preallocate many arrays of the largest possible size. Instead, we can just preallocate one large array and use `strdup` to duplicate it into dynamically allocated memory. This has the further advantage of using the heap for string storage rather than the stack, which is usually much more limited in size than the heap. (We'll discuss the memory layout of a process, including the heap and stack, in Section 14.6.)

3.3.7 Splitting a String into Tokens

Many programs need to split a string into its component tokens. In the context of a given program, a *token* is a meaningful unit, similar to a word in speech. Tokens in a string aren't necessarily delimited by spaces; almost any character can be a delimiter.

The `strtok` and `strtok_r` Functions

We use the `strtok` and `strtok_r` functions to retrieve the first and subsequent tokens sequentially from a string.

```
#include <string.h>

char *strtok (char *s1, const char *s2);

char *strtok_r (char *s1, const char *s2, char **lasts);
```
Both return: see text

We use the `strtok` function to split the string pointed to by *s1* into a sequence tokens. Each token is delimited by one or more of the characters in *s2* (the set of delimiting characters specified by *s2* may be different from call to call). The first call to `strtok`, with *s1* pointing to the string to be tokenized, returns a pointer to the first character of the first token. A NUL character is written into *s1* immediately following the last character of the returned token.

Subsequent calls to `strtok` (which keeps track of its position within *s1* between function calls), with *s1* being a NULL pointer, return successive tokens in *s1* until no more tokens remain, in which case a NULL pointer is returned.

The `strtok_r` is a thread-safe version of `strtok`. It works the same as `strtok`, except that *lasts* is a pointer to a string placeholder, which is used to keep track of the next substring in which to search for the next token.

Example: Tokenizing using `strtok_r`

Program 3.10 uses the `strtok_r` function to split lines into tokens.

—— *utils/strtok_r.c*
```
 1 #include <stdio.h>
 2 #include <string.h>
 3 #include "ssp.h"

 4 int main (int argc, char **argv)
 5 {
 6     char buf [LINE_LEN];
 7     char *c;
 8     char *ptr;

 9     if (argc != 2)
10         err_quit ("Usage: strtok_r characters");

11     while (fgets (buf, LINE_LEN, stdin) != NULL) {
12         buf [strlen (buf) - 1] = '\0';
13         if ((c = strtok_r (buf, argv [1], &ptr)) != NULL) {
14             printf ("Tokens found: '%s'", c);
15             while ((c = strtok_r (NULL, argv [1], &ptr)) != NULL)
16                 printf (", '%s'", c);
17             printf ("\n");
18         }
19     }

20     return (0);
21 }
```
—— *utils/strtok_r.c*

Program 3.10 Splitting lines into tokens.

Tokenize standard input

11–19 One or more lines from standard input are read and tokenized; the characters used to delimit the tokens are specified on the command line. We call `strtok_r` with the first argument set to `buf` to find the first token in the line. Then we loop through the remaining tokens on the line by calling `strtok_r` with the first argument set to NULL.

When we run Program 3.10, we get the results below.

```
$ cat /tmp/test_file
This is the first line.
No pain, no gain.
Are you for or against?
This is the last line.
$ ./strtok_r " ,.?" < /tmp/test_file
Tokens found: 'This', 'is', 'the', 'first', 'line'
Tokens found: 'No', 'pain', 'no', 'gain'
Tokens found: 'Are', 'you', 'for', 'or', 'against'
Tokens found: 'This', 'is', 'the', 'last', 'line'
```

Note that we've tokenized the English words, using white space and punctuation characters to delimit them.

The `bufsplit` Function

We use the `bufsplit` function when we want to tokenize a whole string at once.

```
cc [ flag ... ] file ... -lgen [ library ... ]
#include <libgen.h>

size_t bufsplit (char *buf, size_t n, char **a);
```
Returns: see text

The `bufsplit` function has a similar effect as multiple calls to `strtok`. A pointer to each of the first *n* tokens in *buf* is stored in the array *a*. If *buf* is not NULL, `bufsplit` returns the number of tokens assigned to the array *a*; otherwise, 0 is returned and *buf* is unchanged. If there are fewer than *n* tokens in *buf*, the remaining elements in *a* will point to the address of the NUL character at the end of *buf*. The delimiting characters in *buf* are changed to NULs by `bufsplit`.

By default, the tokens are delimited by tab or newline characters, but the delimiting characters may be changed by calling `bufsplit` with *buf* pointing to a string that contains the new delimiting characters, setting *n* to zero, and making *a* NULL.

Example: Tokenizing using `bufsplit`

Program 3.11 is essentially a reimplementation of Program 3.10, using `bufsplit` instead of `strtok_r`.

Compiling and running Program 3.11 gives results similar to Program 3.10.

```
$ ./bufsplit " ,.?" < /tmp/test_file
5 tokens found: 'This', 'is', 'the', 'first', 'line'
5 tokens found: 'No', 'pain', '', 'no', 'gain'
5 tokens found: 'Are', 'you', 'for', 'or', 'against'
5 tokens found: 'This', 'is', 'the', 'last', 'line'
```

It is interesting to observe how `bufsplit` handles two or more consecutive delimiters. In the second line of our output, the repeated delimiter (in this case, the space after the comma) is tokenized into a zero-length string. The are two reasons for this:

1. The `bufsplit` function is usually used to tokenize files with a fixed number of fields with only one delimiter between them. An example of this would be `/etc/passwd`, in which empty fields are represented by two adjacent colons. Another example would be a comma-separated value (CSV) file, which might get output from a database or spreadsheet dumping program. With these sorts of files, it's important to be able to recognize empty fields, and hence zero-length strings are returned for adjacent delimiters.

```
 1 #include <stdio.h>
 2 #include <string.h>
 3 #include <libgen.h>
 4 #include "ssp.h"

 5 #define NUM_TOKENS 10

 6 int main (int argc, char **argv)
 7 {
 8     char buf [LINE_LEN];
 9     char *tokens [NUM_TOKENS];
10     int c;
11     int i;

12     if (argc != 2)
13         err_quit ("Usage: bufsplit characters");

14     bufsplit (argv [1], 0, NULL);

15     while (fgets (buf, LINE_LEN, stdin) != NULL) {
16         buf [strlen (buf) - 1] = '\0';
17         if ((c = bufsplit (buf, NUM_TOKENS, tokens)) != NULL) {
18             printf ("%d tokens found: '%s'", c, tokens [0]);
19             for (i = 1; i < c; i++)
20                 printf (", '%s'", tokens [i]);
21             printf ("\n");
22         }
23     }

24     return (0);
25 }
```

Program 3.11 Another method of splitting a line into tokens.

2. Ignoring multiple occurrences of the delimiter characters loses information (the fact that there are multiple delimiters). It is fairly trivial, in subsequent processing, to treat empty strings as absent if that is what we want.

3.3.8 Functions for Transforming Strings

Solaris provides five functions for transforming strings: two copy a string while compressing escape codes; two copy a string while expanding control characters to their C language escape sequence; and the last is a general string transformation routine, which substitutes certain characters when copying the string.

The `strccpy` and `strcadd` Functions

We use the `strccpy` and `strcadd` functions to copy a string while compressing escape codes.

```
cc [ flag ... ] file ... -lgen [ library ... ]
#include <libgen.h>

char *strccpy (char *output, const char *input);

char *strcadd (char *output, const char *input);
```

Both return: output

The `strccpy` function copies the *input* string to the *output* string, compressing C language escape sequences to their equivalent character (the terminating NUL character is copied without being compressed), returning a pointer to the result (i.e., *output*). Buffer overflows are not checked for, but if the buffer pointed to by *output* is the same size as that pointed to by *input*, it is guaranteed to be big enough.

The `strcadd` function is the same as `strccpy`, except that it returns a pointer to the NUL character at the end of the result.

The `strecpy` and `streadd` Functions

We use the `strecpy` and `streadd` functions to copy a string while expanding control character codes.

```
cc [ flag ... ] file ... -lgen [ library ... ]
#include <libgen.h>

char *strecpy (char *output, const char *input, const char *exceptions);

char *streadd (char *output, const char *input, const char *exceptions);
```

Both return: output

The `strecpy` function copies the *input* string to the *output* string, expanding nongraphic characters (i.e., those characters for which `isgraph` (see Section 3.2.1) returns false) to their C language escape sequences (the terminating NUL character is copied without being expanded), returning a pointer to the result (i.e., *output*). Buffer overflows are not checked for, but if the buffer pointed to by *output* is four times the size as that pointed to by *input*, it is guaranteed to be big enough (each character could potentially be expanded to \ and three digits). Characters in the string pointed to by *exceptions* are not expanded; if *exceptions* is a NULL pointer, all nongraphic characters are expanded.

The `streadd` function is the same as `strecpy`, except that it returns a pointer to the NUL character at the end of the result.

The `strtrns` Function

Another function we can use to transform a character string is `strtrns`.

```
cc [ flag ... ] file ... -lgen [ library ... ]
#include <libgen.h>

char *strtrns (const char *string, const char *old, const char *new,
    char *result);
```

Returns: result

The `strtrns` function copies a string from *string* to *result*, transforming characters as it does so. If the character being copied appears in *old*, it is replaced by the character in the same position in *new*. The pointer *result* is returned.

Example: Simple string encryption

Program 3.12 uses `strtrns` to encrypt strings using rot13, a simple encryption mechanism that replaces every character in a string with the 13th next character, wrapping around at the end of the alphabet. For example, the letter "A" becomes "N", "B" becomes "O", and so on.

utils/rot13.c

```
 1 #include <stdio.h>
 2 #include <string.h>
 3 #include <libgen.h>
 4 #include "ssp.h"

 5 int main (int argc, char **argv)
 6 {
 7     char buf [LINE_LEN];
 8     char *old = "ABCDEFGHIJKLMNOPQRSTUVWXYZabcdefghijklmnopqrstuvwxyz";
 9     char *new = "NOPQRSTUVWXYZABCDEFGHIJKLMnopqrstuvwxyzabcdefghijklm";
10     char result [LINE_LEN];

11     if (argc != 1)
12         err_quit ("Usage: %s", argv [0]);

13     while (fgets (buf, LINE_LEN, stdin) != NULL) {
14         buf [strlen (buf) - 1] = '\0';
15         strtrns (buf, old, new, result);
16         printf ("%s\n", result);
17     }

18     return (0);
19 }
```

utils/rot13.c

Program 3.12   String encryption using rot13.

Set up transformation buffers

8–9 Two buffers are set up that contain the transformation characters. A character in *old* is replaced by the character in the corresponding position in *new*.

Transform the string

15 We use `strtrns` to translate the string for us.

Running Program 3.12 on a new test file gives us the following results:

```
$ cat /tmp/test_file
A strongly encrypted message.
A dog is a man's best friend.
$ ./rot13 < /tmp/test_file
N fgebatyl rapelcgrq zrffntr.
N qbt vf n zna'f orfg sevraq.
```

Note that rot13 is not useful for real world encryption needs: it is trivial to decrypt.

3.3.9 Converting Strings to Numbers

A number of functions enable us to convert a string to a number. Seven of these convert a string to an integer, and the remaining two convert a string to a floating-point number.

The `strtol`, `strtoll`, `strtoul`, and `strtoull` Functions

We use these functions to convert a string to a signed or unsigned long or long long integer. In the ILP32 data model (see Section 1.12.1), a long integer is a 32-bit quantity, and a long long integer is a 64-bit quantity. In the LP64 data model, both longs and long longs are 64-bit quantities.

```
#include <stdlib.h>

long strtol (const char *str, char **endptr, int base);

long long strtoll (const char *str, char **endptr, int base);

unsigned long strtoul (const char *str, char **endptr, int base);

unsigned long long strtoull (const char *str, char **endptr, int base);
```
                                                              All four return: see text

The `strtol` function is used to convert the initial part of the string *str* to a long integer. The string is broken down to three sections: the first section consists of zero or more white space characters (see the `isspace` function in Section 3.2.1), and the second section is the sequence to be interpreted as an integer in the radix *base*. The final section is the remainder of the string (including the terminating NUL), consisting of one or more unrecognized characters.

> The *radix* of a number is the number of distinct digits in a fixed radix number system. These digits represent the integers in the range of zero to one less than the radix. For example, we usually count using a number system that has a radix (or base) of 10, and uses the digits 0 to 9 inclusive. Bases in excess of 10 use letters of the alphabet to represent digits over 9 (A for 10, B for 11, and so on). The radix of a number is sometimes indicated by means of a subscript, e.g., 256_{10} or 100_{16}. Historically, binary (base 2) numbers were sometimes prefixed with a % sign, and hexadecimal (base 16) numbers were sometimes prefixed with a $ sign.
>
> Unless context dictates otherwise, numbers without an explicit radix are in base 10.

If *base* is 0, the section to be interpreted is expected to be either a positive or negative decimal (base 10), octal (base 8), or hexadecimal (base 16) constant. A decimal constant is a sequence of decimal digits (0 to 9), with the proviso that the first digit is not 0. An octal constant consists of an initial 0 followed by a sequence of digits from 0 to 7. A hexadecimal constant consists of an initial 0x (or 0X) followed by a sequence of decimal digits and the letters A to F (or a to f) for the values 10 to 15 respectively.

If *base* is between 2 and 36, the section to be interpreted is expected to be either a positive or negative constant in the radix *base*. The constant must consist of a sequence of decimal digits and the letters A to Z (or a to z) for the values 10 to 35 respectively. Only letters whose values are less than *base* are permitted (if *base* is 16, the characters "0x" or "0X" may precede the constant, after any sign that is present).

If *endptr* is not NULL, a pointer to the final section of the string (i.e., the section of the original string following the section to be converted) is stored in the object it points to.

If the value to be converted is empty or invalid, no conversion is performed, and the value of *str* is stored in the object pointed to by *endptr*, provided that the latter is not NULL. We might be tempted to use the following to check for errors from strtol:

```
char *ptr;

value = strtol (str, &ptr, 0);
if ((ptr == str) || (*ptr != '\0')) {
    /* Handle error */
}
```

While this code catches some errors, more stringent error checking is required to catch them all (we'll show an example of this in Program 3.13).

The strtoll function is the same as strtol, except it converts a string to a long long integer.

Similarly, the strtoul and strtoull functions are similar to strtol and strtoll, except they convert a string to an unsigned long integer or unsigned long long integer respectively.

If we are converting hexadecimal numbers, we should usually use strtoul or strtoull in preference to their signed counterparts. This is because strtol will fail if the number to be converted is greater than or equal to 2^{31}.

Example: Using strtol to convert numbers of various bases

Program 3.13 uses the strtol function to convert numbers in three different bases to their integer representation.

Here's what we get when we run Program 3.13:

```
$ ./strtol
1010101 base 2 is 85 base 10
12345 base 10 is 12345 base 10
Deadbeef base 16 is 2147483647 base 10
Deadbeef is out of range
```

```
 1 #include <stdio.h>
 2 #include <stdlib.h>
 3 #include <errno.h>
 4 #include <limits.h>
 5 #include "ssp.h"

 6 int main (void)
 7 {
 8     char *bin = "1010101";
 9     char *dec = "12345";
10     char *hex = "Deadbeef";
11     char *ptr;
12     long val;

13     printf ("%s base 2 is %ld base 10\n", bin, strtol (bin, NULL, 2));
14     printf ("%s base 10 is %ld base 10\n", dec, strtol (dec, NULL, 10));
15     printf ("%s base 16 is %ld base 10\n", hex, strtol (hex, NULL, 16));

16     errno = 0;

17     val = strtol (hex, &ptr, 16);

18     if ((val == 0) && ((errno != 0) || (ptr == hex))) {
19         err_quit ("No conversion took place for %s", hex);
20     }
21     else if ((errno != 0) && ((val == LONG_MAX) || (val == LONG_MIN))) {
22         err_quit ("%s is out of range", hex);
23     }
24     else
25         printf ("%s base 16 is %ld base 10\n", hex, val);

26     return (0);
27 }
```

Program 3.13 Converting numbers using `strtol`.

Notice that the first time we attempt to convert the hexadecimal number 0xdeadbeef, an undetected overflow occurs. Because all of the possible return values are legal, the only way to detect an error condition when using any of these functions (assuming a conversion took place) is to set `errno` to 0 before calling the desired function, and then check `errno`'s value when the function returns. If `errno` is non-zero, it is safe to assume that an error has occurred.

The `atol`, `atoll`, and `atoi` Functions

These functions provide a less generic and easier-to-use set of methods to convert a string to an integer.

```
#include <stdlib.h>

long atol (const char *str);

long long atoll (const char *str);

int atoi (const char *str);
```
                                                                                    All three return: the converted number

The `atol` function converts the initial part of the string *str* to a long integer. The string is converted in a similar manner to that described for `strtol` in the preceding section. In fact, with the exception of the error handling,

```
num = atol (str);
```

is the same as

```
num = strtol (str, NULL, 10);
```

The function `atoll` is similar to `atol`, except it converts *str* to a long long integer, and

```
num = atoll (str);
```

is equivalent to

```
num = strtoll (str, NULL, 10);
```

Finally, `atoi` converts *str* to an integer.

```
num = atoi (str);
```

is the same as

```
num = (int) strtol (str, NULL, 10);
```

Detecting errors when using these functions is impossible; although all possible return values are legal, they do not set `errno` in the event of an error. We therefore recommend that new applications use the `strtol` family of functions in preference to these.

The `strtod` and `atof` Functions

Solaris also provides two functions for converting a string to a floating-point number.

```
#include <stdlib.h>

double strtod (const char *str, char **endptr);

double atof (const char *str);
```
                                                                                        Both return: the converted number

The `strtod` function is the floating-point analogue of `strtol`, in that it converts the initial part of the the string *str* to a floating-point number. The string is broken down into three sections: the first section consists of zero or more white space characters (see the `isspace` function in Section 3.2.1), and the second section is the sequence to be interpreted as a floating-point number. The final section is the remainder of the string (including the terminating NUL), which consists of one or more unrecognized characters.

The first part of the sequence that is to be converted is an optional + or − sign, followed by a series of one or more digits (which may optionally contain a decimal point), followed by an optional exponent part. The exponent part consists of the letter "E" or "e", an optional sign, and a series of one or more digits. The decimal point character is defined by the LC_NUMERIC category of the locale of the calling process. In the POSIX locale, or a locale where the decimal point is not defined, it defaults to a period (.). We'll have more to say about locales in Appendix A.

If *endptr* is not NULL, a pointer to the final section of the string (i.e., the section of the original string following the section to be converted) is stored in the object it points to.

If the value to be converted is empty or invalid, no conversion is performed, and the value of *str* is stored in the object pointed to by *endptr*, provided the latter is not NULL.

The atof function is equivalent to calling strtod with a NULL *endptr*. That is,

```
num = atof (str);
```

is the same as

```
num = strtod (str, NULL);
```

3.3.10 Converting Numbers to Strings

Besides converting strings to numbers, Solaris provides two functions to do the opposite: converting a number to a string.

```
#include <stdlib.h>

char *lltostr (long long value, char *endptr);

char *ulltostr (unsigned long long value, char *endptr);
```
                                        Both return: a pointer to the converted number

The lltostr function converts the long long integer *value* into a string and returns a pointer to the beginning of it; *endptr* must point to the byte immediately following the buffer into which the string is to be placed. The number gets converted, with the low order digit of the result being stored in the memory position (*endptr* - 1). The string created is not NUL terminated, and no leading zeros are produced (if *value* is zero, a single 0 digit is produced).

The ulltostr function is the same as lltostr, except that *value* is an unsigned long long.

As we'll see in Chapter 5, we can also use the sprintf function to convert a number to a string. In fact, we *must* use this function (or one of its variants) if we want to convert a number to a hexadecimal or octal string.

3.4   Manipulating Byte Arrays

A byte array is similar to a string, except that they are not NUL terminated. Unlike a string, a byte array may contain one or more zero bytes anywhere within the buffer.

Because byte arrays have no terminating character, we must pass the size of the array to the functions that manipulate them.

The Solaris operating environment provides several functions for manipulating byte arrays, although there aren't quite as many as for manipulating strings. Just like their string counterparts, the functions we discuss in this section fall into a number of categories; we can compare two byte arrays, copy them, search them, and initialize them.

3.4.1 Comparing Byte Arrays

Comparing two byte arrays is much the same as comparing two strings, apart from the fact that the idea of one byte array being lexicographically less than or more than another is at best dubious (what does it mean if one array of structures is greater than another?). For this reason, although they can distinguish between equal to, greater than, or less than, the memory comparison functions are usually just used to test for equality.

We use the memcmp function to compare two byte arrays.

```
#include <string.h>

int memcmp (const void *s1, const void *s2, size_t n);
```
Returns: see text

The memcmp function compares the first *n* bytes of the two byte arrays pointed to by *s1* and *s2*. The bytes are interpreted as unsigned chars, and the function returns an integer less than, equal to, or greater than 0, if *s1* is lexicographically less than, equal to, or greater than *s2*.

3.4.2 Copying Byte Arrays

Copying byte arrays is also very similar to copying strings, except we can't rely on a NUL byte to terminate the array. Instead, these functions are passed the number of bytes that are to be copied.

```
#include <string.h>

void *memcpy (void *dst, const void *src, size_t n);

void *memccpy (void *dst, const void *src, int c, size_t n);

void *memmove (void *dst, const void *src, size_t n);
```
All three return: see text

The memcpy function copies *n* bytes from the byte array pointed to by *src* to the buffer pointed to by *dst*, and returns *dst*. If the two buffers overlap, the result is undefined for the overlapping portion (use memmove to copy overlapping regions safely).

Despite this limitation, memcpy is the preferred method of copying a region of memory; the algorithm used by memmove may be slower on some architectures.

The memccpy function copies bytes from the byte array pointed to by *src* to the buffer *dst*, stopping after *n* bytes have been copied or the first occurrence of *c* (which gets converted to an unsigned character). If *c* was found in the first *n* bytes of *src*, memccpy returns a pointer to the byte after the copy of *c* in *dst*. Otherwise, it returns a NULL pointer.

The memmove function also copies *n* bytes from the byte array pointed to by *src* to the buffer pointed to by *dst*, and returns *dst*. However, unlike memcpy, memmove correctly handles overlapping memory buffers.

3.4.3 Searching Byte Arrays

We can search a byte array for the first occurrence of a byte with a given value; we can also search for the first bit that is set in an integer.

The memchr Function

This function is used to find the first occurrence of a byte in a byte array.

```
#include <string.h>

void *memchr (void *s, int c, size_t n);
```
                                                                                    Returns: see text

The memchr function returns a pointer to the first occurrence of *c* (converted to an unsigned char) in the first *n* bytes of the byte array pointed to by *s* (each byte is interpreted as an unsigned char). If *c* does not appear in the searched area, a NULL pointer is returned.

The ffs Function

We use the ffs function to search for the first bit set in an integer.

```
#include <strings.h>

int ffs (const int i);
```
                                                                                    Returns: see text

The ffs function returns the index of the first bit set in *i*, starting with the least significant bit (which has an index value of one). If *i* is 0, then 0 is returned. For example, if *i* is equal to 34 (which is 100010 in binary), ffs will return 2.

3.4.4 Initializing Byte Arrays

We use the `memset` function to initialize all the bytes in a byte array to the specified value.

```
#include <string.h>

void *memset (void *s, int c, size_t n);
```
Returns: *s*

The `memset` function sets the first *n* bytes of the byte array pointed to by *s* to the value *c* (which is converted to an unsigned char), and returns *s*.

3.5   Dynamic Memory

In our previous examples, we used static character arrays to store our data (when we say static in this context, we mean that the arrays are fixed in size, rather than static in the sense of the C reserved word). Static arrays are fine for small examples and have many uses in bigger programs, but the fact that their size is fixed at compile time can be a limitation or lead to inefficiencies: an array that is too small will not be able to hold all the data a user wants it to, and an array that is big enough for all foreseeable circumstances will needlessly waste memory.

The answer to this dilemma is to use dynamic memory instead of static arrays. The `malloc` and `free` functions provide a simple, general purpose memory allocation package.

3.5.1 Memory Alignment

Before we talk about memory allocation, we should first understand the concepts of memory alignment. When we say a memory location is *aligned*, we mean that the address of the memory is an integral multiple of the alignment value. For example, if we have an address that is 4-byte aligned, that address will be a multiple of four. Some architectures require that multibyte accesses are suitably aligned, e.g., UltraSPARC half word (16-bit) accesses must be aligned on 2-byte boundaries, 32-bit word accesses (including instruction fetches) must be 4-byte aligned, double word (64-bit) accesses must be aligned on an 8-byte boundary, and quad word (128-bit) accesses must be aligned on a 16-byte boundary [Weaver and Germond 1994].

Figure 3.1 illustrates the alignments of bytes, half words, words, double words, and quad words.

Figure 3.1 shows that accesses to 4-byte words are only permitted from addresses that are an exact multiple of four (e.g., 1000, 1024, and 32768); attempts to access a 4-byte word from address 1002 will fail, since it is not exactly divisible by four. Misaligned reads or writes almost always cause a bus error followed by a core dump.

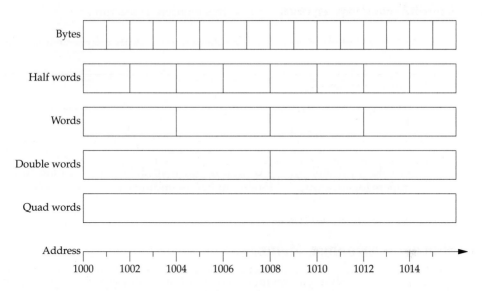

Figure 3.1 Alignment of various word sizes.

Compilers will automatically pad structure members so that they are suitably aligned. This can cause the size of a structure to change depending on the ordering of its members. For example, the size of the following structure is 12 bytes:

```
struct {
    char foo;
    int bar;
    char baz;
};
```

Figure 3.2 shows the memory layout for this structure.

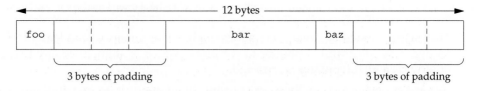

Figure 3.2 Memory layout of our structure.

By reordering the members, we can shrink the structure's memory requirements down to just eight bytes:

```
struct {
    int bar;
    char foo;
    char baz;
};
```

Figure 3.3 shows the memory layout for this reordered structure.

Figure 3.3 Memory layout of our reordered structure.

Two good rules of thumb when designing our own data structures are to keep similar sized members together and to store them in descending size order.

3.5.2 Allocating Dynamic Memory

Before we can use dynamic memory, we must first allocate it to our process. Solaris provides a number of functions to allocate memory, the most common of which is `malloc`.

The `malloc` Function

We use the `malloc` function to allocate a block of memory from the heap of a process (we'll discuss the memory layout of a process in Section 14.6).

```
#include <stdlib.h>

void *malloc (size_t size);
```
                              Returns: a pointer to the allocated memory if OK, NULL on error

The `malloc` function attempts to allocate a block of memory of at least *size* bytes. If the request was successful, a pointer to the block, which is aligned for any use, is returned; otherwise, a NULL pointer is returned.

A common error (especially when porting older code) is to cast the return value from `malloc` and its related functions. Although this was necessary in the pre-ISO C days, the correct use of function prototypes dispenses with the need to cast. In fact, casting the value returned by `malloc` can hide subtle bugs in our programs. Consider what would happen if we didn't include `<stdlib.h>` and therefore didn't have a function prototype for `malloc`. We would cast the value returned to a pointer (recall that unless the compiler is told otherwise, all functions in C return an `int`), which would be OK for a 32-bit process because pointers and `int`s are the same size, but would result in a truncated pointer for a 64-bit process. (The `malloc` function returns a 64-bit pointer, which is truncated to a 32-bit integer because we haven't told the compiler to do otherwise. We then cast the 32-bit integer back to a 64-bit pointer, which results in information loss. Because of the cast, the compiler does not alert us to this problem.)

The moral of all this is to make sure that we always include the correct header files, and never cast the value returned by `malloc` and its related functions.

The `calloc` Function

The memory allocated by `malloc` is not initialized in any way; a read from the allocated memory will return whatever happens to be in that location from the last time it was used. One way around this problem would be to use `memset` to initialize the memory after it had been allocated. Another would be to use `calloc` to allocate the memory instead of `malloc`.

```
#include <stdlib.h>

void *calloc (size_t nelem, size_t elsize);
```
                        Returns: a pointer to the allocated memory if OK, NULL on error

The `calloc` function attempts to allocate enough memory to hold at least *nelem* elements of *elsize* bytes each. If the allocation was successful, a pointer to the memory (which is initialized to zeros) is returned; otherwise, a NULL pointer is returned. When we say the memory gets initialized to zeros, we mean that all the bits in the memory region are set to zero, rather than the number zero represented as an integer or floating-point number (both of which may have very different representations than a number of bytes whose bits are all zero).

The `memalign` and `valloc` Functions

The memory allocated by the functions we have just discussed (`malloc` and `calloc`) align the memory on a boundary that is suitable for any purpose. However, there are times when we want to have the memory aligned on a specific boundary. To do this, we use either the `memalign` or `valloc` function.

```
#include <stdlib.h>

void *memalign (size_t alignment, size_t size);

void *valloc (size_t size);
```
                    Both return: a pointer to the allocated memory if OK, NULL on error

The `memalign` function returns a pointer to a block of memory of at least *size* bytes that is aligned on an address that is guaranteed to be an even multiple of *alignment* (which must be a power of two and no smaller than a word).

The `valloc` function allocates a block of memory that is at least *size* bytes in size and is aligned on a page boundary. In other words

```
valloc (size);
```

is the same as

```
memalign (sysconf (_SC_PAGESIZE), size);
```

We discuss the `sysconf` function in Section 8.3.

The `realloc` Function

If for some reason we want to change the size of a region of memory that we have allocated, we can use the `realloc` function.

```
#include <stdlib.h>

void *realloc (void *ptr, size_t size);
```
                              Returns: a pointer to the allocated memory if OK, NULL on error

We use the `realloc` function to change the size of the memory block pointed to by *ptr* to *size* bytes; a pointer to the new region (that might have been moved to accommodate the change in size) is returned. If *size* is at least as big as the block's current size, its contents will be unchanged. If *size* is smaller than the current size, the data that doesn't fit into the new region are lost. If *ptr* is not NULL, the block of memory must have been previously allocated using `malloc` or one of its related functions; if *ptr* is NULL, `realloc` has the same behaviour as a `malloc` of the same size. If *ptr* is not NULL, and *size* is 0, `realloc` has the same behaviour as `free` (which we discuss in Section 3.5.3).

If `realloc` returns NULL when it was called with *size* greater than 0, the memory block pointed to by *ptr* is left intact.

A failure of `realloc` can cause problems in code like the following:

```
ptr = realloc (ptr, new_size);
```

The original value of `ptr` will be lost, so if we plan to try to recover from this situation (rather than just printing an error and terminating), we must save its value in a temporary pointer before calling `realloc`.

The `alloca` Function

All of the memory allocation functions we have discussed so far allocate memory from a segment of the process' virtual memory space called the heap (we discuss the memory layout of a process in Section 14.6). The `alloca` function allocates memory from the stack frame of the caller.

```
#include <alloca.h>

void *alloca (size_t size);
```
                              Returns: a pointer to the allocated memory if OK, NULL on error

The `alloca` function allocates *size* bytes from the caller's stack frame and returns a pointer to it. This allocation is temporary, and is returned to the process when the caller returns. If the allocated block is beyond the current stack limit, the result is undefined. Note that the `alloca` function is very machine–, compiler–, and system dependent; its use is strongly discouraged.

3.5.3 Freeing Dynamic Memory

We have described several functions that allocate dynamic memory to a process. If we are to avoid memory leaks in our (long running) processes, we should free any memory we allocate once we have finished using it.

The `free` Function

The primary method of returning memory to a process is to call `free`. As we noted in our discussion of dynamic memory allocation, `realloc` can also be used to free memory, but `free` is by far the most common method and the one we recommend.

```
#include <stdlib.h>

void free (void *ptr);
```

The `free` function frees memory pointed to by *ptr* that was dynamically allocated by a previous invocation of `malloc`, `calloc`, or `realloc` (or even other functions, such as `strdup`) by returning it to the calling process; if *ptr* is NULL, `free` returns without taking any action. The freed memory is available for reuse by the process but not the operating system. Memory freed by a process is not returned to the operating system until a process terminates.

Even though memory isn't returned to the operating system until the demise of a process, it is good programming practice to free blocks of dynamic memory when we are finished with them to avoid memory leaks in long-running processes.

Also, a freed memory block may be returned to the application unchanged (although this behaviour is not guaranteed). This can be abused in code segments similar to the following when freeing linked lists:

```
while (ptr) {
    free (ptr);
    ptr = ptr -> next;
}
```

Strictly speaking, the memory is no longer valid after it has been freed, so its contents should not be relied on as in this example. The correct way to implement this code would be something like this:

```
while (ptr) {
    next = ptr -> next;
    free (ptr);
    ptr = next;
}
```

Here, we get a pointer to the next item in the list *before* we call `free` to free the current item. Although the memory that `ptr` pointed to is no longer valid, the memory pointed to by `next` is.

3.6   Other Memory Management Packages

The dynamic memory management functions we discussed in Section 3.5 are provided by the standard C library, `libc.so`. They are the standard, fully SPARC Compliance Definition (SCD; see [SPARC International 1999]) compliant versions, which are a compromise between space efficiency and performance. Most of the time this is the desired behaviour, but there are times when we would prefer better performance at the expense of space efficiency, or vice versa. Solaris provides a number of alternative memory allocation libraries for this reason. These are the `malloc`, `bsdmalloc`, and `mapmalloc` libraries. (There is also the `mtmalloc` library, which is intended for high performance multithreaded applications. A close look at at multithreaded programming is beyond the scope of this text, so we won't discuss the `mtmalloc` library further.) Another shared object, `watchmalloc.so`, is useful for debugging purposes.

> Solaris 9 4/03 introduced `libumem`, which is a library of functions that provide fast, scalable, object caching memory allocation with multithreaded application support. This library also provides extensive debugging support, including detection of memory leaks, buffer overflows, multiple frees, use of uninitialized data, use of freed data, and many other common programming errors. Unfortunately, we don't have space to describe this library in any further detail, but interested readers are referred to the `libumem` and related manual pages.

3.6.1 The `malloc` Library

We use the `malloc` library when space efficiency is of more importance than performance. The functions provided by this library are much the same as the default one, except that memory that is freed is explicitly made unavailable (although this can be overridden by using the `mallopt` function we discuss next). To make use of these functions, our programs must be compiled with the `-lmalloc` flag specified on the command line. Notice also that although some of these functions are prototyped in `<malloc.h>`, we must also include `<stdlib.h>` for the remaining function prototypes.

As well as providing memory allocation and deallocation functions (i.e., `malloc`, `realloc`, `calloc`, and `free`), the `malloc` library also provides two other functions.

The `mallopt` Function

The `mallopt` function allows us to exercise some control over the allocation algorithm used.

```
cc [ flag ... ] file ... -lmalloc [ library ... ]
#include <malloc.h>

int mallopt (int cmd, int value);
```
Returns: 0 if OK, not zero on error

We use the `mallopt` function to control some aspects of the allocation algorithm. The *cmd* parameter selects the option we want to affect, and *value* is an optional value for *cmd*. Three variables private to the library may be tuned. The `maxfast` variable defines the maximum number of bytes that will be allocated from a large block of like-sized units. Each of these large blocks contains `numblks` blocks. Finally, all memory requests smaller than `maxfast` bytes are rounded up to the nearest multiple of `grain`. Three of the four *cmd* values are used to tune these variables.

M_MXFAST	This option sets the value of `maxfast`, which defaults to 24, to *value*.
M_NLBLKS	We use this *cmd* to set the `numblks` variable to *value*. The default value for `numblks` is 100, and it must be greater than zero.
M_GRAIN	Using this *cmd* we can set the value of `grain` to *value*, which must also be greater than zero. The default value of `grain` is the smallest number of bytes that will allow for the alignment of any data type; *value* is rounded up to a multiple of the default when setting `grain`.
M_KEEP	By default, memory that is freed using the `malloc` library version of `free` is destroyed, i.e., its contents are no longer available. Using this value of *cmd* forces data in the freed block to be preserved until the next allocation using `malloc`, `calloc`, or `realloc`. This option is provided for compatibility with the old version of `malloc` and is not recommended for new programs.

The `mallopt` function may be called several times to set different options, but it may not be called after the first small block has been allocated, even if all the memory allocated by `malloc` is subsequently freed.

The `mallinfo` Function

We can use the `mallinfo` function to get information about the memory space usage.

```
cc [ flag ... ] file ... -lmalloc [ library ... ]
#include <malloc.h>

struct mallinfo mallinfo (void);
```
Returns: a <code>mallinfo</code> structure

The `mallinfo` function returns a `mallinfo` structure that describes the memory space usage of the library. The `mallinfo` structure has the following members:

```
struct mallinfo {
      unsigned long arena;         /* Total space in arena */
      unsigned long ordblks;       /* Number of ordinary blocks */
      unsigned long smblks;        /* Number of small blocks */
      unsigned long hblks;         /* Number of holding blocks */
      unsigned long hblkhd;        /* Space in holding block headers */
      unsigned long usmblks;       /* Space in small blocks in use */
      unsigned long fsmblks;       /* Space in free small blocks */
      unsigned long uordblks;      /* Space in ordinary blocks in use */
      unsigned long fordblks;      /* Space in free ordinary blocks */
      unsigned long keepcost;      /* Cost of enabling keep option */
};
```

Most members of the `mallinfo` structure are straightforward, but some need a little further explanation. The number of ordinary blocks, `ordblks`, is the number of blocks used to hold the small blocks of memory plus the number of larger allocation blocks (recall from our discussion of the `mallopt` function that requests for memory that are smaller than `maxfast` bytes are satisfied from a pool of like-sized blocks). The number of small blocks, `smblks`, is a multiple of `numblks`, which we can tune using the `M_NLBLKS` command of `mallopt`. The space used by the small blocks in use, `usmblks`, is a multiple of `maxfast`, which we can tune using the `M_MXFAST` command of `mallopt`. Finally, the total amount of memory occupied by the allocation pool (except for that represented by `freecost`), `arena`, is equal to the sum of `hblkhd`, `usmblks`, `fsmblks`, `uordblks`, and `fordblks`.

3.6.2 The `bsdmalloc` Library

We use the `bsdmalloc` library (which despite its name is not part of the BSD Source Compatibility Package) when performance is of more importance than space efficiency. The library provides just three functions, which are incompatible with the functions provided in the standard C library (use of the `bsdmalloc` functions renders an application non-SCD compliant, so it should not be used unless memory allocation and deallocation is proven to be a significant performance bottleneck).

The functions provided by the `bsdmalloc` library are `malloc`, `realloc`, and `free`. To make use of the functions in this library, our programs must be compiled with the `-lbsdmalloc` flag specified on the command line.

```
cc [ flag ... ] file ... -lbsdmalloc [ library ... ]

char *malloc (size);
unsigned size;

char *realloc (ptr, size);
char *ptr;
unsigned size;

                    Both return: a pointer to the allocated memory if OK, NULL on error

int free (ptr);
char *ptr;
```

The fact that a header file to include is missing from the prototypes we list above is not an omission; no header file defines these functions (hence our use of the K&R style function prototypes).

They have the same functionality as their standard library counterparts but have slightly different interfaces. Also, the pointer returned by the bsdmalloc versions of malloc and realloc should always be cast to an appropriate type. This in contrast to the same functions in the standard library, whose returned pointers should never be cast.

3.6.3 The mapmalloc Library

As we have noted previously, the memory allocation functions (with the exception of alloca) deal with memory that is part of the heap of a process. When one of the allocation functions needs to acquire more heap space from the process, it uses the sbrk system call (see Section 14.8); the routines in the mapmalloc library use the mmap system call instead.

The four functions in the mapmalloc library (malloc, calloc, realloc, and free) are provided for the occasion where we need our programs to call sbrk directly and need to call other library routines that might call malloc.

The functions are prototyped in <stdlib.h>, and programs wishing to use this library must be linked with the -lmapmalloc flag specified on the command line. The algorithms used are not very sophisticated, and no memory is reclaimed.

3.6.4 The watchmalloc Shared Object

The functions provided by the watchmalloc.so shared object are alternative versions of the dynamic memory management functions provided in the standard C library. They provide a much stricter interface than the standard versions, and enable enforcement of the various interfaces through the watchpoint facility of the /proc file system (see Section 8.8).

Any dynamically linked application can be run with these functions instead of the standard ones by placing the following string in the environment:

```
LD_PRELOAD=watchmalloc.so.1
```

Each function has the same prototype as the standard ones we describe in Section 3.5, but certain laxities they allow are not permitted when the watchpoint facility is enabled:

- Memory may not be freed more than once.
- A pointer to freed memory may not be used in a call to `realloc`.
- A call to `malloc` immediately following a call to `free` will not return the same space.
- Any reference to memory that has been freed yields undefined results.

Using the watchpoint facility has a considerable performance penalty, so as a way of partially enforcing the above restrictions, freed memory is overwritten with the pattern 0xdeadbeef. The memory allocated by one of the `malloc` functions is initialized to 0xbaddcafe as a precaution against applications relying on a previously freed buffer's contents. Like its standard library namesake, the space returned by `calloc` is always zero filled.

Watchpoints

A process may apply the watchpoint facility of `/proc` to itself (we discuss the `/proc` file system in Section 8.8). The functions in the `watchmalloc.so` shared object use watchpoints if the `MALLOC_DEBUG` environment variable is set to either `RW` or `WATCH`. A third value, `STOP`, may also be part of the the `MALLOC_DEBUG` environment variable, provided that the variable also contains `RW` or `WATCH`. Options are enabled by using a comma-separated string of options, for example, `MALLOC_DEBUG=RW,STOP`.

The valid options for `MALLOC_DEBUG` are as follows:

RW	Every block of freed memory is covered by `WA_READ` and `WA_WRITE` watched areas. An attempt to read from or write to the freed memory will result in a watchpoint trap, which results in a `SIGTRAP` signal being sent to the process (the default action when a `SIGTRAP` is delivered to a process is to produce a core dump). Requesting this level of watchpoint detection incurs such an overhead that applications may be slowed down by a factor of up to 1000.
STOP	Rather than dumping core as a result of a `SIGTRAP`, the process will stop, showing a `FLTWATCH`, should the process trigger a watchpoint trap. This allows us to attach a debugger to the live process to determine what caused the watchpoint

trap. It also allows us to use the various /proc tools to examine the stopped process.

WATCH　　　　　　　Every block of freed memory is covered by a WA_WRITE watched area. Any attempt to write to the freed memory will result in a watchpoint trap, and a SIGTRAP being sent to the process. Requesting this level of watchpoint detection incurs such an overhead that applications may be slowed down by a factor of between 10 and 100.

Should both RW and WATCH be specified, RW takes precedence, but at least one of them must be specified for the watchpoint facility to be enabled.

A header is maintained for each block of allocated memory. This header is covered with a watched area, thereby providing a red zone before each block of allocated memory.

> A *red zone* is an area of memory owned by a process that is marked as being neither readable nor writable. The idea is to protect memory that shouldn't be accessed even though it is part of the address space of a process.

> Suppose we have a version of malloc that allocates memory only in multiples of 8 KB chunks, and we ask for a 6 KB chunk. Although a whole 8 KB chunk gets allocated to our process, it would be an error for our program to attempt to access the last 2 KB. So, the last 2 KB gets covered by a red zone, which traps inadvertent reads or writes to it. We show this in Figure 3.4. (Note that a red zone trap is different to a segmentation violation, which traps attempts to access memory that is not part of the address space of our process.)

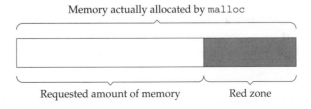

Figure 3.4　Red zones.

The headers for subsequent allocations are used as the trailing red zone for the preceding memory block. These red zones ensure that writes to just before or just after the memory block returned by malloc will trigger a watchpoint trap. (Strictly speaking, this isn't necessarily the case for writes beyond the end of a block of memory. This is because the size of the blocks allocated by malloc get rounded up to the worst-case alignment size, which is 8 bytes for 32-bit processes and 16 bytes for 64-bit processes. Accessing the extra space is technically a memory violation, but these violations are not detected by the watchpoint facility.)

3.6.5 Comparing the `malloc` Libraries

The comparative features of the `bsdmalloc`, `malloc`, and `libc` versions of `malloc` are:

- The `bsdmalloc` routines offer greater performance at the expense of space efficiency and SCD compatibility.
- The `malloc` routines tend to be more space efficient but have slower performance.
- The standard, fully SCD-compliant routines supplied in `libc` are a trade-off between performance and space efficiency. They should always be used unless there are demonstrably good reasons not to.

Example: Comparing the performance of the different versions of `malloc`

We've listed the comparative features of the different versions of `malloc`, but how do they compare in practice? Specifically, what effect do they have on a program's size and its performance? Program 3.14 goes through a number of iterations of allocating and freeing two dissimilar-sized chunks of memory.

Figure 3.5 tabulates the results we get running Program 3.14 on a Sun Blade 100 when linked with each of the different `malloc` libraries.

Version of `malloc`	Time	Size
`libc`	3	15752
`malloc`	13	20768
`bsdmalloc`	2	21000
`mapmalloc`	910	1000
`watchmalloc`	110069	15776

Figure 3.5 Results from running Program 3.14.

The Time column shows the execution time of the program in seconds (as printed from the program itself), and the Size column shows the amount of virtual memory used by the process in kilobytes. We obtained the latter number by running the following command after the run time had been printed out:

```
$ ps -eo vsz,comm | grep malloc
15752 ./malloc
```

Notice how much slower `mapmalloc` and especially `watchmalloc` are compared to the other versions of `malloc`. Using `watchmalloc` has a *huge* performance impact, taking more than 30 hours to run, compared to 3 seconds for the `libc` version. Its use should therefore be reserved for debugging purposes; fortunately, we do not need to relink our applications to use it. Simply setting the `LD_PRELOAD` environment variable appropriately is all that's required.

—— *utils/malloc.c*

```
 1 #include <stdio.h>
 2 #include <unistd.h>
 3 #include <stdlib.h>
 4 #include <sys/types.h>
 5 #include <time.h>
 6 #include "ssp.h"

 7 #define NUM_CHUNKS 10000
 8 #define CHUNK_SIZE1 1152
 9 #define CHUNK_SIZE2 1500
10 #define NUM_ITERS 100

11 int main (void)
12 {
13     int i;
14     int j;
15     void *ptrs [NUM_CHUNKS];
16     time_t start;
17     time_t fin;

18     start = time (NULL);

19     for (i = 0; i < NUM_ITERS; i++) {
20         printf ("Iteration = %d\n", i);
21         for (j = 0; j < NUM_CHUNKS; j++) {
22             if ((ptrs [j] = malloc (CHUNK_SIZE1)) == NULL)
23                 err_msg ("malloc fails");
24         }

25         for (j = 0; j < NUM_CHUNKS; j++)
26             free (ptrs [j]);

27         for (j = 0; j < NUM_CHUNKS; j++) {
28             if ((ptrs [j] = malloc (CHUNK_SIZE2)) == NULL)
29                 err_msg ("malloc fails");
30         }

31         for (j = 0; j < NUM_CHUNKS; j++)
32             free (ptrs [j]);
33     }

34     fin = time (NULL);

35     printf ("Run time = %ld seconds\n", fin - start);
36     pause ();

37     return (0);
38 }
```

—— *utils/malloc.c*

Program 3.14 Comparing the different versions of malloc.

3.7   Temporary Files

There are times when our processes need to make use of temporary files. In this context, a *temporary file* is one that is no longer needed once the process that created it has exited (or at the very least will be removed soon after the process that created it exits). For example, compilers often use temporary intermediary files between the different stages of compilation.

Solaris provides several functions for naming and creating temporary files: four for generating a unique temporary filename, and two for creating uniquely named temporary files.

3.7.1   Generating Temporary Filenames

Sometimes we need to know the name of a temporary file we create (the functions we describe in Section 3.7.2 are ideal when we don't need to know the name). Rather than using a hard-coded filename and hoping that is sufficient, we can use one of the four functions we describe in this section to create a filename safely.

The `mktemp` Function

We use the `mktemp` function to make a unique filename.

```
#include <stdlib.h>

char *mktemp (char *template);
```
                                                          Returns: a pointer to *template*

The `mktemp` function replaces the string *template* with a unique filename, returning *template*. It does this by replacing the six trailing Xs with a character string that can be used to create a unique filename (as few as three Xs may be the trailing characters, but this severely limits the algorithm; it's best to use six). If a unique name cannot be created, an empty string is returned.

The `tmpnam` and `tmpnam_r` Functions

We use these functions to generate a filename that has a prefix of `P_tmpdir`. On Solaris, `P_tmpdir` is defined as `/var/tmp`.

```
#include <stdio.h>

char *tmpnam (char *s);

char *tmpnam_r (char *s);
```
                                                                  Both return: see text

The `tmpnam` function generates a unique filename. The path prefix of the generated name is `P_tmpdir`. If *s* is not NULL, it is assumed to point to a buffer of at least `L_tmpnam` bytes in size (both `P_tmpdir` and `L_tmpnam` are defined in `<stdio.h>`). The resulting filename is copied to the supplied buffer, and *s* is returned.

If *s* is NULL, the filename is copied to a static buffer, and a pointer to this buffer is returned. Subsequent calls to `tmpnam` will overwrite the contents of the buffer.

The `tmpnam_r` function does the same as the `tmpnam` function, with the exception that if *s* is NULL, a NULL pointer is returned.

The `tempnam` Function

The `tempnam` function is also used to create a temporary filename, but allows us to specify the directory the file is to reside in and a prefix for it.

```
#include <stdio.h>

char *tempnam (const char *dir, const char *pfx);
```
                                                                 Returns: see text

Using `tempnam` allows us to have some control over which directory the file should be located in, and a file prefix. The directory we want the file's name to start with is pointed to by *dir*; if *dir* is NULL, the `P_tmpdir` constant is used instead. If `P_tmpdir` cannot be accessed, `/tmp` will be used. If the environment variable `TMPDIR` contains the name of a directory that the process can write to, it will be used, taking precedence over *dir*. If `TMPDIR` is not writable by the process, `P_tmpdir` will be used.

By setting *pfx* to at most five characters, processes can ensure that temporary files have a certain initial character sequence. This allows our applications to use a consistent naming scheme.

The filename generated by `tempnam` is stored in a buffer created by `malloc`; a pointer to this buffer is returned upon success; otherwise, a NULL pointer is returned.

3.7.2 Creating Temporary Files

The problem with creating a temporary file by using one of the functions we discussed in Section 3.7.1 to name the file and using another (e.g., `open` or `fopen`) to create it is that a race condition exists between generating the name of the file and actually creating it (after testing for its existence). Fortunately, Solaris provides two functions that atomically generate a filename and then create that file. The first, `mkstemp`, returns a file descriptor for the temporary file, and the second, `tmpfile`, returns a pointer to a FILE structure.

The `mkstemp` Function

We use the `mkstemp` function to name and open a temporary file.

```
#include <stlib.h>

int mkstemp (char *template);
```
                                              Returns: a file descriptor if OK, −1 on error

The `mkstemp` function creates and opens a temporary file, returning the file descriptor of the newly created file. Like the `mktemp` function, *template* is used to create a unique filename. The trailing six X characters of *template* are replaced by a string that uniquely identifies the file (if a unique filename can't be generated, a NULL pointer is returned). The resulting filename is then opened for reading and writing, thus avoiding the race hazard that would result if we performed the tasks ourselves.

The `tmpfile` Function

The `tmpfile` function can be used to create and open a temporary file.

```
#include <stdio.h>

FILE *tmpfile (void);
```
                                                 Returns: a file pointer if OK, NULL on error

Unlike `mkstemp`, this function arranges for the temporary file to be deleted when all references to it are closed. This is accomplished by the `tmpfile` code calling the `unlink` function (see Section 10.15) internally before returning the file pointer. The file created is opened for reading and writing.

The fact that `tmpfile` automatically deletes files is the main reason why using it is preferred over `mkstemp`, especially when using it for transient files that have no need for existence beyond the life of the current process.

3.8   Parsing Command Line Arguments

The majority of non-trivial programs would be pretty useless if their I/O was restricted to standard input and output, or if everything was hard coded. Fortunately, UNIX allows us to pass arguments to our processes when they are started; these arguments are called *command line arguments*, because most commands are invoked from a command line (although `exec` is used behind the scenes).

The generic form of a command is

    command-name *options* *operands*

where `command-name` is the name of the command, *options* are the optional command line arguments, and *operands* are the optional command operands. Commands and their arguments conventionally follow a number of rules that can be enumerated as follows:

1. Command names ideally should be between two and nine characters in length.
2. Command names ideally should consist of lower case letters and digits only.
3. Options ideally should be preceded by a dash (–).
4. Option names ideally should consist of a single character.
5. Options with no arguments may be grouped together after a single –. In other words, –x –y –z is the same as –xyz.
6. If an option has arguments, those arguments must be mandatory. This means that we can't allow both –o and –o foo.
7. The first option argument following an option ideally should be preceded by a space or tab character, so –o foo is OK, but –ofoo is not.
8. Groups of option arguments must either be comma separated or quoted and separated by a space or tab character, i.e., –o foo,bar,baz or –o "foo bar baz".
9. The relative order of options should be unimportant, such that –xyz means the same as –zyx.
10. All options must precede any operands on the command line. So, command –x foo –y would be illegal, whereas command –xy foo would be allowed.
11. A pair of dashes (––) may be used to indicate the end of the options.
12. The relative order of a command's operands may be significant in ways determined by the command. An example of this would be the mv(1) command, which moves a file from the first operand to the second. If we reverse the two arguments, the meaning of the command is completely different.
13. A dash surrounded by space or tab characters should only be used to indicate standard input.

Most old commands, with one or two exceptions (like find), implement these rules; new programs should always implement them. Solaris provides two functions to help us implement these rules: getopt, which parses command lines that adhere to the rules just listed, and getsubopt, which parses command line arguments that follow rule eight.

The getopt Function

When a process starts executing, the kernel passes it three variables: the number of command line arguments, a list of those arguments, and the list of environment variables. Traditionally, these variables are called argc, argv, and envp respectively. We'll say more about process invocation and environment variables in Chapter 14, but for now we'll just say that portable applications should not use envp; the external global variable environ should be used instead.

Between them, argc and argv specify the command line arguments. We can use the getopt function to parse the command line options in a standard manner.

```
#include <unistd.h>

int getopt (int argc, char * const argv [], const char *optstring);
extern char *optarg;
extern int optind;
extern int opterr;
extern int optopt;
```

Returns: see text

The getopt function returns the next command line option letter from *argv* that matches a letter in *optstring* while enforcing the command line option rules we discussed previously. The returned letter is also stored in optopt.

The letters to be recognized as command line options are listed in *optstring*; if an option has one or more arguments, a colon (:) must follow the option letter. If a command line option is encountered that requires an argument (indicated in *optstring* by a colon following the letter), optarg will point to the start of the first argument when getopt returns. When all of the command line options have been processed (i.e., when the first non-option argument, or −− is encountered), getopt returns EOF (the −− is skipped if it was what signaled the end of the options).

The optind external variable contains the index of the *argv* array that is being examined and it has an initial value of 1 (the first element in the *argv* array, *argv [0]*, contains the name of the program).

If an error occurs (i.e., an option is encountered that isn't specified by *optstring*, or the argument expected from an option is missing), getopt prints an error message to the standard error stream and returns a question mark (?). Printing the error message (if we want to use our own standard of error reporting, for example) can be disabled by setting opterr to 0.

The Solaris implementation of getopt has a couple of weaknesses. The first is that getopt doesn't fully check for mandatory arguments. Given an *optstring* of "x:y" and the input "−x −y", getopt assumes that −y is the argument to −x rather than the more probable case that −y is a separate option, and −x is missing its mandatory argument.

The second weakness is that getopt allows options that require an argument to be grouped with options that don't, even though this is a violation of the command syntax rules we discussed previously. In other words, even though the current implementation allows commands such as

    command -xyz *filename*

where x and y are options, z is an option that requires an argument, and *filename* is z's argument, this syntax should be avoided because it may not be supported in future releases of Solaris. The technically correct syntax for this command is

    command -xy -z *filename*

It is worth noting that in addition to the getopt function, Solaris also provides the getopts(1) command, which performs the same task as getopt, but for shell scripts. There is also a getopt command, but its use is deprecated.

The `getsubopt` Function

The `getsubopt` function is used to parse suboptions in the argument of an option that was previously parsed by `getopt`.

```
#include <stdlib.h>

int getsubopt (char **optionp, char * const *tokens, char **valuep);
```
Returns: see text

The suboptions parsed by the `getsubopt` function consist of a list of comma-separated tokens or token-value pairs. Token-value pairs consist of a token and a value separated by an equals sign (=). Because the suboptions are comma delimited, commas are not permitted in the token or token value (space and tab characters are permitted, provided they are quoted).

The following example uses the `mount`(1M) command, which allows us to specify mount suboptions using the −o option, to illustrate this syntax.

```
mount -o rw,hard,bg,wsize=1024 host:/space /mnt
```

Here we show four suboptions: `rw`, `hard`, `bg`, and `wsize` which has an associated value of `1024`.

The option string to be parsed is pointed to by *optionp*, and *tokens* points to an array of strings that contain the list of valid suboptions. If a suboption matches one of those in *tokens*, the index of the matching suboption is returned, and a non-NULL value for *valuep* indicates that the suboption processed had an associated value (in which case *valuep* points to the first character of the value). If a suboption does not match one of those specified in *tokens*, −1 is returned, and *valuep* points to the first character of the unrecognized token. In either case, *optionp* will point to the next suboption to be processed; a value of NULL indicates that all suboptions have been processed.

Example: Parsing arguments using `getopt` and `getsubopt`

Program 3.15 shows an example of how we can use these functions in our programs to parse command line arguments. The program could form the basis of an image-generation utility. We select what shape we want by using the −c (circle), −r (rectangle), or −t (triangle) command line options. Each is mutually exclusive, and if none is specified, a square is used by default. We may specify an output filename by using the −f option, and we use the −o option to specify one of the following suboptions: the foreground colour, the background colour, and whether the shape is solid or not. The foreground and background colour suboptions require an argument (the colour to use), whereas the solid suboption does not.

Define our suboptions

7–12 Define the list of suboptions.

utils/getopt.c

```
 1 #include <stdio.h>
 2 #include <stdlib.h>
 3 #include "ssp.h"

 4 #define BG 0
 5 #define FG 1
 6 #define SOLID 2

 7 char *subopts [] = {
 8     "bg",
 9     "fg",
10     "solid",
11     NULL
12 };

13 int main (int argc, char **argv)
14 {
15     int c;
16     int circle;
17     int rectangle;
18     int triangle;
19     int err_flag;
20     char *options;
21     char *value;

22     circle = 0;
23     rectangle = 0;
24     triangle = 0;
25     err_flag = 0;

26     while ((c = getopt (argc, argv, "cf:o:rt")) != EOF) {
27         switch (c) {
28             case 'c':
29                 if (rectangle || triangle)
30                     err_flag++;
31                 else {
32                     printf ("Circle\n");
33                     circle++;
34                 }
35                 break;

36             case 'f':
37                 printf ("Filename is %s\n", optarg);
38                 break;

39             case 'o':
40                 options = optarg;
41                 while (*options != '\0') {
42                     switch (getsubopt (&options, subopts, &value)) {
43                         case BG:
44                             if (value != NULL)
45                                 printf ("Background colour is %s\n", value);
46                             else
47                                 printf ("Missing background colour\n");
48                             break;
```

```
49                      case FG:
50                          if (value != NULL)
51                              printf ("Foreground colour is %s\n", value);
52                          else
53                              printf ("Missing foreground colour\n");
54                          break;

55                      case SOLID:
56                          printf ("Solid\n");
57                          break;

58                      default:
59                          printf ("Unknown option: %s\n", value);
60                          break;
61                  }
62              }
63              break;

64          case 'r':
65              if (circle || triangle)
66                  err_flag++;
67              else {
68                  printf ("Rectangle\n");
69                  rectangle++;
70              }
71              break;

72          case 't':
73              if (circle || rectangle)
74                  err_flag++;
75              else {
76                  printf ("Triangle\n");
77                  triangle++;
78              }
79              break;

80          default:
81              err_flag++;
82              break;
83          }
84      }

85      if (!circle && !rectangle && !triangle)
86          printf ("Square\n");

87      if (err_flag)
88          err_quit ("Usage: getopt [-c | -r | -t] [-f filename] [-o options]");

89      for (; optind < argc; optind++)
90          printf ("Operand: %s\n", argv [optind]);

91      return (0);
92 }
```

utils/getopt.c

Program 3.15 Using getopt and getsubopt.

Parse command line arguments

26–84 The `while` statement uses `getopt` to iterate over each command line argument we pass to the program, stopping when `getopt` returns `EOF`, which indicates that all the command line arguments have been exhausted. We use a `switch` statement to determine the course of action, depending on what option letter is returned by `getopt`.

Handle the `-c` option

28–35 We first check to make sure that another of the shape-setting options hasn't been used (setting an error flag if one has been set), and then print out a message telling the user that a circle was selected. Lines 64 to 79 are similar, but for rectangles and triangles.

Handle the `-f` option

36–38 We print out the filename the user selected.

Handle the `-o` option and its suboptions

39–63 This section of code handles the parsing of suboptions by using the `getsubopt` function.

43–48 Handle the "bg" suboption by checking that a value is associated with it; if there is, we print out its name, and if there isn't, we print an error message.

48–54 Perform the same function for the "fg" suboption.

54–56 Handle the "solid" suboption by printing out the word "solid".

58–60 These lines implement the catch all case by printing an error message.

Set default shape if required

85–86 We select a square as the required shape if none has been explicitly specified.

Print command operands

89–90 Iterate through the operands of the command (if any), printing out the value of the operand.

When we run Program 3.15, these are the sort of results we get.

```
$ ./getopt -r -f rectangle.out a b
Rectangle
Filename is rectangle.out
Operand: a
Operand: b
$ ./getopt -c -o bg=white,fg=red,solid
Circle
Background colour is white
Foreground colour is red
Solid
$ ./getopt -tx
Triangle
./getopt: illegal option -- x
Usage: getopt [-c | -r | -t] [-f filename] [-o options]
```

The second line of output from the third invocation of Program 3.15 was produced by `getopt`; we can disable this behaviour by setting the external variable `opterr` to 0 before calling `getopt`.

3.9   Error Reporting

We've noted previously that it's good programming practice to check for errors when we make function calls. Nearly all the system calls and library functions provided by Solaris return a certain value that is used to indicate an error. This is usually −1 in the case of functions that return a numerical result, or NULL for functions that return a pointer. When an error is indicated in this manner, the reason for the error is stored in a global non-negative integer called errno. We should note that although errno may be set by many functions, it is not cleared if a function completes successfully.

Each of the different errno values is documented in <sys/errno.h>, and the manual page for each system call and library function describes what errno values are pertinent to them.

The symbolic name for each value of errno starts with an "E", e.g., EPERM for permission denied, ENOENT for a missing file or directory, etc. When talking about error notification, we sometimes say that a function returns one of these errno values. For example, we might say that a call to open failed, returning ENOENT. This is a conversational shorthand for saying that the call to open failed; it returned −1 after setting errno to ENOENT.

These errno values, as well as being somewhat system dependent, are not very useful to the people running our programs. To print out an appropriate error message in a portable manner, Solaris provides two functions: perror and strerror.

The `perror` Function

The perror function outputs a message on standard error describing the last error that occurred in a system or library call.

```
#include <stdio.h>
#include <errno.h>

void perror (const char *s);
extern int errno;
```

If s is not NULL and does not point to a zero-length string, the error message printed by perror is preceded by s, a colon, and a space character. In either case, a newline character is appended to the error message. The error message printed corresponds to the current value of errno. The name of the program reporting the error is conventionally at least part of s.

The `strerror` Function

The perror function we have just described is useful, but is a bit inflexible with respect to formatting the error message. For example, if we want to include the name of a file that gave rise to the error, we must first place the desired message in a buffer and pass that to perror. The following code segment is an example of this.

```
if ((fd = open (filename, O_RDONLY)) == -1) {
    saved_errno = errno;
    sprintf (buf, "progname: %s", filename);
    errno = saved_errno;
    perror (buf);
}
```

We save and restore errno around our call to sprintf, because there are circumstances under which sprintf will change the value of errno.

If we assume that the open failed because filename does not exist, this code would print out the familiar

```
progname: foo: No such file or directory
```

The strerror function gives us a little more flexibility with the way we report errors.

```
#include <string.h>

char *strerror (int errnum);
```

Returns: a pointer to an error message if OK, NULL on error

The strerror function returns a pointer to the error message that corresponds to *errnum*, or a NULL pointer if *errnum* is out of range.

This means that our example code segment can be simplified to the following:

```
if ((fd = open (filename, O_RDONLY)) == -1) {
    fprintf (stderr, "progname: %s: %s", filename, strerror (errno));
}
```

Notice that with this method of reporting the error, we don't need to define a buffer to hold the error message.

Assertions

Another way we can detect and report run time errors in our programs is to use assertions. An *assertion* is the evaluation of a Boolean expression that is expected to be true at run time; if the expression evaluates to false, the assertion fails. If the assertion fails, an error message is printed to standard error, and the process aborts.

Although they can be used anywhere we would normally perform error checking, assertions are best used only in "impossible" scenarios.

To test for an assertion, we simply call the assert macro, passing it the expression we want to test.

```
#include <assert.h>

void assert (int expression);
```

Because assert is implemented as a macro, *expression* must not contain string literals.

Defining the preprocessor symbol NDEBUG before including <assert.h> will prevent assertions from being compiled into our program. This is useful if we want to leave the assertions in the source code for later debugging if necessary.

Example: Using an assertion to check for a NULL pointer

Program 3.16 attempts to allocate MAXLONG bytes of memory using malloc.

———————————————————————————————— *utils/assert.c*

```
 1  #include <assert.h>
 2  #include <stdio.h>
 3  #include <stdlib.h>
 4  #include <values.h>

 5  int main (void)
 6  {
 7      char *ptr;

 8      ptr = malloc (MAXLONG);

 9      assert (ptr != NULL);

10      printf ("Allocated %ld bytes of memory\n", MAXLONG);

11      return (0);
12  }
```

———————————————————————————————— *utils/assert.c*

Program 3.16 Using an assertion to check for a NULL pointer.

If the machine on which we test Program 3.16 has less than MAXLONG bytes of virtual memory available, the call to malloc will fail, returning a NULL pointer. This in turn causes the assertion to fail:

```
$ ./assert
Assertion failed: ptr != NULL, file assert.c, line 11
Abort(coredump)
```

Running Program 3.16 on another machine that has sufficient virtual memory doesn't cause the assertion to fail:

```
$ ./assert
Allocated 2147483647 bytes of memory
```

3.10 Suspending a Process

On occasion we want to temporarily suspend the execution of our process. Solaris provides a number of functions that provide this functionality, which can be divided into two groups: pauses for a specified amount of time, and pauses until a signal arrives. Next we describe the sleep function, which we can use for the former; in Chapter 17 we'll describe several functions that suspend the calling process until it receives a signal.

The `sleep` Function

The `sleep` function is used to suspend a process for a given number of seconds.

```
#include <unistd.h>

unsigned int sleep (unsigned int seconds);
```

Returns: the number of unslept seconds

Calling the `sleep` function will suspend the current process for *seconds* seconds (in a multithreaded process, only the invoking thread is suspended). If a signal being caught is delivered to the process, `sleep` will return after the signal's catching routine has been executed. There may also be an unpredictable extension to the suspension, because of other activity on the system. The unslept number of seconds is equal to the requested time minus the amount of time actually slept.

The `sleep` function is implemented using the `alarm` function (see Section 17.13); the previous state of the alarm signal is saved and restored. If the calling process has set up an alarm before calling `sleep`, and *seconds* exceeds the remaining time for the alarm, then `sleep` will return when the alarm signal would have occurred. If *seconds* is shorter than the alarm period, however, then the alarm time is reset to go off at the time it would have without the intervening `sleep`.

3.11   Summary

In this chapter we discussed many of the utility functions available to the Solaris programmer. We first looked at the way we can manipulate strings and byte arrays, and character classes. We then talked about the facilities provided by Solaris for allocating and freeing dynamic memory, including some alternative implementations that offer a choice between space efficiency and run time performance.

We then turned our attention to temporary files, covering the generation of temporary filenames, and the creation of temporary files. We then talked about the rules for command line arguments and how to parse them using functions that enforce those rules. We then showed how to print error messages in a standard manner (including a discussion about assertions) before ending the chapter by describing how to put our processes to sleep for a specified amount of time.

Exercises

3.1 Consider the pros and cons of NUL-terminated strings versus counted stings. In which circumstances would the fact that a NUL-terminated string has to be scanned to determine its length become a matter of concern?

3.2 Write a set of library routines for counted strings that has the same functionality as the `str` family of functions we discuss in this chapter.

3.3   We can use the `strtol` family of functions to convert a string that represents a number in an arbitrary base to an integer, but Solaris doesn't provide a function to do the opposite. Write a function that will output the string representation of an integer in any supplied base from 2 to 36.

4

Basic File I/O

4.1　Introduction

In this chapter we examine low level file I/O. Low level I/O is sometimes referred to as *unbuffered file I/O*, because the functions we discuss in this chapter do not do any buffering, unlike those in the standard I/O library (which we discuss in Chapter 5). Although this is technically correct, it can be a little misleading, as it is possible to use the standard I/O library, which is normally buffered, in unbuffered mode. It is also possible that the kernel may internally buffer "unbuffered" I/O.

We first describe file descriptors and then describe the functions that most UNIX I/O operations rely on, like `open`, `close`, `read`, `write`, and `lseek`. We then examine the effect of application buffer size on I/O efficiency, and the data structures associated with file sharing. After talking about atomic operations, we describe the `dup`, `fcntl`, and `ioctl` functions. We end the chapter by looking at the `/dev/fd` file system.

4.2　File Descriptors

File descriptors are the fundamental way of accessing files from a user process. A file descriptor, which is a positive integer, is actually the offset into the per process file table. Each process has a process file table associated with it, and it is this table which provides a mapping between file descriptors (i.e., the process' idea of the file), and vnodes (i.e., the kernel's native description of a file). Each basic file I/O function takes a file descriptor as an argument or returns one.

The first three file descriptors for a process (i.e., descriptors 0, 1, and 2) are usually associated with its standard input, standard output, and standard error. Instead of these magic numbers, newer programs should use the POSIX constants `STDIN_FILENO`, `STDOUT_FILENO`, and `STDERR_FILENO`, which are defined in `<unistd.h>`.

File descriptors are an attribute of a process, not a thread. Hence, they are allocated per process, not per thread.

4.3   The `open` Function

Before we can do any I/O with a file, we must open it for reading or writing (or both). To open a file, we use the `open` function.

```
#include <sys/types.h>
#include <sys/stat.h>
#include <fcntl.h>

int open (const char *path, int oflag, /* mode_t mode */...);
```
Returns: file descriptor if OK, −1 on error

The name of the file we want to open is stored in the buffer pointed to by *path*, and *oflag* specifies what sort of access to the file we want (i.e., read only, write only, or read and write). The *oflag* argument also specifies any optional flags we want to use. If the call to `open` causes a file to be created, it is created with the permissions in *mode*, modified by the process' umask. If the call to `open` is successful, the file's file descriptor is returned; otherwise, −1 is returned, and `errno` is set appropriately. The file descriptor returned is guaranteed to be the lowest unused one available.

We open a file for reading, writing, or both, by setting *oflag* to one of the following mutually exclusive constants:

O_RDONLY	Open the file for reading only.
O_WRONLY	Open the file for writing only.
O_RDWR	Open the file for reading and writing. The result of applying this flag when opening a FIFO is undefined. (A FIFO (first in, first out) is a type of file similar to a pipe, and is used for interprocess communications; we describe pipes and FIFOs in more detail in Chapter 19.)

We may also specify other options by bitwise-ORing one or more of the following constants with *oflag*:

O_APPEND	Sets the file offset to the end of the file prior to each write. This is useful if, for example, more than one process is updating the file, because the writes won't overwrite each other.
O_CREAT	If the file exists, this flag has no effect unless O_EXCL is also specified, q.v. Otherwise, the file is created, with the file's owner set to the effective user ID of the process. If the directory in which the file is being created has the S_ISGID bit set, the group ID of the file is set to the directory's;

| | otherwise, the file's group ID is set to the process' effective group ID. The access permission bits of the file are set by *mode*, as modified by the process' umask. We discuss file permissions in Section 10.7. |

O_DSYNC

Write operations on the file descriptor do not complete until the data is transferred to the physical storage medium. Normally, a call to `write` returns once the data has been copied to a buffer in the kernel; it has no idea whether the data actually was stored on the physical medium. The kernel buffering we have just alluded to is not related to the buffering that happens in the standard I/O library. In Chapter 1 we referred to I/O using `read` and `write` as unbuffered I/O. More precisely, the I/O is not buffered in the process (unlike the standard I/O library, which has its own internal buffering in addition to that provided by the kernel).

O_EXCL

If this and the O_CREAT flags are set, the call to `open` will fail if the file to be opened exists. The check, and the subsequent creation of the file if it doesn't exist, are atomic with respect to other processes trying the same operation on the same file. We talk about atomicity in Section 4.13. The effect of setting O_EXCL but not O_CREAT is undefined.

O_LARGEFILE

Setting this option will set the maximum offset for the file to the largest value that can be stored in an `off64_t`, regardless of the compilation model. If this flag is not set, the maximum allowable offset is restricted to the largest value that will fit into an `off_t`. Specifying O_LARGEFILE is necessary only in programs using the transitional large file interfaces, because large file aware 32-bit processes and 64-bit processes do not distinguish between large and small files.

> This flag was introduced in Solaris 2.6 as part of the large files feature set. In releases of Solaris prior to 2.6, files were limited to 2 GB in size.

O_NOCTTY

If the file to open is a terminal device, setting this flag will prevent the terminal from becoming the controlling terminal for the process. See Section 16.6 for a description of controlling terminals.

O_NONBLOCK or

O_NDELAY

These flags affect future reads or writes to the file. If the file to be opened is a FIFO, then setting either O_NONBLOCK or O_NDELAY will cause a read-only `open` to return without delay; a write-only `open` will fail if no process currently has the FIFO open for reading. If both O_NONBLOCK and O_NDELAY are clear, then a read-only `open` will block until a process opens the FIFO for writing. Similarly, a write-only open of a FIFO will block until a process opens it for reading.

If the file to be opened is a block or character special file that supports nonblocking opens, then setting either O_NONBLOCK or O_NDELAY will cause open to return without waiting for the device to get ready; the subsequent behaviour is device specific. (We talk about character and block special files in Section 10.26.) If both O_NONBLOCK and O_NDELAY are clear, then the open will block until the device is ready before returning.

O_RSYNC   If this flag is set, reading the data will block until any pending writes that affect the data are complete. Consider the situation where we want to read a block of data that another process is updating. If this flag is not set, it is indeterminate whether the data returned will be that which is on the disk, or that which is scheduled to be written.

O_SYNC   The result of setting this flag is similar to setting O_DSYNC, except that the write blocks until the data to be transferred is written to the physical medium *and* the on-disk file attributes are updated.

O_TRUNC   If the file exists and is successfully opened for writing, setting this flag will cause the file's length to be truncated to 0 bytes. Any data that the file contained are discarded.

O_XATTR   The relative path named in *path* is interpreted as an extended attribute of the current working directory (extended attributes must be referenced with a relative path, because providing an absolute path results in a normal file reference). We talk about extended file attributes in Section 13.38.

This flag was introduced in Solaris 9 as part of the extended file attributes feature set.

Figure 4.1 summarizes the availability of these flags.

4.4   The `creat` Function

The creat function is another way of creating a file.

```
#include <sys/types.h>
#include <sys/stat.h>
#include <fcntl.h>

int creat (const char *path, mode_t mode);
```
                                              Returns: file descriptor if OK, −1 on error

Flag	2.5	2.5.1	2.6	7	8	9	ISO C	SVID	POSIX	SUSv1	SUSv2
O_RDONLY	•	•	•	•	•	•		•	•	•	•
O_RDWR	•	•	•	•	•	•		•	•	•	•
O_WRONLY	•	•	•	•	•	•		•	•	•	•
O_APPEND	•	•	•	•	•	•		•	•	•	•
O_CREAT	•	•	•	•	•	•		•	•	•	•
O_DSYNC	•	•	•	•	•	•					•
O_EXCL	•	•	•	•	•	•		•	•	•	•
O_LARGEFILE			•	•	•	•					
O_NDELAY	•	•	•	•	•	•		•			
O_NOCTTY	•	•	•	•	•	•		•	•	•	•
O_NONBLOCK	•	•	•	•	•	•		•	•	•	•
O_RSYNC	•	•	•	•	•	•			•		•
O_SYNC	•	•	•	•	•	•		•	•	•	•
O_TRUNC	•	•	•	•	•	•		•	•	•	•
O_XATTR						•					

Figure 4.1 Availability of open flags.

The name of the file to create is pointed to by *path*. If the file is successfully created, its permission bits are set to *mode*, as modified by the process' umask. The `creat` function is equivalent to

```
open (path, O_WRONLY | O_CREAT | O_TRUNC, mode);
```

> In early versions of UNIX, the *oflag* option to `open` allowed only three values: 0, 1, and 2 (for read-only, write-only, and read-write respectively—in Solaris, these are the values for O_RDONLY, O_WRONLY, and O_RDWR), hence the need for `creat`. Since support for O_CREAT and O_TRUNC was added to `open`, the use of `creat` has become less necessary.

> The decision to call this function `creat` instead of `create` was arbitrary. Ken Thompson, one of the original authors of UNIX, was once asked what he would do differently if he were redesigning the UNIX operating system. His reply was, "I'd spell `creat` with an e" [Kernighan and Pike 1984].

4.5   The `close` and `closefrom` Functions

The `close` function closes an open file.

```
#include <unistd.h>

int close (int fildes);
```

Returns: 0 if OK, −1 on error

The *fildes* argument should be a file descriptor that was previously returned by `open`, `creat`, `dup`, `dup2`, or `pipe`. When a process closes a file, any locks it may have on the file are released. We discuss file locking in greater detail in Chapter 13.

When a process exits, all of its files are automatically closed, a fact taken advantage of by many programmers. It is considered good programming practice to close a file when we are finished with it, as file descriptors are a finite resource.

We should also note that ignoring the return value from close is a common, but bad, practice. Because of the kernel's internal buffering, it is possible that a previously successful write may cause close to fail when the data is flushed to disk. In this case, the close would return −1 because the buffer flush failed.

The closefrom Function

Starting with Solaris 9, we can use the closefrom function to close a range of open file descriptors.

```
#include <stdlib.h>

void closefrom (int lowfd);
```

The closefrom function closes all open file descriptors greater than or equal to *lowfd*. With two exceptions, calling closefrom is the same as the following code:

```
#include <sys/resource.h>

int i;
struct rlimit limits;

getrlimit (RLIMIT_NOFILE, &limits);

for (i = lowfd; i < limits.rlim_max; i++)
    close (i);
```

The two differences between calling closefrom and this code are:

1. If we call closefrom, close is called only for file descriptors that are actually open, rather than for every possible file descriptor between *lowfd* and limits.rlim_max.

2. Calling closefrom causes *all* open file descriptors that are greater than or equal to *lowfd*, even those that are greater than limits.rlim_max (should any exist).

Provided we are targeting Solaris 9 and newer, closefrom can be used to great effect in daemons and other programs to ensure that all unnecessary file descriptors are closed. (We discuss daemons in Chapter 18.)

4.6   The lseek and llseek Functions

Every open file has an associated *file offset*, which determines where the next read or write operation will start from. The file offset is set to 0 when a file has been opened, and it is automatically increased after each successful read or write. Reads from a file descriptor start from the current file offset, as do writes, unless the O_APPEND flag was set when the file was opened (in which case the file offset is set to the end of the file at the start of every write). Because file descriptors are a per process attribute, any thread (in a multithreaded process) that changes the file offset will affect all the other threads using that file descriptor.

We can change the file offset for an open file by using either the lseek or llseek functions.

```
#include <sys/types.h>
#include <unistd.h>

off_t lseek (int fildes, off_t offset, int whence);

offset_t llseek (int fildes, offset_t offset, int whence);
```
                                    Both return: new file offset if OK, –1 on error

How the value of *offset* is interpreted depends on the value of the *whence* argument.

- If *whence* is SEEK_SET, the file pointer is set to *offset* bytes, relative to the start of the file.
- If *whence* is set to SEEK_CUR, the file pointer is set to its current location plus *offset*.
- If *whence* is SEEK_END, the file pointer is set to the end of the file plus *offset*.

The constants SEEK_SET, SEEK_CUR, and SEEK_END are defined in <unistd.h> and have the values of 0, 1, and 2 respectively, for compatibility with older code.

> The 1 in lseek's name stands for "long integer". The lseek system call was added to UNIX in Version 7, the same time that the long data type was introduced to C. Similarly, the ll in llseek's name stands for "long long integer".

As we discussed in Section 1.12, the size of an off_t depends on the compilation model. In a 64-bit process, and in a large file aware 32-bit process, off_t is a 64-bit quantity. In a 32-bit process that is not large file aware, off_t is a 32-bit quantity. This is fine if we expect to treat all our files in the same manner. But there are times when we might need to mix code that is large file aware with code that isn't (we do *not* recommend doing this, but it is sometimes unavoidable with legacy code). If we need to do this, we must use the transitional large file interfaces. Solaris provides the llseek function for this purpose, which stores the desired offset in an offset_t rather than an off_t. An offset_t is large enough to hold the largest supported file offset of any file, regardless of the compilation model.

Portable code should avoid using llseek. Instead, we should ensure that it is fully 64-bit clean, uses the standards compliant lseek function, and uses the large file compilation environment (i.e., define -D_FILE_OFFSET_BITS=64 on the compiler command line) if necessary.

We can use the following code to position the file pointer at the beginning of a file:

```
lseek (fildes, 0, SEEK_SET);
```

Similarly, we can use the following code to position the file pointer at the end of a file:

```
lseek (fildes, 0, SEEK_END);
```

Notice that off_t and offset_t are signed quantities. This means that negative offsets may be specified, although attempts to seek before the start of a file result in an error.

It is possible to use lseek to seek beyond the end of a file. When we next write to the file, it gets extended, creating a hole between the old end of file and the offset of the write. These holes are read back as 0. A file with holes in it is called a *sparse file*. An interesting characteristic of sparse files is that depending on the file system they reside on, the holes may not actually occupy any disk blocks (some file systems do, however, fill holes). This is why the sum of all the file sizes on a disk (as shown by using ls -l) can exceed the disk's capacity.

Example: Creating a sparse file

Program 4.1 creates a sparse file.

file_io/sparse.c

```
 1 #include <sys/types.h>
 2 #include <sys/stat.h>
 3 #include <fcntl.h>
 4 #include <unistd.h>
 5 #include "ssp.h"

 6 int main (void)
 7 {
 8     int fd;
 9     char buf1 [] = "DEADBEEF";
10     char buf2 [] = "COFFEE12";

11     if ((fd = creat ("sparse_file", FILE_PERMS)) == -1)
12         err_msg ("creat error");

13     if ((write (fd, buf1, 8)) != 8)
14         err_msg ("buf1 write error");

15     if ((lseek (fd, 36, SEEK_SET)) == -1)
16         err_msg ("lseek error");

17     if ((write (fd, buf2, 8)) != 8)
18         err_msg ("buf2 write error");

19     close (fd);

20     return (0);
21 }
```

file_io/sparse.c

Program 4.1 Creating a sparse file.

Create the file

11–12 We create the file that we will be using.

Write to file and create hole

13-14 We write out the contents of the first buffer, buf1, using the write function, which we discuss in Section 4.9. At this point, the file offset is 8.

15-16 We extend the file by moving the file pointer to beyond the end of the file. The file offset is now 36.

17-18 We write out the contents of the second buffer, buf2, which creates a hole between bytes 8 and 32 of the file. At this point, the file offset is 44.

```
$ ./sparse
$ ls -l sparse_file                        Check the file's size
-rw-r--r--   1 rich      staff              44 Jan 25 15:42 sparse_file
$ od -c sparse_file                        Look at the file's contents
0000000   D   E   A   D   B   E   E   F  \0  \0  \0  \0  \0  \0  \0  \0
0000020  \0  \0  \0  \0  \0  \0  \0  \0  \0  \0  \0  \0  \0  \0  \0  \0
0000040  \0  \0  \0  \0   C   O   F   F   E   E   1   2
0000054
```

We use the od (octal dump) command to print out the contents of the file. The -c flag tells od to print the bytes as single characters, except certain nonprintable characters, which appear as C language escapes. The \0 characters in the output represent the bytes that were read as 0 (because of the hole we created). The seven digit number at the beginning of each line of the od output is the file offset represented in octal (base 8).

4.7   The tell Function

The tell function is used to get the current file offset for a file descriptor.

```
#include <unistd.h>

off_t tell (int fd);
```
Returns: file offset if OK, –1 on error

Notice that the return type is an off_t (which is a 32-bit quantity in 32-bit processes that are not large file aware). This means that we cannot safely use it in the transitional large file environment for files that were opened with the O_LARGEFILE flag specified, because the file's offset may be too large to fit into an off_t. Instead, we should use the transitional interface, tell64. An even better approach would be to make our code fully 64-bit clean and use the large file compilation environment if necessary.

The call

```
offset = tell (fd);
```

is equivalent to

```
offset = lseek (fd, 0, SEEK_CUR);
```

4.8   The read and pread Functions

We use the read and pread functions to read data from an open file.

```
#include <unistd.h>

ssize_t read (int fildes, void *buf, size_t nbyte);

ssize_t pread (int fildes, void *buf, size_t nbyte, off_t offset);
```
                Both return: number of bytes read if OK (0 if end of file), −1 on error

The `read` function reads up to *nbyte* bytes from the open file referred to by *fd* into the buffer pointed to by *buf*. If the read is successful, the number of bytes read is returned, unless we are at the end of file, in which case 0 is returned.

It's possible that `read` will read less than the number of bytes we requested with *nbyte*. There are several reasons why this could happen.

- We are reading from a regular file, and we encounter the end of file before reading the number of requested bytes. For example, if only 64 bytes remain until the end of file, and we request 128 bytes, `read` will return 64. The next time we try to read from the file, 0 will be returned (assuming that no other process has written to the file in the meantime).

- Reading from a terminal usually happens one line at a time.

- Reading from a TCP socket may return any number of bytes, depending on how packets are received.

The read operation starts at the file's current offset, which is incremented by the number of bytes read before a successful return.

The `pread` function is identical to `read`, except that `pread` read operations start at the specified *offset* without changing the file pointer. (In other words, even though internal seek operations may be required to read the data from the specified file offset, the file's file pointer is unchanged after `pread` returns.) Attempting to perform a `pread` on a file that is incapable of seeking (for example, a FIFO or a socket) results in an error.

4.9   The `write` and `pwrite` Functions

We use the `write` and `pwrite` functions to write data to an open file.

```
#include <unistd.h>

ssize_t write (int fildes, const void *buf, size_t nbyte);

ssize_t pwrite (int fildes, const void *buf, size_t nbyte, off_t offset);
```
                        Both return: number of bytes written if OK, −1 on error

The `write` function writes up to *nbyte* bytes to the open file referred to by *fd* from the buffer pointed to by *buf*. If the write is successful, the number of bytes written is returned.

Normally, a write operation starts at the file's current offset, which is incremented by the number of bytes written before a successful return. However, if the O_APPEND flag is set, the file pointer is set to the end of the file before the buffer is written. The moving of the file pointer and the writing of the data are performed atomically.

The pwrite function is identical to write, except pwrite write operations start at the given *offset* without changing the file pointer. As with pread, attempting to perform a pwrite on a file that is incapable of seeking results in an error.

Example: Copying a file using read and write

Program 4.2 copies a file from standard input to standard output using only the read and write functions.

————————————————————————— file_io/copy.c

```
 1 #include <stdio.h>
 2 #include <unistd.h>
 3 #include <stdlib.h>
 4 #include "ssp.h"

 5 int main (int argc, char **argv)
 6 {
 7     char *buf;
 8     int buf_size;
 9     ssize_t n;
10     ssize_t res;
11     char *ptr;

12     if (argc != 2)
13         buf_size = 8192;
14     else
15         buf_size = atoi (argv [1]);

16     if ((buf = malloc (buf_size)) == NULL)
17         err_msg ("malloc failed");

18     while ((n = read (STDIN_FILENO, buf, buf_size)) > 0) {
19         ptr = buf;
20         while ((n > 0) && ((res = write (STDOUT_FILENO, ptr, n)) > 0)) {
21             ptr += res;
22             n -= res;
23         }

24         if (res == -1)
25             err_msg ("write failed");
26     }

27     if (n == -1)
28         err_msg ("read failed");

29     return (0);
30 }
```

————————————————————————— file_io/copy.c

Program 4.2 Copy a file using read and write.

There are a couple of observations we can make about this 30-line program.

- We dynamically allocate the buffer we use for copying the file. This allows us to experiment with different buffer sizes without recompiling the program.

- We `read` from standard input and `write` to standard output, thus avoiding the need to `open` any files.

- We take advantage of the convention that the system opens standard input and standard output on file descriptors `STDIN_FILENO` and `STDOUT_FILENO`.

- We enclose the `writes` in a loop, which ensures that `write` is called as many times as is necessary for the whole buffer to be written. The loop terminates only when all the data has been written or if an error occurs while writing the data.

4.10 The `readn` and `writen` Functions

We saw in the previous section how to handle the fact that sometimes `write` might legitimately return a number that's smaller than the request. Although this isn't an error, we must detect this condition so that we can write the remainder of the buffer. A similar problem can occur when we call `read`; fewer bytes than we request may be returned even though no error has occurred.

Both of these scenarios can occur with network devices, terminals, and STREAMS devices, but we should never see it happen with disk I/O.

Rather than writing verbose loops like the one in Program 4.2 every time we want to read or write some data, we have written two functions, called `readn` and `writen`, to handle the details for us.

```
#include "ssp.h"

ssize_t readn (int fd, void *buf, size_t num);

ssize_t writen (int fd, const void *buf, size_t num);

                    Both return: number of bytes read or written if OK, –1 on error
```

Throughout the text, we'll use this notation for our own functions, i.e., those that aren't supplied by Solaris. We use dashed rather than solid lines for the box around the function prototype and return values. Our header file, `ssp.h`, contains the function prototype for all of our exported functions (i.e., those that aren't private to examples). We show this header file in Program D.1.

In nearly all of the examples from now on, We'll use `writen` whenever we need to write some data. Even though we needn't take this precaution when performing disk I/O, it helps to be consistent and ensures that we won't forget to handle short writes when we *do* write to network or terminal device (e.g., when we write to standard output).

None of the examples in this text use our `readn` function (we're willing to accept whatever we get), but we mention it here for the sake of completeness. (Some programs, especially those that need to handle network I/O, have stricter requirements when it comes to reading data; for these programs, `readn` is invaluable.) We show the source code for both of these functions in Program D.5.

4.11 I/O Efficiency

In Program 4.2, we copied a file in buf_size sized chunks, which defaults to 8192 bytes. But why did we chose this number? Did we randomly pick it out of the air, or was there some reason for it?

When we read from or write to a file, the kernel buffers the data as an efficiency measure. Although we may request a given number of bytes in a read or a write, the kernel buffers the data for us. reads and writes will be most efficient if their size is the same as the kernel's buffers.

buf_size	Real	User	Sys	Iterations
1	140.00	27.08	112.77	10485760
2	70.13	13.63	56.24	5242880
4	35.37	6.44	28.70	2621440
8	17.96	3.70	14.03	1310720
16	9.29	1.77	7.22	655360
32	4.95	0.82	3.78	327680
64	2.78	0.48	1.98	163840
128	1.89	0.22	1.19	81920
256	1.89	0.08	0.82	40960
512	1.86	0.02	0.67	20480
1024	1.84	0.01	0.30	10240
2048	1.82	0.02	0.32	5120
4096	1.87	0.00	0.24	2560
8192	1.85	0.01	0.21	1280
16384	1.86	0.00	0.19	640
32768	1.82	0.00	0.18	320
65536	1.87	0.00	0.15	160
131072	1.85	0.00	0.20	80
262144	1.84	0.01	0.24	40
524288	1.86	0.00	0.23	20
1048576	1.92	0.00	0.19	10

Figure 4.2 The effect of buffer size on file I/O.

To demonstrate this, Figure 4.2 shows the results of running Program 4.2 with several different values for buf_size when copying a 10 MB file. The values of buf_size we use are powers of two that range from 1 byte to 1 megabyte. The real time is the amount of time the program took to execute, and is sometimes referred to as the wall clock time. The user column is the amount of time the CPU was executing our code, and the sys column us the amount of time the kernel spent executing code on behalf of our process. The total amount of time the CPU spends executing our code is obtained by adding the real time to the sys time. On a single-CPU system, the difference between the total CPU time and the real time is the amount of time the process was waiting for resources; in this example, the resource being waited for is the NFS-mounted file system. On a system with multiple CPUs, it's quite possible that the total CPU time will exceed the real time. On one system the author uses (a dual-processor SPARCstation 20), running the catman command gave the following results:

```
$ time catman
real    3h41m35.56s
user    3h11m52.74s
sys     1h1m47.65s
```

We can see that in this example, the total CPU time exceeded the real time by about 32 minutes.

Notice that with a very small buffer size, the amount of time waiting for I/O is small compared to our CPU time (especially the sys time, almost all of which can be attributed to the overhead incurred when making a system call). As the buffer size increases, the real time for the process drops dramatically, and on the system the author used for this test, once the buffer exceeded 128 bytes, the amount of time spent waiting for I/O is significantly more than the time spent executing our code.

Processes that spend a large proportion of their run time waiting for I/O are said to be *I/O bound*; those processes that spend relatively little time waiting for I/O are said to be *CPU bound*. If a process is I/O bound, there is little point in investing in a faster CPU; similarly, if a process is CPU bound, there's not much point investing in a faster I/O subsystem (faster and/or more disks). A well-tuned system will try to balance the CPU and I/O bandwidth.

4.12 File Sharing

Before we discuss the dup and dup2 functions, we must first talk about file sharing and atomicity. Let's examine the various kernel data structures associated with open files. Figure 4.3 shows the data structures for a process that has two files open on descriptors one and three. The dashed box represents the process' private kernel address space (the proc structure) and shows the elements we're interested in. The structures that we talk about in this section (i.e., user, uf_entry, file, and vnode) contain more members than we show here; we have shown only the ones that concern our discussion. (To see the complete structure definitions, look in <sys/user.h> for the definitions of user and uf_entry, <sys/file.h> for the definition of file, and <sys/vnode.h> for the definition of vnode.) One of the user structure's members is u_flist, which points to the process' file descriptor table.

The file descriptor table is an array of uf_entry structures, which is dynamically allocated (in multiples of NFPCHUNK on Solaris 7 and earlier; from Solaris 8, the file table always has 2^n entries). The uf_ofile member of the uf_entry structure points to a file structure, and the uf_pofile member contains the per process file descriptor flags. Notice that the file structure is outside of the process' private kernel memory (it is part of the shared kernel memory). This means, as we shall show later, that multiple processes can share the same file descriptor.

The f_flag member contains the flags which we opened the file with (or the flags that we apply to an open file using the fcntl function that we discuss in Section 4.15), and the f_offset contains the file descriptor's current offset. The f_vnode points to a vnode, which contains all the file system independent information about a file. When we need to make a distinction between the two types of open file flags, we refer to the

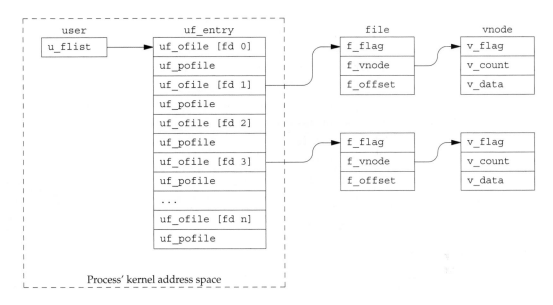

Figure 4.3 Kernel structures used for open files.

`uf_pofile` flags as the *file descriptor flags* (or sometimes the *per process file descriptor flags*), and the `f_flag` flags as the *file status flags*.

The `vnode` is the focus of all file activity in UNIX; one is allocated for each active file or directory, each current directory, each mounted on directory, and the root directory.

The `v_flag` member contains the flag that the `vnode` was created with, and `v_count` is a reference count, which indicates how many open files refer to this `vnode`. Finally, `v_data` is a pointer to the file system specific data for the file (which we don't show). Vnodes are also in the shared kernel memory, and so may be (and in fact, are) shared by more than one process.

To show how vnodes are shared among processes, Figure 4.4 shows the arrangement when two processes open the same file.

In this example, process 1 has has opened the file on descriptor 3, and process 2 has opened the file on descriptor 1. Although both processes share the same vnode (so its `v_count` will be two instead of one), they each have their own `file` structure, and so each process has a different set of flags and a different file offset.

Now that we are cognizant of the kernel's data structures for open files, we can make the following observations:

- When a `read` or a `write` function call completes, it is the `f_offset` member of `file` structure that's pointed to by *n*th `uf_ofile` pointer in the calling process' `uf_entry`, where *n* is the file descriptor passed to the `read` or `write`. If a `write` to a file causes the offset to exceed the file size as recorded in the file's inode (which is pointed to by `v_data`), then the inode is updated to reflect the new file size.

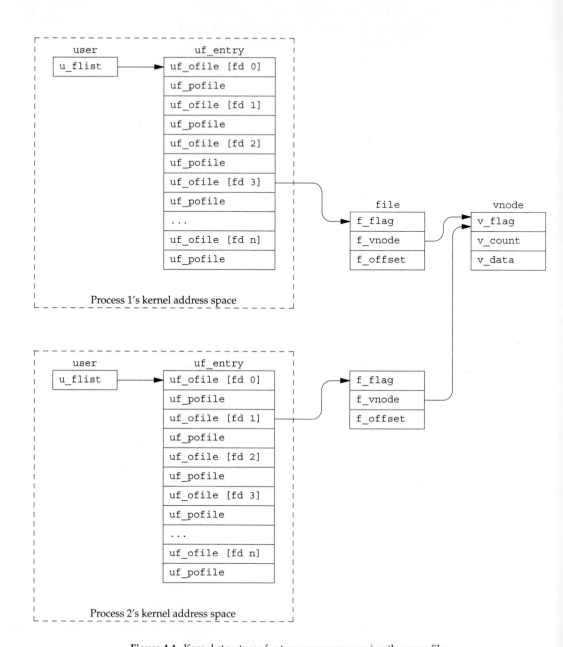

Figure 4.4 Kernel structures for two processes opening the same file.

- If the O_APPEND flag is set in a file's f_flag, the f_offset is set to the end of the file (by setting it to the file size as indicated in the file's inode) before the data transfer takes place.

- Changing the file offset by calling lseek results in no I/O; just the f_offset member is changed to the desired value. If a seek to the end of the file is requested, the offset is set to the file size as specified by the inode.

We'll have more to say about inodes in Section 10.3, when we discuss the stat function.

Although we don't show it in any of our examples, it is possible for more than one of a process' uf_ofile pointers to point to the same file. This is what the dup and dup2 functions do. File descriptors also are copied when a process forks a copy of itself (we discuss fork in detail in Section 15.3).

All of our discussion above works fine when only a single process is writing to a file, or if all the processes accessing the file are only reading from it. But if two or more processes are sharing write access to the same file, the processes' I/O needs to be coordinated in such a manner that undesirable results are avoided. This requires that certain file operations be atomic; we discuss atomicity in the next section.

4.13 Atomic Operations

When we say that an operation is *atomic*, we mean that the steps that make up the operation are indivisible (in the context of user processes, we mean that the operation is indivisible by everything outside the kernel. Atomic operations in the kernel really are indivisible.) Either all of the steps required to perform a task are completed, or none of them are. It must not be possible for only some of the required steps to be performed.

Example: Creating a file

Recall our discussion of the open function in Section 4.3, where we stated that specifying both the O_CREAT and O_EXCL flags would cause the file to be created unless the file already existed, in which case an error would be returned. We also stated that the check for the file's existence and the creation of the new one was atomic.

If there was no O_EXCL flag at our disposal, we might try to implement this with the following code segment:

```
if ((fd = open (file, O_WRONLY)) == -1) {
    if (errno == ENOENT) {
        if ((fd = creat (file, perms)) == -1)
            err_msg ("creat error");
    }
    else
        err_msg ("open error");
}
```

The first thing this code does is try to open the required file. If an error occurs, we check errno to see if the error was ENOENT (which means that file doesn't exist). If this is the case, we call creat to create the file for us; otherwise, we report an error.

The problem with this code is that the two steps of detecting the failed open and creating the file are not atomic. If the process that was executing this code is put to sleep for any reason (e.g., the scheduler decides that the process has used up enough CPU time for now), another process could create the file before the call to creat in our example code. If the second process then writes some data to the file, the data will be lost when the first process calls creat, because creat truncates files to 0 bytes if they exist at the time of the function call. On a machine with multiple CPUs, the problem is exacerbated, because the first process doesn't even need to be put to sleep for the problem to occur.

Example: Appending to a file

In Section 4.3, we also said that specifying O_APPEND when we open a file causes all writes (that use the resulting file descriptor) to be appended at the end of the file. Without the O_APPEND flag, we would have to call lseek before every write.

```
if (lseek (fd, 0, SEEK_END) == -1)
    err_msg ("lseek error");
if (write (fd, buf, 200) != 200)
    err_msg ("write error");
```

Again, this is fine if only one process is accessing the file. But if more than one process wants to access the file (for example, multiple instances of a program writing to a log file) in append mode, we run into problems.

Suppose both processes want to ensure that all of their writes are appended to the end of the file; without the O_APPEND flag, they'd both use code like we show above. After both processes have opened the file, their data structures would look similar to what we show in Figure 4.4. The first process calls lseek to position the file pointer to the end of the file (say offset 1000), but before it can call write, the kernel switches context to the second process, and it manages to call both lseek (also to offset 1000) and write, writing 200 bytes. The end of the file is now at an offset of 1200 (the inode is also updated to reflect the new size of the extended file), but when the first process resumes execution, the f_offset member of its file structure is only set to 1000, so the write that was supposed to append to the file actually overwrites what the second process wrote. This is because the lseek and write calls are not atomic with respect to each other.

Had both processes specified the O_APPEND flag when they opened the file, this problem would have been avoided because the moving of the file pointer and the writing of the data would have happened atomically in the same function call (the write). By using O_APPEND, the call to lseek can be eliminated.

4.14   The dup and dup2 Functions

We use the dup and dup2 functions to duplicate open file descriptors.

```
#include <unistd.h>

int dup (int fildes);

int dup2 (int fildes, int fildes2);
```

Both return: new file descriptor if OK, −1 on error

The dup function duplicates the file descriptor *fildes* and guarantees that the file descriptor returned will be the lowest one available. Because a file descriptor is copied, the new descriptor refers to the same file that the original descriptor does. The descriptors also share the same file pointer and access mode (i.e., read, write, or read/write).

As we showed in Figure 4.3, each open file has two sets of flags associated with it: the f_flag member of the file structure and the uf_pofile member of the uf_entry structure. After a successful call to dup, the close on exec flag for the new descriptor, FCLOSEXEC, is cleared so that it will remain open across an exec. (Very briefly, the exec function is how a new program is run in the UNIX environment; the image of the new program overlays the current process. Open file descriptors that do not have their FCLOSEXEC flag set remain open in the new process. Conversely, file descriptors that have their FCLOSEXEC flag set will not be open in the new process. We'll take a closer look at process creation in Chapter 15.) Unlike most flags for open files, the FCLOSEXEC flag is stored in the per process file descriptor flags, uf_pofile, rather than the file structure's f_flag.

The call

```
new_fd = dup (old_fd);
```

is the same as

```
new_fd = fcntl (old_fd, F_DUPFD, 0);
```

(We discuss the fcntl function in the next section.)

Figure 4.5 shows the kernel data structures after file descriptor 1 has been duped; the diagram assumes that file descriptor 3 was the lowest one available.

The dup2 function is similar to dup, except that the file descriptor *fildes* is copied to the file descriptor *fildes2*. If *fildes2* is not the same as *fildes*, and refers to a file that is already open, that file will be closed before the duplication occurs. If *fildes2* is the same as *fildes* (or if *fildes* is not a valid file descriptor), then *fildes2* will not be closed first.

The call

```
result = dup2 (old_fd, new_fd);
```

is functionally the same as

```
close (new_fd);
result = fcntl (old_fd, F_DUPFD, new_fd);
```

The only difference is that when we use dup2, the closing of *new_fd* and the duplication of *old_fd* to it happen atomically, whereas the preceding example has two discrete function calls (one to close and one to fcntl). An event (for example, the delivery of a signal) could occur between the two function calls that changes the state of the descriptors.

There's more than one way to get the behaviour of the dup2 function. The call

```
result = dup2 (old_fd, new_fd);
```

is the same as

```
result = fcntl (old_fd, F_DUP2FD, new_fd);
```

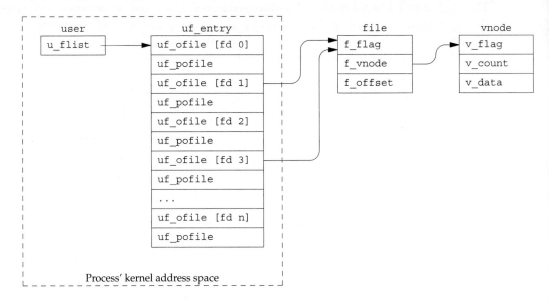

Figure 4.5 Kernel structures after dup.

In fact, this is exactly how Solaris implements dup2. We talk about the fcntl function in the next section.

4.15 The `fcntl` Function

The fcntl function allows us to manipulate and interrogate an open file descriptor.

```
#include <sys/types.h>
#include <unistd.h>
#include <fcntl.h>

int fcntl (int fildes, int cmd, /* arg */...);
```
                                        Returns: depends on *cmd* if OK, −1 on error

The *cmd* argument specifies which operation is to be performed by fcntl, and *fildes* indicates which file descriptor to use. The optional *arg* argument has its type, value, and use determined by *cmd*. There are seven different classes of *cmd* values:

- Duplicate a file descriptor
- Free file storage space
- Get or set file descriptor flags
- Get or set file access flags
- Get or set file locks

- Get or set asynchronous I/O ownership
- Obtain or release file share reservations

We summarize these in Figure 4.6.

Value of *cmd*	Category
F_DUPFD, F_DUP2FD	Duplicate a file descriptor
F_FREESP	Free file storage space
F_GETFD, F_SETFD	Get or set file descriptor flags
F_GETFL, F_GETXFL, F_SETFL	Get or set file access flags
F_GETLK, F_GETLK64, F_SETLK, F_SETLK64, F_SETLKW, F_SETLKW64	Get or set file locks
F_GETOWN, F_SETOWN	Get or set asynchronous I/O ownership
F_SHARE, F_UNSHARE	Obtain or release file share reservations

Figure 4.6 Categories of fcntl *cmd* arguments.

We now describe each of the values of *cmd*.

F_DUPFD   This *cmd* duplicates the file descriptor *fildes*, returning the lowest available descriptor that is greater than or equal to *arg*. The new file descriptor refers to the same file description as *fildes* and shares any locks. The FD_CLOEXEC flag for the new descriptor is cleared, which prevents the file from being closed across an exec.

F_DUPFD with *arg* equal to 0 is the same as dup (*fildes*).

F_DUP2FD   This is similar to F_DUPFD, except that it always returns *arg*. If *arg* refers to an open file, it will first be closed unless *arg* is the same as *fildes*. (Closing the old file and duplicating *fildes* to *arg* is an atomic operation.)

F_DUP2FD is the same as dup2 (*fildes*, *arg*).

F_FREESP   If *fildes* refers to an ordinary file, this command frees a section of the storage space associated with it. The section to be freed is specified by an flock structure, which is pointed to by *arg*. The fields of the flock structure that are used for F_FREESP are shown below (the flock structure has several other members that we don't show here).

```
typedef struct flock {
    short l_whence;      /* Base indicator */
    off_t l_start;       /* Starting offset */
    off_t l_len;         /* Length */
} flock_t;
```

The l_whence member may be one of SEEK_SET, SEEK_CUR, or SEEK_END. The starting offset, l_start, starts from the base indicator, and l_len specifies the size of the section; a value of 0 means "to the end of the file".

F_GETFD This *cmd* gets the value of the per process file descriptor flags stored in uf_pofile. Note that the only supported flag we may retrieve is FD_CLOEXEC, the close on exec flag.

F_SETFD This *cmd* sets the per process file descriptor flags that are stored in uf_pofile to *arg*. The only currently supported flag we may set is FD_CLOEXEC. Setting it to 0 will cause the file descriptor to remain open across a call to exec; if *arg* is not zero, the file descriptor will be closed upon a successful exec.

F_GETFL This *cmd* sets the file status flags and access modes that are associated with *fildes*. The access modes can be extracted from the returned value by bitwise-ANDing it with O_ACCMODE. The file status flags are a subset of those that may be passed to open, and are listed in Figure 4.7.

File access flag	Description
O_RDONLY	Open for read only
O_RDWR	Open for reading and writing
O_WRONLY	Open for write only
O_APPEND	Append writes to end of file
O_DSYNC	Synchronous data writes
O_LARGEFILE	Allow large files
O_NDELAY	Nonblocking I/O
O_NONBLOCK	Nonblocking I/O (POSIX)
O_RSYNC	Reads synchronize with writes
O_SYNC	Synchronous data and file attribute writes

Figure 4.7 File access flags.

F_GETXFL This *cmd* gets the file status flags, access modes, and file creation and assignment flags associated with *fildes*. (In other words, the F_GETXFL *cmd* can be used to retrieve all the flags passed to open, not just a subset.) The access modes can be extracted from the returned value by bitwise-ANDing it with O_ACCMODE.

F_SETFL This sets the file status flags associated with *fildes* to those specified in *arg*. The flags that may be set are: O_APPEND, O_DSYNC, O_RSYNC, O_SYNC, O_LARGEFILE, O_NDELAY, and O_NONBLOCK.

F_GETLK

This gets the first lock that blocks the lock described by the flock structure pointed to by *arg*. We describe file locking in detail in Chapter 13.

F_GETLK64

This is the transitional large file compilation environment version of F_GETLK. The *arg* argument points to a flock64_t structure. We describe file locking in detail in Chapter 13.

F_SETLK

This is used to set or clear a file lock according to the flock structure pointed to by *arg*. If the requested lock cannot be set, −1 will be returned. We describe file locking in detail in Chapter 13.

F_SETLK64

This is the transitional large file compilation environment version of F_SETLK. The *arg* argument points to a flock64_t structure. We describe file locking in detail in Chapter 13.

F_SETLKW

This is equivalent to F_SETLK, except that if the requested lock cannot be set, the process will wait until the request can be satisfied. We describe file locking in detail in Chapter 13.

F_SETLKW64

This is the transitional large file compilation environment version of F_SETLKW. The *arg* argument points to a flock64_t structure. We describe file locking in detail in Chapter 13.

F_GETOWN

If *fildes* refers to a socket, this returns the process or process group ID that will receive SIGURG signals when high priority (out-of-band) data is available. A positive value indicates a process ID, whereas a negative value (other than −1) indicates a process group ID, whose value is equal to the absolute value returned.

F_SETOWN

If *fildes* refers to a socket, this sets the process or process group ID that will receive SIGURG signals when high priority (out-of-band) data is available to *arg*. A positive value for *arg* indicates a process ID, and a negative value (other than −1) indicates a process group ID, whose value is equal to the absolute value of *arg*.

F_SHARE

This sets a share reservation on *fildes*. A share reservation is placed on the entire file to allow cooperating processes to coordinate access to it. The access mode and types of denied access are specified in the fshare structure pointed to by *arg*. The definition of the fshare structure is shown in the following code.

F_UNSHARE

This *cmd* removes an existing share reservation.

File share reservations are an advisory form of access control that allows cooperating processes, both local and on remote systems, to coordinate access to files. They are most often used by MS-DOS or Windows emulators and MS-DOS or Windows-based NFS clients, but UNIX applications may also use this form of access control.

A share reservation is described by an `fshare_t`, which has the following members:

```
typedef struct fshare {
    short f_access;      /* Access requested */
    short f_deny;        /* Access to deny to other processes */
    long f_id;           /* Process unique ID */
} share_t;
```

The `f_access` member specifies the type of access to be requested, `f_deny` specifies what access to deny to other processes if the share request is successful, and the `f_id` member is an identifier unique to the process that can be used to allow a single process to have several nonconflicting reservations. It is the `f_id` member that specifies which share reservation is to be released by using a F_UNSHARE *cmd*; the other two members (i.e., `f_access` and `f_deny`) are ignored.

The valid values for `f_access` are:

F_RDACC	Request a read-only file reservation.
F_RWACC	Request a file reservation for read and write access.
F_WRACC	Request a write-only file reservation.

The valid values for `f_deny` are:

F_COMPAT	Set the file share to old MS-DOS compatibility mode.

> Share reservations existed in MS-DOS before it understood networking. Consequently, the semantics were inadequate when the network-aware Windows appeared. To handle old MS-DOS based applications, which did not understand the new semantics, the compatibility mode was created and has the same numeric value that MS-DOS programs used. The actual semantics are beyond the scope of this text; with the creation of the Win32 API and the removal of MS-DOS, this flag is virtually never used, and may be removed from future releases of Solaris.

F_NODNY	Do not deny access to other processes.
F_RDDNY	Deny read access to other processes.
F_RWDNY	Deny read and write access to other processes.
F_WRDNY	Deny write access to other processes.

Figure 4.8 summarizes the availability of the `fcntl` *cmd*s.

Value of *cmd*	2.5	2.5.1	2.6	7	8	9	ISO C	SVID	POSIX	SUSv1	SUSv2
F_DUPFD	•	•	•	•	•	•		•	•	•	•
F_DUP2FD			•	•	•	•					
F_FREESP	•	•	•	•	•	•					
F_GETFD	•	•	•	•	•	•		•	•	•	•
F_SETFD	•	•	•	•	•	•		•	•	•	•
F_GETFL	•	•	•	•	•	•		•	•	•	•
F_GETXFL						•					
F_SETFL	•	•	•	•	•	•		•	•	•	•
F_GETLK	•	•	•	•	•	•		•	•	•	•
F_GETLK64			•	•	•	•					
F_SETLK	•	•	•	•	•	•		•	•	•	•
F_SETLK64			•	•	•	•					
F_SETLKW	•	•	•	•	•	•		•	•	•	•
F_SETLKW64			•	•	•	•					
F_GETOWN	•	•	•	•	•	•					
F_SETOWN	•	•	•	•	•	•					
F_SHARE			•	•	•	•					
F_UNSHARE			•	•	•	•					

Figure 4.8 Availability of fcntl *cmd*s.

Example: Displaying the file status flags

The next couple of examples print out the file status flags for a file descriptor by using the print_fsflags function we show in Program 4.3.

Print the file access mode

6–18 We determine the access mode of the file by bitwise-ANDing the flags with O_ACCMODE and print out the result.

Print the file status flags that are set

19–46 We check each file flag in turn, printing out its name if the flag is set. Notice that the check for O_LARGEFILE is conditionally compiled using the C preprocessor's #ifdef directive. This is because releases of Solaris prior to 2.6 don't support this feature. Similarly, the check for O_XATTR is conditionally compiled because this feature wasn't supported prior to Solaris 9.

Program 4.4 prints out the access mode and file status flags for a given file descriptor.

Get number of file descriptor to check

11–14 Check the number of command line arguments. If all is well, get the file descriptor number we are to check; otherwise, flag an error.

Get and print the file's flags

15–16 Retrieve the current access mode and file flags.

17–18 Print the file flags by using our print_fsflags function.

————————————————————————————————— file_io/print_fsflags.c

```
 1 #include <stdio.h>
 2 #include <fcntl.h>
 3 #include "ssp.h"

 4 void print_fsflags (int flags)
 5 {
 6     switch (flags & O_ACCMODE) {
 7         case O_RDONLY:
 8             printf ("O_RDONLY");
 9             break;

10         case O_WRONLY:
11             printf ("O_WRONLY");
12             break;

13         case O_RDWR:
14             printf ("O_RDWR");
15             break;

16         default:
17             err_dump ("Unrecognised file status flag: %d", flags & O_ACCMODE);
18     }

19     if (flags & O_APPEND)
20         printf (", O_APPEND");
21     if (flags & O_CREAT)
22         printf (", O_CREAT");
23     if (flags & O_DSYNC)
24         printf (", O_DSYNC");
25     if (flags & O_EXCL)
26         printf (", O_EXCL");
27 #ifdef O_LARGEFILE
28     if (flags & O_LARGEFILE)
29         printf (", O_LARGEFILE");
30 #endif
31     if (flags & O_NOCTTY)
32         printf (", O_NOCTTY");
33     if (flags & O_NDELAY)
34         printf (", O_NDELAY");
35     if (flags & O_NONBLOCK)
36         printf (", O_NONBLOCK");
37     if (flags & O_RSYNC)
38         printf (", O_RSYNC");
39     if (flags & O_SYNC)
40         printf (", O_SYNC");
41     if (flags & O_TRUNC)
42         printf (", O_TRUNC");
43 #ifdef O_XATTR
44     if (flags & O_XATTR)
45         printf (", O_XATTR");
46 #endif

47     printf ("\n");
48 }
```

————————————————————————————————— file_io/print_fsflags.c

Program 4.3   Print file status flags.

file_io/file_flags.c

```
 1 #include <stdio.h>
 2 #include <stdlib.h>
 3 #include <sys/types.h>
 4 #include <unistd.h>
 5 #include <fcntl.h>
 6 #include "ssp.h"

 7 extern void print_fsflags (int flags);

 8 int main (int argc, char **argv)
 9 {
10     int flags;
11     int fd;

12     if (argc != 2)
13         err_quit ("Usage: file_flags <file descriptor>");

14     if ((fd = atoi (argv [1])) == -1)
15         err_msg ("atoi failed");

16     if ((flags = fcntl (fd, F_GETFL)) == -1)
17         err_msg ("Can't get file status flags");

18     printf ("Flags for FD %d = ", fd);
19     print_fsflags (flags);

20     return (0);
21 }
```

file_io/file_flags.c

Program 4.4 Print out the file access mode and status flags.

The following shows the output of Program 4.4 for various file descriptors when run from the Korn shell:

```
$ ./file_flags 0
Flags for FD 0 = O_RDWR
$ ./file_flags 1
Flags for FD 1 = O_RDWR
$ ./file_flags 2
Flags for FD 2 = O_RDWR
$ ./file_flags 0 < /dev/tty
Flags for FD 0 = O_RDONLY, O_LARGEFILE
$ ./file_flags 1 > foo
$ cat foo
Flags for FD 1 = O_WRONLY, O_LARGEFILE
$ ./file_flags 1 >> bar
$ cat bar
Flags for FD 1 = O_WRONLY, O_APPEND, O_LARGEFILE
$ ./file_flags 3 3<> /dev/tty
Flags for FD 3 = O_RDWR, O_LARGEFILE
```

The first three lines are interesting; they show that standard input, standard output, and standard error are opened for reading and writing, despite there being only one logical direction for each of them (read-only for standard input, and write-only for standard output and standard error). This leads us to the conclusion that the Korn shell probably opens one file descriptor for reading and writing, and then calls dup two times for the remaining file descriptors. The next three lines show that simple redirection works as we would think: redirecting standard input causes the file to be opened in read-only mode, and redirecting standard output causes the file to be opened write-only (the append redirection example shows that the O_APPEND flag gets correctly set). The final line shows that when a file descriptor gets redirected by using the < > operator, the named file is opened for reading and writing. In this example, it is file descriptor 3 that we are redirecting.

Example: Displaying the extended flags for a file descriptor

Program 4.5 is similar to Program 4.4, except that it prints out the extended file descriptor flags for a file it opens, as well as the regular flags. We print the flags twice so that we can compare the output results for the same file. (The flags we use in Program 4.5 don't make sense for a real application. We're just using them for illustrative purposes.)

file_io/file_xflags.c

```
 1 #include <stdio.h>
 2 #include <sys/types.h>
 3 #include <unistd.h>
 4 #include <fcntl.h>
 5 #include "ssp.h"

 6 extern void print_fsflags (int flags);

 7 int main (int argc, char **argv)
 8 {
 9     int flags;
10     int fd;

11     if ((fd = open ("/tmp/rich", O_RDONLY | O_APPEND | O_DSYNC | O_RSYNC |
12         O_SYNC | O_CREAT | O_TRUNC | O_LARGEFILE, FILE_PERMS)) == -1) {
13         err_msg ("Open failed");
14     }

15     if ((flags = fcntl (fd, F_GETFL)) == -1)
16         err_msg ("Can't get file status flags");

17     printf ("Flags for FD %d = ", fd);
18     print_fsflags (flags);

19     if ((flags = fcntl (fd, F_GETXFL)) == -1)
20         err_msg ("Can't get extended file status flags");

21     printf ("Extended flags for FD %d = ", fd);
22     print_fsflags (flags);

23     return (0);
24 }
```

file_io/file_xflags.c

Program 4.5 Print the extended and regular file descriptor flags.

Let's run Program 4.5 and take a look at the results (we've had to wrap one of the lines to fit it on to the page).

```
$ ./file_xflags
Flags for FD 3 = O_RDONLY, O_APPEND, O_DSYNC, O_LARGEFILE, O_RSYNC, O_SYNC
Extended flags for FD 3 = O_RDONLY, O_APPEND, O_CREAT, O_DSYNC, O_LARGEFILE,
    O_RSYNC, O_SYNC, O_TRUNC
```

We can see that the line showing the extended flags prints out all the flags we passed to open, not just a subset.

Example: Setting or clearing file status flags

There are occasions when we want to set or clear various file flags. Program 4.6 shows our function set_fsflag, which allows us to set file flags.

─── *lib/file_flags.c*

```
 1 #include <fcntl.h>
 2 #include "ssp.h"

 3 int set_fsflag (int fd, int new_flags)
 4 {
 5     int flags;

 6     if ((flags = fcntl (fd, F_GETFL)) == -1)
 7         return (-1);

 8     flags |= new_flags;

 9     if ((flags = fcntl (fd, F_SETFL, flags)) == -1)
10         return (-1);

11     return (0);
12 }
```
─── *lib/file_flags.c*

Program 4.6   A function to set file flags.

Get the current file status flags

6–7 The current file status flags are retrieved using the F_GETFL fcntl.

Set the specified flags

8 The new flags get bitwise-ORed with the current ones. If we just set the flags without performing this step, we may inadvertently clear a flag that we want to be set.

Set the file status flags

9–10 The new set of file status flags is applied to the file descriptor using the F_SETFL fcntl.

We can write a similar function that clears flags by changing line 8 to

```
flags &= ~new_flags;
```

Here we bitwise-AND the existing flags with the one's complement of the new flags.

For example, if we insert

```
set_fsflag (STDOUT_FILENO, O_SYNC);
```

into Program 4.2 just before the outer while loop, synchronous writing will be enabled. Normally, the write function will return once the data to be written has been scheduled to be written. Turning on the O_DSYNC flag will cause write to block until the data has been written to the storage medium. Databases and other programs that want to ensure the integrity of their data would make use of this flag. The O_SYNC flag is similar, except that the write blocks until the data is written and the on-disk file attributes are updated.

Because writes with the O_SYNC flag set wait for the storage medium before returning, we expect performance to drop somewhat when the flag is enabled. To investigate the impact of synchronous writes on performance, we use two variations of Program 4.7 to copy a 10 MB file. The first has the O_SYNC flag set, and the other sets the O_DSYNC flag.

————————————————————————— file_io/copy_test.c

```
 1 #include <stdio.h>
 2 #include <unistd.h>
 3 #include <fcntl.h>
 4 #include "ssp.h"

 5 int main (void)
 6 {
 7     char buf [BUF_SIZE];
 8     ssize_t n;

 9     if (set_fsflag (STDOUT_FILENO, O_SYNC) == -1)
10         err_msg ("set_fsflag failed");

11     while ((n = read (STDIN_FILENO, buf, BUF_SIZE)) > 0) {
12         if (writen (STDOUT_FILENO, buf, n) == -1)
13             err_msg ("writen failed");
14     }

15     if (n == -1)
16         err_msg ("read failed");

17     return (0);
18 }
```

————————————————————————— file_io/copy_test.c

Program 4.7 Copy a file using synchronous writes.

Figure 4.9 tabulates the results, showing the timings for copying the same file without using O_DSYNC or O_SYNC as a reference.

Operation	Real	User	Sys
Copy file using default flags	1.40	0.00	0.33
Copy file using O_DSYNC	35.53	0.00	0.79
Copy file using O_SYNC	35.26	0.02	0.86

Figure 4.9 The effect of O_DSYNC and O_SYNC on file copy times.

In the first line, we see that the process spent about 1.1 seconds waiting for the writes to be scheduled. When we set the O_DSYNC flag, the system time (i.e., the time spent in the kernel) is more than doubled from 0.33 seconds to 0.79 seconds. However, the process spends 34 more seconds waiting for the writes to be committed to disk. The final line shows the further increase in system and user time caused by the kernel waiting for the on-disk file attributes to be updated.

This example shows how useful the fcntl function is. The process may have no control over how the file is opened (because its parent opens the files for it before the process starts running), but processes can dynamically change the O_SYNC and other flags as appropriate for the data they are dealing with.

In Section 4.18, we'll see how the use of direct I/O can also affect file I/O performance, particularly sequential file I/O.

4.16   The ioctl Function

The ioctl function is used for a variety of control functions on devices and STREAMS. To perform an ioctl on a device, we must open the file associated with it, which is conventionally in the /dev directory. The specific ioctl commands we can issue to non-STREAMS devices are device specific and beyond the scope of this text. However, we do discuss some of the ioctl operations that can be performed on STREAMS devices in Chapter 13.

```
#include <unistd.h>
#include <stropts.h>

int ioctl (int fildes, int request, /* arg */...);
```
                                             Returns: depends on *request* if OK, −1 on error

The *request* argument selects which function is to be performed on the file descriptor *fildes*, which refers to the device file. Some *request*s require an optional argument; if so, *arg* is used for this.

In the preceding function prototype, we have shown only the header files that need to be included for the ioctl function itself. Other header files may have to be included to actually use it. For example, the STREAMS ioctls require that <sys/conf.h> and <sys/types.h> are also included, and the terminal I/O ioctls need <termio.h> or <termios.h>. We'll have more to say about the terminal I/O ioctls in Chapter 12.

There are several different categories of ioctl requests. Some are private to software like Solaris Volume Manager (so we won't document them in this book), while others are available for public use. We'll just mention some categories here and save discussion about the specifics for later chapters. The categories of ioctls include: terminal I/O, STREAMS, sockets, and various hardware-specific ones.

4.17   The fdwalk Function

At times, we want to perform certain tasks on some (or all) of the file descriptors a process has open. Prior to Solaris 9, our only options were to use global variables for our file descriptors, or manually parse the file descriptors from the /proc file system.

Solaris 9 introduced a function called fdwalk that makes this task easier for us.

```
#include <stdlib.h>

int fdwalk (int (*func) (void *cd, int fd), void *cd);
```
                                    Returns: the last result from *func*, 0 if *func* was never called

The `fdwalk` function takes a snapshot of all the currently open file descriptors, and then calls the user-defined function *func* for every descriptor in the list. The file descriptors are processed in numerical order starting with the lowest numbered one. Two arguments are passed to the user-defined function: *cd*, which is a pointer to the callback data, and *fd*, which is the number of the current file descriptor.

If *func* returns a non-zero value, the iteration through the list is terminated, and `fdwalk` returns the value returned by *func*. Otherwise, `fdwalk` returns 0 after calling *func* for every file descriptor in the list.

Example: Implementing the `closefrom` function using `fdwalk`

Program 4.8 shows how we can implement the `closefrom` function from Section 4.5 using `fdwalk`.

file_io/closefrom.c

```
 1 #include <unistd.h>
 2 #include <stdlib.h>

 3 static void ssp_closefrom (int lowfd);
 4 static int close_func (void *lowfd, int fd);

 5 int main (void)
 6 {
 7     ssp_closefrom (0);

 8     return (0);
 9 }

10 static void ssp_closefrom (int lowfd)
11 {
12     fdwalk (close_func, &lowfd);
13 }

14 static int close_func (void *lowfd, int fd)
15 {
16     if (fd >= *(int *)lowfd)
17         close (fd);

18     return (0);
19 }
```

file_io/closefrom.c

Program 4.8 Implementing the `closefrom` function.

As with the real version of `closefrom`, errors from `close` are ignored. Consequently, it is possible for some file descriptors to remain open when `closefrom` returns. We should also add that injudicious use of `closefrom` can have disastrous results.

4.18 Direct I/O

By default, file I/O is performed in conjunction with the kernel's caches. When a process reads from a file, the data are first cached in the kernel's memory and then copied into the buffer supplied by the process. If the kernel detects that the process is reading sequentially from a file, it will asynchronously read ahead from the file so that the data is available immediately for the next `read`.

Similarly, when a process writes to a file, the data is first cached in the kernel's memory and is then written to the device later. To increase performance, the `write` function returns when the data has been cached; the data is later written asynchronously to the device. When possible, these writes are clustered into large chunks and written to the device is a single operation.

If we want to change the default behaviour, we have two choices. We can do this for a whole file system by using the `forcedirectio` mount option (provided the file system supports this option), or we can do it on a per file descriptor basis by using the `directio` function.

```
#include <sys/types.h>
#include <sys/fcntl.h>

int directio (int fildes, int advice);
```
Returns: 0 if OK, −1 on error

The `directio` function provides advice to the kernel about the process' expected behaviour when accessing the file associated with the file descriptor specified by *fildes*. The kernel uses this information to help optimize accesses to the file's data.

The *advice* argument specifies the expected file access behaviour, and can be one of the following values:

DIRECTIO_OFF   Applications get the default system behaviour, as described in the preceding paragraphs.

DIRECTIO_ON   This advises the system that the process is not going to reuse the file's data in the near future. The causes the file data not to be cached in the kernel's memory pages.

When possible, file I/O operations are performed directly between the application's buffer and the device when the data is accessed using `read` or `write`. When this type of transfer is not possible, the system switches back to the default behaviour for that operation. Generally, these transfers are possible when the application's buffer is aligned on a short (i.e., two-byte) boundary, the file offset is on a device sector boundary, and the size of the operation is a multiple of device sectors.

This value of *advice* is ignored while the file associated with *fildes* is mapped (using the `mmap` function we describe in Section 13.25).

We should aware of the fact that the *advice* argument is kept systemwide per file. The last caller of `directio` sets the *advice* for all applications using the file associated with *fildes*.

Small sequential I/O usually performs best with `DIRECTIO_OFF`. Large sequential I/O usually performs best with `DIRECTIO_ON`, except when a file is sparse or is being extended and has the `O_SYNC` or `O_DSYNC` flags specified.

Example: Investigating the performance impact of direct I/O

Let's investigate how the use of direct I/O affects sequential file access. Program 4.9 copies a 10 MB file; by changing lines 17 and 19, we can turn direct I/O on or off for the reading and writing file descriptors.

Figure 4.10 summarizes the results we get after running Program 4.9 four times.

Operation	Real	User	Sys
Copy file, input direct I/O off, output direct I/O off	0.45	0.00	0.32
Copy file, input direct I/O off, output direct I/O on	0.56	0.01	0.29
Copy file, input direct I/O on, output direct I/O off	2.15	0.01	0.29
Copy file, input direct I/O on, output direct I/O on	2.00	0.01	0.24

Figure 4.10 Summary of how direct I/O affects sequential file I/O.

This example clearly shows the impact of disabling the read ahead performed by the kernel when we're performing sequential input. Using direct I/O for output causes a measurable delay, but not as big as the delay for reading. Notice that the CPU times for all four examples are very similar; the differences in real times can be attributed to the waits for the disk.

As with all tuning optimizations, the recommended way of determining what works best for our applications is to measure the performance of the different optimizations we try and compare the results.

4.19 The `/dev/fd` File System

The `/dev/fd` file system is a pseudo file system that allows a process to refer to its file descriptors using filenames. A *pseudo file system* is one that represents various abstractions as files, as opposed to a regular file system that uses blocks on a disk, or a network file system, which allows files on a remote server to appear to be local. In addition to the `/dev/fd` file system, `fdfs`, other pseudo file systems include `doorfs` (which is part of the door interprocess communication facility), `procfs` (for `/proc`), and `mntfs`, which provides read-only access to the table of the file systems mounted on the current host.

—————————————————————————————————————— *file_io/directio.c*

```
 1 #include <stdio.h>
 2 #include <unistd.h>
 3 #include <fcntl.h>
 4 #include "ssp.h"

 5 int main (void)
 6 {
 7     char buf [BUF_SIZE];
 8     ssize_t n;
 9     int in_fd;
10     int out_fd;

11     snprintf (buf, BUF_SIZE, "/space/directio");
12     if ((in_fd = open (buf, O_RDONLY)) == -1)
13         err_msg ("open failed");

14     snprintf (buf, BUF_SIZE, "/space/directio.out");
15     if ((out_fd = open (buf, O_WRONLY | O_TRUNC | O_CREAT, FILE_PERMS)) == -1)
16         err_msg ("open failed");

17     if (directio (in_fd, DIRECTIO_OFF) == -1)
18         err_msg ("directio failed");
19     if (directio (out_fd, DIRECTIO_OFF) == -1)
20         err_msg ("directio failed");

21     while ((n = read (in_fd, buf, BUF_SIZE)) > 0) {
22         if (writen (out_fd, buf, n) == -1)
23             err_msg ("writen failed");
24     }

25     if (n == -1)
26         err_msg ("read failed");

27     return (0);
28 }
```
—————————————————————————————————————— *file_io/directio.c*

Program 4.9 Investigating how direct I/O affects sequential file I/O.

Each entry in /dev/fd is a number that refers to the corresponding file descriptor. For example, /dev/fd/0 refers to file descriptor 0, and /dev/fd/4 refers to file descriptor 4. Three other files conveniently refer to standard input, standard output, and standard error. These are /dev/stdin, /dev/stdout, and /dev/stderr, which are synonyms for /dev/fd/0, /dev/fd/1, and /dev/fd/2 respectively.

If a file descriptor, x, is open, then

```
fd = open ("/dev/fd/x", mode);
```

has the same effect as

```
fd = dup (x);
```

Calling creat is equivalent to calling open, and the mode is ignored.

Because opening a file in the /dev/fd file system is the same as calling dup, both files share the same file data structure, and hence have the same access mode, file status flags, and file offset (see Figure 4.5).

The /dev/fd file system is most useful in shell pipelines when we want to use a program that uses command-line-supplied filenames. Some programs allow a filename of – to represent standard input, but this is a bit of a kludge, as it could possibly be confused with a command line argument. Using /dev/fd allows us to dispense with this, and gives us a uniform way to refer to files. For example, instead of saying

```
$ cat file1 - > file2
```

to concatenate some arbitrary data from standard input with file1, we can say

```
$ cat file1 /dev/fd/0 > file2
```

and dispense with the special handling of –.

4.20 Summary

In this chapter, we talked about the functions used for unbuffered I/O. We wrote a program that copied data from its standard input to its standard output, and examined the effect of the buffer size on the program's efficiency. We also talked about sparse files and showed how to create them.

We then examined the kernel data structures associated with files and saw how file sharing was implemented. We discussed the important concept of atomic operations, and then described the dup, fcntl, and ioctl functions. Finally, we had a look at direct I/O and the /dev/fd file system.

Exercises

4.1   In Program 4.2, we used a buffer size of 8192 bytes, despite our finding that a 128-byte buffer was sufficient to make our process I/O bound. Why?

4.2   Throughout the chapter, we've stated that the file I/O we're talking about is unbuffered. Is the file I/O we've talked about in this chapter really unbuffered? Explain your answer.

4.3   Modify Program 4.2 to copy files named on the command line instead of from standard input to standard output.

4.4   Write a program that opens a file for writing, dups the resulting descriptor, and then performs an lseek and write on both descriptors. Explain what the output file would look like. How does using the O_APPEND flag when we open the file affect the results?

5

The Standard I/O Library

5.1 Introduction

In this chapter we talk about the standard I/O library, which provides facilities for performing buffered I/O. The library takes care of allocating buffers and performing I/O in optimally sized chunks, freeing us from worrying about details like the ideal buffer size. The standard I/O library also provides some convenience functions that make it easier for us to perform formatted I/O.

The standard I/O library was written by Dennis Ritchie around 1975 as a major revision of the portable I/O library written by Mike Lesk. Very little has changed in the standard I/O library since its inception.

5.2 File Streams, Data Types, and Constants

The functions we described in Chapter 4 operate on file descriptors. A successful open of a file returns a file descriptor, which is then used in all subsequent operations on that file. The functions we describe in this chapter operate on file streams. We should be careful not to confuse the term *file stream* with the STREAMS I/O subsystem (details on STREAMS programming can be found in [Rago 1993]).

When we open a file using functions provided by the standard I/O library, we say that we have associated a stream with that file. A successful open returns a pointer to a FILE object. A FILE object is a structure that contains all the information required to manage the stream, including the next character in the buffer, the number of characters available in the buffer, a pointer to the buffer, various flags (e.g., end of file and error), and the file descriptor used for the actual I/O.

> A 32-bit process can only use file descriptors 0 to 255 for a file stream, but 64-bit processes are not subject to this restriction, so they can use any open file descriptor for a file stream.

The members of the FILE object are private to the implementation and may change from one release of Solaris to another. Hence, FILE objects should be treated as opaque objects, that is, applications should not directly manipulate the structure members. Instead, we pass a pointer to a FILE object (i.e., a FILE *) to one of the functions in the standard I/O library; in this text we refer to the object we pass as a *file pointer*.

In addition to file streams and FILE objects, we need to know about five manifest constants.

BUFSIZ	This is the default buffer size used by the standard I/O library functions. It is also useful for declaring character arrays for use as buffers.
EOF	This value is returned by most functions that return an integer when an end of file condition is detected. It typically has the value of −1.
FILENAME_MAX	This constant specifies the number of bytes needed to hold the longest pathname allowed by the implementation.
FOPEN_MAX	This constant specifies the minimum number of files that Solaris guarantees can be open simultaneously.
NULL	This value (which represents a NULL pointer) is returned by most functions that return a pointer when an error condition is detected. Even though NULL is defined as 0 (although it is arguable that "(void *) 0" would be a better definition), the C run time system treats any pointer below a certain threshold as NULL. For 32-bit processes, this value is 64K; for 64-bit processes, it is 4G.

These constants, as well as the FILE object, are defined in <stdio.h>.

There are two other manifest constants we should know about:

MAXNAMELEN	This is the maximum length of each component of a pathname, including the terminating NUL. That is, it is the maximum length of a filename or a directory name.
MAXPATHLEN	This is the maximum length of an absolute pathname, including the terminating NUL.

These constants are defined in <sys/param.h>.

5.3   Standard Input, Standard Output, and Standard Error

As we mentioned in Section 1.5, when a process is started by a shell, the first three file descriptors (STDIN_FILENO, STDOUT_FILENO, and STDERR_FILENO) are reserved for standard I/O. (We qualify this by specifying processes started by a shell because other programs that create a process may close one or more of these file descriptors before calling `fork`, so they won't be open in the new process.) Similarly, three file streams are automatically available for use by a process: standard input, standard output, and standard error.

These three file streams refer to the same files as the `STDIN_FILENO`, `STDOUT_FILENO`, and `STDERR_FILENO` file descriptors and can be accessed using the predefined file pointers `stdin`, `stdout`, and `stderr`, which are defined in `<stdio.h>`.

Standard input, standard output, and standard error are usually associated with the terminal at which the program's user is sitting, although this won't be the case if we redirect any of them. When we run multiple processes in a pipeline, the standard output of one process is fed into the standard input of the next process in the pipeline.

5.4   Opening a File Stream

Before we can perform any I/O using the standard I/O library, we must first open a file stream. Solaris provides three functions to do this: `fopen`, `freopen`, and `fdopen`.

The `fopen` Function

The `fopen` function is the one we use most often to open a file stream.

```
#include <stdio.h>

FILE *fopen (const char *filename, const char *mode);
```
Returns: a file pointer if OK, NULL on error

The `fopen` function opens the file *filename* for the access specified by *mode*. If *filename* was successfully opened, a file stream is associated with it, and a pointer to the file stream is returned.

The *mode* argument specifies how the file is to be opened, and should be one of six combinations of the characters +, a, r, and w. Figure 5.1 describes the allowed values of *mode*.

mode	Description
a	Open or create the file write only, writing at end of file (append).
r	Open the file for read only.
w	Open the file for write only; truncate it to 0 bytes or create it as necessary.
a+	Open or create the file for update (reading and writing); append writes.
r+	Open the file for update.
w+	Open the file for update; truncate it to 0 bytes or create it as necessary.

Figure 5.1   The effect of the values of *mode* on `fopen`, `freopen`, and `fdopen`.

Some operating systems differentiate between ASCII and binary files. The character b can be added to any of the values of *mode* we show in Figure 5.1 to indicate a binary file. Solaris, and in fact all versions of UNIX, treats all files as a stream of bytes, so using the character b has no effect; in fact, we recommend against using it.

A read-only fopen of a file will fail if it doesn't exist. Writes to a file that is opened in append mode will be forced to the current end of file. Moving the file pointer and writing the data is an atomic operation, so different processes appending to the same file may do so without worrying about overwriting data written by another process; the data will be intermixed in the file in the order in which it was written.

When a file is opened in update mode, both reads and writes may be performed with the associated stream. There are some restrictions to this, however. Writes must not be directly followed by a read—the stream must be flushed by calling fflush, or one of the file positioning functions we discuss in Section 5.9 must be called first. Similarly, reads must not be followed by a write without calling a file positioning function, unless the read operation encounters the end of the file.

If it can be determined that it does not refer to a terminal device, an open stream is fully buffered (a terminal device is opened in line buffered mode). We talk about the different buffering modes in Section 5.11.

Notice that unlike the open function we discussed in Section 4.3, we can't specify the permissions for a file we create with fopen. Instead, files are created with read and write permission for the owner, the owner's group, and others (i.e., 0666 in octal), subject to modification by the umask value of the process. (Briefly, the bits that are *set* in a process' umask value are *cleared* when a file is created; we'll discuss this in more detail in Section 10.9 when we discuss the umask function.)

The freopen Function

In addition to redirecting a file stream using the shell redirection operators, we can also redirect an open file stream to a file by using the freopen function.

```
#include <stdio.h>

FILE *freopen (const char *filename, const char *mode, FILE *stream);
```
Returns: a file pointer if OK, NULL on error

The freopen function flushes the file stream, *stream*, and then closes the file descriptor associated with it. It then opens the file *filename* and associates *stream* with it. The *mode* argument is used to determine how to open the new file, in the same manner as the *mode* argument of the fopen function. Although it is most frequently used with the stdin, stdout, and stderr file streams, the freopen function is not restricted to these three streams; *stream* may point to any open file stream.

The fdopen Function

We may want to associate a file stream with a file descriptor that we have already opened. This would usually be because the file descriptor was obtained by one of the network-communication or pipe-opening functions, which don't offer interfaces that return a file stream. We can use the `fdopen` function to do this for us.

```
#include <stdio.h>

FILE *fdopen (int fildes, const char *mode);
```
Returns: a file pointer if OK, NULL on error

The `fdopen` function associates a file stream with the file descriptor *fildes*. Like `fopen` and `freopen`, *mode* specifies the access required. Although we can specify the access type for the file stream using *mode*, the actual access granted will be no more permissive than that of the underlying file descriptor. For example, if *fildes* is open in read-only mode, and *mode* requests update access, only read permission will be granted.

If the *mode* requested by `fdopen` includes write access, the file will not be truncated. Also, the file cannot be created by `fdopen`, as the presence of a file descriptor implies that the file has already been opened, and hence it must already exist.

5.5 Closing a File Stream

When finished with a file stream, we should close it using the `fclose` function.

```
#include <stdio.h>

int fclose (FILE *stream);
```
Returns: 0 if OK, EOF on error

The `fclose` function flushes and closes the file stream *stream*, and closes the file descriptor associated with it by calling the `close` function we discussed Section 4.5.

When a process terminates, it implicitly or explicitly calls the `exit` function. One of the many tasks performed by the `exit` function is to flush and close any open file streams. That said, it is good programming practice to close file streams when we are finished with them, because file streams are a finite resource (especially in 32-bit processes).

5.6 Reading and Writing

We can perform three types of unformatted I/O with a file stream:

- Character I/O, which treats the I/O as an unstructured stream of bytes
- Line I/O, where we perform I/O a line at a time
- Binary I/O, which we use to read or write arbitrary bytes to or from a file stream (The ISO C standard refers to this as Direct I/O.)

The standard I/O library also provides functions for performing formatted I/O, which we discuss in Section 5.8.

5.6.1 Character Input Functions

Most of the character input functions are concerned with reading a character from a file stream, but the standard I/O library also has a provision for pushing a character that we read back in to the input stream.

Reading a Character

With one exception, the four functions we describe in this section are used to read one character at a time from a file stream (the exception reads a 32-bit word at a time).

```
#include <stdio.h>

int fgetc (FILE *stream);

int getc (FILE *stream);

int getchar (void);
```

>   All three return: the next available character if OK, EOF on end of file or error

```
int getw (FILE *stream);
```

>   Returns: the next available word if OK, EOF on end of file or error

The fgetc function retrieves the next character from the input stream, *stream*, and advances the file position indicator associated with it. The character is read as an unsigned char and converted to an int. The reason for the conversion is so that characters with the most significant bit set are not interpreted as a negative number. The input functions return EOF on error or end of file, which is usually defined as –1. If legal characters could return –1, there would be no way to use –1 as an error indicator.

The getc routine also obtains the next character from *stream*, but it may be implemented as a macro rather than a function (which is the case with the Solaris implementation). This means that it runs faster than fgetc (by avoiding the overhead associated with a function call), but it also takes up more space as macros are expanded inline. Being a macro also means that getc can't be passed as an argument to a function call.

Similarly, getchar is a macro that expands to

```
getc (stdin)
```

Because it is a macro, getchar is subject to the same advantages and disadvantages as getc.

The getw function reads the next word from *stream*. Unlike a character, which is an 8-bit quantity, a word is the same size as an int. In Solaris, an int is always a 32-bit quantity, on both the SPARC and x86 platforms, and in 32-bit and 64-bit processes. Note that getw makes no assumptions as to the alignment of the word that is read from the file.

Pushing a Character Back into the Input Stream

We can push a character onto an input file stream by using ungetc.

```
#include <stdio.h>

int ungetc (int c, FILE *stream);
```
                                        Returns: the character pushed if OK, EOF on error

The `ungetc` function pushes the character *c* onto the input stream *stream*. Pushed-back characters will be returned by subsequent reads in the reverse order that they were pushed, although a successful call to a file positioning function (see Section 5.9) for *stream* will discard any pushed-back characters for that stream.

Although *c* is usually the most recently read character from the stream, this is not obligatory; we can push any character back onto the input stream using `ungetc`.

Solaris guarantees four characters of push back per stream, although the ISO C standard only requires a minimum of one. Portable applications should therefore not rely on having more than one push-back character available.

The ability to push a character back into the input stream is often useful if we are parsing a string or breaking it into tokens, because sometimes the action a program must take for the current character depends on what the next character is. Without the ability to push a character back, we would have to store the most recently read character in a temporary location and use a flag to determine if the next read should be satisfied from our temporary copy or the input stream.

5.6.2 Character Output Functions

The Solaris implementation of the standard I/O library provides us with three functions to write a character to a file stream and another function to write a 32-bit word.

```
#include <stdio.h>

int fputc (int c, FILE *stream);

int putc (int c, FILE *stream);

int putchar (int c);
```
                                  All three return: the character written if OK, EOF on error
```
int putw (int w, FILE *stream);
```
                                        Returns: 0 if OK, non-zero on error

The `fputc` function writes the character *c* (which is converted to an `unsigned char`) to the output stream *stream*. The character is appended to *stream* if the stream is incapable of file positioning, or if it was opened in append mode.

The `putc` and `putchar` routines are much like their input analogues, `getc` and `getchar`, in that they may be (and in Solaris, are) implemented as macros, not functions. They execute faster, but take up more space and cannot be used as an argument to a function call.

The `putchar` macro expands to

```
putc (c, stdout)
```

The `putw` function writes the word (i.e., `int`) w to the stream *stream*. A word is a 32-bit quantity on both SPARC and x86 platforms, for both 32-bit and 64-bit processes. No alignment of w within the stream is assumed or enforced.

5.6.3 Line Input Functions

As its name suggests, line-orientated I/O reads or writes whole lines at a time rather than a character at a time.

Two functions are provided for performing line-orientated input.

```
#include <stdio.h>

char *gets (char *s);

char *fgets (char *s, int n, FILE *stream);
```

Both return: see text

The `gets` function reads characters from the standard input stream and places them in the buffer *s* until a newline character is read or an end of file condition is detected. The newline character is replaced by a NUL character, terminating the string.

Note that `gets` is deprecated, and it should *never* be used in new programs. This is because `gets` will read an arbitrary number of characters, allowing the input to overflow the buffer we provide, with potentially disastrous results.

The `fgets` function reads at most $n - 1$ characters from the stream, *stream* and places them in the buffer *s*, stopping when a newline character is read or an end of file condition is detected. If the input length exceeds n, a subsequent call to `fgets` will return up to the next $n - 1$ characters. Unlike `gets`, the newline character is copied to *s*. A NUL character is appended to the string, terminating it.

> When using `fgets` to fill a buffer one character at a time, we should be aware that we can inadvertently create an infinite loop, as shown in this code fragment:
>
> ```
> char c;
>
> while (fgets (&c, 1, stdin) != NULL) {
>     /*
>      * This will loop for ever
>      */
> }
> ```
>
> To avoid this problem, the second argument of `fgets` should be 2 rather than 1.

Both functions return *s* if successful. A NULL pointer is returned if no characters have been read and an end of file condition is detected. If a read error occurs, a NULL pointer is returned and the error indicator for the stream is set. Finally, if an end of file condition is detected, the EOF indicator for the stream is set.

5.6.4 Line Output Functions

Two functions are provided to perform line-orientated output.

```
#include <stdio.h>

int puts (const char *s);

int fputs (const char *s, FILE *stream);
```
                              Both return: number of characters written if OK, EOF on error

The `puts` function writes the string stored in the buffer *s*, followed by a newline character, to the standard output stream.

Similarly, the `fputs` function writes the string stored in the buffer *s* to the standard output stream without appending a newline character. Neither function writes the terminating NUL character.

Even though both functions are designed for line-orientated output, there is no requirement that the last character of *s* must be a newline character.

Unlike the `gets` function, `puts` is not unsafe, but to avoid confusion over the handling of newlines, we'll just use `fgets` and `fputs`, which requires us to handle the newline characters for both input and output. There's also the added benefit of us being less likely to accidentally use the unsafe `gets` function.

5.6.5 Binary I/O

The functions we discussed in the preceding sections are fine when we want to read or write characters or character strings, but they are not useful when we want to perform I/O on arbitrary binary data. We can't, for example, use `fputs` to write an arbitrary buffer to a file, because the buffer might contain NUL characters; `fputs` stops writing when it encounters a NUL character. The same problem exists with reading; `fgets` stops when a NUL character is encountered.

We could use `fgetc` and `fputc` in loops to read or write an arbitrary byte stream, but it would be tedious, inefficient, and possibly error prone. Fortunately, two functions perform binary I/O for us: `fread` and `fwrite`.

The `fread` Function

We use the `fread` function to read arbitrary bytes from a file stream.

```
#include <stdio.h>

size_t fread (void *ptr, size_t size, size_t nitems, FILE *stream);
```
                                                        Returns: number of items read

The `fread` function reads up to *nitems* items of *size* bytes from the file stream *stream* and stores them in the buffer pointed to by *ptr*. If an error occurs or end of file is detected, `fread` stops reading data. The number of items read is returned.

The `fwrite` Function

```
#include <stdio.h>

size_t fwrite (const void *ptr, size_t size, size_t nitems, FILE *stream);
```
                                                      Returns: number of items written

The `fwrite` function writes at most *nitems* items of *size* bytes to the file stream *stream* from the buffer pointed to by *ptr*. Writing stops when *nitems* have been written or an error condition is encountered.

One problem with `fwrite` is that if the writes are performed in buffered mode, `fwrite` might return success even though the call to the underlying `write` function fails. This can cause unpredictable results, so we should either use `fwrite` in unbuffered mode (see Section 5.11) or use `write` directly.

We should be wary of using `fread` and `fwrite` to read and write data structures in a heterogeneous environment. Different architectures (and even different compilers on the same architecture) represent data in different ways, so data we write on one platform will be meaningless on another. We can use two methods to transfer data portably between dissimilar machines: send all the data as ASCII strings, or use External Data Representation (XDR), which is described in RFC 1832 [Srinivasan 1995].

5.7   Stream Status

In Section 5.2 we mentioned that a file stream has at least two flags associated with it: an end of file indicator and an error flag. We also saw in the preceding sections that some functions in the standard I/O library return the constant EOF on error *or* end of file. The only way we can determine which condition actually caused EOF to be returned is to call one of two functions: `ferror` or `feof`.

The `ferror` Function

We can use the `ferror` function to determine whether an error as occurred on a file stream.

```
#include <stdio.h>

int ferror (FILE *stream);
```
                            Returns: non-zero if an error has occurred on *stream*, 0 otherwise

The `ferror` function returns a non-zero value when an error has occurred on the stream *stream*, or 0 if no error has occurred.

The `clearerr` Function

We can use the `clearerr` function to clear the error and EOF flags.

```
#include <stdio.h>

void clearerr (FILE *stream);
```

The `clearerr` function clears the error and end of file flags for *stream*. Some programs use Control-D to indicate the end of user input, which isn't the same as being finished with the program. The `mailx(1)` command is an example of this. In these programs, subsequent reads from the terminal would return immediately because the end of file flag was set. By calling `clearerr` to clear the end of file flag, the program is able to read from the terminal again.

The `feof` Function

We can use the `feof` function to determine whether or not an end of file condition has been detected on *stream*.

```
#include <stdio.h>

int feof (FILE *stream);
```
                            Returns: non-zero if EOF has been detected on *stream*, 0 otherwise

The `feof` function returns a non-zero value when an end of file condition has been detected on *stream*, or 0 if not.

The `fileno` Function

As we mentioned previously, each file stream has an underlying file descriptor. It is sometimes useful to know which file descriptor is being used by a stream. For example, if we wanted to manipulate the file flags using the `fcntl` function we discussed in Section 4.15, we would first need to ascertain which file descriptor to manipulate. We can use the `fileno` function to find out.

```
#include <stdio.h>

int fileno (FILE *stream);
```
                                    Returns: the file descriptor associated with *stream*

The `fileno` function returns the file descriptor associated with the stream *stream*.

5.8   Formatted I/O

All of the functions we have discussed so far perform unformatted I/O. Although we can perform I/O a character at a time, a line at a time, or for an arbitrary number of bytes, we still have no control over the data format. Fortunately, the standard I/O library provides the `printf` family of functions to perform formatted output, and the `scanf` family to perform formatted input.

The formatted I/O functions are driven by a format string, which contains three types of character:

1. Regular characters, which are passed through verbatim
2. Format conversion specifications, which we discuss in the next section
3. C language escape sequences, which represent nongraphic characters (We discuss these in Section 5.8.4.)

Because all of the formatted I/O functions use the same format strings to specify the conversions to be performed, we'll examine the conversion specifications after we've looked at the individual functions.

5.8.1   Formatted Output

Formatted output is handled by the four functions in the `printf` family. Two functions output to a file stream, and the other two place their output into a user-supplied buffer.

The `printf` and `fprintf` Functions

These two functions output to a file stream.

```
#include <stdio.h>

int printf (const char *format, /* args */...);

int fprintf (FILE *stream, const char *format, /* args */...);
```
                    Both return: the number of bytes output if OK, negative value on error

The `printf` function interprets the string *format* as we outlined in Section 5.8 and outputs the result on the standard output stream, `stdout`.

The `fprintf` function does the same thing as `printf`, but places the output onto the file stream *stream*.

The `sprintf` and `snprintf` Functions

These two functions place their output into a user-supplied buffer.

```
#include <stdio.h>

int sprintf (char *s, const char *format, /* args */...);
```
                      Returns: the number of bytes stored in buffer if OK, negative value on error
```
int snprintf (char *s, size_t n, const char *format, /* args */...);
```
                      Returns: the number of characters formatted if OK, negative value on error

The `sprintf` function places the output, as determined by the string *format* and followed by a terminating NUL character, into consecutive bytes starting at *s*. No checking for buffer overflows occurs, hence `sprintf` should be used with caution.

The `snprintf` is the same as `sprintf`, except that *n* specifies the size of the buffer. The output of `snprintf` will never exceed the buffer size and will always be NUL terminated. The `snprintf` function returns the number of characters formatted; this is the number of characters that would have been written to the buffer if it were large enough.

Each function has a variant that takes an argument of type `va_list` instead of a variable number of arguments (the . . . in the function prototypes).

The `vprintf` and `vfprintf` Functions

The `vprintf` and `vfprintf` functions are the same as `printf` and `fprintf`, except they are called with an argument list.

```
#include <stdio.h>
#include <stdarg.h>

int vprintf (const char *format, va_list ap);

int vfprintf (FILE *stream, const char *format, va_list ap);
```
                      Both return: the number of bytes output if OK, negative value on error

See Section 7.3 of [Kernighan and Ritchie 1988] for all the details of how variable-length argument lists work.

The `vsprintf` and `vsnprintf` Functions

The `vsprintf` and `vsnprintf` functions are the same as `sprintf` and `snprintf`, except they are called with an argument list.

```
#include <stdio.h>
#include <stdarg.h>

int vsprintf (char *s, const char *format, va_list ap);
```
                     Returns: the number of bytes stored in buffer if OK, negative value on error
```
int vsnprintf (char *s, size_t n, const char *format, va_list ap);
```
                     Returns: the number of characters formatted if OK, negative value on error

We use the `vsnprintf` function in our error routines described in Appendix D.

5.8.2 Formatted Input

Formatted input is handled by the three functions in the `scanf` family. Two functions read from a file stream, and the third reads from a string.

The `scanf` and `fscanf` Functions

These two functions read from a file stream.

```
#include <stdio.h>

int scanf (const char *format, ...);

int fscanf (FILE *stream, const char *format, ...);
```
                     Both return: the number of successfully matched items if OK, EOF on error

The `scanf` function reads bytes from the standard input file stream, `stdin`, interprets them according to *format*, and stores the results in its arguments. The format conversion specifications are the same as for the `printf` family of functions, except as noted in Section 5.8.3.

The `fscanf` function is the same as `scanf`, but reads from *stream* instead of `stdin`.

The `sscanf` Function

This functions reads from the supplied string.

```
#include <stdio.h>

int sscanf (const char *s, const char *format, ...);
```
                     Returns: the number of successfully matched items if OK, EOF on error

The `sscanf` function is the same as `scanf`, but reads from the buffer *s* instead of a file stream.

It is usually better to use a combination of `fgets` and `sscanf` than it is to use `scanf` or `fscanf`. If we use the latter two functions, data previously buffered in the file stream will be interpreted. By using `fgets` and `sscanf`, we have more control over which set of data is interpreted.

The `vscanf`, `vfscanf`, and `vsscanf` Functions

A variant of each `scanf` function takes an argument of type `va_list` instead of a variable number of arguments (the . . . in the function prototypes).

```
#include <stdio.h>
#include <stdarg.h>

int vscanf (const char *format, va_list arg);

int vfscanf (FILE *stream, const char *format, va_list arg);

int vsscanf (const char *s, const char *format, va_list arg);
```
                    All three return: the number of successfully matched items if OK, EOF on error

These three functions are analogous to the `vfprintf` functions, in that they are the same as `scanf`, `fscanf`, and `sscanf` respectively, but are called with an argument list.

5.8.3 Format Conversion Specifications

There are two methods of introducing a format conversion. The most usual method of starting a format conversion is to use the percent character (%), which applies the conversion to the next unused function argument. An alternative is to use the sequence %*n*$ to introduce a format conversion, where *n* is a decimal integer in the range of 1 to `NL_ARGMAX` (which is defined in `<limits.h>`); this alternative format was introduced by SUSv1. In this case, the conversion applies to the *n*th function argument after the format string. This allows us to define format strings that select arguments in an order appropriate for a specific language. In a given format string, the conversion characters cannot be mixed (the exception to this is the use of %% to convert a percent character). In this text, we will use the normal % conversion character.

Conversion specifications contain several fields, a number of which are optional. After the introductory % or %*n*$, the following appear in sequence:

- Zero or more flags (in any order), which modify the meaning of the conversion specification. The flags and their meanings are discussed later in this section.

- An optional minimum field width. If the converted value has fewer bytes than the field width, it will be padded by spaces. By default, the field will be left padded, but specifying the − flag will cause the field to be right padded. The field width takes the form of an integer or an asterisk (*).

A small field width does not cause a field to be truncated; if the result of a conversion is wider than the field width, the field is simply expanded to contain the conversion result.

- An optional precision that has a different meaning for different conversion characters. The precision takes the form of a period (.) followed by *, or an optional decimal digit string (a null string is treated as 0).

- An optional size modifier that varies depending on the data type being modified.

- A conversion character that indicates the type of conversion to be performed.

The details of all these specification fields are discussed throughout this section. We'll start our investigation of conversion specifications by looking at the conversion characters, and build up more complicated examples later.

Conversion Characters

There are a large number of conversion characters, each taking zero or more arguments. These characters can be divided into five categories: integers, floating-point numbers, characters and character strings, pointers, and pass through.

The integer conversion characters and their meanings are:

d	The int argument is converted to a signed decimal number in the format [–]*ddd*. The default precision is 1, and the result of converting 0 with an explicit precision of 0 is no characters.
i	This is exactly the same as the d conversion character.
o	The unsigned int argument is converted to an unsigned octal number in the format *ddd*. The default precision is 1, and the result of converting 0 with an explicit precision of 0 is no characters.
u	The unsigned int argument is converted to an unsigned decimal number in the format *ddd*. The default precision is 1, and the result of converting 0 with an explicit precision of 0 is no characters.
x	The unsigned int argument is converted to an unsigned hexadecimal number in the format *ddd*; the letters abcdef are used to represent values from 10 decimal to 15 decimal. The default precision is 1, and the result of converting 0 with an explicit precision of 0 is no characters.
X	This is the same as the x conversion character, except that the letters ABCDEF are used instead of abcdef. This conversion character is used for output only.

The floating-point conversion characters and their meanings are:

e	The double argument is converted to decimal notation in the format [–]*d.ddd*e±*dd*, where there is one digit before the radix character (which will be non-zero if the argument is non-zero), and the number of digits

after it is equal to the precision (which defaults to 6). If the precision is 0 and the # flag is not specified, no radix character will be printed. The value is rounded to the appropriate number of digits, and the exponent always contains at least two digits.

E   This is the same as the e conversion character, except the format for the converted number is [−]$d.dddE\pm dd$. This conversion character is used for output only.

f   The `double` argument is converted to decimal notation in the format [−]$ddd.ddd$, where the number of digits after the radix character is equal to the precision (which defaults to 6). If the precision is 0 and the # flag is not specified, no radix character will be printed. If a radix character appears, at least 1 digit will appear before it. The value is rounded to the appropriate number of digits.

g   The `double` argument is printed in the style of the e or f conversion character, with the precision specifying the number of significant digits. If the precision is 0, it is taken as being 1. The style used depends on the value converted; the style of the e conversion character will be used only if the exponent is less than −4 or greater than or equal to the precision. Trailing zeros are removed from the fractional part of the result, and the radix character appears only if it is followed by a digit.

G   This is the same as the g conversion character, except the format of the E conversion character will be used instead of the one for e. This conversion character is used for output only.

If the floating-point value is the internal representation for infinity, the output will be [±]*Infinity*, where *Infinity* is either "Infinity" or "Inf" depending on the desired output string length. The printing of the sign follows the rules just described.

If the floating-point value is the internal representation for "not a number", the output will be [±]NaN. Again, the printing of the sign follows the rules just described.

The character and character string conversion characters and their meanings are:

c   The `int` argument is converted to an `unsigned char`, and the result is printed.

             If the l size modifier is present, the `wint_t` argument is converted as if by an ls conversion specification with no precision and an argument that points to an array of two `wchar_t` elements, the first of which contains the `wint_t` argument to the ls conversion specification, and the second of which is a NUL wide character.

C   This is the same as specifying lc.

s   The argument must be a pointer to an array of `char`s. Bytes from the array are written up to (but not including) the terminating NUL. If a precision is specified, a standard-conforming application will write only the number of bytes specified by the precision; an application that is not standard-conforming will write only the portion of the string that will display in the number of screen columns specified by the precision. If the precision is not specified, it is taken to be infinite, so all bytes up to the first NUL will be printed.

If the l size modifier is present, the argument must be a pointer to an array of wchar_ts. Wide characters from the array are converted to characters up to and including a terminating NUL character. The resulting characters up to (but not including) the terminating NUL are printed.

S   This is the same as specifying ls.

wc   The int argument is converted to a wide character (wchar_t), and the resulting wide character is printed.

ws   The argument must be a pointer to an array of wchar_ts. Bytes from the array are written up to (but not including) the terminating NUL. If a precision is specified, only the portion of the wide character array that will display in the number of screen columns specified by the precision will be written. If the precision is not specified, it is taken to be infinite, so all wide characters up to the first NUL will be printed.

The pointer conversion characters and their meanings are:

n   The argument must be a pointer to an int, into which is written the number of bytes written to the standard output I/O stream so far by this call to one of the printf functions. No arguments are converted.

p   The argument must be a pointer to a void. The value of the pointer is converted to a set of sequences of printable characters.

The scan set conversion character and its meaning is:

[This conversion character introduces a scan set. A scan set matches all the characters between [and the closing], unless the first character is a caret (^), in which case, all characters *not* in the scan set will be matched. A] can be matched by making it the first character (after the ^, if any). The normal rule of white space ending a conversion specification is suppressed. The argument must be a pointer to an array of chars, which must be big enough to hold the expected sequence and a terminating NUL, which will be added automatically. This conversion character is used for input only.

The pass through conversion character and its meaning is:

%   Print a % sign. No argument is converted, and the entire conversion specification must be %%.

Figure 5.2 summarizes these conversion characters.

Character	Argument type	Target format
d	int	Decimal integer
i	int	Decimal integer
o	unsigned int	Octal integer
u	unsigned int	Decimal integer
x	unsigned int	Hexadecimal integer (using abcdef)
X	unsigned int	Hexadecimal integer (using ABCDEF)
e	double	Decimal exponent notation (using e)
E	double	Decimal exponent notation (using E)
f	double	Decimal notation
g	double	Decimal or decimal exponent notation (using e)
G	double	Decimal or decimal exponent notation (using E)
c	int	A character (unsigned char)
C	wint_t	Two wchar_ts
s	array of chars	String
S	array of wchar_ts	Wide character string
wc	int	Wide character (wchar_t)
ws	array of wchar_ts	Wide character string
n	int *	None
p	void *	The value of the pointer
[	array of chars	All characters between [and] (or not if first character is ^)
%	None	% character

Figure 5.2 Conversion characters.

Example: Simple conversion specifications

Program 5.1 prints out the results of several simple conversion specifications. As we add more detail to our discussion of conversion specifications, we'll modify this example to show the results of the changes we discuss.

This is the output we get from Program 5.1:

```
$ ./printf1
i = '12345'
f = '1.234568e+03'
f = '1234.567871'
f = '1234.57'
s = 'This string is 34 characters long.'
```

We've enclosed the results in single quotes to show the effect of some of the modifiers later. The three lines showing the value of f illustrate three of the floating-point formats.

standard_io/printf1.c

```
1 #include <stdio.h>

2 int main (void)
3 {
4     int i = 12345;
5     float f = 1234.56789123456789;
6     char *s = "This string is 34 characters long.";

7     printf ("i = '%d'\n", i);
8     printf ("f = '%e'\n", f);
9     printf ("f = '%f'\n", f);
10    printf ("f = '%g'\n", f);
11    printf ("s = '%s'\n", s);

12    return (0);
13 }
```

standard_io/printf1.c

Program 5.1 Simple conversion specifications.

Example: Using the alternate conversion introducer

Program 5.2 shows how we can use the alternative sequence of characters to introduce a conversion specification (i.e., how we can use %*n*$ instead of just %).

standard_io/printf2.c

```
1 #include <stdio.h>

2 int main (void)
3 {
4     char *one = "one";
5     int two = 2;
6     char *three = "three";

7     printf ("%1$s %2$d %3$s %1$s\n", one, two, three);

8     return (0);
9 }
```

standard_io/printf2.c

Program 5.2 Using the alternative conversion introducer.

This is the output we get when we run Program 5.2:

```
$ ./printf2
one 2 three one
```

Note that numbered arguments can be referenced more than once.

Precision Modifiers

The precision modifier determines the precision and the number of significant digits to be displayed.

For the d, i, o, u, x, and X conversion characters, the precision specifies the minimum number of digits to appear (the field is padded with leading zeros).

For the e, E, and f conversion characters, it specifies the number of digits to appear after the radix character.

For the g and G conversion characters, it specifies the maximum number of significant digits, and for the s or S conversion characters, it specifies the maximum number of bytes to be printed.

We stated previously that a field width and/or precision may be indicated by an asterisk. In this case, an int argument supplies the field width or precision. Arguments specifying the field width, the precision, or both must appear in that order before the argument, if any, to be converted. In format strings using the %*n*$ form of conversion specification, a field width or precision may be indicated by the sequence **m$ where *m* is a decimal integer from 1 to NL_ARGMAX, giving the position in the argument list (after the format string) of an integer argument containing the field width or precision.

The precision modifiers are summarized in Figure 5.3.

Conversion characters	Description
d, i, o, u, x, and X	Minimum number of digits (pad with leading zeros)
e, E, and f	Number of digits after the radix character
g and G	Maximum number of significant digits
s and S	Maximum number of bytes to print

Figure 5.3   Precision modifiers.

Example: Adding precision modifiers

Program 5.3 adds some precision modifier characters to Program 5.1.

standard_io/printf3.c

```
 1 #include <stdio.h>

 2 int main (void)
 3 {
 4     int i = 12345;
 5     float f = 1234.56789123456789;
 6     char *s = "This string is 34 characters long.";

 7     printf ("i = '%15.9d'\n", i);
 8     printf ("f = '%.9e'\n", f);
 9     printf ("f = '%.9f'\n", f);
10     printf ("f = '%.9g'\n", f);
11     printf ("s = '%30.20s'\n", s);

12     return (0);
13 }
```

standard_io/printf3.c

Program 5.3   Adding precision modifiers.

Running our new program gives the following results:

```
$ ./printf3
i = '       000012345'
f = '1.234567871e+03'
f = '1234.567871094'
f = '1234.56787'
s = '            This string is 34 ch'
```

We can see that the first line has been padded with zeros to make it nine characters long and placed in a field that is 15 characters wide. The floating-point numbers are also accurate to more significant digits. The string output is interesting. Here we've said that at most 20 characters are to be printed in a field that is 30 characters wide. Note that by default, when we specify a field width, the output is right-aligned in that field.

Conversion Specification Flag Characters

There are seven conversion specification flag characters. These are:

'   The integer portion of a decimal conversion will be formatted with thousands grouping characters.

−   The result of the conversion will be left-justified within the field (right justification is the default).

+   The result of a signed conversion will always begin with a + or − sign. By default, only negative values are preceded by a sign.

" "   The space conversion specification flag character specifies that if the first character of a signed conversion is not a sign or if a signed conversion results in no characters, a space will be placed before the result. The flag is overridden by the + flag.

Convert the value to an alternate form (this flag has no effect with the c, d, i, s, and u conversion characters). If the conversion character is o, the precision is increased (if necessary) to force the first digit of the result to be zero.

   If the conversion character is x or X, a non-zero result will have "0x" or "0X" prepended to it.

   If the conversion character is e, E, f, g, or G, the result will always contain a radix character, even if no digits follow the radix character. By default, the radix character is only printed if one or more digits follow it.

0   If the conversion character is d, e, E, f, g, G, i, o, u, x, or X, leading zeros are printed (after any sign indicator) to pad to the field width (no space padding is performed). The − flag takes precedence over the 0 flag if both are specified.

   If the conversion character is d, i, o, u, x, or X, and a precision is specified, the 0 flag will be ignored. If both the 0 and ' flags appear, the grouping characters are inserted before the zero padding.

    *   Suppress an assignment (input only). This will cause the conversion specification to be matched, but the results of the match will not be stored. This is useful for skipping fields when we are performing formatted input.

Figure 5.4 summarizes the conversion specification flag characters.

Flag	Description
'	Format with thousands grouping characters
–	Left justify
+	Always print a + or – sign
" "	Print a space if no sign or output
#	Convert the value to an alternate form
0	Pad with leading zeros
*	Suppress assignment

Figure 5.4 Conversion specification flag characters.

Example: Adding conversion specification flags

Program 5.4 introduces some specification flags into our program.

———— standard_io/printf4.c

```
 1 #include <stdio.h>

 2 int main (void)
 3 {
 4     int i = 12345;
 5     float f = 1234.56789123456789;
 6     char *s = "This string is 34 characters long.";

 7     printf ("i = '%09d'\n", i);
 8     printf ("f = '%.9e'\n", f);
 9     printf ("f = '%+.9f'\n", f);
10     printf ("f = '%.9g'\n", f);
11     printf ("s = '%-30.20s'\n", s);

12     return (0);
13 }
```
———— standard_io/printf4.c

Program 5.4 Adding conversion specification flags.

Let's take a look at the effect of these flags on our output:

```
$ ./printf4
i = '000012345'
f = '1.234567871e+03'
f = '+1234.567871094'
f = '1234.56787'
s = 'This string is 34 ch            '
```

Notice that this time our truncated string is left aligned within its field. Also, the middle floating-point number is preceded by a + sign.

Size Modifiers

There are four size modifiers. These are:

h   The following d, i, o, u, x, or X conversion character will be interpreted as an
    unsigned short int or a short int. The following n conversion character
    will be interpreted as a pointer to a short int.

l   (This character is a lower case L, not the number one.) The following d, i, o, u, x,
    or X conversion character will be interpreted as an unsigned long int or a
    long int. The following n conversion character will be interpreted as a pointer
    to a long int. The following c conversion character will be interpreted as a
    wint_t, and the following s conversion character is interpreted as a wchar_t.

ll (These characters are lower case Ls, not the number one.) The following d, i, o, u,
    x, or X conversion character will be interpreted as an unsigned long long or
    a long long. The following n conversion character will be interpreted as a
    pointer to a long long.

L   The following e, E, f, g, or G conversion character will be interpreted as a long
    double.

The size modifiers are summarized in Figure 5.5.

Size modifier	Conversion characters	Interpretation
h	d, i, o, u, x, and X n	unsigned short int or short int pointer to a short int
l	d, i, o, u, x, and X n c s	unsigned long int or long int pointer to a long int wint_t wchar_t
ll	d, i, o, u, x, and X n	unsigned long long or long long pointer to a long long
L	e, E, f, g, and G	long double

Figure 5.5 Size modifiers.

Example: Adding size modifiers

The last program in this section, Program 5.5, shows how we use size modifiers.

Running Program 5.5 shows why size modifiers are necessary:

```
$ ./printf5
ll = '11'                              This is wrong
ll = '50000000000'
```

In the first line of output, where we do not specify the size of ll, its value is incorrectly
printed as 11. This is because the only the first 32 bits (which are called the *high order*

standard_io/printf5.c
```
1 #include <stdio.h>

2 int main (void)
3 {
4     long long ll = 50000000000;

5     printf ("ll = '%d'\n", ll);
6     printf ("ll = '%lld'\n", ll);

7     return (0);
8 }
```
standard_io/printf5.c

Program 5.5 Adding size modifiers.

word; the remaining 32 bits are called the *low order word*) of the 64-bit value are used, and the value of the high order word is 11.

5.8.4 C Language Escape Sequences

Several escape sequences built into the C language are commonly used in format strings for the `printf` family of functions. The sequences are not processed by the `printf` functions, but are converted by the compiler. The escape sequences and their meanings are:

\a	Alert. Ring the bell.
\b	Backspace. Move the printing position to one character before the current position, unless the current position is the start of a line.
\f	Form feed. Move the printing position to the start of the next logical page.
\n	Newline. Move the printing position to the start of the next line.
\r	Carriage return. Move the printing position to the start of the current line.
\t	Tab. Move the printing position to the next implementation-defined horizontal tab position on the current line. Tab stops are usually set in multiples of eight.
\v	Vertical tab. Move the printing position to the start of the next implementation-defined vertical tab position. Vertical tabs are usually one line.
\\	Back slash. Print a back slash character (\).

In addition to these escape sequences, we can also specify arbitrary octal or hexadecimal number sequences. This syntax is more frequently used to represent the NUL character as "\0", which is identical to the numerical constant 0. Using this notation, an octal number is assumed, unless the sequence begins with x (X is not allowed).

5.9   Positioning a Stream

One of the pieces of information kept about a file stream is its current position indicator, or offset. Solaris provides seven functions to get or set a file stream's position indicator.

Getting the File Position Indicator

We can retrieve the current file position indicator using either the `ftell` or `fgetpos` functions.

```
#include <stdio.h>

long ftell (FILE *stream);

off_t ftello (FILE *stream);
```
                                    Both return: the current file offset if OK, −1 on error

The `ftell` function returns the current value of the file position indicator for the stream *stream*. The `ftello` function is identical to `ftell`, except it returns an `off_t` rather than a `long`.

The offset is measured in bytes from the beginning of the file.

ISO C introduced the `fgetpos` function.

```
#include <stdio.h>

int fgetpos (FILE *stream, fpos_t *pos);
```
                                             Returns: 0 if OK, non-zero on error

The `fgetpos` function stores the value of the current file position indicator for the stream *stream* in the object pointed to by *pos*. The value stored contains unspecified information usable by `fsetpos` for repositioning the stream to its position at the time of the call to `fgetpos`.

Setting the File Position Indicator

We can set the current file position indicator by using either the `fseek` or `fseeko` functions.

```
#include <stdio.h>

int fseek (FILE *stream, long offset, int whence);

int fseeko (FILE *stream, off_t offset, int whence);
```
                                               Both return: 0 if OK, −1 on error

```
void rewind (FILE *stream);
```

The `fseek` function sets the file position indicator for the stream *stream*. The `fseeko` function is identical, except that *offset* is of type `off_t` rather than a `long`.

The new position is measured in bytes from the beginning of the file, and is obtained by adding *offset* to the position specified by *whence*.

The permitted values for *whence* are:

`SEEK_SET`	Set the position equal to *offset* bytes.
`SEEK_CUR`	Set the position equal to the current location plus *offset*.
`SEEK_END`	Set the position to EOF plus *offset*.

If the stream is to be used with the wide character functions, *offset* must either be 0 or a value returned by a previous call to `ftell` on the same stream, and *whence* must be `SEEK_SET`.

A successful call to `fseek` clears the end of file indicator for *stream* and undoes any `ungetc` on the same stream.

Positioning the file pointer beyond the end of file and writing data will result in the creating of a sparse file (see Section 4.6).

The `rewind` function resets the file position indicator for the stream *stream*. The call

```
rewind (stream);
```

is the same as

```
fseek (stream, 0L, SEEK_SET);
```

except that `rewind` also clears the error indicator for *stream*.

ISO C also introduced the `fsetpos` function.

```
#include <stdio.h>

int fsetpos (FILE *stream, const fpos_t *pos);
```
Returns: 0 if OK, non-zero on error

The `fsetpos` function sets the file position indicator for the stream *stream* according to the value of the object *pos*, which must have been obtained from a prior call to `fgetpos` on the same stream.

A successful call to `fsetpos` clears the end of file indicator for *stream* and undoes the effects of any `ungetc` on the same stream.

5.10 File Stream Locking

The standard I/O functions we have talked about so far guarantee that when two threads in the same process are writing to the same file, the individual writes are atomic. This means that although an individual write will not be interfered with by a write from another thread, multiple writes issued by more than one process will appear in an unpredictable order.

For example, suppose we have an application that stores records in a file, and that each record consists of several lines. A function to write the records could consist of a few fprintf lines, one for each item in the record. If only one thread is calling the record output function, the lines will appear in the file in the order in which they were written. However, if we have two threads calling the record output function, we have no way of predicting the order in which the lines will be printed (although the lines themselves will be whole and complete).

The reason why the standard I/O function can guarantee the atomicity of the writes is because the functions lock the file stream before writing the data, and unlock it when they have written the data. The standard I/O library provides two functions to lock a file stream, and one function to unlock a file stream.

The `flockfile` and `ftrylockfile` Functions

The flockfile and ftrylockfile functions are used to acquire a file stream lock.

```
#include <stdio.h>

void flockfile (FILE *stream);

int ftrylockfile (FILE *stream);
```

Returns: 0 if lock acquired, non-zero if not

The flockfile function acquires an internal lock on the file stream *stream*. If the lock has already been acquired by another thread, the thread calling flockfile will block until the lock is available. If the file stream lock is available, flockfile not only acquires the lock, but keeps track of how many times it has been called by the current thread. This means that a file stream lock can be acquired more than once by the same thread.

The ftrylockfile function also acquires an internal lock on the file stream *stream*, but unlike flockfile, ftrylockfile will return immediately should the file stream lock be unavailable. In other words, it is a nonblocking version of flockfile.

Note that these functions acquire internal (i.e., process specific) locks on the stream. They therefore can't be used for interprocess advisory locking (unlike the functions we describe in Chapter 13).

The `funlockfile` Function

The funlockfile function is used to release a previously acquired file stream lock.

```
#include <stdio.h>

void funlockfile (FILE *stream);
```

The funlockfile function releases the lock (that was previously acquired by either flockfile or ftrylockfile) that the current thread has on the file stream *stream*. If the current thread has locked the file stream recursively, `funlockfile` must be called the same number of times that `flockfile` or `ftrylockfile` was called before the file stream lock is available for other threads to acquire.

Example: Writing records with and without a file stream lock

Program 5.6 is a multithreaded program. Each thread writes a record, using `fprintf` statements for each line. Each line also contains the thread ID, so that we can see which thread the line corresponds to.

We use POSIX threads (Pthreads) in this example; see [Butenhof 1997] for details. This means that we must link our program with the Pthreads library, by specifying `-lpthread` on the command line.

Before we run Program 5.6, let's take a closer look at its implementation.

Set thread concurrency

16 Set the thread concurrency to two. This is advising the Pthreads library that we have (at least) two processors available, so two threads can run concurrently. In this example there's no reason to set the thread concurrency any higher, as we only have two threads that do anything useful. This step is unnecessary starting with Solaris 9 because of the new default thread library. This alternative thread library was first available with Solaris 8, but it was not the default.

Start each thread

17–18 Each of these lines creates a thread and starts it running. Whether these threads run concurrently is determined by the number of processors in the machine, how busy they are, and the relative priority of other threads running on the machine.

Wait for both threads to finish

19–20 These lines ensure that both threads have finished before ending the program (the `main` function also runs in the context of its own thread).

Get our thread ID

27 We retrieve our thread ID so that we can print it as part of printing part of a record.

Let's run Program 5.6 on a workstation with two processors.

```
$ ./flockfile1
$ cat records.dat
5: Name
5: Address
5: City
5: Province
5: Post Code
5: Phone
4: Name
4: Address
4: City
4: Province
5: Fax
5: Email
```

standard_io/flockfile1.c

```
 1 #include <stdio.h>
 2 #include <unistd.h>
 3 #include <stdlib.h>
 4 #include <pthread.h>

 5 #define RECORD_FILE "records.dat"

 6 FILE *fp;

 7 static void *write_record (void *arg);

 8 int main (void)
 9 {
10     pthread_t thread1;
11     pthread_t thread2;

12     if ((fp = fopen (RECORD_FILE, "w")) == NULL) {
13         perror ("Can't open " RECORD_FILE);
14         exit (1);
15     }

16     pthread_setconcurrency (2);
17     pthread_create (&thread1, NULL, write_record, NULL);
18     pthread_create (&thread2, NULL, write_record, NULL);

19     pthread_join (thread1, NULL);
20     pthread_join (thread2, NULL);

21     fclose (fp);

22     return (0);
23 }

24 static void *write_record (void *arg)
25 {
26     pthread_t thread_id;

27     thread_id = pthread_self ();

28     fprintf (fp, "%u: Name\n", thread_id);
29     fprintf (fp, "%u: Address\n", thread_id);
30     fprintf (fp, "%u: City\n", thread_id);
31     fprintf (fp, "%u: Province\n", thread_id);
32     fprintf (fp, "%u: Post Code\n", thread_id);
33     fprintf (fp, "%u: Phone\n", thread_id);
34     fprintf (fp, "%u: Fax\n", thread_id);
35     fprintf (fp, "%u: Email\n", thread_id);

36     return (NULL);
37 }
```

standard_io/flockfile1.c

Program 5.6   Two threads writing a record without file locking.

```
4: Post Code
4: Phone
4: Fax
4: Email
```

The number before the colon is the thread ID. Its value is not important, except to show which thread wrote a particular line. We can see that in this case, with no file locking, the output from the two threads is unpredictably intermingled.

When we add the calls to `flockfile` and `funlockfile` (i.e., lines 28 and 37 in Program 5.7, which we've highlighted in the listing), we can see that the records aren't intermingled (although the order of their appearance is still unpredictable).

```
$ ./flockfile2
$ cat records.dat
4: Name
4: Address
4: City
4: Province
4: Post Code
4: Phone
4: Fax
4: Email
5: Name
5: Address
5: City
5: Province
5: Post Code
5: Phone
5: Fax
5: Email
```

5.10.1 Unlocked File Stream I/O

If performance is an issue with reading or writing characters using the standard I/O library, versions of the character I/O routines that don't perform any locking are available.

The `getc_unlocked` and `getchar_unlocked` Routines

These two routines implement unlocked character input.

```
#include <stdio.h>

int getc_unlocked (FILE *stream);

int getchar_unlocked (void);
```
              Both return: the next byte from the input stream if OK, EOF on end of file or error

The `getc_unlocked` and `getchar_unlocked` routines are variants of `getc` and `getchar` respectively that do not lock the stream. It is the caller's responsibility to acquire a stream lock using `flockfile` (or `ftrylockfile`) before calling these routines, and to unlock it using `funlockfile` afterward. Both routines are implemented as macros.

———————————————————————————————————— standard_io/flockfile2.c

```
 1 #include <stdio.h>
 2 #include <unistd.h>
 3 #include <stdlib.h>
 4 #include <pthread.h>

 5 #define RECORD_FILE "records.dat"

 6 FILE *fp;

 7 static void *write_record (void *arg);

 8 int main (void)
 9 {
10     pthread_t thread1;
11     pthread_t thread2;

12     if ((fp = fopen (RECORD_FILE, "w")) == NULL) {
13         perror ("Can't open " RECORD_FILE);
14         exit (1);
15     }

16     pthread_setconcurrency (2);
17     pthread_create (&thread1, NULL, write_record, NULL);
18     pthread_create (&thread2, NULL, write_record, NULL);

19     pthread_join (thread1, NULL);
20     pthread_join (thread2, NULL);

21     fclose (fp);

22     return (0);
23 }

24 static void *write_record (void *arg)
25 {
26     pthread_t thread_id;

27     thread_id = pthread_self ();
28     flockfile (fp);
29     fprintf (fp, "%u: Name\n", thread_id);
30     fprintf (fp, "%u: Address\n", thread_id);
31     fprintf (fp, "%u: City\n", thread_id);
32     fprintf (fp, "%u: Province\n", thread_id);
33     fprintf (fp, "%u: Post Code\n", thread_id);
34     fprintf (fp, "%u: Phone\n", thread_id);
35     fprintf (fp, "%u: Fax\n", thread_id);
36     fprintf (fp, "%u: Email\n", thread_id);
37     funlockfile (fp);

38     return (NULL);
39 }
```

———————————————————————————————————— standard_io/flockfile2.c

Program 5.7   Two threads writing a record with file locking.

The following code sample illustrates the use of these functions.

```
flockfile (fp);
while (!feof (fp))
    *buf++ = getc_unlocked (fp);
funlockfile (fp);
```

In this sample, fp is a file pointer to a file that has been opened, and buf is a character array that is assumed to be big enough to store the input.

The `putc_unlocked` and `putchar_unlocked` Routines

These two routines implement unlocked character output.

```
#include <stdio.h>

int putc_unlocked (int c, FILE *stream);

int putchar_unlocked (int c);
```
                                    Both return: the character written if OK, EOF on error

The putc_unlocked and putchar_unlocked routines are variants of putc and putchar respectively that do not lock the stream. It is the caller's responsibility to acquire a stream lock using flockfile (or ftrylockfile) before calling these routines, and to unlock it using funlockfile afterward. Both routines are implemented as macros.

The following code sample illustrates the use of these functions.

```
flockfile (fp);
while (*buf)
    putc_unlocked (*buf++, fp);
funlockfile (fp);
```

In this sample, fp is a file pointer to a file that has been opened, and buf is a character array that holds the characters to output.

In the next section, we'll examine how much of an effect on performance these functions have.

5.11 Buffering

One of the design goals of the standard I/O library was to minimize the number of read and write system calls (recall our discussion of I/O efficiency in Section 4.11 comparing the amount of CPU time required to perform I/O with different buffer sizes). The buffering of each file stream is provided automatically.

There are three buffering modes.

1. Fully buffered. When I/O is fully buffered, no actual I/O takes place until the buffer allocated by the standard I/O library fills up. The memory for the buffer is allocated dynamically the first time I/O is performed on the stream. By default, all standard I/O with disk-based files occurs in this mode.

   When a standard I/O buffer is written to disk, we say that it has been *flushed*. A buffer is flushed automatically when it is filled, or can be flushed manually using the `fflush` function we discuss further on. Flush is another one of those terms that is overloaded in UNIX programming. In the context of standard I/O, flushing means writing out the buffer to a file (whether or not the buffer is full), but in the context of terminal I/O (see Chapter 12), flushing means throwing away any pending I/O already in a buffer.

2. Line buffered. When I/O is line buffered, the standard I/O library defers performing the I/O until a newline character is encountered. This allows us to use character I/O (e.g., `fputc`) knowing that no I/O will occur until we read or write a newline. File streams connected to an interactive terminal (e.g., standard input and standard output) are usually line buffered (the notable exception being standard error, which is unbuffered).

   There are two things to bear in mind with line buffered I/O. The first is that since the buffer allocated by the standard I/O library to collect the line is a fixed size, actual I/O might take place before a newline is encountered. The second is that bytes are intended to be transmitted from all line buffered streams when input is requested from an unbuffered stream, or when input is requested from a line buffered stream that requires the transmission of bytes.

3. Unbuffered. In this mode, the standard I/O library does not buffer the file stream. For example, if we write a number of characters to a file, we would expect all of those characters to be written immediately (probably by using the `write` function).

   By default standard error is unbuffered. This is so that error messages are displayed as quickly as possible regardless of whether they contain newline characters. However, using `freopen` on standard error will cause it to become fully buffered or line buffered.

In summary:

- Standard error always defaults to unbuffered mode.
- All other file streams are fully buffered unless they refer to a terminal device, in which case they are by default line buffered.

The `setbuf` and `setvbuf` Functions

If we don't like the defaults for a given stream, we can use a number of functions to change them.

```
#include <stdio.h>

void setbuf (FILE *stream, char *buf);

int setvbuf (FILE *stream, char *buf, int type, size_t size);
```
Returns: 0 if OK, non-zero on error

The `setbuf` function can be used to change the buffering used for the stream *stream*. The call to `setbuf` must occur after the file has been successfully opened, but before any I/O is performed using the stream. If *buf* is not NULL, the array it points to will be used as a buffer instead of an automatically allocated one. The array pointed to by *buf* must always be `BUFSIZ` bytes in size; if it is larger, space will be wasted, and if it is smaller than `BUFSIZ`, other memory may be overwritten. If *buf* is a NULL pointer, I/O performed on *stream* will be completely unbuffered.

The `setvbuf` functions can also be used to change the buffering used for the stream *stream*. The call to `setvbuf` must occur after the file has been successfully opened, but before any I/O is performed using the stream. If *buf* is not a NULL pointer, the array it points to will be used as a buffer instead of an automatically allocated one. The type of buffering performed is determined by *type*. The legal values for *type* are:

`_IOFBF`	I/O performed on *stream* will be fully buffered.
`_IOLBF`	I/O performed on *stream* will be line buffered. The buffer will be flushed when a newline is written, the buffer is full, or input is requested.
`_IONBF`	I/O performed on *stream* will be completely unbuffered.

The *size* argument specifies the size in bytes of the buffer to be used.

If unbuffered I/O is selected, *buf* and *size* are ignored.

Something to be aware of when allocating our own buffer is to make sure that the buffer is still in scope when we attempt to use or close the file. We should either use one of the `malloc` functions to allocate memory for the buffer (remembering to free the memory later when we close the stream) or let the standard I/O library allocate the memory for us. If the buffer is allocated by the standard I/O library, it is automatically freed when we close the stream. Also, parts of the array pointed to by *buf* are used for internal bookkeeping of the stream, so *buf* will contain less than *size* bytes when full. Unless we have specific reasons to do otherwise, it's a good idea to let the standard I/O library handle the buffer allocation for us when we use `setvbuf`.

The `setbuffer` and `setlinebuf` Functions

We can use two other functions to modify the type of buffering used with a file stream. These are `setbuffer` and `setlinebuf`.

```
#include <stdio.h>

void setbuffer (FILE *iop, char *abuf, size_t asize);

int setlinebuf (FILE *iop);
```

Returns: no useful value

The setbuffer function is essentially the same as setbuf, except we must also specify the size of the buffer we supply in the *asize* argument. Because it is more standard, we recommend the use of setbuf over setbuffer.

The setlinebuf function is used to change the buffering for the file stream specified by *iop* from block buffered or unbuffered to line buffered. It is essentially the same as calling setvbuf like this:

```
setvbuf (fp, NULL, _IOLBF, BUFSIZ);
```

Unlike setbuffer, setbuf, and setvbuf, setlinebuf can be called whenever *iop* is valid (not just prior to performing I/O). However, despite this small advantage, we recommend using the more standard setvbuf function in preference to setlinebuf.

The fflush Function

As we mentioned earlier, the fflush function is used to flush a stream.

```
#include <stdio.h>

int fflush (FILE *stream);
```

Returns: 0 if OK, EOF on error

If *stream* points to an output stream (or an update stream in which the most recent operation was not input), the fflush function causes any unwritten data for that stream to be written to the file to which it refers.

If *stream* is a NULL pointer, fflush will perform this flushing action on all streams that are as defined above. Also, an input stream (or an update stream in which the most recent operation was input) is also flushed if it is seekable and is not already at the end of the file.

Flushing an input stream discards any buffered input and adjusts the file pointer such that the next input operation accesses the byte after the last one read.

5.12   Standard I/O Efficiency

In Section 4.11 we examined the effect of buffer size on I/O efficiency. It's instructive to perform a similar analysis on the standard I/O library.

Program 5.8 copies a file from standard input to standard output using fgetc and fputc. We use the time command to see how long it takes to copy our test file using different buffer sizes. The test file we used is about 10 MB in size; it's an ASCII file with 156,396 lines.

———————————————————————————— standard_io/cp_fgetc.c

```
 1 #include <stdio.h>
 2 #include <stdlib.h>
 3 #include "ssp.h"

 4 int main (int argc, char **argv)
 5 {
 6     int c;
 7     int buf_size;
 8     char *stdin_buf;
 9     char *stdout_buf;

10     if (argc != 2)
11         buf_size = 1024;
12     else
13         buf_size = atoi (argv [1]);

14     if ((stdin_buf = malloc (buf_size)) == NULL)
15         err_msg ("malloc failed");
16     if ((stdout_buf = malloc (buf_size)) == NULL)
17         err_msg ("malloc failed");

18     setvbuf (stdin, stdin_buf, _IOFBF, buf_size);
19     setvbuf (stdout, stdout_buf, _IOFBF, buf_size);

20     while ((c = fgetc (stdin)) != EOF)
21         if (fputc (c, stdout) == EOF)
22             err_msg ("fputc failed");

23     if (ferror (stdin))
24         err_msg ("fgetc failed");

25     return (0);
26 }
```

———————————————————————————— standard_io/cp_fgetc.c

Program 5.8 Copy standard input to standard output using fgetc and fputc.

We also have two variations of Program 5.8; one uses getc and putc, and the other uses getc_unlocked and putc_unlocked (we don't show the source code for these trivial changes). The latter pairs of routines are implemented as macros rather than functions.

Program 5.9 also copies a file from standard input to standard output, but it uses fgets and fputs to do the copying.

Figure 5.6 tabulates the results for fgetc, fputc and getc, putc; Figure 5.7 shows the results for fgets, fputs and getc_unlocked, putc_unlocked. All times are in seconds.

The lines where buf_size is 0 show the results for unbuffered I/O. We did this by changing the lines that read

```
    setvbuf (stdin, stdin_buf, _IOFBF, buf_size);
    setvbuf (stdout, stdout_buf, _IOFBF, buf_size);
```

to the following:

standard_io/cp_fgets.c

```
1 #include <stdio.h>
2 #include <stdlib.h>
3 #include "ssp.h"

4 int main (int argc, char **argv)
5 {
6     int buf_size;
7     char buf [LINE_LEN];
8     char *stdin_buf;
9     char *stdout_buf;

10    if (argc != 2)
11        buf_size = 1024;
12    else
13        buf_size = atoi (argv [1]);

14    if ((stdin_buf = malloc (buf_size)) == NULL)
15        err_msg ("malloc failed");
16    if ((stdout_buf = malloc (buf_size)) == NULL)
17        err_msg ("malloc failed");

18    setvbuf (stdin, stdin_buf, _IOLBF, buf_size);
19    setvbuf (stdout, stdout_buf, _IOLBF, buf_size);

20    while (fgets (buf, LINE_LEN, stdin) != NULL)
21        if (fputs (buf, stdout) == EOF)
22            err_msg ("fputs failed");

23    if (ferror (stdin))
24        err_msg ("fgets failed");

25    return (0);
26 }
```

standard_io/cp_fgets.c

Program 5.9 Copy standard input to standard output using `fgets` and `fputs`.

```
setvbuf (stdin, NULL, _IONBF, 0);
setvbuf (stdout, NULL, _IONBF, 0);
```

The lines where the value of `buf_size` is "Default" were obtained by deleting the calls to `setvbuf` completely.

Figure 5.8 summarizes the results. The times are in seconds, and the Size column shows the size of the executable program in bytes. This is so that we can see the effect of inline macro expansion on the size of a program compared to using function calls. We also show two times for copying the same file using `read` and `write`; the first is for copying one byte at a time, and the second is for copying the file 8192 bytes at a time. We do this so that we can compare the efficiency of the standard I/O library with the `read` and `write` system calls.

When we look at the results of copying the file using the standard I/O library, we can make several interesting observations. The first is that for this type of program, nonbuffered I/O is substantially slower than buffered I/O—by more than an order of magnitude, in fact. The second thing we can see is that different buffer sizes have a much

fgetc and fputc			
buf_size	Real	User	Sys
0	130.92	38.10	92.51
1	2.32	1.85	0.25
2	2.29	1.83	0.26
4	2.36	1.87	0.24
8	2.29	1.90	0.20
16	18.72	6.57	11.98
32	7.60	3.42	3.99
64	4.59	2.37	1.97
128	3.35	2.03	1.11
256	2.80	1.87	0.71
512	2.55	1.94	0.33
1024	2.32	1.82	0.29
2048	2.19	1.90	0.09
4096	2.19	1.85	0.13
8192	2.23	1.85	0.12
Default	2.26	1.89	0.13

getc and putc			
buf_size	Real	User	Sys
0	122.27	34.10	87.97
1	1.72	1.33	0.22
2	1.67	1.24	0.22
4	1.67	1.18	0.25
8	1.71	1.28	0.20
16	16.65	5.18	11.14
32	6.67	2.44	4.00
64	3.92	1.98	1.71
128	2.67	1.32	1.13
256	2.17	1.49	0.45
512	1.90	1.28	0.40
1024	1.72	1.17	0.32
2048	1.64	1.28	0.17
4096	1.61	1.24	0.12
8192	1.61	1.14	0.15
Default	1.47	0.85	0.08

Figure 5.6 The effect of buffer size on standard (character) I/O.

fgets and fputs			
buf_size	Real	User	Sys
0	62.66	22.07	40.46
1	1.74	0.52	0.91
2	1.73	0.58	0.90
4	1.75	0.52	0.98
8	1.76	0.62	0.87
16	16.02	5.27	10.52
32	6.26	1.85	4.18
64	3.80	1.14	2.41
128	2.54	0.65	1.62
256	2.04	0.50	1.28
512	1.83	0.55	1.09
1024	1.72	0.57	0.91
2048	1.73	0.49	0.96
4096	1.74	0.53	0.93
8192	1.70	0.50	0.91
Default	1.45	0.25	0.12

getc_unlocked and putc_unlocked			
buf_size	Real	User	Sys
0	122.51	32.93	89.35
1	1.70	1.17	0.23
2	1.73	1.19	0.23
4	1.70	1.24	0.22
8	1.73	1.15	0.30
16	16.67	5.19	11.20
32	6.66	2.70	3.77
64	3.82	1.73	1.80
128	2.70	1.34	1.03
256	2.15	1.45	0.47
512	1.94	1.30	0.36
1024	1.73	1.20	0.23
2048	1.64	1.17	0.21
4096	1.61	1.22	0.12
8192	1.54	1.18	0.15
Default	1.45	0.91	0.11

Figure 5.7 The effect of buffer size on standard (line and unlocked) I/O.

less dramatic effect on the outcome than when we use read and write. The final item
of note is the anomalous results when buf_size is 16 bytes (and to a lesser extent, when
it is 32 bytes). Each of these values is between four and ten times slower than the average
speed of the other values of buf_size.

Functions	Real	User	Sys	Size
`fgetc` and `fputc`	2.26	1.89	0.13	9844
`getc` and `putc`	1.47	0.85	0.08	9976
`fgets` and `fputs`	1.45	0.25	0.12	9684
`getc_unlocked` and `putc_unlocked`	1.45	0.91	0.11	10032
read and `write` (one byte at time)	108.83	20.86	87.72	9780
read and `write` (8192 bytes at time)	1.49	0.01	0.13	

Figure 5.8 Summary results from Programs 5.8 and 5.9.

By using the `truss(1)` utility, we can see the size of the I/O associated with a given standard I/O buffer size. Figure 5.9 tabulates the results.

buf_size	I/O size
1	1024
2	1024
4	1024
8	1024
9	1
10	2
16	8
32	24
64	56

buf_size	I/O size
128	120
256	248
512	504
1024	1016
2048	2040
4096	4088
8192	8184
Default	8192

Figure 5.9 I/O buffer sizes for different values of `buf_size`.

The evidence suggests that the standard I/O library rejects buffer size requests of less than 8 bytes, and uses a 1024-byte buffer instead. There is an 8-byte overhead associated with each buffer (presumably for internal house keeping), which is included in the buffer size we allocate. This is why the I/O size is always exactly 8 bytes less than the buffer size we set using `setvbuf`.

Looking at the summary results in Figure 5.8, we can make some other observations. The first is that the size of the programs that use macros are slightly larger than those that use functions. The second is that the user time for the programs that use macros is less than those that use functions. This is because functions calls have a small but finite overhead associated with them. With at least 20 million function calls (10 million calls to `fgetc` and 10 million calls to `fputc`), this overhead becomes noticeable. The system time is roughly the same because the same number of system calls are made.

Comparing the CPU time of the line-at-a-time copying with the character-at-a-time copying, we can see that the former is more efficient than the latter. Because there are only about 300,000 function calls (instead of about 20 million), this makes sense, until we start thinking about how `fgets` and `fputs` are implemented. If they were implemented using `getc` and `putc`, we would expect the line-at-a-time CPU usage to be higher than the character-at-a-time method, because there will be 20 million macro invocations on top of the 300,000 function calls. Line-at-a-time I/O is faster because the functions internally use the `memccpy` function, which is very efficient—much more so than using `getc` and `putc`. The last item of interest is when we compare the results of copying using the standard I/O library character-at-a-time functions with the 1-byte-at-a-time `read` and `write` method. Even compared to the function versions of the routines, using `read` and `write` one character at a time is nearly two orders of magnitude slower. This is because although the same number of function calls (about 20 million) are made, using `read` and `write` also invokes a system call for every function call. In other words, in addition to the 20 million function calls, there are also 20 million system calls. The overhead of a system call is much higher than that of a normal function call (recall Figure 1.2), hence the huge increase in the time required to perform the copy. As we might expect, using `read` and `write` 8192 bytes at a time is much faster than any method that copies one character at a time.

One thing to be aware of is that these results are only valid for the test system. A different compiler or release of Solaris (or changing platforms) could produce different results, although it would be fair to add that the trends illustrated here would still be valid. The preceding notwithstanding, it is instructive to have a set of figures and discuss the different results so that we can better understand the trade offs involved with different approaches to solving the same problem. One basic fact we can ascertain is that the standard I/O library is not that much slower than using `read` and `write` (in our examples here, less than three seconds when copying a 10 MB file). For most non-trivial applications, the CPU time required by I/O is small compared to that required by the application itself.

5.13   Summary

In this chapter we talked about the standard I/O library. We first discussed the concepts of a file stream and the `FILE` object, and introduced some constants that are used by the standard I/O library. We then talked about the three streams that are automatically opened for our processes (standard input, standard output, and standard error). After showing how to open and close a file stream, we talked about the three types of I/O we can perform using the library: character-at-a-time I/O, line-at-a-time I/O, and binary I/O.

Next we looked at how to retrieve the stream status (e.g., the end of file and error flags), and discussed formatted I/O. We then talked about positioning a stream's file position indicator, and file stream locking. After discussing the different types of buffering offered by the standard I/O library, we performed an analysis of the efficiency of the standard I/O library.

Exercises

5.1   Implement the `setbuf` function using `setvbuf`.

5.2   Compile and run Program 5.9, omitting the calls to `setvbuf` and using a `LINE_LEN` of 8. What happens if you attempt to copy lines that exceed this length, and why?

5.3   What is wrong with the following code fragment?

```
#include <stdio.h>

int main (void)
{
    char c;

    while ((c = getchar ()) != EOF)
        putchar (c);
}
```

5.4   Our shell programs from Chapter 1 (Programs 1.5 and 1.7) print prompts that do not include a newline character. Given that we also don't call `fflush`, what causes the prompts to be displayed?

6

Date and Time Operations

6.1   Introduction

As we mentioned in Chapter 1, Solaris measures time in the number of seconds since the epoch, which was at 00:00:00 UTC on Thursday, January 1st, 1970, and stores this value in a variable whose type is `time_t` (we call this the *calendar time*). Keeping track of time this way is a simple concept and easy to implement, but is not very user-friendly.

Many systems programming applications need to convert from calendar time to something we can easily understand, and vice versa. For example, the `ls -l` command prints out the time a file was last modified, and the `touch` command allows us to set a file's modification time to a time of our choosing.

In this chapter, we look at the various time representations, and how we can convert between them.

6.2   The Complexities of Converting Time

Converting the number of seconds since the epoch into something more comprehensible to humans is a non-trivial undertaking. If everyone used UTC, the problem would be more straightforward to solve. There are 86,400 seconds in a day, so if we take the number of seconds since the epoch and divide it by 86,400, we will get the number of days and a remainder. If we divide the remainder by 3600 (the number of seconds in an hour), we get the hour and a remainder. Dividing this remainder by 60 gives us the minute, and the remainder is the number of seconds.

If we divide the number of days by 365, we get the year. Working out the month and day from the remainder is relatively easy.

Unfortunately, life isn't that simple. Every four years we have a leap year that has 366 days, and occasionally we have leap seconds and (even more occasionally) double leap seconds. Also, not everyone uses UTC, which is the time of day at the prime meridian. (The prime meridian passes through Greenwich, England, hence the name Greenwich Mean Time, or GMT.)

Although "every four years" is an acceptable definition of the frequency of leap years for everyday conversation, it is inaccurate. Strictly speaking, a leap year is every four years, unless the year is divisible by 100, in which case it isn't, unless the year is also divisible by 400. For example, the year 2000 was a leap year, but 1900 was not.

For a given year, y, we can represent this in C as:

```
if (y % 4 == 0)
    if (y % 100 == 0)
        if (y % 400 == 0)
            ly = 1;
        else
            ly = 0;
    else
        ly = 1;
else
    ly = 0;
```

The variable `ly` will be 1 if y is a leap year, or 0 otherwise. We can express this more succinctly using C's ternary operator, as we show in Program 6.1.

Example: Determining a leap year

Program 6.1 determines whether the specified year is a leap year.

─── *date_and_time/leap_year.c*

```
 1 #include <stdio.h>
 2 #include <stdlib.h>
 3 #include "ssp.h"

 4 int main (int argc, char **argv)
 5 {
 6     int y;
 7     int ly;

 8     if (argc != 2)
 9         err_quit ("Usage: leap_year year");

10     y = atoi (argv [1]);

11     ly = (y % 4 == 0) ? ((y % 100 == 0) ? ((y % 400 == 0) ? 1 : 0) : 1) : 0;

12     printf ("%d %s a leap year\n", y, (ly == 0) ? "is not" : "is");

13     return (0);
14 }
```
─── *date_and_time/leap_year.c*

Program 6.1 Determining a leap year.

Let's try our program on a few years to test it:

```
$ for i in 1900 1967 1996 2000; do
> ./leap_year $i
> done
1900 is not a leap year
1967 is not a leap year
1996 is a leap year
2000 is a leap year
```

Notice how we use the shell's looping construct to run Program 6.1 for several different years. For each iteration through the loop, the shell variable, i, is assigned the value of the year we want to test. The $i is replaced with the value of i.

The local time in different parts of the world is determined by adding or subtracting an offset from UTC. If the location is east of Greenwich, the offset is positive (meaning that local time is later than UTC), and if the location is west of Greenwich, the offset is negative (i.e., local time is earlier than UTC). For example, Kelowna is eight hours earlier than UTC, so if it's 08:00 (8:00 a.m.) in Kelowna, it's already 16:00 (4:00 p.m.) in Greenwich.

Each offset is called a *time zone*. The purpose of a time zone is to allow us to change the clock so that it agrees with local day and night. If we didn't use time zones, 10:00 a.m. would be in daylight in Greenwich, but in Kelowna it would still be dark. So Kelowna shifts its local time by eight hours to compensate.

The offset from UTC in most time zones is an integer, but some places, like Saint John's, Newfoundland (off Canada's eastern coast), have a fractional offset (in the case of Saint John's, the local time is two and a half hours behind UTC).

As if all this wasn't complicated enough, humans have invented the concept of Daylight Savings Time (DST), which shifts clocks an hour forward in the spring, and restores the "correct" time in the autumn. (One way to remember which way round this is is to recite the following phrase: clocks spring forward in spring, and fall backward in fall.) The idea was to help farmers and other people who work outside by giving them an extra hour of daylight in the evening. Of course, the day doesn't actually get longer: bedtime is just shifted, giving the illusion of a longer day. Unfortunately, not all countries observe the shift to and from DST on the same date, and some countries (or parts thereof) don't observe it at all.

All of these variables and rules make the conversion of Solaris time to calendar time (and vice versa) a very difficult problem. Fortunately for us, Solaris comes with library routines to handle the conversions for us.

6.3   Getting the Current Time

We can use four functions to obtain the current time: time, gethrtime, gethrvtime, and gettimeofday.

The time Function

The time function returns the number of seconds elapsed since the epoch.

```
#include <sys/types.h>
#include <time.h>

time_t time (time_t *tloc);
```
                                    Returns: number of seconds since the epoch if OK, −1 on error

If *tloc* is not NULL, the return value is also stored in the location to which it points.

The `gettimeofday` Function

The `gettimeofday` function is also used to get the current time.

```
#include <sys/time.h>

int gettimeofday (struct timeval *tp, void *);
```
                                                    Returns: 0 if OK, −1 on error

The `gettimeofday` function (not to be confused with the function of the same name in the BSD Compatibility Library) also gets the elapsed time since the epoch. Unlike the `time` function, which has a one-second granularity, `gettimeofday` expresses the time in seconds and microseconds since the epoch (the actual resolution is hardware dependent). The time is stored in the `timeval` structure pointed to by *tp*, which has the following members:

```
struct timeval {
    time_t      tv_sec;     /* Seconds */
    suseconds_t tv_usec;    /* Microseconds */
};
```

The second argument should be NULL, as it isn't used.

The `gethrtime` and `gethrvtime` Functions

Unlike the `time` and `gettimeofday` functions, which return the elapsed time since the epoch, the `gethrtime` and `gethrvtime` functions return the value of a high-resolution timer, which is measured in nanoseconds since some arbitrary time in the past (usually when the system booted).

```
#include <sys/time.h>

hrtime_t gethrtime (void);

hrtime_t gethrvtime (void);
```
                                    Both return: number of nanoseconds since the timer started

The `gethrtime` function returns the number of nanoseconds elapsed since the system booted. Although the value returned is measured in nanoseconds, the granularity isn't necessarily one nanosecond. Two sufficiently proximate calls to gethrtime could return the same value. However, the value returned is guaranteed to be monotonic (i.e., it won't decrease in value, and it won't periodically wrap) and linear (i.e., it won't occasionally speed up or slow down). The gethrtime is ideally suited to performance measurement tasks, where cheap, accurate interval timing is required. We showed an example of using gethrtime in Program 1.8.

The gethrvtime function is similar to gethrtime, except that it returns the current high-resolution Light Weight Process (LWP) virtual time, which is the total number of nanoseconds of execution time. Using this function requires that microstate accounting has been enabled with the ptime utility.

6.3.1 The difftime Function

We can determine the difference between two times by using the difftime function.

```
#include <time.h>

double difftime (time_t time1, time_t time0);
```
                                   Returns: the difference between the two times

The difference between *time1* and *time0* (i.e., *time1* − *time0*) is calculated and returned as a double. This function is provided because there are no arithmetic operations defined for the time_t data type (not all computers use a long for time_t).

6.4   Setting the Current Time

A privileged process can change the system's idea of the current time by calling either stime or settimeofday. The system clock can also be adjusted by calling adjtime.

The stime Function

We can set the current time by using the stime function.

```
#include <unistd.h>

int stime (const time_t *tp);
```
                                        Returns: 0 if OK, −1 on error

The stime function allows a privileged process to set the current time to the value specified in the location pointed to by *tp*. The value pointed to by *tp* is the number of seconds since the epoch.

Although a time_t is a signed quantity, we are not allowed to set the date to be prior to the epoch.

The `settimeofday` Function

The `settimeofday` function can also be used to set the current time.

```
#include <sys/time.h>

int settimeofday (struct timeval *tp, void *);
```

Returns: 0 if OK, −1 on error

The `settimeofday` function (not to be confused with the function of the same name in the BSD SCP) allows us to specify the time with a granularity of one microsecond (although the actual granularity honoured is hardware dependent).

The *tp* argument points to a `timeval` structure, which holds the new time value in seconds and microseconds since the epoch. As with `gettimeofday`, the second argument is ignored, so it should be NULL.

The `adjtime` Function

The `stime` and `settimeofday` functions allow us to set the time to an arbitrary value. If we want to adjust the time slowly (for example, to synchronize with another machine), we can use the `adjtime` function.

```
#include <sys/time.h>

int adjtime (struct timeval *delta, struct timeval *olddelta);
```

Returns: 0 if OK, −1 on error

The `adjtime` function gradually adjusts the system's notion of the current time by advancing or retarding it by the amount specified by the `timeval` structure pointed to by *delta*.

The adjustment is made by speeding up or slowing down the system clock by a small percentage, usually less than 1 percent. Even if the change specified by *delta* is negative, the system clock will always be monotonic.

Setting *delta* to 0 will return the status of the effects of a previous call to `adjtime`. If *olddelta* is not NULL, the `timeval` structure it points to will be filled with the number of seconds and microseconds still to be corrected. Using `adjtime` in this manner has no effect on the time correction.

6.5   Getting the Current Time Zone

We now know how to determine the elapsed time since the epoch, but how can we determine our current time zone?

The `TZ` environment variable contains a string that is the name of the local time zone (e.g., Canada/Pacific or US/Eastern). However, C programs should call the `tzset` or ftime functions to determine information about their time zone. (We describe the latter in Appendix B.)

The `tzset` Function

The tzset function sets four external variables that describe the current time zone.

```
#include <time.h>

void tzset (void);
extern time_t timezone;
extern time_t altzone;
extern int daylight;
extern char *tzname [2];
```

The tzset function uses the value of the TZ environment variable to override the values of timezone, altzone, daylight, and tzname (by default, these variables contain values that describe UTC).

The timezone variable contains the difference in seconds between UTC and local standard time, and the altzone variable contains the difference in seconds between UTC and the local alternate time zone (DST). The daylight variable is set to zero if DST is not in effect, or non-zero if it is. Finally, the tzname array contains the names of the local standard time zone and DST. The first element contains the local standard time, and the second contains the DST time zone name.

Example: Displaying information about the local time zone

Program 6.2 uses the tzset function to set the timezone, altzone, daylight, and tzname external variables.

Running Program 6.2 on one of the author's systems gives the following results.

```
$ ./tzset
Time zone = Canada/Pacific
   timezone difference = 28800 seconds
   altzone difference = 25200 seconds
   daylight = 1
   tzname [0] = PST
   tzname [1] = PDT
```

Note that the tzname variables contain the abbreviated name of the time zone (PST) rather than the full name (Canada/Pacific).

6.6   Converting between UNIX Time and Calendar Time

The concept of "number of seconds since the epoch" is easy for computers to implement and work with, but it doesn't translate very easily to the calendar we normally use.

---
date_and_time/tzset.c

```
 1 #include <stdio.h>
 2 #include <time.h>
 3 #include <stdlib.h>
 4 #include "ssp.h"

 5 int main (void)
 6 {
 7     char *tz;

 8     if ((tz = getenv ("TZ")) == NULL)
 9         err_quit ("TZ is not in environment\n");

10     tzset ();

11     printf ("Time zone = %s\n", tz);
12     printf ("  timezone difference = %ld seconds\n", timezone);
13     printf ("  altzone difference = %ld seconds\n", altzone);
14     printf ("  daylight = %d\n", daylight);
15     printf ("  tzname [0] = %s\n", tzname [0]);
16     printf ("  tzname [1] = %s\n", tzname [1]);

17     return (0);
18 }
```
date_and_time/tzset.c

Program 6.2 Displaying information about the local time zone.

Solaris provides the tm structure, which handily encapsulates a calendar date and time for us. The tm structure has the following members:

```
struct tm {
    int tm_sec;      /* Seconds after the minute (0 - 61) */
    int tm_min;      /* Minutes after the hour (0 - 59) */
    int tm_hour;     /* Hours after midnight (0 - 23) */
    int tm_mday;     /* Day of month (1 - 31) */
    int tm_mon;      /* Months since January (0 - 11) */
    int tm_year;     /* Years since 1900 */
    int tm_wday;     /* Days since Sunday (0 - 6) */
    int tm_yday;     /* Days since January 1st (0 - 365) */
    int tm_isdst;    /* Daylight savings in effect? */
};
```

The reason why tm_yday and tm_sec have maximum values of 365 and 61 respectively (instead of 364 and 59) is to allow for leap years, leap seconds, and double leap seconds. Notice also that tm_year contains the number of years since 1900, *not* the actual year. For example, this member would have a value of 104, rather than 2004, if a date in 2004 was being represented. (Line 15 in Program 6.4 reinforces this point.)

Solaris provides two functions for converting a time_t into a tm structure (localtime and gmtime) and one for performing the opposite conversion (mktime).

Figure 6.1 shows the relationship between the various representations of time, and the functions that we can use to convert from one to another. Some of the lines in Figure 6.1 are dashed; these lines show that the conversion being depicted may take into account the local time zone.

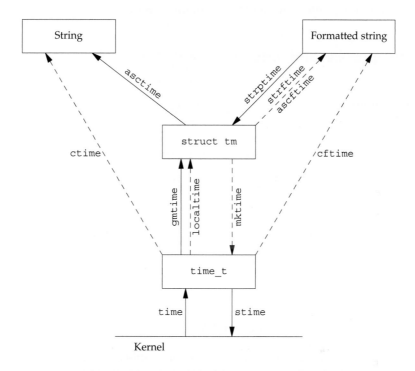

Figure 6.1 The relationship of the various time functions.

6.6.1 The `localtime` and `localtime_r` Functions

The `localtime` function converts a time expressed as the number of seconds since the epoch into a representation broken into its constituent parts.

```
#include <time.h>

struct tm *localtime (const time_t *clock);

struct tm *localtime_r (const time_t *clock, struct tm *res);
```
                                    Both return: a pointer to the converted time

The `localtime` function converts the date and time specified by buffer pointed to by *clock* to a `tm` structure, and returns a pointer to the result. The result is stored in a statically allocated buffer and is corrected for the current time zone.

The `localtime_r` function has the same functionality as `localtime`, except the result is stored in the caller-supplied buffer pointed to by *res*.

6.6.2 The `gmtime` and `gmtime_r` Functions

The `gmtime` function can also be used to convert the number of seconds since the epoch into a more human-friendly representation.

```
#include <time.h>

struct tm *gmtime (const time_t *clock);

struct tm *gmtime_r (const time_t *clock, struct tm *res);
```
                                          Both return: a pointer to the converted time

The `gmtime` function performs the same conversion as `localtime`, but the result is not corrected for the current time zone. Instead, the result is presented in UTC.

The `gmtime_r` function does likewise, but the result is stored in the caller-supplied buffer pointed to by *res*.

Example: Using the `gmtime` function

We might be tempted to wonder what the utility of `gmtime` is, given that we have `localtime` that automatically corrects for our current time zone. One situation in which the former would be useful is when we want to display the difference between two times (e.g., we might want to calculate a session length, given log in and log out times). We can use `difftime` to calculate the difference between the two times, and then use `gmtime` to convert it to a readable format. Program 6.3 shows how we can do this.

Running Program 6.3 gives the following result:

```
$ ./gmtime
Session length is 1 days, 3 hours, 46 minutes, and 40 seconds
```

Another use for the `gmtime` function would be when we have an application where we specifically want the time to be in GMT no matter what the current time zone.

6.6.3 The `mktime` Function

The `mktime` function performs the opposite conversion to `localtime`: it converts a `tm` structure into the number of seconds since the epoch.

———————————————————————————— date_and_time/gmtime.c

```
 1 #include <stdio.h>
 2 #include <time.h>

 3 int main (void)
 4 {
 5     struct tm *tp;
 6     time_t login;
 7     time_t logout;
 8     time_t session_length;

 9     login = 100000;
10     logout = 200000;
11     session_length = (time_t) difftime (logout, login);

12     tp = gmtime (&session_length);

13     printf ("Session length is %d days, %d hours, %d minutes, "
14         "and %d seconds\n", tp -> tm_yday, tp -> tm_hour, tp -> tm_min,
15         tp -> tm_sec);

16     return (0);
17 }
```

———————————————————————————— date_and_time/gmtime.c

Program 6.3   Printing login session length using gmtime.

```
#include <time.h>

time_t mktime (struct tm *timeptr);
```
Returns: number of seconds since the epoch if OK, −1 on error

---

The mktime function converts the time represented by the tm structure pointed to by *timeptr* into a calendar time (i.e., the number of seconds since the epoch). Also, the supplied tm structure is normalized. The original values for the tm_wday and tm_yday members are ignored, and the other members are not restricted to the ranges indicated in Section 6.6. On successful completion, tm_wday and tm_yday are set to appropriate values, and the others are set to represent the specified calendar time, but with their values forced to be within the appropriate ranges. For example, setting tm_mon to −2 means two months before January of tm_year.

If tm_isdst is greater than zero, the original values are assumed to be in the alternate time zone (i.e., DST). If the alternate time zone is not valid for the computed calendar time, then the components are adjusted to the main time zone. Similarly, if tm_isdst is zero, the original values are assumed to be in the main time zone. If the main time zone is not valid for the computed calendar time, then the components are adjusted to the alternate time zone. Finally, if tm_isdst is less than zero, the mktime function attempts to determine if the alternate time zone is in effect for the specified time.

Local time zone information is used as if tzset had been called by mktime.

Example: On what day of the week was September 18th, 1967?

Program 6.4 uses the `mktime` function to determine what day of the week September 18th, 1967, was on.

——————————————————————————————————— *date_and_time/mktime.c*

```
 1 #include <stdio.h>
 2 #include <time.h>

 3 int main (void)
 4 {
 5     struct tm tp;
 6     char *wday [] = {
 7         "Sunday", "Monday", "Tuesday", "Wednesday",
 8         "Thursday", "Friday", "Saturday", "Unknown"
 9     };

10     tp.tm_sec = 1;
11     tp.tm_min = 0;
12     tp.tm_hour = 0;
13     tp.tm_mday = 18;
14     tp.tm_mon = 9 - 1;
15     tp.tm_year = 1967 - 1900;
16     tp.tm_isdst = -1;

17     if (mktime (&tp) == -1)
18         tp.tm_wday = 7;

19
20     printf ("September 18th, 1967 was a %s.\n", wday [tp.tm_wday]);

21     return (0);
22 }
```

——————————————————————————————————— *date_and_time/mktime.c*

Program 6.4 Using `mktime` to determine what day of the week a given date is.

Running Program 6.4, we can see that September 18th, 1967, was a Monday:

```
$ ./mktime
September 18th, 1967 was a Monday.
```

At the time of this writing (mid 2004), the time zone data files used by Solaris do not transition past 03:14:07 on Tuesday, January 19th, 2038. Therefore, 64-bit processes might not yield correct results when converting times past this date. (As we previously discussed, 64-bit processes have no problem representing dates beyond this, as a `time_t` is a 64-bit quantity in a 64-bit process.)

6.7 Formatted Date I/O

Now that we know how to convert from calendar time to a `tm` structure and vice versa, we need to know how to read or write dates and times formatted for human consumption. Solaris provides several functions for converting a date to a string and several for converting a string into one of the internal date representations (i.e., either a `time_t` or a `tm` struct).

6.7.1 Converting a Date to a Formatted String

We can use a variety of functions for converting a date to a formatted string. Which one we use depends on how much control over the formatting we require, whether we want the output be localized, and what format the date we are converting is in (a time_t or a tm structure).

The `ctime` and `asctime` Functions

These two functions convert a date to a fixed-length string.

```
#include <time.h>

char *ctime (const time_t *clock);

char *asctime (const struct tm *tm);
```
Both return: a pointer to the converted time

The `ctime` functions converts the calendar time pointed to by *clock* to a 26-character string after applying time zone and daylight savings corrections. The string is formatted as follows, with constant-width fields:

```
Tue May 21 12:12:12 2002\n\0
```

(This is the same as the output of the `date` command, but without the time zone.)

The `asctime` function converts the tm structure pointed to by *tm* to a 26-character string that has exactly the same format as that for `ctime`. Indeed,

```
ctime (clock);
```

is the same as

```
asctime (localtime (clock));
```

The `ctime_r` and `asctime_r` Functions

These are reentrant versions of `ctime` and `asctime` for use in multithreaded programs.

```
#include <time.h>

char *ctime_r (const time_t *clock, char *buf, int buflen);

char *asctime_r (const struct tm *tm, char *buf, int buflen);

cc [ flag ... ] file ... -D_POSIX_PTHREAD_SEMANTICS [ lib ... ]

char *ctime_r (const time_t *clock, char *buf);

char *asctime_r (const struct tm *tm, char *buf);
```
All four return: a pointer to the converted time if OK, NULL on failure

These two functions have the same functionality as their non-reentrant counterparts, except that the caller must supply the buffer in which the result should be placed. The buffer is pointed to by *buf* and must be at least 26 characters in length. The length of the buffer is specified by *buflen*, but the POSIX versions of these functions omit this argument.

The `strftime`, `cftime`, and `ascftime` Functions

The `strftime`, `cftime`, and `ascftime` functions convert a date to a human-readable string with arbitrary formatting.

```
#include <time.h>

size_t strftime (char *s, size_t maxsize, const char *format,
    const struct tm *timeptr);

int cftime (char *s, const char *format, const time_t *clock);

int ascftime (char *s, const char *format, const struct tm *timeptr);
```
All three return: the number of bytes copied if OK, 0 on error (<code>strftime</code> only)

Each of these three functions places characters into the array pointed to by *s* (in the case of `strftime`, the number of bytes is limited to *maxsize*). What is placed in *s* is determined by the format string pointed to by *format*, which we discuss later in this section. If *format* is NULL, then the locale's default format is used (`%c` is the default format for `strftime`; `cftime` and `ascftime` use `%C` as their default format, having first tried the value of the `CFTIME` environment variable). Note that we should exercise caution when using `cftime` and `ascftime` because, unlike `strftime`, they don't prevent the buffer *s* from overflowing.

For `strftime` and `ascftime`, the *timeptr* argument points to the `tm` structure that represents the date to be formatted. Similarly, the *clock* argument for `cftime` specifies the calendar time to be formatted.

Regular characters in the *format* string are copied to *s* unchanged, but conversion specifications (introduced by a % character) are replaced by the appropriate characters as described in the following list. The appropriate characters are determined by the `LC_TIME` category of the process' locale and the appropriate member of *timeptr* or *clock*.

The conversion specifications and their meanings are as follows:

`%%`	A literal % sign
`%a`	The locale's abbreviated weekday name
`%A`	The locale's full weekday name
`%b`	The locale's abbreviated month name
`%B`	The locale's full month name
`%c`	The locale's appropriate date and time representation
`%C`	(Default) The locale's date and time representation as produced by the `date` command

%C	(Standards conforming) The century number (i.e., the year divided by 100 and truncated to an integer as a decimal number from 1 to 99. Single digits are preceded by a 0.)
%d	The day of the month from 1 to 31 (Single digits are preceded by a 0.)
%D	The same as %m/%d/%y
%e	The day of the month from 1 to 31 (Single digits are preceded by a space.)
%g	The week-based year within a century from 0 to 99
%G	The week-based year including the century from 0 to 9999
%h	The locale's abbreviated month name.
%H	The hour using a 24-hour clock from 0 to 23 (Single digits are preceded by a 0.)
%I	The hour using a 12-hour clock from 1 to 12 (Single digits are preceded by a 0.)
%j	The day number of the year from 1 to 366 (Single digits are preceded by a 0.)
%k	The hour using a 24-hour clock from 0 to 23 (Single digits are preceded by a space.)
%l	The hour using a 12-hour clock from 1 to 12 (Single digits are preceded by a space.)
%m	The month number from 1 to 12 (Single digits are preceded by a 0.)
%M	The minute from 0 to 59 (Single digits are preceded by a 0.)
%n	Inserts a newline
%p	The locale's equivalent of AM or PM
%r	The locale's appropriate time representation using a 12-hour clock with %p
%R	The time as %H:%M
%S	The seconds from 0 to 61 (Single digits are preceded by a 0.)
%t	Inserts a tab
%T	The time as %H:%M:%S
%u	The weekday as a decimal number from 1 to 7, with 1 representing Monday
%U	The week number of the year as a decimal number from 0 to 53, with Sunday as the first day of week one
%V	The ISO 8601 week number of the year as a decimal number from 1 to 53 (Weeks begin on Monday in the ISO 8601 week-based system, and week one of the year is the week that includes both January 4th and the first Thursday of the year. If the first Monday of January is the 2nd, 3rd, or 4th, the preceding days are part of the last week of the previous year.)

%w	The weekday as a decimal number from 0 to 6, with 0 representing Sunday
%W	The week number of the year as a decimal number from 0 to 53, with Monday as the first day of week one
%x	The locale's appropriate date representation
%X	The locale's appropriate time representation
%y	The year within the century from 0 to 99 (Single digits are preceded by a 0.)
%Y	The year, including the century
%Z	The time zone name or abbreviation, or no bytes if no time zone information exists

The difference between the %U and %W conversion specifications (and the %OU and %OW alternate conversion specifications) lies in which day is considered to be the first of the week. For %U, week one is the first week in January starting with a Sunday; for %W, week one is the first week in January starting with a Monday. Week 0 contains those days before the first Sunday or Monday in January for %U or %W respectively.

Some conversion specifications can be modified by using the E or O modifiers to indicate that an alternate format or specification should be used. If the alternate format or specification does not exist in the current locale, then the unmodified specification will be used.

The alternate conversion specifications and their meanings are as follows:

%Ec	The locale's alternate appropriate date and time representation
%EC	The name of the base year (period) in the locale's alternate specification
%Eg	The offset from %EC of the week-based year in the locale's alternate representation
%EG	The full alternate representation of the week-based year
%Ex	The locale's alternate date representation
%EX	The locale's alternate time representation
%Ey	The offset from %EC (year only) in the locale's alternate representation
%EY	The full alternate year representation
%Od	The day of the month, using the locale's alternate numeric symbols
%Oe	The same as %Od
%Og	The week-based year (offset from %C) in the locale's alternate representation, using the locale's alternate numeric symbols
%OH	The hour, using a 24-hour clock and the locale's alternate numeric symbols
%OI	The hour, using a 12-hour clock and the locale's alternate numeric symbols

%Om	The month, using the locale's alternate numeric symbols
%OM	The minutes, using the locale's alternate numeric symbols
%OS	The seconds, using the locale's alternate numeric symbols
%Ou	The weekday as a number, using the locale's alternate numeric symbols
%OU	The week number of the year (with Sunday as the first day of the week), using the locale's alternate numeric symbols
%Ow	The number of the weekday (with Sunday = 0), using the locale's alternate numeric symbols
%OW	The week number of the year (with Monday as the first day of the week), using the locale's alternate numeric symbols
%Oy	The year (offset from %C) in the locale's alternate representation, using the locale's alternate numeric symbols

Local time zone information is used as though `tzset` had been called. The conversion specification for %V was changed in the Solaris 7 release. The old behaviour was such that if the week containing January 1st had fewer than four days in the new year, it became week 53 of the previous year. Solaris 7 also added the %g, %G, %Eg, %EG, and %Og conversion specifications.

In Solaris 8, the %u conversion specification was also changed. Previous releases specified that a value of 1 represented Sunday rather than Monday.

Example: Converting the current time to various formats

Program 6.5 uses the `strftime` function to print out the current time in various different formats.

Running Program 6.5 gives us the following results:

```
$ ./strftime
%A, %B %e, %Y, %H:%M:%S     Sunday, May 26, 2002, 17:52:39
%I:%M %p, %d-%b-%y          05:52 PM, 26-May-02
%x %X                       05/26/02 17:52:39
%C                          Sun May 26 17:52:39 PDT 2002
%c                          Sun May 26 17:52:39 2002
```

6.7.2 Converting a Formatted String to a Date

To perform conversions in the other direction (i.e., from text to a tm structure), we can use either the `strptime` or `getdate` functions, which we discuss next.

The `strptime` Function

The `strptime` function is used to convert a text string to a tm structure.

date_and_time/strftime.c

```
 1 #include <stdio.h>
 2 #include <time.h>

 3 int main (void)
 4 {
 5     struct tm *tp;
 6     time_t now;
 7     int i;
 8     char buf [BUFSIZ];
 9     char *formats [] = {
10         "%A, %B %e, %Y, %H:%M:%S",
11         "%I:%M %p, %d-%b-%y",
12         "%x %X",
13         "%C",
14         "%c",
15         NULL
16     };

17     now = time (NULL);
18     tp = localtime (&now);

19     for (i = 0; formats [i] != NULL; i++) {
20         strftime (buf, BUFSIZ, formats [i], tp);
21         printf ("%-30s %s\n", formats [i], buf);
22     }

23     return (0);
24 }
```

date_and_time/strftime.c

Program 6.5 Using `strftime` to convert the time to various formats.

```
#include <time.h>

char *strptime (const char *buf, const char *format, struct tm *tm);
```
                         Returns: a pointer to the byte after the last byte parsed if OK, NULL on error

---

The `strptime` function converts the character string pointed to by *buf* to values stored in the `tm` structure pointed to by *tm*, using the format specified by *format*.

The format specifications are the same as those listed for `strftime`, with the following exceptions:

%a   The locale's weekday name (Either the full name or the abbreviated name may be specified.)

%A   The same as %a

%b   The locale's month name (Either the full name or the abbreviated name may be specified.)

%B   The same as %b

%C   The century number (i.e., the year divided by 100 and truncated to an integer as a decimal number. Single digits are preceded by a 0. If %C is used without the %y specifier, `strptime` assumes the year offset is zero in whatever century is specified. Note that this behaviour is not specified by any standards document, so portable applications should not depend on it.)

%d	The day of the month (A leading 0 is permitted but not required.)
%e	The same as %d
%h	The same as %b
%H	The hour, using a 24-hour clock (A leading 0 is permitted but not required.)
%I	The hour, using a 12-hour clock (A leading 0 is permitted but not required.)
%j	The day number of the year (Leading 0s are permitted but not required.)
%m	The month number (A leading 0 is permitted but not required.)
%M	The minute (A leading 0 is permitted but not required.)
%n	Any white space
%S	The seconds (A leading 0 is permitted but not required.)
%t	Any white space
%U	The week number of the year as a decimal number (A leading 0 is permitted but not required.)
%W	The week number of the year as a decimal number, with Monday as the first day of the week (A leading 0 is permitted but not required.)
%y	The year within the century (When a century is not otherwise specified, values in the range 69 to 99 refer to years in the 20th century (i.e., 1969 to 1999 inclusive), and values in the range 0 to 68 refer to years in the 21st century (i.e., 2000 to 2068 inclusive). Leading 0s are permitted but not required.)

In addition to the preceding changes, the following format specifications are not supported: %g, %G, %k, %l, %u, and %v. Like `strftime`, the `strptime` function supports alternate conversion specifications by using the E or O modifiers. The same alternate conversion specifications supported for `strftime` are supported for `strptime`, with the exception of %Eg, %EG, %Og, and %Ou.

The month and weekday names, as well as the alternate numeric symbols, can be any combination of upper- and lower case letters.

The Solaris version of `strptime` provides a number of extensions. The behaviour of most of these extensions depends on whether _STRPTIME_DONTZERO was defined when <time.h> was included.

Regardless of whether _STRPTIME_DONTZERO is defined, the following extensions apply:

- If %j is specified, tm_yday is set. If the year is given, and the month and day are not, then tm_mon, tm_mday, and tm_year are calculated and set.

- If %U or %W is specified, and if the weekday and year are given but the month and day of month are not, then tm_mon, tm_mday, tm_wday, and tm_year are calculated and set.

The following extensions apply if _STRPTIME_DONTZERO is not defined:

- The tm structure is zeroed on entry, and strptime updates the members of the tm struct associated with the specifiers in the format string.
- If %C is specified and %y is not, then 0 is assumed as the year offset, and the year is calculated and assigned to tm_year.

The following extensions apply if _STRPTIME_DONTZERO is defined:

- The tm structure is not zeroed on entry. Also, for some format specifiers, some values of the input tm structure will be used to recalculate the date and will be reassigned to the appropriate members of the tm structure.
- If %C is specified and %y is not, the year offset is assumed to be the value of the tm_year member of the input tm structure. The year is then calculated and reassigned to tm_year.
- If %j is specified, but %y, %Y, nor %C are specified, and neither the month nor the day of the month are specified, then the year is assumed to be the value of the tm_year member of the input tm structure. In addition to setting tm_yday, the day of year and year values are used to calculate the month and day of the month, which are then assigned to tm_mon and tm_mday respectively.
- If %U or %W is specified, and if the weekday or the year are not given, and the month and day of month are not given, then the weekday value or the year value (or both) will be assumed to be the values of the tm_wday or tm_year members of the input tm structure. Then the month and day of month are calculated and assigned to tm_mon and tm_wday.
- If %p is specified, but the hour is not, then the tm_hour member of the input tm structure will be referenced, and if necessary, updated. If the AM or PM input is the latter, and the input tm_hour is between 0 and 11 inclusive, 12 hours will be added, and tm_hour will be updated with the new value. Similarly, if the AM or PM input is the former, and the input tm_hour is between 13 and 23 inclusive, then 12 hours will be subtracted, and tm_hour will be updated with the new value.

These extensions may be changed at any time, and should not be relied upon by portable applications. The use of several "same as" formats, as well as the handling of white space, makes it easier for us to use the same format strings for strftime and strptime.

The `strptime` function tries to calculate `tm_year`, `tm_mon`, and `tm_mday` when given incomplete input. This allows the resulting `tm` structure to be passed to `mktime` to produce a `time_t` for dates that are representable by a `time_t`.

The `getdate` Function

We can also use the `getdate` function to convert the textual representation of a date to a `tm` structure.

```
#include <time.h>

struct tm *getdate (const char *string);
extern int getdate_err;
```
                             Returns: a pointer to the converted time if OK, NULL on error

The `getdate` function uses user-supplied template files to convert the time specified by *string* to a `tm` structure.

The template file to use is specified by the DATEMSK environment variable. Each line of the template file represents an acceptable date specification, using conversion format specifiers similar to those used by `strftime` and `strptime`. The first line in the template file that matches the input specification is used to interpret *string* and is converted into the internal time format.

The format conversion specifiers may be any that are used by `strftime`, with the following omissions: `%g`, `%G`, `%u`, `%Eg`, and `%EG`. Also, both `%n` and `%t` are interpreted as any white space.

The following rules are applied when converting *string* to a `tm` structure:

- If only the weekday is given, then today is assumed if the given day is the same as the current day, and next week if it is less.

- If only the month is given, the current month is assumed if the given month is the same as the current one, and next year if it is less and no other year is given. Also, the first day of the month is assumed if no other day is specified.

- If only the year is given, the values of the `tm_mon`, `tm_mday`, `tm_yday`, `tm_wday`, and `tm_isdst` are indeterminate.

- If the century is given, but not the year within the century, the current year within the century is assumed.

- If no hour, minute, and second are given, then the current hour, minute, and second are assumed.

- If no date is given, today is assumed if the given hour is greater than the current hour, and tomorrow is assumed otherwise.

If an error occurs, getdate returns NULL and sets the global variable getdate_err to indicate the cause of the error. Subsequent calls to getdate will alter the contents of getdate_err.

6.8   Summary

In this chapter we discussed the various representations of time: calendar time (the number of seconds since the epoch), the tm structure (which holds a time that's been broken down into its component parts), and an arbitrarily formatted text string that we humans are most familiar with. We have also shown how we can convert from one of these representations to another.

Exercises

6.1   Set your TZ environment variable to a different value, and rerun Program 6.2 to see what happens.

6.2   Modify Program 6.5 to print each of the formats in several different locales (e.g., POSIX, French, German, Italian, and Swedish). Hint: the setlocale function we discuss in Appendix A might be useful.

6.3   Write a program to show the current time in different time zones around the world. Include both northern and southern hemisphere locations.

7

Users and Groups

7.1 Introduction

As we stated in Chapter 1, every process, file, and system resource in a UNIX system belongs to a particular user and group: there is no such thing as an anonymous file or resource. Solaris maintains several pieces of information about each user: a user name, a user ID, and one or more group IDs. This information is used to keep track of the privileges associated with each process (for example, which files may be opened and how, how many resources it may consume, and so on), who is logged in, when each user last logged in, etc. In this chapter we examine the information maintained by the operating system about each user, and what this information can be used for.

7.2 User Names

When an account is created on a UNIX system, one of the attributes it has is a user name. A *user name* is a string that is used to uniquely identify an account. (We say account here, rather than user, because some user names are associated with nonuser accounts, e.g., daemon, bin, and nobody.) A user name consists of one to eight characters from the following set: alphanumerics, the period (.), the underscore (_), and the hyphen (–). The first character should be alphabetic, and at least one of the characters should be a lower case alphabetic character. (We recommend that all alphabetics be lower case to prevent user confusion.)

> The useradd command will issue a warning if an attempt is made to add a user name that violates these rules. We can avoid the warning by using other methods to add users, but we strongly recommend against this practice. In fact, the Solaris useradd man page goes so far as to say that user names not meeting these requirements may not work in future releases of Solaris. We recommend that only user names following these rules be used.

In some places in this text, we shall refer to a login name. A *login name* is a user name specifically associated with a login session. As we shall see, it is possible for us to log in as one person, and then assume the identity of another. When we say "login name", we specifically mean the person who we logged in as, which may or may not be the same as the person we are currently running processes as.

Probably the two most important uses of our user name are when we log in and when we receive email. As we mentioned in Chapter 1, logging in usually requires us to authenticate ourselves by supplying our user name and password (although there are alternatives to this, such as ssh sessions that use keys to authenticate us).

Although is has recently become popular to allow email to be addressed as "firstname.lastname@domain", all email addresses eventually resolve to a user name on a machine. For example, "joe.r.luser@example.com" might be mapped to the user name "jrl" internally.

Other uses for user names include identifying print outs, changing file permissions, and editing file system quotas.

One important thing to realize is that the kernel does not use the user name. Instead, the kernel uses our user ID (see the next section) to identify us. The reason for this is that it is much easier and quicker to compare two numbers than it is to compare two strings. The former can be accomplished with one CPU instruction, but the latter requires a whole subroutine. Since the kernel checks permissions very frequently (e.g., whenever a file is opened), it is vital that these checks are performed as efficiently as possible.

The getlogin and getlogin_r Functions

We can use three functions to determine the user name a process is running as. The first two are called getlogin and getlogin_r.

```
#include <unistd.h>

char *getlogin (void);

char *getlogin_r (char *name, int namelen);

                                     Both return: user name if OK, NULL on error

cc [ flag ... ] file ... -D_POSIX_PTHREAD_SEMANTICS [ lib ... ]

int getlogin_r (char *name, size_t namesize);

                                            Returns: 0 if OK, errno on error
```

The getlogin function searches the file /var/adm/utmpx for the entry that matches the current controlling terminal, and it returns a pointer to the login name for that entry. Prior to Solaris 8, the file /var/adm/utmp was searched; we'll describe both of these files later in this chapter. The pointer points to a static area whose contents are overwritten on the next call to getlogin.

If getlogin is called from a process that has no controlling terminal (e.g., programs run remotely using the rsh command, or programs left running after the user has logged out), there will be no entry in /var/adm/utmpx, so a NULL pointer will be returned. The cuserid function we discuss next is more robust in this regard.

The getlogin_r function performs the same task as getlogin, but *name* must point to a buffer *namelen* bytes in size, where the result will be stored. This buffer must be at least _POSIX_LOGIN_NAME_MAX (which is defined in <limits.h>) characters in size.

The POSIX version of getlogin_r is the same as the non-POSIX version, except the last argument is of type size_t, and the return value is different. The POSIX version of getlogin_r returns 0 on success or the error number on failure.

The non-POSIX version of getlogin_r is deprecated, so new code should use the POSIX version.

Example: Using the getlogin function

Program 7.1 uses getlogin to determine the login name of the user that invoked it.

——————————————————————————————— users_and_groups/getlogin.c

```
 1 #include <stdio.h>
 2 #include <unistd.h>
 3 #include "ssp.h"

 4 int main (void)
 5 {
 6     char *user;

 7     sleep (5);

 8     if ((user = getlogin ()) == NULL)
 9         err_quit ("Not in /var/adm/utmp[x]");
10     else
11         printf ("Login name = %s\n", user);

12     return (0);
13 }
```

——————————————————————————————— users_and_groups/getlogin.c

Program 7.1 Using getlogin.

Program 7.1 sleeps for five seconds to give us time to close the terminal window before getlogin is called.

Let's see what happens when we run Program 7.1 a couple of times:

```
$ su
Password:
# id
uid=0(root) gid=1(other)
# ./getlogin
Login name = rich
# nohup ./getlogin &
18682
# Sending output to nohup.out
# $                             Type Control-D twice to close terminal window
$ cat nohup.out                 We run this command in another window
Not in /var/adm/utmp[x]
```

Note that we become `root` before running Program 7.1. This is to demonstrate that our login name and the user we are currently running commands as do not have to be the same.

> In this example (and some later ones), we needed to become `root` to demonstrate how something works. If you do not have superuser privileges on your system, you won't be able to duplicate these examples completely.

The first time we run Program 7.1, our login name is printed. The second time we run it, however, we run it in the background and use the `nohup(1)` command to prevent `SIGHUP` signals from being delivered. The `nohup` command arranges for the standard output and standard error file streams to be redirected to a file called `nohup.out` in the current directory.

Once we've closed the terminal window in which we ran Program 7.1, we must view the contents of `nohup.out` in another. This time, we see that we have no controlling terminal, and hence, no entry in `/var/adm/utmpx`.

The `cuserid` Function

The `cuserid` function is another way we can determine the user name a process is running as.

```
#include <unistd.h>

char *cuserid (char *s);
```
Returns: see text

The `cuserid` function also generates a character string representation of the login name under which the owner of the current process is logged in. If `s` is a NULL pointer, the login name is stored in an internal static buffer whose address is returned. If `s` is not NULL, it is assumed to point to a buffer at least `L_cuserid` (which is defined in `<stdio.h>`) characters in size, and the login name is placed in it.

The difference between `getlogin` and `cuserid` is that if the latter can't find an appropriate entry in `/var/adm/utmpx`, it will perform a user name lookup of the effective user ID of the process (we'll see how in Section 7.6).

Example: Using the `cuserid` function

Program 7.2 uses `cuserid` to determine the login ID that invoked the program.

These are the results we get when we run Program 7.2 in the same ways as Program 7.1.

```
$ su
Password:
# id
uid=0(root) gid=1(other)
# ./cuserid
```

users_and_groups/cuserid.c

```
 1 #include <stdio.h>
 2 #include <unistd.h>
 3 #include "ssp.h"

 4 int main (void)
 5 {
 6     char *user;

 7     sleep (5);

 8     if ((user = cuserid (NULL)) == NULL)
 9         err_quit ("Not in /var/adm/utmp[x]");
10     else
11         printf ("Login name = %s\n", user);

12     return (0);
13 }
```

users_and_groups/cuserid.c

Program 7.2 Using `cuserid`.

```
Login name = rich
# nohup ./cuserid &
18682
# Sending output to nohup.out
# $                                  Type Control-D twice to close terminal window
$ cat nohup.out                      We run this command in another window
Login name = root
```

Notice that this time, despite having no controlling terminal, a user name is written to `nohup.out` the second time we run Program 7.2.

It is important to realize that neither `getlogin` nor `cuserid` should be trusted by programs that must know the name of the user executing them. This is especially true of programs that rely on this information for permissions or authorization checking. The trouble with these functions is that they rely on the contents of `/var/adm/utmpx` first: whatever is written in there is taken to be correct. On some UNIX platforms (although not Solaris), `/var/adm/utmpx` is writable by anyone, so malicious users could change their entry to that of an authorized user, and our program would be none the wiser. Programs that must know the true identity of the executing user should use only the user ID to identify that user. If we need to know the user's name, we can look it up in the password file. We'll see how to accomplish both of these tasks later in this chapter.

7.3   User IDs

A *user ID* (UID) is an integer that identifies an account on the system. User IDs are usually unique to a given account (it is possible and permissible to set up multiple accounts that share the same user ID).

Every process running on a Solaris system has three user IDs associated with it: a real user ID, an effective user ID (EUID), and a saved set-user-ID. The real user ID is usually who we logged in as, and is used for accounting purposes. Only privileged processes can change their real user ID. The effective user ID is the user ID that is used for permissions checks. Any process can change its effective user ID, provided it has appropriate privilege. That is, the effective user ID of the process is 0, or the set-user-ID (SUID) bit (see Section 10.5) on the program's executable is set. The saved set-user-ID is only used in set-user-ID executables, and is set to the value of the effective user ID just after an `exec` of a set-user-ID program (we discuss the `exec` function in Section 15.11). The saved set-user-ID allows a process to alternate its effective user ID between the value obtained by running a set-user-ID program and the value of the executing user's real user ID.

The `getuid` and `geteuid` Functions

The `getuid` and `geteuid` functions enable a process to determine its user ID and effective user ID respectively.

```
#include <sys/types.h>
#include <unistd.h>

uid_t getuid (void);

uid_t geteuid (void);
```

Both return: see text

The `getuid` function returns the real user ID of the calling process; the `geteuid` function returns the effective user ID. Since all processes have an owner, no errors are defined for either function. Note that although we can obtain the current user ID and effective user ID, there is no way for a process to determine its current saved set-user-ID.

The `setuid` and `seteuid` Functions

The `setuid` and `seteuid` functions enable a suitably privileged process to set its user ID and effective user ID respectively.

```
#include <sys/types.h>
#include <unistd.h>

int setuid (uid_t uid);

int seteuid (uid_t euid);
```

Both return: 0 if OK, −1 on error

If the effective user ID of the calling process is zero (i.e., the `root` user), the `setuid` function sets the real, effective, and saved set-user-IDs of the calling process to *uid*. If the effective user ID of the calling process is not zero, but *uid* is either the real user ID or the saved set-user-ID, the effective user ID is set to *uid*.

Example: Getting and setting user IDs

Program 7.3 illustrates the rules for getting and setting the real and effective user IDs of a process.

users_and_groups/getuid.c

```
1 #include <stdio.h>
2 #include <sys/types.h>
3 #include <unistd.h>
4 #include "ssp.h"

5 static void print_uids (void);

6 int main (void)
7 {
8     print_uids ();

9     printf ("Trying seteuid (1)...\n");
10    if (seteuid (1) == -1)
11        err_ret ("seteuid failed");
12    print_uids ();

13    printf ("Trying seteuid (2)...\n");
14    if (seteuid (2) == -1)
15        err_ret ("seteuid failed");
16    print_uids ();

17    printf ("Trying seteuid (0)...\n");
18    if (seteuid (0) == -1)
19        err_ret ("seteuid failed");
20    print_uids ();

21    printf ("Trying setuid (1)...\n");
22    if (setuid (1) == -1)
23        err_ret ("setuid failed");
24    print_uids ();

25    printf ("Trying seteuid (0)...\n");
26    if (seteuid (0) == -1)
27        err_ret ("seteuid failed");
28    print_uids ();

29    printf ("Trying setuid (0)...\n");
30    if (setuid (0) == -1)
31        err_ret ("setuid failed");
32    print_uids ();

33    return (0);
34 }

35 static void print_uids (void)
36 {
37    printf ("UID = %ld, EUID = %ld\n", (long) getuid (), (long) geteuid ());
38 }
```

users_and_groups/getuid.c

Program 7.3 Getting and setting real and effective user IDs.

Let's run Program 7.3 a couple of times and observe the results:

```
$ ls -l getuid
-rwxr-xr-x   1 rich     staff         9668 Sep 19 17:13 getuid
$ ./getuid
UID = 1001, EUID = 1001
Trying seteuid (1)...
seteuid failed: Not owner
UID = 1001, EUID = 1001
Trying seteuid (2)...
seteuid failed: Not owner
UID = 1001, EUID = 1001
Trying seteuid (0)...
seteuid failed: Not owner
UID = 1001, EUID = 1001
Trying setuid (1)...
setuid failed: Not owner
UID = 1001, EUID = 1001
Trying seteuid (0)...
seteuid failed: Not owner
UID = 1001, EUID = 1001
Trying setuid (0)...
setuid failed: Not owner
UID = 1001, EUID = 1001
$ su
Password:                              Become root
# chown root getuid
# chmod u+s getuid
#                                      Type Control-D to exit shell
$ ls -l getuid
-rwsr-xr-x   1 root     staff         9668 Sep 19 17:13 getuid
$ ./getuid
UID = 1001, EUID = 0
Trying seteuid (1)...
UID = 1001, EUID = 1
Trying seteuid (2)...
seteuid failed: Not owner
UID = 1001, EUID = 1
Trying seteuid (0)...
UID = 1001, EUID = 0
Trying setuid (1)...
UID = 1, EUID = 1
Trying seteuid (0)...
seteuid failed: Not owner
UID = 1, EUID = 1
Trying setuid (0)...
setuid failed: Not owner
UID = 1, EUID = 1
```

The first time we run Program 7.3, we run it with the default file permissions. Running as regular user means that we can't change either our user ID or our effective user ID. We then become `root` and change the file ownership and permissions to make Program 7.3 a set-user-ID `root` executable.

Running Program 7.3 again as a regular user, we see that when the program starts, its real user ID is 1001 and its effective user ID is 0. Because the effective user ID is 0, the process can change its user ID and effective user ID to whatever it wants. Note that when we try to change our effective user ID to 2 (from 1), we can't. However, we can change it to 0. This is because 0 is our saved set-user-ID. Also notice that after calling `setuid` the first time, our real, effective, and saved set-user-IDs are irrecoverably changed to 1.

The `setreuid` Function

Another function we can use to change the effective and real user IDs of a process is `setreuid`.

```
#include <sys/types.h>
#include <unistd.h>

int setreuid (uid_t ruid, uid_t euid);
```
Returns: 0 if OK, −1 on error

The `setreuid` function sets the real and effective user IDs of the calling process to the values specified by *ruid* and *euid* respectively. If *ruid* is −1, the real user ID is not changed, and if *euid* is −1, the effective user ID is not changed.

If the effective user ID of the calling process is zero, the real and effective user IDs can be set to any legal value. If the effective user ID of the calling process is not zero, either the real user ID can be set to the effective user ID, or the effective user ID can be set to the saved set-user-ID or the real user ID.

In either case, if the real user ID is being changed (i.e., *ruid* is not −1), or the effective user ID is being changed to a value not equal to the real user ID, the saved set-user-ID is set to the value of the new effective user ID.

Using this function allows us to set the real and effective user IDs to different values in the same function call.

7.4   Group IDs

A *group ID* (GID) is an integer that identifies a group on the system.

As well as the real, effective, and saved set-user-IDs, each process also has a real, effective, and saved set-group-ID. Unlike user IDs, group IDs usually are used only for checking file access permissions. User IDs are also used to determine whether a process has sufficient permission to perform privileged operations, and for accounting purposes. group IDs are also used in some limited situations beyond file access control. For example, the `pm` (power management) driver allows processes whose group ID is 0 to change power state, and the kernel allows processes whose group ID is 0 to change the priority of IA class processes (the latter capability is used by `Xsun`).

The rules for changing group IDs are analogous to those for user IDs.

The `getgid` and `getegid` Functions

The `getgid` and `getegid` functions enable a process to determine its group ID and effective group ID (EGID) respectively.

```
#include <sys/types.h>
#include <unistd.h>

gid_t getgid (void);

gid_t getegid (void);
```
                                                                    Both return: see text

The `getgid` function returns the real group ID of the calling process; the `getegid` returns the effective group ID. Since all processes have at least one group associated with them, no errors are defined for either function. Note that although we can obtain the current group ID and effective group ID, there is no way for a process to determine its current saved set-group-ID.

The `setgid` and `setegid` Functions

The `setgid` and `setegid` functions enable a suitably privileged process to set its group ID and effective group ID respectively.

```
#include <sys/types.h>
#include <unistd.h>

int setgid (gid_t gid);

int setegid (gid_t egid);
```
                                                            Both return: 0 if OK, −1 on error

If the effective user ID of the calling process is zero (i.e., the `root` user), the `setgid` function sets the real, effective, and saved set-group-IDs of the calling process to *gid*. If the effective user ID of the calling process is not zero, but *gid* is either the real group ID or the saved set-group-ID, the effective group ID is set to *gid*.

The `setregid` Function

Another function we can use to change the effective and real group IDs of a process is `setregid`.

```
#include <sys/types.h>
#include <unistd.h>

int setregid (gid_t rgid, gid_t egid);
```

Returns: 0 if OK, −1 on error

The setregid function sets the real and effective group IDs of the calling process to the values specified by *rgid* and *egid* respectively. If *rgid* is −1, the real group ID is not changed, and if *egid* is −1, the effective group ID is not changed.

If the effective user ID of the calling process is zero, the real and effective group IDs can be set to any legal value. If the effective user ID of the calling process is not zero, either the real group ID can be set to the effective group ID, or the effective group ID can be set to the saved set-group-ID or the real group ID.

In either case, if the real group ID is being changed (i.e., *rgid* is not −1), or the effective group ID is being changed to a value not equal to the real group ID, the saved set-group-ID is set to the value of the new effective group ID.

Using this function allows us to set the real and effective group IDs to different values in the same function call.

Figure 7.1 shows the relationship among the functions we've described that modify the three user IDs associated with a process.

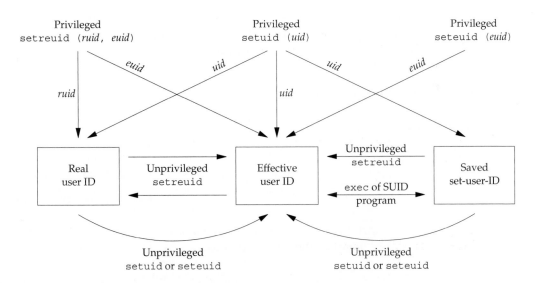

Figure 7.1 Relationship between the functions that modify the different user IDs.

Figure 7.2 summarizes the different ways the three user IDs associated with a process (i.e., the real, effective, and saved set-user-ID) can be changed.

User ID	exec		setuid (*uid*)	
	SUID bit off	SUID bit on	Privileged	Unprivileged
Real	Unchanged	Unchanged	Set to *uid*	Unchanged
Effective	Unchanged	Set to program file's owner	Set to *uid*	Set to *uid*
Saved	Copied from effective user ID	Copied from effective user ID	Set to *uid*	Unchanged

Figure 7.2   The different ways to change the three user IDs.

An analogous relationship exists between the functions that modify the three group IDs associated with a process.

7.5   Group Membership

When we log in, our group ID is set to the one found for our user in /etc/passwd (or other naming service). This group ID is called our *primary group ID*. We can, however, be a member of more than one group at a time. These other groups are called *supplementary groups*, and the union of the primary and secondary groups is called a *group set*. The supplementary groups are for permissions checks only; objects such as files are created with their group set to the process' current effective group ID. Each user can be a member of a maximum of NGROUPS_MAX groups, which is defined in <limits.h>.

Three functions let us manipulate the current group set; one gets the list of supplementary groups, and the other two set it.

The getgroups Function

The getgroups function gets the current list of supplementary groups.

```
#include <unistd.h>

int getgroups (int gidsetsize, gid_t *grouplist);
```
                              Returns: number of supplementary groups if OK, –1 on error

The getgroups function gets the current list of supplementary group IDs for the calling process and stores them in the buffer pointed to by *grouplist*. This buffer contains *gidsetsize* members; the number of members cannot exceed NGROUPS_MAX.

If *gidsetsize* is 0, the number of groups to which the calling process belongs is returned, and the buffer pointed to by *grouplist* is unchanged. This allows us to determine the size of the buffer we need to allocate for *grouplist*.

The `setgroups` Function

The `setgroups` function allows a privileged process to set its list of supplementary group IDs.

```
#include <unistd.h>

int setgroups (int ngroups, const gid_t *grouplist);
```
                                                      Returns: 0 if OK, −1 on error

If the effective user ID of the calling process is 0, the `setgroups` function sets the supplementary group list to those specified in the buffer pointed to by *grouplist*. The number of entries in the list is specified by *ngroups*, which cannot exceed NGROUPS_MAX.

Example: Getting and setting the list of supplementary groups

Program 7.4 prints the current group set, and then attempts to change it.

Let's take a look at it in action:

```
$ ./getgroups
10
setgroups failed: Not owner
$ su
Password:
# ./getgroups
1, 0, 2, 3, 4, 5, 6, 7, 8, 9, 12
10, 11, 12, 13, 14, 15, 16, 17, 18, 19, 20, 21, 22, 23, 24, 25
```

Note that when we run Program 7.4 as a regular user, we can't set our group set. Running the program as `root` shows that `root` is a member of several groups by default and that it can change its group membership at will.

The `initgroups` Function

We initialize a user's group membership list by using the `initgroups` function.

```
#include <grp.h>
#include <sys/types.h>

int initgroups (const char *name, gid_t basegid);
```
                                                      Returns: 0 if OK, −1 on error

The `initgroups` function reads the group file to get the group membership for the user specified by *name* and initializes the supplementary group access list of the calling process (using the `getgrnam` and `setgroups` functions we discussed earlier in this

─── *users_and_groups/getgroups.c*

```
 1 #include <stdio.h>
 2 #include <sys/types.h>
 3 #include <unistd.h>
 4 #include <limits.h>
 5 #include "ssp.h"

 6 static void print_groups (int ngroups, const gid_t *groups);

 7 int main (void)
 8 {
 9      int ngroups;
10      int i;
11      gid_t groups [NGROUPS_MAX];

12      if ((ngroups = getgroups (NGROUPS_MAX, groups)) == -1)
13          err_msg ("getgroups failed");

14      print_groups (ngroups, groups);

15      for (i = 0; i < NGROUPS_MAX; i++)
16          groups [i] = 10 + i;

17      if (setgroups (NGROUPS_MAX, groups) == -1)
18          err_msg ("setgroups failed");

19      if ((ngroups = getgroups (NGROUPS_MAX, groups)) == -1)
20          err_msg ("getgroups failed");

21      print_groups (ngroups, groups);

22      return (0);
23 }

24 static void print_groups (int ngroups, const gid_t *groups)
25 {
26      int i;

27      if (ngroups > 0) {
28          printf ("%ld", (long) groups [0]);
29          for (i = 1; i < ngroups; i++)
30              printf (", %ld", (long) groups [i]);
31          printf ("\n");
32      }
33 }
```
─── *users_and_groups/getgroups.c*

Program 7.4 Getting and setting the current group set.

chapter). The *basegid* group ID is also included in the supplementary group access list. This is typically the real group ID from the password (user) file.

While scanning the group file, if the number of groups, including *basegid*, exceeds NGROUPS_MAX, subsequent group entries are ignored.

Setting the list of supplementary groups is a privileged operation, so this function will fail if the effective user ID of the calling process is not 0.

7.6   The Password File

The password file, /etc/passwd, stores most of the commonly maintained information about each account on the system, including the user name, user ID, primary group ID, home directory, and preferred login shell.

> Older versions of UNIX (including SunOS) stored the user's encrypted password in the password file (hence its name). This is inherently insecure, because /etc/passwd being readable by everyone makes it easier for unscrupulous users to run dictionary attacks on other users' passwords. Because of this, passwords were moved to the shadow password file we talk about in the next section, which is readable only by root.

Each line in /etc/passwd stores the information for one user and is broken into several colon-delimited fields. Programs manipulating entries in the password file do so using the passwd structure (defined in <pwd.h>), which has the following members:

```
struct passwd {
    char    *pw_name;        /* User's user name */
    char    *pw_passwd;      /* No longer used */
    uid_t   pw_uid;          /* User's user ID */
    gid_t   pw_gid;          /* User's primary group ID */
    char    *pw_age;         /* Not used */
    char    *pw_comment;     /* Not used */
    char    *pw_gecos;       /* Typically user's full name */
    char    *pw_dir;         /* User's home directory */
    char    *pw_shell;       /* User's login shell */
};
```

Each structure member has the following definition:

pw_name	This is the user name associated with the account.
pw_passwd	Historically, this field was the user's encrypted password. It is no longer used, as passwords are now stored in the shadow password file (see next section).
pw_uid	This is the user's user ID.
pw_gid	This is the user's primary group ID. The user's supplementary group membership is defined by the groups file, which we describe in Section 7.9.
pw_age	Historically, this field was used by some versions of UNIX for password aging, but the shadow password file has superseded it.
pw_comment	This field is also not used. In fact, despite being around since Version 7, to the author's knowledge it has never been used.
pw_gecos	This field is used to store comments—usually the user's full name. It derives its name from its original use at Bell Labs to define an accounting identifier used to submit remote jobs to a General Electric mainframe. The operating system on the mainframe was called GECOS (General Electric

Comprehensive Operating System). Although the computer division of General Electric was later bought by Honeywell (who renamed GECOS to GCOS), this field has retained its original name.

pw_dir   This is the absolute pathname of the user's home directory.

pw_shell   This is the user's login shell, which is the program that will be run when the user logs in. If this field is blank, the Bourne shell, /bin/sh, will be used by default.

We can search the password file three ways:

1. We can search for a given user name.

2. We can search for a given user ID.

3. We can search through the file one entry at a time.

With two exceptions, each of the functions used to read the password file searches the sources specified in the file /etc/nsswitch.conf (see nsswitch.conf(4)).

The `getpwnam` and `getpwnam_r` Functions

The getpwnam and getpwnam_r functions enable us to search the password file by user name.

```
#include <pwd.h>

struct passwd *getpwnam (const char *name);

struct passwd *getpwnam_r (const char *name, struct passwd *pwd,
    char *buffer, int buflen);

                            Both return: password entry if OK, NULL on error

cc [ flag...] file... -D_POSIX_PTHREAD_SEMANTICS [ library... ]

int getpwnam_r (const char *name, struct passwd *pwd, char *buffer,
    size_t bufsize, struct passwd **result);

                            Returns: 0 if OK, errno on error
```

The getpwnam function searches for an entry in the password file that has a user name matching the one in the buffer pointed to by *name*. If a match is found, a pointer to a passwd structure is returned that contains the broken-down password file entry. The pointer returned refers to an internal static buffer that will be overwritten the next time the function is called.

The getpwnam_r function also searches for an entry in the password file whose user name matches the one in the buffer pointed to by *name*, but places the resulting passwd structure in the buffer pointed to by *pwd*. Most of the members are pointers to character strings. These strings are stored in the caller-supplied buffer, which is pointed to by *buffer* and has a size of *buflen* bytes.

The POSIX version of getpwnam_r is similar to the non-POSIX version, except for the return type and the type of the *bufsize* argument. Also, a pointer to the modified passwd structure is returned in the buffer pointed to by *result*.

The non-POSIX version of getpwnam_r is deprecated, so new code should use the POSIX version.

Example: Searching by user name

Program 7.5 illustrates the use of getpwnam by searching for the password file entries for the users specified on the command line. If a match is found, the pertinent details are printed; otherwise, a message stating that the user couldn't be found is printed.

—————————————————— users_and_groups/getpwnam.c

```
 1 #include <stdio.h>
 2 #include <pwd.h>

 3 int main (int argc, char **argv)
 4 {
 5     struct passwd *pwd;
 6     int i;

 7     for (i = 1; i < argc; i++) {
 8         if ((pwd = getpwnam (argv [i])) == NULL)
 9             printf ("%s: No such user\n", argv [i]);
10         else {
11             printf ("User name: %s\n", pwd -> pw_name);
12             printf ("User ID: %ld\n", (long) pwd -> pw_uid);
13             printf ("Group ID: %ld\n", (long) pwd -> pw_gid);
14             printf ("GECOS: %s\n", pwd -> pw_gecos);
15             printf ("Home directory: %s\n", pwd -> pw_dir);
16             printf ("Login shell: %s\n", pwd -> pw_shell);
17             printf ("\n");
18         }
19     }

20     return (0);
21 }
```

—————————————————— users_and_groups/getpwnam.c

Program 7.5 Searching by user name.

Running Program 7.5 gives us the following results:

```
$ ./getpwnam rich
User name: rich
User ID: 1001
Group ID: 10
GECOS: Rich Teer
Home directory: /home/rich
Login shell: /bin/ksh
```

The `getpwuid` and `getpwuid_r` Functions

The `getpwuid` and `getpwuid_r` functions let us to search the password file by user ID.

```
#include <pwd.h>

struct passwd *getpwuid (uid_t uid);

struct passwd *getpwuid_r (uid_t uid, struct passwd *pwd, char *buffer,
    int buflen);
```
                                        Both return: password entry if OK, NULL on error
```
cc [ flag...] file... -D_POSIX_PTHREAD_SEMANTICS [ library... ]

int getpwuid_r (uid_t uid, struct passwd *pwd, char *buffer, size_t bufsize,
    struct passwd **result);
```
                                                      Returns: 0 if OK, `errno` on error

The `getpwuid` function searches for an entry in the password file that has a user ID matching the one specified by *uid*. If a match is found, a pointer is returned to a `passwd` structure that contains the broken-down password file entry. The pointer returned refers to an internal static buffer that will be overwritten the next time the function is called.

The `getpwuid_r` function also searches for an entry in the password file whose user ID matches the one specified by *uid*, but places the resulting `passwd` structure in the buffer pointed to by *pwd*. Most of the members are pointers to character strings. These strings are stored in the caller-supplied buffer, which is pointed to by *buffer* and has a size of *buflen* bytes.

The POSIX version of `getpwuid_r` is similar to the non-POSIX version, except for the return type and the type of the *bufsize* argument. Also, a pointer to the modified `passwd` structure is returned in the buffer pointed to by *result*.

The non-POSIX version of `getpwuid_r` is deprecated, so new code should use the POSIX version.

The `setpwent`, `getpwent`, `getpwent_r`, and `endpwent` Functions

If we want to search the password file sequentially (i.e., enumerate) rather than searching for a specific user name or user ID, we can use the `setpwent`, `getpwent`, `getpwent_r`, and `endpwent` functions.

```
#include <pwd.h>

void setpwent (void);

void endpwent (void);

struct passwd *getpwent (void);

struct passwd *getpwent_r (struct passwd *pwd, char *buffer, int buflen);
```
                                                                Both return: see text

The `setpwent` function sets (or resets) the enumeration of the password file to the beginning of the entries. It should be called before the first call to `getpwent` or `getpwent_r`.

Successive calls to `getpwent` return either successive entries in the password file, or NULL on error or when all of the password entries have been enumerated. The pointer returned by `getpwent` refers to a static internal buffer that will be overwritten the next time the function is called.

Successive calls to `getpwent_r` also return either successive entries in the password file, or NULL on error or when all of the password entries have been enumerated. However, the results are stored in the `passwd` structure pointed to by *pwd*. The strings pointed to by the various members of *pwd* are stored in the buffer pointed to by *buffer*, which is *buflen* bytes in size.

The `endpwent` function is used to tell the system that we are finished using the password file. The password file being used is closed, and any resources it was using are deallocated.

Example: Listing all the users

Program 7.6 uses the `setpwent`, `getpwent`, and `endpwent` functions to list all of the accounts on the system.

users_and_groups/lusers.c

```
1 #include <stdio.h>
2 #include <pwd.h>
3 #include "ssp.h"

4 int main (void)
5 {
6     struct passwd *pwd;

7     setpwent ();

8     while ((pwd = getpwent ()) != NULL) {
9         if (*pwd -> pw_gecos == '\0') {
10            printf ("\"%s\" is %s (%ld, %ld)\n", pwd -> pw_name,
11                pwd -> pw_name, (long) pwd -> pw_uid, (long) pwd -> pw_gid);
12        }
13        else {
14            printf ("\"%s\" is %s (%ld, %ld)\n", pwd -> pw_gecos,
15                pwd -> pw_name, (long) pwd -> pw_uid, (long) pwd -> pw_gid);
16        }
17    }

18    endpwent ();

19    return (0);
20 }
```

users_and_groups/lusers.c

Program 7.6 List all the users.

Running Program 7.6 on one of the author's machines gives the following results:

```
$ ./lusers
"Super-User" is root (0, 1)
"daemon" is daemon (1, 1)
"bin" is bin (2, 2)
"sys" is sys (3, 3)
"Admin" is adm (4, 4)
"Line Printer Admin" is lp (71, 8)
"uucp Admin" is uucp (5, 5)
"uucp Admin" is nuucp (9, 9)
"SendMail Message Submission Program" is smmsp (25, 25)
"Network Admin" is listen (37, 4)
"Nobody" is nobody (60001, 60001)
"No Access User" is noaccess (60002, 60002)
"SunOS 4.x Nobody" is nobody4 (65534, 65534)
"Tape backup user" is backup (500, 3)
"Rich Teer" is rich (1001, 10)
"Jenny Teer" is jenny (1002, 10)
"Accounting user" is accting (1003, 10)
```

The numbers in parentheses after each user name are the user's user ID and group ID.

The `fgetpwent` and `fgetpwent_r` Functions

All the functions we've discussed so far in this section use the name service selection file, /etc/nsswitch.conf, to determine which repositories (e.g., files, LDAP, NIS, or NIS+) are used to look up password file entries. There are, however, two functions that bypass /etc/nsswitch.conf: fgetpwent and fgetpwent_r.

```
#include <pwd.h>

struct passwd *fgetpwent (FILE *fp);

struct passwd *fgetpwent_r (FILE *fp, struct passwd *pwd, char *buffer,
    int buflen);
```

Both return: see text

The fgetpwent function is much the same as getpwent, except that it reads and parses the next line from the file associated with *fp*, which is assumed to have the same format as /etc/passwd. A successful call to fgetpwent returns a pointer to a passwd structure, which is stored in a static internal buffer that will be overwritten the next time the function is called.

The fgetpwent_r function also reads and parses the next line from the file associated with *fp*, but it places the result in the passwd structure pointed to by *pwd*. The strings pointed to by the various members of *pwd* are stored in the buffer pointed to by *buffer*, which is *buflen* bytes in size.

Both functions return a NULL pointer on error or when the end of the file has been reached.

Writing a Password File Entry

The functions we've discussed so far in this section have been concerned with getting information from the password file. We can use another function to write a password file entry (although updating the password file using this function is discouraged).

```
#include <pwd.h>

int putpwent (const struct passwd *pwd, FILE *fp);
```
Returns: 0 if OK, non-zero on error

The `putpwent` function is the inverse of `fgetpwent`; the `passwd` structure pointed to by *pwd* is written to the file associated with *fp*. The format of the written data matches the format of `/etc/passwd`. Note that because this function also bypasses `/etc/nsswitch.conf`, it is of limited utility.

Programs modifying the password or shadow password files (see the next section) should lock them before modifying them, then unlock them when the modifications are complete.

```
#include <shadow.h>

int lckpwdf (void);

int ulckpwdf (void);
```
Both return: 0 if OK, −1 on error

The `lckpwdf` function attempts to obtain an exclusive lock on the file `/etc/.pwd.lock`. This file is used to coordinate modification access to the password databases `/etc/passwd` and `/etc/shadow`.

The `ulckpwdf` unlocks the password database lock file.

Because these two functions are intended for internal use only, compatibility is not guaranteed.

7.7 The Shadow Password File

As we stated earlier, users' encrypted passwords formerly were stored in the password file. Because of the security problems inherent in a world-readable password file, modern UNIX variants store the encrypted passwords in a file that only `root` can read. This file is referred to as the *shadow password file* and is called `/etc/shadow` on Solaris.

Besides storing encrypted passwords, the shadow password file also stores information used to implement password aging. The idea behind password aging is that users are periodically forced to change their passwords, so that even if an attacker guesses a user's password, that knowledge will not be useful for ever. Password aging is optional; by default it is not used.

Each line in /etc/shadow stores the encrypted password and password-aging information for one user, and is broken into several colon-delimited fields. Programs manipulating entries in the shadow password file do so using the spwd structure, which is defined in <shadow.h>. It has the following members:

```
struct spwd {
    char          *sp_namp;    /* Login name */
    char          *sp_pwdp;    /* Encrypted password */
    int           sp_lstchg;   /* Date of last change */
    int           sp_min;      /* Minimum days to password change */
    int           sp_max;      /* Maximum days to password change */
    int           sp_warn;     /* Warning period */
    int           sp_inact;    /* Maximum inactive days */
    int           sp_expire;   /* Account expiry date */
    unsigned int  sp_flag;     /* Not used */
};
```

Each structure member has the following definition:

sp_namp   This is the user name associated with the account.

sp_pwdp   This is the user's encrypted password, a *lock string* (*LK*) to indicate that the account is locked, or empty, which means that there is no password for the account.

Prior to Solaris 9 Update 2 (i.e., Solaris 9 12/02), the encrypted password was a 13-character string generated by a one-way encryption algorithm. Starting with Solaris 9 12/02, it is possible to use different encryption algorithms, that result in a different (and longer) encrypted password format (the details of the encrypted password formats are not important). A number of alternative encryption algorithms are available, including Blowfish and several variations of MD5.

sp_lstchg   This is the number of days since January 1, 1970, and the date the password was last modified. This field is part of the password-aging implementation and may be blank if password aging is not being used.

sp_min   The minimum number of days required to pass between password changes. This is provided to prevent a user from defeating the password-aging system by changing their password to something new, and then immediately changing it back. The passwd program does not allow us to "change" our password to our current password. This field is part of the password-aging implementation and may be blank if password aging is not being used.

sp_max   This is the maximum number of days the current password is valid. This field is part of the password-aging implementation and may be blank if password aging is not being used.

sp_warn	This is the number of days before the current password expires that the user is warned of its expiration. This warning period is important because we typically can't think of a good password without prior notice. This field is part of the password-aging implementation and may be blank if password aging is not being used.
sp_inact	This is the number of days of inactivity allowed for this user. Accounts inactive for more than this number of days are disabled (locked) so that an attacker can't use them. This field is part of the password-aging implementation and may be blank if password aging is not being used.
sp_expire	This is the absolute date (in UNIX time format) that the account will expire. After this time, the login may no longer be used. This field is part of the password-aging implementation and may be blank if password aging is not being used.
sp_flag	This field is reserved for future use and is set to zero. It is not currently used.

We can search the shadow password file two ways:

1. We can search for a given user name.

2. We can search through the file one entry at a time.

With two exceptions, each of the functions used to read the shadow password file search the sources specified in the file /etc/nsswitch.conf.

The getspnam and getspnam_r Functions

The getspnam and getspnam_r functions enable a privileged process to search the shadow password file by user name.

```
#include <shadow.h>

struct spwd *getspnam (const char *name);

struct spwd *getspnam_r (const char *name, struct spwd *result, char *buffer,
    int buflen);
```
Both return: shadow password entry if OK, NULL on error

The getspnam function searches for an entry in the shadow password file that has a user name matching the one in the buffer pointed to by *name*. If a match is found, a pointer to a spwd structure is returned that contains the broken-down shadow password file entry. The pointer returned refers to an internal static buffer that will be overwritten the next time the function is called.

The getspnam_r function also searches for an entry in the shadow password file whose user name matches the one in the buffer pointed to by *name*, but places the resulting spwd structure in the buffer pointed to by *result*. Two of the spwd structure members are pointers to character strings. These strings are stored in the caller-supplied buffer, which is pointed to by *buffer* and has a size of *buflen* bytes.

Example: Searching by user name

Program 7.7 illustrates the use of getspnam by searching for the shadow password file entries for the users specified on the command line. If a match is found, the pertinent details are printed; otherwise, a message stating that the user couldn't be found is printed.

users_and_groups/getspnam.c

```
 1 #include <stdio.h>
 2 #include <shadow.h>
 3 #include <errno.h>
 4 #include "ssp.h"

 5 int main (int argc, char **argv)
 6 {
 7     struct spwd *spwd;
 8     int i;

 9     for (i = 1; i < argc; i++) {
10         if ((spwd = getspnam (argv [i])) == NULL)
11             if (errno == 0)
12                 printf ("%s: No such user\n", argv [i]);
13             else
14                 err_ret ("getspnam failed");
15         else {
16             printf ("User name: %s\n", spwd -> sp_namp);
17             printf ("Encrypted password: %s\n", spwd -> sp_pwdp);
18             printf ("Last change: %d\n", (int) spwd -> sp_lstchg);
19             printf ("Min: %d\n", (int) spwd -> sp_min);
20             printf ("Max: %d\n", (int) spwd -> sp_max);
21             printf ("Warn: %d\n", (int) spwd -> sp_warn);
22             printf ("Inact: %d\n", (int) spwd -> sp_inact);
23             printf ("Expires: %d\n", (int) spwd -> sp_expire);
24             printf ("Flags: %d\n", (int) spwd -> sp_flag);
25             printf ("\n");
26         }
27     }

28     return (0);
29 }
```

users_and_groups/getspnam.c

Program 7.7 Searching the shadow password file by user name.

Running Program 7.7 on one of the author's machines gives the following results:

```
$ ./getspnam rich
getspnam failed: Permission denied
$ su
Password:
# ./getspnam rich
User name: rich
Encrypted password: $md5$MyAudiTT$/I/GbTrJO9TTEOnZRackH0
Last change: 11954
Min: -1
Max: -1
Warn: -1
Inact: -1
Expires: -1
Flags: 0
```

Note that we must become `root` to successfully run Program 7.7.

From the format of the encrypted passwords, we can see that `rich` is using a password encrypted with an MD5 message digest algorithm rather than the traditional UNIX crypt algorithm.

The `setspent`, `getspent`, `getspent_r`, and `endspent` Functions

If we want to search the shadow password file sequentially (i.e., enumerate) rather than searching for a specific user name, we can use the `setspent`, `getspent`, `getspent_r`, and `endspent` functions.

```
#include <shadow.h>

void setspent (void);

void endspent (void);

struct spwd *getspent (void);

struct spwd *getspent_r (struct spwd *result, char *buffer, int buflen);
```
Both return: see text

The `setspent` functions sets (or resets) the enumeration of the shadow password file to the beginning of the entries. It should be called before the first call to `getspent` or `getspent_r`.

Successive calls to `getspent` return either successive entries in the shadow password file, or NULL on error or when all of the shadow password entries have been enumerated. The pointer returned by `getspent` refers to a static internal buffer that is overwritten the next time the function is called.

Successive calls to `getspent_r` also return either successive entries in the shadow password file, or NULL on error or when all of the shadow password entries have been enumerated. However, the results are stored in the `spwd` structure pointed to by *result*. The strings pointed to by two of the members of *result* are stored in the buffer pointed to by *buffer*, which is *buflen* bytes in size.

The endspent function is used to tell the system that we are finished using the shadow password file. The shadow password file being used is closed, and any resources it was using are deallocated.

Example: Listing all the users' passwords

Program 7.8 uses the setspent, getspent, and endspent functions to list all the accounts on the system with their encrypted passwords.

————————————————————————— users_and_groups/lusersp.c

```
 1 #include <stdio.h>
 2 #include <shadow.h>
 3 #include <errno.h>
 4 #include "ssp.h"

 5 int main (void)
 6 {
 7     struct spwd *spwd;

 8     setspent ();

 9     while ((spwd = getspent ()) != NULL)
10         printf ("%s: %s\n", spwd -> sp_namp, spwd -> sp_pwdp);

11     endspent ();

12     return (0);
13 }
```

————————————————————————— users_and_groups/lusersp.c

Program 7.8   Listing all the passwords.

Running Program 7.8 on one of the author's machines gives the following results:

```
$ ./lusersp
$ su
Password:
# ./lusersp
root: KPxyZZybg3JZw
daemon: NP
bin: NP
sys: NP
adm: NP
lp: NP
uucp: NP
nuucp: NP
smmsp: NP
listen: *LK*
nobody: NP
noaccess: NP
nobody4: NP
backup: *LK*
rich: $md5$MyAudiTT$/I/GbTrJO9TTEOnZRackH0
jenny: R2D2O8t.qLi/2
accting: PCSh1tvw.QS96
```

Notice that again we had to become root to successfully run Program 7.8.

From the format of the encrypted passwords, we can see that `rich` is using a password encrypted with an MD5 message digest algorithm, whereas `root`, `jenny`, and `accting` are using passwords encrypted with the traditional UNIX crypt algorithm. The users whose passwords are either `*LK*` or `NP` are locked; it is impossible for someone to log in as one of these users.

The `fgetspent` and `fgetspent_r` Functions

All of the functions we've discussed so far in this section use the name service selection file, `/etc/nsswitch.conf`, to determine which repositories (e.g., files, LDAP, NIS, or NIS+) are used to look up shadow password file entries. There are, however, two functions that bypass `/etc/nsswitch.conf`. These are `fgetspent` and `fgetspent_r`.

```
#include <shadow.h>

struct spwd *fgetspent (FILE *fp);

struct spwd *fgetspent_r (FILE *fp, struct spwd *result, char *buffer,
    int buflen);
```
Both return: see text

The `fgetspent` function is much the same as `getspent`, except that it reads and parses the next line from the file associated with *fp*, which is assumed to have the same format as `/etc/shadow`. A successful call to `fgetspent` returns a pointer to a `spwd` structure, which is stored in a static internal buffer that will be overwritten the next time the function is called.

The `fgetspent_r` function also reads and parses the next line from the file associated with *fp*, but it places the result in the `spwd` structure pointed to by *result*. Two of the `spwd` structure members are pointers to character strings. These strings are stored in the buffer pointed to by *buffer*, which is *buflen* bytes in size.

Both functions return a NULL pointer on error or when the end of the file has been reached.

Writing a Shadow Password File Entry

All the functions so far in this section have been concerned with getting information from the shadow password file. Another function lets us write a shadow password file entry (although updating the shadow password file using this function is discouraged).

```
#include <shadow.h>

int putspent (const struct spwd *spwd, FILE *fp);
```
Returns: 0 if OK, non-zero on error

The `putspent` function is the inverse of `fgetspent`; the `spwd` structure pointed to by *spwd* is written to the file associated with *fp*. If any of the `sp_min`, `sp_max`, `sp_lstchg`, `sp_warn`, `sp_inact`, or `sp_expire` members of the `spwd` structure are −1, or if `sp_flag` is 0, the corresponding field in the file is cleared.

The format of the written data matches the format of `/etc/shadow`. Note that because this function also bypasses `/etc/nsswitch.conf`, it is of limited utility.

Updating the shadow password file using this function is ill-advised; programs doing so should use the password database locking functions we discussed in Section 7.6 to avoid potential file corruption.

7.8   Reading and Encrypting Passwords

We've talked about encrypted passwords and alluded to the fact that one-way encryption algorithms are used. One thing we haven't addressed, though, is how we compare passwords. Passwords are stored as strings, so we can use the `strcmp` function we discussed in Chapter 3. But obviously we can't compare the unencrypted password we enter with the one stored in the shadow password file; they will always be different. Because passwords are encrypted using a one-way algorithm, we must encrypt the password we enter before comparing it to the one stored in the shadow password file.

Before we do that, however, we must get a password from the user.

The `getpass` and `getpassphrase` Functions

Reading a password from an interactive user is straightforward, but we shouldn't just use `fgets` or the like. This is because echoing is enabled by default, and echoing a user's plain-text password is not a good idea. We could write our own function using the facilities described in Chapter 12, but using the ones supplied with the OS is easier.

```
#include <stdlib.h>

char *getpass (const char *prompt);

char *getpassphrase (const char *prompt);
```
                              Both return: the password typed if OK, NULL on error

The `getpass` function opens the controlling terminal of the process, writes out the NUL-terminated prompt pointed to by *prompt*, and then reads the next line of newline or EOF terminated characters. After reading the line of text, the terminal state is restored and the controlling terminal is closed. (We'll take a closer look controlling terminals and how to change terminal state in Chapter 12.) Of the characters read from the user, at most PASS_MAX (which is defined in `<limits.h>`) characters are returned to the caller.

The `getpassphrase` function is the same as `getpass`, except it reads and returns a string up to 256 characters in length.

Upon successful completion, both functions return a pointer to a static internal buffer that is overwritten the next time the function is called.

Once we have read in a password, we need to encrypt it.

The `crypt` Function

We use the `crypt` function to encrypt a password.

```
#include <unistd.h>

char *crypt (const char *key, const char *salt);
```
Returns: the encrypted password if OK, NULL on error

The `crypt` function encrypts a block of 0s, using the string pointed to by *key* as the encryption key. The encryption algorithm used depends on the release of Solaris and the value of *salt*.

Prior to Solaris 9 12/02, the `crypt` function was based on a one-way data encryption algorithm, called DES (Data Encryption Standard), with variations intended to frustrate the use of hardware implementations of a key search (among other things). Only the first eight characters of *key* are used to encrypt a block of bytes whose values are 0; the rest are ignored. The *salt* argument points to a two-character string that is used to perturb the hashing algorithm in one of 4096 different ways.

Although it is somewhat secure, computer processing speed has increased significantly since the introduction of DES in 1977, making brute force cracking of DES encrypted passwords a real threat. Solaris 9 12/02 implemented a new encryption infrastructure. Several strong encryption algorithms were provided, including the BSD Blowfish algorithm and several varieties of the MD5 message digest algorithm. (These algorithms, because of their increased key length and complexity, are much more computationally intensive to process, so the brute force breaking of passwords enrypted with them requires several orders of magnitude more time than passwords encrypted using DES.) For new passwords, which algorithm gets used depends on the contents of the files `/etc/security/crypt.conf` and `/etc/security/policy.conf`; old passwords also use the current salt to determine the encryption algorithm.

It is generally accepted that Blowfish is stronger than the BSD and Linux variants of the MD5 algorithm, but given a sufficient key length, which algorithm is "strongest" is a moot point. Having said this, the Sun MD5 algorithm has some changes intended to increase resistance to brute force cracking (via speed optimization) and dictionary lookup attacks.

If the traditional encryption algorithm is used, the value returned from `crypt` is a pointer to a 13-character string, the first two characters of which are those of *salt*. Starting with Solaris 9 12/02, the length of the string returned by `crypt` depends on the algorithm used to encrypt *key*; the number of characters used for *salt*, which is generated by the `crypt_gensalt` function, is also dependent on the encryption algorithm.

The `crypt_gensalt` Function

Introduced with Solaris 9 12/02, the `crypt_gensalt` function is used to generate a salt value suitable for use by the `crypt` function.

```
#include <crypt.h>

char *crypt_gensalt (const char *oldsalt, const struct passwd *userinfo);
```
                                    Returns: a pointer to the new salt if OK, NULL on error

If *oldsalt* is NULL, the `crypt_gensalt` function uses the algorithm defined by the `CRYPT_DEFAULT` variable in `/etc/security/policy.conf` to generate the new salt.

If *oldsalt* is not NULL, the `crypt_gensalt` function determines if the algorithm specified by *oldsalt* is allowed by checking the `CRYPT_ALGORITHMS_ALLOW` and `CRYPT_ALGORITHMS_DEPRECATE` variables in `/etc/security/policy.conf`. If the algorithm is allowed, an appropriate salt is generated. If the algorithm is not allowed, or there is no entry for it in `/etc/security/crypt.conf`, the default algorithm is used to generate the new salt.

Example: Encrypting passwords the traditional way

Program 7.9 prompts for a password, and then encrypts it using a fixed salt (real applications would be more likely to generate the salt randomly than use a fixed one). Note that we use the `getpassphrase` function, rather than `getpass`. We do this to show that only the first eight characters of the key are significant.

————————————————————— users_and_groups/old_crypt.c

```
 1 #include <stdio.h>
 2 #include <stdlib.h>
 3 #include <unistd.h>

 4 int main (void)
 5 {
 6     char *pass;
 7     char *salt;
 8     char *secret;

 9     pass = getpassphrase ("Password: ");
10     salt = "RT";
11     secret = crypt (pass, salt);

12     printf ("Password = \"%s\"\n", pass);
13     printf ("Salt = \"%s\"\n", salt);
14     printf ("Secret = \"%s\"\n", secret);

15     return (0);
16 }
```
————————————————————— users_and_groups/old_crypt.c

Program 7.9 Traditional style password encryption.

Running program 7.9 a couple of times gives the following results:

```
$ ./old_crypt
Password:
Password = "verylongpassword"
Salt = "RT"
Secret = "RThqLEGigQGr."
$ ./old_crypt
Password:
Password = "verylongindeed"
Salt = "RT"
Secret = "RThqLEGigQGr."
```

Notice that despite using different keys, the generated encrypted string is the same both times.

Example: Encrypting passwords the new way

Program 7.10 also prompts for a password and then encrypts it using the salt returned by crypt_gensalt. Notice that the password file entry for the user specified on the command line is also used to help create the new salt.

Running program 7.10 a few times gives the following results:

```
$ ./new_crypt rich
Password:
Password = "verylongpassword"
Salt = "$md5$wVMPV4bR$"
Secret = "$md5$wVMPV4bR$p9VBNzbTcg2N4VsMW6KXn/"
$ ./new_crypt rich
Password:
Password = "verylongindeed"
Salt = "$md5$nQdTvP2C$"
Secret = "$md5$nQdTvP2C$oX5vQ2ma50XDiluAUB2OR1"
$ ./new_crypt rich
Password:
Password = "verylongpassword"
Salt = "$md5$nT8Ud9ix$"
Secret = "$md5$nT8Ud9ix$4MwF/AZ0bH2U7ok4g9.al0"
```

We can make two observations from this output:

1. One of the MD5 message digest algorithms was used.
2. Using the same password twice generates a different salt, and hence, a different encrypted password.

Although it is implied by the output of Program 7.10 (but can't be proven because of our second observation), all the characters we typed for the password are significant. We can test this on a system using one of the new algorithms by choosing a password longer than eight characters. All characters of the password must be correct for us to be authenticated. On traditional systems, we need to type only the first eight correctly.

—————————————————————————————— *users_and_groups/new_crypt.c*

```
 1 #include <stdio.h>
 2 #include <stdlib.h>
 3 #include <crypt.h>
 4 #include <pwd.h>
 5 #include "ssp.h"

 6 extern char *crypt_gensalt (const char *salt, const struct passwd *userinfo);

 7 int main (int argc, char **argv)
 8 {
 9     char *pass;
10     char *salt;
11     char *secret;
12     struct passwd *pwd;

13     if (argc !=2)
14         err_quit ("Usage: new_crypt username");

15     if ((pwd = getpwnam (argv [1])) == NULL)
16         err_quit ("%s: No such user", argv [1]);

17     pass = getpassphrase ("Password: ");
18     salt = crypt_gensalt (NULL, pwd);
19     secret = crypt (pass, salt);

20     printf ("Password = \"%s\"\n", pass);
21     printf ("Salt = \"%s\"\n", salt);
22     printf ("Secret = \"%s\"\n", secret);

23     return (0);
24 }
```
—————————————————————————————— *users_and_groups/new_crypt.c*

Program 7.10   New style password encryption.

Example: Comparing passwords

Frequently, the next thing we want to do once we've encrypted a password is compare it
to the user's current one. Program 7.11 compares the password we enter to the one
stored in the shadow password file for a given user.

Running Program 7.11 a few times gives the following results:

```
$ ./passwd_comp rich
Password:
Password = "password"
Can't get shadow database entry for rich: Permission denied
$ su
Password:
# ./passwd_comp rich
Password:
Password = "password"
Passwords match
# ./passwd_comp rich
Password:
Password = "passwordthatshouldbewrong"
Passwords match
```

——————————————————————————————— users_and_groups/passwd_comp.c

```
 1 #include <stdio.h>
 2 #include <stdlib.h>
 3 #include <unistd.h>
 4 #include <shadow.h>
 5 #include <string.h>
 6 #include "ssp.h"

 7 static boolean_t compare_passwd (const char *user, const char *passwd);

 8 int main (int argc, char **argv)
 9 {
10     char *pass;

11     if (argc !=2)
12         err_quit ("Usage: passwd_comp username");

13     pass = getpassphrase ("Password: ");
14     printf ("Password = \"%s\"\n", pass);

15     if (compare_passwd (argv [1], pass))
16         printf ("Passwords match\n");
17     else
18         printf ("Passwords don't match\n");

19     return (0);
20 }

21 static boolean_t compare_passwd (const char *user, const char *passwd)
22 {
23     struct spwd *shadow_ent;
24     char *secret;

25     if ((shadow_ent = getspnam (user)) == NULL)
26         err_msg ("Can't get shadow database entry for %s", user);

27     secret = crypt (passwd, shadow_ent -> sp_pwdp);

28     return (strcmp (secret, shadow_ent -> sp_pwdp) == 0);
29 }
```

——————————————————————————————— users_and_groups/passwd_comp.c

Program 7.11 Comparing passwords.

Note that because we need to read the shadow password file, we must run Program 7.11 as root. Also notice that only the first eight characters of the password are significant. This is because the user rich is currently using a password with traditional UNIX encryption.

If we edit /etc/security/policy.conf so that a different encryption algorithm is used (and run the passwd command so that the algorithm takes effect) and rerun Program 7.11, we get the following results:

```
$ su
Password:
# ./passwd_comp rich
Password:
Password = "password"
```

```
Passwords match
# ./passwd_comp rich
Password:
Password = "passwordthatshouldbewrong"
Passwords don't match
```

This time, we can see that all characters in the password are significant.

7.9   The Group File

The group file, /etc/group, stores the information about each group on the system, including the group's name, its group ID, and the list of users who are members of the group.

Each line in /etc/group stores the information for one group and is broken into several colon-delimited fields. The last field is a comma-separated list of the group's members. Programs manipulating entries in the group file do so using the group structure (defined in <grp.h>), which has the following members:

```
struct group {
    char    *gr_name;       /* Name of the group */
    char    *gr_passwd;     /* The encrypted group password */
    gid_t   gr_gid;         /* The group's group ID */
    char    **gr_mem;       /* The group's members */
};
```

Each structure member has the following definition:

gr_name	This is the name of the group.
gr_passwd	This field is usually empty. If it isn't empty, it contains an encrypted password. When we run the newgrp command, if a password is present, we must enter that password to gain access to the group.
	With the advent of supplementary groups, where we can be members of several groups simultaneously, the use of group passwords has become somewhat antiquated and obsolete.
gr_gid	This is the group ID of the group.
gr_mem	This is an array or pointers to strings. Each string contains the user name of one of the members of the group. The list is terminated by a NULL pointer.

We can search the group file three ways:

1. We can search for a given group name.
2. We can search for a given group ID.
3. We can search through the file one entry at a time.

With two exceptions, each of the functions used to read the group file searches the sources specified in the file /etc/nsswitch.conf (see nsswitch.conf(4)).

The `getgrnam` and `getgrnam_r` Functions

The `getgrnam` and `getgrnam_r` functions enable us to search the group file by group name.

```
#include <grp.h>

struct group *getgrnam (const char *name);

struct group *getgrnam_r (const char *name, struct group *grp, char *buffer,
    int buflen);
```

Both return: group entry if OK, NULL on error

```
cc [ flag...] file... -D_POSIX_PTHREAD_SEMANTICS [ library... ]

int getgrnam_r (const char *name, struct group *grp, char *buffer,
    size_t bufsize, struct group **result);
```

Returns: 0 if OK, errno on error

The `getgrnam` function searches for an entry in the group file that has a group name matching the one in the buffer pointed to by *name*. If a match is found, a pointer to a `group` structure is returned that contains the broken-down group file entry. The pointer returned refers to an internal static buffer that will be overwritten the next time the function is called.

The `getgrnam_r` function also searches for an entry in the group file whose group name matches the one in the buffer pointed to by *name*, but places the resulting `group` structure in the buffer pointed to by *grp*. Most of the members are pointers to character strings. These strings are stored in the caller-supplied buffer, which is pointed to by *buffer* and has a size of *buflen* bytes. The maximum size needed for this buffer can be determined with the `_SC_GETGR_R_SIZE_MAX` sysconf parameter, which we discuss in Chapter 8.

The POSIX version of `getgrnam_r` is similar to the non-POSIX version, except for the return type and the type of the *bufsize* argument. Also, a pointer to the modified `group` structure is returned in the buffer pointed to by *result*.

The non-POSIX version of `getgrnam_r` is deprecated, so new code should use the POSIX version.

Example: Searching by group name

Program 7.12 illustrates the use of `getgrnam` by searching for the group file entries for the groups specified on the command line. If a match is found, the pertinent details are printed; otherwise, a message stating that the group couldn't be found is printed.

Running Program 7.12 gives us the following results:

```
$ ./getgrnam sys
Group name: sys
Password: ""
```

users_and_groups/getgrnam.c

```
 1 #include <stdio.h>
 2 #include <grp.h>

 3 int main (int argc, char **argv)
 4 {
 5     struct group *grp;
 6     char *member;
 7     int i;

 8     for (i = 1; i < argc; i++) {
 9         if ((grp = getgrnam (argv [i])) == NULL)
10             printf ("%s: No such user\n", argv [i]);
11         else {
12             printf ("Group name: %s\n", grp -> gr_name);
13             printf ("Password: \"%s\"\n", grp -> gr_passwd);
14             printf ("Group ID: %ld\n", (long) grp -> gr_gid);
15             printf ("Members:");
16             while ((member = *grp -> gr_mem++) != NULL)
17                 printf (" %s", member);
18             printf ("\n");
19         }
20     }

21     return (0);
22 }
```

users_and_groups/getgrnam.c

Program 7.12 Searching by group name.

```
Group ID: 3
Members: root bin sys adm
```

The `getgrgid` and `getgrgid_r` Functions

Two functions enable us to search the group file by group ID.

```
#include <grp.h>

struct group *getgrgid (gid_t gid);

struct group *getgrgid_r (gid_t gid, struct group *grp, char *buffer,
    int buflen);

                              Both return: group entry if OK, NULL on error

cc [ flag...] file... -D_POSIX_PTHREAD_SEMANTICS [ library... ]

int getgrgid_r (gid_t gid, struct group *grp, char *buffer, size_t bufsize,
    struct group **result);

                                           Returns: 0 if OK, errno on error
```

The `getgrgid` function searches for an entry in the group file that has a group ID matching the one specified by *gid*. If a match is found, a pointer is returned to a group structure that contains the broken-down group file entry. The pointer returned refers to an internal static buffer that will be overwritten the next time the function is called.

The `getgrgid_r` function also searches for an entry in the group file whose group ID matches the one specified by *gid*, but places the resulting `group` structure in the buffer pointed to by *grp*. Most of the members are pointers to character strings. These strings are stored in the caller-supplied buffer, which is pointed to by *buffer* and has a size of *buflen* bytes. The maximum size needed for this buffer can be determined with the `_SC_GETGR_R_SIZE_MAX` sysconf parameter, which we discuss in Chapter 8.

The POSIX version of `getgrgid_r` is similar to the non-POSIX version, except for the return type and the type of the *bufsize* argument. Also, a pointer to the modified `group` structure is returned in the buffer pointed to by *result*.

The non-POSIX version of `getgrgid_r` is deprecated, so new code should use the POSIX version.

The `setgrent`, `getgrent`, `getgrent_r`, and `endgrent` Functions

If we want to search the group file sequentially (i.e., enumerate) rather than searching for a specific group name or group ID, we can use the `setgrent`, `getgrent`, `getgrent_r`, and `endgrent` functions.

```
#include <grp.h>

void setgrent (void);

void endgrent (void);

struct group *getgrent (void);

struct group *getgrent_r (struct group *grp, char *buffer, int buflen);
```
                                                                    Both return: see text

The `setgrent` function sets (or resets) the enumeration of the group file to the beginning of the entries. It should be called before the first call to `getgrent` or `getgrent_r`.

Successive calls to `getgrent` return either successive entries in the group file, or NULL on error or when all of the group entries have been enumerated. The pointer returned by `getgrent` refers to a static internal buffer that will be overwritten the next time the function is called.

Successive calls to `getgrent_r` also return either successive entries in the group file, or NULL on error or when all of the group entries have been enumerated. However, the results are stored in the `group` structure pointed to by *grp*. The strings pointed to by the various members of *grp* are stored in the buffer pointed to by *buffer*, which is *buflen* bytes in size. The maximum size needed for this buffer can be determined with the `_SC_GETGR_R_SIZE_MAX` sysconf parameter, which we discuss in Chapter 8.

The `endgrent` function is used to tell the system that we are finished using the group file. The group file being used is closed, and any resources it was using are deallocated.

Example: Listing all the groups

Program 7.13 uses the `setgrent`, `getgrent`, and `endgrent` functions to list all of the groups on the system.

users_and_groups/lgroups.c

```
1 #include <stdio.h>
2 #include <grp.h>
3 #include "ssp.h"

4 int main (void)
5 {
6     struct group *grp;

7     setgrent ();

8     while ((grp = getgrent ()) != NULL)
9         printf ("%s is group %ld\n", grp -> gr_name, (long) grp -> gr_gid);

10    endgrent ();

11    return (0);
12 }
```

users_and_groups/lgroups.c

Program 7.13   List all the groups.

Running Program 7.13 on one of the author's machines gives the following results:

```
$ ./lgroups
root is group 0
other is group 1
bin is group 2
sys is group 3
adm is group 4
uucp is group 5
mail is group 6
tty is group 7
lp is group 8
nuucp is group 9
staff is group 10
daemon is group 12
sysadmin is group 14
smmsp is group 25
nobody is group 60001
noaccess is group 60002
nogroup is group 65534
```

The `getgrent` and `getgrent_r` functions may not support all sources of groups, so they should be used with caution.

The `fgetgrent` and `fgetgrent_r` Functions

So far in this section, all of the functions we've discussed use the name service selection file, /etc/nsswitch.conf, to determine which repositories (e.g., files, LDAP, NIS, or NIS+) are used to look up group file entries. There are, however, two functions that bypass /etc/nsswitch.conf. These are fgetgrent and fgetgrent_r.

```
#include <grp.h>

struct group *fgetgrent (FILE *fp);

struct group *fgetgrent_r (FILE *fp, struct group *grp, char *buffer,
    int buflen);
```
Both return: see text

The fgetgrent function is much the same as getgrent, except that it reads and parses the next line from the file associated with *fp*, which is assumed to have the same format as /etc/group. A successful call to fgetgrent returns a pointer to a group structure, which is stored in a static internal buffer that will be overwritten the next time the function is called.

The fgetgrent_r function also reads and parses the next line from the file associated with *fp*, but it places the result in the group structure pointed to by *grp*. The strings pointed to by the various members of *grp* are stored in the buffer pointed to by *buffer*, which is *buflen* bytes in size. The maximum size needed for this buffer can be determined with the _SC_GETGR_R_SIZE_MAX sysconf parameter, which we discuss in Chapter 8.

Both functions return a NULL pointer on error or when the end of the file has been reached.

7.10 The `utmpx` and `wtmpx` Files

The files /var/adm/utmpx (utmpx) and /var/adm/wtmpx (wtmpx) contain extended user access and accounting information for commands such as who, finger, and write. Prior to Solaris 8, another pair of files, /var/adm/utmp and /var/adm/wtmp contained similar, but abbreviated, information; we'll discuss these obsolete files in the next section.

The utmpx file contains records that describe the current state of the system. This includes one record for each logged-in user, the system boot time, and the last run level change. The login command writes a record to utmpx every time a user logs in; the record is removed when the user logs out.

The `wtmpx` file contains historical data in the same format as `utmpx`. Each time a user logs in, a record is written to the file; when the user logs out, the same record is written again, except the user name field is empty, and the time stamp contains the log-out time instead of the log-in time.

The information about the execution of certain systems processes (e.g., a change of run level) is not stored in `wtmpx`.

The record format for the `utmpx` and `wtmpx` files is described by the `utmpx` structure, which is defined in `<utmpx.h>`.

```
struct utmpx {
    char                 ut_user [32];    /* User login name */
    char                 ut_id [4];       /* /etc/inittab id */
    char                 ut_line [32];    /* Device name */
    pid_t                ut_pid;          /* Process ID */
    short                ut_type;         /* Entry type */
    struct exit_status   ut_exit;         /* Process exit status */
    struct timeval       ut_tv;           /* Time of the entry */
    int                  ut_session;      /* Session ID */
    int                  pad [5];         /* Reserved for future use */
    short                ut_syslen;       /* Significant length of ut_host */
    char                 ut_host [257];   /* Remote hostname */
};
```

The members have the following definitions:

`ut_user`	This is the user's login name. Sometimes known as `ut_name`.
`ut_id`	This is the id field from `/etc/inittab` for a process spawned by the `init` program. The id field is the first field in `/etc/inittab`.
`ut_line`	This is the name of the device on which the user is logged in. The pathname for the device can be obtained by concatenating this string with `"/dev/"`.
`ut_pid`	This is the process ID of the process this entry describes.
`ut_type`	This indicates the type of data in this record. Legal values for this field are:

`EMPTY`	The record is empty.
`RUN_LVL`	This type of record indicates a change in the system run level. The `ut_id` field contains the new run level.
`BOOT_TIME`	This type of record is stored when the system boots. The time is recorded in the `ut_tv` field.
`OLD_TIME`	Changing the system time creates two records in `utmpx`: `OLD_TIME` and `NEW_TIME`. The `OLD_TIME`

	record type stores the time prior to the change.
NEW_TIME	This record type stores the the time after it was changed using the date command.
INIT_PROCESS	This record type is used for processes spawned by init. The name of the process is stored in ut_user, and its process ID is stored in ut_pid.
LOGIN_PROCESS	This is used for processes waiting for a user to log in. There is usually one of these for each terminal attached to the system.
USER_PROCESS	This is a user login session.
DEAD_PROCESS	This is a process that has terminated. The exit status and return code are stored in ut_exit.
ACCOUNTING	Although designed for designating an accounting record, this type is not actually implemented.

ut_exit   This is the termination and exit status of a process recorded in a DEAD_PROCESS record type. This information is stored in a exit_status structure, which has the following members:

```
struct exit_status {
    short   e_termination;   /* Termination status */
    short   e_exit;          /* Exit status */
};
```

We'll discuss how to set this field in Chapter 15.

ut_tv   This is the time this record was last modified.

ut_session   This is the session ID number. We talk about session IDs in Chapter 16.

ut_pad   This is just padding reserved for future use.

ut_syslen   This is the length, including the terminating NUL, of the hostname in the ut_host field.

ut_host   This is the hostname of the remote host if the user is logged in over the network.

Manipulating the utmpx and wtmpx files directly is strongly discouraged. Instead, we should use the functions we discuss next to ensure that the files are maintained consistently.

The `setutxent`, `getutxent`, and `endutxent` Functions

If we want to search the entries in the `utmpx` file sequentially (i.e., enumerate), we can use the `setutxent`, `getutxent`, and `endutxent` functions.

```
#include <utmpx.h>

void setutxent (void);

void endutxent (void);

struct utmpx *getutxent (void);
```

                               Returns: a pointer to a `utmpx` structure if OK, NULL on error

The `setutxent` function sets (or resets) the `utmpx` input stream to the beginning. This should be done before each search for a new entry if it is intended that the entire file be examined.

Successive calls to `getutxent` return either successive entries in the `utmpx` file, or NULL on error or when all the `umptx` entries have been enumerated. The pointer returned by `getutxent` refers to a static internal buffer that will be overwritten the next time the function is called.

The `endutxent` function is used to tell the system we are finished with the current `utmpx` file. The file is closed, and any resources it was using are deallocated.

Example: Listing the logged-in users

Program 7.14 shows our implementation of a program that is similar to `who`. The difference is that our program prints out the user's real name (the GECOS field from the password file).

For each login record in `utmpx` (which is identified by having its `ut_type` field set to `USER_PROCESS`), the `getpwnam` function is called to determine the user's real name (the GECOS field). We print the login time using the `ctime` function we discuss in Section 6.7 (the "+ 4" on line 22 is to skip the first four characters of the time (i.e., the day)).

Running Program 7.14 gives results like the following:

```
$ ./ssp_who
Login      Name            Line      Time            Host
========================================================
jenny      Jenny Teer      console   Sep 21 17:59:31  :0
rich       Rich Teer       dtremote  Sep 21 12:52:13  zaphod:0
rich       Rich Teer       pts/3     Sep 21 12:52:24  zaphod:0.0
rich       Rich Teer       pts/5     Sep 21 15:19:27  zaphod:0.1
rich       Rich Teer       pts/4     Sep 21 12:52:25  zaphod:0.0
rich       Rich Teer       pts/6     Sep 21 16:14:35  zaphod:0.1
jenny      Jenny Teer      pts/11    Sep 21 17:59:40  :0.0
rich       Rich Teer       pts/15    Sep 21 12:52:24  zaphod:0.0
rich       Rich Teer       pts/2     Sep 21 12:52:24  zaphod:0.0
jenny      Jenny Teer      pts/9     Sep 21 17:59:39  :0.0
jenny      Jenny Teer      pts/10    Sep 21 17:59:40  :0.0
```

users_and_groups/ssp_who.c

```
 1 #include <stdio.h>
 2 #include <utmpx.h>
 3 #include <pwd.h>
 4 #include <time.h>
 5 #include "ssp.h"

 6 int main (void)
 7 {
 8     struct utmpx *utmpx;
 9     struct passwd *pwd;
10     char name [17];

11     printf ("Login      Name                 Line      Time             Host\n");
12     printf ("================================================================\n");

13     setutxent ();

14     while ((utmpx = getutxent ()) != NULL) {
15         if (utmpx -> ut_type != USER_PROCESS)
16             continue;

17         if ((pwd = getpwnam (utmpx -> ut_user)) != NULL)
18             snprintf (name, 17, "%s", pwd -> pw_gecos);
19         else
20             snprintf (name, 17, "#%ld", (long) pwd -> pw_uid);

21         printf ("%-8s  %-16s  %-8s  %15.15s", utmpx -> ut_user, name,
22             utmpx -> ut_line, ctime (&utmpx -> ut_tv.tv_sec) + 4);
23         if (utmpx -> ut_syslen > 0)
24             printf ("  %s", utmpx -> ut_host);

25         printf ("\n");
26     }

27     endutxent ();

28     return (0);
29 }
```

users_and_groups/ssp_who.c

Program 7.14 Listing the logged-in users.

In this example, the user `jenny` is logged in on the console and has a couple of terminal windows open. The user `rich` has logged in over the network using XDMCP from the machine called `zaphod` and also has several terminal windows open. Note that the lines for `pts/3` and `pts/5` have different numbers on the end of the remote hostname. This is because `zaphod` is a dual-headed workstation: the sessions whose hostname ends with "0.0" were started from one monitor, and those ending in "0.1" were started on the other.

Running Program 7.14 on another machine gives these results:

```
$ ./ssp_who
Login       Name            Line        Time            Host
===========================================================
rich        Rich Teer       pts/1       Sep 21 15:52:52 grover
```

This time, `rich` logged in remotely from the machine called `grover`.

The easiest way to see the type of information stored in the other types of `utmpx` record is to run the command `who -a`.

The `getutxid` Function

We can search for a given `utmpx` record type by using the `getutxid` function.

```
#include <utmpx.h>

struct utmpx *getutxid (const struct utmpx *id);
```
Returns: a pointer to a <code>utmpx</code> structure if OK, NULL on error

The `getutxid` function searches forward from the current location in the `utmpx` file until it finds an entry with a `ut_type` that matches *id* `-> ut_type`, if the type specified is either `RUN_LVL`, `BOOT_TIME`, `OLD_TIME`, or `NEW_TIME`. If the type specified by *id* is one of `INIT_PROCESS`, `LOGIN_PROCESS`, `USER_PROCESS`, or `DEAD_PROCESS`, then a pointer will be returned to the first entry whose type is one of these four and whose `ut_id` field is the same as *id* `-> ut_id`.

The `getutxline` Function

We can search for a `utmpx` record associated with a given line by using the `getutxline` function.

```
#include <utmpx.h>

struct utmpx *getutxline (const struct utmpx *line);
```
Returns: a pointer to a <code>utmpx</code> structure if OK, NULL on error

The `getutxline` function searches forward from the current location in the `utmpx` file until it finds an entry whose `ut_type` is either `LOGIN_PROCESS` or `USER_PROCESS` and also has a `ut_line` string that matches *line* `-> ut_line`.

The `pututxline` Function

We can write a `utmpx` entry using `pututxline`.

```
#include <utmpx.h>

struct utmpx *pututxline (const struct utmpx *utmpx);
```
Returns: a pointer to a <code>utmpx</code> structure if OK, NULL on error

The `pututxline` function writes the `utmpx` structure pointed to by *utmpx* into the `utmpx` file. If the function determines that it is not already at the correct place in the file, it calls `getutxid` to search forward for the proper place. If no such entry exists, the entry is added to the end of the file.

If pututxline is called by a user whose effective user ID is not zero, a set-user-ID root program (/usr/lib/utmp_update) is invoked to verify and write the entry. (We talk about set-user-ID programs in Section 10.5.) This is because the utmpx file normally is writable only by root. In this event, the ut_user member must correspond to the actual user name associated with the process, the ut_type member must be either USER_PROCESS or DEAD_PROCESS, and the ut_line member must be a device special file (see Section 10.4) that is writable by the user.

The utmpxname Function

We can change the name of the utmpx file we use using the utmpxname function.

```
#include <utmpx.h>

int utmpxname (const char *file);
```
                                                        Returns: 1 if OK, 0 on error

The utmpxname function allows us to change the name of the utmpx file from /var/adm/utmpx to any other filename (more often than not, the alternative name is /var/adm/wtmpx). The old file is closed if it is open, but the new one is not opened (although the filename is saved). The new filename must end with an "x" to allow the name of the corresponding utmp file to be easily obtainable (we talk about utmp files in the next section).

The getutmp and getutmpx Functions

We can convert between the utmpx and utmp record types by using either getutmp or getutmpx.

```
#include <utmpx.h>

void getutmp (struct utmpx *utmpx, struct utmp *utmp);

void getutmpx (struct utmp *utmp, struct utmpx *utmpx);
```

The getutmp function copies the information stored in the utmpx structure pointed to by *utmpx* to the corresponding members of the utmp structure pointed to by *utmp*. If the information in any member of *utmpx* does not fit into the corresponding *utmp* member, the data is silently truncated.

The getutmpx function performs the opposite transformation, that is, it copies the information stored in the utmp structure pointed to by *utmp* to the corresponding members of the utmpx structure pointed to by *utmpx*.

The updwtmp and updwtmpx Functions

We can update the historical wtmpx files using the updwtmp and updwtmpx functions.

```
#include <utmpx.h>

void updwtmp (char *wfile, struct utmp *utmp);

void updwtmpx (char *wfilex, struct utmpx *utmpx);
```

These two functions have slightly different functionality depending on what release of Solaris is being used. We'll describe the current behaviour first, and then describe the behaviour in earlier versions of Solaris.

From Solaris 8, the updwtmp function could be used in one of two ways:

1. If *wfile* is /var/adm/wtmp, the utmp structure pointed to by *utmp* is converted to a utmpx structure, and the file /var/adm/wtmpx is updated. This is because starting with Solaris 8, the utmp file no longer exists, and operations on wtmp are converted to operations on wtmpx by the library functions.

2. If *wfile* is not /var/adm/wtmp, it is assumed to be an old file in utmp format and is updated directly with the utmp record pointed to by *utmp*.

The updwtmpx function writes the contents of the utmpx structure pointed to by *umptx* to the file whose name is in the buffer pointed to by *wnamex*.

Prior to Solaris 8, the updwtmp function checked for the existence of *wfile* and its parallel file, whose name is obtained by adding an "x" to *wfile*. If only one of the files exists, the other is created and initialized to reflect the state of the existing file. Then the utmp structure pointed to by *utmp* is written to *wfile*, and the corresponding utmpx structure is written to the parallel file.

Similarly, the updwtmpx function checked for the existence of *wfilex* and its parallel file, whose name is obtained by removing the final "x" from *wfilex*. If only one of the files exists, the other is created and initialized to reflect the state of the existing file. Then the utmpx structure pointed to by *utmpx* is written to *wfilex*, and the corresponding utmpx structure is written to the parallel file.

7.11   The utmp and wtmp Files

On systems running Solaris 7 or earlier, the files /var/adm/utmp (utmp) and /var/adm/wtmp (wtmp) contain user access and accounting information similar to that stored in the utmpx and wtmpx files. However, these files are not present from Solaris 8 and should be considered obsolete.

The record format for the utmp and wtmp files is a subset of that for the utmpx and wtmpx files and is described by the utmp structure, which is defined in <utmp.h>.

```
struct utmp {
    char                ut_user [8];    /* User login name */
    char                ut_id [4];      /* /etc/inittab id */
    char                ut_line [12];   /* Device name */
    short               ut_pid;         /* Process ID */
    short               ut_type;        /* Entry type */
    struct exit_status  ut_exit;        /* Exit status of process */
    time_t              ut_time;        /* Time of the entry */
};
```

The members of this structure have the same meaning as their namesakes in the utmpx structure, with the following exceptions:

ut_user	This field is used for the login name, but is limited to eight characters in length (this should not be a problem, however, as Solaris does not support user names longer than this). Be aware that if the user name is exactly eight characters long, it will not be NUL terminated.
ut_line	This is the device on which the user logged in, but is limited to 12 characters.
ut_pid	The type of the process ID is a short rather than a pid_t.
ut_time	The time stamp is stored in a time_t rather than a timeval structure.

There is a set of functions virtually identical to the ones we discussed for utmpx, which are prototyped in <utmp.h>. These take and return utmp structures rather than utmpx structures.

Given that the utmp file and its associated data structure is obsolete, and because the utmpx interfaces are available on all versions of Solaris, the older functions should not be used by new code. In fact, because the utmpx and wtmpx functions also update the utmp and wtmp files on older versions of Solaris, there's never a need to call the old functions.

7.12 The lastlog File

The file /var/adm/lastlog (lastlog) keeps track of the last login time for each user and is maintained by the login command. The lastlog file is indexed by user ID and contains one lastlog structure for each user that has logged in. The lastlog structure has the following members:

```
struct lastlog {
    time_t  ll_time;        /* Time stamp */
    char    ll_line [8];    /* Device name */
    char    ll_host [16];   /* Hostname */
};
```

The members have the following definitions:

`ll_time`	This is the time the user last logged in. Note that in the 64-bit programming environment, the type of this member is `time32_t`, which means that it will overflow in 2038.
`ll_line`	This is the name of the terminal device the user last logged in on. As with the `utmpx` file, the pathname of the device can be obtained by concatenating this string with "/dev/".
`ll_host`	This is the hostname from where the user last logged in.

Example: Printing the last login times for users

Program 7.15 shows our implementation of a function called `getllnam` that returns a pointer to a `lastlog` structure for the given user name (a NULL pointer is returned in the event of an error) and a program that uses it.

Running Program 7.15 on one of the author's systems gives the following results:

```
$ ./lastlog rich jenny adm
rich       dtremot    zaphod:0        Sat Sep 21 12:52:13 2002
jenny      console    :0              Sat Sep 21 17:59:30 2002
adm        never logged in
```

7.13 The `shells` File

The shells file, `/etc/shells` (`shells`), contains a list of the shells on the system. This allows applications like `ftp` to determine whether a user's shell is valid; if the user's shell is not listed in the `shells` file, the user is denied access.

The `/etc/shells` file is just a list of the absolute pathnames of the permitted shells. However, if the `shells` file is not present, then the default list of shells of used. The shells contained in the default list vary depending on the release, but typically include `/bin/ksh`, `/bin/sh`, and `/bin/csh`. Blank lines in the `shells` file are ignored, as are the characters after a hash mark (#).

Three functions enable us to read the `shells` file in a portable manner: `setusershell`, `getusershell`, and `endusershell`.

```
void setusershell (void);

void endusershell (void);

char *getusershell (void);
```
                                    Returns: a pointer to a legal shell if OK, NULL on error

The `setusershell` function sets or resets the list of shells to the beginning.

users_and_groups/lastlog.c

```
 1 #include <stdio.h>
 2 #include <unistd.h>
 3 #include <sys/types.h>
 4 #include <sys/stat.h>
 5 #include <fcntl.h>
 6 #include <lastlog.h>
 7 #include <time.h>
 8 #include <pwd.h>
 9 #include "ssp.h"

10 static struct lastlog *getllnam (const char *name);

11 int main (int argc, char **argv)
12 {
13     struct lastlog *ll_entry;
14     int i;

15     if (argc < 2)
16         err_quit ("Usage: lastlog username ...");

17     for (i = 1; i < argc; i++) {
18         if ((ll_entry = getllnam (argv [i])) == NULL)
19             continue;

20         if (ll_entry -> ll_time != 0)
21             printf ("%-8s  %-8s  %-16s  %s", argv [i], ll_entry -> ll_line,
22                 ll_entry -> ll_host, ctime (&ll_entry -> ll_time));
23         else
24             printf ("%-8s  never logged in\n", argv [i]);
25     }

26     return (0);
27 }

28 static struct lastlog *getllnam (const char *name)
29 {
30     static struct lastlog ll_entry;
31     struct passwd *pwd;
32     int fd;

33     if ((fd = open ("/var/adm/lastlog", O_RDONLY)) == -1)
34         return (NULL);

35     if ((pwd = getpwnam (name)) == NULL)
36         return (NULL);

37     pread (fd, &ll_entry, sizeof (struct lastlog),
38         pwd -> pw_uid * sizeof (struct lastlog));
39     close (fd);

40     return (&ll_entry);
41 }
```

users_and_groups/lastlog.c

Program 7.15 Printing users' last login times.

Successive calls to the `getusershell` return either successive entries in the `shells` file (or list), or NULL on error or when all of the shells have been enumerated. The pointer returned by `getusershell` refers to a static internal buffer that will be overwritten the next time the function is called.

The `endusershell` function is used to tell the system we are finished with the `shells` file. The file is closed, and any resources it was using are deallocated.

Example: Listing the legal shells

Program 7.16 lists the valid shells on the system.

users_and_groups/list_shells.c

```
 1 #include <stdio.h>

 2 extern char *getusershell (void);
 3 extern void setusershell (void);
 4 extern void endusershell (void);

 5 int main (void)
 6 {
 7     char *shell;

 8     setusershell ();

 9     while ((shell = getusershell ()) != NULL)
10         printf ("%s\n", shell);

11     endusershell ();

12     return (0);
13 }
```

users_and_groups/list_shells.c

Program 7.16   Listing the legal shells.

If we run Program 7.16 on a Solaris 9 system, we get the following results:

```
$ cat /etc/shalls
cat: cannot open /etc/shalls
$ ./list_shells
/usr/bin/sh
/usr/bin/csh
/usr/bin/ksh
/usr/bin/jsh
/bin/sh
/bin/csh
/bin/ksh
/bin/jsh
/sbin/sh
/sbin/jsh
/usr/bin/pfsh
/usr/bin/pfcsh
/usr/bin/pfksh
/usr/bin/bash
/usr/bin/tcsh
```

```
/usr/bin/zsh
/bin/pfsh
/bin/pfcsh
/bin/pfksh
/bin/bash
/bin/tcsh
/bin/zsh
/usr/xpg4/bin/sh
$ su
Password:
# echo /bin/ksh > /etc/shells
# ./list_shells
/bin/ksh
```

7.14 Summary

In this chapter, we've had a long look at users and groups. First we looked at user names, then took a closer look at user IDs, group IDs, and supplementary groups.

Next we took a look at the password file, /etc/passwd; the shadow password file, /etc/shadow; and showed how to encrypt and compare passwords.

After taking a look at the /etc/group file, we discussed the utmpx and wtmpx files and the obsolete utmp and wtmp files.

Finally, we looked at the /var/adm/lastlog and /etc/shells files.

Exercises

7.1   Why do we advise against updating the password and shadow password files using putpwent and putspent respectively?

7.2   What are the pros and cons of using the new password encryption algorithms supplied by Solaris 9 12/02 and newer?

7.3   Implement a function called getlluid that returns a pointer to a lastlog structure for the given user ID.

8

System Information and Resource Limits

8.1 Introduction

Solaris is a very scalable operating system capable of running on tiny uniprocessor workstations with as little as 16 MB of RAM (such as the SPARCstation 2) or large servers with more than 100 multicore processors and more than 512 GB of RAM (for example, the Sun Fire 25K). Remarkably, all this is achieved with complete binary compatibility throughout the whole range. Because of this, applications can't make any assumption about the capabilities of the machine they are running on.

Solaris has a number of facilities that enable a process to gather information about the kind of machine it is running on, like the number of processors, the amount of memory, and the architecture. Most of the facilities offered by Solaris are also available on other flavours of UNIX, although some of the specifics may vary.

UNIX has always offered a number of parameters that can be tuned by the system administrator, so that systems perform better under a particular workload. Some of these parameters are configured into the kernel, and on some versions of UNIX, changing them requires the kernel to be recompiled. Solaris, however, does not need to be recompiled if a kernel parameter is changed. Given that access to the Solaris source code outside of Sun is very restricted, this is a good thing. Instead, Solaris kernel tuning is performed by editing the file /etc/system (the details of which are beyond the scope of this text) and rebooting.

Historically, many of the adjustable parameters were defined in header files. This meant that whenever they were changed, the programs using them had to be recompiled. As the number of third party programs grew, it became clear that this idea wasn't very flexible. Instead, many of the parameters could be determined (and in some cases, changed) by using standard library calls.

The various UNIX standardization efforts (like POSIX, the Open Group, and the Single UNIX Specification) have also helped this situation by specifying standard interfaces and resource names.

In this chapter, we look at the facilities available to systems programmers that allow their programs to determine information about the machine they are running on. We'll also discuss how to get or set systemwide and per-process resource limits, and how a process can determine how much of a resource it has consumed.

8.2   System Information and Identification

We can call a number of functions to ascertain information about the machine a process is running on. Depending on the function called, we can retrieve the machine's hostname, its hostid, the OS version, and so on.

The `uname` Function

Each UNIX system maintains a number of pieces of information about itself, including the hostname, the operating system name and version, and the hardware type. We can use the uname function to obtain this information.

```
#include <sys/utsname.h>

int uname (struct utsname *name);
```
                                         Returns: non-negative if OK, −1 on error

The uname function stores information identifying the current operating system and machine in the utsname structure pointed to by *name*. The utsname structure has the following members:

```
struct utsname {
    char     sysname [SYS_NMLN];      /* Name of OS */
    char     nodename [SYS_NMLN];     /* Hostname */
    char     release [SYS_NMLN];      /* The OS release */
    char     version [SYS_NMLN];      /* The OS version */
    char     machine [SYS_NMLN];      /* The machine type */
};
```

The structure members have the following definitions:

sysname	This is a NUL-terminated string containing the name of the operating system. On machines running Solaris, this field will be "SunOS".
nodename	This is the NUL-terminated name of the machine as it is known on the network (i.e., its hostname).
release	This is a NUL-terminated string containing the release number. On machines running Solaris, this field will be the SunOS version number (e.g., 5.9).

versionThis is a NUL-terminated string containing the operating system version. On machines running Solaris, this field contains the string "Generic", possibly followed by a number that specifies the kernel jumbo patch (KJP) number and revision. An example would be "Generic_112233-12", which is a Solaris 9 machine running revision 12 of the Solaris 9 KJP.

machineThis is a NUL-terminated string identifying the type of hardware (i.e., the machine architecture). On Sun hardware, this would typically be something like "sun4u".

The `sysinfo` Function

The uname function can be used to retrieve only some system information. The sysinfo function performs a similar task, but can provide more information and enables some system information to be set.

```
#include <sys/systeminfo.h>

long sysinfo (int command, char *buf, long count);
```
Returns: non-negative if OK, −1 on error

The sysinfo function copies information about the operating system, as requested by *command*, into the buffer pointed to by *buf*. The *count* parameter indicates the size of the buffer (257 is a good value to use for *count*, as it is likely to cover all strings returned). Upon successful completion, sysinfo returns the buffer size (in bytes) required to hold the complete value, including the terminating NUL. If this value is no greater than *count*, the entire string was copied. Otherwise, the string copied into *buf* has been truncated to *count* − 1 bytes, plus the terminating NUL.

The values of *command* are as follows (note that some values of *command* allow system information to be set from *buf*).

SI_SYSNAMECopy the name of the operating system into the buffer pointed to by *buf*. This is the same value returned by uname in the sysname field; on a Solaris system, it will be "SunOS".

SI_HOSTNAMECopy the name of the machine into the buffer pointed to by *buf*. This is the same value returned by uname in the nodename field. The name may or may not be fully qualified. Internet hostnames may be up to 256 bytes in length, plus the terminating NUL.

SI_SET_HOSTNAMEIf the effective user ID of the calling process is zero, this copies the NUL-terminated string pointed to by *buf* into the kernel. Subsequent calls to sysinfo with *command* set to SI_HOSTNAME will return the new value.

SI_RELEASE	Copy the release of the operating system into the buffer pointed to by *buf*. This is the same value returned by uname in the release field.
SI_VERSION	Copy the operating system version into the buffer pointed to by *buf*. This is the same value returned by uname in the version field.
SI_MACHINE	Copy a string that represents the machine type into the buffer pointed to by *buf*. This is the same value returned by uname in the machine field.
SI_ARCHITECTURE	Copy into the buffer pointed to by *buf* a string that represents the basic instruction architecture of the machine. Examples of values returned on a system running Solaris would be "sparc" or "i386".
SI_ISALIST	Copy a string that represents the variant instruction set architectures executable on the current system.
	The names are separated by spaces and are listed in order of performance (from best to worst). In other words, earlier named instruction sets may contain more instructions than later named ones. A program compiled for an earlier named instruction set will likely run faster on that machine than the same program compiled using a later named instruction set.
	For example, given the list "sparcv9 sparcv8 sparcv7", a program compiled for sparcv9 will likely run faster on a machine using the sparcv9 architecture than the same program compiled for sparcv7.
	Programs compiled for an instruction set that does not appear in this list will at best suffer a performance degradation, or at worst will not run at all.
SI_PLATFORM	A string describing the specific hardware model is copied into the buffer pointed to by *buf*. For example, "SUNW,Sun-Blade-100", "SUNW,Ultra-60", "SUNW,S240", or "SUNW,SPARCstation-20".
SI_HW_PROVIDER	This copies the name of the hardware manufacturer into the buffer pointed to by *buf*.
SI_HW_SERIAL	This copies into the buffer pointed to by *buf* a string that is the ASCII representation of the hardware-specific serial number of the machine that executes the function. On Sun hardware, this will usually be the hostid, which is not the same thing as the serial number of the actual machine.

> A commonly asked Solaris programming question is "How do I programmatically obtain the serial number of a given machine?". The answer is: there's no way to do this. The only place the serial number of a machine is stored is on the case. The best we can hope to do is obtain the hostid.

It is not expected that manufacturers will issue the same "serial number" to more than one physical machine, so the pair of strings returned by `SI_HW_PROVIDER` and `SI_HW_SERIAL` is likely to be unique.

SI_SRPC_DOMAIN This copies the Secure Remote Procedure Call domain into the buffer pointed to by *buf*.

SI_SET_SRPC_DOMAIN If the effective user ID of the calling process is zero, this copies the NUL-terminated string pointed to by *buf* into the kernel. Subsequent calls to `sysinfo` with *command* set to `SI_SRPC_DOMAIN` will return the new value.

SI_DHCP_CACHE This copies into the buffer pointed to by *buf* an ASCII string that consists of the ASCII hexadecimal encoding of the name of the interface configured by `boot`(1M) followed by the `DHCPACK` reply from the server. This command is intended for use only by the `dhcpagent`(1M) DHCP client daemon for the purpose of adopting the DHCP maintenance of the interface configured by `boot`.

Not all values for *command* are supported on all versions of Solaris. Figure 8.1 summarizes their availability.

Example: Obtaining system information

Program 8.1 prints out the information obtained by the `uname` and `sysinfo` functions.

Notice how we've used the ISO C string creation operator (#) in our `psysinfo` macro, to generate the string version of each resource. When we say

```
psysinfo (SI_SYSNAME);
```

this is expanded by the C preprocessor to

```
print_sysinfo ("SI_SYSNAME", SI_SYSNAME);
```

Running Program 8.1 on one of the author's systems gave the following results:

```
$ ./sysinfo
Info from uname:
  sysname: SunOS
  nodename: grover
  release: 5.9
  version: Generic_112233-07
  machine: sun4u
```

Command	Solaris version					
	2.5	2.5.1	2.6	7	8	9
SI_SYSNAME	•	•	•	•	•	•
SI_HOSTNAME	•	•	•	•	•	•
SI_SET_HOSTNAME	•	•	•	•	•	•
SI_RELEASE	•	•	•	•	•	•
SI_VERSION	•	•	•	•	•	•
SI_MACHINE	•	•	•	•	•	•
SI_ARCHITECTURE	•	•	•	•	•	•
SI_ISALIST			•	•	•	•
SI_PLATFORM	•	•	•	•	•	•
SI_HW_PROVIDER	•	•	•	•	•	•
SI_HW_SERIAL	•	•	•	•	•	•
SI_SRPC_DOMAIN	•	•	•	•	•	•
SI_SET_SRPC_DOMAIN	•	•	•	•	•	•
SI_DHCP_CACHE					•	•

Figure 8.1 Availability of `sysinfo` commands.

```
Info from sysinfo
   SI_SYSNAME: SunOS
   SI_HOSTNAME: grover
   SI_RELEASE: 5.9
   SI_VERSION: Generic_Patch
   SI_MACHINE: sun4u
   SI_ARCHITECTURE: sparc
   SI_ISALIST: sparcv9+vis sparcv9 sparcv8plus+vis sparcv8plus sparcv8
      sparcv8-fsmuld sparcv7 sparc
   SI_PLATFORM: SUNW,Sun-Blade-100
   SI_HW_PROVIDER: Sun_Microsystems
   SI_HW_SERIAL: 2198662555
   SI_SRPC_DOMAIN:
   SI_DHCP_CACHE:
$ hostid
830ced9b
$ bc
obase=16
2198662555
830CED9B
```

Notice that we had to wrap the `SI_ISALIST` line to fit it onto the page. Also note that we used the `hostid` and `bc` commands to confirm that the serial number returned by the `SI_HW_SERIAL` command is the same as the hostid.

The `gethostname` and `sethostname` Functions

If we are just interested in retrieving the hostname of a machine, we can use the `gethostname` and `sethostname` functions.

———————————————————————————————— *sys_info/sysinfo.c*

```
 1 #include <stdio.h>
 2 #include <sys/utsname.h>
 3 #include <sys/systeminfo.h>
 4 #include "ssp.h"

 5 #define psysinfo(name) print_sysinfo (#name, name)

 6 static void print_sysinfo (const char *name, int command);

 7 int main (void)
 8 {
 9     struct utsname utsname;

10     if (uname (&utsname) == -1)
11         err_msg ("uname failed");
12     printf ("Info from uname:\n");
13     printf ("  sysname: %s\n", utsname.sysname);
14     printf ("  nodename: %s\n", utsname.nodename);
15     printf ("  release: %s\n", utsname.release);
16     printf ("  version: %s\n", utsname.version);
17     printf ("  machine: %s\n\n", utsname.machine);

18     printf ("Info from sysinfo\n");
19     psysinfo (SI_SYSNAME);
20     psysinfo (SI_HOSTNAME);
21     psysinfo (SI_RELEASE);
22     psysinfo (SI_VERSION);
23     psysinfo (SI_MACHINE);
24     psysinfo (SI_ARCHITECTURE);
25 #ifdef SI_ISALIST
26     psysinfo (SI_ISALIST);
27 #endif
28     psysinfo (SI_PLATFORM);
29     psysinfo (SI_HW_PROVIDER);
30     psysinfo (SI_HW_SERIAL);
31     psysinfo (SI_SRPC_DOMAIN);
32 #ifdef SI_DHCP_CACHE
33     psysinfo (SI_DHCP_CACHE);
34 #endif

35     return (0);
36 }

37 static void print_sysinfo (const char *name, int command)
38 {
39     char buf [257];

40     if (sysinfo (command, buf, 257) == -1)
41         err_msg ("sysinfo (%s) failed", name);
42     printf ("  %s: %s\n", name, buf);
43 }
```

———————————————————————————————— *sys_info/sysinfo.c*

Program 8.1 System information provided uname and sysinfo.

```
#include <unistd.h>

int gethostname (char *name, int namelen);

int sethostname (char *name, int namelen);
```

Both return: 0 if OK, −1 on error

The `gethostname` function copies the hostname of the current processor into the buffer pointed to by *name*, which is *namelen* bytes in size. The returned name is NUL-terminated unless insufficient space is provided in *name*.

This is the same value as those returned in the `nodename` member of the `utsname` structure returned by uname, and by calling `sysinfo` using the `SI_HOSTNAME` command.

If the effective user ID of the calling process is zero, the `sethostname` function sets the hostname of the current processor to that in the buffer pointed to by *name*, which is *namelen* bytes in size.

Hostnames are limited to `MAXHOSTNAMELEN` bytes, which is defined in `<netdb.h>`.

The `gethostid` Function

If we are just interested in retrieving the hostid of a machine, we can use the `gethostid` function.

```
#include <unistd.h>

long gethostid (void);
```

Returns: the host's hostid

The `gethostid` function returns the 32-bit identifier for the current host. In Sun machines, this identifier is taken from the CPU board's ID PROM. It is not guaranteed to be unique.

This is the same value as that returned by calling `sysinfo` using the `SI_HW_SERIAL` command.

8.3   System Resource Limits

There are many magic numbers and constants that are defined by a UNIX implementation. Historically, these have been hard coded into programs, or determined in an ad hoc manner. Part of the UNIX standardization effort of POSIX and the SUS was to come up with a more portable method of determining these magic numbers and any implementation-defined constants and limits.

We need to consider three categories:

1. Compile time options. An example of this would be whether job control is supported.

2. Compile time limits. An example of this would be the size of a pointer.

3. Run time limits. An example of this would be the memory page size.

Compile time options and limits can be defined in headers, which can be included when the program is compiled. But run time limits require the process to call a function to determine the value of the requested limit.

Run time limits can be subdivided into two types:

1. Those that are associated with a file or directory

2. Those that are not associated with a file or directory

As an example of the former, consider the maximum length of a filename. Older versions of Solaris supported the System V file system, s5fs, as well as the usual UFS file system. The s5fs file system allows only 14 characters for a filename, whereas UFS allows 256. If we want our code to work with s5fs and UFS, we can't rely on compile time limits, and must use run time limits.

Because there are two types of run time limits, two types of function are used to determine them; sysconf is used to determine run time limits that are not associated with a file or directory, and pathconf and fpathconf are used to determine run time limits that are associated with a file or directory.

The sysconf Function

We use the sysconf function to determine the value of configurable system variables.

```
#include <unistd.h>

long sysconf (int name);
```
                                                                    Returns: see text

The sysconf function returns the current value of a configurable system limit of option (variable). On successful completion, sysconf returns the current value of the variable. This value will not be more restrictive than the corresponding value available at compile time in <limits.h>, <unistd.h>, or <time.h>. The value of most of these variables will not change during the lifetime of the calling process.

In the event of an error, −1 is returned and errno is set appropriately. We should be aware that −1 is also a legal return value when no error occurs, so programs wanting to check for errors should set errno to 0 before calling sysconf, and then check it if −1 is returned.

The parameter *name* specifies the name of the run time limit we are interested in, and must be one of the following values (the values returned are integers unless otherwise stated):

`_SC_2_C_BIND`	This is a Boolean value that indicates whether the POSIX C language bindings are supported. `_POSIX2_C_BIND` is the returned value.
`_SC_2_C_DEV`	This is a Boolean value that indicates whether the POSIX C language development utilities options is supported. The returned value is `_POSIX2_C_DEV`.
`_SC_2_C_VERSION`	This indicates which version of the ISO POSIX.2 standard (Commands) is supported. The returned value is `_POSIX2_C_VERSION`.
`_SC_2_CHAR_TERM`	This is a Boolean value that indicates whether at least one terminal is supported. The returned value is `_POSIX2_CHAR_TERM`.
`_SC_2_FORT_DEV`	This is a Boolean value that indicates whether the FORTRAN development utilities option is supported. `_POSIX2_FORT_DEV` is the returned value.
`_SC_2_FORT_RUN`	This is a Boolean value that indicates whether the FORTRAN run time utilities option is supported. `_POSIX2_FORT_RUN` is the returned value.
`_SC_2_LOCALEDEF`	This is a Boolean value that indicates whether the creation of locales using the `localedef` utility is supported. The returned value is `_POSIX2_LOCALEDEF`.
`_SC_2_SW_DEV`	This is a Boolean value that indicates whether the software development utilities option is supported. `_POSIX2_SW_DEV` is the value returned.
`_SC_2_UPE`	This is a Boolean value that indicates whether the user portability utilities option is supported. `_POSIX2_UPE` is the value returned.
`_SC_2_VERSION`	This indicates which version of the ISO POSIX.2 standard (C language binding) is supported. The returned value is `_POSIX2_VERSION`.
`_SC_AIO_LISTIO_MAX`	This indicates the maximum number of I/O operations in a single call that is supported. The returned value is `AIO_LISTIO_MAX`.
`_SC_AIO_MAX`	This indicates the maximum number of outstanding asynchronous I/O operations that are supported. (We talk about asynchronous I/O in Chapter 13). The returned value is `AIO_MAX`.
`_SC_AIO_PRIO_DELTA_MAX`	This indicates the maximum amount by which a process can decrease its asynchronous I/O priority level from its own scheduling priority. The returned value is `AIO_PRIO_DELTA_MAX`.

_SC_ARG_MAX	This is the maximum size of argv [] plus argp []. The returned value is ARG_MAX.
_SC_ASYNCHRONOUS_IO	This is a Boolean value that indicates whether asynchronous I/O is supported. The returned value is _POSIX_ASYNCHRONOUS_IO.
_SC_ATEXIT_MAX	This is the maximum number of functions that can be registered with atexit. These functions are called when a process terminates. The returned value is ATEXIT_MAX.
_SC_AVPHYS_PAGES	This is the number of physical memory pages not currently in use by the system.
_SC_BC_BASE_MAX	This is the maximum ibase and obase values allowed by the bc command. The returned value is BC_BASE_MAX.
_SC_BC_DIM_MAX	This is the maximum number of elements permitted in an array by the bc command. The returned value is BC_DIM_MAX.
_SC_BC_SCALE_MAX	This is the maximum scale value allowed by the bc command. The returned value is BC_SCALE_MAX.
_SC_BC_STRING_MAX	This is the maximum length of a string constant allowed by the bc command. The returned value is BC_STRING_MAX.
_SC_CHILD_MAX	This is the maximum number of processes allowed to each user ID. The value returned is CHILD_MAX.
_SC_CLK_TCK	This is the number of clock ticks per second. The returned value is CLK_TCK.
_SC_COLL_WEIGHTS_MAX	This is the maximum number of weights that can be assigned to an entry of the LC_COLLATE order keyword in a locale definition file. The returned value is COLL_WEIGHTS_MAX.
_SC_CPUID_MAX	This is the maximum possible processor ID.
_SC_DELAYTIMER_MAX	This is the maximum number of timer expiration overruns. DELAYTIMER_MAX is the returned value.
_SC_EXPR_NEST_MAX	This is the maximum number of parentheses allowed by the expr command. The returned value is EXPR_NEST_MAX.
_SC_FSYNC	This is a Boolean value that indicates whether file synchronization is supported. The returned value is _POSIX_FSYNC.
_SC_GETGR_R_SIZE_MAX	This is the maximum size of the group entry in /etc/nsswitch.conf, the name service switch file. NSS_BUFLEN_GROUP is the returned value.

`_SC_GETPW_R_SIZE_MAX`	This is the maximum size of the password entry in `/etc/nsswitch.conf`, the name service switch file. `NSS_BUFLEN_PASSWD` is the returned value.
`_SC_IOV_MAX`	This is the maximum number of iovec structures available to each process for use with `readv` and `writev`. The returned value is `IOV_MAX`.
`_SC_JOB_CONTROL`	This is a Boolean value that indicates whether job control is supported. The returned value is `_POSIX_JOB_CONTROL`.
`_SC_LINE_MAX`	This is maximum length of an input line. The returned value is `LINE_MAX`.
`_SC_LOGIN_NAME_MAX`	This is the maximum length of a login name, including the terminating NUL. The value returned is `LOGNAME_MAX + 1`.
`_SC_LOGNAME_MAX`	This is the maximum length of a login name, excluding the terminating NUL. The value returned is `LOGNAME_MAX`.
`_SC_MAPPED_FILES`	This is a Boolean value that indicates whether memory-mapped files are supported. The returned value is `_POSIX_MAPPED_FILES`.
`_SC_MAXPID`	This is the maximum value of a process ID.
`_SC_MEMLOCK`	This is a Boolean value that indicates whether memory locking is supported. The returned value is `_POSIX_MEMLOCK`.
`_SC_MEMLOCK_RANGE`	This is a Boolean value that indicates whether range memory locking is supported. The returned value is `_POSIX_MEMLOCK_RANGE`.
`_SC_MEMORY_PROTECTION`	This is a Boolean value that indicates whether memory protection is supported. The returned value is `_POSIX_MEMORY_PROTECTION`.
`_SC_MESSAGE_PASSING`	This is a Boolean value that indicates whether message passing is supported. The returned value is `_POSIX_MESSAGE_PASSING`.
`_SC_MQ_OPEN_MAX`	This is the maximum number of open messages a process can hold. The returned value is `MQ_OPEN_MAX`.
`_SC_MQ_PRIO_MAX`	This is the maximum number of message priorities supported. The returned value is `MQ_PRIO_MAX`.
`_SC_NGROUPS_MAX`	The is the maximum number of groups to which a user can belong. The returned value is `NGROUPS_MAX`.

`_SC_NPROCESSORS_CONF`	This is the number of processors currently configured (i.e., actually installed in the system).
`_SC_NPROCESSORS_MAX`	This is the maximum number of processors supported by the current platform.
`_SC_NPROCESSORS_ONLN`	This is the number of processors currently online.
`_SC_OPEN_MAX`	This is the maximum number of open files per process. The returned value is `OPEN_MAX`.
`_SC_PAGESIZE`	This is the system memory page size. The returned value is `PAGESIZE`.
`_SC_PAGE_SIZE`	This is a synonym for `_SC_PAGESIZE`. The returned value is `PAGESIZE`.
`_SC_PASS_MAX`	This is the maximum number of significant bytes in a password. It does not take into account the extended password lengths available from Solaris 9 12/02 and later, if different encryption algorithms are used. The returned value is `PASS_MAX`.
`_SC_PHYS_PAGES`	This is the number of pages of physical memory in the system.
`_SC_PRIORITIZED_IO`	This is a Boolean value that indicates whether POSIX prioritized I/O is supported. The returned value is `_POSIX_PRIORITIZED_IO`.
`_SC_PRIORITY_SCHEDULING`	This is a Boolean value that indicates whether process scheduling is supported. The returned value is `_POSIX_PRIORITY_SCHEDULING`.
`_SC_RE_DUP_MAX`	This is the maximum number of repeated occurrences of a regular expression permitted when using interval notation {m,n}. The returned value is `RE_DUP_MAX`.
`_SC_REALTIME_SIGNALS`	This is a Boolean value that indicates whether realtime signals are supported. The returned value is `_POSIX_REALTIME_SIGNALS`.
`_SC_RTSIG_MAX`	This is the maximum number of realtime signals reserved for application use. The returned value is `RTSIG_MAX`.
`_SC_SAVED_IDS`	This is a Boolean value that indicates whether saved set-user-IDs are supported. The returned value is `_POSIX_SAVED_IDS`.
`_SC_SEM_NSEMS_MAX`	This is the maximum number of POSIX semaphores available to each process. The returned value is `SEM_NSEMS_MAX`.
`_SC_SEM_VALUE_MAX`	This is the maximum value a POSIX semaphore can have. `SEM_VALUE_MAX` is the returned value.

`_SC_SEMAPHORES`	This is a Boolean value that indicates whether POSIX semaphores are supported. The returned value is `_POSIX_SEMAPHORES`.
`_SC_SHARED_MEMORY_OBJECTS`	This is a Boolean value that indicates whether POSIX shared memory objects are supported. `_POSIX_SHARED_MEMORY_OBJECTS` is the returned value.
`_SC_SIGQUEUE_MAX`	This is the maximum number of queued signals that a process can send and have pending at receivers at a time. The returned value is `SIGQUEUE_MAX`.
`_SC_STACK_PROT`	This is the default stack protection.
`_SC_STREAM_MAX`	This is the maximum number of streams a process can have open at a time. The returned value is `STREAM_MAX`.
`_SC_SYNCHRONIZED_IO`	This is a Boolean value that indicates whether POSIX synchronized I/O is supported. The returned value is `_POSIX_SYNCHRONIZED_IO`.
`_SC_THREAD_ATTR_STACKADDR`	This is a Boolean value that indicates whether the POSIX thread stack address attribute option is supported. The returned value is `_POSIX_THREAD_ATTR_STACKADDR`.
`_SC_THREAD_ATTR_STACKSIZE`	This is a Boolean value that indicates whether the POSIX thread stack size attribute option is supported. The returned value is `_POSIX_THREAD_ATTR_STACKSIZE`.
`_SC_THREAD_DESTRUCTOR_ITERATIONS`	This is the number of attempts to destroy thread-specific data when a thread exits. `PTHREAD_DESTRUCTOR_ITERATIONS` is the returned value.
`_SC_THREAD_KEYS_MAX`	This is the maximum number of data keys per process. `PTHREAD_KEYS_MAX` is the returned value.
`_SC_THREAD_PRIO_INHERIT`	This is a Boolean value that indicates whether the POSIX threads priority inheritance option is supported. `_POSIX_THREAD_PRIO_INHERIT` is the returned value.
`_SC_THREAD_PRIO_PROTECT`	This is a Boolean value that indicates whether the POSIX threads priority protection option is supported. `_POSIX_THREAD_PRIO_PROTECT` is the returned value.
`_SC_THREAD_PRIORITY_SCHEDULING`	This is a Boolean value that indicates whether the POSIX threads execution scheduling option is supported. The returned value is `_POSIX_THREAD_PRIORITY_SCHEDULING`.

`_SC_THREAD_PROCESS_SHARED`	This is a Boolean value that indicates whether the POSIX threads process shared synchronization option is supported. `_POSIX_THREAD_PROCESS_SHARED` is the returned value.
`_SC_THREAD_SAFE_FUNCTIONS`	This is a Boolean value that indicates whether the POSIX threads thread safe functions option is supported. The returned value is `_POSIX_THREAD_SAFE_FUNCTIONS`.
`_SC_THREAD_STACK_MIN`	This is the minimum number of bytes of thread stack storage. `PTHREAD_STACK_MIN` is the returned value.
`_SC_THREAD_THREADS_MAX`	This is the maximum number of threads per process. `PTHREAD_THREADS_MAX` is the value returned.
`_SC_THREADS`	This is a Boolean value that indicates whether POSIX threads are supported. The returned value is `_POSIX_THREADS`.
`_SC_TIMER_MAX`	This is the maximum number of timers per process. The returned value is `TIMER_MAX`.
`_SC_TIMERS`	This is a Boolean value that indicates whether POSIX timers are supported. The returned value is `_POSIX_TIMERS`.
`_SC_TTY_NAME_MAX`	This is the maximum length of a TTY device name. The returned value is `TTYNAME_MAX`.
`_SC_TZNAME_MAX`	This is the maximum number of bytes supported for the name of time zones. The returned value is `TZNAME_MAX`.
`_SC_VERSION`	This indicates which version of POSIX.1 is supported. `_POSIX_VERSION` is the returned value.
`_SC_XBS5_ILP32_OFF32`	This is a Boolean value that indicates whether the X/Open ILP32 with 32-bit file offsets build environment is supported. The returned value is `_XBS_ILP32_OFF32`.
`_SC_XBS5_ILP32_OFFBIG`	This is a Boolean value that indicates whether the X/Open ILP32 with 64-bit file offsets build environment is supported. The returned value is `_XBS5_ILP32_OFFBIG`.
`_SC_XBS5_LP64_OFF64`	This is a Boolean value that indicates whether the X/Open LP64 with 64-bit file offsets build environment is supported. The returned value is `_XBS5_LP64_OFF64`.
`_SC_XBS5_LPBIG_OFFBIG`	This is a synonym for `_SC_XBS5_LP64_OFF64`. The returned value is `_XBS5_LP64_OFF64`.

_SC_XOPEN_CRYPT

This is a Boolean value that indicates whether the X/Open encryption feature group is supported. _XOPEN_CRYPT is the returned value.

_SC_XOPEN_ENH_I18N

This is a Boolean value that indicates whether the X/Open enhanced internationalization feature group is supported. The returned value is _XOPEN_ENH_I18N.

_SC_XOPEN_LEGACY

This is a Boolean value that indicates whether the X/Open legacy feature group is supported. _XOPEN_LEGACY is the returned value.

_SC_XOPEN_REALTIME

This is a Boolean value that indicates whether the X/Open POSIX realtime feature group is supported. _XOPEN_REALTIME. is the returned value.

_SC_XOPEN_REALTIME_THREADS

This is a Boolean value that indicates whether the X/Open POSIX realtime threads feature group is supported. The returned value is _XOPEN_REALTIME_THREADS.

_SC_XOPEN_SHM

This is a Boolean value that indicates whether the X/Open shared memory feature group is supported. The returned value is _XOPEN_SHM.

_SC_XOPEN_UNIX

This is a Boolean value that indicates whether the X/Open CAE Specification, August 1994, System Interfaces and Headers, Issue 4, Version 2 is supported. _XOPEN_UNIX is the returned value.

_SC_XOPEN_VERSION

This indicates which version of the X/Open Portability Guide the implementation conforms to. The returned value is _XOPEN_VERSION.

_SC_XOPEN_XCU_VERSION

This indicates which version of the XCU specification the implementation conforms to. The returned value is _XOPEN_XCU_VERSION.

Some of the preceding values for *name* return −1 without setting errno. This is because no maximum limit can be determined. Although the system supports at least the minimum values, higher values can be supported depending on system resources. Figure 8.2 summarizes the variables this applies to.

We must be aware of a number points when we use the sysconf function:

1. The value of CLK_TCK can be variable, so we should not assume that it is a compile time constant.

Variable	Minimum supported value
`_SC_AIO_MAX`	`_POSIX_AIO_MAX`
`_SC_ATEXIT_MAX`	32
`_SC_THREAD_THREADS_MAX`	`_POSIX_THREAD_THREADS_MAX`
`_SC_THREAD_KEYS_MAX`	`_POSIX_THREAD_KEYS_MAX`
`_SC_THREAD_DESTRUCTOR_ITERATIONS`	`_POSIX_THREAD_DESTRUCTOR_ITERATIONS`

Figure 8.2 Variables that return –1 without setting `errno`.

2. A call to `setrlimit` (see Section 8.4) can cause the value of OPEN_MAX to change.

3. Determining the amount of physical memory (in bytes) in the system by multiplying sysconf (`_SC_PHYS_PAGES`) by sysconf (`_SC_PAGESIZE`) can return a value that exceeds the maximum value representable by a `long` or an `unsigned long` in a 32-bit process. The same applies to determining the amount of free physical memory by multiplying sysconf (`_SC_PAGESIZE`) by sysconf (`_SC_AVPHYS_PAGES`).

   There are two workarounds for this problem. The first is to compile our program as a 64-bit process (so that a `long` is large enough to hold the result of the multiplication), but the disadvantage to this is that the resulting program will run only on a 64-bit kernel. The second workaround is to store the result of the multiplication in a 64-bit quantity, like a `longlong_t`. This has the advantage of working correctly on both 32-bit and 64-bit kernels.

The variables `_SC_CPUID_MAX` and `_SC_NPROCESSORS_MAX` were added in Solaris 9.

Example: Printing CPU and memory information

Program 8.2 shows how we can use the `sysconf` function to determine the total amount of memory installed in a machine and how much is free. It also shows how many CPUs are installed and how many are online.

Running Program 8.2 on a dual-CPU Ultra 60 gives the following results:

```
$ ./sysconf
2 CPUs installed, 2 online
2048 MB physical memory, 1530 MB free
$ su
Password:
# psradm -f 2                          Take CPU 2 offline
# ./sysconf
2 CPUs installed, 1 online
2048 MB physical memory, 1530 MB free
```

—————————————————————————— sys_info/sysconf.c

```
 1 #include <stdio.h>
 2 #include <unistd.h>

 3 #define ONE_MB (1024 * 1024)

 4 int main (void)
 5 {
 6     long num_procs;
 7     long procs_online;
 8     long page_size;
 9     long num_pages;
10     long free_pages;
11     longlong_t mem;
12     longlong_t free_mem;

13     num_procs = sysconf (_SC_NPROCESSORS_CONF);
14     procs_online = sysconf (_SC_NPROCESSORS_ONLN);
15     page_size = sysconf (_SC_PAGESIZE);
16     num_pages = sysconf (_SC_PHYS_PAGES);
17     free_pages = sysconf (_SC_AVPHYS_PAGES);

18     mem = (longlong_t) ((longlong_t) num_pages * (longlong_t) page_size);
19     mem /= ONE_MB;
20     free_mem = (longlong_t) free_pages * (longlong_t) page_size;
21     free_mem /= ONE_MB;

22     printf ("%ld CPU%s installed, %ld online\n", num_procs,
23         (num_procs > 1) ? "s" : "", procs_online);
24     printf ("%lld MB physical memory, %lld MB free\n", mem, free_mem);

25     return (0);
26 }
```

—————————————————————————— sys_info/sysconf.c

Program 8.2   Displaying CPU and memory information.

The `pathconf` and `fpathconf` Functions

As we stated previously, the `pathconf` and `fpathconf` functions are used to determine the value of run time limits associated with a file or directory.

```
#include <unistd.h>

long pathconf (const char *path, int name);

long fpathconf (int fildes, int name);
```
Both return: see text

The `pathconf` function returns the current value of a configurable limit or option (variable) associated with a file or directory identified by *path*.

The `fpathconf` function returns the same information, but for the file associated with the file descriptor *fildes*.

For both functions, the *name* argument represents the name of the variable we are interested in. In the event of an error, −1 is retuned and errno is set appropriately. We should be aware that −1 is also a legal return value when no error occurs, so programs wanting to check for errors should set errno to 0 before calling pathconf or fpathconf, and then check it if −1 is returned.

The parameter *name* specifies the name of the limit we are interested in, and must be one of the following values (the values returned are integers unless otherwise stated):

_PC_FILESIZEBITS	This is the maximum number of bits that can be used to store the size of a file. If *path* or *fildes* refer to a directory, the returned value applies to files within that directory. The actual value returned depends on the underlying file system type. A UFS file system that does not support large files will always return 32. UFS file systems that support large files will return 41, and NFS v3 file systems return whatever is in the maxfilesize member of a successful FSINFO request; FSINFO is a procedure that retrieves nonvolatile file system information and general information about the NFS v3 protocol server implementation.
_PC_LINK_MAX	This is the maximum number of links the file or directory may have. If *path* or *fildes* refers to a directory, the returned value applies to the directory itself. The value returned is LINK_MAX.
_PC_MAX_CANON	This is the maximum number of characters in a line from a terminal in canonical mode (we talk about terminal modes in Chapter 12). If *path* or *fildes* does not refer to a terminal device, the returned value is meaningless; otherwise, the returned value is MAX_CANON.
_PC_MAX_INPUT	This is the maximum number of characters in a terminal input queue. If *path* or *fildes* does not refer to a terminal device, the returned value is meaningless; otherwise, the returned value is MAX_INPUT.
_PC_NAME_MAX	This is the maximum number of characters in a filename. If *path* or *fildes* refers to a directory, the returned value applies to files within that directory.
_PC_PATH_MAX	This is the maximum number of characters in a pathname. If *path* or *fildes* refers to a directory, the returned value is the maximum length of a relative pathname when the specified directory is the working directory.
_PC_PIPE_BUF	This is the maximum number of bytes we can write atomically to a pipe or FIFO. If *path* or *fildes* refers to a

pipe or FIFO, the returned value applies to that pipe or FIFO. If *path* or *fildes* refers to a directory, then the returned value applies to any FIFO that exists or can be created in that directory. In all of the preceding cases, the returned value is `PIPE_BUF`.

`_PC_XATTR_ENABLED` This is a Boolean value that indicates whether the file system containing *path* or *fildes* supports extended file attributes. We talk about extended file attributes in Section 13.38.

`_PC_XATTR_EXISTS` This is a Boolean value that indicates whether *path* or *fildes* has one or more extended file attributes. We talk about extended file attributes in Section 13.38.

`_PC_CHOWN_RESTRICTED` This is a Boolean value that indicates whether unprivileged users may use the `chown` function to change the ownership of files they currently own. If *path* or *fildes* refers to a directory, the returned value applies to any files, other than directories, that exist or can be created within that directory. The returned value is `_POSIX_CHOWN_RESTRICTED`.

`_PC_NO_TRUNC` This is a Boolean value that indicates whether pathnames whose components are longer than `_PC_NAME_MAX` characters will generate an error. If *path* or *fildes* refers to a directory, the returned value applies to filenames within that directory and is `_POSIX_NO_TRUNC`.

`_PC_VDISABLE` This is a Boolean value that indicates whether special terminal input characters can be disabled (see Chapter 12). If *path* or *fildes* does not refer to a terminal device, the returned value is meaningless; otherwise, the returned value is `_POSIX_VDISABLE`.

`_PC_ASYNC_IO` This is a Boolean value that indicates whether asynchronous I/O may be performed on the file. The returned value is `_POSIX_ASYNC_IO`.

`_PC_PRIO_IO` This is a Boolean value that indicates whether prioritized I/O may be performed on the file. If *path* or *fildes* refers to a directory, the returned value is meaningless, otherwise, the returned value is `_POSIX_PRIO_IO`.

`_PC_SYNC_IO` This is a Boolean value that indicates whether synchronous I/O may be performed on the file. The returned value is `_POSIX_SYNC_IO`.

The variables `_PC_XATTR_ENABLED` and `_PC_XATTR_EXISTS` were added in Solaris 9.

Example: Printing some run time file limits

Program 8.3 shows how we can use the `pathconf` function to determine some run time file limits.

——————————————————————— sys_info/pathconf.c

```
1 #include <stdio.h>
2 #include <unistd.h>
3 #include "ssp.h"

4 int main (int argc, char **argv)
5 {
6     long filesize_bits;
7     long max_links;

8     if (argc != 2)
9         err_quit ("Usage: pathconf path");

10    filesize_bits = pathconf (argv [1], _PC_FILESIZEBITS);
11    max_links = pathconf (argv [1], _PC_LINK_MAX);

12    printf ("Maximum file size bits = %ld\n", filesize_bits);
13    printf ("Maximum links to a file = %ld\n", max_links);

14    return (0);
15 }
```

——————————————————————— sys_info/pathconf.c

Program 8.3 Displaying some run time file limits.

Let's see what happens when we run this simple program against a few directories.

```
$ ./pathconf /
Maximum file size bits = 41
Maximum links to a file = 32767
$ ./pathconf /home
Maximum file size bits = -1
Maximum links to a file = 32767
$ ./pathconf /home/rich
Maximum file size bits = 40
Maximum links to a file = 32767
```

The program output shows that the root directory is on a UFS file system that supports large files, /home has essentially no file size limit (although it would be reasonable to assume that file offsets are limited to 64 bits in practice), and that /home/rich is an NFS-mounted directory that limits the size of files to 40 bits. All of the directories tested support up to 32,767 links to a single file. This also means that directories are limited to containing 32,765 subdirectories; two links are reserved for the directory itself and its parent. (There are no limits on how many files a directory may contain, except for the number of directory entries that will fit into a file, and the availability of inodes.)

The `getpagesize` Function

Another way we can get the page size is to use `getpagesize`.

```
#include <unistd.h>

int getpagesize (void);
```
Returns: the number of bytes in a page

The `getpagesize` function returns the number of bytes in a page. This page size is the system page size, which is not necessarily the same size as the underlying hardware.

The page size is the granularity of many memory management functions. However, the value returned by `getpagesize` is not the smallest value that can be allocated by `malloc`.

Calling `getpagesize` is equivalent to calling the `sysconf` function with an argument of `_SC_PAGESIZE` or `_SC_PAGE_SIZE`.

The `getpagesizes` Function

Solaris 9 introduced the feature of multiple user page sizes. We can get a list of the supported user page sizes by using `getpagesizes`.

```
#include <sys/mman.h>

int getpagesizes (size_t pagesize [], int nelem);
```
Returns: the number of page sizes supported or retrieved if OK, −1 on error

We can use the `getpagesizes` function in two ways: we can either determine how many different user page sizes are supported, or we can get a list of the supported user page sizes.

If we call `getpagesizes` with a NULL pointer for *pagesize* and *nelem* set to 0, the number of supported user page sizes is returned. Otherwise, up to *nelem* page sizes are retrieved and placed into successive elements of *pagesize*.

Not all processors support all page sizes or combinations of page sizes with equal efficiency, so we must take this into consideration when using `getpagesizes`.

Example: Listing the supported user page sizes

Program 8.4 lists all the supported user page sizes.

Get the number of user page sizes

11–12 Call `getpagsizes` with *pagesize* and *nelem* set to NULL and 0 respectively to determine the number of supported user page sizes.

Allocate sufficient memory to hold the list

13–14 Call `malloc` to allocate a memory buffer big enough to hold the list of supported user page sizes.

Print the list of supported user page sizes

15–16 Call `getpagesizes` again to retrieve the list of supported user page sizes.

sys_info/getpagesizes.c

```
 1 #include <stdio.h>
 2 #include <stdlib.h>
 3 #include <sys/mman.h>
 4 #include "ssp.h"

 5 int main (void)
 6 {
 7     int num_page_sizes;
 8     int res;
 9     int i;
10     size_t *page_sizes;

11     if ((num_page_sizes = getpagesizes (NULL, 0)) == -1)
12         err_msg ("getpagesizes (NULL, 0) failed");

13     if ((page_sizes = malloc (sizeof (size_t) * num_page_sizes)) == NULL)
14         err_msg ("malloc failed");

15     if ((res = getpagesizes (page_sizes, num_page_sizes)) == -1)
16         err_msg ("getpagesizes failed");

17     printf ("Supported page sizes:");
18     for (i = 0; i < res; i++)
19         printf (" %d", page_sizes [i]);
20     printf ("\n");

21     free (page_sizes);

22     return (0);
23 }
```

sys_info/getpagesizes.c

Program 8.4 Listing the supported user page sizes.

17–20 Print the list we just retrieved.

Running Program 8.4 on one of the author's machines (an Ultra 60) gives the following results:

```
$ ./getpagesizes
Supported page sizes: 8192 65536 524288 4194304
```

Running the command `pagesize -a` confirms these results.

8.4   Per-Process Resource Limits

Beyond the systemwide resource limits we discussed in the previous section, a number of limits are applied on a per-process basis, like the maximum amount of CPU time, the number of file descriptors, and the size of the stack. Many of these limits can be changed by the process, and are intended to prevent a runaway process from consuming all of the machine's resources.

There are two types of limit for each resource: a soft (current) limit, and a hard (maximum) limit. Any process can change soft limits to any value less than or equal to the hard limit, but only privileged process can raise the hard limit. Any process can (permanently) lower its hard limits.

The `ulimit` Function

The `ulimit` function can be used to get and set certain process limits.

```
#include <ulimit.h>

long ulimit (int cmd, /* long newlimit */...);
```
                                    Returns: the value of the requested limit if OK, –1 on error

The `ulimit` function allows a process to get or set some of its limits. The operation performed is determined by the value of the *cmd* argument, which must be one of the following four values:

`UL_GETFSIZE`	This returns the maximum file size in units of 512-byte blocks that the process can create. The number returned is the integer part of the soft limit divided by 512. Note that this limit only affects writing to a file; files of any size can be read, with the exception of a non-large-file-aware program trying to read a large file (see Section 1.12).
`UL_SETFSIZE`	This sets the hard and soft limits for output operations to the value specified by *newlimit*. The file size limits are set to the value of *newlimit* multiplied by 512. The new file size limit is returned.
`UL_GMEMLIM`	This returns the maximum amount of memory the process may use.
`UL_GDESLIM`	This returns the maximum number of file descriptors the process may open.

On successful completion, the requested limit is returned. Otherwise, –1 is returned and the limit is not changed.

The `getrlimit` and `setrlimit` Functions

The `getrlimit` and `setrlimit` functions provide a more general interface for controlling process limits.

```
#include <sys/resource.h>

int getrlimit (int resource, struct rlimit *rlp);

int setrlimit (int resource, const struct rlimit *rlp);
```
                                                    Both return: 0 if OK, –1 on error

The `getrlimit` function gets the hard and soft limits associated with the resource identified by *resource* and places them in the `rlimit` structure pointed to by *rlp*. The `rlimit` structure has the following members:

```
struct rlimit {
    rlim_t  rlim_cur;    /* Soft (current) limit */
    rlim_t  rlim_max;    /* Hard limit (maximum value for rlim_cur) */
};
```

As well as specifying a specific limit, an "infinite" limit may be applied by setting the appropriate member of the `rlimit` structure to the special value of `RLIM_INFINITY`.

The legal values of *resource* are:

RLIMIT_AS   This is a synonym for `RLIMIT_VMEM`.

RLIMIT_CORE   This is the maximum size of a `core` file in bytes that may be created. Setting this limit to 0 will prevent the creation of a `core` file. The writing of the `core` file terminates when it reaches this size, even if it is incomplete.

RLIMIT_CPU   This is the maximum amount of CPU time (measured in seconds) the process is allowed to use. This a soft limit only; there is no hard limit. When the time limit is exceeded, the process is sent a `SIGXCPU` signal (see Chapter 17). If `SIGXCPU` is being held or ignored, the behaviour is scheduling-class defined.

RLIMIT_DATA   This is the maximum size of the process' heap in bytes. The heap is the data segment of a process.

RLIMIT_FSIZE   This is the maximum size of a file in bytes that the process may create. Setting this limit to 0 will prevent the creation of files. When this limit is exceeded, the process is sent a `SIGXFSZ` signal. If this signal is being held or ignored, continued attempts to increase the size of the file will fail with `errno` set to `EFBIG`.

RLIMIT_NOFILE   This is the maximum value that the kernel may assign to a file descriptor, effectively limiting the number of file descriptors (and hence, the number of open files) for the calling process to this number.

RLIMIT_STACK   This is the maximum size of the process' stack in bytes. The kernel will not automatically grow the stack beyond this limit. When this limit is exceeded, a `SIGSEGV` signal is sent to the process. If this signal is being held or ignored, or is being caught without arrangements being made to us an alternate stack, the signal's disposition is set to `SIG_DFL` before it is sent to the process. (We talk about signals in Chapter 17.)

Increasing this limit will increase the size of the stack, but current memory segments will not be moved to allow this growth. The only way we can guarantee that the process' stack will be able to grow to the new limit is to increase the limit before we execute the process in which the new stack is to be used.

In a multithreaded process, setting this limit has no effect if the calling thread is not the main one. Calling `setrlimit` for `RLIMIT_STACK` only impacts the main thread's stack, and should be made only from the main thread, if at all.

RLIMIT_VMEM   This is the maximum size of the process' mapped address space in bytes. When this limit is exceeded, the `malloc` and other memory allocation functions will fail, as will calls to `mmap`. Additionally, the automatic stack growth will fail, with the effects described under `RLIMIT_STACK`.

As we stated previously, setting a limit to `RLIM_INFINITY` means that there is "no limit" on the resource. Requesting a limit of `RLIM_SAVED_MAX` will set the limit to the corresponding saved hard limit. Similarly, requesting a limit of `RLIM_SAVED_CUR` will set the limit to the corresponding saved soft limit.

The current value of two limits affect their corresponding implementation-defined constants. These are summarized in Figure 8.3.

Limit	Constant
RLIMIT_FSIZE	FCHR_MAX
RLIMIT_NOFILE	OPEN_MAX

Figure 8.3   The effect of limits on implementation-defined constants.

Example: Printing the current resource limits

Program 8.5 prints out the current soft and hard resource limits.

Note how we've used the ISO C string creation operator again, as we did in Program 8.1.

Running Program 8.5 gives us the following results:

```
$ ./getrlimit
RLIMIT_AS        unlimited   unlimited
RLIMIT_CORE      unlimited   unlimited
RLIMIT_CPU       unlimited   unlimited
RLIMIT_DATA      unlimited   unlimited
RLIMIT_FSIZE     unlimited   unlimited
RLIMIT_NOFILE          256       65536
RLIMIT_STACK       8388608   unlimited
RLIMIT_VMEM      unlimited   unlimited
```

———————————————————————— sys_info/getrlimit.c

```
 1 #include <stdio.h>
 2 #include <sys/resource.h>
 3 #include "ssp.h"

 4 #define plimit(name) print_limits (#name, name)

 5 static void print_limits (const char *name, int resource);

 6 int main (void)
 7 {
 8     plimit (RLIMIT_AS);
 9     plimit (RLIMIT_CORE);
10     plimit (RLIMIT_CPU);
11     plimit (RLIMIT_DATA);
12     plimit (RLIMIT_FSIZE);
13     plimit (RLIMIT_NOFILE);
14     plimit (RLIMIT_STACK);
15     plimit (RLIMIT_VMEM);

16     return (0);
17 }

18 static void print_limits (const char *name, int resource)
19 {
20     struct rlimit limits;

21     if (getrlimit (resource, &limits) == -1)
22         err_quit ("getrlimit (%s) failed", name);

23     printf ("%-13s  ", name);

24     if (limits.rlim_cur == RLIM_INFINITY)
25         printf ("unlimited  ");
26     else
27         printf ("%9ld  ", limits.rlim_cur);

28     if (limits.rlim_max == RLIM_INFINITY)
29         printf ("unlimited\n");
30     else
31         printf ("%9ld\n", limits.rlim_max);
32 }
```

———————————————————————— sys_info/getrlimit.c

Program 8.5 Print the current soft and hard resource limits.

The `getdtablesize` Function

Another way of determining the maximum number of file descriptors available to a process is by using the `getdtablesize` function.

```
#include <unistd.h>

int getdtablesize (void);
```

Returns: the soft file descriptor limit

The `getdtablesize` function returns the current soft limit of the maximum file descriptor number as if obtained by calling `getrlimit` with *resource* set to `RLIMIT_NOFILE`.

8.5   The Resource Control Facility

Solaris 9 introduced the resource control facility, which provides more general purpose resource control functionality than the `getrlimit` (rlimit) mechanism. (We should note that the resource control facility is supplied in addition to rlimits, not instead of. In fact, the latter is built on top of the former.)

One of the limitations of the rlimit method of resource control is that the granularity of the limits is restricted to processes only. The resource controls facility extends the concept of limits to the task and project entities described in Chapter 6 of [Sun Microsystems 2002a]. Another advantage of the resource control facility is that it can provide information about encountered restraints without necessarily denying access to the requested resource. This information can be used to help the capacity planning process.

Resource Controls

The resource control attributes are set in the final field of the `project` database entry (in a files-based environment, the project database is stored in `/etc/project`). The values associated with each resource control are enclosed in parentheses and appear as plain text separated by commas. The value in parentheses is called an *action clause,* and is made up of a privilege level, a threshold value, and an action associated with the given threshold value. Each resource control can have multiple action clauses, which are also separated by commas. The following example resource control defines a per-process address space limit and a per-task LWP limit on a project entry (note that we had to wrap the line so it fits on the page; each entry must be on one and only one line):

```
dev:100::::task.max-lwps=(privileged,10,deny);
       process.max-address-space=(privileged,209715200,deny)
```

Figure 8.4 lists the standard resource controls available in Solaris 9 (later versions added numerous others).

The resource control threshold values constitute an enforcement point where local or global actions can occur. Each threshold value must be associated with one of the following privilege levels:

- Basic, which can be modified by the owner of the calling process

Control name	Description	Default unit
project.cpu-shares	The number of CPU shares granted to this project for use with the fair-share scheduler	Quantity (shares)
task.max-cpu-time	Maximum CPU time available to this task's processes	Time (milliseconds)
task.max-lwps	Maximum number of LWPs simultaneously available to this task's processes	Quantity (LWPs)
process.max-cpu-time	Maximum CPU time available to this process	Time (milliseconds)
process.max-file-descriptor	Maximum file descriptor index available to this process	Index
process.max-file-size	Maximum file offset available for writing by this process	Size (bytes)
process.max-core-size	Maximum size of a core file that may be created by this process	Size (bytes)
process.max-data-size	Maximum size of heap available to this process	Size (bytes)
process.max-stack-size	Maximum stack memory segment available to this process	Size (bytes)
process.max-address-space	Maximum address space, as summed over segment size, available to this process	Size (bytes)

Figure 8.4 Resource controls available in Solaris 9.

- Privileged, which can be modified only by privileged callers, i.e., `root`
- System, which is fixed for the duration of the OS instance

Each resource control is guaranteed to have at least a system value associated with it. This value represents how much of the resource the current instance of the OS is capable of providing. Any number of privileged values can be defined, but only one basic value is allowed.

The resource value is stored as an unsigned 64-bit quantity. When the resource threshold of a resource is exceeded, one or more actions can be invoked:

1. Requests for an amount of the resource that will exceed the threshold can be denied.

2. A signal can be sent to the violating or observing process if the threshold value is reached.

Resource controls also have associated with them a set of global and local flags, which we discuss below.

From the perspective of a program, resource control blocks are used to implement the resource control facility. Each of these blocks is stored in an opaque data structure called an `rctlblk_t`. (When we say a data structure is opaque, we mean that we have no idea what members it has; the only way we can manipulate the members is to use the functions provided for that purpose.)

The `rctlblk_size` Function

Because a resource control block is implemented as an opaque data structure, we can't simply use something like

```
struct rctlblk rblk;
```

to allocate the correct amount of memory for it. Instead, we must use `malloc`; the number of bytes we need to allocate is given by the `rctlblk_size` function.

```
#include <rctl.h>

size_t rctlblk_size (void);
```
>   Returns: the size of a resource control block

The `rctlblk_size` function returns the size of a resource control block for use in memory allocation. Using `malloc` (or a related function) to allocate the number of bytes returned by `rctlblk_size` is the only safe way to allocate memory for a resource control block.

The `getrctl` Function

We use the `getrctl` function to get resource values.

```
#include <rctl.h>

int getrctl (const char *controlname, rctlblk_t *old_blk, rctlblk_t *new_blk,
    uint_t flags);
```
>   Returns: 0 if OK, −1 on error

The `getrctl` function enables us to retrieve resource control values on active entities on the system, such as processes, tasks, and projects. As we stated earlier, each resource control is an unsigned 64-bit quantity, although a number of flags modify the resource control that is retrieved.

The name of the resource control we are interested in must be stored in the buffer pointed to by *controlname*, and the retrieved resource control is stored in the `rctlblk` structure pointed to by *new_blk*.

The values of *old_blk* and *flags* determine which resource control associated with *controlname* is retrieved (recall that each resource control may have several values associated with it). Setting *old_blk* to NULL and *flags* to `RCTL_FIRST` will retrieve the first value associated with *controlname*. Subsequent resource control values can be retrieved by setting *old_blk* to the previously retrieved value and setting *flags* to `RCTL_NEXT`. When the list of values is exhausted, `getrctl` fails, setting `errno` to `ENOENT`.

The current usage of a controlled resource can be retrieved by setting *flags* to `RCTL_USAGE`.

Once we have retrieved the resource control we are interested in, we can get or modify the values associated with it using the `rctlblk_get` and `rctlblk_set` family of functions discussed next.

The `setrctl` Function

We use the `setrctl` function to set resource values.

```
#include <rctl.h>

int setrctl (const char *controlname, rctlblk_t *old_blk, rctlblk_t *new_blk,
    uint_t flags);
```
Returns: 0 if OK, −1 on error

The `setrctl` function enables us to modify resource control values. In other words, it allows us to create, modify, or delete the action-value pairs of a given resource control.

The name of the resource control we want to operate on is stored in the buffer pointed to by *controlname*. The operation performed on the resource control is determined by the value of *flags*, *old_blk*, and *new_blk*.

If *flags* is set to `RCTL_INSERT`, the resource control block pointed to by *new_blk* is inserted into the sequence. Conversely, if *flags* is set to `RCTL_DELETE`, the resource control block pointed to by *new_blk* is removed from the sequence. Setting *flags* to `RCTL_REPLACE` will cause the resource control matching the one pointed to by *old_blk* to be replaced by the one pointed to by *new_blk*.

We must bear in mind several points when manipulating resource control blocks. Resource control blocks are matched on the privilege as well as the value fields. Resource control operations are performed on the first matching resource control block; multiple blocks of equal privilege and value will likely need to be deleted and reinserted, rather than replaced, to have the desired outcome. The resource control blocks are sorted such that all blocks with the same value that do not have the `RCTL_LOCAL_DENY` flag set precede those that do.

Because the resource control facility is used by both `[gs]etrlimit` and `[gs]etrctl`, the ordering issues we have just discussed and the limit equivalencies we discuss in the next paragraph must be considered if we use both interfaces in the same program (these issues are of no concern if either interface is used exclusively).

As we stated previously, the resource control facility is used to implement the hard and soft process limits made available with `getrlimit` and `setrlimit`. An rlimit has two (and only two) values associated with it, but the `RCTL_INSERT` and `RCTL_DELETE` operations allow a resource control to have an arbitrary number of values associated with it. In the event of the number of values associated with a resource control not being equal to two, the lowest priority resource control value with the `RCTL_LOCAL_DENY` flag set is taken as the soft limit, and the lowest priority resource control value with a priority equal to or exceeding `RCPRIV_PRIVILEGED` with the `RCTL_LOCAL_DENY` flag set is taken as the hard limit. If no identifiable soft limit exists on the resource control, and `setrlimit` is called, a new resource control value will be created. If a resource control does not have the global `RCTL_GLOBAL_LOWERABLE` property set, its hard limit will not allow lowering by unprivileged callers.

Now that we've discussed resource control blocks and how to get and set them, let's take a closer look at the functions we need to manipulate the attributes of a resource control block.

Manipulating a Resource Control's Privilege Level

We mentioned previously that resource control blocks have a privilege level associated with them. We manipulate this privilege level by using the `rctlblk_get_privilege` and `rctlblk_set_privilege` functions.

```
#include <rctl.h>

rctl_priv_t rctlblk_get_privilege (rctlblk_t *rblk);

                                    Returns: resource control block's privilege

void rctlblk_set_privilege (rctlblk_t *rblk, rctl_priv_t privilege);
```

The `rctlblk_get_privilege` returns the privilege level of the resource control block pointed to by *rblk*. Three privilege levels are defined:

`RCPRIV_BASIC`	The resource control can be modified by the owner of the calling process.
`RCPRIV_PRIVILEGED`	The resource control can be modified only by a privileged process (i.e., one whose effective user ID is 0); for other users, the resource limit is read-only. The only exception to this is if the `RCTL_GLOBAL_LOWERABLE` global flag is set for the resource, in which case unprivileged applications can lower the value of the resource limit.
`RCPRIV_SYSTEM`	System resource controls are read-only and are fixed for the duration of the OS instance. They represent the amount of the resource the current instance of the OS is capable of providing.

The `rctlblk_set_privilege` function enables us to set the privilege of the resource control pointed to by *rblk* to the value specified by *privilege* (which must be one of the three values we describe in the previous paragraph). No errors are returned by `rctlblk_set_privilege`; any errors are reported by the `setrctl` function.

Manipulating a Resource Control's Values

The value of a resource control is manipulated using the `rctlblk_get_value`, `rctlblk_get_enforced_value`, and `rctlblk_set_value` functions.

```
#include <rctl.h>

rctl_qty_t rctlblk_get_value (rctlblk_t *rblk);

rctl_qty_t rctlblk_get_enforced_value (rctlblk_t *rblk);

                                        Both return: resource control block's value

void rctlblk_set_value (rctlblk_t *rblk, rctl_qty_t value);
```

The `rctlblk_get_value` function returns the value associated with the resource control block pointed to by *rblk*. The `rctlblk_get_enforced_value` function also returns the value associated with the resource control block pointed to by *rblk*.

Most of the time, the values returned by `rctlblk_get_value` and `rctlblk_get_enforced_value` will be the same. However, in cases where the process, task, or project associated with the control possesses fewer capabilities than allowable by the current value, the value returned by `rctlblk_get_enforced_value` will differ from that returned by `rctlblk_get_value`. An example of when this can happen is if the calling process is using an address space model smaller than the maximum address space model supported by the system (e.g., running a 32-bit process on a 64-bit kernel).

The `rctlblk_set_value` enables us to set the value associated with the resource control block pointed to by *rblk* to the value specified by *value*. No errors are returned by `rctlblk_set_value`; any errors are reported by the `setrctl` function.

Manipulating a Resource Control's Flags

Each resource control has two sets of flags associated with it: the global flags and the local flags. We can manipulate them by using the `rctlblk_get_global_flags`, `rctlblk_get_local_flags`, and `rctlblk_set_local_flags` functions.

```
#include <rctl.h>

int rctlblk_get_global_flags (rctlblk_t *rblk);

int rctlblk_get_local_flags (rctlblk_t *rblk);

                                        Both return: resource control block's flags

void rctlblk_set_local_flags (rctlblk_t *rblk, int flags);
```

The `rctlblk_get_global_flags` function returns the global flags associated with the resource control block pointed to by *rblk*. Global flags are set using the `rctladm` command, and are generally a published property of the control and hence not modifiable. The returned value is the bitwise-OR of zero or more of the following flags:

`RCTL_GLOBAL_DENY_ALWAYS`	The action taken when a control value is exceeded on this control will always include denial of the resource.
`RCTL_GLOBAL_DENY_NEVER`	The action taken when a control value is exceeded on this control will never include denial of the resource, although other actions can also be taken.
`RCTL_GLOBAL_CPU_TIME`	The list of valid signals available as local actions includes `SIGXCPU`.
`RCTL_GLOBAL_FILE_SIZE`	The list of valid signals available as local actions includes `SIGXFSZ`.
`RCTL_GLOBAL_INFINITE`	The resource supports the concept of unlimited value. This is usually true of only accumulation oriented resources, such as CPU time.
`RCTL_GLOBAL_LOWERABLE`	This means that unprivileged callers are able to lower the value of privileged resource control values on this control.
`RCTL_GLOBAL_NOBASIC`	This means that no values with the `RCPRIV_BASIC` are allowed on this control.
`RCTL_GLOBAL_NOLOCALACTION`	No local actions are permitted on this control.
`RCTL_GLOBAL_UNOBSERVABLE`	The resource control (usually on a task- or project-related control) does not support observational control values. A control value with a privilege of `RCPRIV_BASIC` that is placed by a process on the task or process will generate an action only if the value is exceeded by that process.

As its name suggests, the `rctlblk_get_local_flags` returns the local flags associated with the resource control block pointed to by *rblk*. At present, only one local flag is defined:

`RCTL_LOCAL_MAXIMAL`	Setting this flag indicates that this resource control value represents a request for the maximum amount of resource for this control. If the `RCTL_GLOBAL_INFINITE` global flag is set for this resource control, setting the `RCTL_LOCAL_MAXIMAL` flag indicates an unlimited resource control value, which can't be exceeded.

The `rctlblk_set_local_flags` function enables us to set the local flags associated with the resource control block pointed to by *rblk* to the value specified by *flags*. No errors are returned by `rctlblk_set_local_flags`; any errors are reported by the `setrctl` function.

Manipulating a Resource Control's Actions

When a resource control's threshold value is exceeded, one of several actions can be triggered. These actions can be manipulated using the `rctlblk_get_global_action`, `rctlblk_get_local_action`, and `rctlblk_set_local_action` functions.

```
#include <rctl.h>

int rctlblk_get_global_action (rctlblk_t *rblk);

int rctlblk_get_local_action (rctlblk_t *rblk, int *signalp);

                                   Both return: resource control block's actions

void rctlblk_set_local_action (rctlblk_t *rblk, rctl_action_t action,
    int signal);
```

The `rctlblk_get_global_action` function returns the global action associated with the resource control block pointed to by *rblk*. Global actions are set using the `rctladm` command. The returned value will be one of the following values:

RCTL_GLOBAL_NOACTION   No global action will be taken when a resource control value is exceeded on this control.

RCTL_GLOBAL_SYSLOG   A message will be logged using the `syslog` facility when any resource control value on a sequence associated with this control is exceeded.

Similarly, the `rctlblk_get_local_action` function returns the local action associated with the resource control block pointed to by *rblk*. The value returned will be a bitwise-OR of one or more of the following values:

RCTL_LOCAL_DENY   If this action is specified, resource requests that exceed the threshold value associated with the resource control will be denied. If the `RCTL_GLOBAL_DENY_ALWAYS` global flag is set for this control, the local action `RCTL_LOCAL_DENY` will always be set on all values of this control. On the contrary, setting the global flag `RCTL_GLOBAL_DENY_NEVER` for this control will always clear the `RCTL_LOCAL_DENY` action on all values of this control.

RCTL_LOCAL_NOACTION   No local action will be taken when this resource control is exceeded.

RCTL_LOCAL_SIGNAL   The signal specified (see the following paragraph) will be sent to the process that placed this resource control in the value sequence when consumption of the resource exceeds the value associated with the resource control.

If the local action includes sending a signal to the process, the number of the signal that will be sent is stored in the integer pointed to by *signalp*.

The `rctlblk_set_local_action` function enables us to determine the actions that occur when the resource value associated with resource control block pointed to by *rblk* is exceeded. The *action* argument specifies the action to be taken (as described previously), and the *signal* argument enumerates the signal associated with the `RCTL_LOCAL_SIGNAL` action. The set of valid signals is: `SIGABRT`, `SIGXRES`, `SIGHUP`, `SIGSTOP`, `SIGTERM`, and `SIGKILL` (although other signals—specifically `SIGXCPU` and `SIGXFSZ`—may be permitted because of the global properties of a specific control). No errors are returned by `rctlblk_set_local_action`; any errors are reported by the `setrctl` function.

The `rctlblk_get_firing_time` Function

If we want to know if (or when) a resource control has exceeded one of its action values, we can use the `rctlblk_get_firing_time` function.

```
#include <rctl.h>

hrtime_t rctlblk_get_firing_time (rctlblk_t *rblk);
```
                                                                          Returns: see text

The `rctlblk_get_firing_time` function returns the value of `gethrtime` at the moment the action on the resource control pointed to by *rblk* was taken. This time is measured in nanoseconds since the system was booted.

If the action value for the resource control has not been exceeded for its lifetime on the process, `rctlblk_get_firing_time` returns 0.

The `rctlblk_get_recipient_pid` Function

If we want to know which process ID placed a resource control, we use the `rctlblk_get_recipient_pid` function.

```
#include <rctl.h>

id_t rctlblk_get_recipient_pid (rctlblk_t *rblk);
```
                                                                          Returns: see text

The `rctlblk_get_recipient_pid` function returns the process ID that placed the resource control pointed to by *rblk*. The process ID is set automatically by the kernel when a process calls `setrctl`.

The `rctl_walk` Function

We can visit all the registered resource controls on the system by using the `rctl_walk` function.

```
#include <rctl.h>

int rctl_walk (int (*callback) (const char *rctlname, void *walk_data),
    void *init_data);
```
Returns: 0 if OK, −1 on error

The `rctl_walk` function walks through all the active resource controls on the system. For each resource control, the function referred to by *callback* is called and is passed two arguments. The first argument, *rctlname*, is the name of the current resource control. The second argument, *walk_data*, can be used by *callback* to record its own state. The callback function should return a non-zero result in the event of an error or if it wants to prematurely terminate the walk; otherwise, it should return zero.

Upon successful completion, `rctl_walk` returns 0. If *callback* returns a non-zero result, or an error occurs when performing the walk, −1 is returned and `errno` is set to indicate the error.

8.6   Resource Control Examples

This section presents a couple of example programs that illustrate some of the points we've made about resource controls.

The examples in this section use two functions to print out resource control blocks; `print_rctls` prints all the resource control blocks associated with the named resource, and `print_rctl` prints out a single resource control block.

Our `print_rctls` Function

Program 8.6 shows our implementation of `print_rctls`.

Print each resource control block

9–12 Allocate some space for a resource control block, and get the first one that matches the resource control name. Return −1 if either fails.

13–14 Print the name of the resource control and its attributes.

15–16 Print the attributes of all the other resource controls of the same name.

17 Free the memory we previously allocated.

————————————————————————————— sys_info/print_rctl.c

```
 1 #include <stdio.h>
 2 #include <stdlib.h>
 3 #include <signal.h>
 4 #include <rctl.h>

 5 void print_rctl (rctlblk_t *rblk);

 6 int print_rctls (const char *name)
 7 {
 8      rctlblk_t *rblk;

 9      if ((rblk = malloc (rctlblk_size ())) == NULL)
10          return (-1);

11      if (getrctl (name, NULL, rblk, RCTL_FIRST) == -1)
12          return (-1);

13      printf ("%s:\n", name);
14      print_rctl (rblk);

15      while (getrctl (name, rblk, rblk, RCTL_NEXT) != -1)
16          print_rctl (rblk);

17      free (rblk);

18      return (0);
19 }
```

————————————————————————————— sys_info/print_rctl.c

Program 8.6 Our implementation of the print_rctls function.

Our `print_rctl` Function

Program 8.7 shows the implementation of print_rctl.

Print resource control's process ID

24 Print the process ID of the process that placed the resource control. The process ID is retrieved using rctlblk_get_recipient_pid.

Print the resource control's privilege

25–39 Get the privilege level using the rctlblk_get_privilege function, and print out its name.

Print resource control's values

40–41 Print the value and enforced value of the resource control, getting the values by calling rctlblk_get_value and rctlblk_get_enforced_value respectively.

Print resource control's global flags

42–62 Retrieve the global flags using rctlblk_get_global_flags, and print the name of each flag that is set.

Print resource control's global actions

63–69 Print out the global actions, having first retrieved them using the rctlblk_get_global_action function.

— sys_info/print_rctl.c

```
20  void print_rctl (rctlblk_t *rblk)
21  {
22      int tmp;
23      int sig;

24      printf ("  Process ID: %ld\n", (long) rctlblk_get_recipient_pid (rblk));

25      printf ("  Privilege: ");
26      switch (rctlblk_get_privilege (rblk)) {
27          case RCPRIV_BASIC:
28              printf ("RCPRIV_BASIC\n");
29              break;

30          case RCPRIV_PRIVILEGED:
31              printf ("RCPRIV_PRIVILEGED\n");
32              break;

33          case RCPRIV_SYSTEM:
34              printf ("RCPRIV_SYSTEM\n");
35              break;

36          default:
37              printf ("Unknown privilege\n");
38              break;
39      }

40      printf ("  Value: %llu\n", rctlblk_get_value (rblk));
41      printf ("  Enforced value: %llu\n", rctlblk_get_enforced_value (rblk));

42      printf ("  Global flags: ");
43      tmp = rctlblk_get_global_flags (rblk);
44      if (tmp & RCTL_GLOBAL_DENY_ALWAYS)
45          printf ("RCTL_GLOBAL_DENY_ALWAYS ");
46      if (tmp & RCTL_GLOBAL_DENY_NEVER)
47          printf ("RCTL_GLOBAL_DENY_NEVER ");
48      if (tmp & RCTL_GLOBAL_CPU_TIME)
49          printf ("RCTL_GLOBAL_CPU_TIME ");
50      if (tmp & RCTL_GLOBAL_FILE_SIZE)
51          printf ("RCTL_GLOBAL_FILE_SIZE ");
52      if (tmp & RCTL_GLOBAL_INFINITE)
53          printf ("RCTL_GLOBAL_INFINITE ");
54      if (tmp & RCTL_GLOBAL_LOWERABLE)
55          printf ("RCTL_GLOBAL_LOWERABLE ");
56      if (tmp & RCTL_GLOBAL_NOBASIC)
57          printf ("RCTL_GLOBAL_NOBASIC ");
58      if (tmp & RCTL_GLOBAL_NOLOCALACTION)
59          printf ("RCTL_GLOBAL_NOLOCALACTION ");
60      if (tmp & RCTL_GLOBAL_UNOBSERVABLE)
61          printf ("RCTL_GLOBAL_UNOBSERVABLE ");
62      printf ("\n");

63      printf ("  Global actions: ");
64      tmp = rctlblk_get_global_action (rblk);
65      if (tmp & RCTL_GLOBAL_NOACTION)
66          printf ("RCTL_GLOBAL_NOACTION ");
67      if (tmp & RCTL_GLOBAL_SYSLOG)
68          printf ("RCTL_GLOBAL_SYSLOG ");
69      printf ("\n");
```

```
 70     printf ("  Local flags: ");
 71     tmp = rctlblk_get_local_flags (rblk);
 72     if (tmp & RCTL_LOCAL_MAXIMAL)
 73         printf ("RCTL_LOCAL_MAXIMAL ");
 74     printf ("\n");

 75     printf ("  Local actions: ");
 76     tmp = rctlblk_get_local_action (rblk, &sig);
 77     if (tmp & RCTL_LOCAL_DENY)
 78         printf ("RCTL_LOCAL_DENY ");
 79     if (tmp & RCTL_LOCAL_NOACTION)
 80         printf ("RCTL_LOCAL_NOACTION ");
 81     if (tmp & RCTL_LOCAL_SIGNAL) {
 82         printf ("RCTL_LOCAL_SIGNAL ");
 83         switch (sig) {
 84             case SIGABRT:
 85                 printf ("(SIGABRT)");
 86                 break;

 87             case SIGXRES:
 88                 printf ("(SIGXRES)");
 89                 break;

 90             case SIGHUP:
 91                 printf ("(SIGHUP)");
 92                 break;

 93             case SIGSTOP:
 94                 printf ("(SIGSTOP)");
 95                 break;

 96             case SIGTERM:
 97                 printf ("(SIGTERM)");
 98                 break;

 99             case SIGKILL:
100                 printf ("(SIGKILL)");
101                 break;

102             case SIGXCPU:
103                 printf ("(SIGXCPU)");
104                 break;

105             case SIGXFSZ:
106                 printf ("(SIGXFSZ)");
107                 break;

108             default:
109                 printf ("(Illegal signal)");
110                 break;
111         }
112     }
113     printf ("\n");

114     printf ("  Firing time: %llu\n\n", rctlblk_get_firing_time (rblk));
115 }
```
——— *sys_info/print_rctl.c*

Program 8.7 Our implementation of the `print_rctl` function.

Print resource control's local flags

70–74 Get the local flags using the `rctlblk_get_local_flags` function, and if any are set, print their names.

Print resource control's local actions

75–113 Print the local actions after retrieving them using `rctlblk_get_local_action`. If a signal is to be sent to the process, print the name of the signal to be sent.

Print resource control's firing time

114 Get the most recent time the resource control was triggered (using the `rctlblk_get_firing_time` function to retrieve it), and print it out.

Example: Printing the values of resource controls

Program 8.8 prints the details of all the default resource controls.

—————————————————————————— sys_info/rctl_walk.c

```
 1 #include <rctl.h>
 2 #include "ssp.h"

 3 extern int print_rctls (const char *name);
 4 static int callback (const char *name, void *pvt);

 5 int main (void)
 6 {
 7     if (rctl_walk (callback, NULL) == -1)
 8         err_msg ("callback failed");

 9     return (0);
10 }

11 static int callback (const char *name, void *pvt)
12 {
13     return (print_rctls (name));
14 }
```

—————————————————————————— sys_info/rctl_walk.c

Program 8.8 Printing all the resource controls.

When we run Program 8.8, we get results like the following:

```
$ ./rctl_walk
process.max-address-space:
  Process ID: -1
  Privilege: RCPRIV_PRIVILEGED
  Value: 18446744073709551615
  Enforced value: 4294967295
  Global flags: RCTL_GLOBAL_DENY_ALWAYS RCTL_GLOBAL_LOWERABLE
      RCTL_GLOBAL_NOLOCALACTION
  Global actions:
  Local flags: RCTL_LOCAL_MAXIMAL
  Local actions: RCTL_LOCAL_DENY
  Firing time: 0
```

```
      Process ID: -1
      Privilege: RCPRIV_SYSTEM
      Value: 18446744073709551615
      Enforced value: 4294967295
      Global flags: RCTL_GLOBAL_DENY_ALWAYS RCTL_GLOBAL_LOWERABLE
          RCTL_GLOBAL_NOLOCALACTION
      Global actions:
      Local flags: RCTL_LOCAL_MAXIMAL
      Local actions: RCTL_LOCAL_DENY
      Firing time: 0

   process.max-file-descriptor:
      Process ID: 2481
      Privilege: RCPRIV_BASIC
      Value: 256
      Enforced value: 256
      Global flags: RCTL_GLOBAL_DENY_ALWAYS RCTL_GLOBAL_LOWERABLE
      Global actions:
      Local flags:
      Local actions: RCTL_LOCAL_DENY
      Firing time: 0

      ...                                      Output cut for brevity
```

We've had to wrap some of the longer lines so that they will fit onto the page, and trimmed most of the output to save space. There are some points of interest we should note:

1. The enforced values for the `process.max-address-space` resource controls are 4 GB. This is because we compiled Program 8.8 as a 32-bit program. If we recompile Program 8.8 as a 64-bit program, the enforced value of these resource controls reflects the full 64-bit address space.

2. The last block of output from our example is associated with process ID 2481; this is the process ID of the `rctl_walk` program.

Example: Modifying a resource control

Program 8.9 modifies the resource control block for the resource that controls the maximum number of file descriptors for a process: `process.max-file-descriptor`. Our new resource control block replaces the default one, which has a value equal to the current soft limit (256 in our example).

Let's take a closer look at some of the implementation details of Program 8.9.

Allocate memory

17–19 We allocate the memory we need for the two resource control blocks. We need two resource control blocks in this example because of how we've chosen to order the code. If we delete the current resource control before modifying it with our new values, we could use just one resource control block.

——————————————————————————— sys_info/setrctl.c

```
1 #include <stdio.h>
2 #include <stdlib.h>
3 #include <string.h>
4 #include <signal.h>
5 #include <rctl.h>
6 #include <sys/types.h>
7 #include <sys/stat.h>
8 #include <fcntl.h>
9 #include "ssp.h"

10 extern void print_rctl (rctlblk_t *rblk);

11 int main (void)
12 {
13     rctlblk_t *old_rblk;
14     rctlblk_t *new_rblk;
15     char *name = "process.max-file-descriptor";
16     int fd;

17     if (((old_rblk = malloc (rctlblk_size ())) == NULL) ||
18         ((new_rblk = malloc (rctlblk_size ())) == NULL))
19         err_msg ("malloc failed");

20     if (getrctl (name, NULL, old_rblk, RCTL_FIRST) == -1)
21         err_msg ("getrctl failed");

22     memcpy (new_rblk, old_rblk, rctlblk_size ());

23     printf ("Before...\n");
24     print_rctl (old_rblk);

25     rctlblk_set_value (new_rblk, 10);
26     rctlblk_set_local_action (new_rblk, RCTL_LOCAL_DENY | RCTL_LOCAL_SIGNAL,
27         SIGTERM);

28     if (setrctl (name, NULL, old_rblk, RCTL_DELETE) == -1)
29         err_msg ("setrctl (RCTL_DELETE) failed");
30     if (setrctl (name, NULL, new_rblk, RCTL_INSERT) == -1)
31         err_msg ("setrctl (RCTL_INSERT) failed");

32     if (getrctl (name, NULL, new_rblk, RCTL_FIRST) == -1)
33         err_msg ("getrctl failed");

34     printf ("After...\n");
35     print_rctl (new_rblk);

36     for (;;) {
37         fd = open ("/tmp", O_RDONLY);
38         printf ("Returned file descriptor = %d\n", fd);
39     }
40 }
```

——————————————————————————— sys_info/setrctl.c

Program 8.9 Modifying a resource control.

Get the current resource control

20–21 Get the current value of the first resource control matching the one we are interested in.

22 Use the current resource control as a template for our new one.

Print the resource control before changing it

23–24 Call `print_rctl` to print the resource control before we modify it.

Modify the resource control

25 Set the threshold value for this resource control to 10.

26–27 Set up the local action flags to deny access to the resource and to send the signal `SIGTERM` to the process when the threshold limit is exceeded. We must specify the `RCTL_LOCAL_DENY` action because the `process.max-file-descriptor` resource control has the `RCTL_GLOBAL_DENY_ALWAYS` flag set; not doing so will cause the `setrctl` function to fail. We also specify `RCTL_LOCAL_SIGNAL` to arrange for a signal to be sent at the appropriate time (i.e., when an attempt to use more than 10 file descriptors is made by the process).

Replace the resource control

28–31 The original resource control is deleted, and then a new one with our new threshold value and actions is inserted. Note that we must perform this task as two separate steps; although intuition might tell us otherwise, we can't simply replace the original resource control with our new one by passing `RCTL_REPLACE` to the `setrctl` function.

Print the resource control after changing it

34–35 Call `print_rctl` to print the resource control before we modify it.

Use up all available file descriptors

36–39 This infinite loop repeatedly calls `open` to consume file descriptors. When the number of file descriptors exceeds the threshold value (which in this example is 10), a `SIGTERM` signal is sent to the process, terminating it. A real application would likely do something more useful than just terminating, like logging an error or trying to free up some of the overallocated resource.

Although we used `SIGTERM` in this example, `SIGXRES` is a more logical choice. By default, `SIGXRES` is ignored, so we would have to set up a signal handler to do anything useful when the signal is received. We show how to do this in Chapter 17.

Let's see what happens when we run Program 8.9:

```
$ ./setrctl
Before...
  Process ID: 1460
  Privilege: RCPRIV_BASIC
  Value: 256
  Enforced value: 256
  Global flags: RCTL_GLOBAL_DENY_ALWAYS RCTL_GLOBAL_LOWERABLE
  Global actions:
  Local flags:
  Local actions: RCTL_LOCAL_DENY
  Firing time: 0
```

```
After...
  Process ID: 1460
  Privilege: RCPRIV_BASIC
  Value: 10
  Enforced value: 10
  Global flags: RCTL_GLOBAL_DENY_ALWAYS RCTL_GLOBAL_LOWERABLE
  Global actions:
  Local flags:
  Local actions: RCTL_LOCAL_DENY RCTL_LOCAL_SIGNAL (SIGTERM)
  Firing time: 0

Returned file descriptor = 3
Returned file descriptor = 4
Returned file descriptor = 5
Returned file descriptor = 6
Returned file descriptor = 7
Returned file descriptor = 8
Returned file descriptor = 9
Terminated
```

Notice that the enforced value was automatically lowered to match the new value.

8.7   Resource Usage Information

Solaris provides two methods that enable us to monitor our resource consumption: the `times`, `clock`, and `getrusage` functions, and the `/proc` file system.

The `times` Function

We can use the `times` function to determine the CPU usage for the calling process and its children.

```
#include <sys/times.h>
#include <limits.h>

clock_t times (struct tms *buffer);
```

Returns: the elapsed time since the system booted if OK, –1 on error

The `times` function retrieves the system and user CPU time for the calling process and its children, placing the result in the `tms` structure pointed to by *buffer*. The `tms` structure has the following members:

```
struct tms {
    clock_t tms_utime;      /* User time */
    clock_t tms_stime;      /* System time */
    clock_t tms_cutime;     /* User time, children */
    clock_t tms_cstime;     /* System time, children */
};
```

The definition of the members is a follows:

`tms_utime`   This is the amount of CPU time spent executing instructions in the user space of the calling process.

`tms_stime`   This is the amount of CPU time spent executing kernel code on behalf of the calling process (i.e., executing system calls).

`tms_cutime`   This is the sum of the `tms_utime` and `tms_cutime` values for all of the children of the calling process.

`tms_cstime`   This is the sum of the `tms_stime` and `tms_cstime` values for all of the children of the calling process.

All of the times are reported in clock ticks; there are `CLK_TCK` clock ticks per second.

The times of terminated children are included in the `tms_cutime` and `tms_cstime` members of the parent when one of the `wait` functions we describe in Chapter 15 returns the process ID of the terminated child. If a process doesn't `wait` for its children, their times will not be included in its times.

Upon successful completion, the `times` function returns the elapsed real time since some arbitrary point in the past (e.g., the system boot time), in clock ticks. This point does not change from one invocation of `times` in a process to another. If an error occurs, –1 is returned.

Although the Solaris implementation of `times` uses the system boot as its "arbitrary point in the past", this event is not codified by any standards, so portable applications shouldn't rely on it.

Example: Timing the execution of command line arguments

Program 8.10 uses the `system` function we describe in Section 15.13 to run each of its command line arguments, timing how long the command takes to run and printing the results. It also calls the `print_term_status` function we show in Section 15.6.

Running Program 8.10 gives us the following results:

```
$ ./ssp_time "sleep 2" date
Command: sleep 2
  Real:    2.040
  User:    0.000
  Sys:     0.000
  Child user:    0.010
  Child sys:     0.020
Normal termination; exit status = 0

Command: date
Mon Jan 27 12:25:33 PST 2003
  Real:    0.060
  User:    0.000
  Sys:     0.000
  Child user:    0.010
  Child sys:     0.030
Normal termination; exit status = 0
```

sys_info/ssp_time.c

```
 1 #include <stdio.h>
 2 #include <stdlib.h>
 3 #include <unistd.h>
 4 #include <sys/times.h>
 5 #include <limits.h>
 6 #include "ssp.h"

 7 static void proc_cmd (char *cmd);
 8 static void print_times (clock_t real, struct tms *start, struct tms *end);

 9 int main (int argc, char **argv)
10 {
11     int i;

12     for (i = 1; i < argc; i++)
13         proc_cmd (argv [i]);

14     return (0);
15 }

16 static void proc_cmd (char *cmd)
17 {
18     struct tms start_tms;
19     struct tms end_tms;
20     clock_t start;
21     clock_t end;
22     int status;

23     printf ("Command: %s\n", cmd);

24     if ((start = times (&start_tms)) == -1)
25         err_msg ("Start times failed");

26     if ((status = system (cmd)) == -1)
27         err_msg ("system failed");

28     if ((end = times (&end_tms)) == -1)
29         err_msg ("End times failed");

30     print_times (end - start, &start_tms, &end_tms);
31     print_term_status (status);
32     printf ("\n");
33 }

34 static void print_times (clock_t real, struct tms *start, struct tms *end)
35 {
36     static double tps = 0.0;

37     if (tps == 0.0)
38         if ((tps = (double) sysconf (_SC_CLK_TCK)) == -1)
39             err_msg ("sysconf failed");

40     printf ("  Real: %7.3f\n", real / tps);
41     printf ("  User: %7.3f\n", (end -> tms_utime - start -> tms_utime) / tps);
42     printf ("  Sys:  %7.3f\n", (end -> tms_stime - start -> tms_stime) / tps);
43     printf ("  Child user: %7.3f\n",
44         (end -> tms_cutime - start -> tms_cutime) / tps);
```

```
45      printf ("  Child sys:   %7.3f\n",
46          (end -> tms_cstime - start -> tms_cstime) / tps);
47 }
```
─── *sys_info/ssp_time.c*

Program 8.10 Time how long each command line argument takes to run.

Note that in this example, all the CPU time is attributed to the child process. This is because it is the child process that runs the shell and the specified command.

We can compare the output from Program 8.10 to the `time` command:

```
$ time ls -1R > /dev/null

real    0m9.00s
user    0m2.78s
sys     0m1.75s
$ ./ssp_time "ls -1R > /dev/null"
Command: ls -1R > /dev/null
  Real:    6.510
  User:    0.000
  Sys:     0.000
  Child user:   2.270
  Child sys:    1.300
Normal termination; exit status = 0
```

As we expect, the CPU times are very similar. The reason for the disparity with the real time is that the second `ls` command benefits from the fact that the results of the directory lookups from the first command are cached by the kernel.

The `clock` Function

The `clock` function enables us to determine the CPU usage for the caller and its reaped children, starting from a specific event.

```
#include <time.h>

clock_t clock (void);
```
                           Returns: the CPU usage of the caller and its reaped children if OK, −1 on error
---

The `clock` function returns the total amount of user and system CPU time (in microseconds) used since the first call to `clock` in the calling process. The time returned is the sum of the user and system time for the calling process and all of its terminated children that have been waited for. Dividing the value returned by the constant `CLOCKS_PER_SEC` will convert the time into seconds.

Because the value returned is measured in microseconds, it is possible that the counter will wraparound in long-running 32-bit processes; this wraparound will occur after 2147 seconds (about 36 minutes) of CPU time have accumulated.

The `getrusage` Function

A process can determine its resource usage (or that of its terminated children) by calling the `getrusage` function.

```
#include <sys/resource.h>

int getrusage (int who, struct rusage *r_usage);
```
Returns: 0 if OK, –1 on error

The `getrusage` function is used to gather comprehensive process resource usage information. The value of the *who* argument determines which process the resource usage information is gathered for: the calling process, or its children. If *who* is RUSAGE_SELF, then resource usage information for the calling process is returned, and if *who* is RUSAGE_CHILDREN, then resource usage information for the terminated and waited for children of the calling process is returned. If a child is not waited for (for example, if the parent sets SA_NOCLDWAIT or ignores the SIGCHLD signal), the resource usage information for the child is discarded and not included in the resource usage information provided by `getrusage`.

The resource usage information is stored in the `rusage` structure pointed to by *r_usage*. The `rusage` structure has the following members:

```
struct rusage {
        struct timeval  ru_utime;      /* User time */
        struct timeval  ru_stime;      /* System time */
        long            ru_maxrss;     /* Maximum resident set size */
        long            ru_ixrss;      /* Integral shared memory size */
        long            ru_idrss;      /* Integral unshared data size */
        long            ru_isrss;      /* Integral unshared stack size */
        long            ru_minflt;     /* Minor page faults */
        long            ru_majflt;     /* Major page faults */
        long            ru_nswap;      /* Number of swaps */
        long            ru_inblock;    /* Block input operations */
        long            ru_oublock;    /* Block output operations */
        long            ru_msgsnd;     /* Messages sent */
        long            ru_msgrcv;     /* Messages received */
        long            ru_nsignals;   /* Number of signals received */
        long            ru_nvcsw;      /* Voluntary context switches */
        long            ru_nivcsw;     /* Involuntary context switches */
};
```

The members of the `rusage` structure are interpreted as follows:

ru_utime   This is the amount of CPU time spent executing instructions in user space. The time is measured in seconds and microseconds.

ru_stime   This is the amount of CPU time spent executing instructions in the kernel. The time is measured in seconds and microseconds.

`ru_maxrss`	This is the maximum resident set size measured in pages.
`ru_idrss`	This is an "integral" value indicating the amount of memory in use by a process while it is running. This value is the sum of the resident set sizes of the process when a clock tick occurs. The value is given in pages multiplied by clock ticks. It does not take shared pages into account.
`ru_minflt`	This is the number of minor page faults serviced. A *minor page fault* is one that does not require any physical I/O activity. An example of a minor page fault would be when a process starts up and refers to pages already in memory (e.g., those in a shared library like `libc.so`).
`ru_majflt`	This is the number of major page faults serviced. A *major page fault* is one that requires physical I/O activity. An example of a major page fault would be when a process starts up for the first time since the system was booted; the pages of the executable must be paged in from disk before the program can run.
`ru_nswap`	This is the number of times the process was swapped out of physical memory.
`ru_inblock`	This is the number of times the kernel had to perform input when servicing a `read` request.
`ru_oublock`	This is the number of times the kernel had to perform output when servicing a `write` request.
`ru_msgsnd`	This is the number of messages sent over sockets.
`ru_msgrcv`	This is the number of messages received over sockets.
`ru_nsignals`	This is the number of signals that have been delivered.
`ru_nvcsw`	This is the number of voluntary context switches. A voluntary context switch occurs when a process gives up the CPU before its time slice has expired. This is usually because the process is awaiting the availability of a resource.
`ru_nivcsw`	This is the number of involuntary context switches. An involuntary context switch occurs when a higher priority process has become runnable, or because the process has exceeded its time slice.

In the Solaris implementation of `getrusage`, the `ru_maxrss`, `ru_ixrss`, `ru_idrss`, and `ru_isrss` members of the `rusage` structure are set to 0 (these members are present only to maintain backward source compatibility with SunOS 4.x). The `psinfo` object in the `/proc` file system can be read if we want to know the resident set size of a process. (Note that the presence of the `getrusage` functions is mandated by various industry standards, but the information it returns is not.)

The most flexible way to determine the resource usage of a process is to use the `/proc` file system, which we describe next.

8.8   Determining Resource Usage Using the /proc File System

Historically, process data such as that obtained using the ps utility could be obtained only by directly reading kernel memory. The problem with this approach is that as well as being inherently non-portable, it requires the use of superuser privileges. To get around these problems, the /proc file system provides a general interface to the memory image of processes.

The /proc file system contains one directory for each process currently running on the system; the name of the directory is the same as the process ID of the process to which it refers. The owner and group of the directory are set to the real user ID and group ID of the process the directory is associated with. (There is another invisible alias a process can use to refer to itself; opening /proc/self is the same as opening /proc/*PID*, where *PID* is the process ID of the process. /proc/self is invisible in the sense that the name self does not appear in directory listing of /proc.)

Inside each directory is a number of files and subdirectories that contain information about the process. For example, the file as contains the address space of the process, psinfo contains information used by the ps command, and (of most interest to us in this discussion) usage, which contains the resource usage of the process.

One of the directories under /proc/*PID* is called lwp, and it contains one directory for each lightweight process (LWP) associated with the process. Each of those directories contains a number of files holding LWP-specific information.

From the perspective of a user process, a *lightweight process* can be thought of as a virtual CPU. LWPs are actually kernel entities, similar to kernel threads (kthreads). A single threaded program will have exactly one LWP and one kthread in its address space, but there is not necessarily a one-to-one correspondence between the number of threads in a process and the number of LWPs. LWPs maintain a control structure in which they store the hardware context (i.e., CPU registers) when a thread is context-switched off a processor. Readers interested in an in-depth discussion of the Solaris multithreaded architecture are encouraged to read Chapter 8 of [Mauro and McDougall 2001].

Most files in the /proc hierarchy can be opened only for reading, and although process state—and therefore the contents of /proc files—can change from instant to instant, a single read of a file in /proc is guaranteed to be sane. In other words, the read will be atomic with respect to the state of the process. The only exception to this is that atomicity is not guaranteed for I/O applied to the as (address space) file for a running process, or for a process whose address space contains memory shared with other running processes.

Standard system calls are used to interface with the /proc files, including open, close, read, and write.

> Prior to Solaris 2.6, /proc was not a directory hierarchy. Instead, the entries in /proc were files—one for each process. Rather than reading a file to obtain the required information, ioctl commands were used. For example, the PIOCUSAGE command was used to obtain the resource usage of the process. Although the ioctl method of obtaining process information is still supported for binary compatibility reasons, new programs should use the directory hierarchy method we describe in this text.

As we said earlier, each process directory contains a number of files that contain information about the process. The contents of many of these files can be read into a structure (which structure depends of course on the file we are reading). For the purpose of obtaining the resource usage information for a process, we must read the contents of the file usage into a prusage structure. This structure is defined in <sys/procfs.h> (which is included by <procfs.h>), and has the following members:

```
typedef struct prusage {
    id_t       pr_lwpid;      /* LWP ID */
    int        pr_count;      /* Number of contributing LWPs */
    timestruc_t pr_tstamp;    /* Current time stamp */
    timestruc_t pr_create;    /* Process/LWP creation time stamp */
    timestruc_t pr_term;      /* Process/LWP termination time */
    timestruc_t pr_rtime;     /* Total LWP real (elapsed) time */
    timestruc_t pr_utime;     /* User level CPU time */
    timestruc_t pr_stime;     /* System call CPU time */
    timestruc_t pr_ttime;     /* Other system trap CPU time */
    timestruc_t pr_tftime;    /* Text page fault sleep time */
    timestruc_t pr_dftime;    /* Data page fault sleep time */
    timestruc_t pr_kftime;    /* Kernel page fault sleep time */
    timestruc_t pr_ltime;     /* User local wait sleep time */
    timestruc_t pr_slptime;   /* All other sleep time */
    timestruc_t pr_wtime;     /* Wait-CPU (latency) time */
    timestruc_t pr_stoptime;  /* Stopped time */
    timestruc_t filltime [6]; /* Filler for future expansion */
    ulong_t    pr_minf;       /* Minor page faults */
    ulong_t    pr_majf;       /* Major page faults */
    ulong_t    pr_nswap;      /* Swaps */
    ulong_t    pr_inblk;      /* Input blocks */
    ulong_t    pr_oublk;      /* Output blocks */
    ulong_t    pr_msnd;       /* Messages sent */
    ulong_t    pr_mrcv;       /* Messages received */
    ulong_t    pr_sigs;       /* Signals received */
    ulong_t    pr_vctx;       /* Voluntary context switches */
    ulong_t    pr_ictx;       /* Involuntary context switches */
    ulong_t    pr_sysc;       /* System calls */
    ulong_t    pr_ioch;       /* Characters read and written */
    ulong_t    filler [10];   /* Filler for future expansion */
} prusage_t;
```

The members of the prusage structure are interpreted as follows:

pr_lwpid   This is the lightweight process ID. This will be 0 for regular processes.

pr_count   This is the number of LWPs that contribute to the process totals.

pr_tstamp   This is a time stamp; it contains the time at which the read of the prusage structure was performed, measured in seconds and nanoseconds since the last reboot.

pr_create   This is the creation time of the process or LWP, measured in seconds and nanoseconds since the last reboot.

pr_term	This is the termination time of the process or LWP, measured in seconds and nanoseconds since the last reboot.
pr_rtime	This is the total elapsed time of the process or LWP. Like all time values in this structure, the time is measured in seconds and nanoseconds.
pr_utime	This is the amount of CPU time spent executing instructions in user space.
pr_stime	This is the amount of CPU time spent executing instructions in the kernel.
pr_ttime	This is the amount of CPU time spent performing system trap instructions, other than that covered by pr_stime.
pr_tftime	This is the amount of time spent waiting for program text page faults to be serviced.
pr_dftime	This is the amount of time spent waiting for data page faults to be serviced.
pr_kftime	This is the amount of time spent waiting for kernel page faults to be serviced.
pr_ltime	This is the amount of time spent waiting for user locks.
pr_slptime	This is the total amount of time spent sleeping for reasons not covered by pr_tftime, pr_dftime, pr_kftime, and pr_ltime.
pr_wtime	This is the amount of time spent waiting for the CPU (in other words, the CPU latency).
pr_stoptime	This is the amount time the process was stopped for.
pr_minf	This is the number of minor faults serviced.
pr_majf	This is the number of major faults serviced.
pr_nswap	This is the number of times the process was swapped out of physical memory.
pr_inblk	This is the number of blocks of physical input required to service read requests.
pr_oublk	This is the number of blocks of physical output required to service write requests.
pr_msnd	This is the number of messages sent over sockets.
pr_mrcv	This is the number of messages received over sockets.
pr_sigs	This is the number of signals that have been delivered.
pr_vctx	This is the number of voluntary context switches.
pr_ictx	This is the number of involuntary context switches.
pr_sysc	This is the number of system calls that have been made.

pr_ioch   This is the number of characters that have been read or
                           written.

If microstate accounting has not been enabled, the times reported for the various states
are only estimates.

Example: Implementing the `getprusage` function

Program 8.11 shows our implementation of a function similar to `getrusage` called
`getprusage`. Our function takes two arguments. The first is the process ID that we
want to get the resource usage for, and the second is a pointer to a `prusage` structure,
which is used to hold the results. Setting the process ID to −1 will return the resource
usage for the calling process.

If the resource usage for the requested process ID is successfully acquired, `getprusage`
returns 0. Otherwise −1 is returned, and `errno` is set to indicate the error.

Running Program 8.11 to obtain the resource usage information for a long running
process (in this case, `init`) gives the following results:

```
$ ./getprusage1 1
Resource usage for PID 1:
  LWP ID: 0
  Number of LWPs: 1
  Timestamp: 1795343.11543115
  Creation time: 54.248659987
  Termination time: 0.0
  Real (elapsed) time: 1795288.757557953
  User CPU time: 0.230000000
  System CPU time: 0.220000000
  System trap CPU time: 0.0
  Text page fault CPU time: 0.0
  Data page fault CPU time: 0.0
  Kernel page fault CPU time: 0.0
  User lock wait time: 0.0
  Other sleep time: 1795288.310000000
  CPU latency time: 0.0
  Stopped time: 0.0
  Minor faults: 0
  Major faults: 80
  Number of swaps: 0
  Input blocks: 94
  Output blocks: 1
  Messages sent: 0
  Messages received: 0
  Signals received: 6517
  Voluntary context switches: 6519
  Involuntary context switches: 79
  System calls: 143924
  Characters read/written: 13803067
```

We can make a number of observations about these results:

```
 1 #include <stdio.h>
 2 #include <unistd.h>
 3 #include <stdlib.h>
 4 #include <fcntl.h>
 5 #include <sys/types.h>
 6 #include <sys/stat.h>
 7 #include <sys/resource.h>
 8 #include <procfs.h>
 9 #include <limits.h>
10 #include "ssp.h"

11 static int getprusage (pid_t pid, prusage_t *pr_usage);
12 static void print_rusage (pid_t pid, prusage_t *buf);

13 int main (int argc, char **argv)
14 {
15     pid_t pid;
16     prusage_t buf;
17     int i;

18     if (argc == 1) {
19         if (getprusage (-1, &buf) == -1)
20             err_msg ("getprusage failed");
21         print_rusage (getpid (), &buf);
22     }
23     else {
24         for (i = 1; i < argc; i++) {
25             pid = atoi (argv [i]);
26             if (getprusage (pid, &buf) == -1)
27                 err_ret ("getprusage failed");
28             else
29                 print_rusage (pid, &buf);
30         }
31     }

32     return (0);
33 }

34 static int getprusage (pid_t pid, prusage_t *pr_usage)
35 {
36     int fd;
37     char name [PATH_MAX];

38     if (pid == -1)
39         snprintf (name, PATH_MAX, "/proc/self/usage");
40     else
41         snprintf (name, PATH_MAX, "/proc/%ld/usage", (long) pid);

42     if ((fd = open (name, O_RDONLY)) == -1)
43         return (-1);

44     if (read (fd, pr_usage, sizeof (prusage_t)) == -1) {
45         close (fd);
46         return (-1);
47     }
```

```
48      else {
49          close (fd);
50          return (0);
51      }
52  }

53  static void print_rusage (pid_t pid, prusage_t *buf)
54  {
55      printf ("Resource usage for PID %ld:\n", (long) pid);
56      printf ("  LWP ID: %ld\n", (long) buf -> pr_lwpid);
57      printf ("  Number of LWPs: %d\n", buf -> pr_count);
58      printf ("  Timestamp: %ld.%ld\n", buf -> pr_tstamp.tv_sec,
59          buf -> pr_tstamp.tv_nsec);
60      printf ("  Creation time: %ld.%ld\n", buf -> pr_create.tv_sec,
61          buf -> pr_create.tv_nsec);
62      printf ("  Termination time: %ld.%ld\n", buf -> pr_term.tv_sec,
63          buf -> pr_term.tv_nsec);
64      printf ("  Real (elapsed) time: %ld.%ld\n", buf -> pr_rtime.tv_sec,
65          buf -> pr_rtime.tv_nsec);
66      printf ("  User CPU time: %ld.%ld\n", buf -> pr_utime.tv_sec,
67          buf -> pr_utime.tv_nsec);
68      printf ("  System CPU time: %ld.%ld\n", buf -> pr_stime.tv_sec,
69          buf -> pr_stime.tv_nsec);
70      printf ("  System trap CPU time: %ld.%ld\n", buf -> pr_ttime.tv_sec,
71          buf -> pr_ttime.tv_nsec);
72      printf ("  Text page fault CPU time: %ld.%ld\n", buf -> pr_tftime.tv_sec,
73          buf -> pr_tftime.tv_nsec);
74      printf ("  Data page fault CPU time: %ld.%ld\n", buf -> pr_dftime.tv_sec,
75          buf -> pr_dftime.tv_nsec);
76      printf ("  Kernel page fault CPU time: %ld.%ld\n", buf -> pr_kftime.tv_sec,
77          buf -> pr_kftime.tv_nsec);
78      printf ("  User lock wait time: %ld.%ld\n", buf -> pr_ltime.tv_sec,
79          buf -> pr_ltime.tv_nsec);
80      printf ("  Other sleep time: %ld.%ld\n", buf -> pr_slptime.tv_sec,
81          buf -> pr_slptime.tv_nsec);
82      printf ("  CPU latency time: %ld.%ld\n", buf -> pr_wtime.tv_sec,
83          buf -> pr_wtime.tv_nsec);
84      printf ("  Stopped time: %ld.%ld\n", buf -> pr_stoptime.tv_sec,
85          buf -> pr_stoptime.tv_nsec);
86      printf ("  Minor faults: %ld\n", buf -> pr_minf);
87      printf ("  Major faults: %ld\n", buf -> pr_majf);
88      printf ("  Number of swaps: %ld\n", buf -> pr_nswap);
89      printf ("  Input blocks: %ld\n", buf -> pr_inblk);
90      printf ("  Output blocks: %ld\n", buf -> pr_oublk);
91      printf ("  Messages sent: %ld\n", buf -> pr_msnd);
92      printf ("  Messages received: %ld\n", buf -> pr_mrcv);
93      printf ("  Signals received: %ld\n", buf -> pr_sigs);
94      printf ("  Voluntary context switches: %ld\n", buf -> pr_vctx);
95      printf ("  Involuntary context switches: %ld\n", buf -> pr_ictx);
96      printf ("  System calls: %ld\n", buf -> pr_sysc);
97      printf ("  Characters read/written: %ld\n", buf -> pr_ioch);
98  }
```

sys_info/getprusage1.c

Program 8.11 Our implementation of getprusage.

1. The init process started less than one minute after the machine booted. This isn't surprising, because init is the first non-system process created when the Solaris kernel starts running.

2. Despite running for about 20 days, less than one second of CPU time has been consumed by the process.

3. More than 6500 signals have been received, and nearly 144,000 system calls have been made.

Example: Implementing getprusage using the PIOCUSAGE ioctl

Program 8.12 shows another implementation of our getprusage function. This time, however, we have used the PIOCUSAGE ioctl. We've done this to show how to use the older ioctl method of obtaining process information from /proc.

Program 8.12 is almost the same as Program 8.11. The only differences are the implementation of the getprusage function, and that we must include <sys/old_procfs.h> instead of <procfs.h> (if we are compiling Program 8.12 on Solaris 2.5 or Solaris 2.5.1, we must include <sys/procfs.h>; we perform this behind the scenes sleight of hand by checking if NEED_SNPRINTF—which we define only when compiling on Solaris 2.5 or 2.5.1—is defined).

Let's see what happens when we run Program 8.12:

```
$ ./getprusage2 1
getprusage failed: Permission denied
$ ps
   PID TTY       TIME CMD
   503 pts/10   0:01 ksh
 18503 pts/10   0:00 ps
$ ./getprusage2 503
Resource usage for PID 503:
  LWP ID: 0
  Number of LWPs: 1
  Timestamp: 267011.76709783
  Creation time: 1977.486278389
  Termination time: 0.0
  Real (elapsed) time: 265033.589329198
  User CPU time: 0.228333337
  System CPU time: 0.650211029
  System trap CPU time: 0.7082816
  Text page fault CPU time: 0.0
  Data page fault CPU time: 0.0
  Kernel page fault CPU time: 0.0
  User lock wait time: 0.0
  Other sleep time: 265032.598291161
  CPU latency time: 0.109213722
  Stopped time: 0.0
  Minor faults: 0
  Major faults: 8
  Number of swaps: 0
  Input blocks: 8
```

─── *sys_info/getprusage2.c*

```
 1  #include <stdio.h>
 2  #include <unistd.h>
 3  #include <stdlib.h>
 4  #include <fcntl.h>
 5  #include <sys/types.h>
 6  #include <sys/stat.h>
 7  #include <sys/resource.h>
 8  #ifdef NEED_SNPRINTF
 9  #include <sys/procfs.h>
10  #else
11  #include <sys/old_procfs.h>
12  #endif
13  #include <limits.h>
14  #include "ssp.h"

15  static int getprusage (pid_t pid, prusage_t *pr_usage);
16  static void print_rusage (pid_t pid, prusage_t *buf);

17  int main (int argc, char **argv)
18  {
19      pid_t pid;
20      prusage_t buf;
21      int i;

22      if (argc == 1) {
23          if (getprusage (-1, &buf) == -1)
24              err_msg ("getprusage failed");
25          print_rusage (getpid (), &buf);
26      }
27      else {
28          for (i = 1; i < argc; i++) {
29              pid = atoi (argv [i]);
30              if (getprusage (pid, &buf) == -1)
31                  err_ret ("getprusage failed");
32              else
33                  print_rusage (pid, &buf);
34          }
35      }

36      return (0);
37  }

38  static int getprusage (pid_t pid, prusage_t *pr_usage)
39  {
40      int fd;
41      char name [PATH_MAX];

42      if (pid == -1)
43          snprintf (name, PATH_MAX, "/proc/%ld", (long) getpid ());
44      else
45          snprintf (name, PATH_MAX, "/proc/%ld", (long) pid);

46      if ((fd = open (name, O_RDONLY)) == -1)
47          return (-1);
```

```
48     if (ioctl (fd, PIOCUSAGE, pr_usage) == -1) {
49         close (fd);
50         return (-1);
51     }
52     else {
53         close (fd);
54         return (0);
55     }
56 }

57 static void print_rusage (pid_t pid, prusage_t *buf)
58 {
59     printf ("Resource usage for PID %ld:\n", (long) pid);
60     printf ("  LWP ID: %ld\n", (long) buf -> pr_lwpid);
61     printf ("  Number of LWPs: %d\n", (int) buf -> pr_count);
62     printf ("  Timestamp: %ld.%ld\n", buf -> pr_tstamp.tv_sec,
63         buf -> pr_tstamp.tv_nsec);
64     printf ("  Creation time: %ld.%ld\n", buf -> pr_create.tv_sec,
65         buf -> pr_create.tv_nsec);
66     printf ("  Termination time: %ld.%ld\n", buf -> pr_term.tv_sec,
67         buf -> pr_term.tv_nsec);
68     printf ("  Real (elapsed) time: %ld.%ld\n", buf -> pr_rtime.tv_sec,
69         buf -> pr_rtime.tv_nsec);
70     printf ("  User CPU time: %ld.%ld\n", buf -> pr_utime.tv_sec,
71         buf -> pr_utime.tv_nsec);
72     printf ("  System CPU time: %ld.%ld\n", buf -> pr_stime.tv_sec,
73         buf -> pr_stime.tv_nsec);
74     printf ("  System trap CPU time: %ld.%ld\n", buf -> pr_ttime.tv_sec,
75         buf -> pr_ttime.tv_nsec);
76     printf ("  Text page fault CPU time: %ld.%ld\n", buf -> pr_tftime.tv_sec,
77         buf -> pr_tftime.tv_nsec);
78     printf ("  Data page fault CPU time: %ld.%ld\n", buf -> pr_dftime.tv_sec,
79         buf -> pr_dftime.tv_nsec);
80     printf ("  Kernel page fault CPU time: %ld.%ld\n", buf -> pr_kftime.tv_sec,
81         buf -> pr_kftime.tv_nsec);
82     printf ("  User lock wait time: %ld.%ld\n", buf -> pr_ltime.tv_sec,
83         buf -> pr_ltime.tv_nsec);
84     printf ("  Other sleep time: %ld.%ld\n", buf -> pr_slptime.tv_sec,
85         buf -> pr_slptime.tv_nsec);
86     printf ("  CPU latency time: %ld.%ld\n", buf -> pr_wtime.tv_sec,
87         buf -> pr_wtime.tv_nsec);
88     printf ("  Stopped time: %ld.%ld\n", buf -> pr_stoptime.tv_sec,
89         buf -> pr_stoptime.tv_nsec);
90     printf ("  Minor faults: %ld\n", buf -> pr_minf);
91     printf ("  Major faults: %ld\n", buf -> pr_majf);
92     printf ("  Number of swaps: %ld\n", buf -> pr_nswap);
93     printf ("  Input blocks: %ld\n", buf -> pr_inblk);
94     printf ("  Output blocks: %ld\n", buf -> pr_oublk);
95     printf ("  Messages sent: %ld\n", buf -> pr_msnd);
96     printf ("  Messages received: %ld\n", buf -> pr_mrcv);
97     printf ("  Signals received: %ld\n", buf -> pr_sigs);
98     printf ("  Voluntary context switches: %ld\n", buf -> pr_vctx);
99     printf ("  Involuntary context switches: %ld\n", buf -> pr_ictx);
100    printf ("  System calls: %ld\n", buf -> pr_sysc);
101    printf ("  Characters read/written: %ld\n", buf -> pr_ioch);
102 }
```

sys_info/getprusage2.c

Program 8.12 Implementing getprusage using ioctl.

```
Output blocks: 3
Messages sent: 0
Messages received: 0
Signals received: 6
Voluntary context switches: 1169
Involuntary context switches: 686
System calls: 10673
Characters read/written: 178966
```

Notice that when we try to get the resource usage information for init this time, we get an error (Permission denied). This is because the ioctl method of obtaining information from /proc only works for processes whose effective user ID is the same as the program trying to obtain the information (running Program 8.12 as root would of course work around this restriction).

In our example output, we use the ps command to list some processes we can get the resource usage for. We chose the process for our shell, the process ID of which is 503. This time, the program works as expected.

8.9   Determining the System's Load Average

It is sometimes useful to determine the system's current load average. A process can use this information to decided whether to perform a given task. For example, Sendmail can be configured to refuse connections when the load average exceeds a certain threshold. But before we show how to determine the current load average, we need to describe what a load average is.

The *load average* is the number of runnable and running processes (the *load*), averaged over a certain time interval. Solaris (and many other implementations of UNIX) uses time intervals of 60, 300, and 900 seconds (i.e., 1, 5, and 15 minutes respectively) to calculate the load average. Note that the load average does not take into account the number of CPUs the system has; whether or not a given load average is cause for concern is dependant on this piece of information (which we can determine by calling the sysconf function we describe in Section 8.3). For example, a load average of 10 on a uniprocessor machine is likely to be a problem, but that same load average on a 16-CPU system is not an issue. (As a general rule of thumb, a load average that is less than four times the number of CPUs is acceptable.)

From Solaris 7, the load average for the last 60, 300, and 900 seconds can be ascertained by calling the getloadavg function.

```
#include <sys/loadavg.h>

int getloadavg (double loadavg [], int nelem);
```
                              Returns: the number of samples retrieved if OK, −1 on error

The getloadavg function retrieves up to *nelem* load averages, placing them in successive elements of *loadavg*. The system imposes a maximum of three samples, representing the load averaged over the last 1, 5, and 15 minutes respectively.

Three constants defined in `<sys/loadavg.h>` can be used to extract data from the appropriate element of the *loadavg* array. These are LOADAVG_1MIN, LOADAVG_5MIN, and LOADAVG_15MIN.

Example: Printing the system's load averages

Program 8.13 retrieves the current load averages for the system, and then displays them.

——— *sys_info/loadav.c*

```
 1 #include <stdio.h>
 2 #include <sys/loadavg.h>
 3 #include "ssp.h"

 4 int main (void)
 5 {
 6     double load_av [3];

 7     if (getloadavg (load_av, 3) == -1)
 8         err_msg ("getloadavg failed");

 9     printf ("Load averaged over 1 minute: %.2f\n", load_av [LOADAVG_1MIN]);
10     printf ("Load averaged over 5 minutes: %.2f\n", load_av [LOADAVG_5MIN]);
11     printf ("Load averaged over 15 minutes: %.2f\n", load_av [LOADAVG_15MIN]);

12     return (0);
13 }
```
——— *sys_info/loadav.c*

Program 8.13 Displaying the system's load averages.

Running Program 8.13 on a lightly loaded Ultra 60 gave the following results:

```
$ ./loadav
Load averaged over 1 minute: 0.10
Load averaged over 5 minutes: 0.06
Load averaged over 15 minutes: 0.04
```

We can verify these results by examining the output of the `uptime` command:

```
$ uptime
  9:49pm  up 2 day(s),   3:21,   1 user,   load average: 0.10, 0.06, 0.04
```

8.10 Summary

In this chapter, we discussed the various ways a process can discover information about the machine it is running on. This information includes (but is not limited to): the system's hostname, the OS version, the system's CPU architecture, etc.

We then talked about system and per-process resource limits, showing how a process can portably determine the limits of its environment. We also discussed the resource control facility that was introduced with Solaris 9, and showed a couple of examples of how programs can use this facility.

Finally, we discussed how a process can determine its own resource usage by using the `getrusage` function and the newer `procfs` methods, and how to retrieve the system load averaged over 1, 5, and 15 minutes.

Exercises

8.1   Compare the contents of the `uname` section of Program 8.1 and the output from the command `uname -a`.

8.2   If we call `sethostname` to change the system's name, does this new name persist across a reboot?

8.3   Assuming a `CLK_TCK` value of 100 and that `times` returns the number of clock ticks since the system last booted, how long after the system boots will the value returned by `times` first wrap around in a 32-bit process?

9

Secure C Programming

9.1   Introduction

From a programmer's point of view, there are two areas where security is a concern: denial of service attacks, and compromises. The latter can be broken down into two categories:

1. Local compromises, which is where an attack originates from a local user (i.e., one who is logged in to the machine).

2. Remote compromises, which is where an attack originates from a remote machine, be it on the same network or half way around the world.

A *denial of service* (DoS) attack is when an attacker tries to make the services offered by a site unavailable. This could be by either crashing the whole machine, causing one or more applications to crash, or by saturating the network with bogus requests.

A compromise occurs when an unauthorized person gains access to one or more of our machines. The usual target for compromises is the root account, because once an attacker has root access to a machine, they can do more or less what they like with it, from deleting or copying confidential data, to using the machine as a platform to launch attacks on other machines.

While there isn't much an application can do to defend itself against DoS attacks, a well designed and written program can do a lot to defend itself from compromises. Some of the things we can do to protect our programs from compromises are: avoiding buffer overflows, practicing defensive programming, adhering the to principle of least privilege, and being wary of the program's environment.

In the rest of this chapter, we take a closer look at some of these issues and present a checklist of things to consider when writing secure C programs.

9.2   Buffer Overflows

Buffer overflows are one of the most commonly exploited vulnerabilities in C programs. A *buffer overflow* is what happens when a program tries to store more data in a variable than it has been allocated space for. For example, suppose we have a program that prompts the user for their name, and then stores it in a variable called name that has been defined as an array of 10 characters. Because we must allow room for the terminating NUL, the array has enough room to store only 9 characters. A malicious user could send a carefully constructed byte stream to this program, which would build the instructions needed to start a shell on the stack. If the process is running as root, the user would get a shell with root privileges.

The C programming language does not perform any bounds checking at run time, so it is very easy for the user of a badly written program to overflow a buffer. Consider this segment from our hypothetical example program:

```
char name [10];

printf ("Enter your name: ");
fflush (stdout);
gets (name);
```

If we enter a string less than 10 characters in length, all is well. But if we enter a longer string, the buffer defined by the variable name will overflow. The results of the overflow depends on the quantity and contents of the data that caused it. If we are unfortunate, nothing bad will happen most of the time. (This would be unfortunate because our chances of discovering and fixing the bug are diminished.) A more likely result is data corruption and possibly a core dump. A carefully crafted overflow can even cause a shell to be executed, with the same privileges as the effective user ID of the process. If the process is running as root, this would be disastrous.

One way of avoiding buffer overflows is to use buffers so large that "no one will ever overflow them." This is a bad idea, because apart from the obvious waste of memory that will result, it doesn't actually fix the problem. It makes it harder for users to accidentally overflow the buffer, but it doesn't prevent a malicious user from deliberately overflowing it. To do that, we must use functions that let us specify the buffer size when we are performing I/O. In the preceding example, if we change the line that reads

```
gets (name);
```

to

```
fgets (name, 10, stdin);
```

it doesn't matter how many characters we type in response to the prompt, because only the first 9 characters will be copied to the variable *name*. We must also remove the newline character from the end of the name, because unlike gets, the fgets function doesn't remove it for us.

By their very nature, these types of attacks are very processor- and OS-dependent. For example, an exploit designed for Linux on x86 processors will not work on SPARC processors running Solaris. Such an exploit might cause the process being attacked to dump core, resulting in a denial of service, but this is arguably better than the headache caused by a root shell compromise.

Fortunately, Solaris systems administrators (starting with Solaris 2.6) have a line of defence against this method of attack. Putting the following two lines in to /etc/system will help prevent this attack, and provide a warning when an exploit of this type is attempted:

```
set noexec_user_stack = 1
set noexec_user_stack_log = 1
```

Like all changes to /etc/system, a reboot is required before the change takes effect. All systems running Solaris 2.6 or newer have this variable, but it is effective on only sun4u, sun4m, or sun4d architectures.

> Although this technically violates the SPARC-V8 ABI (see page 3-19 of [SCO 1996]), which specifies that the user stack must have read, write, and execute permissions, in reality very few programs are adversely affected. The SPARC-V9 ABI (on page 3P-17 of [SPARC International 1999]) states that the user stack has only read and write permissions. As a consequence of this, 64-bit processes are by default protected against this type of exploit, irrespective of the setting of noexec_user_stack.

The gets function is not the only one vulnerable to this type of problem. Almost all string copying functions are potential sources of buffer overflows, especially when manipulating data from an untrusted source (e.g., user input). The problems with these functions can also be avoided by using safer alternatives; for example, strncpy should be used in favour of strcpy, strncat should be used instead of strcat, and snprintf should replace sprintf.

Related to preventing buffer overflows is the correct calculation of buffer size. All C strings are NUL terminated, so we must remember to include it in our string buffer sizes. If we need a string LEN characters long, we must declare a character array with at least LEN + 1 bytes in it.

9.3   The Program's Environment

A security conscious program should never trust anything in its environment: what directory it was run from (the current working directory), the value of its umask, what file descriptors are open, signal disposition, and even the values of the environment variables passed to it from its parent.

Some of the things we can do to ensure the environmental integrity of our programs are:

- Use the chdir function to change explicitly to a known directory when the program starts.
- Set the umask to an appropriate value. A value of 022 (octal) is a good choice, because it prevents the creation of files that are writable by people other than the user. The chmod function can be used to change the file's permissions explicitly if this is required.
- Ensure that the disposition of signals is sensible.
- Close any file descriptors that are not expected to be open, and similarly, ensure that any file descriptors that are expected to be open are open. The corollary of

this is make sure that the close on exec flag is set on any file descriptor that we don't intend to pass to child processes.

- Erase all but the most essential environment variables, such as TZ (which specifies the current time zone), and the locale variables (e.g., LC_COLLATE, LC_CTYPE, etc.).

- If the program is calling another, consider creating a new environment for it from scratch. This is safer than relying on a sanitized environment, because we have absolute control over it.

- If data confidentiality is an issue, we should ensure that our program can't produce a core dump. This is done by limiting the size of a core dump to 0 bytes, either by using the ulimit command before running the program, or by calling the setrlimit function near the beginning of our program. The latter is preferable, because it is harder to forget or (more importantly) circumvent.

Another thing related to the environment of a process is the user ID and group ID of the invoking user, and what user ID and group ID the program was designed to run as. An example of this is Berkeley Internet Name Domain (BIND), the most commonly used Domain Name System (DNS) server. Recent versions of BIND are designed to run as an unprivileged user rather than root. A program designed to run as an unprivileged user might have security implications if it is run by root, and vice versa (although the former is potentially more dangerous).

9.4   Defensive Programming

Defensive programming is the antithesis of Murphy's Law (i.e., anything that can go wrong, will go wrong). Rigorous sanity checks should be performed on all data read from external sources, and functions (especially those that rely on external data) should bounds-check their inputs. For example, if a function is expecting one of its arguments to be in the range of 1 to 100, it should ensure that the input actually is in that range; it shouldn't just assume that it will be. Boundary conditions (off-by-one errors, etc.) should be carefully tested. In the example here, check that 1 and 100 are accepted, but 0, −1, and 101 are rejected.

Most library functions and system calls return an indication of their success or failure, so we should always check the return value for errors, even when an error seems unlikely. Only by checking for errors can our programs take appropriate action, rather than just crashing.

It follows from this that any functions we write should check for error conditions and return an appropriate error indication.

9.5   The Principle of Least Privilege

The *principle of least privilege* is relatively straightforward: any operation carried out by a program should be done so using the least amount of privilege required to successfully complete the task.

The security model used by Solaris is simple: a process which has an effective user ID of 0 can do almost anything with any system resource; all other user IDs are restricted to what they can do. In this respect, Solaris (and most other variants of UNIX) fail to adhere to the principle of least privilege.

Trusted Solaris uses a different security model whereby the godlike powers entrusted to the superuser are broken down in to a number of distinct privileges. For example, a process can be given the privilege of being able to read any file (for example, a backup program) without all the other privileges a superuser process implies (e.g., being able to write to any file). Solaris 10 introduced this privilege separation model to regular Solaris.

> Trusted Solaris is an enhanced version of the Solaris operating environment with special security features. It meets the requirements of the Common Criteria at the EAL4 level (which is equivalent to the Orange Book B1 level), and lets an organization define and implement a security policy for Sun workstations and servers. Further details can be found at the following URL: http://www.sun.com/trusted-solaris.

Even without the finely grained privilege model of Trusted Solaris, we can still apply the principle of least privilege to a degree. Suppose we have a program that may be invoked by any user, and that program must write to a common file that the users wouldn't ordinarily be able to (an example of this would be the passwd command). It would be tempting to write a set-user-ID root program to accomplish this, but this would give the program far too much privilege for such a simple task. A far better approach would be to allocate a dedicated group to the program and its files, and have the program run set-group-ID to this new group. The common file would be readable by all users, but writable only by the owner and group.

> Solaris 8 introduced to concept of roles, which can also be used in this sort of scenario to avoid set-user-ID root programs.

Related to the principle of least privilege is the concept of privilege bracketing. *Privilege bracketing* is when our programs take on the extra privileges they need to accomplish a task, and then drop them once that task has been completed.

In our shared program example, the program would revert its group ID to that of the invoking user when it starts up, and only set its group ID to the one allocated to it when it needs to open the common file. Once the file is open, the privileges can subsequently be dropped (i.e., the invoking user's group ID is reassumed). Writes to the file will succeed because it was opened with the right privileges.

Example: Using privilege bracketing

Program 9.1 illustrates the use of privilege bracketing by printing the real and effective user and group IDs.

Program 9.1 first turns off any privileges, then prints the real and effective user and group IDs. Then privileges are turned on and the IDs are printed again. Finally, privileges are turned back off, and the IDs are printed one last time.

—————————————————————————— secure_c/bracketing.c

```c
1  #include <stdio.h>
2  #include <sys/types.h>
3  #include <unistd.h>

4  uid_t saved_euid;
5  gid_t saved_egid;

6  static void priv_off (void);
7  static void priv_on (void);
8  static void print_uids (void);

9  int main (void)
10 {
11     priv_off ();
12     print_uids ();

13     priv_on ();
14     print_uids ();

15     priv_off ();
16     print_uids ();

17     return (0);
18 }

19 static void priv_off (void)
20 {
21     static int first_time = 1;

22     if (first_time) {
23         saved_euid = geteuid ();
24         saved_egid = getegid ();
25         first_time = 0;
26     }

27     seteuid (getuid ());
28     setegid (getgid ());
29 }

30 static void priv_on (void)
31 {
32     seteuid (saved_euid);
33     setegid (saved_egid);
34 }

35 static void print_uids (void)
36 {
37     printf ("Real UID = %ld, GID = %ld\n", (long) getuid (), (long) getgid ());
38     printf ("Effective UID = %ld, GID = %ld\n", (long) geteuid (),
39         (long) getegid ());
40 }
```

—————————————————————————— secure_c/bracketing.c

Program 9.1   Using privilege bracketing.

This is what happens when we run Program 9.1 a few times:

```
$ ls -l bracketing
-rwxr-xr-x   1 rich      staff      10088 Feb 14 15:49 bracketing
$ ./bracketing
Real UID = 1001, GID = 10
Effective UID = 1001, GID = 10
Real UID = 1001, GID = 10
Effective UID = 1001, GID = 10
Real UID = 1001, GID = 10
Effective UID = 1001, GID = 10
$ su
Password:                                  Type root's password
# ./bracketing
Real UID = 0, GID = 1
Effective UID = 0, GID = 1
Real UID = 0, GID = 1
Effective UID = 0, GID = 1
Real UID = 0, GID = 1
Effective UID = 0, GID = 1
# chmod 4755 bracketing                    Set the SUID bit
# ls -l bracketing
-rwsr-xr-x   1 rich      staff      10088 Feb 14 15:49 bracketing
# ./bracketing
Real UID = 0, GID = 1
Effective UID = 0, GID = 1
Real UID = 0, GID = 1
Effective UID = 1001, GID = 1
Real UID = 0, GID = 1
Effective UID = 0, GID = 1
```

The first two times we run the program, the `priv_on` and `priv_off` functions have no effect. This is because the program is not set-user-ID. When we set the set-user-ID bit, the third invocation shows that the effective user ID changes when we call `priv_on` and `priv_off`.

If we are writing a daemon that will be started when the system boots, and it is intended that the daemon run as a particular user, then we should also set the real user- and group IDs to the user we want the daemon to run as. If we didn't take this precaution, the process will still retain some of its `root` privileges. This is because although the effective user- and group IDs will be that of the reserved user, the real user- and group IDs will be `root`. Another (perhaps better) way of achieving this is to run the daemon using the `su` command in the start/stop script:

```
/sbin/su $SPECIAL_USER -c /path/to/daemon/executable
```

where `SPECIAL_USER` is a variable in the script that defines the user name the script is to run as. This technique is useful only if the program will never need to use superuser privileges.

9.6   Using `chroot` Jails

Using a `chroot` jail is another way of enhancing a program's security (or at least limiting the damage in the event of a compromise). As we show in Section 10.25, the `chroot` function allows a privileged process to change its notion of the root directory. After a `chroot`, all absolute pathname searches will start from the new directory, not the "real" root. This essentially gives the process a private world from which it cannot (usually) escape.

> Solaris Zones, introduced with Solaris 10, takes the concept of `chroot` jails a lot further.

An example of a program that could make use of a `chrooted` environment is BIND. One of the conventional locations for BIND's configuration and zone files is `/var/named`. In this case, the following code will restrict BIND to this directory:

```
chroot ("/var/named");
```

(We've omitted error checking in this trivial example.) Newer releases of BIND have a command line option to perform a `chroot` to a given directory.

We should consider a few issues when writing a program that will be run in a `chrooted` environment.

1. The `chrooted` directory hierarchy will need access to some devices and shared libraries. An example device is `/dev/zero`, which is used with `mmap` to create zero-filled blocks of memory. Any devices or shared libraries must be copied into the `chrooted` environment's directory tree.

2. Users should not have write access to the `chrooted` environment.

3. If the program intends to use the `syslog` facility for its logging, the `openlog` function should be called before the `chroot` takes place. Failing that, a copy of the `/dev/log` device should exist in the `chrooted` environment.

Example: Breaking out of a `chroot` jail

Although a `chrooted` environment provides a lot of protection for unprivileged programs, it is possible for a privileged process to break out of one. Program 9.2 shows how we can do this.

The reason why Program 9.2 works is because `chroot` does not perform a `chdir` to the desired directory. So, we can keep performing a `chdir` to our parent directory until we reach the real root directory. Program 9.2 does this by comparing the device and inode of the current directory and its parent: if they are the same, we've reached the root directory. The final `chroot` changes the root directory back to the real one, before running a shell. Notice that because programs that can break out of a `chroot` jail must run as `root`, the shell we run is also running as `root`.

Let's run program 9.2, and see what happens.

secure_c/break_chroot.c

```
 1 #include <stdio.h>
 2 #include <sys/types.h>
 3 #include <sys/stat.h>
 4 #include <unistd.h>
 5 #include "ssp.h"

 6 int main (int argc, char **argv)
 7 {
 8     struct stat buf1;
 9     struct stat buf2;

10     if (argc != 2)
11         err_quit ("Usage: break_chroot directory");

12     if (chdir ("/") == -1)
13         err_msg ("Can't chdir to /");

14     if (chroot (argv [1]) == -1)
15         err_msg ("Can't chroot to %s", argv [1]);

16     for (;;) {
17         if (stat (".", &buf1) == -1)
18             err_msg ("Can't stat .");
19         if (stat ("..", &buf2) == -1)
20             err_msg ("Can't stat ..");

21         if ((buf1.st_dev == buf2.st_dev) && (buf1.st_ino == buf2.st_ino))
22             break;

23         if (chdir ("..") == -1)
24             err_msg ("Can't chdir to ..");
25     }

26     chroot (".");

27     switch (fork ()) {
28         case -1:
29             err_msg ("Can't fork");
30             break;

31         case 0:
32             execl ("/sbin/sh", "-sh", NULL);
33             execl ("/bin/sh", "-sh", NULL);
34             printf ("Can't find a shell - exiting.\n");
35             _exit (0);

36         default:
37             break;
38     }

39     return (0);
40 }
```

secure_c/break_chroot.c

Program 9.2 Breaking out of a chroot jail.

```
$ pwd
/space/chroot
$ ls
break_chroot  sbin          usr
$ ./break_chroot usr
Can't chroot to usr: Not owner
$ su                                      Let's try again as root
Password:
# chroot /space/chroot /sbin/sh
# pwd
/
# ls
ls: not found
# echo *                                  We didn't copy ls to our jail, so let's use echo
break_chroot sbin usr
# ./break_chroot usr
# pwd
/
# ls
TT_DB         etc          lib          pcfs         sbin         usr
bin           export       lost+found   platform     share        var
cdrom         floppy       mnt          proc         space        vol
dev           home         net          reconfigure  src          xfn
devices       kernel       opt          root         tmp
```

Some flavours of UNIX (for example, FreeBSD) provide a version of chroot that can't be exploited like this, because calling chroot also does a chdir to the desired directory. Unfortunately, this behaviour breaks standards compliance, so Solaris does not implement it.

Despite the relative ease in which a privileged process can break out of a chroot jail, we still recommend their use, especially in self-contained programs that supply network services. Running these programs as an unprivileged user will prevent attackers from breaking out of the jail, and using the defensive programming techniques we describe in this chapter will help minimize other risks.

9.7   Tips For Writing Secure Programs

Now that we've covered some of the principles of writing secure programs, here are some ideas to be considered when we write programs with a security requirement. Some of these could be considered as recommended practices, regardless of any security needs.

1. Design with security in mind. There's not much point in implementing a design that has inherent security flaws.

2. Keep your code, especially security critical sections, short and simple. Code that is easier to read is easier to understand, and hence, easier to debug than code that is obfuscated by "clever" constructs.

3. Check all arguments. This includes arguments passed on the command line, arguments passed to functions, and arguments passed in environment variables. Make sure that all arguments are of the right type and within the expected bounds.

4. Avoid buffer overflows by not using functions that do not check buffer boundaries. When manipulating strings of arbitrary length, always use a function that specifies the size of the buffer (when one is available). Remember to allow space for the terminating NUL in buffer size calculations.

5. Check all library function and system call return values, even those that are unlikely to fail. If a function does fail, examine `errno` to find out why. If an error is irrecoverable, log a message, delete any temporary files, and exit. Even if the error is recoverable, it might be a good idea to log it somewhere.

   Even programs running as `root` can have unexpected errors with functions like `open` or `chdir`. For example, if the file being opened is on a read-only file system (e.g., a CD-ROM), an open requesting write access will always fail. Similarly, if the directory that is the subject of a `chdir` does not exist, attempts to change to that directory will fail.

6. Include lots of logging. Using the `syslog` facility is a good idea, as this allows users to determine where logging goes. Using different logging levels to control the verbosity of logs is also a good idea, although it's arguably better to have too much logging than too little.

7. Always use fully qualified absolute pathnames for any files that are opened, especially when running new programs using `exec`. Using relative pathnames is dangerous because they are so easy to subvert. It is trivial for users to change to a directory of their own choosing, or worse, change their `PATH` environment variable to include untrusted directories.

8. On the subject of running new programs, avoid the use of `system` and `popen`. Instead, `fork` and `exec` should be used to implement the required functionality. This is because both `system` and `popen` start a shell to run the desired command.

   Avoid using `execlp` and `execvp`; ideally, a program should pass on a carefully crafted environment, rather than trusting the one it inherits from its parent.

9. Do not trust user input. Specifically:

   - Check anything supplied by the user for shell meta characters, especially if it is going to be passed to another program, written to a file, or used as a pathname. Rather than checking for and rejecting known bad characters, decide which characters you deem to be acceptable and reject all others. As firewall administrators know, denial by default is a good security policy.

   - User input should not be used as the format argument for functions like `printf`, `scanf`, `syslog`, and the like.

   - User input from the network (e.g., from a web browser) should be sanitized before being used by our programs. For example, we might employ client-side input validation using JavaScript, but it is trivial for an attacker to bypass these checks by connecting directly to our server and sending malformed HTTP requests.

10. Do not provide shell escapes. With windowing systems and job control shells, they are not as useful as they used to be. Programs that must include this functionality (especially in a set-user-ID or set-group-ID program), then make sure that the process resets its user- and group IDs to the real ones before invoking the shell.

11. Test, test, test, and retest, especially border conditions, and especially after making any changes (no matter how innocuous they may seem).

The ideas in this list are by no means exhaustive, nor do they apply to all programs. Another thing to consider is that most security holes are the result of programming bugs. Fixing security holes has the added benefit of making programs more reliable.

Writing Secure Set-User-ID and Set-Group-ID Programs

A huge number of UNIX security problems are caused by set-user-ID and set-group-ID programs. This is because, at worst, they can allow an unauthorized person to run a `root` shell. It is for this reason that authors of set-user-ID and set-group-ID programs need to be more careful and paranoid than usual.

Because of the inherent risks associated with set-user-ID programs (and to a slightly lesser extent, set-group-ID programs)—especially those that are set-user-ID `root`—the first step in writing a secure set-user-ID program is to reconsider the need for it to be set-user-ID in the first place. If something can be achieved by not using a set-user-ID program, do it that way; most of the time, set-user-ID programs are not necessary.

If, after careful consideration, it is determined that a set-user-ID program is needed, the following rules should be considered, in addition to the general purpose ones we listed previously.

- *Always* adhere to the principle of least privilege. The greatest danger with set-user-ID programs is when they are running as a privileged user. If the amount of time the program spends as a privileged user is minimized, it follows that the risk associated with running as that user are also minimized. Using functions like the ones we presented in Program 9.1 is a good idea.

- Avoid writing set-user-ID shell scripts. Many shells and other scripting languages (e.g., `awk`) are so flexible and powerful that they are easy to trick into doing unintended things.

- If it is appropriate, assign a dedicated user or group to the program, and run as that user rather than `root`.

- If the program is fairly large and only a small subset of it requires superuser privileges, consider writing a small set-user-ID program that does what's needed using a controlled interface with the main program. The main program will no longer need to be set-user-ID `root`, so the size of the code that must be rigorously inspected will be much smaller.

- If possible, we should have one or more colleagues inspect our code (in other words, we should perform peer code reviews whenever possible). Questions asked during code inspections have a way of bringing any design or implementation flaws to light.

- Ensure that the process environment is clean (see Section 9.3).

- Programs that spawn processes should use only `execl`, `execv`, `execle`, or `execve`. Avoid using `execlp` and `execvp`, and *never* use `system` or `popen`. Child processes started in this manner should also have their effective user- and group IDs set to the real ones before being called (programs adhering to the principle of least privilege are, by definition, covered here).

  If the program being run is a shell or uses pipes, make sure that the `IFS` and `PATH` environment variables are set to safe values.

- Use absolute, rather than relative, pathnames for all files. Changing to a known directory, for example /, is also a good idea.

- Check the ownership and permissions by using file descriptors rather than filenames. A favourite technique of some attackers is to run a set-user-ID program that accesses one of their own files. The program uses `access` or `stat` to check ownership and permissions on the file, and then opens it for processing.

  The trouble with this is the window of vulnerability between when the checks are made and when the file is opened. The attacker could stop the process between the check and opening the file, replace the file in question with some other file that they don't usually have permissions to look at, and then restart the program. The program will open the file the symbolic link points to, under the impression that its security checks have already been made. (A similar tactic can be used with temporary files; a carefully crafted symbolic link in /tmp can fool some programs that use `mktemp` and related functions into opening files they shouldn't be able to.)

  The way to avoid this problem is to `open` the file first, and then use `fstat` on the file descriptor to check the ownership and permissions. Using this technique ensures that the checks are performed on the file the program actually uses, rather than one substituted by a malicious user.

Many, if not all, of the tips in the preceding list can be applied to all programs, not just those that are set-user-ID or set-group-ID. A key thing to remember is that when writing a set-user-ID program (especially one that is set-user-ID `root`), there's no such thing as being too paranoid.

9.8   Summary

In this chapter we discussed some of the security concerns programmers must contend with, and how we can overcome some of these problems. We discussed buffer overflows, the program's environment, defensive programming, and the principle of least privilege.

Next we discussed `chroot` jails: their attributes, how we can make one, and perhaps most importantly, how a privileged process can break out of one. We rounded off the chapter by presenting some tips for writing secure programs, and especially secure set-user-ID and set-group-ID programs.

Exercises

9.1   What are some of the things an application can do to help prevent (or at least minimize the impact of) denial of service attacks against a server?

9.2   Assuming the use of dynamically linked programs, what is the minimum set of system files (i.e., those that are supplied as part of Solaris) a `chrooted` environment must contain to run a simple program like "Hello World"?

Part 3

Input/Output

10

Files and Directories

10.1 Introduction

In Chapters 4 and 5 we discussed how to create regular files and perform I/O on them. In this chapter, we'll do the same thing for directories, show how to delete a file or directory, and also take a long look at the `stat` structure, which contains most of a file's attributes.

When we describe the members of the `stat` structure, we'll also look at the functions Solaris provides to manipulate them (e.g., changing file ownership or permissions).

We'll see how a UFS file system is structured, and take a closer look at symbolic links.

However, before we discuss these subjects, we need to take a closer look at pathnames.

10.2 Pathname Components

As we have stated previously, every file and directory in the file system has a name, which is called its pathname. We also stated that a pathname is made up of zero or more components, each of which is separated by a / character.

A pathname consists of two parts: a *basename* (the last component of a pathname), and a parent directory. It is sometimes useful to split a pathname into its component parts. To do this, we use the `dirname` and `basename` functions.

The `dirname` Function

The `dirname` function returns the name of path's parent directory.

```
#include <libgen.h>

char *dirname (char *path);
```
                                        Returns: a pointer to the parent directory of *path*

The dirname function returns a pointer to the name of *path*'s parent directory. If *path* doesn't contain a "/", then a pointer to the string "." is returned. A pointer to the string "." is also returned if *path* is a NULL pointer or points to an empty string.

The dirname function may modify the string pointed to by *path*, and may return a pointer to a static storage area that may be overwritten by subsequent calls to dirname.

The basename Function

The basename function returns the path's last component.

```
#include <libgen.h>

char *basename (char *path);
```
                                        Returns: a pointer to the last component of *path*

The basename function returns a pointer to the last component of *path*, deleting any trailing "/" characters. If *path* consists entirely of "/" characters, then a pointer to the string "." is returned. A pointer to the string "." is also returned if *path* is a NULL pointer or points to an empty string.

The basename function may modify the string pointed to by *path*, and may return a pointer to a static storage area that may be overwritten by subsequent calls to basename.

The basename and dirname functions together yield a complete pathname. The expression

```
dirname (path);
```

obtains the pathname of the directory where

```
basename (path);
```

can be found.

Example: The effect of basename and dirname on various paths

Program 10.1 shows how we can use dirname and basename to split up a path into its component parts.

Figure 10.1 summarizes the results of running Program 10.1 with several different paths.

Notice that dirname shows that "." is the parent directory of "..", even though this is true only for the root directory. We can therefore conclude that dirname and basename merely manipulate strings—they do *not* interpret their arguments as file system pathnames.

files_and_dirs/pathcomp.c

```
 1 #include <stdio.h>
 2 #include <libgen.h>
 3 #include <string.h>
 4 #include <stdlib.h>
 5 #include "ssp.h"

 6 int main (int argc, char **argv)
 7 {
 8      int n;
 9      char *ptr1;
10      char *ptr2;
11      char *dir;
12      char *base;

13      for (n = 1; n < argc; n++) {
14          if ((ptr1 = strdup (argv [n])) == NULL)
15              err_msg ("strdup failed");
16          dir = dirname (ptr1);

17          if ((ptr2 = strdup (argv [n])) == NULL)
18              err_msg ("strdup failed");
19          base = basename (ptr2);

20          printf ("%s:\n", argv [n]);
21          printf ("   dirname = %s\n", dir);
22          printf ("   basename = %s\n\n", base);

23          free (ptr1);
24          free (ptr2);
25      }

26      return (0);
27 }
```

files_and_dirs/pathcomp.c

Program 10.1 Splitting a path into its component parts.

Path	dirname (path)	basename (path)
/	/	/
//	/	/
.	.	.
..	.	..
/usr	/	usr
/usr/lib	/usr	lib
/usr/lib/	/usr	lib
/usr/lib/libc.so	/usr/lib	libc.so

Figure 10.1 The effect of dirname and basename on different paths.

10.3 The stat, fstat, and lstat Functions

Most of the discussion in this chapter revolves around the stat family of functions, and the information they return.

```
#include <sys/types.h>
#include <sys/stat.h>

int stat (const char *path, struct stat *buf);

int lstat (const char *path, struct stat *buf);

int fstat (int fildes, struct stat *buf);
```

                                                    All three return: 0 if OK, −1 on error

The stat function obtains information about the file pointed to by *path* and stores the results in the buffer pointed to by *buf*. Read permission for *path* is not required, but all directories listed in the pathname must be searchable.

The lstat function is much the same as stat, except when *path* refers to a symbolic link (we discuss symbolic links in Section 10.17). If *path* refers to a symbolic link, then the lstat function will store information about the symbolic link in *buf* (in the case of a symbolic link, stat will obtain information about the file the link references).

Finally, the fstat function obtains information about the open file descriptor, *fildes*.

Each of the stat functions stores the information obtained in a stat structure, which includes the following members:

```
struct stat {
    dev_t      st_dev;      /* Directory entry's file system */
    ino_t      st_ino;      /* Inode number */
    mode_t     st_mode;     /* File type and permissions */
    nlink_t    st_nlink;    /* Number of links */
    uid_t      st_uid;      /* User ID of the file's owner */
    gid_t      st_gid;      /* Group ID of the file's group */
    dev_t      st_rdev;     /* ID of device (special files) */
    off_t      st_size;     /* File size in bytes */
    time_t     st_atime;    /* Time of last access */
    time_t     st_mtime;    /* Time of last data modification */
    time_t     st_ctime;    /* Time of last inode modification */
    blksize_t  st_blksize;  /* Preferred I/O block size */
    blkcnt_t   st_blocks;   /* Number of 512 byte blocks allocated */
    char       st_fstype [_ST_FSTYPSZ]; /* File's file system type */
};
```

The description of each member follows:

st_dev   This field uniquely identifies the file system that contains the directory entry for the file. Its value may be used as input to the ustat function to determine more information about the file system. We discuss the ustat function in Section 11.7.

st_ino   This field uniquely identifies the file within a given file system. The st_ino and st_dev pair uniquely identify a regular file.

st_mode   This is the file's type and permissions. If the file is a symbolic link and the function being called is lstat, the field will have the value S_IFLNK.

`st_nlink`	This is the number of links to the file.
`st_uid`	The user ID of the file's owner.
`st_gid`	The group ID of the file's owner.
`st_rdev`	This field, which is valid for only block or character special files, contains the device number of the device the file refers to.
`st_size`	This is the address of the end of the file, which may or may not be the same as the number of bytes in the file (the `st_size` field of a sparse file will be larger than the actual number of bytes occupied by the file). This field is not defined for character or block special files.
`st_atime`	This field is the time (measured in seconds since the epoch) the file data was last accessed. It can be changed by the following functions: `creat`, `mknod`, `open`, `pipe`, `read`, `utime`, and `utimes`.
`st_mtime`	This field is the time (measured in seconds since the epoch) the file data was last modified. It can be changed by the following functions: `creat`, `mknod`, `open`, `pipe`, `utime`, `utimes`, and `write`.
`st_ctime`	This field is the time (measured in seconds since the epoch) the file's inode data was last modified. It can be changed by the following functions: `chmod`, `chown`, `creat`, `link`, `mknod`, `open`, `pipe`, `unlink`, `utime`, `utimes`, and `write`.
`st_blksize`	For regular files, this field is a hint as to the best (i.e., most efficient) unit size for I/O operations. This field is not defined for character or block special files.
`st_blocks`	For regular files, this is the total number of physical 512-byte blocks actually allocated on disk for the file. This field is not defined for character or block special files.
`st_fstype`	This field identifies the type of file system (from the calling program's perspective) that the file resides on.

Probably the most frequent user of the `stat` functions is the `ls -l` command.

10.4 File Types

We've talked about two file types so far in this text: regular files and directories. Regular files and directories account for the vast majority of files found in typical Solaris installations, but there are several other file types.

1. Regular files. These are the most common type of file (a typical installation has many thousands of regular files). They are regarded by the kernel as an unstructured stream of bytes, with no distinction between ASCII and binary files.

Any interpretation of the contents of a regular file is up to the application accessing it.

2. Directories. A directory is a file that contains a table of all the files logically contained within the directory. Each directory entry also contains the file system unique identifier associated with the file (this is the file's inode number). Any process that has read permission on a directory may read the contents of the directory file, but only the kernel can write to a directory file, regardless of the permissions on it (directory files are one of the few examples where the root user cannot override access permissions on a file).

3. Character special files. A *special file* is the interface to a device driver. Unless the device driver implements a new system call, special files are the only way a user process can interact with a device driver. A character special file is intended for character at a time I/O with the device driver (e.g., commands or small items of data).

4. Block special files. This is a special file that performs block-sized transfers to and from a device driver. The most obvious example of a block special file would be those that represent the slices of a disk, e.g., /dev/dsk/c0t0d0s0.

5. FIFOs. Also known as a named pipe, a FIFO is a type of file used for interprocess communications.

6. Sockets. A type of file used for communication between processes, usually across a network.

7. Symbolic links. This is a file that points to (i.e., contains the name of) another file. See Section 10.17.

8. Doors. A door is a mechanism for very fast RPCs to another process on the same host. A door file is how a client opens a door.

The file type is encoded in the st_mode field of the stat structure (which also contains the permission bits and other flags). There are eight macros in <sys/stat.h> we can use to determine the file type, each of which takes the value of st_mode as its argument. Figure 10.2 summarizes these macros.

Macro	Type of file	Character
S_ISREG	Regular file	–
S_ISDIR	Directory	d
S_ISCHR	Character special file	c
S_ISBLK	Block special file	b
S_ISFIFO	FIFO	p
S_ISSOCK	Socket	s
S_ISLNK	Symbolic link	l
S_ISDOOR	Door	D

Figure 10.2 File type macros.

The Character column shows the character that appears in the first column of a file's entry when it is listed with ls -l.

By bitwise-ANDing the value of st_mode with S_IFMT (which is defined in <sys/stat.h>, we can isolate file type part of st_mode.

Example: File types

Program 10.2 loops through each of its command line arguments and prints the file types.

files_and_dirs/file_type.c

```
 1 #include <stdio.h>
 2 #include <sys/types.h>
 3 #include <sys/stat.h>
 4 #include "ssp.h"

 5 int main (int argc, char **argv)
 6 {
 7     struct stat buf;
 8     char *type;
 9     int i;

10     for (i = 1; i < argc; i++) {
11         if (lstat (argv [i], &buf) == -1) {
12             err_ret ("lstat failed: %s", argv [i]);
13             continue;
14         }
15         printf ("%s is a ", argv [i]);

16         if (S_ISREG (buf.st_mode))
17             type = "regular file";
18         if (S_ISDIR (buf.st_mode))
19             type = "directory";
20         if (S_ISCHR (buf.st_mode))
21             type = "character special file";
22         if (S_ISBLK (buf.st_mode))
23             type = "block special file";
24         if (S_ISFIFO (buf.st_mode))
25             type = "FIFO";
26         if (S_ISSOCK (buf.st_mode))
27             type = "socket";
28         if (S_ISLNK (buf.st_mode))
29             type = "symbolic link";
30 #ifdef S_ISDOOR
31         if (S_ISDOOR (buf.st_mode))
32             type = "door";
33 #endif

34         printf ("%s\n", type);
35     }

36     return (0);
37 }
```

files_and_dirs/file_type.c

Program 10.2 Print out the file type for each command line argument.

When we run Program 10.2 on a few files, these are the results we get:

```
$ ./file_type /etc/passwd /etc /devices/pseudo/mm@0:null \
> /devices/pci@1f,0/ide@d/sd@1,0:a /tmp/.X11-pipe/X0 \
> /tmp/.X11-unix/X0 /dev/null /var/run/syslog_door
/etc/passwd is a regular file
/etc is a directory
/devices/pseudo/mm@0:null is a character special file
/devices/pci@1f,0/ide@d/sd@1,0:a is a block special file
/tmp/.X11-pipe/X0 is a FIFO
/tmp/.X11-unix/X0 is a socket
/dev/null is a symbolic link
/var/run/syslog_door is a door
```

In this example, we have used the \ continuation character at the end of the first two lines. The shell responds by printing the > prompt on the next line, indicating that it is expecting more input.

Notice that Program 10.2 uses the lstat function to obtain the data. This is so that we can obtain information about symbolic links. If we used stat instead, we'd only be able to see the result for the file the link points to.

10.5   Set-User-ID and Set-Group-ID

As well as the file access permissions we discuss in Section 10.7, the st_mode field contains three extra flags. These are the set-user-ID (SUID), the set-group-ID (SGID), and the save-text bit (which is historically known as the sticky bit).

Every process has at least six IDs associated with it, in three categories. These are the real user and group IDs, the effective user and group IDs, and the saved set-user and set-group-IDs. The meaning of these is as follows:

- Real user ID. This is who we really are. In the case on an interactive session, it is the user who we logged in as. This normally doesn't change, but a privileged process can change it using one of the functions we describe in Section 7.3.

- Real group ID. This is the primary group associated with the real user ID. It is the group ID from the user's entry in the password database (e.g., /etc/passwd, NIS, LDAP, etc.). This normally doesn't change, but a privileged process can change it using one of the functions we describe in Section 7.4.

- Effective user ID. This is the user ID that is used for file access permission checks (see Section 10.7). It is usually the same as the real user ID.

- Effective group ID. This is the group ID that is used for file access permission checks. It is usually the same as the real group ID.

- Supplementary group IDs. These are the other groups the real user ID is a member of (recall Section 1.8), and are also used for file access permission checks.

- Saved set-user-ID. This is a copy of the effective user ID saved when a program is executed. We described saved set-user-IDs in Section 7.3 when we discussed the setuid function.

- Saved set-group-ID. This is a copy of the effective group ID saved when a program is executed.

Every file has an owner and group; these are stored in the `st_uid` and `st_gid` fields respectively. When a process starts running, the effective user and group IDs are usually the same as the real user and group IDs, but there exists a facility in Solaris that allows a process to assume another identity when it starts.

If the set-user-ID bit is set in `st_mode`, then the effective user ID of the process will become the same as the file's owner (the original effective user ID is preserved in the saved set-user-ID). Setting the set-group-ID bit in `st_mode` will cause the effective group ID of the process to become the same as the file's group (the original effective group ID is preserved in the saved set-group-ID). The set-user-ID and set-group-ID bits can be tested against the constants `S_ISUID` and `S_ISGID` respectively.

The set-user-ID and set-group-ID bits enable unprivileged users to perform privileged tasks in a controlled manner. For example, the password file, `/etc/passwd`, must be readable by everybody. Without the concept of a set-user-ID process, `/etc/passwd` would need write permission for everybody if users are to be allowed to change their own passwords. While it is not unreasonable for users to change their own passwords, allowing everyone to write to `/etc/passwd` is very bad from a security point of view. The solution to this problem is to make the password file writable by the superuser only, and make the password changing program (`/bin/passwd`) set-user-ID `root`. The program will then have the ability to write to the password file, even though the user wouldn't normally be able to.

A process running as another user has the same access permissions as that user, so care must be taken when we write a set-user-ID or set-group-ID program; if the program is to be set-user-ID `root`, extreme care should be taken. Chapter 9 contains some guidance on how to write secure C programs. Security should be a consideration for any program that we write; authors of set-user-ID and set-group-ID programs should be even more vigilant when it comes to writing secure programs.

The set-group-ID bit has another meaning if the group execute bit is not set; we'll look at this in Section 13.3, when we discuss discretionary and mandatory file locking.

If the set-group-ID (`S_ISGID`) bit in the `st_mode` for a directory is set, any files or directories created within that directory will have their group set to the group of the containing directory (if a directory is created within a directory with the set-group-ID set, the new directory will also have its set-group-ID bit set, thus propagating the group ownership down the directory hierarchy).

10.6 The Sticky Bit

The *sticky bit* is one of the flags stored in the `st_mode` member of a `stat` structure, in addition to the file's permissions and the set-user-ID and set-group-ID bits.

It's not unusual for contemporary computers to have hundreds of megabytes of memory, but in the early years of UNIX, computers didn't have the relatively huge amounts of memory that we now take for granted. Also, the virtual memory algorithms were not as sophisticated as they are today; whole processes were swapped in and out.

> The Digital Equipment Corporation (DEC) PDP–7 that the original version of UNIX was developed on had only about 16K 18-bit words. That's less than half the amount of on-chip cache of an UltraSPARC processor.

Historically, when the sticky bit was set for an executable file, a copy of the program's text (i.e., machine instructions) would be saved in the swap area the first time the program ran. This would allow subsequent invocations of the program to start faster because the swap area was treated as a contiguous file, as opposed to the potentially random placement of blocks in a normal file system. The sticky bit was often set for frequently used programs like the shell, the C compiler, and the text editor.

Of course, swap space is a finite resource, so there was a limit as to how many programs could have their sticky bit set. Nevertheless, it was a useful performance enhancing technique. The name "sticky bit" came into being because the program text stuck around in swap until the system was rebooted. Later versions of UNIX referred to it as the *save-text* bit, hence the `st_mode` bit mask constant is `S_ISVTX`.

Modern versions of UNIX, including Solaris, typically run on machines with much more memory, use more efficient file systems, and use more efficient virtual memory systems than the systems of yesteryear, so the need for this use of the sticky bit has all but disappeared.

With its original use obsolescent, the sticky bit now serves two new purposes. A file in a directory that has its sticky bit set may be deleted or renamed by only the user who owns the file or the user who owns the directory. In both cases, the user must have write permission to the directory. This is useful for directories such as `/tmp`, which must be writable by everyone, but should prevent users from arbitrarily deleting or renaming files owned by others.

The other use of the sticky bit is for data files (i.e., those that have no execute bits set). If the sticky bit is set for a data file, the system's page cache will not be used to hold the file's data. Also, inode updates for the file will be asynchronous [Cockcroft and Pettit 1998]. Mostly because of the latter, using the sticky bit on a data file should be approached with caution unless that file is a preallocated fixed size, like a swap file (or other file) created by `mkfile`(1).

Only privileged processes (i.e., those running as `root`) can set the sticky bit on a file, but any user can set the sticky bit on directories they own.

10.7   File Access Permissions

The `st_mode` field also contains the access permissions of a file. Every file (of every type) in Solaris has three sets of permissions for three categories of user associated with it. Each type of access can be specified separately for each category of user. The three type of user associated with a file are:

1. The user who owns the file. The owner of a file is stored in the `st_uid` field of the `stat` structure.

2. The group the file is a member of. The group of a file is stored in the st_gid field of the stat structure.

3. Other users. Any user who is not the owner of the file and is not a member of the file's group.

The chmod(1) command allows us to change the permission bits of a file, and refers to these categories as u, g, and o respectively. Some texts refer to these categories as owner, group, and world, but this is confusing because the chmod command uses o to refer to others, not owner. In this book, we'll use the terms user, group, and others to be consistent with the chmod command.

The three types of access allowed by each of the user categories are:

1. Read permission. For all file types, the contents of the file can be read. Read permission is required for an open that specifies the O_RDONLY or O_RDWR flags to the open function.

2. Write permission. For all file types except directories, this means that the contents of the file may be overwritten or appended to. Write access to a directory means that files may be created or deleted within that directory. No user, not even root, can directly write to a directory file; that privilege is reserved solely for the kernel. Write permission is required for an open that specifies the O_RDWR, O_TRUNC, or O_WRONLY flags to the open function.

> The original Solaris file deletion semantics were "if you own a file or can write to it, then you can remove it" (the BSD semantics were "if you own it, you can remove it"). The Solaris semantics have since been refined to "if you own it, or it's a regular file and you can write to it, then you can remove it". In other words, we can delete any regular file we can write to (regardless of the file's ownership), provided the permissions on the file's directory allow us to.

3. Execute permission. For regular files, the file may be executed (i.e., run). Obviously, it doesn't make sense to execute files that aren't compiled programs or scripts. Ordinary data files should not have any execute permission bits set. As well as potentially causing user confusion, a file with an execute bit set that is not a program will interfere with the virtual memory subsystem (which gives a higher priority to text and data pages associated with an executable than it does to pages associated with data files).

   For a directory, execute permission means that a process may search the directory. Search permission on a directory is required to access files (including subdirectories) within the directory. If a directory has read permission but not execute (search) permission, we can use the ls command to determine the existence of a file, but we will not be able to open it, regardless of the permissions on the file. On the other hand, if a directory has search permission but not read permission, we will only be able to cd into it or access files that we know the name of (if the file's permissions allow us to).

Nine constants defined in `<sys/stat.h>` can be used as masks to be bitwise-ANDed with the `st_mode` field to determine the permissions of a file. They are summarized in Figure 10.3.

st_mode mask	Meaning
S_IRUSR	Readable by user (owner)
S_IWUSR	Writable by user (owner)
S_IXUSR	Executable by user (owner)
S_IRGRP	Readable by group
S_IWGRP	Writable by group
S_IXGRP	Executable by group
S_IROTH	Readable by others
S_IWOTH	Writable by others
S_IXOTH	Executable by others

Figure 10.3 Masks to determine file access permissions.

By bitwise-ANDing the value of `st_mode` with `S_IAMB` (which is defined in `<sys/stat.h>`, we can isolate the file access permission part of `st_mode`. Three other masks defined in `<sys/stat.h>` can be used to extract all of the bits associated with a given category of user. These masks are summarized in Figure 10.4.

st_mode mask	Meaning
S_IAMB	Access mode bits
S_IRWXU	Read, write, and execute by user (owner)
S_IRWXG	Read, write, and execute by group
S_IRWXO	Read, write, and execute by others

Figure 10.4 Other file access permission masks.

When we attempt to open a file, the kernel performs a series of checks to ensure that we have permission to access the file in the manner that we request. For the purpose of these access checks, the effective user and group IDs of the process opening the file are compared with the `st_uid` and `st_gid` fields of the file and all directories in the name of the file, including the current directory whether or not it is explicitly mentioned.

For example, if we want to open the file `/etc/default/passwd` for reading, we would need execute (i.e., search) permission for the `/`, `/etc`, and `/etc/default` directories, as well as read permission on the actual `passwd` file . If `/etc/default` is the current directory when we try to open the `passwd` file for reading, just the execute permission of the current directory (i.e., `/etc/default`) would be checked in addition to read permission for the `passwd` file.

Several steps make up the actual permission checking algorithm:

1. If the effective user ID is 0, the requested access is granted (unless the file is a directory, in which case only read-only opens will be allowed).

2. If the effective user ID of the process is the same as the file's owner, then if the file's user permission bits allow the access requested, the request is allowed; otherwise, the request is denied.

3. If the effective group ID of the process (or one of the supplementary group IDs of the owner of the process) is the same as the file's group ID, then if the file's group permission bits allow the access requested, the request is allowed; otherwise, the request is denied.

4. If the file's other permission bits allow the access requested, the request is allowed; otherwise, the request is denied.

These four steps are tried in sequence, and checking stops after the first success or failure. In other words, if the effective user ID of the process is the same as the file's owner, and the user permission bits deny the requested access, the group and other bits are not tested. Similarly, if the user IDs are not the same, but the file's group matches the effective group ID (or one of the supplementary group IDs) of the process, then only the group permission bits will be used to allow or deny access.

10.8 The access Function

The access function is used to determine the accessibility of a file.

```
#include <unistd.h>

int access (const char *path, int amode);
```
Returns: 0 if access is permitted, −1 on error

The access function checks the file pointed to by *path* for accessibility according to the mode contained in *amode*. Normal file access checks are based on the effective user and group IDs, but the checks performed by the access function use the real user and group IDs. This allows a set-user-ID or set-group-ID process to determine whether the user running the program would have permission to access *path*.

> We should add, however, that using access in this manner is perhaps of limited utility. This is because it is possible that the file's permissions could change between the access check and the time the file is actually opened. If it is important for our applications to open only files that the real user ID or group ID has permissions to, we should call open with the effective user and group IDs set to those that we would have called access with.
>
> In other words, the access function tells us whether we *could* open a file, not whether the open will actually succeed.

The *amode* argument contains the type of access requested, which should either be the bitwise-OR of the access permissions to be checked (i.e., R_OK, W_OK, or X_OK), or the existence test, F_OK.

The meaning of these constants is as follows:

R_OK   Test for read permission.

W_OK   Test for write permission.

X_OK   Test for execute (search) permission.

F_OK   Test for the existence of *path*.

If any access permissions are to be checked, each is checked individually as described in the previous section.

Example: Using the `access` function

Program 10.3 demonstrates the use of the `access` function by first determining if the file given on the command line can be accessed read-only. An attempt is then made to open the same file in read-only mode.

————————————————————————— files_and_dirs/access.c

```
 1 #include <stdio.h>
 2 #include <fcntl.h>
 3 #include <sys/types.h>
 4 #include <sys/stat.h>
 5 #include <unistd.h>
 6 #include "ssp.h"

 7 int main (int argc, char **argv)
 8 {
 9     int fd;

10     if (argc != 2)
11         err_quit ("Usage: access filename");

12     if ((access (argv [1], R_OK)) == 0)
13         printf ("Read access OK\n");
14     else
15         err_ret ("Read access denied");

16     if ((fd = open (argv [1], O_RDONLY)) == -1)
17         err_ret ("Read only open failed");
18     else {
19         printf ("Read only open OK\n");
20         close (fd);
21     }

22     return (0);
23 }
```

————————————————————————— files_and_dirs/access.c

Program 10.3 Demonstrating the `access` function.

Let's see what happens when we run Program 10.3 against a couple of files.

```
$ ls -l access
-rwxr-xr-x   1 rich      staff       9280 Nov 23 10:13 access
$ ./access access
Read access OK
Read only open OK
```

```
$ ls -l /etc/shadow
-r--------   1 root      sys           381 Sep 26 11:30 /etc/shadow
$ ./access /etc/shadow
Read access denied: Permission denied
Read only open failed: Permission denied
$ su
Password:                              Become root
# chown root access                    Change the file's user to root
# chmod u+s access                     Set the SUID bit
# exit                                 Revert to our own user
$ ls -l access                         Check new permissions on our program
-rwsr-xr-x   1 root      staff        9280 Nov 23 10:13 access
$ ./access /etc/shadow
Read access denied: Permission denied
Read only open OK
```

In this example, we see that the access function indicates that our user does not have permission to open the file, even though the open succeeds in the set-user-ID root version of the program.

10.9   The umask Function

In Section 4.3 we said that the permission bits requested for a newly created file are modified by the umask value of the process. (We'll show how to create a directory in Section 10.22.) The umask of a process is a security feature that allows users to specify which permission bits are automatically cleared when a file is created.

```
#include <sys/types.h>
#include <sys/stat.h>

mode_t umask (mode_t cmask);
```
                                                      Returns: the previous umask value

The umask function sets the file creation mask for the process and returns the previous value of the mask. The mask, *cmask*, is created by bitwise-ORing one or more of the constants in Figure 10.3 together (e.g., S_IRUSR, S_IWUSR, etc.). A bit that is *set* in the umask of a process will be *cleared* in the file's mode when it is created.

Example: Using the umask function

Program 10.4 creates two files using two different file creation masks. The mode for each file is the same: read and write permission for the file's owner, the file's group, and others.

Running Program 10.4 gives us the following results:

```
$ umask                                Print our current file creation mask
022
$ ./umask
```

files_and_dirs/umask.c

```
 1 #include <sys/types.h>
 2 #include <sys/stat.h>
 3 #include <fcntl.h>
 4 #include "ssp.h"

 5 #define MASK (S_IRUSR | S_IWUSR | S_IRGRP | S_IWGRP | S_IROTH | S_IWOTH)

 6 int main (void)
 7 {
 8     umask (0);
 9     if (creat ("foo", MASK) == -1)
10         err_ret ("Creation of foo failed");

11     umask (S_IRGRP | S_IWGRP | S_IROTH | S_IWOTH);
12     if (creat ("bar", MASK) == -1)
13         err_ret ("Creation of bar failed");

14     return (0);
15 }
```

files_and_dirs/umask.c

Program 10.4   Using the umask function.

```
$ ls -l foo bar
-rw-------   1 rich      staff          0 Nov 26 16:32 bar
-rw-rw-rw-   1 rich      staff          0 Nov 26 16:32 foo
$ umask                             Check that our file creation mask hasn't changed
022
```

The first file, foo, is created with a umask of 0; no bits are set, which means that none are cleared when the file is created. The second file, bar, is created with umask set to a value that disallows reading and writing for the file's group and others.

The umask command and function are infrequently dealt with by most Solaris users. It is usually set to some value by the shell's start-up file when we log in, and doesn't change.

10.10 The chmod and fchmod Functions

We've shown how to set the file permissions of a file when we create it, but what if we want to change the permissions of a file that already exists? Fortunately, the chmod and fchmod functions fill this niche for us.

```
#include <sys/types.h>
#include <sys/stat.h>

int chmod (const char *path, mode_t mode);

int fchmod (int fildes, mode_t mode);
```

Both return: 0 if OK, −1 on error

The chmod function sets the permission bits of the file pointed to by *path* to those specified by *mode*; similarly, the fchmod function allows us to change the permission bits of a file we have already opened.

The new permissions are specified by bitwise-ORing one or more of the constants in Figure 10.5 together.

mode	Description
S_ISUID	Set-user-ID on execution
S_ISGID	Set-group-ID on execution
S_ISVTX	Sticky bit (save-text bit)
S_IRWXU	Read, write, and execute by user (owner)
S_IRUSR	Readable by user (owner)
S_IWUSR	Writable by user (owner)
S_IXUSR	Executable by user (owner)
S_IRWXG	Read, write, and execute by group
S_IRGRP	Readable by group
S_IWGRP	Writable by group
S_IXGRP	Executable by group
S_IRWXO	Read, write, and execute by others
S_IROTH	Readable by others
S_IWOTH	Writable by others
S_IXOTH	Executable by others

Figure 10.5 Masks to determine file access permissions.

Only processes whose effective user ID is the same as the owner of the file may change the permissions on that file (the superuser is of course exempt from this rule).

Two other rules are enforced:

1. If an unprivileged process tries to set the sticky bit of an ordinary file, the S_ISVTX bit of *mode* will be ignored. Only the superuser can set the sticky bit of an ordinary file.

2. As we mentioned in Section 10.5, if the set-group-ID (S_ISGID) bit is set on a directory, any files or directories created within that directory will have their group set to the group of the containing directory. This means that it is possible for a process to create a file whose group is not one of the primary or supplementary group IDs of the owner. For this reason, an unprivileged process cannot set the set-group-ID bit of a file if the effective group ID of the process, or one of its supplementary group IDs, does not match that of the file. This prevents a user from creating a set-group-ID file owned by a group the user isn't a member of.

Example: Using the `chmod` function

Program 10.5 illustrates the use of the chmod function using the files from the previous example.

————————————————————————————— files_and_dirs/chmod.c

```
1 #include <sys/types.h>
2 #include <sys/stat.h>
3 #include "ssp.h"

4 int main (void)
5 {
6     struct stat buf;

7     if (stat ("foo", &buf) == -1)
8         err_ret ("Stat failed");

9     if (chmod ("foo", (buf.st_mode & ~(S_IWGRP | S_IWOTH)) | S_IXUSR) == -1)
10        err_ret ("Chmod failed for foo");

11    if (chmod ("bar", S_IRUSR | S_IWUSR | S_IRGRP | S_IROTH) == -1)
12        err_ret ("Chmod failed for bar");

13    return (0);
14 }
```

————————————————————————————— files_and_dirs/chmod.c

Program 10.5 Using the chmod function.

Running Program 10.5 on the two files from the previous example gives the following results:

```
$ ls -l foo bar
-rw-------   1 rich      staff         0 Nov 26 16:32 bar
-rw-rw-rw-   1 rich      staff         0 Nov 26 16:32 foo
$ ./chmod
$ ls -l foo bar
-rw-r--r--   1 rich      staff         0 Nov 26 16:32 bar
-rwxr--r--   1 rich      staff         0 Nov 26 16:32 foo
```

For the first file, `foo`, we modify the existing permissions by calling the `stat` function first to determine what the current permissions are, and then set or clear the bits we want to modify. In this example, we set the user execute bit (`S_IXUSR`) and clear the group and other write bits (`S_IWGRP` and `S_IWOTH`). We set the permissions for the second file, `bar`, absolutely, disregarding the current permissions. Notice that the time stamp for the files remained the same. This is because we didn't change the file's contents, only its associated inode, and the `ls -l` command we use shows the last file modification time. If we want to see the last time a file's inode was updated, we would have to pass the `-c` flag to `ls`, e.g., `ls -lc`. (We'll see in Section 10.21 how to examine the various times associated with a file and see which functions affect them.)

10.11 The `chown`, `fchown`, and `lchown` Functions

We can change the owner or group membership of a file by using one of the `chown` functions.

```
#include <unistd.h>
#include <sys/types.h>

int chown (const char *path, uid_t owner, gid_t group);

int lchown (const char *path, uid_t owner, gid_t group);

int fchown (int fildes, uid_t owner, gid_t group);
```

All three return: 0 if OK, −1 on error

The `chown` function sets the user and group IDs of file specified by *path* to *owner* and *group* respectively. If either *owner* or *group* is set to −1, the corresponding ID is not changed.

The `lchown` function performs the same task, except that if *path* refers to a symbolic link, the ownership of the link itself is changed rather than the file the link points to.

Finally, the `fchown` function allows us to change the ownership of a file we have previously opened. In this case, *fildes* is the file descriptor of the open file.

POSIX allows a configuration variable, `_POSIX_CHOWN_RESTRICTED`, to restrict file ownership changes. A kernel variable, `rstchown`, determines whether this is in effect. By default, `rstchown` is 1, enabling `_POSIX_CHOWN_RESTRICTED`. This means that only the superuser can change file ownerships, and non-`root` users can only change a file's group membership to either the effective group ID of the process, or one of the user's supplementary groups, if they own the file.

If `_POSIX_CHOWN_RESTRICTED` is not in effect, any user can change file ownerships of any file they own (but note that this provides a way to defeat file system quotas). To disable `_POSIX_CHOWN_RESTRICTED`, add the following line to `/etc/system`:

```
set rstchown = 0
```

A reboot is required for this to take effect. We can interrogate the value of `_POSIX_CHOWN_RESTRICTED` by using the `pathconf` or `fpathconf` functions we describe in Section 8.3.

If the `chown` functions are called by an unprivileged process, a successful return will clear both the set-user-ID and set-group-ID bits.

10.12 File Size

For regular files, directories, and symbolic links, the `st_size` field of the `stat` structure contains the size of a file in bytes. For a pipe (FIFO), it contains the number of bytes available for reading. For other file types, the value of `st_size` is undefined.

Strictly speaking, the st_size of an ordinary file is not necessarily the same as the number of bytes in the file, because the file might be sparse (see the next section). In the case of a sparse file, we can say that the st_size of a regular file is the address of the end of the file; for a file that is not sparse, this is the same as the number of bytes in the file. A file length of 0 is allowed; any reads from the file will immediately indicate end of file.

The size of a directory file depends on the number of directory entries in the directory and the type of file system that contains the directory. The size of a directory on a UFS file system is always an integral multiple of 512 bytes. We talk about reading directories in Section 10.23.

The st_size of a symbolic link is the number of characters in the name of the file the link points to, *without* a terminating NUL. For example, /bin is a symbolic link to /usr/bin:

```
$ ls -l /bin
lrwxrwxrwx   1 root      root          9 Sep 26 11:04 /bin -> ./usr/bin
```

The size of the link is 9 bytes, which is exactly the number of characters in "./usr/bin".

Related to the size of a file is the st_blocks field, which is a count of how many 512-byte disk blocks are actually allocated to the file. A sparse file that appears to be huge may take up only a few disk blocks.

The st_blksize field is the preferred size of I/O blocks (recall Section 4.11 when we experimented with different sized I/O blocks). The standard I/O library tries to perform I/O in st_blksize chunks for maximum efficiency.

Sparse Files

We saw in Section 4.6 how to create a sparse file: seek beyond the end of the file and write some data, thus creating a hole. Consider the following, where we used a variation of Program 4.1 to create a sparse file. We use the du(1) command to display the number of blocks occupied by the file.

```
$ ls -l sparse_file
-rw-r--r--   1 rich      staff    1012912 Nov 27 21:14 sparse_file
$ du sparse_file
48       sparse_file
```

Although the file is just under a megabyte in size (1012912 bytes), it occupies only 48 512-byte blocks for a total disk usage of 24576 bytes. It clearly contains one or more holes.

We also said that when a hole is read, data bytes equal to 0 are returned. We can illustrate this by using the wc -c command to count the number of characters (bytes) in the file:

```
$ wc -c sparse_file
1012912 sparse_file
```

If we make a copy of the file, for example, using the `cp` command, the 0 bytes read are written out to the file:

```
$ cp sparse_file sparse_file.copy
$ du sparse_file*
48        sparse_file
2000      sparse_file.copy
$ ls -l sparse_file*
-rw-r--r--    1 rich      staff      1012912 Nov 27 21:14 sparse_file
-rw-r--r--    1 rich      staff      1012912 Nov 27 21:24 sparse_file.copy
```

After the copy, the files appear to be the same size, but the copy occupies many more disk blocks than the original. The copy occupies 1024000 bytes (2000 * 512); the difference between the actual size of the file, and the number of the bytes occupied by the disk blocks (in this case, 11088 bytes) results from the overhead of storing files in a file system. Readers interested in the gory details of the UFS implementation for Solaris are encouraged to read Chapter 14 of [Mauro and McDougall 2001].

> As an aside, sparse files are one of the reasons why `ufsdump` and `ufsrestore` should be used to backup and restore UFS file systems in preference to commands like `tar` and `cpio`. The problem with `tar` and `cpio` is that they are not sparse-file aware: they backup and restore files using the `read` and `write` functions, which fill holes with 0 bytes. Commands like `ufsdump` and `ufsrestore` interact directly with the data structures that make up a file system. The lack of sparse-file support is a common cause for backups created using `tar` etc. to run out of disk space when they are restored. Most, if not all, commercial backup utilities are sparse-file aware.
>
> GNU `tar` and `star` are apparently sparse-file aware, but we still recommend the use of `ufsdump` and `ufsrestore`.

10.13 File Truncation

Sometimes we want to truncate a file to a certain length. Truncating a file to 0 bytes (i.e., emptying it) by passing the `O_TRUNC` flag to `open` is a special case of file truncation.

```
#include <unistd.h>

int truncate (const char *path, off_t length);

int ftruncate (int fildes, off_t length);
```
Both return: 0 if OK, −1 on error

The `truncate` function causes the regular file *path* to have a size of *length* bytes. If the file was originally larger than *length*, the extra bytes are lost. If the file was originally smaller than *length*, then a hole will be created in the file to fill the gap between the original length and the new length.

The `ftruncate` function is similar, except that the previously opened file referenced by the file descriptor *fildes* will have its size set to *length* bytes.

10.14 File Systems

Before we can discuss the concept of links, we should have a basic understanding of file system structure. It is also useful to be able to distinguish between an inode, and a directory entry that references an inode.

As we mentioned in Chapter 1, Solaris supports several different types of file system. For the purposes of this discussion, we will confine ourselves to the most common Solaris disk-based file system, UFS. The UFS file system is derived from the Berkeley Fast File System (FFS), although it has had many enhancements over the years (refer to Chapter 7 of [Leffler et al. 1989] for details of the FFS).

Consider a hard drive, which consists of one or more logical slices, as illustrated in Figure 10.6.

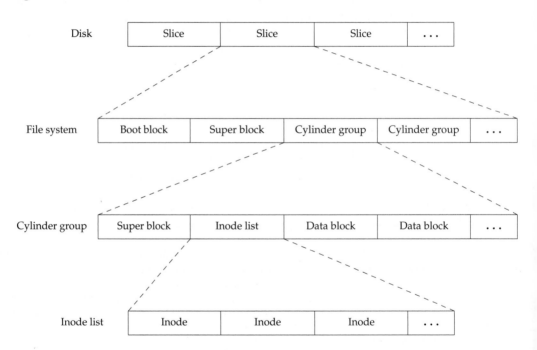

Figure 10.6 Logical layout of file systems, cylinder groups, and inode lists.

Each slice is either raw (i.e., does not have a file system on it), or has a file system on it. Raw slices are used for either spare capacity or database tables.

> The term "partition" is sometimes used as a synonym for slice. While this is fine for everyday conversation, it can cause some confusion. Multiboot PCs with a single hard drive divide the available disk space among the various OSes by partitioning the drive: e.g., a Linux partition and a Solaris partition. These partitions may then be subdivided into slices in an OS-specific manner. For example, a Solaris partition might have /, swap, and /export/home slices.

At the start of every file system is the boot block. The *boot block* is a spare sector reserved for the boot program when the slice is used as a root file system. When the system boots, the boot firmware loads the first sector from the boot device and then executes the code in that block. The boot firmware is file-system-independent, so it has no knowledge about the file system. The code in the file system boot block mounts the root file system. The boot program then passes control to a larger kernel loader, /platform/`uname -m`/ufsboot, which loads the Solaris kernel. (In this pathname, we used the shell "back tick" expression to mean that the output of the command (in this case, uname -m) should replace the back ticks and everything between them. On a sun4u architecture machine, this would expand to /platform/sun4u/ufsboot.)

Immediately after the boot block is the superblock. The *superblock* contains information about the geometry and layout of the file system, and is critical to the file system state. Because of this, a copy of the superblock is stored in each cylinder group of the file system, so that the file system will not be unusable should the superblock become corrupted. The superblock contains a variety of information, including the following:

- The offset of the first cylinder block in the file system
- The offset of the first inode block in the file system
- The offset of the first data block after the first cylinder group
- The number of blocks in the file system
- The last time the superblock was modified
- A magic number (Bill Joy's birthday), to validate the superblock

The file system configuration parameters are also stored in the superblock. The file system parameters are configured when the file system is constructed, and may be changed later by using the tunefs command.

> In the BUGS section of the original BSD version of the tunefs man page, the following humorous quotation appears: "You can tune a file system, but you can't tune a fish". The [nt]roff source code for the SunOS 4.1.1 version of the tunefs man page contains a comment warning against removing the joke: "Take this out and a UNIX Daemon will dog your steps from now until the time_t's wrap around". Unfortunately, both the joke and the comment were removed from the Solaris and SVR4 versions of the man page.

Some of the file system parameters are:

- The minimum percentage of free blocks
- The number of disk revolutions per second
- The optimization preference: space or time
- The maximum number of data blocks per cylinder group

The data blocks in Figure 10.6 can be classified into three categories:

1. Directory blocks. These are blocks used to hold directory entries. For optimum performance, the file system tries to keep all the directory blocks for a given directory together.

2. Data blocks. Data blocks are the blocks allocated to files (other than directories) in the file system. Again for performance reasons, the file system tries to keep up to a configurable number of blocks in the same cylinder group, preferably in contiguous blocks.

3. Free blocks. These are the blocks in the file system that are not currently allocated to a directory or file. When a file's link count reaches zero and all file descriptors that reference the file have been closed, the file's blocks are added to the list of free blocks.

In Section 1.4 we stated that a directory file contains a list of directory entries, each entry being the name of the file, and the inode associated with it. Figure 10.7 illustrates this in the context of a file system (for the sake of simplicity, we have assumed that all the elements we show in Figure 10.7 are in the same cylinder group, but this needn't be the case in a real file system).

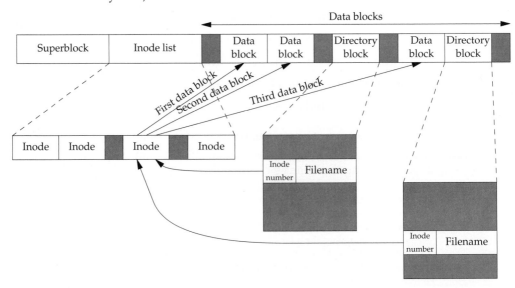

Figure 10.7   File system in more detail.

With reference to Figure 10.7, we can make several observations.

- We have shown two directory entries that point to the same inode. One of the pieces of information stored by every inode is the number of links to the inode. When a directory entry that points to an inode is created, its link count is incremented; similarly, the link count is decremented when a directory entry that points to the inode is removed. The disk blocks for a file are only added to the list of free blocks when the number of links in the file's inode equals zero. It's for this reason that the function to delete a file is called unlink instead of remove or delete. In the stat structure, st_nlink is the name of the member that contains the link count for a file. The type of link that causes a file's st_nlink to increase is called a *hard link*, and is indistinguishable from another hard link to the same file. A file can have at most LINK_MAX (defined in <limits.h>) links to it.

- As we mentioned previously, the other type of link is a soft, or symbolic, link. A symbolic link is marked as such in its inode (its st_mode field is set to S_IFLNK); the file contains the name of the file the link points to.

- All the information about a file (the file's owner, its permissions, the number of links, etc.) is stored in its inode, whereas a file's directory entry contains only its name and its inode number (strictly speaking, there are other fields in a directory entry, but they are used internally and have no effect on this discussion).

- The inode number in a directory entry refers to an inode within the current file system. For this reason, hard links to files can't span file systems; a symbolic link must be used instead.

- Because a file's directory entry points to an inode in the same file system, moving (renaming) a file within a file system just requires the old directory entry to be deleted, and the new one created pointing to the same inode; no data needs to be copied. The file's data needs to be copied only if renaming it places it on to a different file system (this is exactly how the mv command works).

The reference count for directories works in a similar manner, counting the number of directory entries that refer to the directory in question. A directory always has a reference count of at least two: the directory's directory entry in its parent, and the file "." (*dot*) that refers to the current directory (recall Section 1.4, where we said that when a directory is created, the first two directory entries, *dot* and *dot-dot*, are automatically created).

Every subdirectory created in a directory causes its reference count to increment, so a directory containing one subdirectory will have a reference count of three. Figure 10.8 illustrates this after we have created a test directory, called testdir.

The directory block to the right of the inode list in Figure 10.8 is the one for the newly created directory, and the directory block to *its* right is the one for testdir's parent.

10.15 The link and unlink Functions

We can use the link function to create a link to a pre-existing file.

```
#include <unistd.h>

int link (const char *existing, const char *new);
```
                                                                Returns: 0 if OK, −1 on error

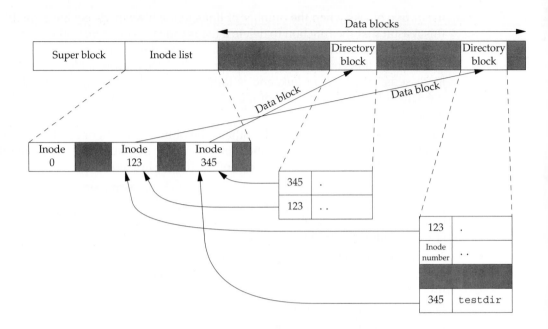

Figure 10.8   File system detail after creating a test directory.

The `link` function creates a new link (directory entry) to the existing file, *existing*. If the creation of the link is successful, the new link will be known by the pathname pointed to by *new*, and the link count of the existing file will be incremented by one. The creation of the directory entry and the incrementing of the inode's link count happen atomically.

Both the existing file and the new link must be on the same file system, and only the superuser can create a link to a directory. The latter restriction is to help prevent loops in a file system, because many utilities that manipulate file systems aren't capable of handling them.

We can use the `unlink` function to remove a link to a file.

```
#include <unistd.h>

int unlink (const char *path);
```
Returns: 0 if OK, −1 on error

The `unlink` function is used to remove a link to the file pointed to by *path*. If *path* is a symbolic link, `unlink` removes the actual symbolic link rather than the file the symbolic link points to.

If the link is successfully removed, the inode's reference count is decremented. As with the `link` function, adjusting the link count and removing the directory entry is an atomic operation.

The data blocks associated with a file are not freed until the file's reference count reaches zero; if the file's reference count falls to zero while a process is using it, the entry in the file system will be removed, but the data blocks associated with the file will not be freed until the last process that references the file exits.

If the superuser uses `unlink` to remove a directory, the directory is unlinked from its parent with no clean-up being performed, even if the directory is not empty (other methods of removing a directory ensure that it is empty before permitting the removal). The disconnected directory will be found the next time the file system is checked with the `fsck` command. The `rmdir` function we discuss in Section 10.22 is the preferred method of removing a directory.

Example: Unlinking a file

Program 10.6 demonstrates the use of `unlink` to remove a file. The temporary file is unlinked, then Program 10.6 goes to sleep for 10 seconds to give us time to run a couple of commands. When the 10 seconds are over, the program exits; it's at this point that the blocks allocated to the file are returned to the free list for the file system.

—————————————————————————————— files_and_dirs/unlink.c
```
 1 #include <stdio.h>
 2 #include <unistd.h>
 3 #include <sys/types.h>
 4 #include <sys/stat.h>
 5 #include <fcntl.h>
 6 #include "ssp.h"

 7 int main (void)
 8 {
 9     int fd;

10     if ((fd = open ("/tmp/test_file", O_RDONLY)) == -1)
11         err_msg ("Can't open test_file");

12     unlink ("/tmp/test_file");

13     sleep (10);

14     printf ("Finished\n");
15     close (fd);

16     return (0);
17 }
```
—————————————————————————————— files_and_dirs/unlink.c

Program 10.6 Unlinking a file.

When we run Program 10.6, this is what we get.
```
$ mkfile 10m /tmp/test_file              Create the temporary file
$ ls -l /tmp/test_file                   Verify the file's existence
-rw-------   1 rich     staff    10485760 Dec 11 15:56 /tmp/test_file
$ du -k /tmp/test_file                   ... and see how many blocks it uses
10240   /tmp/test_file
$ df -k /tmp                             See how many disk blocks are used
Filesystem            kbytes   used   avail capacity  Mounted on
swap                  688448   10584  677864    2%    /tmp
```

```
$ ./unlink &                           Run our program in the background
[1]     7686                           The shell prints out the job and PIDs of our process
$ ls -l /tmp/test_file                 See if the file is still there
/tmp/test_file: No such file or directory
$ df -k /tmp                           See how many disk blocks are used
Filesystem            kbytes    used   avail capacity  Mounted on
swap                  688448   10584  677864     2%    /tmp
$ Finished                             Our program has finished

[1] +  Done                    ./unlink &
$ df -k /tmp                           Confirm that the file's blocks have been freed
Filesystem            kbytes    used   avail capacity  Mounted on
swap                  688416     344  688072     1%    /tmp
```

Notice that even though the file is removed, `df` shows that the blocks are still allocated to the file. Only when Program 10.6 exits are the blocks actually freed. We can confirm this by looking at the "used" column of the `df` output: the difference between the figures before and after the "Finished" message is 10240, which is the number of 1 KB blocks the file occupied (as shown by using the `du` command).

This technique is often used by programs that want to ensure that a temporary file will be removed when the process exits. The file is created using `open` or `creat`, and then immediately unlinked. Because the file is still open, it is not deleted. Only when the file is closed (by the process calling `close`, or by the process terminating) are the blocks allocated to it freed. (The kernel closes all of a process' open files when the process exits.)

10.16 The `remove` and `rename` Functions

The `remove` function can be used to delete a file or directory.

```
#include <stdio.h>

int remove (const char *path);
```
                                                            Returns: 0 if OK, −1 on error

The `remove` function causes the file or empty directory whose name is pointed to by *path* to no longer be accessible by that name.

For files, `remove` is identical to `unlink`; for directories, it is the same as `rmdir`.

> The `remove` function was introduced with ISO C, because many of the platforms that support ISO C don't support the concept of files with multiple links to them.

The `rename` function allows us to change the name of a file.

```
#include <stdio.h>

int rename (const char *old, const char *new);
```
                                                            Returns: 0 if OK, −1 on error

The `rename` function changes the name of the file pointed to by *old* to the new name specified by *new*. There are a couple of scenarios to consider:

1. The *old* pathname refers to a file that is not a directory. In this case, the *new* file must also not be the name of a directory. If the link named by *new* exists, it will be removed and the *old* file will be renamed to *new*. The *new* pathname will remain accessible by other processes throughout the renaming operation, although the contents of the file are indeterminate while the rename operation is in progress (the file will contain either the contents of *new*, or the contents of *old* before the operation began). Write permission is required for the directories that contain *old* and *new*, as both directories must be updated.

2. If the *old* pathname refers to a directory, the the *new* pathname either must not exist, or must be an empty directory. If *new* does refer to an empty directory (i.e., one that only contains entries for *dot* and *dot-dot*), it will be removed before the rename occurs, although as with regular files, other processes will be able to refer to the *new* pathname at all times. Also, the *new* pathname must not contain a path prefix that names *old*. This means that we can't, for example, rename `/home/rich/docs` to `/home/rich/docs/old` because `/home/rich/docs` is a path prefix of `/home/rich/docs/old`, and can't be deleted.

As a special case, if *old* and *new* refer to the same existing file, `rename` does nothing except return successfully.

If the directory containing *old* has the sticky bit set, at least one of the following conditions must be true for the `rename` to succeed:

- The user must own *old*.
- The user must own the directory containing *old*.
- The *old* file must be writable by the user.
- The user is the superuser (i.e., `root`).

If *new* exists and the directory containing *new* is writable and has its sticky bit set, at least one of the following conditions must be true for the `rename` to succeed:

- The user must own *new*.
- The user must own the directory containing *new*.
- The *new* file must be writable by the user.
- The user is the superuser.

Both *old* and *new* must reside on the same file system.

10.17 Symbolic Links

Unlike the hard links we discussed in the previous sections, a *symbolic link* is a file that contains a pointer to another file. The contents of the symbolic link file is the pathname of the file being linked to; the file system code knows that a file is a symbolic link (rather than just an ordinary file that happens to contain a pathname) because the S_IFLNK flag in the st_mode member of the file's inode will be set. Symbolic links were introduced to get around some of the limitations of hard links. First, there are no file system restrictions on symbolic links, i.e., a symbolic link can refer to a file on another file system, unlike hard links, which must link to files on the same file system. Second, any user can create a symbolic link to a directory; the creation of hard links to directories is restricted to superusers only.

When we use functions that refer to files by name, we need to know which functions follow symbolic links and which ones don't. Functions that follow symbolic links will refer to the file the link points to, whereas those that don't will refer to the link itself. (When we talk about symbolic links being followed or not, we are specifically referring to symbolic links that are the last component of a pathname; symbolic links that are not the last component of a pathname are always followed.) Figure 10.9 lists some of the functions (discussed in this and other chapters) that take a pathname as an argument and shows those that follow symbolic links. The rmdir function is not shown, because it returns an error if passed a pathname that is a symbolic link.

Function	Follows symbolic links
access	•
chdir	•
chmod	•
chown	•
creat	•
exec	•
lchown	
link	•
lstat	
mkdir	
mkfifo	•
mknod	
open	•
opendir	•
pathconf	•
readlink	•
remove	
rename	
stat	•
truncate	•
unlink	

Figure 10.9 How symbolic links are handled by various functions.

Although we show link as following symbolic links, the behaviour is actually dependent on which version of the link function we use. The version of link that complies with the SUS standards does follow symbolic links, but the default Solaris version of link doesn't.

If, when we open a file, the pathname passed to open is a symbolic link, the link is followed, and an open of the file the link refers to is attempted (unless the O_EXCL and

O_CREAT flags are specified, in which case the symbolic link will not be followed, and open will return an error). If the file the link points to can't be opened, open returns an error. This can confuse users who are not used to the concept of symbolic links. For example:

```
$ ln -s /no/such/file example          Create a symbolic link
$ ls example
example                                 ls says it's there,
$ cat example                           so try looking at it
cat: cannot open example
$ ls -l example                         Try the -o option
lrwxrwxrwx   1 rich     staff           15 Dec 19 18:18 example -> /no/such/file
```

Two items in the output of ls -l (or ls -o) indicate that the file example is a symbolic link: the l as the first character of the permissions field (which indicates the file type), and the -> /no/such/file following the filename. The name after the arrow is the pathname of the file the symbolic link points to. Another way of determining if a file is a symbolic link is to use the -F flag of the ls command, which appends an "at" sign (@) to the name of a symbolic link:

```
$ ls -F example
example@
```

When we talked about the link function, we mentioned that it is possible to create loops in a file system. We can also create loops using symbolic links. Most functions detect loops created by symbolic links, and set errno to ELOOP when this happens. Consider the following sequence of commands:

```
$ mkdir foo
$ touch foo/bar
$ ln -s ../foo foo/baz
$ ls -l foo
total 48
-rw-r--r--   1 rich     staff           0 Dec 21 15:53 bar
lrwxrwxrwx   1 rich     staff           6 Dec 21 15:53 baz -> ../foo
```

This makes a new directory called foo in the current directory, creates an empty file called bar in that directory, and then creates a symbolic link called baz that points to foo.

Program 10.7 uses the ftw function we discuss in Section 10.23 to recursively list all the files in the given directory.

When we run Program 10.7, these are the results we get:

```
$ ./ftw foo
foo
foo/bar
foo/baz
foo/baz/bar
foo/baz/baz
foo/baz/baz/bar
foo/baz/baz/baz
foo/baz/baz/baz/bar
foo/baz/baz/baz/baz
...                                     Many lines cut
foo/baz/baz/baz/baz/baz/baz/baz/baz/baz/baz/baz/.../baz/baz/baz
```

————————————————————————————————————— files_and_dirs/ftw.c

```
 1 #include <stdio.h>
 2 #include <ftw.h>
 3 #include <sys/types.h>
 4 #include <sys/stat.h>
 5 #include "ssp.h"

 6 static int print (const char *name, const struct stat *stat_buf, int flags);

 7 int main (int argc, char **argv)
 8 {
 9     if (ftw (argv [1], print, 64) != 0)
10         err_msg ("ftw failed");

11     return (0);
12 }

13 static int print (const char *name, const struct stat *stat_buf, int flags)
14 {
15     printf ("%s\n", name);

16     return (0);
17 }
```

————————————————————————————————————— files_and_dirs/ftw.c

Program 10.7 Recursively list all the files in a directory.

Rather than getting stuck in an infinite recursion loop or terminating with an error, Program 10.7 stops after displaying 43 lines. To find out why, we can use the `truss` program to monitor the system calls our program makes:

```
$ truss ./ftw foo
execve("ftw", 0xFFBEF28C, 0xFFBEF298)  argc = 2
mmap(0x00000000, 8192, ..., -1, 0) = 0xFF3A0000
...                                 Several lines cut
stat("foo", 0xFFBEF100)                  = 0
open64("foo", O_RDONLY|O_NDELAY)         = 3
fcntl(3, F_SETFD, 0x00000001)            = 0
fstat64(3, 0xFFBEF008)                   = 0
brk(0x00021208)                          = 0
brk(0x00023208)                          = 0
ioctl(1, TCGETA, 0xFFBEE29C)             = 0
foo
write(1, " f o o\n", 4)                  = 4
getdents64(3, 0x00021220, 1048)          = 96
stat("foo/bar", 0xFFBEF018)              = 0
foo/bar
write(1, " f o o / b a r\n", 8)          = 8
stat("foo/baz", 0xFFBEF018)              = 0
open64("foo/baz", O_RDONLY|O_NDELAY)     = 4
fcntl(4, F_SETFD, 0x00000001)            = 0
fstat64(4, 0xFFBEEF20)                   = 0
foo/baz
write(1, " f o o / b a z\n", 8)          = 8
getdents64(4, 0x00021A58, 1048)          = 96
```

```
stat("foo/baz/bar", 0xFFBEEF30)                = 0
foo/baz/bar
write(1, " f o o / b a z / b a  r\n", 12)      = 12
stat("foo/baz/baz", 0xFFBEEF30)                = 0
open64("foo/baz/baz", O_RDONLY|O_NDELAY)       = 5
fcntl(5, F_SETFD, 0x00000001)                  = 0
fstat64(5, 0xFFBEEE38)                          = 0
foo/baz/baz
write(1, " f o o / b a z / b a  z\n", 12)      = 12
...                                       Many lines cut
stat("foo/baz/baz/baz/.../baz/baz/baz", 0xFFBEDDF8) Err#90 ELOOP
lstat("foo/baz/baz/baz/.../baz/baz/baz", 0xFFBEDDF8) = 0
foo/baz/baz/baz/baz/baz/baz/baz/baz/baz/baz/.../baz/baz/baz
write(1, " f o o / b a z / b a  z /".., 88)    = 88
...                                       Many lines cut
getdents64(3, 0x00021220, 1048)                = 0
close(3)                                        = 0
llseek(0, 0, SEEK_CUR)                         = 764989
_exit(0)
```

We used an ellipsis (...) on some lines to show that we've omitted some output to make it fit on the page. The line that we've highlighted shows that the loop in the file system caused by the recursive symbolic link caused an error. The ftw function caught the error and resorts to using the lstat function instead of stat to read the data about the link.

10.18 Resolving Paths that Might Contain Symbolic Links

It is sometimes useful to know a file's pathname once all symbolic links have been resolved. Solaris provides two functions to do this: resolvepath and realpath.

The resolvepath Function

We can resolve all symbolic links in a pathname by calling resolvepath.

```
#include <unistd.h>

int resolvepath (const char *path, char *buf, size_t bufsiz);
```

                              Returns: the number of bytes placed into *buf* if OK, –1 on error

---

The resolvepath function fully resolves all of the symbolic links in the pathname pointed to by *path*, storing the result in the buffer pointed to by *buf*. The size of the buffer is specified by *bufsiz*. All "." components are removed, as are all nonleading ".." components and their preceding directory component. If leading ".." components resolve to the root directory, they are replaced by "/".

If the number of bytes copied to *buf* is less than *bufsiz*, the contents of the remainder of *buf* are unspecified. Note that the contents of *buf* are not NUL terminated; applications must add their own.

The `realpath` Function

We can also use the `realpath` function to resolve all symbolic links in a pathname.

```
#include <stdlib.h>

char *realpath (const char *file_name, char *resolved_name);
```
Returns: a pointer to the resolved name if OK, NULL on error

The `realpath` function fully resolves all of the symbolic links in the pathname specified by *file_name*, placing the result into the buffer pointed to by *resolved_name* (which must be at least NAME_MAX bytes in size).

The main differences between `realpath` and `resolvepath` is that the former, where possible, resolves its argument to an absolute pathname, and it also NUL terminates the result. For these reasons, and because it is more standard, applications should use `realpath` in preference to `resolvepath`.

Example: Illustrating the difference between `realpath` and `resolvepath`

Program 10.8 shows how we can use `realpath` and `resolvepath` to resolve the symbolic links in a pathname.

files_and_dirs/realpath.c

```
1 #include <stdio.h>
2 #include <unistd.h>
3 #include <stdlib.h>
4 #include <limits.h>
5 #include <string.h>
6 #include "ssp.h"

7 int main (int argc, char **argv)
8 {
9     int n;
10    char buf1 [PATH_MAX];
11    char buf2 [PATH_MAX];

12    for (n = 1; n < argc; n++) {
13        memset (buf1, 0, PATH_MAX);
14        if (resolvepath (argv [n], buf1, PATH_MAX) == -1)
15            err_msg ("resolvepath failed");

16        if (realpath (argv [n], buf2) == NULL)
17            err_msg ("realpath failed");

18        printf ("%s:\n", argv [n]);
19        printf ("  resolvepath = %s\n", buf1);
20        printf ("  realpath = %s\n\n", buf2);
21    }

22    return (0);
23 }
```
files_and_dirs/realpath.c

Program 10.8 Resolving symbolic links using `realpath` and `resolvepath`.

Running Program 10.8 against a few files on one of the author's systems gave the
following results:

```
$ ./realpath realpath ../../src /dev/null
realpath:
  resolvepath = realpath
  realpath = /home/rich/doc/books/ssp/src/files_and_dirs/realpath

../../src:
  resolvepath = ../../src
  realpath = /home/rich/doc/books/ssp/src

/dev/null:
  resolvepath = /devices/pseudo/mm@0:null
  realpath = /devices/pseudo/mm@0:null
```

10.19 The `symlink` and `readlink` Functions

We've shown how to create a symbolic link by using the `ln -s` command, and we've
shown that most functions that deal with files follow a symbolic link or can return
information about the link itself. We can use the `symlink` function to create a symbolic
link in our programs, and the `readlink` function to determine where a symbolic link
points to.

```
#include <unistd.h>

int symlink (const char *name1, const char *name2);
                                              Returns: 0 if OK, –1 on error
```

The `symlink` function creates symbolic link called *name2* that points to the file called
name1. The symbolic link may span file systems, and no check for the existence of *name1*
is performed.

Once a symbolic link has been created, the `readlink` function can be used to read its
contents (i.e., see where it points to).

```
#include <unistd.h>

int readlink (const char *path, char *buf, size_t bufsiz);
                                Returns: number of bytes read if OK, –1 on error
```

The `readlink` function allows us to determine what the symbolic link called *path* points
to. The first *bufsiz* bytes of the pathname will be copied to the user-supplied buffer, *buf*.
When the pathname is copied to *buf*, it is not NUL terminated as we might expect, so we
must add one ourselves.

10.20 File Times

Every file has three times associated with it; each is measured in seconds since the epoch:

st_atime	The st_atime (or just "atime") of a file is the time the file was last accessed (i.e., the last time the file was opened or read from). A file's atime can be seen by using the -u option of the ls command combined with another option that displays file times (e.g., ls -l or ls -o).
	The access time is sometimes used by systems administrators to delete space wasting files (e.g., core files from crashed programs) that haven't been accessed for more than a certain period of time.
st_mtime	This is the last time the contents of the file were modified (written to), and is sometimes called the "mtime". Overwriting a section of a file with the same data that is already there will still update the mtime, even though strictly speaking the file hasn't been modified. The modification time is the one displayed by default when we get a long listing from ls.
st_ctime	The st_ctime (or just "ctime") of a file is the last time the file's inode changed. A file's inode may change under several circumstances, including changing ownership, changing permissions, and changing the number of links. A file's ctime is sometimes mistakenly referred to as the file's creation time. While it is true that creating a file causes a change in its inode, and hence changes the st_ctime, it isn't the only event that changes a file's inode. A file's ctime can be seen by using the -c option when using ls to get a long file listing.

A file's ctime and st_mtime are used when making incremental backups.

Figure 10.10 summarizes the file I/O functions we discuss in this text and how they affect a file's access, modification, and inode modification times (in columns labelled "a", "m", and "c" respectively). (These last two times are sometimes called the "update time" and the "inode update time"). Some functions that modify a directory entry also have the potential to modify some of the times associated with their parent directory; Figure 10.10 shows this too.

Some functions do not access a file's contents or update its inode; we haven't shown these functions in Figure 10.10. For example, the access and stat functions retrieve all their information from a file's inode, and the access time of an inode is not recorded anywhere.

We haven't discussed some of the functions in Figure 10.10 yet: mknod is discussed in Section 10.26, mkdir and rmdir are covered in Section 10.22, and the utime and utimes functions are discussed in the next section.

Function	File or directory			Parent directory			Notes
	a	m	c	a	m	c	
chmod			•				
chown			•				
creat	•	•	•	•		•	When creating a new file
creat		•	•				When truncating an existing file
exec	•						
fchmod			•				
fchown			•				
ftruncate		•	•				Only if the file size is changed
lchown			•				
link			•		•	•	
mkdir	•	•	•		•	•	
mkfifo	•	•	•		•	•	
mknod	•	•	•		•	•	
open	•	•	•	•		•	When creating a new file
open		•	•				When truncating an existing file
pipe	•	•	•				
read	•						
readdir	•						
readlink	•						
remove			•		•	•	When removing a file
remove					•	•	When removing a directory
rename			•		•	•	For both arguments
rmdir					•	•	
symlink	•	•	•		•	•	
truncate		•	•				Only if the file size is changed
unlink			•		•	•	
utime	•	•	•				
utimes	•	•	•				
write		•	•				

Figure 10.10 The effect of functions on a file's access, update, and inode update times.

Example: Displaying a file's times

The ls program allows us to see the access, modification, and inode modification time of
a file, but we have to select which one of these times we want to see. If we want to see
them all, we must run ls three times for each file. Program 10.9 allows to see all three
times associated with a file at the same time.

Program 10.9 uses the ctime function we discuss in Section 6.7 to convert the times
stored in seconds since the epoch to their more familiar representation.

```
$ ./ftimes .
st_atime = Mon Jan 21 14:12:15 2002
st_mtime = Mon Jan 21 12:09:45 2002
st_ctime = Mon Jan 21 12:09:45 2002
```

————————————————————————————————— files_and_dirs/ftimes.c

```
 1 #include <stdio.h>
 2 #include <sys/types.h>
 3 #include <sys/stat.h>
 4 #include <time.h>
 5 #include "ssp.h"

 6 int main (int argc, char **argv)
 7 {
 8     struct stat stat_buf;

 9     if (stat (argv [1], &stat_buf) == -1)
10         err_msg ("stat failed");

11     printf ("st_atime = %s", ctime (&stat_buf.st_atime));
12     printf ("st_mtime = %s", ctime (&stat_buf.st_mtime));
13     printf ("st_ctime = %s", ctime (&stat_buf.st_ctime));

14     return (0);
15 }
```

————————————————————————————————— files_and_dirs/ftimes.c

Program 10.9 Display a file's access, modification, and inode modification times.

10.21 Changing a File's Access and Modification Times

If we need to set a file's access and modifications times to a given value, we can use the utime and utimes functions.

The utime Function

The utime function sets a file's access and modification times.

```
#include <sys/types.h>
#include <utime.h>

int utime (const char *path, const struct utimbuf *times);
```
Returns: 0 if OK, −1 on error

The utime function sets the access and modification times (st_atime and st_mtime respectively) of the file named by *path*, and causes the inode modification time (the st_ctime) to be set to the current time.

If *times* is NULL, then st_atime and st_ctime are set to the current time. The effective user ID of the calling process must be the same as the file's owner, or have write permission to use utime in this way.

If *times* is not NULL, it is interpreted as a pointer to a utimbuf structure, which has the following members:

```
struct utimbuf {
    time_t  actime;     /* Access time */
    time_t  modtime;    /* Modification time */
};
```

Both values are measured in seconds since the epoch.

If the effective user ID of the calling process is the same as the owner of the file (or is root), the file's st_atime and st_mtime will be set to the values specified by the structure pointed to by *times*. Notice that when using utime in this way, it is not sufficient just to have write permission to the file.

The utimes Function

The utimes function also sets a file's access and modification times.

```
#include <sys/time.h>

int utimes (const char *path, const struct timeval times[2]);
```
                                                                    Returns: 0 if OK, −1 on error

The utimes function also sets the access and modification times of the file named by *path*, and causes the inode modification time to be set to the current time. The times are specified in seconds and microseconds since the epoch, but might be rounded to the nearest second, depending on the underlying file system.

If *times* is NULL, then the file's access and modification times are set to the current time. Otherwise, *times* is interpreted as an array of two timeval structures. The first element specifies the last access time, and the second element specifies the last modification time.

Example: Changing a file's access and modification times

Program 10.10 illustrates the use of the utime function.

Before calling utime with a NULL *times* argument to set the file's last access and modification times to the current time, the stat function is called to retrieve the file's previous last access and modification times. After going to sleep for 10 seconds, the file's access and modification times are restored.

Let's see what happens when we run Program 10.10 on a file we created a few days ago.

```
$ ./ftimes ftw
st_atime = Fri Jan  4 11:13:53 2002
st_mtime = Fri Jan  4 11:13:53 2002
st_ctime = Sat Jan 12 13:44:47 2002
$ ./utime ftw &                          Start our program in the background
[1]     8019
$ date
Mon Jan 21 14:44:08 PST 2002
$ ./ftimes ftw
st_atime = Mon Jan 21 14:44:07 2002
st_mtime = Mon Jan 21 14:44:07 2002
st_ctime = Mon Jan 21 14:44:07 2002
[1] +  Done                      ./utime ftw &
```

files_and_dirs/utime.c

```
 1  #include <unistd.h>
 2  #include <sys/types.h>
 3  #include <sys/stat.h>
 4  #include <utime.h>
 5  #include "ssp.h"

 6  int main (int argc, char **argv)
 7  {
 8      struct stat stat_buf;
 9      struct utimbuf times;

10      if (stat (argv [1], &stat_buf) == -1)
11          err_msg ("stat failed");

12      if (utime (argv [1], NULL) == -1)
13          err_msg ("utime failed");

14      sleep (10);

15      times.actime = stat_buf.st_atime;
16      times.modtime = stat_buf.st_mtime;

17      if (utime (argv [1], &times) == -1)
18          err_msg ("utime failed");

19      return (0);
20  }
```

files_and_dirs/utime.c

Program 10.10   Changing a file's access and modification times.

```
$ ./ftimes ftw                              Ten seconds after we started our program
st_atime = Fri Jan  4 11:13:53 2002
st_mtime = Fri Jan  4 11:13:53 2002
st_ctime = Mon Jan 21 14:44:17 2002
```

10.22 Creating and Removing Directories

We stated previously that a directory is really just another file with a certain structure imposed on it. We also said that the kernel prevents all users, even `root`, from writing directly to a directory. Directories are written to only as a side effect of other functions that our programs call.

The `mkdir` function is used to create a directory.

```
#include <sys/types.h>
#include <sys/stat.h>

int mkdir (const char *path, mode_t mode);
```
                                                          Returns: 0 if OK, −1 on error

The `mkdir` function is used to create a new directory called *path*. The new directory is empty (except for the *dot* and *dot-dot* entries, which are created automatically and refer to the new directory and its parent respectively), and its permissions bits are set from *mode* (as modified by the process' file creation mask). Note that unlike most files we create, directories usually have at least one of the execute (search) bits set.

The owner of the new directory is set to the effective user ID of the calling process, and the group ID of the directory is set to the effective group ID of the process, unless the S_ISGID bit is set for the new directory's parent, in which case the new directory inherits its parent's group ID and S_ISGID bit.

An empty directory can be removed by using the rmdir function.

```
#include <unistd.h>

int rmdir (const char *path);
```
Returns: 0 if OK, −1 on error

If the directory named by *path* is empty (i.e., it has no entries other than *dot* and *dot-dot*), it is removed from the file system. However, just like a regular file, the actual disk blocks allocated to the directory are not freed until its reference count drops to zero.

10.23 Reading Directories

Solaris supports several types of file system, each of which might use a different internal directory format. For example, the deprecated s5fs (System V File System) file system limits directory entries to 14 characters, whereas UFS allows up to MAXNAMLEN (which has a value of 512) characters (MAXNAMLEN is defined in <dirent.h>). Because the maximum supported filename length is file system dependent, we should use pathconf (file, _PC_NAME_MAX) rather than relying on compile time constants.

To enable us to avoid writing non-portable file system dependent code, Solaris provides a number of functions to read directories.

The opendir and fdopendir Functions

Before we can read a directory, we must first open it by using one of the opendir or fdopendir functions.

```
#include <sys/types.h>
#include <dirent.h>

DIR *opendir (const char *dirname);

DIR *fdopendir (int fildes);
```
Both return: pointer to a DIR object if OK, NULL on error

The opendir function opens a directory stream that corresponds to the directory named by *dirname*. Directory streams are represented by a DIR structure, whose purpose is analogous to the FILE structure for file streams. The newly opened directory stream is positioned at the first entry, ready to be read by readdir or readdir_r.

The fdopendir function (which was introduced in Solaris 9) performs a similar task, except that it opens a directory stream for the file descriptor *fildes*. The file descriptor should not be used or closed following a successful call to fdopendir.

The readdir and readdir_r Functions

Once we've opened a directory stream using one of the opendir functions, we can read it using readdir or readdir_r (multithreaded applications should use the latter).

```
#include <sys/types.h>
#include <dirent.h>

struct dirent *readdir (DIR *dirp);

struct dirent *readdir_r (DIR *dirp, struct dirent *entry);
```

            Both return: pointer to a DIR object if OK, NULL on error or end of directory

```
cc [ flag ... ] file ... -D_POSIX_PTHREAD_SEMANTICS [ lib ... ]

int readdir_r (DIR *dirp, struct dirent *entry, struct dirent **result);
```

                                        Returns: 0 if OK, error number on error

The readdir function returns a pointer to to a dirent structure that represents the directory entry at the current position in the directory stream specified by *dirp*. When the directory entries have been exhausted, a NULL pointer is returned.

A dirent structure is composed of the following members:

```
typedef struct dirent {
    ino_t           d_ino;      /* Inode number of entry */
    off_t           d_off;      /* Offset of disk directory entry */
    unsigned short  d_reclen;   /* Length of this record */
    char            d_name [1]; /* Name of file */
} dirent_t;
```

Notice that the member for the name of the file, d_name, is declared as an array of one char. This is to allow the structure to be file system independent, by not hard coding a maximum file length into it. Instead, we must allocate a buffer that contains sufficient space for the dirent structure and the maximum allowed length of a file. One way to do this is to use malloc:

```
buf = malloc (sizeof (dirent_t) + MAXNAMLEN - 1);
```

We subtract one from MAXNAMLEN to account for the character already included in the dirent structure.

The pointer returned by readdir points to a buffer that may be overwritten by subsequent calls to readdir on the same directory stream, and hence is not safe to use in a multithreaded program. At the end of the directory stream, both readdir and `readir_r` (discussed next) return a NULL pointer. Because a NULL pointer is also returned on error, the only way to distinguish between the end of the directory stream and an error is to set `errno` to 0 before calling the function, and checking its value if a NULL pointer is returned; if `errno` is non-zero, it is safe to assume that an error occurred.

Because the `readdir` function is not thread safe, multithreaded programs should use `readdir_r` instead. We need to consider two variants of `readdir_r`: one for when we are using Solaris threads, and the other for when we are using POSIX threads (Pthreads).

The Solaris threads version of `readdir_r` initializes the user-allocated `dirent` structure pointed to by *entry* to represent the current directory entry in the directory stream referenced by *dirp*, and positions the directory stream at the next entry.

The Pthreads version of `readdir_r` initializes the user-allocated `dirent` structure pointed to by *entry* to represent the current directory entry in the directory stream referenced by *dirp*, and positions the directory stream at the next entry. If the function was successful, a pointer to the result (which will have the same value as *entry*) is stored in *result*. When the end of the directory stream is reached, *result* will be a NULL pointer.

One thing we must be aware of when using the `readdir` and `readdir_r` functions to read a directory stream sequentially is that the directory entries are not ordered in any way. For example, the familiar alphabetical ordering we see when we run `ls` is performed by the `ls` command itself.

Solaris threads are deprecated, so new applications should use the Pthreads interfaces instead.

The `seekdir`, `rewinddir`, and `telldir` Functions

The `readdir` and `readdir_r` functions read a directory stream linearly; there are times when we might want to reposition the directory stream pointer. We can do this by using `seekdir`.

```
#include <sys/types.h>
#include <dirent.h>

void seekdir (DIR *dirp, long int loc);

void rewinddir (DIR *dirp);
```

The `seekdir` function sets the position for the next `readdir` operation on the directory stream *dirp* to the position specified by *loc*, which must have been obtained by a previous call to `telldir` (see below).

The `rewinddir` function resets the position for the next `readdir` operation on the directory stream *dirp* to the beginning of the directory. It also causes the directory stream to refer to the current state of the directory, just like a call to `opendir` would have done.

As we alluded to in our discussion of the `seekdir` function, `telldir` is used to obtain the current location of a directory stream.

```
#include <dirent.h>

long int telldir (DIR *dirp);
```
                                                          Returns: current location if OK, –1 on error

The `telldir` function returns the current position of the directory stream referenced by *dirp*. The value returned can be supplied as the *loc* argument to `seekdir`.

The result from `telldir` is valid only if there is no intervening `closedir`. In other words, we can use `seekdir` with `telldir` only if they refer to the same `DIR` structure.

The `closedir` Function

When we have finished using a directory stream, we should close it using `closedir`.

```
#include <sys/types.h>
#include <dirent.h>

int closedir (DIR *dirp);
```
                                                              Returns: 0 if OK, –1 on error

The `closedir` function closes the directory stream referred to by *dirp* and closes the file descriptor associated with it.

Example: Count the number of files of each type in a directory

Program 10.11 uses the `opendir`, `readdir`, and `closedir` functions to count the number of files of each file type in the given directories.

Check command line argument is a directory

22–25 If we can't `stat` the current command line argument, try the next one.

26–29 If the current command line argument isn't a directory, try the next one.

30–37 Attempt to open a directory stream for the named directory using `opendir`. If the call to `opendir` was successful, we call our function `process_dir` to process the directory, and then call `closedir` to close the directory stream.

Print the results

38–46 Print the total numbers of each file type for the current directory.

Initialize counters

55–56 Set all the file type counters to 0, making use of the C programming language's ability to assign several variables the same value. We do this because although the variables are global (and are therefore initialized to 0), `process_dir` may be called more than once per program invocation, so we must ensure that the values from the previous invocation are cleared.

files_and_dirs/readdir.c

```
 1 #include <stdio.h>
 2 #include <sys/types.h>
 3 #include <dirent.h>
 4 #include <sys/param.h>
 5 #include <sys/stat.h>
 6 #include "ssp.h"

 7 static int num_reg;
 8 static int num_dir;
 9 static int num_cspec;
10 static int num_bspec;
11 static int num_fifo;
12 static int num_sock;
13 static int num_symlink;
14 static int num_door;

15 static void process_dir (DIR *dirp, const char *file);

16 int main (int argc, char **argv)
17 {
18     struct stat stat_buf;
19     DIR *dirp;
20     int i;

21     for (i = 1; i < argc; i++) {
22         if (stat (argv [i], &stat_buf) == -1) {
23             err_ret ("stat failed: %s", argv [i]);
24             continue;
25         }

26         if (!S_ISDIR (stat_buf.st_mode)) {
27             log_msg ("%s: Not a directory", argv [i]);
28             continue;
29         }

30         if ((dirp = opendir (argv [i])) != NULL) {
31             process_dir (dirp, argv [i]);
32             closedir (dirp);
33         }
34         else {
35             err_ret ("opendir failed: %s", argv [i]);
36             continue;
37         }

38         printf ("Totals for %s:\n", argv [i]);
39         printf ("  Regular files: %d\n", num_reg);
40         printf ("  Directories: %d\n", num_dir);
41         printf ("  Character special files: %d\n", num_cspec);
42         printf ("  Block special files: %d\n", num_bspec);
43         printf ("  FIFOs: %d\n", num_fifo);
44         printf ("  Sockets: %d\n", num_sock);
45         printf ("  Symbolic links: %d\n", num_symlink);
46         printf ("  Doors: %d\n", num_door);
47     }

48     return (0);
49 }
```

```
50 static void process_dir (DIR *dirp, const char *file)
51 {
52     struct stat stat_buf;
53     dirent_t *entry;
54     char path [MAXPATHLEN];

55     num_reg = num_dir = num_cspec = num_bspec = 0;
56     num_fifo = num_sock = num_symlink = num_door = 0;

57     if ((readdir (dirp) != NULL) && (readdir (dirp) != NULL)) {
58         while ((entry = readdir (dirp)) != NULL) {
59             snprintf (path, MAXPATHLEN, "%s/%s", file, entry -> d_name);
60             if (lstat (path, &stat_buf) == -1) {
61                 err_ret ("lstat failed: %s", path);
62                 continue;
63             }
64             switch (stat_buf.st_mode & S_IFMT) {
65                 case S_IFREG:
66                     num_reg++;
67                     break;

68                 case S_IFDIR:
69                     num_dir++;
70                     break;

71                 case S_IFCHR:
72                     num_cspec++;
73                     break;

74                 case S_IFBLK:
75                     num_bspec++;
76                     break;

77                 case S_IFIFO:
78                     num_fifo++;
79                     break;

80                 case S_IFSOCK:
81                     num_sock++;
82                     break;

83                 case S_IFLNK:
84                     num_symlink++;
85                     break;

86                 case S_IFDOOR:
87                     num_door++;
88                     break;
89             }
90         }
91     }
92 }
```

files_and_dirs/readdir.c

Program 10.11 Count the number of each type of file.

Get the next directory entry

57 We use `readdir` to skip over the entries for *dot* and *dot-dot*.

60–92 We get the file status of the current directory entry so that we can determine its type. Note that we use `lstat` instead of `stat` to ensure that symbolic links aren't followed (if symbolic links were followed, we wouldn't be able to count them).

Running Program 10.11 on `/etc` on one of the author's machines gave the following:

```
$ ./readdir /etc
Totals for /etc:
  Regular files: 78
  Directories: 40
  Character special files: 0
  Block special files: 0
  FIFOs: 2
  Sockets: 0
  Symbolic links: 69
  Doors: 0
```

The `ftw` and `nftw` Functions

The `readdir` functions we discussed in the preceding paragraphs are fine if we want to iterate through all the files in a directory and perform some action on them, but are somewhat cumbersome if we want to iterate through a whole directory structure. Instead, we can use one of the file tree walking functions, `ftw` and `nftw`.

```
#include <ftw.h>

int ftw (const char *path, int (*fn) (const char *, const struct stat *, int),
    int depth);

int nftw (const char *path, int (*fn) (const char *, const struct stat *, int,
    struct FTW *), int depth, int flags);

                                                    Both return: see text
```

The `ftw` function recursively descends the directory tree that starts at *path*. For each directory entry in the hierarchy, the user-defined function, *fn*, is called. The function is passed a pointer to the name of the current directory entry, a pointer to a `stat` structure for the directory entry, and an integer. Possible values for the integer are:

FTW_F	The directory entry refers to a file.
FTW_D	The directory entry refers to a directory.
FTW_DNR	The directory entry refers to a directory that cannot be read. Descendants of the directory are not processed.
FTW_NS	The `stat` function failed on the directory entry because of a lack of appropriate permission, or the entry is a symbolic link pointing to a file that doesn't exist.

The `ftw` function looks at all files in a directory before examining any descendants (subdirectories).

For each level descended in the directory tree, `ftw` uses one file descriptor. The *depth* argument allows us to limit the number of file descriptors used. Using a *depth* less than the number of levels in the directory tree will result in some loss of performance, so for best results *depth* should be at least as many levels as we expect.

Once all the files and directories in a directory tree have been visited, `ftw` returns 0. If an error is detected by `ftw`, −1 is returned, and if *fn* returns a non-zero value, the file tree walking operation is halted and `ftw` returns the value returned by *fn*.

One of the problems with `ftw` is that it internally uses the `stat` function to determine a file type. This means that symbolic links are followed, which may not always be what we want. To address this shortcoming, and to make use of additional functionality, we can use the `nftw` function instead of `ftw`.

The `nftw` function performs the task as the `ftw` function we just discussed, but offers more flexibility. This extra flexibility is controlled by the *flags* argument, which is made up by bitwise-ORing one or more of the following constants together:

`FTW_PHYS`	The walk is physical, i.e., does not follow symbolic links.
`FTW_MOUNT`	The walk will not cross a mount point. That is, the walk will be confined to the file system that the initial argument, *path*, is on.
`FTW_DEPTH`	All subdirectories are visited before the directory itself. By default, the files in the current directory are visited before any subdirectories.
`FTW_CHDIR`	The walk changes to each directory before reading it.

The `nftw` function calls the user-defined function, *fn*, with four arguments for each file and directory. The first argument is a pointer to the name of the directory entry, the second is a pointer to a `stat` buffer for the directory entry, the third is an integer that contains more information (listed next), and the fourth is a `FTW` structure.

The values the third argument may have are:

`FTW_F`	The directory entry refers to a file.
`FTW_D`	The directory entry refers to a directory.
`FTW_DP`	The directory entry refers to a directory, and its subdirectories have been visited.
`FTW_SL`	The directory entry is a symbolic link.
`FTW_SLN`	The directory entry is a symbolic link that points to a file that doesn't exist.
`FTW_DNR`	The directory entry refers to a directory that cannot be read. Descendants of the directory are not processed.

FTW_NS   The stat function failed on the directory entry because of a
                              lack of appropriate permission, or the entry is a symbolic link
                              pointing to a file that doesn't exist.

The FTW structure contains the following members:

```
struct FTW {
    int quit;
    int base;
    int level;
};
```

The quit member allows the user-defined function to have some control over the action
of the current object. For example, setting quit to FTW_SKD will cause a directory to be
skipped, and setting it to FTW_PRUNE will cause the file tree walk to be stopped for this
branch of the directory tree. The base member is the offset of the file entry's filename in
the pathname passed to *fn*, and the level member indicates the depth relative to where
the walk started (*path*), where the starting level is 0.

For each level descended in the directory tree, nftw uses one file descriptor. The *depth*
argument allows us to limit the number of file descriptors used. Using a *depth* that is less
than the number of levels in the directory tree will result in some loss of performance, so
for best results *depth* should be at least as many levels as we expect.

Once all the files and directories in a directory tree have been visited, nftw returns 0. If
an error is detected by nftw, −1 is returned, and if *fn* returns a non-zero value, the file
tree walking operation is halted and nftw returns the value returned by *fn*.

Example: Recursively count the number of each file type in a directory tree

Program 10.12 is similar to Program 10.11, with the exception that it counts the number of
each file type recursively for a whole directory tree, rather than a single directory.

Line 24 calls the nftw function, which calls our function, process, for every file in the
directory tree that starts at path. We use the third argument to nftw to allow the
maximum number of file descriptors to be used, and we specify FTW_PHYS as the fourth
argument, to prevent symbolic links from being followed so that we can count them.

Running Program 10.12 for /etc on one of the author's systems gives the following
results:

```
$ ./nftw /etc
Can't read directory: /etc/inet/secret: Permission denied
Can't read directory: /etc/sfw/private: Permission denied
Can't read directory: /etc/openwin/server: Permission denied
Totals for /etc:
  Regular files: 484
  Directories: 77
  Character special files: 0
  Block special files: 0
  FIFOs: 6
  Sockets: 0
  Symbolic links: 101
  Doors: 3
```

files_and_dirs/nftw.c

```
 1 #include <stdio.h>
 2 #include <sys/types.h>
 3 #include <ftw.h>
 4 #include <sys/param.h>
 5 #include <sys/stat.h>
 6 #include <dirent.h>
 7 #include "ssp.h"

 8 static int num_reg;
 9 static int num_dir;
10 static int num_cspec;
11 static int num_bspec;
12 static int num_fifo;
13 static int num_sock;
14 static int num_symlink;
15 static int num_door;

16 static int process (const char *path, const struct stat *stat_buf, int type,
17     struct FTW *ftwp);

18 int main (int argc, char **argv)
19 {
20     int i;

21     for (i = 1; i < argc; i++) {
22         num_reg = num_dir = num_cspec = num_bspec = 0;
23         num_fifo = num_sock = num_symlink = num_door = 0;

24         nftw (argv [i], process, FOPEN_MAX, FTW_PHYS);

25         printf ("Totals for %s:\n", argv [i]);
26         printf ("  Regular files: %d\n", num_reg);
27         printf ("  Directories: %d\n", num_dir);
28         printf ("  Character special files: %d\n", num_cspec);
29         printf ("  Block special files: %d\n", num_bspec);
30         printf ("  FIFOs: %d\n", num_fifo);
31         printf ("  Sockets: %d\n", num_sock);
32         printf ("  Symbolic links: %d\n", num_symlink);
33         printf ("  Doors: %d\n", num_door);
34     }

35     return (0);
36 }

37 static int process (const char *path, const struct stat *stat_buf, int type,
38     struct FTW *ftwp)
39 {
40     switch (type) {
41         case FTW_F:
42             switch (stat_buf -> st_mode & S_IFMT) {
43                 case S_IFREG:
44                     num_reg++;
45                     break;
```

```
46                      case S_IFCHR:
47                          num_cspec++;
48                          break;

49                      case S_IFBLK:
50                          num_bspec++;
51                          break;

52                      case S_IFIFO:
53                          num_fifo++;
54                          break;

55                      case S_IFSOCK:
56                          num_sock++;
57                          break;

58                      case S_IFDOOR:
59                          num_door++;
60                          break;
61                      }
62                  break;

63              case FTW_D:
64                  num_dir++;
65                  break;

66              case FTW_SL:
67              case FTW_SLN:
68                  num_symlink++;
69                  break;

70              case FTW_DNR:
71                  err_ret ("Can't read directory: %s", path);
72                  break;

73              case FTW_NS:
74                  err_ret ("Can't stat %s", path);
75                  break;
76          }

77      return (0);
78  }
```

files_and_dirs/nftw.c

Program 10.12   Recursively count the number of each type of file.

10.24 The `chdir`, `fchdir`, and `getcwd` Functions

In Section 1.4 we mentioned that every process has a current working directory associated with it. When we log in to a Solaris system, the current directory is set from our user's entry in /etc/passwd (or some other password database, e.g., LDAP or NIS). A process can change its current working directory by using one of the chdir or fchdir functions.

```
#include <unistd.h>

int chdir (const char *path);

int fchdir (int fildes);
```

                                                          Both return: 0 if OK, –1 on error

The chdir function causes the directory named by *path* to become the current working directory of the process if the process has execute (search) permission for the directory. The current working directory of a process is the starting point for relative path searches, i.e., those that do not start with /.

Alternatively, we can call the fchmod function, passing it the file descriptor for a directory we have previously opened in *fildes*.

Example: Changing directory

Program 10.13 changes the current working directory, and then exits.

———————————————————————————————————— *files_and_dirs/chdir.c*
```
 1 #include <stdio.h>
 2 #include <unistd.h>
 3 #include "ssp.h"

 4 int main (void)
 5 {
 6     if (chdir ("/tmp") != 0)
 7         err_msg ("chdir failed");

 8     printf ("chdir to /tmp was successful\n");

 9     return (0);
10 }
```
———————————————————————————————————— *files_and_dirs/chdir.c*

Program 10.13   Change the current working directory.

Running Program 10.13 gives these results:
```
$ pwd
/home/rich/doc/books/ssp/src/files_and_dirs
$ ./chdir
chdir to /tmp was successful
$ pwd
/home/rich/doc/books/ssp/src/files_and_dirs
```

The current working directory is one of the attributes of a process that is inherited by its children, but there is no way that a process can modify the current working directory of its parent. This is why Program 10.13 doesn't work how we might expect it to. It is also for this reason that the cd command that we type in a shell session is built into the shell rather than being a separate executable.

A process can determine its current working directory by using the getcwd function.

```
#include <unistd.h>

char *getcwd (char *buf, size_t size);
```

                                                        Returns: *buf* if OK, NULL on error

The getcwd function places the absolute pathname of the current working directory into the buffer pointed to by *buf*, which must have a size of *size* bytes. If *buf* is a NULL pointer, getcwd will allocate *size* bytes using malloc and return a pointer to the space allocated. To prevent memory leaks, memory allocated in this manner should be freed when we are finished with it.

Example: Printing the current working directory

Program 10.14 changes the current working directory and then calls getcwd to display it.

————————————————————————————————————— *files_and_dirs/getcwd.c*

```
 1 #include <stdio.h>
 2 #include <unistd.h>
 3 #include <stdlib.h>
 4 #include <sys/param.h>
 5 #include "ssp.h"

 6 int main (void)
 7 {
 8     char *cwd;

 9     if (chdir ("/lib/nfs") != 0)
10         err_msg ("chdir failed");

11     if ((cwd = getcwd (NULL, MAXPATHLEN)) == NULL) {
12         err_msg ("getcwd failed");
13         exit (1);
14     }

15     printf ("CWD = %s\n", cwd);

16     free (cwd);

17     return (0);
18 }
```

————————————————————————————————————— *files_and_dirs/getcwd.c*

Program 10.14   Print the current working directory.

When we run Program 10.14 (which changes to the directory /lib/nfs), we get the following results:

```
$ ./getcwd
CWD = /usr/lib/nfs
$ ls -l /lib
lrwxrwxrwx   1 root      root           9 Jan  7 17:59 /lib -> ./usr/lib
```

We let `getcwd` allocate the memory for the buffer and free it once we've printed its contents. In such a short program, the latter step isn't necessary, but we show it to encourage good programming habits. Also notice that although `chdir` followed the symbolic link from `/lib` to `/usr/lib` (which, from Figure 10.9, is what we would expect), the `getcwd` function is unaware of this fact and returns the true, nonsymbolic linked pathname of the directory. This one way mapping is one of the attributes of symbolic links.

10.25 The `chroot` and `fchroot` Functions

We stated in Section 1.4 that absolute pathnames are resolved from the root directory of the process. A privileged process has the ability to change its notion of the root directory by calling either of the `chroot` functions.

```
#include <unistd.h>

int chroot (const char *path);

int fchroot (int fildes);
```
                                                          Both return: 0 if OK, −1 on error

The `chroot` function causes the directory specified by *path* to become the root directory for the calling process, if it is suitably privileged.

Similarly, the `fchmod` function causes the directory associated with the file descriptor specified by *fildes* to become the root directory for the calling process, if it is suitably privileged. This function is usually used to change back to the system root directory.

Neither function causes the process' current working directory to be changed, which can cause security problems; in Section 9.6 we saw how to break out of a `chrooted` jail by using the `chroot` function.

10.26 Special Files

A *special file* is a file that, rather than containing data, provides a mechanism for mapping physical devices to filenames in a file system. Each device supported by the system is represented by at least one special file. When a request to read or write a special file is made, the operation is handled by the device driver for the device. Device drivers are beyond the scope of this text, so we only give a very brief description here.

A *device driver* is a section of kernel resident code that handles all interaction with a given device. When a special file is read from or written to, the I/O is performed on the device associated with the underlying device driver rather than the file itself as is the usual case.

There are two types of special file: block and character. Block special files are associated with block structured devices, such as disks. Data transfers to or from a block special file are buffered by the kernel and are flushed periodically by `fsflush`.

Data transfers via a character special file are passed directly between the device driver and the controlling process, without any buffering. For this reason, character special files are sometimes referred to as the raw interface to a device.

In much the same manner as a vnode represents a file inside the kernel, each device is associated with a unique number, called the device number. A *device number* is made up from two components: a major number and a minor number. In other words, the major-minor pair makes up the device number.

Returning to the `stat` structure, each file has one or two devices associated with it. The first of these is stored in the `st_dev` member, and is the device number for the file system that contains the file. This member is valid for all files. Given that each file system has its own device number, and that inodes on a given file system occur only once, we can see that the combination of the `st_dev` and `st_ino` members uniquely identifies a file.

The other member of the `stat` structure associated with a device number is `st_rdev`. This member, which is valid only for character and block special files, holds the device number of the device associated with the file.

In other words, the `st_dev` member is the device number of the file system that contains the filename and inode of a file, and the `st_rdev` member is the device number for the actual device associated with a character or block special file.

We just stated that a device number is composed of two parts: a major number and a minor number. Given a device number, we can use two functions to determine the major and minor components: `major` and `minor`.

```
#include <sys/types.h>
#include <sys/mkdev.h>

major_t major (dev_t device);

minor_t minor (dev_t device);
```
                              Both return: major or minor component if OK, NODEV on error

The `major` function returns the major component of the device number *device*. Similarly, the `minor` function returns the minor component of the device number *device*.

The `makedev` function performs the opposite task.

```
#include <sys/types.h>
#include <sys/mkdev.h>

dev_t makedev (major_t maj, minor_t min);
```
                                    Returns: device number if OK, NODEV on error

The `makedev` function makes a device number from its major and minor components, *maj* and *min* respectively. The resulting device number is suitable for passing to the `mknod` function.

The `mknod` function is used to create special files.

```
#include <sys/stat.h>

int mknod (const char* path, mode_t mode, dev_t dev);
```

Returns: 0 if OK, −1 on error

The mknod function is used to make a special file, a directory, or a regular file that is to be known by the pathname pointed to by *path*, and with the permissions specified by *mode*. The *mode* argument is also used to specify the type of file to create, in exactly the same way that the st_mode member of the stat structure does.

The S_IFMT bits of the *mode* argument specify the type of file to create, and may be one of the following values:

S_IFBLK	Create a block special file.
S_IFCHR	Create a character special file.
S_IFDIR	Create a directory.
S_IFIFO	Create a FIFO.
S_IFREG	Create a regular file.

If the type of file to be created is either a character or block special file, the *dev* argument specifies the device number of the new file (*dev* is ignored for all other file types).

The use of mknod to create FIFOs, directories, or regular files is somewhat deprecated these days: mkfifo, mkdir, and open or creat should be used instead.

Example: Printing the device numbers of a file

Program 10.15 prints the st_dev field for every file on the command line, and also prints the st_rdev field for character and block special files.

Running Program 10.15 on some files gives the following results:

```
$ ./devs / devs /dev/null
/: st_dev = 136, 0
devs: st_dev = 236, 25
/dev/null: st_dev = 136, 0 (st_rdev = 13, 2)
$ df -k /
Filesystem              kbytes    used    avail capacity  Mounted on
/dev/dsk/c0t0d0s0       2307374  947577 1313650    42%     /
$ ls -1L /dev/dsk/c0t0d0s0 /dev/null
brw-r-----   1 root      sys       136,   0 Jan  7 18:19 /dev/dsk/c0t0d0s0
crw-rw-rw-   1 root      sys        13,   2 Feb  3 19:17 /dev/null
```

As we expect, the first two files we use, / and devs, only have an st_dev field associated with them. The last file, /dev/null, has an st_rdev field associated with it because it is a character special file.

We can see that the the st_dev numbers for / and /dev/null are the same (both files are on the same file system). We use the df command to see the device the root file system is mounted on, and then use ls to confirm the st_rdev numbers for /dev/null

files_and_dirs/devs.c

```
 1 #include <stdio.h>
 2 #include <sys/types.h>
 3 #include <sys/stat.h>
 4 #include <sys/mkdev.h>
 5 #include "ssp.h"

 6 int main (int argc, char **argv)
 7 {
 8     struct stat buf;
 9     int i;

10     for (i = 1; i < argc; i++) {
11         if (stat (argv [i], &buf) == -1) {
12             err_ret ("stat failed: %s", argv [i]);
13             continue;
14         }

15         printf ("%s: st_dev = %ld, %ld", argv [i],
16             (long) major (buf.st_dev), (long) minor (buf.st_dev));

17         if ((S_ISCHR (buf.st_mode)) || (S_ISBLK (buf.st_mode)))
18             printf (" (st_rdev = %ld, %ld)",
19                 (long) major (buf.st_rdev), (long) minor (buf.st_rdev));

20         printf ("\n");
21     }

22     return (0);
23 }
```

files_and_dirs/devs.c

Program 10.15 Print the st_dev and st_rdev fields of a file.

and the root file system's device. Note that we make use of the ls command's −L option, which follows symbolic links. We do this because on Solaris, the files in /dev are just symbolic links to the real device special files in /devices.

10.27 The sync and fsync Functions

Traditional UNIX implementations set aside an area of system memory to act as a buffer cache for pending I/O transactions. This allows data reads and writes to occur faster because they are asynchronous with respect to the underlying disks, which are much slower (by several orders of magnitude) than RAM.

Solaris differs from traditional UNIX implementations somewhat because rather than allocating a fixed area of memory as a buffer cache, the Solaris kernel treats all memory that is not in use by processes or the kernel itself as a buffer cache. This is because of the way the virtual memory subsystem works: no distinction is made between pages of application code and data, and data from disk-based files.

> Actually, this is not strictly true under all circumstances. Although pages from disk files are
> treated the same as application text and data, the priority paging algorithm introduced in
> Solaris 7 (and subsequent changes to the virtual memory subsystem in Solaris 8 and beyond)
> gives application text and data a higher priority when system memory starts becoming scarce.
> The pages of memory used to buffer files are freed before those of any application.
>
> For this reason, it is important that data files do not have any execution bits set; pages mapped
> from files with an execute bit set are deemed to be from a program (and hence higher priority)
> so they won't be paged out when they should. They will, of course, be paged out eventually
> when memory is sufficiently low, but this interferes with the virtual memory algorithms.

The pages used to buffer file accesses are periodically flushed to disk by a kernel process
called `fsflush`. Kernel processes are created when the system first boots and run
completely within the kernel; they have no user space code, and are all descendants of
the first process created when the system boots, `sched`. All other processes are direct or
indirect descendants of `init`, which has a process ID of 1.

Although `fsflush` flushes file updates every 30 seconds or so, this still leaves a large (by
computer time standards) time for potential loss resulting from power failures, etc.
Fortunately we can use the `sync` function to flush any dirty file buffers (a *dirty buffer* is
one that has been written to since the last flush to disk).

```
#include <unistd.h>

void sync (void);

int fsync (int fildes);
```
                                                              Returns: 0 if OK, −1 on error

As well as flushing dirty file buffers, the `sync` function writes all other information in
memory that should be on disk, including modified superblocks and modified inodes.
One thing to bear in mind when using the `sync` function (and the `sync` command,
which just calls the `sync` function) is that unlike `fsync`, the writes scheduled by `sync`
are not waited for, which means that they may not be complete when `sync` returns.

The `fsync` function writes all modified data and file attributes associated with the file
descriptor *fildes* to backing storage (disk). Unlike the `sync` function, `fsync` does not
return until the data has been written to a physical medium.

We can compare the use of `fsync` and passing the `O_SYNC` flag to `open`; calling `fsync`
causes dirty buffers to be written at the time of invocation, whereas `O_SYNC` forces *all* file
updates to be synchronous.

10.28 Putting It All Together

As a way of wrapping up our discussion of the `stat` structure and its fields,
Program 10.16 prints out the values for all the `stat` structure fields for the named files,

including the final member of the structure, `st_fstype`. The `st_fstype` field is just a text string that identifies, from the point of view of the calling process, the type of file system the file is on. It is possible that the same file will have different strings in `st_fstype`; for example, if the file is being shared via NFS, then `st_fstype` will be "nfs" on a client that has mounted the file system containing the file, and "ufs" on the server where the file physically resides.

There's nothing new in Program 10.16 except in the function `print_formatted`, which prints out a formatted version of the `stat` structure. (By using the `-r` command line argument, Program 10.16 will also provide a raw dump of the `stat` structure.)

In `print_formatted` we obtain the user name and group of the file by calling the `getpwuid` and `getgrgid` functions respectively. We talk more about these functions in Chapter 7.

Let's see what happens when we run Program 10.16 on `/tmp`.

```
$ ./stat /tmp
/tmp:
  File system device: 0, 2
  Inode: 35489
  File type: Directory
  Permissions: rwxrwxrwx, sticky bit
  Number of links: 7
  User ID: root
  Group ID: sys
  File size: 1693
  Last access time: Tue Feb  5 20:14:28 2002
  Last modification time: Tue Feb  5 20:04:04 2002
  Last inode change: Tue Feb  5 20:04:04 2002
  Preferred block size: 8192
  Number of blocks: 16
  File system type: tmpfs
```

A raw dump of the same file yields the following:

```
$ ./stat -r /tmp
/tmp:
  st_dev: 2
  st_ino: 35489
  st_mode: 41777
  st_nlink: 7
  st_uid: 0
  st_gid: 3
  st_rdev: 0
  st_size: 1693
  st_atime: 1012968868
  st_mtime: 1012968244
  st_ctime: 1012968244
  st_blksize: 8192
  st_blocks: 16
  st_fstype: tmpfs
```

files_and_dirs/stat.c

```
 1 #include <stdio.h>
 2 #include <unistd.h>
 3 #include <stdlib.h>
 4 #include <sys/types.h>
 5 #include <sys/stat.h>
 6 #include <sys/mkdev.h>
 7 #include <sys/param.h>
 8 #include <time.h>
 9 #include <pwd.h>
10 #include <grp.h>
11 #include "ssp.h"

12 static void print_formatted (struct stat *buf, char *path);
13 static void print_type (int type, char *path);
14 static void print_perms (int perms);
15 static void print_raw (struct stat *buf);

16 int main (int argc, char **argv)
17 {
18     char arg_char;
19     boolean_t err_flag;
20     boolean_t raw_flag;
21     struct stat buf;

22     opterr = 0;
23     err_flag = B_FALSE;
24     raw_flag = B_FALSE;

25     while ((arg_char = getopt (argc, argv, "r")) != EOF) {
26         switch (arg_char) {
27             case 'r':
28                 raw_flag = B_TRUE;
29                 break;

30             default:
31                 err_flag = B_TRUE;
32                 break;
33         }
34     }

35     if (err_flag)
36         err_quit ("Usage: stat [-r] file ...");

37     while (optind != argc) {
38         if (lstat (argv [optind], &buf) != 0) {
39             err_ret ("stat: Can't lstat %s", argv [optind]);
40             continue;
41         }

42         printf ("%s:\n", argv [optind]);
43         if (raw_flag)
44             print_raw (&buf);
45         else
46             print_formatted (&buf, argv [optind]);
47         optind++;
48     }
```

```
49      return (0);
50 }

51 static void print_formatted (struct stat *buf, char *path)
52 {
53      struct passwd *pwd;
54      struct group *grp;

55      printf ("  File system device: %ld, %ld\n",
56          (long) major (buf -> st_dev), (long) minor (buf -> st_dev));
57      printf ("  Inode: %lld\n", (long long) buf -> st_ino);
58      print_type (buf -> st_mode & S_IFMT, path);
59      print_perms (buf -> st_mode);
60      printf ("  Number of links: %ld\n", (long) buf -> st_nlink);

61      if ((pwd = getpwuid (buf -> st_uid)) == NULL)
62          printf ("  User ID: %ld\n", (long) buf -> st_uid);
63      else
64          printf ("  User ID: %s\n", pwd -> pw_name);

65      if ((grp = getgrgid (buf -> st_gid)) == NULL)
66          printf ("  Group ID: %ld\n", (long) buf -> st_gid);
67      else
68          printf ("  Group ID: %s\n", grp -> gr_name);

69      if ((S_ISCHR (buf -> st_mode)) || (S_ISBLK (buf -> st_mode)))
70          printf ("  Special file device numbers: %ld, %ld\n",
71              (long) major (buf -> st_rdev), (long) minor (buf -> st_dev));

72      printf ("  File size: %lld\n", (long long) buf -> st_size);
73      printf ("  Last access time: %s", ctime (&(buf -> st_atime)));
74      printf ("  Last modification time: %s", ctime (&(buf -> st_mtime)));
75      printf ("  Last inode change: %s", ctime (&(buf -> st_ctime)));
76      printf ("  Preferred block size: %ld\n", (long) buf -> st_blksize);
77      printf ("  Number of blocks: %ld\n", (long) buf -> st_blocks);
78      printf ("  File system type: %s\n", buf -> st_fstype);
79 }

80 static void print_type (int type, char *path)
81 {
82      char link_buf [MAXPATHLEN];
83      int n;

84      printf ("  File type: ");
85      switch (type) {
86          case S_IFREG:
87              printf ("Regular file\n");
88              break;

89          case S_IFDIR:
90              printf ("Directory\n");
91              break;

92          case S_IFCHR:
93              printf ("Character special\n");
94              break;
```

```
 95            case S_IFBLK:
 96                printf ("Block special\n");
 97                break;

 98            case S_IFIFO:
 99                printf ("FIFO\n");
100                break;

101            case S_IFSOCK:
102                printf ("Socket\n");
103                break;

104            case S_IFLNK:
105                if ((n = (readlink (path, link_buf, MAXPATHLEN))) == -1)
106                    snprintf (link_buf, MAXPATHLEN, "<Indeterminate>");
107                else
108                    link_buf [n] = '\0';
109                printf ("Symbolic link to %s\n", link_buf);
110                break;

111            case S_IFDOOR:
112                printf ("Door\n");
113                break;

114            default:
115                printf ("Unrecognised\n");
116                break;
117        }
118 }

119 static void print_perms (int perms)
120 {
121     printf ("  Permissions: ");

122     if (perms & S_IRUSR)
123         printf ("r");
124     else
125         printf ("-");
126     if (perms & S_IWUSR)
127         printf ("w");
128     else
129         printf ("-");
130     if (perms & S_IXUSR)
131         printf ("x");
132     else
133         printf ("-");

134     if (perms & S_IRGRP)
135         printf ("r");
136     else
137         printf ("-");
138     if (perms & S_IWGRP)
139         printf ("w");
140     else
141         printf ("-");
```

```
142     if (perms & S_IXGRP)
143         printf ("x");
144     else
145         printf ("-");

146     if (perms & S_IROTH)
147         printf ("r");
148     else
149         printf ("-");
150     if (perms & S_IWOTH)
151         printf ("w");
152     else
153         printf ("-");
154     if (perms & S_IXOTH)
155         printf ("x");
156     else
157         printf ("-");

158     if (perms & S_ISUID)
159         printf (", set UID");
160     if (perms & S_ISGID) {
161         if (perms & S_IXGRP)
162             printf (", set GID");
163         else
164             printf (", mandatory locking");
165     }

166     if (perms & S_ISVTX)
167         printf (", sticky bit");

168     printf ("\n");
169 }

170 static void print_raw (struct stat *buf)
171 {
172     printf ("   st_dev: %ld\n", (long) buf -> st_dev);
173     printf ("   st_ino: %lld\n", (long long) buf -> st_ino);
174     printf ("   st_mode: %ld\n", (long) buf -> st_mode);
175     printf ("   st_nlink: %ld\n", (long) buf -> st_nlink);
176     printf ("   st_uid: %ld\n", (long) buf -> st_uid);
177     printf ("   st_gid: %ld\n", (long) buf -> st_gid);
178     printf ("   st_rdev: %ld\n", (long) buf -> st_rdev);
179     printf ("   st_size: %lld\n", (long long) buf -> st_size);
180     printf ("   st_atime: %ld\n", buf -> st_atime);
181     printf ("   st_mtime: %ld\n", buf -> st_mtime);
182     printf ("   st_ctime: %ld\n", buf -> st_ctime);
183     printf ("   st_blksize: %ld\n", (long) buf -> st_blksize);
184     printf ("   st_blocks: %ld\n", (long) buf -> st_blocks);
185     printf ("   st_fstype: %s\n", buf -> st_fstype);
186 }
```

files_and_dirs/stat.c

Program 10.16 Print the entire contents of the stat structure.

10.29 Summary

In this chapter we took a long look at the members of the `stat` structure and discussed the functions that can be used to manipulate them. We looked at the structure of the UFS file system, and symbolic links.

After discussing the various file times, we described the functions we use to manipulate directories, including how to create and remove them, how to read them, how to change the current working directory, and how to change the root directory.

Finally, after talking about special files and the functions we can use to flush dirty buffers to disk, we wrote a program that prints out an interpreted version of all the fields of the `stat` structure for a file.

Exercises

10.1 Why must the file `/etc/passwd` be readable by all users on the system?

10.2 What happens if you set your file creation mask to 0777? Use the `umask` command to verify the results.

10.3 What happens if we rerun Program 10.4 after creating the files `foo` and `bar`?

10.4 In Section 10.12 we stated that the `st_size` member is valid for regular files, symbolic links, and directories; we also said that regular files can have a length of 0. Is it possible for a directory or symbolic link to ever have a length of 0?

10.5 Write a version of `cp` that is sparse-file aware (i.e., 0 bytes should not be written to the output file).

10.6 How can we use the `utime` function to modify only one of the two time values it sets?

11

Working with File Systems

11.1 Introduction

In our discussion of file I/O so far, we have made an implicit assumption that the file we are reading or writing resides on a file system that is mounted. This may not always be the case, and although we could run the `mount` command to mount the file system, it is sometimes desirable to do it programmatically.

In this chapter, we'll discuss how to interrogate the mounted file system table (`/etc/mnttab`), the file system defaults (`/etc/vfstab`), and how to obtain the status of a mounted file system. We'll also show how to mount and unmount a file system, and discuss the data structures used to implement the UFS file system.

11.2 Disk Terminology

Before we take a closer look at the files and functions that enable our programs to interact with file systems, and the data structures that make up a file system, it is instructive to review the how a disk drive works. Understanding this also helps us understand some of the optimizations used in the UFS implementation (e.g., cylinder groups).

A disk drive contains one or more platters. A *platter* is a circular piece of metal (or glass) with an oxide coating on both sides (the outer surfaces of the top and bottom platters are not normally used). The oxide is similar to the material used in video and audio tapes, and responds to magnetic fields. The platters are stacked on a spindle with a small gap between each of them.

The gap between the platters is for the read/write heads. There is one read/write head for each surface, and they are usually mounted on a common assembly that moves all the heads back and forth together. During a read or write operation, the heads are held stationary over the platters while they rotate at high speed (several thousand RPM).

On one of the surfaces of a single platter, the area that can be read or written without moving the read/write heads is called a track. *Tracks* are a series of concentric rings, composed of a number of 512-byte sectors. A *sector* is the smallest addressable unit on a disk drive; even if we try to read or write one byte to or from the disk, 512 bytes will be transferred. The term *disk block* is sometimes used as a synonym for sector, but this can lead to confusion with file system blocks.

If we extend a track vertically through all the platters in the disk, we have what is called a *cylinder*. A single disk drive may contain several hundred to several thousand cylinders.

Before a disk I/O can take place, the disk must be positioned in the correct place. To do this, the disk must be told the head number, the track number, and the sector number. Once the heads are positioned in the correct cylinder, the disk must wait for the correct sector to pass by the read/write heads. Only when this happens can a data transfer take place.

Three main factors determine the performance of a single disk:

1. The *seek time* or *access time*. This is the amount of time required to position the head assembly in the correct cylinder. For our purposes, we also include the settle time in the seek time. The *settle time* is the time the head assembly takes to settle once it arrives at the right cylinder.

2. The *latency time*. This the amount of time it takes for the right sector to arrive under the read/write heads.

3. The *transfer rate*. Also known as the *internal transfer rate*, this is the rate at which the drive can transfer data to or from the disk surface, assuming the heads are in the correct position.

Other factors beyond the control of the manufacturer also have an effect on disk drive performance. These include the speed of bus connecting the drive to the computer, and the speed of the host bus adapter (the latter is frequently referred to as the SCSI controller, but strictly speaking this is wrong; technically, "controller" is the term used for the intelligent electronics located in the target peripheral device—in this case, the drive).

The intended use of a disk may have an influence on choosing which model to use. Lots of random accesses to the disk (e.g., a database or email system) will probably benefit more from a faster seek time than a higher transfer rate, whereas a system that performs large sustained I/O (e.g., an image file server, where the images can become quite large) may benefit more from a higher transfer rate than a fast seek time.

11.3 The Mounted File System Table

The file /etc/mnttab contains information about each mounted file system. Each line in /etc/mnttab refers to one file system, and consists of several fields. These fields include the name of the device that holds the file system, the name of the file system (i.e., its mount point), the type of file system, the mount options, and the time the file system was mounted. The entries in /etc/mnttab are maintained in chronological order (i.e., the first mounted file system is first in the list, and the most recently mounted file system is the last).

Prior to Solaris 8, /etc/mnttab was a regular plain text file. Starting with Solaris 8, however, /etc/mnttab is implemented as a read-only file system.

We can use several functions to obtain information about mounted file systems, most of which make use of the mnttab structure. This structure has the following members, each of which corresponds to a field in /etc/mnttab:

```
struct mnttab {
    char    *mnt_special;    /* Name of mounted resource */
    char    *mnt_mountp;     /* The mount point */
    char    *mnt_fstype;     /* Type of file system mounted */
    char    *mnt_mntopts;    /* Options for this mount */
    char    *mnt_time;       /* File system mount time */
};
```

Each structure member has the following definition:

mnt_special   This is the name of the mounted resource. This will either be the pathname of the block special device that holds the file system (in the case of local UFS file system mounts), or a string of the form host:/path/to/resource for file systems mounted from remote servers. For loopback mounts, this field contains the pathname of the loopback mounted directory.

mnt_mountp   This is the mount point (i.e., where abouts in the file system hierarchy the mount appears). The mount point must exist as a directory at the time of the mount operation, and any files in the mounted-on directory will be inaccessible once the mount operation successfully completes.

mnt_fstype   This is the type of file system mounted. Examples include ufs, nfs, and tmpfs.

mnt_mntopts   This is a list of comma-separated options for this mount. The legal values are file system dependent, but common options include rw, readonly, largefiles, logging, and nosuid.

mnt_time   This is the time the file system was mounted (in seconds since the epoch).

Applications intended to be used on releases prior to Solaris 8 should obtain a read lock on /etc/mnttab before trying to read it; this provides a consistent access to other processes trying to access it. Similarly, processes wanting to write to /etc/mnttab should first obtain a write lock for it. Neither of these precautions need to be taken from Solaris 8, as user processes can't write to /etc/mnttab.

A read from the beginning of /etc/mnttab causes a snapshot to be taken; this is used to populate the file. If another file system is mounted after /etc/mnttab has been read from, the information for that file system will not appear in /etc/mnttab until another read from offset 0 has taken place. Note that we should use the functions provided (discussed next) to interrogate /etc/mnttab rather than trying to parse it manually.

Now that we've described the mnttab structure and mentioned some precautions we must take if our target release is Solaris 7 or earlier, we can take a look at the functions that obtain information about the contents of /etc/mnttab.

The getmntent, getmntany and getextmntent Functions

Three functions obtain information about the contents of /etc/mnttab. These are getmntent, getmntany, and getextmntent.

```
#include <stdio.h>
#include <sys/mnttab.h>

int getmntent (FILE *fp, struct mnttab *mp);

int getmntany (FILE *fp, struct mnttab *mp, struct mnttab *mpref);

int getextmntent (FILE *fp, struct extmnttab *mp, int len);
```
All three return: see text

The getmntent function reads a line (starting at the current file offset) from the file pointed to by *fp*, and populates the mnttab structure pointed to by *mp* with the information found. Successive calls to getmntent can be used to search through the list of mounted file systems.

The getmntany function searches the file referenced by *fp* until a match is found between a line in the file and the mnttab structure pointed to by *mpref*. A match occurs if all the non-NULL fields in *mpref* match the corresponding fields in the file. If a match is found, the mnttab structure pointed to by *mp* is populated with the data from the file.

The getextmntent function was introduced with Solaris 8 and is similar to the getmntent function, but it returns the major and minor device numbers of the mounted resource in addition to the information that getmntent provides. Notice that getextmntent populates an extmnttab structure, which has the following members:

```
struct extmnttab {
    char    *mnt_special;    /* Name of mounted resource */
    char    *mnt_mountp;     /* The mount point */
    char    *mnt_fstype;     /* Type of file system mounted */
    char    *mnt_mntopts;    /* Options for this mount */
    char    *mnt_time;       /* File system mount time */
    uint_t  mnt_major;       /* Major number of mounted device */
    uint_t  mnt_minor;       /* Minor number of mounted device */
};
```

The first five members are the same as in the mnttab structure so that the hasmntopt function will work properly when its *mnt* argument is a suitably cast pointer to an extmnttab structure.

For the `getextmntent` function to work properly, it must be notified whenever `/etc/mnttab` has been reopened or rewound since a previous call to `getextmntent`. This is done by calling the `resetmnttab` function we discuss further on in this section. Apart from this, `getextmntent` behaves exactly the same as `getmntent` (the *len* argument is ignored).

Each of these functions returns 0 if an entry is successfully read (or a match is found in the case of `getmntany`). If EOF is encountered, they return −1, and if an error occurs, one of the following values will be returned:

`MNT_TOOLONG`	A line in the file exceeds the internal buffer size, which is `MNT_LINE_MAX` bytes.
`MNT_TOOMANY`	A line in the file contains too many fields.
`MNT_TOOFEW`	A line in the file does not contain enough fields.

Example: Printing a formatted version of `/etc/mnttab`

Program 11.1 uses the `getmntent` and `getmntany` functions to obtain information about the mounted file systems, then prints it out. The program is essentially the same as the `mount` command without any arguments but uses a different display format. Also, we can specify on the command line the name of the file systems we are interested in.

Program 11.1 checks the number of command line arguments. If there aren't any, information about all currently mounted file systems is printed. However, if there are arguments, they are taken as being the mount point of file systems we are interested in. Notice that we call `rewind` after printing out the details of individual file systems. This is because the `getmntent` and `getmntany` functions do not automatically rewind the file pointer for `/etc/mnttab`, and the file systems on the command line may not be listed in chronological order.

This what we get when we run Program 11.1:

```
$ ./mnttab / /proc /etc/mnttab /home/rich
Mount point: /
  Mounted from: /dev/dsk/c0t0d0s0
  File system type: ufs
  Mount options: rw,intr,largefiles,logging,xattr,onerror=panic,suid,
      dev=2200000                      Line wrapped to fit on the page
  Mount time: Mon Jan  7 19:57:44 2002

Mount point: /proc
  Mounted from: /proc
  File system type: proc
  Mount options: dev=38c0000
  Mount time: Mon Jan  7 19:57:44 2002

Mount point: /etc/mnttab
  Mounted from: mnttab
  File system type: mntfs
  Mount options: dev=3980000
  Mount time: Mon Jan  7 19:57:44 2002
```

————————————————————————————————— *file_systems/mnttab.c*

```
 1 #include <stdio.h>
 2 #include <stdlib.h>
 3 #include <sys/mnttab.h>
 4 #include "ssp.h"

 5 static void print_mnttab (struct mnttab *mp);

 6 int main (int argc, char **argv)
 7 {
 8     FILE *fp;
 9     struct mnttab mp;
10     struct mnttab mpref;
11     int ret;
12     int i;

13     if ((fp = fopen ("/etc/mnttab", "r")) == NULL)
14         err_msg ("Can't open /etc/mnttab");

15     if (argc == 1) {
16         while ((ret = getmntent (fp, &mp)) == 0)
17             print_mnttab (&mp);

18         if (ret != -1)
19             err_quit ("Bad /etc/mnttab file.\n");
20     }
21     else {
22         for (i = 1; argc-- > 1; i++) {
23             mpref.mnt_mountp = argv [i];
24             mpref.mnt_special = NULL;
25             mpref.mnt_fstype = NULL;
26             mpref.mnt_mntopts = NULL;
27             mpref.mnt_time = NULL;

28             switch (getmntany (fp, &mp, &mpref)) {
29                 case -1:
30                     rewind (fp);
31                     break;

32                 case 0:
33                     print_mnttab (&mp);
34                     rewind (fp);
35                     break;

36                 default:
37                     err_quit ("Bad /etc/mnttab file.\n");
38                     break;
39             }
40         }
41     }

42     return (0);
43 }

44 static void print_mnttab (struct mnttab *mp)
45 {
46     time_t mount_time;
```

```
47      mount_time = atol (mp -> mnt_time);
48      printf ("Mount point: %s\n", mp -> mnt_mountp);
49      printf ("  Mounted from: %s\n", mp -> mnt_special);
50      printf ("  File system type: %s\n", mp -> mnt_fstype);
51      printf ("  Mount options: %s\n", mp -> mnt_mntopts);
52      printf ("  Mount time: %s\n", ctime (&mount_time));
53  }
```
────────────────────────────────── file_systems/mnttab.c

Program 11.1 Displaying information about mounted file systems.

```
Mount point: /home/rich
  Mounted from: zen:/export/home/rich
  File system type: nfs
  Mount options: xattr,dev=3b00050
  Mount time: Sun May 26 22:38:52 2002
```

The `hasmntopt` Function

We can search the `mnt_mntopts` member of a `mnttab` structure for a specific mount option by using the `hasmntopt` function.

```
#include <stdio.h>
#include <sys/mnttab.h>

char *hasmntopt (struct mnttab *mnt, char *opt);
```
                    Returns: the address of the matching substring if found, NULL if not

The `hasmntopt` function scans the `mnt_mntopts` member of the `mnttab` structure pointed to by *mnt* for a substring that matches *opt*. Substrings are delimited by commas and the end of the `mnt_mntopts` string.

Example: Listing file systems mounted with a specific option

Program 11.2 lists all the file systems mounted with the option specified on the command line.

When we run Program 11.2, we get results similar to the following:

```
$ ./hasmntopt logging
/
/space
```

In the UNIX tradition of combining tools to make new ones, we can use Programs 11.1 and 11.2 to print the details of all file systems mounted with a given option. For example:

```
$ ./mnttab `./hasmntopt logging`
Mount point: /
  Mounted from: /dev/dsk/c0t0d0s0
  File system type: ufs
  Mount options: rw,intr,largefiles,logging,xattr,onerror=panic,suid,
     dev=2200000
  Mount time: Mon Jan  7 19:57:44 2002
```

file_systems/hasmntopt.c

```
 1 #include <stdio.h>
 2 #include <sys/mnttab.h>
 3 #include "ssp.h"

 4 int main (int argc, char **argv)
 5 {
 6     FILE *fp;
 7     struct mnttab mp;
 8     int ret;

 9     if (argc != 2)
10         err_quit ("Usage: hasmntopt mount_option");

11     if ((fp = fopen ("/etc/mnttab", "r")) == NULL)
12         err_msg ("Can't open /etc/mnttab");

13     while ((ret = getmntent (fp, &mp)) == 0) {
14         if (hasmntopt (&mp, argv [1]))
15             printf ("%s\n", mp.mnt_mountp);
16     }

17     if (ret != -1)
18         err_quit ("Bad /etc/mnttab file.\n");

19     return (0);
20 }
```

file_systems/hasmntopt.c

Program 11.2 Listing file systems mounted with a given option.

```
Mount point: /space
  Mounted from: /dev/dsk/c0t0d0s7
  File system type: ufs
  Mount options: rw,intr,largefiles,logging,xattr,onerror=panic,suid,
     dev=2200007
  Mount time: Tue May 21 19:43:42 2002
```

Once again, we've had to wrap some of the lines so that they can fit on the page. Notice also that we've used command substitution on the first line. Everything between back ticks (`) and the back ticks themselves is replaced with the output of the command they surround. In this case, the back ticks and everything between them are replaced by the output of the command "./hasmntopt logging". Another way of doing this would be to use the construct "./mnttab $(./hasmntopt logging)".

The `resetmnttab` Function

We mentioned earlier that the getextmntent function should be notified if /etc/mnttab is reopened or rewound between successive calls to it; we do this by calling resetmnttab.

```
#include <stdio.h>
#include <sys/mnttab.h>

void resetmnttab (FILE *fp);
```

This function was also introduced with Solaris 8.

The putmntent Function

For releases of Solaris prior to Solaris 8, the putmntent function can be used to add an entry to /etc/mnttab.

```
#include <stdio.h>
#include <sys/mnttab.h>

int putmntent (FILE *iop, struct mnttab *mp);
```
                                   Returns: the number of bytes written if OK, −1 on error

The putmntent function formats the contents of the mnttab structure pointed to by *mp* and writes it the file associated with *fp* (which should be opened in append mode).

Since Solaris 8, this function is obsolete and does nothing except return −1 to indicate an error. Mounting a file system (by using the mount command or one of the functions we discuss in Section 11.6) is now the only way to add an entry to /etc/mnttab.

11.4   The mntfs File System ioctl commands

Coincident with the Solaris 8 implementation of /etc/mnttab as a read-only file system is a set of three new commands to be used with the ioctl function. Before we take a closer look at them, let's review ioctl's function prototype.

```
#include <unistd.h>
#include <stropts.h>
#include <sys/mntio.h>

int ioctl (int fildes, int request, /* arg */...);
```
                                   Returns: depends on *request* if OK, −1 on error

Two of the ioctl requests (MNTIOC_SETTAG and MNTIOC_CLRTAG) make use of a mnttagdesc structure, which has the following members:

```
struct mnttagdesc {
    uint_t  mtd_major;      /* Major number of mounted resource */
    uint_t  mtd_minor;      /* Minor number of mounted resource */
    char    *mtd_mntpt;     /* Mount point for mounted resource */
    char    *mtd_tag;       /* Tag to set or clear */
};
```

Once we've obtained a file descriptor for /etc/mnttab, we can issue an ioctl with the *request* argument set to one of the following:

MNTIOC_NMNTS   This returns the number of mounted resources in the current snapshot in the uint32_t pointed to by *arg*.

MNTIOC_GETDEVLIST   This returns an array of uint32_t's that has twice as many elements as the number returned by MNTIOC_NMNTS. Each pair of array elements contains the major and minor device number for the file system at the corresponding line in the /etc/mnttab snapshot. The *arg* argument points to the buffer in which the array should be written.

MNTIOC_SETTAG   This request sets a tag word into the options list for a mounted file system. A tag is a notation that appears in the options string of a mounted file system, but is not recognized or interpreted by the file system code. The *arg* argument points to a suitably populated mnttagdesc structure. If the tag already exists, it is marked as set but not re-added. Tags can be at most MAX_MNTOPT_TAG bytes long.

MNTIOC_CLRTAG   This marks a tag in the options list for a mounted file system as not set. The *arg* argument points to a mnttagdesc structure, which identifies the file system and tag to be cleared.

Example: Setting a tag on a mounted file system

Program 11.3 uses the MNTIOC_SETTAG ioctl to set a tag on the file system identified by the command line arguments.

Let's use Program 11.3 to add our own tag to a file system.

```
$ ./mnttab /home
Mount point: /home
  Mounted from: auto_home
  File system type: autofs
  Mount options: indirect,ignore,nobrowse,dev=3b40002
  Mount time: Mon Jan  7 19:57:53 2002

$ ./settag /home ssp_tag
$ ./mnttab /home
Mount point: /home
  Mounted from: auto_home
  File system type: autofs
  Mount options: indirect,ignore,nobrowse,ssp_tag,dev=3b40002
  Mount time: Mon Jan  7 19:57:53 2002
```

Notice that the tag we added, ssp_tag, was placed between nobrowse and dev=3b40002. Tags are ignored by the OS, but one example of their use is for noting which project or Zone a file system is associated with.

file_systems/settag.c

```
 1 #include <stdio.h>
 2 #include <unistd.h>
 3 #include <string.h>
 4 #include <sys/mnttab.h>
 5 #include <sys/stat.h>
 6 #include <sys/mntio.h>
 7 #include "ssp.h"

 8 int main (int argc, char **argv)
 9 {
10     FILE *fp;
11     int fd;
12     struct extmnttab mp;
13     struct mnttagdesc dp;
14     int ret;

15     if (argc != 3)
16         err_quit ("Usage: settag filsystem tag");

17     if ((fp = fopen ("/etc/mnttab", "r")) == NULL)
18         err_msg ("Can't open /etc/mnttab");

19     fd = fileno (fp);

20     while ((ret = getextmntent (fp, &mp, 0)) == 0) {
21         if (strcmp (mp.mnt_mountp, argv [1]) == 0) {
22             dp.mtd_major = mp.mnt_major;
23             dp.mtd_minor = mp.mnt_minor;
24             dp.mtd_mntpt = mp.mnt_mountp;
25             dp.mtd_tag = argv [2];
26             if (ioctl (fd, MNTIOC_SETTAG, &dp) == -1)
27                 err_msg ("ioctl failed");
28             break;
29         }
30     }

31     if (ret > 0)
32         err_quit ("Bad /etc/mnttab file.\n");

33     return (0);
34 }
```

file_systems/settag.c

Program 11.3 Setting a tag on a mounted file system.

11.5 File System Defaults

The file /etc/vfstab contains information about the defaults for each file system. Each line in /etc/vfstab refers to one file system and consists of several fields. The fields include the name of the device to mount (a block device), the name of the device to check with fsck (a character device), the name of the mount point, the type of file system, the number used by fsck to determine when to check the file system, a flag to say that the file system should be mounted automatically when the system boots, and a list of the mount options. A hyphen is used to indicate that a field doesn't apply to the file system associated with the current line.

We can use several functions to obtain information about file system defaults, each of which uses the `vfstab` structure. This structure has the following members, each of which corresponds to a field in `/etc/vfstab`:

```
struct vfstab {
      char     *vfs_special;     /* The device to mount */
      char     *vfs_fsckdev;     /* The device to fsck */
      char     *vfs_mountp;      /* The file system's mount point */
      char     *vfs_fstype;      /* The type of file system */
      char     *vfs_fsckpass;    /* Pass number to run fsck */
      char     *vfs_automnt;     /* Mount at boot flag */
      char     *vfs_mntopts;     /* The mount options */
};
```

Each structure member has the following definition:

`vfs_special`	This is the name of the resource to be mounted. In the case of local file systems, this is the name of the block device on which the file system resides. Remote resources are specified using a sting of the form `host:/path/to/resource`.
`vfs_fsckdev`	This is the name of the character device on which the file system resides. This is the device used by `fsck` when it checks the integrity of the file system at system boot.
`vfs_mountp`	This is the name of the file system's mount point in the file system hierarchy, i.e., the directory the file system is to be mounted on.
`vfs_fstype`	This is the file system type. Examples include `ufs`, `nfs`, and `tmpfs`.
`vfs_fsckpass`	When `fsck` runs as the system boots, certain file systems (e.g., `/` and `/usr`) must be checked before others. This field indicates which pass of `fsck` should check this file system.
`vfs_automnt`	This is a flag that specifies whether the file system is to be automatically booted when the system boots.
`vfs_mntopts`	This is a list of comma-separated options for this file system. The legal values are file system dependent, but common options include `rw`, `readonly`, `largefiles`, `logging`, and `nosuid`.

Fields that don't apply to the file system in question are NULL.

Now that we've described the `vfstab` structure, we can take a look at the functions we use to obtain information about the contents of `/etc/vfstab`. As with `/etc/mnttab`, we should use the functions provided to interrogate `/etc/vfstab` rather than parsing it manually.

The `getvfsent` Family of Functions

Four functions let us obtain information about the contents of `/etc/vfstab`. These are `getvfsent`, `getvfsfile`, `getvfsspec`, and `getvfsany`.

```
#include <stdio.h>
#include <sys/vfstab.h>

int getvfsent (FILE *fp, struct vfstab *vp);

int getvfsfile (FILE *fp, struct vfstab *vp, char *file);

int getvfsspec (FILE *fp, struct vfstab *vp, char *spec);

int getvfsany (FILE *fp, struct vfstab *vp, struct vfstab *vref);
```

All four return: see text

The getvfsent function reads a line (starting at the current file offset) from the file specified by *fp*, populating the vfstab structure pointed to by *vp* with the information found. Successive calls to getvfsent can be used to search through the entire file.

The getvfsfile function searches the file referenced by *fp* until a mount point matching *file* is found. When a match is found, the vfstab structure pointed to by *vp* is filled with the fields from the file corresponding to the matching line.

The getvfsspec function searches the file referenced by *fp* until a special device matching *spec* is found, and fills the vfstab structure pointed to by *vp* with the information from the file. The function will try to match the *spec* argument on the device type (block or character), and the major and minor device numbers. If a match cannot be found in this manner, then getvfsspec will compare strings.

The getvfsany function searches the file referenced by *fp* until a match is found between a line in the file and the vfstab structure pointed to by *vref*. A match occurs if all the non-NULL fields in *vref* match the corresponding fields in the file. If a match is found, the vfstab structure pointed to by *vp* is populated with the data from the file.

Each of these functions returns 0 if an entry is successfully read (or, in the case of getvfsany, a match is found). If EOF is encountered, they return −1, and if an error occurs, one of the following values will be returned:

VFS_TOOLONG	A line in the file exceeds the internal buffer size, which is VFS_LINE_MAX bytes.
VFS_TOOMANY	A line in the file contains too many fields.
VFS_TOOFEW	A line in the file does not contain enough fields.

Example: Printing a formatted version of /etc/vfstab

Program 11.4 uses the getvfsent and getvfsfile functions to obtain information about the file systems listed in /etc/vfstab and then prints it out. We can specify on the command line the name of the file system we are interested in.

Program 11.4 checks the command line arguments. If there aren't any, information about all file systems in /etc/vfstab is printed. However, if there are arguments, they are taken as being the name of the file systems we are interested in. Notice that we call rewind after printing out the details of individual file systems. This is because the

file_systems/vfstab.c

```
 1 #include <stdio.h>
 2 #include <sys/vfstab.h>
 3 #include "ssp.h"

 4 static void print_vfstab (struct vfstab *vp);

 5 int main (int argc, char **argv)
 6 {
 7     FILE *fp;
 8     struct vfstab vp;
 9     int ret;
10     int i;

11     if ((fp = fopen ("/etc/vfstab", "r")) == NULL)
12         err_msg ("Can't open /etc/vfstab");

13     if (argc == 1) {
14         while ((ret = getvfsent (fp, &vp)) == 0)
15             print_vfstab (&vp);

16         if (ret != -1)
17             err_quit ("Bad /etc/vfstab file.\n");
18     }
19     else {
20         for (i = 1; argc-- > 1; i++) {
21             switch (getvfsfile (fp, &vp, argv [i])) {
22                 case -1:
23                     rewind (fp);
24                     break;

25                 case 0:
26                     print_vfstab (&vp);
27                     rewind (fp);
28                     break;

29                 default:
30                     err_quit ("Bad /etc/vfstab file.\n");
31                     break;
32             }
33         }
34     }

35     return (0);
36 }

37 static void print_vfstab (struct vfstab *vp)
38 {
39     printf ("Mount point: %s\n", (vp -> vfs_mountp) ?
40         vp -> vfs_mountp : "-");
41     printf (" Mounted from: %s\n", (vp -> vfs_special) ?
42         vp -> vfs_special : "-");
43     printf (" Device to fsck: %s\n", (vp -> vfs_fsckdev) ?
44         vp -> vfs_fsckdev : "-");
45     printf (" File system type: %s\n", (vp -> vfs_fstype) ?
46         vp -> vfs_fstype : "-");
47     printf (" Fsck pass number: %s\n", (vp -> vfs_fsckpass) ?
48         vp -> vfs_fsckpass : "-");
```

```
49     printf ("  Mount at boot: %s\n", (vp -> vfs_automnt) ?
50         vp -> vfs_automnt : "-");
51     printf ("  Mount options: %s\n\n", (vp -> vfs_mntopts) ?
52         vp -> vfs_mntopts : "-");
53 }
```
—— *file_systems/vfstab.c*

Program 11.4 Displaying information from /etc/vfstab.

getvfsent and getvfsfile functions do not automatically rewind the file pointer for /etc/vfstab, and the file systems on the command line may not be listed in the order in which they appear in /etc/vfstab.

This is what we get when we run Program 11.4:

```
$ ./vfstab / /install /tmp
Mount point: /
  Mounted from: /dev/dsk/c0t0d0s0
  Device to fsck: /dev/rdsk/c0t0d0s0
  File system type: ufs
  Fsck pass number: 1
  Mount at boot: no
  Mount options: logging

Mount point: /src
  Mounted from: zen:/export/install
  Device to fsck: -
  File system type: nfs
  Fsck pass number: -
  Mount at boot: yes
  Mount options: -

Mount point: /tmp
  Mounted from: swap
  Device to fsck: -
  File system type: tmpfs
  Fsck pass number: -
  Mount at boot: yes
  Mount options: -
```

Adding an Entry to /etc/vfstab

The functions we have just described allow us to get information from /etc/vfstab. If we want to update that file, we can use the putvfsent function.

```
#include <stdio.h>
#include <sys/vfstab.h>

int putvfsent (FILE *fp, struct vfstab *vp);
```
                                    Returns: the number of bytes written if OK, −1 on error

The putvfsent function writes the vfstab structure pointed to by *vp* to the file associated with the file pointer *fp*. The file should be opened in append mode so that new entries are added to the end of the file (which minimizes the potential interaction with other functions reading the file).

If any members of the `vfstab` structure are NULL, they are output as hyphens.

11.6 Mounting and Unmounting File Systems

Before we can access the data stored in a file system, we must first make it available (this also applies to creating new files in a file system). We do this by mounting the file system at some point in the directory hierarchy. The file system's mount point must be a directory; any files within the mount point directory are inaccessible once a file system has been mounted on it.

Mounting or unmounting a file system is a privileged activity, so only processes with an effective user ID of 0 can do so.

The `mount` Function

The `mount` function is used to mount a file system, adding it to the local directory hierarchy.

```
#include <sys/types.h>
#include <sys/mount.h>
#include <sys/mntent.h>

int mount (const char *spec, const char *dir, int mflag, char *fstype,
    char *dataptr, int datalen, char *optptr, int optlen);
```
Returns: 0 if OK, −1 on error

The `mount` function requests that the file system contained on the device specified by *spec* be mounted on the directory identified by *dir*.

The *mflag* argument specifies the file system independent mount flags, which are constructed from a bitwise-OR of flags from the following list:

`MS_DATA`	The *dataptr* and *datalen* arguments describe a block of file system specific binary data starting at the address *dataptr* with a length of *datalen* bytes. If the file system being mounted does not require this data, *dataptr* should be NULL, and *datalen* should be 0.
`MS_GLOBAL`	If the system is configured and booted as part of a cluster, this mounts the file system globally.
`MS_NOSUID`	This flag prevents programs that are marked set-user-ID or set-group-ID from executing. It also causes `open` to return `ENXIO` when attempting to open a block or character special file.
`MS_OPTIONSTR`	The *optptr* and *optlen* arguments describe a character buffer at the address specified by *optaddr* that has a length of *optlen* bytes. The buffer should contain a NUL-terminated string of

comma-separated file system specific options. Options that have values (as opposed to binary options like `"logging"` or `"nologging"`) are separated by an equals sign (e.g., `"dev=2200000"`). The maximum value *optlen* can have is `MAX_MNTOPT_STR`. The buffer should be long enough to contain more options than were passed in, because the state of any default options not passed in the input option string may also be returned in the recognized options list returned.

`MS_OVERLAY`   This allows the file system to be mounted over an existing file system already mounted on *dir*, making the underlying file system inaccessible. If this flag is not specified, an attempt to mount a file system on a pre-existing file system will fail.

`MS_RDONLY`   This mounts the file system for reading only. This flag should also be specified for file systems incapable of writing (e.g., a CD-ROM). Without this flag, writing is permitted according to the permissions on individual files and directories.

`MS_REMOUNT`   This flag remounts a read-only file system as read-write.

The *fstype* argument is used to indicate the file system type. Figure 11.1 lists the standard file system types.

fstype	String	Description
MNTTYPE_UFS	ufs	UNIX file system
MNTTYPE_NFS	nfs	Network file system
MNTTYPE_NFS3	nfs3	Network file system version 3
MNTTYPE_CACHEFS	cachefs	Cache file system
MNTTYPE_PCFS	pcfs	PC (MS-DOS FAT) file system
MNTTYPE_LOFS	lofs	Loopback file system
MNTTYPE_HSFS	hsfs	High Sierra (ISO 9660) file system
MNTTYPE_SWAP	swap	Swap file system
MNTTYPE_TMPFS	tmpfs	Volatile file system for temporary files
MNTTYPE_AUTOFS	autofs	Automounter file system

Figure 11.1 Standard file system types.

The *dataptr* and *datalen* arguments describe a file system specific binary buffer, which starts at the address specified by *dataptr* and has a size of *datalen* bytes. If there is no file system specific data, *dataptr* should be NULL and *datalen* should be 0. Otherwise, the `MS_DATA` flag should be set in *mflag*.

The *optptr* and *optlen* arguments describe a character buffer, which starts at the address specified by *optptr* and has a length of *optlen* bytes. The buffer should contain a NUL-terminated string of comma-separated options, with a length of no more than `MAX_MNTOPT_STR` characters. If no mount options are to be used, *optptr* should be NULL and *optlen* should be 0. Otherwise, the `MS_OPTIONSTR` flag should be set in *mflag*.

Figure 11.2 describes the standard mount options.

Option	String	Description
MNTOPT_ACDIRMAX	acdirmax	Maximum attribute cache timeout for directories
MNTOPT_ACDIRMIN	acdirmin	Minimum attribute cache timeout for directories
MNTOPT_ACREGMAX	acregmax	Maximum attribute cache timeout for files
MNTOPT_ACREGMIN	acregmin	Minimum attribute cache timeout for files
MNTOPT_ACTIMEO	actimeo	Attribute cache timeout in seconds
MNTOPT_BG	bg	Do mount retries in the background
MNTOPT_DEV	dev	Device ID of mounted file system
MNTOPT_DFRATIME	dfratime	Defer access time updates
MNTOPT_DIRECT	direct	Automount direct map mount
MNTOPT_DISABLEDIRECTIO	disabledirectio	Disable DirectIO `ioctls`
MNTOPT_FG	fg	Do mount retries in the foreground
MNTOPT_FORCEDIRECTIO	forcedirectio	Force DirectIO on all files
MNTOPT_GLOBAL	global	Cluster-wide global mount
MNTOPT_GRPID	grpid	System V compatible group ID on create
MNTOPT_HARD	hard	Hard mount
MNTOPT_IGNORE	ignore	Ignore this entry
MNTOPT_INDIRECT	indirect	Automount indirect map mount
MNTOPT_INTR	intr	Allow NFS operations to be interrupted
MNTOPT_LARGEFILES	largefiles	Allow large files
MNTOPT_LLOCK	llock	Local locking (no lock manager)
MNTOPT_LOGGING	logging	Enable logging
MNTOPT_MAP	map	Automount map
MNTOPT_MULTI	multi	Do multi-component lookup
MNTOPT_NBMAND	nbmand	Allow nonblocking mandatory locks
MNTOPT_NOAC	noac	Don't cache attributes at all
MNTOPT_NOATIME	noatime	Do not update inode access time
MNTOPT_NOCTO	nocto	No close-to-open consistency
MNTOPT_NODFRATIME	nodfratime	Don't defer access time updates
MNTOPT_NOFORCEDIRECTIO	noforcedirectio	No force DirectIO
MNTOPT_NOGLOBAL	noglobal	Mount local to a single node
MNTOPT_NOINTR	nointr	Don't allow NFS operations to be interrupted
MNTOPT_NOLARGEFILES	nolargefiles	Don't allow large files
MNTOPT_NOLOGGING	nologging	Disable logging
MNTOPT_NONBMAND	nonbmand	Disallow nonblocking mandatory locks
MNTOPT_NOPRINT	noprint	Do not print messages
MNTOPT_NOQUOTA	noquota	Don't check quotas
MNTOPT_NOSETSEC	nosec	Do not allow setting of security attributes
MNTOPT_NOSUB	nosub	Disallow mounts on subdirectories
MNTOPT_NOSUID	nosuid	Set-user-ID and set-group-ID not allowed
MNTOPT_NOXATTR	noxattr	Disable extended attributes
MNTOPT_ONERROR	onerror	Action to be taken on error
MNTOPT_PORT	port	NFS server port number
MNTOPT_POSIX	posix	Get static `pathconf` for mount
MNTOPT_PROTO	proto	Protocol network_id indicator
MNTOPT_PUBLIC	public	Use NFS public file handles
MNTOPT_QUOTA	quota	Check quotas
MNTOPT_REMOUNT	remount	Change mount options
MNTOPT_RETRANS	retrans	Maximum retransmissions for soft mounts
MNTOPT_RETRY	retry	Number of mount retries
MNTOPT_RO	ro	Read only

Figure 11.2 The standard mount options.

Option	String	Description
MNTOPT_RQ	rq	Read/write with quotas
MNTOPT_RSIZE	rsize	Maximum NFS read size in bytes
MNTOPT_RW	rw	Read/write
MNTOPT_SEC	sec	Security flavour indicator
MNTOPT_SECURE	secure	Secure (AUTH_DES) mounting
MNTOPT_SEMISOFT	semisoft	Partial soft mount (uncommitted interface)
MNTOPT_SOFT	soft	Soft mount
MNTOPT_SUID	suid	Set-user-ID and set-group-ID allowed
MNTOPT_SYNCDIR	syncdir	Synchronous local directory operations
MNTOPT_TIMEO	timeo	NFS timeout in 1/10ths of a second
MNTOPT_VERS	vers	Protocol version number
MNTOPT_WSIZE	wsize	Maximum NFS write size in bytes
MNTOPT_XATTR	xattr	Enable extended attributes

Figure 11.2 The standard mount options (continued).

If the mount is successful, all references to the mount point *dir* refer to the root directory of the mounted file system. The mounted file system is also added to the kernel's list of all mounted file systems, which can be examined by reading /etc/mnttab.

Note that some *mflag* bits set file system options that can also be passed in an option string. Options in the option string are set first, then those specified by *mflags* are applied (i.e., the options specified by *mflags* take precedence over those specified by the option string).

Example: Mounting a local file system

Program 11.5 shows an example of how to mount a local UFS file system.

Mounting a UFS file system requires us to pass a ufs_args structure to the mount system call, which means that we must specify the MS_DATA flag. We also use the option arguments to pass the logging option (so we must also specify MS_OPTIONSTR).

Running Program 11.5 gives us the following results (we've wrapped some of the lines so they will fit on the page):

```
$ ./mnttab /space
Mount point: /space
  Mounted from: /dev/dsk/c0t0d0s7
  File system type: ufs
  Mount options: rw,intr,largefiles,logging,xattr,onerror=panic,suid,
     dev=2200007
  Mount time: Fri Jun  7 15:00:42 2002
$ su
Password:                              We type our root password here
# umount /space
# ./sspmount /dev/dsk/c0t0d0s7 /space
Options = ro,intr,largefiles,logging,noquota,xattr,nodfratime, onerror=panic,
   nosuid
```

—————————————————————————— file_systems/sspmount.c

```
 1 #include <stdio.h>
 2 #include <sys/types.h>
 3 #include <sys/mount.h>
 4 #include <sys/mntent.h>
 5 #include <sys/fs/ufs_mount.h>
 6 #include "ssp.h"

 7 int main (int argc, char **argv)
 8 {
 9     char options [MAX_MNTOPT_STR];
10     struct ufs_args args;

11     if (argc != 3)
12         err_quit ("Usage: sspmount special dir");

13     snprintf (options, MAX_MNTOPT_STR, "logging");
14 #ifdef UFSMNT_LARGEFILES
15     args.flags = UFSMNT_LARGEFILES;
16 #else
17     args.flags = 0;
18 #endif

19     if (mount (argv [1], argv [2], MS_DATA | MS_NOSUID | MS_OPTIONSTR |
20         MS_RDONLY, MNTTYPE_UFS, &args, sizeof (args), options,
21         MAX_MNTOPT_STR) == -1) {
22         err_msg ("Can't mount %s on %s", argv [1], argv [2]);
23     }
24     printf ("Options = %s\n", options);

25     return (0);
26 }
```

—————————————————————————— file_systems/sspmount.c

Program 11.5 Mounting a UFS file system.

```
# ./mnttab /space
Mount point: /space
  Mounted from: /dev/dsk/c0t0d0s7
  File system type: ufs
  Mount options: ro,intr,largefiles,logging,xattr,onerror=panic,nosuid,
      dev=2200007
  Mount time: Sat Jun  8 10:09:01 2002
```

Notice that several options (i.e., intr, largefiles, xattr, onerror, and dev) are automatically added for us. Most of these automatically added options can be changed by using an option string or by setting the appropriate flags in the ufs_args structure.

The umount and umount2 Functions

Once we've finished using a file system, we can make its contents unavailable by unmounting it. We do this by using either the umount or umount2 function calls.

```
#include <sys/mount.h>

int umount (const char *file);

int umount2 (const char *file, int mflag);
```
Both return: 0 if OK, −1 on error

The umount function makes a request to unmount a previously mounted file system. The *file* argument specifies the absolute pathname of the mount point to be unmounted. If the unmount operation is successful, the contents of the underlying directory are available once again.

Introduced with Solaris 8, the umount2 function is exactly the same as umount, except it has the additional capability of unmounting a file system even if it is busy. The *mflag* argument governs this behaviour and must be set to one of the following two values:

0   This performs a normal unmount, like the umount function. An error is returned (EBUSY) if the file system is busy at the time of the request.

MS_FORCE   This forcibly unmounts the file system, even if it is busy. A forced unmount might result in the loss of some data, so it should be used only when a regular unmount request is unsuccessful. If the underlying file system does not support forced unmounts, an error is returned (currently, only the UFS and NFS file systems support MS_FORCE).

Unless portability is a concern, the umount2 function is preferred over umount, because it provides greater functionality.

Example: Unmounting a file system

Program 11.6 attempts to unmount a file system. If the file system is busy, we are asked if we want to force the unmount operation.

Let's see what happens when we run Program 11.6 on a busy file system:

```
$ su
Password:                           Become root
# cp sspumount /space
# cd /space
# ./sspumount /space
The file system mounted on /space is busy.
Do you want to force the unmount?  y
# pwd
/space
# ls
.: Not a directory
# cd /
# mount | grep space
#
```

file_systems/sspumount.c

```
 1 #include <stdio.h>
 2 #include <sys/mount.h>
 3 #include <errno.h>
 4 #include "ssp.h"

 5 int main (int argc, char **argv)
 6 {
 7     char resp;

 8     if (argc != 2)
 9         err_quit ("Usage: sspumount dir");

10     if (umount2 (argv [1], 0) == -1) {
11         if (errno == EBUSY) {
12             printf ("The file system mounted on %s is busy.\n", argv [1]);
13             printf ("Do you want to force the unmount?  ");
14             resp = fgetc (stdin);
15             if (resp == 'y') {
16                 if (umount2 (argv [1], MS_FORCE) == -1)
17                     err_msg ("Forced umount failed");
18             }
19         }
20         else
21             err_msg ("umount failed");
22     }

23     return (0);
24 }
```

file_systems/sspumount.c

Program 11.6 Unmounting a file system.

Notice that when we force the /space file system to unmount, our current directory is no longer valid. Running the mount command confirms that /space is no longer mounted.

11.7   Obtaining the Status of a File System

It is often useful to obtain statistics and other information about a mounted file system. Programs used by system administrators might be interested in the available space on a file system, or the number of files. We can use two functions to obtain these and other statistics about a file system: statvfs and fstatvfs (there is also an obsolete function, ustat, which we discuss for the sake of completeness).

The statvfs and fstatvfs Functions

The statvfs and fstatvfs functions are used to obtain information about a mounted file system.

```
#include <sys/types.h>
#include <sys/statvfs.h>

int statvfs (const char *path, struct statvfs *buf);

int fstatvfs (int fildes, struct statvfs *buf);
```
Both return: 0 if OK, −1 on error

The `statvfs` function obtains information about the file system in which the file pointed to by *path* resides, and places it in the `statvfs` structure pointed to by *buf*.

The `statvfs` structure has the following members:

```
typedef struct statvfs {
    unsigned long   f_bsize;                /* Block size */
    unsigned long   f_frsize;               /* Fragment size */
    fsblkcnt_t      f_blocks;               /* Number of blocks */
    fsblkcnt_t      f_bfree;                /* Total free blocks */
    fsblkcnt_t      f_bavail;               /* Available blocks */
    fsfilcnt_t      f_files;                /* Number of inodes */
    fsfilcnt_t      f_ffree;                /* Total free inodes */
    fsfilcnt_t      f_favail;               /* Available inodes */
    unsigned long   f_fsid;                 /* File system ID */
    char            f_basetype [_FSTYPSZ];  /* File system type */
    unsigned long   f_flag;                 /* Bit mask of flags */
    unsigned long   f_namemax;              /* Max filename length */
    char            f_fstr [32];            /* File system string */
    unsigned long   f_filler [16];          /* Reserved */
} statvfs_t;
```

The `statvfs` structure's members are defined as follows:

`f_bsize`	This is the preferred file system block size. Reads and writes to the file system should use this block size for optimum performance. By default Solaris uses a block size of 8192 bytes (i.e., 8 KB).
`f_frsize`	The fragment size—the fundamental file system block size—is the smallest amount of space that can be consumed by a file. If a file has a size less than this value, it will still consume a block of this size on the disk. The default fragment size for Solaris is 1024 bytes (i.e., 1 KB).
`f_blocks`	This is the total number of `f_frsized` blocks that can be used in the file system. In other words, this field contains the size of the file system.
`f_bfree`	This is the total number of free blocks in the file system. A number of the free blocks can be allocated only by a privileged process.
`f_bavail`	The number of free blocks available to unprivileged processes. Early releases of Solaris reserved 10 percent of the file system's space for privileged processes, but starting with

	Solaris 8, the amount reserved depends on the size of the file system. This is in recognition of the average file system size having grown considerably since the days when a 100 MB disk was considered large.
`f_files`	This is the total number files that can be created on the file system (i.e., the number of inodes in the file system).
	This value may not be valid for NFS-mounted file systems.
`f_ffree`	This is the total number of free inodes in the file system.
	This value may not be valid for NFS-mounted file systems.
`f_favail`	This is the number of free inodes available to unprivileged processes.
	This value may not be valid for NFS-mounted file systems.
`f_fsid`	This is the file system identifier. Currently, this is the device number the file system resides on.
`f_basetype`	This is the name of the file system type, as a NUL-terminated string.
`f_flag`	This is a bit mask of flags.
`f_namemax`	This is the maximum length of filename permitted by the file system.
`f_fstr`	This is a file system specific string, which is only used by the kernel.
`f_filler`	This is just a padding field reserved for future expansion.

The value of `f_flag` is a bit mask constructed by bitwise-ORing one or more of the following values together:

`ST_RDONLY`	This is a read-only file system.
`ST_NOSUID`	The file system does not support set-user-ID and set-group-ID semantics.
`ST_NOTRUNC`	The file system does not truncate filenames longer than `f_namemax`.

The `fstatvfs` function obtains the same information about a file system as `statvfs`. The only difference is that `fstatvfs` obtains information about the file system in which the file associated with the file descriptor *fildes* resides.

Example: Printing file system statistics

Program 11.7 obtains the statistics for the file system in which the file given on the command line resides, and then prints them out.

Running Program 11.7 on a local file system gives the following results:

file_systems/statvfs.c

```
 1 #include <stdio.h>
 2 #include <sys/types.h>
 3 #include <sys/statvfs.h>
 4 #include "ssp.h"

 5 int main (int argc, char **argv)
 6 {
 7     struct statvfs buf;

 8     if (argc != 2)
 9         err_quit ("Usage: statvfs file");

10     if (statvfs (argv [1], &buf) == -1)
11         err_msg ("statvfs of %s failed", argv [1]);

12     printf ("File system containing: %s\n", argv [1]);
13     printf ("  Block size: %lu\n", buf.f_bsize);
14     printf ("  Fragment size: %lu\n", buf.f_frsize);
15     printf ("  Total blocks: %lu\n", buf.f_blocks);
16     printf ("  Free blocks: %lu\n", buf.f_bfree);
17     printf ("  Available blocks: %lu\n", buf.f_bavail);
18     printf ("  Total inodes: %lu\n", buf.f_files);
19     printf ("  Free inodes: %lu\n", buf.f_ffree);
20     printf ("  Available inodes: %lu\n", buf.f_favail);
21     printf ("  File system ID: %lu\n", buf.f_fsid);
22     printf ("  File system type: %s\n", buf.f_basetype);

23     printf ("  Flags: ");
24     if (buf.f_flag == 0)
25         printf ("0\n");
26     else {
27         if (buf.f_flag & ST_RDONLY)
28             printf ("ST_RDONLY ");
29         if (buf.f_flag & ST_NOSUID)
30             printf ("ST_NOSUID ");
31         if (buf.f_flag & ST_NOTRUNC)
32             printf ("ST_NOTRUNC ");
33         printf ("\n");
34     }

35     printf ("  Maximum filename length: %lu\n", buf.f_namemax);
36     printf ("  File system string: %s\n", buf.f_fstr);

37     return (0);
38 }
```

file_systems/statvfs.c

Program 11.7 Printing file system statistics.

```
$ ./statvfs /space
File system containing: /space
  Block size: 8192
  Fragment size: 1024
  Total blocks: 4383734
  Free blocks: 3457638
  Available blocks: 3413801
```

```
Total inodes: 555904
Free inodes: 500163
Available inodes: 500163
File system ID: 35651584
File system type: ufs
Flags: ST_NOTRUNC
Maximum filename length: 255
File system string:
```

The `ustat` Function

Older programs might use the `ustat` function to obtain information about a mounted file system.

```
#include <sys/types.h>
#include <ustat.h>

int ustat (dev_t dev, struct ustat *buf);
```

Returns: 0 if OK, −1 on error

The `ustat` function obtains information about the mounted file system specified by *dev*, and stores it in the `ustat` structure pointed to by *buf*.

The `ustat` structure has the following members:

```
struct ustat {
    daddr_t f_tfree;        /* Total free blocks */
    ino_t   f_tinode;       /* Number of free inodes */
    char    f_fname [6];    /* File system name */
    char    f_fpack [6];    /* File system pack name */
};
```

The number of free blocks is measured in 512-byte blocks, and the file system name and file system pack name don't usually contain anything useful (they are usually empty).

The `ustat` function is obsolete; new programs should use the replacement function, `statvfs` (or `fstatvfs`).

Example: Obtaining file system information using `ustat`

Program 11.8 uses the `ustat` function to obtain information about the file system in which the file specified on the command line resides.

When we run Program 11.8, we get the following results:

```
$ ./ustat /space
File system containing: /space
  Total free blocks: 6915196
  Total free inodes: 500162
  File system name:
  File system pack name:
```

After adjusting for the different units (i.e., 512-byte blocks versus 8192-byte blocks), these results are the same as we get from Program 11.7.

```
 1 #include <stdio.h>
 2 #include <sys/types.h>
 3 #include <sys/stat.h>
 4 #include <ustat.h>
 5 #include "ssp.h"

 6 int main (int argc, char **argv)
 7 {
 8     struct stat sbuf;
 9     struct ustat buf;

10     if (argc != 2)
11         err_quit ("Usage: ustat file");

12     if (stat (argv [1], &sbuf) == -1)
13         err_msg ("stat of %s failed", argv [1]);
14     if (ustat (sbuf.st_dev, &buf) == -1)
15         err_msg ("ustat of %s failed", argv [1]);

16     printf ("File system containing: %s\n", argv [1]);
17     printf ("   Total free blocks: %lu\n", buf.f_tfree);
18     printf ("   Total free inodes: %lu\n", buf.f_tinode);
19     printf ("   File system name: %s\n", buf.f_fname);
20     printf ("   File system pack name: %s\n", buf.f_fpack);

21     return (0);
22 }
```

Program 11.8 Obtaining file system information using `ustat`.

11.8 Reading File System Data Structures

Sometimes it is useful to be able to read the raw data structures that make up a file system. For example, the `ufsdump` program reads the file system to make a backup that efficiently handles sparse files. Interpreting the raw data is not inherently difficult, but requires that we must be cognizant of the underlying data structures.

Recall our discussion of a file system's structure in Section 10.14, where we said that a file system consists of several items:

1. A boot block, which is reserved for the boot program when the partition on which the file system resides is to be used as a root file system

2. The superblock, which contains information about the geometry and layout of the file system, and is critical to the file system state

3. The inode list, which is spread throughout the file system's cylinder groups

4. Data blocks, which are used to store actual file and directory data, and take up most of the file system

5. Cylinder groups, which are groups of data blocks, an inode list, and a copy of the superblock, that are in close physical proximity to each other on the disk (The space in a file system is arranged into cylinder groups for reasons of efficiency.)

In the next few sections, we'll take a closer look at the data structures used to implement the superblock, the cylinder group, and the inode list for UFS file systems (other file systems will be similar).

The Superblock

As we mentioned in Section 10.14, the superblock contains information about the geometry and layout of the file system, and is critical to the file system state. Because the superblock is so important (it is arguably *the* most important part of a file system), it is replicated in each cylinder group of the file system. The replica can be used should the original become corrupted. The replicas are put in place when the file system is first created, but because the critical information doesn't change during the lifetime of the file system, the replicas don't need to be updated.

The superblock of a UFS file system is defined by the `fs` structure (which is declared in `<sys/fs/ufs_fs.h>`) and contains the following members:

```
struct fs {
        uint32_t        fs_link;
        uint32_t        fs_rlink;
        daddr32_t       fs_sblkno;
        daddr32_t       fs_cblkno;
        daddr32_t       fs_iblkno;
        daddr32_t       fs_dblkno;
        int32_t         fs_cgoffset;
        int32_t         fs_cgmask;
        time32_t        fs_time;
        int32_t         fs_size;
        int32_t         fs_dsize;
        int32_t         fs_ncg;
        int32_t         fs_bsize;
        int32_t         fs_fsize;
        int32_t         fs_frag;
        int32_t         fs_minfree;
        int32_t         fs_rotdelay;
        int32_t         fs_rps;
        int32_t         fs_bmask;
        int32_t         fs_fmask;
        int32_t         fs_bshift;
        int32_t         fs_fshift;
        int32_t         fs_maxcontig;
        int32_t         fs_maxbpg;
        int32_t         fs_fragshift;
        int32_t         fs_fsbtodb;
        int32_t         fs_sbsize;
        int32_t         fs_csmask;
        int32_t         fs_csshift;
        int32_t         fs_nindir;
        int32_t         fs_inopb;
        int32_t         fs_nspf;
        int32_t         fs_optim;
```

```
        int32_t           fs_npsect;
        int32_t           fs_interleave;
        int32_t           fs_trackskew;
        int32_t           fs_id [2];
        daddr32_t         fs_csaddr;
        int32_t           fs_cssize;
        int32_t           fs_cgsize;
        int32_t           fs_ntrak;
        int32_t           fs_nsect;
        int32_t           fs_spc;
        int32_t           fs_ncyl;
        int32_t           fs_cpg;
        int32_t           fs_ipg;
        int32_t           fs_fpg;
        struct csum       fs_cstotal;
        char              fs_fmod;
        char              fs_clean;
        char              fs_ronly;
        char              fs_flags;
        char              fs_fsmnt [MAXMNTLEN];
        int32_t           fs_cgrotor;
        union {
            uint32_t      fs_csp_pad [MAXCSBUFS];
            struct csum *fs_csp;
        } fs_u;
        int32_t           fs_cpc;
        short             fs_opostbl [16] [8];
        int32_t           fs_sparecon [52];
        int32_t           fs_logbno;
        int32_t           fs_reclaim;
        int32_t           fs_sparecon2;
        int32_t           fs_state;
        quad_t            fs_qbmask;
        quad_t            fs_qfmask;
        int32_t           fs_postblformat;
        int32_t           fs_nrpos;
        int32_t           fs_postbloff;
        int32_t           fs_rotbloff;
        int32_t           fs_magic;
        uchar_t           fs_space [1];
    };
```

In the following paragraphs we show the definition of each structure member. For the sake of presentation, we've not listed them strictly in the order they are defined in the structure.

Many of the members in the fs structure are no longer used, but are kept as padding for backward compatibility. Also, most of the fields are used by the kernel to implement the file system and are of little use outside of this context.

fs_link   Historically, this and the fs_rlink members were used to maintain the in core list of superblocks. In Solaris, they are just used for padding.

`fs_sblkno`	This is the address of the superblock in the file system.
`fs_cblkno`	This is the offset of the cylinder group blocks in the file system.
`fs_iblkno`	This is the offset of the inode blocks in the file system.
`fs_dblkno`	This is the offset of the first data block after the cylinder group.
`fs_cgoffset`	This is the cylinder group offset in the cylinder.
`fs_cgmask`	This is used to calculate mod `fs_ntrak`.
`fs_time`	This is the last time the file system was written to.
`fs_size`	This is the total number of blocks in the file system, measured in fragment-sized blocks. This includes the overhead required to maintain the file system, and the data blocks.
`fs_dsize`	This is the number of fragment-sized data blocks in the file system.
`fs_ncg`	This is the number of cylinder groups in the file system. We discuss cylinder groups in the next section.
`fs_bsize`	This is the size of a file system block, and is a multiple of the sector size. Solaris uses a block size of 8192 bytes.
`fs_fsize`	This is the file system fragment size. Fragments are the smallest allocatable chunks in the file system, and were introduced to reduce wasted disk space. The larger block size used by UFS makes I/O more efficient, but can waste a lot of space for small files. For example, given an 8192-byte block size, a 1192-byte file would waste 7000 bytes. By splitting a block into eight equal sized fragments of 1024 bytes each, only 856 bytes will be wasted. The other six fragments in the fragmented block can be used by other files.
`fs_frag`	This is the number of fragments in a file system block. This can be calculated easily using the previous two members, but is precalculated and stored here for speed.
`fs_id`	This is a unique ID for this file system. Solaris neither uses nor maintains this member.
`fs_csaddr`	This is the block address of the cylinder group summary area.
`fs_cssize`	This is the size of the cylinder group summary area.
`fs_cgsize`	This is the size of a cylinder group.
`fs_ncyl`	This is the number of cylinders in the file system.
`fs_cstotal`	This is the cylinder group summary information. It is stored in a `csum` structure, which we discuss later.
`fs_fmod`	This is a flag that indicates whether the superblock has been modified.

`fs_clean`	This holds the file system state. Figure 11.3 summarizes the valid values for `fs_clean`.
`fs_ronly`	A flag indicating that the file system was mounted read only.
`fs_flags`	These are file system flags. At the time of writing, the only valid flag is `FSLARGEFILES`, which means that one or more large files are or have been on the file system.
`fs_fsmnt`	This is the name of the directory the file system is mounted on. If the file system is not mounted, it contains the last point on which it was mounted.
`fs_cgrotor`	This is the last cylinder group searched.
`fs_u`	This is a pointer to the cylinder group summary information. Prior to Solaris 2.6, this was an array limited to `MAXCSBUFS` entries; Solaris 2.6 removes this limit.
`fs_cpc`	This is the number of cylinders per cycle in the position table.
`fs_opostbl`	This is the head of the old rotation block list.
`fs_sparecon`	This space is reserved for future constants.
`fs_logbno`	This is the block number of the embedded log.
`fs_reclaim`	This is used for reclaiming open deleted files.
`fs_sparecon2`	This is reserved for a future constant.
`fs_state`	This is the file system state time stamp.
`fs_qbmask`	This is the value of `~fs_bmask`, for use with a quad word size.
`fs_qfmask`	This is the value of `~fs_fmask`, for use with a quad word size.
`fs_postblformat`	This holds the format of the position layout tables.
`fs_nrpos`	This is the number of rotational positions.
`fs_postbloff`	This is the rotation block list head.
`fs_rotbloff`	This is the blocks for each rotation.
`fs_magic`	This is a magic number that identifies a superblock. It is a reference to Bill Joy's birthday (January 19, 1954).
`fs_space`	This is the list of blocks for each rotation.

The following members are configuration parameters:

`fs_minfree`	This is the minimum percentage of free blocks. Once the number of free blocks goes below this value, only privileged processes may increase the size of files or create new ones.
`fs_rotdelay`	This is the optimal number of milliseconds to wait for the next block. With today's faster drives, this field is usually 0.

`fs_rps`	This is how fast the disk rotates in revolutions per second.
`fs_maxcontig`	This is the maximum number of contiguous blocks in a file.
`fs_maxbpg`	This is the maximum number of blocks per cylinder group.
`fs_optim`	This is the optimization preference. A value of `FS_OPTTIME` means that allocation time is to be minimized, and a value of `FS_OPTSPACE` means that disk fragmentation should be minimized.

The following members can be computed from the others:

`fs_bmask`	This is used in the `blkoff` macro to calculate block offsets.
`fs_fmask`	This is used by the `fragoff` macro to calculate fragment offsets.
`fs_bshift`	This is used by the `lblkno` macro to calculate the logical block number.
`fs_fshift`	This is used in the `numfrags` macros to calculate the number of fragments.
`fs_fragshift`	This is used in the block to fragment shift calculation.
`fs_fsbtodb`	This is the shift constant used in the `fsbtodb` and `dbtofsb` macros.
`fs_sbsize`	This is the actual size of the superblock.
`fs_csmask`	This is the cylinder group summary information block offset.
`fs_csshift`	This is the cylinder group summary information block number.
`fs_nindir`	This is the value returned by the `NINDIR` macro.
`fs_inopb`	This is the value returned by the `INOPB` macro.
`fs_nspf`	This is the value returned by the `NSPF` macro.
`fs_cpg`	This is the number of cylinders per cylinder group.
`fs_ipg`	This is the number of inodes per cylinder group. Multiplying this number by `fs_ncg` gives the number of inodes in the file system, and hence, the maximum number of distinct files the file system may contain.
`fs_fpg`	This is the number of fragments per cylinder group (i.e., the number of blocks per cylinder group * `fs_frag`).

The following members are derived from the hardware:

`fs_npsect`	This is the number of sectors per track, including spares. On little-endian machines (e.g., x86-based PCs), this member and `fs_state` have their positions reversed. This is to allow read-only compatibility with SVR4 file systems.

fs_interleave   This is the hardware sector interleave.

fs_trackskew   This is the sector 0 skew, per track.

fs_ntrak   This is the number of tracks per cylinder.

fs_nsect   This is the number of sectors per track.

fs_spc   This is the number of sectors per cylinder.

fs_clean	Interpretation
FSACTIVE	The file system may have fsck inconsistencies
FSCLEAN	The file system has successfully unmounted (implies everything is OK)
FSSTABLE	There were no fsck inconsistencies, but no guarantee on user data
FSBAD	The file system is mounted from a partition that is neither FSCLEAN nor FSSTABLE
FSSUSPEND	Clean flag processing is temporarily disabled
FSLOG	This is a logging file system
FSFIX	The file system is being repaired while mounted

Figure 11.3 Values of fs_clean.

The cylinder group summary information is stored in a csum structure, which has the following members:

```
struct csum {
    int32_t cs_ndir;    /* Number of directories */
    int32_t cs_nbfree;  /* Number of free blocks */
    int32_t cs_nifree;  /* Number of free inodes */
    int32_t cs_nffree;  /* Number of free fragments */
};
```

We can use a number of constants to help us read or write a superblock; these are summarized in Figure 11.4.

Constant	Description
BBSIZE	The size of the boot block, in bytes
SBSIZE	The size of the superblock, in bytes
BBOFF	The absolute disk address of the boot block, in byte offset form
SBOFF	The absolute disk address of the superblock, in byte offset form
BBLOCK	The absolute disk address of the boot block, as a disk block number
SBLOCK	The absolute disk address of the superblock, as a disk block number

Figure 11.4 Constants that help with superblock I/O.

By using these constants, reading a superblock (or the boot block) is as straightforward as reading SBSIZE bytes from the disk offset SBOFF. The byte offset forms of addressing are preferred, as they don't imply a sector size.

Given a file system fs and a block number b, we can convert a file system block number to a disk block number by using the fsbtodb macro:

```
disk_block = fsbtodb (fs, b);
```

Similarly, we can perform the opposite conversion by using the `dbtofsb` macro:

```
fs_block = dbtofsb (fs, b);
```

The Inode Table

We mentioned in Chapter 10 that an inode is where all the important information about a file (e.g., the file type, the owner's user ID and group ID, the file's permission, the number of links, etc.) is stored. The inode also stores the addresses of all the disk blocks that contain the file's data.

There is one inode for each unique file in the file system. Inodes are allocated when the file system is created, which means that the maximum number of files a file system can hold is determined at the time the file system was created. Because of this, it is possible that we will be unable to create new files on a file system, despite there being sufficient free space (however, running out of data blocks is more common). If we have an idea of how a file system we create is to be used, we can vary the inode density, i.e., specify fewer or more bytes per inode. The higher the bytes-per-inode number is, the lower the number of allocated inodes is. Conversely, if we require more inodes, we should reduce the number of bytes per inode (the default for UFS file systems is 2048).

There are a number of structures associated with inodes. One is stored on disk, and the others are stored in memory for use by the kernel. The common parts of the inode are stored in a `icommon` structure, while the on-disk inode is stored in a `dinode` structure.

The `icommon` structure has the following members:

```
struct icommon {
        o_mode_t                ic_smode;       /* Mode and type of file */
        short                   ic_nlink;       /* Number of links to file */
        o_uid_t                 ic_suid;        /* Owner's UID */
        o_gid_t                 ic_sgid;        /* Owner's GID */
        u_offset_t              ic_lsize;       /* Number of bytes in file */
#ifdef _KERNEL
        struct timeval32        ic_atime;       /* Last access time */
        struct timeval32        ic_mtime;       /* Last modification time */
        struct timeval32        ic_ctime;       /* Last inode change time */
#else
        time32_t                ic_atime;       /* Last access time */
        int32_t                 ic_atspare;
        time32_t                ic_mtime;       /* Last modification time */
        int32_t                 ic_mtspare;
        time32_t                ic_ctime;       /* Last inode change time */
        int32_t                 ic_ctspare;
#endif
        daddr32_t               ic_db [NDADDR]; /* Direct block addresses */
        daddr32_t               ic_ib [NIADDR]; /* Indirect blocks */
        int32_t                 ic_flags;       /* Status, not used */
        int32_t                 ic_blocks;      /* Blocks actually held */
        int32_t                 ic_gen;         /* Generation number */
        int32_t                 ic_shadow;      /* Shadow inode */
```

```
    uid_t               ic_uid;         /* Long EFT version of UID */
    gid_t               ic_gid;         /* Long EFT version of GID */
    uint32_t            ic_oeftflag;    /* Reserved */
};
```

The inode structure was enhanced to support SVR4 Extended Fundamental Types (EFTs). This was to allow 32-bit user and group IDs, and a 32-bit device number. The current inode structure is 100 percent backward compatible with the previous one if no user ID or group ID exceeds USHRT_MAX, and no major or minor number of a device number in an inode exceeds 255.

The dinode structure has the following members:

```
struct dinode {
    union {
        struct icommon  di_icom;
        char            di_size [128];
    } di_un;
};
```

To simplify our code, the following synonyms are defined in <sys/fs/ufs_inode.h>:

```
#define di_ic        di_un.di_icom
#define di_mode      di_ic.ic_smode
#define di_nlink     di_ic.ic_nlink
#define di_uid       di_ic.ic_uid
#define di_gid       di_ic.ic_gid
#define di_smode     di_ic.ic_smode
#define di_suid      di_ic.ic_suid
#define di_sgid      di_ic.ic_sgid
#define di_size      di_ic.ic_lsize
#define di_db        di_ic.ic_db
#define di_ib        di_ic.ic_ib
#define di_atime     di_ic.ic_atime
#define di_mtime     di_ic.ic_mtime
#define di_ctime     di_ic.ic_ctime
#define di_cflags    di_ic.ic_flags
#ifdef _LITTLE_ENDIAN
#define di_ordev     di_ic.ic_db [1]
#else
#define di_ordev     di_ic.ic_db [0]
#endif
#define di_shadow    di_ic.ic_shadow
#define di_blocks    di_ic.ic_blocks
#define di_gen       di_ic.ic_gen
```

Most of the members of the icommon structure are self-explanatory. The di_mode, di_nlink, di_uid, di_gid, di_size, di_atime, di_mtime, and di_ctime members are copied to the stat structure when one of the stat family of functions is called.

However, we need to explain the di_db and di_ib members in more detail.

The disk blocks for each file are represented by disk address pointers in the file's inode. There are two types of block referenced by these pointers: direct and indirect. A *direct block* is one that can be accessed directly from a reference in an inode. The di_db member is an array of direct blocks.

If we use just the direct blocks, each file is limited to NDADDR (which has the value of 12 on Solaris) direct blocks of 8 KB each, which is 96 KB. Once the file exceeds 96 KB in size, we must start using indirect blocks.

An *indirect block* must be accessed through one or more levels of indirection. The data blocks pointed to by the inode do not contain file data; instead, they contain another list of directory blocks, and it is those blocks that contain the actual file data. The *di_ib* member is an array of indirect blocks.

Assuming an 8 KB block size, each indirect block can hold up to 2048 block addresses, which greatly increases the maximum file size. Solaris also supports the notion of double and triple indirect blocks. In the case of double indirect blocks, the double indirect block points to a block that contains the addresses of 2048 indirect blocks, each of which contains a list of 2048 blocks. The blocks referenced by the latter set of directory blocks are the data blocks for the file. Similarly, the triple indirect blocks pointer refers to a block that contains the block addresses of 2048 double indirect blocks, which in turn contain a list of 2048 indirect blocks. Each of those indirect blocks contains a list of 2048 data block addresses, which are used to store the file's data. Figure 11.5 illustrates the use of direct, indirect, double indirect, and triple indirect blocks.

We mentioned earlier that the UFS file system allocates file space as fragments. Assuming an 8 KB block size, we can make the following observations:

1. The first 12 direct blocks allow for 12 blocks, which is 98,304 bytes (96 KB).

2. The first level of indirection allows a full block of disk addresses. This means that an 8 KB block can hold 2048 32-bit disk addresses, which gives us 12 + 2048 (2060) blocks, or 16,875,520 bytes (about 16 MB).

3. Using double indirect blocks allows for $12 + 2048 + 2048^2$ (4,196,364) blocks, which is 34,376,613,888 bytes (about 32 GB).

4. Using triple indirect blocks allows for $12 + 2048 + 2048^2 + 2048^3$ (8,594,130,956) blocks, which is 70,403,120,791,552 bytes (about 64 TB).

The above notwithstanding, there is a limit on the maximum offset in each disk address, which is expressed as a number of file system fragments. Using the default fragment size of 1 KB, the maximum offset for each block is $2^{31} * 1$ KB, which is 2 TB. However, the size of a UFS file system is limited to 1 TB.

> Solaris 9 8/03 introduced support for multiterabyte UFS file systems, which allows the creation of UFS file systems up to 16 TB in size. Multiterabyte UFS support can be added to earlier releases of Solaris 9 via patches.
>
> The minimum fragment size on these multiterabyte file systems is 8 KB.

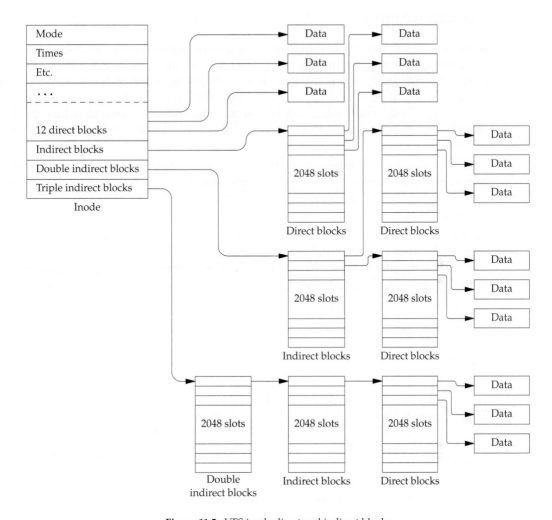

Figure 11.5 UFS inode direct and indirect blocks.

Given a pointer to a superblock fs and an inode number x, a number of macros can help us translate an inode number into something more useful. They each have the following format:

```
func (fs, x)
```

where func is the name of the macro. Figure 11.6 summarizes these macros.

Macro	Description
itoo	Converts an inode number to a file system block offset
itog	Converts an inode number to a cylinder group number
itod	Converts an inode number to a file system block address

Figure 11.6 Macros for handling inode numbers.

Cylinder Groups

In the original UNIX file system, the inodes were stored on disk immediately after the superblock, and the data blocks were immediately after the inodes. This arrangement makes for an easy implementation, but it results in a lot of head movement when accessing files. Because the time to move the heads is by far the most significant part of the time required to perform a disk I/O, something had to be done to reduce the amount of head movements required. The solution was to divide the disk into several cylinder groups.

Each cylinder group contains a backup copy of the superblock, some inode structures, and some data blocks. There's also some bookkeeping information stored in each cylinder group. This bookkeeping information includes a list of the used inodes in the cylinder group and a list of the cylinder group's free blocks.

Subject to certain restraints, the system attempts to store the contents of a file in the same cylinder group as its inode. To prevent one file from monopolizing the space in a cylinder group, files that exceed a given size are split into several cylinder groups.

The cylinder group information is stored in a cg structure, which has the following members:

```
struct cg {
        uint32_t     cg_link;               /* Not used */
        int32_t      cg_magic;              /* Magic number */
        time32_t     cg_time;               /* Time last written */
        int32_t      cg_cgx;               /* We are the cgx'th cg */
        short        cg_ncyl;              /* Number of cyls in this cg */
        short        cg_niblk;             /* Number of inode blocks in cg */
        int32_t      cg_ndblk;             /* Number of data blocks in cg */
        struct csum  cg_cs;                /* Cylinder summary info */
        int32_t      cg_rotor;             /* Position of last used block */
        int32_t      cg_frotor;            /* Position of last used fragt */
        int32_t      cg_irotor;            /* Position of last used inode */
        int32_t      cg_frsum [MAXFRAG];   /* Counts of available frags */
        int32_t      cg_btotoff;           /* Block totals per cylinder */
        int32_t      cg_boff;              /* (short) Free block positions */
        int32_t      cg_iusedoff;          /* (char) Used inode map */
        int32_t      cg_freeoff;           /* (uchar_t) Free block map */
        int32_t      cg_nextfreeoff;       /* (uchar_t) Next avail space */
        int32_t      cg_sparecon [16];     /* Reserved for future use */
        uchar_t      cg_space [1];         /* Space for cg maps */
};
```

Example: Obtaining the disk usage for each user

Now that we've had a look at some of the low level data structures used by a UFS file system, let's see how we can use this information in a practical example. Program 11.9 calculates the total disk usage for each user on the given file system, then sorts the results before printing them.

Before we look at the output of Program 11.9, let's take a look at some of the details.

```
 1  #include <stdio.h>
 2  #include <unistd.h>
 3  #include <limits.h>
 4  #include <pwd.h>
 5  #include <sys/fs/ufs_fs.h>
 6  #include <sys/fs/ufs_inode.h>
 7  #include <sys/vfstab.h>
 8  #include <sys/types.h>
 9  #include <sys/stat.h>
10  #include <sys/param.h>
11  #include <fcntl.h>
12  #include <stdlib.h>
13  #include <string.h>
14  #include <errno.h>
15  #include "ssp.h"

16  #define sb sbu.sblock
17  #define SSP_MAXUID USHRT_MAX     /* Default MAXUID requires too much space! */

18  union sb_union {
19      struct fs sblock;
20      char pad [SBSIZE];
21  };

22  struct usage {
23      uid_t uid;
24      size_t blocks;
25      size_t inodes;
26  };

27  static int diskuse (const char *device, struct usage *use_by_uid);
28  static void print_results (char *mountp, char *dev, struct usage *use_by_uid);
29  static int blk_compare (const void *a, const void *b);

30  int main (int argc, char **argv)
31  {
32      int i;
33      int j;
34      struct usage use_by_uid [SSP_MAXUID];
35      FILE *fp;
36      struct vfstab vfstab;

37      if (argc < 2)
38          err_quit ("Usage: diskuse file_system ...");

39      if ((fp = fopen (VFSTAB, "r")) == NULL)
40          err_quit ("Can't open %s", VFSTAB);

41      for (j = 1; j < argc; j++) {
42          rewind (fp);

43          if (getvfsfile (fp, &vfstab, argv [j]) == -1) {
44              log_msg ("%s: Not found in %s", argv [j], VFSTAB);
45              continue;
46          }

47          memset (use_by_uid, 0, sizeof (use_by_uid));
48          for (i = 0; i < SSP_MAXUID; i++)
49              use_by_uid [i].uid = i;
```

```
50        if (diskuse (vfstab.vfs_fsckdev, use_by_uid) == -1)
51            continue;

52        qsort (use_by_uid, SSP_MAXUID, sizeof (struct usage), blk_compare);

53        print_results (vfstab.vfs_mountp, vfstab.vfs_fsckdev, use_by_uid);
54    }

55    fclose (fp);

56    return (0);
57 }

58 static int diskuse (const char *device, struct usage *use_by_uid)
59 {
60    ino_t inode;
61    daddr32_t inode_blk;
62    int i;
63    int fd;
64    int num_inodes;
65    struct dinode inode_tab [MAXBSIZE / sizeof (struct dinode)];
66    union sb_union sbu;

67    if ((fd = open (device, O_RDONLY)) == -1) {
68        err_ret ("diskuse: %s", device);
69        return (-1);
70    }

71    sync ();

72    if (pread (fd, &sb, SBSIZE, ldbtob (SBLOCK)) == -1) {
73        close (fd);
74        return (-1);
75    }

76    num_inodes = sb.fs_ipg * sb.fs_ncg;

77    for (inode = 0; inode < num_inodes;) {
78        inode_blk = fsbtodb (&sb, itod (&sb, inode));
79        if (pread (fd, inode_tab, sb.fs_bsize, ldbtob (inode_blk)) == -1) {
80            close (fd);
81            return (-1);
82        }

83        for (i = 0; i < INOPB (&sb) && inode < num_inodes; i++, inode++) {
84            if (inode < UFSROOTINO)
85                continue;

86            if ((inode_tab [i].di_mode & IFMT) == 0)
87                continue;

88            use_by_uid [inode_tab [i].di_uid].blocks +=
89                inode_tab [i].di_blocks;
90            use_by_uid [inode_tab [i].di_uid].inodes++;
91        }
92    }

93    return (0);
94 }
```

```
 95 static void print_results (char *mountp, char *dev, struct usage *use_by_uid)
 96 {
 97     int i;
 98     struct passwd *pwd;

 99     printf ("%s (%s):\n", mountp, dev);

100     for (i = 0; i < SSP_MAXUID; i++) {
101         if (use_by_uid [i].blocks == 0)
102             continue;

103         if ((pwd = getpwuid (use_by_uid [i].uid)) == NULL)
104             printf ("  %-10ld", (long) use_by_uid [i].uid);
105         else
106             printf ("  %-10s", pwd -> pw_name);

107         printf ("%10d", use_by_uid [i].blocks / 2);

108         printf ("%10d\n", use_by_uid [i].inodes);
109     }

110     printf ("\n");
111 }

112 static int blk_compare (const void *a, const void *b)
113 {
114     struct usage *x;
115     struct usage *y;

116     x = (struct usage *) a;
117     y = (struct usage *) b;

118     return (y -> blocks - x -> blocks);
119 }
```
——— *file_systems/diskuse.c*

Program 11.9 Print the disk and inode use for each user.

Define our data structures

18–21 We need to define a union to hold the superblock, because it takes up a whole disk block, but the structure itself is not actually that big.

22–26 We keep track of disk space and inode usage in a usage structure. We need to save the user ID in this structure because later we'll be sorting it by the number of blocks used.

Check command line arguments and open /etc/vfstab

37–38 Quit with an error if we don't have at least two command line arguments (including the command name itself).

39–40 Open /etc/vfstab, quitting if there's an error.

Process each file system named on the command line

42 Rewind the file stream used to access /etc/vfstab. This is so that the file pointer is in the correct position every time around the while loop (one iteration for each file system specified on the command line).

43–46 Look up the file system in /etc/vfstab so we can determine which character device to use.

47–49 We prepare our array of usage counters by setting the memory where the counters are stored to zero, and then initializing the user ID member of each element.

50–51 Calculate the disk usage of each user on the current file system.

52 Call `qsort` to sort the results into descending order.

53 Call our function `print_results` to print the results.

Open the file system's character special file

67–70 Open the character special device associated with the file system we're calculating the totals for.

Flush dirty I/O buffers

71 Call `sync` to make sure that all pending file system I/O is flushed to the disk.

Read in the superblock

72–75 We call `pread` to read in the superblock, which we use in several places. Notice that we use the `ldbtob` macro (which is defined in `<sys/param.h>`) to convert the superblock's disk block number into a byte offset into the file system. We do this because `pread` works with byte offsets, not disk block numbers.

Calculate the number of inodes

76 Calculate the total number of inodes we have by multiplying the number of cylinder groups by the number of inodes per group.

Calculate the disk and inode usage for each user ID

78–82 We read in the inode table for the current cylinder group. The `fsbtodb` macro converts a file system block number to a disk block number, and the `itod` macro converts an inode number to its file system block number.

83–91 For each inode in the block we've just read in, add up the number of disk blocks and inodes used, and add it to the totals for the owner of the file. Notice that we skip inodes less than `UFSROOTINO`; inode 0 can't be used for normal purposes, and inode 1 was historically used to link bad blocks. We also skip unallocated inodes.

Print the results

99 Print the name of the mount point and its character special file.

Iterate through each user ID

101–102 Skip the users who aren't using any disk blocks.

103–106 Look up the login name associated with the current user ID. If we find one, we print it out. Otherwise, we just use the user ID.

107 We print the number of 1 KB blocks owned by the user ID. The number we have is in 512-byte (actually `DEV_BSIZE`) blocks, so we convert it to kilobytes by dividing it by two.

108 Print the number of inodes used by the user ID.

Compare the number of blocks

112–119 Calculate the difference between two sets of disk block usage. This function is used by `qsort` to compare two users' disk block usage.

Let's see what happens when we run Program 11.9 (note that we must run it as `root`):

```
$ su
Password:
# ./diskuse / /space
/ (/dev/rdsk/c0t0d0s0):
    root            980337        56625
    rich               360           22
    uucp                55            5
    adm                 41            4
    lp                  13           13
    jenny               12           28
    accting              8            8
    daemon               4            5
    smmsp                2            2

/space (/dev/rdsk/c0t0d0s7):
    rich           3821998        13190
    root                 9            2
```

The first column is the user name, the second is the number of 1 KB blocks used, and the last column is the number of inodes consumed by the user.

Program 11.9 is an example of a program that must be large file aware if we want to use it with file systems that exceed 2 GB in size. We must either build it as a 64-bit program, or specify the `-D_FILE_OFFSET_BITS=64` compile time option.

Apart from its speed, Program 11.9 has another advantage over the alternative ways we could use to find out the same information; it works just as well on unmounted file systems as mounted ones.

11.9 Summary

In this chapter we showed how to read the mounted file system and file system defaults tables. We also showed how to mount and unmount a file system, and showed how to obtain the status of a mounted file system.

We then examined the disk-based data structures that implement a UFS file system (the superblock, the inode, and the cylinder group), and finished the chapter with a program that calculates the disk and inode usage for every user on a file system.

Exercises

11.1 From Solaris 8, `/etc/mnttab` is implemented as a read-only file system rather than a text file. What are the advantages of this?

11.2 If we remove a file while a process is running, that process is still able to access the file contents, provided it had opened the file prior to its deletion. We can also mount a file system on any directory. If we mount a file system on top of a file a process has open, can that process still access the file's contents? If so, what are the possible ramifications?

11.3 If we forcibly umount a file system while we have a file within it open, can we still access the file's contents?

11.4 Add to Program 11.9 the ability to sort based on the number of inodes used by each user.

12

Terminal I/O

12.1 Introduction

Terminal I/O is probably the messiest topic in UNIX systems programming. Part of the problem is the plethora of devices that can be connected to a serial interface: terminals, printers, modems, and other specialized bits of hardware. Although there is much overlap, each of these different device types has its own special needs. Because of this, the number of options has grown so large (Solaris currently supports nearly 60 options; as a result the `termio` man page that describes them exceeds 27 pages) that it can be very difficult to know which ones to use with any given device.

Another problem with terminal I/O is that there has historically been two different, incompatible interfaces. The original version was developed for Version 7, and was based on the `stty` and `ioctl` functions. BSD adopted and extended this interface, while System III introduced a new interface. This new interface was carried forward to all releases of System V, including SVR4. POSIX (and later, the SUS) resolved these differences and is now the preferred method of terminal I/O.

In this chapter, we'll take a close look at the terminal control functions. We'll start with a high-level overview so that we can introduce some concepts that are necessary for understanding the rest of the chapter. We'll then examine each of the options in detail, and show how to get and set them.

12.2 Overview of Terminal I/O

Terminal I/O is performed in one of two modes: canonical and non-canonical. They have the following characteristics:

Canonical mode

In *canonical mode*, the terminal input is processed as lines. The terminal driver returns at most one line per read. Lines are delimited by a newline character (ASCII LF), an end of file character (ASCII EOT), or an end of line character (which is user defined). Processes attempting to read from the terminal will be suspended until an entire line has been typed. Also, it doesn't matter how many characters are requested by the read, because at most only one line will be returned. If the number of characters we request is fewer than the number of characters in the line, only as many characters as we requested will be returned (subsequent characters will be returned by the next read). However, it is important to realize that the first read, regardless of its size, will not be satisfied until an entire line has been read.

Certain keyboard characters enable special processing (e.g., character deletion, line erase, and so on). Because the input is processed one line at a time, the terminal driver handles all the special characters, which means that our programs don't have to. We talk about these in Section 12.3.

The input processing performed in canonical mode also enables certain keyboard sequences to generate signals that are sent to the processes in the terminals process group (more on this in Section 16.6). How these signals are handled depends on the signal's disposition (see Chapter 17).

Canonical mode also enables certain output processing, such as the conversion of tabs to spaces; the generation of delays after newlines, tabs, and form feeds; and the conversion of lower case letters to upper case (to support very old upper case only terminals).

Non-canonical mode

In *non-canonical mode*, the terminal input is not assembled into lines, and input processing is not performed. Signal generation and output processing are still performed, but they may be disabled.

Input characters are returned to the reading process after a minimum number of characters have been typed, after a maximum time has passed, or some combination of these.

Older versions of UNIX used the terms "cooked" instead of canonical and "raw" instead of non-canonical. Many people still use these terms today, even though they don't really apply to the systems they use. There was also a "cbreak" mode.

Cooked mode

Cooked mode corresponds to the canonical mode we just described. Input is processed as lines, input editing and signal generation are enabled, and output processing is performed.

Cbreak mode	*Cbreak mode* can be thought of as a sort of "half-cooked" mode. Input editing is disabled, and reads are satisfied one character at a time (i.e., the input is not buffered). However, signal generation and output processing are still performed.
Raw mode	*Raw mode* is much the same as non-canonical mode, except that signal generation and output processing are also disabled. Read requests are satisfied one character at a time.

By default, canonical mode is used. This is OK most of the time, but consider the case of a screen editor, for example, `vi`. Programs like `vi` must use non-canonical mode, because their commands may be single letters and are not terminated by newlines. Also, input processing of the special characters is undesirable, because the special characters may be used as commands in the program. For example, `vi` uses Control-D to scroll down half a page, but Control-D is often the terminal's end of file character.

There are a number of special input characters, most of which we can change. We've already used some of these in this text, like Control-D for end of file, Control-Z to suspend a process, and Control-C to kill a process. Each of these characters, and how we can change them, is described in Section 12.3.

A terminal device is controlled by a kernel-resident device driver. Each terminal device has a pair of queues associated with it: an input and an output. We show this arrangement in Figure 12.1.

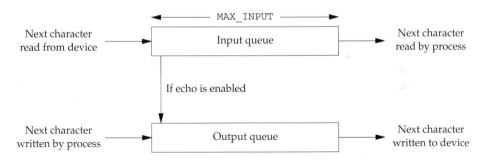

Figure 12.1 Terminal device input and output queues.

With reference to Figure 12.1, we can make several observations:

- If echoing is enabled, characters read from the device are placed at the tail of the input and output queues.

- The size of the input queue is `MAX_INPUT` bytes. What happens when the queue becomes full is implementation-dependent, but Solaris echos the BEL character to the terminal device.

- There is another limit associated with the input queue that we don't show: `MAX_CANON`. This is the maximum number of bytes in the canonical mode input line.

- The output queue also has a maximum size, but there are no constants defining its size that are accessible by our programs. This is because when the queue starts to fill up, the writing process is put to sleep by the kernel until more room is available.

- We'll show later how we can flush either the input queue or the output queue. We'll also discuss how to examine and change the attributes of a terminal device.

In Solaris, the STREAMS module `ldterm` implements all the canonical processing. This module sits between the kernel's generic read and write functions and the terminal device. We show this in Figure 12.2, and discuss STREAMS more in Section 13.9.

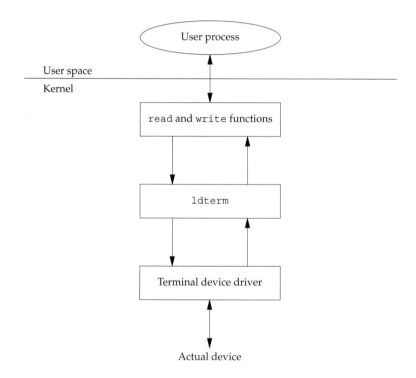

Figure 12.2 Terminal line discipline.

As we just mentioned, we can examine and modify some characteristics of a terminal device. These characteristics are stored in the `termios` structure, which is defined in `<termios.h>`. The `termios` structure has the following members:

```
struct termios {
    tcflag_t    c_iflag;        /* Input modes */
    tcflag_t    c_oflag;        /* Output modes */
    tcflag_t    c_cflag;        /* Control modes */
    tcflag_t    c_lflag;        /* Line discipline modes */
    cc_t        c_cc [NCCS];    /* Control characters */
};
```

The input modes control the input of characters by the terminal device driver, for example, map CR to NL, ignore parity errors, or strip off the eighth bit. The output modes control the driver's output, e.g., mapping lower case to upper case, perform output processing, or expanding tabs to spaces. The control modes control the flags that affect the RS-423 (or RS-232) serial interface lines, like the number of bits in a character, the number of stop bits, or flow control. The line discipline modes control how the driver interfaces with the user, for example, canonical mode, echoing, or terminal-generated signals. We summarize each of these modes in Figure 12.3, and discuss them in more detail in Section 12.5.

The c_cc member is an array of NCCS characters, which contains all the special control characters we can change. SUSv2 defines 11 special characters (nine of which we can change); Solaris defines another seven. We discuss these special characters in the next section.

> SunOS and pre-SVR4 versions of System V used a termio structure to hold the terminal options, which is defined in termio.h. POSIX added a trailing s to their names to differentiate them from their legacy versions. Interestingly enough, on Solaris it is the termio man page (rather than the termios man page) that describes the option flags and special characters used by Solaris, even though they are stored in a termios structure.

Given the large number of options in Figure 12.3, a good question would be how do we examine and change them? Thirteen functions, which we can split into five groups, enable us to do this.

The first group consists of two functions used to manipulate the terminal options shown in Figure 12.3. These two functions manipulate nearly 60 different flags. The large number of options and the difficulty in determining which options are best for a given device complicates the handling of terminal devices.

The second group consists of four functions that allow us to get and set the input and output baud rates. We can also do this using the functions from the first group, but these functions are preferred because they are easier to use and are more portable.

The next group of four functions are the line control functions. Some of their uses include flow control, input and output queue flushing, and sending a BREAK to the device on the other end of the serial line.

The fourth group of two functions are used to get and set the foreground process group ID associated with a terminal, and the fifth group, containing just one function, is used to get the terminal's session ID. We'll discuss these three functions in Chapter 16.

Figure 12.4 summarizes these 13 functions.

A number of ioctl commands can be used to operate on terminal devices, but the preferred interface is to use one of the functions summarized in Figure 12.4.

The relationships between the functions in Figure 12.4 and the terminal device are shown in Figure 12.5. Notice that although we show the input and output baud rates as part of the termios structure, it is undefined where in this structure the speeds are stored. Hence, we should use only the documented interfaces to manipulate the baud rate of the terminal interface.

Field	Flag	Description
c_iflag	BRKINT	Generate SIGINT on BREAK
	ICRNL	Map CR to NL on input
	IGNBRK	Ignore BREAK condition
	IGNCR	Ignore CR
	IGNPAR	Ignore characters with parity errors
	IMAXBEL	Echo BEL on input line too long
	INLCR	Map NL to CR on input
	INPCK	Enable input parity check
	ISTRIP	Strip eighth bit off input characters
	IUCLC	Map upper case to lower case on input
	IXANY	Enable any character to restart output
	IXOFF	Enable start/stop input flow control
	IXON	Enable start/stop output flow control
	PARMRK	Mark parity errors
c_oflag	BSDLY	Mask to select backspace delay
	CRDLY	Mask to select CR delay
	FFDLY	Mask to select form feed delay
	OCRNL	Map CR to NL on output
	OFDEL	Fill is DEL, else NUL
	OFILL	Use fill characters for delay
	OLCUC	Map lower case to upper case on output
	ONLCR	Map NL to CR-NL on output
	ONLRET	NL performs CR function
	ONOCR	No CR output at column 0
	OPOST	Perform output processing
	NLDLY	Mask to select NL delay
	TABDLY	Mask to select horizontal tab delay or expansion
	VTDLY	Mask to select vertical tab delay
c_cflag	CBAUD	Mask to select the output baud rate
	CBAUDEXT	Bit to indicate output speed > 38400
	CIBAUD	Mask to select the input baud rate, if different from output rate
	CIBAUDEXT	Bit to indicate input speed > 38400
	CLOCAL	Ignore modem status lines
	CREAD	Enable receiver
	CRTSCTS	Enable outbound hardware flow control
	CRTSXOFF	Enable inbound hardware flow control
	CSIZE	Mask to select character size
	CSTOPB	Send two stop bits, else one
	HUPCL	Hang up on last close
	PARENB	Parity enable
	PAREXT	Extended parity for mark and space parity
	PARODD	Odd parity, else even
c_lflag	ECHO	Enable echo
	ECHOCTL	Echo control characters as ^char
	ECHOE	Echo erase character as error correcting backspace
	ECHOK	Echo KILL
	ECHOKE	Visually erase entire line on line kill
	ECHONL	Echo NL
	ECHOPRT	Echo erase character as character erased
	FLUSHO	Output is being flushed
	ICANON	Canonical input mode
	IEXTEN	Enable extended functions
	ISIG	Enable terminal-generated signals
	NOFLSH	Disable flush after interrupt or quit
	PENDIN	Retype pending input at next read or input character
	TOSTOP	Send SIGTTOU for background output
	XCASE	Canonical upper/lower presentation

Figure 12.3 Terminal flag summary.

2.5	2.5.1	2.6	7	8	9	ISO C	SVID	POSIX	SUSv1	SUSv2	Flag
•	•	•	•	•	•		•	•	•	•	BRKINT
•	•	•	•	•	•		•	•	•	•	ICRNL
•	•	•	•	•	•		•	•	•	•	IGNBRK
•	•	•	•	•	•		•	•	•	•	IGNCR
•	•	•	•	•	•		•	•	•	•	IGNPAR
•	•	•	•	•	•						IMAXBEL
•	•	•	•	•	•		•	•	•	•	INLCR
•	•	•	•	•	•		•	•	•	•	INPCK
•	•	•	•	•	•		•	•	•	•	ISTRIP
•	•	•	•	•	•		•		•	•	IUCLC
•	•	•	•	•	•		•		•	•	IXANY
•	•	•	•	•	•		•	•	•	•	IXOFF
•	•	•	•	•	•		•	•	•	•	IXON
•	•	•	•	•	•		•	•	•	•	PARMRK
•	•	•	•	•	•		•		•	•	BSDLY
•	•	•	•	•	•		•		•	•	CRDLY
•	•	•	•	•	•		•		•	•	FFDLY
•	•	•	•	•	•		•		•	•	OCRNL
•	•	•	•	•	•		•				OFDEL
•	•	•	•	•	•		•		•	•	OFILL
•	•	•	•	•	•		•		•	•	OLCUC
•	•	•	•	•	•		•		•	•	ONLCR
•	•	•	•	•	•		•		•	•	ONLRET
•	•	•	•	•	•		•		•	•	ONOCR
•	•	•	•	•	•		•	•	•	•	OPOST
•	•	•	•	•	•		•		•	•	NLDLY
•	•	•	•	•	•		•		•	•	TABDLY
•	•	•	•	•	•		•		•	•	VTDLY
•	•	•	•	•	•						CBAUD
•	•	•	•	•	•						CBAUDEXT
•	•	•	•	•	•						CIBAUD
•	•	•	•	•	•						CIBAUDEXT
•	•	•	•	•	•		•	•	•	•	CLOCAL
•	•	•	•	•	•		•	•	•	•	CREAD
•	•	•	•	•	•						CRTSCTS
•	•	•	•	•	•						CRTSXOFF
•	•	•	•	•	•		•	•	•	•	CSIZE
•	•	•	•	•	•		•	•	•	•	CSTOPB
•	•	•	•	•	•		•	•	•	•	HUPCL
•	•	•	•	•	•		•	•	•	•	PARENB
•	•	•	•	•	•						PAREXT
•	•	•	•	•	•		•	•	•	•	PARODD
•	•	•	•	•	•		•	•	•	•	ECHO
•	•	•	•	•	•						ECHOCTL
•	•	•	•	•	•		•	•	•	•	ECHOE
•	•	•	•	•	•		•	•	•	•	ECHOK
•	•	•	•	•	•						ECHOKE
•	•	•	•	•	•		•	•	•	•	ECHONL
•	•	•	•	•	•						ECHOPRT
•	•	•	•	•	•						FLUSHO
•	•	•	•	•	•		•	•	•	•	ICANON
•	•	•	•	•	•		•	•	•	•	IEXTEN
•	•	•	•	•	•		•	•	•	•	ISIG
•	•	•	•	•	•		•	•	•	•	NOFLSH
•	•	•	•	•	•						PENDIN
•	•	•	•	•	•		•	•	•	•	TOSTOP
•	•	•	•	•	•		•		•	•	XCASE

Figure 12.3   Terminal flag summary (continued).

Function	Description	Section
tcgetattr	Get terminal attributes	12.4
tcsetattr	Set terminal attributes	12.4
cfgetispeed	Get input baud rate	12.6
cfgetospeed	Get output baud rate	12.6
cfsetispeed	Set input baud rate	12.6
cfsetospeed	Set output baud rate	12.6
tcdrain	Wait for all output to be transmitted	12.7
tcflow	Suspend/restart data transmission or reception	12.7
tcflush	Flush pending input and/or output	12.7
tcsendbreak	Send a BREAK	12.7
tcgetpgrp	Get the foreground process group ID	16.7
tcsetpgrp	Set the foreground process group ID	16.7
tcgetsid	Get the session ID	16.8

Figure 12.4   Summary of terminal I/O functions.

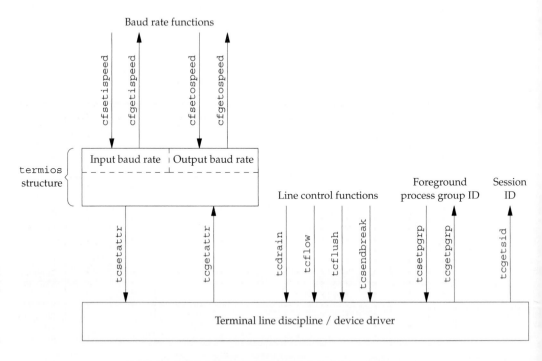

Figure 12.5   Relationship between the terminal device functions.

12.3 Special Input Characters

A number of characters are handled specially on input. They are summarized in Figures 12.6 and 12.7. (Although we show it in Figure 12.6, BREAK is not really a character at all, but a condition. More on this later.)

Character	Description	Subscript	Enabled by	Default
BREAK	Break condition	N/A	N/A	
CR	Carriage return	N/A	ICANON	\r
DISCARD	Discard input	VDISCARD	IEXTEN	^O
DSUSP	Delayed suspend	VDSUSP	ISIG	^Y
EOF	End of file	VEOF	ICANON	^D
EOL	End of line	VEOL	ICANON	NUL
EOL2	Alternate end of line	VEOL2	ICANON	
ERASE	Backspace one character	VERASE	ICANON	DEL
INTR	Interrupt signal	VINTR	ISIG	^C
KILL	Erase line	VKILL	ICANON	^U
LNEXT	Literal next character	VLNEXT	IEXTEN	
NL	Newline (Line feed)	N/A	ICANON	\n
QUIT	Quit signal	VQUIT	ISIG	^\
REPRINT	Reprint all input	VREPRINT	ICANON	^R
START	Resume output	VSTART	IXON/IXOFF	^Q
STOP	Stop output	VSTOP	IXON/IXOFF	^S
SUSP	Suspend signal	VSUSP	ISIG	^Z
SWTCH	Obsolete	VSWTCH	IEXTEN	
WERASE	Backspace one word	VWERASE	ICANON	^W

Figure 12.6 Summary of special input characters.

We can modify most of these characters by changing the appropriate entry in the c_cc array. We can use the manifest constants shown in the Subscript column of Figure 12.8 to refer to the desired array element. However, we can't modify the carriage return and newline characters, so we show their subscript as "N/A".

We can also disable a special input character by storing the value _POSIX_VDISABLE in the appropriate entry in the c_cc array.

Next we describe each special input character in detail. Even though we call them special input characters, two (START and STOP) are also handled specially on output. Most special characters are processed by the terminal driver and then discarded; they are not returned to the reading process. The exceptions to this are CR, EOL, EOL2, and NL.

BREAK   The BREAK character is not really a character as such, but a condition that can occur during asynchronous serial communications. A BREAK is a special kind of framing error that consists only of bits whose value is zero. (In serial communications, a framing error is caused by the absence of stop bits in received data.) The entire sequence of zero-valued

Character	2.5	2.5.1	2.6	7	8	9	ISO C	SVID	POSIX	SUSv1	SUSv2
BREAK	•	•	•	•	•	•		•	•	•	•
CR	•	•	•	•	•	•		•	•	•	•
DISCARD	•	•	•	•	•	•					
DSUSP	•	•	•	•	•	•					
EOF	•	•	•	•	•	•			•		•
EOL	•	•	•	•	•	•			•	•	•
EOL2	•	•	•	•	•	•					
ERASE	•	•	•	•	•	•		•	•	•	•
INTR	•	•	•	•	•	•		•	•	•	•
KILL	•	•	•	•	•	•		•	•	•	•
LNEXT	•	•	•	•	•	•					
NL	•	•	•	•	•	•		•	•	•	•
QUIT	•	•	•	•	•	•		•	•	•	•
REPRINT	•	•	•	•	•	•					
START	•	•	•	•	•	•		•	•	•	•
STOP	•	•	•	•	•	•		•	•	•	•
SUSP	•	•	•	•	•	•		•	•	•	•
SWTCH	•	•	•	•	•	•					
WERASE	•	•	•	•	•	•					

Figure 12.7 Availability of special input characters.

bits is considered a single BREAK. Most terminals have a key labelled BREAK that transmits a BREAK sequence, which is why many people think of BREAK as a regular character. We'll see in Section 12.7 how to send a BREAK.

CR This is the carriage return character, and we can't change it. It is recognized on input in canonical mode. When both the ICANON (canonical mode) and ICRNL (translate CR to NL) flags are set, and the IGNCR (ignore CR) flag is clear, the character is translated to NL and has the same effect as the NL character.

This character is returned to the reading process (maybe after being translated to an NL character).

DISCARD This is the discard character, which causes all subsequent output to be discarded. Output is discarded until another DISCARD character is typed, more input arrives, or the condition is cleared using the FLUSHO flag.

This character is discarded when processed (i.e., it is not passed to the reading process).

DSUSP This is the delayed suspend character. It is recognized on input in extended mode (IEXTEN) when the ISIG flag is set. Like the SUSP character, a SIGTSTP signal is sent to all processes in the foreground process group, but the signal is sent when a process in the foreground process group attempts to read from the controlling terminal rather than when it is typed.

This character is discarded when processed (i.e., it is not passed to the reading process).

EOF

This is the end of file character, and is recognized on input in canonical mode (ICANON). When this character is typed, all characters waiting to be read are immediately passed to the reading process without waiting for a newline. If there are no characters waiting (i.e., the EOF occurred at the beginning of a line), a count of 0 is returned, which is the standard end of file indication. Note that despite its name, UNIX does *not* mark the end of a file with this—or any other—character (unlike MS-DOS, which marks the end of a file with a ^Z character; a dubious trait it inherited from CP/M).

This character is discarded when processed in canonical mode (i.e., it is not passed to the reading process).

EOL

This is an additional line delimiter, like NL. It is recognized on input in canonical mode (ICANON).

This character is not normally used and is returned to the reading process.

EOL2

This is an additional line delimiter, like NL. It is recognized on input in canonical mode (ICANON).

This character is not normally used and is returned to the reading process.

ERASE

This is the backspace character. This character is recognized on input in canonical mode (ICANON) and erases the preceding character in the line. It does not erase beyond the beginning of a line, as delimited by an EOF, EOL, EOL2, or NL character.

This character is discarded when processed in canonical mode (i.e., it is not passed to the reading process).

INTR

This is the interrupt character. If the ISIG flag is set, it is recognized on input, causing a SIGINT signal to be sent to all the processes in the foreground process group associated with the terminal.

This character is discarded when processed (i.e., it is not passed to the reading process).

KILL

This character deletes an entire line, as delimited by an EOF, EOL, EOL2, or NL character. (The name KILL is a bit of a misnomer; LERASE (for line erase) would have been a better name.) It is recognized on input in canonical mode (ICANON).

This character is discarded when processed (i.e., it is not passed to the reading process).

LNEXT

This is the literal next character. In extended mode (IEXTEN), it is recognized on input, and causes the special meaning of the next character to be ignored. It allows us to input any special characters mentioned in this section that would otherwise be interpreted by the system. (The EOF, ERASE, and KILL characters can be escaped by preceding them with a backslash (\) character.)

The LNEXT character is discarded when processed, but the next character entered is passed to the reading process.

NL

This is the newline character, which is the normal line delimiter. It is recognized on input in canonical mode (ICANON), and we can't change or escape it.

This character is returned to the reading process.

QUIT

This is the quit character. If the ISIG flag is set, it is recognized on input, causing a SIGQUIT signal to be sent to all the processes in the foreground process group associated with the terminal. The difference between the QUIT and KILL characters is that the former causes the terminated processes to produce a core dump, whereas the latter doesn't.

This character is discarded when processed (i.e., it is not passed to the reading process).

REPRINT

This character causes all unread input to be output (reechoed), preceded by a newline. It is recognized in extended mode (IEXTEN).

This character is discarded when processed (i.e., it is not passed to the reading process).

START

The start character is used to resume output that has been suspended by the STOP character. It is recognized on input if output has been suspended by STOP, and the IXON flag is set.

This character is discarded when processed (i.e., it is not passed to the reading process).

If the IXOFF flag is set, the terminal driver automatically generates a START character to resume input it had previously stopped with a STOP character, when the input queue has drained sufficiently.

STOP

This character is recognized on input if the IXON flag is set. If the IXON flag is set when it is received, output is temporarily suspended; output is resumed when a START character is received.

This character is discarded when processed (i.e., it is not passed to the reading process).

If the `IXOFF` flag is set, the terminal driver automatically generates a STOP character to prevent the input queue from overflowing.

SUSP

This is the suspend character. It is recognized on input when the `ISIG` flag is set. A `SIGTSTP` signal is sent to all processes in the foreground process group.

This character is discarded when processed (i.e., it is not passed to the reading process).

SWTCH

This special character was used for System V's "layers" job control facility, which was abandoned by POSIX in favour of BSD-style job control (we discuss job control in Section 16.9). This rendered the SWTCH character obsolete; header file symbols related to it are present only for compatibility purposes. No special action is taken, and the character is discarded (i.e., it is not passed to the reading process).

WERASE

This is the word erase character. It is recognized on input in extended canonical mode (both the `ICANON` and the `IEXTEN` flags are set) and erases the preceding word. This is accomplished by deleting any spaces or tabs at the end of the word, and then deleting backward until the white space preceding the erased word is reached. The cursor is positioned at the location where the first character of the word was located. WERASE does not erase beyond the beginning of a line, as delimited by an EOF, EOL, EOL2, or NL character.

This character is discarded when processed (i.e., it is not passed to the reading process).

Example: Changing special input characters

We mentioned earlier that we can change the key combination required to generate a given special character, and that we can disable a special character. Program 12.1 illustrates both of these scenarios, by changing the INTR character to Control-L, and disabling the KILL character.

We used the `tcgetattr` and `tcsetattr` functions we discuss in the next section to change the special characters. Notice also our use of the CTRL macro, which returns the value of a given control character. This handy macro is defined in `<termios.h>`.

These are the results we get when we run this 14 line program:

```
$ ./change_char
$ Testing INTR^C^C^C^L
$ Testing KILL^U^U^U
```

After running Program 12.1, we can restore the original INTR and KILL characters by using the `stty` program we discuss in Section 12.5.

——————————————————————————————————— terminal_io/change_char.c

```
 1 #include <unistd.h>
 2 #include <termios.h>
 3 #include "ssp.h"

 4 int main (void)
 5 {
 6     struct termios term;

 7     if (tcgetattr (STDIN_FILENO, &term) == -1)
 8         err_msg ("Can't get terminal attributes");

 9     term.c_cc [VINTR] = CTRL('l');          /* INTR is now Control-L */
10     term.c_cc [VKILL] = _POSIX_VDISABLE;    /* Disable KILL */

11     if (tcsetattr (STDIN_FILENO, TCSANOW, &term) == -1)
12         err_msg ("Can't set terminal attributes");

13     return (0);
14 }
```

——————————————————————————————————— terminal_io/change_char.c

Program 12.1 Changing the INTR and KILL special input characters.

12.4 Getting and Setting Terminal Attributes

We use two functions to get and set a `termios` structure: `tcgetattr` and `tcsetattr`. These functions are how we examine and modify the various flags and special characters to make the terminal device work how we want it to.

```
#include <termios.h>

int tcgetattr (int fildes, struct termios *termios_p);

int tcsetattr (int fildes, int opt, const struct termios *termios_p);
```
Both return: 0 if OK, –1 on error

The `tcgetattr` function gets the parameters associated with the terminal device referred to by *fildes* and stores them in the `termios` structure pointed to by *termios_p*.

If the terminal device supports different input and output baud rates, both are stored in the `termios` structure, even if they are the same. Otherwise, the actual baud rate being used is returned as the output baud rate, and the input baud rate returned is 0.

The `tcsetattr` function sets the parameters associated with the terminal device referred to by *fildes* from the `termios` structure pointed to by *termios_p*. The *opt* argument lets us specify when we want the changes to take place, and must be one of the following constants:

TCSANOW   The change occurs immediately.

TCSADRAIN   The change will occur after all output written to *fildes* has been transmitted. This option should be used when changing output parameters.

TCSAFLUSH   The change will occur after all output written to *fildes* has
                          been transmitted, and all input so far received but not read
                          will be discarded (flushed) before the change is made.

One thing we should be wary of when using tcsetattr is that a successful return will
occur if *any* of the requested changes were able to be made. The only way we can be sure
that all of our changes took place is to call tcgetattr and compare the terminal's actual
attributes to the desired ones.

Further, rather than just calling tcsetattr with the attributes we want, we should first
call tcgetattr to get the current terminal attributes, make the changes we want to the
resulting termios structure, and then apply them using tcsetattr. Testing the
changes using a subsequent call to tcgetattr is always a good idea.

Example: Getting and setting terminal attributes

Before we examine the flags in detail, let's take a look at how we can get and set the
terminal settings. Program 12.2 shows how we use the tcgetattr and tcsetattr
functions to retrieve the current character size, and set it to a new value.

Let's see what happens when we run Program 12.2 a couple of times.

```
$ ./char_size
Old size is 8 bits/character
New size is 8 bits/character
$ stty cs7                           Change character size to 7 bits
$ ./char_size
Old size is 7 bits/character
New size is 8 bits/character
```

Notice that we used the stty command we discuss in Section 12.5 to change the
character size.

12.5 Terminal Option Flags

In Figure 12.3 we summarized the terminal option flags. In this section, we'll tale a closer
look at each of these flags. For ease of reference, we've listed the flags in alphabetical
order, indicating the field in which they appear.

All of these flags set or clear one or more bits, except those that we call a mask. A mask
defines multiple bits, and as well as the mask name, we define each of the valid values.
For example, to set the character size, we first clear the appropriate bits using the
character size mask CSIZE, and then set them to either CS5, CS6, CS7, or CS8 (we show
this in Program 12.2).

BRKINT   (c_lflag) If this flag is set and IGNBRK is clear, a BREAK
                          condition detected on input will cause the input and output
                          queues to be flushed, and a SIGINT signal will be sent to the
                          terminal's foreground process group if the terminal is the
                          controlling terminal for that group (we talk about process
                          groups and controlling terminals in Chapter 16).

terminal_io/char_size.c

```
 1 #include <stdio.h>
 2 #include <unistd.h>
 3 #include <termios.h>
 4 #include "ssp.h"

 5 static char *print_csize (int size);

 6 int main (void)
 7 {
 8     struct termios term;
 9     int size;

10     if (tcgetattr (STDIN_FILENO, &term) == -1)
11         err_msg ("Can't get terminal attributes");
12     size = term.c_cflag & CSIZE;
13     printf ("Old size is %s\n", print_csize (size));

14     term.c_cflag &= ~CSIZE;     /* Clear the size bits */
15     term.c_cflag |= CS8;        /* Set 8 bits per character */

16     if (tcsetattr (STDIN_FILENO, TCSANOW, &term) == -1)
17         err_msg ("Can't set terminal attributes");

18     if (tcgetattr (STDIN_FILENO, &term) == -1)
19         err_msg ("Can't get terminal attributes");
20     size = term.c_cflag & CSIZE;
21     printf ("New size is %s\n", print_csize (size));

22     return (0);
23 }

24 static char *print_csize (int size)
25 {
26     switch (size) {
27         case CS5:
28             return ("5 bits/character");

29         case CS6:
30             return ("6 bits/character");

31         case CS7:
32             return ("7 bits/character");

33         case CS8:
34             return ("8 bits/character");

35         default:
36             return ("unknown");
37     }
38 }
```

terminal_io/char_size.c

Program 12.2 Using `tcgetattr` and `tcsetattr` to change the character size.

If BRKINT and IGNBRK are not set, then a BREAK condition will be read as a single NUL character unless PARMRK is set, in which case the BREAK will be read as the three byte sequence 0xff, 0x00, 0x00 (i.e., \377, \0, \0).

BSDLY

(c_oflag) This is the backspace delay mask. The permissible values are BS0 and BS1.

CBAUD

(c_cflag) This is the output baud rate mask. There are a number of legal values: B0 (hang up), B50, B75, B110, B134, B150, B200, B300, B600, B1200, B1800, B2400, B4800, B9600, B19200, B38400, B57600, B76800, B115200, B153600, B230400, B307200, B460800, EXTA, and EXTB. The last two are synonyms for B19200 and B38400 respectively, from very early versions of Solaris that did not directly support speeds in excess of B9600; they should not be used in new programs.

The other values set the baud rate to the number after the B (so B38400 selects a baud rate of 38400, and so on). If B0 is specified, the data terminal ready (DTR) signal is not asserted, which usually disconnects the line.

Values not supported by the underlying hardware are ignored, and those in excess of 38400 must be set in conjunction with the BAUDEXT field. If the input and output baud rates are not the same, the CIBAUD and CIBAUDEXT must be used to set the input baud rate.

CBAUDEXT

This field is used in conjunction with CBAUD to select an output baud rate in excess of 38400.

The following code segment can be used to retrieve the output speed (os) from the termios structure pointed to by t:

```
if (t -> c_cflag & CBAUDEXT)
    os = (t -> c_cflag & CBAUD) + CBAUD + 1;
else
    os = t -> c_cflag & CBAUD;
```

Similarly, we can use the following code segment to set the output speed:

```
if (os > CBAUD) {
    t -> c_cflag |= CBAUDEXT;
    os -= ((CBAUD + 1);
}
else
    t -> c_cflag &= ~CBAUDEXT;
t -> c_cflag = (t -> c_cflag & ~CBAUD) |
    (os & CBAUD);
```

That said, the cfgetospeed and cfsetospeed functions
are the preferred methods of getting and setting the output
baud rate.

CIBAUD

If both this field and the CIBAUDEXT field are zero, the input
baud rate is the same as the output baud rate. Otherwise, this
field sets the input baud rate in much the same way that
CBAUD sets the output baud rate.

Values not supported by the underlying hardware are
ignored, and those in excess of 38400 must be set in
conjunction with the CIBAUDEXT field.

CIBAUDEXT

This field is used in conjunction with CIBAUD to select an
input baud rate in excess of 38400.

The following code segment can be used to retrieve the input
speed (is) from the termios structure pointed to by t:

```
if (t -> c_cflag & CIBAUDEXT)
    is = ((t -> c_cflag & CIBAUD) >> IBSHIFT) +
    (CIBAUD >> IBSHIFT) + 1;
else
    is = (t -> c_cflag & CIBAUD) >> IBSHIFT;
```

Similarly, we can use the following code segment to set the
input speed:

```
if (is == 0) {
    is = t -> c_cflag & CBAUD;
    if (t -> c_cflag & CBAUDEXT)
        is += (CBAUD + 1);
}
if ((is << IBSHIFT) > CIBAUD) {
    t -> c_cflag |= CIBAUDEXT;
    is -= ((CIBAUD >> IBSHIFT) + 1);
}
else
    t -> c_cflag &= ~CIBAUDEXT;
t -> c_cflag = (t -> c_cflag & ~CIBAUD) |
    ((is << IBSHIFT) & CIBAUD);
```

Again, the tcgetispeed and tcsetispeed functions are
the preferred methods of getting and setting the input speed.

CLOCAL

(c_cflag) If this flag is set, the modem status lines are
ignored, which usually means that the device is directly
attached. If this flag is clear, an open of the terminal device
will usually sleep until the modem is answered.

CRDLY

(c_oflag) This is the carriage return (CR) delay mask. The
permissible values are CR0, CR1, CR2, and CR3.

CREAD

(c_cflag) Setting this flag enables the receiver, allowing
characters to be received.

CRTSCTS	(c_cflag) Setting this flag enables outbound hardware flow control, using the request to send (RTS) and clear to send (CTS) pins of the interface.
CRTSXOFF	(c_cflag) Setting this flag enables inbound hardware flow control using the RTS pin of the interface.
CSIZE	(c_cflag) This is the character size mask, which is used to set the number of bits per character for transmission and reception, excluding and parity bits. The permissible values are CS5, CS6, CS7, or CS8, for 5, 6, 7, or 8 bits per character respectively.
CSTOPB	(c_cflag) Setting this flag causes two stop bits per character to be sent. If it is clear, only one stop bit per character is sent.
ECHO	(c_lflag) Setting this flag enables echoing. This means that received characters are echoed back to the terminal device. Echoing can be enabled in both canonical and non-canonical modes.
ECHOCTL	(c_lflag) If this and the ECHO flags are set, ASCII control characters (those in the range of 0 to 31 inclusive) are echoed as ^X, where X is the character formed by adding 64 to the control character. In other words, the ASCII Control-A character (which has a value of 1) will be echoed as ^A. The exceptions to this rule are the TAB, NL, START, STOP, and DELETE characters. The latter is echoed as ^?, the others are echoed as themselves or interpreted, depending on the character.
	If this flag is not set, the control characters are echoed as themselves. Echoing control characters can be enabled in both canonical and non-canonical modes.
ECHOE	(c_lflag) If this flag and the ICANON flags are set, the ERASE character erase the last character in the current line of the display. This is done by the terminal driver writing the three character sequence backspace, space, backspace.
	Setting the ECHOE flag also causes the WERASE character to erase the previous word, using one or more of the same three character sequence.
	The actions we describe for this flag assume that the ECHOPRT flag is not set.
ECHOK	(c_lflag) Setting this flag when the ICANON flag is also set causes the KILL character to be echoed, followed by a NL character.
	The actions we describe for this flag assume that the ECHOKE flag is not set.

ECHOKE	(c_lflag) Setting this flag when the ICANON flag is also set causes the KILL character to erase each character on the current line. How the characters are erased is determined by the ECHOE and ECHOPRT flags.
ECHONL	(c_lflag) Setting this flag when the ICANON flag is also set will cause the NL character to be echoed, even when the ECHO flag is clear.
ECHOPRT	(c_lflag) Setting this flag when the ICANON and ECHO flags are also set causes the ERASE and WERASE characters to erase characters by echoing the character being erased. This can be useful on hardcopy terminals, where it would otherwise be hard to see which characters were being erased.
FFDLY	(c_oflag) This is the form feed delay mask. The permissible values are FF0 and FF1.
FLUSHO	(c_lflag) If this flag is set, output is being flushed. This flag is set by typing the DISCARD character and is cleared when another DISCARD character is typed. We can also set or clear this condition by setting or clearing this flag.
HUPCL	This is the hang up on close flag. Setting it causes the modem control lines to be lowered when the last process closes the device (i.e., the modem connection is broken).
ICANON	(c_lflag) When this flag is set, canonical processing is enabled. This causes input characters to be assembled into lines, and enables the EOF, EOL, EOL2, ERASE, KILL, REPRINT, STATUS, and WERASE characters.
	If this flag is clear, the terminal device is in non-canonical mode. Read requests are satisfied directly from the input queue. A read is not satisfied until at least MIN bytes have been received or the timeout value TIME has expired between characters.
	See Section 12.9 for more information about canonical mode, and Section 12.10 for more details about non-canonical mode.
ICRNL	(c_iflag) If this flag is set and IGNCR is clear, received CR characters are converted to NL characters.
IEXTEN	(c_lflag) If this flag is set, various implementation-defined special characters are recognized and processed. Solaris recognizes the following special characters when the IEXTEN flag is set: DISCARD, DSUSP, EOL2, LNEXT, REPRINT, SWTCH, and WERASE.
IGNBRK	(c_iflag) If this flag is set, a BREAK condition on input is ignored. See the BRKINT entry at the beginning of this list to see how to get a BREAK condition to generate a SIGINT signal or be read as data.

IGNCR	(c_iflag) Setting this flag causes CR input characters to be ignored. If this flag is clear, then translating CR characters to NL is possible by setting INLCR.
IGNPAR	(c_iflag) If this flag is set, an input character with a framing error (other than BREAK) or parity error is ignored.
IMAXBEL	(c_iflag) Setting this flag causes the BEL character to be echoed if the input queue is full.
INLCR	(c_iflag) Setting this flag causes input NL characters to be translated to CR characters.
INPCK	(c_iflag) When this flag is set, input parity checking is enabled; otherwise, it is disabled.
ISIG	(c_lflag) If this flag is set, input characters that match one of the signal-generating special characters (i.e., INTR, QUIT, SUSP, and DSUSP) cause the appropriate signal to be generated.
ISTRIP	(c_iflag) If this flag is set, the eighth bit is stripped (that is, set to 0) from valid input characters. Otherwise, all eight bits are processed.
IUCLC	(c_iflag) Setting this flag causes upper case input characters to be mapped to lower case.
IXANY	(c_iflag) If this flag is set, any character will restart output.
IXOFF	(c_iflag) When this flag is set, software input flow control is enabled. When the input queue starts getting full, the terminal driver outputs a STOP character. This should cause the sending device to stop transmitting. Once the terminal driver has processed the characters in the input queue, it outputs a START character, which causes the sending device to resume data transmission.
IXON	(c_iflag) When this flag is set, software output flow control is enabled. When a STOP character is received by the terminal driver, it stops sending data until the next START character is received. If this flag is clear, the START and STOP characters are read by the process as normal characters.
NLDLY	(c_oflag) This is the newline delay mask. The permissible values are NL0 and NL1.
NOFLSH	(c_lflag) If this flag is clear (the default), when the SIGINT and SIGQUIT signals are generated by the terminal driver, both the input and output queues are flushed. Also, when the SIGSUSP signal is generated, the input queue is flushed. We can override this behaviour by setting the NOFLSH flag: the input and output queues will not be flushed when these signals are generated.

OCRNL	(c_oflag) Setting this flag causes output CR characters to be translated to NL characters.
OFDEL	(c_oflag) If this flag is set, the output fill character is set to ASCII DEL; otherwise, it is ASCII NUL. See the OFILL flag for more information.
OFILL	(c_oflag) Setting this flag causes a fill character (either ASCII DEL or ASCII NUL) to be transmitted for a delay rather than using a timed delay. This flag applies to the six delay masks, i.e., BSDLY, CRDLY, FFDLY, NLDLY, TABDLY, and VTDLY.
OLCUC	(c_oflag) Setting this flag causes lower case output characters to be translated to upper case.
ONLCR	(c_oflag) Setting this flag causes output NL characters to be translated to CR-NL character sequences.
ONLRET	(c_oflag) If this flag is set, the NL character is assumed to perform the carriage return function on output.
ONOCR	If this flag is set, a CR is not output at column 0.
OPOST	(c_oflag) Setting this flag enables output processing. The processing performed is controlled by the flags in the c_oflag section of Figure 12.3.
PARENB	(c_cflag) If this flag is set, parity generation is enabled for outgoing characters, and parity checking is performed on incoming characters. The state of the PARODD flag determines whether odd or even parity is used.
	We should note that parity "generation and detection" and "input parity checking" are two different things. As we said, setting the PARENB flag causes the terminal driver to generate parity for outgoing characters, and to check the parity of incoming characters (the parity type being determined by PARODD). If an input character arrives with the wrong parity, the INPCK flag is checked. If it is set, the IGNPAR flag is checked to see if the character should be ignored. If the character should not be ignored, then the PARMRK flag is checked to see what characters should be passed to the reading process.
PAREXT	(c_cflag) Setting this flag enables extended parity for mark and space parity.
PARMRK	(c_iflag) When this flag is set, and IGNPAR is clear, an input character with a framing or parity error (other than BREAK) is passed to the reading program as the three character sequence 0xff, 0x00, X, where X is the character that was received in

error. If `ISTRIP` is not set, a valid 0xff is passed to the reading program as 0xff, 0xff. If neither `IGNPAR` nor `PARMRK` is set, an input character with a framing or parity error (other than BREAK) is passed to the reading program as a single ASCII NUL character.

PARODD
(`c_cflag`) Setting this flag causes the incoming and outgoing characters to use odd parity; otherwise, even parity is used. Note that this flag only has an effect if parity generation and checking is enabled using the `PARENB` flag.

PENDIN
(`c_lflag`) If this flag is set, any pending input that as not been read by the process is reprinted by the terminal driver when the next character is input. This action is similar to what happens when we type the REPRINT character.

TABDLY
(`c_oflag`) This is the horizontal tab delay mask. The permissible values are `TAB0`, `TAB1`, `TAB2`, `TAB3`, and `XTABS`.

The last two values cause tabs to be expanded into spaces. Tab stops every eight columns are assumed, and we can't change this assumption.

TOSTOP
(`c_lflag`) If this flag is set, a `SIGTTOU` signal is generated and sent to the process group of a background process that tries to write to its controlling terminal. By default, this signal stops all process in the process group. The signal is not generated by the terminal driver if the writing process is either blocking or ignoring `SIGTTOU`.

VTDLY
(`c_oflag`) This is the vertical tab delay mask. The permissible values are `VT0` and `VT1`.

XCASE
(`c_lflag`) Setting this flag when the `ICANON` flag is also set causes the terminal driver to assume that an upper case only terminal is being used, and all input is converted to lower case. If we want to input an upper case character, we must precede it with a backslash (\). Similarly, an output upper case character is preceded by a backslash. This flag is arguably obsolete, as upper case only terminals have all but disappeared.

We mentioned that two flags control hardware flow control: `CRTSCTS` and `CRTSXOFF`. The four combinations of these flags and their interactions are described below:

1. `CRTSCTS` off, `CRTSXOFF` off. In this case, hardware flow control is disabled.

2. `CRTSCTS` off, `CRTSXOFF` on. In this case, only inbound hardware flow control is enabled. The state of the RTS signal is used to do inbound flow control. It is expected that input will be suspended if RTS is low, and resumed when it is high.

3. CRTSCTS on, CRTSXOFF off. In this case, only outbound hardware flow control is enabled. The state of the CTS signal is used to do outbound flow control. It is expected that output will be suspended if CTS is low, and resumed when it is high.

4. CRTSCTS on, CRTSXOFF on. In this case both inbound and outbound flow control are enabled. The state of the CTS signal is used to handle outbound flow control, and the state of the RTS signal is used to do inbound flow control.

The stty Command

All of the options we have just discussed can be manipulated from the command line using the stty command. The stty command is a front end to the first six functions in Figure 12.4. Running it with the -a option displays all the current terminal settings:

```
$ stty -a
speed 9600 baud;
rows = 48; columns = 132; ypixels = 634; xpixels = 934;
csdata ?
eucw 1:0:0:0, scrw 1:0:0:0
intr = ^c; quit = ^\; erase = ^h; kill = ^u;
eof = ^d; eol = <undef>; eol2 = <undef>; swtch = <undef>;
start = ^q; stop = ^s; susp = ^z; dsusp = ^y;
rprnt = ^r; flush = ^o; werase = ^w; lnext = ^v;
parenb -parodd cs7 -cstopb hupcl cread -clocal -loblk -crtscts -crtsxoff
    -parext
-ignbrk brkint ignpar -parmrk -inpck istrip -inlcr -igncr icrnl -iuclc
ixon -ixany -ixoff imaxbel
isig icanon -xcase echo echoe echok -echonl -noflsh
-tostop echoctl -echoprt echoke -defecho -flusho -pendin iexten
opost -olcuc onlcr -ocrnl -onocr -onlret -ofill -ofdel
```

Note that we've wrapped some of the lines so that they will fit on the page. The first line shows the baud rate our terminal is connected at. However, because we ran the command in virtual terminal, the baud rate is meaningless. The second line shows the dimensions of our terminal window; we'll discuss this in Section 12.11. Lines 5 to 8 show the settings for the special input characters, and the remaining lines show the settings of the terminal options. Those preceded by a hyphen are disabled.

12.6 Baud Rate Functions

The term "baud rate" is somewhat obsolescent, being replaced by the phrase "bits per second". (Technically, *baud rate* is the number of times per second a data transmission channel changes state.) Although most terminal devices use the same baud rate for input and output, some support the use of different input and output speeds. Because of this, Solaris provides functions to manipulate both the input baud rate and the output baud rate.

```
#include <termios.h>

speed_t cfgetispeed (const struct termios *termios_p);

speed_t cfgetospeed (const struct termios *termios_p);
```

                                                        Both return: the baud rate value

```
int cfsetispeed (struct termios *termios_p, speed_t speed);

int cfsetospeed (struct termios *termios_p, speed_t speed);
```

                                                        Both return: 0 if OK, −1 on error

The cfgetispeed function extracts the input baud rate from the termios structure pointed to by *termios_p*. This means that we must first call tcgetattr to populate the termios structure with the information for the current terminal device. Depending on the baud rate, the return value will be one of the following constants: B0, B50, B75, B110, B134, B150, B200, B300, B600, B1200, B1800, B2400, B4800, B9600, B19200, B38400, B57600, B76800, B115200, B153600, B230400, B307200, or B460800.

The cfgetospeed function performs the same task, but for the output baud rate.

The cfsetispeed function sets the input baud rate in the termios structure pointed to by termios_p to the rate specified by *speed*. The *speed* argument must be one of the values we listed previously as possible return values from cfgetispeed.

It is important to realize that these functions just set the baud rate in the termios structure; the do not take effect until the terminal's attributes are updated using the tcsetattr function.

The cfsetospeed performs the same task as cfsetispeed, but for the output baud rate. An output baud rate of B0 means "hang up". Specifying B0 as the output baud rate will cause the modem's control signals to be asserted no longer when the terminal's attributes are updated using tcsetattr.

We can't assume that a successful return from either cfsetispeed or cfsetospeed means that the attached device supports the selected speed. The only way we can be sure is to call tcgetattr and check the baud rate after we've called tcsetattr to update the terminal's attributes.

Example: Changing the input baud rate

Program 12.3 sets the input speed to 115,200 baud.

Running Program 12.3 in a dtterm window gives the following results:

```
$ stty -a | grep speed              Check current speed
speed 9600 baud;
$ ./cfsetispeed
$ stty -a | grep speed              Recheck current speed
ispeed 115200 baud; ospeed 9600 baud;
```

terminal_io/cfsetispeed.c

```
 1 #include <unistd.h>
 2 #include <termios.h>
 3 #include "ssp.h"

 4 int main (void)
 5 {
 6     struct termios term;

 7     if (tcgetattr (STDIN_FILENO, &term) == -1)
 8         err_msg ("Can't get terminal attributes");

 9     if (cfsetispeed (&term, B115200) == -1)
10         err_msg ("Can't set output baud rate");

11     if (tcsetattr (STDIN_FILENO, TCSANOW, &term) == -1)
12         err_msg ("Can't set terminal attributes");

13     if (tcgetattr (STDIN_FILENO, &term) == -1)
14         err_msg ("Can't get terminal attributes");

15     if (cfgetispeed (&term) != B115200)
16         err_msg ("115200 baud not supported");

17     return (0);
18 }
```

terminal_io/cfsetispeed.c

Program 12.3 Changing the input baud rate.

We use the stty program to verify the results. Notice that the output from stty changes when the input and output baud rates differ.

12.7 Line Control Functions

Four functions provide line control capability for terminal devices. These are tcdrain, tcflow, tcflush, and tcsendbreak.

The tcdrain Function

The tcdrain function waits for all output to be transmitted.

```
#include <termios.h>

int tcdrain (int fildes);
```
                                                    Returns: 0 if OK, −1 on error

The tcdrain function waits until all the output written to the terminal device associated with the file descriptor *fildes* is transmitted.

The `tcflow` Function

The `tcflow` function gives us control over input and output flow control.

```
#include <termios.h>

int tcflow (int fildes, int action);
```
                                                              Returns: 0 if OK, –1 on error

The `tcflow` function suspends or restarts transmission or reception of data on the terminal device associated with the file descriptor *fildes*, depending on the action of *action*. The *action* argument must be one of the following four values:

TCOOFF	Output is suspended.
TCOON	Previously suspended output is restarted.
TCIOFF	A STOP character is transmitted, which is intended to cause the terminal device to stop sending data.
TCION	A START character is transmitted, which is intended to cause the terminal device to resume sending data.

When a terminal device is first opened, neither its input nor its output are suspended.

The `tcflush` Function

We can use the `tcflush` function to flush the input and output queues.

```
#include <termios.h>

int tcflush (int fildes, int queue_selector);
```
                                                              Returns: 0 if OK, –1 on error

Depending on the value of *queue_selector*, the `tcflush` function discards (flushes) data written to (but not yet transmitted from) the terminal device associated with *fildes*, or data received but not read (or both). In other words, data in the input queue or the output queue (or both) associated with *fildes* is discarded. The *queue_selector* argument must be one of the following constants:

TCIFLUSH	The input queue is flushed.
TCOFLUSH	The output queue is flushed.
TCIOFLUSH	The input and output queues are flushed.

The `tcsendbreak` Function

We use the `tcsendbreak` function to send a BREAK.

```
#include <termios.h>

int tcsendbreak (int fildes, int duration);
```

Returns: 0 if OK, −1 on error

If the terminal associated with *fildes* is using asynchronous serial data transmission, the tcsendbreak function causes a transmission of a continuous stream of zero bits for the specified duration. If the *duration* argument is 0, the BREAK condition will last for at least 0.25 seconds, but no more than 0.5 seconds. If *duration* is non-zero, then tcsendbreak behaves in a manner similar to tcdrain.

> Different versions of UNIX have different actions when *duration* is not zero. From a portability point of view, setting *duration* to 0 is strongly recommended.

12.8 Terminal Identification

When we talk about terminal identification, we are talking about the answer to one of three different questions:

1. What is the name of our controlling terminal?
2. Is a given file descriptor associated with a terminal device?
3. What is the pathname of the terminal device associated with a given file descriptor?

These questions can be answered by calling one of the following functions: ctermid, isatty, or ttyname.

The cTermid and ctermid_r Functions

Historically, the name of the controlling terminal in most versions of UNIX has been /dev/tty, and Solaris is no different. However, rather than hard coding this name into our programs, we can use the ctermid function to determine the name of the controlling terminal at run time.

```
#include <stdio.h>

char *ctermid (char *s);

char *ctermid_r (char *s);
```

Both return: see text

The ctermid function determines the pathname of controlling terminal for the calling process, and places it into a buffer, as determined by *s*.

If *s* is NULL, the pathname of the controlling terminal is stored in an internal static area whose address is returned to the caller and whose contents are overwritten at the next call to `ctermid`. If *s* is not NULL, it is assumed to point to an array of at least `L_ctermid` bytes. The controlling terminal's pathname is stored in this array, and the value of *s* is returned to the caller.

The `ctermid_r` is the same as `ctermid` except that it returns NULL if *s* is a NULL pointer.

The `isatty` Function

We can determine whether a file descriptor refers to a terminal device by using `isatty`.

```
#include <unistd.h>

int isatty (int fildes);
```
Returns: 1 if fildes refers to a terminal device, 0 otherwise

The `isatty` function returns 1 if the file descriptor *fildes* is associated with a terminal device. If it is not (or an error occurs), 0 is returned. In the event of an error, `errno` will be set to indicate the error.

Example: Implementing `isatty`

Program 12.4 shows one way the `isatty` function could be implemented.

terminal_io/isatty.c

```
 1 #include <stdio.h>
 2 #include <termios.h>

 3 static int ssp_isatty (int fd);

 4 int main (void)
 5 {
 6     int i;

 7     for (i = 0; i < 3; i++)
 8         printf ("fd %d: %s a tty\n", i, (ssp_isatty (i)) ? "is" : "is not");

 9     return (0);
10 }

11 static int ssp_isatty (int fd)
12 {
13     struct termios term;

14     return (tcgetattr (fd, &term) != -1);
15 }
```

terminal_io/isatty.c

Program 12.4 Our implementation of `isatty`.

Our implementation of `isatty` just calls one of the terminal-specific functions and returns an indication as to whether the operation was successful. Which function we use is unimportant as long as it doesn't change anything (in this case, we're using tcgetattr).

Running Program 12.4 gives us the following results:

```
$ ./isatty < /dev/null 2> /dev/null
fd 0: is not a tty
fd 1: is a tty
fd 2: is not a tty
```

The `ttyname` and `ttyname_r` Functions

We can determine the pathname of the terminal associated with a given file descriptor by using the ttyname function.

```
#include <unistd.h>

char *ttyname (int fildes);

char *ttyname_r (int fildes); char *name, int namelen);

cc [ flag ... ] file ... -D_POSIX_PTHREAD_SEMANTICS [ lib ... ]

int ttyname_r (int fildes); char *name, size_t namesize);
```

                                                                All three return: see text

The ttyname function returns a pointer to the NUL-terminated pathname of the terminal device associated with *fildes*. The pathname is stored in an internal static area whose contents are overwritten on the next call to ttyname. In the event of an error, a NULL pointer is returned.

The ttyname_r function performs the same task as ttyname, but *name* must point to a buffer (that is of *length* bytes in size) which will store the result. This buffer must be at least _POSIX_PATH_MAX (which is defined in <limits.h>) bytes in size.

The POSIX version of ttyname_r is the same as the non-POSIX version, except the last argument is of type size_t, and the return value is different. The POSIX version of ttyname_r returns 0 on success, or the error number on failure.

The non-POSIX version of ttyname_r is deprecated, so new code should use the POSIX version.

Example: Implementing `ttyname_r`

The ttyname_r function is more complicated to implement than isatty. This is partly because we must search through the /dev directory hierarchy to find the terminal's pathname. Program 12.5 shows one way the POSIX version of ttyname_r could be implemented.

Our version of ttyname_r is not very sophisticated; it merely recursively traverses the /dev directory hierarchy until a file is found that matches the terminal device.

terminal_io/ttyname.c

```
 1 #include <stdio.h>
 2 #include <unistd.h>
 3 #include <limits.h>
 4 #include <termios.h>
 5 #include <strings.h>
 6 #include <sys/types.h>
 7 #include <sys/stat.h>
 8 #include <dirent.h>
 9 #include <errno.h>
10 #include "ssp.h"

11 static int ssp_ttyname_r (int fd, char *name, size_t namesize);
12 static int dir_search (char *dir, struct stat *fd_stat, char *name);

13 int main (void)
14 {
15     int i;
16     char buf [_POSIX_PATH_MAX];

17     for (i = 0; i < 3; i++) {
18         if (ssp_ttyname_r (i, buf, _POSIX_PATH_MAX) == 0)
19             printf ("fd %d: %s\n", i, buf);
20         else
21             printf ("fd %d: Not a TTY\n", i);
22     }

23     return (0);
24 }

25 static int ssp_ttyname_r (int fd, char *name, size_t namesize)
26 {
27     struct stat fd_stat;
28     char buf [_POSIX_PATH_MAX];

29     if (isatty (fd) == 0)
30         return (ENOTTY);
31     if (fstat (fd, &fd_stat) == -1)
32         return (errno);
33     if (namesize < _POSIX_PATH_MAX)
34         return (ERANGE);

35     if (dir_search ("/dev/", &fd_stat, buf) == 0) {
36         strcpy (name, buf);
37         return (0);
38     }
39     else
40         return (errno);
41 }

42 static int dir_search (char *dir, struct stat *fd_stat, char *name)
43 {
44     struct stat dev_stat;
45     DIR *dp;
46     struct dirent *dirp;
47     char buf [_POSIX_PATH_MAX];
```

```
48      if ((dp = opendir (dir)) == NULL)
49          return (-1);

50      if ((readdir (dp) == NULL) || (readdir (dp) == NULL)) {
51          closedir (dp);
52          return (-1);
53      }
54      while ((dirp = readdir (dp)) != NULL) {
55          snprintf (buf, _POSIX_PATH_MAX, "%s%s", dir, dirp -> d_name);
56          if (stat (buf, &dev_stat) == -1)
57              continue;
58          if (S_ISDIR (dev_stat.st_mode)) {
59              strcat (buf, "/");
60              if (dir_search (buf, fd_stat, name) == 0) {
61                  closedir (dp);
62                  return (0);
63              }
64          }
65          else {
66              if ((dev_stat.st_ino == fd_stat -> st_ino) &&
67                  (dev_stat.st_dev == fd_stat -> st_dev) &&
68                  (dev_stat.st_rdev == fd_stat -> st_rdev)) {
69                  strcpy (name, buf);
70                  closedir (dp);
71                  return (0);
72              }
73          }
74      }
75      closedir (dp);
76      errno = EINVAL;
77      return (-1);
78  }
```

terminal_io/ttyname.c

Program 12.5   Our implementation of `ttyname_r`.

Let's take a closer look at some of the code in Program 12.5.

Print results for standard input, standard output, and standard error

17–22 Iterate through the first three file descriptors. For each one, call our function `ssp_ttyname_r` and print the results.

Perform sanity checks on arguments

29–34 We perform three tests to eliminate common errors:

1. The file descriptor is not associated with a terminal device.

2. We can't get the status of the file descriptor.

3. The supplied buffer is not large enough to hold the result.

35–41 Call our function `dir_search` to perform the task of actually searching for a match, returning 0 if we find one, or the value of `errno` otherwise.

Open directory stream

48–49 Open a directory stream using the `opendir` function we discussed in Section 10.23.

50–53 Call `readdir` twice, discarding the results. This is a more efficient method of skipping the *dot* and *dot-dot* entries than using `strcmp` in the `while` loop, because we are guaranteed that the first two directory entries will always be *dot* and *dot-dot*.

Examine each directory entry

55 Create the pathname to `stat` by concatenating the current filename to the directory we're searching.

56–64 Perform the `stat` on the resulting pathname; if the current file we're checking is a directory, we append a slash to its pathname and recursively call `dir_search`.

65–73 If the current file we're checking is not a directory, we compare its inode number, the device of the file system that contains the directory entry for the file, and its device number with those of the terminal device. If they match, we have found the pathname we are looking for, and return.

75–78 If we get this far, the file we're looking for isn't in the current directory, so we return a negative result.

Running Program 12.5 gives us the following results.

```
$ ./ttyname < /dev/console 2> /dev/null
fd 0: /dev/console
fd 1: /dev/pts/7
fd 2: Not a TTY
```

12.9 Canonical Mode

Canonical mode is specified by turning on the `ICANON` flag in the `c_lflag` member of the `termios` structure. Interacting with a terminal device in canonical mode is straightforward: we issue a read, and the terminal driver returns when a line has been entered. Several conditions cause a read to return:

1. The number of bytes we requested have been read. Although the terminal driver delivers data in line-sized chunks, we don't have to read the whole line at once. If we read only part of the line, no information is lost, because the next read starts where the previous one stopped.

2. A line delimiter is encountered. In Section 12.2 we said that the following characters are interpreted as end of line in canonical mode: EOF, EOL, EOL2, and NL. Also, as we stated in Section 12.5, if the `ICRNL` flag is set and `IGNCR` is clear, then the CR character also terminates a line since it acts just like the NL character.

   The EOF character is discarded by the terminal driver when it is processed. The other four are retuned to the reading process as the last character of the line.

3. A signal is caught and the function is not automatically restarted (we discuss interrupted system calls in Section 17.9).

Example: Reading a password

Sometimes we need to read a password from the user of our program. For obvious reasons, it is undesirable for the user's password to be echoed on the screen while they type it. Program 12.6 shows our implementation of a function to read a user's password safely (as we saw in Chapter 7, Solaris supplies the `getpass` and `getpassphrase` functions to do this for us).

Let's take a closer look at Program 12.6.

Our `main` function

14–15 Call our `readpass` function to read a password from the user.

16 Print the password the user entered. This just lets us confirm that canonical mode line editing (i.e., the ERASE and KILL characters) works as intended. In a real program, we would most likely encrypt the password here (we saw in Section 7.8 how to do this).

17–18 Destroy the cleartext version of the password. The *cleartext* version of a password is the unencrypted form. The reason why we clear it is to make sure the cleartext password is not in the memory image of the process. If we did not take this precaution, the cleartext password would be visible in any `core` file that might be produced.

Open the controlling terminal

28–29 Open the controlling terminal. Note that we use the `ctermid` function to determine its name rather than hard coding /dev/tty into our program.

We open the controlling terminal for reading and writing, but other conventions exist. For example, Solaris reads from the controlling terminal while writing to standard error.

Change the terminal's attributes

30–31 After getting the current terminal attributes, we use a structure copy to populate the `new_term` structure.

32–33 We disable echoing by clearing all the echo flags the `termios` structure. We then apply the new set of terminal flags, flushing the input queue at the same time.

Print the prompt

34 Print out the supplied prompt.

Read in the password

35 Clear the buffer that will hold the string to ensure that it will be NUL terminated.

36 Read at most `PASS_MAX` characters from the controlling terminal.

37 Echo a newline.

38–40 If the last character of the password string is the newline character, we replace it with a NUL. We must do this because the newline character is returned by `read` unless the line is longer than `PASS_MAX` characters.

Restore the terminal's attributes and return

41–43 After restoring the terminal's attributes, the file descriptor for the controlling terminal is closed, and we return a pointer to the password string.

terminal_io/readpass.c

```
 1 #include <stdio.h>
 2 #include <unistd.h>
 3 #include <termios.h>
 4 #include <limits.h>
 5 #include <string.h>
 6 #include <sys/types.h>
 7 #include <sys/stat.h>
 8 #include <fcntl.h>
 9 #include "ssp.h"

10 static char *readpass (const char *prompt);

11 int main (void)
12 {
13     char *pass;

14     if ((pass = readpass ("Enter password: ")) == NULL)
15         err_msg ("readpass error");
16     printf ("Password = %s\n", pass);

17     while (*pass)
18         *pass++ = '\0';

19     return (0);
20 }

21 static char *readpass (const char *prompt)
22 {
23     struct termios old_term;
24     struct termios new_term;
25     int fd;
26     static char buf [PASS_MAX + 1];
27     int n;

28     if ((fd = open (ctermid (NULL), O_RDWR)) == -1)
29         return (NULL);

30     tcgetattr (fd, &old_term);
31     new_term = old_term;
32     new_term.c_lflag &= ~(ECHO | ECHOE | ECHOK | ECHONL);
33     tcsetattr (fd, TCSAFLUSH, &new_term);

34     writen (fd, prompt, strlen (prompt));

35     memset (buf, 0, PASS_MAX + 1);
36     read (fd, buf, PASS_MAX);
37     writen (fd, "\n", 1);
38     n = strlen (buf) - 1;
39     if (buf [n] == '\n')
40         buf [n] = '\0';

41     tcsetattr (fd, TCSAFLUSH, &old_term);
42     close (fd);

43     return (buf);
44 }
```

terminal_io/readpass.c

Program 12.6   A function to read a user's password.

One problem with the `readpass` function in Program 12.6 is that it does not block signals. (This is because we don't cover signals until Chapter 17.) For this reason, typing the INTR character will cause the program to exit, leaving echoing disabled. Similarly, the SUSP character would suspend the program, returning to the shell with echoing disabled.

Some shells (e.g., `ksh`) turn echoing back on whenever they read interactive input. These shells provide command line editing and therefore manipulate the terminal's state every time we enter an interactive command. Shells that don't offer interactive command editing (like `sh` and `csh`) do not restore the terminal's mode. If we interrupt our program in one of these shells, we can restore echoing by using the `stty` command.

12.10 Non-Canonical Mode

Non-canonical mode is specified by turning off the `ICANON` flag in the `c_lflag` member of the `termios` structure. In non-canonical mode, the input data is not assembled into lines, and the following special characters are not processed: CR, EOF, EOL, EOL2, ERASE, KILL, NL, REPRINT, and WERASE.

As we stated previously, input in canonical mode is straightforward; data is returned a line at a time. But how does the system know when to return data in non-canonical mode? One way would be to return every byte as it is read. But as we saw in Figure 4.2, performing I/O one character at a time is very inefficient because the system call overhead is excessive. Returning a fixed number of bytes at a time won't work either because sometimes we don't know how much data we need to read until we start reading it.

Solaris solves these problems by allowing us to tell the system to return after either of two conditions have been satisfied:

1.   The specified amount of data has been read.

2.   At least the specified amount of time has passed.

Two variables in the `c_cc` array of the `termios` structure are used to facilitate this: MIN and TIME. They are indexed using the constants `VMIN` and `VTIME` respectively.

MIN specifies the minimum number of bytes before a read returns, and TIME specifies the amount of time to wait for data to arrive. The time is specified in multiples of 0.1 seconds. Using the MIN and TIME variables gives us four cases to consider:

Case A: MIN > 0, TIME > 0

In this case, TIME serves as an intercharacter timer that is started only after the first character is received. Because it is an intercharacter timer, it is reset after each character is received. If MIN characters are received before the timer expires, the read is satisfied, returning MIN characters. If the timer expires before MIN characters are received, the characters received up to that point are returned to the caller. (At least one character will be returned if the timer expires, because it isn't started until the first character is received.)

The read operation sleeps until the MIN and TIME mechanisms are activated by the first character. If the number of characters read is less than the number available, the timer is not reactivated and the subsequent read is satisfied immediately.

Case B: MIN > 0, TIME == 0

The read does not return until MIN characters have been received. Programs using this case to read terminal I/O may block indefinitely.

Case C: MIN == 0, TIME > 0

In this case, since MIN is zero, TIME is no longer used as an intercharacter timer. Instead, it serves as a read timer that is activated as soon as the read function is called. The read is satisfied as soon as a character is received or the timer expires. Note that if the timer expires, no characters will be returned.

Case D: MIN == 0, TIME == 0

In this case, the read returns immediately. If some data is available, the minimum of either the number of characters requested or the number of characters currently available is returned without waiting for more input. If no data is available, the read is satisfied immediately, returning 0 characters.

Note that in all these cases, MIN is only a minimum. If we request more than MIN characters, it's possible to receive up to that amount.

Figure 12.8 summarizes the four different cases for non-canonical input. In this figure, *nbyte* refers to the third argument of the read function, which is the maximum number of bytes to return, and the entries between square brackets indicate a range.

	MIN > 0	MIN == 0
TIME > 0	A: read returns [MIN, *nbytes*] before timer expires; read returns [1, MIN] if timer expires. (TIME = intercharacter timer. Caller can block indefinitely.)	B: read returns [1, *nbytes*] before timer expires; read returns 0 if timer expires. (TIME = read timer.)
TIME == 0	C: read returns [MIN, *nbytes*] when available. (Caller can block indefinitely.)	D: read returns [0, *nbytes*] immediately.

Figure 12.8 The four cases for non-canonical input.

There's a potential problem we need to be aware of when changing from non-canonical mode to canonical mode. The c_cc array subscripts VMIN and VTIME can have the same values as VEOF and VEOL respectively (indeed, this is the case on Solaris). If we set MIN to its typical value of 1 in non-canonical mode, the EOF character will become Control-A when we switch back to canonical mode. The best way to avoid this problem is to save the entire `termios` structure when entering non-canonical mode, and restore it when switching back to canonical mode.

Example: Implementing the cbreak and raw modes

In Section 12.2 we mentioned that older versions of UNIX used cooked, cbreak, and raw modes instead of canonical and non-canonical. Program 12.7 defines five functions we can use to set the terminal to each of these modes.

Let's take a closer look at some of the implementation details of Program 12.7.

Global variables

2–8 We set up three global variables that let us keep track of state between the various functions. We use `saved_fd` to keep track of the terminal's file descriptor, `saved_term` to save the original terminal attributes, and `term_state` to keep track of the terminal's current state. Note that these global variables are defined as `static`, so they have no scope outside their source file.

The `tty_cbreak` function

12–13 Save the terminal's current attributes so that we can restore them later.

14–19 We use a structure copy to populate the `term` structure. Then we clear the `ECHO` and `ICANON` flags, arrange to receive one character at a time (with no timer), and apply these new attributes to the terminal.

20–22 We set our `term_state` variable to reflect the fact that we are now emulating cbreak mode, save the number of the file descriptor we altered, and return.

The `tty_raw` function

27–28 Save the terminal's current attributes so that we can restore them later.

29–38 We use a structure copy to populate the `term` structure. Then we set up raw mode:

- The `BRKINT`, `ICRNL`, `INPCK`, `ISTRIP`, and `IXON` flags are cleared. This turns off `SIGINT` on BREAK, CR to NL input translation, input parity checking, and input flow control. Also, we don't strip the eighth bit.

- We clear the `OPOST` flag to disable output processing.

- The `CSIZE` and `PARENB` flags are cleared, clearing the character size mask and disabling parity checking. Then we select eight bits per character (`CS8`).

- The `ECHO`, `ICANON`, `IEXTEN`, and `ISIG` flags are cleared. This turns off echoing, canonical mode, extended input mode, and disables the processing of the signal generating characters.

- We arrange to receive one character at a time with no timer.

The new attributes are then applied to the terminal.

39–41 We set our `term_state` variable to reflect the fact that we are now emulating raw mode, save the number of the file descriptor we altered, and return.

terminal_io/modes.c

```
 1 #include <termios.h>

 2 static int saved_fd = -1;
 3 static struct termios saved_term;
 4 static enum {
 5     RESET,
 6     RAW,
 7     CBREAK
 8 } term_state = RESET;

 9 int tty_cbreak (int fd)
10 {
11     struct termios term;

12     if (tcgetattr (fd, &saved_term) == -1)
13         return (-1);

14     term = saved_term;
15     term.c_lflag &= ~(ECHO | ICANON);
16     term.c_cc [VMIN] = 1;
17     term.c_cc [VTIME] = 0;
18     if (tcsetattr (fd, TCSAFLUSH, &term) == -1)
19         return (-1);

20     term_state = CBREAK;
21     saved_fd = fd;

22     return (0);
23 }

24 int tty_raw (int fd)
25 {
26     struct termios term;

27     if (tcgetattr (fd, &saved_term) == -1)
28         return (-1);

29     term = saved_term;
30     term.c_iflag &= ~(BRKINT | ICRNL | INPCK | ISTRIP | IXON);
31     term.c_oflag &= ~(OPOST);
32     term.c_cflag &= ~(CSIZE | PARENB);
33     term.c_cflag |= CS8;
34     term.c_lflag &= ~(ECHO | ICANON | IEXTEN | ISIG);
35     term.c_cc [VMIN] = 1;
36     term.c_cc [VTIME] = 0;
37     if (tcsetattr (fd, TCSAFLUSH, &term) == -1)
38         return (-1);

39     term_state = RAW;
40     saved_fd = fd;

41     return (0);
42 }
```

```
43 int tty_reset (int fd)
44 {
45     if (term_state == RESET)
46         return (0);

47     if (tcsetattr (fd, TCSAFLUSH, &saved_term) == -1)
48         return (-1);

49     term_state = RESET;
50     saved_fd = -1;

51     return (0);
52 }

53 void tty_atexit (void)
54 {
55     if (saved_fd != -1)
56         tty_reset (saved_fd);
57 }

58 struct termios *tty_getoldattr (void)
59 {
60     return (&saved_term);
61 }
```
——— *terminal_io/modes.c*

Program 12.7 Set terminal to cbreak or raw mode.

The `tty_reset` function

45–46 If the current terminal state is already RESET, we just return.

47–48 We restore the terminal's original attributes.

49–51 We reset our `term_state` variable, set `saved_fd` to −1, and return.

The `tty_atexit` function

53–57 If we have previously called one of these functions to change the terminal's state (i.e., `saved_fd` is not −1), then call `tty_reset`, passing it the saved file descriptor as an argument.

The `tty_getoldattr` function

58–61 This function just returns a pointer to the structure in which we saved the terminal's attributes (in either `tty_cbreak` or `tty_raw`).

We can test our implementation of the raw and cbreak modes in Program 12.7 by using Program 12.8.

Notice that in Program 12.8 we set up a signal handler for three signals: SIGINT, SIGQUIT, and SIGTERM. We arrange to catch these signals so that we can reset the terminal's attributes before terminating.

For this reason, as a rule of thumb, whenever we write a program that changes the terminal's attributes, we should catch most signals.

terminal_io/test_modes.c

```
 1 #include <stdio.h>
 2 #include <unistd.h>
 3 #include <stdlib.h>
 4 #include <termios.h>
 5 #include <signal.h>
 6 #include "ssp.h"

 7 extern int tty_cbreak (int fd);
 8 extern int tty_raw (int fd);
 9 extern int tty_reset (int fd);
10 static void sig_handler (int sig);

11 int main (void)
12 {
13     int i;
14     char c;

15     if (sigset (SIGINT, sig_handler) == SIG_ERR)
16         err_msg ("sigset error");
17     if (sigset (SIGQUIT, sig_handler) == SIG_ERR)
18         err_msg ("sigset error");
19     if (sigset (SIGTERM, sig_handler) == SIG_ERR)
20         err_msg ("sigset error");

21     if (tty_raw (STDIN_FILENO) == -1)
22         err_msg ("tty_raw error");

23     printf ("Enter raw mode characters, end with Backspace\n");
24     while ((i = read (STDIN_FILENO, &c, 1)) == 1) {
25         if ((c &= 255) == 0x08)
26             break;
27         printf ("%d\n", c);
28     }

29     if (tty_reset (STDIN_FILENO) == -1)
30         err_msg ("tty_reset");
31     if (i <= 0)
32         err_msg ("read error");

33     if (tty_cbreak (STDIN_FILENO) == -1)
34         err_msg ("tty_cbreak error");

35     printf ("\nEnter cbreak mode characters, end with INTR\n");
36     while ((i = read (STDIN_FILENO, &c, 1)) == 1) {
37         c &= 255;
38         printf ("%d\n", c);
39     }

40     if (tty_reset (STDIN_FILENO) == -1)
41         err_msg ("tty_reset");

42     if (i <= 0)
43         err_msg ("read error");

44     return (0);
45 }
```

```
46 static void sig_handler (int sig)
47 {
48     tty_reset (STDIN_FILENO);
49     exit (0);
50 }
```
——————————————————————————————— *terminal_io/test_modes.c*

Program 12.8 Testing our raw and cbreak modes.

Running program 12.8 gives results like the following:

```
$ ./test_modes
Enter raw mode characters, end with Backspace
                                             3
                                             4
                                            72
                                           101
                                          108
                                         108
                                        111
                                       33
                                      13
                                                    Type Backspace
Enter cbreak mode characters, end with INTR
4                                                   Type Control-D
8                                                   Type Backspace
10                                                  Type Return
$                                                   Type INTR key
```

In raw mode, the characters we typed were Control-C (3), Control-D (4), H (72), e (101), l (108), l (108), o (111), ! (33), and Return (13). Notice that with output processing turned off (i.e., the OPOST flag is clear), we don't get a carriage return after every character; we just get a newline.

Also notice that special input character handling is disabled in cbreak mode. This means that Control-D and Backspace are not handled specially, but terminal-generated signals are still processed. Another interesting thing to observe is that the return character (13) got translated to a newline character (10).

12.11 Terminal Window Size

With the widespread use of the X Window System on UNIX platforms, a terminal device is more likely to be a terminal emulator like xterm or dtterm (a *pseudo terminal*) than a real hardware terminal attached to a serial port. Because the window size of a pseudo terminal is usually easy to change, it is useful to know what the current window size is, and when a size change occurs. (Some hardware terminals also support different screen sizes, but they are less likely to be changed during an interactive session.) To facilitate this, the kernel maintains a winsize structure for every terminal and pseudo terminal. The winsize structure contains the following members:

```
struct winsize {
    unsigned short ws_row;    /* Rows, in characters */
    unsigned short ws_col;    /* Columns, in characters */
```

```
        unsigned short ws_xpixel;    /* Horizontal size, in pixels */
        unsigned short ws_ypixel;    /* Vertical size, in pixels */
    };
```

We can populate a `winsize` structure with the current values by calling `ioctl` with the *cmd* argument set to `TIOCGWINSZ` and the *arg* argument pointing to a `winsize` structure.

We can also store a set of values in the kernel by using a `TIOCSWINSZ ioctl`. If the new set of values is different from the current set, a `SIGWINCH` signal is sent to the foreground process group. As we shall see when we discuss signals in Chapter 17, `SIGWINCH` signals are ignored by default.

Other than storing the current values of the structure and generating a signal when the values change, the kernel does nothing with the contents of the `winsize` structure. Any interpretation of the structure's contents is entirely up to the application.

The reason why a signal is sent when the structure changes is so that applications are notified when the screen size changes. Text editors like `vi` make use of this information by redrawing their screen.

Example: Printing the effect of window size changes

After establishing a new signal handler for the `SIGWINCH` signal, Program 12.9 prints out the terminal window's current dimensions and goes to sleep. When a `SIGWINCH` is caught, the window's new dimensions are printed, and the program goes back to sleep. (We discuss the `pause` function in Chapter 17.)

Running Program 12.9 in a `dtterm` gives the following results:

```
$ ./winsize
132 columns by 48 rows (934 pixels by 634 pixels)
SIGWINCH received                          Change window size
105 columns by 48 rows (745 pixels by 634 pixels)
SIGWINCH received                          Change window size again
80 columns by 24 rows (570 pixels by 322 pixels)
^C$                                        Type Control-C to quit
```

12.12 Device-Independent Terminal Control

Any discussion about terminal I/O would be incomplete without mentioning `termcap`, `terminfo`, and the `curses` library.

One of the problems when dealing with terminal I/O is how to handle the plethora of different terminal types. Each of these terminals has many different attributes and capabilities that programs will want to interrogate. The `termcap` (which stands for "terminal capability") facility was developed at Berkeley to support the `vi` editor. It consists of the text file `/etc/termcap` and a set of functions to read this file. The `/etc/termcap` file contains descriptions of all the supported terminal types and the features they support (like how many rows and columns the screen has, and does the terminal use software flow control), as well as how to make the terminal perform certain

terminal_io/winsize.c

```
 1  #include <stdio.h>
 2  #include <unistd.h>
 3  #include <termios.h>
 4  #include <signal.h>
 5  #include "ssp.h"

 6  static volatile sig_atomic_t got_sigwinch;

 7  static void print_winsize (int fd);
 8  static void sigwinch (int sig);

 9  int main (void)
10  {
11      if (sigset (SIGWINCH, sigwinch) == SIG_ERR)
12          err_msg ("sigset");

13      got_sigwinch = 0;
14      print_winsize (STDIN_FILENO);

15      for (;;) {
16          pause ();
17          if (got_sigwinch) {
18              printf ("SIGWINCH received\n");
19              print_winsize (STDIN_FILENO);
20              got_sigwinch = 0;
21          }
22      }
23  }

24  static void print_winsize (int fd)
25  {
26      struct winsize size;

27      if (ioctl (fd, TIOCGWINSZ, &size) == -1)
28          err_msg ("ioctl failed");

29      printf ("%d columns by %d rows (%d pixels by %d pixels)\n",
30          size.ws_col, size.ws_row, size.ws_xpixel, size.ws_ypixel);
31  }

32  static void sigwinch (int sig)
33  {
34      got_sigwinch = 1;
35  }
```

terminal_io/winsize.c

Program 12.9 Print window size changes.

actions (like position the cursor at a given location on the screen, delete a line, or clear the screen). By placing all this information into an editable text file (rather than in the vi executable), new terminals can be easily added without recompiling vi or other programs that use the termcap facility.

The functions that vi used to handle the termcap file were removed and placed into a separate curses library. Many features were added to this library to make it useful for any program that wanted to perform device-independent screen manipulation.

One of the problems with the termcap scheme is that was implemented as a plain text file. This file had to be searched linearly when a terminal's capabilities were being looked up. Also, termcap uses two character names to identify a terminal's characteristics. To work around these deficiences, the terminfo scheme and its associated curses library were developed. The terminfo facility uses a compiled version of the textual terminal descriptions. This makes searching them much faster.

A detailed discussion of curses programming is beyond the scope of this text. Interested readers are referred to [Goodheart 1991] for a description of terminfo and the curses library, or [Strang 1986], which describes the original Berkeley version of the curses library. For a description of the termcap and terminfo files, see [Strang, Mui, and O'Reilly 1991].

Neither termcap nor terminfo by themselves address the problems we've discussed in this chapter (i.e., changing the terminal's mode, changing the special characters, handling the screen size, etc.). But they do provide a way to perform typical operations, like clearing the screen or moving the cursor, on a wide variety of terminals. The curses library does, however, provide some functions that help us handle some of the details we've talked about in this chapter, like setting raw or cbreak mode, enabling or disabling echoing, and so on.

Given the wide use of GUI-based workstations these days, the character-oriented curses style of screen programming is becoming deprecated in favour of graphical applications using the X Window System, or written in Java.

12.13 Summary

In this chapter we've talked about the many features and options associated with terminal I/O. We've talked about how to change the special input characters, and discussed several functions that enable us to manipulate a terminal's attributes.

We've shown the two input modes, canonical and non-canonical, and we've also implemented functions that allow us to use the historical cbreak and raw modes. We then showed how to get and set the kernel's record of a terminal's window size, and discussed termcap, terminfo, and the curses library.

Exercises

12.1 Open two terminal windows and start vi in one of them. In the other, run the command stty -a, redirecting standard input to read from the terminal you started vi in. What values are printed for "min" and "time", what do they mean, and why are they set to these values?

12.2 Write and run a program that calls tty_raw and then exits (without restoring the terminal settings). What happens, and what can we do to restore normal terminal operation?

13

Advanced I/O

13.1 Introduction

In this chapter we take a look at some of the more advanced or esoteric I/O capabilities offered by the Solaris operating environment.

Some of the topics we cover are nonblocking I/O, record locking, STREAMS, memory mapped I/O, access control lists, and extended file attributes.

13.2 Nonblocking I/O

There are two types of system call: those that are "slow", and all others. A *slow system call* is one that could potentially block for ever. Examples of slow system calls include:

- Reads or writes to files that can block the caller for ever if there is no data present or can't be accepted immediately (e.g., terminals, pipes, and network devices)
- Opens of files that block until a condition occurs (e.g., opening a terminal device that waits for an attached modem to answer the phone)
- Certain ioctl operations
- The pause and wait functions
- Some of the interprocess communication functions (see Chapters 19, 20, and 21)
- Reads and writes to files that have mandatory locking enabled

One exception to these slow system calls is anything related to disk I/O, even though a disk read or write can cause the caller to temporarily block. This is because disk I/O operations always return and unblock the caller quickly (hardware errors notwithstanding).

Nonblocking I/O allows us to issue I/O requests (e.g., open, read, or write) that will not block indefinitely. If the requested operation cannot be completed, an error is returned to the caller, which notes that the operation would have blocked.

There are two ways to specify nonblocking I/O for a file descriptor:

1. Specify either O_NONBLOCK or O_NDELAY when we open it using the open function.

2. If the file is already open, we can call fcntl to turn on the O_NONBLOCK or O_NDELAY flags for the relevant file descriptor. We showed a suitable function for doing this in Program 4.6.

Although they are mostly the same, there are subtle differences in the semantics of O_NONBLOCK and O_NDELAY. Historically, the O_NDELAY flag was used to specify nonblocking mode. A value of 0 was returned for a read that would block, but this overlaps with a return value of 0, meaning end of file. POSIX cleaned this up somewhat by providing nonblocking I/O with a different name (O_NONBLOCK) and semantics. Solaris supports both the older O_NDELAY and the newer O_NONBLOCK, although the former is really provided only for compatibility reasons. New programs should use O_NONBLOCK.

The differences in semantics between the two flags is most apparent when using the read and write system calls. Figure 13.1 summarizes the differences between the two flags for the read function.

File type	O_NONBLOCK	O_NDELAY
Regular	Returns −1, errno = EAGAIN	Returns −1, errno = EAGAIN
Pipe or FIFO	Returns −1, errno = EAGAIN	Returns 0
Terminal file	Returns −1, errno = EAGAIN	Returns 0
Other socket or STREAM	Returns −1, errno = EAGAIN	Returns −1, errno = EAGAIN

Figure 13.1 The effect of O_NONBLOCK and O_NDELAY on a blocking read.

With reference to Figure 13.1, there are a number of points to consider:

- When we're attempting to perform a nonblocking read on a regular file that has mandatory file locking set on it, and there is a write lock owned by another process on the segment to be read, the read will fail.

- When attempting to read from an empty pipe or FIFO that another process has open for writing, a nonblocking read will fail.

- A nonblocking read from a terminal or other socket or STREAM will fail when there is no data currently available.

Figure 13.2 summarizes the differences between the two flags for the write function.

With reference to Figure 13.2, there are a number of points to consider:

File type	O_NONBLOCK	O_NDELAY
Regular	Returns −1, errno = EAGAIN	Returns −1, errno = EAGAIN
Pipe or FIFO	Returns −1, errno = EAGAIN	Returns 0
Socket or STREAM	Returns −1, errno = EAGAIN	Returns −1, errno = EAGAIN
Socket or STREAM	Returns number of bytes written	Returns number of bytes written
Other file descriptor	Returns −1, errno = EAGAIN	Returns −1, errno = EAGAIN

Figure 13.2   The effect of O_NONBLOCK and O_NDELAY on a blocking write.

- When we're attempting a nonblocking write on a regular file that has mandatory file locking set on it, and there is a write lock owned by another process on the segment to be written, the write will fail.

- When attempting to write to a STREAM when it cannot accept any data, the write will fail.

- When attempting to write to a STREAM when part of the buffer has already been written, and a condition occurs which prevents the STREAM from accepting additional data, the write will fail.

- If some other file descriptor supports nonblocking writes, and it cannot accept the data immediately, the write will fail.

Example: Nonblocking I/O in use

Let's take a look at nonblocking I/O in action. Program 13.1 reads 100,000 bytes in from standard input, and attempts to write them to standard output, which is set to use nonblocking I/O. The nonblocking I/O flag is set using the set_fsflag function we wrote in Program 4.6.

The writes to standard output are performed in a loop as many times as is necessary to write out the whole buffer.

The first time we run Program 13.1, standard output is a regular file.

```
$ ls -l ssp.ps                        See how big the file is
-rw-r--r--    1 rich      staff      1565588 Feb 17 14:51 ssp.ps
$ ./nonblock < ssp.ps > foo
Read 100000 bytes
Wrote 100000 bytes
$ ls -l foo                           Check how big the new file is
-rw-r--r--    1 rich      staff      100000 Feb 22 16:43 foo
```

The second time we run Program 13.1, standard output is our terminal, where we might expect flow control to interfere with the output.

```
$ ./nonblock < ssp.ps 2> errors
                                    Lots of output deleted
$ cat errors
Read 100000 bytes
Wrote 1000000 bytes
```

advanced_io/nonblock.c

```
 1 #include <stdio.h>
 2 #include <sys/types.h>
 3 #include <unistd.h>
 4 #include <fcntl.h>
 5 #include "ssp.h"

 6 #define BUFFER_SIZE 100000

 7 static char buf [BUFFER_SIZE];

 8 int main (void)
 9 {
10     ssize_t n;
11     ssize_t res;
12     char *ptr;
13     int errs;

14     errs = 0;
15     n = read (STDIN_FILENO, buf, BUFFER_SIZE);
16     log_msg ("Read %d bytes", n);

17     set_fsflag (STDOUT_FILENO, O_NONBLOCK);

18     while (n > 0) {
19         ptr = buf;
20         while ((n > 0) && ((res = write (STDOUT_FILENO, ptr, n)) > 0)) {
21             if (errs > 0) {
22                 err_ret ("write failed %d times", errs);
23                 errs = 0;
24             }
25             log_msg ("Wrote %d bytes", res);
26             ptr += res;
27             n -= res;
28         }
29         if (res == -1)
30             errs++;
31     }
32     clear_fsflag (STDOUT_FILENO, O_NONBLOCK);

33     return (0);
34 }
```

advanced_io/nonblock.c

Program 13.1 Using nonblocking I/O.

In both cases, a single write was sufficient to output all the data. This is because of the amount of buffering the STREAMS subsystem provides. By changing BUFFER_SIZE to 1,000,000 and recompiling Program 13.1, we can force the STREAMS buffers to overflow, and hence require more than one write to copy the whole buffer. Let's see what happens now:

```
$ ./nonblock < ssp.ps 2> errors
```
                              Lots of output deleted

```
$ cat errors
Read 1000000 bytes
Wrote 327680 bytes
write failed 58000 times: Resource temporarily unavailable
Wrote 65536 bytes
write failed 80463 times: Resource temporarily unavailable
Wrote 65536 bytes
write failed 63252 times: Resource temporarily unavailable
Wrote 65536 bytes
write failed 59524 times: Resource temporarily unavailable
Wrote 65536 bytes
write failed 59974 times: Resource temporarily unavailable
Wrote 65536 bytes
write failed 73725 times: Resource temporarily unavailable
Wrote 65536 bytes
write failed 63639 times: Resource temporarily unavailable
Wrote 65536 bytes
write failed 73789 times: Resource temporarily unavailable
Wrote 65536 bytes
write failed 80606 times: Resource temporarily unavailable
Wrote 65536 bytes
write failed 73560 times: Resource temporarily unavailable
Wrote 65536 bytes
write failed 67110 times: Resource temporarily unavailable
Wrote 16960 bytes
```

This time, the first 327,680 bytes are written immediately. The next 58,000 writes fail because they would block (the string "Resource temporarily unavailable" is the error message associated with EAGAIN), then 65,536 bytes are written. This carries on for several cycles until all 1,000,000 bytes are written. The number of failed writes between each successful one varies because the buffers drain at a varying rate depending on how busy the machine is at the time.

The technique used in this example, called *polling*, is very wasteful of CPU time. It took only 12 successful writes to copy the 1,000,000 bytes to the terminal. The number of failed writes in our example exceeds 750,000; we'll see later in this chapter how I/O multiplexing with nonblocking descriptors is a more efficient way to do this sort of thing.

13.3 Record Locking

Until now, we have only considered file accesses when only one person or process is updating it. But what happens when two or more people (or processes) want to update the same file at the same time? Without taking any precautions, the version written last will be the one that prevails. Changes made by the previous writer may be lost.

Some applications need to allow multiple users to update a file without any data loss or corruption. The way we solve the problem of multiple simultaneous access to a file is to use record locking.

Record locking is when a section of a file (possibly the whole file) is locked for the use of the process that owns the lock. More than one section of a file may be locked (as long as the sections don't overlap), and different processes may own the locks.

The term "record locking" is a bit of a misnomer in the context of Solaris files, because all files in Solaris are unstructured: any interpretation of the file is application-dependent. A better term would be "section locking", "byte range locking", or "region locking".

There are two types of lock: shared and exclusive. When a section of a file has a shared lock on it, other processes are able to acquire a shared lock on the same section, or a part of it. A shared lock prevents any other process from acquiring an exclusive lock on any portion of the locked area. A process wanting to acquire a shared lock on a file must have the file open for reading at a minimum (i.e., O_RDONLY or O_RDWR).

An exclusive lock prevents any other process from acquiring a shared or exclusive lock on the locked section. A process wanting to acquire an exclusive lock on a file must have the file open for writing at a minimum (i.e., O_WRONLY or O_RDWR).

Shared locks can be thought of as read locks, and exclusive locks can be thought of as write locks. This makes sense because although there is no harm in having multiple readers of the same file section, we don't want to allow access to a section that is currently being updated (i.e., protected by a write lock). Figure 13.3 summarizes the interoperability of shared and exclusive locks.

Current lock on section	Lock request	
	Shared	Exclusive
None	Allowed	Allowed
One or more shared	Allowed	Denied
One exclusive	Denied	Denied

Figure 13.3 The interoperability of different lock types.

A shared or exclusive lock is either advisory or mandatory. An *advisory lock* is one that does not affect I/O operations; a process is not stopped from accessing a section of a file locked by another process unless it elects to do so. In other words, advisory locking requires processes to cooperate with each other with respect to locks.

A *mandatory lock* is one that is enforced during I/O operations; a process that attempts to access a section of a file locked by another will not be able to do so until the lock is removed. Mandatory locks do not need processes to cooperate with each other. Because of the checks that must be performed for each read or write, mandatory locks have a performance penalty associated with them.

By default, all locks are advisory. Mandatory locking is enabled on a per-file basis by setting the file's set-group-ID bit and clearing its group execute bit. Once mandatory locking is enabled for a file, all locks on that file are mandatory.

We should emphasize that the distinction between advisory and mandatory locks only applies to I/O operations. The kernel manages all lock information, and will block processes trying to use fcntl if necessary.

The kernel automatically joins or splits locks owned by the same process as required. For example, if we have locked bytes 100 to 200 of a file, and then subsequently lock bytes 201 to 300, the two locks will be combined into one, spanning bytes 100 to 300. If we then went on to unlock bytes 250 to 260, the kernel will create two locked regions: one covering bytes 100 to 249, and another covering bytes 261 to 300.

Record locking should not be used in combination with the functions from the standard I/O library (e.g., `fopen`, `fread`, etc.). This is because unexpected results might occur in processes than do buffering in the user address space; data that is or was locked may be read or written. Instead, the nonbuffered functions (e.g., `open`, `read`, etc.) should be used.

NFS locking is the same as we have just described, with the following exceptions:

1. Unless the whole file is locked, the kernel does not cache slow I/O. If this were not imposed, the kernel would have difficulty managing lock requests for the same page from two (or more) different clients.

2. Locking a file and mapping parts of it into the process' address space using `mmap` is not allowed.

3. Failed clients can cause locks to be held for ever.

4. NFS does not support mandatory locking, as this would hang all the `lockd` threads on the server (`lockd` is the NFS lock manager daemon).

5. If the `lockd` process on the server runs out of threads, attempts to acquire a lock will fail, setting `errno` to `ENOLOCKS`.

We can use two functions to acquire a lock on a file: `fcntl` and `lockf`. We'll look at `fcntl` locking first, followed by `lockf` (which is implemented using `fcntl`).

13.4   Record Locking Using `fcntl`

Before we describe `fcntl` record locking, let's take another look at the function prototype for `fcntl`.

```
#include <sys/types.h>
#include <unistd.h>
#include <fcntl.h>

int fcntl (int fildes, int cmd, flock_t *lockp);
```

Returns: depends on *cmd* if OK, −1 on error

The `fcntl` function can be used to get or set lock information for the file descriptor *fildes* depending on the value of *cmd*. The *lockp* argument is a pointer to an `flock` structure.

The `flock` structure contains the following members:

```
typedef struct flock {
    short   l_type;      /* Lock operation type */
    short   l_whence;    /* Lock base indicator */
    off_t   l_start;     /* Starting offset from base */
    off_t   l_len;       /* Lock length; 0 means until end of file */
    int     l_sysid;     /* System ID running process holding lock */
    pid_t   l_pid;       /* Process ID of process holding lock */
} flock_t;
```

The l_type member determines the lock operation type, and may be one of four values: F_RDLCK to create a shared read lock, F_WRLCK to create an exclusive write lock, F_UNLCK to remove a lock or locks, or F_UNLKSYS to remove remote locks for a given system (the latter is not used, being an old lockd specific operation).

The value of l_whence indicates where the relative offset of l_start starts from. A value of SEEK_SET means the offset is measured from the start of the file, SEEK_CUR means relative to the current position, and SEEK_END means relative to the end of the file. The value of l_len specifies the number of consecutive bytes to be locked. A value of 0 means to lock until the end of the file; if the file is extended, the lock will also be extended as the file is written. By setting l_whence to SEEK_SET, l_start to 0, and l_len to 0, the whole file may be locked. Note that a lock may start and extend beyond the current end of file, but cannot start or extend before the beginning of the file.

The l_pid and l_sysid members are used only when *cmd* is either F_GETLK or F_GETLK64 to return the process ID of the process holding a blocking lock and to indicate which system is running that process. Note that l_sysid is an internal integer that can't easily be converted to a hostname or IP address.

The *cmd* argument may be one of the following values:

F_GETLK	This command is used to get information about the first lock which blocks the lock described by the flock structure pointed to by *lockp*. If such a lock exists, its information overwrites that pointed to by *lockp*. Otherwise, the structure pointed to by *lockp* is left unchanged, except that its l_type member is set to F_UNLCK.
F_GETLK64	This is the 64-bit transitionary interface equivalent of F_GETLK. The *lockp* argument points to an flock64 structure rather than an flock structure.
F_SETLK	This command is used to set or clear the lock specified by *lockp*. If the requested lock cannot be immediately granted (for example, it is denied by the rules in Figure 13.3), fcntl will return −1 and set errno to EAGAIN.
F_SETLK64	This is the 64-bit transitionary interface equivalent of F_SETLK. The *lockp* argument points to an flock64 structure rather than an flock structure.
F_SETLKW	This command is similar to F_SETLK except that if the lock specified by *lockp* is not immediately obtainable, the calling process is put to sleep until the request can be satisfied. If a signal is caught while the process is sleeping, fcntl will be interrupted. When the signal handler returns, fcntl will return −1, errno will be set to EINTR, and the lock operation will not be done.

F_SETLKW64   This is the 64-bit transitionary interface equivalent of
                      F_SETLKW. The *lockp* argument points to an `flock64`
                      structure rather than an `flock` structure.

One thing we should be aware of is that testing for a lock using F_GETLK and then trying
to acquire it using one of the F_SETLK variants is not an atomic operation (in much the
same way that testing for the existence of a file using `access` before opening it using
`open` is not atomic). It is possible that between the two `fcntl` calls, another process
could acquire the lock. If we don't want to wait for the lock to become available, we
must be prepared to handle errors from F_SETLK.

Example: Requesting and releasing a lock

If our program does a lot of work with locks, it can become tedious to allocate and fill in
an `flock` structure each time. Program 13.2 shows the `ssp_lock` function, which
handles all the details for us.

lib/lock.c

```
 1 #include <fcntl.h>

 2 int ssp_lock (int fd, int cmd, short type, short whence, off_t start,
 3     off_t len)
 4 {
 5     flock_t lock;

 6     lock.l_type = type;
 7     lock.l_whence = whence;
 8     lock.l_start = start;
 9     lock.l_len = len;

10     return (fcntl (fd, cmd, &lock));
11 }
```

lib/lock.c

Program 13.2 Our function to acquire or release a lock.

By using the function in Program 13.2, we can write some more specific macros to acquire
or release a lock.

```
#define ssp_rlock(fd, whence, start, len) \
    ssp_lock (fd, F_SETLK, F_RDLCK, whence, start, len)
#define ssp_rlockw(fd, whence, start, len) \
    ssp_lock (fd, F_SETLKW, F_RDLCK, whence, start, len)
#define ssp_wlock(fd, whence, start, len) \
    ssp_lock (fd, F_SETLK, F_WRLCK, whence, start, len)
#define ssp_wlockw(fd, whence, start, len) \
    ssp_lock (fd, F_SETLKW, F_WRLCK, whence, start, len)
#define ssp_unlock(fd, whence, start, len) \
    ssp_lock (fd, F_SETLK, F_UNLCK, whence, start, len)
```

We'll use some of these macros (which for convenience we have defined in our header
file, `ssp.h`) in later examples.

Example: Testing for a lock

Program 13.3 shows another function that we can use to hide the tedious handling the
flock structure, this time testing for the existence of a lock.

advanced_io/ssp_lock_test.c

```
 1 #include <sys/types.h>
 2 #include <unistd.h>
 3 #include <fcntl.h>
 4 #include "ssp.h"

 5 typedef struct {
 6     int sysid;
 7     pid_t pid;
 8 } ssp_lowner_t;

 9 ssp_lowner_t *ssp_lock_test (int fd, short type, short whence, off_t start,
10     off_t len)
11 {
12     flock_t lock;
13     static ssp_lowner_t lock_owner;

14     lock.l_type = type;
15     lock.l_whence = whence;
16     lock.l_start = start;
17     lock.l_len = len;

18     if (fcntl (fd, F_GETLK, &lock) == -1)
19         err_quit ("fcntl failed");

20     if (lock.l_type == F_UNLCK)
21         return (NULL);

22     lock_owner.sysid = lock.l_sysid;
23     lock_owner.pid = lock.l_pid;

24     return (&lock_owner);
25 }
```

advanced_io/ssp_lock_test.c

Program 13.3 Our function to test for a lock.

If no lock exists that would block the request specified by the arguments,
ssp_lock_test returns a NULL pointer. If such a lock does exist, however, then a
pointer to a structure is returned. The structure contains the system and process IDs of
the process holding the lock.

As with ssp_lock, we can write some macros to make using ssp_lock_test even
easier.

```
#define ssp_is_rlock(fd, whence, start, len) \
    ssp_lock_test (fd, F_RDLCK, whence, start, len)
#define ssp_is_wlock(fd, whence, start, len) \
    ssp_lock_test (fd, F_WRLCK, whence, start, len)
```

In Chapter 18, we'll show another example of file locking that ensures that only one copy
of a program runs at a given time.

13.5 Record Locking Using `lockf`

The `lockf` function can also be used to establish and test for locks on a section of an open file.

```
#include <unistd.h>

int lockf (int fildes, int function, off_t size);
```
Returns: 0 if OK, −1 on error

The `lockf` function also allows us to acquire or test for the presence of locks on a file, although it is less flexible than using `fcntl`. Any lock created by `lockf` is an exclusive (write) lock, hence, the file to which *fildes* refers must have been opened with at least write permission (i.e., O_RDWR or O_WRONLY).

The *function* argument determines the action to be taken, and may be one of the following values:

F_ULOCK   This is used to unlock a previously locked section of the file. The section unlocked is *size* bytes from the current file offset. If *size* is 0, any locks between the current offset and the end of the file will be released.

F_LOCK   This *function* is used to acquire an exclusive write lock of *size* bytes from the current file offset. If *size* is 0, then the file will be locked from the current offset to the end of the file. If *size* is negative, the preceding bytes up to but not including the current offset are locked.

           If the requested lock can't be acquired, the calling process is put to sleep until it can be.

F_TLOCK   This *function* is the same as F_LOCK, except when the lock can't be acquired. In this case, `lockf` will return −1, and `errno` will be set to EAGAIN.

F_TEST   This is used to test for the presence of locks on the indicated section, i.e., *size* bytes from the current file offset. If no such lock exists, `lockf` will return 0; otherwise, it will return −1 and set `errno` to EAGAIN.

13.6 Deadlock and Livelock

One thing we need to be aware of when locking files is deadlock. *Deadlock* occurs when two (or more) processes that share multiple resources get stuck waiting for the other to release a resource they need. Because locked files are a shared resource, they are a potential source of deadlock. Deadlocked processes are sometimes said to be in a "deadly embrace".

The canonical example of deadlock is called the *dining philosophers problem*. A number of philosophers are sitting at a circular table (we'll use five in this example, but it can be any number greater than one). Each philosopher spends his life alternatively thinking and eating. At the centre of of the table is a large bowl of noodles, and between each philosopher is a chopstick. A philosopher must have two chopsticks in his possession before he can eat some noodles: one from his immediate right, and one from his immediate left.

When a philosopher is hungry, he reaches for the chopstick on his right. If it is not there, he thinks some more. If the chopstick is there, he holds it, and reaches for the chopstick on his left. If the left chopstick is there, he eats some noodles, replaces both chopsticks, and thinks some more. If the left chopstick is not there, he waits for it while still holding the right chopstick.

Depending on how long the philosophers spend thinking, this quickly leads to deadlock: each philosopher has a chopstick in his right hand, and is waiting for the philosopher on his left to put down their chopstick so that he can eat. However, that philosopher is waiting for the one on *his* left to put down his chopstick. The end result is that all the philosophers are deadlocked waiting for a resource another one has, and die of starvation.

Deadlock must be detected or avoided. In the dining philosophers problem, deadlock can be avoided by numbering the chopsticks from one to five clockwise around the table, and changing the rules such that rather than starting with the chopstick on his right, each philosopher must start with the lowest numbered adjacent chopstick. Using these rules, most of the philosophers will take the right-hand chopstick, except for the one between chopsticks one and five; he will try to take chopstick number one, which is on his left, not his right. This philosopher and the one between numbers one and two now reach for the same chopstick first. Whoever gets it can now take the other one; the other philosopher must wait for the first to release the first chopstick. Deadlock is not possible.

Another way of avoiding deadlock is to release all resources we have locked so far if we can't lock all the ones we need. In other words, if the philosophers put down their chopstick if they can't get the other, that would also avoid deadlock. The trouble with this solution is that it might give rise to a livelock condition.

Livelock is an active variant of mutual resource deprivation, whereby two (or more) processes that share multiple resources perform the following tasks endlessly:

- Acquire a free resource.
- Be deprived of acquiring other resources by other another process.
- Release all held resources to avoid deadlock.

In the context of our dining philosophers, livelock would be the situation where a philosopher picks up a chopstick after thinking for a while, reaches for another chopstick, and puts down his chopstick if he can't acquire the second one. It's possible that some philosophers will do this ad infinitum, and starve to death. So, although releasing all held resources is one way of avoiding deadlock, it isn't the best way, because it introduces the problem of livelock.

Example: Avoiding deadlock

Let's look at an example that illustrates deadlock in the context of a locked file. Deadlock might occur if a process that holds a lock is put to sleep while trying to acquire a lock on another section that is held by some other process.

Program 13.4 opens a file for writing, creating it if necessary, and then writes 2 bytes to it. The process then forks, so that we have two processes trying to lock the file. The child process locks byte 0 of the file, goes to sleep for a second (this is so that the parent process gets a chance to run), and then attempts to lock byte 1 of the file. The parent behaves similarly, except that the bytes are locked in the reverse order: byte 1 is locked, followed by byte 0.

Let's see what happens when we run Program 13.4 a couple of times.

```
$ ./deadlock
Child: Got a lock on byte 0
Parent: Got a lock on byte 1
Child: Can't get write lock: Deadlock situation detected/avoided
Parent: Got a lock on byte 0
$ ./deadlock
Child: Got a lock on byte 0
Parent: Got a lock on byte 1
Parent: Can't get write lock: Deadlock situation detected/avoided
$ Child: Got a lock on byte 1
```

The output we show highlights the fact that either the parent or the child can be deadlocked: which one is indeterminate. The kernel detects that a deadlock situation is about to occur, and avoids it by unlocking one of the sections under contention (this is the same idea as the philosophers who must put down the chopstick they have if they can't immediately get the other).

The prompt appears on the last line of the second run before the message the child saying that it got the lock on byte 1 because the parent exits before the child, and hence the shell prints a prompt before the child prints its message.

13.7   Lock Inheritance and Release

Unlike file descriptors, locks are never inherited by the child process created by `fork`; if the child process wants to acquire a lock on the file descriptor, it must call either `fcntl` or `lockf` itself. This makes sense, because locks are designed to protect files from simultaneous updates from multiple processes, and a child and parent are different processes despite their relationship with each other. If this were not the case, both the parent and the child processes could write to the same file at the same time.

However, file locks are maintained across calls to one of the `exec` functions, assuming that the associated file descriptor doesn't have its close on exec flag (`FD_CLOEXEC`) set.

A lock is removed explicitly by calling either `fcntl` or `lockf`. Locks are implicitly removed when a file descriptor is closed; when a file descriptor is closed, all locks on the file referenced by the descriptor which are owned by the process closing the file are released, even if the process has associated another file descriptor with the file. (In other

```
1 #include <stdio.h>
2 #include <sys/types.h>
3 #include <unistd.h>
4 #include <fcntl.h>
5 #include "ssp.h"

6 static void lock_byte (const char *proc, int fd, int byte);

7 int main (void)
8 {
9     int fd;

10    if ((fd = open ("tmpfile", O_RDWR | O_CREAT | O_TRUNC, FILE_PERMS)) == -1)
11        err_msg ("Can't create temp file");

12    if (writen (fd, "xx", 2) != 2)
13        err_msg ("Write error");

14    switch (fork ()) {
15        case -1:
16            err_msg ("Can't fork");
17            break;

18        case 0:
19            lock_byte ("Child", fd, 0);
20            sleep (1);
21            lock_byte ("Child", fd, 1);
22            _exit (0);

23        default:
24            lock_byte ("Parent", fd, 1);
25            sleep (1);
26            lock_byte ("Parent", fd, 0);
27            break;
28    }

29    return (0);
30 }

31 static void lock_byte (const char *proc, int fd, int byte)
32 {
33    if (ssp_wlockw (fd, SEEK_SET, byte, 1) != 0)
34        err_msg ("%s: Can't get write lock", proc);

35    printf ("%s: Got a lock on byte %d\n", proc, byte);
36 }
```

Program 13.4 Deadlock detection when file locking.

words, locks are released on the first close of the file descriptor, not the last.) The corollary of this is that when a process terminates, all of its locks are released.

Less obviously, the following code will release the lock acquired for the first descriptor, even though the second descriptor is the one being closed.

```
fd1 = open ("/some/path/name", ...);
ssp_rlock (fd1, ...);
fd2 = dup (fd1);
close (fd2);
```

We get the same result if we replace the dup with an open, so that we open the same file on another descriptor.

```
fd1 = open ("/some/path/name", ...);
ssp_rlock (fd1, ...);
fd2 = open ("/some/path/name", ...);
close (fd2);
```

13.8 Mandatory Versus Advisory Locking

As we stated in Section 13.3, there are two types of I/O operation lock: mandatory and advisory. The latter requires the use of cooperating processes, i.e., those that abide by the locking rules voluntarily. But there's nothing to stop some other, uncooperating process from ignoring the locks and writing whatever it wants to the file whenever it wants to.

Mandatory locks, on the other hand, force the kernel to check every open, read, or write to ensure that the calling process isn't violating a lock on the file being accessed.

What happens to a process that tries to open, read, or write a file that has mandatory locking enabled and the specified part of the file is locked by another process depends on three things: the type of operation being performed, the type of lock (shared read or exclusive write), and whether the file descriptor is nonblocking. Figure 13.4 shows the possibilities.

Operation being performed	Type of lock on section	
	Shared	Exclusive
Blocking open with O_CREAT or O_TRUNC	EAGAIN	EAGAIN
Blocking read	OK	blocks
Blocking write	blocks	blocks
Nonblocking open with O_CREAT or O_TRUNC	EAGAIN	EAGAIN
Nonblocking read	OK	EAGAIN
Nonblocking write	EAGAIN	EAGAIN

Figure 13.4 The effect of mandatory locking on I/O by other processes.

It is interesting to note that both a blocking and a nonblocking open fail immediately if O_CREAT or O_TRUNC are specified. Failing if O_TRUNC is specified makes sense because a file can't be truncated if a section of it is locked by another process. But failing if O_CREAT is specified doesn't make sense; the idea of O_CREAT is to create the file if it doesn't exist, in which case no lock can be associated with it.

Even using mandatory locks doesn't prevent all interaction with a locked file. For example, if one process has a mandatory lock on a file, another process will not be prevented from removing the file using the unlink function and then replacing it with another file (provided the permissions on the file's directory allow it).

Another potential problem with files with mandatory locking is that they might be the target of a denial of service attack. Suppose we have a database file that is readable by everyone and has mandatory locking enabled. A malicious user could open the database file and create a read lock on the whole file, and never release that lock, thereby denying authorized users from updating the database file.

Another problem with mandatory locks is that they are not supported by NFS. If a file on an NFS server has mandatory locking enabled, processes on NFS clients will not be able to open it.

Example: How mandatory locking affects file I/O performance

Mandatory locks impose a slight performance penalty on open, read, and write function calls. Program 13.5 measures this by copying a 10,240,000-byte file in 1024-byte chunks (thereby requiring 10,000 reads of the file). Before the file is copied, a read lock is placed on the whole file. A child process is then created to perform the actual copy (the child does no locking).

We run Program 13.5 twice: once when mandatory locking is enabled for the source file, and another time when it isn't. Figure 13.5 shows the results we get.

Mandatory locking	Real	User	Sys
Disabled	6.75	0.05	2.54
Enabled	6.83	0.08	2.79

Figure 13.5 Effect of mandatory locking on file I/O performance.

The overall penalty of mandatory locking is not that great: just 0.03 seconds more of User time, and 0.25 seconds more of System time. We expect the greater increase of System time because the mandatory lock checks are performed by the kernel as part of the read system call.

Another interesting observation is that if we remove lines 16 and 17 of Program 13.5 and rerun the resulting program on the same file with mandatory locking enabled, there is no significant variation of the times. This is because the read system call still has to check for locks on the file, even though there aren't any. (Which makes sense, because the only way the kernel can determine if a lock exists for a particular section is to test for it. On the other hand, we have the benefit of knowing that the file has no locks on it.)

The bottom line of all this discussion about mandatory locking is that it is perhaps best avoided, and advisory locks with cooperating processes should be used instead wherever possible.

advanced_io/lock_perf.c

```
1  #include <stdio.h>
2  #include <unistd.h>
3  #include <stdlib.h>
4  #include <sys/types.h>
5  #include <sys/wait.h>
6  #include <fcntl.h>
7  #include "ssp.h"

8  int main (void)
9  {
10     int fd1;
11     int fd2;
12     char buf [1024];
13     int status;

14     if ((fd1 = open ("tmpfile", O_RDONLY, 0)) == -1)
15         err_msg ("Can't open temp file");

16     if (ssp_rlockw (fd1, SEEK_SET, 0, 0) != 0)
17         err_msg ("Can't get read lock");

18     switch (fork ()) {
19         case -1:
20             err_msg ("Can't fork");
21             break;

22         case 0:
23             if ((fd2 = open ("tmpfile.out", O_RDWR | O_CREAT | O_TRUNC,
24                 FILE_PERMS)) == -1) {
25                 err_msg ("Can't open output file");
26             }

27             while (read (fd1, buf, 1024) != 0)
28                 writen (fd2, buf, 1024);

29             _exit (0);

30         default:
31             wait (&status);
32             close (fd1);
33             break;
34     }

35     return (0);
36 }
```

advanced_io/lock_perf.c

Program 13.5 Copying a file that has a read lock on it.

13.9   The STREAMS I/O Subsystem

The STREAMS I/O subsystem (not to be confused with the file streams used by the standard I/O library) provides a framework for interfacing device drivers into the kernel. A detailed look at STREAMS (including the kernel resident APIs) is beyond the scope of this text, (interested readers are referred to [Rago 1993]), but we need to have at least some familiarity with them to understand terminal I/O and I/O multiplexing using the `poll` function.

The fundamental STREAMS unit is the stream. A *stream* is a full-duplex data path between a process and a STREAMS device driver. A stream, created when a process opens a STREAMS device, consists of three parts: a stream head, zero or more modules, and a driver. When a STREAMS device is first opened, the stream consists of just the stream head and a driver, unless we use the `autopush` command to configure a list of modules that are to be automatically pushed onto the stream when it is created.

The *stream head* is the end of the stream nearest the user process, and is the interface between the stream and the process. When our processes make system calls with a STREAMS file descriptor, the stream head routines are invoked, resulting in data copying, message generation, or control operations being performed. The stream head is the only part of a stream that is able to copy data between our processes and the kernel.

A STREAMS *module* is a set of kernel-resident functions and data structures that processes data that passes through it. Modules are pushed onto a stream by using an `ioctl`. We say that a module is pushed onto the stream because the new module is inserted just below the stream head, pushing down any other modules. The top module (immediately below the stream head) may be popped off the stream by using another `ioctl`.

A STREAMS *driver* is at the end of the stream furthest away from the user process, below the stream head and any modules that might have been pushed onto the stream. The driver can interface with an external device, or it can be a pseudo device driver, which is an internal device that exists in software only.

All I/O is performed in STREAMS by passing messages along queues. (Strictly speaking, it is pointers to messages that are passed along the queues, to avoid the costly overhead of data copying.) Each stream head, module, and driver has two queues: a read queue and a write queue. When a message is passed from one module's read queue to the next module's read queue, it is said to be travelling upstream. Conversely, messages passed from one module's write queue to the next module's write queue are said to be travelling downstream. In other words, data that we write to the stream head travels downstream, and data that we read from the device travels upstream. Figure 13.6 illustrates this arrangement.

The arrows in Figure 13.6 between the stream head and STREAMS module (and from the module to the driver) represent the message queues. We use dashed lines for the module to show that it is optional, and that more than one may be pushed on to a given stream.

We interact with a stream by using the `open`, `close`, `read`, `write`, and `ioctl` functions we described in Chapter 4, plus the five functions we will introduce later in this section:

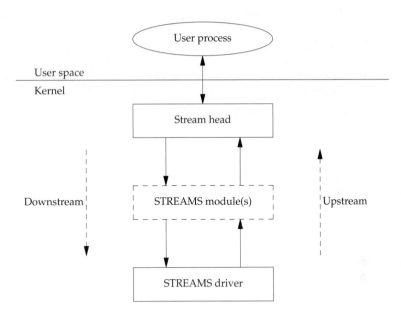

Figure 13.6 Anatomy of a simple stream.

poll, getmsg, putmsg, getpmsg, and putpmsg. The pathname that we open for a stream usually lives in /dev or one of its subdirectories, but there is no way of determining whether a file is a STREAMS device by just using ls. However, all STREAMS devices are character special files.

The isastream Function

We can use the isastream function to determine whether a file descriptor refers to a STREAMS device.

```
#include <stropts.h>

int isastream (int fildes);
```
                                                    Returns: 0 or 1 if OK, −1 on error

The isastream function determines if the file descriptor *fildes* refers to a STREAMS device. If *fildes* is a STREAMS device, isastream returns 1; if it isn't, isastream returns 0. In the event of an error, −1 is returned.

Example: Using isastream

Program 13.6 illustrates the use of the isastream function.

advanced_io/isastream.c

```
 1  #include <stdio.h>
 2  #include <stropts.h>
 3  #include <sys/types.h>
 4  #include <sys/stat.h>
 5  #include <fcntl.h>
 6  #include "ssp.h"

 7  int main (int argc, char **argv)
 8  {
 9      int fd;
10      int i;

11      if (argc < 2)
12          err_quit ("Usage: isastream file ...");

13      for (i = 1; i < argc; i++) {
14          if ((fd = open (argv [i], O_RDONLY)) == -1) {
15              err_ret ("Can't open %s", argv [i]);
16              continue;
17          }

18          printf ("%s %s a STREAMS device\n", argv [i],
19              (isastream (fd)) ? "is" : "is not");
20      }

21      return (0);
22  }
```

advanced_io/isastream.c

Program 13.6 Using `isastream`.

Running Program 13.6 against a couple of files in /dev gives us the following results:

```
$ ./isastream /dev/tty /dev/null
/dev/tty is a STREAMS device
/dev/null is not a STREAMS device
```

13.10 STREAMS Messages

As we stated previously, all STREAMS I/O is performed using messages. The stream head and user process exchange messages using the read, write, ioctl, getmsg, putmsg, getpmsg, and putpmsg functions. Messages are also passed up and down the stream between the stream head, any modules, and the device driver. Each module has two input queues: one for downstream messages and one for upstream messages.

Each message on a stream has a priority associated with it. A message is either a high priority message (the highest priority), a priority band message (the band is a number from 1 to 255, with a higher band specifying a higher priority), and ordinary messages, (which are the lowest priority). Ordinary messages are priority band messages with a band of 0.

Messages are queued for processing by an input queue in priority order. Messages of the same priority are queued chronologically.

Simple messages are composed of one message block. More complicated messages can be created by linking multiple message blocks. These are then treated logically as a single larger message. The data in one message block are considered to be contiguous with the data in the next message block. The message structure is usually transparent to our processes, the exception being when we deal with a complex message that includes both control and data parts.

Messages between user processes and the stream head consist of three parts:

1. A message type

2. Optional control information

3. Optional data

The control information and data are each specified by `strbuf` structures:

```
struct strbuf {
    int     maxlen;     /* Size of buffer in bytes */
    int     len;        /* Number of bytes in buffer */
    caddr_t buf;        /* Pointer to data */
};
```

The `buf` member points to the data portion of the message. When we call `getmsg` or `getpmsg`, `maxlen` specifies the maximum size of the buffer (to prevent overflows); it is not used with `putmsg` or `putpmsg`. When a message is sent using `putmsg` or `putpmsg`, `len` specifies the number of bytes in the buffer. When we receive a message using `getmsg` or `getpmsg`, the actual number of bytes in the message is stored in `len`. Zero length messages are OK, and a `len` of −1 means there is no data.

The Solaris STREAMS subsystem uses about 30 messages, but only a few are passed between the stream head and user processes. The rest are just passed up and down the stream, and are only of interest to people writing STREAMS modules and drivers.

We are interested in three messages:

M_DATA	Regular data for I/O. This is the most common message type, and is used to package any data we want to send downstream (the stream head does the packaging for us).
M_PROTO	Protocol control information. This message type is used to send or receive control information. Control information is usually specific to a particular module or driver on the stream, and is usually not transmitted past the component that interprets it.
M_PCPROTO	High priority protocol control information. A version of M_PROTO used for high priority control information, like interface acknowledgements.

We show in Figure 13.7 how different arguments to `write`, `putmsg`, and `putpmsg` cause these different messages to be generated.

13.11 The `putmsg` and `putpmsg` Functions

Two functions enable us to write a message to a stream: `putmsg` and `putpmsg`. The two functions are the same, except that `putpmsg` enables us to specify a priority band for the message.

```
#include <stropts.h>

int putmsg (int fildes, const struct strbuf *ctlptr, const struct strbuf *dataptr,
    int flags);

int putpmsg (int fildes, const struct strbuf *ctlptr,
    const struct strbuf *dataptr, int band, int flags);
```
Both return: 0 if OK, −1 on error

The `putmsg` function creates a message from the control information specified by *ctlptr* and the data specified by *dataptr*, and sends it to the STREAMS device referenced by the file descriptor *fildes*. The actual semantics of each part is determined by the STREAMS module that receives the message. Setting *ctlptr* to NULL or setting *ctlptr* -> `len` to −1 indicates that there is no control information. Similarly, setting *dataptr* to NULL or setting *dataptr* -> `len` to −1 indicates that there is no data portion.

The value of *flags* determines what type of message is sent. If *flags* is 0, an ordinary message is sent, unless there is no control information and no data, in which case no message is sent. If *flags* is set to `RS_HIPRI`, a high priority message is sent.

The `putpmsg` function is the same as `putmsg`, except for two things:

1. The *band* argument specifies the priority band of the message.
2. The *flags* argument is a bitmask with two mutually exclusive values: `MSG_HIPRI` and `MSG_BAND` (setting *flags* to 0 will result in an error).

   If *flags* is set to `MSG_HIPRI`, *band* must be set to 0, and a control part must be specified. This results in a high priority message being sent.

   If *flags* is set to `MSG_BAND`, a message in the priority band specified by *band* will be sent, unless there is no control information and no data, in which case no message is sent.

Writing to a stream using `write` is the same as calling `putmsg` with no control information and setting *flags* to 0.

Figure 13.7 summarizes the message type sent for the different combinations of the arguments to `putmsg` and `putpmsg`, and the `write` function.

A "Yes" in the Control or Data column of Figure 13.7 means that *ctlptr* (or *dataptr*) is not NULL, and that *ctlptr* -> `len` (or *dataptr* -> `len`) is greater than or equal to zero. A "No" in those columns means that either *ctlptr* (or *dataptr*) is NULL, or that *ctlptr* -> `len` (or *dataptr* -> `len`) is −1. "Don't care" in those columns means that we don't care whether the control information or data is supplied.

Function	Control	Data	*band*	*flags*	Generated message type
write	N/A	Yes	N/A	N/A	M_DATA (ordinary)
putmsg	No	No	N/A	0	None, returns 0
putmsg	No	Yes	N/A	0	M_DATA (ordinary)
putmsg	Yes	Don't care	N/A	0	M_PROTO (ordinary)
putmsg	Yes	Don't care	N/A	RS_HIPRI	M_PCPROTO (high priority)
putmsg	No	Don't care	N/A	RS_HIPRI	None, returns EINVAL
putpmsg	Don't care	Don't care	0–255	0	None, returns EINVAL
putpmsg	No	No	0–255	MSG_BAND	None, returns 0
putpmsg	No	Yes	0	MSG_BAND	M_DATA (ordinary)
putpmsg	No	Yes	1–255	MSG_BAND	M_DATA (priority band)
putpmsg	Yes	Don't care	0	MSG_BAND	M_PROTO (ordinary)
putpmsg	Yes	Don't care	1–255	MSG_BAND	M_PROTO (priority band)
putpmsg	Yes	Don't care	0	MSG_HIPRI	M_PCPROTO (high priority)
putpmsg	No	Don't care	0	MSG_HIPRI	None, returns EINVAL
putpmsg	Don't care	Don't care	non-zero	MSG_HIPRI	None, returns EINVAL

Figure 13.7 STREAMS message type created by write, putmsg, and putpmsg.

13.12 The `getmsg` and `getpmsg` Functions

STREAMS messages can be read from the stream head by using the getmsg and getpmsg functions.

```
#include <stropts.h>

int getmsg (int fildes, struct strbuf *ctlptr, struct strbuf *dataptr, int *flagsp);

int getpmsg (int fildes, struct strbuf *ctlptr, struct strbuf *dataptr, int *bandp,
    int *flagsp);
```

                                                                    Both return: see text

The getmsg retrieves the first message from the stream head read queue of the STREAMS device referenced by the file descriptor *fildes,* and places the contents in the user specified buffer(s). The control information part of the message (if any) is placed into the strbuf structure pointed to by *ctlptr,* and any data is placed into the strbuf structure pointed to by *dataptr.* As with putmsg and putpmsg, the semantics of each part of the message is defined by the module that generated it.

The *flagsp* argument points to an integer that determines the message to retrieve. If that integer is RS_HIPRI, the next message will be processed, but only if it is a high priority message. Setting the integer to 0 will result in the first available message being retrieved from the stream head. Once the message is received, the integer will be 0 if a normal priority message was retrieved, or RS_HIPRI if the message was high priority.

The getpmsg function is the same as getmsg, but provides finer control over the messages received. The integer pointed to by *flagsp* is an integer that must be set to one of the following values:

MSG_HIPRI   This retrieves the first message from the stream head, but only if it is a high priority message. The integer pointed to by *bandp* must be set to 0.

MSG_BAND   This retrieves the first message from the stream head, but only if it is in a priority band greater than or equal to that specified by the integer pointed to by *bandp*, or if it a high priority message.

MSG_ANY   This retrieves the first message from the stream head regardless of priority. The integer pointed to by *bandp* should be set to 0. If the message retrieved was a high priority message, the integer pointed to by *flagsp* will be set to MSG_HIPRI, and the one pointed to by *bandp* will be set to 0. Otherwise, the integer pointed to by *flagsp* will be set to MSG_BAND, and the one pointed to by *bandp* will be set to the priority band of the message.

Subject to the provisos in Section 13.14, reading from a stream using read is the same as calling getmsg with *flagsp* set to 0.

Figure 13.8 summarizes the message type retrieved from the stream head for different combinations of the arguments to getmsg and getpmsg.

Function	*bandp*	*flagsp*	To be retrieved, first message must be
read	N/A	N/A	Doesn't matter
getmsg	N/A	0	Doesn't matter
getmsg	N/A	RS_HIPRI	A high priority message
getpmsg	0	0	Error, returns EINVAL
getpmsg	0	MSG_HIPRI	A high priority message
getpmsg	1–255	MSG_HIPRI	Error, returns EINVAL
getpmsg	0–255	MSG_BAND	In a priority band that is >= *bandp*, or high priority
getpmsg	0–255	MSG_ANY	Doesn't matter

Figure 13.8   STREAMS message type retrieved by read, getmsg, and getpmsg.

In Figure 13.8, where we say "Doesn't matter", we mean that the first message is retrieved regardless of its priority band. Also, the values in the columns called *bandp* and *flagsp* refer to the values of the integer pointed to by these arguments.

Both functions return a non-negative value upon successful completion. A return value of 0 means that the entire message was read successfully. A return value of MORECTL means that more control information needs to be retrieved, and a return value of MOREDATA indicates that more data needs to be retrieved. These two values are not mutually exclusive, so a return value of MORECTL | MOREDATA means that more control information and more data must be retrieved. Further calls to getmsg or getpmsg can be used to retrieve the remainder of the message, unless a message of higher priority is received by the stream head, in which case the higher priority message will be retrieved before the remainder of the incomplete message is retrieved.

Example: Copying a file using getmsg and write

Program 13.7 is a reimplementation of Program 4.2 that uses getmsg and write to copy a file from standard input to standard output, rather than read and write.

Let's see what happens when we run Program 13.7 a few times.

```
$ echo "Hello, world!" | ./copy
flags = 0, control.len = -1, data.len = 14
Hello, world!
flags = 0, control.len = 0, data.len = 0
$ ./copy
This is the first line
flags = 0, control.len = -1, data.len = 23
This is the first line
This is the second line
flags = 0, control.len = -1, data.len = 24
This is the second line
^D                                      We type Control-D to quit
flags = 0, control.len = -1, data.len = 0
$ ./copy < /etc/passwd > /dev/null
Can't getmsg: Not a stream device
$ ls -l /etc/passwd
-r--r--r--    1 root      sys            919 Jan  7 19:15 /etc/passwd
$ cat /etc/passwd | ./copy > /dev/null
flags = 0, control.len = -1, data.len = 919
flags = 0, control.len = 0, data.len = 0
$ ls -l ../../file_io.ps
-rw-r--r--    1 rich     staff       205927 Oct 22 12:54 ../../file_io.ps
$ cat ../../file_io.ps | ./copy > /dev/null
getmsg returns MOREDATA           The file is so large that MOREDATA is returned
flags = 0, control.len = -1, data.len = 8192
flags = 0, control.len = -1, data.len = 2048
flags = 0, control.len = -1, data.len = 5120
flags = 0, control.len = -1, data.len = 5120
...                               Several identical lines omitted
flags = 0, control.len = -1, data.len = 5120
flags = 0, control.len = -1, data.len = 3899
flags = 0, control.len = 0, data.len = 0
```

The first two invocations rely on the fact that Solaris pipes and terminals are implemented using STREAMS. When a STREAMS hangup is received, flags, control.len, and data.len are equal to 0. Note that when we type Control-D, a STREAMS hangup is not generated. (I.e., a terminal EOF is not the same as a STREAMS hangup.) The third invocation shows that getmsg does not work when the file being referenced is not a STREAMS device. The last invocation shows what happens when getmsg cannot return all the data in the message in one piece. We redirect standard output to /dev/null in some of the examples to prevent the screen from being cluttered with output.

Program 13.7 is, of course, a somewhat contrived example to show what happens when there is more data at the stream head than can be transferred in one getmsg operation. A real-life application would probably not be using getmsg to read a file through a pipe.

advanced_io/copy.c

```
 1  #include <stdio.h>
 2  #include <unistd.h>
 3  #include <stdlib.h>
 4  #include <stropts.h>
 5  #include "ssp.h"

 6  static char control_buf [BUF_SIZE];
 7  static char data_buf [BUF_SIZE];

 8  int main (void)
 9  {
10      int n;
11      int flags;
12      struct strbuf control;
13      struct strbuf data;

14      control.buf = control_buf;
15      control.maxlen = BUF_SIZE;
16      data.buf = data_buf;
17      data.maxlen = BUF_SIZE;

18      for (;;) {
19          flags = 0;

20          n = getmsg (STDIN_FILENO, &control, &data, &flags);

21          switch (n) {
22              case -1:
23                  err_msg ("Can't getmsg");
24                  break;

25              case MORECTL:
26                  log_msg ("getmsg returns MORECTL");
27                  break;

28              case MOREDATA:
29                  log_msg ("getmsg returns MOREDATA");
30                  break;

31              case MORECTL | MOREDATA:
32                  log_msg ("getmsg returns MORECTL | MOREDATA");
33                  break;
34          }

35          log_msg ("flags = %d, control.len = %d, data.len = %d", flags,
36              control.len, data.len);

37          if (data.len == 0)
38              exit (0);
39          if (data.len > 0)
40              if (writen (STDOUT_FILENO, data.buf, data.len) != data.len)
41                  err_msg ("Can't write");
42      }
43  }
```

advanced_io/copy.c

Program 13.7 Copy a file using getmsg and write.

13.13 STREAMS `ioctl` Operations

Solaris defines more than 40 `ioctl` operations in `<sys/stropts.h>`, each of which starts with `I_` and is documented in the `streamio` man page. Before we take a closer look at some of them, let's repeat the function prototype for the `ioctl` function.

```
#include <unistd.h>
#include <stropts.h>

int ioctl (int fildes, int request, /* arg */...);
```
Returns: depends on request if OK, −1 on error

The *request* argument specifies which operation to perform, and the option third argument, *arg*, depends on which operation is being performed. We don't show a type for *arg* because sometimes it's an integer and sometimes it's a pointer.

The *request*s we are interested in are:

`I_CANPUT`	This checks that the priority band specified by *arg* is writable. The `ioctl` function returns 0 if the priority band is flow controlled, 1 if it is writable, or −1 on error.
`I_LIST`	This *request* allows us to get either a list of all the module names on the stream referenced by *fildes,* or a count of the number of modules (including the topmost driver) on that stream. (We say topmost driver because a multiplexing driver may have more than one driver. Multiplexing drivers are discussed in Chapter 12 of [Rago 1993].) If *arg* is NULL, the number of modules is returned.

If *arg* is not NULL, it must be a pointer to a `str_list` structure, which has the following definition:

```
struct str_list {
    int             sl_nmods;
    struct str_mlist    *sl_modlist;
};
```

The `sl_nmods` member contains the number of entries in the array, and `sl_modlist` points to the array of module names. The module names are stored as an array of `str_mlist` structures, which is defined as follows:

```
struct str_mlist {
    char    l_name [FMNAMESZ + 1];
};
```

The constant `FMNAMESZ` is defined in `<sys/conf.h>`, which is automatically included by `<stropts.h>`. We show an example of how to use the `I_LIST` *request* in Program 13.8.

`I_GRDOPT`	This allows us to get the current read mode options. When this `ioctl` successfully returns, the current read mode is

stored in the integer pointed to by *arg*. We discuss the read mode in the next section.

I_SRDOPT   This *request* allows us to set the read mode to that specified by the integer pointed to by *arg*. Rather than setting the read mode to an absolute value, we should retrieve the current value and modify it.

I_GWROPT   This *request* retrieves the write mode for the stream and places it into the the integer pointed to by *arg*. We discuss the write mode in the next section.

I_SWROPT   This *request* allows us to set the write mode to that specified by the integer pointed to by *arg*. Rather than setting the write mode to an absolute value, we should retrieve the current value and modify it.

Example: Listing the modules on a stream

Program 13.8 uses the I_LIST ioctl *request* to list the names of the modules and topmost driver associated with a STREAMS device.

When we run Program 13.8 for a couple of devices, we get the following:

```
$ ./list_mods /dev/tty
Number of modules = 4
  Module: ttcompat
  Module: ldterm
  Module: ptem
  Driver: pts
$ ./list_mods /dev/tcp
Number of modules = 2
  Module: tcp
  Driver: ip
```

The pts driver in the first invocation of Program 13.8 is the pseudo terminal server, because this example was run using a network login. We talk about pseudo terminals in Chapter 23. The second invocation illustrates how prior to Solaris 10 the TCP protocol was layered on top of the IP protocol.

13.14 STREAMS I/O Using `read` and `write`

Instead of using getmsg and getpmsg to read from a stream and putmsg and putpmsg to write to a stream, we can also use the read and write functions.

Reading From a STREAMS Device

Reading from a stream poses two questions:

advanced_io/list_mods.c

```c
 1  #include <stdio.h>
 2  #include <stdlib.h>
 3  #include <unistd.h>
 4  #include <sys/types.h>
 5  #include <sys/stat.h>
 6  #include <fcntl.h>
 7  #include <stropts.h>
 8  #include "ssp.h"

 9  int main (int argc, char **argv)
10  {
11      int fd;
12      int i;
13      int num_modules;
14      struct str_list modules;

15      if (argc != 2)
16          err_quit ("Usage: list_mods pathname");

17      if ((fd = open (argv [1], O_RDONLY)) == -1)
18          err_msg ("Can't open %s", argv [1]);

19      if ((num_modules = ioctl (fd, I_LIST, NULL)) == -1)
20          err_msg ("Can't get number of modules");

21      printf ("Number of modules = %d\n", num_modules);

22      if ((modules.sl_modlist = calloc (num_modules,
23          sizeof (struct str_mlist))) == NULL) {
24          err_msg ("Can't calloc memory");
25      }

26      modules.sl_nmods = num_modules;

27      if (ioctl (fd, I_LIST, &modules) == -1)
28          err_msg ("Can't get list of module names");

29      for (i = 1; i <= num_modules; i++) {
30          if (i == num_modules)
31              printf ("  Driver: %s\n", (char *) modules.sl_modlist++);
32          else
33              printf ("  Module: %s\n", (char *) modules.sl_modlist++);
34      }

35      close (fd);

36      return (0);
37  }
```

advanced_io/list_mods.c

Program 13.8 Listing the modules on a STREAMS device using `ioctl`.

1. What happens to the record boundaries associated with STREAMS messages?

2. How do we handle a message's control information when using `read` to read the message?

How these questions are answered depends on the stream's read mode, which can be set using the I_SRDOPT ioctl.

There are three modes that determine the answer to our first question. These are selected by setting the *arg* argument of the I_SRDOPT ioctl to one of the following constants:

RNORM	This selects normal byte stream mode, which is the default read mode. Data is read from the stream until the requested number of bytes has been transferred, or there is no more data. STREAMS message boundaries are ignored.
RMSGD	Message discard mode. Data is read from the stream until the requested number of bytes has been transferred, or a message boundary in encountered. If read retrieves a partial message, the remainder of the message is discarded.
RMSGN	Message nondiscard mode. This is much the same as message discard mode, except that if only a partial message is read, the remainder of the message is left on the stream for a subsequent read.

As for our second question, by default read will return with an error if there is a control (or protocol) message at the stream head. We can change the default behaviour by setting the *arg* argument of the I_SRDOPT ioctl to one of the following constants:

RPROTNORM	Normal protocol mode, which is the default. If a control message is at the front of the stream head's read queue, read will fail, returning EBADMSG.
RPROTDAT	Protocol data mode. The control portion of the message is delivered as data when a read of the STREAMS device is issued.
RPROTDIS	Protocol discard mode. The control portion of the message is discarded, but any data in the message is retrieved.

Writing to a STREAMS Device

Writing to a STREAMS device is relatively straightforward, but two questions arise:

1. What happens when we write a zero-length message?
2. What happens when an error or hangup condition occurs?

The answers to these questions depend on the stream's write mode, and in the case of our first question, the type of device associated with the stream. The stream's write mode can be set using the I_SWROPT ioctl, with the *arg* argument set to one of the following constants:

SNDZERO   If the device is not a pipe or FIFO, a zero-length write will
                   result in a zero-length message being sent downstream.
                   However, by default zero-length writes are ignored by pipes
                   and FIFOs. We can change this by using the SNDZERO write
                   mode, which causes a zero-length message to be sent
                   downstream when a zero-length write is performed on a pipe
                   or FIFO.

SNDPIPE   By default, errors cause write or putmsg to return −1, but by
                   setting the stream to SNDPIPE write mode, we can change
                   this. In this mode, a SIGPIPE signal is sent to the calling
                   process if an error occurs when writing to the stream, or the
                   stream is in hangup mode. (This write mode applies to
                   write, putmsg, and putpmsg.) We use this mode to support
                   BSD socket semantics over STREAMS.

13.15 I/O Multiplexing

In our discussions of I/O so far, we have considered only the scenario in which we read
from only one file descriptor at a time. For example, consider the following code extract
from a program that copies a file from one file descriptor to another in a while loop:

```
while ((n = read (fd1, buf, BUF_SIZE)) > 0)
    if (write (fd2, buf, n) != n)
        err_msg ("Can't write");
```

In this example, read blocks until data is available on fd1. But we can't use this
technique if we want to read from multiple file descriptors at the same time; data might
become available for one file descriptor while our process is blocked in read on another
file descriptor. In this situation, we need to use something else.

Let's consider the talk program, which allows two users to carry on a realtime
conversation, possibly over a network connection. The in.talkd daemon coordinates
the conversation for us. Figure 13.9 shows the arrangement when both users are logged
into the same machine.

Figure 13.9 Overview of the talk program.

The in.talkd process has two inputs and two outputs, The process can't do a blocking
read on either of the inputs, because there's no way of knowing which of the inputs will
get data first.

One solution to this problem would be to implement the daemon as two processes (child and parent), each of which handles data transfer in one direction. Figure 13.10 shows how this would be arranged.

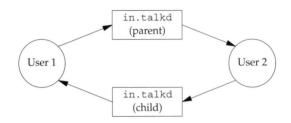

Figure 13.10 The `talk` program using two processes.

Using two processes allows us to use blocking `read`s, but introduces another problem when the users exit the program. If User 1 terminates the `talk` session, the parent must notify the child somehow (for example, send it a signal). If User 2 terminates the session, the child process will die, and the parent will be notified (by the kernel sending it a `SIGCHLD` signal). Correctly handling these signals complicates the program a bit.

> We could also use two threads, rather than two processes, to solve the problem of reading from several file descriptors. Using threads would also obviate the need for the signal handling we just mentioned.

Another solution to our problem would be to use nonblocking I/O in a single process (thus avoiding the signal handling complications we mentioned previously). Each of the file descriptors used for input would be opened in nonblocking mode, and then we would attempt to `read` from the first descriptor. If data is present, it will be read and processed. If no data is present, `read` will return immediately. We then repeat this process for the other input file descriptor. We repeat this process indefinitely, alternating between the two descriptors.

The problem with this method, called *polling*, is that it is very wasteful of CPU time. Even if we pause between the pairs of `read`s for a short time, most of the time there will be no data to read, so a large number of `read` system calls will be needlessly performed, wasting CPU resources that could be used by another process. If we are the only user on the system, this waste of CPU time may be of little consequence. But on a typical Solaris system with many concurrent users, it should be avoided.

One other technique we can use in this situation is called *asynchronous I/O*. Solaris provides two types of asynchronous I/O: one that is provided in the `libaio` library, and another that is supplied in the realtime library, `librt` (the latter is available only in Solaris 2.6 and newer releases). Section 13.19 talks about the `libaio` asynchronous I/O.

One final technique we can use is *I/O multiplexing*, which is where we build a list of the descriptors we are interested in, and then call a function that doesn't return until an event happens on one or more of the descriptors. We are told when the function returns which file descriptors had an event happen on them.

We can perform I/O multiplexing by three mechanisms:

1. Use the `select` function.
2. Use the `poll` function.
3. Starting with Solaris 7, use the `/dev/poll` device driver.

Let's take a closer look at these three mechanisms.

13.16 The `select` Function

The `select` function allows us to do I/O multiplexing on a set of file descriptors.

```
#include <sys/time.h>

int select (int nfds, fd_set *readfds, fd_set *writefds, fd_set *errorfds,
    struct timeval *timeout);
```
                           Returns: the number of ready file descriptors, 0 on timeout, −1 on error
```
void FD_SET (int fd, fd_set *fdset);

void FD_CLR (int fd, fd_set *fdset);

void FD_ZERO (fd_set *fdset);

int FD_ISSET (int fd, fd_set *fdset);
```
                           Returns: non-zero if *fd* is set in *fdset*, 0 otherwise

The `select` function is used to perform synchronous multiplexed I/O on a number of file descriptors. The *nfds* argument determines the range of file descriptors to be tested, which are in the range of 0 to *nfds* −1. We can either determine for ourselves the value to use for *nfds*, or we could just use the `FD_SETSIZE` constant defined in `<sys/select.h>` (which is automatically included when we include `<sys/types.h>`). The default `FD_SETSIZE` for a 32-bit process is 1024, but this can be increased at compile time by defining a larger value for it before including any system-supplied header. The maximum supported `FD_SETSIZE` is 65,536, which is the default value for 64-bit processes. Unnecessarily checking this large number of descriptors wastes CPU time, so supplying our own value for *nfds* is preferred over using `FD_SETSIZE`. If we do supply our own value for *nfds*, we must make sure that it never exceeds `FD_SETSIZE`.

Each of the *readfds, writefds,* and *errorfds* arguments points to a file descriptor set. The descriptor sets tell the `select` function the events we are interested in for each file descriptor; *readfds* is the list of descriptors we are interested in reading from, *writefds* is the set of descriptors we are interested in writing to, and *errorfds* is the list of descriptors we are interested in receiving exception conditions from.

Any of these pointers may be NULL (indicating that we are not interested in any of the events associated with the argument); if they are not NULL, they point to an `fd_set` data type. An `fd_set` is an opaque data type that we can think of as array of bits—one bit for each file descriptor, as we show in Figure 13.11.

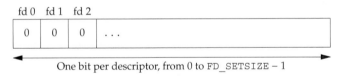

Figure 13.11   Visualization of the `fd_set` data type.

Each of the bits is either 0 or 1; 0 means we are not interested in the file descriptor, and 1 means we are. The only way we should manipulate an `fd_set` (apart from declaring a variable, or assigning one `fd_set` to another) is to use one of the following four macros:

`FD_ZERO`	This clears all the bits in the descriptor set pointed to by *fdset*. Once we have declared a descriptor set, we must clear it using this macro.
`FD_SET`	This turns on (sets) the bit for *fd* in the descriptor set pointed to by *fdset*.
`FD_CLR`	This turns off (clears) the bit for *fd* in the descriptor set pointed to by *fdset*.
`FD_ISSET`	We can use this macro to determine if the bit for *fd* is set in the descriptor set pointed to by *fdset*.

The *readfds*, *writefds*, and *errorfds* arguments must be reinitialized before each call to the `select` function.

Example: Manipulating `fd_set` data types

Program 13.9 shows a trivial example of how we can use the `FD_ZERO`, `FD_SET`, and `FD_ISSET` macros.

Here's the output we get when we run Program 13.9:

```
$ ./fd_set
read_set:
   bit 0 is set
   bit 1 is clear
   bit 2 is set
   bit 3 is clear
write_set:
   bit 0 is clear
   bit 1 is set
   bit 2 is clear
   bit 3 is set
```

Returning to the `select` function, the last argument, *timeout*, determines how long `select` will wait for something to happen on one of the file descriptors we are interested

advanced_io/fd_set.c

```
1 #include <stdio.h>
2 #include <string.h>
3 #include <sys/types.h>

4 int main (void)
5 {
6     fd_set read_set;
7     fd_set write_set;
8     int i;

9     FD_ZERO (&read_set);
10    FD_ZERO (&write_set);

11    FD_SET (0, &read_set);
12    FD_SET (1, &write_set);
13    FD_SET (2, &read_set);
14    FD_SET (3, &write_set);

15    printf ("read_set:\n");
16    for (i = 0; i < 4; i++) {
17        printf ("  bit %d is %s\n", i,
18            (FD_ISSET (i, &read_set)) ? "set" : "clear");
19    }

20    printf ("write_set:\n");
21    for (i = 0; i < 4; i++) {
22        printf ("  bit %d is %s\n", i,
23            (FD_ISSET (i, &write_set)) ? "set" : "clear");
24    }

25    return (0);
26 }
```

advanced_io/fd_set.c

Program 13.9 Using fd_sets.

in. The object pointed to by *timeout* is a timeval structure, which has the following members:

```
struct timeval {
    time_t      tv_sec;      /* Time in seconds */
    suseconds_t tv_usec;     /* and microseconds */
};
```

We need to consider three conditions:

1. The *timeout* argument is NULL.

   This will cause select to wait for ever; it will only return when at least one of the descriptors is ready, or when a signal is caught. In the latter case, select will return −1 and set errno to EINTR.

2. *timeout* -> tv_sec equals 0 and *timeout* -> tv_usec equals 0.

   In this case, all the descriptors are tested, and select returns immediately. This allows us to poll multiple file descriptors without blocking in select.

3. *timeout* -> `tv_sec` is not 0 or *timeout* -> `tv_usec` is not 0.

    This specifies a timeout value of the given number of seconds and microseconds. The `select` function will return only when the timeout expires, unless one of the descriptors becomes ready, in which case it returns immediately. If the timeout expires, `select` returns 0. It is also possible that a signal will interrupt the wait.

If the *readfds*, *writefds*, and *errorfds* arguments are all NULL, we can use `select` to implement a version of `sleep` that has a sub-second granularity.

The `select` function returns one of three types of value:

1. If −1 is returned, an error has occurred. For example, a signal might have been caught, or one of the descriptors to be tested does not refer to a valid open file.

2. A return value of 0 indicates that no descriptors are ready. This happens if the time limit specified by *timeout* expires before any of the descriptors are ready.

3. A positive value indicates the number of descriptors that are ready. In this case, the descriptor sets are cleared, except that for each file descriptor less than *nfds*, the corresponding bit will be set if it was set when `select` was called, and the associated condition is true for that file descriptor.

The meaning of "ready" in the previous paragraphs depends on which descriptor set we are talking about.

A descriptor in the *readfds* descriptor set is ready if a `read` from that descriptor will not block. A descriptor in the *writefds* descriptor set is ready if a `write` to that descriptor will not block. A descriptor in the *errorfds* descriptor set is ready if there is an error condition pending on that descriptor.

One thing we should point out about `select` is that it doesn't matter if the file descriptors being monitored by `select` are blocking or not. If one of the descriptors in the *readfds* descriptor set is in nonblocking mode and we specify a *timeout* of two seconds, `select` will block for up to two seconds. The `select` will only return early in the event of an error, or if data is ready for one of the selected descriptors. The same thing will happen if we specify an infinite wait time (by setting *timeout* to NULL).

Many people are under the misconception that end of file represents an error condition as far as `select` is concerned, but this is not true. If end of file is detected for a file descriptor in the *readfds* descriptor set, it is considered readable by `select`. A subsequent call to `read` on that descriptor will return 0, which is the normal way to signify end of file in Solaris programming.

Because it is more efficient, the `poll` function is preferred over `select`, and *must* be used when the number of file descriptors exceeds FD_SETSIZE (indeed, the Solaris implementation of `select` is built on top of `poll`). Another reason why we recommend `poll` over `select` is the former's ease of use. For example, `select` will tell us that one or more of the file descriptors is invalid, but `poll` will also tell us which ones.

> The reason why there are two functions that essentially perform the same task (i.e., multiplexed I/O) is historical; `select` is from BSD, and `poll` comes from System V.

13.17 The `poll` Function

The `poll` function can also be used to perform multiplexed I/O.

```
#include <poll.h>

int poll (struct pollfd fds[], nfds_t nfds, int timeout);
```
Returns: the number of ready file descriptors, 0 on timeout, −1 on error

The `poll` function provides another mechanism by which applications can perform synchronous multiplexed I/O over a set of file descriptors, but does it in a way that is more efficient than `select`. Instead of building three arrays of `fd_set` structures (one for each condition: readability, writability, and error condition) and then checking each file descriptor from 0 to *nfds*, with `poll` we build an array of `pollfd` structures, each of which has the following members:

```
struct pollfd {
    int     fd;        /* File descriptor to poll */
    short   events;    /* Events of interest on fd */
    short   revents;   /* Events that occurred on fd */
};
```

We pass the array of `pollfd` structures to `poll` in the *fds* argument. The number of elements in the array is specified in *nfds*.

The `fd` member specifies an open file descriptor that we are interested in (compare this with the `select` function, where the file descriptor is implied by its position in an array), and the `events` member is a bitmask that specifies which events we are interested in for this file descriptor. Similarly, the `revents` member is a bitmask that specifies which events have occurred on the file descriptor when `poll` returns.

The `events` member is constructed by bitwise-ORing any of the following events:

POLLIN	Data other than high priority data may be read without blocking. If `fd` refers to a STREAMS device, this flag is set in `revents` even if the message is zero length.
POLLRDNORM	Normal data (priority band 0) may be read without blocking. If `fd` refers to a STREAMS device, this flag is set in `revents` even if the message is zero length.
POLLRDBAND	Data from a non-zero priority band may be read without blocking. If `fd` refers to a STREAMS device, this flag is set in `revents` even if the message is zero length.
POLLPRI	High priority data may be received without blocking. If `fd` refers to a STREAMS device, this flag is set in `revents` even if the message is zero length.
POLLOUT	Normal data (priority band 0) may be written without blocking.
POLLWRNORM	This is the same as POLLOUT.

POLLWRBAND   Data in a non-zero priority band may be written. This event examines only priority bands that have been written to at least once.

The first four events (i.e., POLLIN, POLLRDNORM, POLLRDBAND, and POLLPRI) test for readability, and the last three (that is, POLLOUT, POLLWRNORM, and POLLWRBAND) test for writability. The following flags test for errors, and are valid only in the revents member; they are not used by the events member:

POLLERR   An error has occurred on the device or stream.

POLLHUP   A hangup has occurred on the stream. This event and POLLOUT are mutually exclusive; a stream cannot be writable if a hangup has occurred. However, there may still be data to read from the descriptor, so this event and POLLIN, POLLRDNORM, POLLRDBAND, or POLLPRI are not mutually exclusive.

POLLNVAL   The descriptor specified by fd does not refer to an open file.

As with select, the last argument, *timeout*, specifies how long poll will wait for one of the events before timing out. There are three cases to consider:

1. The value of timeout is –1.

    This causes poll to wait for ever. The poll function will return only when one of the descriptors is ready, or when the calling process catches a signal. In the latter case, poll returns –1 and sets errno to EINTR. Instead of using a value of –1 for *timeout*, we can also use the constant INFTIM, which is defined in <stropts.h>.

2. *timeout* equals 0.

    In this case, all descriptors are tested, and poll returns immediately. This enables us to find out the status of multiple file descriptors without blocking in poll.

3. *timeout* is greater than 0.

    This specifies a timeout period of *timeout* milliseconds. The poll function will return only when the timeout expires, unless one of the descriptors becomes ready, in which case it returns immediately. If the timeout period expires, poll returns 0. It is also possible that a signal will interrupt the wait.

As with select, whether a file descriptor is blocking has no effect on whether poll will block.

We must also be cognizant of the difference between an end of file condition and a hangup. If end of file is detected, POLLIN will be set in revents (not POLLHUP), and a subsequent read will return 0. We'll receive a POLLHUP notification if we're reading from something like a modem and the telephone line is hung up.

Example: Copying a file using `poll` and nonblocking I/O

Recall from our discussion of nonblocking I/O in Section 13.2, where we showed an example of copying a file using nonblocking file descriptors. When we tried to `write` a buffer that was larger than the buffering provided by the STREAMS subsystem, the call would fail thousands of times in a tight loop before subsequent writes would succeed. Our example wasted a lot of CPU time by calling the `write` system call more than 750,000 time unnecessarily.

Program 13.10 also copies a file using nonblocking I/O, but it uses the `poll` function to wait until the `write` would succeed.

Let's see what happens when we run Program 13.10.

```
$ ./poll < ssp.ps 2> errors
                                    Lots of output deleted
$ cat errors
Read 1000000 bytes
Wrote 327680 bytes
Wrote 65536 bytes
Wrote 65536 bytes
Wrote 65536 bytes
Wrote 65536 bytes
Wrote 65536 bytes
Wrote 65536 bytes
Wrote 65536 bytes
Wrote 65536 bytes
Wrote 65536 bytes
Wrote 65536 bytes
Wrote 16960 bytes
```

As a result of using `poll`, more than 72,000 system calls are eliminated, and the CPU time is significantly reduced. We'll see in the next section how much of a performance improvement using `poll` gives us.

13.18 The `/dev/poll` Device Driver

Solaris 7 introduced the `/dev/poll` device driver, which we can use to poll large numbers of file descriptors efficiently. We use the device by opening `/dev/poll` and writing an array of suitably defined `pollfd` structures to the file descriptor returned by open. We then use one of two `ioctl` commands defined in `<sys/devpoll.h>` to interface with the device (see Section 13.13 for the `ioctl` function's prototype), as illustrated here:

```
ioctl (int fd, DP_POLL, struct dvpoll *arg);
ioctl (int fd, DP_ISPOLLED, struct pollfd *arg);
```

The `DP_POLL` command is used to retrieve the poll events that occurred on the file descriptors in the descriptor set that is monitored by *fd*. The *arg* argument is a pointer to a `dvpoll` structure, which has the following members:

advanced_io/poll.c

```
 1 #include <stdio.h>
 2 #include <sys/types.h>
 3 #include <unistd.h>
 4 #include <fcntl.h>
 5 #include <poll.h>
 6 #include "ssp.h"

 7 #define BUFFER_SIZE 1000000

 8 static char buf [BUFFER_SIZE];

 9 int main (void)
10 {
11     ssize_t n;
12     ssize_t res;
13     char *ptr;
14     int errs;
15     struct pollfd fds;

16     errs = 0;
17     n = read (STDIN_FILENO, buf, BUFFER_SIZE);
18     log_msg ("Read %d bytes", n);

19     set_fsflag (STDOUT_FILENO, O_NONBLOCK);

20     fds.fd = STDOUT_FILENO;
21     fds.events = POLLOUT;
22     fds.revents = 0;

23     ptr = buf;
24     while (n > 0) {
25         if (poll (&fds, 1, -1) == -1)
26             err_msg ("Can't poll");

27         while ((n > 0) && ((res = write (STDOUT_FILENO, ptr, n)) > 0)) {
28             if (errs > 0) {
29                 err_ret ("write failed %d times", errs);
30                 errs = 0;
31             }

32             log_msg ("Wrote %d bytes", res);
33             ptr += res;
34             n -= res;
35         }
36     }

37     clear_fsflag (STDOUT_FILENO, O_NONBLOCK);

38     return (0);
39 }
```

advanced_io/poll.c

Program 13.10   Using `poll` and nonblocking I/O to copy a file.

```
struct dvpoll {
    pollfd_t    *dp_fds;        /* Array of pollfd structures */
    nfds_t      dp_nfds;        /* Number of pollfd structures in dp_fds */
    int         dp_timeout;     /* Timeout in milliseconds */
};
```

The dp_fds member points to a buffer holding an array of pollfd structures that is returned by the DP_POLL command. The dp_nfds member specifies the number of pollfd structures in the buffer pointed to by dp_fds (and hence, the maximum number of file descriptors from which poll information can be obtained). The dp_timeout member specifies how long (in milliseconds) the ioctl will wait for an event we are interested in before timing out. Like the poll function, setting dp_timeout to –1 will cause the ioctl to wait indefinitely for an event we are interested in unless an interrupt is caught (in which case, ioctl will return –1), and setting it to 0 will cause the ioctl to return immediately after the descriptors have been checked. If the polling times out, ioctl returns 0.

If an event that we are interested in occurs, ioctl returns the number of valid pollfd entries in dp_fds. For each valid pollfd entry, the fd member indicates on which file descriptor the polled event happened. As with the poll function, the events member contains the events we are interested in, and the revents member contains the events that actually occurred.

We can use the DP_ISPOLLED command to check whether a file descriptor is already in the set of monitored descriptors represented by *fd*. The fd member of the pollfd structure is set to the file descriptor we are interested in. On a successful return, ioctl returns 0 if the file descriptor is not in the set, or 1 if it is. In the latter case, the events member contains the events that are being polled for, and the revents member is set to 0.

Example: Copying a file using /dev/poll and nonblocking I/O

Program 13.11 is a reimplementation of Program 13.10, which uses the /dev/poll device rather then the poll function.

When we run Program 13.11, we get the same results as when we run Program 13.10:

```
$ ./devpoll < ssp.ps 2> errors
```
                              Lots of output deleted
```
$ cat errors
Read 1000000 bytes
Wrote 327680 bytes
Wrote 65536 bytes
Wrote 65536 bytes
Wrote 65536 bytes
Wrote 65536 bytes
Wrote 65536 bytes
Wrote 65536 bytes
```

```
 1 #include <stdio.h>
 2 #include <sys/types.h>
 3 #include <unistd.h>
 4 #include <fcntl.h>
 5 #include <sys/devpoll.h>
 6 #include "ssp.h"

 7 #define BUFFER_SIZE 1000000

 8 static char buf [BUFFER_SIZE];

 9 int main (void)
10 {
11     ssize_t n;
12     ssize_t res;
13     char *ptr;
14     int errs;
15     struct pollfd fds;
16     int fd;
17     dvpoll_t devpoll;

18     errs = 0;
19     n = read (STDIN_FILENO, buf, BUFFER_SIZE);
20     log_msg ("Read %d bytes", n);

21     set_fsflag (STDOUT_FILENO, O_NONBLOCK);

22     if ((fd = open ("/dev/poll", O_RDWR)) == -1)
23         err_msg ("Can't open /dev/poll");

24     fds.fd = STDOUT_FILENO;
25     fds.events = POLLOUT;
26     fds.revents = 0;

27     devpoll.dp_fds = &fds;
28     devpoll.dp_nfds = 1;
29     devpoll.dp_timeout = -1;

30     if (write (fd, &fds, sizeof (struct pollfd)) != sizeof (struct pollfd))
31         err_msg ("Can't write pollfd structure");

32     ptr = buf;
33     while (n > 0) {
34         if (ioctl (fd, DP_POLL, &devpoll) == -1)
35             err_msg ("DP_POLL ioctl failed");

36         while ((n > 0) && ((res = write (STDOUT_FILENO, ptr, n)) > 0)) {
37             if (errs > 0) {
38                 err_ret ("write failed %d times\n", errs);
39                 errs = 0;
40             }

41             log_msg ("Wrote %d bytes", res);
42             ptr += res;
43             n -= res;
44         }
45     }
```

```
46        clear_fsflag (STDOUT_FILENO, O_NONBLOCK);

47        return (0);
48   }
```
——— *advanced_io/devpoll.c*

Program 13.11 Using `/dev/poll` and nonblocking I/O to copy a file.

```
Wrote 65536 bytes
Wrote 65536 bytes
Wrote 65536 bytes
Wrote 65536 bytes
Wrote 16960 bytes
```

Figure 13.12 compares the time to run Program 13.11, Program 13.10 as we show in the listing, and Program 13.10 with lines 25 and 26 commented out. The file we copied was only 1,841,652 bytes in size.

Operation	Real	User	Sys
Copy the file without using `poll` or `/dev/poll`	15.84	1.96	3.04
Copy the file using `poll` to throttle `writes`	8.98	0.01	0.05
Copy the file using `/dev/poll` to throttle `writes`	6.99	0.00	0.05

Figure 13.12 The effect of `poll` and `/dev/poll` on nonblocking I/O efficiency.

We can see that using `poll` and `/dev/poll` in these examples has a dramatic effect: the Real time is halved, and the User and System CPU times are reduced by about two orders of magnitude. Using `/dev/poll` in this example shows a small performance gain over using the `poll` function, but we are polling only a single file descriptor. We would expect the difference to be more noticeable when polling many file descriptors.

When we use the `/dev/poll` device, the best performance gains over using the `poll` function will be realized if the list of polled descriptors rarely changes.

File descriptors that are closed should be removed from the set of monitored descriptors. Otherwise, if the file descriptor is reused, we will be polling events on the file associated with the reused file descriptor, not the original file.

The `/dev/poll` driver caches the list of polled file descriptors on a per-process basis. Therefore, the descriptor associated with `/dev/poll` that is inherited by a child process should be closed, and `/dev/poll` should be reopened if required.

13.19 Asynchronous I/O

The `select` and `poll` functions just described provide a synchronous method of I/O notification. That is, the kernel doesn't tell us about a pending I/O event until we ask for it. There are times, however, when we would like to be notified of an I/O event asynchronously (i.e., without specifically asking). Signals, which we discuss in Chapter 17, provide an asynchronous method for the kernel to notify our process that something has happened.

Solaris provides three asynchronous I/O mechanisms: one that can only be used with STREAMS devices, another that can be used with almost any file, and a third that is part of the realtime library and can be used by almost any file.

13.20 Asynchronous I/O With STREAMS Device Files

A process that wants to use asynchronous I/O on a STREAMS device must issue an I_SETSIG command to that device's stream head by using the ioctl function. This instructs the stream head to send the calling process a SIGPOLL signal when a particular event has occurred on the stream associated with the open file descriptor. The optional argument, *arg*, is a bitmask that specifies which events we are interested in. It is the bitwise-OR of any of the following constants (which are defined in <stropts.h>):

S_INPUT	This deprecated event is for when any message other than M_PCPROTO arrives at the stream head read queue. The event is triggered even if the message is of zero length.
S_RDNORM	An ordinary (nonpriority) message has arrived at the stream head read queue. The event is triggered even if the message is of zero length.
S_RDBAND	A priority band message (where the band is > 0) has arrived at the stream head read queue. The event is triggered even if the message is of zero length.
S_HIPRI	This means that a high priority message is present at the stream head read queue. The event is triggered even if the message is of zero length.
S_OUTPUT	The write queue just below the stream head is no longer full, which means that we can write more data downstream.
S_WRNORM	This is the same as S_OUTPUT.
S_WRBAND	A priority band > 0 of a queue downstream exists and is writable.
S_MSG	A STREAMS signal message that contains the SIGPOLL signal has reached the front of the stream head read queue.
S_ERROR	This event means that an M_ERROR message has reached the stream head.
S_HANGUP	This event means that an M_HANGUP message has reached the stream head.
S_BANDURG	When used with S_RDBAND, a SIGURG signal is generated instead of SIGPOLL when a priority message reaches the front of the stream head read queue.

If we set *arg* to 0, the calling process will be unregistered and will not receive further SIGPOLL signals.

Because this method of asynchronous I/O sends a SIGPOLL (or SIGURG if we specify the S_BANDURG argument) signal to our process when one of the events we are interested in happens, we must establish a signal handler for it. The default action for SIGPOLL is to terminate the process, so we should establish the new signal handler before calling ioctl (by default, SIGURG is ignored).

13.21 Asynchronous I/O With Other Files

A more general purpose asynchronous I/O facility is provided by the asynchronous I/O library. We initiate an asynchronous I/O operation by calling either aioread or aiowrite, and can be notified of the completion of the operation either synchronously by using the aiowait function we discuss further on, or asynchronously by installing a signal handler for the SIGPOLL signal (the manual pages talk about using SIGIO, but that signal is just an alias for SIGPOLL). If no handler for SIGPOLL is installed, then asynchronous notification is disabled, and only synchronous notification using aiowait is possible.

The results of an asynchronous I/O operation are stored in a aio_result_t structure, which has the following members:

```
typedef struct aio_result_t {
    ssize_t aio_return;    /* Return value of read or write */
    int     aio_errno;     /* The errno generated by the I/O */
} aio_result_t;
```

When the I/O operation is complete, both the aio_return and aio_errno members are set to reflect the results of the operation. We can set aio_return to AIO_INPROGRESS (a value otherwise not used by the OS) before calling aioread or aiowrite, and then detect a change of state by checking aio_return.

The aioread and aiowrite Functions

The aioread and aiowrite functions are used to initiate an asynchronous read or write respectively.

```
cc [ flag  ... ] file ... -laio [ library ... ]
#include <sys/types.h>
#include <sys/asynch.h>

int aioread (int fildes, char *bufp, int bufs, off_t offset, int whence,
    aio_result_t *resultp) ;

int aiowrite (int fildes, const char *bufp, int bufs, off_t offset, int whence,
    aio_result_t *resultp) ;
```

> Both return: 0 if OK, −1 on error

The aioread function (which should not be confused with the aio_read function in the realtime library) initiates an asynchronous operation to read *bufs* bytes of data from the file descriptor *fildes* into the buffer pointed to by *bufp,* and returns control to the calling function; the read happens concurrently with other activity in the calling process. Similarly, the `aiowrite` function initiates an asynchronous operation to write *bufs* bytes of data from the buffer pointed to by *bufp* to the file descriptor *fildes*, and returns control to the calling function. As with `aioread`, the write happens concurrently with other activity in the calling process.

If the file specified by *fildes* is capable of seeking, the read or write operation starts at the position specified by *whence* and *offset*. As with `lseek` and other functions, setting *whence* to `SEEK_SET` will cause the read or write to start at *offset* bytes into the file, `SEEK_CUR` will start the read or write at *offset* bytes relative to the current location, and `SEEK_END` will start the read or write at *offset* bytes relative to the end of the file.

If the file is not capable of seeking, the read or write operation starts at the current file position, and the *whence* and *offset* parameters are ignored.

As we stated previously, the result of the operation is stored in the `aio_result_t` structure pointed to by *resultp*.

We should be aware of a few things when using these functions. The first is that neither `aioread` nor `aiowrite` update the file pointer for files capable of seeking. This means that if we want to perform sequential asynchronous I/O operations on these devices, we must manage the file pointer ourselves by using the *whence* and *offset* parameters.

Second, we should not refer to the buffer pointed to by *bufp* until the operation is complete. This is because the buffer is in use by the OS.

Third, each outstanding I/O request should use a different result buffer. Once an operation is complete, its result buffer may be reused.

Finally, calls to `close`, `exit`, and `execve` will block until all pending asynchronous I/O operations can be cancelled by the OS.

The `aiowait` Function

We can wait for an asynchronous I/O operation to complete by calling the `aiowait` function.

```
cc [ flag  ... ] file ... -laio [ library ... ]
#include <sys/asynch.h>
#include <sys/time.h>

aio_result_t *aiowait (const struct timeval *timeout);
```
                    Returns: a pointer to the result if OK, 0 if the timeout expires, or −1 on error

The `aiowait` function suspends the calling process until one of its outstanding asynchronous I/O operations completes.

The *timeout* argument specifies how long `aiowait` should wait for the operation to complete. If *timeout* is a NULL pointer, `aiowait` will block indefinitely; otherwise, it should be a pointer to a `timeval` structure (which we described in Section 13.16). A poll can be performed by setting the members of the `timeval` structure to 0.

Calling `aiowait` is the only way to remove an asynchronous notification from its queue. It can be called by the main program or the `SIGPOLL` signal handler. We should also note that one `SIGPOLL` signal may represent several queued events.

The `aiocancel` Function

We can cancel a pending asynchronous I/O operation by using the `aiocancel` function.

```
cc [ flag  ... ] file ... -laio [ library ... ]
#include <sys/asynch.h>

int aiocancel (aio_result_t *resultp);
```
                                                    Returns: 0 if OK, −1 on error

The `aiocancel` function cancels the asynchronous I/O operation associated with the result buffer pointed to by *resultp*. If the operation in progress cannot immediately be cancelled, `aiocanel` will not wait.

If an asynchronous I/O operation is successfully cancelled, the calling process will not receive the `SIGPOLL` completion signal.

Although the `aioread`, `aiowrite`, `aiowait`, and `aiocancel` functions are specific to Solaris, they have POSIX-defined analogues called `aio_read`, `aio_write`, `aio_waitn`, and `aio_cancel` respectively. Portable applications should use the POSIX functions in preference to the ones we describe here; however, they are part of the realtime library, and are therefore beyond the scope of this text.

13.22 The `readv` and `writev` Functions

We can perform I/O on data in several noncontiguous buffers in a single logical transaction. We could either issue multiple `read`s and `write`s, or we could use the `readv` and `writev` functions. Using these functions allows us to perform operations known as *scatter read*s and *gather write*s.

```
#include <sys/uio.h>

ssize_t readv (int fildes, const struct iovec *iov, int iovcnt);

ssize_t writev (int fildes, const struct iovec *iov, int iovcnt);
```
                    Both return: number of bytes read or written if OK, −1 on error

The `readv` function reads data from the file descriptor *fildes*, which is placed in the buffers specified by the array of `iovec` structures pointed to by *iov*. The `iovec` structure has two members:

```
typedef struct iovec {
    void    *iov_base;      /* Points to the buffer */
    size_t  iov_len;        /* The size of the buffer */
} iovec_t;
```

The number of `iovec` structures in the *iov* array is specified by *iovcnt*, which should be between 1 and `IOV_MAX` inclusive. The constant `IOV_MAX` is defined in `<limits.h>`. Figure 13.13 illustrates this arrangement.

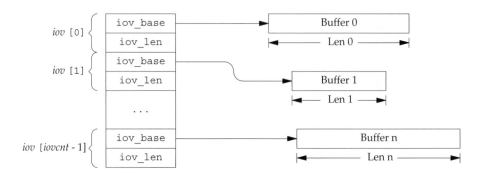

Figure 13.13 Details of the array of `iovec` structures used by `readv` and `writev`.

Each buffer is completely filled before the next is used. Upon successful completion, `readv` returns the number of bytes read; 0 is returned when the end of file is reached and there is no more data.

The `writev` function writes the data in the buffers to the file descriptor *fildes*. Each buffer is fully written before the next is used. On success, `writev` returns the number of bytes written, which would normally be the sum of all the `iov_len` members.

Example: Comparing `writev` to multiple `writes` and buffer copies

Suppose we have a program that writes data from multiple buffers in a single logical transaction. For example, we could have a function that writes out a variable length record and precedes it with another record that contains the length of the variable length record. (We might do this because we want to be able to optimize the searching of records linearly without encoding the record length in the record itself.) We can accomplish this three ways:

1. We could call `write` twice: once for each buffer.
2. We could allocate a new buffer big enough for both items of data, copy both buffers to the new one, and call `write` once to write the new buffer to disk.
3. We could call `writev`, writing both buffers in one transaction.

Program 13.12 implements the third of these options.

When we run Program 13.12, we end up with a file 26 million bytes in size. Let's compare the three methods of writing the two buffers. Figure 13.14 tabulates the times taken to run the three versions (we don't show the listings for the other two methods; we just changed `write_buf` function).

advanced_io/writev.c

```
 1 #include <sys/types.h>
 2 #include <sys/stat.h>
 3 #include <fcntl.h>
 4 #include <unistd.h>
 5 #include <sys/uio.h>
 6 #include "ssp.h"

 7 static void write_buf (int fd, char *buf, int buf_size);

 8 int main (void)
 9 {
10     int fd;
11     char buf [256];
12     int i;

13     if ((fd = open ("/tmp/test", O_RDWR | O_CREAT | O_TRUNC,
14         FILE_PERMS)) == -1) {
15         err_msg ("Can't open temp file");
16     }

17     for (i = 0; i < 100000; i++)
18         write_buf (fd, buf, sizeof (buf));

19     close (fd);
20     return (0);
21 }

22 static void write_buf (int fd, char *buf, int buf_size)
23 {
24     struct iovec iov [2];

25     iov [0].iov_base = (char *) &buf_size;
26     iov [0].iov_len = sizeof (int);
27     iov [1].iov_base = buf;
28     iov [1].iov_len = buf_size;

29     if (writev (fd, iov, 2) != sizeof (int) + buf_size)
30         err_msg ("writev failed");
31 }
```

advanced_io/writev.c

Program 13.12   Using writev to write multiple buffers.

Method	Real	User	Sys
Using writev	1.30	0.12	1.11
Using two writes	1.82	0.28	1.48
Copy to a buffer, then one write	1.25	0.24	0.94

Figure 13.14   Timing results for different methods of writing two buffers.

By adding up the User and Sys time for each result, we can calculate the total CPU time required for each method. Using writev and copying the two buffers to a new buffer and calling write once took roughly the same amount of time: 1.23 seconds for writev, and 1.18 seconds for the buffer copy and `write` (issuing two writes took a total of 1.76 seconds).

As we would expect, calling `write` twice increases the Sys time overhead by about 50 percent. Interestingly, the time for using `writev` is nearly the same as copying to a buffer and using one `write` (at least it is in this simple example, where we just declared a local array of `chars` big enough to hold the result; a real program might use `malloc` to allocate the buffer instead). This is probably because in our simple example we only had two buffers to copy. A real-life application might have several buffers that form a single logical transaction. In this case, we would expect the difference in CPU time between copying buffers with a single `write` and using `writev` to be larger.

Although superior performance is the main reason for preferring `writev` over copying buffers and calling `write`, another reason is that using `writev` is more straightforward, and hence, less error prone.

13.23 The `sendfile` and `sendfilev` Functions

Sometimes it is useful to copy the contents of a file (or several files) to a file descriptor. An example of when we might want to send a file might be an FTP server, and an example of when we might want to send several files efficiently is an HTTP server. In the case of the HTTP server, we might want to send all of the local files referenced in the page we're sending (e.g., images, JavaScript source, or Java applets). From Solaris 8 7/01, we can use the `sendfile` and `sendfilev` functions to perform these tasks.

The `sendfile` Function

We can copy a file to a file descriptor by using the `sendfile` function.

```
cc [ flag  ... ] file ... -lsendfile [ library ... ]
#include <sys/sendfile.h>

ssize_t sendfile (int out_fd, int in_fd, off_t *off, size_t len);
```

Returns: number of bytes written if OK, −1 on error

The `sendfile` function copies *len* bytes of data from the file descriptor specified by *in_fd* to the file descriptor specified by *out_fd*, starting from the offset specified by *off*. The *in_fd* argument must be a file descriptor associated with a regular file that has been opened for reading, and *out_fd* must be file descriptor that has been opened for writing, or a connected AF_INET or AF_INET6 socket of type SOCK_STREAM. (For details about programming with sockets, see [Stevens, Fenner, and Rudoff 2004].)

When we call `sendfile`, the *off* argument points to a variable that holds the file offset from which data will be read. Upon successful completion, this variable will be set to the offset of the byte following the last byte that was read. The current file offset of *in_fd* is not modified by `sendfile`, but the file offset for *out_fd* is modified if *out_fd* is associated with a regular file.

We can also use the sendfile function to send buffers by setting *in_fd* to SFV_FD_SELF and pointing *off* to the buffer to be copied.

Example: Copying a file using sendfile

Program 13.13 shows how we can use sendfile to copy a file.

—— *advanced_io/sendfile1.c*

```
 1 #include <stdio.h>
 2 #include <unistd.h>
 3 #include <sys/sendfile.h>
 4 #include <sys/types.h>
 5 #include <sys/stat.h>
 6 #include <fcntl.h>
 7 #include "ssp.h"

 8 int main (int argc, char **argv)
 9 {
10     struct stat buf;
11     int in_fd;
12     int out_fd;
13     off_t off;
14     ssize_t res;

15     if (argc != 3)
16         err_quit ("Usage: sendfile1 source_file dest_file");

17     if ((in_fd = open (argv [1], O_RDONLY)) == -1)
18         err_msg ("Can't open %s", argv [1]);
19     if (fstat (in_fd, &buf) == -1)
20         err_msg ("Can't stat %s", argv [1]);

21     if ((out_fd = open (argv [2], O_WRONLY | O_TRUNC | O_CREAT,
22         FILE_PERMS)) == -1) {
23         err_msg ("Can't open %s", argv [2]);
24     }

25     off = 0;
26     if ((res = sendfile (out_fd, in_fd, &off, buf.st_size)) == -1)
27         err_msg ("sendfile failed");
28     else
29         printf ("Copied %d bytes\n", res);

30     close (in_fd);
31     close (out_fd);

32     return (0);
33 }
```

—— *advanced_io/sendfile1.c*

Program 13.13 Copying a file using sendfile.

Open the input file

17–18 Open the file we're copying for reading.

19–20 Get the status of the file we just opened. We do this to determine the file's length.

Open the output file

21–24 Open the output file for writing, creating or truncating it as necessary.

Copy the file

25 Initialize the file offset to 0.

26–29 Call `sendfile` to copy the file, printing the number of bytes copied if `sendfile` successfully completed.

Close file descriptors

30–31 Close the file descriptors we previously opened.

Let's run Program 13.13 to copy a file:

```
$ ./sendfile1 sendfile1.c foo
Copied 797 bytes
$ ls -l foo
-rw-r--r--   1 rich     staff          797 Jun 18 19:31 foo
$ diff sendfile1.c foo
```

The files are the same, indicating a successful copy.

Example: Copy a buffer using `sendfile`

Program 13.14 is a trivial example of how we can write a buffer to a file descriptor using `sendfile`.

Program 13.14 is similar to Program 13.13; the differences are that we only open an output file, and we use `SFV_FD_SELF` for the source file descriptor.

Running Program 13.14 gives us the following results:

```
$ ./sendfile2 foo
Copied 14 bytes
$ ls -l foo
-rw-r--r--   1 rich     staff           14 Jun 18 20:04 foo
$ cat foo
Hello, World!
```

Although using `sendfile` in this manner appears to offer little advantage over using `write`, it does avoid costly buffer copies between the process and the kernel. This technique comes into its own when we have several buffers and files we want to copy to a file descriptor (the `writev` function we described in the previous section only works with multiple buffers; it does not work with file descriptors). And for *that* we need the `sendfilev` function.

The `sendfilev` Function

We can copy several buffers and files to a file descriptor by using the `sendfilev` function.

advanced_io/sendfile2.c

```
 1 #include <stdio.h>
 2 #include <unistd.h>
 3 #include <sys/sendfile.h>
 4 #include <sys/types.h>
 5 #include <sys/stat.h>
 6 #include <fcntl.h>
 7 #include "ssp.h"

 8 static char buf [LINE_LEN];

 9 int main (int argc, char **argv)
10 {
11     int out_fd;
12     off_t off;
13     ssize_t len;
14     ssize_t res;

15     if (argc != 2)
16         err_quit ("Usage: sendfile2 dest_file");

17     if ((out_fd = open (argv [1], O_WRONLY | O_TRUNC | O_CREAT,
18         FILE_PERMS)) == -1) {
19         err_msg ("Can't open %s", argv [1]);
20     }

21     len = snprintf (buf, LINE_LEN, "Hello, World!\n");

22     off = (off_t) buf;
23     if ((res = sendfile (out_fd, SFV_FD_SELF, &off, len)) == -1)
24         err_msg ("sendfile failed");
25     else
26         printf ("Copied %d bytes\n", res);

27     close (out_fd);

28     return (0);
29 }
```

advanced_io/sendfile2.c

Program 13.14 Writing a buffer using sendfile.

```
cc [ flag  ... ] file ... -lsendfile [ library ... ]
#include <sys/sendfile.h>

ssize_t sendfilev (int *fildes*, const struct sendfilevec *vec*, int *sfvcnt*,
    size_t *xferred*);
```

Returns: number of bytes written if OK, –1 on error

The sendfilev function attempts to write the data from the *vec* array of buffers to the file descriptor *fildes*. The number of elements in *vec* is specified by *sfvcnt*, and *fildes* must refer to a file descriptor that has been opened for writing, or a connected AF_NCA,

AF_INET, or AF_INET6 socket of type SOCK_STREAM. The *xferred* argument points to a buffer into which the number of bytes written to *fildes* is stored.

We can think of sendfilev as being conceptually like a combination of sendfile and writev, the difference being that sendfilev can send data from buffers or file descriptors, whereas writev is limited to just writing multiple buffers.

The *vec* argument points to an array of *sfvcnt* sendfilevec structures, which consists of the following members:

```
typedef struct sendfilevec {
    int     sfv_fd;     /* Input file descriptor */
    uint_t  sfv_flag;   /* Reserved for flags; set to 0 */
    off_t   sfv_off;    /* The offset to start reading from */
    size_t  sfv_len;    /* The amount of data to write */
} sendfilevec_t;
```

To send a file, sfv_fd must be a file descriptor associated with a regular file that has been opened for reading, sfv_off should be set to the offset from which data will be read, and sfv_len should be set to the number of bytes to transfer. The sfv_flag member is reserved and should be set to 0.

To send a buffer, we must set sfv_fd to SFV_FD_SELF, sfv_off should point to the data buffer to be written, and sfv_len should be set to the size of the buffer.

Example: Copying buffers and a file using sendfilev

Program 13.15 shows how we can use sendfilev to write a file and some buffers to a file descriptor.

Initialize first vector

19–22 We set up the first vector by setting the sfv_fd member to SFV_FD_SELF, which indicates that this vector is associated with a buffer rather than a file descriptor. We also set the flags to 0 and arrange for the buffer to point to our header string.

Initialize second vector

23–26 We open the requested input file and get its status. We do this so that we can later determine the file's length.

27–29 Set the flag and offset to 0, and set the length to the file's length, limited to 100 bytes.

Initialize the third vector

30–35 Set up the third vector in a similar manner to the first, except we use a different buffer.

Open the output file

34–37 Open the output file for writing, creating or truncating it as necessary.

Copy the vectors

38–41 Call sendfilev to write out the vectors, printing the number of bytes copied if sendfilev successfully completed.

Close file descriptors

42–43 Close the file descriptors we previously opened.

advanced_io/sendfilev.c

```
 1 #include <stdio.h>
 2 #include <unistd.h>
 3 #include <sys/sendfile.h>
 4 #include <sys/types.h>
 5 #include <sys/stat.h>
 6 #include <fcntl.h>
 7 #include "ssp.h"

 8 static char header_buf [LINE_LEN];
 9 static char trailer_buf [LINE_LEN];
10 int main (int argc, char **argv)
11 {
12     struct stat buf;
13     int out_fd;
14     ssize_t res;
15     size_t xferred;
16     sendfilevec_t vec [3];

17     if (argc != 3)
18         err_quit ("Usage: sendfilev source_file dest_file");

19     vec [0].sfv_fd = SFV_FD_SELF;
20     vec [0].sfv_flag = 0;
21     vec [0].sfv_off = (off_t) header_buf;
22     vec [0].sfv_len = snprintf (header_buf, LINE_LEN, "*** Header ***\n");

23     if ((vec [1].sfv_fd = open (argv [1], O_RDONLY)) == -1)
24         err_msg ("Can't open %s", argv [1]);
25     if (fstat (vec [1].sfv_fd, &buf) == -1)
26         err_msg ("Can't stat %s", argv [1]);
27     vec [1].sfv_flag = 0;
28     vec [1].sfv_off = 0;
29     vec [1].sfv_len = (buf.st_size > 100) ? 100 : buf.st_size;

30     vec [2].sfv_fd = SFV_FD_SELF;
31     vec [2].sfv_flag = 0;
32     vec [2].sfv_off = (off_t) trailer_buf;
33     vec [2].sfv_len = snprintf (trailer_buf, LINE_LEN, "\n*** Trailer ***\n");

34     if ((out_fd = open (argv [2], O_WRONLY | O_TRUNC | O_CREAT,
35         FILE_PERMS)) == -1) {
36         err_msg ("Can't open %s", argv [2]);
37     }

38     if ((res = sendfilev (out_fd, vec, 3, &xferred)) == -1)
39         err_msg ("sendfilev failed");
40     else
41         printf ("Wrote %d bytes\n", res);

42     close (vec [1].sfv_fd);
43     close (out_fd);

44     return (0);
45 }
```

advanced_io/sendfilev.c

Program 13.15 Copying a file and two buffers using sendfilev.

Running Program 13.15 gives the following results:

```
$ ./sendfilev sendfilev.c foo
Wrote 132 bytes
$ cat foo
*** Header ***
#include <stdio.h>
#include <unistd.h>
#include <sys/sendfile.h>
#include <sys/types.h>
#include <sy
*** Trailer ***
```

13.24 Memory Mapped I/O

Memory mapped I/O is what we do when we map a file on disk into the address space of a process. Once this mapping is established, a process can access the contents of the file as though it were memory (e.g., using pointer, array subscripts, etc.). When we read bytes from the mapping, the corresponding bytes from the file are paged in, hence the term *demand paged*. If the mapped pages are modified, the corresponding bytes are automatically written to the file. In other words, using this technique lets us perform file I/O without using read or write, which is usually (but not always) more efficient than reading the whole file into memory, especially if we use only a small part of the file.

One of the most important uses for memory mapped files is the implementation of dynamically shared libraries. Rather than copying all the library routines into the executable program (which is what happens when we use *static linking*), the appropriate part of the shared library is mapped into the address space of the process.

Another important use for memory mapped files is for randomly accessing binary data in a large file, for example, the index file for a database. If we need to retrieve only a small number of items from the database, it is a waste of resources to read the whole index into memory. Using a memory map so that only the parts we need are paged in is more efficient, making our program run faster and putting less load on the system.

Two processes can share memory by mmapping the same file. This method of sharing memory is easier to use than either of the two alternatives (POSIX and System V shared memory).

An example of when using memory mapping is less efficient than using read or write is when we perform heavy random I/O in large chunks. Using a memory mapping may result in the chunks being read in several transactions (as each part is paged in), whereas a single read might request the whole of the chunk in one transaction (from the point of view of the process, that is. Internally, read is converted into getpage calls.).

13.25 The mmap and munmap Functions

The first thing we must do if we want to perform memory mapped I/O is to map a portion of the file into a region of memory using the mmap function.

```
#include <sys/mman.h>

void *mmap (void *addr, size_t len, int prot, int flags, int fildes, off_t off);
```
                    Returns: starting address of mapped region if OK, MAP_FAILED on error

The mmap function establishes a mapping between the file descriptor *fildes* and the address space of the calling process. The mapping for the file starts at the offset *off* for *len* bytes. The start address in the process' address space of the region is returned by a successful call to mmap, and is determined by *addr* and *flags*. The region is *len* bytes in size. Figure 13.15 illustrates this arrangement.

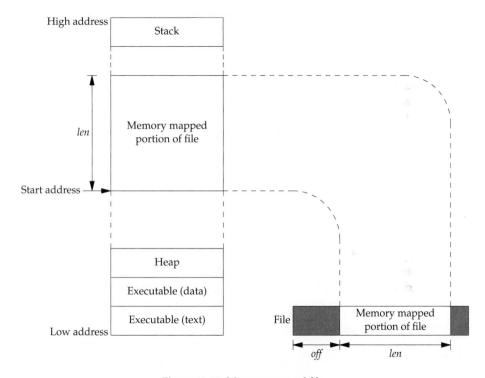

Figure 13.15 Memory mapped file.

The *prot* argument determines the protections on the memory mapped file segment, and should be a bitwise-OR of one or more of the following constants:

PROT_READ   Data from the region can be read.

PROT_WRITE   Data from the region can be written.

PROT_EXEC   Data from the region can be executed.

PROT_NONE   Data from the region cannot be accessed. This is mutually exclusive with the other values *prot* may have.

If `PROT_WRITE` is specified, the file represented by *fildes* must have been open for writing, unless `MAP_PRIVATE` is specified in *flags*.

The *flags* argument provides other information about the handling of the mapped region, and should be a bitwise-OR of one or more of the following constants:

`MAP_SHARED`	Changes to the data in the region are shared. This means that data written to the mapped region will be written to the underlying file. Either this flag or `MAP_PRIVATE` (see the following) must be specified, but not both.
`MAP_PRIVATE`	Changes to the data in the region are private. The first time part of the private region is written to, a private copy of the page is created, and the write (and subsequent writes) is redirected to the copy. Further references to the page are satisfied from the copy. One example of where this copy on write behaviour would be useful is a debugger. Any instructions that get patched will be updated in the private copy of the page rather than the file. Either this flag or `MAP_SHARED` must be specified, but not both.
`MAP_FIXED`	Interpret *addr* exactly. If the `MAP_FIXED` is successful, the `mmap` function returns *addr*. Use of this flag is discouraged, however, since it hinders portability and may prevent the OS from making the most efficient use of the system's resources.
	If `MAP_FIXED` is not specified, a non-zero *addr* is used as a hint to the kernel as to where to place the mapped region in the address space of the process.
	Specifying an *addr* of 0 is preferred because it allows the kernel to place the region wherever it deems best.
	`MAP_FIXED` and `MAP_ALIGN` are mutually exclusive flags.
`MAP_NORESERVE`	Do not reserve swap space. If this flag is not specified, the creation of a writable `MAP_PRIVATE` mapping reserves an amount of swap space equal to the size of the mapping. When the mapped region is written to, the reserved swap space is used to hold the private copies of the data.
	The result of writing to a `MAP_PRIVATE` region with the `MAP_NORESERVE` flag specified depends on the current availability of swap space. If sufficient swap space is available, the write succeeds, and a private copy of the written page will be created. However, if sufficient swap space is not available, the write will fail, and a `SIGBUS` or `SIGSEGV` signal will be delivered to the writing process.
`MAP_ANON`	Map anonymous memory. When this (new with Solaris 8) flag is set and *fildes* is equal to −1, the `mmap` function provides a direct method of providing zero-filled anonymous pages to

	the caller. Using this flag is the same as passing an open file descriptor that is associated with /dev/zero to mmap, with MAP_ANON removed from the *flags* argument.
MAP_ALIGN	Interpret *addr* as the required alignment for the memory mapped region. This must be 0, or a power of two multiple of the page size as returned by sysconf (which we discuss in Section 8.3). If *addr* is 0, the kernel chooses a suitable alignment. This flag was introduced with Solaris 8.

MAP_ALIGN and MAP_FIXED are mutually exclusive flags.

The value of *off* and *addr* (if MAP_FIXED is specified) must be aligned on a page boundary (a suitable value can be obtained by passing _SC_PAGESIZE or _SC_PAGE_SIZE to the sysconf function we discuss in Section 8.3). As *addr* and *len* are frequently set to 0, this limitation presents no problems.

Partial pages at the end of a mapped object are zero filled, so if we mmap a 192-byte file on a machine that uses an UltraSPARC processor (which has a page size of 8192 bytes), the remaining 8000 bytes will be read as zero. Any changes we make to the last page beyond the end of the mapped region are not written to the underlying object.

We can't use mmap to extend a file; the shared memory region (i.e., *len*) cannot be bigger than the size of the file we're mmapping. We can use ftruncate to work around this restriction (as we do in Program 13.16).

Memory mapped regions are inherited by children across a fork, but not an exec.

When we mmap a file, its reference count is incremented. Closing the file does not decrement the reference count, which means that we can close the file descriptor we passed to mmap if we have no further use for it.

There are two ways to decrement the reference count:

1. Terminate the process (which causes all memory mapped regions to be automatically unmapped).
2. Call munmap to unmap the region.

The munmap function has the following prototype:

```
#include <sys/mman.h>

int munmap (void *addr, size_t len);
                                              Returns: 0 if OK, −1 on error
```

The munmap function removes the mapping for pages in the range from *addr* to *addr* + *len*. The *len* argument is rounded up to the next multiple of the system's page size.

Example: Copying a file using mmap and memcpy

Program 13.16 copies a file by using the mmap and memcpy function calls (this is in fact how the cp command works).

advanced_io/mcopy.c

```
 1 #include <stdio.h>
 2 #include <sys/types.h>
 3 #include <sys/stat.h>
 4 #include <fcntl.h>
 5 #include <unistd.h>
 6 #include <string.h>
 7 #include <sys/mman.h>
 8 #include "ssp.h"

 9 int main (int argc, char **argv)
10 {
11     int src_fd;
12     int dest_fd;
13     char *src_ptr;
14     char *dest_ptr;
15     struct stat stat_buf;
16     off_t len;

17     if (argc != 3)
18         err_quit ("Usage: mcopy src dest");

19     if ((src_fd = open (argv [1], O_RDONLY)) == -1)
20         err_msg ("Can't open source file %s", argv [1]);

21     if (fstat (src_fd, &stat_buf) == -1)
22         err_msg ("Can't fstat");
23     len = stat_buf.st_size;

24     if ((dest_fd = open (argv [2], O_RDWR | O_TRUNC | O_CREAT,
25         FILE_PERMS)) == -1) {
26         err_msg ("Can't open destination file %s", argv [2]);
27     }

28     if (ftruncate (dest_fd, len) == -1)
29         err_msg ("Can't ftruncate");

30     if ((src_ptr = mmap (0, len, PROT_READ, MAP_SHARED,
31         src_fd, 0)) == MAP_FAILED) {
32         err_msg ("Can't mmap source file");
33     }

34     if ((dest_ptr = mmap (0, len, PROT_WRITE, MAP_SHARED,
35         dest_fd, 0)) == MAP_FAILED) {
36         err_msg ("Can't mmap destination file");
37     }

38     close (src_fd);
39     close (dest_fd);

40     memcpy (dest_ptr, src_ptr, len);

41     return (0);
42 }
```

advanced_io/mcopy.c

Program 13.16 Copy a file using mmap and memcpy.

Open source file

19–20 We open the source for reading.

21–23 Use fstat to determine the file size. We need this so that we can make the destination file the right size and mmap the correct-sized region.

Open destination file

24–27 Open the destination file for writing, truncating or creating it as necessary.

Set the size of the destination file

28–29 Force the size of the destination file to be the correct size by using the ftruncate function. If we didn't do this, the file copy would fail.

Copy the file

30–37 Map the files into the address space of our process.

38–39 Close the file descriptors we previously opened. We do this for two reasons: the first is to show that it is possible to do so, and the second is because it is good practice to close file descriptors when we no longer require them. Despite our closing of the files, the memory mapping is still valid, so the program works as expected.

40 This line actually performs the copy. Bytes read from the buffer pointed to by src_ptr are read from the file, and similarly, bytes written to the dest_ptr buffer are written out to the destination file.

Something to be aware of when copying files using mmap and memcpy is that should the partition to which we are copying become full before the memcpy completes, a SIGSEGV or SIGBUS signal will be sent to our process. We'll see in Chapter 17 how we can catch these signals so that we can handle this error condition gracefully.

In Chapter 4, we used Program 4.2 to copy a file using read and write. Let's compare the time it takes Programs 4.2 and 13.16 to copy the same 10 megabyte file (using a buffer size of 8192 bytes in the case of Program 4.2). Figure 13.16 shows the results.

Method	Real	User	Sys
Using read and write	0.14	0.01	0.13
Using mmap and memcpy	0.03	0.00	0.03

Figure 13.16 Comparing the time to copy a file using Programs 4.2 and 13.16.

Looking at the results, the total CPU time (i.e., User + Sys) makes up the majority of the time when we run Program 4.2 (the fact that we used a tmpfs file system to eliminate variations because of the network explains this). However, the total CPU time for Program 13.16 is only 0.03 seconds. This is significantly faster than Program 4.2 because the kernel is doing I/O directly to and from the memory mapped buffers. When we use read and write, the kernel must copy the data from its own buffers to those of our process.

The difference between the two results would be more apparent if we used a bigger data set or a slower CPU (a 450 MHz UltraSPARC II processor was used for this test).

Example: Memory mapping `/dev/zero`

We'll see in Section 20.5 how unrelated processes can share a segment of memory, but if related process (i.e., those that share a common ancestor) want to share memory segments, we can use another technique: mapping `/dev/zero`.

Reading from `/dev/zero` gives us an infinite stream of 0 bytes, and anything written to `/dev/zero` is accepted and silently discarded. It also has three interesting properties when it is memory mapped:

- A memory region is created whose size is that of the second argument to `mmap`, rounded up to the next page boundary.
- This memory region is initialized to 0.
- Multiple related processes can share the region if a common ancestor passed the `MAP_SHARED` flag to `mmap`.

Program 13.17 shows an example of how we can use this device.

Map `/dev/zero` into our address space

13–19   We open `/dev/zero` and map it into our address space, specifying the size of an integer. Once the region is successfully mapped, we close the file descriptor.

Increment shared counter, alternating between parent and child

20–21   Initialize our parent and child synchronization facility. (We describe this and why it's needed in Section 15.10.)

25–44   The parent and child take turns in incrementing the counter. The memory mapped region is initialized to 0 by `mmap`. The parent increments it to 1, then the child increments it to 2, then the parent runs again, incrementing it to 3. This continues until we are finished.

One of the advantages of using `/dev/zero` like this is that an actual file doesn't need to exist before we call `mmap`. Mapping `/dev/zero` causes a mapped region of the specified size to be created automatically.

From Solaris 8, we can achieve exactly the same results by passing `mmap` a file descriptor value of −1 and setting the `MAP_ANON` flag. Memory mapped in this manner is sometimes called *anonymous memory*, because it is not associated with a pathname via a file descriptor. If we wanted to change Program 13.17 to use anonymous memory, we could replace lines 13 to 19 with the following:

```
if ((ptr = mmap (0, sizeof (int), PROT_READ | PROT_WRITE,
    MAP_SHARED | MAP_ANON, -1, 0)) == MAP_FAILED) {
    err_msg ("mmap failed");
}
```

We could then also remove the calls to `open` and `close`, and delete the variable `fd`; they no longer serve any useful purpose.

advanced_io/devzero.c

```
1 #include <unistd.h>
2 #include <fcntl.h>
3 #include <sys/mman.h>
4 #include "ssp.h"

5 #define NUM_ITERS 1000

6 int main (void)
7 {
8     int i;
9     int fd;
10    int counter;
11    pid_t pid;
12    int *ptr;

13    if ((fd = open ("/dev/zero", O_RDWR)) == -1)
14        err_msg ("open failed");
15    if ((ptr = mmap (0, sizeof (int), PROT_READ | PROT_WRITE, MAP_SHARED,
16        fd, 0)) == MAP_FAILED) {
17        err_msg ("mmap failed");
18    }
19    close (fd);

20    if (ssp_tell_wait_init () == -1)
21        err_msg ("ssp_tell_wait_init failed");

22    switch (pid = fork ()) {
23        case -1:
24            err_msg ("Can't fork");

25        case 0:
26            for (i = 1; i < NUM_ITERS + 1; i += 2) {
27                if (ssp_wait_parent () == -1)
28                    err_msg ("ssp_wait_parent failed");
29                if ((counter = (*ptr)++) != i)
30                    err_quit ("Child: Got %d, expected %d", counter, i);
31                ssp_tell_parent (getppid ());
32            }
33            _exit (0);

34        default:
35            for (i = 0; i < NUM_ITERS; i += 2) {
36                if ((counter = ((*ptr)++)) != i)
37                    err_quit ("Parent: Got %d, expected %d", counter, i);
38                if (ssp_tell_child (pid) == -1)
39                    err_msg ("ssp_tell_child failed");
40                if (ssp_wait_child () == -1)
41                    err_msg ("ssp_wait_child failed");
42            }
43            break;
44    }

45    return (0);
46 }
```

advanced_io/devzero.c

Program 13.17 Sharing memory between related processes using /dev/zero.

13.26 The `mprotect` Function

Once we have established a memory mapped region using `mmap`, we can change its protection using the `mprotect` function.

```
#include <sys/mman.h>

int mprotect (void *addr, size_t len, int prot);
```
Returns: 0 if OK, −1 on error

The `mprotect` function changes the access protections on the memory mapped region specified by the range *addr* to *addr* + *len* to those specified by *prot*. The *len* argument is rounded up to the next multiple of the page size, and the valid values of *prot* are the same as those for the *prot* argument of the `mmap` function.

If `mprotect` should fail, it is possible that some of the specified pages will have had their protections changed. The pages affected are those from *addr* to the page immediately before the one that caused the failure.

13.27 The `madvise` Function

The kernel is responsible for paging a mapped file into memory. To make this more efficient, we can use the `madvise` function to give hints to the kernel about how we will use the mapped region, and hence how to best page it in.

```
#include <sys/types.h>
#include <sys/mman.h>

int madvise (void *addr, size_t len, int advice);
```
Returns: 0 if OK, −1 on error

The `madvise` function tells the kernel that the memory mapped region in the range from *addr* to *addr* + *len* will be accessed in the type of pattern specified by *advice*.

The *advice* argument must be one of the following nine constants.

`MADV_NORMAL`	No special treatment. This is the default characteristic for mapped pages, where accessing memory in the address range causes data to be read in from the mapped file. The kernel tries to read in as much data from the file as is reasonable on the assumption that other accesses will be in the same locality.
	The pages are kept in a cache until they are either freed or stolen by other processes. This page stealing happens quite regularly, but only has an adverse affect on system performance if a large amount of memory is being accessed.

MADV_RANDOM   Expect random page accesses. This tells the kernel to only read in a minimum amount of data from the file in any one access. The likelihood of another reference in the same locality is smaller because of the random page access pattern, so there's no point in reading data in advance.

MADV_SEQUENTIAL   Expect sequential page accesses, i.e., that the pages in this range are likely to be accessed only once, so the resources consumed by pages that have already been accessed can be freed. We could use this option in Program 13.16 to increase performance on systems with limited memory resources.

MADV_WILLNEED   We will need these pages. The kernel starts reading the specified range into memory as soon as possible. This allows programs to access data for the first time faster, because the need to read the file in from a file first will be reduced if not eliminated. Usually, the file isn't read until the associated memory locations are accessed (the read aheads described above notwithstanding); using this option reads in the file before the associated memory is accessed.

MADV_DONTNEED   This tells the kernel that we no longer need these pages, so it starts freeing the resources associated with the address range.

MADV_FREE   This tells the kernel that the contents of the address range are no longer important and will be overwritten. When there is a demand for memory, the kernel will free pages associated with the address range. The next time the data is accessed, the page referenced will be zero filled. If MADV_FREE is not specified, freed pages that are accessed again will contain their old data.

                     This value can't be used on mappings that have underlying file objects.

MADV_ACCESS_LWP   This tells the kernel that the next LWP that accesses the specified range will access it most heavily. The kernel uses this information to allocate memory and other resources for the specified range and LWP accordingly. This flag was introduced with Solaris 9 12/02.

MADV_ACCESS_MANY   This tells the kernel that many processes or LWPs (or both) will access the specified range randomly across the machine. As a result, the kernel tries to allocate memory and other resources for the specified range accordingly. This flag was introduced with Solaris 9 12/02.

MADV_ACCESS_DEFAULT This resets the kernel's expectation for how the specified range will be accessed to the default. This flag was introduced with Solaris 9 12/02.

If we know how our programs will access memory mapped objects, we should use madvise to increase system performance. This is especially true for very busy systems or those with limited resources.

13.28 The msync Function

When we memory map an object, there are potentially two copies of that object: the one in memory, and the one in *backing storage*. Memory mapped objects require backing storage so that their pages can be stolen should the system get short of memory. The data in the stolen pages is stored in its backing store until it is read in again.

The backing storage for a MAP_SHARED mapping is the file associated with the mapping, and MAP_PRIVATE regions use their swap space as their backing storage. The kernel periodically synchronizes the in memory regions with their backing storage, but some programs need to ensure that the backing storage is in a known state. In much the same way that the fsync function we discussed in Section 10.27 synchronizes file buffers to disk, we can use the msync function to synchronize memory regions to with its backing store.

```
#include <sys/mman.h>

int msync (void *addr, size_t len, int flags);
```
Returns: 0 if OK, −1 on error

The msync function writes all modified pages in the range from *addr* to *addr* + *len* to their backing storage, or invalidates any copies so that further references to the pages will be obtained from their backing storage.

The *flags* argument determines the action to be taken, and is made up from a bitwise-OR of one or more of the following constants:

MS_ASYNC   The backing store is synchronized with the current contents of the region using asynchronous writes. Once all the writes have been scheduled, msync returns.

All write references to the memory region prior to the call to msync are visible by subsequent reads from the file, but writes to the same part of the file prior to the call may or may not be visible by reads from the mapped memory region.

Pages in the specified range that are not modified are written to the backing storage.

MS_SYNC   This option is the same as MS_ASYNC, except that synchronous writes are used to synchronize the backing storage with the region. The `msync` function only returns when all of the writes have been completed.

`MS_INVALIDATE`   This value of *flags* causes the contents of memory to be synchronized with the backing storage (i.e., the opposite to `M_ASYNC` and `M_SYNC`, which cause the backing store to be synchronized with the memory region). All writes to the mapped section of the file made prior to the call to `msync` are visible to subsequent reads from the memory region, and all writes prior to the function call (by any process) to memory regions mapped to the same portion of the file using `MAP_SHARED` are visible to subsequent reads from the region.

As we said before, normal system activity can cause pages to be written to disk, so there is no guarantee that `msync` is the only control over when pages are written to disk or not.

13.29 Locking Pages in Memory

We stated previously that when the system gets short of memory, some pages are written to swap space and reused. Some pages (e.g., those belonging to the text part of an executable) needn't be written to swap, as they are already available from backing storage. When the page is referenced again, it is paged back in from its backing storage. This paging in and out is normal, and if the system isn't very heavily loaded, the performance impact is relatively small.

The `mlock` and `munlock` Functions

To avoid this paging and lock some of our pages in memory, we use the `mlock` function.

```
#include <sys/mman.h>

int mlock (const void *addr, size_t len);

int munlock (const void *addr, size_t len);
```
                                                                   Both return: 0 if OK, −1 on error

The `mlock` function locks the pages in the range *addr* to *addr* + *len* in memory, and the `munlock` function unlocks them. If a writable `MAP_PRIVATE` page is written to, the lock will be transferred to the newly created copy.

A page may be locked more than once by calling `mlock` with different mappings, although locks within a process do not nest; multiple locks on the same memory mapping in the same process will be undone by a single `munlock`. Conversely, two or more processes can establish a lock on a region of memory, and the region will not be unlocked until all processes remove their locks.

If the mapping through which an `mlock` has been performed is removed, an implicit `munlock` is performed. Pages are also unlocked when a page is deleted because of file deletion or truncation.

Locks acquired using mlock are not inherited by child processes across a fork.

Because of their potential impact on system resources, mlock and munlock are available only to privileged processes.

The mlockall and munlockall Functions

The mlock function we just discussed allows us to lock a range of pages. To lock all the pages mapped by an address space, we use mlockall.

```
#include <sys/mman.h>

int mlockall (int flags);

int munlockall (void);
```
                                                              Both return: 0 if OK, −1 on error

The *flags* argument determines which mappings are locked, and should be a bitwise-OR of one or both of the following values:

MCL_CURRENT	Lock all current mappings.
MCL_FUTURE	Lock all future mappings as they are added to the address space, or replace existing mappings if sufficient memory is available.

Locks established using mlockall are not inherited by child processes across a fork.

Memory mappings locked using mlockall (using either option) may be unlocked using the munlockall function, which removes address space locks and locks on mappings in the address space.

Because of their potential impact on system resources, mlockall and munlockall are available only to privileged processes.

The plock Function

Another method we can use to lock all or part of a process in memory is the plock function.

```
#include <sys/lock.h>

int plock (int op);
```
                                                                    Returns: 0 if OK, −1 on error

The plock function locks the segments of the calling process specified by *op* into memory, making them immune to all normal swapping.

The *op* argument specifies the operation to be performed.

PROCLOCK   Lock both the text and the data segments into memory. This is called a *process lock*.

TXTLOCK   Lock the text segment in memory. This is called a *text lock*.

DATLOCK   Lock the data segment in memory. This is called a *data lock*.

PUNLOCK   Remove any locks previously acquired using plock.

The mlock and mlockall functions are the preferred methods of process locking. Because of the potential impact on system resources, plock is available only to privileged processes.

Example: Locking a file in memory

We've seen how an application can lock its own pages in memory. But what if we want to lock a file in memory when the application we're using doesn't do it for us, and we don't have the source code to make to necessary changes? Program 13.18 provides one solution for us.

Program 13.18 opens the file specified on the command line, and then creates a read-only MAP_SHARED memory mapping. The pages of the mapped memory are then locked into memory by using the mlock function, and then the program goes to sleep until a signal is delivered to it. (Because of this, we must run Program 13.18 in the background or in another terminal window.) When a signal is delivered, Program 13.18 terminates, automatically unlocking and unmapping the memory region.

When we run Program 13.18, these are the results we get:

```
$ ./mlock foo
Can't lock file in memory: Not owner
$ su
Password:                               Type in our root password
# ./mlock foo &
1394
# pmap 1394
1394:   ./mlock foo
00010000       8K r-x--  /home/rich/doc/books/ssp/src/advanced_io/mlock
00020000       8K rwx--  /home/rich/doc/books/ssp/src/advanced_io/mlock
FE800000   10240K r--s-  dev:236,58 ino:462942
FF280000     680K r-x--  /usr/lib/libc.so.1
FF33A000      32K rwx--  /usr/lib/libc.so.1
FF380000      16K r-x--  /usr/platform/sun4u/lib/libc_psr.so.1
FF3A0000       8K r-x--  /usr/lib/libdl.so.1
FF3B0000       8K rwx--    [ anon ]
FF3C0000     152K r-x--  /usr/lib/ld.so.1
FF3F6000       8K rwx--  /usr/lib/ld.so.1
FFBFA000      24K rw---    [ stack ]
 total     11184K
# ls -il foo
   462942 -rw-------   1 rich     staff    10485760 Apr 17 14:58 foo
```

advanced_io/mlock.c

```
 1 #include <sys/types.h>
 2 #include <sys/stat.h>
 3 #include <fcntl.h>
 4 #include <unistd.h>
 5 #include <sys/mman.h>
 6 #include "ssp.h"

 7 int main (int argc, char **argv)
 8 {
 9     int fd;
10     char *buf;
11     struct stat stat_buf;
12     off_t len;

13     if (argc != 2)
14         err_quit ("Usage: mlock file");

15     if ((fd = open (argv [1], O_RDONLY)) == -1)
16         err_msg ("Can't open %s", argv [1]);

17     if (fstat (fd, &stat_buf) == -1)
18         err_msg ("Can't fstat");
19     len = stat_buf.st_size;

20     if ((buf = mmap (0, len, PROT_READ, MAP_SHARED, fd, 0)) == MAP_FAILED)
21         err_msg ("Can't mmap file");

22     if (mlock (buf, len) == -1)
23         err_msg ("Can't lock file in memory");

24     pause ();

25     return (0);
26 }
```

advanced_io/mlock.c

Program 13.18 Locking a file in memory.

```
# ps -ef | grep mlock
    root  1394     1  0 13:33:48 pts/9    0:00 ./mlock foo
    root  1561  1560  0 13:39:29 pts/9    0:00 grep mlock
# pkill mlock
# ps -ef | grep mlock
    root  1564  1560  0 13:39:29 pts/9    0:00 grep mlock
```

Running the program as our own user doesn't work, so we become root using the su command. We then run Program 13.18 in the background so that we can continue using the same terminal. We use the pmap command to show Program 13.18's address space when it is running. The line that we've highlighted refers to the file we've locked in memory. To confirm this, we use the -i option of the ls command to show the file's inode, which matches the one in the line we highlighted from the pmap output (i.e., the file whose inode number is 462942). We then kill the process using the pkill command. (Prior to Solaris 7, we must use the kill command, passing it the process ID of our mlock process.)

13.30 The `memcntl` Function

The `memcntl` function is used for general purpose memory management control.

```
#include <sys/types.h>
#include <sys/mman.h>

int memcntl (caddr_t addr, size_t len, int cmd, caddr_t arg, int attr, int mask);
```

Returns: 0 if OK, −1 on error

The `memcntl` function allows a process to apply a variety of control operations over the address space identified by the mappings established for the addresses in the range *addr* to *addr + len*.

The *attr* argument allows us to specify page selection and protection criteria. The following two attributes specify page mapping selection criteria:

SHARED	Pages are shared mappings.
PRIVATE	Pages are private mappings.

The following attributes specify the page protection criteria, which is constructed by bitwise-ORing one or more of the following constants:

PROT_READ	Pages can be read from.
PROT_WRITE	Pages can be written.
PROT_EXEC	Pages can be executed.
PROC_TEXT	Pages are part of the process text, i.e., specify all privately mapped segments with read and execute permission.
PROC_DATA	Pages are part of the process data, i.e., specify all privately mapped segments with write permission.

If the operation we want to perform is not to be constrained by the selection criteria, *attr* must have a value of 0.

The *mask* argument is reserved for future use, and must be set to 0.

The *cmd* argument identifies the operation to be performed, which may have an optional argument specified by *arg*. If *arg* is not used, it should be set to 0.

The operation to be performed must be one of the following:

MC_LOCK	Lock all the pages in the address range and attributes specified by *attr* in memory. This is similar to calling `mlock`.
	The *arg* argument is not used, so it should be set to 0.
MC_LOCKAS	Lock all the pages mapped by the address space with the attributes specified by *attr*. The *addr* and *len* arguments are not used, but must be set to NULL and 0 respectively.

The *arg* argument is the bitwise-OR of two flags: MCL_CURRENT (which locks the current mappings) and MCL_FUTURE (which locks future mappings). At least one (or both) of these flags must be specified.

MC_SYNC

Write all modified pages in the given range with the attributes *attr* to their backing storage, optionally invalidating the cache copies.

The *arg* argument is the bitwise-OR of three flags that control the behaviour of the operation: MS_ASYNC causes the write to be performed asynchronously, MS_SYNC causes the write to be performed synchronously, and MS_INVALIDATE causes the cache to be invalidated, forcing further reads from the pages to be sourced from their backing store.

MC_UNLOCK

Unlock all the pages in the specified range with attributes *attr*.

The *arg* argument is not used, so it should be set to 0.

MC_UNLOCKAS

Remove the address space locks and locks on all pages in the address space with attributes *attr*.

The *addr*, *len*, and *arg* arguments are not used, so they should be set to NULL, 0, and 0 respectively.

MC_HAT_ADVISE

This *cmd* is used to advise the kernel how a region of user-mapped memory will be accessed. The *arg* argument is a pointer to a memcntl_mha structure, which has the following members:

```
struct memcntl_mha {
    uint_t  mha_cmd;        /* Command */
    uint_t  mha_flags;      /* Flags */
    size_t  mha_pagesize;   /* Page size */
};
```

The mha_flags member is reserved for future use and should be set to 0. The mha_pagesize member should be a valid page size (e.g., obtained by calling the getpagesizes function we discuss in Section 8.3) or set to 0 to allow the system to choose an appropriate hardware address translation mapping size.

The mha_cmd member must be set to one of the following three values: MHA_MAPSIZE_VA, MHA_MAPSIZE_STACK, or MHA_MAPSIZE_BSSBRK.

Setting mha_cmd to MHA_MAPSIZE_VA sets the preferred hardware address translation mapping size of the region of memory in the range from *addr* to *addr* + *len*. Both *addr* and *len* must be aligned on a mha_pagesize boundary, and the address space must not have any holes in it. (Very briefly, *hardware address translation* (HAT) is the process of translating a virtual address to its corresponding physical address. The kernel manages all these mappings for us, but a detailed discussion of kernel internals is beyond the scope of this text. Readers interested in knowing more about HAT are referred to Section 5.9 of [Mauro and McDougall 2001].)

The `MHA_MAPSIZE_STACK` mha_cmd sets the preferred HAT mapping size of the calling process' main thread stack segment. The *addr* and *len* arguments must be set to NULL and 0 respectively.

The `MHA_MAPSIZE_BSSBRK` mha_cmd sets the preferred HAT mapping size of the calling process' heap. The *addr* and *len* arguments must be set to NULL and 0 respectively.

The *attr* argument must be 0 for all `MC_HAT_ADVISE` operations.

The `MC_HAT_ADVISE` operations were introduced with Solaris 9 and are used to implement the multiple user page size feature. They are intended to improve performance of applications that use large amounts of memory on processors that support multiple HAT mapping sizes.

They should be used with care, however, as not all processors support all sizes with equal efficiency. Using larger sizes may also introduce extra overhead that could reduce performance or available memory; using large sizes for an application may reduce the available resources for other processes and result in slower overall system performance.

Because of the potential impact on system resources, all operations, with the exception of `MC_SYNC`, are restricted to privileged processes.

13.31 Summary of Memory Mapped I/O

Memory mapped I/O has performance and algorithmic advantages to other forms of I/O. It is faster, and in some cases simpler, than reading or writing a file, because we manipulate memory rather than calling `read` or `write`. However, there are limitations to what we can do with memory mapped I/O. We can't copy files between certain devices (e.g., networks or terminals), and we must be careful if the size of the underlying file could change after we map it.

Some of the functions we've discussed in this section may have only a tangential relevance to memory mapped I/O, but we include them here because they affect how a process performs I/O, and the paging in and out of memory mapped into the address space of a process.

13.32 Access Control Lists

The discussion in Section 10.7 describes the traditional UNIX file access permissions, which also apply to Solaris. Solaris 2.5 introduced a finer grained access control mechanism to supplement the standard one, called Access Control Lists (ACLs). ACLs expand the permissions model by allowing us to specify access permission for specific users and groups, in addition to those for the user, group, and others. If a file has no ACL entries for additional users or groups, the ACL is considered to be a *trivial ACL*.

Suppose we had a file that we wanted a few select people to have access to, and all of the people were not in the same group. We could create a new group with these people as the members, but this solution does not scale very well because each user can be a member of at most 16 groups. A better solution would be to assign an ACL to the file, listing each of the individuals we want to be able to access the file.

There are two ways we can determine from the command line if a file has an ACL associated with it:

1. Use the `ls` command with the `-l` or `-o` options.
2. Use the `getfacl` command.

When we use the `ls` command, a plus sign (+) is displayed at the end of the file's permissions if it has an ACL. For example:

```
$ ls -l
-rw-r-----+  1 rich     staff          0 Apr 23 16:58 has_acl
-rw-r-----   1 rich     staff          0 Apr 23 16:58 no_acl
```

We can see that the file called has_acl has an ACL associated with it, whereas the file called no_acl doesn't.

We can confirm this by using the `getfacl` command:

```
$ getfacl *

# file: has_acl
# owner: rich
# group: staff
user::rw-
user:sys:r--            #effective:r--
group::r--              #effective:r--
mask:r--
other:---

# file: no_acl
# owner: rich
# group: staff
user::rw-
group::r--              #effective:r--
mask:r--
other:---
```

The `getfacl` output for no_acl shows what a trivial ACL looks like. It also shows the four types of ACL: user, group, mask, and other.

Both the user and group types can optionally specify a specific user name or group name (if this information is missing, the entry refers to the file's owner and group), and there can be many user or group entries.

The other type has the same meaning as with regular file permissions, and the mask type indicates the maximum permissions allowed to any user except the owner, and to any group entry, including the file's group. In other words, for users apart from the file's owner, the allowed permission is the logical AND of the mask and the user ACL entry for that user.

> When an ACL for a file is first created, a *shadow inode* is created, which points to one or more data blocks that hold the actual ACL entries. The shadow inode does not have a corresponding name in the directory hierarchy namespace (i.e., there is no directory entry that contains the inode number of the shadow inode), and the type of file it refers to is an `IFSHAD`.

In addition to these ACLs, we can set default ACL entries for users and groups. These defaults can be applied only to directories, and are automatically applied to files and directories created in the directory with a default ACL on it (the default ACLs are also applied to new subdirectories, so they are propagated down the directory hierarchy).

One caveat with ACLs is that they are attributes of files stored in a UFS file system. Other file systems, such as `tmpfs`, may not support ACLs. This means that if we copy or restore a file that has an ACL to `/tmp` (which is usually mounted as a `tmpfs` file system), the ACL entries will be lost. Using `/var/tmp` for temporary storage of files with an ACL is safer. We should also ensure that the program we use for backups supports ACLs if we use them. (The native Solaris versions of `cpio`, `tar`, and `ufsdump` all support ACLs; at the time of writing, GNU `tar` did not.)

13.33 The `acl` and `facl` Functions

The `acl` and `facl` functions allow us to get or set a file's ACL programmatically.

```
#include <sys/acl.h>

int acl (char *pathp, int cmd, int nentries, aclent_t *aclbufp);

int facl (int fildes, int cmd, int nentries, aclent_t *aclbufp);
```
Both return: 0 or number of ACLs if OK, –1 on error

The `acl` function is used to get or set the ACL associated with the file whose pathname is pointed to by *pathp*.

The *nentries* argument specifies how many entries ACL entries will fit in the buffer pointed to by *aclbufp*. The buffer is an array of `acl` structures, which has the following members:

```
typedef struct acl {
    int         a_type;     /* The type of this ACL entry */
    uid_t       a_id;       /* The UID or GID for this entry */
    o_mode_t    a_perm;     /* The permissions for this entry */
} aclent_t;
```

The *cmd* argument specifies the operation to be performed and must be one of the following three values:

GETACL   This *cmd* is used to get the file's ACL entries. At most *nentries*
                      ACL entries are stored in the buffer pointed to by *aclbufp*, and
                      the actual number of ACL entries is returned upon successful
                      completion. Read access to the file is not required, but all
                      directories in the pathname must be searchable.

GETACLCNT   This is the number of ACL entries for the file is returned.
                      Read access to the file is not required, but all directories in the
                      pathname must be searchable.

SETACL   The *nentries* ACL entries specified in the buffer *aclbufp* are
                      stored in the file's ACL. If this operation completes
                      successfully, 0 is returned. Read access to the file is not
                      required, but all directories in the pathname must be
                      searchable.

The minimum number of ACL entries returned by GETACL or GETACLCNT is MIN_ACL_ENTRIES (only a file with a trivial ACL will return this value).

When we set a file's ACL, we should populate the *aclbufp* buffer using the aclfromtext function we describe next.

The facl function is the same as acl, except that the ACL for the open file referenced by *fildes* is set or retrieved.

13.34 The aclfromtext and acltotext Functions

We can use two functions to convert an ACL from human-readable textual representation to a format that's more machine friendly, and vice versa. These are the aclfromtext and acltotext functions respectively.

```
cc [ flag ... ] file ... -lsec [ library ... ]
#include <sys/acl.h>

aclent_t *aclfromtext (char *acltextp, int *aclcnt);
```
                              Returns: a pointer to the list of ACL entries if OK, NULL on error
```
char *acltotext (aclent *aclbufp, int aclcnt);
```
                              Returns: a pointer to a text string if OK, NULL on error

The aclfromtext function converts the external (human-readable) ACL representation pointed to by *acltextp* and returns a pointer to a malloced array of acl structures (to avoid memory leaks, we should free the buffer returned when we are finished with it). The *aclcnt* argument is a pointer to an integer, which upon successful conversion contains the number of ACLs found.

The external representation of ACLs consists of one or more comma-delimited ACL entries. Each ACL entry has two or three colon-delimited fields. The first field corresponds to the a_type member of the acl structure, and is the ACL's tag type. The second field corresponds to the `a_id` member of the `acl` structure, and is the ACL's ID entry. The final field corresponds to the `a_perm` member of the `acl` structure, and contains the ACL's access permissions.

The type is identified by one of the following keywords:

`user`	If the second field is empty, this specifies the access granted to the owner of the file, and is said to be a `USER_OBJ` ACL entry. Otherwise, is specifies the access granted to the user in the ID field, and is said to be a `USER` ACL entry.
`group`	If the second field is empty, this specifies the access granted to the owning group of the file, and is said to be a `GROUP_OBJ` ACL entry. Otherwise, is specifies the access granted to the group in the ID field, and is said to be a `GROUP` ACL entry.
`other`	This specifies the access granted to any user or group who doesn't match any other ACL entry, and is called an `OTHER_OBJ` ACL entry.
`mask`	This specifies the maximum access granted to user or group entries, and is called a `CLASS_OBJ` ACL entry.
	The actual access granted to a given user or group is the logical AND of the `mask` and the ACL entry for that user or group.
`defaultuser`	If the second field is empty, this specifies the default access granted to the owner of the file, and is called a `DEF_USER_OBJ` ACL entry. Otherwise, is specifies the default access granted to the user in the ID field, and is called a `DEF_USER` ACL entry. This may be set only for a directory.
`defaultgroup`	If the second field is empty, this specifies the default access granted to the owning group of the file, and is called a `DEF_GROUP_OBJ` ACL entry. Otherwise, is specifies the default access granted to the group in the ID field, and is called a `DEF_GROUP` ACL entry. This may be set only for a directory.
`defaultother`	This specifies the default access granted to any user of group that doesn't match any other ACL entry, and is said to be a `DEF_OTHER_OBJ` ACL entry. This may be set only for a directory.
`defaultmask`	This specifies the maximum default access granted to user or group entries, and is called a `DEF_CLASS_OBJ` ACL entry. This may be set only for a directory.

The second field is only used for the `user`, `group`, `defaultuser`, and `defaultgroup` types, and is either the user name or group name. If no user name or group name exists, the user ID or group ID will be used instead.

If this field is empty, it is taken to mean the file's owner or the file's owning group.

The final field contains the symbolic access permissions:

r   Read permission

w   Write permission

x   Execute permission

-   No access

The `acltotext` function converts the *aclcnt* ACL entries in the buffer pointed to by *aclbufp* from their internal representation to their external representation. The space for the external string is obtained by calling `malloc`, so it should be freed when we are finished with it to avoid memory leaks.

Example: Printing a file's ACL

Program 13.19 gets the ACL for a file, converts it to text using the `acltotext` function, and then prints it out.

When we run Program 13.19, we get the following results:

```
$ ./get_acl no_acl has_acl
no_acl: Trivial ACL
has_acl: user::rw-,user:sys:r--,group::r--,mask:r--,other:---
```

The first file has no additional ACL entries beyond the usual UNIX permissions, which Program 13.19 reports as a trivial ACL. The second file, however, has an ACL entry that can be broken down like this:

`user::rw-`	The file's owner can read and write the file.
`user:sys:r--`	The user sys can read the file.
`group::r--`	Users in the file's group can read the file.
`other::---`	Other users can't access the file.

This ACL permits the user sys to read the file even though the permissions for others would normally disallow it.

13.35 The `aclcheck` Function

Once we've created an ACL, we can use the `aclcheck` function to check its validity.

```
cc [ flag ... ] file ... -lsec [ library ... ]
#include <sys/acl.h>

int aclcheck (aclent_t *aclbufp, int nentries, int *which);
```

Returns: 0 if OK, non-zero on error

—————————————————————————— advanced_io/get_acl.c

```
 1 #include <stdio.h>
 2 #include <stdlib.h>
 3 #include <sys/acl.h>
 4 #include "ssp.h"

 5 int main (int argc, char **argv)
 6 {
 7     int num_acls;
 8     aclent_t *acl_buf;
 9     char *acl_text;
10     int i;

11     if (argc < 2)
12         err_quit ("Usage: get_acl file ...");

13     for (i = 1; i < argc; i++) {
14         if ((num_acls = acl (argv [i], GETACLCNT, 0, NULL)) == -1)
15             err_ret ("acl (GETACLCNT) failed for %s", argv [i]);

16         if (num_acls == MIN_ACL_ENTRIES) {
17             printf ("%s: Trivial ACL\n", argv [i]);
18         }
19         else {
20             if ((acl_buf = malloc (sizeof (aclent_t) * num_acls)) == NULL)
21                 err_ret ("Malloc failed");

22             if (acl (argv [i], GETACL, num_acls, acl_buf) != num_acls)
23                 err_ret ("acl (GETACL) failed for %s", argv [i]);

24             acl_text = acltotext (acl_buf, num_acls);
25             printf ("%s: %s\n", argv [i], acl_text);

26             free (acl_text);
27             free (acl_buf);
28         }
29     }

30     return (0);
31 }
```

—————————————————————————— advanced_io/get_acl.c

Program 13.19   Printing a file's ACL.

The aclcheck function checks the validity of the *nentries* ACL entries in the buffer pointed to by *aclbufp*. If one or more of the ACL entries is invalid, the integer pointed to by the *which* argument contains the index of the first invalid entry.

For an ACL to be valid, it must adhere to the following rules:

- There must be exactly one USER_OBJ ACL entry.
- There must be exactly one GROUP_OBJ ACL entry.
- There must be exactly one OTHER_OBJ ACL entry.
- If there are any USER ACL entries, the user ID in each must be unique.

- If there are any GROUP ACL entries, the group ID in each must be unique.
- If there are any USER or GROUP ACL entries, there must be exactly one CLASS_OBJ (ACL mask) entry.
- If there are any default ACL entries, the following rules also apply:

  - There must be exactly one DEF_USER_OBJ ACL entry.
  - There must be exactly one DEF_GROUP_OBJ ACL entry.
  - There must be exactly one DEF_OTHER_OBJ ACL entry.
  - If there are any DEF_USER ACL entries, the user ID in each must be unique.
  - If there are any DEF_GROUP ACL entries, the group ID in each must be unique.
  - If there are any DEF_USER or DEF_GROUP ACL entries, there must be exactly one DEF_CLASS_OBJ (default ACL mask) ACL entry.

If the ACL passes all of these tests, aclcheck returns 0. However, if any rule is violated, aclcheck will fail, returning one of the following values:

USER_ERROR	There is more than one USER_OBJ or DEF_USER_OBJ ACL entry.
GRP_ERROR	There is more than one GROUP_OBJ or DEF_GROUP_OBJ ACL entry.
OTHER_ERROR	There is more than one OTHER_OBJ or DEF_OTHER_OBJ ACL entry.
CLASS_ERROR	There is more than one CLASS_OBJ (ACL mask) or DEF_CLASS_OBJ (default ACL mask) ACL entry.
DUPLICATE_ERROR	There are duplicate USER, GROUP, DEF_USER, or DEF_GROUP ACL entries.
ENTRY_ERROR	The entry type is invalid.
MISS_ERROR	An ACL entry is missing (i.e., the number of ACL entries is less than *nentries*). In this case, *which* is set to −1.
MEM_ERROR	The system couldn't allocate any memory. In this case, the *which* parameter is set to −1.

We should use the aclcheck function to verify the validity of all user supplied ACLs before applying them to a file using the acl or facl functions.

Example: Setting a file's ACL

Program 13.20 converts the ACL we specify on the command line into its internal representation using the aclfromtext function, checks its validity using aclcheck, and then applies it to the named files.

advanced_io/set_acl.c

```
 1 #include <stdio.h>
 2 #include <stdlib.h>
 3 #include <sys/acl.h>
 4 #include "ssp.h"

 5 int main (int argc, char **argv)
 6 {
 7     int num_acls;
 8     aclent_t *acl_buf;
 9     int i;
10     int which;

11     if (argc < 3)
12         err_quit ("Usage: set_acl ACL file ...");

13     if ((acl_buf = aclfromtext (argv [1], &num_acls)) == NULL)
14         err_msg ("aclfromtext failed");

15     switch (aclcheck (acl_buf, num_acls, &which)) {
16         case 0:
17             break;

18         case USER_ERROR:
19             err_quit ("Invalid ACL entry: %d: "
20                 "Multiple USER_OBJ or DEF_USER_OBJ entries", which);
21             break;

22         case GRP_ERROR:
23             err_quit ("Invalid ACL entry: %d: "
24                 "Multiple GROUP_OBJ or DEF_GROUP_OBJ entries", which);
25             break;

26         case OTHER_ERROR:
27             err_quit ("Invalid ACL entry: %d: "
28                 "Multiple OTHER_OBJ or DEF_OTHER_OBJ entries", which);
29             break;

30         case CLASS_ERROR:
31             err_quit ("Invalid ACL entry: %d: "
32                 "Multiple CLASS_OBJ or DEF_CLASS_OBJ entries", which);
33             break;

34         case DUPLICATE_ERROR:
35             err_quit ("Invalid ACL entry: %d: "
36                 "Duplicate USER, GROUP, DEF_USER, or DEF_GROUP entries", which);
37             break;

38         case ENTRY_ERROR:
39             err_quit ("Invalid ACL entry: %d: Invalid entry type", which);
40             break;

41         case MISS_ERROR:
42             err_quit ("Missing ACL entries");
43             break;

44         case MEM_ERROR:
45             err_quit ("Out of memory!");
46             break;
```

```
47          default:
48              err_quit ("aclcheck returns unknown error");
49              break;
50      }

51      for (i = 2; i < argc; i++) {
52          if (acl (argv [i], SETACL, num_acls, acl_buf) != 0)
53              err_ret ("acl (SETACL) failed for %s", argv [i]);
54      }

55      free (acl_buf);

56      return (0);
57 }
```
advanced_io/set_acl.c

Program 13.20 Setting a file's ACL.

When we run Program 13.20, we get the following results:

```
$ touch foo
$ ls -l foo
-rw-r--r--   1 rich      staff            0 Apr 27 17:37 foo
$ ./set_acl user::rw-,group::r--,other::---,mask:r--,user:sys:rw- foo
$ ls -l foo
-rw-r-----+  1 rich      staff            0 Apr 27 17:37 foo
$ ./get_acl foo
foo: user::rw-,user:sys:rw-,group::r--,mask:r--,other:---
```

The ACL we apply to the file `foo` allows the user `rich` to read and write the file, allows members of the file's group to read the file, and denies access to all other users. It also allows the user `sys` to read the file, overriding the file's permissions for others. Note that although we specify that the user `sys` can read and write the file, the ACL's mask effectively limits this user's access to read only. We can confirm this by using the `getfacl` command:

```
$ getfacl foo

# file: foo
# owner: rich
# group: staff
user::rw-
user:sys:rw-              #effective:r--
group::r--               #effective:r--
mask:r--
other:---
```

13.36 The `aclfrommode` and `acltomode` Functions

If we want to convert a file's permission bits into an ACL, or vice versa, we can do this using the `aclfrommode` and `acltomode` functions. (In this context, when we refer to a file's permission bits, we mean the regular, non-ACL permissions bits.)

```
cc [ flag ... ] file ... -lsec [ library ... ]
#include <sys/types.h>
#include <sys/acl.h>

int aclfrommode (aclent_t *aclbufp, int nentries, mode_t *modep);

int acltomode (aclent_t *aclbufp, int nentries, mode_t *modep);
```

> Both return: 0 if OK, −1 on error

The aclfrommode function converts the permissions pointed to by *modep* into an ACL pointed to by *aclbufp*. The file's owner permissions are copied to the USER_OBJ ACL entry, and the file's other permissions are copied to the OTHER_OBJ ACL entry. The file's group permissions are copied to the GROUP_OBJ ACL entry, and to the CLASS_OBJ (ACL mask) ACL entry, if one is available.

The acltomode function does the converse; it converts the ACL pointed to by *aclbufp* into the permissions pointed to by *modep*. The USER_OBJ ACL entry is copied to the file's owner permissions, and the OTHER_OBJ ACL entry is copied to the file's other permissions. If there is a CLASS_OBJ (ACL mask) ACL entry, then it is bitwise-ANDed with the GROUP_OBJ ACL entry, and the result is stored in the file's group permissions. Otherwise, the GROUP_OBJ ACL entry is copied to the file's group permissions.

For both functions, the *nentries* argument specifies the number of ACL entries in *aclbufp*. Also, if a USER_OBJ, GROUP_OBJ, or OTHER_OBJ ACL entry cannot be found in the ACL buffer, then the aclfrommode or acltomode function will fail.

13.37 The aclsort Function

We can use the aclsort function to sort an ACL.

```
cc [ flag ... ] file ... -lsec [ library ... ]
#include <sys/acl.h>

int aclsort (int nentries, int calclass, aclent_t *aclbufp);
```

> Returns: 0 if OK, −1 on error

The aclsort function sorts the *nentries* ACL entries in the buffer pointed to by *aclbufp*, and recalculates the CLASS_OBJ (ACL mask) permissions if *calclass* is not zero. The ACL mask is the union of all the ACL permissions, with the exception of the USER_OBJ, CLASS_OBJ, and OTHER_OBJ entries.

The ACL buffer is sorted as follows:

- The ACL entries are sorted into this order: USER_OBJ, USER, GROUP_OBJ, GROUP, CLASS_OBJ (ACL mask) , OTHER_OBJ, DEF_USER_OBJ, DEF_USER, DEF_GROUP_OBJ, DEF_GROUP, DEF_CLASS_OBJ, and DEF_OTHER_OBJ.

- Entries in the USER, GROUP, DEF_USER, and DEF_GROUP classes are sorted in ascending ID order.

The `aclsort` function will return successfully under these conditions:

- There is exactly one ACL entry for each of these types: USER_OBJ, GROUP_OBJ, CLASS_OBJ, and OTHER_OBJ.
- If there are any default entries, then there must be exactly one entry of each of the following types: DEF_USER_OBJ, DEF_GROUP_OBJ, DEF_OTHER_OBJ, and DEF_CLASS_OBJ.
- Entries of type USER, GROUP, DEF_USER, and DEF_GROUP must be unique.

If any of these rules are violated, `aclsort` will return an error.

13.38 Extended File Attributes

A file's attributes are things such as its size, its owner and group, its access and modification times, and its permissions. Solaris 9 introduced the concept of *extended file attributes*, which allow applications to associate arbitrary attributes with a specific file. An example of the use of extended attributes might be a window manager that associates a program with a file. Double clicking on the file would run the associated program, with the filename as an argument (e.g., selecting a document that was written in the StarOffice word processor, StarOffice Writer, would run the StarWrite program and load the document into it). Another example would be the association of an icon with a filename.

The `runat` command runs a command in the attribute namespace associated with a given file. For example, the command

```
runat foo cp /tmp/README README
```

will copy the file /tmp/README into the attribute namespace of the file `foo`. We can use the following command to see the contents of the attribute directory:

```
runat foo ls
```

There are two ways we can determine from the command line if a file has any extended attributes associated with it:

1. Use the `ls` command with the `-@` option.
2. Use the `find` command with the `-xattr` option.

When we use the `ls` command, a commercial "at" sign (@) is displayed at the end of the file's permissions if it has any extended attributes. For example:

```
$ ls -@l
-rw-r--r--@  1 rich     staff           0 Apr 30 10:49 has_attr
-rw-r--r--   1 rich     staff           0 Apr 30 10:46 no_attr
```

We can see that the file called `no_attr` has no extended attributes associated with it, but the file called `has_attr` does.

Because they both use the character at the end of a file's permissions to indicate their presence, the easiest way to show which files have an ACL and extended attributes is to use the find command (we've trimmed the first two fields (i.e., the inode number and the file's size in kilobytes) so that the output will fit on the page):

```
$ find . -xattr -ls
-rw-r-----   1 rich      staff            0 Apr 30 10:27 ./no_acl
-rw-r-----+  1 rich      staff            0 Apr 30 10:29 ./has_acl
-rw-r--r--   1 rich      staff            0 May  1 11:57 ./has_attr
```

Of these three files with extended attributes, only the file called has_acl has an ACL associated with it.

Although conceptually the attribute model is fully general (i.e., attributes may be nested arbitrarily deeply, and can be any type of file), the Solaris 9 implementation allows only regular files as attributes and rejects attempts to place attributes on attributes.

The following operations are not allowed by the current implementation:

link

Any attempt to create links between the attribute namespace and the non-attribute namespace is rejected to prevent security-related or otherwise sensitive attributes from being exposed, and therefore manipulable as regular files.

rename

Any attempt to rename between the attribute namespace and the non-attribute namespace is rejected to prevent an already linked file from being renamed, thereby circumventing the link restriction.

mkdir

An attempt to create a nonregular file in the attribute namespace is rejected to reduce the functionality, and hence the exposure and risk of the initial extended attributes implementation.

symlink

This operation is rejected for the same reason as the mkdir operation.

mknod

This operation is rejected for the same reason as the mkdir and symlink operations.

Extended attributes are stored as files inside a hidden directory that is associated with the target file. The hidden directory has an inode type of IFATTRDIR, and can be manipulated only by attribute-aware applications. Several system utilities are attribute-aware, including cp, cpio, du, find, fsck, fsdb, ls, mv, pax, and tar. We can also write our own attribute-aware applications, using the functions we discuss in the following sections.

13.39 The openat and attropen Functions

As with regular files, the first thing we must do if we want to read or write an attribute file is open it. We can do this by using either the openat or attropen function.

```
#include <sys/types.h>
#include <sys/stat.h>
#include <fcntl.h>

int openat (int fildes, const char *path, int oflag, /* mode_t mode */...);

int attropen (const char *path, const char *attrpath, int oflag,
    /* mode_t mode */...);
```

Both return: file descriptor if OK, −1 on error

The openat function is the same as the open function we discussed in Section 4.3, except that the *path* argument is interpreted relative to the starting point implied by the file descriptor *fildes*. If *fildes* is set to the special value AT_FDCWD, then *path* will be interpreted as being relative to the current working directory. If *path* specifies an absolute pathname, then the *fd* argument is ignored.

The *oflag* and optional *mode* arguments have exactly the same meanings they have for the open function. We should note, however, the meaning of the O_XATTR value for *oflag* in the context of the openat function; the *path* argument is interpreted as a relative path reference to an extended attribute of the file associated with *fildes*.

The attropen function is also similar to the open function, except that it returns a file descriptor for the extended attribute named by *attrpath* for the file indicated by *path*. The *oflag* and *mode* arguments have the same meanings as with the open function, and are applied to the open operation of the attribute file (e.g., we can create a new attribute by specifying the O_CREAT flag).

The O_XATTR flag is set by default using this function, and the *attrpath* argument is always interpreted as a reference to an extended attribute.

Calling attropen like this:

```
attr_fd = attropen (path, attrpath, oflag);
```

is the same as the following:

```
fd = open (path, O_RDONLY);
attr_fd = openat (fd, attrpath, oflag | O_XATTR);
close (fd);
```

Example: Listing a file's extended attributes

Program 13.21 lists the extended attributes for a given file.

Program 13.21 gets a file descriptor for the hidden extended attribute directory using attropen, and then opens a directory stream for that file descriptor. Each entry in the directory stream is printed, except for *dot* and *dot-dot*.

Let's see what happens when we run Program 13.21.

```
$ runat has_attr touch README foo       Make sure the file has some attributes
$ ./list_attrs *
has_attr: README foo
no_attr: Has no extended attributes
```

advanced_io/list_attrs.c

```
 1 #include <stdio.h>
 2 #include <sys/types.h>
 3 #include <sys/stat.h>
 4 #include <fcntl.h>
 5 #include <dirent.h>
 6 #include "ssp.h"

 7 int main (int argc, char **argv)
 8 {
 9     int fd;
10     int i;
11     DIR *dirp;
12     struct dirent *dir;
13     boolean_t no_attrs;

14     if (argc < 2)
15         err_quit ("Usage: list_attrs file ...");

16     for (i = 1; i < argc; i++) {
17         if ((fd = attropen (argv [i], ".", O_RDONLY)) == -1) {
18             err_msg ("list_attrs: %s", argv [i]);
19             continue;
20         }

21         dirp = fdopendir (fd);

22         printf ("%s:", argv [i]);

23         no_attrs = B_TRUE;

24         if ((readdir (dirp) == NULL) || (readdir (dirp) == NULL)) {
25             goto bail;
26         }

27         while ((dir = readdir (dirp)) != NULL) {
28             no_attrs = B_FALSE;
29             printf (" %s", dir -> d_name);
30         }

31 bail:
32         if (no_attrs)
33             printf (" Has no extended attributes\n");
34         else
35             printf ("\n");

36         closedir (dirp);
37     }

38     return (0);
39 }
```

advanced_io/list_attrs.c

Program 13.21 Listing a file's extended attributes.

We can see that the file called no_attr has no extended attributes, and the file called has_attr has two extended attributes: one called README, and the other called foo.

13.40 The `fstatat` Function

We can use the `fstatat` function to get the status of an attribute file.

```
#include <sys/types.h>
#include <sys/stat.h>
#include <unistd.h>
#include <fcntl.h>

int fstatat (int fildes, const char *path, struct stat *buf, int flag);
```

Returns: 0 if OK, −1 on error

The `fstatat` function obtains file status (similar to the `stat` family of functions) for the extended attributes of the file represented by *fildes*. If *path* is relative, it is resolved relative to *fildes* (if *path* is absolute, then *fildes* is ignored).

If *fildes* has the special value `AT_FDCWD`, then relative paths are resolved from the current working directory.

Setting the *flag* argument to `AT_SYMLINK_NOFOLLOW` prevents symbolic links from being followed (like the `lstat` function).

The *buf* argument is a pointer to a `stat` structure, which we described in Section 10.3.

We can think of `fstatat` as a general purpose replacement for the `stat`, `lstat`, and `fstat` functions.

The function call

```
stat (path, buf);
```

is the same as

```
fstatat (AT_FDCWD, path, buf, 0);
```

The function call

```
lstat (path, buf);
```

is the same as

```
fstatat (AT_FDCWD, path, buf, AT_SYMLINK_NOFOLLOW);
```

Finally, the function call

```
fstat (fildes, buf);
```

is the same as

```
fstatat (fildes, NULL, buf, 0);
```

13.41 The `unlinkat` Function

The `unlinkat` function is used to remove an extended attribute file.

```
#include <unistd.h>
#include <fcntl.h>

int unlinkat (int dirfd, const char *path, int flag);
```
                                                              Returns: 0 if OK, −1 on error

If *flag* is 0, the `unlinkat` function is the same as the `unlink` function we discussed in Section 10.15, except for the processing of the *path* argument. If *path* contains an absolute pathname, `unlinkat` behaves exactly the same as `unlink`, and the *dirfd* argument is ignored. If *path* is a relative pathname, it is resolved relative to the directory referenced by *dirfd* unless *dirfd* is the special value `AT_FDCWD`, in which case *path* is resolved relative to the current working directory.

Setting the *flag* argument to `AT_REMOVEDIR` causes the `unlinkat` function to behave the same as the `rmdir` function, except for the processing of *path* as just described.

13.42 The `renameat` Function

We use the `renameat` function to change the name of an extended attribute file.

```
#include <stdio.h>
#include <fcntl.h>

int renameat (int fromfd, const char *old, int tofd, const char *new);
```
                                                              Returns: 0 if OK, −1 on error

The `renameat` function is used to rename a file. If the *old* pathname is relative, it is resolved from the *fromfd* argument. Otherwise, *fromfd* is ignored. Similarly, if it is not absolute, then the *new* pathname is resolved relative to the *tofd* argument.

If either *fromfd* or *tofd* have the value `AT_FDCWD`, then the pathname related to that argument will be resolved relative to the current working directory.

For security reasons, an extended attribute file may not be renamed to a regular file outside of the extended attribute namespace, and vice versa.

13.43 The `fchownat` Function

The group and ownership of an attribute file can be changed using the `fchownat` function.

```
#include <unistd.h>
#include <sys/types.h>
#include <fcntl.h>

int fchownat (int fildes, const char *path, uid_t owner, gid_t group, int flag);
```
Returns: 0 if OK, −1 on error

The `fchownat` function changes the ownership and group membership of the specified file to *owner* and *group* respectively. The file specified by the *fildes* and *path* arguments. If *path* is relative, it is resolved starting at the file associated with *fildes*; otherwise, it is ignored. Setting *fildes* to the special value `AT_FDCWD` will cause *path* to be resolved relative to the current working directory.

Setting *flag* to `AT_SYMLINK_NOFOLLOW` will cause symbolic links to be ignored (i.e., not followed).

We can think of `fchownat` as a general purpose replacement for the `chown`, `lchown`, and `fchown` functions.

The function call

```
chown (path, owner, group);
```

is the same as

```
fchownat (AT_FDCWD, path, owner, group, 0);
```

The function call

```
lchown (path, owner, group);
```

is the same as

```
fchownat (AT_FDCWD, path, owner, group, AT_SYMLINK_NOFOLLOW);
```

Finally, the function call

```
fchown (fildes, owner, group);
```

is the same as

```
fchownat (fildes, NULL, owner, group, 0);
```

13.44 The `futimesat` Function

An extended attribute file's access and modification times can be set using the `futimesat` function.

```
#include <sys/time.h>
#include <fcntl.h>

int futimesat (int fildes, const char *path, const struct timeval times [2]);
```
Returns: 0 if OK, −1 on error

The futimesat function enables us to set the access and modification times of the file specified by *fildes* and *path* to the nearest microsecond.

If *path* is relative, it is resolved relative to the file associated with *fildes*; otherwise, *fildes* is ignored. The *fildes* argument can be set to the special value AT_FDCWD, which causes relative *paths* to be resolved starting at the current working directory.

If *path* is a NULL pointer, the file specified by *fildes* will have its access and modification times changed.

As with the utimes function we discussed in Section 10.21, the *times* argument is an array of two timeval structures. The first member specifies the time of the last access, and the second member specifies the last modification time.

The call

```
utimes (path, times);
```

is the same as

```
futimesat (AT_FDCWD, path, times);
```

13.45 Changing Extended Attribute File Permissions

It is interesting to observe that the Solaris 9 implementation of the extended file attributes API does not include a function for changing the permissions of an extended attribute file. Program 13.22 shows our implementation of a function we call fchmodat that rectifies this shortcoming.

The way fchmodat works is very simple. A file descriptor for the attribute file is acquired by using the openat function. If a read-only open fails, then a write-only open is attempted. If both attempts fail, −1 is returned. The reason why we try to open the file twice is because we don't know what the file's permissions are. If we have only read access to it, opening it for reading and writing will fail, and likewise if we have only write access to it. So we try a read-only open followed by a write-only one, because if we have any permission at all to open the file, one of these attempts will succeed. All we need is a valid file descriptor associated with the file; because we're not going to access the file directly, we don't care what mode it is opened for.

We then call the fchmod function to change the permissions of the file associated with the newly acquired file descriptor. After closing the attribute file, the return value from fchmod is returned.

advanced_io/fchmodat.c

```
 1 #include <stdio.h>
 2 #include <stdlib.h>
 3 #include <unistd.h>
 4 #include <sys/types.h>
 5 #include <sys/stat.h>
 6 #include <fcntl.h>
 7 #include "ssp.h"

 8 static int fchmodat (int fd, const char *path, mode_t mode);

 9 int main (int argc, char **argv)
10 {
11     mode_t mode;
12     int fd;

13     if (argc != 4)
14         err_quit ("Usage: fchmodat mode file attribute");

15     mode = strtol (argv [1], NULL, 8);

16     if ((fd = open (argv [2], O_RDONLY)) == -1)
17         if ((fd = open (argv [2], O_WRONLY)) == -1)
18             err_msg ("Can't open %s", argv [2]);

19     if (fchmodat (fd, argv [3], mode) == -1)
20         err_msg ("fchmodat failed");

21     return (0);
22 }

23 static int fchmodat (int fd, const char *path, mode_t mode)
24 {
25     int attr_fd;
26     int ret_code;

27     if ((attr_fd = openat (fd, path, O_RDONLY | O_XATTR)) == -1)
28         if ((attr_fd = openat (fd, path, O_WRONLY | O_XATTR)) == -1)
29             return (-1);

30     ret_code = fchmod (attr_fd, mode);

31     close (attr_fd);

32     return (ret_code);
33 }
```

advanced_io/fchmodat.c

Program 13.22 Changing permissions on an extended attribute file.

Program 13.22 arranges for our fchmodat function to be called, using arguments from the command line.

Let's see what happens when we run Program 13.22.

```
$ runat has_attr ls -l
total 0
-rw-r--r--   1 rich      staff        0 May  1 11:57 README
-rw-r--r--   1 rich      staff        0 May  5 17:54 foo
```

```
$ ./fchmodat 666 has_attr foo
$ runat has_attr ls -l
total 0
-rw-r--r--   1 rich      staff         0 May  1 11:57 README
-rw-rw-rw-   1 rich      staff         0 May  5 17:54 foo
```

13.46 Summary

In this chapter we covered numerous advanced I/O topics, including:

- Nonblocking I/O
- File and record locking
- The STREAMS I/O subsystem
- I/O multiplexing using `select` and `poll`
- Asynchronous I/O
- Scattered reads and gathered writes using `readv` and `writev` respectively
- Memory mapped I/O
- Access control lists
- Extended file attributes

Exercises

13.1 Modify Program 13.4 so that each process tries to acquire a lock on two shared files. Does the kernel detect and prevent this deadlock?

13.2 Can we implement the parent and child synchronization functions we describe in Section 15.10 using advisory file locking?

13.3 The `fd_set` data structure has default limit on its size. How can we increase this limit so that we can handle 4096 file descriptors?

13.4 How can we determine the capacity of a pipe using `select` or `poll`?

Part 4

Processes and Process Control

14

The Environment of a
UNIX Process

14.1 Introduction

Before we take a close look at process control and how processes relate to each other, we need to understand the environment in which each UNIX process executes. We'll discuss how a process starts up (including how `main` gets called), and process termination. We'll also see how command line arguments are passed to programs, how to manipulate environment variables, and see what the typical layout of a process in memory looks like. Finally, we'll take a look at the `setjmp` and `longjmp` functions, and how they interact with the stack.

14.2 Process Start-Up

With the exception of a small number of system process that are created by hand when the kernel first starts running, the only way to create a process in the Solaris environment is to use one of the `fork` family of functions (which we discuss in Chapter 15). The `fork` functions create a new process by making an exact copy of the calling process. To execute a new program, this new process calls one of the `exec` functions (which we also discuss in Chapter 15), which causes the new program to be read into memory and run.

The `main` Function

Programs written in other languages have their own conventions (which are beyond the scope of this text), but a program written in C starts execution with a function called `main`. The function prototype for `main` is:

```
int main (int argc, char *argv []);
```

The first argument, *argc*, contains the number of command line arguments (including the name of the command). The second argument, *argv*, is an array of pointers to the command line arguments. We describe *argc* and *argv* in more detail in Section 14.4.

In addition to the command line arguments, POSIX defines a global variable, `environ`, which contains the address of an array pointers to environment variables:

```
extern char **environ;
```

We discuss environment variables in Section 14.5.

> Applications that don't require access to their command line arguments can use this function prototype for `main`:
>
> ```
> int main (void);
> ```
>
> Historically, most UNIX systems (including Solaris) have provided a third argument to `main`, which is the address of the list of environment variables (q.v.):
>
> ```
> int main (int argc, char *argv [], char *envp []);
> ```
>
> However, ISO C specifies that `main` has two arguments, and POSIX specifies that `environ` should be used in preference to the possible third argument. Applications wishing to access a specific environment variable should use the `getenv` and `putenv` functions we discuss in Section 14.5, but accessing the entire list of environment variables requires the use of `environ`.
>
> The function prototype for `main` is frequently written like this:
>
> ```
> int main (int argc, char **argv);
> ```
>
> In fact, this is the style we use in this text.
>
> A common mistake made by novice C programmers is to declare `main` as a `void` function. This problem is exacerbated by at least one C programming text book known to the author, which declares `main` to be `void` in all of its examples. Although this gets rid of compiler warnings (something like "warning: Function has no return statement"), it is contrary to what is specified by ISO C and POSIX, and should not be done.

Strictly speaking, when a C program is started by the kernel (using the `exec` function we alluded to earlier), `main` is not the first function called. Instead, a special start-up routine is called. This start-up routine takes the list of command line arguments and environment variables supplied by the kernel, sets things up so that `main` can be called as we showed previously, and then calls `main`.

Once control is passed to the `main` function, the process continues to run (subject to the time slicing whims of the scheduler) until it terminates.

14.3 Process Termination

All good things must come to an end, and the life of a process is no exception. There are two categories of process termination: normal or abnormal. Both can happen for one of several reasons. A process may terminate normally for one of these four reasons:

1. The process explicitly or implicitly returns from `main`. An implicit return from `main` happens if the code "falls off the end" of `main`.

2. The process called `exit`.

3. The process called `_exit`.

4. The last thread in the process called `pthread_exit`. This has the same effect as `exit(0)`.

Two events will cause abnormal termination:

1. The process calls `abort`.
2. The process is terminated by a signal.

(Although a process ceases to run when the power suddenly goes off, this is not an example of process termination as we are describing it here.) We discuss the `abort` function and signals in Chapter 17.

The start-up code we mentioned previously is written so that if `main` returns, the `exit` function is called. The start-up routine is usually written in assembler, but if it were written in C, the call to `main` would look something like this:

```
exit (main (argc, argv));
```

The `exit` and `_exit` Functions

As we stated before, two functions cause a process to terminate normally: `exit` and `_exit`. The `_exit` function terminates the calling process immediately, whereas the `exit` performs certain cleanup processing before actually terminating the process.

```
#include <stdlib.h>

void exit (int status);

#include <unistd.h>

void _exit (int status);
```

The `exit` function performs some cleanup processing, and then terminates the calling process. The cleanup processing performed is as follows:

- Any exit handlers that were registered using the `atexit` function (see further on) are called in the reverse order of their registration. Each function is called as many times as it was registered.

  If one of the exit handlers does not return, the remaining functions are not called, and the rest of the `exit` processing is not completed.
- All standard I/O library output file streams are flushed.
- All standard I/O library file streams are closed.
- All temporary files created using the `tmpfile` function are deleted.

Once this cleanup processing is complete, the `_exit` function is called.

The `_exit` function actually terminates the calling process. This has the effect of (among others) closing all file descriptors and directory streams, unmapping each memory mapped object, and detaching each shared memory segment.

Both the exit and _exit functions accept an integer argument, *status*. The value of this argument is called the *exit status* of the process, and this value can be retrieved by its parent (more on this in Chapter 15). In the case of simple commands run at the command line, the shell is the parent process; most shells have a method of examining the exit status of a process.

If either function is called with an explicit *status*, or if main falls off the bottom (or performs a return with no argument), the exit status of a process is undefined. This means that the traditional "hello world" example program is incomplete:

```
#include <stdio.h>

main ()
{
    printf ("Hello, World!\n");
}
```

Not only is main incompletely prototyped, but the program falls off the bottom without returning an exit status. A complete and correct version of this program is:

```
#include <stdio.h>

int main (void)
{
    printf ("Hello, World!\n");
    return (0);
}
```

Some programmers and texts prefer to use exit to return from main, so that they can use grep to locate all exit statements in a program. While this approach does have some merit, we'll just use a return statement to return from main. (This also has the added benefit of keeping the compiler and lint quiet.) Some would also argue that we should include the definitions of *argc* and *argv* in our function prototype for main, but this gives rise to warnings about variables that are defined but not used. In this text we use the convention of declaring main with no arguments, unless we explicitly want to access the command line arguments.

The atexit Function

We stated previously that when a process calls exit, one of the actions taken is to call the exit handlers. Exit handlers are registered using the atexit function.

```
#include <stdlib.h>

int atexit (void (*func) (void));
```

Returns: 0 if OK, non-zero on error

The atexit function registers the function pointed to by *func* to be called on normal termination of the process, or when the object defining the function is unloaded. No arguments are passed to *func*, and no return value is expected.

The number of functions that can be registered with atexit is limited only by the available memory, although at least 32 functions can be registered. We can use the _SC_ATEXIT_MAX argument of sysconf to determine the maximum number of exit handlers, but there is no way for an application to determine how many exit handlers are currently installed.

Although no return value is expected, the exit handlers must return to ensure that all registered functions are called (specifically, the exit handlers must *not* call one of the exit functions).

Figure 14.1 shows the relationship of the exit handlers and the exit and _exit functions in the context of a process.

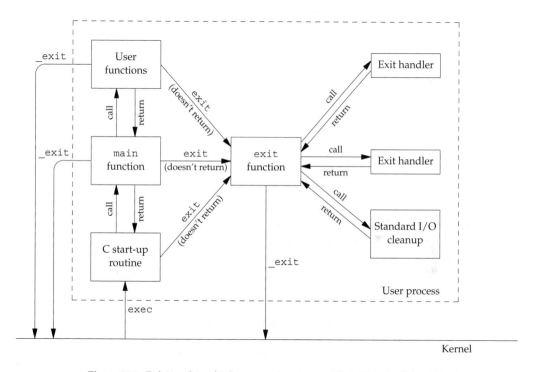

Figure 14.1   Relationship of a C program's start-up and termination functions.

Figure 14.1 shows that the only way to start a new program is by using the exec function. It also shows that _exit is the function that ultimately handles normal process termination. We show two exit handlers in Figure 14.1, but subject to the availability of machine resources, we can have as many or as few as we like.

A process can also be abnormally terminated by a signal, but we don't show this in Figure 14.1.

Example: Using exit handlers

Program 14.1 shows how we set up exit handlers.

———————————————————————————————————— *proc_env/atexit.c*

```
 1 #include <stdio.h>
 2 #include <stdlib.h>
 3 #include "ssp.h"

 4 static void eh1 (void);
 5 static void eh2 (void);

 6 int main (void)
 7 {
 8     if (atexit (eh2) != 0)
 9         err_msg ("Can't register eh2");
10     if (atexit (eh2) != 0)
11         err_msg ("Can't register eh2");

12     if (atexit (eh1) != 0)
13         err_msg ("Can't register eh1");

14     printf ("Returning from main\n");
15     return (0);
16 }

17 static void eh1 (void)
18 {
19     printf ("First exit handler\n");
20 }

21 static void eh2 (void)
22 {
23     printf ("Second exit handler\n");
24 }
```

———————————————————————————————————— *proc_env/atexit.c*

Program 14.1   Example of how to use exit handlers.

Running Program 14.1 gives the following results:

```
$ ./atexit
Returning from main
First exit handler
Second exit handler
Second exit handler
```

14.4   Command Line Arguments

When running a new program, the process calling exec can pass command line arguments to the new program. We've seen in many examples of this in earlier chapters. In Section 3.8, we showed how to parse command line arguments.

Each program is passed two arguments: argc and argv. The first of these is a count of the command line arguments (including the name of the program), and the second is a NULL-terminated list of the program's arguments.

Example: Echoing command line arguments

Program 14.2 echoes all of its command line arguments to standard output. Note that unlike the standard UNIX command, echo, Program 14.2 echoes the zeroth argument.

proc_env/ssp_echo.c
```
1 #include <stdio.h>

2 int main (int argc, char **argv)
3 {
4     int i;

5     for (i = 0; i < argc; i++)
6         printf ("argv [%d] = %s\n", i, argv [i]);

7     return (0);
8 }
```
proc_env/ssp_echo.c

Program 14.2   Echo command line arguments to standard output.

Running Program 14.2 gives results like this:
```
$ ./ssp_echo one two three
argv [0] = ./ssp_echo
argv [1] = one
argv [2] = two
argv [3] = three
```
It's worth noting that because ISO C and POSIX guarantees that argv [argc] is a NULL pointer, we can rewrite line 5 as the following:
```
for (i = 0; argv [i]; i++)
```

The getexecname Function

The first argument passed to a process (i.e., argv [0]) is usually its name (we say *usually* because this value is set by whatever called exec to run the program, and setting it to the program's name is merely a convention). If we don't declare argv or don't pass it to a function, we can still determine the name of a process by calling getexecname.

```
#include <stdlib.h>

const char *getexecname (void);
```
                    Returns: a pointer to the executable's pathname if OK, NULL on error

The pathname returned by getexecname is usually an absolute pathname, because the majority of commands are executed by a shell that appends the command name to the user's PATH. If the pathname returned by getexecname is not an absolute path, we can prepend it with the output of the getcwd function we describe in Section 10.24 to get an absolute path. (This assumes that the process or one of its ancestors hasn't changed its root or current directory since the last successful call to exec.)

Example: Using the `getexecname` function

Program 14.3 determines its executable's absolute pathname, prepending it with the current directory if necessary.

proc_env/getexecname.c

```
 1  #include <stdio.h>
 2  #include <unistd.h>
 3  #include <stdlib.h>
 4  #include <limits.h>
 5  #include "ssp.h"

 6  int main (void)
 7  {
 8      char *cwd;
 9      const char *path;

10      if ((path = getexecname ()) == NULL)
11          err_msg ("getexecname failed");

12      if (*path != '/') {
13          if ((cwd = getcwd (NULL, PATH_MAX)) == NULL)
14              err_msg ("getcwd failed");

15          printf ("exec name = %s/%s\n", cwd, path);
16          free (cwd);
17      }
18      else
19          printf ("exec name = %s\n", path);

20      return (0);
21  }
```

proc_env/getexecname.c

Program 14.3   Determining our executable's pathname.

Let's run Program 14.3 a couple of times:

```
$ ./getexecname
exec name = /home/rich/doc/books/ssp/src/proc_env/getexecname
$ su
Password:
# cp getexecname /sbin
# exit
$ getexecname
exec name = /sbin/getexecname
```

First we run Program 14.3 from the current directory. This results in a relative pathname being returned by getexecname, so we prepend the current working directory to it. The second time we run Program 14.3, we copy it to /sbin first, which is our PATH. This time, getexecname returns an absolute pathname, so we don't need to prepend the current directory to it.

14.5   Environment Variables

We mentioned in Section 14.2 that processes are also passed a list of environment variables in the global variable, `environ`. Like the list of command line arguments, the list of environment variables is a pointer to an array of pointers, each of which points to a NUL-terminated string.

We can visualize the environment variable list as shown in Figure 14.2:

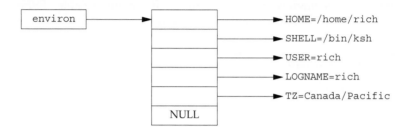

Figure 14.2   An example environment variable list.

By convention, environment variables are upper case only, but this is not a requirement.

Each environment variable consists of a name and value pair separated by an equals sign (=), as Figure 14.2 shows. An environment variable can be set without having a value; this is not the same thing as a variable being unset.

Something that we should be cognizant of is that the kernel doesn't look at the environment variables; they are used only by applications. A number of environment variables are set by the shell, and others are set automatically when we log in. Environment variables that are not automatically set when we log in are usually set in a shell-specific initialization file (e.g., `.profile` for sh and ksh, and `.login` and `.cshrc` for csh). For example, PATH is often configured in a shell initialization file because the default PATH doesn't contain many directories.

If we need to access the entire list of environment variables, we must use `environ`. However, to access individual environment variables, we should use the `getenv` and `putenv` functions.

The `getenv` Function

The `getenv` function is used to fetch the value associated with a given environment variable.

```
#include <stdlib.h>

char *getenv (const char *name);
```
              Returns: a pointer to the value associated with *name*, NULL if not found

The `getenv` function searches the environment variables for the string pointed to by *name*. The string must be of the form *name=value*, and if it is present, a pointer to *value* in the current environment is returned. If such a string is not present, `getenv` returns a NULL pointer.

The `putenv` Function

There are times when we want to set an environment variable. Either we want to change the value of an existing variable, or we want to add a new one. To do this, we use the `putenv` function.

```
#include <stdlib.h>

int putenv (char *string);
```
Returns: 0 if OK, non-zero on error

The `putenv` function places the string pointed to by *string* into the environment, where *string* must be of the form *name=value* (rather surprisingly, perhaps, there can be no spaces around the = sign). If *name* already exists in the environment, it is replaced. In either case, the string pointed to by *string* becomes part of the environment, so changing the string will change the environment.

The *string* argument should not be an automatic variable. This is because calling `putenv` with a pointer to an automatic variable may cause problems when the function calling `putenv` exits; the automatic variable will go out of scope, even though it is still part of the environment.

If the current memory allocated to the environment is insufficient to hold *string*, the `malloc` function is called to allocate more.

After `putenv` is called, the order of the environment variables is undefined. That is, the alphabetical listing seen by the `set` shell command will not necessarily be preserved.

Finally, we should note that a process can only modify its own environment or that of its children. There is no way to modify the environment of a parent or unrelated process. (We discuss the relationship of all these different processes in Chapter 16.)

Example: Manipulating environment variables

Program 14.4 displays, modifies, and redisplays the value of an environment variable.

Running Program 14.4 gives us the following results:

```
$ echo $HOME
/home/rich
$ ./getenv
Before putenv, HOME is /home/rich
After putenv, HOME is where the heart is
$ echo $HOME
/home/rich
```

```
                                                                    proc_env/getenv.c
1 #include <stdio.h>
2 #include <stdlib.h>
3 #include "ssp.h"

4 int main (void)
5 {
6     char *s;
7     char buf [LINE_LEN];

8     if ((s = getenv ("HOME")) == NULL)
9         err_quit ("HOME is not in the environment");
10    printf ("Before putenv, HOME is %s\n", s);

11    snprintf (buf, LINE_LEN, "HOME=where the heart is");
12    if (putenv (buf) == -1)
13        err_msg ("putenv failed");

14    if ((s = getenv ("HOME")) == NULL)
15        err_quit ("HOME is not in the environment");
16    printf ("After putenv, HOME is %s\n", s);

17    return (0);
18 }
```
                                                                    proc_env/getenv.c

Program 14.4 Getting and setting environment variables.

We show the value of HOME before and after running Program 14.4. Notice that although
we can change the value of HOME in the environment of our process, the changes we
make are not propagated to our shell's environment.

14.6 The Memory Layout of a C Program

In this text (and others), we sometimes see references to the program's text, or its stack or
heap. What are these things, and how do they relate to the environment of a process?

A C program is made up from several pieces: the text segment, the initialized and
uninitialized data segments, the stack, and the heap.

- Text segment. The text segment contains the machine code instructions executed
  by the CPU. The text segment is sharable so that only one copy need be in
  memory no matter how many copies of a program are running simultaneously.
  This can result in substantial memory savings on systems with many users
  executing the same program (e.g., the shell, vi, or a C compiler). The
  permissions on the text segment are read and execute; this means that programs
  can't accidentally (or otherwise) overwrite their own instructions.

- Initialized data segment. Often just called the data segment, the initialized data
  segment contains a program's variables that are specifically initialized. This
  means that declarations like

      int foo = 100;

cause the variable `foo` to be placed in the initialized data segment. The permissions on the initialized data segment are read, write, and execute.

The text and initialized data segments are stored in the program's file; the other segments are not stored in the program's file, and only exist for the life time of the process.

- Uninitialized data segment. This segment, also frequently called the BSS (derived from an ancient assembler directive that stood for "Block Started by Symbol") segment, contains the global variables that are not initialized, as well as any uninitialized static variables (initialized global and static variables are, of course, placed in the initialized data segment).

  The C language guarantees any variables in the BSS will be set to 0 by the time the program starts running.

- Stack. The stack is where automatic variables are stored, along with information saved each time a function is called. This information includes the address of the next instruction to be executed once the current function returns, and information about the caller's environment (e.g., processor registers). When a new function is called, sufficient space is allocated for the function's local variables and any temporary space the C compiler might reserve. Using the stack in this way allows functions to be recursive.

  Processes that conform to the SPARC-V9 ABI use a stack whose permissions are read and write (i.e., execute permission is disabled, preventing certain buffer overflow attacks). Processes conforming to previous versions of the SPARC ABI use a stack that has read, write, and execute permissions by default. As we showed in Chapter 9, we can set the kernel variable `noexec_user_stack` to 1 in `/etc/system` to override this default at a systemwide level, or use a loader mapfile to disable stack execution on a per-application level.

  As a rule, stacks grow "down" in memory, that is, from higher addresses to lower ones.

- Heap. The heap is where dynamically allocated memory is placed. The heap is located above the uninitialized data (BSS) segment, and grows "up" in memory.

On SPARC processors, some space above the stack is reserved for kernel context (on non-UltraSPARC processors) and the Open Boot PROM (OBP). Also, the virtual memory below the program's text is not mapped. This means that NULL pointer dereferences will cause a segmentation fault rather than return whatever happens to be at the bottom of the address space. This is a good idea, as NULL pointer dereferences are almost always an error; some platforms map 0 into these low address spaces, masking these errors.

> The only reason there's a 4 MB mapping at the top of Figure 14.3 on UltraSPARC processors is to simplify the virtual address arithmetic: it doesn't have to worry that the result of page + address will overflow the 4 GB boundary.

Figure 14.3 shows the arrangement of these segments for a 32-bit process on a sun4u architecture machine. The arrangement differs a bit on other architectures, but what we show in Figure 14.3 is sufficient for our needs.

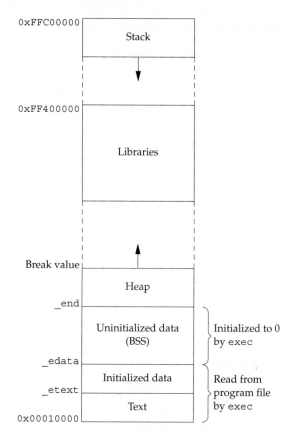

Figure 14.3 Address space for 32-bit SPARC sun4u processes.

One notable difference on x86 processors is that the stack is placed *below* the program's text, growing toward the bottom of memory.

As we stated previously (and as Figure 14.3 shows), a program's file on disk contains only the text and initialized data segments. We can use the `size` command to show the sizes of the text, initialized data, and BSS segments of a program. For example:

```
$ size /bin/ksh
194690 + 3000 + 5419 = 203109
```

In this example, /bin/ksh has a text size of 194,690 bytes, an initialized data segment size of 3000 bytes, and BSS segment size of 5419 bytes.

Finding the Last Locations in a Program

We can use three external variables to find the addresses of various parts of a program: _etext, _edata, and _end. These names refer neither to functions nor to locations with interesting contents; only their addresses are meaningful.

_etext	The address of _etext is the first location after the program text.
_edata	The address of _edata is the first location after the initialized data segment.
_end	The address of _etext is the first location after the uninitialized data segment (i.e., the BSS).

We show each of these addresses in Figure 14.3.

When a process begins execution, its break value coincides with _end. The *break value* of a process is the address of the first location beyond the end of its data segment (i.e., the heap). The break value may be changed by one of several functions, so the current break value should be determined as follows:

```
break_value = sbrk (0);
```

We discuss the sbrk function in Section 14.8.

14.7 Shared Objects

Figure 14.3 has a region of memory labelled "Libraries". These libraries contain functions that are used by the program, but are not implemented in the program itself. Examples of library functions include printf, open, stat, etc. Including a copy of all these functions in every program that used them would waste a lot of disk space, so they are placed in libraries that can be shared by multiple programs. Using shared objects also has the advantage of reducing the memory requirements of a system: the code for each library needs to be loaded only once (the data is of course private to each process). Another big advantage of using shared objects is that if we replace them with a newer version (for bug fixes or additional functionality), every program that uses the library will have access to the new version immediately, assuming that the function prototypes haven't changed. No relinking will be necessary.

One disadvantage with shared objects is that they have a small amount of run-time overhead when the program is first started or the first time a library function is called. This is because the run time linker must resolve the addresses of references to the functions in the library.

A program that uses shared objects is said to be *dynamically linked*. It is sometimes possible to link the library code directly into the executable program; such programs are said to be *statically linked*. Dynamically linked programs are produced by default on Solaris, and are by far the most preferred.

In addition to increased program size, static linking has another drawback: programs statically linked with the system libraries may fail when the system is upgraded or patched. From Solaris 10, linking statically with the system libraries is not an option, because the required files are not supplied.

Example: Comparing dynamic and static linking

Program 14.5 shows the standard "hello world" program.

proc_env/hello.c

```
1 #include <stdio.h>

2 int main (void)
3 {
4     printf ("Hello, World!\n");

5     return (0);
6 }
```

proc_env/hello.c

Program 14.5 The ubiquitous "hello world" program.

First we compile Program 14.5 using static linking.

```
$ cc -dn -o hello hello.c
$ file hello
hello:        ELF 32-bit MSB executable SPARC Version 1, statically linked,
    not stripped
$ ls -l hello
-rwxr-xr-x   1 rich     staff      373560 Dec 14 12:18 hello
$ size hello
220469 + 6297 + 2991 = 229757
```

> If we use gcc to compile our examples, we must use the -static command line option instead of -dn. So to compile our "hello world" program, we would use the following command line:
>
>   gcc -static -o hello hello.c
>
> The results we get are independent of the compiler we use.

Let's compile Program 14.5 again, but this time we'll use dynamic linking.

```
$ cc -o hello hello.c
$ file hello
hello:        ELF 32-bit MSB executable SPARC Version 1, dynamically linked,
    not stripped
$ ls -l hello
-rwxr-xr-x   1 rich     staff        5300 Dec 14 12:28 hello
$ size hello
1715 + 348 + 8 = 2071
```

(We had to wrap some lines so that they would fit on the page.) Notice how the size of the program file is drastically reduced when we use dynamic linking.

14.8   Memory Allocation

As we mentioned in our discussion of the memory allocation functions in Chapter 3, the memory pool used by `malloc` is allocated from the heap. When the amount of memory requested exceeds the space left in the heap, the heap is expanded using the `sbrk` function.

The `sbrk` Function

The size of a process' heap can be increased or decreased using the `sbrk` function.

```
#include <unistd.h>

void *sbrk (intptr_t incr);
```
Returns: prior break value if OK, (void *) -1 on error

The `sbrk` function is used to dynamically change the heap size of the calling process. This is accomplished by changing the break value of the process. The amount of allocated space increases as the break value increases. Newly allocated space is set to zero; however, memory reallocated to the same process has undefined contents. The original break value is set by `exec`; it is set to the highest location defined by the program text and data storage areas.

The `sbrk` function increases or decreases the break value by *incr* bytes. If *incr* is positive, the break value is increased (which increases the allocated space), and if it is negative, the break value is decreased (thereby decreasing the allocated space).

We should note that although `malloc` uses `sbrk` to increase the size of the heap, `free` does not use `sbrk` to decrease its size.

The `brk` Function

The `brk` function enables us to set the heap size of the calling process.

```
#include <unistd.h>

int brk (void *endds);
```
Returns: 0 if OK, -1 on error

The `brk` function is also used to change the heap size of the calling process dynamically. It does this by changing the break value to that specified by *endds*.

Using either of these functions and the `malloc` family of functions in the same process is at best ill advised, as the interaction between the two sets of functions is unspecified. The use of `mmap` (see Section 13.25) is preferred because it can be used portably with all other memory allocation functions.

14.9   The `setjmp` and `longjmp` Functions

C supports the notion of a local (i.e., within the same function) unconditional branch: the
`goto` statement. When used judiciously, the `goto` statement can make error checking
inside deeply nested loops somewhat easier to understand. For example, consider the
following code fragment:

```
while (...) {
    if (error)
        goto err;
    for (...) {
        if (error)
            goto err;
        while (...) {
            if (error)
                goto err;
        }
    }
}
...
err:    /* Handle error conditions */
```

If we didn't use `goto`, we would have to set flags and test them inside each loop. While
this is certainly doable, it would arguably obfuscate the code more than the use of `goto`
would. (In other words, although it is best avoided in structured programming, even
`goto` has its place when used appropriately.)

We can't use `goto` to perform an unconditional branch to a label in another function. If
we want to use a similar technique to handle nonfatal errors in deeply nested functions,
we must use the two functions provided for this purpose: `setjmp` and `longjmp`.

In Section 14.6, we said that the stack is used to store the local automatic variables and
return address for each function. This information is stored in a stack frame; there's one
stack frame for each function. Program 14.6 shows a simple program with nested
functions.

The `main` function in Program 14.6 reads a line from standard input and passes it to
`process_line`. This function calls `get_token` to return the first token, which is
assumed to be some sort of command. A switch statement is used to determine the
function to be called, depending which token is input. In this example, only one token is
recognized, which results in the function `do_foo` being called.

The code in Program 14.6 is typical for programs that read a command, determine which
command it is, and then call a function to process it (an example of this type of program
would be a shell). Figure 14.4 shows what the stack for Program 14.6 would look like
when in the function `do_foo`.

The size of the stack frame depends on how many local automatic variables the function
has, which is why the stack frames in Figure 14.4 have different sizes. The arrow below
`do_foo`'s stack frame indicates that the stack grows down in memory. While this
arrangement is typical, it is not mandatory.

proc_env/nested.c

```
1  #include <stdio.h>
2  #include "ssp.h"

3  #define FOO_CMD 1

4  static char *token_ptr;

5  static void process_line (char *line);
6  static void do_foo (void);
7  static int get_token (void);

8  int main (void)
9  {
10     char buf [LINE_LEN];

11     while (fgets (buf, LINE_LEN, stdin) != NULL)
12         process_line (buf);

13     return (0);
14 }

15 static void process_line (char *line)
16 {
17     int token;

18     token_ptr = line;
19     while ((token = get_token ()) != -1) {
20         switch (token) {
21             case FOO_CMD:
22                 do_foo ();
23                 break;
24         }
25     }
26 }

27 static void do_foo (void)
28 {
29     int token;

30     token = get_token ();
31     /* Other processing for this function */
32 }

33 static int get_token (void)
34 {
35     /*
36      * Get next token from line pointed to
37      * by token_ptr, and return its number.
38      */

39     return (0);
40 }
```

proc_env/nested.c

Program 14.6 A program using nested functions.

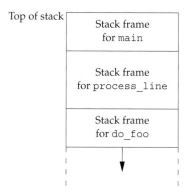

Figure 14.4 Stack frames after do_foo has been called.

A problem often encountered in programs like Program 14.6 is how to handle errors that aren't fatal. Suppose an error is encountered in do_foo, and that the appropriate course of action for the error is to discard the rest of the input line (maybe printing an error message) and read another. When we're nested several levels down from main, this can be hard to do in C. Each function would have to check for and return some sentinel value, which would become cumbersome and error prone.

In the same way that goto can help us in this situation within a function, a nonlocal goto, using setjmp and longjmp, helps us neatly solve this problem across function boundaries.

```
#include <setjmp.h>

int setjmp (jmp_buf env);

                    Returns: 0 if called directly, non-zero if returning from a call to longjmp

void longjmp (jmp_buf env, int val);
```

The setjmp function saves its stack environment in the buffer pointed to by *env* for later use by longjmp. The buffer pointed to by *env* is usually a global variable, because we must be able to reference it in another function.

The longjmp function restores the environment saved by the last call to setjmp with the corresponding *env* argument. When the longjmp is complete, program execution continues as if the corresponding call to setjmp had just returned *val*. (The exception to this is if *val* is set to 0; in this case, 1 will be returned by setjmp.) One caveat is that the function that called the corresponding setjmp must not have returned in the interim. At the time of this return from setjmp, all external and static variables have values as of the time longjmp was called.

We call setjmp from the place we want to return to; in our example program, that would be just before the while loop in main.

When we encounter an error (for example, in do_foo), we call longjmp to return to the location where we called setjmp. Because the second parameter of longjmp determines the value returned by setjmp, we can use different values to identify the location we're returning from if we want to. For example, we could return 1 from process_line, 2 from do_foo, and so on.

Returning to our example, Program 14.7 highlights the modifications we've made to implement this error handling. To save space, we've removed two functions (process_line and get_token) from the listing that haven't changed.

proc_env/setjmp.c

```
 1 #include <stdio.h>
 2 #include <setjmp.h>
 3 #include "ssp.h"

 4 #define FOO_CMD 1

 5 static char *token_ptr;
 6 static jmp_buf main_context;

 7 static void process_line (char *line);
 8 static void do_foo (void);
 9 static int get_token (void);
10 int main (void)
11 {
12     char buf [LINE_LEN];

13     if (setjmp (main_context) != 0)
14         printf ("Error\n");

15     while (fgets (buf, LINE_LEN, stdin) != NULL)
16         process_line (buf);

17     return (0);
18 }

       . . .

31 static void do_foo (void)
32 {
33     int token;

34     if ((token = get_token ()) == -1)
35         longjmp (main_context, 1);

36     /* Other processing for this function */
37 }
```

proc_env/setjmp.c

Program 14.7 Our example changed to use setjmp and longjmp.

This time, we call setjmp in main, which records the information required for a later return in the global buffer, main_context, and returns 0. The while loop is entered, which calls process_line, which in turn calls do_foo. For the sake of this discussion, let's assume that an error occurs when we call get_token. Just before longjmp gets called, the stack will look like Figure 14.4. However, calling longjmp causes the stack to be unwound back to main, discarding the stack frames for do_foo and process_line. In main, the longjmp results in setjmp returning the non-zero value passed in the second argument to longjmp. This in turn results in an error message being printed before the while loop is entered again.

Automatic, Register, and Volatile Variables

After a longjmp, the valued of global and static variables is unchanged, but what happens to the variables that are local to the target of a longjmp? Are the values rolled back to their values at the time of the setjmp, or do they have the same values as when longjmp was called? The short answer is "it depends". The long answer is that the value of automatic variables after a longjmp is indeterminate if three conditions are met:

1. They are local to the function containing the corresponding setjmp invocation.
2. They are not declared with the volatile type qualifier.
3. They are changed between the setjmp invocation and the call to longjmp.

From the preceding list, it is clear that if we want to be sure that the value of a local variable won't be rolled back, we must declare it to be volatile. Otherwise, the value is indeterminate, and may even be affected by compiler optimizations.

Example: The effect of optimization on automatic variables after a longjmp

Program 14.8 demonstrates the effect of longjmp on automatic, register, and volatile variables.

The results from running Program 14.8 depend on whether optimizations were turned on when we compiled it. Running Program 14.8 without any compiler optimizations gives the following results:

```
$ cc -o longjmp longjmp.c
$ ./longjmp
Before setjmp: var1 = 1, var2 = 20, var3 = 300
In func1: var1 = 1000, var2 = 20000, var3 = 300000
After longjmp: var1 = 1000, var2 = 20000, var3 = 300000
```

However, rerunning Program 14.8 after enabling the compiler's optimizer gives us different results:

```
$ cc -O -o longjmp longjmp.c
$ ./longjmp
Before setjmp: var1 = 1, var2 = 20, var3 = 300
In func1: var1 = 1000, var2 = 20000, var3 = 300000
After longjmp: var1 = 1, var2 = 20, var3 = 300000
```

Note that both times we run Program 14.8, the value of var3 is unchanged, verifying our earlier assertion that the value of volatile variables is not rolled back after a longjmp. Looking at the values for var1 and var2, we can see that these variables are not rolled back in the unoptimized version of Program 14.8, but they are in the optimized version. This suggests that they are stored in registers rather than on the stack. If this is the case,

proc_env/longjmp.c

```
 1 #include <stdio.h>
 2 #include <stdlib.h>
 3 #include <setjmp.h>

 4 static jmp_buf main_context;

 5 static void func1 (int i, int j, int k);
 6 static void func2 (void);

 7 int main (void)
 8 {
 9     int var1;
10     register int var2;
11     volatile int var3;

12     var1 = 1;
13     var2 = 20;
14     var3 = 300;

15     printf ("Before setjmp: var1 = %d, var2 = %d, var3 = %d\n", var1,
16         var2, var3);
17     if (setjmp (main_context) != 0) {
18         printf ("After longjmp: var1 = %d, var2 = %d, var3 = %d\n",
19             var1, var2, var3);
20         exit (0);
21     }

22     var1 = 1000;
23     var2 = 20000;
24     var3 = 300000;

25     func1 (var1, var2, var3);

26     return (0);
27 }

28 static void func1 (int i, int j, int k)
29 {
30     printf ("In func1: var1 = %d, var2 = %d, var3 = %d\n", i, j, k);
31     func2 ();
32 }

33 static void func2 (void)
34 {
35     longjmp (main_context, 1);
36 }
```

proc_env/longjmp.c

Program 14.8 The effect of longjmp on automatic, register, and volatile variables.

then we can also deduce that the hint to store var2 in a register was ignored by the compiler in the unoptimized version.

From this simple example, it is impossible to tell whether variables stored in registers are explicitly preserved or not—our previous results could be just circumstantial. A more complicated program that made more use of register variables might not roll back the register values after a longjmp.

The bottom line with all this discussion is that the only behaviour that can be relied on is that volatile variables will not be rolled back after a longjmp. Everything else is system dependent, and should not be relied on in portable code.

The _setjmp and _longjmp Functions

One of the problems with setjmp and longjmp is that their interaction with the signal mask of the calling process is undefined. To rectify this shortcoming, the _setjmp and _longjmp functions were introduced.

```
#include <setjmp.h>

int _setjmp (jmp_buf env);
```

            Returns: 0 if called directly, non-zero if returning from a call to _longjmp

```
void _longjmp (jmp_buf env, int val);
```

The _setjmp and _longjmp functions are identical to setjmp and longjmp respectively, except that the former functions explicitly do *not* save the caller's signal mask.

In Solaris, _setjmp is actually a synonym for setjmp, and _longjmp is a synonym for longjmp. However, this may not be the case in other implementations, so portable applications should not rely on this information.

When we talk about signals in Chapter 17, we'll describe two other functions that perform nonlocal branches. These two functions, called sigsetjmp and siglongjmp, are essentially the same as setjmp and longjmp, except they explicitly have the ability to save and restore the caller's signal mask if requested. Because of this additional functionality (that is defined in various standards including POSIX and the SUS), we recommend that new applications use them in preference to the _setjmp, setjmp, _longjmp, and longjmp functions we describe in this section.

A Common Error When Using Automatic Variables

We've seen that automatic variables are stored on the stack in stack frames. A golden rule of C programming is that automatic variables should never be referenced after the function that declared them has returned.

Program 14.9 shows a function that returns a temporary filename. The returned pathname is based on the name passed to the function and the process ID of the calling process.

The problem with Program 14.9 is that when the tmp_name function returns, the space it used on the stack to store the automatic variable name will be used by the stack frame for the next function that is called. The function that called tmp_name will try to use the pointer returned (presumably passing it to open or fopen), with potentially disastrous results. To correct this problem, the space for the resulting name should be allocated from global memory. There are two ways to do this:

proc_env/tmp_name.c

```
1 #include <stdio.h>
2 #include <unistd.h>
3 #include <sys/param.h>

4 char *tmp_name (const char *base)
5 {
6     char name [MAXPATHLEN];

7     snprintf (name, MAXPATHLEN, "/tmp/%s%d", base, getpid ());
8     return (name);
9 }
```

proc_env/tmp_name.c

Program 14.9   Incorrect usage of an automatic variable.

1. Define name to be either a `static` or an `extern` variable.
2. Allocate the memory dynamically, using one of the `malloc` functions.

Fortunately, some compilers warn that a function returns the address of a local variable, reminding us when we have made this error.

14.10 Resource Limits

A part of the environment of every process is the set of resource limits applied to it. We discussed resource usage in detail in Chapter 8, but to summarize, we can retrieve and set resource limits using the `getrlimit` and `setrlimit` functions. Solaris 9 also introduced the new resource control facility, which allows for finer grained resource control than the older rlimit mechanism does.

In Chapter 8 we also showed how the `/proc` file system (and to a lesser extent, the `getrusage` function) can be used to retrieve the current resource usage of a process.

It is important to appreciate the difference between resource limits and resource usage. The former is the maximum amount of a resource the process may consume, and the latter is the amount of the resource that has actually been consumed by the process.

14.11 Summary

This chapter has described the environment in which every C program running on UNIX executes. Understanding this is key to understanding the UNIX process controls.

In this chapter we saw some of what happens behind the scenes when a process starts: how the `main` function gets called, and how the command line arguments and environment variables are passed to the process. (We explained that the command line arguments and environment variables are not interpreted by the kernel in any way; they are merely passed to the process from the caller of exec.) We also described how a process terminates.

We described the memory layout of a C program (including a brief diversion comparing statically and dynamically linked processes), showing how allocating dynamic memory can increase the size of a process.

We then looked at how we can use the setjmp and longjmp functions to perform nonlocal unconditional branches within a process, and mentioned some of the problems and pitfalls we should be aware of. We concluded the chapter with a brief recap of our discussion of resource limits in Chapter 8.

Exercises

14.1 Is it possible for a function called by main to access the command line arguments, assuming that main doesn't copy them to global variables or pass them to the called function?

14.2 Why doesn't the size command we showed in Section 14.6 display the sizes of the stack and the heap?

14.3 Why don't the totals from the size command in Section 14.7 equal the size of the files as shown by ls?

14.4 Looking at the file sizes shown by the ls of Program 14.5 in Section 14.7, why is there such a large difference between the statically and dynamically linked versions, given how trivial the program is?

15

Process Control

15.1 Introduction

Now that we've discussed the environment in which a process executes, let's take a look at the process control functions provided by Solaris. Process control includes process creation, new program execution, and process termination. We'll also discuss concepts such as process identifiers, file sharing, and race conditions (including how to avoid the latter).

Interpreter files and the `system` function are also discussed. We end the chapter with a look at process accounting and process times, which give us a different perspective of the process control functions.

15.2 Process Identifiers

Every process on a UNIX system has a unique, positive integer associated with it; this number is known as the process ID (PID) of the process. Most process IDs are arbitrarily assigned on a first come, first served basis. The exceptions are so-called system processes created as part of the kernel's initialization process.

The first of these system processes is the scheduler. It has a process ID of 0 and is called `sched`. The second system process is `init`; we'll have more to say about this system process shortly. Process IDs 2 and 3 are reserved for the `pageout` and `fsflush` system processes respectively. The former is run when free memory falls below a certain value (the exact value is determined by the amount of RAM in the machine, which version of Solaris is being used, and whether priority paging is enabled), and the latter is run periodically (usually every 30 seconds) to flush dirty file system pages to disk.

The `init` system process, whose process ID is 1, is a special case of the system processes, because it is the only one that has a corresponding executable program on disk (the other system processes exist only as routines within the kernel). The name of this program in the Solaris operating environment is `/sbin/init`. The init process is responsible for bringing up the system once the kernel has been initialized. This is accomplished by running the appropriate `/sbin/rc?` scripts, which are determined by the current run level (in turn, these scripts call the scripts in `/etc/rc?.d`, each of which performs a specific task, like mounting file systems, configuring network interfaces, and starting various system services). It is also the only "system" process that runs as a regular user process that is no different from any other. Under normal circumstances, the init process never dies. We'll see later in this chapter how init inherits any orphaned child processes.

The `getpid` Function

A process can ascertain its process ID by calling `getpid`.

```
#include <unistd.h>

pid_t getpid (void);
```
                                                     Returns: the process ID of the calling process

The `getpid` function returns the process ID of the calling process. No errors are defined for this function.

The `getppid` Function

In addition to the unique process ID, every process has a parent process ID (PPID). A process' parent is usually the process that called one of the `fork` functions to create the process. A process can determine the process ID of its parent by calling `getppid`.

```
#include <unistd.h>

pid_t getppid (void);
```
                                                  Returns: the parent process ID of the calling process

The `getppid` function returns the parent process ID of the calling process (i.e., the process ID of the calling process' parent). No errors are defined for this function.

Each process has only one parent, but a process can be a parent of multiple children simultaneously. We'll talk more about parent process IDs in the next section.

15.3   The `fork` and `fork1` Functions

Using one of the `fork` functions is the *only* way to create a process in the UNIX environment.

```
#include <sys/types.h>
#include <unistd.h>

pid_t fork (void);

pid_t fork1 (void);
```

                                   Both return: 0 in child, process ID of child in parent, −1 on error

The `fork` function creates a new process. The new process, called the *child process*, is an exact copy of the calling process, which is called the *parent process*. Assuming there are no errors when creating the child process, the `fork` function returns twice: once in the parent, and another in the child. The `fork` function returns the process ID of the newly created child to the parent process, and 0 to the child (which can easily obtain its process ID by calling `getpid`, or `getppid` to get the process ID of its parent).

Both the child and the parent continue executing with the instruction after the call to `fork`. This leads to this frequently used idiom:

```
switch (child_pid = fork ()) {
    case -1:
        /* Handle error condition */
        break;

    case 0:
        /* Child specific code */
        break;

    default:
        /* Parent specific code */
        break;
}
```

Another common idiom when using `fork` is the use of multiple `if` statements:

```
if ((child_pid = fork ()) == -1) {
    /* Handle error condition */
}

if (child_pid == 0) {
    /* Child specific code */
}
else {
    /* Parent specific code */
}
```

We stated that the child is a copy of the parent. This means that the parent's text, data, and stack pages are copied (note that although read-only text segments may be shared, the data segments are actually copied; they are not shared). As an optimization measure, not all of the data pages are actually copied (fork is often followed by an exec, which would render useless the copied pages). Instead, the pages are marked *copy on write* (COW). When either process tries to write to a page marked COW, it is first copied so that the other process' view of the page is unchanged.

As well as copying the memory pages of the parent, the child process inherits the following attributes from its parent:

- The real and effective user and group IDs
- The environment
- The close on exec flags (see Section 15.11)
- The disposition of all signals
- Supplementary group IDs
- The set-user-ID and set-group-ID mode bits
- The profiling status (on or off)
- The nice value and scheduler class
- All attached shared memory segments
- The process group ID
- The session ID
- The root and current working directories
- The file creation mask (i.e., the umask value)
- The resource limits
- The controlling terminal
- The saved set-user-ID and saved set-group-ID
- The task ID and project ID
- Processor bindings
- Processor set bindings
- Any preferred hardware address translation sizes

The differences between a child and its parent are as follows:

- The process IDs are different. The child has a unique process ID which does not match any active process group ID.
- The two processes have different parent process IDs: the parent process ID of the child is set to the process ID of the parent; the parent process ID of the parent doesn't change.

- The value returned by `fork`.

- The child process has its own copy of the parent's file descriptors. Each of the child's file descriptors shares a common file pointer with the corresponding file descriptor of the parent. We'll talk about this more later.

- Each shared memory segment remains attached, and the value of `shm_nattach` is incremented by one.

- All of the `semadj` values are cleared.

- All process locks, text locks, data locks, and other memory locks held by the parent are not inherited by the child.

- The `tms` structure of the child process is cleared; `tms_utime`, `tms_stime`, `tms_cutime`, and `tms_cstime` are set to 0.

- The child process' resource usages are set to 0.

- Pending alarms are cleared for the child, and the `it_value` and `it_interval` values for the `ITIMER_REAL` timer are set to 0.

- The set of pending signals for the child is initialized to the empty set.

- No asynchronous I/O operations are inherited by the child.

- File locks set by the parent are not inherited by the child.

We haven't covered many of these features yet; we'll discuss them in later chapters.

Most of the time, `fork` and `fork1` behave the same. However, if Solaris threads are being used in preference to POSIX threads, there is a subtle distinction between the two. When Solaris threads are being used, `fork` duplicates in the child process all of the threads and LWPs in the parent. The `fork1` function, on the other hand, duplicates only the calling thread in the child process.

If POSIX threads are used, `fork` has the same semantics as `fork1` (i.e., only the calling thread is duplicated in the child).

> From Solaris 10, `fork` always has the same semantics as just described for `fork1`, and a new function, called `forkall`, has the same semantics as just described for `fork`.

Example: Using the `fork` function

Program 15.1 demonstrates the use of the `fork` function. The program is quite straightforward; the child process increments the two variables, and the parent sleeps for two seconds. Both parent and child then print out their process IDs and the values of the variables before terminating.

The reason why the parent sleeps is to try to ensure that the child runs first. Which process starts running first after returning from a `fork` is indeterminate, and there's no guarantee that a two-second sleep will be sufficient.

proc_control/fork.c

```
 1 #include <stdio.h>
 2 #include <unistd.h>
 3 #include <string.h>
 4 #include "ssp.h"

 5 int global_var = 123;
 6 char buf [] = "A write to stdout.\n";

 7 int main (void)
 8 {
 9     int local_var;

10     local_var = 456;
11     if (writen (STDOUT_FILENO, buf, strlen (buf)) != strlen (buf))
12         err_msg ("writen failed");
13     printf ("Before fork...\n");

14     switch (fork ()) {
15         case -1:
16             err_msg ("Can't fork");
17             break;

18         case 0:             /* Child */
19             global_var++;
20             local_var++;
21             break;

22         default:            /* Parent */
23             sleep (2);
24             break;
25     }

26     printf ("PID = %ld, global_var = %d, local_var = %d\n", (long) getpid (),
27         global_var, local_var);

28     return (0);
29 }
```

proc_control/fork.c

Program 15.1 An example of the `fork` function.

Running Program 15.1 gives the following results:

```
$ ./fork
A write to stdout.
Before fork...
PID = 23672, global_var = 124, local_var = 457
PID = 23671, global_var = 123, local_var = 456
$ ./fork > foo
$ cat foo
A write to stdout.
Before fork...
PID = 23674, global_var = 124, local_var = 457
Before fork...
PID = 23673, global_var = 123, local_var = 456
```

Notice that in this example the child's process ID is greater than the parent's. This is not always the case, however. At a certain value (30,000 by default on Solaris), the process IDs wrap around and start at the lowest available one again. Also notice what happens to the variables: they are incremented in the child, but not in the parent.

However, perhaps the most interesting observation we can make is how fork interacts with the I/O functions in Program 15.1. Recall from our discussion in Chapter 1 that write is not buffered, but the standard I/O library is. Because write is called once before the fork, its data is written once to standard output. In Section 5.11 we stated that if the standard I/O library is used, standard output is line buffered if it's connected to a terminal; otherwise, it is fully buffered. When we run Program 15.1 without redirecting standard output, the line printed by the printf on line 13 is printed only once. This is because the standard output buffer is flushed by the newline. However, when we run Program 15.1 with standard output redirected to a file, we get two copies of that line. This is because the line from printf remains in the buffer when fork is called. The buffer is copied to the child process when the parent's data space is copied, so both the parent and the child have a copy of the message in their standard output buffer. The output from the second printf (lines 26 and 27) is appended to the existing buffer in each process. The buffer is finally flushed when each process terminates (that is, when each process terminates, its copy of the buffer is flushed).

One way we can avoid this duplicated output is to call fflush prior to calling fork. Also, because of the problems with standard I/O buffering and the potential interaction with exit handlers, _exit should always be used in preference to exit when terminating the child process before calling exec (or if the call to exec fails).

File Sharing across fork

Another observation we can make about Program 15.1 is that when we redirected the standard output of the parent process, the child's standard output was also redirected. This is because all open file descriptors in the parent are duplicated in the child (our choice of the word "duplicated" is deliberate; the effect is as if the dup function had been called for each file descriptor). The parent and child share a file table entry for each open file descriptor that was open at the time of the fork.

Figure 15.1 illustrates the arrangement for the first three file descriptors of a parent and child once fork returns.

Notice that in Figure 15.1, the parent and child share the same file offset. This has to be the case; otherwise, data written by one process might be overwritten by writes by the other. For example, let's say that both processes normally write to standard output, which has been redirected. The child can write to standard output while the parent was waiting for it. Once the child terminates, the parent can write to standard output, knowing that its output will be appended to the child's. Without a shared file offset, this sort of interaction would be much harder to implement, and would require explicit actions by the parent.

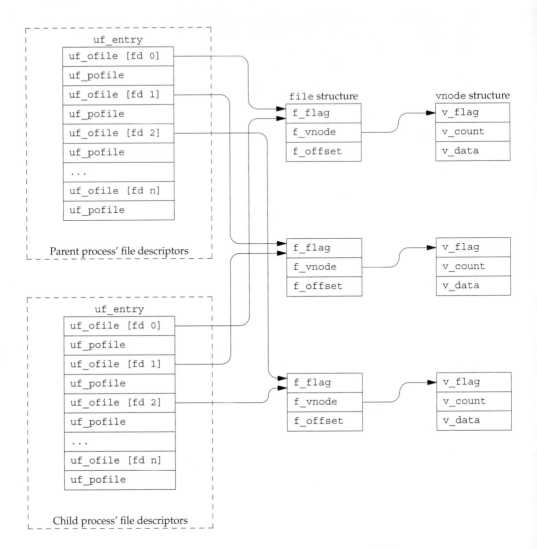

Figure 15.1 Sharing of open files between parent and child.

We saw in Program 15.1 that both processes can also write to the same file descriptor without any form of synchronization. In this case, the output of the two processes gets intermixed in an unpredictable manner. However, this is not how file descriptors are normally handled after a `fork`.

After a `fork`, file descriptors are usually handled in one of two ways:

1. The parent waits for the child to complete (this is the case we alluded to previously). In this case, the parent doesn't need to do anything with its file descriptors. When the child terminates, the file offsets of all the descriptors the child performed I/O on will be updated accordingly.

2. The parent and child each do their own thing. After the fork, both the parent and child close the descriptors they don't need. This way, there's no way one process can interfere with the other's open file descriptors. This is the modus operandi often used in network servers.

There are two main reasons why a fork might fail: the first is that there is insufficient virtual memory to create a copy of the calling process, and the second is that the number of processes per user limit has been reached. Passing the argument _SC_CHILD_MAX to the sysconf function will return the value of latter.

The fork function is used in one of two ways:

1. When a process wants to duplicate itself so that the parent and child can execute different sections of code at the same time (a sort of coarse-grained multithreading). This is common for network servers (recall our discussion of the in.talkd daemon from Section 13.15); the parent waits for services requests from clients, and when one arrives, the parent calls fork and lets the child handle the request. Meanwhile, the parent goes back to listening for further requests from clients.

2. When a process wants to run a different program (this a very frequent occurrence in shells). In this case, once the child returns from the fork, it invokes one of the exec functions to execute the new program (see Section 15.11).

Some OSes (for example, VMS) combine the steps from option 2 into a single operation called a *spawn*. UNIX keeps the two steps separate because there are numerous uses for fork without an exec. Keeping the two steps separate also allows us to change per-process attributes, such as signal disposition, I/O redirection, user ID, and so on.

> Version 3 of the Single UNIX Specification introduced the posix_spawn function, which does combine the two operations. However, SUSv3 is not supported by any of the versions of Solaris we cover in this text, so we'll say no more about this function.

15.4   The vfork Function

Even with the efficiency gained by using COW shared pages, fork is an expensive operation that is mostly wasted if all the child does is call exec. In this scenario, it is more efficient to create the child process using vfork.

```
#include <unistd.h>

pid_t vfork (void);
```
                                Returns: 0 in child, process ID of child in parent, –1 on error

Like fork, the vfork function creates a new process. However, vfork does not fully copy the address space of the parent process; the child process borrows the parent's memory and thread of control until a call to exec is made or the process terminates (either abnormally or by calling _exit).

Another difference between fork and vfork is that the latter guarantees that the child will run before the parent (in fact, the parent is suspended while the child uses its resources). When the child calls exec or _exit, the parent resumes execution. This can lead to deadlock if the child requires a resource that is held by the parent before calling either of these functions.

> We have to be careful here: although Solaris guarantees that the parent is suspended until the child calls exec or _exit, this behaviour is not mandated by any standards, so portable programs should not rely on it.

Example: Using the `vfork` function

Program 15.2 is a reimplementation of Program 15.1, with the call to fork replaced by a call to vfork. We've also removed the call to sleep from the parent (as we are guaranteed that the child will run first) and the write to standard output. We've added an explicit call to _exit at the end of the code for the child.

proc_control/vfork.c

```c
 1 #include <stdio.h>
 2 #include <unistd.h>
 3 #include <string.h>
 4 #include <stdlib.h>
 5 #include "ssp.h"

 6 static int global_var = 123;

 7 int main (void)
 8 {
 9     int local_var;

10     local_var = 456;
11     printf ("Before vfork...\n");

12     switch (vfork ()) {
13         case -1:
14             err_msg ("Can't vfork");
15             break;

16         case 0:                    /* Child */
17             global_var++;
18             local_var++;
19             _exit (0);
20     }

21     printf ("PID = %ld, global_var = %d, local_var = %d\n", (long) getpid (),
22         global_var, local_var);

23     return (0);
24 }
```

proc_control/vfork.c

Program 15.2 An example of the vfork function.

Running Program 15.2 gives the following results:

```
$ ./vfork
Before vfork...
PID = 27193, global_var = 124, local_var = 457
$ ./vfork > foo
$ cat foo
Before vfork...
PID = 27195, global_var = 124, local_var = 457
```

Notice how this time the variables in the parent are incremented by one. This is because the child is now executing in the address space of the parent, and hence has access to the parent's variables. (Contrast this to Program 15.1, where the values of the parent's variables remained unchanged.)

Notice that we've also used _exit to terminate the child rather than using exit. As we stated in Section 14.3, _exit does not flush the standard I/O buffers, but the exit function does. If we replace the call to _exit with a call to exit, the output from Program 15.2 now becomes this:

```
$ ./vfork
Before vfork...
PID = 27206, global_var = 124, local_var = 457
$ ./vfork > foo
$ cat foo
Before vfork...
```

Notice that when we call exit instead of _exit, the output from the second printf doesn't appear when we redirect standard output to a file. This is because when the child calls exit, the standard I/O library file streams are flushed and closed. Even though this happens in the child process, it's done in the parent's address space, so the parent's file streams are affected. When the parent later calls printf, its output is not flushed when main returns (because the redirected standard output stream is fully buffered rather than line buffered), and hence the second message isn't printed.

There are other, potentially far more damaging, side effects of using exit when terminating a child that was created by using vfork; the bottom line is that _exit should always be used in this situation instead of exit.

15.5   The exit and _exit Functions

As we described in Section 14.3, there are three ways a process may terminate normally and two ways a process may terminate abnormally.

The three methods of normal termination are:

1. Executing a return from the main function. This can be done explicitly by using the return keyword, or implicitly by falling off the end of main. Either is equivalent to calling exit.

2. Calling exit. This performs certain cleanup processing, including calling any exit handlers that were registered using atexit, the flushing and closing of all standard I/O streams, and deleting any temporary files created using tmpfile.

3. Calling the _exit function. This function (which eventually is called by exit) closes all file descriptors and directory streams, unmaps each memory mapped object, and detaches each shared memory segment.

The two methods of abnormal process termination are:

1. Calling the abort function. This is actually just a special case of the next item, because it causes a SIGABRT signal to be sent to the calling process.

2. Receiving certain signals. The signal can be generated by the process itself (e.g., by calling the abort function), another process (by using the kill function), or by the kernel. Examples of signals generated by the kernel include SIGSEGV, which is generated when a process attempts to reference a memory location that isn't within its address space, and SIGFPE, which can be generated when a process attempts to divide by zero (among other things).

Regardless of how a process terminates, the same code in the kernel eventually executes. It's this code that closes the file descriptors and frees up the resources the process was using.

No matter how a process terminates, it is useful for the terminating process to be able to notify its parent how it terminated. For the exit and _exit functions (as well as the return statement), this is done by passing an exit status as the argument. However, if the process terminates abnormally, the kernel—not the process—generates a termination status that indicates why the process terminated abnormally. In any of these cases, the parent process can obtain the termination status by using one of the wait functions we discuss in the following sections. The act of retrieving the termination status of a process is known as *reaping*.

Notice how we differentiate between the "exit status" and the "termination status" of a process. The *exit status* is the argument passed to exit or _exit, or the return value from main, and is converted into a termination status by the kernel. The *termination status* is a combination of the reason why a process terminated and its exit status (the latter is present only if the process exited normally). A process can retrieve the termination status of its children by calling one of the wait functions we discuss in the next section.

When a new process is created using fork, the newly created process has a parent that can interrogate its termination status. But what happens if the parent process terminates before the child? The answer is that the init process inherits the child process, becoming its parent. Whenever a process terminates, the kernel searches the list of active process to see if the terminating process is the parent of any of them. If so, the parent process ID of the still-active process is set to 1 (the process ID of init). Doing this ensures that every process has a valid parent.

Something else we need to consider is what happens when a child process terminates before its parent. If all traces of the child were removed, there would be no way to retrieve its termination status. What happens is that the kernel frees up most of the resources allocated to the child; what remains is enough information to be useful: the termination status, the process ID, and the amount of CPU time consumed.

A process that has terminated, but whose parent has not yet waited for it, is called a *zombie*. Zombies can be identified in the output of the ps command as processes whose command name (the CMD column) is <defunct>. There's nothing inherently wrong with zombies, because the amount of resources they consume is negligible. But a large number of zombies is indicative that some buggy software is being run (the software is buggy in that it should be reaping the termination status of its children). We'll see in Section 15.7 how zombies can be avoided.

Solaris 9 introduced the preap command, which forces the parent of the specified zombie process to reap its defunct child. The preap command should be used sparingly, however, as injudicious use might damage the parent process in unpredictable ways.

There's one last scenario we need to consider: what happens when a process that has been inherited by init terminates? We might be tempted to think that the terminating process becomes a zombie, but that isn't the case. When one of init's children terminates (whether they are inherited or direct descendents), init calls one of the wait functions to reap the termination status, preventing the system from being overwhelmed by zombies.

15.6 The `wait` Function

We can use several functions to reap the termination status of a process. The simplest of these is called wait.

```
#include <sys/types.h>
#include <sys/wait.h>

pid_t wait (int *stat_loc);
```
Returns: process ID if OK, –1 on error

The wait function suspends the calling process until the termination status of one its children becomes available. If a child has already terminated (i.e., it is a zombie), wait returns immediately.

If wait returns because the status of a terminated child is available and *stat_loc* is not NULL, the termination status of the terminated process is stored in the integer it points to. The termination status can be examined by using one of the following macros (each macro takes the value pointed to by *stat_loc* as its argument, which we'll call *status* for brevity):

WIFEXITED	This macro evaluates to a non-zero value (i.e., true) if *status* was returned for a child that terminated normally.
WEXITSTATUS	If the value of WIFEXITED (*status*) is true, then this macro evaluates to the exit status of the process (i.e., the argument passed to exit or _exit, or returned from main).
WIFSIGNALED	This macro evaluates to true if *status* was returned for a child that terminated due to the receipt of a signal.

WTERMSIG	If the value of WIFSIGNALED (*status*) is true, then this macro evaluates to the number of the signal that caused the process to terminate.
WCOREDUMP	If the value of WIFSIGNALED (*status*) is true, then this macro evaluates to true if a core file was created when the child terminated.
WIFSTOPPED	This macro evaluates to true if *status* was returned for a child that is currently stopped.
WSTOPSIG	If the value of WIFSTOPPED (*status*) is true, then this macro evaluates to the number of the signal that caused the process to stop.
WIFCONTINUED	This macro evaluates to true if *status* was returned for a child that has continued.

Example: Printing the termination status of a process

The function print_term_status (Program 15.3) prints a description of the termination status passed to it. Notice how we use the strsignal function to translate the signal numbers returned by WTERMSIG and WSTOPSIG to more descriptive strings.

———————————————————————————— lib/term_status.c

```
 1 #include <stdio.h>
 2 #include <string.h>
 3 #include <sys/wait.h>

 4 void print_term_status (int status)
 5 {
 6     if (WIFEXITED (status))
 7         printf ("Normal termination; exit status = %d\n",
 8             WEXITSTATUS (status));
 9     else if (WIFSIGNALED (status))
10         printf ("Abnormal termination; signal = %s%s\n",
11             strsignal (WTERMSIG (status)),
12             WCOREDUMP (status) ? " (core dumped)" : "");
13     else if (WIFSTOPPED (status))
14         printf ("Child stopped; signal = %s\n",
15             strsignal (WSTOPSIG (status)));
16 }
```

———————————————————————————— lib/term_status.c

Program 15.3   Describe the termination status of a process.

Program 15.4 demonstrates our print_term_status function by calling it for different termination reasons.

Running Program 15.4 gives the following results:

```
$ ./term_status
Normal termination; exit status = 123
Abnormal termination; signal = Abort (core dumped)
Abnormal termination; signal = Arithmetic Exception (core dumped)
```

proc_control/term_status.c

```
1  #include <stdio.h>
2  #include <stdlib.h>
3  #include <sys/wait.h>
4  #include <sys/types.h>
5  #include <unistd.h>
6  #include "ssp.h"

7  int main (void)
8  {
9      int status;

10     switch (fork ()) {
11         case -1:
12             err_msg ("Can't fork");

13         case 0:
14             _exit (123);
15     }

16     if (wait (&status) == -1)
17         err_msg ("wait error");
18     print_term_status (status);

19     switch (fork ()) {
20         case -1:
21             err_msg ("Can't fork");

22         case 0:
23             abort ();
24     }

25     if (wait (&status) == -1)
26         err_msg ("wait error");
27     print_term_status (status);

28     switch (fork ()) {
29         case -1:
30             err_msg ("Can't fork");

31         case 0:
32             status /= (getpid () - getpid ());
33     }

34     if (wait (&status) == -1)
35         err_msg ("wait error");
36     print_term_status (status);

37     return (0);
38 }
```

proc_control/term_status.c

Program 15.4 Demonstrating different termination statuses.

15.7 The waitpid Function

The wait function we have just described is adequate if we have only one child process
or if we don't mind blocking until one of our children terminates. But if we have several

children and want to wait for a specific one to terminate—or if we just want to see if a child process has terminated without blocking—then the wait function can no longer meet our needs. Fortunately, the waitpid function addresses these shortcomings.

```
#include <sys/types.h>
#include <sys/wait.h>

pid_t waitpid (pid_t pid, int *stat_loc, int options);
```

Returns: 0 or process ID if OK, –1 on error

The waitpid function also suspends the calling process until the termination status of one of its children becomes available.

The *pid* argument specifies the process to wait for, and is interpreted thus:

pid == –1	This causes waitpid to wait for any child process (i.e., the same as wait).
pid > 0	This waits for the child whose process ID is equal to *pid*.
pid == 0	This waits for any child that is in the same process group as the caller (i.e., any child whose process group ID is equal to that of the caller).
pid < –1	This waits for any child whose process group ID is equal to the absolute value of *pid*.

(We describe process groups in Section 16.4.) The *options* argument can be used to further control the operation of waitpid, and is constructed from the bitwise-OR of zero or more of the following flags:

WCONTINUED	The status of any child specified by *pid* that has been continued (whose status has not already been reported) is returned.
WNOHANG	This causes waitpid not to block the calling process if the status of one of the child processes specified by *pid* is not immediately available. If no status available, waitpid returns 0.
WNOWAIT	This keeps the process whose status was returned in a waitable state. The process may be waited for again with identical results.
WUNTRACED	The status of any child process specified by *pid* that has been stopped, and whose status has not yet been reported since it stopped, is returned. We can use the WIFSTOPPED macro to determine whether the return value corresponds to a stopped process.

As with wait, if *stat_loc* is not NULL, the termination status (if any) of the terminated child will be placed in the integer pointed to by it. The same macros we described for the wait function can be used to examine the termination status.

Example: Avoiding zombies

Suppose we want to write a program that forks a child, but we don't want to wait for the child to complete and we don't want it to become a zombie? Besides the technique involving signals that we'll discuss in Section 17.2, we can call fork twice; Program 15.5 shows how.

—— *proc_control/no_zombie.c*

```
1  #include <stdio.h>
2  #include <unistd.h>
3  #include <stdlib.h>
4  #include <sys/types.h>
5  #include <sys/wait.h>
6  #include "ssp.h"

7  int main (void)
8  {
9      pid_t pid;

10     switch (pid = fork ()) {
11         case -1:
12             err_msg ("Can't fork");
13             break;

14     case 0:                /* First child */
15         switch (fork ()) {
16             case -1:
17                 err_msg ("Can't fork");
18                 break;

19             case 0:     /* Second child */
20                 sleep (2);
21                 printf ("In second child; PPID = %ld\n", (long) getppid ());
22                 _exit (0);

23             default:
24                 _exit (0);
25         }
26         _exit (0);

27     default:               /* Parent */
28         if (waitpid (pid, NULL, 0) == -1)
29             err_msg ("waitpid failed");
30         break;
31     }

32     return (0);
33 }
```

—— *proc_control/no_zombie.c*

Program 15.5 Avoiding zombies by calling fork twice.

Create first child

10–13 Call fork to create our first child.

First child

14–18 The first thing we do in the first child is call `fork` again to create another child (the grandchild of the first process, as it were).

Second child

19–22 In the second child, we call `sleep` before printing the parent process ID. We go to sleep because there's no way to determine which process will execute first. Without the `sleep`, the second child could conceivably print the process ID of our first process, which would be misleading because that process will terminate very soon after the message was printed.

Back in the first child

23–26 After calling `fork` to create the second child, the first child exits.

Reap status of first child

27–31 Back in the parent, we reap the status of the first child by calling `waitpid`, passing it the first child's process ID.

Running Program 15.5 gives us the following:

```
$ ./no_zombie
$ In second child; PPID = 1
```

Notice how the shell prints its prompt when the original process terminates, which is before the second child prints its parent's process ID.

15.8   The `wait3` and `wait4` Functions

We can use two other functions to reap the termination status of a terminated process: `wait3` and `wait4`.

```
#include <sys/wait.h>
#include <sys/time.h>
#include <sys/resource.h>

pid_t wait3 (int *statusp, int options, struct rusage *rusage);

pid_t wait4 (pid_t pid, int *statusp, int options, struct rusage *rusage);
```
Both return: process ID or 0 if OK, –1 on error

The `wait3` function is similar to the `wait` function, except that we can pass it a pointer to an `rusage` structure. If *statusp* is not a NULL pointer, the status of one of the terminated children is placed in the buffer. If *rusage* is not NULL, a summary of the resources used by the process waited for and all if its children will be stored in the buffer provided. However, only the system time and user time used are currently available (compare this with the `getrusage` function we discussed in Section 8.7).

The *options* argument can be used to further control the operation of these two functions. It is constructed from the bitwise-OR of zero or more of the following flags:

WNOHANG   This causes `wait3` and `wait4` not to block the calling process
                    if the status of one of the child processes specified by *pid* is not
                    immediately available. If no status available, `wait3` and
                    `wait4` return 0.

WUNTRACED   The status of any child process specified by *pid* that has been
                    stopped, and whose status has not yet been reported since it
                    stopped, is returned.

The `wait4` function is the same as `wait3`, except we specify the process ID of the process
we are interested in by using the *pid* argument. If *pid* is equal to 0, `wait4` is identical to
`wait3`. If *pid* is non-zero, then the status is returned for the indicated process, but not for
any other.

The status that is returned in *statusp* can be examined using the same macros we
described for the `wait` function.

15.9 The `waitid` Function

Related to the `wait` functions we've already discussed is the `waitid` function.

```
#include <wait.h>

int waitid (idtype_t idtype, id_t id, siginfo_t *infop, int options);
```
                                                     Returns: 0 if OK, −1 on error

The `waitid` function suspends the calling process until one of its children changes state,
returning immediately if a child process changed state prior to the call. The state of a
child process will change if it terminates, stops because of a signal, becomes trapped, or
reaches a breakpoint. The current status of the child is recorded in the buffer pointed to
by *infop*.

The *idtype* and *id* arguments specify which children are to be waited for, as follows:

- If *idtype* is P_PID, then `waitid` waits for the child whose process ID is equal to
  id.

- If *idtype* is P_PGID, then `waitid` waits for any child whose process group ID is
  equal to *id*.

- If *idtype* is equal to P_ALL, then `waitid` waits for any child, and *id* is ignored.

The *options* argument is used to specify which state changes are to be waited for. It is
constructed from the bitwise-OR of one or more of the following flags:

WCONTINUED   Return the status of any child, whose status has not already
                    been reported, that was stopped and has been continued.

WEXITED   Return the status of any child that has terminated. If such
                    child exists, `waitid` will block until a child terminates.

WNOHANG   Return immediately if the status of any children cannot be
                        determined.

WNOWAIT   This keeps the process whose status was returned in a
                        waitable state.

WSTOPPED   This returns the status of any child that has stopped as a result
                        of receiving a signal, blocking if necessary.

WTRAPPED   This waits for any child process to become trapped or reach a
                        breakpoint.

If `waitid` returns because a child process was found that satisfies the conditions indicated by *idtype* and *options*, then the `siginfo` structure pointed to by *infop* will be populated with the status of the process. We'll discuss this structure in Chapter 17, but for now we only need to know about two members: `si_signo` and `si_pid`. The `si_signo` member will always be equal to `SIGCHLD`. If the `WNOHANG` flag is set in *options*, `waitid` will return 0 immediately, whether or not a child has changed state. If the `si_pid` member is 0, then no children have changed state.

Calling `waitid` with *idtype* set to `P_ALL` and *options* set to `WEXITED | WTRAPPED` is equivalent to calling `wait`.

15.10 Race Conditions

A *race condition* (sometimes called a *race hazard*) is the name given to the situation where the outcome of several operations depends on the order in which they are performed, but the order in which they are actually performed is indeterminate.

In the context of our discussion, a race condition occurs if any logic after a `fork` depends (either explicitly or implicitly) on whether the parent or child runs first. We have no way of determining which process (child or parent) will run first after a `fork`, and even if we did, the continued running of each process would be subject to the scheduling algorithm.

We saw an example of a race condition in Program 15.5, when the second child prints out the process ID of its parent. If the second child runs before the first, then its parent will still be the first child when it calls `getppid`. However, if the first child runs first and has enough time to `exit`, then `init` will become the parent of the second child.

We inelegantly worked around the race condition by calling `sleep`. We say inelegantly because even a two second `sleep` gives us no guarantees; on a heavily loaded system, the second child could resume after `sleep` returns, before the first child has had a chance to run and `exit`. Problems like this can be very hard to track down, because they tend to work "most of the time".

If a process wants to wait for its child to terminate before it continues, the solution is quite straightforward; calling one of the `wait` functions will suffice. However, a process waiting for its parent to terminate is more problematic. One solution would be to use a loop like this:

```
while (getppid () != 1)
    sleep (1);
```

The trouble with this approach (called *polling*) is that it wastes CPU time, because the child is woken up every second to perform the test.

To avoid race conditions and polling, the processes need some sort of asynchronous method of notifying each other that they are ready. Signals are a candidate for this sort of operation, as we'll see in Section 17.23. Other sorts of interprocess communication (IPC) facilities are available; we discuss them in Part 5 of this text.

In a parent-child relationship, there is often a need for each process to do something, waiting for the other to accomplish its task before continuing to do its own thing. For example, the parent might record the process ID of the child in a log file, and the child might create a file for the parent. The child would wait for the parent to update its log, which would then wait for the child to create the file. In pseudocode, this scenario would look something like this:

```
fork ();
if (child) {
    wait for parent
    do stuff in child
    tell parent we're finished
    do other stuff in child
    exit
}

do stuff in parent          (parent goes first)
tell child we're finished
wait for child
do other stuff in parent
exit
```

We can see from the pseudocode that we need four routines: one to wait for the child, another to wait for the parent, a third to tell the child we're done, and one more to tell the parent we're done. Although it's not readily apparent from our pseudocode, we also need another routine to initialize the others, and another to finish. We'll call these routines (which can be functions or macros) `ssp_wait_child`, `ssp_wait_parent`, `ssp_tell_child`, and `ssp_tell_parent`. We'll call the other two routines `ssp_tell_wait_init` and `ssp_tell_wait_fin` respectively.

We'll show how to implement these routines in a later chapter, but for now let's look at an example that uses them.

Example: Avoiding race conditions

Program 15.6 illustrates a typical race condition by printing two strings: one from the parent and one from the child. The race condition is present because although the intention is for each process to print a complete string one after the other, the actual output we get depends on which process runs first and the whims of the scheduler.

The `main` function

5–19 Our `main` function creates a new process, and then both the parent and the child call `print_chars` to print a string.

proc_control/race1.c

```
 1 #include <sys/types.h>
 2 #include <unistd.h>
 3 #include "ssp.h"

 4 static void print_chars (const char *string);

 5 int main (void)
 6 {
 7     switch (fork ()) {
 8         case -1:
 9             err_msg ("Can't fork");
10             break;

11         case 0:
12             print_chars ("Hello from child\n");
13             _exit (0);

14         default:
15             print_chars ("Hello from parent\n");
16             break;
17     }

18     return (0);
19 }

20 static void print_chars (const char *string)
21 {
22     const char *c;

23     for (c = string; *c; c++)
24         writen (STDOUT_FILENO, c, 1);
25 }
```

proc_control/race1.c

Program 15.6   Program with a race condition.

The `print_chars` function

20–25 The function `print_chars` prints its argument (which is assumed to be a pointer to a NUL-terminated string) one character at a time. We print each character by calling `write`. The idea is to try to get the kernel to switch between the two processes as often as possible to demonstrate the race condition (the return from a system call is usually one of the places the kernel decides which process to run next). Even doing this doesn't guarantee that we'll see erroneous output, thus hiding the race condition.

The following output shows how the results can vary. We ran Program 15.6 on a dual-processor machine to exacerbate the race condition (on a single-processor Ultra 1, the race condition didn't manifest itself).

```
$ ./race1
Hello from child
Hello from parent
$ ./race1
HeHello from child
llo from parent
```

```
$ ./race1
HHello from child
ello from parent
```

Today's faster processors also help mask race conditions like this, because the CPU can perform more work in the process' time slice.

To avoid this race condition, we need to use the `ssp_wait` and `ssp_tell` functions we discussed earlier. Program 15.7 is a reimplementation of Program 15.6 that does this; we've highlighted the new lines.

proc_control/race2.c

```
 1 #include <sys/types.h>
 2 #include <unistd.h>
 3 #include "ssp.h"

 4 static void print_chars (const char *string);

 5 int main (void)
 6 {
 7     pid_t pid;

 8     if (ssp_tell_wait_init () == -1)
 9         err_msg ("ssp_tell_wait_init failed");

10     switch (pid = fork ()) {
11         case -1:
12             err_msg ("Can't fork");
13             break;

14         case 0:
15             if (ssp_wait_parent () == -1)
16                 err_msg ("ssp_wait_parent failed");
17             print_chars ("Hello from child\n");
18             _exit (0);

19         default:
20             print_chars ("Hello from parent\n");
21             if (ssp_tell_child (pid) == -1)
22                 err_msg ("ssp_tell_child failed");
23             break;
24     }

25     return (0);
26 }

27 static void print_chars (const char *string)
28 {
29     const char *c;

30     for (c = string; *c; c++)
31         writen (STDOUT_FILENO, c, 1);
32 }
```

proc_control/race2.c

Program 15.7 Reimplementation of Program 15.6 avoiding race condition.

Initialize our synchronization mechanism

8–9 Call `ssp_tell_wait_init` to perform whatever initialization it needs to.

Create a new process

10–13 Create a new process by calling `fork`.

Child process

15–16 Wait for the parent to notify us that we can continue.

17–18 Call `print_chars` to print a message.

Parent process

20 Call `print_chars` to print a message.

21–23 Tell the child that we're finished, so it can do what it needs to.

The `print_chars` function

27–32 The function `print_chars` prints its argument (which is assumed to be a pointer to a NUL-terminated string) one character at a time, by calling `write`.

When we run Program 15.7, the output is as we expect: there is no intermingling of the output from the two processes.

In Program 15.7, the child is well behaved and lets the parent go first. By changing lines 14 to 23 to

```
case 0:
    print_chars ("Hello from child\n");
    ssp_tell_parent (getppid ());
    break;

default:
    ssp_wait_child ();
    print_chars ("Hello from parent\n");
    break;
```

we can make the child more rebellious by insisting that its parent wait for it.

15.11 The `exec` Functions

As we mentioned in Section 15.3, `fork` (or one of its variants) is the only way to create a new process in the UNIX environment. Similarly, calling one of the six `exec` functions is the only way to run a new program. The process calling `exec` is completely replaced by the new one, which starts executing at its `main` function (assuming the program was written in C). Note that the process ID doesn't change across the `exec`. This is because no new process is created; the calling process is merely replaced by the one on disk. The new process image is constructed from a regular executable file, which is called the *new process image file*. This file is either an executable object file or a data file for an interpreter (more on these later).

We've already mentioned that the process ID doesn't change after an `exec`, but we need to consider other properties of the process:

- Any file descriptors open in the calling process remain open after the `exec`, except for those whose close on exec (`FD_CLOEXEC`) flag is set. The attributes of the file descriptors that stay open remain the same. Note that the default is for file descriptors to remain open across an `exec` unless we specifically set the `FD_CLOEXEC` flag using `fcntl`.

- Directory streams, on the other hand, are closed across an `exec`. This is usually done by the `opendir` function calling `fcntl` to set the `FD_CLOEXEC` flag for the file descriptor associated to the directory stream.

- The preferred hardware address translation size for the stack and heap of the new process image are set to the default system page size.

- Signals that are ignored (`SIG_IGN`) or set to the default action (`SIG_DFL`) in the calling process image keep the same disposition in the new process image. Signals that were set to be caught by a signal handler in the calling process image will be set to the default action in the new process image. Alternate signal stacks are not preserved, and the `SA_ONSTACK` flag is cleared for all signals. (We talk about these concepts in Chapter 17.)

- Any exit handlers previously registered with `atexit` are discarded (i.e., they are no longer registered).

- The real user ID and real group ID remain unchanged after the `exec`, but the values of the effective user ID and effective group ID depend on the permissions of the new process image file and the mount options for the file system containing the new process image file.

  If the file system is mounted with the `ST_NOSUID` bit set (i.e., it was mounted with the `nosuid` option specified), then the effective user ID and effective group ID are unchanged in the new process image. However, if this is not the case, then the effective user ID and effective group ID depend on the set-user-ID and set-group-ID bits of the new process image file's permissions. If the set-user-ID flag for the program file is set, then the effective user ID of the new process image will be set to the owner of the file. The effective group ID is handled similarly.

  The effective user ID and and effective group ID are saved (as the saved set-user-ID and the saved set-group-ID respectively) for use by `setuid`.

- Any shared memory segments attached to the calling process image will not be attached to the new process image.

- Memory mappings established through `mmap` are not preserved across an `exec`.

- Memory locks established by calls to `mlockall` or `mlock` in the calling process image are removed. If locked pages in the address space of the calling process are also mapped into the address space of other processes and are locked by those processes, the locks established by the other processes will be unaffected by the call by this process to the `exec` function.

- If `_XOPEN_REALTIME` is defined and has a value other than −1, then any named semaphores open in the calling process are closed as if by appropriate calls to `sem_close`. We talk about semaphores in Chapter 20.

- Profiling is disabled for the new process.
- Timers created by the calling process using the `timer_create` function are deleted before the current process image is replaced with the new one.
- If the `SCHED_FIFO` or `SCHED_RR` scheduling policies are in effect, the policy and priority settings remain the same in the new process image. (The default scheduling policy is `SCHED_IA`.)
- All open message queue descriptors in the calling process are closed in the new process image, as though closed by appropriate calls to `mq_close`.
- Any outstanding asynchronous I/O operations may be cancelled. Uncancelled asynchronous I/O operations will complete as if the `exec` function had not yet occurred, but any associated signal notifications will be suppressed.

We've already stated that the new process image inherits the calling image's process ID (the parent process ID is also inherited), but the new process image also inherits several other attributes from the calling process:

- The `nice` value
- The scheduler class and priority
- The process ID and parent process ID
- The process group ID (We'll talk about process groups in Chapter 16.)
- The task ID
- The supplementary group IDs
- The `semadj` values of semaphores
- The session ID
- The real user ID and real group ID
- The Project ID
- The trace flag
- The time left until an alarm clock signal
- The root and current working directories
- The file creation mask
- The resource limits
- The `tms_utime`, `tms_stime`, `tms_cutime`, and `tms_cstime` values
- File locks
- The controlling terminal
- The process signal mask
- The pending signals
- The processor bindings
- The processor set bindings

We haven't covered many of these features yet; we'll discuss them in later chapters.

A call to exec from a multithreaded process results in all threads in that process being terminated and the new executable image being loaded and executed. No destructor functions are called.

There are actually six different exec functions. Unless we need to be explicit, we'll just refer to "the exec function", on the understanding that any of the six exec functions can be used. Each of the six exec functions performs the same task: overlaying the calling process image with another. We describe the particulars of each function below.

The `execl` Function

The first exec function is called execl.

```
#include <unistd.h>

int execl (const char *path, const char *arg0, ..., const char *argn,
    char * /* NULL */);
```
Returns: −1 on error, no return on success

The execl function overlays the calling process with the new process image file specified by *path*. The arguments *arg0* to *argn* are pointers to NUL-terminated strings, which constitute the argument list available to the new process image (recall our discussion in Section 14.4). By convention, *arg0* points to a filename that is associated with the process being started. Notice that the list of arguments is terminated by a NULL pointer.

The environment variables of the calling process are passed to the new process.

The `execv` Function

The second exec function is called execv.

```
#include <unistd.h>

int execv (const char *path, char *const argv []);
```
Returns: −1 on error, no return on success

The execv function also overlays the calling process with the new process image file specified by *path*. The *argv* argument points to an argument vector (i.e., an array of NUL-terminated strings), which constitute the argument list available to the new process image. The last element of the *argv* array must be a NULL pointer, which terminates the argument list, and conventionally, *argv* [0] points to a filename that is associated with the process being started.

The environment variables of the calling process are passed to the new process.

The `execle` Function

The next exec function is called `execle`.

```
#include <unistd.h>

int execle (const char *path, const char *arg0, ..., const char *argn,
    char * /* NULL */, char *const envp []);
```

Returns: −1 on error, no return on success

The `execle` function is the same as the `execl` function, except that we specify the environment variables to be passed to the new process image in the vector pointed to by *envp*. The last element of *envp* must be a NULL pointer, which terminates the list.

Explicitly setting up a controlled environment is important for security critical programs. There are also times when specifying a certain environment (rather than just inheriting the environment of the calling process) makes sense. For example, the `login` program defines a small number of environment variables, like LOGNAME, TERM, and USER. Other variables (e.g., PATH and the prompt) are added to the environment by the shell's start-up file, and some are properties of the shell itself (e.g., ksh's RANDOM and SECONDS).

The `execve` Function

The fourth exec function is called `execve`.

```
#include <unistd.h>

int execve (const char *path, char *const argv [], char *const envp []);
```

Returns: −1 on error, no return on success

The `execve` function is the same as the `execv` function, except that we specify the environment variables to be passed to the new process image in the vector pointed to by *envp*. The last element of *envp* must be a NULL pointer, which terminates the list.

The `execlp` Function

The fifth exec function is called `execlp`.

```
#include <unistd.h>

int execlp (const char *file, const char *arg0, ..., const char *argn,
    char * /* NULL */);
```

Returns: −1 on error, no return on success

The `execlp` is the same as the `execl` function, with one important difference: the calling process is overlaid with the new process image file specified by *file*. The *file* argument specifies a filename, which is interpreted in one of two ways:

1. If *file* contains a slash character, it is taken as a pathname.
2. If *file* does not contain a slash character, then the named file is searched for in the directories specified by the `PATH` environment variable.

The `PATH` environment variable is a list of colon-separated directories (called path prefixes) that are searched in the order in which they appear. For example, the environment string

```
PATH=/usr/sbin:/usr/bin:.
```

specifies three directories to search: `/usr/sbin`, `/usr/bin`, and the current directory. For security reasons, including the current directory in our `PATH` should only be done with trepidation; `root`'s `PATH` should *never* include the current directory. Chapter 23 of [Garfinkel and Spafford 2003] explains in more detail why the current directory should not be included in our `PATH`.

If the process image file that is found is not a valid executable object, it is assumed to be a shell script. The contents of the file are used as the standard input to the shell. In this case, the shell becomes the new process image. If the application is standards conforming (as defined in the `standards` man page), then `/usr/xpg4/bin/sh` is used as the shell; otherwise, `/usr/bin/sh` is used.

The `execvp` Function

The last `exec` function is called `execvp`.

```
#include <unistd.h>

int execvp (const char *file, char *const argv []);
```
                                            Returns: −1 on error, no return on success

The `execvp` function is the same as the `execv` function, with the exception that the calling process is overlaid with the new process image file specified by *file*. The *file* argument specifies a filename, which is interpreted in one of two ways:

1. If *file* contains a slash character, it is taken as a pathname.
2. If *file* does not contain a slash character, then the named file is searched for in the directories specified by the `PATH` environment variable.

Example: Using the `exec` functions

Program 15.8 demonstrates the use of some of the `exec` functions.

proc_control/execs.c

```
1  #include <unistd.h>
2  #include <stdlib.h>
3  #include <sys/types.h>
4  #include <sys/wait.h>
5  #include "ssp.h"

6  static char *new_env [] = {
7      "USER=richteer",
8      "PATH=/tmp",
9      NULL
10 };

11 int main (void)
12 {
13     switch (fork ()) {
14         case -1:
15             err_msg ("Can't fork");
16             break;

17         case 0:
18             execle ("./echo_all", "echo_all", "arg1", "arg 2", NULL, new_env);
19             err_msg ("execle failed");
20     }

21     if (wait (NULL) == -1)
22         err_msg ("wait failed");

23     switch (fork ()) {
24         case -1:
25             err_msg ("Can't fork");
26             break;

27         case 0:
28             execlp ("echo_all", "echo_all", "only 1 arg", NULL);
29             err_msg ("execlp failed");
30     }

31     return (0);
32 }
```

proc_control/execs.c

Program 15.8 Demonstrating the exec functions.

Create a child

13–16 Call `fork` to create a child process.

First child process

17–20 We call `execle`, which requires us to supply a pathname and a specific environment. If the call to `execle` fails, we print an error message (recall that if an `exec` function is successful, it does not return).

Parent process continues

21–22 Wait for the first child to terminate, discarding its termination status.

Create another child

23–26 Call `fork` again to create another child process.

Second child process

27–30 In the second child, we call `execlp`. This function searches the directories in the PATH environment variable for the given filename and passes the caller's environment to the new process image. The only reason `execlp` works is because the current directory was in our PATH for the duration of this example.

Notice how in both cases we set the first argument to the filename component of the pathname. Some shells set the first argument to the complete pathname.

The `echo_all` program that each child runs is shown in Program 15.9. It's a trivial program that prints out its command line arguments and its environment variables.

—————————————————————————————— *proc_control/echo_all.c*

```
 1 #include <stdio.h>

 2 int main (int argc, char **argv)
 3 {
 4     int i;
 5     char **p;
 6     extern char **environ;

 7     printf ("Command line arguments:\n");
 8     for (i = 0; i < argc; i++)
 9         printf ("  argv [%d]: %s\n", i, argv [i]);

10     printf ("Environment variables:\n");
11     for (p = environ; *p != 0; p++)
12         printf ("  %s\n", *p);

13     return (0);
14 }
```
—————————————————————————————— *proc_control/echo_all.c*

Program 15.9 Echo all the command line arguments and environment variables.

Running Program 15.8 gives us the following results (we've not shown all the environment variables to save space):

```
$ OLD_PATH=$PATH
$ PATH=$PATH:.
$ ./execs
Command line arguments:
  argv [0]: echo_all
  argv [1]: arg1
  argv [2]: arg 2
Environment variables:
  USER=richteer
  PATH=/tmp
$ Command line arguments:
  argv [0]: echo_all
  argv [1]: only 1 arg
Environment variables:
```

```
    USER=rich
    SHELL=/bin/ksh
    HOME=/home/rich
    TERM=dtterm
    TZ=Canada/Pacific
$ PATH=$OLD_PATH
$ ./execs
Command line arguments:
   argv [0]: echo_all
   argv [1]: arg1
   argv [2]: arg 2
Environment variables:
   USER=richteer
   PATH=/tmp
$ execlp failed: No such file or directory
```

Notice that the shell prompt appears before the second occurrence of the string "Command line arguments". This is because the parent program doesn't `wait` for the second child to finish. Also notice that the call to `execlp` failed the second time we ran Program 15.8. This is because the current directory was not in our `PATH`, unlike the first time we ran Program 15.8.

Summary of the `exec` Functions

Remembering which `exec` function to use under different circumstances can be difficult, so we summarize them here:

`execl`	Takes a pathname and a list of arguments to pass to the new process. Passes on the current environment to the new process image.
`execv`	Takes a pathname and an argument vector. Passes on the current environment to the new process image.
`execle`	Takes a pathname and a list of arguments to pass to the new process. The specified environment vector is passed to the new process image.
`execve`	Takes a pathname and an argument vector. The specified environment vector is passed to the new process image.
`execlp`	Takes a filename and uses the `PATH` environment variable to find the executable file, and takes a list of arguments to pass to the new process. Passes on the current environment to the new process image.
`execvp`	Takes a filename and uses the `PATH` environment variable to find the executable file, and an argument vector. Passes on the current environment to the new process image.

The letters in the name after the base `exec` can help us remember which function requires what arguments. The letter `l` means that the function takes an argument list, and is mutually exclusive with the letter `v`, which means that the function takes an argument vector. The letter e means that the function takes an environment vector rather than passing on the current environment. Finally, the letter p means that the function takes a filename (rather than a pathname) argument, and uses the PATH environment variable to find the executable file. Figure 15.2 summarizes these observations.

Function	*path*	*file*	Arg list	Arg vector	Env passed	Env vector
execl	•		•		•	
execv	•			•	•	
execle	•		•			•
execve	•			•		•
execlp		•	•		•	
execvp		•		•	•	
(letter in name)		p	l	v		e

Figure 15.2 Summary of the six exec functions.

The *path* column of Figure 15.2 indicates that the specified function has a pathname argument and ignores the PATH environment variable, and the *file* column of Figure 15.2 indicates that the specified function has a filename argument and searches the directories in the PATH environment variable.

There is a limit on the total size of the argument list and the list of environment variables. This value is given by ARG_MAX, which is defined in <limits.h>. In the Solaris operating environment, 32-bit processes are limited to 1 MB; 64-bit processes have a 2 MB limit.

Astute readers may have noticed that five of the exec functions could be used to transform their arguments into a format suitable for use by the sixth, which is execve. Figure 15.3 shows this arrangement.

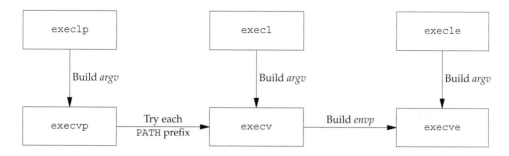

Figure 15.3 Relationship of the six exec functions.

The six exec functions, together with the fork, exit, and wait functions, provide all the process control primitives we need. We create processes with fork, run new programs with exec, terminate a process using exit, and wait for process termination (optionally collecting the termination result) with the wait function. We'll see later how these primitives can be used to build other functions, like system and popen.

15.12 Interpreter Files

We mentioned earlier that the new process image file that is passed to the `exec` function is either a precompiled binary image or an interpreter file. An *interpreter file* is a plain text file whose first line looks like this:

> `#!`*pathname [optional argument]*

The "`#!`" construct is sometimes referred to as a *shebang*, and there can be optional white space between the exclamation mark and the *pathname*. The most common interpreter files are those that start with the line

> `#!/bin/sh`

The *pathname*, which is usually an absolute pathname because no special processing (like using PATH) is performed on it, specifies the name of the interpreter that will interpret the interpreter file. (The recognition of these files occurs in the kernel, as part of the processing of the `exec` system call, so process-level concepts like environment variables are not available.) Note that it is the interpreter specified by *pathname* on the first line that is executed by the kernel, not the interpreter file itself.

The *pathname* is passed to the interpreter as *arg0*; if the optional argument is present, it is passed as *arg1* to the interpreter. The remaining arguments to the interpreter are the original *arg0* to *argn* arguments passed to `exec`. The recognition of interpreter files is not recursive, so the interpreter named by *pathname* must not be an interpreter file.

Although Solaris allows up to MAXPATHLEN characters in the first line of an interpreter file (including the `#!`, the *pathname*, the optional argument, and any spaces), many systems have only a 32-character limit. Hence, portable interpreter files should limit the first line to 32 characters.

Interpreter files are also known as *scripts*, and are further categorized depending on the interpreter used to interpret the script. For example, an interpreter file that is interpreted by one of the shells is known as a *shell script*, one that's interpreted by `awk` is called an *awk script*, and so on.

Example: Passing an interpreter file to `exec`

To illustrate what the kernel does with the `exec` arguments when running an interpreter file, Program 15.10 runs an interpreter file that has an optional argument on the first (and only) line.

The following screen dump shows the contents of our one line interpreter file and the results of running Program 15.10.

```
$ cat script
#!echo_all foo
$ ./exec_int
Command line arguments:
  argv [0]: echo_all
  argv [1]: foo
  argv [2]: ./script
  argv [3]: arg1
```

proc_control/exec_int.c

```
 1  #include <unistd.h>
 2  #include <stdlib.h>
 3  #include <sys/types.h>
 4  #include <sys/wait.h>
 5  #include "ssp.h"

 6  int main (void)
 7  {
 8      switch (fork ()) {
 9          case -1:
10              err_msg ("Can't fork");
11              break;

12          case 0:
13              execle ("./script", "script", "arg1", "arg 2", NULL, NULL);
14              err_msg ("execl failed");
15      }

16      if (wait (NULL) == -1)
17          err_msg ("wait failed");

18      return (0);
19  }
```

proc_control/exec_int.c

Program 15.10 A program the execs an interpreter file.

```
    argv [4]: arg 2
  Environment variables:
```

The echo_all program run by the script is Program 15.9, which just echoes its command line arguments and environment variables. Notice that when the interpreter (echo_all) is execed, argv [0] is the *pathname* of the interpreter, argv [1] is the optional argument from the interpreter file, and the remaining arguments are the *path* (./script) and the third and fourth arguments in the call to execle in Program 15.10. Note that the *path* argument from execle is used rather than the first argument (which is script in this case). This is done based on the assumption that *path* might contain more information than the first argument.

Example: Using the optional argument in an interpreter file

A common use for the optional argument in interpreter files is to specify the -f flag for programs that support it (e.g., awk or sed). For example, an awk program can be run as

```
    awk -f awk_program_file
```

which tells the awk interpreter to read and run the awk program contained in the file awk_program_file.

> To confuse the issue somewhat, many systems, including Solaris, supply two versions of the awk language: the original version, sometimes known as "old awk", which was distributed with Version 7 UNIX; and a newer version, sometimes called "new awk". The latter contains many enhancements to the former, and is described in [Aho, Kernighan, and Weinberger 1988]. One of

the enhancements provided with the new version is access to the command line arguments, which we'll need for this example.

Solaris provides both versions of awk. The two names of the older version are /bin/awk and /bin/oawk, and the two names for the newer version are /usr/xpg4/bin/awk and /bin/nawk (we'll use /bin/nawk in our examples).

Using the -f option in an interpreter file enables us to write

```
#!/bin/nawk -f
```

(The awk program goes here in the interpreter file.)

Program 15.11 shows the interpreter file we'll use in this example. It merely echoes its command line arguments.

———————————————————————————————— *proc_control/awk_eg*

```
1 #!/bin/nawk -f

2 BEGIN {
3     for (i = 0; i < ARGC; i++)
4         printf ("ARGV [%d]: %s\n", i, ARGV [i])
5     exit
6 }
```

———————————————————————————————— *proc_control/awk_eg*

Program 15.11   An awk script as an interpreter file.

Assuming we turn on the execute bit for the file, we can run Program 15.11 with the following results:

```
$ ./awk_eg arg1 "arg 2"
ARGV [0]: /bin/nawk
ARGV [1]: arg1
ARGV [2]: arg 2
```

When /bin/nawk is executed, its command line arguments are

```
/bin/nawk -f ./awk_eg arg1 arg 2
```

The pathname of the interpreter file, ./awk_eg, is passed to the interpreter. When the interpreter file is read by nawk, the first line is ignored because the hash sign (#) is awk's comment character.

We can verify our statements about the command line arguments by replacing /bin/nawk with Program 15.9.

```
$ su
Password:
# mv /bin/nawk /bin/nawk.bak
# cp echo_all /bin/nawk
# suspend                              Suspend the root shell
[1] + Stopped (SIGSTOP)        su
$ ./awk_eg arg1 "arg 2"
Command line arguments:
  argv [0]: /bin/nawk
  argv [1]: -f
  argv [2]: ./awk_eg
  argv [3]: arg1
```

```
argv [4]: arg 2
...
$ fg
su
# mv /bin/nawk.bak /bin/nawk
# exit
```

Environment variable output omitted
Resume the root *shell in the foreground*

In our example, the -f flag (which tells awk what file the program is in) is required. If we remove it from Program 15.11, it no longer works:

```
$ ./awk_eg arg1 "arg 2"
/bin/nawk: syntax error at source line 1
 context is
          >>> . <<< /awk_eg
/bin/nawk: bailing out at source line 1
```

This is because now the command line arguments are

```
/bin/nawk ./awk_eg arg1 arg 2
```

and /bin/nawk is trying to interpret the string ./awk_eg as an awk program. If we couldn't pass at least one optional argument to the interpreter, interpreter files would be usable only by shells.

Interpreter files are not really required, but they do provide a gain in efficiency for the user. This increased efficiency does, however, come at a price: increased overhead in the kernel processing of the exec function. This is because the exec code must specifically look for the shebang every time it is called. Nevertheless, interpreter files are useful for the following reasons:

1. They hide the fact that certain programs are scripts written in some other language. For example, to execute Program 15.11 we can just say

   ```
   ./awk_eg optional arguments
   ```

   instead of needing to know the program was actually a script written in awk that we would otherwise have to run as

   ```
   /bin/nawk -f awk_eg optional arguments
   ```

   Of course, this obfuscation only goes so far, as the file command reveals all:

   ```
   $ file awk_eg
   awk_eg:         executable /bin/nawk script
   ```

2. Despite the overhead in the kernel's exec code, interpreter files provide a gain in efficiency. We could hide the fact that our example program, awk_eg, is an awk script by wrapping it in a shell script:

   ```
   nawk 'BEGIN {
       for (i = 0; i < ARGC; i++)
           printf ("ARGV [%d]: %s\n", i, ARGV [i])
       exit
   }' $*
   ```

   The trouble with this approach is that it is grossly inefficient. First the shell reads the command and tries to exec the filename given. Because the shell script is an executable file, but isn't machine-executable, an internal error occurs in the exec processing and the assumption is made the the filename is a shell script (which in this case, it is). The shell /bin/sh (or /usr/xpg4/bin/sh if the calling program is standards compliant) is execed with the pathname of our script as the argument. The shell correctly runs our script, but to run the awk program it must fork, exec, and wait. All this amounts to much more overhead than the shebang processing performed by exec.

3. Interpreter files enable us to write shell scripts in shells other than /bin/sh. Recall that when exec finds an executable file that is not machine-executable, it invokes /bin/sh (or /usr/xpg4/bin/sh if the calling program is standards compliant) to interpret the file. By using an interpreter file, we can just write

```
#!/bin/ksh
```

(The Korn shell script goes here in the interpreter file.)

to ensure that the script gets interpreted by /bin/ksh. As before, we could wrap all this up in a /bin/sh script that invokes the Korn shell, but more overhead would be required.

None of this would work if the shells and other interpreters like awk didn't use a hash as their comment character.

15.13 The system Function

Although we can perform just about any conceivable task in C with no dependencies on outside programs, there are times when it makes sense to call an external program to do some of the work for us. Consider the task of placing a time stamp into a file. We can take three approaches:

1. We could use the functions we describe in Chapter 6: call time to get the current time since the epoch, call cftime to format the result, and write the resulting string to the file (having previously opened it), being sure to close the file once we've written the time stamp into it.

2. We could fork a child process, redirect its standard output to a file by manipulating the child's file descriptors, and then exec /bin/date.

3. The easiest option is to use the system function:

```
system ("date > file");
```

which handles all the details for us.

Of the three methods, system is the easiest one to use, albeit the least flexible.

```
#include <stdlib.h>

int system (const char *string);
```
                                                                          Returns: see text

If *string* is a NULL pointer, a check is performed to see if the shell that would have been used to interpret *string* (had it not been NULL) exists and is executable. If the shell is available, a non-zero value is returned. Otherwise, 0 is returned. (Which shell is used depends on whether the calling application is standards conforming. A conforming application uses /usr/xpg4/bin/sh; a nonconforming one uses /bin/sh.)

If *string* is not a NULL pointer, the system function causes it to be passed to the shell as input as if *string* had been typed at a terminal. If all goes well, system does not return until the shell has terminated.

Behind the scenes, system uses the vfork, exec, and waitpid functions, so the return value (in the event of a non-NULL *string*) will one of three different types:

1. If either of the fork or waitpid functions fails, −1 is returned.

2. If the exec fails, the return value will be as if the shell had executed the statement exit (127).

3. If the vfork, exec, and waitpid function succeed, the return value will be the shell's termination status in the format specified by waitpid.

The advantage of using system instead of fork and exec is that the former does all the error and signal handling for us.

Example: Implementing the system function

Let's take a look at implementing the system function. Program 15.12 shows our version, which is complete except for the signal handling. We'll add the correct signal handling in Section 17.25.

Before we test our version of the system function, let's take a closer look at some of the implementation details.

Set up the appropriate shell

13–16 Call the sysconf function with an argument of _SC_XOPEN_VERSION, which returns the version of the X/Open Portability Guide (XPG) to which the calling application conforms. If the returned value is less than 4, we are a nonconforming application, and use /bin/sh as the shell.

17–20 Otherwise, we are a conforming application, and use /usr/xpg4/bin/sh. Note that this might fail prior to Solaris 9 if the package SUNWxcu4 isn't installed.

Handle a NULL command string

21–25 If the *string* argument is NULL, and if the access function indicates that we can't execute the appropriate shell, we set the return code to 0 and quit.

26–30 Otherwise, we set the return code to 1 and quit.

Create child process

31–34 If the call to vfork fails, we return −1.

Pass the command string to the shell in child process

35–36 In the child process, we call execl to invoke the appropriate shell. Notice that the first argument we pass to the shell is -c; this tells it to take the next command line argument

proc_control/ssp_system.c

```
 1 #include <sys/types.h>
 2 #include <sys/wait.h>
 3 #include <unistd.h>
 4 #include <errno.h>

 5 int ssp_system (const char *string)
 6 {
 7     int status;
 8     int rc;
 9     int w;
10     pid_t pid;
11     char *shell;
12     char *shell_path;

13     if (sysconf (_SC_XOPEN_VERSION) < 4) {
14         shell = "sh";
15         shell_path = "/bin/sh";
16     }
17     else {
18         shell = "sh";
19         shell_path = "/usr/xpg4/bin/sh";
20     }

21     if (string == NULL) {
22         if (access (shell_path, X_OK) == -1) {
23             rc = 0;
24             goto bail;
25         }
26         else {
27             rc = 1;
28             goto bail;
29         }
30     }

31     if ((pid = vfork ()) == -1) {
32         rc = -1;
33         goto bail;
34     }
35     else if (pid == 0) {
36         execl (shell_path, shell, "-c", string, NULL);
37         _exit (127);
38     }

39     do {
40         w = waitpid (pid, &status, 0);
41     } while ((w == -1) && (errno == EINTR));

42     rc = ((w == -1) ? w : status);

43 bail:
44     return (rc);
45 }
```

proc_control/ssp_system.c

Program 15.12 Our implementation of the system function (without signal handling).

(*string* in this case) as its input rather than reading from standard input or a file. The shell parses the NUL-terminated string, breaking it up into separate tokens for the actual command. The command string we pass to the shell can contain any valid shell commands and metacharacters. This means that we can redirect standard input and standard output by using < and >.

If we didn't invoke the shell to perform this step, we would have to do everything ourselves: parsing the command string into separate arguments, and calling execlp to run the shell. Without a *lot* of extra effort, we would not be able to use the shell's metacharacters.

37 If the call to execl fails, we indicate this by setting the child's exit status to 127. Note that we call _exit instead of exit (recall our discussion in Section 14.3).

Wait for child in parent process

39–41 In the parent process, we call waitpid to wait for the child to terminate. If waitpid returns an error because it was interrupted by a signal, we continue to wait.

42 If waitpid returned successfully, we return the termination status of the child to the caller; otherwise, we return −1.

Program 15.13 tests our implementation of the system function (note that we use the print_term_status function we showed in Program 15.3).

── *proc_control/test_sys.c*

```
 1 #include "ssp.h"

 2 extern int ssp_system (const char *string);

 3 int main (void)
 4 {
 5     int status;

 6     if ((status = ssp_system ("date")) == -1)
 7         err_msg ("system failed");
 8     print_term_status (status);

 9     if ((status = ssp_system ("bad_command")) == -1)
10         err_msg ("system failed");
11     print_term_status (status);

12     if ((status = ssp_system ("date; exit 42")) == -1)
13         err_msg ("system failed");
14     print_term_status (status);

15     return (0);
16 }
```

── *proc_control/test_sys.c*

Program 15.13 Testing our implementation of the system function.

Running Program 15.13 gives the following results:

```
$ ./test_sys
Wed Jan 22 11:53:32 PST 2003
Normal termination; exit status = 0      For first date
sh: bad_command: not found
Normal termination; exit status = 1      For bad_command
Wed Jan 22 11:53:32 PST 2003
Normal termination; exit status = 42     For exit
```

It's interesting to observe how the output from Program 15.13 changes if we compile it as a standards conforming application (we showed how to do this in Section 2.11):

```
$ ./test_sys
Wed Jan 22 12:03:39 PST 2003
Normal termination; exit status = 0
sh: bad_command:  not found              Now using /usr/xpg4/bin/sh
Normal termination; exit status = 127    Exit status is now 127
Wed Jan 22 12:03:40 PST 2003
Normal termination; exit status = 42
```

Notice that this time, /usr/xpg4/bin/sh is used to execute the commands, and that it returns 127 when an error occurs when trying to run the specified command (rather than the 1 returned by sh).

Using system in Set-User-ID and Set-Group-ID Programs

One case that deserves special mention is the use of system in set-user-ID or set-group-ID programs. For security reasons, this should *never* be done. This is because the special permissions of the set-user-ID program will be inherited by the program that is executed by system.

Instead of using system, a set-user-ID (or set-group-ID) program that wants to spawn another process should use fork and exec directly, being sure to drop any privileges (i.e., switch back to the real user ID) after the fork before calling exec.

Even programs that intend to pass on their elevated privileges to their children should not use system. This is because system invokes the desired program by running a shell, and this could have undesirable side effects.

15.14 Process Accounting

Like most UNIX systems, Solaris can be configured to perform process accounting. When process accounting is enabled, the kernel writes a record to the accounting file (usually /var/adm/pacct) every time a process terminates.

Process accounting is turned on by the superuser running the accton command, passing it the name of the accounting file to be used. Running accton with no arguments disables process accounting. The accton command calls a function we don't describe in this text to enable and disable process accounting: acct.

The records written to the accounting file are defined by the `acct` structure, which is defined in `<sys/acct.h>`. The `acct` structure consists of the following members:

```
typedef ushort_t comp_t;     /* "Floating point" number */

struct acct {
    char    ac_flag;         /* Accounting flag */
    char    ac_stat;         /* Termination status */
    uid_t   ac_uid;          /* Accounting (real) UID */
    gid_t   ac_gid;          /* Accounting (real) GID */
    dev_t   ac_tty;          /* Controlling terminal */
    time_t  ac_btime;        /* Beginning time */
    comp_t  ac_utime;        /* User CPU time in clock ticks */
    comp_t  ac_stime;        /* System CPU time in clock ticks */
    comp_t  ac_etime;        /* Elapsed time in clock ticks */
    comp_t  ac_mem;          /* Memory usage in pages */
    comp_t  ac_io;           /* Bytes transferred by read & write */
    comp_t  ac_rw;           /* Number of block reads & writes */
    char    ac_comm [8];     /* Command name */
};
```

The defined type `comp_t` is a pseudo floating-point representation, with a 3-bit base 8 exponent in the high-order bits, and a 13-bit mantissa in the low-order bits.

The `ac_flag` member is used to record certain events during the execution of the process. Figure 15.4 describes these events.

ac_flag	Description
AFORK	Process is the result of a fork, but didn't call exec
ASU	Process used superuser privileges
ACCTF	Record type
AEXPND	Expanded record type; this is the default

Figure 15.4 Values for `ac_flag` in a process accounting record.

The `ac_stat` member, despite its name, does not contain the complete termination status for the process. In the event of abnormal termination, it contains the number of the signal that caused the process to terminate, and a flag that is set if a core dump was produced. If the process terminates normally, this value is 0.

The data required for the accounting records are kept by the kernel, in the process table entry for the process. The entries are initialized when the process is created (i.e., after a fork) and written when the process terminates. This means that the accounting file is written in termination order, not the order in which the processes were started. To ascertain the starting order, we would have to search the entire file, and sort it using the `ac_btime` member as the sort key. But even this wouldn't be ideal, because the start time is stored with a granularity of only one second, and it's possible that several processes could start in the same second.

Even though the elapsed time is measured in clock ticks (usually 100 per second), we don't know the end time of a process. Hence, we can't reconstruct the exact process starting order from the data in the accounting file.

Another thing to bear in mind is that accounting records correspond to processes, not programs; a new record is initialized after a `fork`, not when a new program is run using `exec`. Although the `exec` doesn't create a new accounting record, the command name changes (the `ac_comm` member), and the `AFORK` flag is cleared. This means that if we have a sequence of three programs (i.e., program 1 execs program 2, which then execs program 3, and program 3 exits), only one accounting record will be written. The command name in `ac_comm` will correspond to the name of program 3, but the CPU times and other resource usages will be the sum for all three programs.

Example: Examining process accounting records

Before we can write a program that interprets the process accounting file for us, we need to generate some data to examine. To do that, we'll run Program 15.14, which creates a number of children, each of which does something different and then terminates in one of several ways.

Create first child and sleep

9–14 Create the first child by calling `fork`. The parent sleeps for two seconds and then exits.

First child

16–21 The first child creates the second, and then sleeps for four seconds before calling `abort`. This terminates the first child process, creating a core dump.

Second child

23–28 The second child creates the third, and then execs `/bin/dd`, copying the file `/kernel/genunix` to `/dev/null`.

Third child

30–35 The third child creates the fourth, and then sleeps for eight seconds before terminating.

Fourth child

37–39 The fourth child sleeps for six seconds, and then terminates itself with a signal that doesn't produce a core dump.

Figure 15.5 depicts the process hierarchy for Program 15.14.

Now that we've described the program we're going to use to create the accounting data, let's turn our attention to Program 15.15, which prints selected fields from the accounting file.

Running Programs 15.14 and 15.15 gives us the following results (we've appended a description of the process to each line in italics, to help identify them in the following discussion):

proc_control/gen_acct.c

```
 1 #include <sys/types.h>
 2 #include <unistd.h>
 3 #include <stdlib.h>
 4 #include <signal.h>
 5 #include "ssp.h"

 6 int main (void)
 7 {
 8     pid_t pid;

 9     if ((pid = fork ()) == -1)
10         err_msg ("1st fork failed");
11     else if (pid != 0) {
12         sleep (2);
13         exit (2);
14     }

15     /* In first child */

16     if ((pid = fork ()) == -1)
17         err_msg ("2nd fork failed");
18     else if (pid != 0) {
19         sleep (4);
20         abort ();
21     }

22     /* In second child */

23     if ((pid = fork ()) == -1)
24         err_msg ("3rd fork failed");
25     else if (pid != 0) {
26         execl ("/bin/dd", "dd", "if=/kernel/genunix", "of=/dev/null", NULL);
27         exit (8);
28     }

29     /* In third child */

30     if ((pid = fork ()) == -1)
31         err_msg ("2nd fork failed");
32     else if (pid != 0) {
33         sleep (8);
34         exit (0);
35     }

36     /* In fourth child */

37     sleep (6);
38     kill (getpid (), SIGKILL);
39     return (6);
40 }
```

proc_control/gen_acct.c

Program 15.14 Program to generate some process accounting entries.

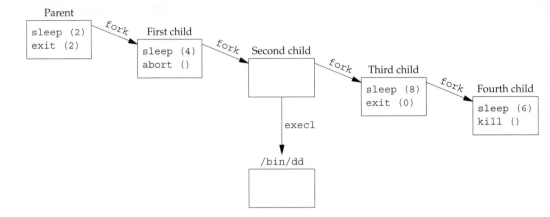

Figure 15.5 Process hierarchy for Program 15.14.

```
$ su
Password:
# /usr/lib/acct/accton /var/adm/pacct
# suspend
[1] + Stopped (SIGSTOP)              su
$ ./gen_acct
3461+1 records in
3461+1 records out
$ fg
su
# /usr/lib/acct/accton
# exit
$ ./pracct
accton     S  etime =       3, io =            0, stat =     0
dd            etime =      33, io =      3544576, stat =     0    Second child
gen_acct      etime =     204, io =          766, stat =     0    Parent
gen_acct   F  etime =     418, io =            0, stat =   134    First child
gen_acct   F  etime =     601, io =            0, stat =     9    Fourth child
gen_acct   F  etime =     801, io =            0, stat =     0    Third child
```

Let's take a closer look at the output from Program 15.15. The first line is the record for the accton command (which is included in the output because process accounting was switched on when the accton process terminated). Note that the S flag was set, indicating that the process used superuser privileges. The first, third, and fourth children have their F flag set, as they did not call exec.

The elapsed time is measured in clock ticks, which on the test system is 100 Hz. So the etime of 418 for the first child means that the process ran for just over four seconds. This is accounted for by the four-second sleep and the processing overhead incurred by the call to abort. Notice that the amount of time a process sleeps for is not exact.

We stated earlier that the ac_stat member does not store the complete process status. The values for the first and fourth children support this. The value of 134 for the first child is 128 + 6; the 128 is the flag that indicates that a core dump was produced, and the 6 is the number of the SIGABRT signal. Similarly, for the fourth child, the value of 9

proc_control/pracct.c

```
 1 #include <stdio.h>
 2 #include <sys/types.h>
 3 #include <sys/stat.h>
 4 #include <sys/acct.h>
 5 #include <unistd.h>
 6 #include <fcntl.h>
 7 #include "ssp.h"

 8 #define ACCT_FILE "/var/adm/pacct"

 9 static unsigned long compt2ulong (comp_t num);

10 int main (void)
11 {
12     int fd;
13     int n;
14     struct acct acct_data;

15     if ((fd = open (ACCT_FILE, O_RDONLY)) == -1)
16         err_msg ("Can't open %s", ACCT_FILE);

17     while ((n = read (fd, &acct_data, sizeof (struct acct))) != 0) {
18         if (n == -1)
19             err_msg ("read failed");

20         printf ("%-8s  %c%c  etime = %6ld, io = %8ld, stat = %3u\n",
21             acct_data.ac_comm, (acct_data.ac_flag & AFORK) ? 'F': ' ',
22             (acct_data.ac_flag & ASU) ? 'S' : ' ',
23             compt2ulong (acct_data.ac_etime), compt2ulong (acct_data.ac_io),
24             (unsigned char) acct_data.ac_stat);
25     }

26     return (0);
27 }

28 static unsigned long compt2ulong (comp_t num)
29 {
30     unsigned long val;
31     int exp;

32     val = num & 017777;          /* 13-bit mantissa */
33     exp = (num >> 13) & 7;       /* 3-bit exponent  */

34     while (exp-- > 0)
35         val *= 8;

36     return (val);
37 }
```

proc_control/pracct.c

Program 15.15 Print selected fields from process accounting file.

corresponds to the SIGKILL signal number. The processes that terminated normally have an ac_stat value of 0; there's no way of knowing from the accounting data what the actual exit status was.

The second child has 3,544,576 bytes of I/O charged to it, which is just under twice the number of bytes in the 1,772,384 /kernel/genunix file. Each byte is read in and written out, which is why the number is approximately twice the number of bytes in the file. The reason why the ac_io field is not exactly twice the size of the file is because of the rounding errors inherent in the pseudo floating-point representation. Note that each byte written is accounted for, even though they are destined for the bit bucket (i.e., /dev/null).

Finally, notice that despite dumping its core, the first child has not had any I/O charged to it. We can therefore deduce that the I/O required to generate a core dump of a process is not charged to that process.

15.15 Summary

An understanding of the process control concepts and functions we've discussed in this chapter is essential for UNIX systems programming. Fortunately, there are only a small number of functions to master: fork, which creates new processes; the exec family, which execute new programs; the exit functions, which terminate a process; and the wait functions, which reap the termination status of a terminated process. These process control primitives are used in many applications, and are used to build other functions, like system. Talking about the fork function also gave us the opportunity to discuss race conditions and how to avoid them.

Next we looked at interpreter files and saw how they operate. Then we looked at the system function; we wrote an implementation of it, and stressed the importance of not using it in set-user-ID programs. Finally, we looked at system accounting, which enabled us to look at fork and exec from a different perspective.

Now that we understand the relationship between a single parent and its children, the next chapter examines the relationship of a process to other processes, including process groups, sessions, and job control.

Exercises

15.1 How can a program obtain its saved set-user-ID?

15.2 Bearing in mind that after a vfork the child process executes in the address space of its parent, what would happen if vfork was called from a function other than main, and the child returns from that function after the vfork? Write a program to verify your hypothesis (drawing a picture of the stack frames might help).

15.3 Write a program that creates a zombie. In another terminal window (or in the program that creates the zombie), run the ps command to verify that a zombie has been created.

16

Process Relationships

16.1 Introduction

We learned in the previous chapter about the relationship a process has with its children and parent. A process can obtain the process ID of its parent, and the parent is notified when the child terminates. The parent can also obtain the child's termination and exit status. We alluded to groups of processes when we talked about the `waitpid` function (in Section 15.7), when we said that we can wait for any process in a process group to terminate.

In this chapter we take a closer look at process groups, as well as sessions (which are groups of process groups). We'll also take a look at the relationship between our login shell and all the processes we start from that shell. We'll also see how our login shell is invoked for us.

We can't talk about these process relationships without mentioning signals, and similarly, a discussion of signals requires an understanding of many of the concepts in this chapter. Readers who are not familiar with the concepts of UNIX signals might want to browse through Chapter 17 before reading this chapter.

16.2 Terminal Logins

Since its inception, UNIX has been a multiuser operating system. Historically, users logged in using dumb terminals connected to the host using RS-232 lines. These terminals were either local (directly connected), or remote (connected through a modem). Either way, these logins were facilitated by a terminal device driver in the kernel. Because each machine had a fixed number of terminal devices, there was a known upper limit on the number of simultaneous logins. We'll now describe what happens behind the scenes when we log in.

When a Solaris system boots into multiuser mode, the Service Access Facility enables terminal logins on those devices that have been configured to perform terminal logins. (How the serial ports and their drivers are installed and configured is beyond the scope of this text.) The `init` program runs `/usr/lib/saf/sac` (the service access controller), which (in the case of terminals) in turn calls `/usr/lib/saf/ttymon` to monitor the serial ports. It is `ttymon` that configures the serial port, displays the login prompt, and collects our user name (it also pushes the required STREAMS modules onto the terminal device's stream). Figure 16.1 illustrates this arrangement.

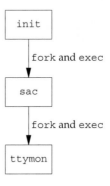

Figure 16.1   Arrangement of process to allow terminal logins.

All of the processes in Figure 16.1 run with real and effective user IDs of 0. Also, the environment of the processes `fork`ed by `init` are empty, except for those entries in `/etc/default/init`.

When we enter our user name, `ttymon` creates a child process, `exec`ing `login`. The `login` process does many things. First it calls `getspnam` to get the shadow file entry for our user name. It then prompts for and reads our password (with echoing disabled). The password we entered is then encrypted by calling `crypt`, and is compared to the password stored in the shadow password file (Solaris uses the Pluggable Authentication Module (PAM) to perform this checking of user credentials). If our user name or password are not correct, even after a number of attempts, `login` exits, and `ttymon` waits for another user name to be entered, starting the cycle again.

If we are correctly authenticated, the ownership of the terminal device is changed to our user, and `login` changes to our home directory. Our group IDs are set by calling `setgid` and `initgroups`. Next the environment is initialized with all the information that `login` has: our home directory (HOME), the default path (PATH), our user's shell (SHELL), and our user name (USER and LOGNAME). Finally, the real and effective user IDs are set to that of our user, and our login shell is invoked. This is done by calling `exec` like this:

```
execl ("/bin/ksh", "-ksh", NULL);
```

The hyphen as the first character of `argv [0]` is a flag to all shells that tells them they are being invoked as a login shell. This lets them modify their start-up behaviour accordingly.

For the sake of brevity, we skipped some of the tasks performed by login. It also checks for new mail, prints the message of the day file (/etc/motd), and several other things.

At this point, our login shell is finally running. Its parent process is the ttymon process that collected our user name. When our login shell exits, ttymon starts listening for another user to enter a user name. File descriptors 0, 1, and 2 for our login shell are set to the terminal device (thus setting up standard input, standard output, and standard error). Figure 16.2 shows the final arrangement.

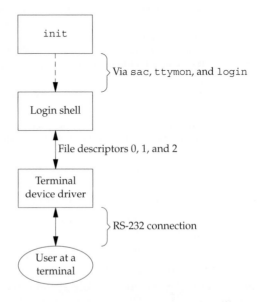

Figure 16.2 Arrangement of processes once we've logged in from a terminal.

Our login shell then reads its start-up files (.profile for the Bourne shell and its derivatives, and .login and .cshrc for the C Shell). These start-up files allow us to customize our environment by changing some variables and adding many others. For example, PATH is often set to include many more directories than the default, and JAVA_HOME is used to identify the base directory for the Java environment. Once the start-up processing is complete, the shell prints a prompt, and we can finally start interacting with it (entering commands and the like).

16.3 Network Logins

More prevalent than terminal logins these days are logins over the network. As the name suggests, rather than coming in from one of a fixed number of terminal devices, network logins arrive through the network device drivers (e.g., the Ethernet driver). We have no way of knowing in advance how many network logins will occur (unlike terminal logins).

There are two ways the OS can listen for network login requests: run a dedicated daemon for each network login protocol, or have one daemon that accepts connections for several different protocols and then runs a protocol specific program to handle the connection. The latter has the advantage of consuming fewer system resources, and is the method used by Solaris. The daemon that waits for these network connections is called `inetd`, and is sometimes referred to as the *Internet superserver*.

> Solaris uses `inetd` for `telnet` and `rsh`, and many other network protocols. However, one network login protocol, `ssh`, has its own daemon, which waits for connection requests. Although it is possible to run the `sshd` (the `ssh` daemon) from `inetd`, running it as a separate process is preferred because `sshd` has a relatively long start-up time. This is because it must create cryptographically secure keys. By starting `sshd` at system boot time, this costly overhead is eliminated for individual `ssh` logins.

> Because it is cryptographically secure, `ssh` is by far the best method of logging in remotely. Both `telnet` and `rsh` are susceptible to eavesdropping attacks and have weak host authentication. When properly configured, `ssh` suffers from neither of these shortcomings.

> From Solaris 9, Sun's version of `ssh` (which is based on OpenSSH) is shipped with the OS; users of previous releases must install and configure `ssh` from elsewhere if they want to use it.

When a Solaris system boots into multiuser mode, the run control scripts, or *rc scripts*, in `/etc/rc2.d` are run in sequence by `/sbin/rc2` to start the system services. One of these rc scripts starts `inetd` in standalone mode, which then reads its configuration file, `/etc/inet/inetd.conf`. The `inetd` process waits for TCP/IP connection requests to arrive as determined by its configuration file. When a connection request arrives, the `inetd` process `forks`, and `execs` the appropriate program to handle the connection.

For the sake of our discussion, let's assume that TELNET is being used as the network login protocol. A user on a remote system that has network connectivity to the TELNET server initiates a TELNET session by using the `telnet` command:

    telnet *host*

(We can use `telnet` to open a network connection to the local host too, but that would serve little purpose.) The `telnet` client opens a TCP connection to *host*. This connection is accepted by `inetd`, which runs the TELNET server, `in.telnetd`. The client and server exchange data using the TELNET protocol, and eventually, if we are correctly authenticated on the remote system, we are logged in to the remote system. Figure 16.3 shows the arrangement of the processes up to the moment when `in.telnetd` starts running. (A connection using `ssh` is similar, except the SSH daemon, `/usr/lib/ssh/sshd`, waits for connection requests rather than `inetd`, and `sshd` spawns a login shell when the user is authenticated.)

Behind the scenes, the `in.telnetd` process opens a pseudo terminal device and `forks` into two processes. (We talk about pseudo terminals in Chapter 23.) One process (the parent) handles the network connection, and the other (the child) `execs` the `login` program. The parent and child processes are connected through the pseudo terminal. Before execing `login`, the child arranges for file descriptors 0, 1, and 2 to be connected to the pseudo terminal. If we correctly authenticate ourselves, `login` performs the same tasks we previously described: it sets the real and effective user and group IDs, changes to our home directory, and sets up the initial environment. The `login` process finally

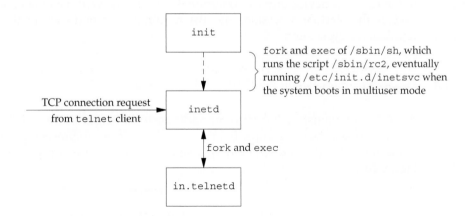

Figure 16.3 Sequence of processes when running the TELNET server.

replaces itself by execing our login shell. Figure 16.4 illustrates the process arrangement at this point.

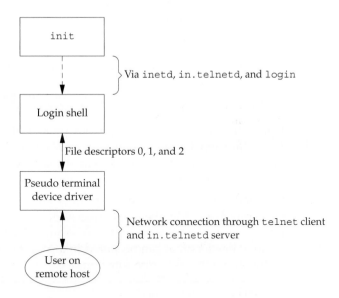

Figure 16.4 Arrangement of processes once we've logged in from the network.

A lot more happens behind the scenes between the pseudo terminal device driver and the user. We'll show all the details when we discuss pseudo terminals in Chapter 23.

The important thing we must understand from the preceding discussion is that whether we log in via a directly connected terminal (Figure 16.2) or the network (Figure 16.4), we have a login shell with its standard input, standard output, and standard error connected to the terminal device or pseudo terminal device. As we'll see in later sections, the login shell is the start of a session, and the terminal or pseudo terminal is the controlling terminal for the session.

16.4 Process Groups

As we've previously alluded to, in addition to having a process ID, each process also belongs to a process group. Before we take a look at process groups, let's remind ourselves of the process structure of a single process and its offspring. We show this in Figure 16.5.

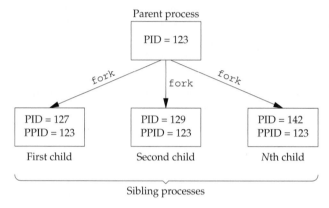

Figure 16.5 Arrangement of a process and its offspring.

Figure 16.5 shows a process (whose process ID is 123) that has created three children. Each child has its own unique process ID, and their parent process IDs are set to the process ID of the process that created them. Child processes related in this manner are called *sibling processes*.

Now let's turn our attention to process groups. A *process group* is a collection of one or more processes. Members of a process group are not necessarily otherwise related. Each process group has a unique process group ID. Process group IDs—like process IDs—are positive integers that can be stored in a pid_t. A process can find out its process group ID by calling the getpgrp function.

```
#include <unistd.h>

pid_t getpgrp (void);
```
Returns: process group ID of calling process

The getpgrp function returns the process group ID of the calling process. Another way a process can ascertain its process group ID (or that of another process) is to use the getpgid function.

```
#include <unistd.h>

pid_t getpgid (pid_t pid);
```
                                          Returns: process group ID of *pid* if OK, −1 on error

The `getpgid` function returns the ID of the process group that the process identified by *pid* is a member of. If *pid* is 0, then the process group ID of the calling process is returned.

Each process group can have a *process group leader*, which is identified by having its process group ID equal to its process ID. We say "can" have a leader, because it is possible for a process to create a process group, and subsequently terminate while other processes are members of the process group. In this scenario, the process group still exists; as long as there is at least one process in the group, the process group will continue to exist. The period of time that begins when a process group is created and ends when the last process in the group leaves is called the *process group lifetime*. A process leaves a process group either by terminating or by joining some other process group. We show a small process group in Figure 16.6.

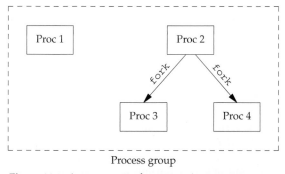

Process group

Figure 16.6 Arrangement of processes in a process group.

Proc 3 and Proc 4 are children of Proc 2. Proc 1 is unrelated to any of these processes, except for being a member of the same process group.

Creating or Joining a Process Group

A process creates a new process group (or joins an existing one) by calling the `setpgid` function. (We'll see in the next section that establishing a new session with `setsid` also creates a new process group.)

```
#include <sys/types.h>
#include <unistd.h>

int setpgid (pid_t pid, pid_t pgid);
```
                                                          Returns: 0 if OK, −1 on error

The `setpgid` function sets the process group ID of the process specified by *pid* to *pgid*. If *pgid* is equal to *pid*, the specified process becomes a process group leader. Otherwise, the process joins an existing process group.

If *pid* is equal to 0, the process ID of the calling process will be used. Finally, if *pgid* is equal to 0, the process specified by *pid* becomes a process group leader.

We should note that a process can change only the process group of itself or one of its children. However, a process can't change the process group ID of one of its children after the child has called `exec`.

Most job control shells call `setpgid` after `forking`: once in the parent to set the process group ID of the newly created child, and another time in the child to set its own process group ID. One of these calls is redundant, but it's the only way to avoid a race condition—the race condition being that the child is placed in its own process group before either process assumes that this has happened. If we only called `setpgid` in the parent or the child, the outcome would depend on which process ran first.

Another function we can use to set the process group ID is `setpgrp`.

```
#include <sys/types.h>
#include <unistd.h>

pid_t setpgrp (void);
```
                                                          Returns: the new process group ID

If the calling process is not already a session leader, the `setpgrp` function makes it one by setting its process group ID and session ID to its process ID; `setpgrp` also releases the caller's controlling terminal. We talk about sessions in the next section, and controlling terminals in Section 16.6.

When we discuss signals in Chapter 17, we'll see that a signal can be sent to a single process or a process group. Similarly, the `waitpid` function we discuss in Section 15.7 allows us to wait for either a single process or a process from the specified process group.

16.5 Sessions

In much the same way that one or more processes can belong to a process group, a group of one or more process groups is called a session. A *session* is a collection of one or more process groups (identified by an identifier called a session ID) capable of establishing a connection with a controlling terminal (we describe controlling terminals in the next section).

Any process that is not a process group leader may create a new session. This process then becomes the session leader of the new session and the process group leader of the process group.

A newly created process joins the session of its parent.

Figure 16.7 shows a hypothetical session that consists of three process groups.

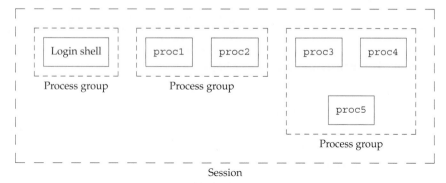

Figure 16.7   A session consisting of three process groups.

The processes in a process group are usually placed in that group by a shell pipeline. For example, the arrangement shown in Figure 16.7 could have been created by running the following shell commands:

```
$ proc1 | proc2 &
$ proc3 | proc4 | proc5
```

Each process is a member of a session; a process is considered to be a member of the session to which its process group belongs. Newly created processes join the session of their parent, although a process can change its session membership using the setsid function we discuss next. Each session has a *session leader*, which is the process that created the session.

We can determine the process group ID of a session leader by using the getsid function.

```
#include <unistd.h>

pid_t getsid (pid_t pid);
```
                                Returns: process group ID of *pid*'s session leader if OK, –1 on error

The getsid function returns the process group ID of the process that is the session leader of the process specified by *pid*. If *pid* is equal to 0, then the process group ID of the process that is the session leader of the calling process is returned.

Creating a New Session

A new session is created by calling the setsid function.

```
#include <sys/types.h>
#include <unistd.h>

pid_t setsid (void);
```
                                     Returns: process group ID of the calling process if OK, −1 on error

If the calling process is not process group leader, the `setsid` function creates a new
session. This causes three things to happen:

1. The calling process becomes the session leader for the new session, and is the
   only process in the new session.

2. A new process group is also created, and the calling process becomes the process
   group leader of the new process group. The process group ID of the new process
   group is equal to the process ID of the calling process.

3. The process has no controlling terminal. If it had one prior to calling `setsid`,
   that association is broken. (We talk about controlling terminals in the next
   section.)

Because calling `setsid` if the calling process is already a process group leader returns an
error, it is usual to call `fork` before calling `setsid`. The parent terminates, and the child
calls `setsid`. By doing this, we are guaranteed that the child is not a process group
leader, because the child gets a new process ID and inherits the process group ID from its
parent; it is impossible for the child's process ID to equal its inherited process group ID.

Note that unlike process groups, there is no way for a process to arbitrarily join a session.

16.6 Controlling Terminal

In addition to those that we've already discussed, there are several other characteristics
of process groups and sessions we need to consider.

- A session can have a *controlling terminal*. If the session has a controlling terminal,
  it is usually the terminal device or pseudo terminal device that we logged in on.
  A session can have no more than one controlling terminal.

- The session leader that establishes the connection to the controlling terminal is
  called the *controlling process*.

- There are two types of process group within a session: a single *foreground process
  group*, and one or more *background process groups*.

- If a session has a controlling terminal, then all but one of the process groups are
  background process groups. The single remaining process group is a foreground
  process group.

- Typing the interrupt key (usually Control-C) causes a `SIGINT` signal to be sent to
  all the processes in the foreground process group. Similarly, typing the quit key
  (usually Control-\) causes a `SIGQUIT` signal to be sent to all the processes in the
  foreground process group.

- If a modem disconnect is detected by the terminal interface, a SIGHUP signal is sent to the controlling process (i.e., the session leader).

- If the session has a controlling terminal, then when the session leader terminates, a SIGHUP signal is sent to all the other processes in the foreground process group associated with the controlling terminal.

Figure 16.8 summarizes these characteristics.

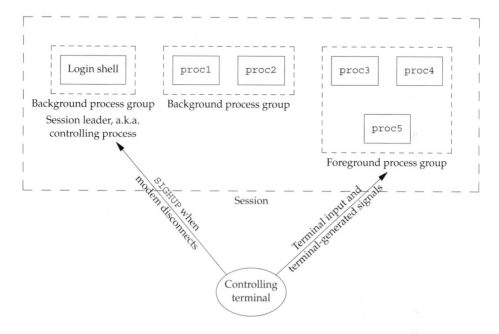

Figure 16.8   A session with three process groups showing the controlling terminal.

Most of the time, we don't have to be concerned about our controlling terminal, because it is usually established for us automatically when we log in. A controlling terminal is allocated for a session when the session leader opens the first terminal device that is not already associated with a session, although this can be prevented by specifying the O_NOCTTY flag in the call to open.

There are times when a program needs talk with the controlling terminal, whether or not standard input or standard output has been redirected. The way a program can guarantee that it is talking to the controlling terminal (if one exists) is to open /dev/tty. This is a special file that is a synonym for the controlling terminal of the calling process. If the calling process doesn't have a controlling terminal, the open of /dev/tty will fail.

An example of a function that does this is getpass, which is used by the passwd and crypt commands, among others. This prevents us from writing a script to change passwords in a noninteractive manner (for example, resetting all the student passwords at the beginning of a new school year). The use of /dev/tty also allows programs like crypt to read passwords from the command lines when standard input and standard output are redirected. (We should note here that the encryption used by crypt is very weak by contemporary standards, and is easily breakable—it is definitely *not* cryptographically secure. It should therefore not be used in situations where confidentiality is very important.)

16.7 The tcgetpgrp and tcsetpgrp Functions

Now that we know what a foreground process group is and what it does, we need a way for a process to determine what a given process' foreground process group ID is, and a way for it to be able to set its own foreground process group ID. This tells the terminal device driver (or pseudo terminal device driver) where to send terminal input and the terminal-generated signals.

We use the tcgetpgrp function to determine a foreground process group ID.

```
#include <sys/types.h>
#include <unistd.h>

pid_t tcgetpgrp (int fildes);
```

Returns: process group ID of the foreground process group if OK, −1 on error

The tcgetpgrp function returns the value of the process group ID of the foreground process group associated with the terminal specified by *fildes*.

If there is no foreground process group associated with *fildes*, tcgetpgrp returns a positive integer that does not match the process group ID of any existing process group.

Contrariwise, a process that has a controlling terminal can set the foreground process group ID associated with that controlling terminal by using the tcsetpgrp function.

```
#include <sys/types.h>
#include <unistd.h>

int tcsetpgrp (int fildes, pid_t pgid_id);
```

Returns: 0 if OK, −1 on error

The tcsetpgrp function sets the foreground process group ID associated with the terminal specified by *fildes* to *pgid_id*. The file associated with *fildes* must be the controlling terminal of the calling process, and the controlling terminal must be currently associated with the session of the calling process. Also, the value of *pgid_id* must be the process group ID of a process group in the same session as the calling process.

Most applications don't call these functions directly; they are normally called by job control shells.

16.8 The tcgetsid Function

We can get the session ID associated with a controlling terminal by calling tcgetsid.

```
#include <termios.h>

pid_t tcgetsid (int fildes);
```
                                            Returns: the session ID associated with *fildes* if OK, −1 on error

The `tcgetsid` function returns the process group ID of the session for which the terminal identified by *fildes* is the controlling terminal. If the file associated with *fildes* is not a terminal, or if it is a terminal but is not a controlling terminal, `tcgetsid` will fail, returning −1.

16.9 Job Control

Job control is a facility that was added to BSD UNIX by Berkeley in the early 1980s. Predating modern windowing systems, it allows us to start several jobs (groups of processes) from a single terminal, and control which jobs can access the terminal, and which jobs run in the background. (SVR3 had the "layers" job control facility, which was abandoned by POSIX in favour of BSD's job control.) Support for job control requires three prerequisites:

1. A shell that supports job control (sometimes called a *job control shell*.)
2. The terminal device driver must support job control.
3. Certain job control signals must be supported.

A job is a collection of one or more processes, often in a pipeline. From a user's perspective, when using a job control shell, a job can be started in either the foreground or the background. For example, the command

```
ls -l
```

starts a job consisting of one process in the foreground. Similarly, the commands

```
make &
wc *ms &
```

start two background jobs. All processes invoked by these background jobs are run in the background.

When we start a job in the background, the shell assigns it a job ID and prints a process ID. The following example runs two background jobs when we use `ksh`.

```
$ wc -w *ms | sort > foo &
[1]     9807
$ make > /dev/null &
[2]     9809
[1]  -   Done            wc -w *ms | sort > foo &
$                         Press Return
[2]  +   Done            make > /dev/null &
```

The `wc` command pipeline was assigned a job ID of 1 by the shell, and the process ID starting process is 9807. The `make` command is job number 2, and its starting process ID is 9809. When a job has finished running, the shell prints a message stating that the job is done. The job ID of the completed job is in square brackets followed by either a + sign or a − sign. The + sign refers to the current job, and the − sign refers to a previous job. The shell only prints the change in job status just before it prints its prompt, which is why we have to press Return to see the notification of the second job's completion. (Some shells, for example `csh` and its derivatives, have an option that when set, notifies the user immediately after a job completes rather then waiting until the prompt is printed.)

The reason why job control requires support from the terminal device driver is because there is a special input character (recall Section 12.3) that we can use to affect the foreground job. This is the suspend key (SUSP, which is usually Control-Z), which causes the terminal driver to send the `SIGTSTP` signal to all processes in the foreground process group (processes that are part of any background job are not affected). The terminal driver looks for three characters, each of which sends a different signal to the foreground process group:

- The interrupt character, INTR. This is usually Control-C, and generates `SIGINT`.
- The quit character, QUIT. This is typically Control-\, and generates `SIGQUIT`.
- The suspend character, SUSP. This is usually Control-Z, and generates `SIGTSTP`.

We show in Chapter 12 how we can change these special characters to whatever we want, and how to disable the terminal driver's processing of them.

Something else the terminal device driver needs to handle correctly when we use job control is terminal I/O. In the case of foreground jobs, terminal is as we expect. But what happens when a background job wants to read or write to the terminal?

Let's consider terminal input first. It is not an error when a background job tries to read from the terminal. Instead, the terminal driver sends a `SIGTTIN` signal to the process when it detects an attempt by a background job to read from the terminal. This signal usually stops the background job, and the shell notifies of this event. We can then bring the job into the foreground so that the read from the terminal can proceed. For example:

```
$ cat > /tmp/foo &
[1]      12212
$
$
[1] + Stopped (SIGTTIN)          cat > /tmp/foo &
$ fg %1
cat > /tmp/foo
Just a test...
$ cat /tmp/foo
Just a test...
```

The shell starts `cat` in the background, but when the `cat` process tries to read from the controlling terminal (i.e., its standard input), the terminal driver sends it a `SIGTTIN` signal. The shell, detecting a change in the status of one of its children (recall our discussion of `waitpid` in Section 15.7), informs us that the job has been stopped. We bring the stopped job into the foreground by using the shell's `fg` command. (The `%1` argument refers to the first job; because this is the only job in this example, we could have just typed `fg` with the same results. Refer to the shell's manual page for more details about its job control commands and how to identify jobs.) This causes the shell to place the job into the foreground process group (by using `tcsetpgrp`) and to send it the continue signal, `SIGCONT`. Now that the job is in the foreground process group, it can read from the controlling terminal.

We've seen what happens when a background job attempts to read from the controlling terminal, but what happens when a background process wants to write to the controlling terminal? The answer is "it depends", because this is something we can optionally allow or disallow. Normally, we do this using the `stty` program we discussed in Section 12.5, but we can also manage this from within our programs. The following is an example of this:

```
$ cat /tmp/foo &
[1]     17278
$ Just a test...
                                                Press Return
[1]  +  Done                  cat /tmp/foo &
$ stty tostop
$ cat /tmp/foo &
[1]     17280
$                                               Press Return
$                                               Press Return
[1] + Stopped (SIGTTOU)       cat /tmp/foo &
$ fg
cat /tmp/foo
Just a test...
```

The first time we run the `cat` command in the background, the output is printed (the default behaviour on Solaris is to allow background jobs to write to the controlling terminal). After we disable this ability (by using the `stty` command), we run `cat` again in the background. This time, however, when the process attempts to write to the controlling terminal, the terminal driver sends it a `SIGTTOU` signal. Once again the shell detects a change in the status of one of its children and informs us the job has been stopped. We resume the job in the foreground (using the `fg` command), which allows it to write to the controlling terminal.

There's quite a lot going on here, so Figure 16.9 summarizes the job control facilities we've described.

The solid lines through the terminal driver box show that the terminal I/O and the terminal-generated signals (i.e., `SIGINT`, `SIGQUIT`, and `SIGTSTP`) are always connected from the actual terminal to the foreground process group. The dashed line through the terminal driver box shows that whether the output from a background process group appears on the terminal is an option.

In these days of workstations running a windowed environment like CDE or GNOME, where we can open almost as many terminals as we want to accomplish our work, it's arguable that job control is no longer necessary. Other people argue that job control is desirable, even in such an environment. One thing is certain though: job control will be a part of UNIX for the foreseeable future.

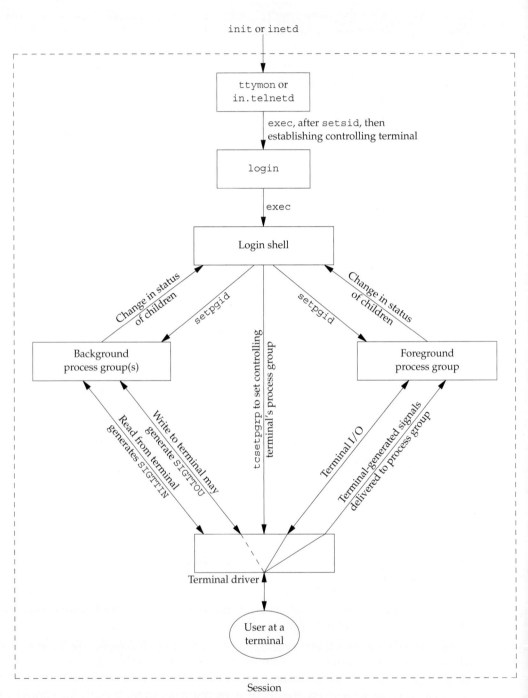

Figure 16.9 Summary of job control features.

16.10 Shell Execution of Programs

Now that we have an understanding of process groups, sessions, and controlling terminals, let's take a look at how shells execute commands, and how this relates to these concepts. To do this, we'll use the ps command. We pass to ps this command line option: -o pid,ppid,pgid,sid,comm. This causes ps to display the process ID, the parent process ID, the process group ID, the session ID, and the command of each process.

First we'll use a shell that doesn't support job control (i.e., /bin/sh), then later we'll use /bin/ksh, which does support job control. Running the ps command gives us the following:

```
$ ps -o pid,ppid,pgid,sid,comm
  PID  PPID  PGID    SID COMMAND
14541 24966 14541 24966 -sh
14547 14541 14541 24966 ps
```

As we would expect, both the sh and the ps processes are in the same session (24966), and the same process group (14541). If we were logged in from a hardwired terminal (or a text console), we would expect the shell's parent process ID to be 1. However, because we're executing these commands in a shell started by a CDE login session, the shell's parent process ID is that of the dtterm the shell is running in. Note that because the shell we're running is effectively a login shell, it has a hyphen as its first character.

Executing the same command in the background gives us the same results, except the process ID of the ps command:

```
$ ps -o pid,ppid,pgid,sid,comm &
  PID  PPID  PGID    SID COMMAND
14541 24966 14541 24966 -sh
14958 14541 14541 24966 ps
```

The background job isn't put into its own process group, because the shell doesn't support job control.

We've looked at single foreground and background processes, so let's see how pipelines are handled. Running a pipeline in the foreground gives us the following:

```
$ ps -o pid,ppid,pgid,sid,comm | ./cat1
  PID  PPID  PGID    SID COMMAND
14977 14541 14541 24966 ./cat1
14541 24966 14541 24966 -sh
14978 14977 14541 24966 ps
```

(We made two links to the cat command, called cat1 and cat2. The reason for the copies is so that we can identify them easily in the following examples.) It's interesting to observe that the last process in the pipeline, rather than the first, has the shell as its parent. Evidently, the shell forks a copy of itself, and this copy then forks once for each of the previous commands in the pipeline.

As before, running the pipeline in the background has the same results, except the process IDs of the ps and cat1 commands change.

```
$ ps -o pid,ppid,pgid,sid,comm | ./cat1 &
   PID  PPID  PGID    SID COMMAND
14979 14541 14541 24966 ./cat1
14541 24966 14541 24966 -sh
14980 14979 14541 24966 ps
```

Because the shell doesn't handle job control, the process group ID of the background processes stays the same (i.e., 14541).

Another facet of job control we need to investigate is the result of a background process trying to read from its controlling terminal.

```
$ cat > /tmp/foo &
17854
```

Recall from our previous discussion that a job control shell would handle this by placing the background job in its own process group, which causes a SIGTTIN signal to be generated if the background job tries to read from the controlling terminal. Without job control, the shell automatically redirects the standard input of a background process to /dev/null if the process doesn't redirect standard input itself. Reading from /dev/null returns EOF, which means that the background cat process immediately terminates normally.

But what happens if the background process thwarts the shell's redirection of standard input by specifically opening /dev/tty, and reads from the resulting file descriptor? Assuming the file called secret contains some data that we've previously encrypted using the crypt command, these are the results we get:

```
$ crypt < secret > cleartext
Enter key:                          We enter our crypt password here
$ cat cleartext
This is a test...
$ crypt < secret > cleartext &
Enter key:19923
$ secret: execute permission denied
$

$ cat cleartext
?£ÜL¶,öwàâ³¯í/Èí$
```

When we run our example in the foreground, the file is decrypted as we expect. But running it in the background has quite different results. What is happening here is that crypt opens /dev/tty, disables echoing, reads from the controlling terminal, and then resets the terminal's characteristics. When we execute this pipeline in the background, the Enter key: prompt is printed by the crypt command on the terminal, but the password we enter is actually read by the shell and taken to be a command to run. The next line we enter to the shell (in this case, we just pressed Return) is taken to be the password, which results in the file not being decrypted correctly. When we run the cat cleartext command, we get junk instead of the decrypted message. What we have here is the result of two processes trying to read from the same device at the same time. The results are indeterminate: if we run this example again, we might get different results.

For one last example, let's examine a three-process pipeline:

```
$ ps -o pid,ppid,pgid,sid,comm | ./cat1 | ./cat2
  PID  PPID  PGID   SID COMMAND
14541 24966 14541 24966 -sh
20196 20195 14541 24966 ps
20197 20195 14541 24966 ./cat1
20195 14541 14541 24966 ./cat2
```

Once again, the last process in the pipeline has the shell as its parent, and is the parent of the other processes in the pipeline. Figure 16.10 shows the arrangement of the processes in this pipeline.

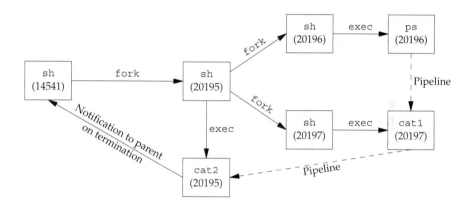

Figure 16.10 Processes in a pipeline when invoked by /bin/sh.

Because the last process in the pipeline is the child of the login shell, the shell is notified when that process (cat2) terminates.

Let's now take a look at the same examples, this time using a job control shell (in these examples, we'll use /bin/ksh). Running the ps command gives us the following:

```
$ ps -o pid,ppid,pgid,sid,comm
  PID  PPID  PGID   SID COMMAND
23389 23387 23389 23389 /bin/ksh
23397 23389 23397 23389 ps
```

(We've highlighted the important changes by using a **bold** font.) We can see in this example that the ps command has been placed in its own process group (23397). The ps command is the process group leader and the only process in the process group. (We also know from our previous discussion that the process group ID associated with the controlling terminal will have been changed to that of the foreground process group (23397), but unfortunately we can't show this using the ps command supplied with Solaris. Although it doesn't help illustrate our examples, this does make sense because the controlling terminal is associated with a process group, not an individual process.) While the ps command executes, our login shell is in a background process group (23389). However, both process groups remain members of the same session (as we'll see in the following examples, the session ID never changes throughout this section).

Executing the ps command in the background gives us

```
$ ps -o pid,ppid,pgid,sid,comm &
[1]      23461
  PID  PPID  PGID    SID COMMAND
23389 23387 23389  23389 /bin/ksh
23463 23389 23463  23389 ps
```

On the surface, these results look the same as the previous example. However, we know from earlier discussion that the ps command has been placed in a background process group this time, and that that process group is no longer associated with the controlling terminal. Instead, the controlling terminal remains associated with the foreground process group (i.e., the login shell).

Let's see how a two-process pipeline is handled:

```
$ ps -o pid,ppid,pgid,sid,comm | ./cat1
  PID  PPID  PGID    SID COMMAND
23389 23387 23389  23389 /bin/ksh
23531 23389 23530  23389 ./cat1
23530 23389 23530  23389 ps
```

In this example, both the cat1 and ps processes are placed into a new foreground process group (23530). Another difference we can see between this example and when we used /bin/sh is that in this example, the login shell is the parent of both processes (as opposed to the shell being the parent of just the last process in the pipeline when we used /bin/sh).

However, running this pipeline in the background has the following results:

```
$ ps -o pid,ppid,pgid,sid,comm | ./cat1 &
[1]      23532
  PID  PPID  PGID    SID COMMAND
23389 23387 23389  23389 /bin/ksh
23532 23389 23532  23389 ./cat1
23533 23532 23532  23389 ps
```

This time we see that the processes are created in the same manner as with /bin/sh. Both processes are placed in the same background process group (23532).

Finally, let's see the results of running our three process pipeline in /bin/ksh.

```
$ ps -o pid,ppid,pgid,sid,comm | ./cat1 | ./cat2
  PID  PPID  PGID    SID COMMAND
23389 23387 23389  23389 /bin/ksh
23534 23389 23534  23389 ps
23536 23389 23534  23389 ./cat2
23535 23389 23534  23389 ./cat1
```

As before, the shell is the parent of all the processes. Figure 16.11 shows the arrangement of the processes in this pipeline.

In this scenario, the parent process (i.e., the login shell) is notified when each of its children terminates.

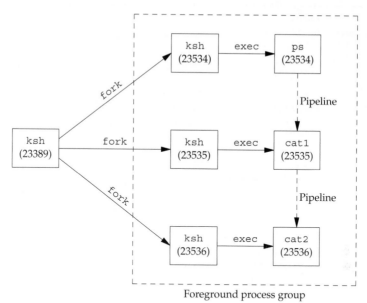

Figure 16.11 Processes in a pipeline when invoked by /bin/ksh.

16.11 Orphaned Process Groups

We stated earlier that a process whose parent terminates is called an orphan, and that it is inherited (adopted) by init. That is, init becomes the parent of the orphaned process. But what happens if an entire process group becomes orphaned?

Suppose we have a process that forks a child and then terminates. What happens if the child is stopped when its parent terminates? How can the child be continued? Does it know that it has been orphaned?

Example: Creating an orphaned process group

Program 16.1 shows an example that will help us answer these questions.

Print IDs for parent process

11 Call our print_ids function, which prints the caller's process ID, its parent process ID, and its process group ID.

Create child

12–15 Call fork, calling our error function if it fails.

proc_rels/pg_orphan.c

```
 1 #include <stdio.h>
 2 #include <unistd.h>
 3 #include <stdlib.h>
 4 #include <sys/types.h>
 5 #include <signal.h>
 6 #include "ssp.h"

 7 static void print_ids (char *proc);

 8 int main (void)
 9 {
10     char c;

11     print_ids ("Parent");

12     switch (fork ()) {
13         case -1:
14             err_msg ("fork failed");
15             break;

16         case 0:
17             print_ids ("Child");
18             sigset (SIGHUP, SIG_IGN);
19             kill (getpid (), SIGTSTP);

20             printf ("Received SIGCONT; continuing...\n");
21             print_ids ("Child");

22             if (read (STDIN_FILENO, &c, 1) != 1)
23                 err_msg ("Read error from controlling terminal");

24             _exit (0);

25         default:
26             sleep (2);
27             exit (0);
28     }

29     return (0);
30 }

31 static void print_ids (char *proc)
32 {
33     printf ("%s: PID = %ld, PPID = %ld, PGID = %ld\n",
34         proc, (long) getpid (), (long) getppid (), (long) getpgrp ());
35     fflush (stdout);
36 }
```

proc_rels/pg_orphan.c

Program 16.1 Creating an orphaned process group.

Child process

17 Call our `print_ids` function to print the IDs associated with the child before the parent terminates.

18 Ignore the SIGHUP signal. We do this because when a new orphaned process group is created, every stopped process in the process group is sent two signals: SIGHUP followed

by SIGCONT. The default action for SIGHUP is to terminate the process, so we change the signal's disposition so that it is ignored. We have a lot more to say about signals in Chapter 17.

19 We send ourselves the SIGTSTP signal, which stops the process until a SIGCONT signal is received (in much the same way that typing the suspend character (Control-Z) on the controlling terminal stops a foreground job). This happens when the parent terminates, creating an orphan process group as we describe further on.

20–21 We print a message stating that we've received a SIGCONT signal and reprint the IDs associated with the child process.

22–24 Attempt to read from standard input. As we saw earlier in this chapter, a read from a background process group causes a SIGTTIN signal to be sent to all the processes in the background process group. However, in this example we have an orphaned process group; if it were to be sent this signal, the processes in the group are unlikely to be continued. Hence, the read fails, with errno set to EIO. In the improbable event that the read succeeds, we call exit to terminate the child.

Parent process

26–27 The parent goes to sleep for two seconds, ensuring (almost) that the child process executes before the parent terminates.

When the parent terminates, the child becomes a member of an orphaned process group An *orphaned process group* is one in which the parent of every member is either itself a member of the group, or is not a member of the group's session. In other words, a process group is *not* orphaned as long as there is a process in the group that has a parent in a different process group but in the same session. If the process group is not orphaned, it is possible that one of those parents in a different process group (but in the same session) will restart a stopped process in the process group that is not orphaned.

In our example, once our original parent terminates, the parent of every process in the process group belongs to another session. Specifically, process 1 (init) becomes the parent of the child process (25074), and init is not a member of our login session.

Figure 16.12 shows the process arrangement after Program 16.1 has started and has created the child process.

Running program 16.1 from a job control shell gives us the following output:

```
$ ./pg_orphan
Parent: PID = 25073, PPID = 24947, PGID = 25073
Child: PID = 25074, PPID = 25073, PGID = 25073
$ Received SIGCONT; continuing...
Child: PID = 25074, PPID = 1, PGID = 25073
Read error from controlling terminal: I/O error
```

Note that the shell's prompt appears with the output from the child. This is because two processes, the shell and the child, are writing to the terminal. As we would expect, the child is adopted by init (i.e., its parent process ID becomes 1).

Recall from the previous section that job control shells place the foreground process into its own process group (25073 in this example), and the shell stays in its own process group (24947). The child process inherits, among other things, the process group ID of its

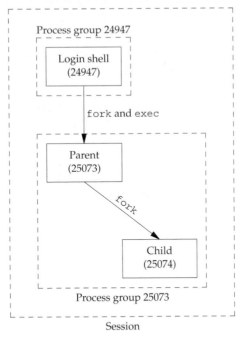

Figure 16.12   Arrangement of processes from Program 16.1.

parent. However, once the parent terminates, the child becomes a background process group.

16.12 Summary

We started this chapter by examing the steps required to start a login shell when we log in from a terminal or over the network. We then described the relationship between groups of processes (process groups) and groups of process groups (sessions). We also described job control, comparing and contrasting the relationship between a shell that supports job control and its children, and a shell that doesn't. We also showed how the controlling terminal for a process, /dev/tty, is involved with these process relationships.

We've made many references in this chapter to the signals used in these process relationships (specifically, SIGCONT, SIGHUP, SIGINT, SIGQUIT, SIGTSTP, SIGTTIN, and SIGTTOU). The next chapter continues our discussion of signals, looking in detail at all the UNIX signals and the functions we can use to manipulate them.

Exercises

16.1 As we stated in Section 16.10, we can't display the process group ID associated with the controlling terminal using the Solaris version of the ps command (because strictly speaking, it isn't a property of a process). Write a program that displays the process group ID associated with a given controlling terminal device.

16.2 Write a program that creates a child, and have that child create a new session. Run the program and verify that the child becomes a process group leader, and that it no longer has a controlling terminal.

17

Signals

17.1 Introduction

Signals are software interrupts that are generated synchronously or asynchronously. Most non-trivial programs have to deal with signals in some way, for example, a user at a terminal typing the interrupt key, the next process in a pipeline terminating unexpectedly, or an event being timed out.

Signals have been a part of the UNIX API since the very early versions (at least as early as Version 6), but the mechanism provided was unreliable: signals could get lost, and it was hard to delay the delivery of a signal when executing a critical region of code. SVR3 and 4.3BSD introduced changes to the signal model, making them reliable (we'll have more to say about this later). Unfortunately, the two reliable signal mechanisms were incompatible, but POSIX has addressed this by standardizing them. Solaris provides the SVR4 and the POSIX reliable signal mechanisms, so we describe both in this chapter.

We'll start with an overview of signals and their associated terminology, and then describe each signal. Then we'll look at the traditional signal mechanism, highlighting its problems, before we describe the reliable signal mechanisms. For pedagogical reasons, this chapter contains several example programs that have various flaws in them. We'll discuss these defects (which arise from naïve or incomplete code), and then show how to correct them.

17.2 Signal Concepts

A signal is said to be *generated* (or sent to a process) when the event associated with that signal first happens. It is possible that the same events will generate signals for multiple processes (e.g., some events send signals to all members of a particular process group).

A signal is *delivered* to a process when the action associated with the signal is actually taken, and a signal is *accepted* when it is selected and returned by one of the `sigwait` functions. After a signal has been generated, but before it is delivered or accepted, the signal is said to be *pending*.

As we said previously, signals may be generated synchronously or asynchronously. Events that are directly caused by the execution of code by a process are referred to as *traps*. Signals generated by traps are said to be synchronously generated. In a multithreaded process, synchronously generated signals initiated by a specific thread will be delivered to and handled by that thread. On the other hand, asynchronously generated signals are not sent to any specific thread.

Every signal has a name and a number. Each signal name starts with the letters `SIG`. For example, `SIGSEGV` is the signal sent to a process that has attempted an operation that would result in a segmentation violation, and `SIGABRT` is an abort signal generated when a process calls the `abort` function. Excluding aliases and a number of signals that are used in realtime programming (which we don't cover in this text), Solaris 9 has 38 different signals. Solaris 2.6, 7, and 8 have 37 different signals, and earlier versions have 36.

The signal names and their corresponding values are defined in the header file `<signal.h>`. The signal numbers are positive integers; no signal has a value of 0. The `kill` function uses a signal value of 0, sometimes called the null signal, for a special case. (We discuss the `kill` function in Section 17.12.)

Several conditions can cause a signal to be generated:

- Hardware exceptions can generate signals. Examples include division by 0, invalid memory references, and so on. These conditions are detected by the hardware, which notifies the kernel. The kernel then generates the appropriate signal and sends it to the process that caused the exception. For example, a `SIGSEGV` signal is sent to processes that attempt an invalid memory reference.

- Software conditions can generate signals when an event happens that the process should know about. For example, when a process attempts to write to a pipe that has no reader, a `SIGPIPE` is sent to it. Other examples include the alarm signal, `SIGALRM`, which is generated when a timer set by the process expires, and `SIGURG`, which is generated when out-of-band data arrives over the network.

- The terminal-generated signals we talked about in Chapter 12 and Chapter 16 occur when users press certain terminal keys. For example, pressing Control-C usually causes the interrupt signal, `SIGINT`, to be sent to a process. This is one way we can stop runaway processes. A *runaway process* is a process that is in an infinite loop, consuming most of the available CPU time. Typing Control-Z in a job control shell usually suspends the foreground process group by sending all the member processes a `SIGTSTP` signal.

- With certain limitations, a process can send any signal to any process or process group by using the `kill` function. Unless our effective user ID is 0, we can only send signals to processes that we own. A process can also send a signal to itself by calling the `raise` function.

- The `kill` command is also used to send signals to other processes. It is just an interface to the `kill` function, and is often used to terminate background processes that have hung or are runaway.

As we stated before, some signals are asynchronous events. This means that they occur at seemingly random times with respect to the process. An analogy that we can use is reading a book when the telephone rings, where reading the book is the executing process, and the phone ringing is the signal. We have no control over timing of the phone ringing, only what we do as a result. This also applies to signals: a process can say to the kernel, "if and when this signal occurs, do the following".

The kernel can handle a signal three ways when it is delivered. What the kernel does with a signal is called the signal's *disposition*, or the *action* associated with the signal. The determination of what action to take happens when the signal is delivered, not when it is generated.

We can set the disposition of a signal to one of the following three actions:

1. The signal can be *caught*. When we say that a signal is caught, we mean that one of our functions gets called by the kernel when the signal occurs. The function that gets called when a signal is caught is called a *signal handler*, and it can do whatever we want to handle the condition. For example, we can catch SIGTERM (the termination signal that is the default signal sent by the `kill` command) to perform an orderly shutdown, like deleting temporary files, etc. A shell could arrange to catch the termination of a child signal, SIGCHLD. The signal handler would call `waitpid` to fetch the process ID of the child and its termination status.

   Two signals cannot be caught (or, as we shall see, blocked or ignored): SIGKILL and SIGSTOP. The reasons why these signals can't be caught is to ensure that there is a way for the superuser to kill or stop any process.

2. A signal can be *ignored*. All signals, with two exceptions, can be ignored. As we just explained, the two signals that can't be ignored are SIGKILL and SIGSTOP. Although it is possible to ignore certain signals generated by hardware exceptions (e.g., dividing by zero), the resulting behaviour of a process doing so is undefined.

3. The signal's default action can apply. The default action for most signals is to terminate the process.

Figure 17.1 summarizes all the signals, their availability, and their default actions.

In Figure 17.1, "Core dump" means that the process terminates, and subject to four conditions being met, a memory image of the process is saved in the file called `core` in the process' current directory. (The name `core` is a left over from when the memory in computers was made from little ferrite rings, called cores.) The `core` file can be used with a debugger to examine the state of the process at the time it terminated (we call this activity *post mortem debugging*). The following conditions must be met for a core dump to be produced:

Name	Description	2.5	2.5.1	2.6	7	8	9
SIGABRT	Abnormal termination	•	•	•	•	•	•
SIGALRM	Alarm clock timeout	•	•	•	•	•	•
SIGBUS	Bus error	•	•	•	•	•	•
SIGCANCEL	Cancellation signal	•	•	•	•	•	•
SIGCHLD	Child status changed	•	•	•	•	•	•
SIGCLD	Alias for SIGCHLD	•	•	•	•	•	•
SIGCONT	Continue stopped process	•	•	•	•	•	•
SIGEMT	Emulator trap	•	•	•	•	•	•
SIGFPE	Arithmetic exception	•	•	•	•	•	•
SIGFREEZE	Check point freeze	•	•	•	•	•	•
SIGHUP	Hangup	•	•	•	•	•	•
SIGILL	Illegal instruction	•	•	•	•	•	•
SIGINT	Terminal interrupt character	•	•	•	•	•	•
SIGIO	Alias for SIGPOLL	•	•	•	•	•	•
SIGIOT	Alias for SIGABRT	•	•	•	•	•	•
SIGKILL	Kill process	•	•	•	•	•	•
SIGLOST	Resource lost			•	•	•	•
SIGLWP	Inter-LWP signal	•	•	•	•	•	•
SIGPIPE	Write to pipe with no readers	•	•	•	•	•	•
SIGPOLL	A pollable event has occurred	•	•	•	•	•	•
SIGPROF	Profiling timer expired	•	•	•	•	•	•
SIGPWR	Power fail or restart	•	•	•	•	•	•
SIGQUIT	Terminal quit character	•	•	•	•	•	•
SIGSEGV	Invalid memory reference	•	•	•	•	•	•
SIGSTOP	Stop	•	•	•	•	•	•
SIGSYS	Bad system call	•	•	•	•	•	•
SIGTERM	Termination	•	•	•	•	•	•
SIGTHAW	Check point thaw	•	•	•	•	•	•
SIGTRAP	Trace or breakpoint trap	•	•	•	•	•	•
SIGTSTP	Terminal stop character	•	•	•	•	•	•
SIGTTIN	Background read from controlling TTY	•	•	•	•	•	•
SIGTTOU	Background write to controlling TTY	•	•	•	•	•	•
SIGURG	Urgent socket condition	•	•	•	•	•	•
SIGUSR1	User defined signal 1	•	•	•	•	•	•
SIGUSR2	User defined signal 2	•	•	•	•	•	•
SIGVTALRM	Virtual timer alarm	•	•	•	•	•	•
SIGWAITING	Concurrency signal	•	•	•	•	•	•
SIGWINCH	Terminal window size change	•	•	•	•	•	•
SIGXCPU	CPU limit exceeded	•	•	•	•	•	•
SIGXFSZ	File size limit exceeded	•	•	•	•	•	•
SIGXRES	Resource control exceeded						•

Figure 17.1 Solaris signal summary.

ISO C	SVID	POSIX	SUSv1	SUSv2	Default action	Name
•	•	•	•	•	Core dump	SIGABRT
	•	•	•	•	Terminate	SIGALRM
	•	•	•	•	Core dump	SIGBUS
					Ignore	SIGCANCEL
	•	•	•	•	Ignore	SIGCHLD
					Ignore	SIGCLD
	•	•	•	•	Ignore	SIGCONT
	•				Core dump	SIGEMT
•	•	•	•	•	Core dump	SIGFPE
					Ignore	SIGFREEZE
	•	•	•	•	Terminate	SIGHUP
•	•	•	•	•	Core dump	SIGILL
•	•	•	•	•	Terminate	SIGINT
					Terminate	SIGIO
					Core dump	SIGIOT
	•	•	•	•	Terminate	SIGKILL
					Terminate	SIGLOST
					Ignore	SIGLWP
	•	•	•	•	Terminate	SIGPIPE
	•		•	•	Terminate	SIGPOLL
			•	•	Terminate	SIGPROF
	•				Ignore	SIGPWR
	•	•	•	•	Core dump	SIGQUIT
•	•	•	•	•	Core dump	SIGSEGV
	•	•	•	•	Stop process	SIGSTOP
	•		•	•	Core dump	SIGSYS
•	•	•	•	•	Terminate	SIGTERM
					Ignore	SIGTHAW
	•		•	•	Core dump	SIGTRAP
	•	•	•	•	Stop process	SIGTSTP
	•	•	•	•	Stop process	SIGTTIN
	•	•	•	•	Stop process	SIGTTOU
			•	•	Ignore	SIGURG
	•	•	•	•	Terminate	SIGUSR1
	•	•	•	•	Terminate	SIGUSR2
			•	•	Terminate	SIGVTALRM
					Ignore	SIGWAITING
	•				Ignore	SIGWINCH
	•		•	•	Core dump	SIGXCPU
	•		•	•	Core dump	SIGXFSZ
					Ignore	SIGXRES

Figure 17.1   Solaris signal summary (continued).

1. The owner of the process must be able to write to the current directory.

2. The process must not be set-user-ID, unless the current user is the file's owner.

3. The process must not be set-group-ID, unless the current user is the file's group owner.

4. The size of the generated file does not exceed the user's limit for `core` files (recall the `RLIMIT_CORE` limit from Section 8.4).

Core files, if created (i.e., they do not already exist), have the credentials of the process and have permissions of 0600 (i.e., only the owner can read or write to the file; everyone else is denied access).

Solaris 8 introduced the `coreadm` command, which enables us to configure global and per-process core file options. Using `coreadm`, we can disable the generation of core files, set up templates for the core filename, specify the directory in which core files will be placed, and override the set-user-ID and set-group-ID restrictions. Because allowing core dumps from set-user-ID or set-group-ID processes is a potential security hazard, core files created by these processes are owned, and are only accessible by, `root`.

> UNIX Version 6 did not check for conditions 2 and 3. The source code for the function that creates the core dump (called, rather appropriately, `core`) contained the comment "If you are looking for protection glitches, there are probably a wealth of them here when this occurs to a suid command". Details can be found in the "Lions Book" [Lions 1977].

The following describes each of the signals in detail:

SIGABRT	This signal is generated by calling the `abort` function, which we discuss in Section 17.24. The process terminates abnormally, producing a core dump.
SIGALRM	This signal is generated when a timer we've previously set using the `alarm` function (see Section 17.13) expires. This signal can also be generated when an interval timer set by the `setitimer` function expires. We talk about the `setitimer` function in Section 17.14.
SIGBUS	This signal is generated by an implementation defined hardware fault. In Solaris, this usually means that a misaligned memory access was attempted (e.g., trying to dereference a pointer stored at an odd address).
SIGCANCEL	This is the thread cancellation signal, which is used internally by the Solaris threads library.
SIGCHLD	Whenever a process changes state (i.e., it terminates or stops), this signal is sent to the process' parent. By default SIGCHLD is ignored, so the parent must arrange to catch this signal if it wants to be notified about a change in the status of one of its children. The normal action in the signal handler is to call one of the `wait` functions to fetch the child's process ID and termination status, thus avoiding zombies.

SIGCLD

In Solaris, this signal is an alias for SIGCHLD. However, releases of System V prior to SVR3 had a signal called SIGCLD which had non-standard semantics. The exact behaviour of a process that receives a SIGCLD signal depends on which function was used to establish the signal's disposition. We'll defer our discussion of these subtle nuances until Section 17.11, noting that new applications should avoid SIGCLD and use the standard SIGCHLD signal instead.

SIGCONT

This is a job control signal that is sent to a stopped process when it is continued. If the process is not stopped, the default action is to ignore the signal; otherwise, the default action is to continue the process. We'll talk about job control signals in more detail in Section 17.27.

SIGEMT

This signal (which gets its name from the PDP-11 "emulator trap" instruction) is generated by an implementation-defined hardware fault. In Solaris, the SIGEMT signal is used by the CPU performance counters library to indicate that a counter has overflowed.

SIGFPE

This signal, which gets its name from "floating-point exception", is generated when an arithmetic exception, such as dividing by zero, floating point overflow, etc. Note that despite its name, this signal is also generated when nonfloating-point exceptions occur.

SIGFREEZE

This signal is used by the CPR (suspend and resume) facility of Solaris. During the suspend operation, the SIGFREEZE signal is sent to all processes to allow them to do any special processing in response to a suspend operation. Most applications, however, do not need to do any special processing.

SIGHUP

This is the hangup signal, and is sent to the session leader (i.e., the controlling process) associated with a terminal if a disconnect is detected by the terminal driver. Note, however, that a SIGHUP is only generated for this condition if the terminal's CLOCAL flag is not set. (Recall from Section 12.5 that a terminal's CLOCAL flag is set if the attached terminal is local. If the flag is set, the modem control lines are ignored.)

Note that the session leader receives the signal, even if it is executing in the background. This is in contrast to the other terminal-generated signals (i.e., SIGINT, SIGQUIT, and SIGTSTP), which are always delivered to the foreground process group.

Another condition that generates this signal is when the session leader terminates. In this case, the signal is sent to each process in the foreground process group.

The SIGHUP signal is often used to notify daemon processes to reread their configuration files. The reason why SIGHUP is used in preference to some other signal is because a daemon process does not (or at least should not) have a controlling terminal, and would therefore never receive this signal. We'll talk about daemons in detail in Chapter 18.

SIGILL   This signal is sent when the CPU attempts to execute an illegal instruction.

SIGINT   This signal is sent to all processes in the foreground process group by the terminal driver when the terminal's interrupt key (typically Control-C) is pressed (refer to Figure 16.8). It is often used to stop a runaway process, especially one that is filling our screen with unwanted output.

SIGIO   This signal is an alias for SIGPOLL. Portable applications should use the latter.

SIGIOT   This deprecated signal gets its name from the PDP-11 instruction IOT (I/O trap). Early versions of System V used to generate this signal from the abort function, but SIGABRT is now used for this purpose. In Solaris, SIGIOT is an alias for SIGABRT; new applications should use the latter.

SIGKILL   This signal is used to terminate a process. It cannot be caught, blocked, or ignored. Its purpose is to provide systems administrators with a sure way to kill any process.

SIGLOST   This signal is sent to a process by the NFS lock daemon, lockd, when it fails to reacquire a previously granted lock on behalf of that process. This could happen if the lock daemon on the server restarted for some reason.

SIGLWP   This signal is used internally by the Solaris threads library.

SIGPIPE   This signal is generated when we write to a pipe that has no reader (we describe pipes in Chapter 19). A SIGPIPE signal will also be generated when we write to a socket when the other end has terminated.

SIGPOLL   This signal is generated when an event occurs on a pollable device. It is used in conjunction with the asynchronous I/O functions we describe in Section 13.19 (not, as its name would suggest, the poll function).

SIGPROF   This signal is generated when the profiling interval timer set by the setitimer function expires.

SIGPWR   The main use for the SIGPWR signal is on systems that are connected to an uninterruptible power supply (UPS). If the main power fails, the UPS takes over, running the systems it is connected to on its battery power reserves. When this happens, the UPS can notify some software running on the host it is connected to, although nothing needs to be done at this point. If the power outage is extended, such that the batteries run down, the UPS notifies the software of this condition. At this point, the UPS monitoring software should send the `SIGPWR` signal to the `init` process, so that it can perform a relatively orderly shutdown before the battery power also fails.

`SIGQUIT`   This signal is sent by the terminal driver to all processes in the foreground process group when the terminal's quit key (usually Control-\) is pressed (see Figure 16.8). This signal not only causes the processes in the foreground process group to terminate, it also causes them to generate a core dump.

`SIGSEGV`   This signal is generated when an invalid memory reference is attempted (e.g., trying to access memory that has not been mapped into the address space of the process). The signal's name derives from the term "segmentation violation".

`SIGSTOP`   This is a job control signal that stops a process. It is the same as the interactive user stop signal, `SIGTSTP`, apart from the fact that `SIGSTOP` cannot be caught, blocked, or ignored. This is so that systems administrators have a sure way to stop any process.

`SIGSYS`   This signal is delivered to a process that attempts to make an invalid system call. The kernel was somehow cajoled into executing a system call trap, but the trap's parameters indicate the system call was invalid.

`SIGTERM`   This is the default signal generated by the `kill` command, the intention being to terminate the recipient process.

`SIGTHAW`   This signal is used by the CPR (suspend and resume) facility of Solaris. During the resume operation, the `SIGTHAW` signal is sent to all processes to allow them to do any special processing in response to a resume operation. Most applications, however, do not need to do any special processing.

`SIGTRAP`   This signal (which gets its name from the PDP-11 TRAP instruction) is generated by an implementation-defined hardware fault. In Solaris, this signal is generated when a process is being traced by a debugger and encounters a breakpoint. This causes the traced process to stop and its parent (the debugger) to be notified. If the process receiving `SIGTRAP` is not being traced, the default action is to terminate the process with a core dump.

`SIGTSTP`   This job control signal is sent by the terminal driver to all processes in the foreground process group when the terminal's suspend key (usually Control-Z) is pressed. (Here we see an unfortunate example of the overloading of terminology. When we talk about job control, we talk about stopping and continuing jobs. However, terminal drivers have historically used the term "stop" in the context of stopping and starting terminal output by using the Control-S and Control-Q keys (i.e., software flow control). As a result of this, terminal drivers refer to the character that generates SIGTSTP as the suspend character, not the stop character.) This signal is also called the interactive stop signal.

SIGTTIN

This job control signal is sent by the terminal driver to a process in a background process group when the process attempts to read from its controlling terminal. However, if either of the following two conditions is true, a read from a background process will not generate a SIGTTIN signal:

1. The reading process is either ignoring or blocking SIGTTIN.

2. The process group to which the reading process belongs is an orphaned process group.

Instead, the read operation will fail, setting errno to EIO.

SIGTTOU

This job control signal is optionally sent by the terminal driver to a process in a background process group when the process attempts to write to its controlling terminal. We showed how to change this option in Chapter 12.

If background writes are not allowed, then if either of the following two conditions is true, a write from a background process will not generate a SIGTTOU signal:

1. The reading process is either ignoring or blocking SIGTTOU.

2. The process group to which the writing process belongs is an orphaned process group.

Instead, the write operation will fail, setting errno to EIO.

Whether or not background writes are allowed, certain other functions can also cause a SIGTTOU signal to be generated. These functions are: tcdrain, tcflow, tcflush, tcsendbreak, tcsetattr, and tcsetpgrp. We described these functions in Chapter 12.

SIGURG

This signal is generated when an urgent condition has occurred. It can be generated optionally when out-of-band data arrives on a network connection.

SIGUSR1	This is the first user-defined signal. It can be used for any purpose we define.
SIGUSR2	This is the second user-defined signal. It can be used for any purpose we define.
SIGVTALRM	This signal is generated when a virtual interval timer set by the `setitimer` function expires.
SIGWAITING	This signal is used internally by the Solaris threads library.
SIGWINCH	This signal is generated whenever the size of the window associated with a terminal or pseudo terminal changes if the change is because of a `TIOCSWINSZ` `ioctl`. If generated, the `SIGWINCH` signal is sent to every process that is a member of the foreground process group associated with the window that changed size.
SIGXCPU	This signal is generated if the process exceeds its soft CPU time limit. We discussed limits in Section 8.4.
SIGXFSZ	This signal is generated if the process exceeds its soft file size limit. We discussed limits in Section 8.4.
SIGXRES	This signal is generated if the process exceeds the limit of a resource control. We describe resource controls in Section 8.5.

We can use a number of functions to manipulate the disposition of a signal, the simplest being `signal` and `sigset`.

17.3   The `signal` Function

The `signal` function is the oldest method of changing a signal's disposition.

```
#include <signal.h>

void (*signal (int sig, void (*disp) (int))) (int);
```
Returns: the previous disposition of sig if OK, SIG_ERR on error

The `signal` function changes the disposition of the signal specified by *sig* to that specified by *disp*. The *disp* argument can be one of three values:

1. The constant SIG_IGN. Setting to disposition of *sig* to this value causes the signal to be ignored. (Recall from our previous discussion that we cannot ignore SIGKILL or SIGSTOP.)

2. The constant SIG_DFL. Setting to disposition of *sig* to this value causes the action associated with the signal to be set to that in the default action column of Figure 17.1.

3. The address of the function that is to be called when the signal is delivered; this function is called the *signal handler*. When we specify a signal handler to be

called when the signal is delivered, we call this *catching* the signal. Again, there are two signals we can't catch: `SIGKILL` and `SIGSTOP`.

The function prototype for the `signal` function can be a bit intimidating at first. Translating it to plain English, `signal` is a function that take two arguments. The first is an integer, and the second is a pointer to a function that has one argument: an integer. The function prototype also tells us the `signal` returns a pointer to a function that has one argument, which is an integer.

Although a signal handler usually has only one argument, we'll see later how we can arrange for the signal handler to be called with more than one argument.

Example: Using `signal` to catch signals

Program 17.1 is a simple program that catches the two user-defined signals, printing out the name of the signal that's caught. Program 17.1 uses the `pause` function, which we talk about in Section 17.7.

Let's take a look at some of Program 17.1's implementation details.

Set up signal handlers

9–10 Establish a signal handler to catch `SIGUSR1`.

11–12 Establish a signal handler to catch `SIGUSR2`.

Print the name of the received signal

14 Call the `pause` function. This puts our process to sleep until it receives a signal.

15–18 Print the name of the signal we received.

Signal handler

23–26 If the signal we've caught is one we're expecting, set the global variable `sig` to the number of the signal we caught. Otherwise, report an error.

To test Program 17.1, we run it in the background. Notice that we use the `kill` command to send signals to our process. (We might argue that "kill" is a bit of a misnomer, because what actually happens to the process depends on the disposition of the signal we send it. Termination is but one of the options.) Running Program 17.1 gives us these results:

```
$ ./signal &
[1]     11218
$ kill -USR1 11218
$ Received SIGUSR1
                                      Type Return
$ kill -USR2 11218
$ Received SIGUSR2
                                      Type Return again
$ kill 11218
[1] + Terminated          ./signal &
```

—————————————————————————————— signals/signal.c
```
 1 #include <stdio.h>
 2 #include <unistd.h>
 3 #include <signal.h>
 4 #include "ssp.h"

 5 static volatile sig_atomic_t sig;

 6 static void sigusr (int sig_num);

 7 int main (void)
 8 {
 9     if (signal (SIGUSR1, sigusr) == SIG_ERR)
10         err_msg ("Can't catch SIGUSR1");
11     if (signal (SIGUSR2, sigusr) == SIG_ERR)
12         err_msg ("Can't catch SIGUSR2");

13     for (;;) {
14         pause ();
15         if (sig == SIGUSR1)
16             printf ("Received SIGUSR1\n");
17         else
18             printf ("Received SIGUSR2\n");
19     }
20 }

21 static void sigusr (int sig_num)
22 {
23     if ((sig_num == SIGUSR1) || (sig_num == SIGUSR2))
24         sig = sig_num;
25     else
26         err_dump ("Received signal %d", sig_num);
27 }
```
—————————————————————————————— signals/signal.c

Program 17.1 Catching the signals SIGUSR1 and SIGUSR2 by using signal.

The last kill command sends our process a SIGTERM signal, which terminates it (because we didn't change the disposition of the signal from the default).

We might be tempted to wonder why we go to all the trouble of setting a global variable, and printing the name of the signal from inside our loop in main, rather than just printing the name of the signal we received in the signal handler. For now we'll just say that calling printf (or indeed, any function in the standard I/O library) inside a signal handler is not good programming practice. We'll revisit this in Section 17.10.

Notice that the type of our global variable is sig_atomic_t, which is defined by ISO C as being an integral object that can be accessed as an atomic entity, even in the presence of asynchronous interrupts. This means that variables of this type must be accessed with one machine instruction and cannot extend across page boundaries. We always use the volatile type qualifier for variables of this data type too. We do this because the variable is accessed from at least two different threads of control: the main function and the asynchronous signal handler.

Process Start-Up

We must consider the disposition of signals when a process is first execed. As we stated in Section 15.11, signals that are ignored or have their default disposition prior to the exec have the same disposition after the exec. Signals that are being caught have their disposition reset to the default. This makes sense, because the address of the signal handler is very likely to be meaningless after an exec.

An example of this sort of behaviour in action is when we run a process in the background using a shell that doesn't support job control. In this case, the shell sets the disposition of SIGINT and SIGQUIT so that they are ignored. Subsequently typing Control-C or Control-\ will affect only the foreground process, leaving our background process intact. If this changing of signal disposition didn't take place, typing the interrupt character would terminate all the background processes (unless they change the disposition of SIGINT themselves), as well as the foreground process.

Many interactive programs use code that resembles the following when catching these two signals:

```
if (signal (SIGINT, SIG_IGN) != SIG_IGN)
    signal (SIGINT, sigint);
if (signal (SIGQUIT, SIG_IGN) != SIG_IGN)
    signal (SIGQUIT, sigquit);
```

By using code like this, the signals are caught only if they're not currently being ignored. (In our example code, sigint and sigquit are the names of our two signal handling functions.)

This example also illustrates one of the limitations of the signal function: we can't determine the current disposition of a signal without changing it. We'll see later in this chapter how we can achieve this by using the sigaction function.

Related to the preceding discussion is the question of signal handling when a process forks. In this case, the child inherits all of the parent's signal dispositions. Under these circumstances, the address of the signal handler is still meaningful, because the memory image of the child is the same as its parent's.

17.4 Unreliable Signals

Signal handling using the signal function has another disadvantage: it is unreliable. *Unreliable signals* are a throwback to the very early versions of UNIX. When we talk about unreliable signals, we mean that they can get lost; a signal could occur, and the process would not know about it.

Another problem with unreliable signals is that the disposition of a signal is reset to the default each time the signal occurs. Astute readers will notice that we sidestepped this detail by catching each signal only once. Let's rerun Program 17.1, sending it the same signal twice:

```
$ ./signal &
[1]     25065
```

Type Return

```
$ kill -USR1 25065
$ Received SIGUSR1
```

Type Return again

```
$ kill -USR1 25065
$
[1] + User Signal 1              ./signal &
```

Notice that when we send the second SIGUSR1 to Program 17.1, its process just terminates (Figure 17.1 confirms that the default action for SIGUSR1 is to terminate the process).

Historically, the only way we could deal with this was to have the signal handler reestablish itself early its code. The resulting code would resemble this, assuming we were writing a handler for the interrupt signal:

```
static void sigint (int signum)
{
    signal (SIGINT, sigint);

    /* Rest of signal processing here */
}
```

The problem with this code is that it has a race condition. There is a window of time between the signal being generated and the signal handler being reestablished in sigusr. Should a second interrupt signal be sent to the process during this time window, the signal's default action will happen (i.e., the process will terminate). Like most race hazards, this is one of those conditions that works correctly most of the time, causing us to think that it is correct when it isn't. Debugging problems in code like this can be hard.

Another problem with unreliable signals is that we can't defer the processing of a signal. All we can do is ignore it. There are occasions, however, where it would be useful to say "don't deliver the signal for now, but remember that it has occurred". An example of a situation where this would be useful is shown in the following code, which sets a flag in the signal handler to let the process know that the signal has occurred (in a similar manner to Program 17.1).

```
static void sigint (int sig);
static volatile sig_atomic_t sigflag;

int main (void)
{
    ...
    signal (SIGINT, sigint);
    ...
    while (sigflag == 0)
        pause ();
    ...
}

static void sigint (int sig)
{
    signal (SIGINT, sigint);
    sigflag = 1;
}
```

In this example code, the process puts itself to sleep until a signal occurs by calling pause. If the signal causes the signal handler, sigint, to be executed, the flag sigflag is set to 1, which causes the while loop in main to terminate. Otherwise, pause is called again.

Unfortunately, there is a window for things to go awry. If a SIGINT signal arrives just after the test for sigflag being equal to 0, but before the call to pause, the process could sleep for ever (assuming that another SIGINT doesn't arrive). The occurrence of the signal is lost. This is another example of code that works most of the, despite being incorrect.

Because it doesn't handle signals reliably, the obsolescent signal function should not be used in new programs. One of the reliable alternatives we discuss in the following sections should be used instead.

17.5   Reliable Signals

Reliable signals were first introduced in 4.2BSD to solve the problems we alluded to in the previous section. SVR3 also provided reliable signals, but the implementation was different to BSD's. Solaris uses the SVR4 signal implementation, which is based on the one from SVR3.

Reliable signals make two changes to the way signals are handled:

1. Signal dispositions are not reset when a signal handler is called. The disposition of a signal is modified only when the process specifically changes it.

2. Processes have the ability to *block* or *hold* signals. Blocking a signal is similar to ignoring it, in that it is not immediately delivered to the process.

When we block a signal, instead of just discarding it (which is what happens when we ignore a signal), the kernel places it on a queue of pending signals to be delivered to the process. If the process ever unblocks (or releases) the signal, it will be delivered to the process at that time. Blocking signals is useful in programs that have critical sections that must not be interrupted, but otherwise want to process the signals. Two signals cannot be blocked: SIGKILL and SIGSTOP.

If a blocked signal is generated for a process and the signal is not being ignored, then the signal remains pending until the process either unblocks it or changes the signal's disposition such that the signal is ignored. The action for a signal is determined when it is delivered to a process, not when it is generated. This means that we can change the disposition of a signal before we accept it for delivery. We can use the sigpending function (which we discuss in Section 17.18) to determine which signals are blocked and pending.

Signals that are generated synchronously should not be blocked. POSIX states that the result is undefined if such a signal is delivered when it is blocked; if a synchronously generated signal is delivered when it is blocked on a Solaris system, the receiving process is killed.

We need to consider two other scenarios:

1.   What happens when multiple occurrences of a blocked signal are generated?
2.   What happens when more than one signal is waiting to be delivered to a process?

The answer to our first question is that the result is system-dependent. The signals can either be queued so that the process receives all the duplicated signals, or all of the duplicate signals can be discarded so that the process receives only one instance of the signal. Solaris takes the latter approach.

As to our second question, the answer is that there is no specified order in which the signals are delivered. However, POSIX does suggest that signals related to the current state of the process (e.g., SIGSEGV) be delivered before other signals.

Each process has a *signal mask* that defines the set of signals currently being blocked. We can think of this signal mask as simply being a set of bits—one bit for each signal. If a bit is set, then the signal associated with that bit is currently being blocked by the process; conversely, if a bit is clear, then the signal associated with that bit will be delivered to the process. A process can examine and change its current signal mask by using the sigprocmask function we describe in Section 17.17.

In the following sections, we'll examine the functions and facilities that are part of the reliable signals feature set.

17.6   The sigset Function

The sigset function is the signal function's reliable counterpart.

```
#include <signal.h>

void (*sigset (int sig, void (*disp) (int))) (int);
```
                                   Returns: the previous disposition of *sig* if OK, SIG_ERR on error

The sigset function changes the disposition of the signal specified by *sig* to that specified by *disp*. The *disp* argument can be one of four values:

1.   The constant SIG_IGN. Setting to disposition of *sig* to this value causes the signal to be ignored. (Recall from our previous discussion that we cannot ignore SIGKILL or SIGSTOP.)

2.   The constant SIG_HOLD. This causes *sig* to be added to the signal mask of the process; the signal's disposition remains unchanged.

3.   The constant SIG_DFL. Setting to disposition of *sig* to this value causes the action associated with the signal to be set to that in the default action column of Figure 17.1.

4.   The address of the function that is to be called when the signal is delivered; this function is called the *signal handler*. When we specify a signal handler to be called when the signal is delivered, we call this *catching* the signal. Again, there are two signals we can't catch: SIGKILL and SIGSTOP.

When `sigset` is used to change the disposition of *sig*, and *disp* is the address of a signal handler, the kernel adds *sig* to the signal mask of the calling process before calling the specified signal handler. When the signal handler returns, the process' signal mask is restored to its state prior to the delivery of the signal.

The BSD version of `signal` is reliable. When porting programs that use `signal` from BSD, it is usually sufficient to add the line

```
#define signal sigset
```

to the top of the program. The only case where we can't do this is when we are working with `SIGCHLD`. Properly handling `SIGCHLD` requires the use of the `sigaction` function we describe later.

Example: Using `sigset` to catch signals

Program 17.2 is a reimplementation of Program 17.1; it catches the `SIGUSR1` and `SIGUSR2` signals using `sigset` instead of `signal`. We've highlighted the lines that have changed.

Running Program 17.2 gives us the following results:

```
$ ./sigset &
[1]     25805
$ kill -USR1 25805
$ Received SIGUSR1
                                          Type Return
$ kill -USR1 25805
$ Received SIGUSR1
                                          Type Return again
$ kill 25805
[1] + Terminated              ./sigset &
```

Notice that this time, the `SIGUSR1` signal is caught reliably. We have to send a termination signal explicitly to Program 17.2 kill it; sending it two `SIGUSR1` signals is not enough.

17.7 The `pause` Function

There are times when we want to suspend a process until a signal arrives. To do this, we use the `pause` function.

```
#include <unistd.h>

int pause (void);
```
                                          Returns: −1 with errno set to EINTR

signals/sigset.c

```
1 #include <stdio.h>
2 #include <unistd.h>
3 #include <signal.h>
4 #include "ssp.h"

5 static volatile sig_atomic_t sig;

6 static void sigusr (int sig_num);

7 int main (void)
8 {
9     if (sigset (SIGUSR1, sigusr) == SIG_ERR)
10         err_msg ("Can't catch SIGUSR1");
11    if (sigset (SIGUSR2, sigusr) == SIG_ERR)
12         err_msg ("Can't catch SIGUSR2");

13    for (;;) {
14        pause ();
15        if (sig == SIGUSR1)
16            printf ("Received SIGUSR1\n");
17        else
18            printf ("Received SIGUSR2\n");
19    }
20 }

21 static void sigusr (int sig_num)
22 {
23     if ((sig_num == SIGUSR1) || (sig_num == SIGUSR2))
24         sig = sig_num;
25     else
26         err_dump ("Received signal %d", sig_num);
27 }
```

signals/sigset.c

Program 17.2 Catching the signals SIGUSR1 and SIGUSR2 by using sigset.

The pause function suspends the calling process until it receives a signal that it is not currently ignoring. The only time pause returns is if a signal handler is executed and returns, in which case −1 is returned and errno is set to EINTR. The process then continues executing from the point of suspension.

If the disposition of the received signal is to terminate the process, pause does not return, and the process terminates (possibly dumping core).

17.8 The sighold, sigrelse, sigignore, and sigpause Functions

Solaris provides a set of four functions for simplified reliable signal management. These are sighold, sigrelse, sigignore, and sigpause.

```
#include <signal.h>

int sighold (int sig);

int sigrelse (int sig);

int sigignore (int sig);

int sigpause (int sig);
```
All four return: 0 if OK, −1 on error

The `sighold` function adds the signal specified by *sig* to the calling process' signal mask. Executing

```
sighold (sig);
```

is the same as executing

```
sigset (sig, SIG_HOLD);
```

Neither of these variants support nesting, so we should take care to avoid this.

The `sigrelse` function does the converse; it removes the signal specified by *sig* from the calling process' signal mask.

The `sigignore` function changes the disposition of the signal specified by *sig* to `SIG_IGN`. Executing

```
sigignore (sig);
```

is the same as executing

```
sigset (sig, SIG_IGN);
```

The `sigpause` function removes the signal specified by *sig* from the calling process' signal mask, and then suspends the calling process until a signal is received that the process is not currently ignoring. Conceptually,

```
sigpause (sig);
```

is the same as

```
sigrelse (sig);
pause ();
```

with one important difference: `sigpause` is an atomic operation that cannot be interrupted between the change in the calling process' signal mask and suspending the process.

We can use these functions to solve the second problem we identified with unreliable signals in Section 17.4 (i.e., the problem of deferring the handling of signals until we are ready for them). For example:

```
static void sigint (int sig);
static volatile sig_atomic_t sigflag;

int main (void)
{
    ...
    sighold (SIGINT);
    sigset (SIGINT, sigint);
    ...
```

```
            while (sigflag == 0)
                sigpause (SIGINT);
            ...
    }

    static void sigint (int sig)
    {
        sigflag = 1;
    }
```

In this example, the call to `sighold` adds `SIGINT` to the process' signal mask, which prevents the signal from being delivered until we are ready for it. After we've set up the signal handler (using `sigset`), we call `sigpause` to remove `SIGINT` from our signal mask and suspend our process until a signal is delivered. Because we blocked `SIGINT`, there's no window in which a `SIGINT` can arrive between testing the flag `sigflag` and suspending the process.

17.9 Interrupted System Calls

Historically, if a process caught a signal while blocked in a "slow" system call, the system call was interrupted. The system call would return an error and set `errno` to `EINTR`. The thinking behind this is that if a signal arrives and the process is catching it, there is a good chance that the event is significant enough to justify interrupting the system call.

> This is one of the few instances in this text where we must differentiate between a system call and a function. When we talk about interrupted system calls, we are specifically referring to system calls running in the kernel that are interrupted when a signal is caught.

There are two categories of system calls: those that are slow, and those that aren't. A *slow system call* is one that could potentially block for ever. Examples of this category include:

- Opens of files that block until some condition occurs (e.g., an open of a terminal device that waits until a modem answers the phone)
- Reads from certain types of file that can block the caller for ever if data isn't present (e.g., pipes, terminal devices, and network connections)
- Writes to these same types of file that can block caller indefinitely if the data cannot be accepted immediately
- The `pause` system call, which by definition blocks until a signal arrives
- The `wait` family of system calls, which block until a child process terminates
- Certain `ioctl` operations
- Some of the IPC (interprocess communications) functions

One notable exception to these slow system calls is anything to do with disk I/O. Despite these operations being slow compared to memory references (by several orders of magnitude), and despite the fact that they can block the caller temporarily while the device driver queues and fulfills the request, the I/O operation always returns and unblocks the caller relatively quickly unless a hardware error occurs.

An example of the sort of situation interrupted system calls handle is that of a user at a terminal. If a process initiates a read from the user's terminal device when the user will be away for an extended period, the process could be blocked for hours or days. Without interruptible system calls, the only way to kill the process would be to reboot the system.

One problem with interrupted system calls (the cloud associated with the silver lining, so to speak) is that we must explicitly handle them in our code. For example, assuming we're performing a read operation that we want to be restarted should it be interrupted, we must write our code like this:

```
again:
    if ((n = read (fd, buf, sizeof (buf))) == -1) {
        if (errno == EINTR)
            goto again;
        /* Handle other errors */
    }
```

To relieve programmers from this somewhat onerous task, 4.2BSD introduced the automatic restarting of certain interrupted system calls. The system calls that were automatically restarted when interrupted are `ioctl`, `read`, `readv`, `write`, `writev`, `wait`, and `waitpid`. (The first five functions in this list are interrupted only if they are operating on a slow device; `wait` and `waitpid` are always interrupted when a signal is caught.) The trouble is, although it eliminated the need to write code like the preceding example, it broke many applications that relied on system calls not being restarted. Because of this, 4.3BSD allowed the process to disable this feature on a per-signal basis.

Historically, System V has never restarted system calls. However, SVR4 introduced the ability to restart interrupted system calls optionally. (The default was to not restart system calls, so as to preserve backward compatibility.) We'll see how to do this when we discuss the `sigaction` function in Section 17.19.

Figure 17.2 summarizes the different signal handling functions.

Function	Signal handler remains installed	Ability to block signals	Restart interrupted system calls
signal			No
sigset	•	•	No
sighold	•	•	No
sigrelse	•	•	No
sigignore	•	•	No
sigpause	•	•	No
sigaction	Optional	•	Optional
sigprocmask	•	•	N/A
sigpending	•	N/A	N/A
sigsuspend	•	N/A	N/A

Figure 17.2 Features provided by the different signal handling functions.

We'll discuss the last four functions (`sigaction`, `sigprocmask`, `sigpending`, and `sigsuspend`) in later sections of this chapter.

17.10 Reentrant Functions

Any discussion of signal handling would be incomplete without talking about reentrant functions. As the name suggests, a *reentrant function* is one that can be safely called more than once simultaneously, either recursively or by another thread. (The POSIX and SUS definition of a reentrant function is "a function whose effect, when called by two or more threads, is guaranteed to be as if the threads each executed the function one after another in an undefined order, even if the actual execution is interleaved".)

Let's review what happens when a process catches a signal. The current sequence of instructions being executed by the process is temporarily interrupted by the signal handler. The process continues to execute, running the instructions of the signal handler. When the signal handler returns (assuming that the interrupt handler doesn't call `exit` or `longjmp`), the instruction sequence interrupted when the signal was caught continues executing. (Hardware interrupts have a similar effect, although at a much lower level.)

The signal handler has no way of knowing what the process was doing immediately prior to receiving the signal. For example, if the process was in the middle of allocating some memory using `malloc`, what would happen if we called `malloc` from inside our signal handler? Since `malloc` maintains a linked list of all its allocated areas, chaos is likely to ensue because the original `malloc` might have been updating those links when the signal arrived. Another situation which can cause mayhem is when a signal is delivered when the process is executing a function that stores its result in an internal static buffer, for example, `localtime`, and the signal handler calls the same function. The buffer being used by the normal program flow would be overwritten by the signal handler.

To avoid these hazards, we should call only those functions that we know to be reentrant (although POSIX and the Sun documentation prefer the term "Async-Signal-Safe") in our signal handlers. Both POSIX and the SVID specify which functions can be safely called in a signal handler (i.e., are guaranteed to be reentrant). The reentrant functions provided by Solaris are a superset of those specified by POSIX. However, some of the functions specified as being safe for use in signal handlers by the SVID are not specifically annotated as such in the Solaris documentation. The functions in question are `abort`, `chroot`, `exit`, `longjmp`, `signal`, and `ustat`.

Figure 17.3 lists the functions that are safe to use in Solaris signal handlers.

Most of the functions that are missing from Figure 17.3 are excluded because they fall into one or more of the three following categories:

1. They use static internal data structures.
2. They call `malloc` or `free`.
3. They are part of the standard I/O library. (The standard I/O library uses global data structures in a non-reentrant manner.)

Something to be aware of is that even if we just call the functions listed in Figure 17.3, there is still just one global `errno` variable per process. It's possible that one of the

_exit	fork	rmdir	tcflush
access	fstat	sem_post	tcgetattr
aio_error	fsync	sema_post	tcgetpgrp
aio_return	getegid	setgid	tcsendbreak
aio_suspend	geteuid	setpgid	tcsetattr
alarm	getgid	setsid	tcsetpgrp
cfgetispeed	getgroups	setuid	thr_kill
cfgetospeed	getpgrp	sigaction	thr_sigsetmask
cfsetispeed	getpid	sigaddset	time
cfsetospeed	getppid	sigdelset	timer_getoverrun
chdir	getuid	sigemptyset	timer_gettime
chmod	kill	sigfillset	timer_settime
chown	link	sigismember	times
clock_gettime	lseek	sigpending	umask
close	mkdir	sigprocmask	uname
creat	mkfifo	sigqueue	unlink
dup	open	sigsuspend	utime
dup2	pathconf	sleep	wait
execle	pause	stat	waitpid
execve	pipe	sysconf	write
fcntl	read	tcdrain	
fdatasync	rename	tcflow	

Figure 17.3   Reentrant functions that can be called from a signal handler.

functions we call from our signal handler will change the value of errno. For example, suppose we call a function that sets errno, and a signal that we handle arrives prior to our testing errno's value. If calling one of the safe functions from Figure 17.3 causes errno to be set to a different value, the original value will be lost. To guard against this sort of information loss, we should save and restore the value of errno.

Another thing we should be cognizant of is that although the SVID states that longjmp is safe to use in signal handlers, there are still occasions where it would be unsafe. For example, we might be updating one of our own linked lists. Using longjmp instead of returning from the signal handler might leave our data structure in an indeterminate state. If we are doing this sort of thing in our applications, we should block the signals that would cause us to call longjmp while we're performing tasks susceptible to this kind of problem.

Example: Calling non-reentrant functions from a signal handler

Program 17.3 shows how *not* to write a signal handler. Not only does the signal handler call a function in the standard I/O library (printf), but it also calls getpwent, which uses a static internal data buffer.

Catch SIGALRM

12 Arrange to catch the the SIGALRM signal. We do this because the interval timer we set up in the next few lines generates periodic SIGALRM signals.

—————————————————— signals/bad_handler.c

```
 1  #include <stdio.h>
 2  #include <string.h>
 3  #include <signal.h>
 4  #include <pwd.h>
 5  #include <sys/time.h>
 6  #include "ssp.h"

 7  static void sigalrm (int sig);

 8  int main (void)
 9  {
10      struct passwd *buf;
11      struct itimerval interval;

12      sigset (SIGALRM, sigalrm);
13      interval.it_interval.tv_sec = 0;
14      interval.it_interval.tv_usec = 1000;
15      interval.it_value.tv_sec = 0;
16      interval.it_value.tv_usec = 1000;
17      setitimer (ITIMER_REAL, &interval, NULL);

18      for (;;) {
19          if ((buf = getpwnam ("rich")) == NULL)
20              err_msg ("getpwnam failed");
21          if (strcmp ("rich", buf -> pw_name) != 0)
22              printf ("Buffer corrupted, pw_name = %s\n", buf -> pw_name);
23      }
24  }

25  static void sigalrm (int sig)
26  {
27      struct passwd *buf;

28      printf ("In signal handler\n");
29      if ((buf = getpwnam ("root")) == NULL)
30          err_msg ("getpwnam (root) failed");
31  }
```

—————————————————— signals/bad_handler.c

Program 17.3 Calling non-reentrant functions from a signal handler.

Set up the interval timer

13–16 Set up an interval timer, such that it generates a SIGALRM signal every 1000 microseconds after an initial 1-microsecond delay.

17 Set up an interval timer that decrements in real time. We describe the setitimer function in Section 17.14.

Infinite loop

18–23 In an infinite loop, get the password file entry for the user "rich", and then compare the user name of the retrieved password entry with "rich". If the strings differ, it means that the static internal buffer used by getpwnam has been corrupted by the signal handler.

Signal handler

28 Print a message stating that the signal handler is executing. Again for emphasis, we
should not normally call any function in the standard I/O library, including printf.

29–30 Get the password file entry for the user "root", doing nothing with the results. What
we're trying to do here is overwrite getpwnam's static internal buffer.

Running Program 17.3 gives us results like the following:

```
$ ./bad_handler
In signal handler
In signal handler
In signal handler
In signal handler
Buffer corrupted, pw_name = root
In signal handler
In signal handler
In signal handler
In signal handler
In signal handler
Buffer corrupted, pw_name = root
In signal handler
```

The number of times no corruption was observed far exceeds the number of times the
buffer was corrupted. This example shows that when we call a non-reentrant function
from a signal handler, the results are unpredictable. Once again, these sorts of bugs can
be very hard to reproduce, and hence can be hard to fix.

17.11 Comparing the SIGCHLD and SIGCLD Signals

Two signals, SIGCHLD and SIGCLD, have historically been a constant source of confusion
for programmers. The former, SIGCHLD, derives from BSD, and was adopted by POSIX
and the Single UNIX Specification. System V has a similar signal, called SIGCLD, which
has different semantics to SIGCHLD. In Solaris, SIGCLD is an alias for SIGCHLD, but the
behaviour of a process receiving this signal depends which function was used to
establish the signal's disposition. New applications should avoid SIGCLD and instead
use the standard SIGCHLD.

In some System V-based versions of UNIX, using either signal or sigset to set the
disposition of SIGCHLD causes the semantics of the old SIGCLD to apply. These are:

1. If the signal's disposition is set to SIG_IGN, then children of the calling process
will not become zombies when they terminate. Instead, the termination status of
any terminated children is discarded. If the calling process subsequently waits
for its children, it blocks until all of its children have terminated. The waiting
function then returns –1 and sets errno to ECHILD.

Note that the default disposition of this signal is to be ignored (see Figure 17.1).
However, the default behaviour will not cause the above semantics to occur.
Instead, we must specifically set the signal's disposition to SIG_IGN.

2. If the process establishes a signal handler for the signal, the kernel immediately checks if there are any terminated children to be waited for, and if so, calls the signal handler. In a sense, this behaviour makes the signal retroactive; processes that terminated before the signal's disposition was changed can result in the handler being called. As we shall see, this item changes the way we must write signal handlers if we catch SIGCHLD using the signal function.

The second of these semantics does *not* apply to program compiled on Solaris. However, we should be aware of this behaviour, especially when porting older programs.

If we use sigaction (see Section 17.19) to change the disposition of SIGCHLD, then the standard SIGCHLD semantics will apply.

Example: An incorrect SIGCLD signal handler

Program 17.4 shows an example of a SIGCLD signal handler that works as expected on Solaris, but can be problematic on other versions of UNIX.

The problem with Program 17.4 arises from our reestablishing of the signal handler inside the handler. The second SIGCLD semantic we described previously means that as soon as we call the signal function from inside our handler, another SIGCLD signal is sent to the process, recursively calling the signal handler. Eventually, the process will run out of stack space and terminate abnormally. This happens because there are still children that need to be waited for.

We can work around this by calling wait to reap the child's termination status before calling signal to reestablish the signal handler. This has the advantage of avoiding infinite recursion; another SIGCLD signal will be sent only if another child terminates. The disadvantage with this solution is that a larger window of time exists between the signal's disposition being reset to its default when the signal is delivered, and the signal handler reestablishing itself.

Compiling and running Program 17.4 on Solaris behaves as we would intuitively expect:

```
$ ./sigcld
Received SIGCLD
Child PID = 12345
```

We'll talk a bit more about the SIGCHLD signal when we discuss the sigaction function in Section 17.19.

17.12 The kill, killpg, raise, sigsend, and sigsendset Functions

So far, our discussion of signals has concentrated on their delivery. But how do we programmatically send a specific signal to a process or group of processes? There are five functions we use to do this: kill, killpg, raise, sigsend, and sigsendset.

signals/sigcld.c

```
 1 #include <stdio.h>
 2 #include <unistd.h>
 3 #include <sys/types.h>
 4 #include <signal.h>
 5 #include <sys/wait.h>
 6 #include "ssp.h"

 7 static void sigcld (int sig);

 8 int main (void)
 9 {
10     pid_t pid;

11     if (signal (SIGCLD, sigcld) == SIG_ERR)
12         err_msg ("signal failed");

13     if ((pid = fork ()) == -1)
14         err_msg ("fork failed");

15     if (pid == 0) {
16         sleep (1);
17         _exit (0);
18     }

19     pause ();
20     return (0);
21 }

22 static void sigcld (int sig)
23 {
24     pid_t pid;
25     int status;

26     printf ("Received SIGCLD\n");

27     if (signal (SIGCLD, sigcld) == SIG_ERR)
28         err_msg ("signal failed");

29     if ((pid = wait (&status)) == -1)
30         err_msg ("wait failed");

31     printf ("Child PID = %ld\n", (long) pid);
32 }
```

signals/sigcld.c

Program 17.4 A SIGCLD signal handler than can be problematic.

The `kill` Function

The `kill` function is used to send a signal to a process or group of processes.

```
#include <sys/types.h>
#include <signal.h>

int kill (pid_t pid, int sig);
```
                                                            Returns: 0 if OK, −1 on error

The `kill` function sends the signal specified by *sig* to the process or process group specified by *pid*. The signal specified by the *sig* argument must be either one of the values from Figure 17.1, or 0. If *sig* is 0 (the *null signal*), then the normal error checking is performed, but no signal is actually sent. We can use this feature to determine the validity of *pid*. There is one caveat with respect to this feature: process IDs are periodically recycled, so the existence of a process with a given process ID is not necessarily indicative that the process is the one we think it is.

The *pid* argument determines which process or process group is sent the signal, and may be one of the following four values.

pid > 0   The signal is sent to the process whose process ID is equal to *pid*.

pid == 0   The signal is sent to all non-system processes in the same process group as the sender (i.e., those processes whose process group ID is the same as the process group ID of the sender) and for which the sender has permission to send the signal.

          Permission to send a signal is granted only if the real or effective user ID of the sending process matches the real or saved user ID of the receiving process. Privileged processes (those whose effective user ID is 0) can send a signal to any process.

pid < 0   The signal is sent to all non-system processes whose process group ID is the same as the absolute value of *pid* and for which the sender has permission to send the signal.

pid == −1   The signal will be sent to a group of processes that is determined by the effective user ID of the sender. If the effective user ID of the sending process is 0, then *sig* will be sent to all non-system processes. Otherwise, *sig* will be sent to all non-system processes whose real user ID is the same as the effective user ID of the sending process.

There is one special case for permissions testing: if *sig* is `SIGCONT`, then a process may send the signal to any process that is a member of the same session.

If the call to `kill` causes *sig* to be generated for the sending process, and if *sig* is not being blocked or being `sigwaited` for, then either *sig* or at least one other pending unblocked signal will be delivered to the sending thread before `kill` returns.

The `killpg` Function

The `killpg` function is used to send a signal to a process group.

```
#include <signal.h>

int killpg (pid_t pgrp, int sig);
```
Returns: 0 if OK, −1 on error

The `killpg` function sends the signal specified by *sig* to the process group specified by *pgrp*. This function is subject to the same permissions checks and restrictions as `kill`.

The call

```
kill (-pgrp, sig);
```

is the same as

```
killpg (pgrp, sig);
```

The `raise` Function

The `raise` function can be used to send a signal to the calling process.

```
#include <signal.h>

int raise (int sig);
```
Returns: 0 if OK, −1 on error

The `raise` function sends the signal specified by *sig* to the calling process. The call

```
raise (sig);
```

is the same as

```
kill (getpid (), sig);
```

This function was defined by ISO C, which has no concept of multiple processes, so it can't specify a function like `kill`, which requires a process ID as an argument.

The `sigsend` and `sigsendset` Functions

Two functions give us more control over which set of processes a signal is sent to: `sigsend` and `sigsendset`.

```
#include <signal.h>

int sigsend (idtype_t idtype, id_t id, int sig);

int sigsendset (procset_t *psp, int sig);
```

Both return: 0 if OK, −1 on error

The `sigsend` function provides a more versatile way of sending signals to a process or group of processes than that provided by `kill`. It sends the signal specified by *sig* to the process or group of processes specified by *idtype* and *id*. The signal specified by *sig* must be one of the values shown in Figure 17.1, or 0. In the latter case, the normal error checking is performed, but no signal is actually sent; this enables us to check the validity of *idtype* and *id*.

The *idtype* argument determines how the corresponding *id* argument is interpreted. The legal values for *idtype* are as follows:

P_ALL	The signal specified by *sig* will be sent to all non-system processes; *id* is ignored.
P_CID	The signal specified by *sig* will be sent to any process whose scheduler class ID is the same as *id*.
P_GID	The signal specified by *sig* will be sent to any non-system process whose effective group ID is equal to *id*.
P_PGID	The signal specified by *sig* will be sent to any non-system process whose process group ID is equal to *id*.
P_PID	The signal specified by *sig* will be sent to the process whose process ID is equal to *id*.
P_PROJID	The signal specified by *sig* will be sent to all processes whose project ID is equal to *id*. This value of *idtype* was introduced with Solaris 8 6/00.
P_SID	The signal specified by *sig* will be sent to any non-system process whose session ID is equal to *id*.
P_TASKID	The signal specified by *sig* will be sent to all processes whose task ID is equal to *id*. This value of *idtype* was introduced with Solaris 8 6/00.
P_UID	The signal specified by *sig* will be sent to any non-system process whose effective user ID is equal to *id*.

If *id* is P_MYID, then the value of *id* is taken to be the process ID of the calling process.

System processes (those processes whose process ID is equal to 0) are always excluded, as is the `init` process, unless *idtype* is set to P_PID.

The `sigsendset` function provides us with another interface for sending signals to sets of processes. The signal to be sent is specified by *sig*, and the set of processes is specified by the `procset` structure pointed to by *psp*. The `procset_t` type is a structure which has the following members:

```
typedef struct procset {
    idop_t       p_op;        /* Operation to be performed */
    idtype_t     p_lidtype;   /* ID type of "left" set of processes" */
    id_t         p_lid;       /* ID of "left" set of processes */
    idtype_t     p_ridtype;   /* ID type of "right" set of processes */
    id_t         p_rid;       /* ID of "right" set of processes */
} procset_t;
```

The `p_lidtype` and `p_lid` members specify the ID type and ID for one of the set of processes (the "left" set), and the `p_ridtype` and `p_rid` members specify the other set of processes (the "right" set). The ID types and IDs are specified as they are for the `sigsend` function.

The `p_op` member specifies the operation to be performed on the two sets of processes; the result of this operation is the set of processes to which the signal specified by *sig* is sent. The valid values for `p_op` and the processes they specify are as follows:

POP_AND   Set intersection: processes in both the left and right sets.

POP_DIFF   Set difference: processes in the left set that are not in the right set.

POP_OR   Set union: processes in the left set, the right set, or both sets.

POP_XOR   Set exclusive-OR: processes in the left set, the right set, but not both sets.

For both `sigsend` and `sigsendset`, the signal will be sent only to processes to which the sending process has permission to send, using the same permission rules we described for the `kill` function.

17.13 The `alarm` Function

We saw earlier how we can use the `pause` and `sigpause` functions to suspend a process (potentially for ever) until a signal is delivered to the process. There are also times when we want to arrange for a signal to be sent to our process at some point in the future without suspending our process.

The `alarm` enables us to set a timer that will expire at a specified number of seconds in the future.

```
#include <unistd.h>

unsigned int alarm (unsigned int sec);
```
                                  Returns: the previous number of remaining alarm clock seconds

The `alarm` function arranges for the alarm signal, `SIGALRM`, to be sent to the calling process after *sec* seconds of real time have elapsed, returning the previously remaining number of seconds in the alarm clock for the calling process. (Be aware that although the signal will be generated at the required time, scheduling delays could prevent the process from receiving the signal immediately.) Any previously set alarms are overridden, and setting *sec* to 0 will cause any previous alarm requests to be cancelled. Alarms are cleared in the child process by the `fork` function, but are preserved across calls to `exec`. Note that once an alarm has been set, the process continues to execute (i.e., calling `alarm` does not suspend the calling process).

Only one of these alarm clocks is available to each process. Careless use of different functions that use the `SIGALRM` signal can cause problems.

Prior to Solaris 9, a multithreaded process calling `alarm` had two semantics:

1. The alarm in a process that uses Solaris threads but not POSIX threads (i.e., is linked with `-lthread` but not `-lpthread`) will be delivered to the LWP that called `alarm`.

2. If the multithreaded process is linked with `-lpthread`, the alarm signal will be sent to the process but not necessarily the calling thread.

From Solaris 9, only the per-process semantics specified by POSIX.1c are available.

Example: Implementing the `sleep` function

Program 17.5 shows our implementation of the `sleep` function, which we call `ssp_sleep`. Like `sleep`, our function suspends the calling process for a number of seconds. (We discussed the `sleep` function in Section 3.10.) As we shall see, there are a number of problems with our naïve implementation.

Let's take a look at some of the implementation details of Program 17.5.

Set up `SIGALRM` signal handler

6–7 Establish the signal handler for `SIGALRM`, returning the number of seconds we were supposed to sleep for if there's an error.

Set the alarm

8 Arrange for an alarm signal to be sent to the calling process in the specified number of seconds.

9 Suspend the process until a signal arrives. Normally, the first signal to be sent to the process will be `SIGALRM`, but the process will wake up when any signal is delivered to it.

10 Turn off the timer and return the number of seconds we didn't sleep for.

Signal handler

13–15 Do nothing. This signal handler doesn't need to do anything. We supply one only so that we can safely return from `pause`.

As we stated previously, there are a number of problems with our implementation of `sleep`. These are:

signals/ssp_sleep1.c

```
 1 #include <unistd.h>
 2 #include <signal.h>

 3 static void sigalrm (int sig);

 4 unsigned int ssp_sleep (unsigned int sec)
 5 {
 6     if (sigset (SIGALRM, sigalrm) == SIG_ERR)
 7         return (sec);

 8     alarm (sec);
 9     pause ();
10     return (alarm (0));
11 }

12 static void sigalrm (int sig)
13 {
14     /* Do nothing */
15 }
```

signals/ssp_sleep1.c

Program 17.5 Our first attempt at implementing `sleep`.

- We change the disposition of the SIGALRM signal. If we had previously set up our own signal handler for this signal, it would be lost once we called `ssp_sleep`. What we should do, especially if we are expecting others to use our function as part of a library, is save SIGALRM's disposition and restore it when our function returns.

- If the caller has already scheduled an alarm using the `alarm` function, that alarm is erased by the call to `alarm` in our function. We can address this shortcoming by saving the return value from `alarm`. If the return value indicates that the original alarm would have gone off before ours, then we should only wait for that amount of time. If the original alarm was set to go off after ours, then we should arrange for this alarm to happen at its designated time.

- There is a race condition between the call to `alarm` and the call to `pause`. Given a short enough sleep time and a sufficiently busy system, it is conceivable that the alarm could go off after the call to `alarm`, but before the call to `pause`. If this happens, the caller will be suspended until the next signal arrives—which could be never.

There are two ways we can fix the third problem:

1. Use `setjmp` and `longjmp`, as we show in Program 17.6.
2. Use the `sigprocmask` and `sigsuspend` functions, which we describe in Sections 17.17 and 17.22.

Example: Avoiding the `sleep` race condition by using `setjmp` and `longjmp`

Program 17.6 shows our reimplementation of the `sleep` function, using `setjmp` and `longjmp` to avoid the race condition we described earlier. We've highlighted the lines that have changed. Also, to save space, we don't solve the first two problems we identified earlier.

————————————————— signals/ssp_sleep2.c

```
 1 #include <unistd.h>
 2 #include <signal.h>
 3 #include <setjmp.h>

 4 static jmp_buf alrm_env;

 5 static void sigalrm (int sig);

 6 unsigned int ssp_sleep (unsigned int sec)
 7 {
 8     if (sigset (SIGALRM, sigalrm) == SIG_ERR)
 9         return (sec);

10     if (setjmp (alrm_env) == 0) {
11         alarm (sec);
12         pause ();
13     }

14     return (alarm (0));
15 }

16 static void sigalrm (int sig)
17 {
18     longjmp (alrm_env, 1);
19 }
```

————————————————— signals/ssp_sleep2.c

Program 17.6 Avoiding the race condition in our first version of `sleep`.

The race condition is avoided in Program 17.6 because even if `pause` is never called, the `longjmp` from the signal handler ensures that `ssp_sleep` returns.

There is, however, another problem with our function. If our process receives a `SIGALRM` signal while it is executing the signal handler for another signal, the `longjmp` we use to return from the `SIGALRM` signal handler will abort the other signal handler; Program 17.7 shows an example of this.

The loop in the `SIGINT` signal handler was designed to run for longer than two seconds on the system used by the author. It doesn't matter exactly how long the loop runs for, as long as it takes longer to execute than the amount of time we sleep for. We declare the variable `j` as being `volatile` to prevent the compiler's optimizer from discarding the loop. Running Program 17.7 gives us the following results:

```
$ ./sleep_test
^C                                        Type our interrupt character
Starting SIGINT signal handler
ssp_sleep returned 0
```

We can see that although the `SIGINT` signal handler started executing, as a side effect of our using `longjmp` to return from the `SIGALRM` signal handler, it did not have a chance to finish.

————————————————————————— signals/sleep_test.c

```
 1 #include <stdio.h>
 2 #include <unistd.h>
 3 #include <signal.h>
 4 #include "ssp.h"

 5 extern unsigned int ssp_sleep (unsigned int sec);
 6 static void sigint (int sig);

 7 int main (void)
 8 {
 9     unsigned int unslept;

10     if (sigset (SIGINT, sigint) == SIG_ERR)
11         err_msg ("sigset failed");

12     unslept = ssp_sleep (2);
13     printf ("ssp_sleep returned %u\n", unslept);

14     return (0);
15 }

16 static void sigint (int sig)
17 {
18     int i;
19     volatile int j;

20     printf ("\nStarting SIGINT signal handler\n");
21     for (i = 0; i < 10000000; i++)
22         j += i * i;
23     printf ("Returning from SIGINT signal handler\n");
24 }
```

————————————————————————— signals/sleep_test.c

Program 17.7   Calling `ssp_sleep` from a program that catches other signals.

We should emphasize that the purpose of the last two examples is to illustrate the kind of problems naïvely written signal handlers can cause. In later sections we'll see how to avoid all these problems so that we can handle signals without interfering with other code.

Example: Timing out operations

We've seen how the `alarm` function can be used to implement a function to suspend a process for a certain period of time. But another common use for `alarm` is to implement timeouts on operations that can block (i.e., to put an upper time limit on how long those operations can take), for example, reading from a slow device (we use the term "slow" here as we described in Section 17.9). Program 17.8 shows how we might use such a timeout when collecting input from a user.

Let's look at some of the implementation details of Program 17.8.

Set up signal handler

12–13 We arrange to catch the SIGALRM signal using the `sigset` function.

―――――――――――――――――――――――――――――――― *signals/timeout1.c*

```
 1 #include <stdio.h>
 2 #include <unistd.h>
 3 #include <signal.h>
 4 #include <string.h>
 5 #include "ssp.h"

 6 static volatile sig_atomic_t flag = 0;

 7 static void sigalrm (int sig);

 8 int main (void)
 9 {
10     char buf [BUFSIZ];
11     char *def_string = "Hello, World!";

12     if (sigset (SIGALRM, sigalrm) == SIG_ERR)
13         err_msg ("sigset failed");

14     alarm (10);

15     printf ("Enter a greeting: ");
16     if (fgets (buf, sizeof (buf), stdin) != NULL)
17         buf [strlen (buf) - 1] = '\0';

18     alarm (0);

19     if (flag == 1) {
20         strcpy (buf, def_string);
21         printf ("\n");
22     }

23     printf ("Using greeting: \"%s\"\n", buf);

24     return (0);
25 }
26 static void sigalrm (int sig)
27 {
28     flag = 1;
29 }
```

―――――――――――――――――――――――――――――――― *signals/timeout1.c*

Program 17.8 Collecting user input with a timeout.

Start the timer

14 Call the alarm function with a parameter of 10 to start a 10-second timeout.

Read a line from the user

15 Print the prompt, asking for user input.

16–17 Read the line of input using fgets. If the timeout expires (i.e., fgets is interrupted), fgets returns a NULL pointer. In this event, we do not want to try to change the last character of buf to '\0'. Because it is an uninitialized variable on the stack, the contents of buf are indeterminate if fgets is interrupted, and hence the strlen operation for it is meaningless. On the other hand, if fgets does not return a NULL pointer, the user has input some data, so we overwrite the newline character at the end with a NUL character.

Disable the alarm

18 We reset the alarm clock. If the timeout expired, this call has no effect (as the alarm has already expired), but if it hasn't, this line disables it. If we get to this point without the timer expiring, the user has input something, so we don't want to use the default.

Copy default string if appropriate

19–22 If `flag` is equal to 1, the timeout expired, and we must copy the default string to the buffer we're about to use.

Signal handler

27–29 Our signal handler merely sets the global variable `flag` to 1, indicating that the timeout expired.

Running Program 17.8 gives the following results:

```
$ ./timeout1
Enter a greeting: Aloha!
Using greeting: "Aloha!"
$ ./timeout1
Enter a greeting:
Using greeting: "Hello, World!"
```

Unfortunately, there are two problems with Program 17.8:

1. A race condition similar to that in Program 17.5 exists in this program; if the kernel blocks between the first call to `alarm` and the call to `fgets` for longer than the period of the timeout, the `fgets` could potentially block for ever. That said, most operations of this type use a long timeout period (like a minute or two), so this event is unlikely. But the race condition still exists.

2. If system calls are automatically restarted, the `fgets` is not interrupted when the `SIGALRM` signal handler returns (although `fgets` is not itself a system call, internally it calls `read`, which is a system call). In this case, the timeout has no effect. The code we show works OK on Solaris, but may not work as expected on other versions of UNIX.

What we want here is some portable way to guarantee that slow system calls can be restarted. As we'll see in Section 17.19, the `sigaction` function gives us the means to do this. We show another solution to this problem in the next example.

Example: Timing out operations with aid of `setjmp` and `longjmp`

Program 17.9 shows another version of the previous example, which uses `setjmp` and `longjmp` to avoid problems if slow system calls are automatically restarted.

This version of our timeout program will work most of the time on any type of UNIX system, regardless of whether or not system calls are automatically restarted when they are interrupted. Unfortunately, as it stands, Program 17.9 has yet another subtle problem, because we are using the `sigset` function to establish the signal handler.

Recall from Section 17.6 that `sigset` is the reliable analogue of `signal`. When our signal handler is called, the kernel adds `SIGALRM` to the process' signal mask. Because

signals/timeout2.c

```c
 1 #include <stdio.h>
 2 #include <unistd.h>
 3 #include <signal.h>
 4 #include <string.h>
 5 #include <setjmp.h>
 6 #include "ssp.h"

 7 static jmp_buf alrm_env;

 8 static void sigalrm (int sig);

 9 int main (void)
10 {
11     char buf [BUFSIZ];
12     char *def_string = "Hello, World!";

13     if (sigset (SIGALRM, sigalrm) == SIG_ERR)
14         err_msg ("sigset failed");

15     if (setjmp (alrm_env) == 0) {
16         alarm (10);

17         printf ("Enter a greeting: ");
18         if (fgets (buf, sizeof (buf), stdin) != NULL)
19             buf [strlen (buf) - 1] = '\0';

20         alarm (0);
21     }
22     else {
23         strcpy (buf, def_string);
24         printf ("\n");
25     }

26     printf ("Using greeting: \"%s\"\n", buf);

27     return (0);
28 }

29 static void sigalrm (int sig)
30 {
31     longjmp (alrm_env, 1);
32 }
```

signals/timeout2.c

Program 17.9 Collecting user input with a timeout, helped by setjmp and longjmp.

our handler doesn't return in the conventional manner (it uses longjmp instead), SIGALRM continues to be blocked once we're finished with the signal handler. This means that the process will no longer be able to receive SIGALRM signals.

There are two ways we can deal with this problem:

1. Call sigrelse inside the signal handler before calling longjmp. This will remove SIGALRM from the process' signal mask, allowing subsequent SIGALRM signals to be delivered correctly.

2. Use the functions `sigsetjmp` and `siglongjmp` instead of `setjmp` and `longjmp`. We'll discuss these functions in Section 17.21.

Another problem with using `setjmp` and `longjmp` is the undesirable interaction with other signal handlers, like we discussed in one of our previous examples.

With the caveats we've mentioned, the timeout mechanism we describe is a viable alternative. However, the `select` and `poll` functions we described in Section 13.16 and Section 13.17 are probably better for this type of work.

17.14 Interval Timers

Although the alarm facility we've just described has its uses, it does have a couple of drawbacks. First, the `alarm` function only provides us with timers with a one-second granularity, and second, it only provides one type of timer: one that runs in real time. To overcome these limitations, BSD introduced a facility called *interval timers*, which have been carried forward into Solaris.

The interval timers provided by Solaris have a resolution of one microsecond (subject to the resolution of the system's on-board clock), and there are two functions for working with interval timers: `getitimer` and `setitimer`.

```
#include <sys/time.h>

int getitimer (int which, struct itimerval *value);

int setitimer (int which, const struct itimerval *value,
    struct itimerval *ovalue);
```
Both return: 0 if OK, −1 on error

The `getitimer` function stores the current value of the interval timer specified by *which* in the `itimerval` structure pointed to by *value*.

There are four interval timers per process. The *which* argument specifies which one we are interested in, and must be one of the following values:

ITIMER_REAL	This interval timer decrements in real time. When it expires, a `SIGALRM` signal is delivered to the process.
ITIMER_VIRTUAL	This interval timer decrements in process virtual time (i.e., it only runs while the process is executing). When it expires, a `SIGVTALRM` signal is delivered to the process.
ITIMER_PROF	This interval timer decrements in both process virtual time and when the system is running on behalf of the process. It is designed to be used by interpreters when statistically profiling the execution of interpreted programs. When the timer expires, a `SIGPROF` signal is delivered to the process.
ITIMER_REALPROF	This interval timer decrements in real time. It is designed to be used for real-time profiling of multithreaded programs.

When the timer expires, one counter in a set of counters maintained by the system for each LWP is incremented. Each of these counters corresponds to the state of the LWP at the time the timer expired. All LPWs executing in user mode when the timer expires are interrupted into system mode. When each LWP resumes execution in user mode, a `SIGPROF` signal is delivered to the process if any of the elements in its set of counters are not equal to zero.

If a `SIGPROF` signal is delivered to the process as a result of an `ITIMER_REALPROF` interval timer expiring, a `siginfo_t` structure (which is defined in `<sys/siginfo.h>`) is associated with the signal, which includes the following members:

```
typedef struct {
    int          si_signo;     /* Signal number */
    int          si_code;      /* Signal code */
    int          si_errno;     /* Error number */
    caddr_t      si_faddr;     /* Last fault address */
    timestruc_t  si_tstamp;    /* High resolution time stamp */
    short        si_syscall;   /* Current syscall */
    char         si_nsysarg;   /* Number of syscall arguments */
    char         si_fault;     /* Last fault type */
    long         si_sysarg []; /* Actual syscall arguments */
    int          si_mstate []; /* Ticks in each microstate */
} siginfo_t;
```

The `si_mstate` member keeps track of a number of LWP microstates, which can be enumerated thus:

`LMS_USER`	Running in user mode
`LMS_SYSTEM`	Running in a syscall or page fault
`LMS_TRAP`	Running in some other trap
`LMS_TFAULT`	Asleep in user text page fault
`LMS_DFAULT`	Asleep in user data page fault
`LMS_KFAULT`	Asleep in kernel page fault
`LMS_USER_LOCK`	Asleep waiting for user mode lock
`LMS_SLEEP`	Asleep for any other reason
`LMS_WAIT_CPU`	Waiting for CPU (latency)
`LMS_STOPPED`	Stopped (by /proc, job control, `lwp_stop`)

These manifest constants are defined in `<sys/msacct.h>`. We'll have more to say about the `siginfo_t` structure in Section 17.19.

The other argument to `getitimer`, *value*, is a pointer to an `itimerval` structure. This structure is used to define a timer value, and has the following members:

```
struct itimerval {
    struct timeval  it_interval;   /* Timer interval */
    struct timeval  it_value;      /* Current value */
};
```

The `it_value` member indicates, in seconds and microseconds, the amount of time remaining until the timer expires. The `it_interval` member specifies the value to be used when reloading `it_value` when the timer expires.

The `setitimer` function sets the value of the interval timer specified by *which* to the value specified by the `itimerval` structure pointed to by *value*. If *ovalue* is not NULL, then the previous value of the specified timer is stored in the `itimerval` structure pointed to by *ovalue*. Setting the `it_value` member of the structure pointed to by *value* to 0 disables the timer, regardless of the value of `it_interval`, and setting `it_interval` to 0 disables the timer after its next expiration.

Note that although `setitimer` is independent of the `alarm` function, we should not use interval timers of type `ITIMER_REAL` with the `sleep` function. This is because `sleep` wipes out knowledge of the user signal handler for `SIGALRM`.

Example: Using an interval timer to timeout user input

Program 17.10 shows another version of our program that reads a line from the user. However, this example use an interval timer to set the timeout to (about) π (pi) seconds.

Program 17.10 is the same as Program 17.9, except the calls to `alarm` have been replaced with the appropriate code to implement an interval timer.

Initialize the interval timer

18–21 We set the interval to 0 (meaning that we want the counter to expire only once), and the value to 3 seconds and 141593 microseconds (i.e., 3.141593 seconds).

22 We call the `setitimer` function to start the interval timer, which counts down in real time.

Disable the interval timer

26–27 Set the value of the interval timer to 0, ready to disable it.

28 Call the `setitimer` function with the new value, disabling it.

17.15 POSIX Signals

POSIX introduced a much more complicated mechanism for processing signals. The added complexity also comes with significant new functionality based on the 4.2BSD signal handling functions. Although the concepts and functionality are similar, the functions and their arguments are very different.

The functionality offered by the POSIX signal mechanism is a superset of that offered by the traditional (SVR4) UNIX mechanism (i.e., the signal handling functions we've discussed so far in this chapter), although there are some parallels we can draw between the two. Figure 17.4 compares them.

signals/timeout3.c

```
 1 #include <stdio.h>
 2 #include <unistd.h>
 3 #include <signal.h>
 4 #include <string.h>
 5 #include <setjmp.h>
 6 #include <sys/time.h>
 7 #include "ssp.h"

 8 static jmp_buf alrm_env;

 9 static void sigalrm (int sig);

10 int main (void)
11 {
12     char buf [BUFSIZ];
13     char *def_string = "Hello, World!";
14     struct itimerval itimer;

15     if (sigset (SIGALRM, sigalrm) == SIG_ERR)
16         err_msg ("sigset failed");

17     if (setjmp (alrm_env) == 0) {
18         itimer.it_interval.tv_sec = 0;
19         itimer.it_interval.tv_usec = 0;
20         itimer.it_value.tv_sec = 3;
21         itimer.it_value.tv_usec = 141593;
22         setitimer (ITIMER_REAL, &itimer, NULL);

23         printf ("Enter a greeting: ");
24         if (fgets (buf, sizeof (buf), stdin) != NULL)
25             buf [strlen (buf) - 1] = '\0';

26         itimer.it_value.tv_sec = 0;
27         itimer.it_value.tv_usec = 0;
28         setitimer (ITIMER_REAL, &itimer, NULL);
29     }
30     else {
31         strcpy (buf, def_string);
32         printf ("\n");
33     }

34     printf ("Using greeting: \"%s\"\n", buf);

35     return (0);
36 }

37 static void sigalrm (int sig)
38 {
39     longjmp (alrm_env, 1);
40 }
```

signals/timeout3.c

Program 17.10 Collecting user input with an interval timer timeout.

SVR4	POSIX	Description
`signal`	`sigaction`	Signal management
`sigset`	`sigaction`	Signal management
`sighold`	`sigprocmask`	Add a signal to the signal mask
`sigrelse`	`sigprocmask`	Remove a signal from the signal mask
`sigignore`	`sigaction`	Ignore a signal
`sigpause`	`sigsuspend`	Block until a signal arrives

Figure 17.4 Similarities between SVR4 and POSIX signal mechanisms.

Although the functionality offered by the POSIX functions is broadly similar to that offered by the SVR4 functions, many details differ. We should also add that the signal handling functions we've discussed so far are adequate for most needs (unless POSIX-compliance is a requirement), and that they are likely to be found on older systems. These days, however, most systems are POSIX-compliant, so the POSIX signal mechanism is worth being familiar with because of the additional functionality.

17.16 Signal Sets

Many of the functions that make up the POSIX signal handling interface use signal sets rather than individual signals. A *signal set* is a bit mask, with one bit for each signal. If a bit is 1, the corresponding signal is a member of the set; if a bit is 0, the corresponding signal is not a member of the set. The number of different signals might exceed the number of bits in an `int`, so signal sets are described by the `sigset_t` data type, which is defined in `<signal.h>`.

We can manipulate signal sets with five functions.

```
#include <signal.h>

int sigemptyset (sigset_t *set);

int sigfillset (sigset_t *set);

int sigaddset (sigset_t *set, int signo);

int sigdelset (sigset_t *set, int signo);
```

All four return: 0 if OK, −1 on error

```
int sigismember (sigset_t *set, int signo);
```

Returns: 1 if true, 0 if false

The `sigemptyset` function initializes the signal set pointed to by *set* so that all defined signals are excluded (i.e., it initializes the set to the empty set). The `sigfillset` function initializes the signal set pointed to by *set* so that all defined signals are included (i.e., it initializes the set to the value of "all signals"). All applications must first call one of these two functions for each signal set before otherwise using the set, even if they are global or static. This is because we can't assume that the initialization value of external and static variables in a C program (0) is meaningful in the context of a given system's implementation of signal sets.

Once we've initialized a signal set (using either sigemptyset or sigfillset), we can add or delete specific signals to or from the set. The sigaddset function adds the single signal specified by *signo* to the signal set pointed to by *set*. Conversely, the sigdelset function deletes the single signal specified by *signo* from the signal set pointed to by *set*.

The sigismember function returns an indication of whether the signal specified by *signo* is a member of the signal set pointed to by *set*. If *sig* is a member of *set*, then sigismember returns 1; otherwise, it returns 0.

17.17 The sigprocmask Function

We stated previously that a signal mask is the set of signals that are currently blocked from delivery to a process. A process can manipulate its signal mask by using the sigprocmask function.

```
#include <signal.h>

int sigprocmask (int how, const sigset_t *set, sigset_t *oset);
```
Returns: 0 if OK, −1 on error

The sigprocmask function enables us to examine or change (or both) our signal mask. If *oset* is not NULL, then a successful call to sigprocmask will result in the current signal mask being stored in the signal set it points to.

If *set* is not NULL, then the signal mask is modified. The nature of the modification is determined by the value of *how*:

SIG_BLOCK	The signal set pointed to by *set* is added to the current signal mask.
SIG_UNBLOCK	The signal set pointed to by *set* is removed from the current signal mask.
SIG_SETMASK	The signal set pointed to by *set* replaces the current signal mask.

If there are any pending unblocked signals after the call to sigprocmask, then at least one of those signals will be delivered before sigprocmask returns. Also, calling sigprocmask from a multithreaded program impacts only the calling thread's signal mask.

Synchronously generated signals should not be blocked. If such a signal is blocked and delivered, the receiving process will be killed.

Example: Display the current signal mask

Program 17.11 prints the name of signals currently blocked. Note that to save space, we check for only the first four signals from Figure 17.1.

Print current signal mask

9 Call our `print_proc_mask` function to print the current signal mask.

Block the signals SIGABRT and SIGALRM

10–12 Create an empty signal set, then add SIGABRT and SIGALRM to it.

13–14 Set the signal mask to the newly defined set. We use the SIG_SETMASK operation to overwrite the current signal mask with our new one. Note that rather than setting up a signal set and then calling sigprocmask to set the signal mask, we could have theoretically used two calls to sighold to block SIGABRT and SIGALRM instead. However, as we stated earlier, mixing two signal mechanisms is probably best avoided.

Print new signal mask

15 Call `print_proc_mask` to print the new signal mask.

The `print_proc_mask` function

22 Save the current value of errno. This is because this function might be called by a signal handler.

23–24 Retrieve the current signal mask.

25–26 If one is supplied, print the message that is to accompany the names of the blocked signals.

27–28 If SIGABRT is a member of the current signal mask, print its name.

29–35 Repeat for the other signals.

36 Restore the previous value of errno.

Running Program 17.11 gives us the following results:

```
$ ./procmask
Before:
After: SIGABRT SIGALRM
```

We'll revisit `print_proc_mask` in Exercise 17.6.

17.18 The `sigpending` Function

We stated previously that a signal generated but yet to be delivered (i.e., is blocked) is said to be pending. We can obtain the set of pending signals by using the sigpending function.

```
#include <signal.h>

int sigpending (sigset_t *set);
```
Returns: 0 if OK, −1 on error

signals/procmask.c

```
 1 #include <stdio.h>
 2 #include <signal.h>
 3 #include <errno.h>
 4 #include "ssp.h"

 5 int print_proc_mask (const char *msg);

 6 int main (void)
 7 {
 8     sigset_t set;

 9     print_proc_mask ("Before");

10     sigemptyset (&set);
11     sigaddset (&set, SIGABRT);
12     sigaddset (&set, SIGALRM);
13     if (sigprocmask (SIG_SETMASK, &set, NULL) == -1)
14         err_msg ("sigprocmask failed");

15     print_proc_mask ("After");

16     return (0);
17 }

18 int print_proc_mask (const char *msg)
19 {
20     sigset_t set;
21     int old_errno;

22     old_errno = errno;
23     if (sigprocmask (0, NULL, &set) == -1)
24         return (-1);

25     if (msg)
26         printf ("%s: ", msg);

27     if (sigismember (&set, SIGABRT))
28         printf ("SIGABRT ");
29     if (sigismember (&set, SIGALRM))
30         printf ("SIGALRM ");
31     if (sigismember (&set, SIGBUS))
32         printf ("SIGBUS ");
33     if (sigismember (&set, SIGCANCEL))
34         printf ("SIGCANCEL ");

35     printf ("\n");

36     errno = old_errno;

37     return (0);
38 }
```

signals/procmask.c

Program 17.11 Printing the current signal mask.

The sigpending function retrieves the set of signals that have been sent to the calling process, but are being blocked from delivery by the signal mask of the process. The resulting signal set is stored in the buffer pointed to by *set*.

Example: Demonstration of blocked and pending signals

Program 17.12 ties together some of the ideas we've discussed about blocked and
pending signals.

————————————————————————————————— signals/pending.c

```
 1 #include <stdio.h>
 2 #include <signal.h>
 3 #include <unistd.h>
 4 #include "ssp.h"

 5 static void sigint (int sig);

 6 int main (void)
 7 {
 8     sigset_t old_mask;
 9     sigset_t new_mask;
10     sigset_t pending_mask;

11     if (sigset (SIGINT, sigint) == SIG_ERR)
12         err_msg ("sigset failed");

13     sigemptyset (&new_mask);
14     sigaddset (&new_mask, SIGINT);
15     if (sigprocmask (SIG_BLOCK, &new_mask, &old_mask) == -1)
16         err_msg ("sigprocmask failed");
17     printf ("SIGINT blocked\n");

18     sleep (5);

19     if (sigpending (&pending_mask) == -1)
20         err_msg ("sigpending failed");
21     if (sigismember (&pending_mask, SIGINT))
22         printf ("\nSIGINT is pending\n");

23     if (sigprocmask (SIG_SETMASK, &old_mask, NULL) == -1)
24         err_msg ("sigpromask failed");
25     printf ("SIGINT unblocked\n");

26     sleep (5);

27     return (0);
28 }

29 static void sigint (int sig)
30 {
31     printf ("Caught SIGINT\n");
32 }
```

————————————————————————————————— signals/pending.c

Program 17.12 Example of signal sets, sigprocmask, and sigpending.

Change the disposition of SIGINT

11–12 Catch SIGINT so that our signal handler is called when the signal is received.

Block SIGINT

13–14 Create a new signal set that consists of just SIGINT.

15–17 Block SIGINT by adding it to the current signal mask. We keep a copy of the previous signal mask so that we can restore it later.

Sleep for five seconds

18 Suspend our process for five seconds. Any interrupt signals sent to our process while it is asleep will remain pending until we later unblock the signal.

Check if a SIGINT is pending

19–20 Get the set of currently pending signals.

21–22 If SIGINT is in the set of pending signals, print a message saying so.

Restore old signal mask

23–25 Set the signal mask to be the same as before we added SIGINT to it. We use SIG_SETMASK rather than SIG_UNBLOCK because although it isn't the case in our example, it's possible that the caller of our function had specifically blocked SIGINT before calling our function. Using SIG_UNBLOCK would unexpectedly (from the caller's perspective) unblock the signal. By using SIG_SETMASK, we ensure that when we exit the function, the signal mask is the same as when our function was entered.

Sleep for another five seconds

26 Suspend the process for another five seconds. This time, any interrupt signals sent to our process will be delivered.

Signal handler

31 Print a message stating that we've caught a SIGINT signal. As we said in Section 17.10, calling a function in the standard I/O library from a signal handler is not good practice; however, we can get away with it in our trivial example.

Let's run Program 17.12 a couple of times:

```
$ ./pending
SIGINT blocked
^C                              Generate signal once (before 5 seconds are up)
SIGINT is pending               After the first sleep returns
Caught SIGINT
SIGINT unblocked
^CCaught SIGINT                 Generate signal again
$ ./pending
SIGINT blocked
^C^C^C^C^C^C^C^C                Generate signal several times
SIGINT is pending
Caught SIGINT                   Signal is only delivered once
SIGINT unblocked
^CCaught SIGINT                 Generate signal again
```

The first time we run Program 17.12, we type the interrupt character (Control-C) once before the first sleep returns. Because SIGINT is currently blocked, the signal is added to the set of pending signals. We then unblock SIGINT, which immediately results in the pending signal being delivered to our process, and the signal handler is called. When the signal handler returns, the message stating that we've unblocked SIGINT is printed (recall from our discussion of sigprocmask, where we said that if a pending signal is unblocked, it would be delivered to the process before sigprocmask returns). Typing

Control-C during the second `sleep` causes the signal handler to be called immediately and the process to be terminated. The remaining sleep time is lost, because `sleep` is not one of the system calls that is automatically restarted.

The second time we run Program 17.12, we type Control-C several times. However, only one `SIGINT` signal is delivered to the process, demonstrating that Solaris does not queue signals.

17.19 The `sigaction` Function

The `sigaction` function is the main workhorse of the POSIX signal mechanism. It enables us to examine, modify, or examine and modify the action associated with a given signal.

```
#include <signal.h>

int sigaction (int sig, const struct sigaction *act, struct sigaction *oact);
```

Returns: 0 if OK, -1 on error

The signal we want to examine or modify is specified by *sig*, and can be any signal shown in Figure 17.1, with the exception of `SIGKILL` and `SIGSTOP`. In a multithreaded process, `SIGCANCEL`, `SIGLWP`, and `SIGWAITING` are also disallowed.

If *act* is not NULL, it points to a `sigaction` structure, which specifies the new action to be taken when *sig* is delivered to process. Similarly, if *oact* is not NULL, it points to a `sigaction` structure in which the action previously associated with *sig* will be stored when the `sigaction` function returns. The `sigaction` structure consists of the following members:

```
struct sigaction {
    int         sa_flags;
    void        (*sa_handler) ();
    void        (*sa_sigaction) (int, siginfo_t *, void *);
    sigset_t    sa_mask;
}
```

Each structure member has the following definition:

`sa_flags`	This member specifies a set of flags used to modify the delivery of the signal. We describe these flags further on.
`sa_handler`	This member specifies the action associated with *sig* if the SA_SIGINFO flag in `sa_flags` is clear. It may be one of the values `SIG_DFL`, `SIG_IGN`, or `SIG_HOLD`, or it may be the address of the user-specified signal handler.
	This member must not be used with sa_sigaction simultaneously.
`sa_sigaction`	This member specifies the action associated with *sig* if the SA_SIGINFO flag in `sa_flags` is set. Its value is the address of the user-specified signal handler.

This member must not be used with `sa_handler` simultaneously.

`sa_mask` This member specifies the set of signals to be blocked while the signal handler is executing. Upon entry to the signal handler, this set of signals is added to the set of signals already being blocked when the signal was delivered. The signal that caused the handler to be executed will also be blocked, unless the `SA_NODEFER` flag is set in `sa_flags`.

The `sa_flags` member is formed by a bitwise-OR of zero or more of the following values:

`SA_ONSTACK` If this flag is set and the signal is caught, and if the thread that is chosen to process the delivered signal has declared an alternate stack using the `sigaltstack` function, then the signal will be processed on the alternate stack.

If this flag is not set, then the signal will be processed using the thread's normal stack.

`SA_RESETHAND` If this flag is set and the signal is caught, then the disposition of the signal is reset to `SIG_DFL` and the signal will not be blocked upon entry to the signal handler. Using this flag allows the old, unreliable signal semantics to be obtained.

`SA_NODEFER` If this flag is set and the signal is caught, the signal will not be automatically blocked by the kernel while the signal handler is executing. Using this flag allows the old, unreliable signal semantics to be obtained.

`SA_RESTART` If this flag is set and the signal is caught, then certain system calls interrupted by the execution of the signal handler are transparently restarted by the system when the signal handler returns. The following functions are restarted automatically: `fcntl`, `ioctl`, `wait`, and `waitpid`. The following functions are also restarted automatically when they are operating on "slow" devices: `getmsg`, `getpmsg`, `putmsg`, `putpmsg`, `pread`, `read`, `readv`, `pwrite`, `write`, `writev`, `recv`, `recvfrom`, `recvmsg`, `send`, `sendto`, and `sendmsg`.

If this flag is not set, interrupted system calls will fail, setting `errno` to `EINTR`.

`SA_SIGINFO` If this flag is clear and the signal is caught, then *sig* is the only argument passed to the signal handler specified by `sa_handler`; this is the same as signal handlers that are established by `signal` and `sigset`.

If this flag is set and the signal is caught, then the signal handler specified by `sa_sigaction` will be called with three arguments. The first argument is *sig*. The second argument, if it is not NULL, points to a `siginfo_t` structure, which contains the reason why the signal was generated (see further on). The third argument points to a `ucontext_t` structure (which is defined in `<sys/ucontext.h>`), which contains the context of the receiving process when the signal was delivered (see the code following this list).

`SA_NOCLDWAIT`   If this flag is set and *sig* is equal to `SIGCHLD`, then zombie processes will not be created when children of the calling process terminate. If the calling process subsequently calls `wait`, it blocks until all of the calling process' children terminate, and then returns –1 with `errno` set to `ECHILD`. This flag, in conjunction with `SA_NOCLDSTOP`, allows the older System V `SIGCLD` semantics to be obtained.

`SA_NOCLDSTOP`   If this flag is set and *sig* is equal to `SIGCHLD`, then `SIGCHLD` signals will not be sent to the calling process when its children stop or continue.

`SA_WAITSIG`   If this flag is set and *sig* is equal to `SIGWAITING`, then the generation of `SIGWAITING` signals (when all the process' LWPs are blocked) is enabled. This flag is reserved for use by the threads library.

If we set the `SA_SIGINFO` flag, we can use a function prototype like the following to declare the signal handler:

```
void handler (int sig, siginfo_t *sip, ucontext_t *uap);
```

The context of the receiving process is defined by the `ucontext_t` structure pointed to by *uap*.

The `siginfo_t` Structure

The `siginfo_t` structure provides information about why a given signal was generated. If a process is monitoring its children, it can ask the kernel to tell it why a child changed state. In either case, this information is stored in a `siginfo_t` structure, which includes the following members:

```
typedef struct {
    int             si_signo;
    int             si_errno;
    int             si_code;
    pid_t           si_pid;
    uid_t           si_uid;
    union sigval    si_value;
    clock_t         si_utime;
    int             si_status;
    clock_t         si_stime;
    void            *si_addr;
    int             si_trapno;
    caddr_t         si_pc;
```

```
    int             si_fd;
    long            si_band;
    caddr_t         si_faddr;
    timestruc_t     si_tstamp;
    short           si_syscall;
    char            si_nsysarg;
    char            si_fault;
    long            si_sysarg [8];
    int             si_mstate [10];
    int32_t         si_entity;
} siginfo_t;
```

Only the first three members of this structure are always present. The others are stored in a union, and their availability is signal-specific (we showed an example of this when we discussed interval timers in Section 17.14).

Each structure member has the following definition:

si_signo	This member contains the system-generated signal number; when used with the waitid function, si_signo is always SIGCHLD.
si_code	This member contains a code that identifies the cause of the signal. If the value of si_code is SI_NOINFO, then only the si_signo member of this structure is meaningful. We describe the other values of si_code following this list.
si_errno	If this member is not zero, it contains the error number associated with this signal.
si_pid	This member is the process ID of the process that sent the signal. It is valid only if si_signo is equal to SIGCHLD, or if the signal was generated by a user process (using either kill, _lwp_kill, sigqueue, abort, or raise).
si_uid	This member is the real user ID of the process that sent the signal. It is valid only if the signal was generated by a user process.
si_value	This member is the signal value. It is valid only if the signal was generated by a user process.
si_utime	This member is the amount of CPU time the child spent executing instructions in user space. It is valid only if si_signo is equal to SIGCHLD.
si_status	If si_code is equal to CLD_EXITED, then this member is the termination status of the child process. Otherwise, it is equal to the number of the signal that caused the process to change state. This member is valid only if si_signo is equal to SIGCHLD.
si_stime	This member is the amount of CPU time the child spent executing kernel code. It is valid only if si_signo is equal to SIGCHLD.

`si_addr`	This member is the address of the faulting instruction or memory reference. It is valid only if `si_signo` is equal to `SIGBUS`, `SIGFPE`, `SIGILL`, `SIGSEGV`, or `SIGTRAP`.
`si_trapno`	This member is the illegal trap number. It is valid only if `si_signo` is equal to `SIGBUS`, `SIGFPE`, `SIGILL`, `SIGSEGV`, or `SIGTRAP`.
`si_pc`	This member is the address of the illegal instruction. It is valid only if `si_signo` is equal to `SIGBUS`, `SIGFPE`, `SIGILL`, `SIGSEGV`, or `SIGTRAP`.
`si_fd`	This member is the file descriptor associated with the signal. It is valid only if `si_signo` is equal to `SIGXFSZ`.
`si_band`	This member is the band event associated with the signal. It is valid only if `si_signo` is equal to `SIGXFSZ`, and `si_code` is equal to `POLL_IN`, `POLL_OUT`, or `POLL_MSG`.
`si_faddr`	This member is the last fault address. It is valid only if `si_signo` is equal to `SIGPROF`.
`si_tstamp`	This member is a high resolution time stamp. It is valid only if `si_signo` is equal to `SIGPROF`.
`si_syscall`	This member is the number of the current system call. It is valid only if `si_signo` is equal to `SIGPROF`.
`si_nsysarg`	This member is the number of arguments to the current system call. It is valid only if `si_signo` is equal to `SIGPROF`.
`si_fault`	This member is the last fault type. It is valid only if `si_signo` is equal to `SIGPROF`.
`si_sysarg`	This member is an array of the actual system call arguments. It is valid only if `si_signo` is equal to `SIGPROF`.
`si_mstate`	This member is an array that keep track of the number of ticks spent in each microstate. It is valid only if `si_signo` is equal to `SIGPROF`.
`si_entity`	This member is the type of entity exceeding a resource limit. It is valid only if `si_signo` is equal to `SIGXRES`, and hence, is not available prior to Solaris 9.

If the value of `si_code` is less than or equal to zero, then the signal was generated by a user process (using `kill`, `_lwp_kill`, `sigqueue`, `sigsend`, `abort`, or `raise`). If this is the case, then `si_uid` will contain the user ID of the process that sent the signal, and `si_pid` will contain the process ID of the process that sent the signal.

If the value of `si_code` is less than or equal to zero, it will be one of the following values:

`SI_ASYNCIO`	The signal was generated by the completion of an asynchronous I/O request.

SI_LWP   The signal was sent by the `_lwp_kill` function.

SI_MESGQ   The signal was generated by the arrival of a message on an empty message queue. This is used in realtime programming.

SI_QUEUE   The signal was sent by the `sigqueue` function, which is used in realtime programming.

SI_TIMER   The signal was generated by the expiration of a realtime timer created by the `timer_settime` function.

SI_USER   The signal was generated by one of the following functions: `abort`, `kill`, `raise`, or `sigsend`.

If `si_code` is `SI_ASYNCIO`, `SI_MESGQ`, `SI_TIMER`, or `SI_QUEUE`, then `si_value` will contain the application specified value which is passed to the application's signal handler.

Positive values of `si_code` indicate that the signal was generated by the system (as opposed to being user-generated). The meaning of `si_code` is signal-specific, as shown in Figure 17.5.

Resource controls were a new feature with Solaris 9, so `SIGXRES` is not available in earlier releases.

Example: Implementing `signal` by using `sigaction`

Program 17.13 shows our implementation of the `signal` function, including its unreliable semantics.

Initialize signal action

7 Set the signal's action to that specified by the `func` argument.

8 Set the signal's flags so that when the signal handler is called, the signal's disposition reverts to `SIG_DFL`, and the signal that caused the handler to be called is not blocked while the handler is executing.

We could implement BSD's more reliable `signal` semantics by setting `sa_flags` to 0 on this line.

9 Specify that no signals are to be blocked while the signal handler is executing.

Implement `SIGCLD` semantics

10–14 If the signal we are changing the disposition of is `SIGCHLD`, then we implement the System V `SIGCLD` semantics (recall that `SIGCLD` is an alias for `SIGCHLD`).

Arrange for system calls to be restarted

15–16 If the signal we are manipulating is `SIGTSTP`, `SIGTTIN`, or `SIGTTOU`, then set the `SA_RESTART` flag so that "slow" system calls that were interrupted are automatically restarted.

Set the new signal action

17–21 Call `sigaction` to set the new action associated with the signal. If all goes well, return the old signal handler. Otherwise, return `SIG_ERR`.

Signal	si_code	Reason
SIGILL	ILL_ILLOPC	Illegal opcode
	ILL_ILLOPN	Illegal operand
	ILL_ILLADR	Illegal addressing mode
	ILL_ILLTRP	Illegal trap
	ILL_PRVOPC	Privileged opcode
	ILL_PRVREG	Privileged register
	ILL_COPROC	Co-processor error
	ILL_BADSTK	Internal stack error
SIGFPE	FPE_INTDIV	Integer divide by zero
	FPE_INTOVF	Integer overflow
	FPE_FLTDIV	Floating-point divide by zero
	FPE_FLTOVF	Floating-point overflow
	FPE_FLTUND	Floating-point underflow
	FPE_FLTRES	Floating-point inexact result
	FPE_FLTINV	Invalid floating-point operation
	FPE_FLTSUB	Subscript out of range
SIGSEGV	SEGV_MAPERR	Address not mapped to object
	SEGV_ACCERR	Invalid permissions for mapped object
SIGBUS	BUS_ADRALN	Invalid address alignment
	BUS_ADRERR	Non-existent physical address
SIGTRAP	TRAP_BRKPT	Process breakpoint
	TRAP_TRACE	Process trace trap
SIGCHLD	CLD_EXITED	Child has terminated normally
	CLD_KILLED	Child was killed
	CLD_DUMPED	Child has terminated abnormally
	CLD_TRAPPED	Traced child has trapped
	CLD_STOPPED	Child has stopped
	CLD_CONTINUED	Child has continued
SIGPOLL	POLL_IN	Data input available
	POLL_OUT	Output buffers are available
	POLL_MSG	Input messages are available
	POLL_ERR	I/O error
	POLL_PRI	High priority input is available
	POLL_HUP	Device has disconnected
SIGXRES	SI_RCTL	Resource control generated signal

Figure 17.5   Values of si_code for system-generated signals.

Example: Signal information

Program 17.14 shows a signal handler that prints out some of the signal information it is passed when the SA_SIGINFO flag is set.

Initialize signal action

11 Set the signal handler to be our function, sigterm.

12 Set the SA_SIGINFO flag so that our signal handler is called with the additional arguments we need.

signals/ssp_signal.c

```
 1 #include <signal.h>
 2 #include <errno.h>

 3 void (*ssp_signal (int sig, void (*func) (int))) (int)
 4 {
 5     struct sigaction new_action;
 6     struct sigaction old_action;

 7     new_action.sa_handler = func;
 8     new_action.sa_flags = SA_RESETHAND | SA_NODEFER;
 9     sigemptyset (&new_action.sa_mask);

10     if (sig == SIGCHLD) {
11         new_action.sa_flags |= SA_NOCLDSTOP;
12         if (func == SIG_IGN)
13             new_action.sa_flags |= SA_NOCLDWAIT;
14     }

15     if ((sig == SIGTSTP) || (sig == SIGTTIN) || (sig == SIGTTOU))
16         new_action.sa_flags |= SA_RESTART;

17     if (sigaction (sig, &new_action, &old_action) == -1)
18         return (SIG_ERR);
19     else
20         return (old_action.sa_handler);
21 }
```

signals/ssp_signal.c

Program 17.13   Our implementation of signal using sigaction.

13 Specify that no signals are to be blocked while the signal handler is executing.

Set the new signal action

14–15 Call sigaction to set the new action associated with SIGTERM.

Wait for a signal

16–17 Print a message stating that we're waiting, then call pause. This puts our process to sleep until it receives a signal.

Signal handler

20–33 If there is no signal information, we return. If there is, then if we can find an entry for the user ID that sent us the signal in the password file, we print out a message using the user name associated with the user ID. Otherwise, we print a message using the user ID.

Note that we shouldn't be calling functions in the standard I/O library from a signal handler. However, in this simple example, there's no danger in doing so.

Running Program 17.14 gives us the following results:

```
$ ./siginfo &                          Run in background so we can type other commands
[1]     2883
$ Waiting...
                                        Type Return
$ kill %1
Ack!  Killed by user rich, from process 29966
[1] + Done                     ./siginfo &
```

signals/siginfo.c

```
 1 #include <stdio.h>
 2 #include <signal.h>
 3 #include <unistd.h>
 4 #include <ucontext.h>
 5 #include <pwd.h>
 6 #include "ssp.h"

 7 static void sigterm (int sig, siginfo_t *info, void *uap);

 8 int main (void)
 9 {
10     struct sigaction action;

11     action.sa_sigaction = sigterm;
12     action.sa_flags = SA_SIGINFO;
13     sigemptyset (&action.sa_mask);

14     if (sigaction (SIGTERM, &action, NULL) == -1)
15         err_msg ("sigaction failed");

16     printf ("Waiting...\n");
17     pause ();

18     return (0);
19 }

20 static void sigterm (int sig, siginfo_t *info, void *uap)
21 {
22     struct passwd *pwent;

23     if (info -> si_code != SI_NOINFO) {
24         if ((pwent = getpwuid (info -> si_uid)) == NULL) {
25             printf ("Ack!  Killed by user %ld, from process %ld\n",
26                 (long) info -> si_uid, (long) info -> si_pid);
27         }
28         else {
29             printf ("Ack!  Killed by user %s, from process %ld\n",
30                 pwent -> pw_name, (long) info -> si_pid);
31         }
32     }
33 }
```

signals/siginfo.c

Program 17.14 Printing signal information in a signal handler.

```
$ ps
   PID TTY        TIME CMD
  2994 pts/8     0:00 ps
 29966 pts/8     0:00 ksh
```

The output of the ps command shows that the process ID of our shell is 29966, which is
the same as the process ID of the process that killed our program (kill is a built in
command in ksh).

17.20 The `sigfpe` Function

If our application is floating-point intensive, it might be desirable to establish a separate signal handler for each possible floating-point exception. Using the functions we've described so far, we can't do this; we would have to have a single signal handler common to all the floating-point exceptions we want to trap, and handle each exception appropriately within it. The `sigfpe` function enables us to work around this shortcoming by allowing us to establish a signal handler for each of the different floating-point exceptions.

```
#include <floatingpoint.h>
#include <siginfo.h>

sigfpe_handler_type sigfpe (sigfpe_code_type code, sigfpe_handler_type hdl);
                                    Returns: the previous handler of code if OK, BADSIG on error
```

The `sigfpe` function associates the handler specified by *hdl* with the floating point exception specified by *code*. There are five IEEE 754-related floating-point exceptions:

FPE_FLTRES	Inexact floating-point result
FPE_FLTDIV	Floating-point division by zero
FPE_FLTUND	Floating-point underflow
FPE_FLTOVF	Floating-point overflow
FPE_FLTINV	Invalid floating-point operations

Readers interested in the details of IEEE 754 floating-point arithmetic are referred to [IEEE 1985].

> Although the Solaris man page for `sigfpe` says that BADSIG is returned on error, at the time of this book's writing there was no such constant on any of the systems used by the author.

The *hdl* argument can be either the address of the function which is to handle the exception, or one of the following three constants:

SIGFPE_ABORT	Dump core.
SIGFPE_DEFAULT	Use the default handling (which is to dump core using abort).
SIGFPE_IGNORE	Ignore the exception.

Once we have established our signal handlers using `sigfpe`, we must enable the relevant IEEE 754 traps in the hardware. We can do this by either writing our own functions in assembler, or by using the two functions `fpgetmask` and `fpsetmask`. The `sigfpe` function itself does not alter floating-point hardware to enable these traps.

Once we have established our signal handlers and enabled the relevant floating-point traps in hardware, performing a floating-point operation that generates one of the intended exceptions will result in our exception handler being called.

Example: Setting up a floating-point exception handler

Program 17.15 demonstrates how we could trap an invalid operation floating-point exception.

Establish our handler

20–21 Set the address of the invalid floating point operation handler to be that of our function.

Modify the FSR

22–23 Get the current set of traps that are enabled in the FSR, and enable the bit we are interested in (i.e., the invalid operand exception).

> Depending on which document we refer to, the acronym FSR expands to either floating-point status register, or floating-point state register. The former is used in Sun's UltraSPARC User Manuals (for example, [Sun Microsystems 1996]), whereas the latter is used in the SPARC Architecture Manuals (e.g., [Weaver and Germond 1994]), which are published by Prentice Hall.

Generate a floating-point exception

24–25 Generate a value of infinity and assign it to another floating-point variable. If we don't perform this assignment, no trap will be generated.

Restore floating-point environment

26–27 We restore the saved FSR exception mask and the previous handler for the invalid operand exception. In our example program this step is unnecessary, because we never return from our exception handler. However, for the sake of illustration, we show the code here.

Exception handler

30–52 Set up a message string appropriate for the exception. We do this because we have chosen to have one handler for all the exceptions. In a real application, we would likely have a different function for each exception we are interested in.

53–54 Print the name of the exception and call the `abort` function.

Running Program 17.15 gives us results very much how we would expect:

```
$ ./sigfpe
FP exception caught: Invalid operand
Abort(coredump)
```

17.21 The `sigsetjmp` and `siglongjmp` Functions

Recall our discussion of `setjmp` and `longjmp` in Section 14.9, where we said that these functions are used to perform nonlocal branches. We said that `longjmp` is often used to return to the main loop of a program from a signal handler, instead of returning from the

—————————————————————————— signals/sigfpe.c

```
 1 #include <stdio.h>
 2 #include <unistd.h>
 3 #include <stdlib.h>
 4 #include <math.h>
 5 #include <floatingpoint.h>
 6 #include <siginfo.h>
 7 #include <ucontext.h>
 8 #include <ieeefp.h>
 9 #include "ssp.h"

10 #ifndef BADSIG
11 #define BADSIG ((void (*)(void)) -1)
12 #endif

13 static void handler (int sig, siginfo_t *sip, ucontext_t *uap);

14 int main (void)
15 {
16     float infinity;
17     float num;
18     fp_except saved_fsr;
19     sigfpe_handler_type saved_handler;

20     if ((saved_handler = sigfpe (FPE_FLTINV, handler)) == BADSIG)
21         err_msg ("sigfpe failed");

22     saved_fsr = fpgetmask ();
23     fpsetmask (saved_fsr | FP_X_INV);

24     infinity = 1.0 / (float) (getpid () - getpid ());
25     num = infinity / infinity;

26     fpsetmask (saved_fsr);
27     sigfpe (FPE_FLTINV, saved_handler);

28     return (0);
29 }

30 static void handler (int sig, siginfo_t *sip, ucontext_t *uap)
31 {
32     char *exception;

33     switch (sip -> si_code) {
34         case FPE_FLTINV:
35             exception = "Invalid operand";
36             break;

37         case FPE_FLTRES:
38             exception = "Inexact";
39             break;

40         case FPE_FLTDIV:
41             exception = "Division by 0";
42             break;

43         case FPE_FLTUND:
44             exception = "Underflow";
45             break;
```

```
46          case FPE_FLTOVF:
47              exception = "Overflow";
48              break;

49          default:
50              exception = "Unknown";
51              break;
52      }

53      printf ("FP exception caught: %s\n", exception);
54      abort ();
55  }
```

signals/sigfpe.c

Program 17.15 Trapping invalid operation floating-point exceptions.

handler. We also said that using `longjmp` in this way can be problematic. This is because when a signal is caught, it is automatically added to the signal mask of the process when the signal handler is called (assuming we are using reliable signals). If we use `longjmp` to return from the signal handler, the signal will remain blocked. To solve this problem, we should always use `sigsetjmp` and `siglongjmp` when branching from a signal handler.

```
#include <setjmp.h>

int sigsetjmp (sigjmp_buf env, int savemask);
```
                    Returns: 0 if called directly, non-zero if returning from a call to `siglongjmp`
```
void siglongjmp (sigjmp_buf env, int val);
```

The only difference between these two functions and `setjmp` and `longjmp` is that `sigsetjmp` has an additional argument, *savemask*. If *savemask* is not zero when `sigsetjmp` is called, then the signal mask and scheduling parameters of the calling process are stored in *env*, in addition to the data that is saved by `setjmp`.

The `siglongjmp` function is similar to `longjmp`, except that if the environment pointed to by *env* was initialized by a call to `sigsetjmp` with a non-zero *savemask* argument, then the saved signal mask and scheduling parameters are also restored.

Because of their increased functionality, we recommend that new applications use these functions rather than the ones we describe in Section 14.9.

Example: The interaction of `sigsetjmp` and `siglongjmp` with signal masks

Program 17.16 shows how the signal that causes a signal handler to be called is automatically added to the signal mask of a process. It also shows how the `sigsetjmp` and `siglongjmp` functions interact with the signal mask.

Set up signal handlers

16–17 Catch SIGUSR1.

signals/siglongjmp.c

```
 1 #include <stdio.h>
 2 #include <unistd.h>
 3 #include <stdlib.h>
 4 #include <setjmp.h>
 5 #include <signal.h>
 6 #include <sys/types.h>
 7 #include <time.h>
 8 #include "ssp.h"

 9 static sigjmp_buf buf;
10 static volatile sig_atomic_t can_jump;

11 static void sigusr1 (int sig);
12 static void sigalrm (int sig);
13 extern int print_proc_mask (const char *msg);

14 int main (void)
15 {
16     if (sigset (SIGUSR1, sigusr1) == SIG_ERR)
17         err_msg ("sigset (SIGUSR1) failed");
18     if (sigset (SIGALRM, sigalrm) == SIG_ERR)
19         err_msg ("sigset (SIGALRM) failed");

20     print_proc_mask ("Starting main");

21     if (sigsetjmp (buf, 1) != 0) {
22         print_proc_mask ("Exiting main");
23         exit (0);
24     }

25     can_jump = 1;

26     for (;;)
27         pause ();
28 }

29 static void sigusr1 (int sig)
30 {
31     time_t now;

32     if (!can_jump)
33         return;

34     print_proc_mask ("Starting sigusr1");

35     alarm (2);

36     now = time (NULL);
37     for (;;)
38         if (time (NULL) > now + 5)
39             break;

40     print_proc_mask ("Exiting sigusr1");

41     can_jump = 0;
42     siglongjmp (buf, 1);
43 }
```

```
44 static void sigalrm (int sig)
45 {
46     print_proc_mask ("In sigalrm");
47 }
```
—————————————————————————————— signals/siglongjmp.c

Program 17.16 How `sigsetjmp` and `siglongjmp` interact with signal masks.

18–19 Catch `SIGALRM`.

Print initial signal mask

20 Call `print_proc_mask`, which prints the process' initial signal mask.

Initialize the buffer for use with `siglongjmp`

21–24 Call `sigsetjmp` to initialize the buffer we'll use later to return from the `SIGUSR1` signal handler using `siglongjmp`. When `sigsetjmp` returns as a result of a call to `siglongjmp`, a non-zero value is returned. In this event, we print the process' signal mask one last time and exit.

Set the `siglongjmp` flag

25 We set the global variable, `can_jump`, to a non-zero value. We check the value of this flag in the `SIGUSR1` signal handler, returning immediately if the flag is zero. This technique provides protection from the signal handler inadvertently being called at some earlier or later time, when the jump buffer isn't properly initialized. We should use this idiom whenever `siglongjmp` is used to return from a signal handler.

In our trivial program this is of little consequence, because we terminate soon after the `siglongjmp`. However, in a non-trivial program it is likely that the signal handler will remain installed long after `siglongjmp` has been called. We don't usually need this type of protection in normal code (i.e., code that is not a signal handler), but we need it here because a signal can occur at any time.

Wait for signals

26–27 We call `pause` in an infinite loop, waiting for the user to send us a signal.

`SIGUSR1` signal handler

32–33 If the flag we discussed above is not set, return immediately.

Print the signal mask on entry to the handler

34 Print the signal mask members when the handler starts executing.

Set an alarm

35 Arrange for a `SIGALRM` to be sent to our process in two seconds.

Wait for the alarm signal

36–39 Use a busy wait loop to delay our process for five seconds. We can't use `sleep` or an interval timer, because they both interfere with `SIGALRM`.

Print the signal mask on exit from the handler

40 Print the process' signal mask again prior to returning.

Return using the jump buffer

41 Reset the `can_jump` flag so that this handler isn't called again until we're ready for it.

42 Use `siglongjmp` to return from the signal handler. Execution resumes after the `sigsetjmp` associated with `buf`, as though `sigsetjmp` had returned 1.

Let's take a look at the results of running Program 17.16:

```
$ ./siglongjmp &
[1]     16417
$ Starting main:
                                           Type Return
$ kill -USR1 %1
Starting sigusr1: SIGUSR1
$ In sigalrm: SIGALRM SIGUSR1
Exiting sigusr1: SIGUSR1
Exiting main:
                                           Type Return again
[1] + Done                     ./siglongjmp &
```

To help us understand what is going on when we run Program 17.16, consider the function trace and time line in Figure 17.6.

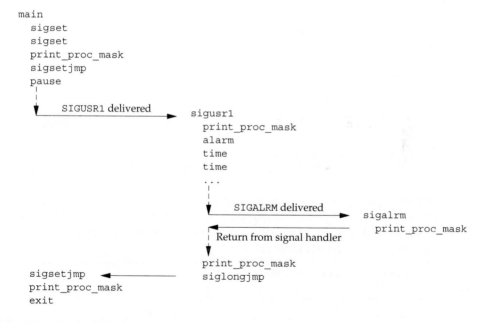

Figure 17.6 Time line for Program 17.16.

We can conceptually divide Figure 17.6 into three parts: the left (which corresponds to `main`), the middle (the `SIGUSR1` signal handler), and the right, which is the `SIGALRM` signal handler. While Program 17.16 is executing in the left part, no signals are blocked (i.e., the process' signal mask is 0). While Program 17.16 is executing in the middle part, its signal mask is `SIGUSR1`. Finally, while Program 17.16 is executing in the right part, its signal mask is `SIGUSR1 | SIGALRM`.

The output from Program 17.16 confirms our expectations. Notice that not only does the signal being caught get blocked when the signal handler is invoked, but the signal mask is restored when the signal handler returns. Note also that `siglongjmp` restores the signal mask that was saved by `sigsetjmp`.

If we make the necessary changes to Program 17.16 to use `setjmp` and `longjmp` instead of `sigsetjmp` and `siglongjmp`, the output is the same, except for the last line, which becomes

```
Exiting main: SIGUSR1
```

This means that `main` is executing with `SIGUSR1` blocked when `setjmp` returns, which is probably not what we intended.

17.22 The `sigsuspend` Function

We've seen how we can protect critical regions of code from being interrupted by signals by manipulating the process' signal mask (by blocking and unblocking selected signals). But suppose we want to execute a critical region of code and then specifically wait for a previously blocked signal to occur? Assuming that the signal is `SIGINT`, one way to do this would be:

```
sigemptyset (&new_mask);
sigaddset (&new_mask, SIGINT);

if (sigprocmask (SIG_BLOCK, &new_mask, &old_mask) == -1)
    err_msg ("sigprocmask (SIG_BLOCK) failed");

/*
 * Critical code region
 */

if (sigprocmask (SIG_SETMASK, &old_mask, NULL) == -1)
    err_msg ("sigprocmask (SIG_SETMASK) failed");
pause ();
```

Unfortunately, this code has a race condition. If the signal occurs between the unblocking and the `pause`, it will be lost. What we need is a function that will unblock the signal and suspend the calling process in one atomic operation. The `sigsuspend` function provides us with this feature.

```
#include <signal.h>

int sigsuspend (const sigset_t *set);
```
                                                              Returns: −1 with errno set to EINTR

The `sigsuspend` function replaces the signal mask of the calling process with the signal set pointed to by *set*. The caller is then suspended until a signal is delivered whose action is either to execute a signal handler or to terminate the process.

If the signal is caught, `sigsuspend` returns after the signal handler returns, and the signal mask is restored to its value before `sigsuspend` was called. On the other hand, if the signal's action is to terminate the process, `sigsuspend` does not return.

Because sigsuspend may suspend the caller indefinitely, there is no successful return value. If it returns to the caller, sigsuspend always returns −1, usually setting errno to EINTR.

Example: Protecting critical code from a specific signal

Program 17.17 shows the correct way to protect a critical region of code from a specific signal.

Set up signal handler

13–14 Catch SIGINT.

Print initial signal mask

15 Call print_proc_mask to print the initial signal mask.

Create an empty signal set

16 Create an empty signal set for later use.

Block SIGINT signals

17 Create an empty signal set.

18 Add SIGINT to the signal set we just created.

19–20 Add the signal set we've just created to the set of signals currently being blocked by the process.

Critical region of code

21 This is the section of code that executes with SIGINT blocked. In our example, we just print the signal mask to show that SIGINT is blocked.

Wait for a signal to be delivered

22–24 Suspend the calling process until a signal arrives. We specify an empty signal mask so that the arrival of any signal will wake us up.

25 Print the signal mask of the process when sigsuspend returns. Note that the signal mask has been restored to what it was when we called sigsuspend (i.e., SIGINT is blocked).

Reset the signal mask

26–27 Restore the previously saved signal mask (old_mask).

28 Print the signal mask one more time before terminating.

Signal handler

31–34 Print the signal mask. As we would expect, SIGINT is blocked while the interrupt handler is executing.

Running Program 17.17 gives us the following output:

```
$ ./critical
Before:
In critical code region: SIGINT
```

signals/critical.c

```
 1 #include <stdio.h>
 2 #include <signal.h>
 3 #include <unistd.h>
 4 #include <errno.h>
 5 #include "ssp.h"
 6 static void sigint (int sig);
 7 extern int print_proc_mask (const char *msg);

 8 int main (void)
 9 {
10     sigset_t old_mask;
11     sigset_t new_mask;
12     sigset_t empty_mask;

13     if (sigset (SIGINT, sigint) == SIG_ERR)
14         err_msg ("sigset failed");

15     print_proc_mask ("Before");

16     sigemptyset (&empty_mask);

17     sigemptyset (&new_mask);
18     sigaddset (&new_mask, SIGINT);
19     if (sigprocmask (SIG_BLOCK, &new_mask, &old_mask) == -1)
20         err_msg ("sigprocmask failed");

21     print_proc_mask ("In critical code region");

22     if (sigsuspend (&empty_mask) == -1)
23         if (errno != EINTR)
24             err_msg ("sigsuspend failed");
25     print_proc_mask ("After sigsuspend returns");

26     if (sigprocmask (SIG_SETMASK, &old_mask, NULL) == -1)
27         err_msg ("sigpromask failed");
28     print_proc_mask ("After");

29     return (0);
30 }
31 static void sigint (int sig)
32 {
33     print_proc_mask ("\nIn SIGINT signal handler");
34 }
```

signals/critical.c

Program 17.17 Protecting a critical region of code from a signal.

```
^C                                    Type our interrupt character
In SIGINT signal handler: SIGINT
After sigsuspend returns: SIGINT
After:
```

Note that the signal mask is empty before and after the critical region of code is executed.

Example: Waiting for a global variable to be set

We can also use sigsuspend to wait for a global variable to be set from a signal handler. Program 17.18 catches both SIGINT and SIGQUIT. In this example, each signal invokes

a common signal handler, but we only want to wake up main when we receive
SIGQUIT.

Install signal handlers

13–14 Set up the signal handler for SIGINT.

15–16 Set up the signal handler for SIGQUIT.

Initialize signal sets and process mask

17 Create an empty signal set.

18–21 Install a signal mask that blocks SIGQUIT.

Wait for flag to be set

22–26 While the global flag is 0, call sigsuspend to suspend our process until any signal
arrives.

SIGQUIT has been caught; do something

27 When we get to this point, a SIGQUIT signal has been received (and is currently
blocked), so we do something. In this example, we just set the global flag to 0, which
clears it.

Restore the old signal mask

28–29 Restore the original signal mask, which unblocks SIGQUIT.

Signal handler

34–37 If the signal we received was SIGINT, then print a message to that effect; otherwise, if
the signal received was SIGQUIT, then set the global flag to 1.

Running Program 17.18 gives us results like the following:

```
$ ./setvar
^C                                      Type our interrupt character
Received SIGINT
^C                                      Type our interrupt character again
Received SIGINT
^\$                                     Type out quit character
```

Note that our process terminates only when we type the quit character.

The sigsuspend function is OK if all we want to do is sleep until a signal occurs, but
what if we want to call other functions while we're waiting for the signal to arrive? On
the supposition that we want to wait for the arrival of a SIGINT or a SIGUSR1 signal
while we call select to wait for I/O on a set of file descriptors, the best we can is
something like the following:

```
if (int_flag)
    handle_sigint ();
if (usr_flag)
    handle_sigusr ();

while (select (...) == -1) {
    if (errno == EINTR) {
        if (int_flag)
            handle_sigint ();
```

signals/setvar.c

```
 1 #include <stdio.h>
 2 #include <signal.h>
 3 #include <unistd.h>
 4 #include <errno.h>
 5 #include "ssp.h"

 6 static volatile sig_atomic_t flag;

 7 static void sig_handler (int sig);

 8 int main (void)
 9 {
10     sigset_t old_mask;
11     sigset_t new_mask;
12     sigset_t empty_mask;

13     if (sigset (SIGINT, sig_handler) == SIG_ERR)
14         err_msg ("sigset (SIGINT) failed");
15     if (sigset (SIGQUIT, sig_handler) == SIG_ERR)
16         err_msg ("sigset (SIGQUIT) failed");

17     sigemptyset (&empty_mask);

18     sigemptyset (&new_mask);
19     sigaddset (&new_mask, SIGQUIT);
20     if (sigprocmask (SIG_BLOCK, &new_mask, &old_mask) == -1)
21         err_msg ("sigprocmask failed");

22     while (flag == 0) {
23         if (sigsuspend (&empty_mask) == -1)
24             if (errno != EINTR)
25                 err_msg ("sigsuspend failed");
26     }

27     flag = 0;

28     if (sigprocmask (SIG_SETMASK, &old_mask, NULL) == -1)
29         err_msg ("sigpromask failed");

30     return (0);
31 }

32 static void sig_handler (int sig)
33 {
34     if (sig == SIGINT)
35         printf ("\nReceived SIGINT\n");
36     else if (sig == SIGQUIT)
37         flag = 1;
38 }
```

signals/setvar.c

Program 17.18 Waiting for a global variable to be set.

```
            if (usr_flag)
                handle_sigusr ();
        }
        else {
            /* Some other error */
        }
    }
```

We test each of our global flags before calling select, and again if that function was interrupted. The problem with our code is that there is a race condition between our flag tests and when we call select. If either signal is caught in this gap, it will be lost. This is because the signal handler will be called (thus setting the appropriate global variable), but the select never returns unless one of the file descriptors is ready to be read or written to.

In an ideal world, we'd like to perform the following steps:

1. Block the signals we are interested in (in this case, SIGINT and SIGUSR1).
2. Test the global flags to see if one of the signals has occurred, and if so, call the appropriate handler.
3. Call the function we want to use and unblock the signals we previously blocked in one atomic operation.

Unfortunately, there is no foolproof method of implementing this. However, the sigsuspend function can help us—but only if we want to put our process to sleep.

17.23 The sigwait Function

Two of the problems with sigsuspend is that we must install at least an empty signal handler for each signal we're suspending for, and that we're not told which signal arrived to wake us up. The sigwait function provides us with a neat solution to these problems.

```
#include <signal.h>

int sigwait (sigset_t *set);
```
                                    Returns: signal number that woke us if OK, –1 on error

```
cc [ flag ... ] file ... -D_POSIX_PTHREAD_SEMANTICS [ library...]

#include <signal.h>

int sigwait (const sigset_t *set, int *sig);
```
                                                    Returns: 0 if OK, –1 on error

---

The `sigwait` function selects a signal from the set specified by *set* that is pending for the calling thread. If no signal in *set* is pending, then `sigwait` blocks until such a signal becomes pending. The selected signal is then cleared from the calling thread's set of pending signals, and the signal number is returned to the caller. The selection of a signal is independent of the current signal mask. This means that we can synchronously wait for signals being blocked. To ensure that only the caller receives the signals in *set*, all threads should have the signals in *set* blocked, including the calling thread (a side effect of this is that the signal handler for the received signal, if any, will not be executed).

The behaviour we just described applies to the default version of `sigwait`. The POSIX version is the same, except that that the number of the selected signal is stored in the integer pointed to by *sig*, and 0 is returned on success.

The default version of `sigwait` is obsolescent, so new applications should use the POSIX version.

Example: Synchronizing parent and child processes

Recall from Section 15.10 how we used six functions to synchronize a parent and its child. Program 17.19 shows a signals-based implementation of these six functions (i.e., `ssp_tell_wait_init`, `ssp_tell_child`, `ssp_tell_parent`, `ssp_wait_child`, `ssp_wait_parent`, and `ssp_tell_wait_fin`). The functions use two signals; SIGUSR1 is sent from the parent to the child, and SIGUSR2 is sent from the child to its parent.

Let's look a bit closer at these useful functions.

The `ssp_tell_wait_init` function

7 Create an empty signal set.

8–9 Create a signal set that consists of the signals SIGUSR1 and SIGUSR2.

10 Establish the new signal mask, saving the old one.

The `ssp_tell_child` function

12–15 Send the signal SIGUSR1 to the specified process, which should be a child of the calling process.

The `ssp_tell_parent` function

16–19 Send the signal SIGUSR2 to the specified process, which should be the parent of the calling process.

The `ssp_wait_child` function

20–24 Wait until one of the signals in our mask (i.e., SIGUSR1 or SIGUSR2) becomes pending. When `sigwait` returns, the signal that engendered the return will no longer be pending.

In Program 17.19, the `ssp_wait_parent` function is the same as `ssp_wait_child`. This may not be the case in other implementations of these functions, which might use another form of synchronization other than signals.

signals/tell_wait.c

```
 1 #include <sys/types.h>
 2 #include <signal.h>

 3 static sigset_t new_mask;
 4 static sigset_t old_mask;

 5 int ssp_tell_wait_init (void)
 6 {
 7     sigemptyset (&new_mask);
 8     sigaddset (&new_mask, SIGUSR1);
 9     sigaddset (&new_mask, SIGUSR2);
10     return (sigprocmask (SIG_BLOCK, &new_mask, &old_mask));
11 }

12 int ssp_tell_child (pid_t pid)
13 {
14     return (kill (pid, SIGUSR1));
15 }

16 int ssp_tell_parent (pid_t pid)
17 {
18     return (kill (pid, SIGUSR2));
19 }

20 int ssp_wait_child (void)
21 {
22     int sig;

23     return (sigwait (&new_mask, &sig));
24 }

25 int ssp_wait_parent (void)
26 {
27     int sig;

28     return (sigwait (&new_mask, &sig));
29 }

30 int ssp_tell_wait_fin (void)
31 {
32     return (sigprocmask (SIG_SETMASK, &old_mask, NULL));
33 }
```

signals/tell_wait.c

Program 17.19 Functions that enable a child and parent to synchronize using signals.

The `ssp_tell_wait_fin` function

30–33 Restore the saved signal mask.

17.24 The `abort` Function

As we've mentioned previously, the abort function causes a process to terminate abnormally.

```
#include <stdlib.h>

void abort (void);
```
This function never returns

The `abort` function sends a `SIGABRT` signal to the calling process, which causes it to terminate abnormally. The exception to this is if `SIGABRT` is being caught by the process, and the signal handler does not return (i.e., it calls `_exit`, `exit`, `longjmp`, or `siglongjmp`). The `abort` function overrides any blocking or ignoring of `SIGABRT`.

Allowing a process to catch `SIGABRT` is intended to provide us with a portable means to abort processing, without any interference from any implementation-defined library functions.

Example: Implementing the `abort` function

Program 17.20 shows our implementation of the `abort` function.

We need to consider several different scenarios, so let's take a closer look at the code for Program 17.20.

Get the current signal action

8 Get the current action associated with `SIGABRT`. Note that at this point, we don't change the action.

Check for user signal handler being installed

9–21 If a user signal handler is installed, then get the current signal mask. If `SIGABRT` is not a member of the set of masked signals, call `raise` to send ourselves a `SIGABRT` signal. Otherwise, get the set of pending signals, and if `SIGABRT` is not one of them, send ourselves the signal. We then remove `SIGABRT` from the signal mask; this will result in `SIGABRT` being delivered and the calling of the user-supplied signal handler.

Flush standard I/O streams

22 If `SIGABRT` was not being caught, flush the standard I/O streams. This line is also where our `abort` function resumes execution when the user-supplied signal handler returns, if one was installed and it returns normally.

Send ourselves the signal that terminates the process

24–25 Make sure that `SIGABRT`'s disposition is set to its default.

26–28 To be safe, mask all signals, except for `SIGABRT`.

29 Send ourselves a `SIGABRT` signal, which will abnormally terminate the process, and produce a core dump if the permissions and configuration allow it.

17.25 The `system` Function Revisited

In Section 15.13 we showed an implementation of the `system` function. As we noted at the time, that version does not handle signals correctly. A correct implementation of the

signals/abort.c

```
 1  #include <stdio.h>
 2  #include <signal.h>
 3  #include <unistd.h>

 4  void abort (void)
 5  {
 6      sigset_t set;
 7      struct sigaction action;

 8      sigaction (SIGABRT, NULL, &action);
 9      if ((action.sa_handler != SIG_DFL) && (action.sa_handler != SIG_IGN)) {
10          sigprocmask (0, NULL, &set);
11          if (sigismember (&set, SIGABRT)) {
12              sigpending (&set);
13              if (!sigismember (&set, SIGABRT))
14                  raise (SIGABRT);
15              sigfillset (&set);
16              sigdelset (&set, SIGABRT);
17              sigprocmask (SIG_SETMASK, &set, NULL);
18          }
19          else
20              raise (SIGABRT);
21      }

22      fflush (NULL);

23      for (;;) {
24          action.sa_handler = SIG_DFL;
25          sigaction (SIGABRT, &action, NULL);

26          sigfillset (&set);
27          sigdelset (&set, SIGABRT);
28          sigprocmask (SIG_SETMASK, &set, NULL);

29          raise (SIGABRT);
30      }
31  }
```

signals/abort.c

Program 17.20 Our implementation of the abort function.

system function ignores SIGINT and SIGQUIT, and blocks SIGCHLD. Before we show our implementation of system that handles signals correctly, let's see why we need to be concerned about signal handling.

Example: Executing the ex editor

Program 17.21 uses our incorrect version of system from Section 15.13 to invoke the ex editor. We use ex because it is an interactive program that catches SIGINT and SIGQUIT, and is line-orientated (rather than screen-orientated, like vi).

Catch signals

9–10 Catch SIGINT.

11–12 Catch SIGCHLD.

signals/system1.c

```
 1 #include <stdio.h>
 2 #include <signal.h>
 3 #include "ssp.h"

 4 extern int ssp_system (const char *string);
 5 static void sigint (int sig);
 6 static void sigchld (int sig);

 7 int main (void)
 8 {
 9     if (sigset (SIGINT, sigint) == SIG_ERR)
10         err_msg ("sigset (SIGINT) failed");
11     if (sigset (SIGCHLD, sigchld) == SIG_ERR)
12         err_msg ("sigset (SIGCHLD) failed");

13     if (ssp_system ("/bin/ex") == -1)
14         err_msg ("ssp_system failed");

15     return (0);
16 }

17 static void sigint (int sig)
18 {
19     printf ("Caught SIGINT\n");
20 }

21 static void sigchld (int sig)
22 {
23     printf ("Caught SIGCHLD\n");
24 }
```

signals/system1.c

Program 17.21   Using ssp_system to invoke ex.

Invoke ex

13–14 Invoke ex, using our ssp_signal function.

Signal handler for SIGINT

19 Print a message saying that we've caught the signal.

Signal handler for SIGCHLD

23 Print a message saying that we've caught the signal.

Running Program 17.21 gives us the following results:

```
$ ./system1
:a                                     Enter append mode
This is some example text.
And this is some more.
.                                      A period on its own exits append mode
:%p                                    Print the contents of the editor's buffer
This is some example text.
And this is some more.
:q!                                    Quit without saving
Caught SIGCHLD
```

The problem we're seeing here is that when the editor terminates, a SIGCHLD signal is delivered to the parent process (i.e., to system1). We catch the signal, but if we are catching SIGCHLD, we should be doing so because we're creating our own child processes and want to know when they have terminated. (Strictly speaking, system creates a child process, but when we talk about child processes here, we mean processes that we explicitly create using fork, rather than the implicit children created by system.) For correct operation, SIGCHLD must be blocked during the call to system; if this is not the case, then the caller of system would think that one of its own children had terminated.

Let's rerun Program 17.21, but this time we'll send an interrupt signal to the editor.

```
$ ./system1
:a
Antidisestablishmentarianism is a very long word.
.
:%p
Antidisestablishmentarianism is a very long word.
:^C                                    Type out interrupt character
Interrupt                              Editor catches signal, and prints this message
:Caught SIGINT                         As does the parent process
q!
Caught SIGCHLD
```

What's happening here is that when we type the interrupt character, SIGINT is sent to all processes in the foreground process group (recall Section 16.6). Figure 17.7 shows the process arrangement when the editor is running.

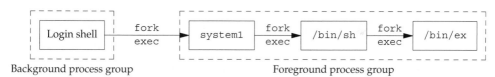

Figure 17.7 Process groups for Program 17.21.

The output from Program 17.21 confirms that the interrupt signal is sent to all three processes in the foreground process group (the shell ignores it). However, when we run another program using system, both processes should not catch terminal-generated signals. Because the command executed by system might be interactive, and since the caller of system gives up control while the program executes and waits for it to finish, the caller of system should not receive SIGINT and SIGQUIT. Hence POSIX and the SUS state that these signals should be ignored while system is executing.

Example: A correct implementation of the system function

Program 17.22 shows an implementation of system that correctly handles signals.

Use the correct shell

22-29 Use /bin/sh or /bin/ksh, depending on whether we're a standards compliant application.

signals/ssp_system.c

```
 1 #include <sys/types.h>
 2 #include <sys/wait.h>
 3 #include <unistd.h>
 4 #include <string.h>
 5 #include <errno.h>
 6 #include <signal.h>

 7 int ssp_system (const char *string)
 8 {
 9     int status;
10     int rc;
11     int w;
12     pid_t pid;
13     char *shell;
14     char *shell_path;
15     struct sigaction def_action;
16     struct sigaction ignore;
17     struct sigaction chld;
18     struct sigaction intr;
19     struct sigaction quit;
20     sigset_t mask;
21     sigset_t saved_mask;

22     if (sysconf (_SC_XOPEN_VERSION) < 4) {
23         shell = "sh";
24         shell_path = "/bin/sh";
25     }
26     else {
27         shell = "ksh";
28         shell_path = "/bin/ksh";
29     }

30     if (string == NULL) {
31         if (access (shell_path, X_OK) == -1) {
32             rc = 0;
33             goto bail;
34         }
35         else {
36             rc = 1;
37             goto bail;
38         }
39     }

40     sigemptyset (&mask);
41     sigaddset (&mask, SIGCHLD);
42     sigprocmask (SIG_BLOCK, &mask, &saved_mask);

43     memset (&def_action, 0, sizeof (def_action));
44     def_action.sa_handler = SIG_DFL;
45     sigaction (SIGCHLD, &def_action, &chld);

46     memset (&ignore, 0, sizeof (ignore));
47     ignore.sa_handler = SIG_IGN;
48     sigaction (SIGINT, &ignore, &intr);
49     sigaction (SIGQUIT, &ignore, &quit);
```

```
50      switch (pid = vfork ()) {
51          case -1:
52              rc = -1;
53              break;

54          case 0:
55              sigaction (SIGINT, &intr, NULL);
56              sigaction (SIGQUIT, &quit, NULL);
57              sigprocmask (SIG_SETMASK, &saved_mask, NULL);

58              execl (shell_path, shell, "-c", string, NULL);
59              _exit (127);

60          default:
61              do {
62                  w = waitpid (pid, &status, 0);
63              } while ((w == -1) && (errno == EINTR));

64              rc = ((w == -1) ? w : status);
65              break;
66      }

67      sigaction (SIGINT, &intr, NULL);
68      sigaction (SIGQUIT, &quit, NULL);
69      sigaction (SIGCHLD, &chld, NULL);
70      sigprocmask (SIG_SETMASK, &saved_mask, NULL);

71 bail:
72      return (rc);
73 }
```

signals/ssp_system.c

Program 17.22 An implementation of system that handles signals correctly.

Check for shell's existence

30–39 If we don't pass a string to be executed by the shell, return an indication of whether we can execute the appropriate shell.

Handle SIGCHLD

40–42 Block SIGCHLD so that caller's signal handler, if any, is not called.

43–45 Set SIGCHLD's action to SIG_DFL in case the caller is ignoring SIGCHLD.

Ignore the interrupt and quit signals

46–49 Ignore SIGINT and SIGQUIT. Many texts show this step as something like this:

```
if ((pid = fork ()) == -1)
    err_msg ("Can't fork");
else if (pid == 0) {
    execl (...);
    _exit (127);
}

old_intr = sigset (SIGINT, SIG_IGN);
old_quit = sigset (SIGQUIT, SIG_IGN);
waitpid (pid, &status, 0);
sigset (SIGINT, old_intr);
sigset (SIGQUIT, old_quit);
```

The problem with this code is that it contains a race condition. Because we have no guarantee that the child will run first, it's possible that an interrupt signal can be generated before the parent can change the signal's disposition.

As an example of defensive programming, we change the disposition of these two signals before forking in Program 17.22, even though in our case it isn't strictly necessary. This is because unlike `fork`, `vfork` on Solaris guarantees that the parent will be suspended until the child process calls `exec`.

Create the child process

50–53 Call `vfork` to create the child process. If `vfork` fails, set the return code to –1.

Child process

55–57 Restore the dispositions of `SIGINT` and `SIGQUIT`. This allows `exec` to change their dispositions to the default, based on the caller's dispositions (recall our description of this in Section 15.11).

58–59 Invoke the shell to run the given program string. If `exec` returns, indicate that an error has occurred.

Parent process

61–63 Wait for the child process to terminate, and retrieve its termination status.

64 Set the return code based on the child's termination status.

Restore caller's signal actions and mask

67–69 Restore the caller's signal actions for `SIGINT`, `SIGQUIT`, and `SIGCHLD`.

70 Restore the caller's signal mask.

Let's see how our version of `system` from Program 17.22 performs. The program called `system2` is the same as Program 17.21, except that it uses our improved version of `ssp_system`.

```
$ ./system2
:a
Hello, World!
.
:%p
Hello, World!
:^c                              Type our interrupt character
Interrupt                        Editor catches signal, and prints this message
:q!
```

Notice that this time, the signal interaction is as we would expect: when we type our interrupt character, only the child process (ex) receives the `SIGINT` signal, and the parent does not receive a `SIGCHLD` when ex terminates.

The Return Value from `system`

Something we must be wary of is the return value from `system`. The value returned by `system` is the termination status of the shell, which is not necessarily the same as the termination status of the command string. We saw some examples of this with Program 15.13, but what happens when we consider signals in this scenario?

Example: How signals affect the return value from `system`

Program 17.23 is a simple program that passes its command line argument to the `system` function, and prints the termination status.

—————————————————————————— signals/run_sys.c

```
 1 #include <stdio.h>
 2 #include <stdlib.h>
 3 #include "ssp.h"

 4 int main (int argc, char **argv)
 5 {
 6     int status;

 7     status = system (argv [1]);
 8     print_term_status (status);

 9     return (0);
10 }
```

—————————————————————————— signals/run_sys.c

Program 17.23   Execute the command line argument using `system`.

Let's run Program 17.23 and send the command it executes some signals.

```
$ ./run_sys "echo Hello, World!"
Hello, World!
Normal termination; exit status = 0
$ ./run_sys "sleep 10"
^CNormal termination; exit status = 130   Type our interrupt key
$ ./run_sys "sleep 10"
^\Quit - core dumped                      Type our quit key
Normal termination; exit status = 131
```

The termination status of the first command is as we would expect. But when we terminate the `sleep` with an interrupt signal, our `print_term_status` function (see Program 15.3) thinks that it terminated normally. The same thing happens when we terminate `sleep` using the quit signal. What we're witnessing here is the effect of a poorly documented feature of the Bourne shell: when the command it was executing is terminated by a signal, the shell's termination status is 128 plus the number of the terminating signal. (The Korn shell also has this feature.) On Solaris, `SIGINT` has a value of 2, and `SIGQUIT` has a value of 3. Hence we get the termination statuses of 130 and 131 respectively. We can observe this by running the Bourne shell interactively.

```
$ sh -c "sleep 10"
^C$                                       Type out interrupt character
$ echo $?                                 Print termination status of last command
130
$ sh -c "sleep 10"
^\Quit - core dumped                      Type our quit character
$ echo $?                                 Print termination status of last command
131
```

Another experiment we can perform is seeing what happens to the return value of
system if we send a signal directly to the shell.

```
$ ./run_sys "sleep 10" &              Start our program in the background this time
[2]      19685
$ ps
   PID TTY       TIME CMD
 19686 pts/8    0:00 sh
 19688 pts/8    0:00 ps
 19685 pts/8    0:00 run_sys
 19687 pts/8    0:00 sleep
 19299 pts/8    0:00 ksh
$ kill -KILL 19686                        Kill the shell
$ Abnormal termination; signal = Killed

[2] +  Done                       ./run_sys "sleep 10" &
```

Here we can see that system only reports an abnormal termination if the shell itself
abnormally terminates. When we write programs that use system, it is important that
we correctly interpret the return value. Note that if we use fork, exec, and wait
ourselves, the termination status will be different than if we call system. If anything, the
return value we get when we call the separate functions ourselves will more likely be
what we're expecting.

17.26 The `sleep` Function Revisited

We described the sleep function in Section 3.10, and we've used it in many of our
examples. We also showed a couple of flawed implementations of it in Program 17.5 and
Program 17.6. To recap, sleep suspends the calling process until either of these events
occur:

1. The specified amount of time has elapsed. If the system is very busy, the actual
   return time may be later than that requested.

2. A signal is caught by the process and the signal handler returns.

In case 1, sleep returns 0; in case 2, the return value is the number of unslept seconds
(i.e., the requested time minus the amount of time actually slept).

If we implement sleep using alarm (as we do here), there are a number of interactions
between these two functions that POSIX leaves unspecified. For example, if we arrange
for an alarm to go off in ten seconds, and then five seconds later do a sleep (3), what
happens? The sleep will return after three seconds (assuming no other signal is
delivered in the meantime), but whether or not another SIGALRM is delivered two
seconds later is implementation-defined.

Ideally, we should avoid any mixing of sleep and alarm (or any other timing function)
in our applications.

Example: A correct implementation of the `sleep` function

Program 17.24 shows our final implementation of the `sleep` function. It doesn't use any nonlocal branching, and it avoids the race condition in Program 17.5 by handling signals reliably. Because of this, there is no effect on other signal handlers that might be executing when our `SIGALRM` is handled.

Assuming that *sleep_time* is the amount of time to sleep for, then if the caller of our function has an alarm set to go off *n* seconds from now, we must consider three cases:

1. If *sleep_time* is greater than or equal to *n*, then sleep for *n* seconds and cause the caller's previously installed alarm signal handler to be executed, then return the amount of unslept time to the caller (i.e., *sleep_time* − *n*).

2. If *sleep_time* is less than *n*, then sleep for *sleep_time* seconds. Then, reset the alarm to go off when it would have anyway.

3. If the process is woken up while it is sleeping by any caught signal, then we reset any prior alarm and return the number of unslept seconds.

Let's look at the implementation details.

Initialize the alarm signal action

20 Stop the current alarm clock, if any, and make a note of how much time it has left before it expires.

21–24 Install a new signal handler for `SIGALRM`, namely our "do nothing" function.

Initialize variables

25 Set the alarm flag to 0. We use this flag to indicate that an alarm clock was already ticking.

26 Set the remainder to 0.

Handle any previously set alarm

27–39 If the number of seconds to the next alarm timeout (the "alarm time") is not zero, then there is an existing alarm clock we must handle. If the alarm time exceeds the time we are to sleep for, then we reduce the remaining alarm time by the sleep time and set a flag. Otherwise, we arrange to sleep for the alarm time, reinstate the saved `SIGALRM` handler, and set a flag.

Sleep for the required time

40–42 Add `SIGALRM` to the signal mask.

43–44 Create a signal set that consists of the previously blocked signals minus `SIGALRM`.

45–47 Set an alarm clock to expire at the appropriate time. Then suspend the process until a signal arrives. When the signal handler returns, make a note of how much time (if any) remains on our alarm clock.

---

signals/ssp_sleep3.c

```
 1 #include <unistd.h>
 2 #include <signal.h>

 3 static void sigalrm (int sig)
 4 {
 5     /* Do nothing */
 6 }

 7 unsigned int ssp_sleep (unsigned int sleep_time)
 8 {
 9     int alarm_flag;
10     unsigned int unslept;
11     unsigned int alarm_time;
12     unsigned int remainder;
13     struct sigaction act;
14     struct sigaction saved_act;
15     sigset_t alarm_mask;
16     sigset_t set;
17     sigset_t saved_set;

18     if (sleep_time == 0)
19         return (0);

20     alarm_time = alarm (0);
21     act.sa_handler = sigalrm;
22     act.sa_flags = 0;
23     sigemptyset (&act.sa_mask);
24     sigaction (SIGALRM, &act, &saved_act);

25     alarm_flag = 0;
26     remainder = 0;

27     if (alarm_time != 0) {
28         if (alarm_time > sleep_time) {
29             alarm_time -= sleep_time;
30             alarm_flag = 1;
31         }
32         else {
33             remainder = sleep_time - alarm_time;
34             sleep_time = alarm_time;
35             alarm_time = 0;
36             alarm_flag = -1;
37             sigaction (SIGALRM, &saved_act, NULL);
38         }
39     }

40     sigemptyset (&alarm_mask);
41     sigaddset (&alarm_mask, SIGALRM);
42     sigprocmask (SIG_BLOCK, &alarm_mask, &saved_set);

43     set = saved_set;
44     sigdelset (&set, SIGALRM);
45     alarm (sleep_time);
46     sigsuspend (&set);
47     unslept = alarm (0);
```

```
48         sigprocmask (SIG_SETMASK, &saved_set, NULL);

49         if (alarm_flag >= 0)
50             sigaction (SIGALRM, &saved_act, NULL);

51         if ((alarm_flag > 0) || ((alarm_flag < 0) && (unslept != 0)))
52             alarm (alarm_time + unslept);

53         return (remainder + unslept);
54     }
```

signals/ssp_sleep3.c

Program 17.24 Our final implementation of `sleep`.

Reset the signal mask

48 Restore the previously saved signal mask.

Restore previous alarm action

49–50 If a previous alarm was set to expire after we wake up from our sleep, or there was no previously set alarm, then restore the previous `SIGALRM` signal action.

Install a new alarm clock, if required

51–52 If a previous alarm was set to expire after we wake up from our sleep, or if the alarm was due to expire before we woke up and we didn't sleep for the full duration, then start a new alarm clock that will expire at the appropriate time.

Return the unslept time

53 Return the unslept time, i.e., the number of requested seconds minus the amount of time we actually slept for.

Even taking into account the additional functionality we provide in Program 17.24, we can see that it takes much more code to write a reliable version of `sleep` than the unreliable versions in Programs 17.5 and 17.6.

17.27 Job Control Signals

Six of the signals listed in Figure 17.1 are considered to be job control signals. These are:

SIGCHLD	Child process has changed state (i.e., has terminated or stopped).
SIGCONT	Continue stopped process.
SIGSTOP	Stop signal. This signal can't be caught or ignored.
SIGTSTP	Interactive stop signal.
SIGTTIN	Read from the controlling terminal by a member of a background process group.
SIGTTOU	Write to the controlling terminal by a member of a background process group.

Most of the time, our programs don't need to handle these signals, as the shell usually does all the work for us. For example, typing the suspend character (usually Control-Z) results in a SIGTSTP signal being sent to all processes in the foreground process group. Conversely, when we instruct the shell to resume a job, each of the processes in the job is sent SIGCONT. Finally, if SIGTTIN or SIGTTOU is delivered to a process, the process is stopped by default, and the shell (assuming it is a job control shell) recognizes this and informs us.

But there are times when we must override the default behaviour. Consider, for example, the vi editor. It needs to know when the user suspends or continues the process so that it may manage the terminal correctly. The terminal's state must be saved when the process is stopped, and it must be restored (and the screen redrawn) when it is continued in the foreground.

There are some interactions between the job control signals we should be cognizant of. The first is that when any of the stop signals (SIGSTOP, SIGTSTP, SIGTTIN, or SIGTTOU) is generated for a process, any pending continue signal (SIGCONT) for that process is discarded. Similarly, when a continue signal is generated for a process, any pending stop signals for that process are discarded.

The default action for SIGCONT is to continue the process if it is stopped; otherwise, it is ignored. We usually don't have to do anything with SIGCONT: if it is generated for a stopped process, that process is continued, even if it is blocking or ignoring the signal.

Example: A typical SIGTSTP handler

Program 17.25 shows the typical code sequence used when a program handles job control.

Catch SIGTSTP

8–9 If we are running from a job control shell, catch SIGTSTP. We do this because if the program is started by a shell that doesn't support job control, then SIGTSTP should be ignored.

Wait for our handler to set a flag

10–11 While the flag is equal to 0, suspend our process until a signal arrives.

Signal handler

18 Print a newline character. This is where we would normally do any terminal related processing, like resetting its mode and moving the cursor to the lower-left corner, etc.

19–21 Unblock SIGTSTP, because it's automatically blocked while we're handling it.

22 Reset SIGTSTP's disposition to its default.

23 Send ourselves a SIGTSTP signal. The raise function won't return until we continue our process (i.e., send it a SIGCONT signal).

24 When we've been continued, reestablish our signal handler.

25 Set our flag to be non-zero, which will cause our loop in the main function to terminate the next time a signal is delivered to our process. This is where we would normally do any terminal-related processing, like resetting its mode and redrawing the screen.

signals/sigtstp.c

```
1 #include <stdio.h>
2 #include <signal.h>
3 #include <unistd.h>

4 static volatile sig_atomic_t flag;

5 static void sigtstp (int sig);

6 int main (void)
7 {
8      if (sigset (SIGTSTP, SIG_IGN) == SIG_DFL)
9          sigset (SIGTSTP, sigtstp);

10     while (flag == 0)
11         pause ();

12     printf ("Program continued - we're done.\n");

13     return (0);
14 }

15 static void sigtstp (int sig)
16 {
17     sigset_t mask;

18     printf ("\n");

19     sigemptyset (&mask);
20     sigaddset (&mask, SIGTSTP);
21     sigprocmask (SIG_UNBLOCK, &mask, NULL);

22     sigset (SIGTSTP, SIG_DFL);
23     raise (SIGTSTP);
24     sigset (SIGTSTP, sigtstp);

25     flag++;
26 }
```

signals/sigtstp.c

Program 17.25 Handling SIGTSTP.

Notice that we don't catch SIGCONT. This is because its default action is to continue the process, and when this happens, Program 17.25 continues as though it had returned from raise.

Running Program 17.25 gives us the following results:

```
$ ./sigtstp
^z                                          Type our suspend character
[1] + Stopped (SIGTSTP)           ./sigtstp
$ fg                                        Continue our job in the foreground
./sigtstp
Program continued - we're done.
```

We saw another way to handle the suspend job control character in Chapter 12, where we recognize the character ourselves rather than using the SIGTSTP signal.

17.28 Software Signals

Solaris provides a software signal facility that is similar to that provided by `signal`. Unlike regular signals, software signals are intraprocess only. That is, a process can send a software signal to only itself and not to any other process.

The software signal facility is available for any of our own purposes and consists of two functions: `ssignal` and `gsignal`.

The `ssignal` Function

The `ssignal` function is the software signal analogue of the `signal` function.

```
#include <signal.h>

void (*ssignal (int sig, int (*action) (int))) (int);
```
                                    Returns: the previous disposition of *sig* if OK, SIG_DFL on error

The `ssignal` function associates the function specified by *action* with the software signal *sig*, which must be an integer in the range from 1 to 17 inclusive. The *action* argument must be one of the following three values:

1. The constant `SIG_IGN`, which causes the software signal to be ignored

2. The constant `SIG_DFL`, which causes the default action to be taken, which, in the case of software signals, is nothing (The difference between `SIG_DFL` and `SIG_IGN` is the return value from `gsignal`, which we discuss next.)

3. The address of the function that is to be called when the signal is generated by `gsignal`

On success, the `ssignal` function returns the previous action associated with *sig*. On error, of if no action was previously associated with *sig*, `ssignal` returns `SIG_DFL` (compare this with `signal`, which returns `SIG_ERR` on error).

The `gsignal` Function

The `gsignal` function is the software signal analogue of the `raise` function.

```
#include <signal.h>

int gsignal (int sig);
```
                                                                          Returns: see text

The `gsignal` function raises the software signal specified by *sig*.

If an action function has been established for *sig*, then that software signal's action is reset to `SIG_DFL`, and the action function is called with an argument of *sig*. If the action function returns, `gsignal` returns the value returned to it by the action function.

If the action for *sig* is SIG_IGN, then gsignal returns 1 and takes no other action.

If the action for *sig* is SIG_DFL, or *sig* is illegal, or no action was ever specified for *sig*, then gsignal returns 0 and takes no other action.

Example: Using software signals

Program 17.26 demonstrates the use of software signals.

signals/ssignal.c

```
 1 #include <stdio.h>
 2 #include <signal.h>

 3 #undef SIG_DFL
 4 #undef SIG_IGN
 5 #define SIG_DFL (int (*) ()) 0
 6 #define SIG_IGN (int (*) ()) 1

 7 static int ssig_action (int sig);

 8 int main (void)
 9 {
10     int sig;

11     ssignal (1, SIG_IGN);
12     ssignal (2, ssig_action);
13     ssignal (3, SIG_IGN);
14     ssignal (4, ssig_action);
15     ssignal (5, SIG_DFL);

16     for (sig = 1; sig < 10; sig++)
17         printf ("gsignal (%d) returns %d\n", sig, gsignal (sig));

18     return (0);
19 }

20 static int ssig_action (int sig)
21 {
22     printf ("Received software signal %d\n", sig);

23     return (sig);
24 }
```

signals/ssignal.c

Program 17.26   Using software signals.

Redefine SIG_DFL and SIG_IGN

3–6 We remove the definitions of SIG_DFL and SIG_IGN we get from including <signal.h> and replace them with our own. We have to do this because the function prototype for the software signal handler is different to that for regular signals. Unfortunately, Solaris doesn't provide suitable manifest constants for use with software signals, so we create our own. (Our program will work correctly if we omit this step, but the compiler will emit warnings about the second argument of ssignal being passed an incompatible pointer type.)

Initialize software signal actions

11–15 Set up our software signal actions. We ignore two software signals (numbers 1 and 3), and associate two with our software signal action function (numbers 2 and 4). We also explicitly ignore one software signal (number 5) to show that there is no difference between explicitly setting a software signal's action to be ignored, and not associating an action with a signal (in other words, we implicitly set the software signal's action to be the default).

16–17 Raise each of the first nine software signals in sequence, and print the value of the result returned by gsignal.

Software signal action

20–24 Print a message saying which software signal we received, and then return that number.

Running Program 17.26 gives us the following:

```
$ ./ssignal
gsignal (1) returns 1
Received software signal 2
gsignal (2) returns 2
gsignal (3) returns 1
Received software signal 4
gsignal (4) returns 4
gsignal (5) returns 0
gsignal (6) returns 0
gsignal (7) returns 0
gsignal (8) returns 0
gsignal (9) returns 0
```

Notice that gsignal returns the same value if we never set a software signal's action, or if we set it to SIG_DFL.

17.29 Alternate Signal Stacks

There are times when it is desirable for our signal handlers to execute in the context of a different stack. For example, on a machine with limited memory resources (e.g., an embedded system), we might want to set up an alternate stack for signals so that we can be sure that our signal handlers will have enough stack space to operate in. Also, the only way we can catch a SIGSEGV caused by a stack overflow is to use an alternate signal stack.

Solaris provides two functions for manipulating alternate signal stacks: the preferred interface, sigaltstack, and the obsolescent sigstack.

The sigaltstack Function

We can manipulate alternate stacks by using the sigaltstack function.

```
#include <signal.h>

int sigaltstack (const stack_t *ss, stack_t *oss);
```

Returns: 0 if OK, −1 on error

The `sigaltstack` function enables a thread to define and examine the properties of an alternate stack on which signals are processed. If *ss* is not NULL, then it must point to a `sigaltstack` structure, which contains the size and address of the new stack to use. When a signal is delivered, its handler will execute on the alternate stack if the SA_ONSTACK flag is set by using the `sigaction` function.

If *oss* is not NULL, then it it must point to a `sigaltstack` structure, into which the attributes of the alternate signal stack that was in effect prior to the call to `sigaltstack` are placed.

The `sigaltstack` structure has the following members:

```
typedef struct sigaltstack {
    void    *ss_sp;     /* Base address of stack */
    size_t  ss_size;    /* Size of stack */
    int     ss_flags;   /* Flags */
} stack_t;
```

When we specify a new stack using `sigaltstack`, the `ss_sp` and `ss_size` members are automatically adjusted for direction of stack growth and alignment.

The `ss_flags` member is constructed by bitwise-ORing zero or more of the following constants together:

SS_DISABLE   If this flag is set, the stack is to be disabled, and `ss_sp` and `ss_size` are ignored. Otherwise, the stack will be enabled.

SS_ONSTACK   If this flag is set, it means that the calling thread is currently executing on the alternate signal stack. Attempts to modify the alternate signal stack while it is in use will fail. This flag will be present only in the `sigaltstack` structure pointed to by *oss*.

Two manifest constants are defined in `<signal.h>` to help us set the stack size. These are SIGSTKSZ and MINSIGSTKSZ. The former is the number of bytes that should be used to cover the usual case when allocating an alternate stack, and the latter is the minimum stack size for a signal handler. If we don't use SIGSTKSZ, then to allow for the OS overhead, we should add MINSIGSTKSZ to the value we want to use.

Example: Using an alternate stack

Program 17.27 demonstrates the use of an alternate stack for a signal handler.

signals/altstack.c

```
 1 #include <stdio.h>
 2 #include <unistd.h>
 3 #include <fcntl.h>
 4 #include <sys/stat.h>
 5 #include <signal.h>
 6 #include <sys/mman.h>
 7 #include "ssp.h"

 8 static void sigusr (int sig);
 9 static void print_stack_info (const char *msg, stack_t *stack);

10 int main (void)
11 {
12     struct sigaction act;
13     stack_t alt_stack;
14     int fd;

15     act.sa_handler = sigusr;
16     sigemptyset (&act.sa_mask);
17     act.sa_flags = 0;
18     if (sigaction (SIGUSR1, &act, NULL) == -1)
19         err_msg ("sigaction failed");

20     printf ("Using default stack\n");
21     raise (SIGUSR1);

22     if ((fd = open ("/dev/zero", O_RDWR)) == -1)
23         err_msg ("open failed");
24     if ((alt_stack.ss_sp = mmap (NULL, SIGSTKSZ, PROT_READ | PROT_WRITE,
25         MAP_PRIVATE, fd, 0)) == MAP_FAILED) {
26         err_msg ("mmap failed");
27     }
28     close (fd);
29     alt_stack.ss_size = SIGSTKSZ;
30     alt_stack.ss_flags = 0;
31     if (sigaltstack (&alt_stack, NULL) == -1)
32         err_msg ("sigaltstack failed");

33     act.sa_flags = SA_ONSTACK;
34     if (sigaction (SIGUSR1, &act, NULL) == -1)
35         err_msg ("sigaction failed");

36     printf ("\nUsing alternate stack\n");
37     raise (SIGUSR1);

38     return (0);
39 }

40 static void sigusr (int sig)
41 {
42     stack_t alt_stack;

43     if (sigaltstack (NULL, &alt_stack) == -1)
44         err_msg ("sigaltstack failed");

45     print_stack_info ("  Handler", &alt_stack);
46 }
```

```
47 static void print_stack_info (const char *msg, stack_t *stack)
48 {
49     printf ("%s stack base: %p\n", msg, stack -> ss_sp);
50     printf ("%s stack size: %ld\n", msg, (long) stack -> ss_size);
51     if (stack -> ss_flags == 0)
52         printf ("%s stack flags: 0\n", msg);
53     else {
54         printf ("%s stack flags: ", msg);
55         if (stack -> ss_flags & SS_DISABLE)
56             printf ("SS_DISABLE ");
57         if (stack -> ss_flags & SS_ONSTACK)
58             printf ("SS_ONSTACK");
59         printf ("\n");
60     }
61 }
```
signals/altstack.c

Program 17.27   Using an alternate stack for a signal handler.

Catch SIGUSR1

15–17 Set up the parameters for our new signal handler.

18–19 Install the new signal handler.

Send ourselves a signal

20–21 Send ourselves SIGUSR1 so that our interrupt handler is called.

Set up the alternate signal stack

22–28 Allocate SIGSTKSZ bytes of anonymous memory.

29–30 Set the size of the alternate stack and clear its flags.

31–32 Activate the alternate signal stack.

Modify the action for SIGUSR1

33 Set the SA_ONSTACK flag, which indicates that the handler for the specified signal should run on the alternate signal stack.

34–35 Install the modified signal handler.

Send ourselves another signal

36–37 Send ourselves another SIGUSR1 signal.

Signal handler

43–44 Retrieve the state of the current alternate signal stack.

45 Print the alternate signal stack's state by calling print_stack_info.

The print_stack_info function

47–61 Print the alternate signal stack's base address, size, and flags.

Running Program 17.27 gives us the following:

```
$ ./altstack
Using default stack
  Handler stack base: 0
  Handler stack size: 0
  Handler stack flags: SS_DISABLE
```

```
Using alternate stack
  Handler stack base: ff3a0000
  Handler stack size: 8192
  Handler stack flags: SS_ONSTACK
```

The results for the default stack show that no alternate stack is being used; it has a base address and size of 0, and its SS_DISABLE flag is set. The results for the alternate stack show that we have an 8 KB stack which has a base address of 0xff3a0000, and that we are currently executing on the alternate stack.

We got these results by running Program 17.27 as a 32-bit process on an Ultra 60. Running it on different architectures or as a 64-bit process will give us different results resulting from changes in the process' memory map.

The `sigstack` Function

We can also use the `sigstack` function to manipulate an alternate signal stack.

```
#include <signal.h>

int sigstack (struct sigstack *ss, struct sigstack *oss);
```
                                                              Returns: 0 if OK, −1 on error

---

The `sigstack` function enables a process to define and examine an alternate stack on which signals are processed.

If *ss* is not a NULL pointer, it must point to a `sigstack` structure, which contains the address of the new stack to use, which must be at least SIGSTKSZ bytes in size. When a signal is delivered, its handler will execute on the alternate stack if the SA_ONSTACK flag is set by using the `sigaction` function.

If *oss* is not NULL, then it must point to a `sigstack` structure, into which the attributes of the alternate stack that was in effect prior to the call to `sigstack` are placed.

The `sigstack` structure has the following members:

```
struct sigstack {
    void   *ss_sp;        /* Base address of stack */
    int     ss_onstack;   /* In use flag */
}
```

The ss_onstack member of *oss* will be non-zero if the calling process is currently executing on the alternate stack.

There are a couple of problems with using `sigstack` to install an alternate signal stack:

1. The direction of stack growth is not indicated in the `sigstack` structure. The only way we can portably establish a stack pointer is if the application determines the direction of stack growth, or if we allocated a block of memory and set the stack pointer to the middle.

2. We should not use the `longjmp` function to return from a signal handler that is executing on alternate stack established with `sigstack`; if we do, the stack may

be disabled for future use. Instead, we should use `siglongjmp`, `setcontext`, or `swapcontext` to abnormally return from a signal handler. These functions fully support switching from one stack to another.

Because of its deficiences (including the requirement for the application to have knowledge about the underlying system's stack architecture), `sigstack` should not be used. The `sigaltstack` function we discussed previously should be used instead.

17.30 System Signal Messages

We described earlier how we can use `perror` and `strerror` to print the message associated with an error number. Solaris provides us with two functions that perform the same task, but for signal names. These are `psignal` and `strsignal`.

The `psignal` Function

The `psignal` function is to signal messages as `perror` is to error messages.

```
#include <siginfo.h>

void psignal (int sig, const char *s);
```

The `psignal` function outputs the string pointed to by *s*, followed by a colon and a blank, followed by a string describing the signal specified by *sig*, on standard error.

We could use `psignal` to print the name of the current signal in a generic signal handler, like this:

```
void sig_handler (int sig)
{
    psignal (sig, "progname");
}
```

The `strsignal` Function

The `strsignal` function is the signal analogue of `strerror`.

```
#include <string.h>

char *strsignal (int sig);
```
                                    Returns: a pointer to the signal message if OK, NULL on error

The `strsignal` function returns a pointer to the description of the signal specified by *sig*. It uses the same set of descriptions as `psignal`. We would use this function when we want more flexibility in the message than that provided by `psignal`.

The `psiginfo` Function

We can use the `psiginfo` function to print more information about a signal.

```
#include <siginfo.h>

void psiginfo (siginfo_t *pinfo, char *s);
```

The `psiginfo` function outputs the string pointed to by *s*, followed by a colon and a space, followed by a string containing some of the information contained in the `siginfo_t` structure pointed to by *pinfo*, on standard error.

Example: Printing signal information

Program 17.28 demonstrates the use of the signal message functions we've described in this section.

Establish signal handlers

11–13 Set up our `sigaction` structure. Because we want to be passed extra information about the signal, we set the `SA_SIGINFO` flag.

14–15 Install the signal handler for `SIGUSR1`.

16–17 Install the signal handler for `SIGUSR2`.

Wait for signals

18–19 Loop for ever, waiting for signals to be delivered to our process.

Signal handler

21–27 If the signal we received was `SIGUSR1`, then print the signal message using `psignal`. Otherwise, call `psiginfo` to print the signal information.

Running Program 17.28 gives us the following results:

```
$ ./psignal &
[1]     12977
$ kill -USR1 12977
$ Received signal: User Signal 1
                                        Type Return
$ kill -USR2 12977
$ Received signal : User Signal 2 ( from process  1167 )
                                        Type Return again
$ kill 12977
$                                       Type Return again
[1] + Terminated              ./psignal &
```

We showed an alternative to using `psiginfo` in Program 17.14.

17.31 The `sig2str` and `str2sig` Functions

The functions we described in the previous section work well if we want to print a description of a given signal number, but what if we want to translate the more

signals/psignal.c

```
 1  #include <stdio.h>
 2  #include <unistd.h>
 3  #include <signal.h>
 4  #include <siginfo.h>
 5  #include <sys/ucontext.h>
 6  #include "ssp.h"

 7  static void sigusr (int sig, siginfo_t *info, void *ucp);

 8  int main (void)
 9  {
10      struct sigaction act;

11      act.sa_sigaction = sigusr;
12      sigemptyset (&act.sa_mask);
13      act.sa_flags = SA_SIGINFO;

14      if (sigaction (SIGUSR1, &act, NULL) == -1)
15          err_msg ("sigaction (SIGUSR1) failed");
16      if (sigaction (SIGUSR2, &act, NULL) == -1)
17          err_msg ("sigaction (SIGUSR2) failed");

18      for (;;)
19          pause ();
20  }

21  static void sigusr (int sig, siginfo_t *info, void *ucp)
22  {
23      if (sig == SIGUSR1)
24          psignal (sig, "Received signal");
25      else
26          psiginfo (info, "Received signal");
27  }
```

signals/psignal.c

Program 17.28 Printing signal information using `psignal` and `psiginfo`.

mnemonic signal names, like `SIGINT` and `SIGSEGV`? Solaris provides us with two functions to perform these translations: `sig2str` and `str2sig`.

```
#include <signal.h>

int sig2str (int signum, char *str);

int str2sig (const char *str, int *signum);
```
                                                    Both return: 0 if OK, −1 on error

The `sig2str` function translates the signal number specified by *signum* to the mnemonic symbol for that signal, without the "`SIG`" prefix. The resulting string is stored in the buffer pointed to by *str*, which must be large enough to hold the symbol and a terminating NUL character. The manifest constant, `SIG2STR_MAX`, which is defined in `<signal.h>`, gives the maximum size in bytes required.

The `str2sig` function performs the opposite translation: the signal name specified by *str* is translated to a signal number, which is stored in the buffer pointed to by *signum*. The signal name can be either the mnemonic symbol for that symbol (without the `"SIG"` prefix) or a decimal number.

Example: Implementing the `kill` command

Program 17.29 shows our implementation of the `kill` command, which sends the specified signal to the specified process. For the sake of brevity, we don't implement all of the `kill` command's functionality.

Initialize variables

16–19 Set all our flags, and the external variable, `opterr`, to 0. We do the latter to prevent error messages being printed by `getopt`.

Parse command line arguments

20–37 We step through each command line argument, taking the appropriate action for each one. If the `l` argument is specified, then if we haven't already processed an `s` argument, we set the list signals flag. Otherwise, we set the error flag.

If the `s` argument is specified, then if we haven't already processed an `s` argument or an `l` argument, we set the signal specified flag and make a copy of the signal number specified.

If we don't recognize the argument, we set the error flag.

Perform some error checking

38–39 If neither command line option has been used, set the error flag.

40–41 If we have specified a signal but no process IDs, or if we indicated that we want a list of signals but have extra arguments on the command line, then set the error flag.

42–46 If the error flag is set, print a usage message and quit.

List signals

47–53 If we are printing a list of signals, then call `sig2str` for each valid signal and print the string returned.

Send signal to designated processes

54–61 Call `str2sig` to translate the signal name given on the command line to its signal number. Then, for each remaining command line argument, send the requested signal to the indicated process, reporting any errors.

Let's run Program 17.29 with a few arguments to see what we get.

```
$ ./ssp_kill -l
EXIT HUP INT QUIT ILL TRAP ABRT EMT FPE KILL BUS SEGV SYS PIPE ALRM TERM USR1
    USR2 CLD PWR WINCH URG POLL STOP TSTP CONT TTIN TTOU VTALRM PROF XCPU XFSZ
    WAITING LWP FREEZE THAW CANCEL LOST XRES RTMIN RTMIN+1 RTMIN+2 RTMIN+3
    RTMAX-3 RTMAX-2 RTMAX-1 RTMAX
$ sleep 30 &                          Sleep in background so we have a killable process
[1]    20892
```

signals/ssp_kill.c

```
 1 #include <stdio.h>
 2 #include <stdlib.h>
 3 #include <unistd.h>
 4 #include <sys/types.h>
 5 #include <signal.h>
 6 #include "ssp.h"

 7 int main (int argc, char **argv)
 8 {
 9     int c;
10     int sig;
11     int s_flag;
12     int l_flag;
13     int err_flag;
14     char buf [SIG2STR_MAX];
15     pid_t pid;

16     s_flag= 0;
17     l_flag =0;
18     err_flag = 0;
19     opterr = 0;

20     while ((c = getopt (argc, argv, "ls:")) != EOF) {
21         switch (c) {
22             case 'l':
23                 if (s_flag)
24                     err_flag++;

25                 l_flag++;
26                 break;

27             case 's':
28                 if ((l_flag) || (s_flag))
29                     err_flag++;

30                 s_flag++;
31                 snprintf (buf, SIG2STR_MAX - 1, "%s", optarg);
32                 break;

33             default:
34                 err_flag++;
35                 break;
36         }
37     }

38     if ((!l_flag) && (!s_flag))
39         err_flag++;

40     if (((s_flag) && (optind == argc)) || ((l_flag) && (optind != argc)))
41         err_flag++;

42     if (err_flag) {
43         log_msg ("Usage: ssp_kill -l");
44         log_msg ("       ssp_kill -s signal PID");
45         exit (1);
46     }
```

```
47     if (l_flag) {
48         for (sig = 0; sig <= MAXSIG; sig++) {
49             sig2str (sig, buf);
50             printf ("%s ", buf);
51         }
52         printf ("\n");
53     }
54     else {
55         if (str2sig (buf, &sig) == -1)
56             err_quit ("ssp_kill: %s: No such signal", buf);
57         for (; optind < argc; optind++) {
58             pid = atoi (argv [optind]);
59             if (kill (pid, sig) == -1)
60                 err_ret ("Can't kill PID %d", pid);
61         }
62     }
63     return (0);
64 }
```
signals/ssp_kill.c

Program 17.29 Our implementation of the `kill` command.

```
$ ./ssp_kill -s TERM 1 2 3 4 20892
Can't kill PID 1: Not owner
Can't kill PID 2: Not owner
Can't kill PID 3: Not owner
Can't kill PID 4: No such process
$                                         Type Return
[1] + Terminated              sleep 30 &
```

Notice that we had to wrap the list of signals so that they would fit on the page. Also note that because we're not running as a privileged user, we can't kill processes we don't own.

17.32 Summary

This has been a long chapter, and we've covered a lot of material. We started by describing the signal mechanism's concepts and each signal in turn. Then we described the problems with the older, unreliable, signal implementations and how they manifest themselves. Armed with this knowledge, we discussed the POSIX reliable signal mechanism and its many related functions.

Next we showed how we could implement various functions that have an interaction with signals, including `abort`, `sleep`, and `system`. We finished our discussion about signals by describing job control signals, software signals, alternate signal stacks, and system signal messages.

Exercises

17.1 What happens if we remove the `for (;;)` loop from Program 17.1? Why does this happen?

17.2 Draw pictures of the stack frames when Program 17.7 is executing.

17.3 Write a set of functions that allow a process to set any number of timers. Use only a single timer, using either `alarm` or `setitimer`.

17.4 If we set the `SA_SIGINFO` flag using `sigaction`, one of the items of information we are passed is the real user ID of the sending process. Why isn't the effective user ID passed?

17.5 In our implementation of the `abort` function (Program 17.20), why do we go to the trouble of setting the disposition of `SIGABRT` and sending ourselves that signal instead of just calling `_exit`?

17.6 Modify the `print_proc_mask` function from Program 17.11 so that it is not so verbose (in other words, replace the repeated `if` statements with something more elegant).

18

Daemon Processes

18.1 Introduction

Daemons are processes that run for a long time. Often, they are started when the system is booted and terminate only when the system shuts down. Daemons run in the background and have no controlling terminal (in fact, they are typically not associated with *any* terminal). Solaris has a large number of daemons that perform day-to-day activities; the exact number depends on which release of Solaris is in use, the set of packages installed, and which daemons have been disabled by the system administrator for security purposes.

The reason why daemons run independently of any terminals is so that we can start them from a terminal, but be able to use that terminal for other tasks. We don't want the daemon's output appearing on our terminal, nor do we want any interrupt signals we type to affect it. We also want the daemon to continue running after we have logged out and not interfere with the next user of our terminal. We could just start our daemon in the background by ending the command line with an ampersand, but daemons should automatically put themselves into the background and also disassociate themselves from any terminal.

There are a number of ways a daemon can be started:

1. When the system boots, many daemons are started by scripts (called run control scripts, or just rc scripts) in /etc/init.d, which are linked to from the directories /etc/rc?.d. Examples of the daemons started in this manner include the mail server, sendmail; the automounter, automountd; and the inetd superserver.

2. The majority of network service daemons are started by the inetd superserver. This daemon, which is itself started by one of the start-up scripts we mentioned

previously, listens for connection requests for the services specified in its configuration file (e.g., finger, FTP, TELNET, and so on). When one of these requests arrives, `inetd` invokes the correct daemon to deal with the request.

3. The `cron` daemon is used to execute programs on a regular basis; these programs are run as daemons. Like the `inetd` superserver, the `cron` daemon is started by one of the rc scripts we mentioned previously.

4. If we want to run a job at one time in the future, we use the `at` command to arrange for this to happen. The `cron` daemon facilitates these so-called "at jobs", so when their time comes to run, they run as daemons.

5. As we alluded to earlier, daemons can be started by a user at a terminal. These invocations can run the daemon either in the foreground or the background, and is often done when a daemon is being tested or restarted after it has terminated for some reason.

In this chapter we'll take a look at the characteristics of daemons, how to write them, and how we can perform error logging, given that a daemon has no controlling terminal.

18.2 Characteristics of Daemons

Let's take a look at some of the daemons that run on a typical Solaris system and see how they relate to the concepts of process groups, controlling terminals, and sessions we discussed in Chapter 16. We'll use the command

```
ps -efjc
```

to show the information we need for our discussion. The options for the `ps` command that we've selected list information about all processes (`-e`), generate a full listing (`-f`), print the session ID and process group ID (`-j`), and display the scheduler properties (`-c`).

Running the `ps` command on one of the author's systems gives the following:

```
$ ps -efjc
   UID   PID  PPID  PGID   SID  CLS  TTY  CMD
  root     0     0     0     0  SYS  ?    sched
  root     1     0     0     0   TS  ?    /etc/init -
  root     2     0     0     0  SYS  ?    pageout
  root     3     0     0     0  SYS  ?    fsflush
  root   237     1   237   237   TS  ?    /usr/lib/saf/sac -t 300
  root   460     1   460   460   TS  ?    /usr/sbin/nscd
  root   104     1   104   104   TS  ?    /usr/sbin/rpcbind
  root   125     1   125   125   TS  ?    /usr/sbin/inetd -s
  root   162     1   162   162   TS  ?    /usr/sbin/syslogd
  root   240   237   237   237   TS  ?    /usr/lib/saf/ttymon
  root   175     1   175   175   TS  ?    /usr/sbin/cron
```

We've shown only the first few processes, and we've removed three columns that are not important to our discussion: the priority of the process (PRI), the start time of the process (STIME), and the process' cumulative execution time (TIME). In order, the columns we show are: the user ID, the process ID, the parent process ID, the process group ID, the session ID, the scheduling class, the controlling terminal, and the command string.

Processes 0, 1, 2, and 3 are the ones we described in Section 15.2. The scheduling class of most of these processes is SYS, which means that they are system process. The only exception is process 1, init, which is in the TS (time sharing) scheduling class. We show this to emphasize the fact that despite its being "hand crafted" by process 0 when the system boots, there is nothing inherently special about init.

As for the other daemons we've shown, sac is the service access controller, which, together with ttymon, monitors terminal lines for attempted logins. The name service cache daemon, nscd, provides a cache for the most common name service requests. RPC program numbers are converted to universal addresses by rpcbind. We discussed inetd in Section 16.3; it listens for incoming requests for various network services. The syslogd daemon can be used by any process to log messages to the console, a file, or even in an email. We describe the syslog facility in Section 18.5. Finally, cron is the daemon responsible for running programs regularly.

Notice that all the daemons run as root. The only exception to this in a default Solaris installation is one we don't list, statd, which runs as the user daemon. Other applications might install daemons that also don't run with superuser privileges.

None of the daemons has a controlling terminal (as indicated by the question mark in the TTY column); this is most likely because of the daemon calling setsid. With the exception of init, sac, and ttymon, all the daemons are process group leaders and session leaders; they are also the only processes in their process group and session. The init process is in the same session and process group as the system processes, whereas sac and ttymon are in the same process group and session, with sac being the session leader.

Finally, with the exception of ttymon, all of these daemons have init as their parent.

18.3 Error Logging

One of the problems with daemons is how to log error messages. We can't simply write to standard error like we would in a normal interactive program, because daemons have no controlling terminal. Each daemon could write its errors to a separate log file, but the number of files would quickly become burdensome on a system that runs many daemons. Having each daemon write its errors to the console is also problematic; the console on many systems is used as a GUI desktop, and as there is no persistent storage, messages will be lost once they scroll off the screen. Also, because neither of these two solutions allow for centralized logging, some sort of daemon logging facility is required; Solaris provides two such facilities.

18.4 The STREAMS log Driver

The first of the logging facilities provided by Solaris is the STREAMS log driver. It has interfaces for STREAMS error logging, STREAMS event tracing, and console logging. It is the facility by which kernel-based STREAMS modules and drivers log their error messages (although the details of this are beyond the scope of this text), and can be used by user processes to log their errors (although the syslog facility we discuss next is usually used). Figure 18.1 depicts the overall structure of this facility.

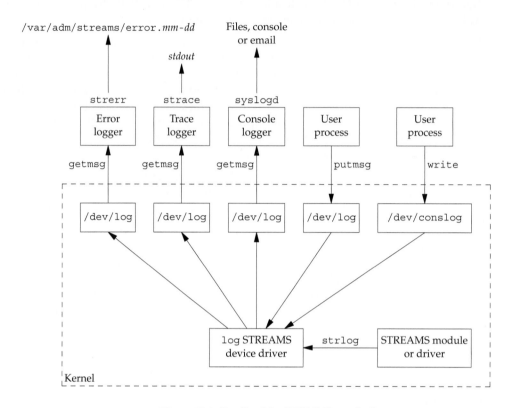

Figure 18.1   Details of the STREAMS log facility.

Each log message generated is destined for one of the three loggers: the error logger, the trace logger, or the console logger. If we want to send a log to more than one logger, we must send it to each logger separately.

Figure 18.1 shows that there are three ways to generate a log message:

1. Functions in the kernel can call strlog to generate messages. This is primarily used by STREAMS modules and drivers to generate error messages or trace messages (the latter are often used to aid in the debugging of STREAMS modules and drivers). Kernel programming is beyond the scope of this text, so we won't discuss the strlog function or this type of message generation any further.

2. User processes (including daemons) can putmsg to /dev/log. The message can be sent to any of the three loggers.

3. User processes (including daemons) can write to /dev/conslog. The message is only sent to the console logger.

Each log message contains other information apart from the message itself. Messages sent upstream from the log driver contain information about what generated the message (if the message was generated by a STREAMS module or driver), a level, some flags, and the time the message was generated; the log(7d) man page has all the details. As we'll see in the examples, we can set some of these fields if we're generating a message using putmsg, but if we're calling write to write to a message to the console logger (through /dev/conslog), then we can send only a message string.

If the appropriate type of logger isn't running when a log message of a given type is generated, the log driver silently discards the message.

Log messages are stored in a log_ctl structure, which has the following members:

```
struct log_ctl {
    short    mid;       /* STREAMS module ID */
    short    sid;       /* Internal sub ID */
    char     level;     /* Tracing level */
    short    flags;     /* Flags */
    clock_t  ltime;     /* Generation time in ticks since boot */
    time_t   ttime;     /* Generation time in secs since the epoch */
    int      seq_no;    /* Sequence number */
    int      pri;       /* Priority */
};
```

A fully populated log_ctl structure is delivered to a logger process, but when we generate a log message, we can specify only the level and flags members (the others are automatically filled in for us). The level member is an application-specific number used to determine the level for tracing. The flags member is made up of a bitwise-OR of one or more of the following:

SL_FATAL	Indicates a fatal error has occurred.
SL_NOTIFY	The logger must notify the system administrator.
SL_ERROR	Include the generated log message in the error log.
SL_TRACE	Include the generated log message in the trace log.
SL_CONSOLE	Include the generated log message in the console log.
SL_WARN	Generate a warning message.
SL_NOTE	Generate a notice message.

We'll see an example of how we can use the flags further on.

Figure 18.1 also shows three ways to read log messages:

1. The usual error logger is strerr. It appends the messages it receives to a file in /var/adm/streams. The name of the file is error.*mm -dd*, where *mm* and *dd* are the month and day of the month the message was generated respectively.

2. The usual trace logger is strace. It can selectively write trace messages to its standard output. Using strace is where being able to specify the level member of the log_ctl structure comes in handy.

3. The standard console logger is syslogd, which we describe in the next section.

Although we don't show it in Figure 18.1, we can replace any or all of these standard programs with ones that we write ourselves. Doing so requires our process to register itself with the /dev/log device as a logger using the ioctl function. Log messages are then read from /dev/log by using the getmsg function.

Example: Logging to the STREAMS error log

Program 18.1 demonstrates how we can generate a message for the trace and STREAMS error logs.

daemons/genlog.c

```
 1 #include <stdio.h>
 2 #include <sys/types.h>
 3 #include <sys/stat.h>
 4 #include <fcntl.h>
 5 #include <stropts.h>
 6 #include <sys/strlog.h>
 7 #include <sys/stream.h>
 8 #include <sys/log.h>
 9 #include <string.h>
10 #include "ssp.h"

11 int main (void)
12 {
13     int fd;
14     struct strbuf control;
15     struct strbuf data;
16     struct log_ctl log;
17     char *message = "Danger Will Robinson!";

18     if ((fd = open ("/dev/log", O_WRONLY)) == -1)
19         err_msg ("Can't open /dev/log");

20     control.maxlen = sizeof (log);
21     control.len = sizeof (log);
22     control.buf = (caddr_t) &log;

23     data.maxlen = strlen (message);
24     data.len = strlen (message);
25     data.buf = message;

26     log.level = 42;
27     log.flags = SL_TRACE | SL_ERROR | SL_FATAL;

28     if (putmsg (fd, &control, &data, 0) == -1)
29         err_msg ("putmsg failed");

30     return (0);
31 }
```

daemons/genlog.c

Program 18.1 Generating a log message.

Open /dev/log

18–19 Open /dev/log; because we will only be generating a log message, we open the device in write-only mode.

Initialize STREAMS message control information

20–22 Set the size and the maximum size of the control portion of the message to be equal to the size of a log_ctl structure, and make the control buffer point to that structure.

Initialize STREAMS message data

23–25 Set the size and the maximum size of the data part of the message to be equal to the length of the message string, and make the data buffer point to the message string.

Initialize the log_ctl structure

26 Set the log level to 42. This is just some random number we've chosen.

27 Set the flags. Setting the SL_TRACE and the SL_ERROR flags means that our message should be logged whether we use strerr or strace as the logger. We set the fatal flag so that we can see its effect on the logger's output.

Log the message

28–29 Send the message we've just generated to the logging device by calling putmsg.

Let's start the error logger, strerr, and run Program 18.1.

```
$ su
Password:
# /usr/sbin/strerr &                    Start the error logger in the background
2321
# ./genlog
# cat /var/adm/streams/error.05-17
000005 17:35:01 0adb9f92 F.T 44 0 Danger Will Robinson!
# kill 2321
2321 Terminated
# $                                     Type Control-D to exit superuser shell
```

The output of the error logger has seven fields: the sequence number (our message was the fifth one generated since this machine was booted), the time this record was generated, the time in the number of clock ticks since the machine was booted that this message was generated (expressed as a hexadecimal number), some flags (the F means that the error was marked as fatal, and the T means that the message was also sent to the trace log), the module ID and sub-ID numbers of the source that generated the message, and finally, our message that we wanted logged.

Note that we must run strerr and our program as root. This is because of the permissions on /dev/log, which is writable only by root or members of the group sys. The need to run as root (or at the very least, in the group sys) might explain why the STREAMS log driver isn't frequently used by user code; the syslog facility we discuss next is much more prevalent.

18.5   The `syslog` Facility

The `syslog` facility has been widely used since 4.2BSD. Most Solaris daemons use this facility, eschewing the STREAMS `log` driver we described in the previous section. (Directly at least; the Solaris implementation of the `syslog` facility internally uses the STREAMS `log` driver.) Figure 18.2 shows the overall structure of this facility.

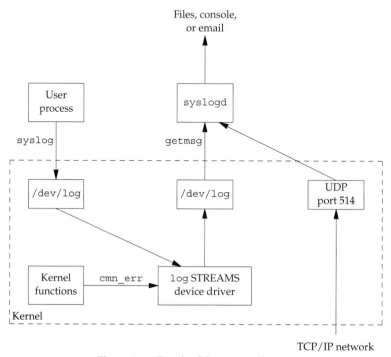

Figure 18.2   Details of the `syslog` facility.

Figure 18.2 shows three sources of log messages:

1. Functions in the kernel can call `cmn_err` to generate messages. There are also other functions that are used by kernel routines to generate log message, including `printf` and `strlog`, which we discussed in the previous section. Unlike its standard I/O library namesake, the kernel resident version of `printf` does not write to standard output (such a concept is meaningless in the kernel); instead, formatted messages are passed to `syslogd` for dissemination as appropriate. Kernel programming is beyond the scope of this text, so we won't discuss this method of message generation any further.

2. User processes (including daemons) can call the `syslog` function to generate a log message (we describe the arguments to this function below). This causes `putmsg` to be called, which sends a message to to the `log` driver, `/dev/log`.

3. Remote (or local) user processes can send a log message to UDP (User Datagram Protocol) port 514. Note that the `syslog` function never generates these UDP

datagrams itself. They must be sent either explicitly by the application generating the log message using network programming, or implicitly by configuring the syslogd daemon to forward them to a remote syslog server.

For security reasons, some versions of the syslogd daemon, including the one supplied with Solaris, can be configured not to listen for these remote UDP datagrams. This disables syslogd's ability to log remote messages, but also prevents attacks through that channel.

The syslog.conf man page describes how to configure the syslogd configuration file, and [Stevens, Fenner, and Rudoff 2004] contains details on UNIX network programming.

Each syslog message has an associated facility and severity that determine its disposition. The *facility* gives an indication of the application or system component generating the message (e.g., the authentication subsystem, the cron daemon, or the mail subsystem), and the *severity* is an indication of how critical the message is.

There are 18 different facilities:

LOG_AUTH	This is used by messages from the authentication subsystem, e.g., login, su, and ttymon.
LOG_CRON	This is used by messages from the cron and at subsystem: crontab, at, and cron.
LOG_DAEMON	This is used by messages from system daemons, like in.ftpd and xntpd.
LOG_KERN	This is used by messages generated by the kernel. These cannot be generated by user processes; attempts to do so will result in the facility being changed to LOG_USER.
LOG_LOCAL0	This is reserved for local use.
LOG_LOCAL1	This is reserved for local use.
LOG_LOCAL2	This is reserved for local use.
LOG_LOCAL3	This is reserved for local use.
LOG_LOCAL4	This is reserved for local use.
LOG_LOCAL5	This is reserved for local use.
LOG_LOCAL6	This is reserved for local use.
LOG_LOCAL7	This is reserved for local use.
LOG_LPR	This is used by messages generated by the line printer spooling system (e.g., lp, lpr, and lpc).
LOG_MAIL	This is used by messages generated by the mail subsystem (e.g., sendmail and mail.local).
LOG_NEWS	This is reserved for messages generated by the Usenet network news system.
LOG_SYSLOG	This is used by messages generated internally by syslogd.

`LOG_USER`	This is used by messages generated by other user processes. This is the default facility used if none is specified.
`LOG_UUCP`	This is reserved for messages generated by the UUCP (UNIX to UNIX copy) system (which doesn't currently use `syslog`).

There are eight different severity levels. In order, they are:

`LOG_EMERG`	An emergency condition exists; the system is unusable. This is the highest severity.
`LOG_ALERT`	A condition exists that must be fixed immediately, such as a corrupted system database.
`LOG_CRIT`	A critical condition exists (for example, a hard device error).
`LOG_ERR`	This is used for noncritical error conditions.
`LOG_WARNING`	This is used to issue warnings.
`LOG_NOTICE`	This is used to note normal, but significant, conditions.
`LOG_INFO`	This is used to log informational messages.
`LOG_DEBUG`	This is used to generate messages that are normally only of use when debugging a program. This is the lowest severity.

The interface to the `syslog` facility is through four functions: `openlog`, `syslog`, `closelog`, and `setlogmask`.

```
#include <syslog.h>

void openlog (const char *ident, int logopt, int facility);

void syslog (int priority, const char *message, /* arguments */...);

void closelog (void);

int setlogmask (int maskpri);
```
                                                      Returns: previous log priority mask

The `openlog` function is optionally used to initialize the process attributes that affect subsequent calls to `syslog`. The *ident* argument is prepended to each generated message. This is usually the name of the program, for example, `in.ftpd` or `xntpd`.

The *logopt* argument specifies the logging options, if any. Values for *logopt* are made up from a bitwise-OR of zero or more of the following constants:

`LOG_CONS`	Write log messages to the system console if they can't be sent to `syslogd`. This option is safe to use in daemons that have no controlling terminal, because `syslog` forks a new process before opening the console.
`LOG_NDELAY`	Open the connection to `syslogd` immediately. Normally, the connection isn't opened until the first message is logged. This

option is useful for programs that need to manage the allocation order of their file descriptors.

LOG_NOWAIT
Don't wait for child processes that have been forked to log messages to the system console. This option should be used only by processes that enable notification of child termination using SIGCHLD. This is because syslog may otherwise block, waiting for a child whose exit status has already been reaped.

LOG_ODELAY
Delay opening the connection to syslogd until syslog is called. This option can safely be omitted, because delaying the opening of the connection is the default behaviour. If this flag and LOG_NDELAY are specified, the latter takes precedence.

LOG_PID
Log the process ID of the calling process with each message. This is useful for identifying the specific instance of a daemon that logged a message when the daemon forks a child to handle different requests.

The *facility* argument specifies the default facility to be assigned to all messages that don't already have their own facility explicitly assigned to them. It must be one of the values we described previously. The initial default facility is LOG_USER.

The closelog function merely closes any file descriptors allocated by previous calls to openlog or syslog. Calling this function is optional, but it is good programming practice to do so once we have finished using the syslog facility.

The syslog function sends a message to syslogd, which dispatches it according to its configuration file, /etc/syslog.conf.

The *priority* argument is formed by bitwise-ORing one of the facilities we described previously with with one of the severities we described previously. If the facility part is omitted, then the default one established with openlog will be used.

The *message* and *arguments* arguments define the actual message that is logged; *message* is interpreted in the same way as a format string to printf would be, except that occurrences of %m in the format string will be replaced by the error message string associated with the current value of errno.

The setlogmask function sets the log priority mask for the calling process to *maskpri*. If *maskpri* is equal to 0, then the current log priority mask is not changed. Once a log mask is established, calls by the current process to syslog with a severity not set in *maskpri* will be silently ignored.

There are two macros that help us calculate values for *maskpri*: LOG_MASK and LOG_UPTO. The mask for an individual severity is given by

    LOG_MASK (*pri*)

and the mask for all severities up to and including *toppri* is given by

    LOG_UPTO (*toppri*)

The default log mask allows all severities to be logged.

Example: Demonstrating the `syslog` facility

Program 18.2 shows an example of how we could use the `syslog` facility.

―― *daemons/syslog.c*

```
 1 #include <syslog.h>

 2 int main (void)
 3 {
 4     openlog ("ssp", LOG_CONS | LOG_PID, LOG_USER);

 5     syslog (LOG_ALERT, "Before changing log mask");
 6     syslog (LOG_ERR, "Before changing log mask");

 7     setlogmask (LOG_MASK (LOG_ERR));

 8     syslog (LOG_ALERT, "After changing log mask");
 9     syslog (LOG_ERR, "After changing log mask");

10     closelog ();

11     return (0);
12 }
```

―― *daemons/syslog.c*

Program 18.2   Using the `syslog` facility.

Open the connection to `syslogd`

4 Open the connection to `syslogd`, using "ssp" as our identifier, and set the options that will log the process ID of our process with each message and log to the console if we can't connect to `syslogd`. We also set the default facility to be LOG_USER.

Generate two log messages

5–6 We generate two log messages at different priorities to show the effect of the `setlogmask` function. If we had not performed the `openlog`, we could have written these lines like this:

```
syslog (LOG_USER | LOG_ALERT, "Before changing logmask");
```

Here we specify the *priority* argument as a combination of a facility and a severity. Note that if we did this, the LOG_CONS and LOG_PID options would not be in effect.

Change the process log mask

7 Call `setlogmask` so that only messages whose severity is equal to LOG_ERR are logged.

Generate two more log messages

8–9 We generate another two messages at different priorities to show the effect of the different process log mask on logging.

Close the connection to `syslogd`

10 We've finished using the `syslog` facility, so we close our connection to `syslogd`.

Let's run Program 18.2 and see what happens:

```
$ ./syslog
$ tail /var/adm/messages
```

```
May 22 11:41:13 zaphod ssp[15876]: [ID 675410 user.alert] Before
    changing log mask
May 22 11:41:13 zaphod ssp[15876]: [ID 675410 user.error] Before
    changing log mask
May 22 11:41:13 zaphod ssp[15876]: [ID 903760 user.error] After
    changing log mask
```

(We've had to wrap some lines so that they'd fit on to the page.) The contents of /var/adm/messages clearly shows that despite being a higher priority, the second LOG_ALERT message is not sent to syslogd.

If we're using a default /etc/syslog.conf, these three lines are also printed on the console.

The functions we've just described are fine for use in C programs, but what about shell scripts? Fortunately, Solaris provides us with the logger utility, which enables noninteractive shell scripts to send log messages to the syslog facility. The logger command allows us to specify the same information that is given by the *ident*, *facility*, and *priority* arguments to the openlog and syslog functions.

18.6 Becoming a Daemon

We must follow a number of rules when becoming a daemon. Some are mandatory, and some are optional. The exact set of rules we need to follow depends on whether our program is a standalone daemon or one that is started from inetd. Our job is easier if our daemon is being started by inetd, because inetd takes care of most of the work. We've written a function called daemon_init to handle all the details.

```
#include "ssp.h"

void daemon_init (const char *prog_name, int inetd);
```

The *prog_name* argument is passed to the openlog function as its first argument, and *inetd* is a flag that the caller should set to 0 if we are a standalone daemon (i.e., we were not invoked by inetd).

Program 18.3 shows the implementation of our function. It can be used by standalone daemons or those started by inetd.

The first four steps of becoming a daemon are not performed if daemon_init is told that the process was started by inetd. We do this by calling daemon_init with the *inetd* argument set to a non-zero value.

Create the first child

16–19 The first thing we do is call fork and have the parent terminate. If the process was started from the command line, this will cause the shell to think that the command has finished. Meanwhile, the child continues to execute in the background. The child inherits the process group ID from its parent, but gets its own unique process ID. This ensures that the child is not a process group leader, which is a prerequisite for a successful call to setsid.

daemons/daemon_init.c

```
 1 #include <sys/types.h>
 2 #include <unistd.h>
 3 #include <stdlib.h>
 4 #include <sys/stat.h>
 5 #include <fcntl.h>
 6 #include <sys/resource.h>
 7 #include <syslog.h>
 8 #include "ssp.h"

 9 extern int daemon_proc;

10 void daemon_init (const char *prog_name, int inetd)
11 {
12     pid_t pid;
13     int fd;
14     struct rlimit limits;

15     if (!inetd) {
16         if ((pid = fork ()) == -1)
17             err_msg ("fork failed");
18         else if (pid != 0)
19             _exit (0);

20         setsid ();

21         if ((pid = fork ()) == -1)
22             exit (1);
23         else if (pid != 0)
24             _exit (0);

25         close (0);
26         fd = open ("/dev/null", O_RDWR);
27         dup2 (fd, 1);
28         dup2 (fd, 2);
29     }

30     daemon_proc = 1;

31     getrlimit (RLIMIT_NOFILE, &limits);
32     if (limits.rlim_cur < limits.rlim_max)
33         limits.rlim_cur = limits.rlim_max;
34     setrlimit (RLIMIT_NOFILE, &limits);

35     for (fd = 3; fd <= limits.rlim_cur; fd++)
36         close (fd);

37     chdir ("/");

38     umask (0);

39     openlog (prog_name, LOG_PID, LOG_DAEMON);
40 }
```

daemons/daemon_init.c

Program 18.3 Our daemon_init function.

Create a new session

20 The first child calls `setsid` to create a new session. This causes the calling process to become the new session leader and the process group leader of a new process group, and to have no controlling terminal (we talked about sessions and process groups in Chapter 16).

Create the second child

21–24 We call `fork` again to create a second-generation child (a grandchild, so to speak). The parent (the first child) terminates, leaving the second child running. The reason why we call `fork` again is to guarantee that our daemon can't automatically acquire a controlling terminal should it open a terminal device some time in the future. Recall from our discussion in Section 16.6 that when a session leader without a controlling terminal opens a terminal device that is not currently the controlling terminal for some other session, that terminal becomes the controlling terminal for that session. By calling `fork` a second time, we guarantee that our daemon is no longer a session leader, so it can't acquire a controlling terminal. If we were to omit this step, then we would have to specify the `O_NOCTTY` flag whenever we open a terminal device. Performing the second `fork` relieves us of this burden.

Establish file descriptors for standard input, standard output, and standard error

25–28 We first close file descriptor 0 (standard input), and then open `/dev/null` for reading and writing. Because we've just closed file descriptor 0, we are guaranteed that that file descriptor will be used when we open `/dev/null` (i.e., standard input will be associated with `/dev/null`). We then duplicate the resulting file descriptor to descriptors 1 and 2 (standard output and standard error respectively) so that all three refer to `/dev/null`. (If either of these descriptors is already open, `dup2` will close them before duplicating descriptor 0.) By doing this, we guarantee that a read from any of these descriptors returns 0 (EOF), and that writes to them will be discarded by the kernel. We do this so that any library function called by our daemon that assumes that it can read from standard input, or write to standard output or standard error, will not fail.

Some daemons do not perform this step, perhaps opening a log file and duplicating the resulting descriptor to standard input and standard output. Also, daemons invoked by `inetd` should *not* perform this step (or any others up to this point). This is because `inetd` sets up standard input, standard output, and standard error to refer to the network connection, and also performs the necessary `fork`ing and session manipulation for us. We handle this in our `daemon_init` function by only performing the preceding steps if the *inetd* argument is 0.

Set the flag for our error functions

30 We set the global variable, `daemon_proc`, to a non-zero value. This variable is used by our error logging functions; if its value is not zero, the error logging functions call `syslog` to log the message rather than `fprintf`. This saves us from having two sets of logging functions (one for use by daemons and another for use by non-daemons) and also means we don't need to make any changes when our program is not being run as a daemon (when we're testing it, for example).

Close any open file descriptors

31–34 Get the current hard and soft number of file descriptor limits. If the soft limit is lower than the hard limit, we set the soft limit to be the same as the hard limit. We do this to make sure that the file descriptor limit is "high enough" for us to be able to close all open file descriptors.

35–36 In a loop, we close all open file descriptors, apart from the first three. We skip these because we've already dealt with them (either implicitly if we are being invoked by inetd, or explicitly if we're not). Most of the file descriptors we try to close are not likely to be open. Unfortunately, there is no easy way we can determine the number of the highest open file descriptor. The only method we could use would be to look for the highest number in /proc/self/fd, which is probably more effort that it's worth (see Exercise 18.4).

If we don't mind restricting our daemon to Solaris 9 and newer, we can replace lines 31 to 36 inclusive with a call to closefrom, like this:

```
closefrom (3);
```

Change the current working directory

37 We change directory to the root directory, which ensures that our daemon doesn't keep any directories in use. If we didn't do this, we would not be able to unmount the directory from which we started the daemon, as it will be busy for the lifetime of the daemon process. Rather than changing to the root directory, some daemons change to a directory that is important to their operation. For example, a DNS server might change to the directory in which its configuration files are stored, or a printer daemon might change to its spool directory. Should a daemon ever produce a core file, it will be created in its current directory, unless (on Solaris 8 and newer) we've used the coreadm command to modify this behaviour.

Clear the file mode creation mask

38 We set the file mode creation mask to 0 so that if the daemon creates any files, the permission bits will be set as expected (i.e., the file mode creation mask the daemon inherits from its parent does not affect the permissions bits of the new files).

Use the syslog facility for errors

39 The last thing we do is call openlog to initialize the syslog facility. The first argument is set by the caller of daemon_init and is usually the name of the program (e.g., argv [0]). We specify that the daemon's process ID should be added to each logged message, and that we're using the LOG_DAEMON facility.

Because daemons have no controlling terminal, they should never receive a SIGHUP signal from the kernel. For this reason, many daemons use this signal as a notification that their configuration file has changed (by the system administrator) and should be reloaded. Two other signals a daemon should never receive are SIGINT and SIGWINCH, so we can also use these to notify our daemon of an event.

Example: Testing our `daemon_init` function

Program 18.4 demonstrates the use of our `daemon_init` function.

————————————————————————————— daemons/test_daemon.c

```
1 #include <unistd.h>
2 #include "ssp.h"

3 int main (int argc, char **argv)
4 {
5     daemon_init (argv [0], 0);
6     pause ();

7     return (0);
8 }
```

————————————————————————————— daemons/test_daemon.c

Program 18.4   Testing our `daemon_init` function.

Program 18.4 is trivial; it merely calls our `daemon_init` function to become a daemon, and then waits for us to send it a signal by calling `pause`. When a signal is received, the daemon will terminate. Let's run Program 18.4 and verify that it has indeed become a daemon:

```
$ ./test_daemon
$ ps -efjc
    UID    PID  PPID  PGID    SID  CLS  TTY  CMD
    rich 19677     1 19676  19676   IA   ?     ./test_daemon
```

As before, we've removed the three columns that don't interest us, and we've deleted all other processes except the one we're testing. The `ps` output shows that our daemon has been initialized correctly.

18.7   Starting One Copy of a Daemon

Sometimes we want only one copy of a program to be running, and this is frequently a requirement of a daemon.

> Note that we're drawing a distinction between running only one copy of a program, and having only one instance of a program. Many daemons (e.g., the Apache daemon, `httpd`) cause several instances of themselves to run even though they allow only one copy to be started. What we're discussing in this section is writing a program that can be run only one copy at a time regardless of how many instances that one copy makes of itself.

There are a number of ways we can ensure that only one copy of a program is running; we can use a semaphore, use a door, we can use a lock file, or we can acquire a lock on a file that's specific to our program.

The difference between the last two is that a lock file implies a lock just by its very existence, whereas the latter requires that we lock the file using one of the locking mechanisms we discussed in Section 13.4. The problem with using a lock file is that they can cause false positives. If the process that created the lock file abruptly terminates without being able to remove the lock file (e.g., the process might have been sent a SIGKILL signal), then the lock file will still exist the next time we try to run the program.

Abrupt termination is not a problem if we lock a file, because when a process terminates, all its locks are automatically released. We've written a function called one_copy to handle all these details for us.

```
#include "ssp.h"

int one_copy (const char *pid_file);
                            Returns: 1 if the caller is already running, 0 if it isn't, −1 on error
```

Program 18.5 shows the implementation of this function. The *pid_file* argument is the name of a file in which the caller's process ID will be placed should the program not already be running.

Open and lock a file

13–14 The first thing we do is attempt to open the file in which our process ID is to be stored, creating it if necessary. Note that the mere presence of the file is not enough to prove that the program is already running.

15–20 We attempt to acquire a write lock on the whole file, using the ssp_wlock function we wrote in Section 13.4. If the lock is not granted, it means that either an error occurred or another copy of the program is already running. We can discern between these two possibilities by testing the value of errno.

Write our process ID into the file

21–25 We truncate the file to 0 bytes, and then copy our process ID to a buffer. The reason why we truncate the file is that the process ID of the previous copy of the program might have more digits in it than our current process ID (i.e., the previous process ID might be 20175 and the current one might only be 42). If we just wrote the line without truncating the file, the contents of the file would be 42\n75\n instead of 42\n. Although the first line would still contain the correct process ID, it is cleaner and less confusing to avoid the second line by truncating the file before we write to it.

Set the close on exec flag

26–30 We set the close on exec flag, FD_CLOEXEC, for the process ID file's file descriptor. This is because there is no need for this file to remain open in child processes. This is especially pertinent in daemons, which often fork and exec new processes.

We can use both functions at the beginning of a daemon that should have only one copy running like this:

daemons/one_copy.c

```
 1 #include <stdio.h>
 2 #include <unistd.h>
 3 #include <sys/types.h>
 4 #include <sys/stat.h>
 5 #include <fcntl.h>
 6 #include <errno.h>
 7 #include "ssp.h"

 8 int one_copy (const char *pid_file)
 9 {
10     int fd;
11     char buf [20];
12     int num;

13     if ((fd = open (pid_file, O_WRONLY | O_CREAT, FILE_PERMS)) == -1)
14         return (-1);

15     if (ssp_wlock (fd, 0, SEEK_SET, 0) == -1) {
16         if ((errno == EACCES) || (errno == EAGAIN))
17             return (1);
18         else
19             return (-1);
20     }

21     if (ftruncate (fd, 0) == -1)
22         return (-1);

23     num = snprintf (buf, sizeof (buf), "%d\n", getpid ());
24     if (writen (fd, buf, num) == -1)
25         return (-1);

26     if ((num = fcntl (fd, F_GETFD, 0)) == -1)
27         return (-1);
28     num |= FD_CLOEXEC;
29     if ((num = fcntl (fd, F_SETFD, 0)) == -1)
30         return (-1);

31     return (0);
32 }
```

daemons/one_copy.c

Program 18.5 Our one_copy function.

```
daemon_init (argv [0], 0);

if ((res = one_copy ("/var/run/our_daemon.pid")) == -1)
    err_msg ("one_copy failed");

if (res == 1)
    err_quit ("%s: Already running\n", argv [0]);

/*
 * Rest of daemon code here
 */
```

Example: Testing our one_copy function

Program 18.6 demonstrates the use of our one_copy function.

daemons/only_one.c

```
 1 #include <stdio.h>
 2 #include <unistd.h>
 3 #include <stdlib.h>
 4 #include "ssp.h"

 5 int main (void)
 6 {
 7     int res;

 8     if ((res = one_copy ("/tmp/macleod")) == -1)
 9         err_msg ("one_copy failed");

10     if (res == 1) {
11         log_msg ("There can be only one!");
12         exit (1);
13     }

14     pause ();

15     return (0);
16 }
```

daemons/only_one.c

Program 18.6   Testing our one_copy function.

Program 18.6 is quite straightforward. It calls one_copy to check if it is already running. If the returned value is 1, it means that a copy of the program is already running, so a suitable message is printed. Otherwise, pause is called, suspending the process until a signal is delivered to it.

Running Program 18.6 gives us the following:

```
$ ./only_one &                          Start the first copy
[1]     1518
$ cat /tmp/macleod                      Check the PID written to the file
1518
$ ./only_one                            Try to run a second copy
There can be only one!
```

Note that in this example, we create the file we lock in /tmp. The usual place for these types of file is either /tmp, /etc, or, starting with Solaris 8, /var/run. From Solaris 8, the /var/run directory is actually implemented as a tmpfs file system that is writable only by root. (This is not as problematic as it may seem, because most daemons are started by root when the system boots.) The former means that /var/run has the advantage of being cleared automatically when the system is booted, and the latter prevents attacks via symbolic links.

18.8 Summary

Daemons are processes that run in the background all the time, independent of any terminals. Because they have no terminal to write diagnostics to, daemons usually log messages via the `syslog` facility, which is itself implemented as a daemon (`syslogd`). The system administrator has control over the disposition of these messages by tailoring the contents of `syslogd`'s configuration file, `/etc/syslog.conf`, as necessary. Log messages can be routed depending on their source and severity. We also discussed the STREAMS `log` device, which can also be used by daemons (but is more usually used by kernel resident code to log messages).

Writing a daemon takes some care and an understanding of the process relationships we discussed in Chapter 16. We described our implementation of a function, called `daemon_init`, which takes care of all the details for us: calling `fork` to run in the background, establishing a new session (by calling `setsid`) and becoming the session leader, `forking` again so as to avoid obtaining a controlling terminal in the future, closing all unnecessary files (making sure that standard input, standard output, and standard error refer to valid files), changing to the root directory so that our daemon doesn't make the file system from which it was started unmountable, and clearing the file mode creation mask.

Daemons are an example of programs that want only one copy (as opposed to one instance) of themselves running, so we wrote a function called `one_copy` that determines whether or not a copy of the caller is already running. It does this by attempting to acquire a write lock on the specified file. If the attempt succeeds, then the caller is the only copy of the program currently running.

Exercises

18.1 Figure 18.2 shows that when the `syslog` facility is used, the device file `/dev/log` has to be opened. What happens if the process using the `syslog` facility calls `chroot` before calling `openlog` or `syslog`?

18.2 Make a note of all the active daemons on your system and identify their purpose.

18.3 If we write a daemon that uses our `daemon_init` function, should the command line argument processing and error reporting appear before or after the call to `daemon_init`? What is the reason for your answer?

18.4 Write a function that returns the number of the highest open file descriptor. It should determine this by examining the `/proc` file system.

18.5 Can we use a technique similar to the one we used in Exercise 18.4 to close only the open file descriptors (as opposed to closing all file descriptors between 1 and the highest number, whether or not they refer to an open file)? What is the reason for your answer?

18.6 In Program 18.5 we call `ftruncate` to set the size of the file to 0 bytes. Why don't we instead just specify the `O_TRUNC` flag when we `open` the file?

18.7 In our pseudo code of a daemon that uses `daemon_init` and `one_copy` to ensure that only one copy of itself can run at a time, why do we perform the check for multiple copies after becoming a daemon rather than before?

Part 5

Interprocess Communication

19

Interprocess Communication Using Pipes and FIFOs

19.1 Introduction

We saw how to create multiple processes in Chapter 15. Apart from passing file descriptors across `fork` and `exec`, or using the file system, the only way these processes can communicate is by using signals, as we describe in Chapter 17. We'll now describe a number of other techniques processes can use to communicate with each other. These techniques are collectively called *interprocess communication*, or IPC.

There are four types of IPC: pipes and FIFOs, message queues, shared memory, and semaphores. Complicating this somewhat is the fact that there are two variants of the last three methods on this list. These variants are called System V IPC and POSIX IPC. We describe the use of pipes and FIFOs in this chapter, saving message queues, shared memory, and semaphores for the next chapter.

There are also some advanced IPC features, like file descriptor passing, which we discuss in Chapter 21.

The IPC we discuss in this text is restricted to two processes on the same host. Readers interested in communications between processes on different hosts (i.e., network programming) are referred to [Stevens, Fenner, and Rudoff 2004].

19.2 Pipes

The oldest and most widely available form of UNIX IPC are pipes. A problem with pipes is that they can be used only between processes that have a common ancestor. Normally, a pipe is created by a process, which then calls `fork`, and the pipe is used between the parent and the child.

Another problem that afflicts older implementations of pipes is that they are half duplex; data only flows in one direction. The pipes in Solaris (and other UNIX variants based on SVR4), being STREAMS based, are full duplex. POSIX pipes are also half duplex.

We'll see later how FIFOs can work around this limitation.

We create a pipe by calling the pipe function.

```
#include <unistd.h>

int pipe (int fildes [2]);
```
                                                                    Returns: 0 if OK, −1 on error

The pipe function creates a pipe, which is associated with two file descriptors, *fildes* [0] and *fildes* [1]. Both file descriptors refer to a stream (in the STREAMS sense of the word), both of which are open for reading and writing. The O_NDELAY, O_NONBLOCK, and FD_CLOEXEC flags for both descriptors are cleared.

A read from *fildes* [0] will access the data written by *fildes* [1] on a FIFO basis. Similarly, A read from *fildes* [1] will access the data written by *fildes* [0], also on a FIFO basis.

Figure 19.1 shows a conceptual picture of a pipe.

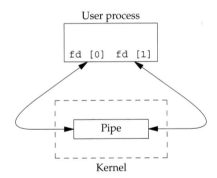

Figure 19.1 Conceptual representation of a pipe.

Half-duplex pipes are similar, except that the arrowhead going into the pipe from fd [0] would be removed, as would the one going into fd [1] from the pipe.

SVR4 pipes, including those in Solaris, are implemented using STREAMS. They are just two stream heads connected together, as shown in Figure 19.2. This means, as we'll show later, that we can push any STREAMS module onto either end of the pipe.

If we call the fstat function from Section 10.3 with the file descriptor of either end of the pipe as an argument, the type of the file associated with the file descriptor will be a FIFO. We can test for this using the S_ISFIFO macro. The size of the file is the number of bytes available for reading.

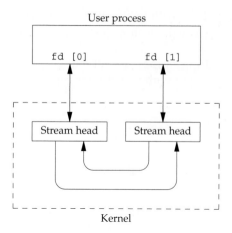

Figure 19.2 Arrangement of SVR4 STREAMS pipes.

With half-duplex pipes, the size returned by `fstat` for `fd [0]` (the read end) returned the number of bytes available for reading from that file descriptor, and the size returned by `fstat` for `fd [1]` (the write end) was also the number of bytes available for reading from `fd [0]`.

A pipe in a single process is not very useful, so the process that created the pipe usually calls `fork`. This creates an IPC channel between the parent and the child, and vice versa. Figure 19.3 shows the arrangement immediately after the call to `fork`.

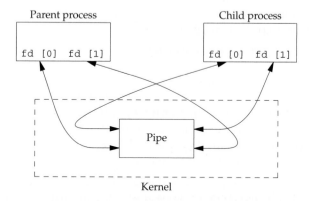

Figure 19.3 Arrangement of a pipe after `fork`.

However, we can't just leave things like this. If we did, then if the parent writes something to `fd [1]`, either the parent or the child would be able to read the data from `fd [0]`; which process will successfully read the data is indeterminate, unless the processes coordinate access to the pipe. Because it is unlikely that a process would want to read something it has just written, the parent and child usually close one of the file descriptors. The file descriptor closed must be different for each process; if the parent closes `fd [0]`, then the child must close `fd [1]`.

Figure 19.4 shows the resulting file descriptor arrangement. (Although it makes our diagram more complicated, closing the file descriptors like this (rather than closing fd [1] in the parent and fd [0] in the child) make our code portable to versions of UNIX that have only half-duplex pipes. Recall that with full-duplex pipes we can read or write from either descriptor, but with half-duplex pipes, we can only write to fd [1] and read from fd [0].)

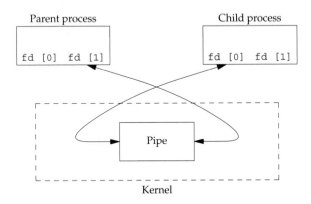

Figure 19.4 Arrangement of a pipe between parent and child.

If we're concerned about porting to a version of UNIX that only supports half-duplex pipes, then if we wanted to communicate from the child to the parent, we'd close fd [0] in the child and fd [1] in the parent.

We need to be aware of two rules when one end of a pipe is closed:

1. Reading from a pipe when the other end is not open for writing will return 0 (indicating end of file) after all data that was written by that end has been read. This rule applies no matter how many writers are associated with the other end, although it is normal for there to be only one reader and one writer for each pipe. (The exception to this, as we'll see in Section 19.5, is for FIFOs; it is not uncommon for a FIFO to have several writers.)

2. Writing to a pipe when the other end is not open for reading results in a SIGPIPE signal being generated for the writing process. The write function will fail, setting errno to EPIPE if this signal ignored or if it is being caught and the signal handler returns.

The constant PIPE_BUF specifies the maximum number of bytes that can be atomically written to a pipe (or FIFO). A write of PIPE_BUF bytes or less will not be interleaved with those from other processes. However, a write that exceeds PIPE_BUF bytes might be interleaved with data from other writers.

Example: Sending data from parent to child over a pipe

Program 19.1 shows how we can use a pipe to send data from one process to its child.

pipes_and_fifos/pipe.c

```
 1 #include <unistd.h>
 2 #include <sys/types.h>
 3 #include <sys/stat.h>
 4 #include <fcntl.h>
 5 #include <sys/wait.h>
 6 #include "ssp.h"

 7 int main (void)
 8 {
 9     int fd [2];
10     char buf [LINE_LEN];
11     ssize_t n;

12     if (pipe (fd) == -1)
13         err_msg ("pipe failed");

14     switch (fork ()) {
15         case -1:
16             err_msg ("fork failed");

17         case 0:
18             close (fd [1]);
19             n = read (fd [0], buf, LINE_LEN);
20             writen (STDOUT_FILENO, "Child reads: ", 13);
21             writen (STDOUT_FILENO, buf, 15);
22             _exit (0);

23         default:
24             close (fd [0]);
25             writen (fd [1], "Hello, World!\n", 15);
26             wait (NULL);
27             break;
28     }

29     return (0);
30 }
```

pipes_and_fifos/pipe.c

Program 19.1 Sending data from parent to child over a pipe.

Create the pipe

12–13 Call the `pipe` function to create the pipe.

Call `fork`

14–16 Call `fork` to create a child process.

Child process

18 Close the file descriptor we're not using.

19 Read from the pipe; the call to read will block until the parent writes something to the pipe.

20–22 Write the data we received from the parent process to standard output.

Parent process

24 Close the file descriptor we're not using.

25 Write a message to the pipe.

26 Wait for the child process to terminate.

Running Program 19.1 gives us the results we'd expect:

```
$ ./pipe
Child reads: Hello, World!
```

The previous example used read and write directly with the file descriptors returned by the pipe function. Although using pipes like this has its uses, it is often more useful to duplicate the pipe's file descriptors onto standard input or standard output. The child usually execs some other program, which either reads from or writes to the pipe. In fact, this is exactly the mechanism used by shells when we create a shell pipeline like the following:

```
cat foo | more
```

Example: Sending email through a pipe

Suppose we have a program that wants to send some email (for example, a monitoring program that sends an email to the system administrator when a service becomes unavailable). Rather than writing an SMTP engine to handle the transaction, it makes more sense to use an existing program. (SMTP is the Simple Mail Transfer Protocol, which is the standard protocol used to transfer email messages.) The program we'll use is sendmail; we could use other programs like mail or mailx, but these usually just talk to sendmail anyway. Also, some of the features they provide (for example, shell escapes) are undesirable from a security point of view.

For this example we'll build up the message we send in memory; another approach would be to specify the name of a file we want to send on the command line.

Program 19.2 shows the code for this example.

Initialize email message

16–26 Set up the email message we'll be sending. The empty string on line 18 is a place holder for the "To:" string we construct later in the program.

Determine the recipient of the mail

27–30 If the environment variable MAIL_USER is set, the recipient is set to its value. Otherwise, we call cuserid to determine the user name we logged in as. If cuserid returns a user

pipes_and_fifos/pipemail.c

```
 1  #include <stdio.h>
 2  #include <unistd.h>
 3  #include <stdlib.h>
 4  #include <sys/types.h>
 5  #include <sys/stat.h>
 6  #include <sys/wait.h>
 7  #include <string.h>
 8  #include "ssp.h"

 9  #define DEF_USER "root"

10  int main (void)
11  {
12      int fd [2];
13      char *user;
14      char buf [LINE_LEN];
15      int i;
16      char *msg [] = {
17          "From: Solaris Systems Programming <nobody@localhost>\n",
18          "",
19          "Subject: Test email from pipemail\n\n",
20          "Hi there,\n\n",
21          "This email was sent from the pipemail\n",
22          "program to show how to send data to an\n"
23          "external program through a pipe.\n\n",
24          "Bye.\n",
25          NULL
26      };

27      if ((user = getenv ("MAIL_USER")) == NULL) {
28          if ((user = cuserid (NULL)) == NULL)
29              user = DEF_USER;
30      }

31      snprintf (buf, LINE_LEN, "To: %s\n", user);
32      msg [1] = buf;

33      if (pipe (fd) == -1)
34          err_msg ("pipe failed");

35      switch (fork ()) {
36          case -1:
37              err_msg ("fork failed");

38          case 0:
39              close (fd [1]);
40              if (dup2 (fd [0], STDIN_FILENO) != STDIN_FILENO)
41                  err_msg ("dup to standard input failed");
42              close (fd [0]);

43              execl ("/usr/lib/sendmail", "sendmail", "-t", NULL);
44              err_msg ("Can't exec sendmail");

45          default:
46              close (fd [0]);
```

```
47                    for (i = 0; msg [i] != NULL; i++) {
48                        if (writen (fd [1], msg [i], strlen (msg [i])) == -1)
49                            err_msg ("Can't write to sendmail");
50                    }
51                    close (fd [1]);
52                    wait (NULL);
53                    break;
54            }
55        return (0);
56 }
```
                                                                    pipes_and_fifos/pipemail.c

Program 19.2 Sending email through a pipe.

name, the recipient is set to its value; if not, the recipient is set to the user defined by the `DEF_USER` manifest constant.

The use of an environment variable to override a hard coded default value is both common and useful.

31–32 Create the "To:" header and make the second line of the email message array point to it.

Create the pipe

34–34 Create the pipe we'll use to talk to sendmail.

Call `fork`

35–37 Call `fork` to create a child process.

Child process

39 Close the file descriptor we're not using.

40–41 Duplicate the pipe's other file descriptor to standard input. Anything written by the parent will be readable from the child's standard input.

42 Close the pipe's other file descriptor, as we don't need it after calling dup2.

43–44 Invoke the `sendmail` command to send the email. Notice that we pass the -t flag to `sendmail`; this tells it to read the message for the list of recipients.

Parent process

46 Close the file descriptor we're not using.

47–50 Write out each line of the message, including the headers, to the pipe.

51–54 Close the pipe's other file descriptor and wait for the child process to terminate.

Running Program 19.2, which must be run on a machine that is set up to send and receive email, gives results like the following:

```
$ ./pipemail
$ tail -13 /var/mail/rich
From: Solaris Systems Programming <nobody@rite-group.com>
To: rich@zen.rite-group.com
Subject: Test email from pipemail
Content-Length: 127
```

```
Hi there,

This email was sent from the pipemail
program to show how to send data to an
external program through a pipe.

Bye.
```

The amount of time it takes to deliver the message depends on the load of the email server.

Example: Synchronizing parent and child processes

Recall from Section 15.10 how we used six functions (ssp_tell_wait_init, ssp_wait_child, ssp_wait_parent, ssp_tell_child, ssp_tell_parent, and ssp_tell_wait_fin) to avoid race conditions by synchronizing parent and child processes. In Program 17.19 we show an implementation of these functions using signals. Program 19.3 shows an implementation using pipes.

The ssp_tell_wait_init function

6–15 Create two pipes: one to communicate from the parent to the child, and the other to communicate from the child to the parent. Figure 19.5 illustrates the arrangement.

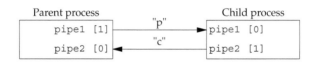

Figure 19.5 Arrangement of pipes for synchronizing parent and child processes.

Note that we must use two pipes in this situation. The full-duplex nature of pipes is of no use to us, as we want to make sure that the correct process reads from the pipe.

In this simple implementation, each pipe has an extra reader (which for clarity we don't show in Figure 19.5). This is OK, however, because each process tries to read from only one of the pipes. The child reads only from the first pipe, and the parent reads only from the second.

Notice that if an error occurs when we create either of these pipes, we only close the first pipe. This is because in the event of an error, the first pipe is the only one that has any possibility of being open: if an error occurs when creating the first pipe, we don't even attempt to create the second, and if we fail to create the second pipe, then its file descriptors are not open by definition.

The ssp_tell_child function

16–19 Write the character "p" to the pipe we're using to communicate from the parent to the child.

The ssp_tell_parent function

20–23 Write the character "c" to the pipe we're using to communicate from the child to the parent.

pipes_and_fifos/tell_wait.c

```
 1 #include <unistd.h>
 2 #include <sys/types.h>
 3 #include "ssp.h"

 4 static int pipe1 [2];
 5 static int pipe2 [2];

 6 int ssp_tell_wait_init (void)
 7 {
 8     if ((pipe (pipe1) == -1) || (pipe (pipe2) == -1)) {
 9         close (pipe1 [0]);
10         close (pipe1 [1]);
11         return (-1);
12     }
13     else
14         return (0);
15 }

16 int ssp_tell_child (pid_t pid)
17 {
18     return (writen (pipe1 [1], "p", 1));
19 }

20 int ssp_tell_parent (pid_t pid)
21 {
22     return (writen (pipe2 [1], "c", 1));
23 }

24 int ssp_wait_child (void)
25 {
26     char c;

27     if (read (pipe2 [0], &c, 1) == -1)
28         return (-1);

29     return ((c == 'c') ? 0 : -1);
30 }

31 int ssp_wait_parent (void)
32 {
33     char c;

34     if (read (pipe1 [0], &c, 1) == -1)
35         return (-1);

36     return ((c == 'p') ? 0 : -1);
37 }

38 int ssp_tell_wait_fin (void)
39 {
40     close (pipe1 [0]);
41     close (pipe1 [1]);
42     close (pipe2 [0]);
43     close (pipe2 [1]);

44     return (0);
45 }
```

pipes_and_fifos/tell_wait.c

Program 19.3 Functions that enable a child and parent to synchronize using pipes.

The ssp_wait_child function

24–30 Read a character from the pipe the child uses to communicate to the parent. The read blocks until data (from the child) is available. If the character isn't the one we're expecting (in this case, the letter "c"), return an error indication.

The ssp_wait_parent function

31–37 Read a character from the pipe the parent uses to communicate to the child. The read blocks until data (from the parent) is available. If the character isn't the one we're expecting (in this case, the letter "p"), return an error indication.

The ssp_tell_wait_fin function

38–45 We close both ends of both pipes.

We can test the code in Program 19.3 by linking it with Program 15.7 (we've had to wrap one of the lines so that it would fit onto the page):

```
$ make race2
cc -I../lib -D__EXTENSIONS__ -v -o race2 race2.c \
    ../pipes_and_fifos/tell_wait.o ../lib/ssp.a
$ ./race2
Hello from parent
Hello from child
```

19.3   The popen and pclose Functions

We saw in Section 15.13 how the convenience function, system, combined the use of fork and exec to invoke a program. An analogous pair of functions exists for pipes: popen and pclose.

```
#include <stdio.h>

FILE *popen (const char *command, const char *mode);

                                    Returns: file pointer if OK, NULL on error

int pclose (FILE *stream);

                        Returns: termination status of the shell if OK, −1 on error
```

The popen function creates a pipe between the calling process and the program specified by *command*. The calling process can either read from, or write to, the pipe, as determined by the *mode* argument. If *mode* is "r", we read from the pipe, which is connected to the standard output of *command*. We show this in Figure 19.6.

Figure 19.6 Result of fp = popen (*command*, "r").

Conversely, if *mode* is "w", we write to the pipe, which is connected to the standard input of *command*. We show this in Figure 19.7.

Figure 19.7 Result of `fp = popen (command, "w")`.

The *command* string is executed by a shell. This means that any shell metacharacters will be interpreted, allowing us to use wildcards like "*" and "?", as well as the redirection operators. Which shell executes *command* depends on whether the calling application is standards conforming. A nonconforming application uses the Bourne shell to invoke *command*:

```
execl ("/usr/bin/sh", "sh", "-c", command, NULL);
```

A conforming application uses `/usr/xpg4/bin/sh` to invoke *command*:

```
execl ("/usr/xpg4/bin/sh", "sh", "-c", command, NULL);
```

When we're finished with the stream created by `popen`, we must close it by calling `pclose`. This closes the pipe, waits for *command* to terminate, and returns the termination status of the shell, rather than that of *command*; this behaviour is the same as the `system` function we describe in Section 15.13.

Example: Sending email through a pipe

Let's rewrite Program 19.2 using `popen`. Program 19.4 shows the code, which is substantially less than when we used the `pipe` function.

With the exception of some header files, Program 19.4 is the same as Program 19.2 up to the point where we determine the email's recipient. Because of this, we'll only describe the code from Program 19.4 after the recipient has been determined.

Call popen

28–29 Call `popen` to invoke `sendmail`. Notice that we use "w" mode, because we'll be writing to the `sendmail` process.

Write out the email message

30–33 Write out each line of the email message, including the headers, to the stream connected to the `sendmail` process.

Close the pipe

34 Call `pclose`, which closes the pipe and reaps the status of the child process.

As we can see by comparing Program 19.2 and Program 19.4, using `popen` reduces the amount of code we have to write. However, as with the `system` function, this reduction is code quantity has a price: less flexibility, and potential security risks.

pipes_and_fifos/popenmail.c

```
 1 #include <stdio.h>
 2 #include <stdlib.h>
 3 #include "ssp.h"

 4 #define DEF_USER "root"

 5 int main (void)
 6 {
 7     FILE *fp;
 8     char *user;
 9     char buf [LINE_LEN];
10     int i;
11     char *msg [] = {
12         "From: Solaris Systems Programming <nobody@localhost>\n",
13         "",
14         "Subject: Test email from popenmail\n\n",
15         "Hi there,\n\n",
16         "This email was sent from the popenmail\n",
17         "program to show how to send data to an\n",
18         "external program through a pipe.\n\n",
19         "Bye.\n",
20         NULL
21     };

22     if ((user = getenv ("MAIL_USER")) == NULL) {
23         if ((user = cuserid (NULL)) == NULL)
24             user = DEF_USER;
25     }

26     snprintf (buf, LINE_LEN, "To: %s\n", user);
27     msg [1] = buf;

28     if ((fp = popen ("/usr/lib/sendmail -t", "w")) == NULL)
29         err_msg ("popen failed");

30     for (i = 0; msg [i] != NULL; i++) {
31         if (fputs (msg [i], fp) == EOF)
32             err_msg ("Can't fputs to sendmail");
33     }

34     pclose (fp);

35     return (0);
36 }
```

pipes_and_fifos/popenmail.c

Program 19.4 Sending email through a pipe using popen.

Example: Implementing the `popen` and `pclose` functions

For pedagogical reasons, we present the source code to these functions in three sections. First we show the code for our version of popen, next we show our implementation of pclose, and finally we show the support functions required by the first two functions.

Program 19.5 shows our implementation of popen. Note that for the sake of brevity, we do not set errno when an error is detected.

pipes_and_fifos/popen.c

```
 1 #include <stdio.h>
 2 #include <unistd.h>
 3 #include <stdlib.h>
 4 #include <errno.h>
 5 #include <sys/types.h>
 6 #include <sys/wait.h>

 7 typedef struct entry {
 8     struct entry *next;
 9     pid_t pid;
10     int fd;
11 } entry_t;

12 static entry_t *list_head = NULL;

13 static int add_entry (pid_t pid, int fd);
14 static pid_t del_entry (int fd);
15 static void close_other_pipes (void);

16 FILE *ssp_popen (const char *command, const char *mode)
17 {
18     char *shell;
19     FILE *fp;
20     pid_t pid;
21     int fd [2];
22     int parent_fd;
23     int child_fd;
24     int std_io;

25     if ((((mode [0] != 'r') && (mode [0] != 'w')) || (mode [1] != 0))
26         return (NULL);

27     if (pipe (fd) == -1)
28         return (NULL);

29 #ifndef _LP64
30     if ((fd [0] >= 256) || (fd [1] >= 256)) {
31         close (fd [0]);
32         close (fd [1]);
33         return (NULL);
34     }
35 #endif

36     parent_fd = (*mode == 'r') ? fd [0] : fd [1];
37     child_fd = (*mode == 'r') ? fd [1] : fd [0];

38     switch (pid = fork ()) {
39         case -1:
40             close (parent_fd);
41             close (child_fd);
42             return (NULL);

43         case 0:
44             close_other_pipes ();

45             close (parent_fd);
46             std_io = (*mode == 'r') ? 1 : 0;
```

```
47                  if (child_fd != std_io) {
48                      dup2 (child_fd, std_io);
49                      close (child_fd);
50                  }

51                  if (sysconf (_SC_XOPEN_VERSION) < 4)
52                      shell = "/bin/sh";
53                  else
54                      shell = "/usr/xpg4/bin/sh";

55                  if (access (shell, X_OK) == -1)
56                      _exit (127);

57                  execl (shell, "sh", "-c", command, NULL);
58                  _exit (1);

59          default:
60                  close (child_fd);

61                  if (add_entry (pid, parent_fd) == -1) {
62                      close (parent_fd);
63                      return (NULL);
64                  }

65                  if ((fp = fdopen (parent_fd, mode)) == NULL) {
66                      close (parent_fd);
67                      return (NULL);
68                  }

69                  return (fp);
70      }
71 }
```
——————————————————————————————————— *pipes_and_fifos/popen.c*

Program 19.5 Our implementation of popen.

Check validity of *mode*

25–26 If the first character of *mode* is not "r" or "w", or *mode* is more than one character long, return EINVAL.

Create the pipe

27–28 Call pipe to create the pipe.

Check that file descriptors are in range

29–35 If _LP64 is not defined (i.e., we are compiling a 32-bit process), check that both of the pipe's file descriptors are less than 256. We must do this because the SPARC-V8 version of the FILE structure uses only 1 byte to hold the file descriptor, thus restricting it to 255. The SPARC-V9 version of the FILE structure removes this limitation by storing the file descriptor in an int.

Determine which file descriptor is used for what

36–37 Determine which of the pipe's file descriptors the parent performs I/O with, and do similarly for the child.

Call `fork`

38–42 Call `fork`, closing the pipe if `fork` fails.

Child process

43–44 Call our function `close_other_pipes` (Program 19.7) to close all the other pipes that were created by calling `popen` in the same process.

45 Close the parent's file descriptor, as we no longer need it.

46–50 Determine which of standard input or standard output should be connected to the pipe. If necessary, call `dup2` to duplicate the pipe's remaining file descriptor to standard input or standard output.

51–54 Call `sysconf` with an argument of `_SC_XOPEN_VERSION` to see if we are a conforming application. If we are, use `/usr/xpg4/bin/sh` as the shell; otherwise, use `/bin/sh`. Note that as with our implementation of `system` (Program 15.12 and Program 17.22), this will not work as written prior to Solaris 9 if the package `SUNWxcu4` is not installed. In this case, `/bin/ksh` should be used.

55–56 If the caller's real user ID doesn't have permission to execute the shell, return an error.

57–58 Invoke the *command* string using the appropriate shell.

Parent process

60 Close the child's file descriptor, as we no longer need it.

61–64 Call our function `add_entry` (Program 19.7) to keep track of which file descriptor is associated with which child process.

65–68 Associate a standard I/O file stream with the parent's end of the pipe, and return a pointer to it to the caller.

Program 19.6 shows our version of `pclose`.

———————————————————————————————— *pipes_and_fifos/popen.c*
```
72 int ssp_pclose (FILE *fp)
73 {
74     pid_t pid;
75     int status;

76     pid = del_entry (fileno (fp));

77     fclose (fp);

78     if (pid == -1)
79         return (-1);

80     while (waitpid (pid, &status, 0) == -1) {
81         if (errno != EINTR)
82             return (-1);
83     }

84     return (status);
85 }
```
———————————————————————————————— *pipes_and_fifos/popen.c*

Program 19.6 Our implementation of `pclose`.

Remove the process and file descriptor association

76 Call our function del_entry to stop keeping track of which file descriptor is associated with the child process.

Close the pipe

77 Close the file stream associated with the pipe, which has the side effect of closing the file descriptor.

Reap status of child process

78–79 Return an error indication if there was a problem reported by del_entry.

80–83 Call waitpid to reap the termination status of the child process. If a signal arrives while we're waiting for the child to terminate, call waitpid again.

84 If no errors were reported by waitpid, return the termination status of the child process.

Our implementation of popen and pclose makes use of three support functions: add_entry, del_entry, and close_other_pipes. Program 19.7 shows the code for these functions.

Because popen may be called several times from one process, we have to keep track of which process is associated with which pipe. Each child looks after its own end of the pipe, so the parent needs to keep track of the file descriptor for only *its* end of the pipe. There are two approaches we can take to store this information. The first method is to use an array. Each array element stores the process ID it is associated with; for simplicity, we can say that the array index is equal to the file descriptor number. The problem with this approach is that not only is it wasteful (the number of pipes is unlikely to be the same as the number of available file descriptors), but the size of the array could become unwieldy if there is a huge number of available descriptors.

If we restrict our functions to just using the first 256 file descriptors, this wouldn't be such an issue. However, we won't impose this artificial limit because of its effect on 64-bit processes.

The second option, which is the one we use, is to store the associations in a dynamically managed linked list. At the expense of a slight increase in complexity, we can avoid all the problems we identified with the array method. Each item in the linked list stores the file descriptor for the parent's end of the pipe, and its associated process ID.

The first two functions in Program 19.7 manage the linked list.

The add_entry function

91–92 Initialize the pointers, ready to traverse the linked list.

93–96 Traverse the linked list. New entries are added to the end of the list (a simple, unordered linked list is sufficient for our purposes).

97–98 Allocate memory for the new list entry.

99–101 Initialize the new list entry.

102–105 Add the new entry to the list. If the list is currently empty, the new entry becomes the list head; otherwise, the new entry is added to the end of the list.

pipes_and_fifos/popen.c

```
 86 static int add_entry (pid_t pid, int fd)
 87 {
 88     entry_t *prev;
 89     entry_t *current;
 90     entry_t *new;

 91     prev = list_head;
 92     current = list_head;

 93     while (current != NULL) {
 94         prev = current;
 95         current = current -> next;
 96     }

 97     if ((new = malloc (sizeof (entry_t))) == NULL)
 98         return (-1);

 99     new -> pid = pid;
100     new -> fd = fd;
101     new -> next = NULL;

102     if (list_head == NULL)
103         list_head = new;
104     else
105         prev -> next = new;

106     return (0);
107 }

108 static pid_t del_entry (int fd)
109 {
110     entry_t *prev;
111     entry_t *current;
112     pid_t pid;

113     prev = list_head;
114     current = list_head;

115     while (current != NULL) {
116         if (current -> fd == fd) {
117             if (current == list_head)
118                 list_head = current -> next;
119             else
120                 prev -> next = current -> next;

121             pid = current -> pid;
122             free (current);

123             return (pid);
124         }

125         prev = current;
126         current = current -> next;
127     }

128     return (-1);
129 }
```

```
130 static void close_other_pipes (void)
131 {
132     entry_t *current;

133     current = list_head;

134     while (current != NULL) {
135         close (current -> fd);
136         current = current -> next;
137     }
138 }
```
————————————————————————————————————— pipes_and_fifos/popen.c

Program 19.7 Support functions for popen and pclose.

The del_entry function

113–114 Initialize the pointers, ready to traverse the linked list.

115–127 Traverse the linked list. If the file descriptor of the current entry is the same as the one we're interested in, remove it. The process ID associated with the file descriptor is returned.

The third function in Program 19.7 closes all the currently opened file descriptors that were opened by our ssp_popen function.

The close_other_pipes function

130–138 Traverse the linked list, closing each file descriptor encountered. (Closing all other open file descriptors associated with pipes opened by calling popen is a POSIX requirement.)

Let's test our implementation of popen and pclose. We'll write a program that prompts the user for some text, then reads a line from standard input. We'll use our version of popen to run another program that filters the text we input before the calling process reads it. The filter we'll use in this example is a modified version of our rot13 program from Chapter 3.

Program 19.8 shows the code for the modified version of rot13.

The code for our new version of rot13 is simple enough, although we'll defer our explanation of why we fflush standard output after writing a newline until the next section.

Program 19.9 prompts the user for a line of text, which is filtered by rot13. It then displays the filtered version.

The code in Program 19.9 is also quite simple. The reason why we fflush standard output after printing the prompt is because standard output is usually line buffered, and our prompt doesn't contain a newline character.

Running Program 19.9 gives the results we'd expect:

```
$ ./test_popen
Enter some text: Hello, World!
Uryyb, Jbeyq!
Enter some text: ^D
```

pipes_and_fifos/rot13.c

```
 1 #include <stdio.h>
 2 #include <string.h>
 3 #include <libgen.h>
 4 #include "ssp.h"

 5 int main (void)
 6 {
 7     char buf [2];
 8     char *old = "ABCDEFGHIJKLMNOPQRSTUVWXYZabcdefghijklmnopqrstuvwxyz";
 9     char *new = "NOPQRSTUVWXYZABCDEFGHIJKLMnopqrstuvwxyzabcdefghijklm";
10     char result [2];

11     buf [1] = '\0';
12     result [1] = '\0';

13     while ((buf [0] = getchar ()) != EOF) {
14         strtrns (buf, old, new, result);

15         if (putchar (result [0]) == EOF)
16             err_msg ("putchar failed");

17         if (buf [0] == '\n')
18             fflush (stdout);
19     }

20     return (0);
21 }
```

pipes_and_fifos/rot13.c

Program 19.8 Our modified version of rot13.

19.4   Coprocesses

We've seen how we can construct pipelines using filters. In this context, a *filter* is a program that reads from its standard output and writes to its standard output, usually transforming the data before writing it (the rot13 program from the previous section is an example of a filter). In shell pipelines, filters are usually connected linearly. When the same process reads from, and writes to, a filter, the filter is then called a *coprocess*.

Using popen gives us a one-way pipe to either read from the standard output or write to the standard input of some other processes. When we use coprocesses, we can have either two one-way pipes or one full-duplex pipe. Figure 19.8 shows the arrangement when two pipes are used.

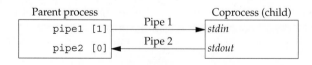

Figure 19.8 Driving a coprocess by using two one-way pipes.

pipes_and_fifos/test_popen.c

```
 1 #include <stdio.h>
 2 #include "ssp.h"

 3 extern FILE *ssp_popen (const char *command, const char *mode);
 4 extern int ssp_pclose (FILE *fp);

 5 int main (void)
 6 {
 7     char buf [LINE_LEN];
 8     FILE *fp;

 9     if ((fp = ssp_popen ("./rot13", "r")) == NULL)
10         err_msg ("ssp_popen failed");

11     for (;;) {
12         printf ("Enter some text: ");
13         fflush (stdout);

14         if (fgets (buf, LINE_LEN, fp) == NULL)
15             break;

16         if (printf ("%s", buf) == EOF)
17             err_msg ("printf to pipe failed");
18     }

19     if (ssp_pclose (fp) == -1)
20         err_msg ("ssp_pclose failed");
21     printf ("\n");

22     return (0);
23 }
```

pipes_and_fifos/test_popen.c

Program 19.9 Invoking `rot13` using our version of `popen` and `pclose`.

Figure 19.9 shows the arrangement when one full-duplex pipe is used, assuming the pipe's file descriptor is duplicated to standard input and standard output.

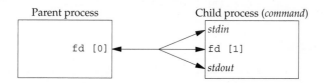

Figure 19.9 Driving a coprocess by using a full-duplex pipe.

We'll use the latter arrangement in our examples, but whichever arrangement we use, the coprocess works in the same manner. We write something to the standard input of the coprocess, which operates on it in some way. The coprocess writes the result to its standard output, which we then read.

Example: Using a coprocess to find the square root of a number

Let's look at an example of coprocesses that is reminiscent of the days before CPUs had intergrated floating-point units.

> Prior to the integration of floating-point units into CPUs in the late 1980s, computers used special-purpose chips to perform floating-point operations. If the floating-point coprocessor was not installed, the computer's operating system would emulate the floating-point operation in software, usually with a considerable performance penalty.

Program 19.10 is a simple coprocess that reads a number from standard input, calculates its square root, and writes the result to standard output.

———————————————————————————————— pipes_and_fifos/sqrt.c

```
 1 #include <stdio.h>
 2 #include <unistd.h>
 3 #include <string.h>
 4 #include <math.h>
 5 #include "ssp.h"

 6 int main (void)
 7 {
 8     double num;
 9     double res;
10     int n;
11     char buf [LINE_LEN];

12     while ((n = read (STDIN_FILENO, buf, LINE_LEN)) > 0) {
13         buf [n] = '\0';
14         if (sscanf (buf, "%lf", &num) == 1) {
15             res = sqrt (num);
16             snprintf (buf, LINE_LEN, "%lf\n", res);
17             n = strlen (buf);
18             if (writen (STDOUT_FILENO, buf, n) == -1)
19                 err_msg ("writen failed");
20         }
21         else {
22             if (writen (STDOUT_FILENO, "Invalid arg\n", 12) == -1)
23                 err_msg ("writen failed");
24         }
25     }

26     return (0);
27 }
```

———————————————————————————————— pipes_and_fifos/sqrt.c

Program 19.10   A simple coprocess to calculate the square root of a number.

We have a program that we can use as our coprocess, so we need a program to drive it. Program 19.11 shows the code for a suitable driver. It reads a number from standard input, writes it to the coprocess, and prints the result.

Catch SIGPIPE

14–15 Catch the SIGPIPE signal.

```
 1 #include <stdio.h>
 2 #include <unistd.h>
 3 #include <stdlib.h>
 4 #include <string.h>
 5 #include <signal.h>
 6 #include <sys/types.h>
 7 #include "ssp.h"

 8 static void sigpipe (int sig);

 9 int main (void)
10 {
11     int fd [2];
12     int n;
13     char buf [LINE_LEN];

14     if (sigset (SIGPIPE, sigpipe) == SIG_ERR)
15         err_msg ("sigset failed");

16     if (pipe (fd) == -1)
17         err_msg ("pipe failed");

18     switch (fork ()) {
19         case -1:
20             err_msg ("fork failed");

21         case 0:
22             close (fd [0]);

23             if (fd [1] != STDIN_FILENO) {
24                 if (dup2 (fd [1], STDIN_FILENO) != STDIN_FILENO)
25                     err_msg ("dup to standard input failed");
26             }

27             if (fd [1] != STDOUT_FILENO) {
28                 if (dup2 (fd [1], STDOUT_FILENO) != STDOUT_FILENO)
29                     err_msg ("dup to standard output failed");
30             }

31             execl ("./sqrt", "sqrt", NULL);
32             err_msg ("exec failed");

33         default:
34             close (fd [1]);

35             printf ("Enter a number: ");
36             fflush (stdout);

37             while (fgets (buf, LINE_LEN, stdin) != NULL) {
38                 n = strlen (buf);
39                 if (writen (fd [0], buf, n) == -1)
40                     err_msg ("writen failed");

41                 if ((n = read (fd [0], buf, LINE_LEN)) == -1)
42                     err_msg ("read from pipe failed");

44                 if (n == 0)
45                     err_msg ("Coprocess closed pipe");
```

```
46                      buf [n] = '\0';
47                      if (fputs (buf, stdout) == EOF)
48                          err_msg ("fputs failed");

49                      printf ("Enter a number: ");
50                      fflush (stdout);
51                  }

52                  if (ferror (stdin))
53                      err_msg ("fgets from standard input failed");

54                  return (0);
55      }
56 }

57 static void sigpipe (int sig)
58 {
59      printf ("Caught SIGPIPE\n");
60      exit (1);
61 }
```
—————————————————————————————— *pipes_and_fifos/coproc.c*

Program 19.11 Program to drive the sqrt coprocess.

Create the pipe

16–17 Call pipe to create the pipe.

Call fork

18–20 Call fork to create the child process.

Child process

22 Close the file descriptor we're not using.

23–26 Duplicate the pipe's remaining file descriptor to standard input.

27–30 Duplicate the pipe's remaining file descriptor to standard output.

31 Call exec to invoke the sqrt coprocess.

Parent process

34 Close the file descriptor we're not using.

35–36 Print a prompt.

37–40 Until the user indicates that they're finished, read a line from standard input and write it to the pipe.

41–42 Read a line from the pipe (i.e., the response from the coprocess).

44–45 If zero bytes were received, the coprocess has closed the pipe.

46–51 Terminate the string we read from the coprocess with a NUL byte and write it to standard output. Print out another prompt and go to the top of the while loop for another iteration.

52–53 If there was a problem reading the line of input from the user, print a message saying so.

Signal handler

57–61 Print a message saying we caught SIGPIPE, and exit with a non-zero status.

Running Program 19.11 gives the results we expect:

```
$ ./coproc
Enter a number: 42
6.480741
Enter a number: 64
8.000000
Enter a number: 4                    Kill the coprocess from another terminal before entering 4
Caught SIGPIPE
```

Notice that when we try to write to the pipe when it has no reader (i.e., the coprocess has terminated), a `SIGPIPE` signal is sent to the parent. (We'll revisit this in Exercise 19.2.)

Example: Rewriting our `sqrt` coprocess to use standard I/O

Our first implementation of the `sqrt` coprocess used the `read` and `write` functions. What happens if we use the function provided by the standard I/O library instead? Program 19.12 shows a version of `sqrt` that uses standard I/O.

pipes_and_fifos/sqrt_stdio.c

```
 1 #include <stdio.h>
 2 #include <math.h>
 3 #include "ssp.h"

 4 int main (void)
 5 {
 6     double num;
 7     double res;
 8     char buf [LINE_LEN];

 9     while (fgets (buf, LINE_LEN, stdin) != NULL) {
10         if (sscanf (buf, "%lf", &num) == 1) {
11             res = sqrt (num);
12             if (printf ("%f\n", res) == EOF)
13                 err_msg ("printf failed");
14         }
15         else {
16             if (printf ("Invalid arg\n") == EOF)
17                 err_msg ("printf failed");
18         }
19     }

20     return (0);
21 }
```

pipes_and_fifos/sqrt_stdio.c

Program 19.12 Another version of `sqrt`, using standard I/O.

If we use the version of `sqrt` we show in Program 19.12 as the coprocess invoked by Program 19.11, it no longer works. The problem is caused by the fact that standard input and standard output are fully buffered, rather than line buffered. This is because they are connected to a pipe, and hence `isatty` is false (recall our discussion of standard I/O library buffering in Section 5.11). While the new version of `sqrt` is blocked reading from its standard input, Program 19.11 is blocked reading from the pipe. In other words, we have deadlock.

In cases like this (where we have access to the source code), we can modify the coprocess to fix this problem. Inserting the following two lines of code before the `while` loop is entered will accomplish this:

```
setbuf (stdin, NULL);
setbuf (stdout, NULL);
```

This causes standard input and standard output to be unbuffered, which has the effect of causing `fgets` to return when a line is available. It also causes `printf` to flush standard output when it prints a newline.

However, if we don't have access to the source code of the program we're using as a coprocess, we can't make these changes. For example, substituting `sqrt` with the following `awk` program will not work:

```
#!/bin/awk -f
{
    printf sqrt
}
```

Once again, the problem is the standard I/O buffering. Given that we don't have the source code for `awk`, how can we get it to work?

The solution is to trick the coprocess (in this case, `awk`) into thinking that it is actually connected to a terminal, and hence use line-buffered I/O. And the way we accomplish that is to use a pseudo terminal; we'll see how to do this in Chapter 23.

19.5 FIFOs

FIFOs, or "named pipes" as they are sometimes called, provide a solution to the problem of pipes being usable only between related processes.

> As we'll see in Chapter 21, it is possible to pass a pipe's (or any other file's) file descriptor to an unrelated process. But for practical purposes, most pipes are used between related processes.

As we stated in Section 10.4, a FIFO is a type of file. We can test whether a file is a FIFO by using the `S_ISFIFO` macro on the `st_mode` member of the `stat` structure.

The reason why FIFOs are sometimes called named pipes is because they exist as files in a file system. We create a FIFO by using the `mkfifo` function.

```
#include <sys/types.h>
#include <sys/stat.h>

int mkfifo (const char *path, mode_t mode);
```
                                                    Returns: 0 if OK, −1 on error

The `mkfifo` function creates a new FIFO, the pathname of which is specified by *path*. The file permission bits of the new FIFO will be set to those specified by *mode*, in the same manner as the `open` function. The FIFO's user and group ownership also follow the rules for the `open` function (when the `O_CREAT` flag is used).

Once we've created a FIFO, we can use any of the normal I/O functions (e.g., open, read, write, etc.) with it. When we open a FIFO, the two nonblocking I/O flags, O_NONBLOCK and O_NDELAY, affect what happens:

- If neither flag is specified, a read-only open will block until another process opens the FIFO for writing. Similarly, a write-only open of a FIFO will block until another process opens it for reading.

- If either flag is set, a read-only open will return immediately. A write-only open will fail if no process has the FIFO open for reading, setting errno to ENXIO.

In either case, a read-write open of a FIFO results in undefined behaviour.

As we might expect, reading from a FIFO whose last writer has closed it generates an EOF for the reader. Also, writing to FIFO after the last reader has closed it will result in a SIGPIPE signal being sent to the writer.

As with regular pipes, the constant PIPE_BUF defines the maximum size of an atomic write to a FIFO. The atomicity of writes is probably more of an issue with FIFOs than regular pipes, because it is not uncommon for FIFOs to have several writers.

There are two typical uses for FIFOs:

1. They are used by shells to pass data from one shell pipeline to another without using intermediate temporary files.

2. They are used by some client server applications to pass data between the two processes.

Let's look at each of these uses.

Using a FIFO to Connect Shell Pipelines

Suppose we have some data that we need to process twice after it has been filtered in some way as shown in Figure 19.10.

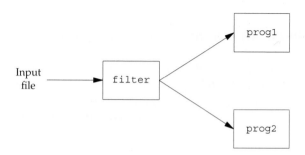

Figure 19.10 Procedure that processes filtered data twice.

We can accomplish this three ways:

1. Save the output of the filtering process in a temporary file, then run each of the processing programs using the temporary file as their input.

2. Construct a pipeline consisting of the filtering program and the first of the processing programs. Repeat as many times as necessary for each processing program.

3. Use the `tee` program to connect the output of the filtering program to one of the processing programs and as many FIFOs as necessary (multiple `tee` processes will be required if there are more than two process programs required). The other processing programs read from the FIFOs.

(The `tee` program copies its standard input to its standard output and the files named on the command line.) The commands we'd use to implement the third of these options are:

```
mkfifo my_fifo
./prog1 < my_fifo &
./filter < input_file | tee myfifo | ./prog2
```

We first create the FIFO, using the `mkfifo` command. Then we start prog2 in the background, reading from the FIFO we just created. Then we start the `filter` program, using `tee` to send its output to the FIFO and prog2. Figure 19.11 shows the resulting process arrangement.

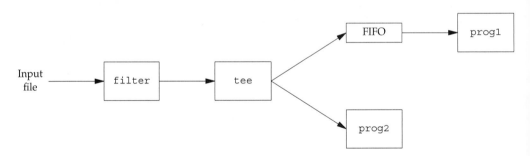

Figure 19.11   Process arrangement when using a FIFO to connect two pipelines.

Using FIFOs in Client-Server Applications

A more common use of FIFOs is sending data between a client and a server. In this scenario, a server that will be contacted by several clients creates a well-known FIFO. (A *well-known FIFO* is one whose pathname is known by all the clients that need to connect to it.) Figure 19.12 shows the arrangement. Because there are multiple clients, each of their requests must be less than PIPE_BUF bytes in size to ensure their atomicity. If a client's request exceeds PIPE_BUF bytes, it is possible that requests from multiple clients could be interleaved.

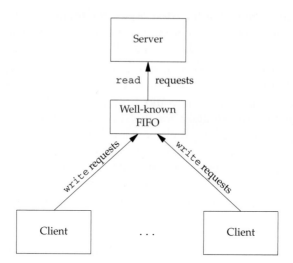

Figure 19.12 Clients sending requests to a server via a well-known FIFO.

The problem with using FIFOs like this is how to get a response from the server back to the client that issued the request. A single FIFO can't be used because the clients wouldn't know when to read the FIFO. There is no way to ensure that the response the client reads is actually intended for it; it could be destined for another client.

Figure 19.13 shows one solution to this problem.

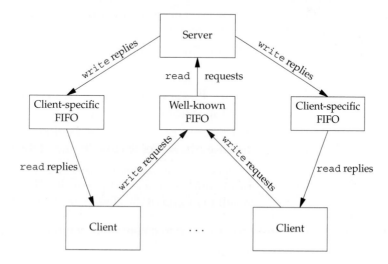

Figure 19.13 Client-server communications using FIFOs.

What happens here is that the client sends a unique identifier (e.g., its process ID) to the server with each request. The first time the server receives a request from a new client, it creates a new FIFO specifically for that client by using a pathname based on the unique identifier the client passed it.

One of the drawbacks of this technique is that there is no way for the server to detect that a client has terminated. This could lead to client-specific FIFOs cluttering up the file system (although the solution for that problem is for the client to unlink its specific FIFO once it has opened it). It also means that the server must catch or ignore SIGPIPE; it's possible a client could send a request to the server and terminate before the server writes the response. This would leave the FIFO with a writer (the server process) but no reader.

Another thing to we need to consider with the arrangement shown in Figure 19.13 is what happens when the number of clients goes from one to zero. If the server opens the well-known FIFO in read-only mode, then EOF will be returned by read when the last client terminates. To save the effort of handling this special case, it is quite common for the server to open its well-known FIFO for reading and writing (see Exercise 19.5).

Example: Client-server communication using FIFOs

Let's take a look at an example that uses FIFOs in the manner we just described. A simple protocol is used for client-to-server communication. The client sends a string to the server with the following format:

    PID command [number]

The first token in the string is the process ID of the client, the second token is the command the client wishes to send, and the third token is an optional number that is used by the sqrt (square root) command.

Our simple server implements only three commands:

open	This should be the first command the client sends to the server. It causes the server to create, and open for writing, the FIFO specific to the client.
quit	This should be the last command the client sends the server. It causes the server to close its end of the FIFO.
sqrt	This command causes the server to calculate the square root of the number the client passes it. The server then writes the result to its end of the client-specific FIFO.

There are no reasons why we couldn't implement more commands should we want to.

Program 19.13 shows the code for FIFO server.

Create the well-known FIFO

26–29 Call unlink to remove the well-known FIFO. This step isn't strictly necessary, but doing so helps ensure that the FIFO is created with the correct ownership and permissions.

30–31 Create the well-known FIFO by using the mkfifo function.

pipes_and_fifos/fifo_server.c

```
 1  #include <stdio.h>
 2  #include <unistd.h>
 3  #include <stdlib.h>
 4  #include <sys/types.h>
 5  #include <sys/stat.h>
 6  #include <fcntl.h>
 7  #include <sys/param.h>
 8  #include <errno.h>
 9  #include <string.h>
10  #include <math.h>
11  #include <signal.h>
12  #include "ssp.h"

13  #define WELL_KNOWN_FIFO "/tmp/ssp_fifo"

14  static void rm_fifo (void);

15  int main (void)
16  {
17      int n;
18      int fd;
19      int *fd_pid;
20      char buf [LINE_LEN];
21      char cmd [LINE_LEN];
22      char path [MAXPATHLEN];
23      pid_t pid;
24      double num;
25      double res;

26      if (unlink (WELL_KNOWN_FIFO) == -1) {
27          if (errno != ENOENT)
28              err_msg ("unlink failed");
29      }

30      if (mkfifo (WELL_KNOWN_FIFO, FIFO_PERMS) == -1)
31          err_msg ("mkfifo failed");

32      if (atexit (rm_fifo) == -1)
33          err_msg ("atexit failed");

34      if ((fd = open (WELL_KNOWN_FIFO, O_RDONLY)) == -1)
35          err_msg ("open failed");

36      if ((fd_pid = calloc (MAXPID, sizeof (int))) == NULL)
37          err_msg ("calloc failed");

38      if (sigset (SIGPIPE, SIG_IGN) == SIG_ERR)
39          err_msg ("sigset failed");

40      while ((n = read (fd, buf, LINE_LEN)) > 0) {
41          buf [n] = '\0';
42          sscanf (buf, "%ld %s %lf", (long *) &pid, cmd, &num);

43          if (strcmp (cmd, "open") == 0) {
44              if (fd_pid [pid] == 0) {
45                  snprintf (path, MAXPATHLEN, "%s.%ld", WELL_KNOWN_FIFO,
46                      (long) pid);
```

```
47                      if (unlink (path) == -1) {
48                          if (errno != ENOENT) {
49                              err_ret ("unlink failed");
50                              continue;
51                          }
52                      }

53                      if (mkfifo (path, FIFO_PERMS) == -1) {
54                          err_ret ("mkfifo failed");
55                          continue;
56                      }

57                      if ((fd_pid [pid] = open (path, O_WRONLY)) == -1) {
58                          err_ret ("open failed");
59                          fd_pid [pid] = 0;
60                          continue;
61                      }
62                  }
63              }
64          if (strcmp (cmd, "sqrt") == 0) {
65              res = sqrt (num);
66              snprintf (buf, LINE_LEN, "%lf\n", res);
67              n = strlen (buf);
68              if (writen (fd_pid [pid], buf, n) == -1) {
69                  err_ret ("writen failed");
70                  close (fd_pid [pid]);
71                  fd_pid [pid] = 0;
72              }
73          }
74          if (strcmp (cmd, "quit") == 0) {
75              close (fd_pid [pid]);
76              fd_pid [pid] = 0;
77          }
78      }
79      return (0);
80  }
81  static void rm_fifo (void)
82  {
83      unlink (WELL_KNOWN_FIFO);
84  }
```
—————————————————————————————————————— *pipes_and_fifos/fifo_server.c*

Program 19.13 FIFO server that can handle multiple clients.

Register exit handler

32–33 Register the exit handler using the `atexit` function. The exit handler ensures that the well-known FIFO doesn't clutter up the file system when the server terminates.

Open the well-known FIFO

34–35 Open the well-known FIFO for read only.

Allocate memory for process ID to file descriptor map

36–37 Allocate the memory required for the array that we use to associate a client with its specific FIFO. The server communicates to each client through a FIFO specific to that client. Because each client request includes the client's process ID, we can store the file descriptor for the server's end of the FIFO in an array, the index of which is equal to the process ID the file descriptor is associated with. The last time we had a similar problem (Program 19.7), we used a linked list. This time, for variety, we've used a dynamically allocated array. We use `calloc` to allocate the memory to ensure that each element is set to zero.

Ignore `SIGPIPE`

38–39 Ignore the `SIGPIPE` signal in case a client submits a request but terminates before we've had a chance to reply.

Read a line from the well-known FIFO and process it

40–42 Read a line from the well-known FIFO, NUL terminate it, and parse it using `sscanf`. (Our parser isn't very sophisticated, but is sufficient for our needs in this example.) Parsing the command extracts the process ID, the command string, and the optional number.

Handle the `open` command

43–63 If the command is "open", then if the file descriptor associated with the process ID we got from the command is zero, we should create a client-specific FIFO and open it for writing. With the exception of the FIFO's pathname, and the fact that we open it in write-only mode, the steps we perform are the same as when we opened the well-known FIFO (i.e., remove the FIFO if it already exists, create a new FIFO, and open it for writing.

Handle the `sqrt` command

64–73 If the command is "sqrt", then calculate the square root of the number we parsed from the line we read from the client. Then write the result to the client-specific FIFO, as determined by the process ID associated with the command.

Handle the `quit` command

74–78 If the command is "quit", then close the file descriptor associated with the server's end of the client-specific FIFO. Note that the task of actually removing the client-specific FIFO from the file system is left to the client.

Exit handler

81–84 This function, called automatically when the server process terminates, removes the well-known FIFO.

Now that we have a server process, we need a client that will talk to it. Program 19.14 shows the code for a suitable client. Let's take a look at some of its implementation details.

Open the well-known FIFO

19–20 Open the well-known FIFO in write-only mode.

pipes_and_fifos/fifo_client.c

```
 1  #include <stdio.h>
 2  #include <unistd.h>
 3  #include <sys/types.h>
 4  #include <sys/stat.h>
 5  #include <fcntl.h>
 6  #include <sys/param.h>
 7  #include <errno.h>
 8  #include <string.h>
 9  #include "ssp.h"

10  #define WELL_KNOWN_FIFO "/tmp/ssp_fifo"

11  int main (void)
12  {
13      pid_t pid;
14      int wk_fd;
15      int my_fd;
16      int n;
17      char buf [LINE_LEN];
18      char path [MAXPATHLEN];

19      if ((wk_fd = open (WELL_KNOWN_FIFO, O_WRONLY)) == -1)
20          err_msg ("Can't open well known FIFO");

21      pid = getpid ();

22      snprintf (buf, LINE_LEN, "%d open\n", pid);
23      n = strlen (buf);

24      if (writen (wk_fd, buf, n) == -1)
25          err_msg ("writen failed");

26      snprintf (path, MAXPATHLEN, "%s.%d", WELL_KNOWN_FIFO, pid);

27      while ((my_fd = open (path, O_RDONLY)) == -1) {
28          if (errno != ENOENT)
29              err_msg ("Can't open my FIFO");
30      }

31      if (unlink (path) == -1)
32          err_msg ("unlink failed");

33      printf ("Enter a number: ");
34      fflush (stdout);

35      while (fgets (path, LINE_LEN, stdin) != NULL) {
36          snprintf (buf, LINE_LEN, "%d sqrt %s", pid, path);
37          n = strlen (buf);
38          if (writen (wk_fd, buf, n) == -1)
39              err_msg ("writen failed");

40          if ((n = read (my_fd, buf, LINE_LEN)) == -1)
41              err_msg ("Can't read my FIFO");

42          if (n == 0)
43              err_msg ("Server closed my pipe");

44          buf [n] = '\0';
```

```
45          if (fputs (buf, stdout) == EOF)
46              err_msg ("fputs failed");

47          printf ("Enter a number: ");
48          fflush (stdout);
49      }

50      if (ferror (stdin))
51          err_msg ("fgets from standard input failed");

52      snprintf (buf, LINE_LEN, "%d close\n", pid);
53      n = strlen (buf);

54      if (writen (wk_fd, buf, n) == -1)
55          err_msg ("writen failed");

56      printf ("\n");
57      close (wk_fd);
58      close (my_fd);

59      return (0);
60  }
```
――――――――――――――――――――――――――――――― *pipes_and_fifos/fifo_client.c*

Program 19.14   FIFO client that works with the server in Program 19.13.

Get our process ID

21 Call getpid to get our process ID.

Send an open command to the server

22–25 Send an open command to the server, which will cause it to create a client-specific FIFO for us.

Open client-specific FIFO

26–30 Call open to open the client-specific FIFO for reading. if the FIFO does not exist (i.e., open returns ENOENT), try again. Although the repetitive calling of open arguably wastes CPU cycles, the amount of time we do this should be fairly short unless the machine is very heavily loaded.

Delete the client-specific FIFO

31–32 We remove the client-specific FIFO because we no longer need to refer to it by name. This step saves us from having to register an exit handler to ensure that client-specific FIFOs that are no longer required are not left cluttering up the file system.

The majority of the rest of Program 19.14 is the same as Program 19.11, except that the writes that request the square root processing are written to the well-known FIFO rather than standard output, and the results are read from the client-specific FIFO rather than standard input.

19.6   Iterative Versus Concurrent Servers

The server we show in Program 19.13 is an example of an iterative server. An *iterative server* is one that handles client requests one at a time (i.e., it iterates through them). Each client request is completed before the next is looked at. This means that if multiple clients make a request at the same time, the first one received will be processed to completion before the next one is processed. If each request takes only a short time to process, this approach is acceptable (although it doesn't scale very well). But if some requests take a long time, say a few seconds or longer, the delays become unacceptable.

The solution to this problem is to use a concurrent server. As its name suggests, a *concurrent server* handles multiple client requests concurrently (i.e., at the same time). Client requests are no longer at the mercy of prior requests, the processing of which might take some time.

There are a number of techniques for implementing a concurrent server:

1. Create one child per client. In this type of concurrent server, every time a new request arrives, a process is `forked` to handle it. The child process handles the request, and the parent waits for another to arrive. Something to be aware of with this type of server is that the `fork` overhead can become problematic if the server starts receiving a lot of requests.

2. Create a pool of children. With this technique, which is sometimes referred to as *pre-forking*, a predetermined number of child processes are created before the server starts accepting client requests. When a new request arrives, it is dispatched to an idle process, which handles it to completion.

3. Create one thread per client. This is similar to the first variety, but instead of creating a new process when a client request arrives, a new thread is created to handle the request. Although the overhead of thread creation isn't as great as creating a new process, it can become problematic on busy servers.

4. Create a pool of threads. This is much the same as the second technique, but a number of threads, rather than child processes, are created before the server starts handling requests.

Designers of network servers have the same set of options.

Denial of Service Attacks

We've already mentioned one problem with iterative servers: because each request is processed serially, the amount of time it takes to service a request depends at least in part on how long the previous request takes to service. Another problem is that a malicious client could deliberately tie up the server with a request, denying other clients access to it. For example, if a client of our FIFO server didn't open its end of the client-specific FIFO, the server will block for ever in the code that handles the open request (recall earlier we stated that a write-only open of a FIFO blocks until the other end has a reader). This is called a *denial of service* (DoS) attack.

One way to help mitigate DoS attacks is to use timeouts with any operation that could potentially block for ever. A better solution to this problem is to use a concurrent server, because in this type of attack, only one instance of the server will be blocked—the other instances will be free to continue handling requests. But even a concurrent server isn't immune to DoS attacks. A suitably malicious client could flood the server with requests (valid or otherwise), and cause a denial of service by resource deprivation (in this case, lack of virtual memory or processes).

19.7 Summary

Pipes and FIFOs are fundamental building blocks that are used every day from the command line and for building many applications. We described how to perform IPC using pipes and FIFOs, and how using popen and pclose can be easier (although less flexible and potentially less secure) than using combinations of pipe, fork, close, exec, and waitpid. We showed our implementation of popen and pclose, and described the problems that can be encountered with pipes and the standard I/O library's buffering.

We also described FIFOs (named pipes) and how they can be used to implement communication between unrelated processes. Next we showed an example of a server that communicates with several clients by using a combination of a well-known FIFO and client-specific FIFOs.

Finally, we discussed the client handling options the server designer has: iterative or concurrent. We also described the four types of concurrent server, and finished off the chapter by taking a brief look at denial of service attacks, and how we can try to avoid them.

In the next chapter we'll take a look at the System V and POSIX flavours of message queues, semaphores, and shared memory.

Exercises

19.1 In our close_other_pipes pipes function (Program 19.7), why don't we free the memory used by each linked list entry after we close the file descriptor?

19.2 Program 19.11 catches the SIGPIPE signal. What happens if you remove the signal handler, and then execute the program? After entering a line of input, how can you tell the parent was terminated by a SIGPIPE signal?

19.3 In our implementation of pclose, we used waitpid to reap the status of the shell that executed the command we passed to popen. Why didn't we use wait instead?

19.4 Why is a SIGPIPE signal generated for the writer when we write to a pipe whose reader has terminated, but not for the reader of a pipe or FIFO whose writer has terminated?

19.5 To avoid writing special case code for when the last client of a FIFO server terminates, it is common for the server to open the FIFO for reading and writing. How can we portably do this without blocking?

20

The System V Interprocess Communication Facility

20.1 Introduction

In this chapter we describe message queues, semaphores, and shared memory, which make up the System V interprocess communication (IPC) facility.

> An analogous facility, using a different set of interfaces, is defined by POSIX. However, the Solaris implementation of POSIX IPC places these functions in the realtime library, which we don't describe in this text. A complete description of the POSIX IPC facility can be found in [Stevens 1999].

A *message queue* is a kernel-resident linked list of messages, a *semaphore* is synchronization primitive, and *shared memory* is memory that is shared between two or more processes (i.e., the memory is mapped into the address space of the processes sharing the memory).

20.2 System V IPC Concepts

System V IPC originated in an internal (to Bell Labs) version of UNIX called Columbus UNIX and was added to the commercial UNIX system with System V in the early 1980s. Before we take a closer look at each of the three IPC facilities, there is some background material that we must understand first.

Identifiers and Keys

Every IPC object (message queue, semaphore, and segment of shared memory) is identified by a non-negative integer, called its *identifier*. These identifiers are analogous to file descriptors, because we must obtain an identifier for an IPC object before we can use it (in much the same way that we must first open a file (obtaining a file descriptor) before we can perform any I/O with it).

An identifier is returned whenever we successfully open or create an IPC object by calling msgget, semget, or shmget. We'll describe these functions in the next few sections, but for now we'll just say that one of the arguments to these functions is a *key*. The data type of an IPC key is key_t, which is defined in <sys/types.h>, which is automatically included when we include <sys/ipc.h>. Keys provide a method of enabling client and server applications to use the same IPC objects, and a key can be obtained in one of three ways:

1. The server creates a new IPC object, specifying a key of IPC_PRIVATE. The returned identifier is then stored somewhere where the client can find it, such as a file. The key IPC_PRIVATE guarantees that the server creates a new IPC object (rather than using, perhaps accidentally, one that already exists). However, this technique suffers from the disadvantage that the file system operations are required; the server must write the identifier into a file, and the clients must read this file to retrieve the identifier later.

   We can also use IPC_PRIVATE in a parent and child relationship. After the parent creates the IPC object using a key of IPC_PRIVATE, the resulting identifier is available to the child process after the fork. The child can then pass the identifier to a new program either as a command line argument or by using an environment variable.

2. The client and server can agree on a predetermined key (one way to do this would be in a header file). The server creates the IPC object using this key. The drawback to this approach is that it is possible for the key to already be associated with an (unrelated) IPC object. In this situation, the function the server calls to get the identifier will fail. The server must handle this error; one way to do this is to delete the existing IPC object and try to create it again.

3. The client and server can agree on a pathname and project ID, perhaps by defining them in a shared header file. They would then call the ftok function we describe next to convert these two values into a key. The resulting key is then used as we described in the preceding paragraph.

The ftok Function

We can generate a key from an existing pathname and project ID by using the ftok function.

```
#include <sys/ipc.h>

key_t ftok (const char *path, int id);
                                                    Returns: IPC key if OK, −1 on error
```

The ftok function returns a key based on the file specified by *path* and the identifier specified by the lower 8 bits of *id*. (That is, *id* must be between 1 and 255; the behaviour of `ftok` is unspecified if *id* is 0). This key can be used by subsequent calls to `msgget`, `semget`, and `shmget` to create or open an IPC object.

The file specified by *path* must be an existing file that the calling process is able to `stat` (a common value for *path* is that of the server daemon). Although `ftok` will return the same key value for all *path*s that name the same file (when called with the same *id*), there is no guarantee that some other combination of *path* and *id* will not result in the same key (although it is unlikely). Different values of *id* will return different keys for the same value of *path*, however.

All of this assumes that *path* is not deleted and replaced between two calls to `ftok`. In this event, it is possible that a different key value will be returned despite the two *path*s being the same. This is because `ftok` internally calls `stat` for *path* and combines three values:

1. The lower 8 bits of *id*
2. Information about the device the file specified by *path* resides on (i.e., the `st_dev` member of the `stat` structure)
3. The file's inode number (i.e., the `st_ino` member of the `stat` structure)

If a file is deleted and then recreated, it is likely that it will have a different inode number, and hence `ftok` will return a different key.

> What we have just described applies to the Solaris implementation of `ftok`; there is no guarantee that other flavours of UNIX will use the same algorithm.
>
> Also, many implementations of UNIX, including Solaris, define `IPC_PRIVATE` to have a value of 0. This is because 0 is not a valid inode number.

Another caveat: because the value returned by `ftok` is based on *id* and the inode number of *path*, it is possible that different *path*s on the same large file system might result in the same key being generated.

Example: Using the `ftok` function

Program 20.1 shows the code for a simple program that takes the pathname passed as the command line argument, and calls the `stat` function for that file. It then prints the file's `st_dev` and `st_ino` stat structure members and the key returned by `ftok`. We print the numbers in hexadecimal so that it's easier to see how the key is derived. For the sake of simplicity, we've hard coded an *id* value of 0x42.

Running Program 20.1 on one of the author's Solaris 9 systems gave the following results:

```
$ ./ftok /etc/passwd
st_dev = 2200000, st_ino = 153e1, key = 420003e1
$ ./ftok /home/rich
st_dev = 3e4002e, st_ino = f5200, key = 4202e200
$ ./ftok /
st_dev = 2200000, st_ino = 2, key = 42000002
$ ./ftok /tmp/foo
st_dev = 2, st_ino = 5f6587, key = 42002587
```

── *ipc/ftok.c*

```
1 #include <stdio.h>
2 #include <sys/ipc.h>
3 #include <sys/stat.h>
4 #include <sys/types.h>
5 #include "ssp.h"

6 int main (int argc, char **argv)
7 {
8     struct stat buf;

9     if (argc != 2)
10         err_quit ("Usage: ftok pathname");

11     if (stat (argv [1], &buf) == -1)
12         err_msg ("stat failed");

13     printf ("st_dev = %lx, st_ino = %lx, key = %x\n", (long) buf.st_dev,
14         (long) buf.st_ino, ftok (argv [1], 0x42));

15     return (0);
16 }
```
── *ipc/ftok.c*

Program 20.1   Obtain a System V IPC key based on a pathname.

Judging by these results, the *id* is is stored in the most significant 8 bits of the key, the least significant 12 bits of st_dev are stored in the next 12 bits, and the least significant 12 bits of st_ino are stored in the least significant 12 bits. Other implementations may differ, however, so we should not rely on this combination of information to form the key.

Another observation we can make is that the mapping is one-way. Because only a subset of the st_dev and st_ino bits are used, we can't determine the pathname of a given key even if we know how the key is created.

Creating and Opening IPC Objects

We create or open a System V IPC object by calling one of three functions: msgget, semget, or shmget. We'll describe these function in detail in later sections, but for now all we need to know is that these functions create or open a message queue, a semaphore, or shared memory segment respectively, and they all return an *identifier* if successful. This identifier is used to identify the IPC object for all subsequent operations, and is not related to the ftok function's *id* argument.

One argument all these functions take is a *key*. This key can be created by ftok, it can be some arbitrary number, or it can be the value IPC_PRIVATE. Using a key of IPC_PRIVATE guarantees that a new, unique IPC object is created.

Each of these functions also takes an argument that is used to specify the permission bits (discussed next) and whether a new object is being created or an existing one being referenced. A number of rules determine if an IPC object is created or if an existing object is referenced. These are:

1. Specifying a *key* of IPC_PRIVATE guarantees that a new IPC object will be created; no combination of *path* and *id* exist that will cause ftok to generate a key value that is the same as IPC_PRIVATE.

2. By setting the IPC_CREAT flag, we can specify that a new IPC object is to be created if it does not already exist. If the requested object already exists, a descriptor for that object is returned.

3. Setting both the IPC_CREAT and IPC_EXCL flags causes a new IPC object to be created, but only if it doesn't already exist. If the object does already exist, an error is returned. Setting the IPC_EXCL flag without setting the IPC_CREAT flag is meaningless.

Figure 20.1 summarizes the effect of these flags when *key* is not IPC_PRIVATE.

Flag	*key* does not exist	*key* already exists
None	Error	OK, references existing object
IPC_CREAT	OK, creates new object	OK, references existing object
IPC_CREAT	IPC_EXCL	OK, creates new object	Error

Figure 20.1 The effect of flags when creating or opening an IPC object.

IPC Permissions

The function argument that specifies the flags we described in the preceding paragraphs is also used to specify the permissions for the IPC object. These permissions, and other information about the IPC object, are stored in ipc_perm structures, which are maintained by the kernel.

```
struct ipc_perm {
    uid_t    uid;     /* Owner's user ID */
    gid_t    gid;     /* Owner's group ID */
    uid_t    cuid;    /* Creator's user ID */
    gid_t    cgid;    /* Creator's group ID */
    mode_t   mode;    /* Access modes */
    uint_t   seq;     /* Slot usage sequence number */
    key_t    key;     /* Key */
};
```

The ipc_perm structure, and several other constants used by the System V IPC facility, is defined in <sys/ipc.h>. Other constants used with message queues, semaphores, and shared memory are defined in <sys/msg.h>, <sys/sem.h>, and <sys/shm.h>.

Whenever an IPC object is created, three items of information are saved in its ipc_perm structure:

- Two members, cuid and cgid, are set to the effective user ID and effective group ID of the calling process. These members are called the *creator IDs*.

- Two other members, uid and gid, are also set to the caller's effective user ID and effective group ID. These members are called the *owner IDs*.

- Some bits of the flag argument to the `msgget`, `semget`, and `shmget` functions initialize the IPC object's permissions, which are stored in the least significant 9 bits of the `mode` member of the `ipc_perm` structure. Figure 20.2 summarizes the permission bits for each of the three IPC mechanisms.

Numeric values	Symbolic values			Description
	Message queue	Semaphore	Shared memory	
0400	MSG_R	SEM_R	SHM_R	Readable by user
0200	MSG_W	SEM_A	SHM_W	Writable by user
0040	MSG_R >> 3	SEM_R >> 3	SHM_R >> 3	Readable by group
0020	MSG_W >> 3	SEM_A >> 3	SHM_W >> 3	Writable by group
0004	MSG_R >> 6	SEM_R >> 6	SHM_R >> 6	Readable by others
0002	MSG_W >> 6	SEM_A >> 6	SHM_W >> 6	Writable by others

Figure 20.2 Summary of IPC permissions.

The values in the first column are in octal (base 8), and the >> 3 and >> 6 are standard C notation, meaning that the value is shifted right by three or six bits respectively. Also, the suffix A in the semaphore permissions stands for "alter".

The creator IDs do not change during the lifetime of the object, but it is possible for a process to change the owner ID by using a control function (there is a separate control function for message queues, semaphores, and shared memory). This same control function can also be used to change an IPC object's permissions.

An IPC object's permissions are used to determine process access rights when the object is first opened and each time the object is accessed. (This is in contrast to file access permissions, which are checked only when a process `opens` a file; the resulting file descriptor can be used by any process regardless of whether that process could have opened the file itself.)

When a process attempts to establish a connection to an existing IPC object, the permissions specified are checked to ensure that they are compatible with those specified in the `mode` member of `ipc_perm` (i.e., the new permissions do not specify any bits that are not already set in `mode`). For example, suppose the process that created the object specified read and write access for the owner, but read-only access for the group and others. If a process subsequently tries to allow write access by the group or others, the `msgget`, `semget`, or `shmget` function will fail. This access check is, however, of little use, because the process doesn't know if it falls into the category of user, group, or other. A process can effectively bypass this access check by setting the flag argument to 0 if it knows that the IPC object already exists.

Every time a process attempts to perform an operation using an IPC object, the kernel checks to see if the process has appropriate permission. For example, a process that wants to place a message on a message queue must be able to write to that queue. The following tests are used to determine whether a process has the required permission to perform a given task.

1. If the effective user ID of the process is 0, the requested access is always granted.

2. If the effective user ID of the process is equal to IPC object's `uid` or `cuid`, and the appropriate bit in the IPC object's `mode` is set, then the requested access is granted. By "appropriate bit" we mean that the read bit must be set for a read operation (for example, reading a message from a message queue), and the write bit must be set for a write operation (e.g., placing a message onto a message queue).

3. If the effective group ID of the process is equal to IPC object's `gid` or `cgid`, and the appropriate bit in the IPC object's `mode` is set, then the requested access is granted.

4. If the preceding tests fail, then the appropriate "other" access bit must be set for the requested access to be granted.

The tests are performed in the order shown, and as soon as a test grants access, no further tests are performed.

The `ipcs` and `ipcrm` Programs

System V IPC objects are *kernel persistent*. This means that they persist until they are explicitly removed or the kernel is rebooted.

> There are two other types of IPC object persistence: *process persistent* and *file-system persistent*. An IPC object that is process persistent exists until the last process with that IPC object open closes it, and a file-system persistent IPC object exists until it is explicitly deleted.
>
> An example of a file-system-persistent IPC object is a POSIX IPC message queue (if they are implemented in this manner, which is not a POSIX requirement), and an example of a process-persistent IPC object is a pipe.
>
> Despite residing in the file system, FIFOs are also process persistent. This is because although the actual FIFO file remains until it is deleted, any data remaining in the FIFO is discarded when the last process that has the FIFO open closes it.

Because they do not appear in the file system, we can't use commands like `ls` and `rm` to view or remove them. Instead, we must use one of two commands: `ipcs` and `ipcrm`. The `ipcs` command is used to view the status of active System V IPC facilities, and the `ipcrm` command is used to remove System V IPC objects. The former supports twelve options to determine the information printed about what facility, and the latter has six options to identify the IPC object to remove. Full details about these commands can be found in their manual pages.

20.3 System V Message Queues

As we stated in the introduction to this chapter, a message queue is a kernel-resident linked list of messages. Each message queue is identified by an integer called the message queue identifier (we'll refer to this number as the message queue ID). Any suitably privileged process can place a message onto a queue, and a suitably privileged message can retrieve a message from a queue.

The kernel maintains an `msqid_ds` structure for every message queue in the system. It has the following members:

```
struct msqid_ds {
    struct ipc_perm  msg_perm;      /* Operation permission structure */
    struct msg       *msg_first;    /* Pointer to first message on queue */
    struct msg       *msg_last;     /* Pointer to last message on queue */
    msglen_t         msg_cbytes;    /* Current number of bytes on queue */
    msgqnum_t        msg_qnum;      /* Number of messages on queue */
    msglen_t         msg_qbytes;    /* Maximum number of bytes on queue */
    pid_t            msg_lspid;     /* Process ID of last msgsnd () */
    pid_t            msg_lrpid;     /* Process ID of last msgrcv () */
    time_t           msg_stime;     /* Last msgsnd () time */
    time_t           msg_rtime;     /* Last msgrcv () time */
    time_t           msg_ctime;     /* Last change time */
    short            msg_cv;        /* Internal condition variable */
    short            msg_qnum_cv;   /* Internal condition variable */
};
```

Most of the members of the `msqid_ds` structure are self-explanatory, although the two pointers, `msg_first` and `msg_last`, are meaningless to user space processes (this is because they refer to addresses in the kernel's virtual memory space). The two condition variables, `msg_cv` and `msg_qnum_cv`, are also of no use to user space processes.

A system administrator can adjust a number of variables to change the various kernel limits on System V message queues. Prior to Solaris 7 there were a total of seven tunable variables; more recent versions have only four. Figure 20.3 summarizes these tunables, showing the name used to tune a variable in /etc/system, a description of what the variable limits, and a typical default value for the variable.

Variable	Description	Default
msgsys:msginfo_msgmax	Maximum size of a System V message	2048
msgsys:msginfo_msgmnb	Maximum number of bytes that can be on a message queue	4096
msgsys:msginfo_msgmni	Maximum number of message queues that can be created	50
msgsys:msginfo_msgtql	Maximum number of messages that can be created	40
msgsys:msginfo_msgmap	Number of entries in the message map	100
msgsys:msginfo_msgssz	Segment size of a message	8
msgsys:msginfo_msgseg	Number of message segments	1024

Figure 20.3 System V message queue tunables.

The lower three variables in Figure 20.3 are available only prior to Solaris 7 (later releases used a different implementation that eliminated the need for these variables). From Solaris 10, all of these tunables have been replaced by resource controls.

The `msgget` Function

Before we can do anything with a message queue, we must determine its queue ID, if we don't already know it (e.g., by using `ipcs`). We do this by using `msgget`.

```
#include <sys/msg.h>

int msgget (key_t key, int msgflg);
```
Returns: queue ID if OK, −1 on error

The `msgget` function returns the message queue identifier associated with *key*. We described the rules for converting a *key* into an identifier, and the effect of *msgflg* on this operation, in Section 20.2.

If `msgget` creates a new message queue, the `msqid_ds` structure associated with it is initialized as follows:

- The `msg_perm.cuid`, `msg_perm.uid`, `msg_perm.cgid`, and `msg_perm.gid` members are initialized to the effective user ID and effective group ID of the calling process.
- The least significant 9 bits of `msg_perm.mode` are set to the least significant 9 bits of *msgflg*.
- The `msg_qnum`, `msg_lspid`, `msg_lrpid`, `msg_stime`, and `msg_rtime` members are set to 0.
- The `msg_ctime` member is set to the current time.
- The `msg_qbytes` member is set to the system limit.

Upon successful completion, a non-negative message queue ID is returned. This queue ID is used by most of the other System V message queue functions (the only exception being `msgids`).

> Although it isn't necessary on Solaris, some versions of UNIX require that we also include `<sys/types.h>` and `<sys/ipc.h>` when using `msgget` and its related functions. This also applies to programs using System V semaphores or System V shared memory.

The `msgsnd` Function

Messages are placed on a message queue by using the `msgsnd` function.

```
#include <sys/msg.h>

int msgsnd (int msqid, const void *msgp, size_t msgsz, int msgflg);
```
Returns: 0 if OK, −1 on error

The `msgsnd` function adds a new message to the message queue identified by *msqid*. The message to be added is specified by *msgp*, which is a pointer to a user-defined structure with two members. The first member specifies the message type, which must be a positive `long int`. The second member is the actual data portion of the message, the size of which is specified by the *msgsz* argument, and can be anywhere from 0 to the system-imposed maximum number of bytes.

The following is an example of what the user-supplied structure could look like:

```
struct ssp_msg {
    long    mtype;           /* Message type */
    char    mtext [msgsz];   /* Message data */
};
```

If *msgsz* is 0, there is no message data.

The value of the *msgflg* argument determines what happens if either of the following two conditions is true:

- The queue specified by *msqid* is already full (i.e., the number of bytes on the queue is equal to the msg_qbytes member of the msqid_ds data structure).
- The total number of messages on all of the queues systemwide is equal to the system imposed maximum.

If either of these conditions arises, then if the IPC_NOWAIT flag is set in *msgflg*, the message will not be sent, and msgsnd will immediately return an error of EAGAIN. Conversely, if the IPC_NOWAIT flag is clear , the caller will be put to sleep until one of the following occurs:

- The condition that caused the block ceases to exist (i.e., sufficient memory becomes available, or some other message gets delivered, reducing the number of systemwide messages). In this case, the message will be sent.
- The message queue identified by *msqid* is removed from the system; when this happens, an error of EIDRM is returned.
- The caller receives a signal that gets caught. In this case, an error of EINTR is returned.

When a message is successfully sent, several members of the msqid_ds structure are modified as follows: msg_qnum is incremented by one, msg_lspid is set to the process ID of the caller, and msg_stime is set to the current time.

The msgrcv Function

Messages are retrieved from a message queue by using the msgrcv function.

```
#include <sys/msg.h>

ssize_t msgrcv (int msqid, void *msgp, size_t msgsz, long msgtyp, int msgflg);
```
                                    Returns: number of bytes retrieved if OK, –1 on error

The msgrcv function reads a message from the message queue specified by *msqid*, placing it in the buffer pointed to by *msgp*. The structure of this buffer is the same as for the msgsnd function. The *msgsz* argument specifies the maximum amount of data that can be stored in the buffer, excluding the long message type member.

The message returned is determined by *msgtyp*, as follows:

- If *msgtyp* is 0, the first message on the queue is received. This will be the oldest message on the queue, because messages are maintained in FIFO order.
- If *msgtyp* is greater than 0, the first message whose type equals *msgtyp* is received.
- If *msgtyp* is less than 0, the first message whose type is less than or equal to the absolute value of *msgtyp* is received.

Suppose we have a message queue that contains three messages, the types of which are 10, 20, and 30 respectively. Figure 20.4 shows the message type returned for various values of *msgtyp*.

Value of *msgtyp*	Type of message retrieved
0	10
10	10
20	20
30	30
-10	10
-20	10
-30	10

Figure 20.4 Message type retrieved by `msgrcv` for different values of *msgtyp*.

The value of the *msgflg* arguments determines what action is taken should the requested message type not be available. If the `IPC_NOWAIT` flag is set, then `msgrcv` will immediately return an error of `ENOMSG` if an appropriate message is not available. Otherwise, the caller will block until one of the following occurs:

- A message of the requested type becomes available.
- The message queue identified by *msqid* is removed from the system; when this happens, an error of `EIDRM` is returned.
- The caller receives a signal that is caught. In this case, an error of `EINTR` is returned.

Another flag that determines the behaviour of the `msgrcv` function is `MSG_NOERROR`. If this flag is set, then data that will not fit into *msgp* is silently truncated so that it will fit into the supplied buffer. If `MSG_NOERROR` is not specified, then `msgrcv` will fail, returning an error of `E2BIG` if the message is larger than *msgsz* bytes. In this case, no part of the message is received.

When a message is successfully received, the number of bytes in the message is returned, excluding the space required by the `long` message type that is also stored in the buffer pointed to by *msgp*. Also, several members of the `msqid_ds` structure are modified as follows: `msg_qnum` is decremented by one, `msg_lrpid` is set to the process ID of the caller, and `msg_rtime` is set to the current time.

The `msgctl` Function

The `msgctl` function enables us to perform various control operations on message queues.

```
#include <sys/msg.h>

int msgctl (int msqid, int cmd, struct msqid_ds *buf);
```
Returns: 0 if OK, −1 on error

The `msgctl` function performs a message control operation on the message queue identified by *msqid*. The operation to be performed is specified by *cmd*, which can be one of three values:

IPC_STAT
: A copy of the kernel-maintained `msqid_ds` structure for the message queue identified by *msqid* is placed into the buffer pointed to by *buf*.

IPC_SET
: The following members of the kernel-maintained `msqid_ds` structure associated with the message queue identified by *msqid* are set to the values in the corresponding members of the `msqid_ds` structure pointed to by *buf*: `msg_perm.uid`, `msg_perm.gid`, `msg_perm.mode`, and `msg_qbytes`. This *cmd* can be successfully executed only by a process whose effective user ID is equal to either the `msg_perm.uid` or `msg_perm.cuid` members of the `msqid_ds` structure associated with the message queue, or is equal to that of the superuser. Only the superuser can increase the value of `msg_qbytes`.

IPC_RMID
: The message queue identified by *msqid* is immediately removed from the system. Any data in the queue is discarded, and any process that subsequently tries to use the message queue will get an error of `EIDRM`. This *cmd* can be successfully executed only by a process whose effective user ID is equal to either the `msg_perm.uid` or `msg_perm.cuid` members of the `msqid_ds` structure associated with the message queue, or is equal to that of the superuser. The *buf* argument is ignored.

Example: Using a message queue

Now that we've described the basic System V message queue functions, let's look at an example that uses them. To make this example more meaningful, we'll use a few small programs to manipulate a message queue. We can do this because, as we stated earlier, System V message queues have kernel persistence.

The first program just creates the message queue we'll use in this example. Program 20.2 shows the code for this program, which we'll call `msgcreat`.

ipc/msgcreat.c

```
 1 #include <stdio.h>
 2 #include <unistd.h>
 3 #include <sys/ipc.h>
 4 #include <sys/msg.h>
 5 #include "ssp.h"

 6 int main (int argc, char **argv)
 7 {
 8     int c;
 9     int qid;
10     key_t key;
11     int msgflg;
12     int err_flag;

13     msgflg = MSG_R | MSG_W | (MSG_R >> 3) | IPC_CREAT;
14     opterr = 0;
15     err_flag = 0;

16     while ((c = getopt (argc, argv, "e")) != EOF) {
17         switch (c) {
18             case 'e':
19                 msgflg |= IPC_EXCL;
20                 break;

21             default:
22                 err_flag++;
23                 break;
24         }
25     }

26     if (optind != argc - 1)
27         err_flag++;

28     if (err_flag)
29         err_quit ("Usage: msgcreat [-e] path");

30     if ((key = ftok (argv [optind], 0x42)) == -1)
31         err_msg ("ftok failed");
32     if ((qid = msgget (key, msgflg)) == -1)
33         err_msg ("msgget failed");

34     printf ("Message queue ID = %x\n", qid);

35     return (0);
36 }
```

ipc/msgcreat.c

Program 20.2 Create a System V message queue.

Parse command line options

16–25 Allow a command line option of -e to specify the `IPC_EXCL` flag.

Create the message queue

30–31 Use `ftok` to generate an appropriate key, using the pathname we specified on the command line, and a hard-coded *id* of 0x42.

32–34 Create the message queue using the key we just created, and print the resulting message queue ID.

Program 20.3 shows the code for our next program, called `msgsnd`.

———————————————————————————— ipc/msgsnd.c

```
1 #include <stdio.h>
2 #include <unistd.h>
3 #include <stdlib.h>
4 #include <sys/ipc.h>
5 #include <sys/msg.h>
6 #include "ssp.h"

7 int main (int argc, char **argv)
8 {
9     int qid;
10    key_t key;
11    size_t msgsz;
12    long msgtyp;
13    struct msgbuf *buf;

14    if (argc != 4)
15        err_quit ("Usage: msgsnd path type size");

16    msgtyp = atol (argv [2]);
17    msgsz = atol (argv [3]);

18    if ((key = ftok (argv [1], 0x42)) == -1)
19        err_msg ("ftok failed");
20    if ((qid = msgget (key, MSG_W)) == -1)
21        err_msg ("msgget failed");

22    if ((buf = malloc (sizeof (long) + msgsz)) == NULL)
23        err_msg ("malloc failed");

24    buf -> mtype = msgtyp;

25    if (msgsnd (qid, buf, msgsz, 0) == -1)
26        err_msg ("msgsnd failed");

27    return (0);
28 }
```

———————————————————————————— ipc/msgsnd.c

Program 20.3   Add a message to a System V message queue.

Parse command line arguments

14–17 If the correct number of command line arguments have been supplied, the message type is taken to be the second argument, and the size of the message to send is taken as the third argument.

Open the message queue

18–19 Use `ftok` to generate the correct key, using the pathname we supplied on the command line and a hard-coded value of 0x42.

20–21 Open the message queue using the key we just created.

Allocate memory for the message

22–23 Allocate the memory required to hold the message using `malloc`.

Set message type

24 Set the message type. Notice that we're using the generic message template structure, `msgbuf`, as defined in `<sys/msg.h>`. We don't worry about initializing the rest of the message, because for this example, its contents don't concern us.

Add the message to the queue

25–26 Add the message to the message queue, using the `msgsnd` function.

Now that we can add messages to a message queue, we need some way to retrieve them. Program 20.4 shows the code for our `msgrcv` program, which performs this task.

Define maximum message size

7 There's no easy programmatic way of determining the maximum size of a message, so we define our own constant. We arrived at the number 2048 by examining the "IPC Messages" section of the output from the `sysdef` utility on a Solaris 9 system:

```
$ sysdef
*
* IPC Messages
*
    2048  max message size (MSGMAX)
    4096  max bytes on queue (MSGMNB)
      50  message queue identifiers (MSGMNI)
      40  system message headers (MSGTQL)
```

Parse command line arguments

22–34 Allow command line options of `-n` to specify nonblocking and `-t` to specify the *msgtyp* argument for the `msgrcv` function.

Open the message queue

39–40 Use `ftok` to generate the required key, using the pathname we supplied on the command line, and a hard-coded value of 0x42.

41–42 Open the message queue using the key we just created.

Allocate memory for the message

43–44 Allocate the memory required to hold the largest message we support using the `malloc` function.

Remove the message from the queue

45–47 Call `msgrcv` to retrieve the next appropriate message from the message queue, and print how many bytes were read and the message type.

ipc/msgrcv.c

```
 1 #include <stdio.h>
 2 #include <unistd.h>
 3 #include <stdlib.h>
 4 #include <sys/ipc.h>
 5 #include <sys/msg.h>
 6 #include "ssp.h"

 7 #define MSGMAX (2048 + sizeof (long))

 8 int main (int argc, char **argv)
 9 {
10     int c;
11     int qid;
12     key_t key;
13     int msgflg;
14     int err_flag;
15     long msgtyp;
16     ssize_t n;
17     struct msgbuf *buf;

18     msgflg = MSG_R;
19     msgtyp = 0;
20     opterr = 0;
21     err_flag = 0;

22     while ((c = getopt (argc, argv, "nt:")) != EOF) {
23         switch (c) {
24             case 'n':
25                 msgflg |= IPC_NOWAIT;
26                 break;

27             case 't':
28                 msgtyp = atol (optarg);
29                 break;

30             default:
31                 err_flag++;
32                 break;
33         }
34     }

35     if (optind != argc - 1)
36         err_flag++;
37     if (err_flag)
38         err_quit ("Usage: msgrcv [-n] [-t type] path");

39     if ((key = ftok (argv [optind], 0x42)) == -1)
40         err_msg ("ftok failed");
41     if ((qid = msgget (key, msgflg)) == -1)
42         err_msg ("msgget failed");

43     if ((buf = malloc (MSGMAX)) == NULL)
44         err_msg ("malloc failed");

45     if ((n = msgrcv (qid, buf, MSGMAX, msgtyp, msgflg)) == -1)
46         err_msg ("msgrcv failed");
47     printf ("Read %d bytes, message type = %ld\n", n, buf -> mtype);

48     return (0);
49 }
```

ipc/msgrcv.c

Program 20.4   Remove a message from a System V message queue.

Finally, we need a program to remove a message queue. Program 20.5 shows the code for our program that performs this task, msgrmq.

ipc/msgrmq.c

```
 1 #include <stdio.h>
 2 #include <unistd.h>
 3 #include <sys/msg.h>
 4 #include "ssp.h"

 5 int main (int argc, char **argv)
 6 {
 7     int qid;
 8     key_t key;

 9     if (argc != 2)
10         err_quit ("Usage: msgrmq path");

11     if ((key = ftok (argv [1], 0x42)) == -1)
12         err_msg ("ftok failed");
13     if ((qid = msgget (key, 0)) == -1)
14         err_msg ("msgget failed");

15     if (msgctl (qid, IPC_RMID, NULL) == -1)
16         err_msg ("msgctl failed");

17     return (0);
18 }
```

ipc/msgrmq.c

Program 20.5 Remove a System V message queue.

Program 20.5 is very straightforward. After checking that the correct number of command line arguments were supplied, the message queue ID is determined by calling ftok with the pathname supplied on the command line and the hard-coded value of 0x42. The message queue identified by this identifier is then removed from the system by calling msgctl with a command of IPC_RMID.

Let's take a look at how we might use the four programs we've just presented. The first thing we have to do is create a message queue and put some messages onto it.

```
$ ./msgcreat /tmp/ssp_ipc
ftok failed: No such file or directory
$ touch /tmp/ssp_ipc
$ ./msgcreat /tmp/ssp_ipc
Message queue ID = 150
$ ./msgsnd /tmp/ssp_ipc 10 5
$ ./msgsnd /tmp/ssp_ipc 20 10
$ ./msgsnd /tmp/ssp_ipc 30 15
$ ipcs -qo
IPC status from <running system> as of Wed Aug 27 17:54:20 PDT 2003
T         ID      KEY         MODE         OWNER    GROUP CBYTES  QNUM
Message Queues:
q         150     0x42002159  --rw-r-----  rich     staff    30     3
```

The first time we run msgcreat, the ftok function fails because the pathname we pass to it, /tmp/ssp_ipc, doesn't exist. After creating this file using touch, we create the message queue (the message queue ID is 150). We then place three messages on the message queue. The first message has a type of 10 and a size of 5 bytes, the second has a type of 20 and a size of 10 bytes, and the third message has a type of 30 and a size of 15 bytes. We then run the `ipcs` command to confirm that three messages are on the message queue, and that they total 30 bytes in size.

Now that we have some messages on our message queue, let's retrieve them using `msgrcv`. We'll demonstrate how we can use the `-t` argument to retrieve the messages in an order other than FIFO.

```
$ ./msgrcv -t 20 /tmp/ssp_ipc
Read 10 bytes, message type = 20
$ ./msgrcv -t -30 /tmp/ssp_ipc
Read 5 bytes, message type = 10
$ ./msgrcv /tmp/ssp_ipc
Read 15 bytes, message type = 30
$ ./msgrcv /tmp/ssp_ipc
^C                                        Type Control-C to terminate
$ ./msgrcv -n /tmp/ssp_ipc
msgrcv failed: No message of desired type
$ grep "No message" /usr/include/sys/errno.h
#define ENOMSG   35      /* No message of desired type          */
$ ./msgrmq /tmp/ssp_ipc
$ ipcs -qo
IPC status from <running system> as of Thu Aug 28 11:18:32 PDT 2003
T         ID      KEY        MODE        OWNER     GROUP CBYTES  QNUM
Message Queues:
```

The first time we invoke `msgrcv`, we request a message of type 20, and the second invocation requests a message whose type is less than or equal to 30. The third invocation just requests the first message on the queue, and the fourth invocation demonstrates what happens when no suitable messages are on the queue: the `msgrcv` function blocks, waiting for a suitable message. We interrupt the `msgrcv` process and run the program again, this time specifying the `IPC_NOWAIT` flag. This time, we are immediately informed that no suitable messages are available, and confirm that `errno` is set to `ENOMSG`.

Finally, we remove the message queue from the system by using our `msgrmq` program and verify that it has been removed by using the `ipcs` command. Note that to remove the message queue, we could simply use the `ipcrm` command

```
$ ipcrm -q 150
```

which specifies the message queue ID, or

```
$ ipcrm -Q 0x42002159
```

which specifies the key associated with the message queue.

The `msgsnap` Function

We can get a snapshot of the messages on a message queue by using the `msgsnap` function.

```
#include <sys/msg.h>

int msgsnap (int msqid, void *buf, size_t bufsz, long msgtyp);
```
                                                               Returns: 0 if OK, −1 on error

The `msgsnap` function provides the caller with a snapshot of all of the messages on the message queue identified by *msqid*, placing them into the buffer pointed to by *buf*, which has a size of *bufsz* bytes.

Upon successful return, the first few bytes of *buf* will contain a header defined by the `msgsnap_head` structure:

```
struct msgsnap_head {
    size_t  msgsnap_size;    /* Bytes used or required in the buffer */
    size_t  msgsnap_nmsg;    /* Number of messages in the buffer */
};
```

This header structure is then followed by `msgsnap_nmsg` messages, each of which is preceded by a message header that is defined by the `msgsnap_mhead` structure:

```
struct msgsnap_mhead {
    size_t  msgsnap_mlen;    /* Number of bytes in the message */
    long    msgsnap_mtype;   /* Message type */
};
```

The `msgsnap_mlen` bytes following the message header contain the message data itself. The header for the next message starts at the first byte after the previous message, rounded up to a `sizeof (size_t)` boundary.

If *buf* is not large enough to hold the snapshot header (that is, *bufsz* is less than `sizeof (struct msgsnap_head)`), the `msgsnap` function will fail, returning an error of `EINVAL`. If *buf* is not of a sufficient size to contain all the requested messages, `msgsnap` will return success, but `msgsnap_nmsg` will be set to 0, and `msgsnap_size` will contain the required buffer size.

The types of the messages contained in the snapshot are determined by the *msgtyp* argument:

- If *msgtyp* is 0, all of the messages on the queue are read.
- If *msgtyp* is greater than 0, all messages whose type is equal to *msgtyp* will be read.
- If *msgtyp* is less than 0, all messages whose type is less than or equal to the absolute value of *msgtyp* will be read.

Obtaining a message queue snapshot is a nondestructive operation. That is, no changes are made to the data structures associated with *msqid*. Also, the contents of the message queue can change immediately following a return from `msgsnap`.

The `msgids` Function

We can get a list of all the current message queues by using the `msgids` function.

```
#include <sys/msg.h>

int msgids (int *buf, uint_t nids, uint_t *pnids);
```
Returns: 0 if OK, −1 on error

The `msgids` function returns a list of all the active System V message queues into the buffer pointed to by *buf*, provided that the number of message queue identifiers does not exceed *nids*.

The number of message queue identifiers currently active in the system is stored in the unsigned integer pointed to by *pnids*, regardless of whether *buf* is of a sufficient size to contain them all. If *nids* is 0 or less than the number of active message queues, *buf* is ignored (we can use this fact to correctly size the buffer before attempting to retrieve all of the message queue identifiers).

The list of message queue identifiers returned by `msgids` is a snapshot of the instant the `msgids` function was called. Once `msgids` returns, message queues might be added to or removed from the system.

Example: Listing all the current messages

Program 20.6 prints a snapshot of the messages currently in message queues.

Parse command line arguments

24–36 Allow command line options of -t to specify the message type we're interested in, and -q to specify the message queue identifier.

Call `queue_snapshot` for the requested message queues

41–42 If msqid is not equal to 0, we've specified a specific message queue, so call `queue_snapshot` to print the messages on the requested message queue.

43–56 Otherwise, call `msgids` to get a list of all the message queue identifiers, allocating the required amount of memory (because we are not planning to recover from any errors, we don't save a copy of the pointer we pass to `realloc`). Once the list of message queue identifiers has been retrieved, call `queue_snapshot` to print the messages on each message queue. Finally, free the buffer we previously allocated.

The `queue_snapshot` function

66–68 Allocate a minimum-sized buffer (i.e., one that is the size of a `msgsnap_head` structure).

69–77 Read all of the messages from the specified queue, allocating memory as required (because we are not planning to recover from any errors, we don't save a copy of the pointer we pass to `realloc`).

78–87 Step through each message in the buffer, printing its position in the queue, its size, and its message type.

88 Free the buffer we previously allocated.

Let's take a look at Program 20.6 in action.

—— *ipc/msgls.c*

```
 1  #include <stdio.h>
 2  #include <unistd.h>
 3  #include <stdlib.h>
 4  #include <sys/ipc.h>
 5  #include <sys/msg.h>
 6  #include "ssp.h"

 7  static void queue_snapshot (int msqid, long msgtyp);

 8  int main (int argc, char **argv)
 9  {
10      int c;
11      int err_flag;
12      long msgtyp;
13      int msqid;
14      int *buf;
15      uint_t i;
16      uint_t n;
17      uint_t nids;

18      nids = 0;
19      buf = NULL;
20      msgtyp = 0;
21      msqid = 0;
22      opterr = 0;
23      err_flag = 0;

24      while ((c = getopt (argc, argv, "t:q:")) != EOF) {
25          switch (c) {
26              case 't':
27                  msgtyp = atol (optarg);
28                  break;

29              case 'q':
30                  msqid = atoi (optarg);
31                  break;

32              default:
33                  err_flag++;
34                  break;
35          }
36      }

37      if (optind != argc)
38          err_flag++;
39      if (err_flag)
40          err_quit ("Usage: msgls [-t type] [-q queue ID]");

41      if (msqid != 0)
42          queue_snapshot (msqid, msgtyp);
43      else {
44          for (;;) {
45              if (msgids (buf, nids, &n) == -1)
46                  err_msg ("msgids failed");

47              if (n <= nids)
48                  break;
```

```
49                    nids = n;
50                    if ((buf = realloc (buf, nids * sizeof (int))) == NULL)
51                        err_msg ("realloc failed");
52                }

53            for (i = 0; i < n; i++)
54                queue_snapshot (buf [i], msgtyp);

55            free (buf);
56        }

57        return (0);
58 }

59 static void queue_snapshot (int msqid, long msgtyp)
60 {
61        size_t buf_size;
62        struct msgsnap_head *buf;
63        struct msgsnap_mhead *mhead;
64        size_t i;
65        size_t mlen;

66        buf_size = sizeof (struct msgsnap_head);
67        if ((buf = malloc (buf_size)) == NULL)
68            err_msg ("malloc failed");

69        for (;;) {
70            if (msgsnap (msqid, buf, buf_size, msgtyp) == -1)
71                err_msg ("msgsnap failed");

72            if (buf -> msgsnap_size <= buf_size)
73                break;

74            buf_size = buf -> msgsnap_size;
75            if ((buf = realloc (buf, buf_size)) == NULL)
76                err_msg ("realloc failed");
77        }

78        printf ("Queue ID %d:\n", msqid);
79        mhead = (struct msgsnap_mhead *) (buf + 1);
80        for (i = 0; i < buf -> msgsnap_nmsg; i++) {
81            mlen = mhead -> msgsnap_mlen;
82            msgtyp = mhead -> msgsnap_mtype;

83            printf ("  %d %d bytes, message type = %ld\n", i, mlen, msgtyp);

84            mhead = (struct msgsnap_mhead *)
85                ((char *) mhead + sizeof (struct msgsnap_mhead) +
86                ((mlen + sizeof (size_t) - 1) & ~(sizeof (size_t) - 1)));
87        }

88        free (buf);
89 }
```

ipc/msgls.c

Program 20.6 List all messages currently in System V message queues.

```
$ touch /tmp/ssp_ipc1
$ touch /tmp/ssp_ipc2
$ ./msgcreat /tmp/ssp_ipc1
Message queue ID = 250
$ ./msgcreat /tmp/ssp_ipc2
Message queue ID = 51
$ ./msgsnd /tmp/ssp_ipc1 10 5
$ ./msgsnd /tmp/ssp_ipc1 20 10
$ ./msgsnd /tmp/ssp_ipc1 30 15
$ ./msgsnd /tmp/ssp_ipc2 100 50
$ ./msgsnd /tmp/ssp_ipc2 200 100
$ ./msgsnd /tmp/ssp_ipc2 300 200
$ ipcs -qo
IPC status from <running system> as of Fri Aug 29 15:26:03 PDT 2003
T         ID      KEY         MODE        OWNER     GROUP CBYTES  QNUM
Message Queues:
q         250    0x420020f9 --rw-r-----    rich      staff    30      3
q          51    0x420021b8 --rw-r-----    rich      staff   350      3
$ ./msgls -t 20
Queue ID 250:
  0 10 bytes, message type = 20
Queue ID 51:
$ ./msgls -t -200
Queue ID 250:
  0 5 bytes, message type = 10
  1 10 bytes, message type = 20
  2 15 bytes, message type = 30
Queue ID 51:
  0 50 bytes, message type = 100
  1 100 bytes, message type = 200
$ ./msgls -q 51 -t -200
Queue ID 51:
  0 50 bytes, message type = 100
  1 100 bytes, message type = 200
$ ./msgls
Queue ID 250:
  0 5 bytes, message type = 10
  1 10 bytes, message type = 20
  2 15 bytes, message type = 30
Queue ID 51:
  0 50 bytes, message type = 100
  1 100 bytes, message type = 200
  2 200 bytes, message type = 300
$ ./msgls -q 250
Queue ID 250:
  0 5 bytes, message type = 10
  1 10 bytes, message type = 20
  2 15 bytes, message type = 30
$ ipcs -qo
IPC status from <running system> as of Fri Aug 29 16:15:30 PDT 2003
T         ID      KEY         MODE        OWNER     GROUP CBYTES  QNUM
Message Queues:
q         250    0x420020f9 --rw-r-----    rich      staff    30      3
q          51    0x420021b8 --rw-r-----    rich      staff   350      3
```

The first thing we do is create the files we'll be using to create message queues we create using `msgcreat`. The queue IDs of the queues we create are 250 and 51.

We then populate the two message queues with some messages and use the `ipcs` command to confirm that the messages have been placed in their queues.

Next we run `msqls` several times. The first time we run `msqls` we specify a type of 20. All messages of type 20, no matter what queue they are in, are printed. Next we run `msqls` specifying a type of −200. All messages whose type is less than or equal to 200, no matter what queue they are in, are printed. We then run `msqls` again, specifying the same type as before, but also specifying the queue identifier we're interested in (in this case, the message queue whose queue ID is 51). This results in all messages whose type is less than or equal to 200 being printed, provided they are on the specified message queue.

We run `msqls` two more times. The first time, we print all the messages on all of the message queues, and the second time, we print all the messages on the message queue whose message queue identifier is 250.

Finally, to prove that `msgsnap` is a nondestructive operation, we run `ipcs` again to ensure that all of the messages we added are still on their respective queues.

20.4 System V Semaphores Sets

A *semaphore* is a primitive that is used to provide synchronization between processes or threads within a process. Another way of expressing this is that a semaphore is a counter used to provide access to a shared data resource by multiple threads or processes.

We can perform three operations on semaphores:

1. We can *create* the semaphore. When we create a semaphore, we also specify its initial value.
2. We can *wait* for a semaphore. When a process or thread requires access to the resource controlled by the semaphore, it tests the semaphore's value. If the value of the semaphore is less than or equal to 0, the requester blocks until the semaphore's value is greater than 0. Once access to the resource controlled by the semaphore has been granted, the semaphores value is decremented.

   This operation was originally called *P* by Edsger Dijkstra, from the Dutch word *proberen*, which means "try". It is also known as *lock* and *down* (because the value of the semaphore is decremented).
3. We can *post* to a semaphore. We typically do this when we have finished using the shared resource. Posting to a semaphore increments its value; if the value of the semaphore becomes greater than 0 as a result, any processes waiting for the resource will be woken up.

This operation was originally called *V*, from the Dutch word *verhogen*, which means "increment". It is also known as *signal*, *unlock*, and *up* (because the value of the semaphore is incremented).

A common type of semaphore is called a *binary semaphore*, which controls a single resource and has a value of 0 or 1. Another type of semaphore is called a *counting semaphore*. It is much the same as a binary semaphore, but can have a value between 0 and some system-defined limit. System V semaphores implement sets of counting semaphores. (POSIX semaphores support only the first two types.)

Two other features of System V semaphores add to their complexity:

1. The creation of a semaphore and its initialization are independent (i.e., there is no way to create and initialize a System V semaphore in a single atomic operation). This flaw can lead to race conditions.

2. Like all System V IPC facilities, System V semaphores have kernel persistence. This means that we have to worry about a program that terminates without releasing any semaphores it might have. (The "undo" feature we describe later is designed to handle this situation.)

The kernel maintains a `semid_ds` structure for every semaphore in the system. It has the following members:

```
struct semid_ds {
    struct ipc_perm sem_perm;       /* Operation permission structure */
    struct sem      *sem_base;      /* Pointer to first semaphore in set */
    ushort_t        sem_nsems;      /* Number of semaphores in set */
    time_t          sem_otime;      /* Last semop () time */
    time_t          sem_ctime;      /* Last change time */
    int             sem_binary;     /* Flag indicating semaphore type */
};
```

As with the `msqid_ds` structure, most of the members of the `semid_ds` structure are self-explanatory. Also, the `sem_base` member is not much use to a user space process, because it points to an address in the kernel's virtual memory space. This memory holds an array of `sem` structures, one for each semaphore in the set:

```
struct sem {
    ushort_t    semval;         /* Semaphore value */
    pid_t       sempid;         /* Process ID of last operation */
    ushort_t    semncnt;        /* Num threads awaiting semval > curr value */
    ushort_t    semzcnt;        /* Num threads awaiting semval = 0 */
    ushort_t    semncnt_cv;     /* Internal condition variable */
    ushort_t    semzcnt_cv;     /* Internal condition variable */
};
```

The system administrator can adjust a number of variables to change the various kernel limits on System V semaphores. Prior to Solaris 7 there were a total of nine tunable variables; more recent versions have only eight. Figure 20.5 summarizes these tunables, showing the name used to tune the variable in /etc/system, a description of what the variable limits, and a typical default value for the variable.

Variable	Description	Default
semsys:seminfo_semmni	Maximum number of semaphore identifiers	10
semsys:seminfo_semmns	Maximum number of semaphores on the system	60
semsys:seminfo_semvmx	Maximum value a semaphore can be set to	32,767
semsys:seminfo_semmsl	Maximum number of semaphores per semaphore identifier	25
semsys:seminfo_semopm	Maximum number of operations per semop call	10
semsys:seminfo_semmnu	Maximum number of undo structures in the system	30
semsys:seminfo_semume	Maximum number of undo structures per process	10
semsys:seminfo_semaem	Maximum value for adjustment on exit	16,384
semsys:seminfo_semmap	Number of entries in the semaphore map	10

Figure 20.5 System V semaphore tunables.

The last variable in Figure 20.5 is available only prior to Solaris 7. Later releases used a different implementation that eliminated the need for this variable. From Solaris 10, all of these tunables have been replaced by resource controls.

The semget Function

We create a new, or access an existing, semaphore set by using semget.

```
#include <sys/sem.h>

int semget (key_t key, int nsems, int semflg);
```
                                    Returns: semaphore set ID if OK, −1 on error

The semget function returns the semaphore set identifier associated with *key*. We described the rules for converting a *key* into an identifier, and the effect of *semflg* on this operation, in Section 20.2.

If a new semaphore set is not being created, *nsems* is ignored (it is not possible to change the number of semaphores in a semaphore set once it has been created). If semget creates a new semaphore set, the set will contain *nsems* semaphores, and the semid_ds structure associated with it is initialized as follows:

- The sem_perm.cuid, sem_perm.uid, sem_perm.cgid, and sem_perm.gid members are initialized to the effective user ID and effective group ID of the calling process.
- The least significant 9 bits of sem_perm.mode are set to the least significant 9 bits of *semflg*.
- The sem_nsems member is set equal to the value of *nsems*.
- The sem_otime member is set to 0.
- The sem_ctime member is set to the current time.

Upon successful completion, a non-negative semaphore set ID is returned. This semaphore set ID is used by most of the other System V semaphore functions (the only exception being semids).

As we stated earlier, the actual value of the semaphores in the set is not initialized by semget. The semctl function (see later) must be used instead.

The semop and semtimedop Functions

Once we've opened a semaphore set using semget, we can perform various operations on some or all of the semaphores in the set by using either semop or semtimedop.

```
#include <sys/sem.h>

int semop (int semid, struct sembuf *sops, size_t nsops);

int semtimedop (int semid, struct sembuf *sops, size_t nsops,
    const struct timespec *timeout);
```
Both return: 0 if OK, −1 on error

The semop function atomically performs the semaphore operations, specified by the array of sembuf structures pointed to by *sops*, on the set (or a subset) of semaphores associated with the semaphore set identified by *semid*. The *nsops* argument specifies the number of sembuf structures are in the array pointed to by *sops*.

The sembuf structure has the following members:

```
struct sembuf {
    ushort_t    sem_num;    /* Semaphore number */
    short       sem_op;     /* Semaphore operation */
    short       sem_flg;    /* Semaphore operation flags */
};
```

The sem_num identifies which semaphore in the set the operation is to be performed on, the sem_op member specifies the operation to be performed, and the sem_flg member specifies any flags associated with the operation that is to be performed.

The value of sem_op may be negative, 0, or positive. Each of these has the following meaning:

sem_op < 0   This corresponds to an allocation of resources; the caller waits until the semaphore's value (i.e., the semval member of the semaphore's semid_ds structure) becomes greater than or equal to the absolute value of sem_op.

If the value of the semaphore is greater than or equal to the absolute value of sem_op, the absolute value of sem_op is subtracted from the semaphore's value. Also, if the SEM_UNDO flag is set in sem_flg, the absolute value of sem_op is added to the calling process' semaphore adjustment value for the specified semaphore.

(The adjustment value is used to undo the effect of semaphore operations should the process unexpectedly terminate. The kernel maintains a variable for each process that specifies the SEM_UNDO flag in a semaphore operation.)

If the value of the semaphore is less than the absolute value of sem_op, and the IPC_NOWAIT flag is set in sem_flg, then semop returns immediately.

If the semaphore value is less than the absolute value of sem_op, and the IPC_NOWAIT flag is not set in sem_flg, then semop increments the semncnt member of the semid_ds structure associated with the specified semaphore and suspends the caller until one of the following occurs:

- The semaphore's value becomes greater than or equal to the absolute value of sem_op. When this happens, the semaphore's semncnt value is decremented, and the absolute value of sem_op is subtracted from the semaphore's value. Also, if the SEM_UNDO flag in sem_flg is set, the absolute value of sem_op is added to the caller's semaphore adjustment value for the specified semaphore.

- The semaphore identified by *semid* is removed from the system. In this case, semop fails, setting errno to EIDRM.

- The caller receives a signal that is caught. In this case, the semaphore's semncnt value is decremented, and an error of EINTR is returned.

sem_op = 0

The caller waits for the semaphore's value to be equal to 0. If value of the semaphore is equal to 0, or if it is not equal to 0 and the IPC_NOWAIT flag in sem_flg is set, then semop returns immediately.

If the semaphore's value is not equal to 0 and the IPC_NOWAIT flag in sem_flg is not set, the semaphore's semzcnt value is incremented, and the caller is suspended until one of the three conditions described under sem_op < 0 occurs. (In this case, semzcnt will be set to 0 when the semaphore's value becomes equal to 0. Similarly, semzcnt is decremented when the caller receives a signal that is caught.)

sem_op > 0

This corresponds to a releasing of resources; the value of sem_op is added to the semaphore's value, and, if the SEM_UNDO flag in sem_flg is set, the value of sem_op is subtracted from the calling process' semaphore adjustment value for the specified semaphore.

Upon successful completion, the `sempid` for each specified semaphore is set to the caller's process ID, and the `sem_otime` member of the `semid_ds` structure associated with *semid* is set to the current time.

The `semtimedop` function is the same as `semop`, except for when the caller must be put to sleep. In this eventuality, *timeout* points to a `timespec` structure that specifies the timeout period. If this timeout expires while the caller is suspended, then `semtimedop` will fail, setting `errno` to `EAGAIN`. If *timeout* points to a `timespec` structure that has a value of 0, then `semtimedop` will immediately return with an error if it would have to suspend the caller. If *timeout* is NULL, then `semtimedop` behaves the same as `semop`.

The `semctl` Function

We can perform various control operations on a semaphore by using `semctl`.

```
#include <sys/sem.h>

int semctl (int semid, int semnum, int cmd, /* union semun arg */...);
                                          Returns: see text if OK, −1 on error
```

The `semctl` function performs the semaphore control operation specified by *cmd* on the semaphore identified by *semid*. Some of the operations require the fourth argument to be supplied. In this case, the variable must be a `semun` union, which must be declared by the application (i.e., it does not appear in any system header file).

The `semun` union must have the following members:

```
union semun {
    int                 val;      /* Used by SETVAL only */
    struct semid_ds *buf;         /* Used by IPC_SET and IPC_STAT */
    ushort_t            *array;   /* Used by GETALL and SETALL */
};
```

Notice also that we pass the union by value, not by reference.

The following values of *cmd* operate on the semaphore specified by *semid* and *semnum*.

GETVAL   This returns the value of `semval` (i.e., the current value of the semaphore).

SETVAL   This sets the value of the semaphore to *argv.val*. If this alteration is successful, the adjustment value corresponding to the specified semaphore in all processes is set to 0.

GETPID   This returns the value of `sempid` (i.e., the process ID of the process that performed the last operation on the semaphore).

GETNCNT   This returns the value of `semncnt` (i.e., the number of threads waiting for the semaphore's value to become greater than it is currently).

GETZCNT   Returns the value of `semzcnt` (i.e., the number of threads waiting for the semaphore's value to become equal to 0).

The following two operations get or set every `semval` in the specified semaphore set:

SETALL
: This sets the `semval` of each semaphore according to the array pointed to by *arg.array*. If this alteration is successful, the adjustment value corresponding to each specified semaphore is set to 0.

GETALL
: This places the current values of `semval` of each semaphore into the array pointed to by *arg.array*. Note that we must allocate a buffer large enough to hold as many `unsigned short` integers as there are semaphores in the set, and make *arg.array* point to this buffer.

The following operations are also available:

IPC_STAT
: A copy of the kernel-maintained `semid_ds` structure for the semaphore set identified by *semid* is placed into the buffer pointed to by *arg.buf*.

IPC_SET
: The following members of the kernel-maintained `semid_ds` structure associated with the message queue identified by *semid* are set to the values in the corresponding members of the `semid_ds` structure pointed to by *arg.buf*: `sem_perm.uid`, `sem_perm.gid`, and `sem_perm.mode`. This *cmd* can be successfully executed only by a process whose effective user ID is equal to either the `sem_perm.uid` or `sem_perm.cuid` members of the `semid_ds` structure associated with the semaphore set, or is equal to that of the superuser.

IPC_RMID
: The semaphore set identified by *semid* is immediately removed from the system. This *cmd* can only be successfully executed by a process whose effective user ID is equal to either the `sem_perm.uid` or `sem_perm.cuid` members of the `semid_ds` structure associated with the semaphore set, or is equal to that of the superuser.

Unless stated otherwise, `semctl` returns 0 on success (−1 is always returned on error).

Example: Using a semaphore set

Let's take a look at an example that uses a System V semaphore set. We'll use a few small programs to manipulate a semaphore set; we can do this because System V semaphores have kernel persistence.

The first program just creates the semaphore set we'll use in this example. The `-e` command line option specifies the `IPC_EXCL` flag. The pathname of the file to use to generate the key, and the number of semaphores in the set, are also specified on the command line.

Program 20.7 shows the code for this program, which is called `semcreat`.

ipc/semcreat.c

```
 1 #include <stdio.h>
 2 #include <unistd.h>
 3 #include <stdlib.h>
 4 #include <sys/sem.h>
 5 #include "ssp.h"

 6 int main (int argc, char **argv)
 7 {
 8     int c;
 9     int semid;
10     int num_sems;
11     key_t key;
12     int semflg;
13     int err_flag;

14     semflg = SEM_R | SEM_A | (SEM_R >> 3) | IPC_CREAT;
15     opterr = 0;
16     err_flag = 0;

17     while ((c = getopt (argc, argv, "e")) != EOF) {
18         switch (c) {
19             case 'e':
20                 semflg |= IPC_EXCL;
21                 break;

22             default:
23                 err_flag++;
24                 break;
25         }
26     }

27     if (optind != argc - 2)
28         err_flag++;

29     if (err_flag)
30         err_quit ("Usage: semcreat [-e] path num_sems");

31     num_sems = atoi (argv [optind + 1]);
32     if ((key = ftok (argv [optind], 0x42)) == -1)
33         err_msg ("ftok failed");
34     if ((semid = semget (key, num_sems, semflg)) == -1)
35         err_msg ("semget failed");

36     printf ("Semaphore set ID = %d\n", semid);

37     return (0);
38 }
```

ipc/semcreat.c

Program 20.7 Create a System V semaphore set.

Parse command line arguments

17–26 Allow a command line option of `-e` to specify the `IPC_EXCL` flag.

Create the semaphore set

31 Convert the last command line argument, which specifies the number of semaphores in the set, to an integer.

32–36 Use `ftok` to generate an appropriate key using the pathname we specified on the command line and a hard-coded *id* of 0x42. Then create the semaphore set using the key we just created and print the resulting semaphore set ID.

Program 20.8 shows the code for `semrm`, which we use to remove a semaphore set.

—— *ipc/semrm.c*

```
 1 #include <stdio.h>
 2 #include <unistd.h>
 3 #include <sys/sem.h>
 4 #include "ssp.h"

 5 int main (int argc, char **argv)
 6 {
 7     int semid;
 8     key_t key;

 9     if (argc != 2)
10         err_quit ("Usage: semrm path");
11     if ((key = ftok (argv [1], 0x42)) == -1)
12         err_msg ("ftok failed");
13     if ((semid = semget (key, 0, 0)) == -1)
14         err_msg ("semget failed");

15     if (semctl (semid, IPC_RMID, NULL) == -1)
16         err_msg ("semctl failed");

17     return (0);
18 }
```

—— *ipc/semrm.c*

Program 20.8   Remove a System V semaphore set.

Program 20.9 shows the code for the next program, called `semset`.

Parse command line arguments

20–21 Exit if the wrong number of arguments was supplied.

Open the semaphore set

22–23 Use `ftok` to generate the correct key using the pathname we supplied on the command line and a hard-coded value of 0x42.

24–25 Open the semaphore set using the key we just created.

Check the number of semaphores

26–32 Call `semctl` with a *cmd* of `IPC_STAT` to determine how many semaphores were in the set when it was created. If we haven't specified the same number of semaphores on the command line, exit with an error.

Populate the semaphore set

33–35 Allocate the memory required to hold the semaphore set using `calloc`.

36–37 Convert the remaining command line arguments to integers and use them for the initial semaphore values.

38–39 Call `semctl` with a *cmd* of `SETALL` to set the values of the semaphores.

-- *ipc/semset.c*

```
 1 #include <stdio.h>
 2 #include <unistd.h>
 3 #include <stdlib.h>
 4 #include <sys/sem.h>
 5 #include "ssp.h"

 6 union semun {
 7     int val;
 8     struct semid_ds *buf;
 9     ushort_t *array;
10 };

11 int main (int argc, char **argv)
12 {
13     int semid;
14     int num_sems;
15     key_t key;
16     struct semid_ds sem_info;
17     union semun arg;
18     unsigned short *buf;
19     int i;

20     if (argc < 2)
21         err_quit ("Usage: semset path [values ...]");

22     if ((key = ftok (argv [1], 0x42)) == -1)
23         err_msg ("ftok failed");
24     if ((semid = semget (key, 0, 0)) == -1)
25         err_msg ("semget failed");

26     arg.buf = &sem_info;
27     if (semctl (semid, 0, IPC_STAT, arg) == -1)
28         err_msg ("semctl (IPC_STAT) failed");
29     num_sems = arg.buf -> sem_nsems;
30     if (argc != num_sems + 2)
31         err_quit ("%d semaphores in set, %d values specified", num_sems,
32             argc - 2);

33     if ((buf = calloc (num_sems, sizeof (unsigned short))) == NULL)
34         err_msg ("calloc failed");
35     arg.array = buf;
36     for (i = 0; i < num_sems; i++)
37         buf [i] = atoi (argv [i + 2]);
38     if (semctl (semid, 0, SETALL, arg) == -1)
39         err_msg ("semctl (SETALL) failed");

40     return (0);
41 }
```

-- *ipc/semset.c*

Program 20.9 Set the values of semaphores in a semaphore set.

We also need a program that will display the values of the semaphores in a semaphore set; Program 20.10, `semget`, does this.

ipc/semget.c

```
 1 #include <stdio.h>
 2 #include <unistd.h>
 3 #include <stdlib.h>
 4 #include <sys/sem.h>
 5 #include "ssp.h"

 6 union semun {
 7     int val;
 8     struct semid_ds *buf;
 9     ushort_t *array;
10 };

11 int main (int argc, char **argv)
12 {
13     int semid;
14     int num_sems;
15     key_t key;
16     struct semid_ds sem_info;
17     union semun arg;
18     unsigned short *buf;
19     int i;

20     if (argc != 2)
21         err_quit ("Usage: semget path");

22     if ((key = ftok (argv [1], 0x42)) == -1)
23         err_msg ("ftok failed");
24     if ((semid = semget (key, 0, 0)) == -1)
25         err_msg ("semget failed");

26     arg.buf = &sem_info;
27     if (semctl (semid, 0, IPC_STAT, arg) == -1)
28         err_msg ("semctl failed");
29     num_sems = arg.buf -> sem_nsems;

30     if ((buf = calloc (num_sems, sizeof (unsigned short))) == NULL)
31         err_msg ("calloc failed");
32     arg.array = buf;

33     if (semctl (semid, 0, GETALL, arg) == -1)
34         err_msg ("semctl failed");
35     for (i = 0; i < num_sems; i++)
36         printf ("semval [%d] = %d\n", i, buf [i]);

37     return (0);
38 }
```

ipc/semget.c

Program 20.10 Get the values of semaphores in a semaphore set.

Parse command line arguments

20–21 Check that the correct number of arguments were supplied.

Open the semaphore set

23–25 Use `ftok` to generate the correct key using the pathname we supplied on the command line and a hard-coded value of 0x42. Then open the semaphore set using the key we just created.

Allocate memory for the semaphore set

26–29 Call `semctl` with a *cmd* of `IPC_STAT` to determine the number of semaphores in the set.

30–32 Allocate the appropriate amount of memory using `calloc`.

Print the semaphore values

33–34 Get the values of all the semaphores in the set by calling `semctl` with a *cmd* of `GETALL`.

35–36 Print the value of each semaphore.

Another program we'll need for this example is `semops`, which enables us to perform various operations on our semaphore set.

Program 20.11 shows the code for `semops`.

Parse command line options

19–31 Allow command line options of `-n` to specify nonblocking, and `-u` to specify the undo flag. Note that although we can specify these flags for each operation individually, for the sake of simplicity, we have these flags set the `IPC_NOWAIT` and `SEM_UNDO` flag for all operations respectively.

Allocate memory for the operations

36–43 After generating the correct key and opening the semaphore set, we allocate enough memory to hold the required number of `sembuf` structures. Note that this program does not insist that the number of operations is equal to the number of semaphores; we can specify fewer operations if we want.

Execute the operations

44–48 Initialize the `sembuf` operations structure.

49–50 Execute the array of operations using `semop`.

Let's see how we might use these five programs. First, we need to create a semaphore set and initialize its values.

```
$ touch /tmp/ssp_ipc
$ ./semcreat /tmp/ssp_ipc 3
Semaphore set ID = 0
$ ./semset /tmp/ssp_ipc 10 20 30
$ ./semget /tmp/ssp_ipc
semval [0] = 10
semval [1] = 20
semval [2] = 30
```

```
 1 #include <stdio.h>
 2 #include <unistd.h>
 3 #include <stdlib.h>
 4 #include <sys/sem.h>
 5 #include "ssp.h"

 6 int main (int argc, char **argv)
 7 {
 8     int c;
 9     int i;
10     int semid;
11     key_t key;
12     int semflg;
13     int num_ops;
14     int err_flag;
15     struct sembuf *buf;

16     semflg = 0;
17     opterr = 0;
18     err_flag = 0;

19     while ((c = getopt (argc, argv, "nu")) != EOF) {
20         switch (c) {
21             case 'n':
22                 semflg |= IPC_NOWAIT;
23                 break;

24             case 'u':
25                 semflg |= SEM_UNDO;
26                 break;

27             default:
28                 err_flag++;
29                 break;
30         }
31     }

32     if (argc - optind < 2)
33         err_flag++;
34     if (err_flag)
35         err_quit ("Usage: semops [-nu] path operation ...");

36     if ((key = ftok (argv [optind], 0x42)) == -1)
37         err_msg ("ftok failed");
38     if ((semid = semget (key, 0, 0)) == -1)
39         err_msg ("semget failed");
40     optind++;
41     num_ops = argc - optind;

42     if ((buf = calloc (num_ops, sizeof (struct sembuf))) == NULL)
43         err_msg ("calloc failed");

44     for (i = 0; i < num_ops; i++) {
45         buf [i].sem_num = i;
46         buf [i].sem_op = atoi (argv [optind + i]);
47         buf [i].sem_flg = semflg;
48     }
```

```
49      if (semop (semid, buf, num_ops) == -1)
50          err_msg ("semop failed");

51      return (0);
52 }
```

Program 20.11   Perform operations on a System V semaphore set.

The first thing we do is create the file we'll use with `ftok` to generate the key we'll pass to the `semget` function. We then create a semaphore set that consists of three semaphores using `semcreat`, and initialize the semaphores using `semset`. Finally, we print the semaphore values by using `semget`.

The semaphore set ID is 0, which we can confirm using `ipcs`:

```
$ ipcs -so
IPC status from <running system> as of Tue Sep  9 17:43:50 PDT 2003
T       ID      KEY         MODE        OWNER   GROUP
Semaphores:
s        0   0x420024f9 --ra-r-----    rich    staff
```

Let's now perform some operations on a semaphore set.

```
$ ./semops -n /tmp/ssp_ipc -5 -15 -35
semop failed: Resource temporarily unavailable
$ ./semget /tmp/ssp_ipc
semval [0] = 10
semval [1] = 20
semval [2] = 30
```

We attempt to perform three operations, specifying the nonblocking flag (-n). Each operation decrements a value in the set. The first operation, which decrements the value of the first semaphore by 5, is OK because we can subtract 5 from the value of the first semaphore, which is 10. Similarly, the second operation, which decrements the value of the second semaphore by 15, is OK because we can subtract 15 from the value of the second semaphore, which is 20. But the third operation, decrementing the value of the third semaphore by 35, fails because we can't subtract 35 from the value of the third semaphore, which is only 30. Because the last operation could not be performed, and because we specified the nonblocking flag, an error of EAGAIN is returned. If we hadn't specified the -n flag, the program would have just blocked. We then run `semget` to ensure that none of the semaphore values had been changed. This is the case, even though two of the operations could have been performed successfully. This proves the `semop` function performs the requested operations atomically (i.e., either *all* of the operations are performed, or *none* of them are).

Another aspect of semaphores we can demonstrate is the undo facility.

```
$ ./semset /tmp/ssp_ipc 10 20 30
$ ./semops -u /tmp/ssp_ipc -10 -20 -30
$ ./semget /tmp/ssp_ipc
semval [0] = 10
semval [1] = 20
semval [2] = 30
```

```
$ ./semops /tmp/ssp_ipc -10 -20 -30
$ ./semget /tmp/ssp_ipc
semval [0] = 0
semval [1] = 0
semval [2] = 0
```

The first thing we do is ensure that the semaphores are set to known values. We then run our semops program, specifying three operations: −10, −20, and −30. Although we don't actually see it in the program output, these operations are performed successfully. However, because we passed the -u flag to our program, the semaphore operations were performed with the SEM_UNDO flag set, so when our semops process terminates, the kernel undoes the changes it (the semops process) made. When we rerun our semops program without specifying the -u flag, the semaphore values remain at 0 when the process terminates.

The semids Function

We can get a list of all the current semaphore sets by using the semids function.

```
#include <sys/sem.h>

int semids (int *buf, uint_t nids, uint_t *pnids);
```

Returns: 0 if OK, −1 on error

The semids function returns a list of all the active System V semaphore sets into the buffer pointed to by *buf*, provided that the number of semaphore set identifiers does not exceed *nids*.

The number of semaphore set identifiers currently active in the system is stored in the unsigned integer pointed to by *pnids*, regardless of whether *buf* is of a sufficient size to contain them all. If *nids* is 0 or less than the number of active semaphore sets, *buf* is ignored (we can use this fact to correctly size the buffer before attempting to retrieve all the semaphore set identifiers).

The list of semaphore set identifiers returned by semids is a snapshot of the instant the semids function was called. Once semids returns, semaphore sets might be added to or removed from the system.

Example: Listing all the current semaphore sets

Program 20.12 prints a snapshot of all the semaphore values currently in semaphore sets.

Parse command line arguments

26–35 Allow a command line option of -s to specify the ID of the semaphore set we're interested in.

Call print_sem_set for the requested semaphore sets

40–41 If semid is not equal to 0, we've specified a specific semaphore set, so call print_sem_set to print the value of the semaphores in the requested semaphore set.

ipc/semls.c

```
 1 #include <stdio.h>
 2 #include <unistd.h>
 3 #include <stdlib.h>
 4 #include <sys/sem.h>
 5 #include "ssp.h"

 6 union semun {
 7     int val;
 8     struct semid_ds *buf;
 9     ushort_t *array;
10 };

11 static void print_sem_set (int semid);

12 int main (int argc, char **argv)
13 {
14     int c;
15     int err_flag;
16     int semid;
17     int *buf;
18     uint_t i;
19     uint_t n;
20     uint_t nids;

21     nids = 0;
22     buf = NULL;
23     semid = 0;
24     opterr = 0;
25     err_flag = 0;

26     while ((c = getopt (argc, argv, "s:")) != EOF) {
27         switch (c) {
28             case 's':
29                 semid = atoi (optarg);
30                 break;

31             default:
32                 err_flag++;
33                 break;
34         }
35     }

36     if (optind != argc)
37         err_flag++;
38     if (err_flag)
39         err_quit ("Usage: semls [-s semaphore set ID]");

40     if (semid != 0)
41         print_sem_set (semid);
42     else {
43         for (;;) {
44             if (semids (buf, nids, &n) == -1)
45                 err_msg ("semids failed");

46             if (n <= nids)
47                 break;
```

```
48                    nids = n;
49                    if ((buf = realloc (buf, nids * sizeof (int))) == NULL)
50                        err_msg ("realloc failed");
51                }

52            for (i = 0; i < n; i++)
53                print_sem_set (buf [i]);

54            free (buf);
55        }

56    return (0);
57 }

58 static void print_sem_set (int semid)
59 {
60     int num_sems;
61     struct semid_ds sem_info;
62     union semun arg;
63     unsigned short *buf;
64     int i;

65     arg.buf = &sem_info;
66     if (semctl (semid, 0, IPC_STAT, arg) == -1)
67         err_msg ("semctl failed");
68     num_sems = arg.buf -> sem_nsems;

69     if ((buf = calloc (num_sems, sizeof (unsigned short))) == NULL)
70         err_msg ("calloc failed");
71     arg.array = buf;

72     if (semctl (semid, 0, GETALL, arg) == -1)
73         err_msg ("semctl failed");

74     printf ("Semaphore set ID %d:\n", semid);
75     for (i = 0; i < num_sems; i++)
76         printf ("  semaphore %d = %d\n", i, buf [i]);

77     free (buf);
78 }
```
—————————————————————————————————— ipc/semls.c

Program 20.12   List all the System V semaphore sets.

42–55 Otherwise, call `semids` to get a list of all the semaphore set identifiers, allocating the required amount of memory (because we are not planning to recover from any errors, we don't save a copy of the pointer we pass to `realloc`). Once the list of semaphore set identifiers has been retrieved, call `print_sem_set` to print the value of the semaphores in each set. Finally, free the buffer we previously allocated.

The `print_sem_set` function

65–68 Call `semctl` with a *cmd* of `IPC_STAT` to determine the number of semaphores in the set.

69–71 Allocate the appropriate amount of memory using `calloc`.

72–76 Get the values of all the semaphores in the set by calling `semctl` with a *cmd* of `GETALL`, and print each value.

77 Finally, free the buffer we previously allocated.

Let's create a couple of semaphore sets and see how we might use Program 20.12.

```
$ touch /tmp/ssp_ipc1
$ touch /tmp/ssp_ipc2
$ ./semcreat /tmp/ssp_ipc1 3
Semaphore set ID = 65536
$ ./semcreat /tmp/ssp_ipc2 3
Semaphore set ID = 1
$ ./semset /tmp/ssp_ipc1 5 10 15
$ ./semset /tmp/ssp_ipc2 10 20 30
$ ipcs -sb
IPC status from <running system> as of Thu Sep 81 11:50:40 PDT 2003
T         ID      KEY           MODE         OWNER      GROUP NSEMS
Semaphores:
s         65536   0x42002a70  --ra-r-----     rich       staff     3
s             1   0x42002649  --ra-r-----     rich       staff     3
$ ./semls -s 1
Semaphore set ID 1:
  semaphore 0 = 10
  semaphore 1 = 20
  semaphore 2 = 30
$ ./semls
Semaphore set ID 65536:
  semaphore 0 = 5
  semaphore 1 = 10
  semaphore 2 = 15
Semaphore set ID 1:
  semaphore 0 = 10
  semaphore 1 = 20
  semaphore 2 = 30
$ ipcrm -s 1
$ ipcrm -S 0x42002a70
$ ipcs -so
IPC status from <running system> as of Thu Sep 18 12:00:09 PDT 2003
T          ID     KEY           MODE         OWNER      GROUP NSEMS
Semaphores:
```

We first use `semcreat` to create the files we'll be using to create the semaphore sets. The IDs of the semaphore sets are 65536 and 1 respectively.

We then initialize the values of semaphores in the sets and use the `ipcs` command to confirm that each semaphore set consists of three semaphores.

Next we run `semls` a couple of times. The first time we specify the semaphore set identifier we're interested in (in this case, the semaphore set whose ID is 1). As we would expect, the values of all the semaphores in the semaphore set whose ID is 1 are printed. The second time we run `semls`, we print the semaphore values of all the semaphore sets.

Finally, we remove the semaphore sets by using the `ipcrm` command, and demonstrate this by running `ipcs` once again. We remove the first semaphore set by referring to its semaphore set identifier, and the second set by referring to its key. Note we could have used our `semrm` program to perform this step.

20.5 System V Shared Memory

As its name suggests, *shared memory* is a segment of memory shared between two or more processes. Shared memory is the fastest form of IPC available to us, because it avoids the costly copying of buffers that must be performed by the other forms of IPC.

Consider, for example, what happens when we write some data to a pipe and read from the other end. When the first process writes to the pipe, the data is copied by the kernel from the application's buffer to the kernel's buffer for the pipe. When the second process reads from the pipe, the kernel must copy the data again, this time from the pipe buffer to the second process' data buffer.

Conversely, because the shared memory segment appears in the memory map of both processes (although not necessarily at the same virtual address), data written to the shared memory segment by one process is immediately available to all others, with no further copying required.

Although no data copying takes place, some sort of process synchronization is usually required to coordinate access to the shared memory by the different processes.

The kernel maintains a `shmid_ds` structure for every shared memory in the system. This structure has the following members:

```
struct shmid_ds {
    struct ipc_perm shm_perm;       /* Operation permission structure */
    size_t          shm_segsz;      /* Size of segment in bytes */
    void            *shm_amp;       /* Segment anon_map pointer */
    ushort_t        shm_lkcnt;      /* Number of times it is being locked */
    pid_t           shm_lpid;       /* Process ID of last shmop () */
    pid_t           shm_cpid;       /* Process ID of creator */
    shmatt_t        shm_nattch;     /* Current number attached */
    ulong_t         shm_cnattch;    /* Current number of in core attached */
    time_t          shm_atime;      /* Time of last attach (shmat ()) */
    time_t          shm_dtime;      /* Time of last detach (shmdt ()) */
    time_t          shm_ctime;      /* Time of last change (shmctl ()) */
};
```

Most of the members of the `smhid_ds` structure are self-explanatory, but the `shm_amp` pointer is meaningless to user space processes because it refers to an address in the kernel's virtual memory space.

A system administrator can adjust a number of variables to change the various kernel limits on System V shared memory. Prior to Solaris 9 there were a total of four tunable variables; more recent versions have only two. Figure 20.6 summarizes these tunables, showing the name that is used to tune a variable in `/etc/system`, a description of what the variable limits, and a typical default value for the variable.

The last two variables in Figure 20.6 are only available prior to Solaris 9. Also, starting with Solaris 9, `shminfo_shmmax` defaults to 8,388,608 (8 MB). Finally, there is little point in changing the value of `shminfo_shmmin`. From Solaris 10, all of these tunables have been replaced by resource controls.

Variable	Description	Default
`shmsys:shminfo_shmmax` `shmsys:shminfo_shmmni`	Maximum size of a shared memory segment Maximum number of shared memory identifiers	1,048,576 100
`shmsys:shminfo_shmmin` `shmsys:shminfo_shmseg`	Minimum size of a shared memory segment Max number of attached shared memory segments per process	1 6

Figure 20.6 System V shared memory tunables.

The `shmget` Function

We create a new, or access an existing, shared memory segment by using `shmget`.

```
#include <sys/shm.h>

int shmget (key_t key, size_t size, int shmflg);
```
                                           Returns: shared memory ID if OK, –1 on error

The `shmget` function returns the shared memory identifier associated with *key*. We described the rules for converting a *key* into an identifier, and the effect of *shmflg* on this operation, in Section 20.2.

If `shmget` creates a new shared memory segment it will be of at least *size* bytes, and the `shmid_ds` structure associated with it will be initialized as follows:

- The `shm_perm.cuid`, `shm_perm.uid`, `shm_perm.cgid`, and `shm_perm.gid` members are initialized to the effective user ID and effective group ID of the calling process.
- The least significant 9 bits of `shm_perm.mode` are set to the least significant 9 bits of *shmflg*.
- The `shm_lpid`, `shm_nattch`, `shm_atime`, and `shm_dtime` members are cleared (i.e., set to 0).
- The `shm_ctime` member is set to the current time.
- The `shm_segsz` member is set equal to the value of *size*.

Upon successful completion, a non-negative shared memory ID is returned. This shared memory ID is used by most of the other System V shared memory functions (the only exception being `shmids`).

The `shmat` Function

In order to use a shared memory segment, we must *attach* it to our process (i.e., map the segment into the memory space of our process). To do this, we must use `shmat`.

```
#include <sys/shm.h>

void *shmat (int shmid, const void *shmaddr, int shmflg);
```
Returns: base address of shared memory segment if OK, −1 on error

The shmat function attaches the shared memory segment identified by *shmid* to the data segment of the calling process.

We can set a number of flags in *shmflg* to affect the behaviour of shmat. These are as follows:

SHM_PAGEABLE   If this flag is set, virtual memory resources are shared and the dynamic intimate shared memory (DISM) framework is created. The dynamic memory can be resized dynamically within the size specified by shmget. The resulting shared memory is pageable unless it is locked.

SHM_SHARE_MMU   If this flag is set, virtual memory resources in addition to the shared memory itself are shared among processes that use the same shared memory.

This flag is not available prior to Solaris 8.

SHM_RDONLY   Setting this flag causes the segment to be attached read only; otherwise, the segment will be attached for reading and writing as determined by the segment's permissions.

SHM_RND   This flag determines the rounding applied to the shared memory's base address, as described next.

The shared memory segment is attached to the data segment of the calling process, and the base address of the segment is returned by shmat. The rules for determining this base address are as follows:

- If *shmaddr* is NULL, the kernel selects the address to which the shared memory will be attached.

- If *shmaddr* is NULL, and either SHM_SHARE_MMU or SHM_PAGEABLE is set, then the kernel selects the address to which the shared memory will be attached, and read or write access will be determined by the permissions of the segment.

   These first two options are the preferred methods, the first one being the most portable.

- If *shmaddr* is not NULL and SHM_RND is not set, the segment is attached to the address specified by *shmaddr*.

- If *shmaddr* is not NULL and SHM_RND is set, the segment is attached to the address specified by *shmaddr*, rounded down by the constant SHMLBA. "LBA" is an acronym for "lower boundary address".

Note that we can only access a shared memory segment after we've called shmat; just calling shmget is insufficient.

The `shmdt` Function

When we have finished using a shared memory segment, we detach it from our address space by calling `shmdt`.

```
#include <sys/shm.h>

int shmdt (const void *shmaddr);
```
                                                          Returns: 0 if OK, –1 on error

The `shmdt` function detaches the shared memory segment pointed to by *shmaddr* from the address space of the calling process. When a process terminates, all currently attached shared memory segments are automatically detached.

Note that calling `shmdt` does not delete the shared memory segment. Shared memory segments must be explicitly removed after the last reference to them has been removed; we do this by calling `shmctl` with a command of `IPC_RMID`.

The `shmctl` Function

The `shmctl` function enables us to perform various control operations on a shared memory segment.

```
#include <sys/shm.h>

int shmctl (int shmid, int cmd, struct shmid_ds *buf);
```
                                                          Returns: 0 if OK, –1 on error

The `shmctl` function performs a shared memory control operation on the shared memory segment identified by *shmid*. The operation to be performed is specified by *cmd*, which can be one of five values:

`IPC_STAT`	A copy of the kernel-maintained `shmid_ds` structure for the shared memory segment identified by *shmid* is placed into the buffer pointed to by *buf*.
`IPC_SET`	The following members of the kernel-maintained `shmid_ds` structure associated with the shared memory segment identified by *shmid* are set to the values in the corresponding members of the `shmid_ds` structure pointed to by *buf*: `shm_perm.uid`, `shm_perm.gid`, and `shm_perm.mode`. This *cmd* can be successfully executed only by a process whose effective user ID is equal to either the `shm_perm.uid` or `shm_perm.cuid` members of the `shmid_ds` structure associated with the shared memory segment, or is equal to that of the superuser.
`IPC_RMID`	The shared memory segment identified by *shmid* is immediately removed from the system. This *cmd* can be

successfully executed only by a process whose effective user ID is equal to either the shm_perm.uid or shm_perm.cuid members of the shmid_ds structure associated with the shared memory segment, or is equal to that of the superuser. The *buf* argument is ignored.

SHM_LOCK   The shared memory segment identified by *shmid* is locked in memory. This command, which is a Solaris extension, can be executed only by a process whose effective user ID is that of the superuser (i.e., 0).

SHM_UNLOCK   The shared memory segment identified by *shmid* is unlocked. This command, which is a Solaris extension, can be executed only by a process whose effective user ID is that of the superuser (i.e., 0).

Example: Using shared memory

Let's take a look at an example that uses a System V shared memory segment. We'll use a few small programs to manipulate the shared memory; we can do this because System V IPC objects have kernel persistence.

The first program just creates the shared memory we'll use in this example. As before, the -e command line option specifies the IPC_EXCL flag. The pathname of the file to use to generate the key, and the size of the segment, are also specified on the command line.

Program 20.13 shows the code for this program, which is called shmcreat.

Parse command line arguments

17–26 Allow a command line option of -e to specify the IPC_EXCL flag.

Create the shared memory segment

31 Convert the last command line argument, which specifies the size of the shared memory segment, to an integer.

32–36 Use ftok to generate an appropriate key using the pathname we specified on the command line and a hard-coded *id* of 0x42. Then create the shared memory segment using the key we just created and print the resulting shared memory segment ID.

Having created a shared memory segment, we need to be able to write some data to it. Program 20.14, called shmwrite, does this.

Attach the shared memory segment

14–17 Use ftok to generate a key, and use that key to access the shared memory segment.

18–19 Map the shared memory segment into the address space of our process.

Write to the shared memory

20–23 Call shmctl with a cmd of IPC_STAT to ascertain the size of the shared memory segment.

ipc/shmcreat.c

```
 1 #include <stdio.h>
 2 #include <unistd.h>
 3 #include <stdlib.h>
 4 #include <sys/shm.h>
 5 #include "ssp.h"

 6 int main (int argc, char **argv)
 7 {
 8     int c;
 9     int shmid;
10     size_t size;
11     key_t key;
12     int shmflg;
13     int err_flag;

14     shmflg = SHM_R | SHM_W | (SHM_R >> 3) | IPC_CREAT;
15     opterr = 0;
16     err_flag = 0;

17     while ((c = getopt (argc, argv, "e")) != EOF) {
18         switch (c) {
19             case 'e':
20                 shmflg |= IPC_EXCL;
21                 break;

22             default:
23                 err_flag++;
24                 break;
25         }
26     }

27     if (optind != argc - 2)
28         err_flag++;

29     if (err_flag)
30         err_quit ("Usage: shmcreat [-e] path size");

31     size = atoi (argv [optind + 1]);
32     if ((key = ftok (argv [optind], 0x42)) == -1)
33         err_msg ("ftok failed");
34     if ((shmid = shmget (key, size, shmflg)) == -1)
35         err_msg ("shmget failed");

36     printf ("Shared memory ID = %d\n", shmid);

37     return (0);
38 }
```

ipc/shmcreat.c

Program 20.13 Create a System V shared memory segment.

24–25 Write the pattern 0, 1, 2, ..., 255, 0, 1, etc. to the shared memory.

Detach the shared memory segment

26 Call shmdt to detach the shared memory segment from the caller's address space.

ipc/shmwrite.c

```
 1 #include <stdio.h>
 2 #include <unistd.h>
 3 #include <sys/shm.h>
 4 #include "ssp.h"

 5 int main (int argc, char **argv)
 6 {
 7     int i;
 8     int shmid;
 9     key_t key;
10     char *buf;
11     struct shmid_ds shm_info;

12     if (argc != 2)
13         err_quit ("Usage: shmwrite path");

14     if ((key = ftok (argv [1], 0x42)) == -1)
15         err_msg ("ftok failed");
16     if ((shmid = shmget (key, 0, 0)) == -1)
17         err_msg ("shmget failed");

18     if ((buf = shmat (shmid, NULL, 0)) == (char *) -1)
19         err_msg ("shmat failed");

20     if (shmctl (shmid, IPC_STAT, &shm_info) == -1) {
21         shmdt (buf);
22         err_msg ("shmctl failed");
23     }

24     for (i = 0; i < shm_info.shm_segsz; i++)
25         *buf++ = i % 256;

26     shmdt (buf);

27     return (0);
28 }
```

ipc/shmwrite.c

Program 20.14   Write to a System V shared memory segment.

Next we need a program to read from a shared memory segment; Program 20.15 shows the code for shmread, which does this.

Attach the shared memory segment

15–18 Use ftok to generate a key, and use that key to access the shared memory segment.

19–20 Map the shared memory segment into the address space of our process.

Read from the shared memory

21–24 Call shmctl with a cmd of IPC_STAT to ascertain the size of the shared memory segment.

25–27 Sequentially read from the shared memory segment, verifying the pattern that we wrote with shmwrite.

ipc/shmread.c

```
1 #include <stdio.h>
2 #include <unistd.h>
3 #include <sys/shm.h>
4 #include "ssp.h"

5 int main (int argc, char **argv)
6 {
7      int i;
8      int shmid;
9      key_t key;
10     unsigned char c;
11     char *buf;
12     struct shmid_ds shm_info;

13     if (argc != 2)
14         err_quit ("Usage: shmread path");

15     if ((key = ftok (argv [1], 0x42)) == -1)
16         err_msg ("ftok failed");
17     if ((shmid = shmget (key, 0, 0)) == -1)
18         err_msg ("shmget failed");

19     if ((buf = shmat (shmid, NULL, 0)) == (char *) -1)
20         err_msg ("shmat failed");

21     if (shmctl (shmid, IPC_STAT, &shm_info) == -1) {
22         shmdt (buf);
23         err_msg ("shmctl failed");
24     }

25     for (i = 0; i < shm_info.shm_segsz; i++)
26         if ((c = *buf++) != (i % 256))
27             printf ("buf [%d] = %d (should be %d)\n", i, c, i % 256);

28     shmdt (buf);

29     return (0);
30 }
```

ipc/shmread.c

Program 20.15 Read from a System V shared memory segment.

Detach the shared memory segment

28 Call `shmdt` to detach the shared memory segment from the caller's address space.

Finally, Program 20.16 shows the code for `shmrm`, which is used to remove a shared memory segment.

Parse command line arguments

9–10 Exit if an incorrect number of arguments was supplied.

Remove the shared memory segment

11–14 Use `ftok` to generate a key and use that key to access the requested IPC object.

15–16 Remove the identifier from the system by calling `shmctl` with an *cmd* of `IPC_RMID`.

ipc/shmrm.c

```
 1 #include <stdio.h>
 2 #include <unistd.h>
 3 #include <sys/shm.h>
 4 #include "ssp.h"

 5 int main (int argc, char **argv)
 6 {
 7     int shmid;
 8     key_t key;

 9     if (argc != 2)
10         err_quit ("Usage: shmrm path");

11     if ((key = ftok (argv [1], 0x42)) == -1)
12         err_msg ("ftok failed");
13     if ((shmid = shmget (key, 0, 0)) == -1)
14         err_msg ("shmget failed");

15     if (shmctl (shmid, IPC_RMID, NULL) == -1)
16         err_msg ("shmctl failed");

17     return (0);
18 }
```

ipc/shmrm.c

Program 20.16 Remove a System V shared memory segment.

Let's run these programs and examine the results.

```
$ ./shmcreat /tmp/ssp_ipc 1138
Shared memory ID = 200
$ ipcs -mbo
IPC status from <running system> as of Thu Sep 18 11:38:28 PDT 2003
T         ID      KEY        MODE        OWNER     GROUP NATTCH      SEGSZ
Shared Memory:
m        200    0x420024f9 --rw-r-----   rich      staff     0        1138
```

First we create a shared memory segment that has a size of 1138 bytes. We then run `ipcs` to verify that the segment was created correctly. As we would expect, the SEGSZ columns shows the size of the segment as 1138 bytes, and the NATTCH column shows that no processes are currently attached to the shared segment of memory.

We then write to the shared memory using `shmwrite` and read from it using `shmread` before removing it by using `shmrm`.

```
$ ./shmwrite /tmp/ssp_ipc
$ ./shmread /tmp/ssp_ipc
$ ./shmrm /tmp/ssp_ipc
$ ipcs -mbo
IPC status from <running system> as of Thu Sep 18 11:47:53 PDT 2003
T         ID      KEY        MODE        OWNER     GROUP NATTCH      SEGSZ
Shared Memory:
```

We run the `ipcs` command again to confirm that the shared memory segment has been removed from the system.

The `shmids` Function

We can get a list of the current shared memory segments by using the `shmids` function.

```
#include <sys/shm.h>

int shmids (int *buf, uint_t nids, uint_t *pnids);
```

Returns: 0 if OK, −1 on error

The `shmids` function returns a list of all the active System V shared memory segments into the buffer pointed to by *buf*, provided that the number of shared memory segment identifiers does not exceed *nids*.

The number of shared memory segment identifiers currently active in the system is stored in the unsigned integer pointed to by *pnids*, regardless of whether *buf* is of a sufficient size to contain them all. If *nids* is 0 or less than the number of active shared memory segments, *buf* is ignored (we can use this fact to correctly size the buffer before attempting to retrieve all the shared memory segment identifiers).

The list of shared memory segment identifiers returned by `shmids` is a snapshot of the instant the `shmids` function was called. Once `shmids` returns, shared memory segments might be added to, or removed from, the system.

Example: Listing all the current shared memory segments

Program 20.17 shows the code for our program, `shmls`, which lists the size of all the shared memory segments currently in the system.

Parse command line arguments

21–30 Allow a command line option of `-m` to specify the ID of the shared memory segment we're interested in.

Call `print_shm_seg` for the requested shared memory segments

35–36 If `shmid` is not equal to 0, we've specified a specific shared memory segment, so call `print_shm_seg` to print the size of the requested shared memory segment.

37–50 Otherwise, call `shmids` to get a list of all the shared memory segment identifiers, allocating the required amount of memory (because we are not planning to recover from any errors, we don't save a copy of the pointer we pass to `realloc`). Once the list of shared memory segment identifiers has been retrieved, call `print_shm_seg` to print the size of each shared memory segment. Finally, free the buffer we previously allocated.

The `print_shm_seg` function

56–57 Call `shmctl` with a *cmd* of `IPC_STAT` to get a copy of the kernel-maintained `shmid_ds` structure for the shared memory segment.

58–59 Print the size of the shared memory segment.

Let's create a couple of shared memory segments and see what happens when we run Program 20.17.

```
 1  #include <stdio.h>
 2  #include <unistd.h>
 3  #include <stdlib.h>
 4  #include <sys/shm.h>
 5  #include "ssp.h"

 6  static void print_shm_seg (int shmid);

 7  int main (int argc, char **argv)
 8  {
 9      int c;
10      int err_flag;
11      int shmid;
12      int *buf;
13      uint_t i;
14      uint_t n;
15      uint_t nids;

16      nids = 0;
17      buf = NULL;
18      shmid = 0;
19      opterr = 0;
20      err_flag = 0;

21      while ((c = getopt (argc, argv, "m:")) != EOF) {
22          switch (c) {
23              case 'm':
24                  shmid = atoi (optarg);
25                  break;

26              default:
27                  err_flag++;
28                  break;
29          }
30      }

31      if (optind != argc)
32          err_flag++;
33      if (err_flag)
34          err_quit ("Usage: shmls [-m shared memory segment ID]");

35      if (shmid != 0)
36          print_shm_seg (shmid);
37      else {
38          for (;;) {
39              if (shmids (buf, nids, &n) == -1)
40                  err_msg ("shmids failed");

41              if (n <= nids)
42                  break;

43              nids = n;
44              if ((buf = realloc (buf, nids * sizeof (int))) == NULL)
45                  err_msg ("realloc failed");
46          }
```

```
47          for (i = 0; i < n; i++)
48              print_shm_seg (buf [i]);

49          free (buf);
50      }

51      return (0);
52  }

53  static void print_shm_seg (int shmid)
54  {
55      struct shmid_ds shm_info;

56      if (shmctl (shmid, IPC_STAT, &shm_info) == -1)
57          err_msg ("shmctl failed");

58      printf ("Shared memory segment ID %d:\n", shmid);
59      printf ("  size = %d bytes\n", shm_info.shm_segsz);
60  }
```
—— *ipc/shmls.c*

Program 20.17 List all the System V shared memory segments.

```
$ ./shmcreat /tmp/ssp_ipc1 18091967
Shared memory ID = 400
$ ./shmcreat /tmp/ssp_ipc2 02081997
Shared memory ID = 101
$ ./shmls -m 400
Shared memory segment ID 400:
  size = 18091967 bytes
$ ./shmls
Shared memory segment ID 400:
  size = 18091967 bytes
Shared memory segment ID 101:
  size = 2081997 bytes
$ ./shmrm /tmp/ssp_ipc1
$ ./shmrm /tmp/ssp_ipc2
$ ./shmls
```

We first create two shared memory segments. The first has a size of 18,091,967 bytes, and the second has a size of 2,081,997 bytes (we had to edit /etc/system to increase the maximum size of a shared memory segment, i.e., shminfo_shmmax).

Next we run shmls a couple of times. The first time we run shmls, we're only interested in looking at the shared memory segment whose ID is 400. The second time we run shmls, we print the size of all shared memory segments.

Finally, we remove both shared memory segments and run shmls one last time to confirm that they've been removed.

20.6 Performance Comparisons

Now that we've described the System V IPC facility, let's compare its performance to some of the alternatives. We'll look at two examples: message queues versus pipes, and semaphores versus file locking.

All tests in this section were performed on a 500 MHz Sun Blade 100 running Solaris 9.

Example: Performance comparison of message queues and pipes

To compare the relative performance of System V message queues and pipes, we wrote two programs, each of which copies 100 MB of data. The first program calls `msgget` to access a message queue that we created using our `msgcreat` program, and calls `fork`. Using `msgsnd`, the parent process sends 50,000 messages, each of which has a size of 2000 bytes, and the child process receives these messages using `msgrcv`. Program 20.18 shows the code for this program, which we call `msgperf`.

The second program is similar, but creates a pipe before calling `fork`, and uses `read` and `write` to transfer the data. In this case, the parent process calls `write` 50,000 times, copying a 2000-byte buffer to the pipe each time. We show the code for this program, called `pipeperf`, in Program 20.19.

Figure 20.7 summarizes the times required by both techniques. All times are in seconds.

Method	Real	User	Sys
Message queue	2.82	0.32	2.30
Pipe	2.24	0.24	1.82

Figure 20.7   Performance comparison of message queues and pipes.

These times show that message queues do not offer any performance advantage over pipes; if anything, there is a slight performance degradation. Considering the other problems associated with the System V IPC facility (e.g., their systemwide nature, kernel persistence, and their dedicated name space), we can safely recommend that new applications use pipes rather than System V message queues. (POSIX message queues—as described in [Stevens 1999]—should be used by applications that need the ability to prioritize messages.)

> Despite our general recommendation to use pipes in preference to message queues, there are times when using the latter makes sense. For example, FIFOs don't preserve message boundaries, which means that our protocols might need to be more complicated. Also, FIFOs don't guarantee the atomicity of messages greater than `PIPE_MAX` bytes in size. FIFOs have another disadvantage: their entry in the file system might be removed by errant or malicious processes; this will prevent new connections to that FIFO.

Example: Performance comparison of semaphores and file locking

If we have a single resource that we want to share among several processes, we can use either a semaphore or record locking.

If we use record locking, we can create an empty file and use the first byte of the file as the lock byte. To allocate the shared resource, we obtain a write lock on the byte (recall

ipc/msgperf.c

```
 1 #include <stdio.h>
 2 #include <unistd.h>
 3 #include <stdlib.h>
 4 #include <sys/ipc.h>
 5 #include <sys/msg.h>
 6 #include <signal.h>
 7 #include "ssp.h"

 8 #define MSGMAX (2048 + sizeof (long))
 9 #define BUFFER_SIZE 2000
10 #define NUM_ITERS 50000

11 int main (int argc, char **argv)
12 {
13     int i;
14     pid_t pid;
15     int qid;
16     struct msgbuf *buf;

17     if (argc != 1)
18         err_quit ("Usage: msgperf");

19     if ((qid = msgget (IPC_PRIVATE, MSG_R | MSG_W | IPC_CREAT)) == -1)
20         err_msg ("msgget failed");

21     if ((buf = malloc (MSGMAX)) == NULL)
22         err_msg ("malloc failed");

23     buf -> mtype = 1;

24     switch (pid = fork ()) {
25         case -1:
26             err_msg ("fork failed");

27         case 0:
28             for (;;)
29                 if (msgrcv (qid, buf, MSGMAX, 1, 0) == -1)
30                     err_msg ("msgrcv failed");

31         default:
32             for (i = 0; i < NUM_ITERS; i++)
33                 if (msgsnd (qid, buf, BUFFER_SIZE, 0) == -1)
34                     err_msg ("msgsnd failed");

35             kill (pid, SIGINT);
36             waitpid (pid, NULL, 0);
37             break;
38     }

39     msgctl (qid, IPC_RMID, NULL);

40     return (0);
41 }
```

ipc/msgperf.c

Program 20.18 Copy 100 MB using a System V message queue.

ipc/pipeperf.c

```
1  #include <stdio.h>
2  #include <unistd.h>
3  #include <stdlib.h>
4  #include <signal.h>
5  #include "ssp.h"

6  #define BUFFER_SIZE 2000
7  #define NUM_ITERS 50000

8  int main (int argc, char **argv)
9  {
10     int i;
11     pid_t pid;
12     int fd [2];
13     char *buf;

14     if (argc != 1)
15         err_quit ("Usage: pipeperf");

16     if (pipe (fd) == -1)
17         err_msg ("pipe failed");

18     if ((buf = malloc (BUFFER_SIZE)) == NULL)
19         err_msg ("malloc failed");

20     switch (pid = fork ()) {
21         case -1:
22             err_msg ("fork failed");

23         case 0:
24             close (fd [1]);
25             for (;;)
26                 if (read (fd [0], buf, BUFFER_SIZE) == -1)
27                     err_msg ("read failed");

28         default:
29             close (fd [0]);
30             for (i = 0; i < NUM_ITERS; i++)
31                 if (writen (fd [1], buf, BUFFER_SIZE) == -1)
32                     err_msg ("writen failed");
33             kill (pid, SIGINT);
34             waitpid (pid, NULL, 0);
35             break;
36     }

37     free (buf);

38     return (0);
39 }
```

ipc/pipeperf.c

Program 20.19 Copy 100 MB using a pipe.

that write locks are exclusive), and to release the shared resource, we unlock the byte. One of the attributes of record locks is that they are automatically released by the kernel when a process terminates, so we don't need to worry about it. We show the code for this program, called `lockperf`, in Program 20.20.

ipc/lockperf.c

```
 1 #include <stdio.h>
 2 #include <unistd.h>
 3 #include <stdlib.h>
 4 #include <signal.h>
 5 #include "ssp.h"

 6 #define NUM_ITERS 50000

 7 static void do_ops (int fd);

 8 int main (int argc, char **argv)
 9 {
10     pid_t pid;
11     int fd;
12     FILE *fp;

13     if (argc != 1)
14         err_quit ("Usage: lockperf");

15     if ((fp = tmpfile ()) == NULL)
16         err_msg ("tmpfile failed");
17     fd = fileno (fp);

18     switch (pid = fork ()) {
19         case -1:
20             err_msg ("fork failed");

21         case 0:
22             do_ops (fd);
23             _exit (0);

24         default:
25             do_ops (fd);
26             waitpid (pid, NULL, 0);
27             break;
28     }

29     return (0);
30 }

31 static void do_ops (int fd)
32 {
33     int i;

34     for (i = 0; i < NUM_ITERS; i++) {
35         if (lockf (fd, F_LOCK, 0) == -1)
36             err_msg ("lockf failed");
37         if (lockf (fd, F_ULOCK, 0) == -1)
38             err_msg ("lockf failed");
39     }
40 }
```

ipc/lockperf.c

Program 20.20   Access a shared resource using a lock file.

If we use a semaphore, we can create a semaphore set that consists of one semaphore and initialize its value to 1. To allocate the shared resource, we call semop with a sem_op of −1; to release the shared resource, we call semop again, this time with a sem_op of 1. Note that to handle the case of our process unexpectedly terminating, we specify SEM_UNDO with every operation. (Note that although it is possible to arrange for semaphores to be released in the event of unexpected process termination by specifying SEM_UNDO, it is something that we must explicitly request. Unlike the case of using lock files, automatic lock release does not come "for free" when using semaphores.)

Program 20.21 shows the code for this program, which we call semperf.

In the do_ops function of Program 20.21, we build an array that contains two semaphore operations (both of which operate on the same semaphore): the first operation acquires the resource, and the second immediately releases that resource (this is analogous to the same function in Program 20.20, where we call lockf twice: the first call acquires an exclusive lock on the lock file, and the second releases it).

Figure 20.8 summarizes the times required by both techniques. In each case, the shared resource was acquired and released 50,000 times by two processes simultaneously. All times are in seconds, and are the totals for both processes.

Method	Real	User	Sys
Semaphore	0.46	0.07	0.38
Record locking	1.53	0.32	1.19

Figure 20.8 Performance comparison of semaphores and record locking.

These times show that record locking has an appreciable performance penalty compared to using System V semaphore locking. However, given that record locking is much simpler to use, and that the kernel automatically removes any lingering locks when a process terminates (without us having to specifically arrange for this to happen), record locking is the preferred method of controlling access to a single shared resource, provided the performance hit isn't deemed to be problematic.

20.7 Summary

In this chapter we described the System V IPC facility. We began by describing how every IPC object has an associated identifier, and how keys are used to generate these identifiers. We described the ftok function, which we use to convert a pathname into a key. We also mentioned the special pathname IPC_PRIVATE, which we can use to guarantee that a new IPC object will be created. We explained that although there are some conceptual similarities, IPC identifiers are systemwide values, unlike file descriptors, which are process specific.

We described permissions structure associated with every IPC object, and the ipcs and ipcrm utilities.

ipc/semperf.c

```
 1 #include <stdio.h>
 2 #include <unistd.h>
 3 #include <stdlib.h>
 4 #include <sys/sem.h>
 5 #include "ssp.h"

 6 #define NUM_ITERS 50000

 7 union semun {
 8     int val;
 9     struct semid_ds *buf;
10     ushort *array;
11 };

12 static void do_ops (int semid);

13 int main (int argc, char **argv)
14 {
15     pid_t pid;
16     int semid;
17     union semun arg;

18     if (argc != 1)
19         err_quit ("Usage: semperf");

20     if ((semid = semget (IPC_PRIVATE, 1, SEM_R | SEM_A | IPC_CREAT)) == -1)
21         err_msg ("semget failed");

22     arg.val = 1;
23     if (semctl (semid, 0, SETVAL, arg) == -1)
24         err_msg ("semctl failed");

25     switch (pid = fork ()) {
26         case -1:
27             err_msg ("fork failed");

28         case 0:
29             do_ops (semid);
30             _exit (0);

31         default:
32             do_ops (semid);
33             waitpid (pid, NULL, 0);
34             break;
35     }

36     semctl (semid, IPC_RMID, NULL);

37     return (0);
38 }

39 static void do_ops (int semid)
40 {
41     struct sembuf buf [2];
42     int i;

43     for (i = 0; i < NUM_ITERS; i++) {
44         buf [0].sem_num = 0;
```

```
45              buf [0].sem_op = -1;
46              buf [0].sem_flg = SEM_UNDO;
47              buf [1].sem_num = 0;
48              buf [1].sem_op = 1;
49              buf [1].sem_flg = SEM_UNDO;

50              if (semop (semid, buf, 2) == -1)
51                  err_msg ("semop failed");
52          }
53  }
```
                                                                              ipc/semperf.c

Program 20.21   Access a shared resource using a System V semaphore.

We then described System V message queues, semaphore sets, and shared memory segments, writing several simple programs to demonstrate how to use these facilities.

We then performed a couple of performance comparisons: pipes versus message queues, and semaphores versus lock files. Guided by the results of these comparisons, we can make the following recommendations: pipes and FIFOs are still an important method of IPC, but message queues and semaphore sets should be avoided in new applications. Pipes and file locks should be considered as alternatives, as they are easier to use, and, in the case of pipes, offer a performance increase.

Shared memory is still useful, although new applications might want to consider using the mmap function we describe in Section 13.25 instead.

In the next chapter, we'll take a look at some advanced IPC techniques that enable us to pass file descriptors from one process to another.

Exercises

20.1   Modify Program 20.2 to accept a pathname argument of IPC_PRIVATE, which should create a message queue with a private key. What changes must then be made to Programs 20.3, 20.4, and 20.5?

20.2   Implement the five parent and child synchronization functions we described in Section 15.10, using System V message queues.

20.3   Implement the five parent and child synchronization functions we described in Section 15.10, using System V semaphores.

20.4   Modify Program 20.15 so that it reads a shared memory segment identifier from the command line rather than a pathname to pass to ftok. Use this program to demonstrate that assuming the object's permissions allow it, we only need to know a System V IPC object's identifier to access it.

21

Advanced

Interprocess Communication

21.1 Introduction

In the last two chapters we looked at the traditional UNIX IPC mechanisms: pipes, FIFOs, message queue, semaphores, and shared memory. In this chapter we'll take a look at some advanced forms of IPC and what we can do with them. We'll look at two methods of passing file descriptors: a regular pipe, for use between related processes; and a named pipe, for use between unrelated processes.

Another form of IPC, called *UNIX domain sockets*, uses the same sockets API that is used to communicate between clients and servers on different hosts. However, these networking APIs are beyond the scope of this text; readers interested in UNIX domain sockets are referred to Chapter 15 of [Stevens, Fenner, and Rudoff 2004].

21.2 Passing File Descriptors

One of the things we can do with pipes is pass an open file descriptor from one process to another. This opens up different ways of writing client-server applications. For example, the server could do everything required to open a file or device (e.g., translating a hostname to an IP address, handling lock files, dialing a modem, etc.) and just pass a file descriptor to the client. This file descriptor can be used with all I/O functions, and the client needn't concern itself with the nitty-gritty details of opening the file.

> We should mention that only pipes implemented using STREAMS can pass file descriptors. The older, half-duplex pipes cannot, nor can POSIX pipes.

But what exactly do we mean by "passing an open file descriptor"? Recall Figure 4.4, where we showed two processes that had opened the same file. Although the processes share the same vnode, each process has its own file table entry for the file.

What we want when we pass an open file descriptor from one process to another is for the file table entry to be shared as well as the vnode. Figure 21.1 shows this arrangement.

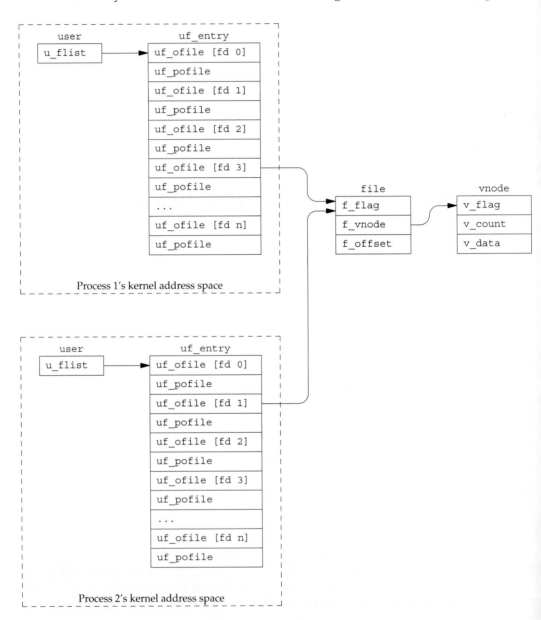

Figure 21.1 Passing a file descriptor from one process to another.

Although we talk about passing a file descriptor, technically we are passing a pointer to a file table entry. This pointer is assigned to the first available file descriptor in the receiving process. In other words, we do *not* pass the descriptor number to the receiving process, despite the impression the term "passing a file descriptor" gives. The number of the file descriptor in the receiving process is usually not the same as the one in the sender. Passing file descriptors is exactly what happens after a fork (recall Figure 15.1).

Once a descriptor has been passed, it is usual for the sender to close it. This doesn't actually close the file or device, and has no effect the receiving process (even if the receiver hasn't actually received the descriptor yet) because the file is still considered open by the kernel.

The send_fd, send_err, and recv_fd Functions

Let's write some functions that we can use to send and receive file descriptors through a pipe. We'll use these function later in this chapter and show their source code later in this section.

```
#include "ssp.h"

int send_fd (int pipe_fd, int fd);

int send_err (int pipe_fd, int status);

                                        Both return: 0 if OK, −1 on error
int recv_fd (int pipe_fd);

                                Returns: file descriptor if OK, < 0 on error
```

A process that wants to send a file descriptor to another process does so by calling send_fd, or send_err if an error occurred when opening the file. The receiving process (i.e., the client) calls recv_fd.

The send_fd function sends the file descriptor specified by *fd* across the pipe *pipe_fd*. Similarly, the send_err function is used to send the error specified by *status* across the pipe *pipe_fd*. The value of *status* must be greater than 0 and is intended to be set to the value of errno.

The recv_fd function is called by the client when it wants to receive a file descriptor from the server. If all is well (i.e., the server called send_fd), the value of the new file descriptor is returned. Otherwise, −1 is returned, and errno is set to the value of *status* that was passed to send_err.

These functions use a simple protocol to talk to each other. The send_fd function sends a 0 byte followed by the actual file descriptor. To send an error, send_err just sends the value of *status*. The read_fd function reads the first byte from the server. If it is equal to 0, recv_fd then reads the actual file descriptor. If the first byte read from the server is not equal to 0, errno is set to the value received, and no file descriptor is read (as there isn't one to receive).

Program 21.1 shows the code for the first two functions, send_fd and send_err.

advanced_ipc/pass_fd.c

```
 1 #include <unistd.h>
 2 #include <errno.h>
 3 #include <stropts.h>
 4 #include "ssp.h"

 5 int send_fd (int pipe_fd, int fd)
 6 {
 7     char buf;

 8     buf = 0;

 9     if (writen (pipe_fd, &buf, 1) != 1)
10         return (-1);

11     if (ioctl (pipe_fd, I_SENDFD, fd) == -1)
12         return (-1);

13     return (0);
14 }

15 int send_err (int pipe_fd, char status)
16 {
17     if (status == 0)
18         status = EINVAL;

19     return (writen (pipe_fd, &status, 1));
20 }
```

advanced_ipc/pass_fd.c

Program 21.1 The send_fd and send_err functions.

The send_fd function

8–10 Set the buffer to 0 and write it to the pipe. This indicates to recv_fd that a file descriptor is to follow.

11–12 Call ioctl with a *request* of I_SENDFD to send the file descriptor to the receiver. The third argument to ioctl is the actual file descriptor we want to send.

The send_err function

15–20 Write the single status byte, which mustn't be 0, to the pipe. This indicates to recv_fd that an error occurred, and no descriptor will follow.

When we want to receive a file descriptor, we use an I_RECVFD ioctl. The third argument is a pointer to a strrecvfd structure, which has the following members:

```
    struct strrecvfd {
        int     fd;         /* New file descriptor */
        uid_t   uid;        /* Effective user ID of sender */
        gid_t   gid;        /* Effective group ID of sender */
        char    fill [8];   /* Filler */
    };
```

Program 21.2 shows the code for our recv_fd function.

Read the status byte from the pipe

27–32 Read the status byte from the pipe. If the number of bytes read is 0, the server has closed the connection.

---
advanced_ipc/pass_fd.c
```
21 int recv_fd (int pipe_fd)
22 {
23     int new_fd;
24     ssize_t n;
25     char buf;
26     struct strrecvfd recvfd;

27     if ((n = read (pipe_fd, &buf, 1)) == -1)
28         err_msg ("read failed");

29     if (n == 0) {
30         err_ret ("Connection close by server");
31         new_fd = -1;
32     }
33     else {
34         if (buf == 0) {
35             if (ioctl (pipe_fd, I_RECVFD, &recvfd) == -1)
36                 return (-1);
37             new_fd = recvfd.fd;
38         }
39         else {
40             errno = buf;
41             new_fd = -1;
42         }
43     }

44     return (new_fd);
45 }
```
advanced_ipc/pass_fd.c

Program 21.2   The recv_fd function.

Receive the file descriptor

33–38 If the status byte is 0, call ioctl with a *request* of I_RECVFD. Return the file descriptor we received to the caller.

39–43 If the status byte is not 0, set errno to the value of the status byte, and return −1 to the caller.

In the next section, we'll use these functions to write an open server.

21.3   An Open Server, Version 1

In this section we'll use the file-descriptor-passing functions we wrote in the previous section to write an open server, that is, a separate program whose only function is to open a file and pass the resulting file descriptor back to its caller. By using an open server, we can add all sorts of extra rules to the standard UNIX permissions. For example, we can restrict access to a file by a given user to certain days of the week. Note that we only pass a file descriptor back to the caller—not the file's contents. This gives us more flexibility and minimizes the amount of data we transfer using IPC: just the pathname and open mode from the client, and the file descriptor (or error status) from the server.

There are several other advantages to writing a separate open server:

1. Because the server is a separate program, it can be contacted by any client (much like a library function). That is, we are not hard coding the functionality into a specific client, but designing a general facility that other programs can use.

2. If we want to change the functionality of the server, we need to modify only one program. (This is the same as one of the advantages shared libraries enjoy over static ones.)

3. As we just alluded to, because the server is a separate program, we can make it a set-user-ID program to give it special privileges the clients won't necessarily have. This is something we can't do in a library function.

In this version of our open server, the client creates a pipe and calls `fork` and `exec` to run the server. The client and server then implement a simple two-step protocol:

1. The client sends a request string to the server. This string has the following format:

   open *pathname mode*\0

   The *pathname* argument specifies the name of the file to open, and the *mode* argument specifies the second argument of the open function (i.e., the *oflag* argument). This argument must be specified as a decimal number. The last byte of the request is a terminating NUL. After sending the request string to the server, it waits for the server's response.

2. If the server successfully opened the requested file, it returns a two-part reply using `send_fd`. The first part is a single byte, the value of which is 0. The second part is the file descriptor itself. If the server cannot open the requested file, a single byte is returned using `send_err`, which contains the value of `errno` resulting from the failed operation.

This first version of our open server just sends a file descriptor between related processes. In Section 21.5 we'll show another version that runs as a standalone daemon, servicing requests from unrelated processes.

Now that we've described how our open server works, let's take a look at its code. There are two programs; the first, called `cs_open1`, is the client. It runs the second program, called `open1`, which is the server. Program 21.3 shows the `main` function for the client.

After checking the command line arguments, the `main` function calls the `cs_open` function to open the file (by using the open server). If the file was successfully opened, we repeatedly read from the file descriptor and write the bytes to standard output.

Program 21.4 shows the code for the `cs_open` (client server open) function.

Open pipe

31–32 Call the `pipe` function to create the pipe we'll use to communicate with the server.

advanced_ipc/cs_open1.c

```
 1 #include <stdio.h>
 2 #include <unistd.h>
 3 #include <fcntl.h>
 4 #include <string.h>
 5 #include <sys/uio.h>
 6 #include "ssp.h"

 7 static int cs_open (char *path, int oflag);

 8 int main (int argc, char **argv)
 9 {
10     int fd;
11     ssize_t n;
12     char buf [BUF_SIZE];

13     if (argc != 2)
14         err_quit ("Usage: cs_open1 path");

15     if ((fd = cs_open (argv [1], O_RDONLY)) == -1)
16         err_msg ("Can't open %s", argv [1]);

17     while ((n = read (fd, buf, BUF_SIZE)) > 0)
18         if (writen (STDOUT_FILENO, buf, n) == -1)
19             err_msg ("write failed");

20     if (n == -1)
21         err_msg ("read failed");

22     close (fd);

23     return (0);
24 }
```

advanced_ipc/cs_open1.c

Program 21.3 The client's main function.

Call `fork`

33–35 Call `fork` to create the child process.

Child process

37 Close the end of the pipe we no longer need.

38–45 Duplicate standard input and standard error to the pipe.

46–47 Call `exec` to run the open server.

Parent process

49 Close the end of the pipe we no longer need.

50–56 Set up the I/O vector for use with `writev`. By using `writev`, we avoid copying the required information to another string (using `snprintf` for example). Besides avoiding the overhead this would incur, we also don't have to worry about the resulting buffer size. We add 1 to the final `iov_len` value to account for the terminating NUL.

advanced_ipc/cs_open1.c

```
25 static int cs_open (char *path, int oflag)
26 {
27     int len;
28     char buf [12];
29     struct iovec iov [3];
30     int pipe_fd [2];

31     if (pipe (pipe_fd) == -1)
32         err_msg ("pipe failed");

33     switch (fork ()) {
34         case -1:
35             err_msg ("fork failed");

36         case 0:
37             close (pipe_fd [0]);
38             if (pipe_fd [1] != STDIN_FILENO) {
39                 if (dup2 (pipe_fd [1], STDIN_FILENO) != STDIN_FILENO)
40                     err_msg ("Can't dup2 stdin");
41             }
42             if (pipe_fd [1] != STDOUT_FILENO) {
43                 if (dup2 (pipe_fd [1], STDOUT_FILENO) != STDOUT_FILENO)
44                     err_msg ("Can't dup2 stdout");
45             }

46             execl ("./opend1", "opend", NULL);
47             err_msg ("exec failed");

48         default:
49             close (pipe_fd [1]);

50             snprintf (buf, 12, " %d", oflag);
51             iov [0].iov_base = "open ";
52             iov [0].iov_len = strlen ("open ");
53             iov [1].iov_base = path;
54             iov [1].iov_len = strlen (path);
55             iov [2].iov_base = buf;
56             iov [2].iov_len = strlen (buf) + 1;

57             len = iov [0].iov_len + iov [1].iov_len + iov [2].iov_len;
58             if (writev (pipe_fd [0], &iov [0], 3) != len)
59                 err_msg ("writev failed");

60             return (recv_fd (pipe_fd [0]));
61     }
62 }
```

advanced_ipc/cs_open1.c

Program 21.4 The cs_open function.

57–59 Calculate the total number of bytes we'll be writing and call `writev` to write the buffers.

60 Call `recv_fd`, returning the resulting file descriptor or error.

Let's now take a look at the code for the first version of our open server, called `opend1`. This is the program that is execed from the child process shown in Program 21.4.

Program 21.5 shows the `main` function for the server.

advanced_ipc/opend1.c

```
 1 #include <unistd.h>
 2 #include <stdlib.h>
 3 #include <string.h>
 4 #include <errno.h>
 5 #include <limits.h>
 6 #include <sys/types.h>
 7 #include <sys/stat.h>
 8 #include <fcntl.h>
 9 #include "ssp.h"

10 static char *path;
11 static int oflag;

12 static void do_request (char *buf, ssize_t n, int pipe_fd);
13 static int buf2args (char *buf);
14 static int parse_args (int argc, char **argv);

15 int main (void)
16 {
17     ssize_t n;
18     char buf [LINE_LEN];

19     for (;;) {
20         if ((n = read (STDIN_FILENO, buf, LINE_LEN)) == -1)
21             err_msg ("read failed");
22         if (n == 0)
23             break;

24         do_request (buf, n, STDOUT_FILENO);
25     }

26     return (0);
27 }
```

advanced_ipc/opend1.c

Program 21.5 The first server's `main` function.

The `main` function consists of an infinite loop that reads a request line from standard input, and passes the resulting line to the `do_request` function. It is this function that actually handles the request.

Program 21.6 shows the code for the `do_request` function.

Check string is NUL terminated

31–34 If the last byte in the buffer is not 0, return an error.

Parse buffer and open the requested file

35–38 Call `buf2args` to convert the string into an `argc`-and-`argv`-like construct.

39–42 Open the specified file. The global variables `path` and `oflag` are set in the function `parse_args`, which we describe further on.

43–44 Send the resulting file descriptor to the client.

Program 21.7 shows the code for the `buf2args` and `parse_args` functions.

―――――――――――――――――――――――――――――― *advanced_ipc/opend1.c*
```
28 static void do_request (char *buf, ssize_t n, int pipe_fd)
29 {
30     int fd;

31     if (buf [n - 1] != '\0') {
32         send_err (pipe_fd, EINVAL);
33         return;
34     }

35     if (buf2args (buf) == -1) {
36         send_err (pipe_fd, EINVAL);
37         return;
38     }

39     if ((fd = open (path, oflag)) == -1) {
40         send_err (pipe_fd, errno);
41         return;
42     }

43     if (send_fd (pipe_fd, fd) == -1)
44         err_msg ("send_fd failed");

45     close (fd);
46 }
```
―――――――――――――――――――――――――――――― *advanced_ipc/opend1.c*

Program 21.6   The do_request function.

The **buf2args** function

52–53 Return an error if the string contains no white space.

54–61 Tokenize the string, storing a pointer to each token in our argv array. We also keep track of how many arguments we've had.

62 Call parse_args to parse the arguments.

The **parse_args** function

66–67 If there aren't three arguments, or the first argument is not "open", then return an error.

68–69 Set the path and oflag global variables. Note that we can safely copy these pointers despite the fact that they will no longer exist once buf2args returns, because they are just pointers into the user-supplied buffer.

Let's see how we can use this open server:

```
$ cat /etc/shadow                          First try viewing /etc/shadow using cat
cat: cannot open /etc/shadow
$ ./cs_open1 /etc/shadow                   Try opening /etc/shadow as a normal user
Can't open /etc/shadow: Permission denied
$ su                                       Become superuser
Password:
# chown root cs_open1                      Make open server be owned by root
# chmod +s cs_open1                        Make open server SUID
# suspend
[1] + Stopped (SIGSTOP)        su
$ ./cs_open1 /etc/shadow                   Try opening /etc/shadow as a normal user again
rich@grover6446# ./cs_open1 /etc/shadow
```

advanced_ipc/opend1.c

```
47 static int buf2args (char *buf)
48 {
49     char *ptr;
50     char *argv [_POSIX_ARG_MAX];
51     int argc;

52     if (strtok (buf, " \t\n") == NULL)
53         return (-1);

54     argc = 0;
55     argv [argc] = buf;
56     while ((ptr = strtok (NULL, " \t\n")) != NULL) {
57         if (++argc >= (_POSIX_ARG_MAX - 1))
58             return (-1);
59         argv [argc] = ptr;
60     }
61     argv [++argc] = NULL;

62     return (parse_args (argc, argv));
63 }

64 static int parse_args (int argc, char **argv)
65 {
66     if ((argc != 3) || (strcmp (argv [0], "open") != 0))
67         return (-1);

68     path = argv [1];
69     oflag = atoi (argv [2]);

70     return (0);
71 }
```

advanced_ipc/opend1.c

Program 21.7 The buf2args and parse_args functions.

```
root:VkCy7hjJIviNE:6445::::::
daemon:NP:6445::::::
bin:NP:6445::::::
sys:NP:6445::::::
adm:NP:6445::::::
lp:NP:6445::::::
uucp:NP:6445::::::
nuucp:NP:6445::::::
smmsp:NP:6445::::::
listen:*LK*::::::
nobody:NP:6445::::::
noaccess:NP:6445::::::
nobody4:NP:6445::::::
rich:nV60Hjh5L.6tI:12281::::::
jenny:4jc09ljhJMZpo:12281::::::
accting:2Ss8Lkjdl9jaI:12281::::::
```

When we try to read /etc/shadow as a normal user, we get a permission denied error. This is correct, because only root has access to this file normally. When we make the open server (i.e., opend1) a set-user-ID root program, we can successfully open /etc/shadow despite running as an unprivileged user.

This example illustrates a subtle fact about UNIX file permissions we should be cognizant of: once a process has an open file descriptor, it can access the file associated with that descriptor in the manner specified when the file was first opened, regardless of whether the effective user ID or effective group ID of the process has access to that file. In other words, the file permission bits are checked only when a process attempts to open a file; the permissions are *not* checked when the process reads from or writes to the file. (Although this is true for normal versions of UNIX, there are at least some versions of "secure UNIX" that check the file permissions on every read or write, as well as when the file is opened.)

With this version of our open server, we have one server per client, which is not very efficient in its use of machine resources. After we look at client-server connections in the next section, we'll rewrite our open server as a standalone daemon that handles requests from all clients.

21.4   Client-Server Connection Functions

The method of passing file descriptors using pipes we discussed in the previous two sections has one significant drawback: it only works between related processes. To circumvent this problem, we need to use a named pipe when we're dealing with unrelated processes.

As we showed in Section 19.5, we can take a pipe and attach a pathname in the file system to either end. A daemon would create one end of the pipe and attach a name to that end. Unrelated processes can then make requests of the daemon by writing messages to the server's end of the pipe. This is a similar situation to the one we show in Figure 19.12, in which we use a well-known FIFO for the clients to send their requests to.

Another, better, approach is to have the server create one end of a pipe with a well-known name, and have the clients *connect* to that end. (The term "connect" is an allusion to the function of the same name that is used in network programming, including UNIX domain sockets.) This has the effect of creating a new pipe between the client and server, which means that the server will be notified each time a client breaks the connection (e.g., by terminating).

The `fattach` and `fdetach` Functions

To attach a pipe to, or detach a pipe from, a pathname, we use the `fattach` and `fdetach` functions respectively.

```
#include <stropts.h>

int fattach (int fildes, const char *path);

int fdetach (const char *path);
```
                                                      Both return: 0 if OK, −1 on error

The `fattach` function attaches the file descriptor specified by *fildes* to the file whose path is specified by *path*. The *fildes* argument must refer to an open file descriptor that is associated with a STREAMS file. Once a file descriptor has been attached to a path, all subsequent operations on *path* will operate on the STREAMS file until it is detached. A STREAMS file may have several names associated with it, i.e., *fildes* can be attached to more than one *path*.

The attributes of the named stream are initialized as follows: the user ID, group ID, and times are set from *path*, the number of links is set to 1, and the size and device identifier are set to those of the STREAMS device associated with *fildes*. If any of these attributes are changed, the underlying file is not affected.

The `fdetach` function performs the opposite task to `fattach`; it detaches a STREAMS file from *path* that was previously attached using `fattach`. A successful call to `fdetach` causes all pathnames that named the attached STREAMS file to again refer to the file to which the STREAMS file was attached. All subsequent operations on *path* will operate on the underlying file rather than the STREAMS file.

All open file descriptors established while the STREAMS file was attached to *path* will still refer to the STREAMS file even after `fdetach` has taken effect.

If there are no open file descriptors or other references to the STREAMS file, then a successful `fdetach` has the same effect as performing the last `close` on the attached file.

We'll use the `fattach` function in the first of our client server connection functions, `srv_listen`.

The `srv_listen` Function

A server announces its willingness to listen for client connections on a well-known name by calling `srv_listen`.

```
#include "ssp.h"

int srv_listen (const char *path);
                                    Returns: file descriptor to listen on if OK, -1 on error
```

The `srv_listen` function is the first of these functions that the server calls. The *path* argument specifies the well-known name, which is used by clients to connect to the server. Upon success, `srv_listen` returns the file descriptor associated with the server's end of the named pipe.

The `srv_accept` Function

After the server has called `srv_listen`, it calls `srv_accept` to wait for new client connections to arrive.

```
    #include "ssp.h"

    int srv_accept (int fd, uid_t *uid);

                                        Returns: new file descriptor if OK, −1 on error
```

The `srv_accept` function waits for clients to connect to the well-known address associated with the STREAMS file descriptor specified by *fd* (which is the file descriptor returned by `srv_listen`). When a client connects, a new pipe is created between the client and server, and the value of this new descriptor is returned to the caller. Also, the effective user ID of the client process is stored in the buffer pointed to by *uid*.

The `cli_connect` Function

To connect to a server, a client calls `cli_connect`.

```
    #include "ssp.h"

    int cli_connect (const char *path);

                                        Returns: file descriptor if OK, −1 on error
```

The `cli_connect` function attempts to connect to a server by using the well-known name specified by *path*. This *path* must be the same as that advertised by the server when it called `srv_listen`. If successful, `cli_connect` returns the file descriptor that refers to the pipe connected to the server.

Let's take a look at the implementation of these functions. Program 21.8 shows the code for the `srv_listen` function.

Although it is quite a short function, a lot happens behind the scenes when we call `srv_listen`, so let's take a closer look at its implementation details.

Create the mount point for `fattach`

11–14 We create the mount point we'll use to attach to the pipe. To ensure that the file we create has the desired permissions (and is of the right type), we delete any file that might have that name first. Note that we create a normal file rather than a FIFO as we did in Chapter 19.

Create pipe and push `connld` module

15–18 We create a pipe and push the `connld` STREAMS module onto one end. It is the `connld` module that provides the unique connections between the server and client processes. Figure 21.2 shows the resulting arrangement.

Attach to mount point

19–20 Using the `fattach` function we attach a pathname (i.e., the mount point) to the end of the pipe that `connld` was pushed onto. Any client process that subsequently opens this pathname is actually referring to the named end of the pipe. When this happens, the following events happen:

—————————————————————————— *advanced_ipc/cs_conn.c*

```
 1 #include <unistd.h>
 2 #include <stropts.h>
 3 #include <sys/types.h>
 4 #include <sys/stat.h>
 5 #include <fcntl.h>
 6 #include "ssp.h"

 7 int srv_listen (const char *path)
 8 {
 9     int fd;
10     int pipe_fd [2];

11     unlink (path);
12     if ((fd = creat (path, FIFO_PERMS)) == -1)
13         return (-1);
14     close (fd);

15     if (pipe (pipe_fd) == -1)
16         return (-1);
17     if (ioctl (pipe_fd [1], I_PUSH, "connld") == -1)
18         return (-1);

19     if (fattach (pipe_fd [1], path) == -1)
20         return (-1);

21     return (pipe_fd [0]);
22 }
```
—————————————————————————— *advanced_ipc/cs_conn.c*

Program 21.8 The srv_listen function.

1. A new pipe is created.

2. One of the new pipe's file descriptors is passed back to the client process as the return value from open.

3. The new pipe's other file descriptor is passed to the server process at the other end of the named pipe (i.e., the end that doesn't have the connld module pushed onto it). The server receives this new file descriptor by using an ioctl with a *cmd* of I_RECVFD.

Let's say that the path of the well-known file the server fattaches to its pipe is /tmp/srv_pipe. Figure 21.3 shows the arrangement after the client has successfully opened this file (by calling cli_connect, for example).

The pipe between the client and the server is the one created when the client opens the well-known file. This is because the file being opened is really a named stream that has connld pushed onto it. The client's file descriptor (fd) is returned by open, and the server's file descriptor (client_fd) is the one received when the server issues an ioctl with a *cmd* of I_RECVFD on the descriptor pipe_fd [0]. The server, once it has pushed connld onto pipe_fd [1] and attached a name to it, never directly uses pipe_fd [1] again.

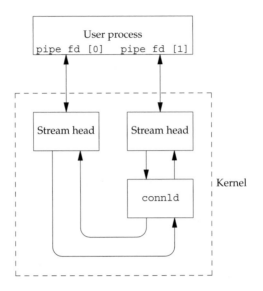

Figure 21.2 Pipe after pushing the `connld` module onto one end.

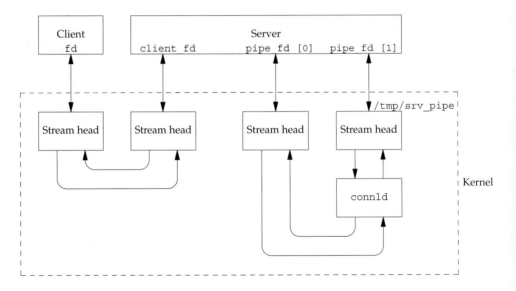

Figure 21.3 Client-server connections on a named pipe.

When the server has advertised its willingness to listen for client connections, it calls `srv_accept` to wait for these connections to arrive. Program 21.9 shows the code for our `srv_accept` function.

---
advanced_ipc/cs_conn.c

```
23 int srv_accept (int fd, uid_t *uid)
24 {
25     struct strrecvfd recvfd;

26     if (ioctl (fd, I_RECVFD, &recvfd) == -1)
27         return (-1);

28     if (uid != NULL)
29         *uid = recvfd.uid;

30     return (recvfd.fd);
31 }
```
advanced_ipc/cs_conn.c

Program 21.9 The srv_accept function.

Wait for a client connection

26–27 We call ioctl with a *cmd* of I_RECVFD. This puts the calling process to sleep until a client has opened the well-known file, which results in the kernel sending our process one of the resulting pipe's file descriptors. With reference to Figure 21.3, the first argument to srv_accept would be pipe_fd [0], and the return value from srv_accept would be client_fd.

28–29 If the caller has supplied a buffer, store the user ID of the connecting process in it.

Clients initiate a connection to the server by calling the cli_connect function, the code for which is shown in Program 21.10.

---
advanced_ipc/cs_conn.c

```
32 int cli_connect (const char *path)
33 {
34     int fd;

35     if ((fd = open (path, O_RDWR)) == -1)
36         return (-1);

37     return ((isastream (fd)) ? fd : -1);
38 }
```
advanced_ipc/cs_conn.c

Program 21.10 The cli_connect function.

This function merely opens the specified file and checks that the returned file descriptor refers to a STREAMS device. We perform this check in case the server isn't running but the well-known pathname exists in the file system anyway.

In the next section, we'll use these functions to write a standalone open server daemon.

21.5 An Open Server, Version 2

In Section 21.3 we wrote an open server that ran as a child of the invoking process by using fork and exec. It showed how to pass a file descriptor from a process to its parent, which is useful, but is also very limited. In this section we'll develop a general purpose open server that runs as a standalone daemon. This daemon will handle requests from all processes. We still use a pipe to pass the file descriptors (although in this case the pipe is the one automatically created by the connld STREAMS module), and the client and server use the same protocol. We'll use the srv_listen, srv_accept, and cli_connect functions we wrote in the previous section, and show how we the server can handle multiple clients by using the poll function we described in Section 13.17.

The client program is very similar to the client we described in Section 21.3. The cs_open function is similar to Program 21.4, but has changes to reflect the fact that we call cli_connect instead of fork and exec. The new version of cs_open is shown in Program 21.11.

advanced_ipc/cs_open2.c

```
26 static int cs_open (char *path, int oflag)
27 {
28     int len;
29     char buf [12];
30     struct iovec iov [3];
31     int fd;

32     if ((fd = cli_connect (CS_PIPE)) == -1)
33         err_msg ("cli_connect failed");

34     snprintf (buf, 12, " %d", oflag);
35     iov [0].iov_base = "open ";
36     iov [0].iov_len = strlen ("open ");
37     iov [1].iov_base = path;
38     iov [1].iov_len = strlen (path);
39     iov [2].iov_base = buf;
40     iov [2].iov_len = strlen (buf) + 1;

41     len = iov [0].iov_len + iov [1].iov_len + iov [2].iov_len;
42     if (writev (fd, &iov [0], 3) != len)
43         err_msg ("writev failed");

44     return (recv_fd (fd));
45 }
```

advanced_ipc/cs_open2.c

Program 21.11 The cs_open function.

The client's main function is the same as Program 21.3, except we add the following line just before the function prototype for cs_open:

```
#define CS_PIPE "/tmp/ssp_cs_open"
```

This defines the server's well-known name.

Let's take a look at the server now. The first section of code, Program 21.12, shows the header files we include, a structure definition, and the function prototypes.

This version of the open server handles connections from multiple clients, so it must keep track of the state of each connection. Because of this requirement, in addition to the usual header file inclusion and definition of function prototypes, we define the entry structure; we use a linked list of these structures to keep track of all the client

advanced_ipc/opend2.c

```
 1  #include <stdio.h>
 2  #include <unistd.h>
 3  #include <stdlib.h>
 4  #include <string.h>
 5  #include <errno.h>
 6  #include <limits.h>
 7  #include <sys/types.h>
 8  #include <sys/stat.h>
 9  #include <fcntl.h>
10  #include <poll.h>
11  #include <sys/stropts.h>
12  #include <sys/resource.h>
13  #include "ssp.h"

14  #define CS_PIPE "/tmp/ssp_cs_open"

15  typedef struct entry {
16      struct entry *next;
17      uid_t uid;
18      int fd;
19  } entry_t;

20  static entry_t *list_head = NULL;
21  static char *path;
22  static int oflag;

23  static void loop (void);
24  static void do_request (char *buf, ssize_t n, int pipe_fd);
25  static int buf2args (char *buf);
26  static int parse_args (int argc, char **argv);
27  static int add_entry (int fd, uid_t uid);
28  static int del_entry (int fd);
```

advanced_ipc/opend2.c

Program 21.12 Preamble for version 2 of our open server.

connections. In Program 21.15 we'll show the code for the two functions that maintain this linked list: add_entry and del_entry.

Program 21.13 shows the code for the open server's main function.

The main function parses the command line options, then calls the loop function (which doesn't return). If the open server is invoked with the -d (debug) option, it runs interactively instead of as a daemon. We can use this option when testing the server (messages will be printed on standard error rather than being sent to the syslog facility).

Program 21.14 shows the code for the loop function.

It is the loop function that waits for new connections from client processes. Let's take a closer look at the code.

Allocate space for pollfd structures

65–67 Get the current (soft) limit for the number of open file descriptors and allocate enough memory to hold that number of pollfd structures. This approach, although it works,

advanced_ipc/opend2.c

```
29 int main (int argc, char **argv)
30 {
31     int c;
32     int debug;
33     int err_flag;

34     debug = 0;
35     err_flag = 0;
36     opterr = 0;

37     while ((c = getopt (argc, argv, "d")) != EOF) {
38         switch (c) {
39             case 'd':
40                 debug = 1;
41                 break;

42             default:
43                 err_flag = 1;
44                 break;
45         }
46     }

47     if (err_flag)
48         err_quit ("Usage: opend2 [-d]");

49     if (debug == 0)
50         daemon_init ("opend2", 0);

51     loop ();

52     return (0);
53 }
```

advanced_ipc/opend2.c

Program 21.13 The second server's main function.

can be problematic if the current file descriptor limit is very high. This is because the system may not have enough virtual memory available for all the structures.

Create server's endpoint for client connections

68–73 Call `srv_listen` to advertise the server's willingness to accept client connections. Note that we use the first `pollfd` structure for `listen_fd`.

Call `poll`, looping for ever

74–76 In an infinite loop, call `poll` to wait for the status of at least one of the file descriptors we're monitoring to change, specifying an infinite timeout. In addition to errors, there are two conditions that can be true after `poll` returns. These are:

1. The file descriptor `listen_fd` could be ready for reading, which means that a client has opened the server's well-known path (i.e., has called `cli_connect`).

2. An existing client's file descriptor could be ready for reading. This means that either the client has terminated, or it has sent a new request.

advanced_ipc/opend2.c

```
54 static void loop (void)
55 {
56     int i;
57     ssize_t n;
58     int listen_fd;
59     int client_fd;
60     int num_fds;
61     char buf [LINE_LEN];
62     uid_t uid;
63     struct pollfd *fds;
64     struct rlimit num_files;

65     getrlimit (RLIMIT_NOFILE, &num_files);
66     if ((fds = calloc (num_files.rlim_cur, sizeof (struct pollfd))) == NULL)
67         err_msg ("Calloc failed");

68     if ((listen_fd = srv_listen (CS_PIPE)) == -1)
69         err_msg ("srv_listen failed");
70     add_entry (listen_fd, 0);
71     fds [0].fd = listen_fd;
72     fds [0].events = POLLIN;
73     num_fds = 0;

74     for (;;) {
75         if (poll (fds, num_fds + 1, INFTIM) == -1)
76             err_msg ("poll failed");

77         if (fds [0].revents & POLLIN) {
78             if ((client_fd = srv_accept (listen_fd, &uid)) == -1)
79                 err_msg ("srv_accept failed");
80             if (add_entry (client_fd, uid) == -1)
81                 err_msg ("add_entry failed");
82             num_fds++;
83             fds [num_fds].fd = client_fd;
84             fds [num_fds].events = POLLIN;
85             log_msg ("New connection: fd = %d, uid = %d", client_fd, uid);
86         }

87         for (i = 1; i <= num_fds; i++) {
88             client_fd = fds [i].fd;
89             if (client_fd == -1)
90                 continue;
91             if (fds [i].revents & POLLHUP)
92                 goto hangup;
93             else if (fds [i].revents & POLLIN) {
94                 if ((n = read (client_fd, buf, LINE_LEN)) == -1)
95                     err_msg ("read error on fd %d", client_fd);
96                 else if (n == 0) {
97 hangup:
98                     log_msg ("Connection closed: fd = %d", client_fd);
99                     del_entry (client_fd);
100                    fds [i].fd = -1;
101                    close (client_fd);
102                }
```

```
103                    else
104                        do_request (buf, n, client_fd);
105                }
106            }
107        }
108 }
```
―――――――――――――――――――――――――――――――― *advanced_ipc/opend2.c*

Program 21.14 The loop function.

Handle a new client connection

77–86 If a new client connection arrives, we call srv_accept to accept the new connection, and then update our linked list of client file descriptors. We also perform some other tasks, like updating the number of file descriptors, updating our array of pollfd structures, and logging the new connection.

Handle existing clients that are ready for reading

87–108 If a client file descriptor is ready for reading, it means that either the client has terminated or has sent a new request. In the case of the former, the POLLHUP field of the revents member of the pollfd structure associated with the file descriptor will be set. When we receive this hangup indicator, we log the fact that a connection has been closed, remove the client's entry in our linked list of connections, mark the appropriate entry in the pollfd array as being invalid, and close the connection. Any data still on the stream (i.e., still in the pipe) is discarded. This is because there is no point in processing the request, as we have no way of sending back a response.

In the event that the client has sent us a new request, we call do_request to handle it. With the exception of the fact that this version of do_request logs the request, version 2 of this function is the same as the one we showed in Program 21.6. The buf2args and parse_args functions are also unchanged (see Program 21.7).

We mentioned a couple of times that the server maintains a linked list of connections. Program 21.15 shows the code for the two functions that do this; add_entry adds an entry to the linked list, and del_entry removes an entry from it.

This completes version 2 of our open server, which uses a single daemon to handle requests from multiple clients.

21.6 Summary

In this chapter we showed how we can pass file descriptors between related processes by using pipe. We then wrote three functions, send_fd, send_err, and recv_fd, which we then used to write an open server. This first version of our open server was invoked directly from the client, using fork and exec.

Next we described how we can attach a pipe to a pathname in the file system by using the fattach function, and how we can use the connld STREAMS module to provide unique connections between unrelated client and server processes. We then described three functions we wrote to transfer a file descriptor between unrelated processes, srv_listen, srv_accept, and cli_connect, and wrote another version of our open

advanced_ipc/opend2.c

```
154 static int add_entry (int fd, uid_t uid)
155 {
156     entry_t *prev;
157     entry_t *current;
158     entry_t *new;

159     prev = list_head;
160     current = list_head;

161     while (current != NULL) {
162         prev = current;
163         current = current -> next;
164     }

165     if ((new = malloc (sizeof (entry_t))) == NULL)
166         return (-1);

167     new -> uid = uid;
168     new -> fd = fd;
169     new -> next = NULL;

170     if (list_head == NULL)
171         list_head = new;
172     else
173         prev -> next = new;

174     return (0);
175 }

176 static int del_entry (int fd)
177 {
178     entry_t *prev;
179     entry_t *current;

180     prev = list_head;
181     current = list_head;

182     while (current != NULL) {
183         if (current -> fd == fd) {
184             if (current == list_head)
185                 list_head = current -> next;
186             else
187                 prev -> next = current -> next;

188             free (current);

189             return (0);
190         }

191         prev = current;
192         current = current -> next;
193     }

194     return (-1);
195 }
```

advanced_ipc/opend2.c

Program 21.15 The add_entry and del_entry functions.

server. The second version of our open server runs as a standalone daemon, which services requests from all clients.

Exercises

21.1 Write a program that uses the `send_fd`, `send_err`, and `recv_fd` functions from this chapter and the process synchronization functions we wrote in Section 15.10. The program should create a child by calling `fork`; the child then opens an existing file and passes the resulting file descriptor back to its parent. The child should then change its offset into the file (printing the new position), and then notify the parent. The parent should then determine the file's current offset and print it. Have the child and parent repeat this a number of times. Do the child and parent file offsets match? Explain your findings.

21.2 There is a relatively easy way we can optimize the `loop` function in Program 21.14. Describe and implement this change.

22

Doors

22.1   Introduction

Introduced with Solaris 2.6, doors provide a mechanism for fast remote procedure calls (RPCs) between clients and servers on the same machine. (For our purposes, the terms "function" and "procedure" are synonymous; we use both terms interchangeably in this text, although some languages use the term "function" to describe a subroutine that returns a single value, and "procedure" to describe a subroutine that has no return value.)

To better understand doors, consider the three types of procedure call scenarios, as illustrated in Figure 22.1. Each of these three types can be described thus:

1. The top scenario is a local function call. A *local procedure call* is the normal sort of function calls we are familiar with. The procedure (function) being called is part of the same process as the caller. This is true if we write both functions, or if one of the functions is in a library.

2. The middle scenario is an RPC where the client and server are on the same host (this is really just a special case of the bottom scenario). A *remote procedure call* is when the function being called and the function calling it are not in the same process. The caller is usually referred to as the client, and the function being called is usually referred to as the server. The client and server can be on either the same host (as is the case here), or on different network connected hosts; *doors* are an optimized version of the former. The server makes a function available to clients by creating a door, which the clients use to call the function. Although not an example of IPC in the traditional sense, we can think of doors as a sort of IPC, because data (e.g., function arguments and return values) are passed between the client and server.

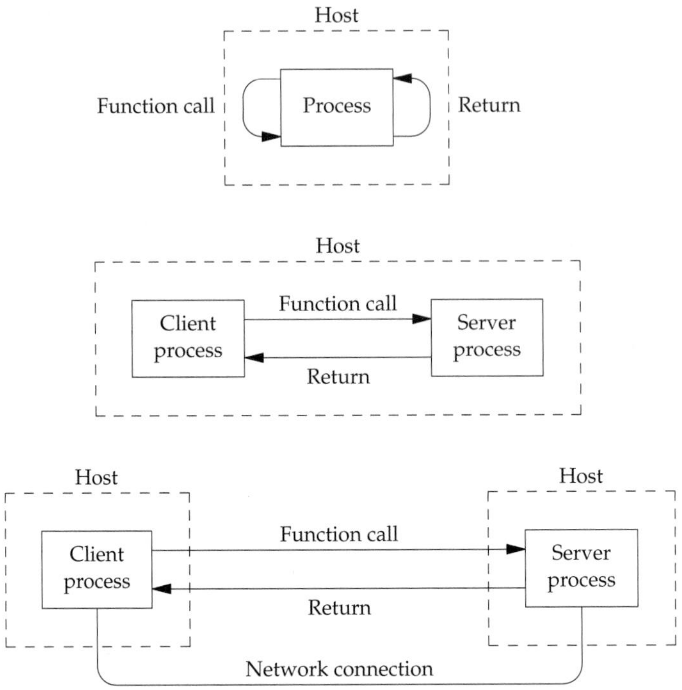

Figure 22.1 The three types of function call scenarios.

3. The bottom scenario illustrates an RPC where the client and server are on different machines. As we mentioned in the preceding paragraph, RPC in general enables a client to call a server function on a different host, provided that there is a network connection between the two machines. Because of the close relationship between general RPC and networking, we won't discuss RPC any further in this text. Interested readers are referred to Chapter 16 of [Stevens 1999].

> Although doors became a supported interface in Solaris 2.6, initially they were developed for Sun's experimental distributed operating system, Spring. They subsequently appeared in Solaris 2.5, although they were unsupported and undocumented (the notes section of the door man page contained the following message: "This manual page is here solely for the benefit of anyone who noticed door_call in truss output and thought, 'Gee, I wonder what that does...'"). At the time of writing this book (mid 2004), the stability of the doors API was still listed as "Evolving", so it's conceivable that changes might occur in future releases of Solaris.
>
> A preliminary version of the doors API is being developed for Linux; details can be found at http://www.rampant.org/doors.

Function calls can be either synchronous or asynchronous. A *synchronous function call* is where the caller does not resume execution until the called function returns. Contrariwise, an *asynchronous function call* is where the caller and the called function execute (or at least appear to execute) at the same time. An example of an asynchronous function call would be the function that is passed as the third argument to `pthread_create`. In this case, the caller can wait for the new thread (i.e., the called function) to complete by calling `pthread_join`. RPCs can be either synchronous or asynchronous; door calls are, however, synchronous.

Inside a process, doors are identified by descriptors. Externally, they may be identified by a pathname in the file system. A server creates a door by calling the `door_create` function we describe next. One of the arguments to this function is a pointer to the function that will be associated with the door, and `door_create`'s return value is a descriptor for the new door. The server then calls the `fattach` function we described in Section 21.4 to associate a pathname with the door. A client opens a door by calling `open` with the door's pathname as its argument; the return value from `open` is the client's door descriptor. The client then calls the server function by using the `door_call` function. Note that door clients and servers are not mutually exclusive; a process that is a server for one door may be a client for another.

As we stated earlier, door calls are synchronous; when a client calls it, `door_call` does not return until the server function returns (or an error occurs). Whenever a client calls a server function, a thread in the server process handles it. The door library usually handles this thread management for us, creating new threads as needed. However, we'll see later how we can manage these threads ourselves. Because each request can potentially execute in its own thread, the server can handle multiple concurrent client requests. We call this a *concurrent server*. This also means that the server functions must be thread safe, because several instances of them could be running simultaneously (with each instance having its own thread).

The client and server can pass both data and descriptors to each other. This means, among other things, that a process can pass a door to some other process. We'll have more to say about this in Section 22.4.

22.2   Basic Door Functions

Now that we've described some of the doors concepts, let's take a look at some of the functions in the doors library.

The `door_create` Function

Before a door can be used, it must be created; to do this, the server calls `door_create`.

```
cc -mt [ flag ... ] file ... -ldoor [ library ... ]
#include <door.h>

int door_create (void (*server_procedure) (void *cookie, char *argp, size_t arg_size,
    door_desc_t *dp, uint_t n_desc), void *cookie, uint_t attributes) ;
```
                                                    Returns: door descriptor if OK, −1 on error

In this function prototype (and all the other prototypes for functions in the door library), we specify the -mt flag on the command line. This flag, which is specific to Sun's compiler, passes -D_REENTRANT to the preprocessor and appends -lthread after all other user-specified libraries on the command line. Users of other compilers can pass these flags "by hand" on the command line.

The door_create function creates a door, associating the function whose address is specified by *server_procedure* with it. The second argument, *cookie*, points to a data item that is associated with the door descriptor, and is the first argument passed to *server_procedure* during an invocation of door_call. This provides us with a mechanism by which the server can pass a pointer to the function every time it is called by a client. The remaining four arguments passed to *server_procedure* (*argp*, *arg_size*, *dp*, and *n_desc*) correspond to the first four members of the door_arg_t structure pointed to by the second argument of the door_call function we describe next.

The final argument to door_create, *attributes*, specifies attributes associated with the newly created door. Valid values for *attributes* are constructed by bitwise-ORing zero or more of the following constants:

DOOR_UNREF
: When the number of references to this door descriptor drops to one, the server function is invoked with the second argument (*argp*) set to DOOR_UNREF_DATA. In this case, *arg_size* and *n_desc* will be set to 0, and *dp* will be a NULL pointer. Note that for this condition to be triggered, more than one reference to this descriptor must have existed at some time in the past. Also, only one unreferenced invocation is delivered on behalf of a door.

DOOR_UNREF_MULTI
: This attribute, introduced in Solaris 7, is similar to DOOR_UNREF, except multiple unreferenced invocations can be delivered on the same door if the number of references to this door descriptor drops to one more than once. Because additional references may have been passed by the time an unreferenced invocation arrives, the DOOR_IS_UNREF attribute returned by the door_info function we describe in Section 22.3 can be used to determine if the door is still unreferenced.

DOOR_PRIVATE
: The doors library maintains a pool of threads in the server process, automatically creating new threads as required to service client requests. By default these new threads are placed into a processwide thread pool and are used to service a client request for any door in the server process.

  This attribute specifies that the doors library should maintain a pool of server threads for this door separate from the processwide pool of server threads. Server threads are associated with a door's private pool by using the door_bind function we describe in Section 22.4.

The *server_procedure* is defined as void because it never returns conventionally (i.e., a return statement is not used, and server functions do not fall off the end). Instead, *server_procedure* must call door_return when it want to return (we describe this function further on).

The descriptor returned to the caller by door_create will have its FD_CLOEXEC (close on exec) flag set. This means that the door descriptor will be closed automatically by the kernel should the server call exec. The fact that the door descriptor remains open across a fork is not problematic, because a door is identified by a process ID and the address of the server function (as we shall see when we describe the door_info function later). The door descriptor must be closed after an exec because although the server's process ID doesn't change, the address of the server function will be meaningless in the new executable.

The door_call Function

To call a server procedure executing in the address space of the server, clients call the door_call function.

```
cc -mt [ flag ... ] file ... -ldoor [ library ... ]
#include <door.h>

int door_call (int d, door_arg_t *params);
```

Returns: 0 if OK, −1 on error

The door_call function invokes the server function associated with the door descriptor *d*. This descriptor is usually the one returned by open, and the pathname opened by the client identifies which server function will be invoked by door_call.

The *params* argument is a pointer to a door_arg_t structure, which contains the function parameters (if any) and any results. Setting *params* to NULL indicates that there are no arguments, and that no results are expected. The door_arg_t structure has the following members:

```
typedef struct door_arg {
    char        *data_ptr;      /* Argument/result buffer pointer */
    size_t      data_size;      /* Size of argument/result buffer */
    door_desc_t *desc_ptr;      /* Argument/result descriptors */
    uint_t      desc_num;       /* Number of argument/result descriptors */
    char        *rbuf;          /* Result buffer */
    size_t      rsize;          /* Result buffer size */
} door_arg_t;
```

(The use of char * for the pointers instead of void * is a little unexpected, and has the undesirable side effect of necessitating casts in our code to avoid warnings from the compiler. Also, the type of desc_num in the Solaris 2.6 definition of this structure is a size_t rather than a uint_t. The last argument of door_return has a corresponding change.) All six members of this structure can change when door_call returns. Note that there are two types of arguments and results: data and descriptors.

The data arguments are an application-defined sequence of `data_size` bytes stored in the buffer pointed to by `data_ptr`. Because both the client and the server must agree on which bytes are used for what, it is useful to encapsulate this information in two structures (one for the arguments and another for the results). These structures could then be defined in a header file that the client and server include. If there are no data arguments, `data_ptr` must be NULL, and `data_size` must be set to 0.

When `door_call` returns, data_ptr points to the data results, and data_size specifies their size. If there are no data results, `data_size` will be 0. In this case, `data_ptr` should be ignored.

The descriptor arguments are an array of `door_desc_t` structures with `desc_num` elements. We describe this structure and descriptor passing in Section 22.4. If there are no descriptor arguments, `desc_ptr` must be a NULL pointer, and `desc_num` must be 0.

When `door_call` returns, desc_ptr points to an array of desc_num door_desc_t structures, each of which contains one descriptor that was passed to the client by the server function. If there are no descriptor results, `desc_num` will be 0. In this case, `desc_ptr` should be ignored.

The results of the door invocation are placed in the buffer pointed to by `rbuf`, the size of which is specified by `rsize`. Using the same buffer for the arguments and the results is allowed (i.e., `data_ptr` and `desc_ptr` can refer to addresses in `rbuf` when `door_call` is called).

Before calling `door_call`, the client must allocate the buffer where the results will be stored, setting `rbuf` to the buffer's address, and `rsize` to its size. When `door_call` returns, data_ptr and desc_ptr usually point inside this buffer.

If the client-supplied `rbuf` is too small to hold the results, the doors library will automatically allocate a new buffer of a sufficient size in the caller's address space (updating `rbuf` and `rsize` accordingly). It is the caller's responsibility to notice when `rbuf` changes, and to return this buffer to the system by calling `munmap` with `rbuf` and `rsize` as arguments when it is no longer required. (We described the `munmap` function in Section 13.25.)

The `door_return` Function

When the server procedure has completed its task, it calls `door_return`. This causes the associated `door_call` in the client to return.

```
cc -mt [ flag ... ] file ... -ldoor [ library ... ]
#include <door.h>

int door_return (char *data_ptr, size_t data_size, door_desc_t *desc_ptr,
    uint_t num_desc);
```
Returns: does not return if OK, –1 on error

The door_return function is used to return from a door invocation. The data results (if any) from the door invocation are passed back to the client in the buffer pointed to by *data_ptr*, which has a size of *data_size* bytes. Similarly, the descriptor results (if any) are returned to the client in the array pointed to by *desc_ptr*, which has *num_desc* elements.

The `door_revoke` Function

A server can revoke access to a door by calling door_revoke.

```
cc -mt [ flag ... ] file ... -ldoor [ library ... ]
#include <door.h>

int door_revoke (int d);
```
Returns: 0 if OK, −1 on error

The door_revoke function revokes access to the door identified by *d*. An implicit call to close is made, marking the door as invalid. Only the process that created the door can revoke it, and any door invocations in progress when door_revoke is called are allowed to complete normally.

Now that we've described the basic door functions, let's take a look at some examples.

Example: A simple door client and server

Our first example is a client that passes a long integer to the server, which squares it and returns the result.

Program 22.1 shows the code for the client.

Open the door

14–17 After checking that the number of command line arguments is correct, we open the door by passing the pathname we specified to open. The returned descriptor is called the *door descriptor*, but for convenience, we'll sometimes just call it the door.

Set up the door arguments and result pointer

18–24 We initialize the door_arg structure, which contains pointers to the arguments and results. The data_ptr member points to the argument buffer, which has a size of data_size bytes. Similarly, the rbuf member points to the result buffer, which has a size of rsize bytes. The desc_ptr and desc_num members are used when passing descriptors, which we cover in Section 22.4.

Call door procedure and print result

25–27 We call the server procedure by calling door_call; we pass the door descriptor and a pointer to the door argument structure as arguments. When door_call returns, we print the result.

—————————————————————————————— doors/door_cli1.c

```
 1 #include <stdio.h>
 2 #include <stdlib.h>
 3 #include <sys/types.h>
 4 #include <sys/stat.h>
 5 #include <fcntl.h>
 6 #include <door.h>
 7 #include "ssp.h"

 8 int main (int argc, char **argv)
 9 {
10     int fd;
11     long num;
12     long res;
13     door_arg_t door_args;

14     if (argc != 3)
15         err_quit ("Usage: door_cli1 path number");

16     if ((fd = open (argv [1], O_RDWR)) == -1)
17         err_msg ("Can't open door");

18     num = atol (argv [2]);

19     door_args.data_ptr = (char *) &num;
20     door_args.data_size = sizeof (long);
21     door_args.desc_ptr = NULL;
22     door_args.desc_num = 0;
23     door_args.rbuf = (char *) &res;
24     door_args.rsize = sizeof (long);

25     if (door_call (fd, &door_args) == -1)
26         err_msg ("door_call failed");

27     printf ("Result = %ld\n", res);

28     return (0);
29 }
```

—————————————————————————————— doors/door_cli1.c

Program 22.1 A simple door client.

Program 22.2 shows the code for the server, which consists of a server procedure called server_proc, and the main function.

Create door descriptor and attach it to a pathname

13–22 After checking the command line arguments, we create a door by calling door_create, passing it the address of our server procedure (we also pass a NULL pointer for the cookie and specify no attributes). Once we've obtained a door descriptor, we must associate it with a pathname in the file system, because this is how clients identify the door. This association is made by creating a regular file, and then calling the fattach function we described in Section 21.4. Note that we unlink the file first, ignoring any errors, in case it exists from a prior run of our server.

—————————————————————————————— *doors/door_srv1.c*

```
 1 #include <unistd.h>
 2 #include <sys/types.h>
 3 #include <sys/stat.h>
 4 #include <fcntl.h>
 5 #include <door.h>
 6 #include "ssp.h"

 7 static void server_proc (void *cookie, char *argp, size_t arg_size,
 8     door_desc_t *dp, uint_t n_desc);

 9 int main (int argc, char **argv)
10 {
11     int door_fd;
12     int tmp_fd;

13     if (argc != 2)
14         err_quit ("Usage: door_srv1 path");

15     if ((door_fd = door_create (server_proc, NULL, 0)) == -1)
16         err_msg ("door_create failed");

17     unlink (argv [1]);
18     if ((tmp_fd = creat (argv [1], FILE_PERMS)) == -1)
19         err_msg ("creat failed");
20     close (tmp_fd);
21     if (fattach (door_fd, argv [1]) == -1)
22         err_msg ("fattach failed");

23     for (;;)
24         pause ();
25 }

26 static void server_proc (void *cookie, char *argp, size_t arg_size,
27     door_desc_t *dp, uint_t n_desc)
28 {
29     long arg;
30     long res;

31     arg = *((long *) argp);
32     res = arg * arg;

33     if (door_return ((char *) &res, sizeof (long), NULL, 0) == -1)
34         err_msg ("door_return failed");
35 }
```

—————————————————————————————— *doors/door_srv1.c*

Program 22.2 A simple door server.

Main thread does nothing

23–24 Now that we've created the door, the main thread blocks in a call to pause. We do this because all of the work from now on is performed by the server procedure, server_proc, in another thread. These other threads are automatically created by the doors library every time a client request arrives.

Server procedure

26–35   Although the server procedure is called with five arguments, in this example we use only argp, which is a pointer to the argument structure the client passes to door_call. The long integer pointed to by argp is obtained and squared. The result is then passed back to the client, using door_return (this also has the effect of allowing the client's door_call to return). The first two arguments specify the location and size of the result buffer, and the last two arguments are used when returning descriptors.

Let's see what happens when we run the door client and server:

```
$ ./door_srv1 /tmp/ssp_door &          Start server in the background
[1]     1234
$ ./door_cli1 /tmp/ssp_door 42         Run the client
Result = 1764
$ ls -l /tmp/ssp_door
Drw-r--r--   1 rich      staff           0 Oct 17 16:45 /tmp/ssp_door
```

The results are what we expect, and the output from the ls command shows that ls uses the letter D in the first column to indicate that a path refers to a door.

Example: Handling a result buffer that is too small

Recall from our description of the door_call function that if the result buffer is too small to hold the result, the door library automatically allocates a new one of a sufficient size. We also stated that it is up to our applications to detect when this happens, and to free the new buffer by calling munmap when it is no longer required.

To illustrate this, Program 22.3 shows the code for our door client that has been modified to show the address and size of the result buffer when door_call returns. Program 22.3 is similar to Program 22.1; we've highlighted the lines that have changed.

Print result

27–29   In this version of the door client, we print the address of our variable, res, the value of data_ptr (which points to the result when door_call returns), and the address and size of the result buffer (i.e., rbuf and rsize respectively). Note that we also print the result by using the data_ptr pointer, rather than using our own variables as we did in Program 22.1.

Let's see what happens when we run our new client, assuming that that the server process is already running:

```
$ ./door_cli2 /tmp/ssp_door 42
Address of res = ffbff938, data_ptr = ffbff938, rbuf = ffbff938, rsize = 4
Result = 1764
```

The results are what we expect: data_buf and rbuf both point to our variable, res, and rsize is 4 bytes (which is the size of a long integer in a 32-bit process). This is because our result buffer was large enough to hold the result.

Let's see what happens when the result buffer isn't large enough. We can ensure this is the case by subtracting one from the size of the result buffer on line 24 of Program 22.3:

```
door_args.rsize = sizeof (long) - 1;
```

doors/door_cli2.c

```
 1 #include <stdio.h>
 2 #include <stdlib.h>
 3 #include <sys/types.h>
 4 #include <sys/stat.h>
 5 #include <fcntl.h>
 6 #include <door.h>
 7 #include "ssp.h"

 8 int main (int argc, char **argv)
 9 {
10     int fd;
11     long num;
12     long res;
13     door_arg_t door_args;

14     if (argc != 3)
15         err_quit ("Usage: door_cli2 path number");

16     if ((fd = open (argv [1], O_RDWR)) == -1)
17         err_msg ("Can't open door");

18     num = atol (argv [2]);

19     door_args.data_ptr = (char *) &num;
20     door_args.data_size = sizeof (long);
21     door_args.desc_ptr = NULL;
22     door_args.desc_num = 0;
23     door_args.rbuf = (char *) &res;
24     door_args.rsize = sizeof (long);

25     if (door_call (fd, &door_args) == -1)
26         err_msg ("door_call failed");

27     printf ("Address of res = %p, data_ptr = %p, rbuf = %p, rsize = %d\n",
28         &res, door_args.data_ptr, door_args.rbuf, door_args.rsize);
29     printf ("Result = %ld\n", *((long *) door_args.data_ptr));

30     return (0);
31 }
```

doors/door_cli2.c

Program 22.3 Door client modified to print address and size of result.

When we run this new version of our client, we can see that a new result buffer has been allocated, and that both `data_ptr` and `rbuf` point to this new buffer.

```
$ ./door_cli2 /tmp/ssp_door 42
Address of res = ffbff938, data_ptr = ff240000, rbuf = ff240000, rsize = 8192
Result = 1764
```

Note that the size of the new buffer is 8192 bytes, which is the page size of the system the author used for this example.

Although it isn't necessary to do so in our simple examples, real applications should be aware of when a new result buffer has been allocated, and free it using munmap when it is no longer required (to avoid memory leaks). The client could also just keep using the new buffer for subsequent door_call invocations.

Example: Unreferenced doors

When we described the `door_create` function, we mentioned that we can specify the `DOOR_UNREF` or `DOOR_UNREF_MULTI` attributes for the newly created door. When the reference count for a door with this attribute drops to one, a special invocation of the door's service function is made. When the server function is called because of this condition, the function's second argument (i.e., the pointer the data arguments, *argp*) is set to the constant `DOOR_UNREF_DATA`.

A door is referenced in three ways:

1. The first reference is the descriptor returned by `door_create`. As a matter of interest, the reason why an unreferenced procedure is triggered when the reference count drops to one, rather than when it drops to zero, is because the server process usually keeps this descriptor open until it terminates.

2. The pathname that the server attaches to the door (using `fattach`) is the second reference. If we call the `fdetach` function (either directly or by running the `fdetach` command) or remove the file by using the `rm` or `unlink` command, we can remove this reference to the door.

3. The third reference is the descriptor returned by `open` when the client opens the door. This reference remains until the client closes the file; this can happen implicitly by the client process terminating, or explicitly by the client calling the `close` function.

We'll write some programs to illustrate each of these. The first program (shown in Program 22.4) shows what happens if the server closes the door descriptor after calling `fattach`.

This server is similar to the one shown in Program 22.2, with a number of small changes.

Close door descriptor

24 Close the door descriptor after `fattach` returns. The server has no use for this descriptor after the `fattach` unless it wants to call `door_bind`, `door_info`, or `door_revoke`.

Recognize an unreferenced invocation

33–37 If the argument pointer is equal to the special value `DOOR_UNREF_DATA`, we are in an unreferenced invocation. The server procedure recognizes this and prints a suitable message. It then returns by calling `door_return` with two NULL pointers and two sizes of 0.

Print status messages

40–42 The server procedure prints status messages so that we can keep track of what happens when. The reason why we sleep for 5 seconds is to make it easier for us to run multiple clients simultaneously.

When we start the server, the first thing we notice is that an unreferenced invocation occurs immediately:

doors/unref_door_srv1.c

```
 1 #include <stdio.h>
 2 #include <unistd.h>
 3 #include <sys/types.h>
 4 #include <sys/stat.h>
 5 #include <fcntl.h>
 6 #include <door.h>
 7 #include "ssp.h"
 8 static void server_proc (void *cookie, char *argp, size_t arg_size,
 9     door_desc_t *dp, uint_t n_desc);
10 int main (int argc, char **argv)
11 {
12     int door_fd;
13     int tmp_fd;

14     if (argc != 2)
15         err_quit ("Usage: unref_door_srv1 path");
16     if ((door_fd = door_create (server_proc, NULL, DOOR_UNREF)) == -1)
17         err_msg ("door_create failed");
18     unlink (argv [1]);
19     if ((tmp_fd = creat (argv [1], FILE_PERMS)) == -1)
20         err_msg ("creat failed");
21     close (tmp_fd);
22     if (fattach (door_fd, argv [1]) == -1)
23         err_msg ("fattach failed");
24     close (door_fd);

25     for (;;)
26         pause ();
27 }
28 static void server_proc (void *cookie, char *argp, size_t arg_size,
29     door_desc_t *dp, uint_t n_desc)
30 {
31     long arg;
32     long res;
33     if (argp == DOOR_UNREF_DATA) {
34         printf ("Door unreferenced\n");
35         if (door_return (NULL, 0, NULL, 0) == -1)
36             err_msg ("door_return failed");
37     }
38     arg = *((long *) argp);
39     res = arg * arg;
40     printf ("Server proc called, arg = %ld\n", arg);
41     sleep (5);
42     printf ("Server proc returning, res = %ld\n", res);
43     if (door_return ((char *) &res, sizeof (long), NULL, 0) == -1)
44         err_msg ("door_return failed");
45 }
```

doors/unref_door_srv1.c

Program 22.4 Door server that handles an unreferenced invocation.

```
$ ./unref_door_srv1 /tmp/ssp_door
Door unreferenced
```

If we keep track of the door reference count, we can understand why this happens. When `door_create` returns, the reference count is one; after the `fattach`, it is two. When the server closes the door, the descriptor count drops to one, thus triggering the unreferenced invocation. The only remaining reference to the door is its pathname in the file system, which is all a client needs to refer to the door. We can demonstrate this by running the client in another window:

```
$ ./door_cli1 /tmp/ssp_door 42
Result = 1764
$ ./door_cli1 /tmp/ssp_door 1138
Result = 1295044
```

By examining the server output, we can see that no further unreferenced invocations occur:

```
Server proc called, arg = 42
Server proc returning, res = 1764
Server proc called, arg = 1138
Server proc returning, res = 1295044
```

Let's change our server back to the more common case where it doesn't close its door descriptor. We do this by removing line 24 from Program 22.4; the rest of the server is unchanged. (Because the change is so minor, we don't show the code for the new version of our server, which is called `unref_door_srv2`.) This time, the "Door unreferenced" message is not printed when we start the server. In another window, we confirm that the door exists, and then delete it:

```
$ ls -l /tmp/ssp_door
Drw-r--r--   1 rich      staff         0 Oct 22 15:39 /tmp/ssp_door
$ rm /tmp/ssp_door
```

As soon as we remove the file, an unreferenced invocation of the server procedure is made:

```
$ ./unref_door_srv2 /tmp/ssp_door
Door unreferenced                           Appears as soon as we delete /tmp/ssp_door
```

Following the reference count for this door, the reference count becomes one when `door_create` returns, and becomes two after the `fattach`. When we deleted the pathname, the reference count dropped back to one, triggering the unreferenced invocation.

In our last example of unreferenced invocations, we'll remove the door's pathname from the file system, but this time we'll start three invocations of our client first. The client and server are unchanged from the previous example. Here's what the client output looks like:

```
$ ./door_cli1 /tmp/ssp_door 42 & ./door_cli1 /tmp/ssp_door 69 & \
    ./door_cli1 /tmp/ssp_door 1138 &
[1]    26163
[2]    26164
[3]    26165
$ rm /tmp/ssp_door                          While the three clients are executing
```

```
$ Result = 1764
Result = 4761
Result = 1295044
```

And here is the output from the server:

```
$ ./unref_door_srv2 /tmp/ssp_door
Server proc called, arg = 42
Server proc called, arg = 69
Server proc called, arg = 1138
Server proc returning, res = 1764
Server proc returning, res = 4761
Server proc returning, res = 1295044
Door unreferenced
```

If we keep track of the door reference count one last time, the reference count is two after door_create and fattach return in the server. As each client opens the door, we might be tempted to think that the reference increments from two to three, three to four, and finally four to five. What actually happens is that the door's reference count remains at two, and the kernel keeps track of each door invocation. So, when we run the client three times, the door's reference count stays at two, but the number of active invocations goes from zero to one, one to two, and from two to three. When we delete the door's pathname in the file system, the door's reference count drops from two to one, but the unreferenced invocation is delayed until the number of active door invocations is zero. As each client terminates, the active invocation count is decremented from three to two, two to one, and finally one to zero. It is the final decrement when the last client terminates that allows the delayed unreferenced invocation to occur.

> Technically speaking, for an unreferenced invocation to be made, the reference count for the door's vnode (v_count) must be one when the reference count for the descriptor (f_count) being closed goes from two to one. This means that there is no way a client can directly cause an unreferenced invocation, because the door's vnode reference count will be at least two while the client is referencing the door (the first reference being the server's door descriptor, and the second and subsequent references being from the file descriptors returned by open in the clients). This becomes clearer when we start considering multiple unreferenced door invocations.

Example: Multiple unreferenced doors

In the previous example, we looked at three ways we could provoke an unreferenced door invocation by setting the DOOR_UNREF attribute when we create the door. But what if we want an unreferenced invocation to be made every time the reference count for the door's descriptor drops from two to one? To do this, we must set the DOOR_UNREF_MULTI attribute when we create the door.

Program 22.5 shows the main function of our server that handles multiple unreferenced invocations.

Define global variables

8–9 We define two global variables: door_fd is the door descriptor, and door_path is the pathname of the door in the file system.

—————————————————————————————— doors/unref_door_srv3.c

```
 1 #include <stdio.h>
 2 #include <unistd.h>
 3 #include <sys/types.h>
 4 #include <sys/stat.h>
 5 #include <fcntl.h>
 6 #include <door.h>
 7 #include "ssp.h"

 8 static int door_fd;
 9 static char *door_path;

10 static void server_proc (void *cookie, char *argp, size_t arg_size,
11     door_desc_t *dp, uint_t n_desc);

12 int main (int argc, char **argv)
13 {
14     int tmp_fd;

15     if (argc != 2)
16         err_quit ("Usage: unref_door_srv3 path");

17     if ((door_fd = door_create (server_proc, NULL, DOOR_UNREF_MULTI)) == -1)
18         err_msg ("door_create failed");

19     door_path = argv [1];
20     unlink (door_path);
21     if ((tmp_fd = creat (door_path, FILE_PERMS)) == -1)
22         err_msg ("creat failed");
23     close (tmp_fd);
24     if (fattach (door_fd, door_path) == -1)
25         err_msg ("fattach failed");

26     for (;;)
27         pause ();
28 }
```

—————————————————————————————— doors/unref_door_srv3.c

Program 22.5 The main function of our multiple unreferenced invocations server.

Create the door

17–18 We create the door by calling door_create. Note that we specify the DOOR_UNREF_MULTI attribute so that we get multiple unreferenced invocations under the right circumstances.

The rest of the main function is essentially the same as Program 22.2.

Program 22.6 shows the server procedure.

Recognize an unreferenced invocation

34–40 If the argument pointer is equal to DOOR_UNREF_DATA, we are in an unreferenced invocation. The server procedure recognizes this and prints a suitable message. We then call fattach, to reattach the door descriptor to a pathname in the file system. We need to do this because in this example we call fdetach to cause the unreferenced invocation. The server procedure then returns by calling door_return with two NULL pointers and two sizes of 0.

——————————————————————————— doors/unref_door_srv3.c
```
29 static void server_proc (void *cookie, char *argp, size_t arg_size,
30     door_desc_t *dp, uint_t n_desc)
31 {
32     long arg;
33     long res;

34     if (argp == DOOR_UNREF_DATA) {
35         printf ("Door unreferenced\n");
36         if (fattach (door_fd, door_path) == -1)
37             err_msg ("fattach failed");
38         if (door_return (NULL, 0, NULL, 0) == -1)
39             err_msg ("door_return failed");
40     }

41     if (fdetach (door_path) == -1)
42         err_msg("fdetach failed");

43     arg = *((long *) argp);
44     res = arg * arg;

45     printf ("Server proc returning, res = %ld\n", res);

46     if (door_return ((char *) &res, sizeof (long), NULL, 0) == -1)
47         err_msg ("door_return failed");
48 }
```
——————————————————————————— doors/unref_door_srv3.c

Program 22.6 The server procedure of our multiple unreferenced invocations server.

Cause an unreferenced invocation to occur

41–42 We call `fdetach` to detach the door descriptor from the pathname in the file system. This causes the door's descriptor's reference count to decrement from two to one, triggering an unreferenced invocation. However, because we are currently in the middle of a client invocation, the door's internal activity count is not zero, so the unreferenced invocation is delayed.

Print status message and return result

43–48 We calculate the square of the argument we were passed, and print a status message before calling `door_return` to pass the result back to the client.

Let's start the server and run the client a few times in another window:

```
$ ./door_cli1 /tmp/ssp_door 42
Result = 1764
$ ./door_cli1 /tmp/ssp_door 69
Result = 4761
$ ./door_cli1 /tmp/ssp_door 1138
Result = 1295044
```

The corresponding server output shows that the server procedure receives multiple unreferenced invocations:

```
$ ./unref_door_srv3 /tmp/ssp_door
Server proc returning, res = 1764
Door unreferenced
Server proc returning, res = 4761
```

```
Door unreferenced
Server proc returning, res = 1295044
Door unreferenced
```

Note that the status message is printed immediately prior to the unreferenced door invocations.

If we change line 17 of our server to read

```
if ((door_fd = door_create (server_proc, NULL, DOOR_UNREF)) == -1)
```

we should only get one unreferenced invocation. We can demonstrate this by restarting the server, and running the client a few times:

```
$ ./door_cli1 /tmp/ssp_door 42
Result = 1764
$ ./door_cli1 /tmp/ssp_door 69
Result = 4761
$ ./door_cli1 /tmp/ssp_door 1138
door_call failed: Bad file number
```

Here is the corresponding server output:

```
$ ./unref_door_srv3 /tmp/ssp_door
Server proc returning, res = 1764
Door unreferenced
Server proc returning, res = 4761
```

As before, the first time we run the client, an unreferenced invocation happens after the server procedure calls `door_return`. One of the things we do when we get an unreferenced invocation is call `fattach` to reattach the door to the file system so the second client invocation works (although this time there isn't another unreferenced invocation after the `door_return`). However, because the door remains unattached, the third invocation of the client fails.

22.3 Door Information Functions

One of the nice features about doors is that the client and server can find out some information about each other. The server can determine the credentials of its clients, and a client can obtain some information about the server it is connected to.

The `door_cred` Function

A server function can obtain the credentials of the client that invoked it by calling `door_cred`.

```
cc -mt [ flag ... ] file ... -ldoor [ library ... ]
#include <door.h>

int door_cred (door_cred_t *info);
```
                                                        Returns: 0 if OK, −1 on error

The door_cred function returns the credentials of the client that invoked the current server function. The credentials are stored in the door_cred structure pointed to by *info*, which has the following members:

```
typedef struct door_cred {
      uid_t   dc_euid;    /* Effective user ID of client */
      gid_t   dc_egid;    /* Effective group ID of client */
      uid_t   dc_ruid;    /* Real user ID of client */
      gid_t   dc_rgid;    /* Real group ID of client */
      pid_t   dc_pid;     /* Process ID of client */
} door_cred_t;
```

We described the difference between real and effective IDs in Section 7.3.

Note that there is no door descriptor argument to this function. The implication of this is that only information about the client of the current invocation can be obtained, so door_cred must be called by the server function or one of the functions the server function calls.

Example: Printing the client's credentials

Program 22.7 shows a new version of our server procedure. We've modified it to print the current client's credentials. The client is the same as Program 22.1, and the server's main function is the same as the one in Program 22.2.

doors/door_srv2.c

```
27 static void server_proc (void *cookie, char *argp, size_t arg_size,
28      door_desc_t *dp, uint_t n_desc)
29 {
30      long arg;
31      long res;
32      door_cred_t info;

33      if (door_cred (&info) == -1)
34          err_msg ("door_cred failed");
35      printf ("Client credentials:\n");
36      printf ("   Effective user ID = %ld\n", info.dc_euid);
37      printf ("   Effective group ID = %ld\n", info.dc_egid);
38      printf ("   Real user ID = %ld\n", info.dc_ruid);
39      printf ("   Real group ID = %ld\n", info.dc_rgid);
40      printf ("   Process ID = %ld\n", info.dc_pid);

41      arg = *((long *) argp);
42      res = arg * arg;

43      if (door_return ((char *) &res, sizeof (long), NULL, 0) == -1)
44          err_msg ("door_return failed");
45 }
```

doors/door_srv2.c

Program 22.7 Server procedure that prints the client's credentials.

Let's start the new version of our server, and then run the client a couple of times:

```
$ ./door_srv2 /tmp/ssp_door &
[1]      11191
$ ./door_cli1 /tmp/ssp_door 42
Client credentials:
  Effective user ID = 1001
  Effective group ID = 10
  Real user ID = 1001
  Real group ID = 10
  Process ID = 11192
Result = 1764
$ su
Password:
# chown root door_cli1
# chmod u+s door_cli1
# ls -l door_cli1
-rwsr-xr-x   1 root       staff      11392 Oct 17 15:31 door_cli1
# exit
$ ./door_cli1 /tmp/ssp_door 42
Client credentials:
  Effective user ID = 0
  Effective group ID = 10
  Real user ID = 1001
  Real group ID = 10
  Process ID = 11197
Result = 1764
```

The first time we run the client, the real and effective user IDs are the same, as we expect. But when we change the client executable's owner to the superuser (i.e., root), set the set-user-ID bit, and run the client again, the real and effective user IDs are different. Again, this is what we expect.

The door_info Function

The client can determine information about the server procedure to which it is connected by calling the door_info function.

```
cc -mt [ flag ... ] file ... -ldoor [ library ... ]
#include <door.h>

int door_info (int d, door_info_t *info);
```
                                                        Returns: 0 if OK, −1 on error

The door_info function returns information associated with the door descriptor specified by d. The information obtained is stored in the door_info structure pointed to by info. This structure has the following members:

```
typedef struct door_info {
    pid_t        di_target;      /* Server process ID */
    door_ptr_t   di_proc;        /* Server procedure */
    door_ptr_t   di_data;        /* Data cookie for server procedure */
    door_attr_t  di_attributes;  /* Attributes associated with door */
    door_id_t    di_uniquifier;  /* Unique number */
} door_info_t;
```

The `di_target` member contains the process ID of the server, or −1 if the server has terminated. The `di_proc` member holds the address of the server procedure, although this is unlikely to be useful to a client, unless the door refers to a service procedure in the calling process. The data cookie that was passed as the first argument to the door procedure is pointed to by `di_data`.

As we mentioned when we described the `door_create` function, each door can have a number of associated attributes. The `di_attributes` member contains the current attributes of the door, which are formed by a bitwise-OR of zero or more of the following constants:

`DOOR_LOCAL`	This attribute specifies that the door descriptor refers to a server procedure that is local to the calling process.
`DOOR_UNREF`	This attribute specifies that the door has requested notification when all but the last reference have been closed.
`DOOR_UNREF_MULTI`	This attribute, introduced in Solaris 7, is similar to `DOOR_UNREF`, except multiple unreferenced notifications may be delivered to the door.
`DOOR_IS_UNREF`	This attribute, introduced in Solaris 7, specifies that only one descriptor currently refers to the door.
`DOOR_REVOKED`	This attribute specifies that the door descriptor refers to a revoked door (i.e., the server has revoked the function associated with the door by calling the `door_revoke` function).
`DOOR_PRIVATE`	This attribute specifies that the door has a private pool of server threads associated with it.

Each door has a systemwide unique number associated with it, which is assigned when the door is created. This number is returned in `di_uniquifier`.

The `door_info` function is usually called by a client to obtain information about the server. However, it is also possible for a server procedure to call this function by setting *d* to `DOOR_QUERY`, which returns information about the calling thread. In this case, `di_proc` and `di_data` contain usable information that might be of interest.

Example: Printing door information

We saw in the previous example how a server procedure can obtain the credentials of its client. In this example we'll write a program that prints information about a door and its server. Program 22.8 shows the code for this program, which we call `doorinfo`.

Open path and check it is a door

12–19 After checking the command line arguments, we open the specified pathname and verify that it refers to a door. We do this by checking the `st_mode` member of the `stat` structure, using the `S_ISDOOR` macro.

—— *doors/doorinfo.c*

```
 1 #include <stdio.h>
 2 #include <sys/types.h>
 3 #include <sys/stat.h>
 4 #include <fcntl.h>
 5 #include <door.h>
 6 #include "ssp.h"

 7 int main (int argc, char **argv)
 8 {
 9     int fd;
10     struct stat stat_buf;
11     door_info_t info;

12     if (argc != 2)
13         err_quit ("Usage: doorinfo path");

14     if ((fd = open (argv [1], O_RDONLY)) == -1)
15         err_msg ("Can't open door");

16     if (fstat (fd, &stat_buf) == -1)
17         err_msg ("stat failed");
18     if (S_ISDOOR (stat_buf.st_mode) == 0)
19         err_quit ("%s: Not a door", argv [1]);

20     if (door_info (fd, &info) == -1)
21         err_msg ("door_info failed");

22     printf ("Door info:\n");
23     printf ("  Server process ID = %ld\n", (long) info.di_target);
24     printf ("  Uniquifier = %lld\n", info.di_uniquifier);
25     printf ("  Attributes =");
26     if (info.di_attributes == 0)
27         printf (" 0");
28     else {
29         if (info.di_attributes & DOOR_LOCAL)
30             printf (" DOOR_LOCAL");
31         if (info.di_attributes & DOOR_UNREF)
32             printf (" DOOR_UNREF");
33 #ifdef DOOR_UNREF_MULTI
34         if (info.di_attributes & DOOR_UNREF_MULTI)
35             printf (" DOOR_UNREF_MULTI");
36         if (info.di_attributes & DOOR_IS_UNREF)
37             printf (" DOOR_IS_UNREF");
38 #endif
39         if (info.di_attributes & DOOR_REVOKED)
40             printf (" DOOR_REVOKED");
41         if (info.di_attributes & DOOR_PRIVATE)
42             printf (" DOOR_PRIVATE");
43     }
44     printf ("\n");

45     return (0);
46 }
```

—— *doors/doorinfo.c*

Program 22.8 Print information about a door.

Get and print door information

20–44 We call `door_info` to retrieve the information about the specified door, and then print it.

Let's see what happens when we run Program 22.8 a couple of times:

```
$ ./doorinfo /var/run/sshd.pid
/var/run/sshd.pid: Not a door
$ ./doorinfo /var/run/name_service_door
Door info:
  Server process ID = 187
  Uniquifier = 6
  Attributes = DOOR_UNREF
$ ./doorinfo /var/run/syslog_door
Door info:
  Server process ID = 169
  Uniquifier = 5
  Attributes = 0
$ ps -f -p 187 -p 169
    UID    PID  PPID  C   STIME TTY      TIME CMD
   root    169     1  0   Oct 17 ?       0:00 /usr/sbin/syslogd
   root    187     1  0   Oct 17 ?       0:02 /usr/sbin/nscd
```

The first time we run Program 22.8, we specify a path that is not a door. We then run the program against two files that are doors associated with system daemons on Solaris 9 (Solaris 8 will also have these files; their paths on previous releases will be `/etc/.name_service_door` and `/etc/syslog_door` respectively). Finally, we use the `ps` command to identify the processes associated with the process IDs printed by `doorinfo`.

22.4 Advanced Door Facilities

The doors library has two facilities that we call advanced. The first is the ability to pass open descriptors from the client to the server, or vice versa. The second advanced facility is the ability of the server to manage its own thread pool (the doors library usually manages them for us).

Passing Descriptors

The doors library provides us with another method of passing an open descriptor from one process to another (recall Section 21.2, where we described the concept of passing an open descriptor). A client passes descriptors across a door to the server by calling `door_call`, setting the `desc_ptr` member of the `door_arg` structure to point to an array of `door_desc` structures, and setting the `desc_num` member to the number of descriptors. A server passes descriptors to the client using the `door_return` function; the third argument points to an array of `door_desc` structures, and the fourth argument specifies the number of elements in the array.

The `door_desc` structure has the following members:

```
typedef struct door_desc {
    door_attr_t d_attributes;              /* Tag for union */
    union {
        struct {                           /* Valid if tag = DOOR_DESCRIPTOR */
            int        d_descriptor;       /* Descriptor number */
            door_id_t  d_id;               /* Unique ID */
        } d_desc;
    } d_data;
} door_desc_t;
```

This structure contains the d_data union; which member of the union is used is determined by the d_attributes member of the door_desc structure. Up to (and including) Solaris 9, only one member of this union is defined (the d_desc structure that describes a descriptor), and the d_attributes tag must be set to DOOR_DESCRIPTOR. (A member called d_handle is also visible inside the kernel. However, kernel programming is beyond the scope of this text, so we'll say no more about this member.)

Example: An open server using doors

Armed with this information, we can write another version of our open server, which passes a file descriptor using a door. As before, the client passes a pathname to the server, which opens the file and returns the resulting file descriptor to the client.

Program 22.9 shows the code for the client.

Check arguments and open the door

18–21 If the correct number of command line arguments has been supplied, open the door using the first argument as the door's pathname (the zeroth argument being the name of the client program itself).

Set up the door arguments and result pointer

22–27 We initialize the door argument structure. The data_ptr member points to the pathname specified in the second command line argument, and the data_size member is set to the length of the pathname string plus one. We add one to the pathname so that the server can add a terminating NUL. The desc_ptr and desc_num arguments are set to NULL and 0 respectively, because we are not passing any descriptors to the server. Finally, rbuf and rsize specify the address and size of the result buffer.

Call door procedure and check result

28–37 We call the door procedure and check that the results are as we expect (i.e., no data and only one descriptor). If data is present, we assume it's an error message that was sent to us by the server, and print it. Note that we also check the attributes of the returned descriptor to ensure that the DOOR_DESCRIPTOR flag is set.

Get the descriptor and copy the file to standard output

38–43 We fetch the file descriptor passed to us by the server, and copy the file to which it refers to standard output.

Program 22.10 shows the server procedure. The server's main function is essentially unchanged from Program 22.2.

————————————————————————— doors/desc_door_cli.c

```
 1 #include <stdio.h>
 2 #include <unistd.h>
 3 #include <stdlib.h>
 4 #include <string.h>
 5 #include <sys/types.h>
 6 #include <sys/stat.h>
 7 #include <fcntl.h>
 8 #include <door.h>
 9 #include "ssp.h"

10 static char buf [BUF_SIZE];
11 static char res_buf [BUF_SIZE];

12 int main (int argc, char **argv)
13 {
14     int fd;
15     int door_fd;
16     ssize_t n;
17     door_arg_t door_args;

18     if (argc != 3)
19         err_quit ("Usage: desc_door_cli1 door_path file_path");

20     if ((door_fd = open (argv [1], O_RDWR)) == -1)
21         err_msg ("Can't open door");

22     door_args.data_ptr = argv [2];
23     door_args.data_size = strlen (argv [2]) + 1;
24     door_args.desc_ptr = NULL;
25     door_args.desc_num = 0;
26     door_args.rbuf = res_buf;
27     door_args.rsize = BUF_SIZE;

28     if (door_call (door_fd, &door_args) == -1)
29         err_msg ("door_call failed");

30     if (door_args.data_size != 0)
31         err_quit ("%.*s", door_args.data_size, door_args.data_ptr);
32     else if (door_args.desc_ptr == NULL)
33         err_quit ("desc_ptr is NULL");
34     else if (door_args.desc_num != 1)
35         err_quit ("desc_num = %d", door_args.desc_num);
36     else if (!(door_args.desc_ptr -> d_attributes & DOOR_DESCRIPTOR))
37         err_quit ("d_attributes = %X", door_args.desc_ptr -> d_attributes);

38     fd = door_args.desc_ptr -> d_data.d_desc.d_descriptor;
39     while ((n = read (fd, buf, BUF_SIZE)) > 0)
40         if (writen (STDOUT_FILENO, buf, n) == -1)
41             err_msg ("writen failed");

42     if (n == -1)
43         err_msg ("read failed");

44     return (0);
45 }
```

————————————————————————— doors/desc_door_cli.c

Program 22.9 Door client for descriptor passing example.

———————————————————————————— doors/desc_door_srv.c
```
29 static void server_proc (void *cookie, char *argp, size_t arg_size,
30     door_desc_t *dp, uint_t n_desc)
31 {
32     int fd;
33     char buf [BUF_SIZE];
34     door_desc_t desc;

35     argp [arg_size - 1] = '\0';
36     if ((fd = open (argp, O_RDONLY)) == -1) {
37         snprintf (buf, BUF_SIZE, "%s: %s", argp, strerror (errno));
38         if (door_return (buf, strlen (buf), NULL, 0) == -1)
39             err_msg ("door_return failed");
40     }

41     printf ("Returning descriptor %d\n", fd);

42     desc.d_attributes = DOOR_DESCRIPTOR;
43     desc.d_data.d_desc.d_descriptor = fd;

44     if (door_return (NULL, 0, &desc, 1) == -1)
45         err_msg ("door_return failed");
46 }
```
———————————————————————————— doors/desc_door_srv.c

Program 22.10 Door server procedure for descriptor passing example.

Open the file specified by the client

35–40 After adding a terminating NUL character to the pathname we received from the client, we try to open the file. If the open was unsuccessful, we send the resulting error message back to the client as a data result.

Send file descriptor to the client

41–46 If the open succeeds, we print the resulting file descriptor's number and return it to the client. In this event, there are no data results.

Let's start the server and run the client a few times:

```
$ ./desc_door_cli /tmp/ssp_door /etc/shadow
/etc/shadow: Permission denied
$ ./desc_door_cli /tmp/ssp_door /etc/auto_master
# Master map for automounter
#
+auto_master
/net            -hosts          -nosuid,nobrowse
/home           auto_home       -nobrowse
/xfn            -xfn
$ ./desc_door_cli /tmp/ssp_door /etc/auto_home
# Home directory map for automounter
#
+auto_home

rich            zen:/export/home/&
jenny           zen:/export/home/&
$ ./desc_door_cli /tmp/ssp_door /etc/passwd
root:x:0:1:Super-User:/root:/sbin/sh
```

```
daemon:x:1:1::/:
bin:x:2:2::/usr/bin:
sys:x:3:3::/:
adm:x:4:4:Admin:/var/adm:
...
```

The first time we run the client, we specify a file that we don't have permission to open, which causes an error return. The next three times work as we expect (we've trimmed the output from /etc/passwd).

Let's take a look at the server's output:

```
$ ./desc_door_srv /tmp/ssp_door
Returning descriptor 4
Returning descriptor 5
Returning descriptor 6
```

As evidenced by the server output, there is a problem when passing descriptors using a door: the server leaks file descriptors. This is because the server can't close the descriptor until after door_return returns (i.e., it has passed the descriptor to the client), but unfortunately door_return doesn't return.

Starting from Solaris 7, we can avoid this problem by specifying the DOOR_RELEASE attribute, which tells the system to close the file once it has been passed to the client. We can verify this by changing line 42 of Program 22.10 as follows:

```
desc.d_attributes = DOOR_DESCRIPTOR | DOOR_RELEASE;
```

If we run the new version of our server, we can see that it no longer leaks file descriptors:

```
$ ./desc_door_srv /tmp/ssp_door
Returning descriptor 4
Returning descriptor 4
Returning descriptor 4
```

If porting our code to Solaris 2.6 is not a concern, we should always specify the DOOR_RELEASE attribute when passing a descriptor using doors.

The door_server_create Function

As we mentioned in Section 22.1, the doors library usually manages the threads required to service client requests as they arrive. The threads created by the library are detached threads with the default thread stack size, thread cancellation disabled, and with a scheduling class and signal mask inherited from the thread that called door_create.

> There are two types of thread: *joinable* (the default) and *detached*. When a joinable thread terminates, its thread ID and exit status are retained until another thread in the process calls pthread_join (in much the same way that when a process terminates, its process ID and exit status are retained until another process reaps its status by calling wait). On the other hand, when a detached thread terminates, all of its resources are released, and we can't wait for it to terminate.

If we want to change any of these characteristics, or if we want to manage the server thread pool ourselves, we must call door_server_create and specify our own server creation function.

```
cc -mt [ flag ... ] file ... -ldoor [ library ... ]
#include <door.h>

typedef void door_server_func_t (door_info_t *);

door_server_func_t *door_server_create (door_server_func_t *create_func);
```
                                        Returns: a pointer to the previous server creation function

Notice that we've used C's `typedef` facility to simplify the function prototype. Our new data type defines a function that takes a single argument (which is a pointer to a `door_info_t`), and has no return value (`void`). The `door_server_create` function registers the function specified by *create_func* and returns a pointer to the previous server creation function.

The function *create_func* is called whenever the server thread pool becomes depleted (i.e., whenever a new thread is required to serve a client request). If the associated door has a private thread pool (i.e., the `DOOR_PRIVATE` attribute was passed to `door_create`), information about which pool is depleted is passed to *create_func* in the form of a pointer to a `door_info` structure. The `di_proc` member contains the address of the server procedure associated with the door, and `di_data` contains the cookie pointer that is passed to the server procedure every time it is called.

The *create_func* creates additional server threads as desired by the design of the program. In other words, as long as there is at least one server thread currently active in the process, *create_func* doesn't necessarily need to create a new thread to handle new requests (if a thread isn't created, the associated `door_call` might block until a server thread becomes available). The converse is also true: subject to the availability of system resources, *create_func* can create as many threads as it wants to handle client requests (for example, creating a new thread for each client request, which is what the door library does by default).

The `door_bind` and `door_unbind` Functions

When we manage our own pool of door server threads, we need a way to associate or disassociate threads with the thread pool. We do this by calling `door_bind` or `door_unbind` respectively.

```
cc -mt [ flag ... ] file ... -ldoor [ library ... ]
#include <door.h>

int door_bind (int d);

int door_unbind (void);
```
                                        Both return: 0 if OK, −1 on error

The `door_bind` function associates (i.e., binds) the calling thread to the private pool of server threads associated with the door identified by *d*. If the calling thread is already bound to a different door, an implicit `door_unbind` is performed.

Conversely, the `door_unbind` function explicitly breaks the association between the calling thread and the door to which it has been bound.

Example: A server that manages its own threads

Let's take a look at a server that manages its own private pool of threads by using the `door_server_create` and `door_bind` functions we have just described. Although our client is unchanged from Program 22.1, we need to add two functions to our server. The first of these, `ssp_create`, is called whenever a new thread needs to be created, and the second function, `ssp_thread`, is the function that first executes in the new thread. When this function calls `door_return`, the calling thread logically appears to continue executing the door server procedure as each client `door_call` is serviced (in our server, `server_proc` is the name of our server procedure).

Program 22.11 shows the new version of `main`.

Let's take a look at some of the details of this version of `main`; it is more complicated than our previous examples.

Define global variables

10–12 This version of our door server program defines three global variables. We've made the door descriptor, `door_fd`, global because we need to refer to it when we call `door_bind` in our thread start function, `ssp_thread`. The mutex `door_lock`, and the condition variable , `door_cv`, are used to coordinate access to the door descriptor.

Register server creation function

22 We register the function that will be called every time a new thread is required.

Create door descriptor

23–30 We first lock the door descriptor mutex. We do this so that we can manipulate it, knowing that some other thread will be unable to. We then call `door_create`, with the attributes argument set to `DOOR_PRIVATE` instead of 0.

Using a private pool of server threads and specifying our own server creation function using `door_server_create` are not mutually exclusive options. Indeed, four combinations are possible:

1. We don't specify a server creation function, and we don't use a private thread pool. The doors library creates threads as they are needed, and they are all added to the processwide thread pool. This is the default scenario.

2. We don't specify a server creation function, but we do use a private thread pool by specifying `DOOR_PRIVATE` when we create the door. The doors library creates threads as they are required and places them into the door's private pool. The threads for doors that were not created with the `DOOR_PRIVATE` attribute still go into the processwide pool of threads.

3. We specify our own server creation function, but we don't use a private thread pool. Our server creation function is called whenever a new thread is required, and the new threads are added to the processwide pool of threads.

doors/door_srv3.c

```
 1 #include <stdio.h>
 2 #include <unistd.h>
 3 #include <sys/types.h>
 4 #include <sys/stat.h>
 5 #include <fcntl.h>
 6 #include <door.h>
 7 #include <pthread.h>
 8 #include <limits.h>
 9 #include "ssp.h"

10 static int door_fd = -1;
11 static pthread_mutex_t door_lock;
12 static pthread_cond_t door_cv;

13 static void ssp_create (door_info_t *info);
14 static void *ssp_thread (void *arg);
15 static void server_proc (void *cookie, char *argp, size_t arg_size,
16     door_desc_t *dp, uint_t n_desc);

17 int main (int argc, char **argv)
18 {
19     int tmp_fd;

20     if (argc != 2)
21         err_quit ("Usage: door_srv3 path");

22     door_server_create (ssp_create);

23     if (pthread_mutex_lock (&door_lock) != 0)
24         err_msg ("Can't lock door");
25     if ((door_fd = door_create (server_proc, NULL, DOOR_PRIVATE)) == -1)
26         err_msg ("door_create failed");
27     if (pthread_cond_signal (&door_cv) == -1)
28         err_msg ("pthread_cond_signal failed");
29     if (pthread_mutex_unlock (&door_lock) != 0)
30         err_msg ("Can't unlock door");

31     unlink (argv [1]);
32     if ((tmp_fd = creat (argv [1], FILE_PERMS)) == -1)
33         err_msg ("creat failed");
34     close (tmp_fd);
35     if (fattach (door_fd, argv [1]) == -1)
36         err_msg ("fattach failed");

37     for (;;)
38         pause ();
39 }
```

doors/door_srv3.c

Program 22.11 The main function of our server that manages its own threads.

4. We specify our own server creation function, and we use a private thread pool. Our server creation function is called whenever a new thread is required. When a thread is created, it should call door_bind to associate itself with the

appropriate private thread pool; otherwise, it will be assigned to the processwide thread pool. This is the scenario we use in this example.

Once we've created the door, we signal the door descriptor condition variable to indicate that the descriptor is now valid. As we shall see later, our thread start function waits for the descriptor to be valid before it calls `door_bind`. Because we've finished manipulating it, we unlock the door descriptor mutex.

Attach door descriptor to a pathname, and do nothing

31–39 As with our previous door servers, we attach the door descriptor to a pathname in the file system, and then suspend the main thread by calling `pause` in an infinite loop.

Program 22.12 shows the code for server creation function, `ssp_create`, which is called whenever a new thread is required to handle a client request.

─── *doors/door_srv3.c*
```
40 static void ssp_create (door_info_t *info)
41 {
42     pthread_t thread_id;
43     pthread_attr_t attr;

44     if (pthread_attr_init (&attr) != 0)
45         err_msg ("pthread_attr_init failed");
46     if (pthread_attr_setscope (&attr, PTHREAD_SCOPE_SYSTEM) != 0)
47         err_msg ("pthread_attr_setscope failed");
48     if (pthread_attr_setdetachstate (&attr, PTHREAD_CREATE_DETACHED) != 0)
49         err_msg ("pthread_attr_setdetachstate failed");
50     if (PTHREAD_STACK_MIN > 8192) {
51         if (pthread_attr_setstacksize (&attr, PTHREAD_STACK_MIN) != 0)
52             err_msg ("pthread_attr_setstacksize failed");
53     }
54     else {
55         if (pthread_attr_setstacksize (&attr, 8192) != 0)
56             err_msg ("pthread_attr_setstacksize failed");
57     }

58     if (pthread_create (&thread_id, &attr, ssp_thread,
59         (void *) info -> di_proc) != 0) {
60         err_msg ("pthread_create failed");
61     }

62     if (pthread_attr_destroy (&attr) != 0)
63         err_msg ("pthread_attr_destroy failed");

64     printf ("ssp_create: Created server thread %d\n", thread_id);
65 }
```
─── *doors/door_srv3.c*

Program 22.12 The server creation function of our server that manages its own threads.

Initialize thread attributes

44–57 We initialize the attributes of the new thread we are about to create. We set the contention scope to `PTHREAD_SCOPE_SYSTEM` and specify that the thread is to run as a detached thread.

A contention scope of PTHREAD_SCOPE_SYSTEM means that the thread will compete against threads in all processes for processor resources. The alternative contention scope, PTHREAD_SCOPE_PROCESS, means that the thread will compete against other threads in the same process only for processor resources. We can't use the latter with doors, because the doors library requires that the kernel LWP performing the door_return must be the same one that originated it. It is possible that an unbound thread (i.e., one whose contention scope is PTHREAD_SCOPE_PROCESS) could change LWPs during execution of the server function.

The reason why we create detached threads is to prevent the system from saving any information about the thread when it terminates. And this is important because we won't be calling pthread_join to reap the thread's status.

We also set the stack size to be the greater of 8192 bytes and PTHREAD_STACK_MIN, which defines the minimum thread stack size.

Create the new thread

58–61 Having created the attributes for the new thread, we call pthread_create to create it. Once the new thread has been created, its thread start function, ssp_thread is called, being passed one argument. This argument is a pointer to the di_proc member of the door_info structure associated with the door that caused the thread to be created. We can use this to differentiate between server procedures for different doors (in the event that our server has multiple doors).

Destroy the thread attributes

62–65 We've finished with the thread attributes, so we destroy them before printing the thread ID of the newly created thread.

Program 22.13 shows the code for the thread start function, ssp_thread. This function is called whenever we create a new thread in ssp_create.

As we stated previously, ssp_thread is the thread start function specified by the call to pthread_create in ssp_create. The argument to this function is a pointer to the door_info structure that was passed by ssp_create. We use this information to verify that the argument references the only server procedure in our server.

Disable thread cancellation

68–69 When a new thread is created by pthread_create, thread cancellation is enabled by default. This means that when a client aborts a door_call that is in progress for some reason, the thread cancellation handlers are called (if there are any), and the thread is terminated. On the other hand, if thread cancellation is disabled and a client aborts a door_call that is in progress, the server procedure is allowed to complete (i.e., the thread is not terminated), and the results from door_return are just thrown away. In this scenario, however, any interruptible system calls in progress in the server will be interrupted.

Because the server thread is terminated when thread cancellation is enabled, and because the server procedure might be in the middle of an operation for the client that ought not to be abruptly terminated (e.g., it might be holding some semaphores or locks), the doors library disables thread cancellation for any thread it creates. If we want our server procedure thread to be cancelled when a client aborts, we must explicitly enable thread cancellation and be prepared to deal with it.

doors/door_srv3.c

```
66 static void *ssp_thread (void *func)
67 {
68     if (pthread_setcancelstate (PTHREAD_CANCEL_DISABLE, NULL) != 0)
69         err_msg ("pthread_setcancelstate failed");

70     if (pthread_mutex_lock (&door_lock) != 0)
71         err_msg ("Can't lock door");
72     while (door_fd == -1) {
73         if (pthread_cond_wait (&door_cv, &door_lock) != 0)
74             err_msg ("pthread_cond_wait failed");
75     }
76     if (pthread_mutex_unlock (&door_lock) != 0)
77         err_msg ("Can't unlock door");

78     if (func == (void *) server_proc) {
79         if (door_bind (door_fd) == -1)
80             err_msg ("door_bind failed");
81         if (door_return (NULL, 0, NULL, 0) == -1)
82             err_msg ("door_return failed");
83     }
84     else
85         err_quit ("ssp_thread: %p: Unknown function", func);

86     return (NULL);
87 }
```

doors/door_srv3.c

Program 22.13 The thread start function of our server that manages its own threads.

Note that unlike the contention scope and attachment status thread attributes (which are specified when we create a thread), the cancellation mode can be set by the thread itself only once it is running. A thread can enable and disable thread cancellation whenever it wants.

Wait for door descriptor to become valid

70–77 Our server creation function is first called when we call door_create from main to create the initial server thread. This call is issued automatically by the doors library, before door_create returns. But the door descriptor (which we use when we call door_bind), door_fd, will not be valid until door_create returns. Because we can't guarantee the thread execution order, we have a timing problem to solve. We do this by using the mutex door_lock and the condition variable door_cv as follows: in the main thread, we lock the mutex prior to calling door_create, signaling the condition variable and unlocking the mutex when door_create returns and the descriptor's value has been stored in door_fd. In the ssp_thread thread, we lock the door mutex (which is likely to block until it has been unlocked in the main thread), wait for the condition variable to be signaled, and then unlock it (the door mutex).

Bind the thread to a door

78–80 By calling door_bind, we bind the calling thread to the private server thread pool associated with the door whose descriptor is stored in the global variable door_fd. The reason why we made door_fd a global variable in this version of our server is because we need to be able to access it to pass it to door_bind.

Make thread available for client requests

81–82 When the thread has finished initializing itself and has been bound to a door, it calls door_return (with two NULL pointers and two lengths of 0 as arguments) to make itself available to service incoming door invocations.

Finally, Program 22.14 shows the code for the server procedure, which is the same as the one we showed in Program 22.2, except for the addition of a 5-second sleep (to make it easier for us to run multiple clients simultaneously) and the printing of the current thread ID.

doors/door_srv3.c
```
 88 static void server_proc (void *cookie, char *argp, size_t arg_size,
 89     door_desc_t *dp, uint_t n_desc)
 90 {
 91     long arg;
 92     long res;

 93     arg = *((long *) argp);
 94     res = arg * arg;

 95     printf ("Server proc called, thread ID = %d, arg = %ld\n",
 96         pthread_self (), arg);
 97     sleep (5);
 98     printf ("Server proc returning, thread ID = %d, res = %ld\n",
 99         pthread_self (), res);

100     if (door_return ((char *) &res, sizeof (long), NULL, 0) == -1)
101         err_msg ("door_return failed");
102 }
```
doors/door_srv3.c

Program 22.14   The server procedure of our server that manages its own threads.

Let's start our new server and run some tests. In each of these tests, we'll use the client we showed in Program 22.1:

```
$ ./door_srv3 /tmp/ssp_door
ssp_create: Created server thread 2
```

Notice that the our server creation procedure is called as soon as the server calls door_create even though we haven't started the client yet. This creates the first thread, which waits for the first client door invocation. Let's run the client a couple of times in another window and see what happens:

```
$ ./door_cli1 /tmp/ssp_door 42
Result = 1764
$ ./door_cli1 /tmp/ssp_door 69
Result = 4761
$ ./door_cli1 /tmp/ssp_door 1138
Result = 1295044
```

Here is the corresponding server output:

```
ssp_create: Created server thread 3
Server proc called, thread ID = 2, arg = 42
Server proc returning, thread ID = 2, res = 1764
Server proc called, thread ID = 2, arg = 69
```

```
Server proc returning, thread ID = 2, res = 4761
Server proc called, thread ID = 2, arg = 1138
Server proc returning, thread ID = 2, res = 1295044
```

We can see here that when the first client request arrives, another thread (thread 3) is created, and then the first thread (thread 2) handles each of the requests. We can deduce from this that the threads library always keeps an extra thread ready.

Let's now run the client three times simultaneously in the background:

```
$ ./door_cli1 /tmp/ssp_door 42 & ./door_cli1 /tmp/ssp_door 69 & \
    ./door_cli1 /tmp/ssp_door 1138 &
[1]      8900
[2]      8901
[3]      8902
$ Result = 1764
Result = 4761
Result = 1295044
```

Here's what the server output looks like this time:

```
Server proc called, thread ID = 2, arg = 42
ssp_create: Created server thread 4
Server proc called, thread ID = 3, arg = 69
ssp_create: Created server thread 5
Server proc called, thread ID = 4, arg = 1138
Server proc returning, thread ID = 2, res = 1764
Server proc returning, thread ID = 3, res = 4761
Server proc returning, thread ID = 4, res = 1295044
```

Here we see that two new server threads are created, threads 4 and 5, and that threads 2, 3, and 4 handle the client requests.

22.5 Premature Termination of a Door Client or Server

In the previous example, we alluded to a problem that we have ignored so far in our investigation of Solaris doors: the premature termination of the server or one of its clients. If the client and server are in the same process (i.e., the local function call we show in Figure 22.1), we don't have to worry about this eventuality, because if either crashes, the whole process crashes. However, if the client and server are implemented in different processes, we must consider what happens if the client or server crashes, and how its peer is notified.

There are two scenarios we need to consider: the premature termination of the server and the premature termination of the client. In both cases, the only time we need to worry about premature termination is during a door_call. Let's start with the server.

Premature Termination of the Server

When a client calls door_call, it blocks until the server sends the results. However, the client needs to be notified if the server thread terminates for some reason before calling door_return. To see what happens, we'll modify our server procedure so that it terminates by calling `pthread_exit`. This just terminates the calling thread, not the whole process. Program 22.15 shows the modified version of the server procedure.

————————————————————————————— doors/term_door_srv1.c
```
27 static void server_proc (void *cookie, char *argp, size_t arg_size,
28     door_desc_t *dp, uint_t n_desc)
29 {
30     long arg;
31     long res;

32     pthread_exit (NULL);

33     arg = *((long *) argp);
34     res = arg * arg;

35     if (door_return ((char *) &res, sizeof (long), NULL, 0) == -1)
36         err_msg ("door_return failed");
37 }
```
————————————————————————————— doors/term_door_srv1.c

Program 22.15 A server procedure that terminates itself.

The rest of the server is the same as Program 22.2, and we use the client shown in Program 22.1. Let's start the server and see what happens when we run the client:

```
$ ./door_cli1 /tmp/ssp_door 42
door_call failed: Interrupted system call
```

We can see that in this case, `door_call` returns an error of `EINTR`.

Interrupting the `door_call` System Call

The `door_call` man page states that this function is not a restartable system call (the `door_call` function in the doors library invokes a system call of the same name; we can see this by running our client using the `truss` utility). This means that we must block any signals that might be generated during a `door_call` from being delivered to our process, because those signals will interrupt `door_call`.

We said that the `door_call` system call can't be restarted, but what if we know that we just caught a signal when we get an error of `EINTR` from `door_call`, and call the server procedure again? Surely this should be safe, because we know that it was the signal we caught that caused `door_call` to fail, rather than the server procedure terminating prematurely? The answer to this question is "it depends"; in this case it depends on whether the server procedure is idempotent.

A function that is *idempotent* is one that can be called any number of times without harm. For example, our server procedure returns the square of its argument. We can call it as many times as we like with no bad side effects; we will always get the correct result. Another example of an idempotent function is `time`; even though we might get a different answer every time we call it (provided we pause for a sufficient period between calls), it is still OK. The canonical example of a nonidempotent function is one that adds or subtracts an amount from a bank account. In this case, calling the function more than once will result in an error.

Example: Demonstrating an idempotent server procedure

Let's demonstrate how our server procedure that squares a number is idempotent.
Program 22.16 shows the server procedure for this example.

———————————————————————————— doors/term_door_srv2.c
```
28 static void server_proc (void *cookie, char *argp, size_t arg_size,
29     door_desc_t *dp, uint_t n_desc)
30 {
31     long arg;
32     long res;

33     arg = *((long *) argp);
34     res = arg * arg;

35     printf ("Server proc called, thread ID = %d\n", pthread_self ());
36     sleep (5);
37     printf ("Server proc returning, thread ID = %d\n", pthread_self ());

38     if (door_return ((char *) &res, sizeof (long), NULL, 0) == -1)
39         err_msg ("door_return failed");
40 }
```
———————————————————————————— doors/term_door_srv2.c

Program 22.16 Server procedure for idempotent server example.

This version of our server procedure prints its thread ID before going to sleep for 5
seconds. It then prints its thread ID again when it returns.

Program 22.17 shows the code for the client.

Declare global variable

11 We declare a global variable that we'll use as a flag to determine whether or not we
received a SIGCHLD signal.

Arrange for a SIGCHLD signal to be delivered

31–38 After install our SIGCHLD signal handler using sigset, we create a child process. This
child goes to sleep for 2 seconds and then terminates. When the child terminates, a
SIGCHLD process will be sent to its parent.

Call door_call in a loop

39–47 We call door_call in a loop as long as the error is an EINTR that was caused by our
signal handler, or until we get a normal return from door_call.

Signal handler

51–54 Our signal handler merely sets the global flag variable to 1 and then returns.

Let's start the server and run the client in another window:

```
$ ./term_door_cli1 /tmp/ssp_door 42
Calling door_call
Calling door_call
Result = 1764
```

doors/term_door_cli1.c

```
 1 #include <stdio.h>
 2 #include <unistd.h>
 3 #include <stdlib.h>
 4 #include <sys/types.h>
 5 #include <sys/stat.h>
 6 #include <fcntl.h>
 7 #include <door.h>
 8 #include <signal.h>
 9 #include <errno.h>
10 #include "ssp.h"

11 static volatile sig_atomic_t flag;

12 static void sig_chld (int sig);

13 int main (int argc, char **argv)
14 {
15     int fd;
16     long num;
17     long res;
18     pid_t pid;
19     door_arg_t door_args;

20     if (argc != 3)
21         err_quit ("Usage: term_door_cli1 path number");

22     if ((fd = open (argv [1], O_RDWR)) == -1)
23         err_msg ("Can't open door");

24     num = atol (argv [2]);

25     door_args.data_ptr = (char *) &num;
26     door_args.data_size = sizeof (long);
27     door_args.desc_ptr = NULL;
28     door_args.desc_num = 0;
29     door_args.rbuf = (char *) &res;
30     door_args.rsize = sizeof (long);

31     if (sigset (SIGCHLD, sig_chld) == SIG_ERR)
32         err_msg ("sigset failed");

33     if ((pid = fork ()) == -1)
34         err_msg ("fork failed");
35     else if (pid == 0) {
36         sleep (2);
37         _exit (0);
38     }

39     for (;;) {
40         printf ("Calling door_call\n");
41         if (door_call (fd, &door_args) == 0)
42             break;
43         if ((errno == EINTR) && (flag == 1))
44             flag = 0;
45         else
46             err_msg ("door_call failed");
47     }
```

```
48      printf ("Result = %ld\n", res);

49      return (0);
50 }

51 static void sig_chld (int sig)
52 {
53      flag = 1;
54 }
```
doors/term_door_cli1.c

Program 22.17 Client that calls `door_call` again when `SIGCHLD` is received.

As we can see, the first invocation of `door_call` is interrupted by our signal handler about 2 seconds after we start the client. The client then invokes `door_call` again, which this time completes successfully, and the expected result is returned.

Looking at the server output confirms that the server procedure is called twice:

```
$ ./term_door_srv2 /tmp/ssp_door
Server proc called, thread ID = 2
Server proc returning, thread ID = 2
Server proc called, thread ID = 3
Server proc returning, thread ID = 3
```

The client's second invocation of `door_call` causes another thread to be created, which subsequently calls the server procedure a second time. Because our server procedure is idempotent, this is OK. However, if our server procedure was not idempotent, this would be problematic.

Premature Termination of a Client

We've seen what happens in the event of premature termination of the server. Let's now take a look at what happens when the client terminates between calling `door_call` and the server returning the result.

Program 22.18 shows the code for the client.

The only change from Program 22.1 is line 26, which is the call to `alarm` immediately before calling `door_call`. This schedules an alarm call (i.e., a `SIGALRM` signal) for about 2 seconds in the future. We don't catch this signal, so client process terminates. This causes the client to terminate before `door_call` returns, because of the 5-second sleep in the door server procedure.

Program 22.19 shows the server procedure and its thread cancellation handler.

Thread cancellation is described in detail Section 5.3 of [Butenhof 1997], and we discussed it briefly in our description of Program 22.13. When a client that has a `door_call` in progress terminates, the server thread handling that call is sent a thread cancellation request. This has one of two results:

1. If cancellation is disabled for the server thread (which is the default), nothing happens, and the thread executes to completion. When the server thread calls `door_return`, the results are discarded.

doors/term_door_cli2.c

```
 1 #include <stdio.h>
 2 #include <unistd.h>
 3 #include <stdlib.h>
 4 #include <sys/types.h>
 5 #include <sys/stat.h>
 6 #include <fcntl.h>
 7 #include <door.h>
 8 #include "ssp.h"

 9 int main (int argc, char **argv)
10 {
11     int fd;
12     long num;
13     long res;
14     door_arg_t door_args;

15     if (argc != 3)
16         err_quit ("Usage: door_cli1 path number");

17     if ((fd = open (argv [1], O_RDWR)) == -1)
18         err_msg ("Can't open door");

19     num = atol (argv [2]);

20     door_args.data_ptr = (char *) &num;
21     door_args.data_size = sizeof (long);
22     door_args.desc_ptr = NULL;
23     door_args.desc_num = 0;
24     door_args.rbuf = (char *) &res;
25     door_args.rsize = sizeof (long);

26     alarm (2);

27     if (door_call (fd, &door_args) == -1)
28         err_msg ("door_call failed");

29     printf ("Result = %ld\n", res);

30     return (0);
31 }
```

doors/term_door_cli2.c

Program 22.18 A client that terminates during a door_call.

2. If the server thread has cancellation enabled, any cleanup handlers are called, and the thread is then terminated.

Enable thread cancellation and register cleanup function

35–36 The first thing we do in our server procedure is to enable thread cancellation by calling pthread_setcancelstate. We have to do this because threads created by the doors library have thread cancellation disabled. Note that we save the current thread cancellation state in the variable prev_state; we'll use this variable to restore the thread cancellation state at the end of the function.

―― *doors/term_door_srv3.c*
```
29 static void server_proc (void *cookie, char *argp, size_t arg_size,
30     door_desc_t *dp, uint_t n_desc)
31 {
32     long arg;
33     long res;
34     int prev_state;

35     if (pthread_setcancelstate (PTHREAD_CANCEL_ENABLE, &prev_state) != 0)
36         err_msg ("pthread_setcancelstate failed");
37     pthread_cleanup_push (server_proc_cleanup, NULL);

38     arg = *((long *) argp);
39     res = arg * arg;

40     sleep (5);
41     pthread_cleanup_pop (0);
42     if (pthread_setcancelstate (prev_state, NULL) != 0)
43         err_msg ("pthread_setcancelstate failed");

44     if (door_return ((char *) &res, sizeof (long), NULL, 0) == -1)
45         err_msg ("door_return failed");
46 }

47 static void server_proc_cleanup (void *arg)
48 {
49     printf ("Server proc cancelled, thread ID = %d\n", pthread_self ());
50 }
```
―― *doors/term_door_srv3.c*

Program 22.19 A server procedure that detects premature client termination.

37 We then call pthread_cleanup_push to register our thread cancellation handler, server_proc_cleanup. When the cleanup handler returns, the thread is terminated.

Sleep for 5 seconds

40 The server procedure goes to sleep for 5 seconds to give the client time to abort while its invocation of door_call is in progress.

Remove cleanup function and restore previous thread cancellation state

41 We remove our cleanup function by calling pthread_cleanup_pop. We pass an argument of 0 to this function, which means that our cleanup handler is removed without being executed.

42–43 We call pthread_setcancelstate again to restore the previously saved thread cancellation state.

Thread cancellation cleanup function

47–50 The thread cancellation cleanup function just prints a message stating that the thread was cancelled, giving the thread ID. However, cleanup functions can do whatever they need to to clean up when a client prematurely terminates, for example, release mutexes or other locks, write a message to a log file, free dynamically allocated memory, and so on. As we said previously, when all of the cancellation handlers have returned (a thread can register more than one cancellation handler), the thread is terminated.

Let's start the server and run the client a couple of times:

```
$ ./term_door_cli2 /tmp/ssp_door 42
Alarm Clock
$ ./term_door_cli2 /tmp/ssp_door 42
Alarm Clock
```

Examining the corresponding server output, we can see that our cleanup handler is called and the server thread is cancelled each time the client terminates prematurely:

```
$ ./term_door_srv3 /tmp/ssp_door
Server proc cancelled, thread ID = 2
Server proc cancelled, thread ID = 3
```

We run the client twice to show each time a server thread is cancelled, the doors library creates a new thread to handle the second client invocation.

22.6   Summary

In this chapter we described the doors API. Doors provide us with a mechanism for fast remote procedure calls when the client and server are processes on the same machine (compared to using regular RPCs when the client and server are on the same machine). We started out by describing door concepts, and the basic doors API: the server creates a door by calling `door_create`, and then attaches this door to a pathname in the file system by calling `fattach`. The client then opens the door and calls `door_call` to invoke the door's server procedure in the server process. The server procedure calls `door_return` to return.

We then showed a number of door clients and servers, starting with a basic pair that just squared a number. Other examples we wrote showed how a client can deal with a result buffer that is too small, and how a server can trigger (and deal with) unreferenced door invocations.

One of the nice features of doors is that the client and server can determine information about their peers. For example, the server can retrieve the client's credentials (i.e., its real and effective user and group IDs) and use this information to decide whether to service the client's request.

We went on to describe some advanced door facilities: the ability of the client and server to exchange descriptors using a door, and how a door server can manage its own thread pool. The doors library usually handles the server's threads automatically, but there are times when it is advantageous for the server to manage them itself. If the server wants its threads to have attributes that are different from the default (for example, a different stack size), it has no choice but to manage its own threads.

When we call a function in another process, we have to worry about the premature termination of the client or server (in the context of doors, a termination is premature if it happens while a `door_call` is in progress). We showed that if the server terminates prematurely, the `door_call` in the client returns an error of `EINTR`, and if the client terminates prematurely, the server thread handling the client's request receives a thread cancellation request. Whether this request is handled is up to the server (if the request isn't handled, the results are silently discarded by `door_return`).

Exercises

22.1 In our description of the `door_create` function in Section 22.2, we stated that the descriptors for doors created using this function have their `FD_CLOEXEC` bit set automatically. However, nothing prevents us from using `fcntl` to clear this bit once `door_create` returns. Suppose we do this in a server, call `exec`, and then try to invoke the server procedure from a client. What happens, and why?

22.2 Remove the mutex and condition variable that protects the global door descriptor, `door_fd`, from Programs 22.11 and 22.13. Run the new server a number of times, and verify that it no longer works. When the new server fails, what is the error message?

22.3 Modify the server procedure in Program 22.2 to call `door_revoke`. Verify that the call in progress completes normally and determine what happens when a client subsequently tries to invoke the server procedure.

22.4 In Program 22.11 (and the solution to the previous exercise), we made the door's descriptor global so that we can access it from the server procedure or the server creation function. What is another (and arguably better, from a software engineering point of view) way of accomplishing this, keeping the door's descriptor local to `main`?

Part 6

Pseudo Terminals

23

Pseudo Terminals

23.1 Introduction

We saw in Chapter 16 that when we log in using a terminal, we do it via the terminal's device driver. Figure 12.2 showed that the terminal line discipline STREAMS module, ldterm, sits between the terminal device and the kernel's generic read and write functions. It is ldterm that implements the canonical processing functionality (e.g., backspace, interrupt processing, etc.). When we log in from the network, however, no terminal line discipline is automatically provided. As Figure 16.4 shows, a pseudo terminal device driver is used. As we shall see, pseudo terminals have uses other than providing network logins. For example, the dtterms and xterms used in a typical windowing system use pseudo terminals, as do programs like expect and script.

In this chapter, we'll write functions to open a pseudo terminal, and write a program called pty that uses them. We'll also show various uses of this program.

23.2 Overview

A *pseudo terminal* is (as its name implies) a device driver that emulates a terminal. To an application program, a pseudo terminal is indistinguishable from a real terminal, except for the name of the device. In the /dev directory, real terminals are represented by files starting with tty (e.g., /dev/ttya), whereas the files for pseudo terminals are in the pts subdirectory (e.g., /dev/pts/13).

Each pseudo terminal is implemented using two devices, called the *master* and the *slave*. The process that is to be the "keyboard" and the "screen" opens the master device; this process is called the *controlling process*. The controlling process (which we should not confuse with a controlling process in the session leader sense of the term) then usually forks, creating a child. The child process creates a new session, opens the corresponding slave device, and duplicates the slave device's file descriptor to be standard input, standard output, and standard error. Finally, exec is called to run the program that is to be connected to the pseudo terminal (the pseudo terminal slave becomes the controlling terminal for the child process). Figure 23.1 shows the typical arrangement of STREAMS modules and processes when we are using a pseudo terminal.

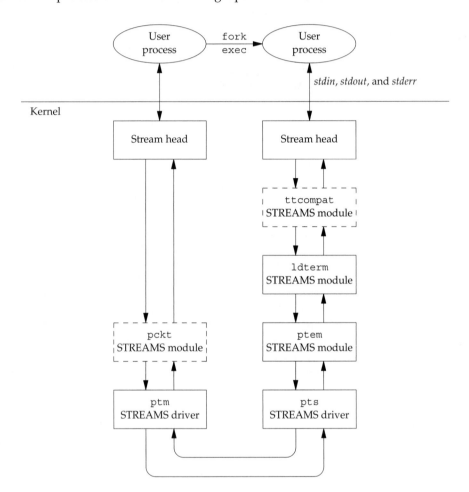

Figure 23.1 Arrangement of pseudo terminals.

When the controlling process writes to the master, the data will appear as input on the slave device. Similarly, when the child process writes to the slave device, the data will appear as input to the controlling process when it reads from the master device.

With reference to Figure 23.1, the left-hand column shows the module and driver associated with the pseudo terminal master, and the right-hand column shows those associated with the pseudo terminal slave. Also, we've shown two STREAMS modules as dashed boxes, indicating that they are optional. The `pckt` module is used to implement packet mode (more on this later), and the `ttcompat` module converts the `ioctls` supported by the older Version 7, 4BSD, and XENIX terminal drivers into the `ioctls` supported by the `termios` interface.

The `ptm` driver implements the pseudo terminal master, and the `pts` driver implements the pseudo terminal slave. The `ptem` (pseudo terminal emulation) module, when used with `ldterm` (the line discipline module), emulates a terminal. All the appropriate messages are processed and acknowledged, but those that don't make sense (e.g., changing the baud rate or parity, or sending a break) are just ignored.

To simplify our figures a bit, we'll group all the modules on the slave side together and just refer to them as the "terminal line discipline" from now on. We'll also use the abbreviation "pty" for pseudo terminal.

Now that we're cognizant of the pseudo terminal concepts, let's take a closer look at some of their typical uses.

X Window Terminal Emulators

Perhaps the most common use for pseudo terminals these days is in X Window terminal emulators like `xterm` or CDE's `dtterm`: it is not uncommon for UNIX workstation users to have several terminals open simultaneously. When an X Window terminal emulator is running, we have the arrangement shown in Figure 23.2.

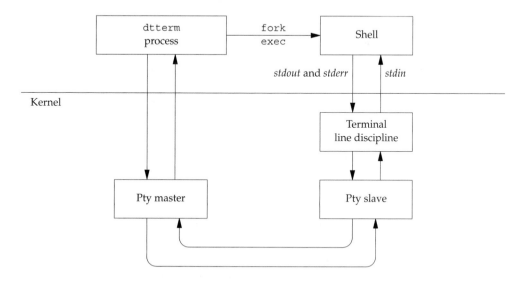

Figure 23.2 Arrangement of processes when using `dtterm`.

The arrangement of processes and STREAMS modules in Figure 23.2 is quite straightforward. However, the picture gets a little more complicated in other situations.

Network Login Servers

After terminal emulators, the next most common use of pseudo terminals is probably network logins. Pseudo terminal handling is built into all network login servers, for example, in.rlogind, in.telnetd, and sshd. We won't concern ourselves with the details of how each of these network login servers work (interested readers are referred to Chapter 15 of [Stevens 1990], which contains all the gory details). Figure 23.3 shows the arrangement once the login shell is running on the remote server. We assume the use of sshd in Figure 23.3; in.rlogind and in.telnetd are similar.

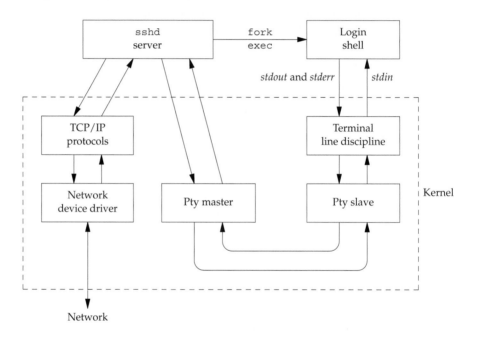

Figure 23.3 Arrangement of processes when using sshd to provide network logins.

An important observation we can make about Figure 23.3 is that the controlling process often performs I/O on another I/O stream at the same time it is driving the pty master. In Figure 23.3, the other I/O stream is the network connection, via the TCP/IP protocol box. This means that the process must be using one of the I/O multiplexing mechanisms we discuss in Section 13.15, or is divided into two processes or threads.

The `script` Program

The script program copies all of a terminal session's input and output to file. It does this by invoking a new copy of our login shell and placing itself between the new copy and the old. Figure 23.4 shows this arrangement, including the shell that we ran script from.

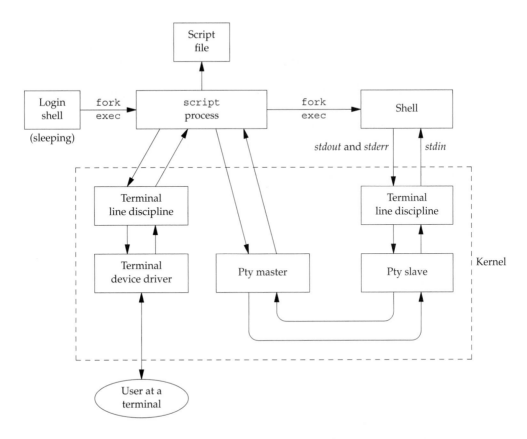

Figure 23.4 Arrangement of processes when running the `script` program.

While the `script` process runs, everything output by the terminal line discipline above the pty slave is copied to the script file, which by default is called `typescript`. Because echoing is usually performed by the terminal line discipline box, any characters we type also are copied to the script file. The only exception to this is when echoing is disabled, for example, when a password is being entered.

With a suitable shell script, we can use the `pty` program we develop in Section 23.5 to emulate the `script` program.

The `expect` Program

Some programs are hardwired to read from or write to a terminal device; the `passwd` command is an example of this. One way to use these programs in batch mode would be to rewrite them, but this is hardly practical. (One example of batch mode processing would be changing the password of numerous users in a script.)

A better method would be to use the expect program written by Don Libes, which uses a pseudo terminal to run other programs in a manner similar to our pty program from Section 23.5. However, expect also provides a programming language so that scripts can make decisions about a program's input based on its output. Using our batch mode password changing example again, we can write an expect script that runs the passwd command for a given user, waits for the "New password: " prompt, passes the desired password to the passwd program, and then repasses the same password when the prompt to re-enter the password is output.

Full details of the expect program can be found in [Libes 1994].

Running Coprocesses

As we saw in Section 19.4, we can't invoke a coprocess that uses the standard I/O library for its standard input and standard output. This is because when standard input and standard output are connected to a pipe, they are not associated with a terminal and are automatically set to fully buffered mode. If we have the source code for the coprocess, we can add calls to fflush to avoid this problem. That, however, is not an option if we don't have access to the coprocess' source code.

Figure 19.8 showed a process driving a coprocess using two half-duplex pipes. If we place a pseudo terminal between the two processes, as shown in Figure 23.5, we can solve the standard I/O buffering problem without access to the source code for the coprocess.

Figure 23.5   Driving a coprocess via a pseudo terminal.

With the arrangement shown in Figure 23.5, the standard input and standard output of the coprocess are connected to a terminal, so the standard I/O library will set these streams to line-buffered mode.

There are two ways we can place a pseudo terminal between the driving process and its coprocess. We can either call the pty_fork function we describe in Section 23.4, rather than calling fork, or we can exec the pty program we describe in Section 23.5, passing the name of the coprocess as its argument.

Watching the Output of Long-Running Programs

If we have a long running program, we can run it in the background, redirecting its standard output to a file. We can monitor the program's output by using the tail -f command on the output file. The trouble with this technique is that the output file will be updated irregularly. Recall our discussion of buffered I/O in Section 5.11, where we stated that all standard I/O streams are fully buffered, except those that are associated with a terminal, which are line buffered. Because our redirected standard output is no longer associated with a terminal, its output is fully buffered, so our file will be updated only when the standard I/O library flushes its buffers.

If we have the inclination, and access to the source code, we could add calls to `fflush` to flush each message as it is printed. Or, we could run the program under our `pty` program, which would make the standard I/O library think that standard output is associated with a terminal, and hence use line buffering. Figure 23.6 shows this arrangement. We've called the long-running program `longrunner`, and shown the `fork` and `exec` arrow as a dashed line to emphasize that the `pty` process is running in the background.

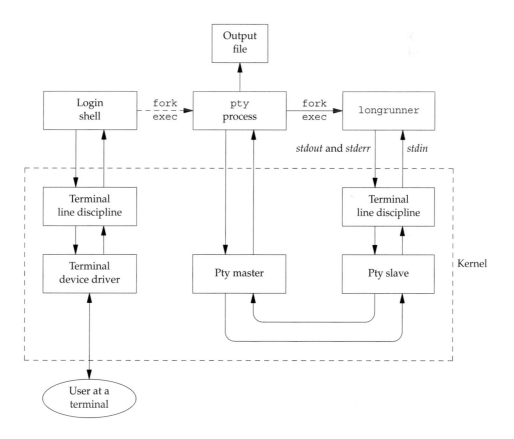

Figure 23.6 Monitoring the output of a long-running program using a pseudo terminal.

23.3   Opening a Pseudo Terminal Device

We can use two methods to open a pseudo terminal device: the older BSD method and the newer SVR4 method. Even though it is obsolete and new programs should not use it, we'll briefly describe the former method for the sake of completeness before turning our attention to the latter method.

Opening BSD-Style Pseudo Terminals

BSD-style pseudo terminal masters have device names like /dev/ptyXN; their corresponding slave devices have names like /dev/ttyXN. In both cases, X is a letter from the set "pqrstuvwxyzPQRST", and N is a hexadecimal digit.

> The number of characters in the set of letters depends on how many pseudo terminals have been configured, and how many entries in /dev have been made for pseudo terminals. By default, Solaris only has the files /dev/ptyp0 to /dev/ptyrf. Many applications that use BSD-style pseudo terminals only use the letters "pqrs" from the set we just mentioned.

The algorithm used to open a pseudo terminal is quite simple: we loop through all possible masters, trying to open them. If the open succeeds, we are finished and can open the corresponding slave device.

There are two reasons why an attempt to open a master device will fail:

1. The master device we are trying to open is already in use. In this case, errno will be set to EIO.

2. The master device we are trying to open does not exist. In this case, errno will be ENOENT, and it is safe to assume that we have exhausted all possible device names.

The code we would use to open a BSD-style pseudo terminal looks like the following:

```
int master_fd;
int slave_fd;
char *ptr1;
char *ptr2;
char master_path [16];
char slave_path [16];

for (ptr1 = "pqrstuvwxyzPQRST"; *ptr1 != ' '; ptr1++) {
    for (ptr2 = "0123456789abcdef"; *ptr2 != ' '; ptr2++) {
        sprintf (master_path, "/dev/pty%c%c", *ptr1, *ptr2);
        if ((master_fd = open (master_path, O_RDWR)) == -1) {
            if (errno == ENOENT)
                /* Bail - no more pseudo terminal devices to try */
            else
                continue;
        }

        sprintf (slave_path, "/dev/tty%c%c", *ptr1, *ptr2);
```

```
            if ((slave_fd = open (slave_path, O_RDWR)) == -1) {
                close (master_fd);
                /* Bail - can't open slave pseudo terminal device */
            }
        }
    }
    if ((*ptr1 == ' ') && (*ptr2 == ' '))
        /* Out of pseudo terminal devices to try */
    ...
```

Among the problems with this code is the race condition between opening the master device and opening the slave device. Also, although we don't show it in the example code above, we should ideally change the ownership of the slave device to that of the user ID of the process, and ensure that the permissions on the device are correct. Only privileged processes can do this, so our program must either be set-user-ID root, or at the very least the functions to open a pseudo terminal must be placed in a separate set-user-ID root executable.

Fortunately for us, using the SVR4 method of opening pseudo terminals neatly sidesteps all these problems.

Opening SVR4-Style Pseudo Terminals

SVR4 pseudo terminals eliminate the race condition by providing a single pseudo terminal master device, /dev/ptmx, which returns a file descriptor associated with an unused pseudo terminal slave. This slave device is automatically locked so that other processes can't use it.

The pseudo terminal master is a STREAMS *clone device*. This means that when we open it, its open routine automatically determines the first available pty master device and opens it.

Before we show a function to open an SVR4-style pseudo terminal, let's look at the three functions we'll need to use: grantpt, unlockpt, and ptsname.

The grantpt Function

Once we've opened the pty master device, we must call grantpt to grant us access to its associated slave device.

```
#include <stdlib.h>

int grantpt (int fildes);
```
                                                          Returns: 0 if OK, −1 on error

The grantpt function grants the calling process access to the pty slave device associated with the pty master device referenced by *fildes*. It does this by calling a set-user-ID root program, which changes the slave device's owner and permissions. The file's owner is changed to the real user ID of the calling process, and the group is set to a reserved group, tty. The file's permissions are set so that it is readable and writable by the owner, and writable by the group (i.e., the permissions are set to 0620). The device is writable by the tty group so that programs like wall and write, which are set-group-ID tty, will work correctly.

The unlockpt Function

Once we have been granted access to the pty slave device, we must unlock it. The unlockpt function accomplishes this for us.

```
#include <stdlib.h>

int unlockpt (int fildes);
```
                                                                    Returns: 0 if OK, −1 on error

The unlockpt function unlocks the pty slave device associated with the master to which *fildes* refers. This function must be called before opening the slave side of the pseudo terminal.

The ptsname Function

When we're ready to open the pty slave device, we need to know its name; we can ascertain this by using the ptsname function.

```
#include <stdlib.h>

char *ptsname (int fildes);
```
                              Returns: pointer to the name of the pseudo terminal device if OK, NULL on error

The ptsname function returns a pointer to a NUL-terminated string that contains the name of the pty slave device associated with the pty master referenced by *fildes*. The pty slave's name is stored in a local static data buffer that is overwritten by each call.

The name of the slave device is of the form /dev/pts/*n*, where *n* is a non-negative integer.

Example: Opening a pseudo terminal master device

Program 23.1 shows our implementation of a function called ptm_open, which opens a pseudo terminal master device.

Open pty master device

13–14 Open the pseudo terminal master clone device, /dev/ptmx, obtaining its file descriptor. Successfully opening the master device automatically locks out access to the corresponding slave device by other processes.

pseudo_terms/pty_fork.c

```
 1 #include <stdio.h>
 2 #include <stdlib.h>
 3 #include <unistd.h>
 4 #include <sys/types.h>
 5 #include <sys/stat.h>
 6 #include <fcntl.h>
 7 #include <stropts.h>
 8 #include <termios.h>
 9 #include "ssp.h"

10 static int ptm_open (void)
11 {
12     int fd;

13     if ((fd = open ("/dev/ptmx", O_RDWR)) == -1)
14         return (-1);

15     if (grantpt (fd) == -1) {
16         close (fd);
17         return (-1);
18     }

19     if (unlockpt (fd) == -1) {
20         close (fd);
21         return (-1);
22     }

23     return (fd);
24 }
```

pseudo_terms/pty_fork.c

Program 23.1 Function to open a pseudo terminal master device.

Change ownership and permissions of slave device

15–18 Call `grantpt` to change the ownership and permissions of the slave device. Internally, `grantpt` runs the set-user-ID `root` program `/usr/lib/pt_chmod` to perform these tasks. This means that programs using pseudo terminals need not be set-user-ID `root` to work correctly (contrast this with BSD-style pseudo terminals).

Clear internal lock on slave device

19–22 Next we call `unlockpt` to clear the internal lock on the slave device. We must do this before we open the slave. We must also determine the name of the slave device, but we defer this step until we call our function to open a pty slave device, `pts_open`.

Example: Opening a pseudo terminal slave device

Program 23.2 shows our function to open a pty slave device, `pts_open`.

Determine the name of the slave device

29–32 Call `ptsname` to obtain the name of the slave device associated with the master device represented by the file descriptor we pass to this function.

pseudo_terms/pty_fork.c

```
25 static int pts_open (int master_fd)
26 {
27     char *name;
28     int slave_fd;

29     if ((name = ptsname (master_fd)) == NULL) {
30         close (master_fd);
31         return (-1);
32     }

33     if ((slave_fd = open (name, O_RDWR)) == -1) {
34         close (master_fd);
35         return (-1);
36     }

37     if (ioctl (slave_fd, I_PUSH, "ptem") == -1) {
38         close (master_fd);
39         close (slave_fd);
40         return (-1);
41     }

42     if (ioctl (slave_fd, I_PUSH, "ldterm") == -1) {
43         close (master_fd);
44         close (slave_fd);
45         return (-1);
46     }

47     if (ioctl (slave_fd, I_PUSH, "ttcompat") == -1) {
48         close (master_fd);
49         close (slave_fd);
50         return (-1);
51     }

52     return (slave_fd);
53 }
```

pseudo_terms/pty_fork.c

Program 23.2 Function to open a pseudo terminal slave device.

Open the pty slave

33–36 Open the device whose name we've just obtained. If the calling process is a session leader and does not already have a controlling terminal, this open will make the slave device the controlling terminal. (We should specify the O_NOCTTY option if we don't want this to happen.)

Push the required modules onto the stream

37–41 Once we've successfully opened the slave device, we must push three STREAMS modules onto the stream. The first is called ptem, which stands for "pseudo terminal emulation module".

42–46 The next module we push onto the stream is the line discipline module, ldterm. This module, together with ptem, makes the stream act like a real terminal.

47–51 The last module we push is called `ttcompat`. This module is optional, and provides compatibility with the older terminal `ioctls`. We push this module onto the stream because console and network logins, as well as X Window terminal emulators, also push it onto the slave's stream (recall the output from Program 13.8, when we ran it against `/dev/tty`).

We can use these two functions to build another that we can call from a real application, which also takes care of creating a child process and establishing a new session leader. We'll call this new function `pty_fork`.

23.4 The `pty_fork` Function

The two functions we wrote in the previous section, `ptm_open` and `pts_open`, are useful, but are insufficient on their own for use in a real application. This is because a real application that uses pseudo terminals must do a number of tasks, in addition to those performed by `ptm_open` and `pts_open`. These include creating a new process, establishing a new session, and setting up the attributes of the pseudo terminal. To accomplish these tasks, we have written a new function called `pty_fork`.

```
#include "ssp.h"

pid_t pty_fork (int master_fdp, const struct termios *slave_termios,
    const struct winsize *slave_winsize);

                        Returns: 0 in child, PID of child in parent, –1 on error
```

The `pty_fork` function combines the functionality of `fork` and our `ptm_open` and `pts_open` functions. The parent process opens the pty master, and the child opens the pty slave. The child process also establishes a new session, initializes the pty slave's terminal attributes and window size (if applicable), and connects its standard input, standard output, and standard error to the pty slave. The values returned by `pty_fork` are the same as those returned by `fork`.

In the parent process, the pty master's file descriptor is returned in the integer pointed to by the *master_fdp* argument.

If the *slave_termios* pointer is not NULL, it must point to a `termios` structure that is used to initialize the attributes of the pty slave. If *slave_termios* is NULL, the kernel will initialize the pty slave to some implementation-defined state. Similarly, if the *winsize* argument is not NULL, it must point to a `winsize` structure that is used to initialize the window size of the pty slave.

Program 23.3 shows the code for our `pty_fork` function.

Let's look at some of `pty_fork`'s implementation details.

Open pty master

60–61 Call `ptm_open` to open the pty master device.

pseudo_terms/pty_fork.c

```
54 pid_t pty_fork (int *master_fdp, const struct termios *slave_termios,
55      const struct winsize *slave_winsize)
56 {
57      int master_fd;
58      int slave_fd;
59      pid_t pid;

60      if ((master_fd = ptm_open ()) == -1)
61          return (-1);

62      switch (pid = fork ()) {
63          case -1:
64              return (-1);

65          case 0:
66              if (setsid () == -1)
67                  err_msg ("setsid failed");

68              if ((slave_fd = pts_open (master_fd)) == -1)
69                  err_msg ("Can't open pty slave");
70              close (master_fd);

71              if (slave_termios != NULL) {
72                  if (tcsetattr (slave_fd, TCSANOW, slave_termios) == -1)
73                      err_msg ("Can't set pty slave's attributes");
74              }

75              if (slave_winsize != NULL) {
76                  if (ioctl (slave_fd, TIOCSWINSZ, slave_winsize) == -1)
77                      err_msg ("Can't set pty slave's window size");
78              }

79              if (dup2 (slave_fd, STDIN_FILENO) != STDIN_FILENO)
80                  err_msg ("Can't dup2 stdin");
81              if (dup2 (slave_fd, STDOUT_FILENO) != STDOUT_FILENO)
82                  err_msg ("Can't dup2 stdout");
83              if (dup2 (slave_fd, STDERR_FILENO) != STDERR_FILENO)
84                  err_msg ("Can't dup2 stderr");
85              if (slave_fd > STDERR_FILENO)
86                  close (slave_fd);

87              _exit (0);

88          default:
89              *master_fdp = master_fd;
90              return (pid);
91      }
92 }
```

pseudo_terms/pty_fork.c

Program 23.3 Our pty_fork function.

Call `fork`

62–64 Call `fork` to create a child process. Return –1 if `fork` fails.

Child process

65–67 Call `setsid`. This has three effects:

1. A new session is established, with the child as the session leader.
2. A new process group is created, with the child as its sole member.
3. The child has no controlling terminal.

68–70 Open the pty slave device. The pseudo terminal becomes the controlling terminal for the child process as a result of this open. We close the file descriptor for the pty master, because the child no longer needs it.

71–74 If the *slave_termios* argument isn't NULL, initialize the attributes of the pty slave.

75–78 If the *slave_winsize* argument isn't NULL, initialize the pty slave's window size.

79–86 Duplicate the pty slave's file descriptor onto standard input, standard output, and standard error. This means that whatever program the child execs will have these three descriptors connected to the pty slave (i.e., its controlling terminal).

We are now finished with the pty slave's file descriptor, so we close it.

87 Return 0 from the child, just like `fork` does.

Parent process

88–91 Store the pty master's file descriptor in the buffer pointed to by *master_fdp*, and return the process ID of the child process (this is also what `fork` does).

In the next section, we'll use our `pty_fork` function in the `pty` program.

23.5 The `pty` Program

In this section we present the code for a command we call `pty`. This program runs the specified command in its own session, connected to a pseudo terminal. Instead of typing

```
prog arg1 arg2 ...
```

we can type

```
./pty prog arg1 arg2 ...
```

Program 23.4 shows the code for the `main` and `disable_echo` functions.

Initialize variables

26–31 The first thing we do is initialize the variables we use to 0. The exceptions to this are `interactive`, the value of which depends on whether standard input is connected to a terminal, and `driver`, which is set to NULL. We set `opterr` to 0 to prevent `getopt` from printing error messages.

pseudo_terms/pty.c

```
 1  #include <stdio.h>
 2  #include <unistd.h>
 3  #include <stdlib.h>
 4  #include <stropts.h>
 5  #include <termios.h>
 6  #include <sys/types.h>
 7  #include <poll.h>
 8  #include "ssp.h"

 9  extern int tty_raw (int fd);
10  extern void tty_atexit (void);
11  static void disable_echo (int fd);
12  static void loop (int master_fd, int ignore_eof);
13  static void run_driver (const char *driver);

14  int main (int argc, char **argv)
15  {
16      int master_fd;
17      int c;
18      int ignore_eof;
19      int interactive;
20      int quiet;
21      int err_flag;
22      pid_t pid;
23      char *driver;
24      struct termios old_termios;
25      struct winsize tty_winsize;

26      ignore_eof = 0;
27      interactive = isatty (STDIN_FILENO);
28      quiet = 0;
29      driver = NULL;
30      err_flag = 0;
31      opterr = 0;

32      while ((c = getopt (argc, argv, "d:eiq")) != EOF) {
33          switch (c) {
34              case 'd':
35                  driver = optarg;
36                  break;

37              case 'e':
38                  ignore_eof++;
39                  break;

40              case 'i':
41                  interactive = 0;
42                  break;

43              case 'q':
44                  quiet++;
45                  break;

46              default:
47                  err_flag++;
48                  break;
```

```
49              }
50          }

51      if ((err_flag) || (optind >= argc))
52          err_quit ("Usage: pty [-d driver] [eiq] command [arg ...]");

53      if (interactive) {
54          if (tcgetattr (STDIN_FILENO, &old_termios) == -1)
55              err_msg ("tcgetattr failed");

56          if (ioctl (STDIN_FILENO, TIOCGWINSZ, &tty_winsize) == -1)
57              err_msg ("TIOCGWINSZ failed");

58          pid = pty_fork (&master_fd, &old_termios, &tty_winsize);
59      }
60      else
61          pid = pty_fork (&master_fd, NULL, NULL);

62      if (pid == -1)
63          err_msg ("pty_fork failed");

64      if (pid == 0) {
65          if (quiet)
66              disable_echo (STDIN_FILENO);

67          if (execvp (argv [optind], &argv [optind]) == -1)
68              err_msg ("pty: %s", argv [optind]);
69      }

70      if ((interactive) && (driver == NULL)) {
71          if (tty_raw (STDIN_FILENO) == -1)
72              err_msg ("tty_raw failed");
73          if (atexit (tty_atexit) == -1)
74              err_msg ("tty_atexit failed");
75      }

76      if (driver)
77          run_driver (driver);

78      loop (master_fd, ignore_eof);

79      return (0);
80  }

81  static void disable_echo (int fd)
82  {
83      struct termios term_attrs;

84      if (tcgetattr (fd, &term_attrs) == -1)
85          err_msg ("tcgetattr failed");

86      term_attrs.c_lflag &= ~(ECHO | ECHOE | ECHOK | ECHOCTL | ECHOKE | ECHONL);
87      term_attrs.c_oflag &= ~(ONLCR);

88      if (tcsetattr (fd, TCSANOW, &term_attrs) == -1)
89          err_msg ("tcsetattr failed");
90  }
```

pseudo_terms/pty.c

Program 23.4 Our pty program's main function.

Parse command line arguments

32–50 We call `getopt` in a `while` loop to parse the command line arguments. We recognize four options:

d   This flag is used to specify a driver script (more on this later). It has an argument, which is the name of the script to use as a driver.

e   Specifying this flag causes `pty` to ignore EOF on standard input.

i   Specifying this flag means that we are not being run interactively. This flag determines whether we initialize the pseudo terminal's attributes and window size, and whether we set the pseudo terminal to raw mode.

q   Specifying this option disables all echoing for the pty slave's line discipline.

51–52 If an error occurred while parsing the command line options, print a usage message.

Call `pty_fork`

53–61 If we are running `pty` interactively, we get the attributes and window size of the current terminal, then call `pty_fork`. The current terminal's attributes and window size are copied to the the pty slave by `pty_fork`. If we are not being run interactively, we just call `pty_fork`, leaving the system to supply suitable default values for the pty slave's attributes and window size.

62–63 If `pty_fork` fails, print an error message.

Child process

64–66 If the `quiet` flag is set, disable echoing form the pty slave's standard input.

67–69 Call the `execvp` function, which runs the command specified on the command line. All the remaining arguments are passed as arguments to the newly `exec`ed program.

Parent process

70–75 If we are running `pty` interactively, and we haven't specified a driver program, set the user's terminal to raw mode. We also register an exit handler to ensure that the user's terminal is reset when `pty` terminates.

76–77 If we have specified a driver program, we call `run_driver` to execute it. We'll describe this function later in this section.

78 We call the `loop` function, which just copies everything received from standard input to the pty master, and everything from the pty master to standard output.

The `disable_echo` function

81–90 We retrieve the current terminal attributes and clear all the echoing flags and the flag that maps newlines to carriage returns on output. Then we apply the new attributes to the terminal so that they take effect immediately.

The `loop` Function

Program 23.5 shows the code for the `loop` function. Because we must read from two input streams simultaneously (input from the user, and output from the pty master), we must implement some sort of multiplexed I/O. We can use two processes, two threads, or a single process using select, /dev/poll, or poll. We'll use the latter method and revisit this problem in Exercise 23.1.

pseudo_terms/pty.c

```
 91 static void loop (int master_fd, int ignore_eof)
 92 {
 93     ssize_t n;
 94     char buf [BUFSIZ];
 95     struct pollfd fds [2];

 96     fds [0].fd = STDIN_FILENO;
 97     fds [0].events = POLLIN;
 98     fds [0].revents = 0;
 99     fds [1].fd = master_fd;
100     fds [1].events = POLLIN;
101     fds [1].revents = 0;

102     for (;;) {
103         if (poll ((struct pollfd *) &fds, 2, INFTIM) == -1)
104             err_msg ("poll failed");

105         if (fds [0].revents & POLLIN) {
106             if ((n = read (STDIN_FILENO, buf, BUFSIZ)) == -1)
107                 err_msg ("read from stdin failed");

108             if (n == 0) {
109                 if (ignore_eof) {
110                     fds [0].events = 0;
111                     continue;
112                 }
113                 else
114                     break;
115             }

116             if (writen (master_fd, buf, n) == -1)
117                 err_msg ("writen to pty master failed");
118         }

119         if (fds [1].revents & POLLIN) {
120             if ((n = read (master_fd, buf, BUFSIZ)) == -1)
121                 err_msg ("read from pty master failed");

122             if (n == 0)
123                 break;

124             if (writen (STDOUT_FILENO, buf, n) == -1)
125                 err_msg ("writen to stdout failed");
126         }
127     }
128 }
```

pseudo_terms/pty.c

Program 23.5 The pty program's loop function.

Initialize pollfd structures

96–101 Initialize our array of pollfd structures so that poll will return when either of the two file descriptors we want to read from has data available. The first element of the array is for standard input, and the second is for the file descriptor associated with the pty master. We then enter an infinite loop, ready to copy the data.

Call `poll`

103–104 Call the `poll` function to wait for either of the two file descriptors we are interested in to become ready for reading. We specify an infinite timeout because we don't mind how long we wait; `poll` will not return until a descriptor is ready for reading (or an interrupt is received).

Handle the event of standard input having data available

105–118 If standard input has data available for reading, then read it. If the number of bytes read is 0, then an EOF condition has been detected. If we're ignoring these EOF conditions, we clear the `events` member of the `pollfd` structure associated with standard input and start another iteration through the infinite loop. If we not ignoring EOF conditions, then we break out of the infinite loop, which causes our `loop` function to return to its caller.

If the number of bytes read from standard input is not 0, then we write the data we read to the pty master's file descriptor.

Handle the event of the pty master having data available

119–126 If the pty master has data available for reading, then read it. If the number of bytes read is 0, then an EOF condition has been detected, so we break out of the infinite loop (thereby causing the `loop` function to return to its caller). Otherwise, we write the data we read to standard output.

23.6   Using the `pty` Program

Now that we've described the basic functionality and implementation of our `pty` program, let's see it in action. We'll use a number of different scenarios to illustrate the use of the various command line options.

Example: Running the `tty` program

Our first example just runs the `tty` command using a pseudo terminal. The `tty` command merely prints the name of its controlling terminal and exits:

```
$ tty
/dev/pts/7
$ who
rich        pts/5        Jul 10 16:20      (zaphod)
rich        pts/6        Jul 10 09:35      (zaphod)
rich        pts/7        Jul 10 09:35      (zaphod)
rich        pts/8        Jul 13 21:33      (zaphod)
$ ./pty tty
/dev/pts/9
```

We first run `tty` from our terminal window so that we can confirm that a new one is being used when we run `pty`. Next we run the `who` command; among other things, this shows us that pts/8 is the highest numbered pseudo terminal in use. When we run tty from pty, we see that we are allocated the next available pty (i.e., /dev/pts/9).

Example: Interaction with job control

If we run a job control shell, for example, ksh, using pty, it works as we would expect. We can run programs in the new shell and use job control as normal. However, if we run an interactive program (other than a job control shell) under pty, things go awry when we type the job control suspend character:

```
$ ./pty cat
echo some stuff
echo some stuff
^z$                              Type our suspend character, then Control-D to quit
```

All is well until we type Control-Z. Instead of suspending the cat command, the job control character is ignored and echoed as ^z.

To understand why this happens, we need to consider all the processes involved, the process groups, and their sessions; Figure 23.7 shows this arrangement.

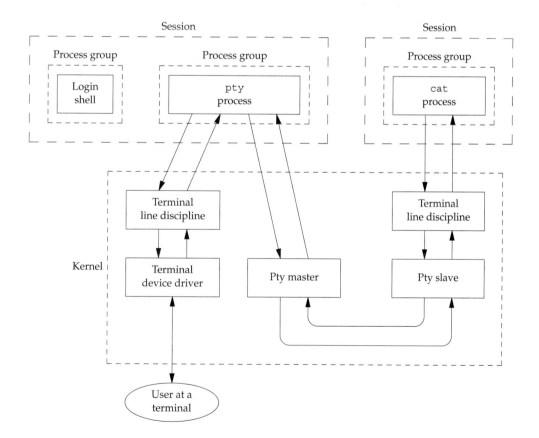

Figure 23.7 Arrangement of processes when running cat from our pty program.

When we type Control-Z, it is recognized by the terminal line discipline module between the pty slave and the cat process rather than by the terminal line discipline module between the user and the pty process. This is because the latter puts its terminal into raw mode. The kernel doesn't suspend the cat process, because it is a member of an orphaned process group (see Section 16.11); the parent of cat is pty, which belongs to another session.

We can use a combination of the truss program and Program 17.25 to determine what happens behind the scenes when we type our suspend character. In one window we run the command

```
./pty ../signals/sigtstp
```

and in another we run the truss command:

```
$ ps -e | grep sigtstp                      Determine which process to truss
 18990 pts/9     0:00 sigtstp
$ truss -p 18990
pause()                               (sleeping...)
    Received signal #24, SIGTSTP, in pause() [caught]
pause()                                         Err#91 ERESTART
ioctl(1, TCGETA, 0xFFBFE68C)                    = 0
fstat64(1, 0xFFBFE5A8)                          = 0
write(1, "\n", 1)                               = 1
sigprocmask(SIG_UNBLOCK, 0xFFBFF500, 0x00000000) = 0
sigaction(SIGTSTP, 0xFFBFF3C0, 0xFFBFF460)      = 0
sigprocmask(SIG_UNBLOCK, 0xFFBFF490, 0xFFBFF480) = 0
getpid()                                        = 18990 [18988]
kill(18990, SIGTSTP)                            = 0
    Received signal #24, SIGTSTP [default]
      siginfo: SIGTSTP pid=18990 uid=1001
sigaction(SIGTSTP, 0xFFBFF3C0, 0xFFBFF460)      = 0
sigprocmask(SIG_UNBLOCK, 0xFFBFF490, 0xFFBFF480) = 0
setcontext(0xFFBFF5D0)
write(1, " P r o g r a m   c o n t".., 32)      = 32
_exit(0)
```

The truss output is showing us that when we type our suspend character, the kernel sends a SIGTSTP signal to our process, which it catches. When the process attempts to really suspend itself (after resetting the SIGTSTP handler to SIG_DFL) by sending itself SIGTSTP using raise, the kernel immediately sends a SIGCONT signal to resume the process. That is, the kernel will not let the process be stopped by using job control.

When we use our pty command to run a job control shell, the jobs the shell invokes can be stopped by typing the suspend character. This is because the jobs never become members of an orphaned process group because the job control shell always belongs to the same session. Hence, the suspend character is sent to the process the shell invokes, not the shell itself.

The only way we can work around this in our pty program would be to add another command line option telling pty to handle job control suspend signals itself rather than just passing the character on to the other line discipline module.

Example: Watching the output of long-running programs

Job control signals can also interact with the pty program in situations like the one shown in Figure 23.6. If we use pty to invoke our long-running program like this:

```
./pty longrunner > longrunner.out &
```

the pty process is stopped as soon as it tries to read from its standard input (i.e., the terminal). This is because it is a background job, meaning that it will be stopped by job control when it tries to read from the terminal (recall Section 17.27). If we try running pty with its standard input redirected so that it doesn't attempt to read from the terminal, like this:

```
./pty longrunner < /dev/null > longrunner.out &
```

then pty will terminate immediately, because it reads an EOF from its standard input. The solution to this problem is to tell pty to ignore EOFs from its standard input by using the –e option:

```
./pty -e longrunner < /dev/null > longrunner.out &
```

This flag causes pty to stop copying from its standard input to the pty master when an EOF on standard input is detected, but it continues copying the pty slave's output to standard output (i.e., the file longrunner.out in this example).

Example: Emulating the `script` program

We can use our pty program in a simple shell script to implement the script utility, as shown in Program 23.6:

pseudo_terms/ssp_script

```
1 #!/bin/sh

2 ./pty "${SHELL:-/bin/sh}" | tee typescript
```

pseudo_terms/ssp_script

Program 23.6 Implementing the script program using pty.

The strange-looking construct in quotation marks on line 2 of Program 23.6 determines which shell is run. What the expression in quotation marks evaluates to depends on the value of the SHELL environment variable. If SHELL evaluates to anything other than an empty string, the result is that value. Otherwise, the value of /bin/sh is used. In this example, we've assumed that SHELL is equal to /bin/ksh.

As we stated earlier, the script program merely makes a copy of anything output by the new shell (and any program it invokes). However, most of what we type also is written to the typescript file because the pty slave usually has echoing enabled.

Figure 23.8 shows the resultant process relationships when we use our shell script to run ksh, which subsequently invokes ps (we run ps so that we can confirm these relationships).

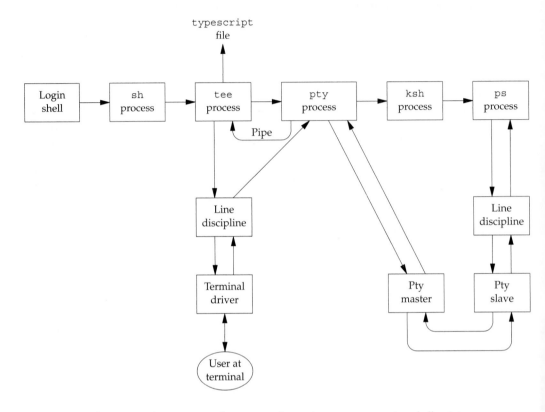

Figure 23.8 Arrangement of processes when using our `ssp_script` shell script.

The horizontal arrowed lines between process boxes in Figure 23.8 represent calls to `fork` and `exec`.

Running Coprocesses

Recall from Section 19.4 how Program 19.12 didn't work because it used standard I/O functions, which by default set standard input and standard output to fully buffered mode when they don't refer to a terminal. We stated that using a pseudo terminal was a good solution to this problem, especially if we don't have access to the source code of the coprocess. We can do this by running the coprocess under `pty` by changing line 31 of Program 19.11 from

```
execl ("./sqrt", "sqrt", NULL);
```

to

```
execl ("./pty", "pty", "-q", "./sqrt", NULL);
```

With this modification in place, Program 19.11 works as expected, even if the coprocess uses standard I/O. Figure 23.9 shows the arrangement when we run a coprocess via a pseudo terminal (Figure 23.9 is a more detailed version of Figure 23.5, showing all the process connections and data flows). The box labelled "Driving program" is Program 19.11 with the execl line modified as we described previously.

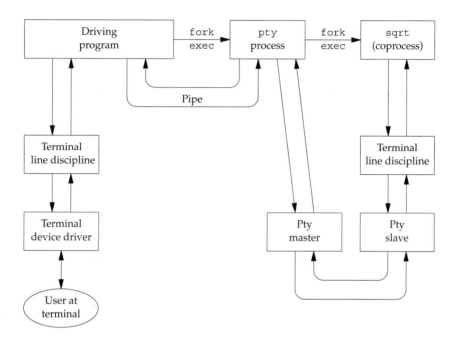

Figure 23.9   Running a coprocess with a pseudo terminal as its input and output.

This example illustrates the need for the -q (quiet) option. The pty program is not running interactively, because its standard input is not connected to a terminal. Line 29 of Program 23.4 sets the interactive flag to false because isatty returns false. As a result of this, the line discipline above the user's terminal remains in canonical mode with echoing enabled. By specifying the -q option, we disable echoing in the terminal line discipline module above the pty slave. If we didn't do this, everything would be echoed twice: once by the line discipline above the user's terminal and once by the line discipline above the pty slave.

The -q command line argument also disables the newline to carriage return on output option (i.e., the ONLCR flag in the termios structure). This prevents all the output from the coprocess from being terminated by a carriage return and a newline.

Running Interactive Programs Noninteractively

The `pty` program works well with noninteractive programs or programs that we use interactively. What it's not so good at, however, is driving interactive programs in batch mode (i.e., noninteractively). This is because `pty` just copies everything read from standard input to the pty master, and everything read from the pty master to its standard output. It makes no attempt to look at what is copied.

An often-cited example of this is running the `passwd` command, perhaps for numerous accounts (e.g., resetting students' accounts to a default password at the start of a new school year). We can run the `passwd` command using `pty` as follows:

```
./pty passwd
```

Invoking `passwd` like this offers no advantage over running directly (i.e., without using `pty`). If we wanted to change a user's password to "changeme", we might be tempted to write the following two lines into a file called `passwords`, knowing that we must enter a password twice with the `passwd` program

```
changeme
changeme
```

and then run `pty` like this:

```
./pty -e < passwords passwd jrluser
```

The only problem with this is that we don't get the results we expect. This is because the two passwords are sent to the `passwd` program before it is ready for them. When we run `passwd` interactively, we wait for the prompts ("New password: ") to be displayed before entering the new password. But the `pty` program doesn't know this, which is why more sophisticated programs, like `expect`, are usually needed to drive an interactive program from a script.

Apart from switching to another program (like `expect`), we have a number of options available to us to solve this problem. We could add a scripting language and interpreter to `pty`, but such an addition would likely be more than an order of magnitude bigger than `pty` currently is. Another option would be to start with a scripting language and use something like our `pty_fork` function to invoke a program (the latter is what `expect` does).

There is a third alternative, which is the one we'll use. We'll add to `pty` the ability to run with a user-specified driver connected to its standard input and standard output rather than the user's terminal (this is the `-d` option). In other words, the standard output of the driver is connected to `pty`'s standard input, and vice versa. Figure 23.10 shows the resulting process arrangement, assuming we're using a driver called `pw_driver` to drive the `passwd` program.

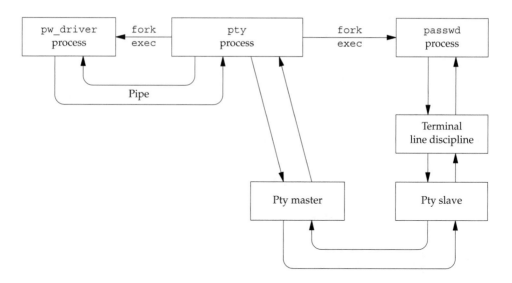

Figure 23.10 Arrangement of processes when using a driver program with pty.

Figure 23.10 differs from our others a bit because pty's standard input and standard output are connected to the pw_driver process via a pipe. Although we have shown two lines in Figure 23.10 for this pipe, it is actually just a single, full-duplex pipe. Each process closes the file descriptor associated with the end of the pipe it is not using.

Program 23.7 shows the code for the run_driver function, which is called from pty's main function when we specify the –d option.

Create pipe

132–133 Call the pipe function to create the pipe we will use to connect the driver's standard input and standard output to ours.

Call fork

134–136 Call fork to create a child process, which will eventually invoke the driver.

Child process

138 Close the half of the pipe we're not interested in.

139–142 Duplicate the remaining pipe file descriptor onto standard input and standard output (note that we don't touch the driver's standard error). This connects the driver's end of the pipe to its parent's standard input and standard output.

143 Close the other file descriptor associated with the pipe. Now that we've duplicated this file descriptor, we're finished with it, so there's no need to keep it open.

144–145 Invoke the specified driver program, printing an error message if the exec fails.

pseudo_terms/pty.c

```
129 static void run_driver (const char *driver)
130 {
131     int fd [2];

132     if (pipe (fd) == -1)
133         err_msg ("pipe failed");

134     switch (fork ()) {
135         case -1:
136             err_msg ("fork failed");

137         case 0:
138             close (fd [1]);

139             if (dup2 (fd [0], STDIN_FILENO) != STDIN_FILENO)
140                 err_msg ("dup2 failed for stdin");
141             if (dup2 (fd [0], STDOUT_FILENO) != STDOUT_FILENO)
142                 err_msg ("dup2 failed for stdout");

143             close (fd [0]);

144             execlp (driver, driver, NULL);
145             err_msg ("pty: %s", driver);

146         default:
147             close (fd [0]);

148             if (dup2 (fd [1], STDIN_FILENO) != STDIN_FILENO)
149                 err_msg ("dup2 failed for stdin");
150             if (dup2 (fd [1], STDOUT_FILENO) != STDOUT_FILENO)
151                 err_msg ("dup2 failed for stdout");

152             close (fd [1]);
153             break;
154     }
155 }
```

pseudo_terms/pty.c

Program 23.7   The run_driver function for the pty program.

Parent process

147 Close the half of the pipe we're not interested in.

148–151 Duplicate the remaining pipe file descriptor onto standard input and standard output. This connects the parent's end of the pipe to the driver's standard input and standard output.

152 Close the other file descriptor associated with the pipe.

Example: Using pty and a driver to change a user's password

Let's look at an example of using pty with a driver. In this example, the shell script we show in Program 23.8 is our driver, but we're not limited to writing drivers as a shell script; we can use any language we want.

```
1 #!/bin/sh

2 NEW_PW="changeme"

3 echo $NEW_PW
4 read junk
5 echo $NEW_PW
6 read junk
7 read junk
```

Program 23.8 Script to drive the passwd program.

The three read lines in Program 23.8 just read (and discard) the prompts from the
passwd program; the echo lines output our desired password to the passwd program.

Let's see this in action:

```
$ su
Password:                                Become superuser
# grep rich /etc/shadow                  Check the current password
rich:$2a$04$s6Nkfz2Dqrpjv4ldWJTi7e5ivQ5/3fIHkMonpeoo5ZPdF8M91pQz2:12252::::::
# ./pty -d ./pw_driver passwd rich       Change the password
# grep rich /etc/shadow                  Check the password got changed
rich:$2a$04$zd.h9Yw1P7eIguoKrmx47.dx5LMyQ.q5WxgxiXu8poBeZoxy1zoxy:12255::::::
```

Note that we must become root; this is because access to /etc/shadow is restricted to
the superuser. It would be trivial to change any number of users' passwords in this
manner by wrapping an invocation of pty with a driver in a script.

Something else that adds to the versatility of using pty with a driver is that although the
driver's standard input and standard output are connected to pty, it can still interact
with the user if required by using /dev/tty. Although our driver solution to the
problem of driving an interactive program noninteractively is not as general as expect,
it is nevertheless a useful option to our pty program, for about 45 lines of code.

23.7 Advanced Features

Pseudo terminals have additional capabilities that we briefly describe here. Readers
interested in all the gory details are referred to [Sun Microsystems 2002b].

Remote Mode

Remote mode is used for applications that perform the canonical line editing functions
normally done by ldterm and ptem. When remote mode is enabled, the slave's line
discipline module doesn't perform any processing of the date it receives from the pty
master, regardless of whether it is in canonical mode (i.e., regardless of the setting of the
ICANON flag in the c_lflag member of the pty slave's termios structure).

Remote mode is enabled or disabled by issuing `TIOCREMOTE ioctl`s on the pty master; if a non-zero parameter is given, remote mode is enabled, and specifying a parameter of 0 will disable remote mode. In other words,

```
ioctl (fd, TIOCREMOTE, 1);
```

will enable remote mode, and

```
ioctl (fd, TIOCREMOTE, 0);
```

will disable it.

Packet Mode

Packet mode is used to inform the controlling process (i.e., the process attached to the pty master) when certain state changes have occurred in the pty slave. We enable packet mode by pushing the `pckt` module onto the pty master (we showed this optional module in Figure 23.1).

When packet mode is enabled, the process reading the pty master will be informed if the following events occur in the pty slave's `ldterm` module: when the read queue is flushed, when the write queue is flushed, when output is stopped using XON/XOFF flow control (e.g., when Control-S is typed), when output is restarted using XON/XOFF flow control (e.g., when Control-Q is typed), when XON/XOFF flow control is enabled after being disabled or vice versa, and when an `ioctl` is performed. Examples of programs that use these events are the `rlogin` client and the `in.rlogind` server.

When we're using packet mode, the process reading the pty master must use `getmsg` (rather than `read`) to fetch messages from the stream head. This is because the `pckt` module converts the events it recognizes into nondata STREAMS messages.

Example: Using packet mode pseudo terminals

Let's take a look at packet mode pseudo terminals in action. To do this we'll need to modify our `pty` program to use packet mode, and we'll need to write a program that causes the events that packet mode notifies us of. Our modified version of `pty` is called `pckt`. The latter is essentially the same as the former, except for some changes to the `loop` function and two additional lines in `main`, just before the call to `loop`. The new lines are:

```
if (ioctl (master_fd, I_PUSH, "pckt") == -1)
    err_msg ("Can't push pckt module");
```

All these two lines do is push the `pckt` STREAMS module onto the pty master's file descriptor. Program 23.9 shows the `pckt` program's `loop` function.

The `loop` function handles all the event notifications, so let's take a look at some of its implementation details.

Initialize `pollfd` structures

105–110 Initialize the array of `pollfd` structures, just like we did in Program 23.5.

———————————————————————— pseudo_terms/pckt.c

```
 91  static void loop (int master_fd, int ignore_eof)
 92  {
 93      ssize_t n;
 94      char buf [BUFSIZ];
 95      struct pollfd fds [2];
 96      char control_buf [BUFSIZ];
 97      char data_buf [BUFSIZ];
 98      int flags;
 99      struct strbuf control;
100      struct strbuf data;
101      struct iocblk *ioc;
102      struct termios *term;
103      unsigned char msg_type;
104      int i;

105      fds [0].fd = STDIN_FILENO;
106      fds [0].events = POLLIN;
107      fds [0].revents = 0;
108      fds [1].fd = master_fd;
109      fds [1].events = POLLIN;
110      fds [1].revents = 0;

111      control.buf = control_buf;
112      control.maxlen = BUFSIZ;
113      data.buf = data_buf;
114      data.maxlen = BUFSIZ;

115      for (;;) {
116          if (poll ((struct pollfd *) &fds, 2, INFTIM) == -1)
117              err_msg ("poll failed");

118          if (fds [0].revents & POLLIN) {
119              if ((n = read (STDIN_FILENO, buf, BUFSIZ)) == -1)
120                  err_msg ("read from stdin failed");

121              if (n == 0) {
122                  if (ignore_eof) {
123                      fds [0].events = 0;
124                      continue;
125                  }
126                  else
127                      break;
128              }

129              if (writen (master_fd, buf, n) == -1)
130                  err_msg ("writen to pty master failed");
131          }

132          if (fds [1].revents & POLLIN) {
133              flags = 0;
134              if ((n = getmsg (master_fd, &control, &data, &flags)) == -1)
135                  err_msg ("getmsg from pty master failed");
```

```
136                 msg_type = control.buf [0];

137             switch (msg_type) {
138                 case M_DATA:
139                     if (writen (STDOUT_FILENO, data.buf, data.len) == -1)
140                         err_msg ("writen to stdout failed");
141                     break;

142                 case M_FLUSH:
143                     fprintf (stderr, "pckt: pty slave flushed its queues\n");
144                     break;

145                 case M_STOPI:
146                     fprintf (stderr, "pckt: pty slave suspended output\n");
147                     break;

148                 case M_STARTI:
149                     fprintf (stderr, "pckt: pty slave resumed output\n");
150                     break;

151                 case M_STOP:
152                     fprintf (stderr, "pckt: pty slave disabled XON/XOFF "
153                         "flow control\n");
154                     break;

155                 case M_START:
156                     fprintf (stderr, "pckt: pty slave enabled XON/XOFF "
157                         "flow control\n");
158                     break;

159                 case M_IOCTL:
160                     ioc = (struct iocblk *) &data.buf [0];
161                     switch (ioc -> ioc_cmd) {
162                         case TCSBRK:
163                             fprintf (stderr, "pckt: pty slave sent BREAK\n");
164                             goto out;

165                         case TCSETS:
166                         case TCSETSW:
167                         case TCSETSF:
168                             fprintf (stderr, "pckt: pty slave changed "
169                                 "terminal attributes\n");
170                             term = (struct termios *)
171                                 &data.buf [sizeof (struct iocblk)];
172                             fprintf (stderr, " term.c_iflag = %04x\n",
173                                 term -> c_iflag);
174                             fprintf (stderr, " term.c_oflag = %04x\n",
175                                 term -> c_oflag);
176                             fprintf (stderr, " term.c_cflag = %04x\n",
177                                 term -> c_cflag);
178                             fprintf (stderr, " term.c_lflag = %04x\n",
179                                 term -> c_lflag);
180                             fprintf (stderr, " term.c_cc = ");
181                             for (i = 0; i < NCCS; i++)
182                                 fprintf (stderr, "%02x ", term -> c_cc [i]);
183                             fprintf (stderr, "\n");
184                             break;
```

```
185                                  default:
186                                      fprintf (stderr, "pckt: Unrecognised ioc_cmd: "
187                                          "%04x\n", ioc -> ioc_cmd);
188                                      fprintf (stderr, "  ioc -> ioc_cmd = %04x\n",
189                                          ioc -> ioc_cmd);
190                                      fprintf (stderr, "  ioc -> ioc_id = %04x\n",
191                                          ioc -> ioc_id);
192                                      fprintf (stderr, "  ioc -> ioc_flag = %04x\n",
193                                          ioc -> ioc_flag);
194                                      fprintf (stderr, "  ioc -> ioc_count = %04x\n",
195                                          ioc -> ioc_count);
196                                      fprintf (stderr, "  ioc -> ioc_rval = %04x\n",
197                                          ioc -> ioc_rval);
198                                      fprintf (stderr, "  ioc -> ioc_error = %04x\n",
199                                          ioc -> ioc_error);
200                                      break;
201                                  }
202                                  break;

203                              default:
204                                  fprintf (stderr, "pckt: Unrecognised message type: "
205                                      "%02x\n", msg_type);
206                                  break;
207                      }
208              }
209      }

210 out:
211      ;
212 }
```
—— *pseudo_terms/pckt.c*

Program 23.9 The pckt program's loop function.

Initialize STREAMS message structures

111–114 Set up the two strbuf structures we'll use to for the STREAMS messages we receive from the stream head when we call getmsg. We then enter an infinite loop, ready to copy the data.

Handle the event of standard input having data available

116–131 In exactly the same manner as for Program 23.5, copy any available data from standard input to the pty master.

Handle the event of the pty master having data available

132–136 If the pty master has data available for reading, then read it using the getmsg function. In other words, retrieve the first available message from the stream head and determine its type.

138–141 If the message type is M_DATA (i.e., an ordinary data message), then write the data associated with the message to standard output.

142–144 If the message type is M_FLUSH, the process connected to the pty slave flushed its input or output queue (or both). Print a message to that effect.

145–147 If the message type is M_STOPI, the pty slave has suspended output (for example, the user typed Control-S).

148–150 If the message type is M_STARTI, the pty slave has resumed output (for example, the user typed Control-Q).

151–154 If the message type is M_STOP, the pty slave has disabled XON/XOFF flow control.

155–158 If the message type is M_START, the pty slave has enabled XON/XOFF flow control.

159–202 If the message type is M_IOCTL, the pty slave has issued an ioctl that affects us. We take the address of the first byte of the buffer and cast it to a pointer to an iocblk structure. With this pointer, we can determine the reason for the ioctl.

If the ioctl's command was TCSBRK, the pty slave sent us a BREAK. This is effectively the same as saying we're done, so we break out of the infinite loop (thereby causing the loop function to return to its caller).

If the ioctl's command was TCSETS, TCSETSW, or TCSETSF, the pty slave has changed the terminal's attributes. We print out a message to that effect and dump the new termios structure.

If we don't recognize the ioctl's command, we print a message saying so and a hex dump of the ioctl message.

203–209 If we don't recognize the type of the message, print out a message and go back to the top of the infinite loop.

The second thing we need to demonstrate packet mode is a program that generates appropriate events. Program 23.10 shows the code for this (somewhat contrived) utility, which we've called tflags.

Get the current terminal attributes

8–10 Call tcgetattr to get the current terminal attributes. We do this so that we can later set them without actually changing anything.

Set the terminal attributes

11–13 Set the terminal attributes. Establish the new ones immediately.

14–16 Set the terminal attributes. Establish the new ones after allowing any outstanding data to be written.

17–19 Set the terminal attributes. Establish the new ones after allowing any outstanding data to be written, and discard any input that has not been read.

Enable XON/XOFF flow control

20–22 Call tcflow with an argument of TCOON to enable XON/XOFF flow control.

Suspend output

23–25 Call tcflow with an argument of TCIOFF to suspend output.

Resume output

26–28 Call tcflow with an argument of TCION to resume output.

Disable XON/XOFF flow control

29–31 Call tcflow with an argument of TCOOFF to disable XON/XOFF flow control.

pseudo_terms/tflags.c

```
 1 #include <stdio.h>
 2 #include <unistd.h>
 3 #include <termios.h>
 4 #include "ssp.h"

 5 int main (void)
 6 {
 7     struct termios term;

 8     printf ("Getting terminal attributes\n");
 9     if (tcgetattr (STDIN_FILENO, &term) == -1)
10         err_msg ("tcgetattr failed");

11     printf ("Setting terminal attributes (TCSANOW)\n");
12     if (tcsetattr (STDIN_FILENO, TCSANOW, &term) == -1)
13         err_msg ("tcgetattr failed");

14     printf ("Setting terminal attributes (TCSADRAIN)\n");
15     if (tcsetattr (STDIN_FILENO, TCSADRAIN, &term) == -1)
16         err_msg ("tcgetattr failed");

17     printf ("Setting terminal attributes (TCSAFLUSH)\n");
18     if (tcsetattr (STDIN_FILENO, TCSAFLUSH, &term) == -1)
19         err_msg ("tcgetattr failed");

20     printf ("Enabling XON/XOFF flow control\n");
21     if (tcflow (STDIN_FILENO, TCOON) == -1)
22         err_msg ("tcflow (TCOON) failed");

23     printf ("Suspending output (^S)\n");
24     if (tcflow (STDIN_FILENO, TCIOFF) == -1)
25         err_msg ("tcflow (TCIOFF) failed");

26     printf ("Resuming output (^Q)\n");
27     if (tcflow (STDIN_FILENO, TCION) == -1)
28         err_msg ("tcflow (TCION) failed");

29     printf ("Disabling XON/XOFF flow control\n");
30     if (tcflow (STDIN_FILENO, TCOOFF) == -1)
31         err_msg ("tcflow (TCOOFF) failed");

32     printf ("Reenabling XON/XOFF flow control\n");
33     if (tcflow (STDIN_FILENO, TCOON) == -1)
34         err_msg ("tcflow (TCOON) failed");

35     printf ("Flushing read and write queues\n");
36     if (tcflush (STDIN_FILENO, TCIOFLUSH) == -1)
37         err_msg ("tcflush failed");

38     return (0);
39 }
```

pseudo_terms/tflags.c

Program 23.10 Program to test packet mode pseudo terminals.

Reenable XON/XOFF flow control

32–34 Call `tcflow` with an argument of `TCOON` to reenable XON/XOFF flow control.

Flush the read and write queues

35–37 Call `tcflush` with an argument of `TCIOFLUSH` to flush the read and write queues.

Let's run Program 23.10 using Program 23.9 and see what happens:

```
$ ./pckt -i ./tflags
Getting terminal attributes
Setting terminal attributes (TCSANOW)
pckt: pty slave changed terminal attributes
  term.c_iflag = 2502
  term.c_oflag = 1805
  term.c_cflag = 00bd
  term.c_lflag = 8a3b
  term.c_cc = 03 1c 7f 15 04 00 00 00 11 13 1a 19 12 0f 17 16 00 00 00
Setting terminal attributes (TCSADRAIN)
pckt: pty slave changed terminal attributes
  term.c_iflag = 2502
  term.c_oflag = 1805
  term.c_cflag = 00bd
  term.c_lflag = 8a3b
  term.c_cc = 03 1c 7f 15 04 00 00 00 11 13 1a 19 12 0f 17 16 00 00 00
Setting terminal attributes (TCSAFLUSH)
pckt: pty slave changed terminal attributes
  term.c_iflag = 2502
  term.c_oflag = 1805
  term.c_cflag = 00bd
  term.c_lflag = 8a3b
  term.c_cc = 03 1c 7f 15 04 00 00 00 11 13 1a 19 12 0f 17 16 00 00 00
Enabling XON/XOFF flow control
Suspending output (^S)
pckt: pty slave suspended output
Resuming output (^Q)
pckt: pty slave resumed output
Disabling XON/XOFF flow control
pckt: pty slave disabled XON/XOFF flow control
pckt: pty slave enabled XON/XOFF flow control
Reenabling XON/XOFF flow control
pckt: pty slave flushed its queues
Flushing read and write queues
pckt: pty slave sent BREAK
```

Notice that we had to specify the `-i` flag to `pckt` to say that we're not running interactively. If we didn't do this, our standard input would be put into raw mode with the effect of our newline characters not being changed to a carriage return and newline sequence.

Also notice that `pckt` did not print a message the first time we enabled XON/XOFF flow control. This is because it was already enabled, and an event is triggered only if the pty slave changes state.

Window Size Changes

We saw in Program 23.3 that we can set the window size of a pty slave by issuing a `TIOCSWINSZ` `ioctl` on the pty slave's file descriptor. The controlling process can also change the pty slave's window size, by issuing a `TIOCSWINSZ` `ioctl` on the pty master's file descriptor. If the new window size is different from the current one, a `SIGWINCH` signal is sent to the foreground process group associated with the pty slave.

Generating Signals

The controlling process can send signals to the process group associated with the pty slave. This is accomplished by issuing an `TIOCSIGNAL` `ioctl` on the pty master's file descriptor, with the third argument set to the signal number. For example,

```
ioctl (fd, TIOCSIGNAL, SIGINT);
```

will send the interrupt signal to the process group associated with the pty slave.

23.8 Summary

We started this chapter by giving an overview of pseudo terminals. We then briefly showed how to open a BSD-style pseudo terminal before writing two functions that open SVR4-style pseudo terminals: `ptm_open` and `pts_open`. We used these two functions as the basis for our generic `pty_fork` function, which can be used in many applications. We then wrote a program called `pty`, which we used to explore the various properties of pseudo terminals.

Pseudo terminals are used daily on most UNIX systems, in the form of X Window terminal emulators, providing network logins, and implementing programs like `script` and `expect`.

Exercises

23.1 Rewrite the `loop` function from Program 23.5 to use two processes (or, if you prefer, two threads).

23.2 Standard input, standard output, and standard error are all open for reading and writing when `pty_fork` returns in the child. Is it possible to change this so that standard input is read-only, and standard output and standard error are write-only? If this change is possible, how would we do it?

23.3 With reference to Figure 23.7, which process groups are in the foreground, which are in the background, and which processes are session leaders?

23.4 The `script` program usually adds a header line with the start time, and a footer with the finish time to the script file. Add this feature to Program 23.6.

23.5 Write a program using `pty_fork` to create a pseudo terminal, and have the child process execute another program, which you must also write. This second program should catch `SIGTERM` and `SIGWINCH`. The signal handler for `SIGTERM` should print a message saying that it has been caught, and the `SIGWINCH` handler should also print the new size of the terminal window. The parent process should send a `SIGTERM` signal to the pty slave's process group. Once you've verified that the signal has been caught, the parent should then change the pty slave's window size. When the parent process terminates, does the child also terminate?

Appendix A

An Internationalization and Localization Primer

A.1   Introduction

All of the examples so far in this text have used English for any messages they have printed. But English isn't the world's only language, so it would be nice if we could make our programs print messages in the users' native language. In this appendix, we'll take a brief look at the internationalization and localization facilities offered by Solaris.

Internationalization is the process of making software portable between languages and regions, and *localization* is the process of adopting software for a specific language or region (each of which is called a *locale*). In other words, internationalization is an engineering process, and localization is a translation one.

> Sometimes software is specifically written to implement locale-specific language processing, text output, and so on. Although this is arguably an engineering process, it is still considered to be a localization one.
>
> Internationalization is frequently abbreviated to I18N. This is because there are 18 letters between the first and last letters of the word "internationalization". Similarly, localization is often abbreviated to L10N, because there are 10 letters between the first and last letters of that word.

The alternative to internationalization and localization is to completely rewrite our applications for each different locale we want to support. But doing this would be a costly maintenance nightmare, as we would have to maintain a separate source tree for each language we support. Internationalized software can be run without change in any supported locale, transparently to the end user.

Basic Steps in Internationalization

Once our application has been internationalized, the program itself (i.e., the executable image) is portable between different locales. We must perform a couple of steps to ensure that our application is internationalized. These are:

- Use appropriate functions to create software whose environment can be modified dynamically without recompilation.
- Separate all message strings from the code. These message strings include anything printable or displayable that the user might see. The message strings are kept in a message catalogue.

Message strings are translated for a given locale as part of the localization process. Related databases that specify formats for time, currency, and numbers are supplied with Solaris, provided that support for that locale has been installed.

To use a localized version of an application, the user sets certain environment variables. The values of these environment variables determine which locale is used to display information like dates, currency, and numbers, as well as the collation (sorting) order.

A.2   Locales

A locale consists of a number of categories that have country-dependent formatting or other specifications. A locale is made up of a base language, the country (or territory) of use, and an optional codeset. For example, the German locale is de (an abbreviation for Deutsch), but the Swiss German's locale is de_CH, the CH being an abbreviation for Confederation Helvetica. This allows for specific differences by country, for example, monetary units.

To allow for regional differences, more than one locale can be associated with a given language. For example, an English-speaking user in Great Britain can select the en_GB locale (English for Great Britain), whereas an English-speaking user in the United States would select en_US (English for the United States).

The naming convention for locales is as follows:

   language[*_territory*][*.codeset*][*@modifier*]

where the two-letter *language* code is from ISO 639, the two-letter *territory* code is from ISO 3166, *codeset* is the name of the codeset being used in the locale, and *modifier* is the name of the characteristic that differentiates the unmodified locale. The items within square brackets are optional. Finally, a single locale can be known by more than one name. For example, the C locale is the same as POSIX.

Locale Categories

The LANG environment variable specifies the default locale if the corresponding environment variable for a particular locale category is unset or empty. There are a number of locale categories, each of which has an associated environment variable. These environment variables are described here:

LC_ALL	If this environment variable is set to a valid non-empty string value, it overrides the values of the LANG and other environment variables described in this list.
LC_COLLATE	This environment variable specifies the character collation (sorting) sequence being used. It is used by the `strcoll` and `strxfrm` functions.
LC_CTYPE	This environment variable specifies the character conversion and widths of multibyte characters. When LC_TYPE is set to a valid non-empty value, the calling utility can display and handle text and pathnames containing valid characters from the specified locale. The default locale, C, corresponds to the 7-bit ASCII character set; only characters from ISO 8859-1 (Latin-1) are valid. This environment variable is used by the functions described in the `ctype` man page, the `mblen` function, and numerous commands, such as `cat`, `ls`, and `vi`.
LC_MESSAGES	This environment variable specifies the locale to be used for displaying messages output by the program. It is used by the `gettxt` and `gettext` functions, and the `exstr`, `gettxt`, `gettext`, and `srchtxt` utilities.
LC_MONETARY	This environment variable specifies the locale to be used for specifying the monetary symbols and delimiters. It is used by the `localeconv` function.
LC_NUMERIC	This environment variable specifies the locale to be used for specifying the decimal and thousands delimiters. It is used by the `localeconv`, `printf`, and `strtod` functions.
LC_TIME	This environment variable specifies the locale to be used for specifying the date and time formats. It is used by many functions (e.g., `strftime` and `getdate`) and commands (e.g., `cal` and `date`).

A.3 The `setlocale` Function

A program can get or set its locale by calling `setlocale`.

```
#include <locale.h>

char *setlocale (int category, const char *locale);
```
                                              Returns: *locale* if OK, NULL on error

The `setlocale` function sets the part of the calling process' locale specified by *category* to the locale specified by *locale*. The *category* argument must be one of the following values: `LC_COLLATE`, `LC_CTYPE`, `LC_MESSAGES`, `LC_MONETARY`, `LC_NUMERIC`, or `LC_TIME`. Additionally, *category* `LC_ALL` can be used to specify all of these. Each category affects the behaviour of the process as described in the previous section.

A value of `C` for *locale* specifies the traditional UNIX behaviour. When a program starts, the equivalent of the following code is executed:

```
setlocale (LC_ALL, "C");
```

Specifying an empty string for *locale* means that the locale should be taken from the environment variable of the same name as *category*. For each category, three variables are checked in order of precedence. Figure A.1 shows which environment variables are checked for each category.

Category	1st env var	2nd env var	3rd env var
LC_COLLATE	LC_ALL	LC_COLLATE	LANG
LC_CTYPE	LC_ALL	LC_CTYPE	LANG
LC_MESSAGES	LC_ALL	LC_MESSAGES	LANG
LC_MONETARY	LC_ALL	LC_MONETARY	LANG
LC_NUMERIC	LC_ALL	LC_NUMERIC	LANG
LC_TIME	LC_ALL	LC_TIME	LANG

Figure A.1 Precedence of environment variables for setting locales.

The easiest way to enable users of our programs to decide which locale they wish to use is to call `setlocale` early in the program:

```
setlocale (LC_ALL, "");
```

The user can then use the `LANG` (or one of the others shown in Figure A.1) environment variable to specify which locale to use.

A.4   Message Catalogues

We stated earlier that one of the steps we must take to create an internationalized application is to separate all the message strings from the program's code. These message strings are stored in locale-specific message catalogues (one message catalogue for each locale the application supports).

Solaris supports three similar (but unfortunately incompatible) types of message catalogue: the SVR4 private scheme using `gettxt`, the XPG3 scheme using `catgets`, and the `gettext` based scheme, which comes from early versions of SunOS. We will concentrate our discussion on the latter.

All three methods provide an interface to message catalogues, but the first two are inflexible when it comes to handling messages identified mnemonically. Because of this, we will follow Sun's lead and recommend that new applications use the `gettext` interfaces, despite the fact that they are not part of an official standard. (If source code portability is a concern, the source for the GNU implementation of `gettext` is freely available. See `http://www.gnu.org/software/gettext/gettext.html`.)

A.5   Creating a Message Catalogue

Many aspects of localization (e.g., formatting and collation) are handled for us by Solaris, but we must perform perhaps the most important task ourselves: that of translating the messages used by our program to the locales we want to support. We do this by creating a message catalogue for each locale.

There are four steps to creating a message catalogue from an internationalized C program. These are:

1. Use the xgettext utility to generate a portable message file. This file, which has a suffix of .po, is a readable text file intended to be edited by the person doing the translation.

2. Edit the portable message file, translating each msgid string. The translation should be placed on the msgstr line directly below the msgid line.

3. When all the messages have been translated, the msgfmt program must be used to create a message object (.mo) file from the portable message file. The message object file is a data file that contains the messages in a machine-friendly format (i.e., one that can be searched quickly). The name of the message file should be *domain*.mo, where *domain* is the name of the text domain we have selected (the default text domain is messages).

4. Install the message object file into the LC_MESSAGES subdirectory of the target locale's directory. The default directory for a locale is /usr/lib/locale/*locale*, although applications can specify their own directory by calling the bindtextdomain function we describe in the next section.

Let's take a closer look at each of these steps, using an internationalized version of the ubiquitous "Hello World" program. (We'll show the code for this program a bit later in this appendix.)

Extracting Text Strings from the Source Code

We first run the xgettext command on our source code, which extracts the (suitably marked) message strings:

```
$ xgettext -d hello hello.c
```

This creates the portable message file, which is called messages.po by default. However, in this example we specified the domain "hello", so the name of our portable message file is hello.po.

Edit the Portable Message File

Now that we've created our portable message file, we need to edit it, adding the translated text. Here's what our portable message file looks like before we edit it:

```
$ cat hello.po
domain "hello"
# File:hello.c, line:8, textdomain("hello");
msgid  "Hello, World!"
msgstr
```

Lines beginning with a number sign (#) are comments, and empty lines are ignored. The other lines are called statement lines, and each statement line consists of a directive and value pair.

The following directives are allowed:

domain *domain_name*   This directive states that all strings up to the next `domain` directive (or the end of the file) are in the domain specified by *domain_name*. Up to the first `domain` directive, all strings are in the default domain, `messages`.

msgid *message_id*   This directive specifies the value of the message identifier associated with the following `msgstr` directive. The *message_id* string is used as the key to retrieve a translated string at retrieval time, and is usually the untranslated message.

msgstr *message_string*   This directive identifies the target string associated with the *message_id* string declared in the immediately preceding `msgid` directive. The *message_string* is usually the translated message.

A translator provides the translations by editing the portable message file, adding the text for the target locale to the `msgstr` lines. For example, if we were targeting the French language, the portable message file would look like this after editing:

```
$ cat hello.po
domain "hello"
# File:hello.c, line:8, textdomain("hello");
msgid  "Hello, World!"
msgstr "Bonjour, Monde!"
```

Once we've finished editing the portable message file, we must create the message object file. (It's a good idea to save a copy of the unedited portable message file to ease the task of supporting additional locales.)

Create the Message Object File

The next step in creating our message catalogue is to create the message object file. We do this by running the `msgfmt` utility, specifying the portable message file's pathname on the command line. For example, this command creates the message object file associated with the portable message file we created in the previous section:

```
$ msgfmt hello.po
```

The `msgfmt` command creates one message object file for each text domain specified in the portable message file or files. In this example, we only have one text domain, so only one message object file is created, called `hello.mo`.

The message object file is suitable for copying into the appropriate LC_MESSAGES subdirectory.

Installing the Message Object File

The last step in creating our message catalogue is to copy the message object file we created in the preceding step into the target locale's LC_MESSAGES directory. In the Solaris operating environment, system messages for libraries and utilities are stored in /usr/lib/locale/*locale*/LC_MESSAGES/*domain*.mo, where *locale* is the specific locale (for example, en_CA for Canadian English), and *domain* is the specific text domain for a given application.

Application-specific message files are best installed in the same directory hierarchy as the application. Here we've decided that message catalogues will be stored in the subdirectory called locale:

```
$ mkdir -p locale/fr/LC_MESSAGES
$ mv hello.mo locale/fr/LC_MESSAGES
```

Applications can associate a directory with a message domain by calling the bindtextdomain function we describe in the next section.

Now that we've described how to make a message catalogue, let's take a look at some of the functions we use in internationalized applications. Prior to Solaris 2.6, applications using the functions we describe in the next three sections must be linked with -lintl.

A.6   The bindtextdomain Function

As we stated earlier, the default location for message files is in /usr/lib/locale. This, however, necessitates that our applications be installed by the superuser. It also makes it more complicated to manage internationalized applications shared across a network. To work around these obstacles, an application can specify its own directory for a given message domain by calling bindtextdomain.

```
#include <libintl.h>

char *bindtextdomain (const char *domainname, const char *dirname);
                                                      Returns: see text
```

The bindtextdomain function binds the directory specified by *dirname* to the message domain specified by *domainname*. The *dirname* argument can specify either an absolute or relative path. In the case of the latter, the path is resolved when gettext, dgettext, or dcgettext are called. If *dirname* is a NULL pointer, a pointer to the name of the directory *domainname* is currently bound to is returned. If *domainname* is NULL or points to an empty string, bindtextdomain returns a NULL pointer. Otherwise, bindtextdomain returns a pointer to *dirname*.

User-defined domain names cannot begin with the string SYS_. These domain names are reserved for use by the system.

A.7   The `gettext`, `dgettext`, and `dcgettext` Functions

When we want to print a message in an internationalized application, we must first retrieve the localized version of the message from the message catalogue. We do this by calling either `gettext`, `dgettext`, or `dcgettext`.

```
#include <libintl.h>

char *gettext (const char *msgid);

char *dgettext (const char *domainname, const char *msgid);

#include <libintl.h>
#include <locale.h>

char *dcgettext (const char *domainname, const char *msgid, int category);
```
All three return: message string if OK, *msgid* on error

The `gettext` function attempts to retrieve the localized version of the message specified by *msgid* from the message catalogue associated with the current text domain.

If we want to retrieve a message from a text domain other than the current one, we use either `dgettext` or `dcgettext`. The `dgettext` function attempts to retrieve the localized version of the message specified by *msgid* from the message catalogue associated with the text domain specified by *domainname*. The `dcgettext` function is the same as `dgettext`, except that the message catalogue searched is in the locale associated with the category specified by *category*, rather than the default, which is `LC_MESSAGES`. The value of *category* must be one of the `LC_` categories we described in Section A.2.

If we are writing a library, we should use `dgettext` rather than `gettext`. This is because we can't guarantee the calling sequence, and different domains may be mixed randomly together.

A.8   The `textdomain` Function

We can get or set the current text domain by calling `textdomain`.

```
#include <libintl.h>

char *textdomain (const char *domainname);
```
Returns: see text

The `textdomain` function gets or sets the name of the current text domain associated with the active `LC_MESSAGES` locale category. The text domain is set to the NUL-terminated string pointed to by *domainname*. If *domainname* is a NULL pointer, `textdomain` returns a pointer to the current text domain without affecting it; if *domainname* points to an empty string, the text domain is set to the default (i.e., `messages`).

Example: An internationalized greeting program

Let's write an internationalized version of the "Hello, World!" program. Program A.1 shows the code.

—————————————————————————————————— i18n_and_l10n/hello.c

```
 1 #include <stdio.h>
 2 #include <locale.h>
 3 #include <libintl.h>

 4 int main (void)
 5 {
 6     setlocale (LC_ALL, "");
 7     textdomain ("hello");
 8     bindtextdomain ("hello", "locale");

 9     printf ("%s\n", gettext ("Hello, World!"));

10     return (0);
11 }
```
—————————————————————————————————— i18n_and_l10n/hello.c

Program A.1 An internationalized version of our greeting program.

Allow environment variables to set locale

6 We call `setlocale`, setting `LC_ALL` to an empty string. This specifies that the locale for each category should be taken from the appropriate environment variable (in this example, we're only interested in the category `LC_MESSAGES`).

Set the text domain

7 We set the text domain to be `hello`. This means that `gettext` will look for messages in the text domain `hello` rather than the default, which is `messages`.

Bind our text domain to our own directory

8 Because we don't want to write our messages for this example into the system directories (i.e., in `/usr/lib/locale`), we bind the local directory called `locale` to the text domain `hello`.

Say hello

9 We call `printf` to print the greeting message. The message printed is determined by `gettext` and the current locale.

Let's run Program A.1 a few times and look at the output:

```
$ for i in C en_CA fr es; do
> LC_MESSAGES=$i
> ./hello
> done
Hello, World!              First the default locale for this system, C
Hello, World, eh?!         How a Canadian might say hello
Bonjour, Monde!            Now in French
¡Hola, Mundo!              And finally, in Spanish
```

If we wanted to add support for more locales, we would just need to create the appropriate directory under `locale` and create a new `hello.mo` file containing a suitably translated message.

A.9   The `strcoll` and `strxfrm` Functions

The string comparison functions we described in Section 3.3.2 assume the default locale, C. Other locales may have a different collation sequence, so internationalized applications can't directly use `strcmp` and friends. Instead, they should use `strcoll`, or call `strxfrm` before calling one of the `strcmp` functions.

```
#include <string.h>

int strcoll (const char *s1, const char *s2);
```
                                                                              Returns: see text

The `strcoll` function can be likened to a locale-aware version of `strcmp`. Like `strcmp`, it compares the strings *s1* and *s2*. If the strings are the same, 0 is returned. If *s1* is lexicographically greater than *s2*, a positive integer is returned; similarly, if *s1* is less than *s2*, a negative integer is returned. The comparison is based on strings interpreted as appropriate to the program's locale for the category `LC_COLLATE`.

The `strcoll` function is intended for use in applications where the number of comparisons per string is small. If the strings are to be compared a number of times, it is more efficient to call `strxfrm` and `strcmp`, because the transformation occurs only once.

The `strxfrm` Function

To transform a string so that it is suitable for use with `strcmp` in an internationalized program, we use `strxfrm`.

```
#include <string.h>

size_t strxfrm (char *s1, const char *s2, size_t n);
```
                                         Returns: length of transformed string if OK, –1 on error

The `strxfrm` function transforms the string pointed to by *s2*, placing at most *n* bytes (including the terminating NUL) of the resulting string into the buffer pointed to by *s1*. The string is transformed such that if `strcmp` is applied to two transformed strings, it returns a value greater than, less than, or equal to 0, corresponding to the result returned by `strcoll` when comparing the two original strings. As with `strcoll`, the transformation function is such that two strings can be ordered by `strcmp` as appropriate to to the collation sequence in the program's locale (i.e., the category `LC_COLLATE`).

If *n* is 0, *s1* is permitted to be a NULL pointer. We can use this fact to determine the required size of the result buffer, like this:

```
size = strxfrm (NULL, s2, 0) + 1;
```

Note that we must add 1 to allow space for the terminating NUL character.

A.10   Checklist for Writing Internationalized Programs

Now that we've described the basic internationalization and localization concepts and API, we present a list of internationalization dos and don'ts.

First the dos:

- Call `setlocale` at the beginning of the `main` function to initialize the language and cultural conventions.
- Make sure that the software is 8-bit clean. Software that is 8-bit clean does not modify the most significant bit of 8-bit bytes.
- Be wary of sign-extension problems; by default, characters are signed when using Sun's compilers or `gcc`.
- Use standard codesets, for example, ISO Latin-1.
- Use the functions described in the `ctype` man page to identify character ranges (we described most of these functions in Chapter 3).
- Remember that many countries use a comma as the decimal separator.
- When printing date and time values, use `strftime` and `cftime` in favour of `ctime`.
- Use the `localeconv` function if local currency formats must be obtained.
- Replace calls to `strcmp` with `strcoll`, unless the strings compared a number of times. In this case, transform the strings using `strxfrm` before comparing them with `strcmp`.
- Rather than just printing user message strings using `printf`, surround them with calls to `gettext`, and create separate message files for each locale. Using this approach avoids the costly maintenance issues that arise when several source trees (one for each locale) are used.
- The buffers required for user messages may change in size after translation, so plan accordingly.
- Where possible, provide translation notes (using comments in the code).
- If there are formatted strings that need to be localized, make sure that all fields are documented. For example, translating the string "%d records deleted" is easy, but translating "%d records %s" is impossible. Adding a comment that the "%s" can become either "deleted" or "inserted" makes the string translatable again.

And now the don'ts:

- Split user message strings; write out whole messages instead.
- Embed graphics in code.
- Use acronyms, abbreviations, or jargon.
- Make assumptions about the order of words in strings.

- Make assumptions about the number of bytes or characters in user messages.
- Test for alphabetic characters by comparing specific characters—for example, "A" and "Z".
- Hard code the decimal character in parsing or calculations.
- Hard code or limit the size of currency and date fields.
- Assume the size of paper on which application output will be printed.
- In menu-driven programs, don't use single-letter commands to represent the first letter of commands (for example, using "q" for "quit").
- Combine the use of different message catalogue schemes. In other words, don't mix the use of `gettext` with either `catgets` or `gettxt`; chose one and use it consistently throughout a program.

Neither of these lists is intended to be complete; they are intended more as "food for thought" to illustrate the sorts of things writers of internationalized software need to think about.

A.11 Summary

In this appendix we've taken a *very* brief look at internationalization and localization. Internationalization is the engineering process of making software portable between languages and regions, and localization is the translation process of adopting software for a specific region or language (i.e., a locale).

We described the six localization categories and how we can create message catalogues for a given locale. We then described the `gettext` API, which is used to retrieve messages for a specific locale from the message catalogue. We followed our description of the API with an internationalized version of the ubiquitous "Hello, World" program.

Finally, we rounded up the appendix with a look at the string collation functions `strcoll` and `strxfrm`, and presented a checklist for writing internationalized programs.

Internationalization and localization is a large and complicated subject. We've only had the briefest of looks at it in this appendix; readers interested in all the gory details are referred to [Tuthill and Smallberg 1997] and [Sun Microsystems 2002c].

Appendix B

The BSD Source
Compatibility Package

B.1 Introduction

As we mentioned in Chapter 2, early versions of SunOS were based on versions of the University of California at Berkeley's flavour of UNIX, called BSD. SVR4, which begat Solaris, includes functionality and APIs from 4.3BSD. Also, binary and source compatibility are very important to Sun and its customers, so to this day Solaris ships with the *BSD Source Compatibility Package* (SCP). The SCP contains the tools, libraries, and header files that weren't merged into the core SVR4 code. Some of these may have SVR4 namesakes that have different functionality. The intention is that old code written to the old BSD interfaces should still be able to be compiled and run on contemporary versions of Solaris. New code should eschew the BSD interfaces in the SCP in favour of the more standard interfaces provided by Solaris.

The SCP is installed into three directories:

- The directory /usr/ucb contains the commands that were located in the /usr/bin, /usr/etc, and /usr/ucb directories under SunOS 4.x. Some Sun old-timers still prefer to place /usr/ucb before /usr/bin in their PATH to get the old pre-Solaris behaviour.

- The /usr/ucbinclude directory contains the header files that were in /usr/include under SunOS 4.x.

- The directory /usr/ucblib contains the libraries that were installed in /usr/lib under SunOS 4.x. These libraries contain the BSD implementation of the functions and system calls provided as part of the SCP. Programs wanting to use the BSD interfaces must be linked with the libraries in this directory.

A number of packages must be installed before applications can use the SCP. These are as follows:

- The SCP utilities and libraries are in SUNWscpu; SUNWscpux must also be installed if 64-bit support is required.
- If archive libraries are required (for static linking), SUNWsra must be installed.
- To compile new programs that use the SCP, the header files must be available. Installing the package SUNWsrh accomplishes this.

(Starting with Solaris 10, SUNWscpux is no longer required for 64-bit support. This is because the 32-bit and 64-bit libraries and utilities have been merged into one package.)

We use the SCP compiler, /usr/ucb/cc, when we want to build C programs using the SCP. (Actually, /usr/ucb/cc is not a complier in itself. It is a wrapper script that runs the unbundled C compiler, passing it the appropriate options to use the SCP headers and libraries.)

The SCP compiler wrapper script sets up the compiler's environment so that the following directories are searched in order:

- User-specified include files and libraries
- The include files and libraries provided by the SCP
- The include files and libraries supplied by the base Solaris installation

Although using the SCP can help us port old applications to Solaris (and enable us to run old applications that have not been updated), using it to develop new code is not recommended for the following reasons:

- The system administrator may not have installed the SCP on every system the application is to be run on. In this case, the application will not execute, because of missing libraries.

- Even if it is installed, programs running under the SCP may suffer a performance degradation. This is because some of the system calls and library functions supplied are emulated, using the base Solaris functionality. Although the cost of this emulation is likely to be small, frequently used functions can suffer a significant accumulated performance penalty.

  Another reason for performance degradation with applications using the SCP is that the majority of Sun's engineering resources are dedicated to enhancing the base software. Performance issues with the SCP aren't likely to be a high priority.

- The SCP is intended to be only a transition tool to aid in the porting of programs from SunOS 4.x to Solaris. As the latter matures and improves, and as the need to support old SunOS 4.x applications diminishes, it is possible (although unlikely, given Sun's commitment to backwards compatibility) that the SCP might be removed from future releases of Solaris.

- Many of the APIs provided by Solaris are more standard than their SunOS 4.x counterparts. By using these more standard interfaces, the portability of our programs is improved.

- It is possible that programs compiled with the SCP will be incompatible with libraries not in the SCP, and hence will fail to run (despite linking without errors). Indeed, the manual pages for functions in the SCP go so far as to state the following: "Use of these interfaces should be restricted to only applications written on BSD platforms. Use of these interfaces with any of the system libraries or in multithreaded applications is unsupported".

None of the examples in this text depend on the SCP, and we strongly discourage its use in new applications.

B.2   Functions That Have Been Removed from the SCP

In Solaris 2.5, a number of functions were removed from the SCP and placed into either `libc` or one of the other base Solaris libraries. We can consider some of these functions as being obsolescent; the others are not. We should avoid functions in the former category, but those in the latter are safe to use.

B.2.1 Obsolescent SCP-Originated Functions

Although these SCP-originated functions are now supported by Sun, some of them are not supported by various standards, or are deprecated in others. For example, `ftime` is not supported by POSIX, and `bcmp`, `bcopy`, and `bzero` are included in the SUSv3's Legacy Option Group (so they may not be available on all platforms that conform to this standard). For this reason, we can consider these functions as being obsolescent.

We now describe these functions, reiterating our warning that new applications should avoid them if possible in favour of their more standard alternatives.

The `bcmp` Function

The `bcmp` function is used to compare two byte arrays.

```
#include <strings.h>

int bcmp (const void *s1, const void *s2, size_t n);
                                         Returns: 0 if the arrays match, 1 otherwise
```

The `bcmp` function is similar to `memcmp` in that it compares the first n bytes of $s1$ and $s2$ for equivalence. The difference between `bcmp` and `memcmp` is that the former only returns an indication of the equality of the two memory arrays. Both arrays are assumed to have a size of n bytes; if n is equal to 0, `bcmp` always returns 0.

The `bcopy` Function

The bcopy function is used to copy memory arrays.

```
#include <strings.h>

void bcopy (const void *src, void *dst, size_t n);
```

The bcopy function copies *n* bytes from the byte array pointed to by *src* to the buffer pointed to by *dst*. Like memmove, bcopy also handles overlapping buffers correctly.

Notice that bcopy's arguments are backwards compared with memcpy and memmove. In other words,

```
bcopy (src, dst, n);
```

is the same as

```
memmove (dst, src, n);
```

The `bzero` Function

The bzero function is used to initialize a byte array to 0.

```
#include <strings.h>

void bzero (void *s, size_t n);
```

The bzero function is similar to the memset function we described in Section 3.3.4, except the first *n* bytes in the byte array pointed to by *s* are initialized to 0. In other words,

```
bzero (s, n);
```

is the same as

```
memset (s, 0, n);
```

The `ftime` Function

We can use the ftime function to get the current time and time zone.

```
#include <sys/timeb.h>

int ftime (struct timeb *tp);
```
                                                                    Returns: 0 if OK, −1 on error

The ftime function fills the members of the timeb structure pointed to by *tp* with the current time and time zone information. The timeb structure has the following members:

```
struct timeb {
    time_t          time;       /* Number of seconds and */
    unsigned short  millitm;    /* milliseconds since the epoch */
    short           timezone;   /* Timezone, minutes West of UTC */
    short           dstflag;    /* Daylight savings in effect? */
};
```

The `ftime` man page says that the contents of the `timezone` and `dstflag` members are unspecified after a successful call, but tests on one of the author's systems indicate that they are correctly set. Having said that, although `ftime` can be used to obtain time zone information, the `tzset` function we described in Section 6.5 is a better choice.

The `getwd` Function

An application can determine its current working directory by calling `getwd`.

```
#include <unistd.h>

char *getwd (char *path_name);

                        Returns: pointer to current working directory if OK, NULL on error
```

The `getwd` function copies the absolute pathname of the current working directory into the buffer pointed to by *path_name*. If the length of the current working directory's pathname exceeds PATH_MAX + 1 bytes, `getwd` fails and returns a NULL pointer.

Upon success, a pointer to *path_name* is returned. Otherwise, a NULL pointer is returned, and the contents of *path_name* are undefined.

New applications should use the `getcwd` function described in Section 10.24 rather than this function.

The `index` and `rindex` Functions

We can find the first or last occurrence of a character in a string by calling `index` or `rindex` respectively.

```
#include <strings.h>

char *index (const char *s, int c);

char *rindex (const char *s, int c);

                        Both return: see text if OK, NULL on error
```

The `index` function returns a pointer to the first occurrence of the character c in the NUL-terminated string pointed to by s. Conversely, `rindex` returns a pointer to the last occurrence of the character c in the NUL-terminated string pointed to by s.

Both functions return a NULL pointer if c does not occur in s.

New applications should use the `strchr` function in preference to `index`; similarly, `strrchr` should be used instead of `rindex`.

The `ualarm` Function

We can generate alarms with subsecond granularity by calling `ualarm`.

```
#include <unistd.h>

useconds_t ualarm (useconds_t useconds , useconds_t interval) ;
```
                          Returns: the previous number of remaining alarm clock microseconds

The `ualarm` function arranges for the `SIGALRM` signal to be sent to the calling process after *useconds* microseconds of real time have elapsed. If the *interval* argument is not 0, then repeated timeout notifications will occur periodically at *interval* microsecond intervals. We should be aware that because of scheduling delays, resumption of the process when the signal is caught may be delayed by an arbitrary amount of time.

The `ualarm` function is a simplified interface to the `setitimer` function we discuss in Section 17.14, and uses the `ITIMER_REAL` interval timer.

The `usleep` Function

We can use the `usleep` function to suspend a process for less than a second.

```
#include <unistd.h>

int usleep (useconds_t useconds) ;
```
                                                        Returns: 0 if OK, −1 on error

Calling the `usleep` function will suspend the calling process for at least *useconds* microseconds by using the process' realtime interval timer. The actual time may be longer than specified because of other system activity, the granularity of the system clock, or the overhead in processing the function. Setting *useconds* to 0 has no effect, and a value of 1,000,000 or more will result in an error.

Each process has only one realtime interval timer, and the `usleep` function will not interfere with a previous setting of it. If *useconds* is greater than or equal to the timer's previous setting, the process will be woken up shortly before the timer was set to expire.

The results of mixing calls to `usleep` and either `alarm` or `sleep` are undefined.

New applications should use the `setitimer` function we discuss in Section 17.14. (Another alternative is the `nanosleep` function from the realtime library. In some circumstances, `nanosleep` is better than `setitimer`, because the former has no effect on the action or blockage of any signal.)

Summary of Obsolescent Functions

Figure B.1 summarizes the SCP-originated obsolescent functions, showing their recommended replacements and the section in which the preferred function is described.

SCP function	Recommended replacement	Section
bcmp	memcmp	3.4.1
bcopy	memmove	3.4.2
bzero	memset	3.4.4
ftime	time or tzset	6.3 or 6.5
getwd	getcwd	10.24
index	strchr	3.3.5
rindex	strrchr	3.3.5
ualarm	setitimer	17.14
usleep	setitimer or nanosleep	17.14

Figure B.1   Obsolescent SCP-originated functions.

B.2.2 SCP-Originated Functions That Are Not Obsolescent

In the preceding section, we described the SCP functions that should be avoided in new software because of their obsolescence. In this section, we'll mention some of the functions that can be safely used (the few functions we don't mention are not within the scope of this text). We consider these functions as being not obsolescent because they are specified by one or more industry standards (e.g., the SUS or POSIX), or because they are *not* specified by a standard, and therefore haven't been categorized as being obsolescent. (Functions that aren't specified by a standard are not necessarily portable, but not being portable is not the same thing as being obsolescent.)

Despite their origin in the SCP, the functions we list here are described elsewhere in this text. (Many other SCP functions have namesakes in the standard Solaris libraries, although these functions have different interfaces and functionality. We do not discuss the SCP version of these functions in this text.)

The non-obsolescent SCP derived functions are briefly described here:

getdtablesize   Gets the file descriptor table size (described in Section 8.4)

gethostid   Gets an identifier for the current host (described in Section 8.2)

gethostname   Gets the name of the current host (described in Section 8.2)

getpagesize   Gets the system page size (described in Section 8.3)

getpriority   Gets the process scheduling priority

getrusage	Gets the resource usage information for the calling process or its children (described in Section 8.7)
killpg	Sends a signal to a process group (described in Section 17.12)
reboot	Reboots or halts the processor
setbuffer	Assigns a buffer to a file stream (described in Section 5.11)
sethostname	Sets the name of the current host (described in Section 8.2)
setlinebuf	Sets a file stream to line buffered (described in Section 5.11)
setpriority	Sets the process scheduling priority
setregid	Sets the real and effective group IDs (described in Section 7.4)
setreuid	Sets the real and effective user IDs (described in Section 7.3)

The preceding list does not contain all of the SCP originated non-obsolescent functions; the few that are missing are beyond the scope of this text.

Summary of Non-Obsolescent Functions

Figure B.2 summarizes the SCP-originated non-obsolescent functions, showing a possible replacement for those functions that aren't specified by an industry standard. If an alternative function is suggested, the section in which that function is described is also shown.

SCP function	Possible alternative	Section
getdtablesize	getrlimit (RLIMIT_NOFILE)	8.4
gethostid	Standard	
gethostname	Standard	
getpagesize	sysconf (_SC_PAGESIZE)	8.3
getpriority	Standard	
getrusage	Standard	
killpg	Standard	
reboot	uadmin	N/A
setbuffer	setbuf	5.11
sethostname	sysinfo (SI_SET_HOSTNAME)	8.2
setlinebuf	setvbuf (_IOLBF)	5.11
setpriority	Standard	
setregid	Standard	
setreuid	Standard	

Figure B.2 SCP-originated functions that are not obsolescent.

If the word "Standard" appears in the second column of Figure B.2, it means that the function in the first column is specified by one or more industry standards.

B.3   Summary

In this appendix we described the BSD SCP. The SCP provides us with the tools, libraries, and header files required to build and execute applications that use the BSD API.

In Solaris 2.5, many functions in the SCP were subsumed into the standard base libraries (presumably, this was at least partially done to align with various industry standards). Some of these functions can be considered as being obsolescent, while others are not. We described the obsolescent functions and stated which functions should be used instead in new applications.

The functions we do not consider obsolescent are described elsewhere in this text, so we just summarized them in this appendix.

Appendix C

Function Summary

C.1 Introduction

This appendix summarizes each of the functions we describe in the text, except for those that we wrote ourselves. It consists of two sections:

- A list of all the function prototypes.
- A list summarizing the availability of the functions, by Solaris release and standard.

C.2 Function Prototypes

This section contains a list of the function prototypes for each function, which contains the required header files, the return value (if any), and the page number containing the description of the function.

Where a POSIX and non-POSIX version of the function is available, only the POSIX function prototype is shown.

```
void _exit (int status);
    <unistd.h>
    This function never returns
```
605

```
void _longjmp (jmp_buf env, int val);
    <setjmp.h>
    This function never returns
```
625

```
int _setjmp (jmp_buf env);                                                       625
    <setjmp.h>
    Returns: 0 if called directly, non-zero if returning from a call to _longjmp

int _tolower (int c);                                                            63
    <ctype.h>
    Returns: the lower case letter corresponding to the argument

int _toupper (int c);                                                            63
    <ctype.h>
    Returns: the upper case letter corresponding to the argument

void abort (void);                                                               776
    <stdlib.h>
    This function never returns

int access (const char *path, int amode);                                        365
    <unistd.h>
    Returns: 0 if OK, −1 on error

int acl (char *pathp, int cmd, int nentries, aclent_t *aclbufp);                 581
    <sys/acl.h>
    Returns: 0 or number of ACLs if OK, −1 on error

int aclcheck (aclent_t *aclbufp, int nentries, int *which);                      584
    <sys/acl.h>
    Returns: 0 if OK, non-zero on error

int aclfrommode (aclent_t *aclbufp, int nentries, mode_t *modep);                589
    <sys/types.h>
    <sys/acl.h>
    Returns: 0 if OK, −1 on error

aclent_t *aclfromtext (char *aclextp, int *aclcnt);                              582
    <sys/acl.h>
    Returns: a pointer to the list of ACL entries if OK, NULL on error

int aclsort (int nentries, int calclass, aclent_t *aclbufp);                     589
    <sys/acl.h>
    Returns: 0 if OK, −1 on error

int acltomode (aclent_t *aclbufp, int nentries, mode_t *modep);                  589
    <sys/types.h>
    <sys/acl.h>
    Returns: 0 if OK, −1 on error

char *acltotext (aclent_t *aclbufp, int *aclcnt);                                582
    <sys/acl.h>
    Returns: a pointer to the ACL string if OK, NULL on error
```

int **adjtime** (struct timeval *delta*, struct timeval *olddelta*);   206

    <sys/time.h>

    Returns: 0 if OK, −1 on error

int **aiocancel** (aio_result_t *resultp*);   553

    <sys/asynch.h>

    Returns: 0 if OK, −1 on error

int **aioread** (int *fildes*, char *bufp*, int *bufs*, off_t *offset*, int *whence*,   551
    aio_result_t *resultp*);

    <sys/types.h>
    <sys/asynch.h>

    Returns: 0 if OK, −1 on error

aio_result_t ***aiowait** (const struct timeval *timeout*);   552

    <sys/asynch.h>
    <sys/time.h>

    Returns: a pointer to the result if OK, 0 if the timeout expires, or −1 on error

int **aiowrite** (int *fildes*, const char *bufp*, int *bufs*, off_t *offset*, int *whence*,   551
    aio_result_t *resultp*);

    <sys/types.h>
    <sys/asynch.h>

    Returns: 0 if OK, −1 on error

unsigned int **alarm** (unsigned int *sec*);   734

    <unistd.h>

    Returns: the previous number of remaining alarm clock seconds

void ***alloca** (size_t *size*);   99

    <stdlib.h>

    Returns: a pointer to the allocated memory if OK, NULL on error

int **ascftime** (char *s*, const char *format*, const struct tm *timeptr*);   214

    <time.h>

    Returns: the number of bytes copied

char ***asctime** (const struct tm *tm*);   213

    <time.h>

    Returns: a pointer to the converted time if OK, NULL on error

char ***asctime_r** (const struct tm *tm*, char *buf*);   213

    <time.h>

    Returns: a pointer to the converted time if OK, NULL on error

void **assert** (int *expression*);   118

    <assert.h>

int **atexit** (void (*_func_) (void));   606
    <stdlib.h>
    Returns: 0 if OK, non-zero on error

double **atof** (const char *_str_);   90
    <stdlib.h>
    Returns: the converted number

int **atoi** (const char *_str_);   90
    <stdlib.h>
    Returns: the converted number

long **atol** (const char *_str_);   90
    <stdlib.h>
    Returns: the converted number

long long **atoll** (const char *_str_);   90
    <stdlib.h>
    Returns: the converted number

int **attropen** (const char *_path_, const char *_attrpath_, int _oflag_, /* mode_t _mode_ */...);   592
    <sys/types.h>
    <sys/stat.h>
    <fcntl.h>
    Returns: file descriptor if OK, −1 on error

char ***basename** (char *_path_);   354
    <libgen.h>
    Returns: a pointer to the final component of _path_

int **bcmp** (const void *_s1_, const void *_s2_, size_t _n_);   1049
    <strings.h>
    Returns: 0 if the arrays match, 1 otherwise

void **bcopy** (const void *_s1_, void *_s2_, size_t _n_);   1050
    <strings.h>

char ***bindtextdomain** (const char *_domainname_, const char *_dirname_);   1041
    <libintl.h>
    Returns: _dirname_ or current binding if _domainname_ is not NULL, NULL otherwise

int **brk** (void *_endds_);   618
    <unistd.h>
    Returns: 0 if OK, −1 on error

size_t **bufsplit** (char *_buf_, size_t _n_, char **_a_);   83
    <libgen.h>
    Returns: the number of tokens assigned to _a_ if _buf_ is not NULL, 0 otherwise

```
void bzero (void *s, size_t n);                                              1050
    <strings.h>

void *calloc (size_t nelem, size_t elsize);                                    97
    <stdlib.h>
    Returns: a pointer to the allocated memory if OK, NULL on error

speed_t cfgetispeed (const struct termios *termios_p);                        485
    <termios.h>
    Returns: a representation of the input baud rate

speed_t cfgetospeed (const struct termios *termios_p);                        485
    <termios.h>
    Returns: a representation of the output baud rate

int cfsetispeed (struct termios *termios_p, speed_t speed);                   485
    <termios.h>
    Returns: 0 if OK, −1 on error

int cfsetospeed (struct termios *termios_p, speed_t speed);                   485
    <termios.h>
    Returns: 0 if OK, −1 on error

int cftime (char *s, char *format, const time_t *clock);                      214
    <time.h>
    Returns: the number of bytes copied

int chdir (const char *path);                                                404
    <unistd.h>
    Returns: 0 if OK, −1 on error

int chmod (const char *path, mode_t mode);                                    368
    <sys/types.h>
    <sys/stat.h>
    Returns: 0 if OK, −1 on error

int chown (const char *path, uid_t owner, gid_t group);                       371
    <unistd.h>
    <sys/types.h>
    Returns: 0 if OK, −1 on error

int chroot (const char *path);                                               406
    <unistd.h>
    Returns: 0 if OK, −1 on error

void clearerr (FILE *stream);                                                169
    <stdio.h>
```

```
clock_t clock (void);                                              322
    <time.h>
    Returns: the CPU time used since the first call to clock if OK, -1 on error

int close (int fildes);                                           127
    <unistd.h>
    Returns: 0 if OK, -1 on error

int closedir (DIR *dirp);                                         396
    <sys/types.h>
    <dirent.h>
    Returns: 0 if OK, -1 on error

void closefrom (int lowfd);                                       128
    <stdlib.h>

void closelog (void);                                             814
    <syslog.h>

int creat (const char *path, int oflag, mode_t mode);             126
    <sys/types.h>
    <sys/stat.h>
    <fcntl.h>
    Returns: file descriptor if OK, -1 on error

char *crypt (const char *key, const char *salt);                  251
    <unistd.h>
    Returns: the encrypted password if OK, NULL on error

char *crypt_gensalt (const char *oldsalt, const struct passwd *userinfo);   252
    <crypt.h>
    Returns: a pointer to the new salt if OK, NULL on error

char *ctermid (char *s);                                          488
    <stdio.h>
    Returns: a pointer to the pathname of the controlling terminal

char *ctermid_r (char *s);                                        488
    <stdio.h>
    Returns: a pointer to the pathname of the controlling terminal if s is not NULL, NULL otherwise

char *ctime (const time_t *clock);                                213
    <time.h>
    Returns: a pointer to the converted time

char *ctime_r (const time_t *clock, char *buf);                   213
    <time.h>
    Returns: a pointer to the converted time if OK, NULL on failure
```

char **cuserid** (char *s);   226

    <stdio.h>

    Returns: a pointer to the username that the owner of the calling process is logged in as

char **dcgettext** (const char *domainname, const char *msgid, int category);   1042

    <libintl.h>
    <locale.h>

    Returns: message string if OK, msgid on error

char **dgettext** (const char *domainname, const char *msgid);   1042

    <libintl.h>

    Returns: message string if OK, msgid on error

double **difftime** (time_t time1, time_t time2);   205

    <time.h>

    Returns: the difference between the two times

int **directio** (int fildes, int advice);   155

    <sys/types.h>
    <sys/fcntl.h>

    Returns: 0 if OK, −1 on error

char **dirname** (char *path);   354

    <libgen.h>

    Returns: a pointer to the parent directory of path

int **door_bind** (int did);   978

    <door.h>

    Returns: 0 if OK, −1 on error

int **door_call** (int d, door_arg_t *params);   955

    <door.h>

    Returns: 0 if OK, −1 on error

int **door_create** (void (*server_procedure) (void *cookie, char *argp,   953
        size_t arg_size, door_desc_t *dp, uint_t n_desc), void *cookie, uint_t attributes);

    <door.h>

    Returns: door descriptor if OK, −1 on error

int **door_cred** (door_cred_t *info);   968

    <door.h>

    Returns: 0 if OK, −1 on error

int **door_info** (int d, struct door_info *info);   970

    <door.h>

    Returns: 0 if OK, −1 on error

int **door_return** (char *$data\_ptr$, size_t $data\_size$, door_desc_t *$desc\_ptr$,   956
    uint_t num_desc);
    <door.h>
    Returns: does not return if OK, −1 on error

int **door_revoke** (int d);   957
    <door.h>
    Returns: 0 if OK, −1 on error

door_server_func_t **door_server_create** (door_server_func_t *$create\_func$);   978
    <door.h>
    typedef void door_server_func_t (door_info_t *);
    Returns: a pointer to the previous server creation function

int **door_unbind** (void);   978
    <door.h>
    Returns: 0 if OK, −1 on error

int **dup** (int $fildes$);   140
    <unistd.h>
    Returns: new file descriptor if OK, −1 on error

int **dup2** (int $fildes$, int $fildes2$);   140
    <unistd.h>
    Returns: new file descriptor if OK, −1 on error

void **endgrent** (void);   259
    <grp.h>

void **endpwent** (void);   240
    <pwd.h>

void **endspent** (void);   247
    <pwd.h>

void **endusershell** (void);   270

void **endutxent** (void);   264
    <utmpx.h>

int **execl** (const char *$path$, const char *$arg0$, ..., const char *$argn$,   655
    char * /* NULL */);
    <unistd.h>
    Returns: does not return if OK, −1 on error

int **execle** (const char *$path$, const char *$arg0$, ..., const char *$argn$,   656
    char * /* NULL */, char * const $envp$ []);
    <unistd.h>
    Returns: does not return if OK, −1 on error

int **execlp** (const char *_file_, const char *_arg0_, ..., const char *_argn_,   656
    char * /* NULL */);
    <unistd.h>
    Returns: does not return if OK, −1 on error

int **execv** (const char *_path_, char * const _envp_ []);   655
    <unistd.h>
    Returns: does not return if OK, −1 on error

int **execve** (const char *_path_, char * const _argv_ [], char * const _envp_ []);   656
    <unistd.h>
    Returns: does not return if OK, −1 on error

int **execvp** (const char *_file_, char * const _envp_ []);   657
    <unistd.h>
    Returns: does not return if OK, −1 on error

void **exit** (int _status_);   605
    <stdlib.h>
    This function never returns

int **facl** (int _fildes_, int _cmd_, int _nentries_, aclent_t *_aclbufp_);   581
    <sys/acl.h>
    Returns: 0 or number of ACLs if OK, −1 on error

int **fattach** (int _fildes_, const char *_path_);   938
    <stropts.h>
    Returns: 0 if OK, −1 on error

int **fchdir** (int _fildes_);   404
    <unistd.h>
    Returns: 0 if OK, −1 on error

int **fchmod** (int _fildes_, mode_t _mode_);   368
    <sys/types.h>
    <sys/stat.h>
    Returns: 0 if OK, −1 on error

int **fchown** (int _fildes_, uid_t _owner_, gid_t _group_);   371
    <unistd.h>
    <sys/types.h>
    Returns: 0 if OK, −1 on error

int **fchownat** (int _fildes_, const char *_path_, uid_t _owner_, gid_t _group_, int _flag_);   596
    <unistd.h>
    <sys/types.h>
    Returns: 0 if OK, −1 on error

int **fchroot** (int *fildes*);   406
    <unistd.h>
    Returns: 0 if OK, −1 on error

int **fclose** (FILE *stream*);   163
    <stdio.h>
    Returns: 0 if OK, −1 on error

int **fcntl** (int *fildes*, int *cmd*, /* *arg* */...);   142
    <sys/types.h>
    <sys/stat.h>
    <fcntl.h>
    Returns: depends on *cmd* if OK, −1 on error

void **FD_CLR** (int *fd*, fd_set *fdset*);   539
    <sys/time.h>

int **FD_ISSET** (int *fd*, fd_set *fdset*);   539
    <sys/time.h>
    Returns: non-zero if *fd* is in *fdset*, 0 otherwise

void **FD_SET** (int *fd*, fd_set *fdset*);   539
    <sys/time.h>

void **FD_ZERO** (int *fd*);   539
    <sys/time.h>

int **fdetach** (const char *path*);   938
    <stropts.h>
    Returns: 0 if OK, −1 on error

FILE *****fdopen** (int *fildes*, const char *mode*);   163
    <stdio.h>
    Returns: file pointer if OK, NULL on error

DIR *****fdopendir** (int *fildes*);   393
    <sys/types.h>
    <dirent.h>
    Returns: pointer to a DIR object if OK, NULL on error

int **fdwalk** (int (*func*) (void *cd*, int *fd*), void *cd*);   154
    <stdlib.h>
    Returns: the last result from *func*, 0 if *func* was never called

int **feof** (FILE *stream*);   169
    <stdio.h>
    Returns: non-zero if EOF has been detected on *stream*, 0 otherwise

int **ferror** (FILE *stream);   168

    <stdio.h>

    Returns: non-zero if an error has occurred on *stream*, 0 otherwise

int **fflush** (FILE *stream);   194

    <stdio.h>

    Returns: 0 if OK, –1 on error

int **ffs** (const int *i*);   93

    <strings.h>

    Returns: the index of the first bit set, 0 if *i* is 0

int **fgetc** (FILE *stream);   164

    <stdio.h>

    Returns: the next available character, EOF on end of file or error

struct group ***fgetgrent** (FILE *f*);   261

    <grp.h>

    Returns: a pointer if OK, NULL on end of enumeration or error

struct group ***fgetgrent_r** (FILE *f*, struct group *grp*, char *buffer*, int *bufsize*);   261

    <grp.h>

    Returns: a pointer if OK, NULL on end of enumeration or error

int **fgetpos** (FILE *stream*, fpos_t *pos*);   184

    <stdio.h>

    Returns: 0 if OK, non-zero on error

struct passwd ***fgetpwent** (FILE *f*);   242

    <pwd.h>

    Returns: a pointer if OK, NULL on end of enumeration or error

struct passwd ***fgetpwent_r** (FILE *f*, struct passwd *pwd*, char *buffer*, int *bufsize*);   242

    <pwd.h>

    Returns: a pointer if OK, NULL on end of enumeration or error

char ***fgets** (char *s*, int *n*, FILE *stream*);   166

    <stdio.h>

    Returns: *s* if OK, NULL on error

struct spwd ***fgetspent** (FILE *fp*);   249

    <shadow.h>

    Returns: a pointer if OK, NULL on end of enumeration or error

struct spwd ***fgetspent_r** (FILE *fp*, struct spwd *result*, char *buffer*, int *buflen*);   249

    <shadow.h>

    Returns: a pointer if OK, NULL on end of enumeration or error

```
int fileno (FILE *stream);                                                  169
    <stdio.h>
    Returns: file descriptor associated with stream if OK, –1 on error

void flockfile (FILE *stream);                                              186
    <stdio.h>

FILE *fopen (const char *filename, const char *mode);                       161
    <stdio.h>
    Returns: file pointer if OK, NULL on error

pid_t fork (void);                                                          631
    <sys/types.h>
    <unistd.h>
    Returns: 0 in child, process ID of child in parent, –1 on error

pid_t fork1 (void);                                                         631
    <sys/types.h>
    <unistd.h>
    Returns: 0 in child, process ID of child in parent, –1 on error

long fpathconf (int fildes, int name);                                      292
    <unistd.h>
    Returns: corresponding value if OK, –1 on error

int fprintf (FILE *stream, const char *format, /* args */...);              170
    <stdio.h>
    Returns: number of bytes output if OK, negative value on error

int fputc (int c, FILE *stream);                                            165
    <stdio.h>
    Returns: the character written if OK, EOF on error

int fputs (const char *s, FILE *stream);                                    167
    <stdio.h>
    Returns: the number of bytes written if OK, EOF on error

int fread (void *ptr, size_t size, size_t nitems, FILE *stream);            167
    <stdio.h>
    Returns: the number of items read

void free (void *ptr);                                                       99
    <stdlib.h>

FILE *freopen (const char *filename, const char *mode, FILE *stream);       162
    <stdio.h>
    Returns: file pointer if OK, NULL on error
```

```
int fscanf (FILE *stream, const char *format, ...);
    <stdio.h>
    Returns: number of successfully matched items if OK, EOF on error
```
172

```
int fseek (FILE *stream, long offset, int whence);
    <stdio.h>
    Returns: 0 if OK, -1 on error
```
184

```
int fseeko (FILE *stream, off_t offset, int whence);
    <stdio.h>
    Returns: 0 if OK, -1 on error
```
184

```
int fsetpos (FILE *stream, const fpos_t *pos);
    <stdio.h>
    Returns: 0 if OK, -1 on error
```
185

```
int fstat (int fildes, struct stat *buf);
    <sys/types.h>
    <sys/stat.h>
    Returns: 0 if OK, -1 on error
```
356

```
int fstatat (int fildes, const char *path, struct stat *buf, int flag);
    <unistd.h>
    <sys/types.h>
    Returns: 0 if OK, -1 on error
```
594

```
int fstatvfs (int fildes, struct statvfs *buf);
    <sys/types.h>
    <sys/statvfs.h>
    Returns: 0 if OK, -1 on error
```
439

```
int fsync (int fildes);
    <unistd.h>
    Returns: 0 if OK, -1 on error
```
410

```
long ftell (FILE *stream);
    <stdio.h>
    Returns: the current file offset if OK, -1 on error
```
184

```
off_t ftello (FILE *stream);
    <stdio.h>
    Returns: the current file offset if OK, -1 on error
```
184

```
int ftime (struct timeb *tp);
    <sys/timeb.h>
    Returns: 0 if OK, -1 on error
```
1050

```
key_t ftok (const char *path, int id);                                    868
```
  `<sys/ipc.h>`
  Returns: an IPC key if OK, −1 on error

```
int ftruncate (int fildes, off_t length);                                 373
```
  `<unistd.h>`
  Returns: 0 if OK, −1 on error

```
int ftrylockfile (FILE *stream);                                          186
```
  `<stdio.h>`
  Returns: 0 if OK, non-zero if the lock couldn't be acquired

```
int ftw (const char *path, int (*fn) (const char *, const struct stat *, int),   399
      int depth);
```
  `<ftw.h>`
  Returns: 0 if tree is exhausted, value returned by *fn* if it is non-zero, −1 on error

```
void funlockfile (FILE *stream);                                          186
```
  `<stdio.h>`

```
int futimesat (int fildes, const char *path, struct timeval times [2]);   597
```
  `<sys/time.h>`
  Returns: 0 if OK, −1 on error

```
int fwrite (const void *ptr, size_t size, size_t nitems, FILE *stream);   168
```
  `<stdio.h>`
  Returns: the number of items written

```
int getc (FILE *stream);                                                  164
```
  `<stdio.h>`
  Returns: the next available character, EOF on end of file or error

```
int getc_unlocked (FILE *stream);                                         189
```
  `<stdio.h>`
  Returns: the next available character, EOF on end of file or error

```
int getchar (void);                                                       164
```
  `<stdio.h>`
  Returns: the next available character, EOF on end of file or error

```
int getchar_unlocked (void);                                              189
```
  `<stdio.h>`
  Returns: the next available character, EOF on end of file or error

```
char *getcwd (char *buf, size_t size);                                    405
```
  `<unistd.h>`
  Returns: *buf* if OK, NULL on error

```
struct tm *getdate (const char *string);
```
<time.h>
Returns: a pointer to the converted time if OK, NULL on error

221

```
int getdtablesize (void);
```
<unistd.h>
Returns: the soft file descriptor limit

302

```
gid_t getegid (void);
```
<sys/types.h>
<unistd.h>
Returns: the effective group ID of the calling process

232

```
char *getenv (const char *name);
```
<stdlib.h>
Returns: a pointer to the value associated with *name* if OK, NULL if not found

611

```
uid_t geteuid (void);
```
<sys/types.h>
<unistd.h>
Returns: the effective user ID of the calling process

228

```
const char *getexecname (void);
```
<stdlib.h>
Returns: a pointer to the executable's pathname if OK, NULL on error

609

```
int getextmntent (FILE *fp, struct extmnttab *mp, int len);
```
<stdio.h>
<sys/mnttab.h>
Returns: 0 if OK, −1 on EOF, MNT_TOOLONG, MNT_TOOMANY, or MNT_TOOFEW on error

420

```
gid_t getgid (void);
```
<sys/types.h>
<unistd.h>
Returns: the real group ID of the calling process

232

```
struct group *getgrent (void);
```
<grp.h>
Returns: a pointer if OK, NULL on end of enumeration or error

259

```
struct group *getgrent_r (struct group *grp, char *buffer, int bufsize);
```
<grp.h>
Returns: a pointer if OK, NULL on end of enumeration or error

259

```
struct group *getgrgid (gid_t gid);
```
<grp.h>
Returns: a pointer if OK, NULL on error

258

int **getgrgid_r** (gid_t *gid*, struct group **grp*, char **buffer*, size_t *bufsize*,   258
      struct group ***result*);

  <grp.h>

  Returns: 0 if OK, error number on error

struct group ****getgrnam** (const char **name*);   257

  <grp.h>

  Returns: a pointer if OK, NULL on error

int **getgrnam_r** (const char **name*, struct group **grp*, char **buffer*, size_t *bufsize*,   257
      struct group ***result*);

  <grp.h>

  Returns: 0 if OK, error number on error

int **getgroups** (int *gidsetsize*, gid_t **grouplist*);   234

  <unistd.h>

  Returns: number of supplementary groups if OK, −1 on error

long **gethostid** (void);   282

  <unistd.h>

  Returns: the host's hostid

int **gethostname** (char **name*, int *namelen*);   282

  <unistd.h>

  Returns: 0 if OK, −1 on error

hrtime_t **gethrtime** (void);   204

  <sys/time.h>

  Returns: the number of nanoseconds since the timer started

hrtime_t **gethrvtime** (void);   204

  <sys/time.h>

  Returns: the number of nanoseconds since the timer started

int **getitimer** (int *which*, struct itimerval **value*);   742

  <sys/time.h>

  Returns: 0 if OK, −1 on error

int **getloadavg** (double *loadavg* [], int *nelem*);   334

  <sys/loadavg.h>

  Returns: the number of samples retrieved if OK, −1 on error

char ****getlogin** (void);   224

  <unistd.h>

  Returns: user name if OK, NULL on error

int **getlogin_r** (char **name*, size_t *namesize*);   224

  <unistd.h>

  Returns: 0 if OK, error number on error

int **getmntany** (FILE *fp, struct mnttab *mp, struct mnttab *mpref);   420
    <stdio.h>
    <sys/mnttab.h>
    Returns: 0 if OK, –1 on EOF, MNT_TOOLONG, MNT_TOOMANY, or MNT_TOOFEW on error

int **getmntent** (FILE *fp, struct mnttab *mp);   420
    <stdio.h>
    <sys/mnttab.h>
    Returns: 0 if OK, –1 on EOF, MNT_TOOLONG, MNT_TOOMANY, or MNT_TOOFEW on error

int **getmsg** (int fildes, struct strbuf *ctlptr, struct strbuf *dataptr, int *flagsp);   529
    <stropts.h>
    Returns: non-negative value if OK, –1 on error

int **getopt** (int argc, char * const argv [], const char *optstring);   112
    <unistd.h>
    Returns: the next option character on the command line, –1 when finished

int **getpagesize** (void);   296
    <unistd.h>
    Returns: the current page size

int **getpagesizes** (size_t pagesize [], int nelem);   296
    <sys/mman.h>
    Returns: the number of supported or retrieved page sizes if OK, –1 on error

char ***getpass** (const char *prompt);   250
    <stdlib.h>
    Returns: the password typed if OK, NULL on error

char ***getpassphrase** (const char *prompt);   250
    <stdlib.h>
    Returns: the password typed if OK, NULL on error

pid_t **getpgid** (pid_t pid);   683
    <unistd.h>
    Returns: the process group ID of pid if OK, –1 on error

pid_t **getpgrp** (void);   682
    <unistd.h>
    Returns: the caller's process group ID

pid_t **getpid** (void);   630
    <unistd.h>
    Returns: the caller's process ID

int **getpmsg** (int *fildes*, struct strbuf **ctlptr*, struct strbuf **dataptr*, int **bandp*,   529
    int **flagsp*) ;

    <stropts.h>

    Returns: non-negative value if OK, –1 on error

pid_t **getppid** (void) ;   630

    <unistd.h>

    Returns: the process ID of the caller's parent

struct passwd ****getpwent** (void) ;   240

    <pwd.h>

    Returns: a pointer if OK, NULL on end of enumeration or error

struct passwd ****getpwent_r** (struct passwd **pwd*, char **buffer*, int *buflen*) ;   240

    <pwd.h>

    Returns: a pointer if OK, NULL on end of enumeration or error

struct passwd ****getpwnam** (const char **name*) ;   238

    <pwd.h>

    Returns: a pointer if OK, NULL on error

int **getpwnam_r** (const char **name*, struct passwd **pwd*, char **buffer*, size_t *bufsize*,   238
    struct passwd ***result*) ;

    <pwd.h>

    Returns: 0 if OK, error number on error

struct passwd ****getpwuid** (uid_t *uid*) ;   240

    <pwd.h>

    Returns: a pointer if OK, NULL on error

int **getpwuid_r** (uid_t *uid*, struct passwd **pwd*, char **buffer*, size_t *bufsize*,   240
    struct passwd ***result*) ;

    <pwd.h>

    Returns: 0 if OK, error number on error

int **getrctl** (const char **controlname*, rctlblk_t **old_blk*, rctlblk_t **new_blk*,   304
    uint_t *flags*) ;

    <rctl.h>

    Returns: 0 if OK, –1 on error

int **getrlimit** (int *resource*), struct rlimit **rlp*) ;   298

    <sys/resource.h>

    Returns: 0 if OK, –1 on error

int **getrusage** (int *who*), struct rusage **r_usage*) ;   323

    <sys/resource.h>

    Returns: 0 if OK, –1 on error

```
char *gets (char *s);
```
<stdio.h>

Returns: *s* if OK, NULL on error

166

```
pid_t getsid (pid_t pid);
```
<unistd.h>

Returns: the process ID of *pid*'s session leader if OK, −1 on error

685

```
struct spwd *getspent (void);
```
<shadow.h>

Returns: a pointer if OK, NULL on end of enumeration or error

247

```
struct spwd *getspent_r (struct spwd *result, char *buffer, int buflen);
```
<shadow.h>

Returns: a pointer if OK, NULL on end of enumeration or error

247

```
struct spwd *getspnam (const char *name);
```
<shadow.h>

Returns: a pointer if OK, NULL on error

245

```
struct spwd *getspnam_r (const char *name, struct spwd *result, char *buffer,
              int buflen);
```
<shadow.h>

Returns: a pointer if OK, NULL on error

245

```
int getsubopt (char **optionp), char * const *tokens, char **valuep);
```
<stdlib.h>

Returns: the index of the matching token if found, −1 on error

113

```
char *gettext (const char *msgid);
```
<libintl.h>

Returns: message string if OK, *msgid* on error

1042

```
int gettimeofday (struct timeval *tp, void *);
```
<sys/time.h>

Returns: 0 if OK, −1 on error

204

```
uid_t getuid (void);
```
<sys/types.h>
<unistd.h>

Returns: the real user ID of the calling process

228

```
char *getusershell (void);
```

Returns: a pointer to a legal shell if OK, NULL on error

270

```
void getutmp (struct utmpx *utmpx, struct utmp *utmp);
```
<utmpx.h>

267

void **getutmpx** (struct utmp *_utmp_, struct utmpx *_utmpx_);   267
    <utmpx.h>

struct utmpx ***getutxent** (void);   264
    <utmpx.h>
    Returns: a pointer if OK, NULL on error

struct utmpx ***getutxid** (const struct utmpx *_id_);   266
    <utmpx.h>
    Returns: a pointer if OK, NULL on error

struct utmpx ***getutxline** (const struct utmpx *_line_);   266
    <utmpx.h>
    Returns: a pointer if OK, NULL on error

int **getvfsany** (FILE *_fp_, struct vfstab *_vp_, struct vfstab *_vref_);   429
    <stdio.h>
    <sys/vfstab.h>
    Returns: 0 if OK, –1 on EOF, VFS_TOOLONG, VFS_TOOMANY, or VFS_TOOFEW on error

int **getvfsent** (FILE *_fp_, struct vfstab *_vp_);   429
    <stdio.h>
    <sys/vfstab.h>
    Returns: 0 if OK, –1 on EOF, VFS_TOOLONG, VFS_TOOMANY, or VFS_TOOFEW on error

int **getvfsfile** (FILE *_fp_, struct vfstab *_vp_, char *_file_);   429
    <stdio.h>
    <sys/vfstab.h>
    Returns: 0 if OK, –1 on EOF, VFS_TOOLONG, VFS_TOOMANY, or VFS_TOOFEW on error

int **getvfsspec** (FILE *_fp_, struct vfstab *_vp_, char *_spec_);   429
    <stdio.h>
    <sys/vfstab.h>
    Returns: 0 if OK, –1 on EOF, VFS_TOOLONG, VFS_TOOMANY, or VFS_TOOFEW on error

int **getw** (FILE *_stream_);   164
    <stdio.h>
    Returns: the next available character, EOF on end of file or error

int **getwd** (char *_path_name_);   1051
    <unistd.h>
    Returns: _path_name_ if OK, NULL on error

struct tm ***gmtime** (const time_t *_clock_);   210
    <time.h>
    Returns: a pointer to the converted time

struct tm ***gmtime_r** (const time_t *_clock_, struct tm *_res_);   210
    <time.h>
    Returns: a pointer to the converted time

```
int grantpt (int fildes);
    <stdlib.h>
    Returns: 0 if OK, −1 on error
```
1005

```
int gsignal (int signal);
    <stdlib.h>
    Returns: the value returned by the action function, if it returns
```
790

```
char *hasmntopt (struct mnttab *mnt, char *opt);
    <stdio.h>
    <sys/mnttab.h>
    Returns: the address of the matching substring if found, NULL if not
```
423

```
char *index (const char *s, int c);
    <strings.h>
    Returns: a pointer if c occurs in s, NULL otherwise
```
1051

```
int initgroups (const char *name, gid_t basegid);
    <grp.h>
    <sys/types.h>
    Returns: 0 if OK, −1 on error
```
235

```
int ioctl (int fildes, int request, /* arg */...);
    <unistd.h>
    <stropts.h>
    Returns: depends on request if OK, −1 on error
```
153

```
int isalnum (int c);
    <ctype.h>
    Returns: non-zero if the classification is true, 0 otherwise
```
61

```
int isalpha (int c);
    <ctype.h>
    Returns: non-zero if the classification is true, 0 otherwise
```
60

```
int isascii (int c);
    <ctype.h>
    Returns: non-zero if the classification is true, 0 otherwise
```
62

```
int isastream (int fildes);
    <stropts.h>
    Returns: 1 if fildes is associated with a STREAMS file, 0 if it isn't, or −1 on error
```
525

```
int isatty (int fildes);
    <unistd.h>
    Returns: 1 if fildes is associated with a terminal, 0 if it isn't, or −1 on error
```
489

```
int iscntrl (int c);
```
    `<ctype.h>`
    Returns: non-zero if the classification is true, 0 otherwise

62

```
int isdigit (int c);
```
    `<ctype.h>`
    Returns: non-zero if the classification is true, 0 otherwise

61

```
int isgraph (int c);
```
    `<ctype.h>`
    Returns: non-zero if the classification is true, 0 otherwise

62

```
int islower (int c);
```
    `<ctype.h>`
    Returns: non-zero if the classification is true, 0 otherwise

60

```
int isprint (int c);
```
    `<ctype.h>`
    Returns: non-zero if the classification is true, 0 otherwise

62

```
int ispunct (int c);
```
    `<ctype.h>`
    Returns: non-zero if the classification is true, 0 otherwise

62

```
int isspace (int c);
```
    `<ctype.h>`
    Returns: non-zero if the classification is true, 0 otherwise

62

```
int isupper (int c);
```
    `<ctype.h>`
    Returns: non-zero if the classification is true, 0 otherwise

60

```
int isxdigit (int c);
```
    `<ctype.h>`
    Returns: non-zero if the classification is true, 0 otherwise

61

```
int kill (pid_t pid, int sig);
```
    `<sys/types.h>`
    `<signal.h>`
    Returns: 0 if OK, −1 on error

731

```
int killpg (pid_t pgrp, int sig);
```
    `<sys/types.h>`
    `<signal.h>`
    Returns: 0 if OK, −1 on error

732

```
int lchown (const char *path, uid_t owner, gid_t group);
    <unistd.h>
    <sys/types.h>
    Returns: 0 if OK, −1 on error
```
371

```
int lckpwdf (void);
    <shadow.h>
    Returns: 0 if OK, −1 on error
```
243

```
int link (const char *existing, const char *new);
    <unistd.h>
    Returns: 0 if OK, −1 on error
```
377

```
offset_t llseek (int fildes, offset_t offset, int whence);
    <sys/types.h>
    <unistd.h>
    Returns: new file offset if OK, −1 on error
```
129

```
char *lltostr (long long value, char *endptr);
    <stdlib.h>
    Returns: a pointer to the converted number
```
91

```
struct tm *localtime (const time_t *clock);
    <time.h>
    Returns: a pointer to the converted time
```
209

```
struct tm *localtime_r (const time_t *clock, struct tm *res);
    <time.h>
    Returns: a pointer to the converted time
```
209

```
int lockf (int fildes, int function, off_t size);
    <unistd.h>
    Returns: 0 if OK, −1 on error
```
517

```
void longjmp (jmp_buf env, int val);
    <setjmp.h>
    This function never returns
```
621

```
off_t lseek (int fildes, off_t offset, int whence);
    <sys/types.h>
    <unistd.h>
    Returns: new file offset if OK, −1 on error
```
129

```
int lstat (const char *path, struct stat *buf);
    <sys/types.h>
    <sys/stat.h>
    Returns: 0 if OK, −1 on error
```
356

int **madvise** (caddr_t *addr*, size_t *len*, int *advice*);   570
>   <sys/types.h>
>   <sys/mman.h>
>   Returns: 0 if OK, −1 on error

major_t **major** (dev_t *device*);   407
>   <sys/types.h>
>   <sys/mkdev.h>
>   Returns: major component if OK, NODEV on error

dev_t **makedev** (major_t *maj*, minor_t *min*);   407
>   <sys/types.h>
>   <sys/mkdev.h>
>   Returns: device number if OK, NODEV on error

struct mallinfo **mallinfo** (void);   102
>   <malloc.h>
>   Returns: a mallinfo structure

void *****malloc** (size_t *size*);   96
>   <stdlib.h>
>   Returns: a pointer if OK, NULL on error

int **mallopt** (int *cmd*, int *value*);   101
>   <malloc.h>
>   Returns: 0 if OK, non-zero on error

void *****memalign** (size_t *alignment*, size_t *size*);   97
>   <stdlib.h>
>   Returns: a pointer if OK, NULL on error

void *****memccpy** (void *$s1$, const void *$s2$, int c, size_t n);   92
>   <string.h>
>   Returns: a pointer if OK, NULL on error

void *****memchr** (const void *s, int c, size_t n);   93
>   <string.h>
>   Returns: a pointer if OK, NULL on error

int **memcmp** (const void *$s1$, const void *$s2$, size_t n);   92
>   <string.h>
>   Returns: a value less than, equal to, or greater than 0 if $s1$ is less than, equal to, or greater than $s2$

int **memcntl** (caddr_t *addr*, size_t *len*, int *cmd*, caddr_t *arg*, int *attr*, int *mask*);   577
>   <sys/types.h>
>   <sys/mman.h>
>   Returns: 0 if OK, −1 on error

void ***memcpy** (const void *_s1_, const void *_s2_, size_t _n_);   92
    <string.h>
    Returns: _s1_

void ***memmove** (const void *_s1_, const void *_s2_, size_t _n_);   92
    <string.h>
    Returns: _s1_

void ***memset** (const void *_s_, int _c_, size_t _n_);   94
    <string.h>
    Returns: _s_

minor_t **minor** (dev_t _device_);   407
    <sys/types.h>
    <sys/mkdev.h>
    Returns: minor component if OK, NODEV on error

int **mkdir** (const char *_path_, mode_t _mode_);   392
    <sys/types.h>
    <sys/stat.h>
    Returns: 0 if OK, −1 on error

int **mkfifo** (const char *_path_, mode_t _mode_);   854
    <sys/types.h>
    <sys/stat.h>
    Returns: 0 if OK, −1 on error

int **mknod** (const char *_path_, mode_t _mode_, dev_t _dev_);   408
    <sys/stat.h>
    Returns: 0 if OK, −1 on error

int **mkstemp** (char *_template_);   110
    <stdlib.h>
    Returns: file descriptor if OK, −1 on error

char ***mktemp** (char *_template_);   108
    <stdlib.h>
    Returns: _template_

time_t **mktime** (struct tm *_timeptr_);   211
    <time.h>
    Returns: the converted time if OK, −1 on error

int **mlock** (const void *_addr_, size_t _len_);   573
    <sys/mman.h>
    Returns: 0 if OK, −1 on error

int **mlockall** (int *flags*);   574
    <sys/mman.h>
    Returns: 0 if OK, –1 on error

void ***mmap** (void **addr*, size_t *len*, int *prot*, int *flags*, int *fildes*, off_t *off*);   563
    <sys/mman.h>
    Returns: a pointer if OK, MAP_FAILED on error

int **mount** (const char **spec*, const char **dir*, int *mflag*, char **fstype*, char **dataptr*,   432
        int *datalen*, char **optptr*, int *optlen*);
    <sys/types.h>
    <sys/mount.h>
    <sys/mntent.h>
    Returns: 0 if OK, –1 on error

int **mprotect** (void **addr*, size_t *len*, int *prot*);   570
    <sys/mman.h>
    Returns: 0 if OK, –1 on error

int **msgctl** (int *msgid*, int *cmd*, struct msqid_ds **buf*);   878
    <sys/msg.h>
    Returns: 0 if OK, –1 on error

int **msgget** (key_t *key*, int *msgflg*);   875
    <sys/msg.h>
    Returns: message queue ID if OK, –1 on error

int **msgids** (int **buf*, uint_t *nids*, uint_t **pnids*);   886
    <sys/msg.h>
    Returns: 0 if OK, –1 on error

ssize_t **msgrcv** (int *msgid*, void **msgp*, size_t *msgsz*, long int*msgtyp*, int *msgflg*);   876
    <sys/msg.h>
    Returns: number of bytes retrieved if OK, –1 on error

int **msgsnap** (int *msgid*, void **buf*, size_t *bufsz*, long *msgtyp*);   885
    <sys/msg.h>
    Returns: 0 if OK, –1 on error

int **msgsnd** (int *msgid*, const void **msgp*, size_t *msgsz*, int *msgflg*);   875
    <sys/msg.h>
    Returns: 0 if OK, –1 on error

int **msync** (void **addr*, size_t *len*, int *flags*);   572
    <sys/mman.h>
    Returns: 0 if OK, –1 on error

int **munlock** (const void *_addr_, size_t _len_);   573

    <sys/mman.h>

    Returns: 0 if OK, −1 on error

int **munlockall** (void);   574

    <sys/mman.h>

    Returns: 0 if OK, −1 on error

int **munmap** (void *_addr_, size_t _len_);   565

    <sys/mman.h>

    Returns: 0 if OK, −1 on error

int **nftw** (const char *_path_, int (*_fn_) (const char *, const struct stat *, int,   399
      struct FTW *), int _depth_, int _flags_);

    <ftw.h>

    Returns: 0 if tree is exhausted, value returned by _fn_ if it is non-zero, −1 on error

int **open** (const char *_path_, int _oflag_, /* mode_t _mode_ */...);   124

    <sys/types.h>
    <sys/stat.h>
    <fcntl.h>

    Returns: file descriptor if OK, −1 on error

int **openat** (int _fildes_, const char *_path_, int _oflag_, /* mode_t _mode_ */...);   592

    <sys/types.h>
    <sys/stat.h>
    <fcntl.h>

    Returns: file descriptor if OK, −1 on error

DIR ***opendir** (const char *_dirname_);   393

    <sys/types.h>
    <dirent.h>

    Returns: pointer to a DIR object if OK, NULL on error

void **openlog** (const char *_ident_, int _logopt_, int _facility_);   814

    <syslog.h>

long **pathconf** (const char *_path_, int _name_);   292

    <unistd.h>

    Returns: corresponding value if OK, −1 on error

int **pause** (void);   720

    <unistd.h>

    Returns: −1 with errno set to EINTR

int **pclose** (FILE *_stream_);   839

    <stdio.h>

    Returns: the termination status of the shell if OK, −1 on error

void **perror** (const char *s);   117
    <stdio.h>

int **pipe** (int *fildes* [2]);   830
    <unistd.h>
    Returns: 0 if OK, −1 on error

int **plock** (int *op*);   574
    <sys/lock.h>
    Returns: 0 if OK, −1 on error

int **poll** (struct pollfd *fds* [], nfds_t *nfds*, int *timeout*);   543
    <poll.h>
    Returns: the number of selected descriptors if OK, 0 on timeout, −1 on error

FILE ***popen** (const char *command*, const char *mode*);   839
    <stdio.h>
    Returns: file pointer if OK, NULL on error

ssize_t **pread** (int *fildes*, void *buf*, size_t *nbyte*, off_t *offset*);   132
    <unistd.h>
    Returns: number of bytes read if OK (0 if end of file), −1 on error

int **printf** (const char *format*, /* *args* */...);   170
    <stdio.h>
    Returns: number of bytes output if OK, negative value on error

void **psiginfo** (siginfo_t *pinfo*, char *s);   798
    <siginfo.h>

void **psignal** (int *sig*, const char *s);   797
    <siginfo.h>

char ***ptsname** (int *fildes*);   1006
    <stdlib.h>
    Returns: a pointer if OK, NULL on error

int **putc** (int *c*, FILE *stream*);   165
    <stdio.h>
    Returns: the character written if OK, EOF on error

int **putc_unlocked** (int *c*, FILE *stream*);   191
    <stdio.h>
    Returns: the character written if OK, EOF on error

int **putchar** (int *c*);   165
    <stdio.h>
    Returns: the character written if OK, EOF on error

```
int putchar_unlocked (int c);
```
    `<stdio.h>`

    Returns: the character written if OK, EOF on error

191

```
int putenv (char *string);
```
    `<stdlib.h>`

    Returns: 0 if OK, non-zero on error

612

```
int putmntent (FILE *iop, struct mnttab *mp);
```
    `<stdio.h>`
    `<sys/mnttab.h>`

    Returns: the number of bytes written if OK, −1 on error

425

```
int putmsg (int fildes, const struct strbuf *ctlptr, const struct strbuf *dataptr,
       int flags);
```
    `<stropts.h>`

    Returns: 0 if OK, −1 on error

528

```
int putpmsg (int fildes, const struct strbuf *ctlptr, const struct strbuf *dataptr,
       int band, int flags);
```
    `<stropts.h>`

    Returns: 0 if OK, −1 on error

528

```
int putpwent (const struct passwd *p, FILE *f);
```
    `<pwd.h>`

    Returns: 0 if OK, non-zero on error

243

```
int puts (const char *s);
```
    `<stdio.h>`

    Returns: the number of characters written if OK, EOF on error

167

```
int putspent (const struct spwd *p, FILE *fp);
```
    `<shadow.h>`

    Returns: 0 if OK, non-zero on error

249

```
struct utmpx *pututxline (const struct utmpx *utmpx);
```
    `<utmpx.h>`

    Returns: a pointer if OK, NULL on error

266

```
int putvfsent (FILE *fp, struct vfstab *vp);
```
    `<stdio.h>`
    `<sys/vfstab.h>`

    Returns: the number of bytes written if OK, −1 on error

431

```
int putw (int c, FILE *stream);
```
    `<stdio.h>`

    Returns: 0 if OK, non-zero on error

165

ssize_t **pwrite** (int *fildes*, const void **buf*, size_t *nbyte*, off_t *offset*) ;   132
     <unistd.h>
     Returns: number of bytes written if OK, –1 on error

int **raise** (int *sig*) ;   732
     <signal.h>
     Returns: 0 if OK, –1 on error

int **rctl_walk** (int (*callback) (const char **rctlname*, void **walk_data*) , void **init_data*) ;   311
     <rctl.h>
     Returns: 0 if OK, –1 on error

rctl_qty_t **rctlblk_get_enforced_value** (rctlblk_t **rblk*) ;   307
     <rctl.h>
     Returns: resource control block's value

hrtime_t **rctlblk_get_firing_time** (rctlblk_t **rblk*) ;   310
     <rctl.h>
     Returns: the time of the most recent action on *rblk*

int **rctlblk_get_global_action** (rctlblk_t **rblk*) ;   309
     <rctl.h>
     Returns: the resource control block's global actions

int **rctlblk_get_global_flags** (rctlblk_t **rblk*) ;   307
     <rctl.h>
     Returns: the resource control block's global flags

int **rctlblk_get_local_action** (rctlblk_t **rblk*, int **signalp*) ;   309
     <rctl.h>
     Returns: the resource control block's local actions

int **rctlblk_get_local_flags** (rctlblk_t **rblk*) ;   307
     <rctl.h>
     Returns: the resource control block's local flags

rctl_priv_t **rctlblk_get_privilege** (rctlblk_t **rblk*) ;   306
     <rctl.h>
     Returns: the resource control block's privilege

id_t **rctlblk_get_recipient_pid** (rctlblk_t **rblk*) ;   310
     <rctl.h>
     Returns: the process ID that placed the resource control

rctl_qty_t **rctlblk_get_value** (rctlblk_t **rblk*) ;   307
     <rctl.h>
     Returns: resource control block's value

void **rctlblk_set_local_action** (rctlblk_t *rblk*, rctl_action_t *action*, int *signal*);   309
    <rctl.h>

void **rctlblk_set_local_flags** (rctlblk_t *rblk*, int *flags*);   307
    <rctl.h>

void **rctlblk_set_privilege** (rctlblk_t *rblk*, rctl_priv_t *privilege*);   306
    <rctl.h>

void **rctlblk_set_value** (rctlblk_t *rblk*, rctl_qty_t *value*);   307
    <rctl.h>

size_t **rctlblk_size** (void);   304
    <rctl.h>
    Returns: resource control block's value

ssize_t **read** (int *fildes*, void *buf*, size_t *nbyte*);   132
    <unistd.h>
    Returns: number of bytes read if OK, 0 if end of file, −1 on error

struct dirent ***readdir** (DIR *dirp*);   394
    <sys/types.h>
    <dirent.h>
    Returns: a pointer if OK, NULL on error or end of directory

int **readdir_r** (DIR *dirp*, struct dirent *entry*, struct dirent **result*);   394
    <sys/types.h>
    <dirent.h>
    Returns: 0 if OK, error number on error

int **readlink** (const char *path*, char *buf*, size_t *bufsiz*);   387
    <unistd.h>
    Returns: 0 if OK, −1 on error

ssize_t **readv** (int *fildes*, const struct iovec *iov*, int *iovcnt*);   553
    <sys/uio.h>
    Returns: number of bytes read if OK, −1 on error

void ***realloc** (void *ptr*, size_t *size*);   98
    <stdlib.h>
    Returns: a pointer to the allocated memory if OK, NULL on error

char ***realpath** (const char *file_name*, char *resolved_name*);   386
    <stdlib.h>
    Returns: a pointer to the resolved name if OK, NULL on error

int **remove** (const char *path*);   380
    <stdio.h>
    Returns: 0 if OK, −1 on error

```
int rename (const char *old, const char *new);                              380
    <stdio.h>
    Returns: 0 if OK, -1 on error

int renameat (int fromfd, const char *old, int tofd, const char *new);      595
    <stdio.h>
    Returns: 0 if OK, -1 on error

void resetmnttab (FILE *fp);                                                425
    <stdio.h>
    <sys/mnttab.h>

int resolvepath (const char *path, char *buf, size_t bufsiz);               385
    <unistd.h>
    Returns: the number of bytes placed in buf if OK, -1 on error

void rewind (FILE *stream);                                                 184
    <stdio.h>

void rewinddir (DIR *dirp);                                                 395
    <sys/types.h>
    <dirent.h>

char *rindex (const char *s, int c);                                       1051
    <strings.h>
    Returns: a pointer if c occurs in s, NULL otherwise

int rmdir (const char *path);                                               393
    <unistd.h>
    Returns: 0 if OK, -1 on error

void *sbrk (intptr_t incr);                                                 618
    <unistd.h>
    Returns: prior break value if OK, -1 on error

int scanf (const char *format, ...);                                        172
    <stdio.h>
    Returns: number of successfully matched items if OK, EOF on error

void seekdir (DIR *dirp, long int loc);                                     395
    <sys/types.h>
    <dirent.h>

int select (int nfds, fd_set *readfds, fd_set *writefds, fd_set *errorfds,  539
        struct timeval *timeout);
    <sys/time.h>
    Returns: the total number of bits set in the bitmasks if OK, 0 on timeout, -1 on error
```

int **semctl** (int *semid*, int *semnum*, int *cmd*, ...);   895
    <sys/types.h>
    <sys/ipc.h>
    <sys/sem.h>
    Returns: non-negative value if OK, −1 on error

int **semget** (key_t *key*, int *nsems*, int *semflg*);   892
    <sys/types.h>
    <sys/ipc.h>
    <sys/sem.h>
    Returns: semaphore set ID if OK, −1 on error

int **semids** (int **buf*, uint_t *nids*, uint_t **pnids*);   904
    <sys/sem.h>
    Returns: 0 if OK, −1 on error

int **semop** (int *semid*, struct sembuf **sops*, size_t *nsops*);   893
    <sys/types.h>
    <sys/ipc.h>
    <sys/sem.h>
    Returns: 0 if OK, −1 on error

int **semtimedop** (int *semid*, struct sembuf **sops*, size_t *nsops*,   893
      const struct timespec **timeout*);
    <sys/types.h>
    <sys/ipc.h>
    <sys/sem.h>
    Returns: 0 if OK, −1 on error

ssize_t **sendfile** (int *out_fd*, int *in_fd*, off_t **off*, size_t *len*);   556
    <sys/sendfile.h>
    Returns: the total number of bytes written if OK, −1 on error

ssize_t **sendfilev** (int *fildes*, const struct sendfilevec **vec*, int *sfvcnt*,   559
      size_t **xferred*);
    <sys/sendfile.h>
    Returns: the total number of bytes written if OK, −1 on error

void **setbuf** (FILE **stream*, char **buf*);   193
    <stdio.h>

void **setbuffer** (FILE **iop*, char **abuf*, size_t *asize*);   194
    <stdio.h>

int **setegid** (gid_t *egid*);   232
    <sys/types.h>
    <unistd.h>
    Returns: 0 if OK, −1 on error

```
int seteuid (uid_t euid);                                                       228
```
    `<sys/types.h>`
    `<unistd.h>`
    Returns: 0 if OK, −1 on error

```
int setgid (gid_t gid);                                                         232
```
    `<sys/types.h>`
    `<unistd.h>`
    Returns: 0 if OK, −1 on error

```
void setgrent (void);                                                           259
```
    `<grp.h>`
    Returns: 0 if OK, −1 on error

```
int setgroups (int ngroups, const gid_t *grouplist);                            235
```
    `<unistd.h>`
    Returns: 0 if OK, −1 on error

```
int sethostname (char *name, int namelen);                                      282
```
    `<unistd.h>`
    Returns: 0 if OK, −1 on error

```
int setitimer (int which, const struct itimerval *value, struct itimerval *ovalue);   742
```
    `<sys/time.h>`
    Returns: 0 if OK, −1 on error

```
int setjmp (jmp_buf env);                                                       621
```
    `<setjmp.h>`
    Returns: 0 if called directly, non-zero if returning from a call to longjmp

```
int setlinebuf (FILE *iop);                                                     194
```
    `<stdio.h>`
    Returns: no useful value

```
char *setlocale (int category, const char *locale);                            1037
```
    `<locale.h>`
    Returns: locale if OK, NULL on error

```
int setlogmask (int maskpri);                                                   814
```
    `<syslog.h>`
    Returns: the previous log mask

```
int setpgid (pid_t pid, pid_t pgid);                                            683
```
    `<sys/types.h>`
    `<unistd.h>`
    Returns: 0 if OK, −1 on error

```
pid_t setpgrp (void);                                                    684
```
    `<sys/types.h>`
    `<unistd.h>`
    Returns: the new process group ID

```
void setpwent (void);                                                    240
```
    `<pwd.h>`

```
int setrctl (const char *controlname, rctlblk_t *old_blk, rctlblk_t *new_blk,    305
        uint_t flags);
```
    `<rctl.h>`
    Returns: 0 if OK, −1 on error

```
int setregid (gid_t rgid, gid_t egid);                                   233
```
    `<unistd.h>`
    Returns: 0 if OK, −1 on error

```
int setreuid (uid_t ruid, uid_t euid);                                   231
```
    `<unistd.h>`
    Returns: 0 if OK, −1 on error

```
int setrlimit (int resource), const struct rlimit *rlp);                 298
```
    `<sys/resource.h>`
    Returns: 0 if OK, −1 on error

```
pid_t setsid (void);                                                     686
```
    `<sys/types.h>`
    `<unistd.h>`
    Returns: 0 if OK, −1 on error

```
void setspent (void);                                                    247
```
    `<shadow.h>`

```
int settimeofday (struct timeval *tp, void *);                           206
```
    `<sys/time.h>`
    Returns: 0 if OK, −1 on error

```
int setuid (uid_t uid);                                                  228
```
    `<sys/types.h>`
    `<unistd.h>`
    Returns: 0 if OK, −1 on error

```
void setusershell (void);                                                270
```

```
void setutxent (void);                                                   264
```
    `<utmpx.h>`

```
int setvbuf (FILE *stream, char *buf, int type, size_t size);            193
```
    `<stdio.h>`
    Returns: 0 if OK, non-zero on error

```
void *shmat (int shmid, const void *shmaddr, int shmflg);                    910
```
    `<sys/types.h>`
    `<sys/shm.h>`

    Returns: start address of attached segment if OK, NULL on error

```
int shmctl (int shmid, int cmd, struct shmid_ds *buf);                       911
```
    `<sys/types.h>`
    `<sys/ipc.h>`
    `<sys/shm.h>`

    Returns: 0 if OK, –1 on error

```
int shmdt (const void *shmaddr);                                             911
```
    `<sys/types.h>`
    `<sys/shm.h>`

    Returns: 0 if OK, –1 on error

```
int shmget (key_t key, size_t size, int shmflg);                            909
```
    `<sys/types.h>`
    `<sys/ipc.h>`
    `<sys/shm.h>`

    Returns: shared memory segment ID if OK, –1 on error

```
int shmids (int *buf, uint_t nids, uint_t *pnids);                          917
```
    `<sys/shm.h>`

    Returns: 0 if OK, –1 on error

```
int sig2str (int signum, char *str);                                        799
```
    `<signal.h>`

    Returns: 0 if OK, –1 on error

```
int sigaction (int sig, const struct sigaction *act, struct sigaction *oact);   752
```
    `<signal.h>`

    Returns: 0 if OK, –1 on error

```
int sigaddset (sigset_t *set, int signo);                                   746
```
    `<signal.h>`

    Returns: 0 if OK, –1 on error

```
int sigaltstack (const stack_t *ss, stack_t *oss);                          793
```
    `<signal.h>`

    Returns: 0 if OK, –1 on error

```
int sigdelset (sigset_t *set, int signo);                                   746
```
    `<signal.h>`

    Returns: 0 if OK, –1 on error

```
int sigemptyset (sigset_t *set);                                            746
```
    `<signal.h>`

    Returns: 0 if OK, –1 on error

int **sigfillset** (sigset_t *set);   746

    <signal.h>
    Returns: 0 if OK, –1 on error

sigfpe_handler_type **sigfpe** (sigfpe_code_type code, sigfpe_handler_type hdl);   761

    <floatingpoint.h>
    <siginfo.h>
    Returns: the previous handler if OK, BADSIG on error

int **sighold** (int sig);   722

    <signal.h>
    Returns: 0 if OK, –1 on error

int **sigignore** (int sig);   722

    <signal.h>
    Returns: 0 if OK, –1 on error

int **sigismember** (sigset_t *set, int signo);   746

    <signal.h>
    Returns: 1 if signo is a member of set, 0 if it isn't, –1 on error

void **siglongjmp** (sigjmp_buf env, int val);   764

    <setjmp.h>
    This function never returns

void *****signal** (int sig, void *disp) (int))) (int);   713

    <signal.h>
    Returns: the previous disposition of sig if OK, SIG_ERR on error

int **sigpause** (int sig);   722

    <signal.h>
    Returns: 0 if OK, –1 on error

int **sigpending** (sigset_t *set);   748

    <signal.h>
    Returns: 0 if OK, –1 on error

int **sigprocmask** (int how, const sigset_t *set, sigset_t *oset);   747

    <signal.h>
    Returns: 0 if OK, –1 on error

int **sigrelse** (int sig);   722

    <signal.h>
    Returns: 0 if OK, –1 on error

int **sigsend** (idtype_t idtype, id_t id, int sig);   733

    <signal.h>
    Returns: 0 if OK, –1 on error

```
int sigsendset (procset_t *psp, int sig);                                    733
```
    `<signal.h>`
    Returns: 0 if OK, −1 on error

```
void *sigset (int sig, void *disp) (int))) (int);                            719
```
    `<signal.h>`
    Returns: the previous disposition of *sig* if OK, `SIG_ERR` on error

```
int sigsetjmp (sigjmp_buf env, int savemask);                               764
```
    `<setjmp.h>`
    Returns: 0 if called directly, non-zero if returning from a call to `siglongjmp`

```
int sigstack (struct sigstack *ss, struct sigstack *oss);                   796
```
    `<signal.h>`
    Returns: 0 if OK, −1 on error

```
int sigsuspend (const sigset_t *set);                                       768
```
    `<signal.h>`
    Returns: −1 with errno set to `EINTR`

```
int sigwait (const sigset_t *set, int *sig);                                773
```
    `<signal.h>`
    Returns: 0 if OK, −1 on error

```
unsigned int sleep (unsigned int seconds);                                  120
```
    `<unistd.h>`
    Returns: the amount of unslept time

```
int snprintf (char *s, size_t n, const char *format, /* args */...);        171
```
    `<stdio.h>`
    Returns: number of characters formatted if OK, negative value on error

```
int sprintf (char *s, const char *format, /* args */...);                   171
```
    `<stdio.h>`
    Returns: number of bytes transmitted if OK, negative value on error

```
int sscanf (const char *s, const char *format, ...);                        172
```
    `<stdio.h>`
    Returns: number of successfully matched items if OK, EOF on error

```
void *ssignal (int sig, int *action) (int))) (int);                         790
```
    `<signal.h>`
    Returns: the previous defined action of *sig* if OK, `SIG_DFL` on error

```
int stat (const char *path, struct stat *buf);                              356
```
    `<sys/types.h>`
    `<sys/stat.h>`
    Returns: 0 if OK, −1 on error

int **statvfs** (const char *_path_, struct statvfs *_buf_);   439
    <sys/types.h>
    <sys/statvfs.h>
    Returns: 0 if OK, −1 on error

int **stime** (const time_t *_tp_);   205
    <unistd.h>
    Returns: 0 if OK, −1 on error

int **str2sig** (const char *_str_, int *_signum_);   799
    <signal.h>
    Returns: 0 if OK, −1 on error

char ***strcadd** (char *_output_, const char *_input_);   85
    <libgen.h>
    Returns: a pointer to the NUL at the end of _output_

int **strcasecmp** (const char *_s1_, const char *_s2_);   70
    <strings.h>
    Returns: a value less than, equal to, or greater than 0 if _s1_ is less than, equal to, or greater than _s2_

char ***strcat** (char *_s1_, const char *_s2_);   71
    <string.h>
    Returns: _s1_

char ***strccpy** (char *_output_, const char *_input_);   85
    <libgen.h>
    Returns: _output_

char ***strchr** (const char *_s_, int _c_);   75
    <string.h>
    Returns: a pointer to the first occurrence of _c_ in _s_

int **strcmp** (const char *_s1_, const char *_s2_);   68
    <string.h>
    Returns: a value less than, equal to, or greater than 0 if _s1_ is less than, equal to, or greater than _s2_

int **strcoll** (const char *_s1_, const char *_s2_);   1044
    <string.h>
    Returns: a value less than, equal to, or greater than 0 if _s1_ is less than, equal to, or greater than _s2_

char ***strcpy** (char *_s1_, const char *_s2_);   73
    <string.h>
    Returns: _s1_

size_t **strcspn** (const char *_s1_, const char *_s2_);   66
    <string.h>
    Returns: the length of the initial segment of _s1_ that consists of characters not from _s2_

char ***strdup** (const char *s1);   81

    <string.h>

    Returns: a pointer a duplicate of s1 if OK, NULL on error

char ***streadd** (char *output, const char *input, const char *exceptions);   85

    <libgen.h>

    Returns: a pointer to the NUL at the end of output

char ***strecpy** (char *output, const char *input, const char *exceptions);   85

    <libgen.h>

    Returns: output

char ***strerror** (int errnum);   118

    <string.h>

    Returns: a pointer to the error messages associated with errnum

int **strfind** (const char *as1, const char *as2);   79

    <libgen.h>

    Returns: the offset of s2 in s1 if OK, −1 on error

size_t **strftime** (char *s, size_t maxsize, const char *format,   214
        const struct tm *timeptr);

    <time.h>

    Returns: the number of bytes copied, 0 on error

size_t **strlcat** (char *dst, const char *src, size_t dstsize);   71

    <string.h>

    Returns: the sum of the lengths of src and dst

size_t **strlcpy** (char *dst, const char *src, size_t dstsize);   73

    <string.h>

    Returns: the sum of the lengths of src and dst

size_t **strlen** (const char *s);   66

    <string.h>

    Returns: the length of s

int **strncasecmp** (const char *s1, const char *s2, size_t n);   70

    <strings.h>

    Returns: a value less than, equal to, or greater than 0 if s1 is less than, equal to, or greater than s2

char ***strncat** (char *s1, const char *s2, size_t n);   71

    <string.h>

    Returns: s1

int **strncmp** (const char *s1, const char *s2, size_t n);   68

    <string.h>

    Returns: a value less than, equal to, or greater than 0 if s1 is less than, equal to, or greater than s2

```
char *strncpy (char *s1, const char *s2, size_t n);                                               73
```
     <string.h>
     Returns: *s1*

```
char *strpbrk (const char *s1, const char *s2);                                                   78
```
     <string.h>
     Returns: a pointer to the first occurrence of a character from *s2* in *s1*

```
char *strptime (const char *buf, const char *format, struct tm *tm);                             218
```
     <time.h>
     Returns: a pointer to the character after the last successfully parsed character if OK, NULL on error

```
char *strrchr (const char *s, int c);                                                             75
```
     <string.h>
     Returns: a pointer to the last occurrence of *c* in *s*

```
char *strrspn (const char *string, const char *tc);                                               78
```
     <libgen.h>
     Returns: a pointer to the character in *string* after the first one not from *tc* (starting from the end)

```
char *strsignal (int sig);                                                                       797
```
     <string.h>
     Returns: a pointer to the error messages associated with *sig* if OK, NULL on error

```
size_t strspn (const char *s1, const char *s2);                                                   66
```
     <string.h>
     Returns: the length of the initial segment of *s1* that consists of characters from *s2*

```
char *strstr (const char *s1, const char *s2);                                                    79
```
     <string.h>
     Returns: a pointer to the first occurrence of *s2* in *s1*

```
double strtod (const char *str, char **endptr);                                                   90
```
     <stdlib.h>
     Returns: the converted number

```
char *strtok (char *s1, const char *s2);                                                          81
```
     <string.h>
     Returns: a pointer until all tokens in *s1* are exhausted, NULL when none remain

```
char *strtok_r (char *s1, const char *s2, char **lasts);                                          81
```
     <string.h>
     Returns: a pointer until all tokens in *s1* are exhausted, NULL when none remain

```
long strtol (const char *str, char **endptr, int base);                                           87
```
     <stdlib.h>
     Returns: the converted number

```
long long strtoll (const char *str, char **endptr, int base);                87
    <stdlib.h>
    Returns: the converted number
```

```
unsigned long strtoul (const char *str, char **endptr, int base);            87
    <stdlib.h>
    Returns: the converted number
```

```
unsigned long long strtoull (const char *str, char **endptr, int base);      87
    <stdlib.h>
    Returns: the converted number
```

```
char *strtrns (const char *string, const char *old, const char *new, char *result);   86
    <libgen.h>
    Returns: new
```

```
size_t strxfrm (char *s1, const char *s2, size_t n);                        1044
    <string.h>
    Returns: the length of the transformed string if OK, −1 on error
```

```
int symlink (const char *name1, const char *name2);                          387
    <unistd.h>
    Returns: 0 if OK, −1 on error
```

```
void sync (void);                                                            410
    <unistd.h>
```

```
long sysconf (int name);                                                     283
    <unistd.h>
    Returns: the current value of the variable name, −1 on error
```

```
long sysinfo (int command, char *buf, long count);                           277
    <sys/systeminfo.h>
    Returns: the size of the buffer required to hold the result if OK, −1 on error
```

```
void syslog (int priority, const char *message, /* arguments */ ...);        814
    <syslog.h>
```

```
int system (const char *string);                                             666
    <stdlib.h>
    Returns: the termination status of the shell if OK, −1 on error
```

```
int tcdrain (int fildes);                                                    486
    <termios.h>
    Returns: 0 if OK, −1 on error
```

```
int tcflow (int fildes, int action);                                         487
    <termios.h>
    Returns: 0 if OK, −1 on error
```

int **tcflush** (int *fildes*, int *queue_selector*) ;   487

    <termios.h>

    Returns: 0 if OK, −1 on error

int **tcgetattr** (int *fildes*, struct termios **termios_p*) ;   474

    <termios.h>

    Returns: 0 if OK, −1 on error

pid_t **tcgetpgrp** (int *fildes*) ;   688

    <sys/types.h>

    <unistd.h>

    Returns: the foreground process group ID associated with *fildes* if OK, −1 on error

pid_t **tcgetsid** (int *fildes*) ;   689

    <termios.h>

    Returns: the session ID associated with *fildes* if OK, −1 on error

int **tcsendbreak** (int *fildes*, int *duration*) ;   488

    <termios.h>

    Returns: 0 if OK, −1 on error

int **tcsetattr** (int *fildes*, int *optional_actions*, const struct termios **termios_p*) ;   474

    <termios.h>

    Returns: 0 if OK, −1 on error

int **tcsetpgrp** (int *fildes*, pid_t *pgid_id*) ;   688

    <sys/types.h>

    <unistd.h>

    Returns: 0 if OK, −1 on error

off_t **tell** (int *fd*) ;   131

    <unistd.h>

    Returns: file offset if OK, −1 on error

long int **telldir** (DIR **dirp*) ;   396

    <dirent.h>

    Returns: the current location of the specified directory stream if OK, −1 on error

char ****tempnam** (const char **dir*, const char **pfx*) ;   109

    <stdio.h>

    Returns: a pointer if OK, −1 on error

char ****textdomain** (const char **domainname*) ;   1042

    <libintl.h>

    Returns: the name of the current text domain

```
time_t time (time_t *tloc);                                               204
    <sys/types.h>
    <time.h>
    Returns: the current time if OK, −1 on error

clock_t times (struct tms *buffer);                                       319
    <sys/types.h>
    <time.h>
    Returns: the elapsed time since the system booted if OK, −1 on error

FILE *tmpfile (void);                                                     110
    <stdio.h>
    Returns: a file pointer if OK, NULL on error

char *tmpnam (char *s);                                                   108
    <stdio.h>
    Returns: s

char *tmpnam_r (char *s);                                                 108
    <stdio.h>
    Returns: s if OK, NULL on error

int toascii (int c);                                                      64
    <ctype.h>
    Returns: the bitwise-AND of c and 0x7f.

int tolower (int c);                                                      63
    <ctype.h>
    Returns: the lower case letter corresponding to the argument if OK, c on error

int toupper (int c);                                                      63
    <ctype.h>
    Returns: the upper case letter corresponding to the argument if OK, c on error

int truncate (const char *path, off_t length);                           373
    <unistd.h>
    Returns: 0 if OK, −1 on error

char *ttyname (int fildes);                                               490
    <unistd.h>
    Returns: a pointer if OK, NULL on error

int ttyname_r (int fildes, char *name, size_t namelen);                  490
    <unistd.h>
    Returns: 0 if OK, error number on error

void tzset (void);                                                        207
    <time.h>
```

useconds_t **ualarm** (useconds_t *useconds*, useconds_t *interval*);   1052
    <unistd.h>
    Returns: the previous number of remaining microseconds

int **ulckpwdf** (void);   243
    <shadow.h>
    Returns: 0 if OK, −1 on error

long **ulimit** (int *cmd*, /* *newlimit* */...);   298
    <ulimit.h>
    Returns: the value of the requested limit if OK, −1 on error

char ***ulltostr** (unsigned long long *value*, char **endptr*);   91
    <stdlib.h>
    Returns: a pointer to the converted number

mode_t **umask** (mode_t *cmask*);   367
    <sys/types.h>
    <sys/stat.h>
    Returns: the previous file creation mask

int **umount** (const char **file*);   437
    <sys/mount.h>
    Returns: 0 if OK, −1 on error

int **umount2** (const char **file*, int *mflag*);   437
    <sys/mount.h>
    Returns: 0 if OK, −1 on error

int **uname** (struct utsname **name*);   276
    <sys/utsname.h>
    Returns: non-negative value if OK, −1 on error

int **ungetc** (int *c*, FILE **stream*);   165
    <stdio.h>
    Returns: the byte pushed if OK, EOF on error

int **unlink** (const char **path*);   378
    <unistd.h>
    Returns: 0 if OK, −1 on error

int **unlinkat** (int *dirfd*, const char **path*, int *flag*);   595
    <unistd.h>
    Returns: 0 if OK, −1 on error

int **unlockpt** (int *fildes*);   1006
    <stdlib.h>
    Returns: 0 if OK, −1 on error

void **updwtmp** (char *wfile, struct utmp *utmp);   268
    <utmpx.h>

void **updwtmpx** (char *wfilex, struct utmpx *utmpx);   268
    <utmpx.h>

int **usleep** (useconds_t useconds);   1052
    <unistd.h>
    Returns: 0

int **ustat** (dev_t dev, struct ustat *buf);   442
    <sys/types.h>
    <ustat.h>
    Returns: 0 if OK, −1 on error

int **utime** (const char *path, const struct utimbuf *times);   390
    <sys/types.h>
    <utime.h>
    Returns: 0 if OK, −1 on error

int **utimes** (const char *path, const struct timeval times [2]);   391
    <sys/time.h>
    Returns: 0 if OK, −1 on error

int **utmpxname** (const char *file);   267
    <utmpx.h>
    Returns: 1 if OK, 0 on error

void ***valloc** (size_t size);   97
    <stdlib.h>
    Returns: a pointer if OK, NULL on error

pid_t **vfork** (void);   637
    <unistd.h>
    Returns: 0 in child, process ID of child in parent, −1 on error

int **vfprintf** (FILE *stream, const char *format, va_list ap);   171
    <stdio.h>
    <stdarg.h>
    Returns: the number of characters transmitted if OK, negative value on error

int **vfscanf** (FILE *stream, const char *format, va_list arg);   173
    <stdio.h>
    <stdarg.h>
    Returns: the number of successfully matched items if OK, EOF on error

int **vprintf** (const char *format, va_list ap);   171
    <stdio.h>
    <stdarg.h>
    Returns: the number of characters transmitted if OK, negative value on error

```
int vscanf (const char *format, va_list arg);                               173
```
    `<stdio.h>`
    `<stdarg.h>`
    Returns: the number of successfully matched items if OK, EOF on error

```
int vsnprintf (char *s, size_t n, const char *format, va_list ap);          172
```
    `<stdio.h>`
    `<stdarg.h>`
    Returns: the number of characters formatted if OK, negative value on error

```
int vsprintf (char *s, const char *format, va_list ap);                     172
```
    `<stdio.h>`
    `<stdarg.h>`
    Returns: the number of characters transmitted if OK, negative value on error

```
int vsscanf (const char *s, const char *format, va_list arg);               173
```
    `<stdio.h>`
    `<stdarg.h>`
    Returns: the number of successfully matched items if OK, EOF on error

```
pid_t wait (int *stat_loc);                                                 641
```
    `<sys/types.h>`
    `<sys/wait.h>`
    Returns: the process ID of the terminated child if OK, −1 on error

```
pid_t wait3 (int *statusp, int options, struct rusage *rusage);             646
```
    `<sys/wait.h>`
    `<sys/time.h>`
    `<sys/resource.h>`
    Returns: the process ID of the terminated child or 0 if OK, −1 on error

```
pid_t wait4 (pid_t pid, int *statusp, int options, struct rusage *rusage);  646
```
    `<sys/wait.h>`
    `<sys/time.h>`
    `<sys/resource.h>`
    Returns: the process ID of the terminated child or 0 if OK, −1 on error

```
int waitid (idtype_t idtype, id_t id, siginfo_t *infop, int options);       647
```
    `<sys/wait.h>`
    Returns: 0 if OK, −1 on error

```
pid_t waitpid (pid_t pid, int *stat_loc, int options);                      644
```
    `<sys/types.h>`
    `<sys/wait.h>`
    Returns: the process ID of the terminated child or 0 if OK, −1 on error

```
ssize_t write (int fildes, const void *buf, size_t nbyte);                  132
```
    `<unistd.h>`
    Returns: number of bytes written if OK, −1 on error

ssize_t **writev** (int *fildes*, const struct iovec **iov*, int *iovcnt*) ;   553

    <sys/uio.h>

    Returns: number of bytes written if OK, −1 on error

C.3   Function Availability

Figures C.1 to C.12 provide alphabetically organized tables that summarize, by Solaris release and standard, the availability of each function we describe in the text, except for those that we wrote. For ease of reference, this summary also shows the page number containing the function description.

In these tables, as in the rest of this text, ISO C refers to the 1989 version of the ISO C standard. Although this has been superseded by the 1999 edition, the versions of Solaris we cover in this text claim conformance to only the former. Similarly, POSIX refers to the 1996 edition of POSIX 1003.1, even though it too has been superseded.

Functions that are not marked in any of the "Standard" columns in these tables are not necessarily Solaris specific, but they are best avoided in portable applications. (At the very least, we should ensure their availability on the platforms we intend to port to.) Having said that, some of them (e.g., strtoll and vsscanf) have been adopted by Version 3 of the Single UNIX Specification or the 1999 version of the ISO C standard. Other functions are widely implemented, despite not being ratified by any standard.

Function	Availability						Standard					Page
	2.5	2.5.1	2.6	7	8	9	ISO C	SVID	POSIX	SUSv1	SUSv2	
_exit	•	•	•	•	•	•		•	•	•	•	605
_longjmp	•	•	•	•	•	•				•	•	625
_setjmp	•	•	•	•	•	•				•	•	625
_tolower	•	•	•	•	•	•		•		•	•	63
_toupper	•	•	•	•	•	•		•		•	•	63
abort	•	•	•	•	•	•	•	•	•	•	•	776
access	•	•	•	•	•	•		•	•	•	•	365
acl	•	•	•	•	•	•						581
aclcheck	•	•	•	•	•	•						584
aclfrommode	•	•	•	•	•	•						589
aclfromtext	•	•	•	•	•	•						582
aclsort	•	•	•	•	•	•						589
acltomode	•	•	•	•	•	•						589
acltotext	•	•	•	•	•	•						582
adjtime	•	•	•	•	•	•		•				206
aiocancel	•	•	•	•	•	•						553
aioread	•	•	•	•	•	•						551
aiowait	•	•	•	•	•	•						552
aiowrite	•	•	•	•	•	•						551
alarm	•	•	•	•	•	•		•	•	•	•	734
alloca	•	•	•	•	•	•						99
ascftime	•	•	•	•	•	•						214

Figure C.1 Function availability (from _exit to ascftime).

Function	Availability						Standard					Page
	2.5	2.5.1	2.6	7	8	9	ISO C	SVID	POSIX	SUSv1	SUSv2	
asctime	•	•	•	•	•	•	•	•	•	•	•	213
asctime_r	•	•	•	•	•	•			•		•	213
assert	•	•	•	•	•	•	•	•	•	•	•	118
atexit	•	•	•	•	•	•	•	•		•	•	606
atof	•	•	•	•	•	•	•	•	•	•	•	90
atoi	•	•	•	•	•	•	•	•	•	•	•	90
atol	•	•	•	•	•	•	•	•	•	•	•	90
atoll	•	•	•	•	•	•						90
attropen						•						592
basename	•	•	•	•	•	•				•	•	354
bcmp	•	•	•	•	•	•				•	•	1049
bcopy	•	•	•	•	•	•				•	•	1050
bindtextdomain	•	•	•	•	•	•						1041
brk	•	•	•	•	•	•				•	•	618
bufsplit	•	•	•	•	•	•						83
bzero	•	•	•	•	•	•				•	•	1050
calloc	•	•	•	•	•	•	•	•	•	•	•	97
cfgetispeed	•	•	•	•	•	•		•	•	•	•	485
cfgetospeed	•	•	•	•	•	•		•	•	•	•	485
cfsetispeed	•	•	•	•	•	•		•	•	•	•	485
cfsetospeed	•	•	•	•	•	•		•	•	•	•	485
cftime	•	•	•	•	•	•						214
chdir	•	•	•	•	•	•		•	•	•	•	404
chmod	•	•	•	•	•	•		•	•	•	•	368
chown	•	•	•	•	•	•		•	•	•	•	371
chroot	•	•	•	•	•	•		•		•	•	406
clearerr	•	•	•	•	•	•	•	•	•	•	•	169
clock	•	•	•	•	•	•	•	•		•	•	322
close	•	•	•	•	•	•		•	•	•	•	127
closedir	•	•	•	•	•	•		•	•	•	•	396
closefrom						•						128
closelog	•	•	•	•	•	•				•	•	814
creat	•	•	•	•	•	•		•	•	•	•	126
crypt	•	•	•	•	•	•		•	•	•	•	251
crypt_gensalt												252
ctermid	•	•	•	•	•	•		•	•	•	•	488
ctermid_r	•	•	•	•	•	•						488
ctime	•	•	•	•	•	•	•	•	•	•	•	213
ctime_r	•	•	•	•	•	•			•		•	213
cuserid	•	•	•	•	•	•		•			•	226
dcgettext	•	•	•	•	•	•						1042
dgettext	•	•	•	•	•	•						1042
difftime	•	•	•	•	•	•	•	•		•	•	205
directio			•	•	•	•						155
dirname	•	•	•	•	•	•				•	•	354
door_bind			•	•	•	•						978
door_call			•	•	•	•						955
door_create			•	•	•	•						953

Figure C.2 Function availability (from asctime to door_create).

Function	Availability						Standard					Page
	2.5	2.5.1	2.6	7	8	9	ISO C	SVID	POSIX	SUSv1	SUSv2	
door_cred			•	•	•	•						968
door_info			•	•	•	•						970
door_return			•	•	•	•						956
door_revoke			•	•	•	•						957
door_server_create			•	•	•	•						978
door_unbind			•	•	•	•						978
dup	•	•	•	•	•	•		•	•	•	•	140
dup2	•	•	•	•	•	•		•	•	•	•	140
endgrent	•	•	•	•	•	•		•		•	•	259
endpwent	•	•	•	•	•	•		•		•	•	240
endspent	•	•	•	•	•	•						247
endusershell	•	•	•	•	•	•						270
endutxent	•	•	•	•	•	•				•	•	264
execl	•	•	•	•	•	•		•	•	•	•	655
execle	•	•	•	•	•	•		•	•	•	•	656
execlp	•	•	•	•	•	•		•	•	•	•	656
execv	•	•	•	•	•	•		•	•	•	•	655
execve	•	•	•	•	•	•		•	•	•	•	656
execvp	•	•	•	•	•	•		•	•	•	•	657
exit	•	•	•	•	•	•	•	•	•	•	•	605
facl	•	•	•	•	•	•						581
fattach	•	•	•	•	•	•		•		•	•	938
fchdir	•	•	•	•	•	•		•		•	•	404
fchmod	•	•	•	•	•	•		•		•	•	368
fchown	•	•	•	•	•	•		•		•	•	371
fchownat						•						596
fchroot	•	•	•	•	•	•						406
fclose	•	•	•	•	•	•	•	•	•	•	•	163
fcntl	•	•	•	•	•	•		•	•	•	•	142
FD_CLR	•	•	•	•	•	•				•	•	539
FD_ISSET	•	•	•	•	•	•				•	•	539
FD_SET	•	•	•	•	•	•				•	•	539
FD_ZERO	•	•	•	•	•	•				•	•	539
fdetach	•	•	•	•	•	•		•		•	•	938
fdopen	•	•	•	•	•	•		•	•	•	•	163
fdopendir						•						393
fdwalk						•						154
feof	•	•	•	•	•	•	•	•	•	•	•	169
ferror	•	•	•	•	•	•	•	•	•	•	•	168
fflush	•	•	•	•	•	•	•	•	•	•	•	194
ffs	•	•	•	•	•	•				•	•	93
fgetc	•	•	•	•	•	•	•	•	•	•	•	164
fgetgrent	•	•	•	•	•	•		•				261
fgetgrent_r	•	•	•	•	•	•						261
fgetpos	•	•	•	•	•	•	•	•		•	•	184
fgetpwent	•	•	•	•	•	•		•				242
fgetpwent_r	•	•	•	•	•	•						242
fgets	•	•	•	•	•	•	•	•	•	•	•	166

Figure C.3 Function availability (from door_cred to fgets).

Function	Availability						Standard					Page
	2.5	2.5.1	2.6	7	8	9	ISO C	SVID	POSIX	SUSv1	SUSv2	
fgetspent	•	•	•	•	•	•						249
fgetspent_r	•	•	•	•	•	•						249
fileno	•	•	•	•	•	•		•	•	•	•	169
flockfile	•	•	•	•	•	•			•		•	186
fopen	•	•	•	•	•	•	•	•	•	•	•	161
fork	•	•	•	•	•	•		•	•	•	•	631
fork1	•	•	•	•	•	•						631
fpathconf	•	•	•	•	•	•		•	•	•	•	292
fprintf	•	•	•	•	•	•	•	•	•	•	•	170
fputc	•	•	•	•	•	•	•	•	•	•	•	165
fputs	•	•	•	•	•	•	•	•	•	•	•	167
fread	•	•	•	•	•	•	•	•	•	•	•	167
free	•	•	•	•	•	•	•	•	•	•	•	99
freopen	•	•	•	•	•	•	•	•	•	•	•	162
fscanf	•	•	•	•	•	•	•	•	•	•	•	172
fseek	•	•	•	•	•	•	•	•	•	•	•	184
fseeko			•	•	•	•					•	184
fsetpos	•	•	•	•	•	•	•	•		•	•	185
fstat	•	•	•	•	•	•		•	•	•	•	356
fstatat						•						594
fstatvfs	•	•	•	•	•	•		•		•	•	439
fsync	•	•	•	•	•	•		•		•	•	410
ftell	•	•	•	•	•	•	•	•		•	•	184
ftello			•	•	•	•					•	184
ftime	•	•	•	•	•	•				•	•	1050
ftok	•	•	•	•	•	•				•	•	868
ftruncate	•	•	•	•	•	•				•	•	373
ftrylockfile	•	•	•	•	•	•			•		•	186
ftw	•	•	•	•	•	•		•		•	•	399
funlockfile	•	•	•	•	•	•			•		•	186
futimesat						•						597
fwrite	•	•	•	•	•	•	•	•	•	•	•	168
getc	•	•	•	•	•	•	•	•	•	•	•	164
getc_unlocked	•	•	•	•	•	•			•		•	189
getchar	•	•	•	•	•	•	•	•	•	•	•	164
getchar_unlocked	•	•	•	•	•	•			•		•	189
getcwd	•	•	•	•	•	•		•	•	•	•	405
getdate	•	•	•	•	•	•		•		•	•	221
getdtablesize			•	•	•	•						302
getegid	•	•	•	•	•	•		•	•	•	•	232
getenv	•	•	•	•	•	•	•	•	•	•	•	611
geteuid	•	•	•	•	•	•		•	•	•	•	228
getexecname			•	•	•	•						609
getextmntent				•	•	•						420
getgid	•	•	•	•	•	•		•	•	•	•	232
getgrent	•	•	•	•	•	•		•		•	•	259
getgrent_r	•	•	•	•	•	•						259
getgrgid	•	•	•	•	•	•		•	•	•	•	258

Figure C.4   Function availability (from fgetspent to getgrgid).

Function	Availability						Standard					Page
	2.5	2.5.1	2.6	7	8	9	ISO C	SVID	POSIX	SUSv1	SUSv2	
getgrgid_r	●	●	●	●	●	●			●		●	258
getgrnam	●	●	●	●	●	●		●	●	●	●	257
getgrnam_r	●	●	●	●	●	●			●		●	257
getgroups	●	●	●	●	●	●		●	●	●	●	234
gethostid	●	●	●	●	●	●				●	●	282
gethostname	●	●	●	●	●	●				●	●	282
gethrtime	●	●	●	●	●	●						204
gethrvtime	●	●	●	●	●	●						204
getitimer	●	●	●	●	●	●		●		●	●	742
getloadavg			●	●	●	●						334
getlogin	●	●	●	●	●	●		●	●	●	●	224
getlogin_r	●	●	●	●	●	●			●		●	224
getmntany	●	●	●	●	●	●						420
getmntent	●	●	●	●	●	●						420
getmsg	●	●	●	●	●	●		●		●	●	529
getopt	●	●	●	●	●	●		●	●	●	●	112
getpagesize			●	●	●	●						296
getpagesizes						●						296
getpass	●	●	●	●	●	●		●				250
getpassphrase			●	●	●	●						250
getpgid	●	●	●	●	●	●		●		●	●	683
getpgrp	●	●	●	●	●	●		●	●	●	●	682
getpid	●	●	●	●	●	●		●	●	●	●	630
getpmsg	●	●	●	●	●	●		●		●	●	529
getppid	●	●	●	●	●	●		●	●	●	●	630
getpwent	●	●	●	●	●	●		●		●	●	240
getpwent_r	●	●	●	●	●	●						240
getpwnam	●	●	●	●	●	●		●	●	●	●	238
getpwnam_r	●	●	●	●	●	●			●		●	238
getpwuid	●	●	●	●	●	●		●	●	●	●	240
getpwuid_r	●	●	●	●	●	●			●		●	240
getrctl						●						304
getrlimit	●	●	●	●	●	●		●		●	●	298
getrusage	●	●	●	●	●	●				●	●	323
gets	●	●	●	●	●	●	●	●	●	●	●	166
getsid	●	●	●	●	●	●		●		●	●	685
getspent	●	●	●	●	●	●						247
getspent_r	●	●	●	●	●	●						247
getspnam	●	●	●	●	●	●						245
getspnam_r	●	●	●	●	●	●						245
getsubopt	●	●	●	●	●	●		●			●	113
gettext	●	●	●	●	●	●						1042
gettimeofday	●	●	●	●	●	●		●		●	●	204
getuid	●	●	●	●	●	●		●	●	●	●	228
getusershell	●	●	●	●	●	●						270
getutmp	●	●	●	●	●	●						267
getutmpx	●	●	●	●	●	●						267
getutxent	●	●	●	●	●	●				●	●	264

Figure C.5 Function availability (from getgrgid_r to getutxent).

Function	Availability						Standard					Page
	2.5	2.5.1	2.6	7	8	9	ISO C	SVID	POSIX	SUSv1	SUSv2	
getutxid	•	•	•	•	•	•				•	•	266
getutxline	•	•	•	•	•	•				•	•	266
getvfsany	•	•	•	•	•	•						429
getvfsent	•	•	•	•	•	•						429
getvfsfile	•	•	•	•	•	•						429
getvfsspec	•	•	•	•	•	•						429
getw	•	•	•	•	•	•						164
getwd	•	•	•	•	•	•				•	•	1051
gmtime	•	•	•	•	•	•	•	•	•	•	•	210
gmtime_r	•	•	•	•	•	•			•		•	210
grantpt	•	•	•	•	•	•		•		•	•	1005
gsignal	•	•	•	•	•	•						790
hasmntopt	•	•	•	•	•	•						423
index	•	•	•	•	•	•				•	•	1051
initgroups	•	•	•	•	•	•		•				235
ioctl	•	•	•	•	•	•				•	•	153
isalnum	•	•	•	•	•	•	•	•	•	•	•	61
isalpha	•	•	•	•	•	•	•	•	•	•	•	60
isascii	•	•	•	•	•	•		•		•	•	62
isastream	•	•	•	•	•	•		•		•	•	525
isatty	•	•	•	•	•	•		•	•	•	•	489
iscntrl	•	•	•	•	•	•	•	•	•	•	•	62
isdigit	•	•	•	•	•	•	•	•	•	•	•	61
isgraph	•	•	•	•	•	•	•	•	•	•	•	62
islower	•	•	•	•	•	•	•	•	•	•	•	60
isprint	•	•	•	•	•	•	•	•	•	•	•	62
ispunct	•	•	•	•	•	•	•	•	•	•	•	62
isspace	•	•	•	•	•	•	•	•	•	•	•	62
isupper	•	•	•	•	•	•	•	•	•	•	•	60
isxdigit	•	•	•	•	•	•	•	•	•	•	•	61
kill	•	•	•	•	•	•		•	•	•	•	731
killpg			•	•	•	•				•	•	732
lchown	•	•	•	•	•	•		•		•	•	371
lckpwdf	•	•	•	•	•	•						243
link	•	•	•	•	•	•		•	•	•	•	377
llseek	•	•	•	•	•	•						129
lltostr	•	•	•	•	•	•						91
localtime	•	•	•	•	•	•	•	•	•	•	•	209
localtime_r	•	•	•	•	•	•			•		•	209
lockf	•	•	•	•	•	•		•		•	•	517
longjmp	•	•	•	•	•	•	•	•	•	•	•	621
lseek	•	•	•	•	•	•		•	•	•	•	129
lstat	•	•	•	•	•	•		•		•	•	356
madvise	•	•	•	•	•	•						570
major	•	•	•	•	•	•						407
makedev	•	•	•	•	•	•						407
mallinfo	•	•	•	•	•	•		•				102
malloc	•	•	•	•	•	•	•	•	•	•	•	96

Figure C.6 Function availability (from `getutxid` to `malloc`).

Function	Availability						Standard					Page
	2.5	2.5.1	2.6	7	8	9	ISO C	SVID	POSIX	SUSv1	SUSv2	
mallopt	•	•	•	•	•	•		•				101
memalign	•	•	•	•	•	•						97
memccpy	•	•	•	•	•	•		•		•	•	92
memchr	•	•	•	•	•	•	•	•		•	•	93
memcmp	•	•	•	•	•	•	•	•		•	•	92
memcntl	•	•	•	•	•	•		•				577
memcpy	•	•	•	•	•	•	•	•		•	•	92
memmove	•	•	•	•	•	•	•	•		•	•	92
memset	•	•	•	•	•	•	•	•		•	•	94
minor	•	•	•	•	•	•						407
mkdir	•	•	•	•	•	•		•	•	•	•	392
mkfifo	•	•	•	•	•	•		•	•	•	•	854
mknod	•	•	•	•	•	•		•		•	•	408
mkstemp	•	•	•	•	•	•				•	•	110
mktemp	•	•	•	•	•	•		•		•	•	108
mktime	•	•	•	•	•	•	•	•	•	•	•	211
mlock	•	•	•	•	•	•		•	•		•	573
mlockall	•	•	•	•	•	•		•	•		•	574
mmap	•	•	•	•	•	•		•		•	•	563
mount	•	•	•	•	•	•		•				432
mprotect	•	•	•	•	•	•		•		•	•	570
msgctl	•	•	•	•	•	•		•		•	•	878
msgget	•	•	•	•	•	•		•		•	•	875
msgids					•	•						886
msgrcv	•	•	•	•	•	•		•		•	•	876
msgsnap					•	•						885
msgsnd	•	•	•	•	•	•		•		•	•	875
msync	•	•	•	•	•	•		•		•	•	572
munlock	•	•	•	•	•	•		•	•		•	573
munlockall	•	•	•	•	•	•		•	•		•	574
munmap	•	•	•	•	•	•		•		•	•	565
nftw	•	•	•	•	•	•		•		•	•	399
open	•	•	•	•	•	•		•	•	•	•	124
openat						•						592
opendir	•	•	•	•	•	•		•	•	•	•	393
openlog	•	•	•	•	•	•				•	•	814
pathconf	•	•	•	•	•	•		•	•	•	•	292
pause	•	•	•	•	•	•		•	•	•	•	720
pclose	•	•	•	•	•	•		•	•	•	•	839
perror	•	•	•	•	•	•	•	•	•	•	•	117
pipe	•	•	•	•	•	•		•	•	•	•	830
plock	•	•	•	•	•	•		•				574
poll	•	•	•	•	•	•		•			•	543
popen	•	•	•	•	•	•		•	•	•	•	839
pread	•	•	•	•	•	•					•	132
printf	•	•	•	•	•	•	•	•	•	•	•	170
psiginfo	•	•	•	•	•	•						798
psignal	•	•	•	•	•	•						797

Figure C.7 Function availability (from `mallopt` to `psignal`).

Function	Availability						Standard					Page
	2.5	2.5.1	2.6	7	8	9	ISO C	SVID	POSIX	SUSv1	SUSv2	
ptsname	•	•	•	•	•	•		•		•	•	1006
putc	•	•	•	•	•	•	•	•	•	•	•	165
putc_unlocked	•	•	•	•	•	•			•		•	191
putchar	•	•	•	•	•	•	•	•	•	•	•	165
putchar_unlocked	•	•	•	•	•	•			•		•	191
putenv	•	•	•	•	•	•		•		•	•	612
putmntent	•	•	•	•	•	•						425
putmsg	•	•	•	•	•	•		•		•	•	528
putpmsg	•	•	•	•	•	•		•		•	•	528
putpwent	•	•	•	•	•	•		•				243
puts	•	•	•	•	•	•	•	•	•	•	•	167
putspent	•	•	•	•	•	•						249
pututxline	•	•	•	•	•	•				•	•	266
putvfsent	•	•	•	•	•	•						431
putw	•	•	•	•	•	•		•		•	•	165
pwrite	•	•	•	•	•	•					•	132
raise	•	•	•	•	•	•	•	•		•	•	732
rctl_walk						•						311
rctlblk_get_enforced_value						•						307
rctlblk_get_firing_time						•						310
rctlblk_get_global_action						•						309
rctlblk_get_global_flags						•						307
rctlblk_get_local_action						•						309
rctlblk_get_local_flags						•						307
rctlblk_get_privilege						•						306
rctlblk_get_recipient_pid						•						310
rctlblk_get_value						•						307
rctlblk_set_local_action						•						309
rctlblk_set_local_flags						•						307
rctlblk_set_privilege						•						306
rctlblk_set_value						•						307
rctlblk_size						•						304
read	•	•	•	•	•	•		•	•	•	•	132
readdir	•	•	•	•	•	•		•	•	•	•	394
readdir_r	•	•	•	•	•	•			•		•	394
readlink	•	•	•	•	•	•		•		•	•	387
readv	•	•	•	•	•	•		•		•	•	553
realloc	•	•	•	•	•	•	•	•	•	•	•	98
realpath	•	•	•	•	•	•		•		•	•	386
remove	•	•	•	•	•	•	•	•	•	•	•	380
rename	•	•	•	•	•	•	•	•	•	•	•	380
renameat						•						595
resetmnttab					•	•						425
resolvepath			•	•	•	•						385
rewind	•	•	•	•	•	•	•	•	•	•	•	184
rewinddir	•	•	•	•	•	•		•	•	•	•	395
rindex	•	•	•	•	•	•				•	•	1051
rmdir	•	•	•	•	•	•		•	•	•	•	393

Figure C.8 Function availability (from ptsname to rmdir).

Function	Availability						Standard					Page
	2.5	2.5.1	2.6	7	8	9	ISO C	SVID	POSIX	SUSv1	SUSv2	
sbrk	•	•	•	•	•	•				•	•	618
scanf	•	•	•	•	•	•	•	•	•	•	•	172
seekdir	•	•	•	•	•	•		•		•	•	395
select	•	•	•	•	•	•				•	•	539
semctl	•	•	•	•	•	•		•		•	•	895
semget	•	•	•	•	•	•		•		•	•	892
semids					•	•						904
semop	•	•	•	•	•	•		•		•	•	893
semtimedop					•	•						893
sendfile					•	•						556
sendfilev					•	•						559
setbuf	•	•		•	•	•	•	•	•	•	•	193
setbuffer			•	•	•	•						194
setegid	•	•	•	•	•	•						232
seteuid	•	•	•	•	•	•						228
setgid	•	•	•	•	•	•		•	•		•	232
setgrent	•	•	•	•	•	•		•			•	259
setgroups	•	•	•	•	•	•		•				235
sethostname	•	•	•	•	•	•						282
setitimer	•	•	•	•	•	•		•		•	•	742
setjmp	•	•	•	•	•	•	•	•		•	•	621
setlinebuf			•	•	•	•						194
setlocale	•	•	•	•	•	•	•	•	•		•	1037
setlogmask	•	•	•	•	•	•				•	•	814
setpgid	•	•	•	•	•	•		•	•	•	•	683
setpgrp	•	•	•	•	•	•		•		•	•	684
setpwent	•	•	•	•	•	•		•		•	•	240
setrctl						•						305
setregid	•	•	•	•	•	•				•	•	233
setreuid	•	•	•	•	•	•				•	•	231
setrlimit	•	•	•	•	•	•		•		•	•	298
setsid	•	•	•	•	•	•		•	•	•	•	686
setspent	•	•	•	•	•	•						247
settimeofday	•	•	•	•	•	•		•				206
setuid	•	•	•	•	•	•		•	•	•	•	228
setusershell	•	•	•	•	•	•						270
setutxent	•	•	•	•	•	•				•	•	264
setvbuf	•	•	•	•	•	•	•	•		•	•	193
shmat	•	•	•	•	•	•		•		•	•	910
shmctl	•	•	•	•	•	•		•		•	•	911
shmdt	•	•	•	•	•	•		•		•	•	911
shmget	•	•	•	•	•	•		•		•	•	909
shmids					•	•						917
sig2str	•	•		•	•	•						799
sigaction	•	•	•	•	•	•		•	•	•	•	752
sigaddset	•	•	•	•	•	•		•	•	•	•	746
sigaltstack	•	•	•	•	•	•		•		•	•	793
sigdelset	•	•	•	•	•	•		•	•	•	•	746

Figure C.9 Function availability (from sbrk to sigdelset).

Function	Availability						Standard					Page
	2.5	2.5.1	2.6	7	8	9	ISO C	SVID	POSIX	SUSv1	SUSv2	
sigemptyset	•	•	•	•	•	•		•	•	•	•	746
sigfillset	•	•	•	•	•	•		•	•	•	•	746
sigfpe	•	•	•	•	•	•						761
sighold	•	•	•	•	•	•		•		•	•	722
sigignore	•	•	•	•	•	•		•		•	•	722
sigismember	•	•	•	•	•	•		•	•	•	•	746
siglongjmp	•	•	•	•	•	•		•	•	•	•	764
signal	•	•	•	•	•	•	•	•		•	•	713
sigpause	•	•	•	•	•	•		•		•	•	722
sigpending	•	•	•	•	•	•		•	•	•	•	748
sigprocmask	•	•	•	•	•	•		•	•	•	•	747
sigrelse	•	•	•	•	•	•		•		•	•	722
sigsend	•	•	•	•	•	•		•				733
sigsendset	•	•	•	•	•	•		•				733
sigset	•	•	•	•	•	•		•		•	•	719
sigsetjmp	•	•	•	•	•	•		•	•	•	•	764
sigstack	•	•	•	•	•	•				•	•	796
sigsuspend	•	•	•	•	•	•		•	•	•	•	768
sigwait	•	•	•	•	•	•				•	•	773
sleep	•	•	•	•	•	•		•	•		•	120
snprintf			•	•	•	•					•	171
sprintf	•	•	•	•	•	•	•	•	•	•	•	171
sscanf	•	•	•	•	•	•	•	•	•	•	•	172
ssignal	•	•	•	•	•	•		•				790
stat	•	•	•	•	•	•		•	•	•	•	356
statvfs	•	•	•	•	•	•		•		•	•	439
stime	•	•	•	•	•	•		•				205
str2sig	•	•	•	•	•	•						799
strcadd	•	•	•	•	•	•						85
strcasecmp	•	•	•	•	•	•				•	•	70
strcat	•	•	•	•	•	•	•	•	•	•	•	71
strccpy	•	•	•	•	•	•						85
strchr	•	•	•	•	•	•	•	•	•	•	•	75
strcmp	•	•	•	•	•	•	•	•	•	•	•	68
strcoll	•	•	•	•	•	•	•	•		•	•	1044
strcpy	•	•	•	•	•	•	•	•	•	•	•	73
strcspn	•	•	•	•	•	•	•	•	•	•	•	66
strdup	•	•	•	•	•	•		•		•	•	81
streadd	•	•	•	•	•	•						85
strecpy	•	•	•	•	•	•						85
strerror	•	•	•	•	•	•	•	•		•	•	118
strfind	•	•	•	•	•	•						79
strftime	•	•	•	•	•	•	•	•	•	•	•	214
strlcat					•	•						71
strlcpy					•	•						73
strlen	•	•	•	•	•	•	•	•	•	•	•	66
strncasecmp	•	•	•	•	•	•				•	•	70
strncat	•	•	•	•	•	•	•	•	•	•	•	71

Figure C.10 Function availability (from sigemptyset to strncat).

Function	Availability						Standard					Page
	2.5	2.5.1	2.6	7	8	9	ISO C	SVID	POSIX	SUSv1	SUSv2	
strncmp	•	•	•	•	•	•	•	•	•	•	•	68
strncpy	•	•	•	•	•	•	•	•	•	•	•	73
strpbrk	•	•	•	•	•	•	•	•	•	•	•	78
strptime	•	•	•	•	•	•				•	•	218
strrchr	•	•	•	•	•	•	•	•	•	•	•	75
strrspn	•	•	•	•	•	•						78
strsignal	•	•	•	•	•	•						797
strspn	•	•	•	•	•	•	•	•	•	•	•	66
strstr	•	•	•	•	•	•	•	•	•	•	•	79
strtod	•	•	•	•	•	•	•	•		•	•	90
strtok	•	•	•	•	•	•	•	•	•	•	•	81
strtok_r	•	•	•	•	•	•			•		•	81
strtol	•	•	•	•	•	•	•	•		•	•	87
strtoll	•	•	•	•	•	•						87
strtoul	•	•	•	•	•	•	•	•		•	•	87
strtoull	•	•	•	•	•	•						87
strtrns	•	•	•	•	•	•						86
strxfrm	•	•	•	•	•	•	•	•			•	1044
symlink	•	•	•	•	•	•		•		•	•	387
sync	•	•	•	•	•	•		•		•	•	410
sysconf	•	•	•	•	•	•		•	•	•	•	283
sysinfo	•	•	•	•	•	•						277
syslog	•	•	•	•	•	•				•	•	814
system	•	•	•	•	•	•	•	•		•	•	666
tcdrain	•	•	•	•	•	•		•	•	•	•	486
tcflow	•	•	•	•	•	•		•	•	•	•	487
tcflush	•	•	•	•	•	•		•	•	•	•	487
tcgetattr	•	•	•	•	•	•		•	•	•	•	474
tcgetpgrp	•	•	•	•	•	•		•	•	•	•	688
tcgetsid	•	•	•	•	•	•		•		•	•	689
tcsendbreak	•	•	•	•	•	•		•	•	•	•	488
tcsetattr	•	•	•	•	•	•		•	•	•	•	474
tcsetpgrp	•	•	•	•	•	•		•	•	•	•	688
tell			•	•	•	•						131
telldir	•	•	•	•	•	•		•			•	396
tempnam	•	•	•	•	•	•		•		•	•	109
textdomain	•	•	•	•	•	•						1042
time	•	•	•	•	•	•	•	•	•	•	•	204
times	•	•	•	•	•	•		•	•	•	•	319
tmpfile	•	•	•	•	•	•	•	•	•	•	•	110
tmpnam	•	•	•	•	•	•	•	•	•	•	•	108
tmpnam_r	•	•	•	•	•							108
toascii	•	•	•	•	•	•		•		•	•	64
tolower	•	•	•	•	•	•	•	•	•	•	•	63
toupper	•	•	•	•	•	•	•	•	•	•	•	63
truncate	•	•	•	•	•	•				•	•	373
ttyname	•	•	•	•	•	•		•	•	•	•	490
ttyname_r	•	•	•	•	•	•			•		•	490

Figure C.11 Function availability (from strncmp to ttyname_r).

Function	Availability						Standard					Page
	2.5	2.5.1	2.6	7	8	9	ISO C	SVID	POSIX	SUSv1	SUSv2	
tzset	•	•	•	•	•	•		•	•	•	•	207
ualarm	•	•	•	•	•	•				•	•	1052
ulckpwdf	•	•	•	•	•	•						243
ulimit	•	•	•	•	•	•		•		•	•	298
ulltostr	•	•	•	•	•	•						91
umask	•	•	•	•	•	•		•	•	•	•	367
umount	•	•	•	•	•	•		•				437
umount2				•	•							437
uname	•	•	•	•	•	•		•	•	•	•	276
ungetc	•	•	•	•	•	•	•	•	•	•	•	165
unlink	•	•	•	•	•	•		•	•	•	•	378
unlinkat						•						595
unlockpt	•	•	•	•	•	•		•		•	•	1006
updwtmp	•	•	•	•	•	•						268
updwtmpx	•	•	•	•	•	•						268
usleep	•	•	•	•	•	•				•	•	1052
ustat	•	•	•	•	•	•		•				442
utime	•	•	•	•	•	•		•	•	•	•	390
utimes	•	•	•	•	•	•				•	•	391
utmpxname	•	•	•	•	•	•						267
valloc	•	•	•	•	•	•				•	•	97
vfork	•	•	•	•	•	•				•	•	637
vfprintf	•	•	•	•	•	•		•		•	•	171
vfscanf						•						173
vprintf	•	•	•	•	•	•	•	•		•	•	171
vscanf						•						173
vsnprintf			•	•	•	•					•	172
vsprintf	•	•	•	•	•	•	•	•		•	•	172
vsscanf						•						173
wait	•	•	•	•	•	•		•	•	•	•	641
wait3			•	•	•	•				•	•	646
wait4				•	•	•						646
waitid	•	•	•	•	•	•		•		•	•	647
waitpid	•	•	•	•	•	•		•	•	•	•	644
write	•	•	•	•	•	•		•	•	•	•	132
writev	•	•	•	•	•	•		•		•	•	553

Figure C.12 Function availability (from tzset to writev).

Appendix D

Miscellaneous Source Code

D.1 Our Header File, `ssp.h`

Almost every example program in this book includes our header file, `ssp.h`, which is shown in Program D.1. This header defines a number of manifest constants, like `BUF_SIZE` (the size of a buffer) and `LINE_LEN` (the length of a line), and several macros. The remainder of the file consists of the function prototypes for all the functions we define in the text that are used in multiple chapters, for example, `err_msg`, `writen`, and `daemon_init`.

————————————————————————————— lib/ssp.h

```
 1 #ifndef _SSP_H
 2 #define _SSP_H

 3 #include <sys/types.h>    /* Required for some of our function prototypes */
 4 #include <sys/termios.h>  /* Required for some of our function prototypes */

 5 #define BUF_SIZE 8192
 6 #define LINE_LEN 256
 7 #define FILE_PERMS (S_IRUSR | S_IWUSR | S_IRGRP | S_IROTH)
 8 #define DIR_PERMS (FILE_PERMS | S_IXUSR | S_IXGRP | S_IXOTH)
 9 #define FIFO_PERMS (FILE_PERMS | S_IWGRP | S_IWOTH)

10 #define ssp_rlock(fd, whence, start, len) \
11     ssp_lock (fd, F_SETLK, F_RDLCK, whence, start, len)
12 #define ssp_rlockw(fd, whence, start, len) \
13     ssp_lock (fd, F_SETLKW, F_RDLCK, whence, start, len)
14 #define ssp_wlock(fd, whence, start, len) \
15     ssp_lock (fd, F_SETLK, F_WRLCK, whence, start, len)
16 #define ssp_wlockw(fd, whence, start, len) \
17     ssp_lock (fd, F_SETLKW, F_WRLCK, whence, start, len)
18 #define ssp_unlock(fd, whence, start, len) \
19     ssp_lock (fd, F_SETLK, F_UNLCK, whence, start, len)
```

```
20 extern void err_dump (const char *text, ...);
21 extern void err_msg (const char *text, ...);
22 extern void err_quit (const char *text, ...);
23 extern void err_ret (const char *text, ...);
24 extern void log_msg (const char *text, ...);
25 extern int set_fsflag (int fd, int new_flags);
26 extern int clear_fsflag (int fd, int new_flags);
27 extern int ssp_lock (int fd, int cmd, short type, short whence, off_t start,
28     off_t len);
29 extern ssize_t readn (int fd, void *buf, size_t num);
30 extern ssize_t writen (int fd, const void *buf, size_t num);
31 extern void print_term_status (int status);
32 #ifdef NEED_SNPRINTF
33 extern int snprintf (char *buf, size_t n, const char *fmt, ...);
34 #endif

35 extern int ssp_tell_wait_init (void);
36 extern int ssp_tell_child (pid_t pid);
37 extern int ssp_tell_parent (pid_t pid);
38 extern int ssp_wait_child (void);
39 extern int ssp_wait_parent (void);
40 extern int ssp_tell_wait_fin (void);
41 extern void daemon_init (const char *prog_name, int inetd);
42 extern int one_copy (const char *pid_file);
43 extern int send_fd (int pipe_fd, int fd);
44 extern int send_err (int pipe_fd, char status);
45 extern int recv_fd (int pipe_fd);
46 extern int srv_listen (const char *path);
47 extern int srv_accept (int fd, uid_t *uid);
48 extern int cli_connect (const char *path);
49 extern pid_t pty_fork (int *master_fdp, const struct termios *slave_termios,
50     const struct winsize *slave_winsize);

51 #endif  /* _SSP_H */
```
—— *lib/ssp.h*

Program D.1 Our header file, `ssp.h`.

D.2 Standard Error Functions

Throughout this text, we've used our own error functions to handle error conditions. The reason why we write our own error functions is so that we can handle errors in a single line of C, as in

```
if (error_condition)
    err_msg (printf-like format with any number of arguments);
```

rather than the more verbose

```
if (error_condition) {
    char err_buf [LINE_LEN];

    snprintf (err_buf, sizeof (buf), printf-like format with any number of arguments);
    perror (err_buf);
    exit (1);
}
```

Our error functions are variadic, which means they have the ability to accept a variable number of arguments, using ISO C's variable length argument facility (refer to Section 7.3 of [Kernighan and Ritchie 1988] for more details).

Figure D.1 summarizes the five error message functions we define. If the global variable daemon_proc is 0, the error message is written to standard error; otherwise, the error is passed to the syslog function with the indicated level (daemon_proc is set to 1 by our daemon_init function, shown in Program 18.3).

Function	strerror (errno)?	Terminate?	syslog level
err_dump	Yes	abort ()	LOG_ERR
err_msg	Yes	exit (1)	LOG_ERR
err_quit	No	exit (1)	LOG_ERR
err_ret	Yes	return	LOG_INFO
log_msg	No	return	LOG_INFO

Figure D.1 Summary of our standard error functions.

Program D.2 shows the code for our standard error functions.

lib/error.c

```
 1 #include <stdio.h>
 2 #include <stdarg.h>
 3 #include <stdlib.h>
 4 #include <string.h>
 5 #include <errno.h>
 6 #include <syslog.h>
 7 #include "ssp.h"

 8 int daemon_proc;

 9 static void err_common (boolean_t flag, int level, const char *text,
10     va_list args);

11 /*
12  * Print an error message preceded by "text",
13  * then dump core and exit.
14  */
15 void err_dump (const char *text, ...)
16 {
17     va_list arg;

18     va_start (arg, text);
19     err_common (B_TRUE, LOG_ERR, text, arg);
20     va_end (arg);
21     abort ();
22 }

23 /*
24  * Print an error message preceded by "text",
25  * then exit.
26  */
```

```
27 void err_msg (const char *text, ...)
28 {
29     va_list arg;

30     va_start (arg, text);
31     err_common (B_TRUE, LOG_ERR, text, arg);
32     va_end (arg);
33     exit (1);
34 }

35 /*
36  * Print "text", then exit.
37  */
38 void err_quit (const char *text, ...)
39 {
40     va_list arg;

41     va_start (arg, text);
42     err_common (B_FALSE, LOG_ERR, text, arg);
43     va_end (arg);
44     exit (1);
45 }

46 /*
47  * Non fatal error: print an error message
48  * preceded by "text", then return.
49  */
50 void err_ret (const char *text, ...)
51 {
52     va_list arg;

53     va_start (arg, text);
54     err_common (B_TRUE, LOG_INFO, text, arg);
55     va_end (arg);
56 }

57 /*
58  * Print the message "text", then return.
59  */
60 void log_msg (const char *text, ...)
61 {
62     va_list arg;

63     va_start (arg, text);
64     err_common (B_FALSE, LOG_INFO, text, arg);
65     va_end (arg);
66 }

67 /*
68  * Common error routine.  Prints a variadic
69  * error message, optionally followed by the
70  * error text associated with errno.
71  */
```

```
72 static void err_common (boolean_t flag, int level, const char *text,
73     va_list args)
74 {
75     int old_errno;
76     int n;
77     char buf [LINE_LEN];

78     old_errno = errno;
79 #ifdef NEED_SNPRINTF
80     n = vsprintf (buf, text, args);
81 #else
82     n = vsnprintf (buf, sizeof (buf), text, args);
83 #endif
84     if (flag)
85         snprintf (buf + n, sizeof (buf) - n, ": %s", strerror (old_errno));
86     strcat (buf, "\n");

87     if (daemon_proc)
88         syslog (level, buf);
89     else {
90         fflush (stdout);
91         fprintf (stderr, "%s", buf);
92         fflush (stderr);
93     }
94 }
```
――――――――――――――――――――――――――――――――――― lib/error.c

Program D.2 Our standard error functions.

D.3   File Status Flags Functions

Several of our example programs modify the file status flags, using either `set_fsflag`
to set one or more flags, or `clear_fsflag` to clear them. These functions avoid any
undesirable side effects by only operating on the specified flags; the other file status flags
are left unchanged.

Program D.3 shows the code for these two functions.

――――――――――――――――――――――――――――――――――― lib/file_flags.c

```
1 #include <fcntl.h>

2 int set_fsflag (int fd, int new_flags)
3 {
4     int flags;

5     if ((flags = fcntl (fd, F_GETFL)) == -1)
6         return (-1);

7     flags |= new_flags;

8     if ((flags = fcntl (fd, F_SETFL, flags)) == -1)
9         return (-1);

10    return (0);
11 }
```

```
12 int clear_fsflag (int fd, int new_flags)
13 {
14     int flags;

15     if ((flags = fcntl (fd, F_GETFL)) == -1)
16         return (-1);

17     flags &= ~new_flags;

18     if ((flags = fcntl (fd, F_SETFL, flags)) == -1)
19         return (-1);

20     return (0);
21 }
```
———————————————————————————————— *lib/file_flags.c*

Program D.3 Our file status flag functions.

D.4   Section Locking Function

Program D.4 shows the code for our convenience function, `ssp_lock`. This function is used by the various section locking macros shown in Program D.1, and can be used to acquire or release a read or write lock on a section of a file.

———————————————————————————————— *lib/lock.c*

```
 1 #include <fcntl.h>

 2 int ssp_lock (int fd, int cmd, short type, short whence, off_t start,
 3     off_t len)
 4 {
 5     flock_t lock;

 6     lock.l_type = type;
 7     lock.l_whence = whence;
 8     lock.l_start = start;
 9     lock.l_len = len;

10     return (fcntl (fd, cmd, &lock));
11 }
```
———————————————————————————————— *lib/lock.c*

Program D.4 Our function to acquire or release a lock on a file section.

D.5   Our `readn` and `writen` Functions

The `read` and `write` functions we describe in Chapter 4 return the actual number of bytes read or written, which may not be the same as the number of bytes requested. Most of the time (particularly when writing data), this is not regarded as an error, but there are times when we need to ensure that a given number of bytes was actually read or written.

To that end, we have written two functions, readn and writen, which are shown in Program D.5. These functions read or write exactly the requested number of bytes, unless an error occurs or an end of file is detected.

————————————————————————————— lib/read_write.c

```
 1 #include <unistd.h>
 2 #include <errno.h>

 3 ssize_t readn (int fd, void *buf, size_t num)
 4 {
 5     ssize_t res;
 6     size_t n;
 7     char *ptr;

 8     n = num;
 9     ptr = buf;
10     while (n > 0) {
11         if ((res = read (fd, ptr, n)) == -1) {
12             if (errno == EINTR)
13                 res = 0;
14             else
15                 return (-1);
16         }
17         else if (res == 0)
18             break;

19         ptr += res;
20         n -= res;
21     }

22     return (num - n);
23 }

24 ssize_t writen (int fd, const void *buf, size_t num)
25 {
26     ssize_t res;
27     size_t n;
28     const char *ptr;

29     n = num;
30     ptr = buf;
31     while (n > 0) {
32         if ((res = write (fd, ptr, n)) <= 0) {
33             if (errno == EINTR)
34                 res = 0;
35             else
36                 return (-1);
37         }

38         ptr += res;
39         n -= res;
40     }

41     return (num);
42 }
```

————————————————————————————— lib/read_write.c

Program D.5 Our readn and writen functions.

D.6   Termination Status Function

Program D.6 shows the code for our function that prints a description of the termination status of a process, `print_term_status`. If the process terminated normally, its exit status is printed. Otherwise, if the process was terminated abnormally, the name of the signal that caused the abnormal termination is printed, along with whether the signal caused the process to dump core. Finally, if the process was stopped, the name of the signal that caused the process to stop is printed.

—————————————————————————————————— lib/term_status.c

```
1 #include <stdio.h>
2 #include <string.h>
3 #include <sys/wait.h>

4 void print_term_status (int status)
5 {
6     if (WIFEXITED (status))
7         printf ("Normal termination; exit status = %d\n",
8             WEXITSTATUS (status));
9     else if (WIFSIGNALED (status))
10        printf ("Abnormal termination; signal = %s%s\n",
11            strsignal (WTERMSIG (status)),
12            WCOREDUMP (status) ? " (core dumped)" : "");
13    else if (WIFSTOPPED (status))
14        printf ("Child stopped; signal = %s\n",
15            strsignal (WSTOPSIG (status)));
16 }
```

—————————————————————————————————— lib/term_status.c

Program D.6 Our function to print the termination status of a process.

D.7   Our Version of `snprintf`

Throughout the text we use `snprintf` because it is safer than `sprintf` (the latter doesn't prevent buffer overflows). Unfortunately, Solaris 2.5 and 2.5.1 don't provide this function, so we must supply our own.

Program D.7 shows our version of `snprintf`, which should be built only on systems running Solaris 2.5 or 2.5.1. Although this function acts like `sprintf` (i.e., it isn't safe), it *does* try to detect and report buffer overflows.

—————————————————————————————————— lib/snprintf.c

```
1 #include <stdio.h>
2 #include <stdarg.h>

3 int snprintf (char *buf, size_t n, const char *fmt, ...)
4 {
5     int len;
6     va_list ap;

7     va_start (ap, fmt);
8     len = vsprintf (buf, fmt, ap);
9     va_end (ap);
```

```
10      if (len >= n)
11          err_quit ("snprintf: \"%s\" caused a buffer overflow", fmt);

12      return (len);
13  }
```
lib/snprintf.c

Program D.7 Our version of `snprintf`.

Appendix E

Solutions to Selected Exercises

Chapter 1

1.1 To verify that *dot* and *dot-dot* refer to different directories except in the root directory, we can use the `ls` command with two arguments in addition to the usual `-l`. The `-d` argument is used to print information about a directory (rather than the files in that directory), and the `-i` argument prints the inode number of the directory entry.

With this in mind, we can execute the following commands:

```
$ ls -ldi /usr/. /usr/..
        7 drwxr-xr-x  31 root     sys          1024 Aug 17 16:53 /usr/.
        2 drwxr-xr-x  26 root     root          512 Aug 17 19:50 /usr/..
$ ls -ldi /. /..
        2 drwxr-xr-x  26 root     root          512 Aug 17 19:50 /.
        2 drwxr-xr-x  26 root     root          512 Aug 17 19:50 /..
```

The number in the first column is the inode number. Notice that the inode numbers of `/usr/.` and `/usr/..` are 7 and 2 respectively, whereas the inode number of both `/.` and `/..` is 2.

1.2 UNIX is a multitasking operating system. Other processes were running at the same time this program was run, and they were assigned these process IDs by the kernel.

1.4 We modified Program 1.10 to `open` and `close` the test file 100,000 times, and then built and ran three variations: a regular 32-bit version, a large-file-aware version, and a 64-bit version. Figure E.1 summarizes the timing results and the resulting file sizes.

Version	Real	User	Sys	Size
32-bit	2.12	0.36	1.58	9384
Large-file-aware	1.77	0.27	1.49	9412
64-bit	2.12	0.41	1.50	12360

Figure E.1 Summary of running different versions of Program 1.10.

We got these results when running Solaris 9 with a 64-bit kernel on a Sun Blade 100. It's interesting to observe that although the times for the 32-bit and 64-bit versions are comparable, the large-file-aware version is significantly faster (we ran each program twice to eliminate any discrepancies caused by the file cache). We can hypothesize that this results from some behind-the-scenes function name mangling, which the large-file-aware version avoids (by calling the large-file-aware version of open directly).

Notice also that the 64-bit version of our program is about 3 KB bigger than the 32-bit versions. This is because long integers and pointers in a 64-bit process are twice as large as their 32-bit counterparts. We must also recompile our library, ssp.a, as a 64-bit library. This also adds to our program's size.

1.5   Program E.1 shows how we can determine the size of a file by using lseek.

——— solutions/file_size.c

```
 1 #include <stdio.h>
 2 #include <unistd.h>
 3 #include <sys/types.h>
 4 #include <sys/stat.h>
 5 #include <fcntl.h>
 6 #include "ssp.h"

 7 #define BIG_FILE "/space/big_file"

 8 int main (void)
 9 {
10     int fd;
11     off_t size;

12     if ((fd = open (BIG_FILE, O_RDONLY)) == -1)
13         err_msg ("Can't open %s", BIG_FILE);

14     if ((size = lseek (fd, 0, SEEK_END)) == -1)
15         err_msg ("lseek failed");

16     printf ("File size is %ld bytes\n", size);
17     close (fd);

18     return (0);
19 }
```

——— solutions/file_size.c

Program E.1 Determine a file's size by using lseek.

Upon success, the `lseek` function returns the new file offset, so if we seek to the end of the file, the offset returned is the file's size.

Chapter 3

3.1 With counted strings, the first few bytes of a string are its length. Assuming we don't want to limit strings to a length of 255 bytes, counted strings take up more space than the equivalent NUL-terminated string. On the other hand, counted strings have the advantage that they can be used to store strings containing NULs (i.e., binary data).

Given today's fast computers, the only time when we should be concerned that a string must be scanned whenever we want to determine its length (for example, when concatenating two strings) is if we perform this task a large number of times.

3.3 Program E.2 shows the code for our function that returns a string containing the representation of a number in any base from 2 to 36.

solutions/ltostr.c

```
15 static char *ltostr (long value, int base)
16 {
17     char *nums = "0123456789abcdefghijklmnopqrstuvwxyz";
18     static char buf [LINE_LEN];
19     long ovalue;
20     char *ptr;
21     char tmp;
22     int mod;
23     int i;
24     int n;

25     if ((base < 2) || (base > 36))
26         return (NULL);

27     ovalue = value;
28     ptr = buf;

29     do {
30         mod = labs (value % base);
31         *ptr++ = nums [mod];
32         value /= base;
33     } while (value != 0);

34     if (ovalue < 0)
35         *ptr++ = '-';
36     *ptr = '\0';

37     n = strlen (buf) - 1;

38     for (i = 0; i < (n / 2); i++) {
39         tmp = buf [i];
40         buf [i] = buf [n - i];
41         buf [n - i] = tmp;
42     }

43     return (buf);
44 }
```

solutions/ltostr.c

Program E.2 Our function to convert an arbitrarily based number to a string.

The do loop builds up a string containing the digits of the converted number in reverse order. After we append a minus sign if necessary and NUL terminate the string, we reverse it in the for loop. When the characters in the string have been reversed, we can return the string to the caller.

Chapter 4

4.1   File I/O will be most efficient if it is performed in multiples of the file system's block size, which is 8192 bytes for UFS file systems (which is the same as the UltraSPARC's page size). Hence, we chose a value of 8192 for the buffer size.

4.2   From the point of view of the process, the I/O is unbuffered. However, as an optimization, the kernel uses memory that isn't otherwise being used as a buffer cache. When recently written data are accessed, the kernel returns the information stored in the buffer cache. This saves the kernel from having to perform costly disk I/O—even the fastest disks are several orders of magnitude slower than RAM. Note that using directio bypasses the buffer cache.

Chapter 15 of [Mauro and McDougall 2001] contains a detailed description of the Solaris buffer cache implementation.

4.4   Duplicated file descriptors share file table entries, so they have a common file offset. This means that when we lseek to a given place in the file and then write some data, the data will be written where we placed the file offset. This is true even if we lseek using one file descriptor and write using the other.

If we specify the O_APPEND flag, all writes to both file descriptors will be appended to the end of the file regardless of how many lseeks are performed on either file descriptor.

Chapter 5

5.2   The program works as expected. This is because fgets reads up to and including the next newline character *or* until the buffer is full. Also, fputs writes everything in the buffer until it gets to a NUL byte, no matter how many (or how few) newlines the buffer contains. If we use a small value for LINE_LEN, both functions still work, but they are called more times than if we had used a larger buffer.

5.3   This code contains a very common error: getchar returns an integer, not a character. The constant EOF is usually defined as −1; if the system we run this code on uses signed characters, the code will work as expected. However, if it uses unsigned characters, the EOF returned by getchar will be stored as an unsigned character, so its value will no longer be −1. As a result of this, the loop will never terminate.

5.4   Standard input and standard output are both line buffered by default when they are connected to a terminal (as is the case when we run these programs interactively). So, when fgets is called, standard output is flushed automatically.

Chapter 6

6.1 Program 6.2 prints information about the caller's timezone. Running it a few times gives us the following:

```
$ ./tzset                              Author's timezone
Time zone = Canada/Pacific
  timezone difference = 28800 seconds
  altzone difference = 25200 seconds
  daylight = 1
  tzname [0] = PST
  tzname [1] = PDT
$ TZ=Canada/Atlantic ./tzset           Eastern Canada
Time zone = Canada/Atlantic
  timezone difference = 14400 seconds
  altzone difference = 10800 seconds
  daylight = 1
  tzname [0] = AST
  tzname [1] = ADT
$ TZ=GB ./tzset
Time zone = GB                         Great Britain
  timezone difference = 0 seconds
  altzone difference = -3600 seconds
  daylight = 1
  tzname [0] = GMT
  tzname [1] = BST
```

Chapter 7

7.1 Using these functions is fine if we *know* that the environment in which they will be used only uses the files password database (i.e., /etc/passwd and /etc/shadow). However, with networked environments being almost ubiquitous and the proliferation of directory protocols like LDAP and NIS, it doesn't make much sense to limit our programs to using the files password database.

7.2 The advantages of using the new password encryption algorithms include:

- The ability to use longer passwords (i.e., those in which more than just the first eight characters are significant). This reduces the ability of other people being able to guess our passwords by observing what we type (assuming we can type fairly quickly).

- Far less chance of a password being broken through a brute force attack (e.g., by using the crack program) should an unauthorized person discover our encrypted password.

- The ability to share password file entries with other systems (e.g., Linux and BSD), provided support for the appropriate encryption scheme has been enabled.

The disadvantages include:

- Lack of interoperability with systems that don't support the new algorithms, including previous releases of Solaris. This can be a real problem in heterogeneous environments or those that need to support older versions of Solaris.

- Migration from the old algorithms to the new requires users to reenter their passwords, because there are no automatic password migration tools (given the one-way nature of the algorithms involved, this is not surprising).

- Support for the new algorithms must be specifically enabled, which can be burdensome if we have a lot of systems to migrate. However, judicious use of Jumpstart scripts or Solaris Flash archives can mitigate this burden somewhat.

7.3   Program E.3 shows the code for a function called getlluid, which returns a pointer to a lastlog structure for a given user ID.

solutions/lastlog.c

```
27 static struct lastlog *getlluid (uid_t uid)
28 {
29     static struct lastlog ll_entry;
30     FILE *fp;

31     if ((fp = fopen ("/var/adm/lastlog", "r")) == NULL)
32         return (NULL);

33     fseek (fp, uid * sizeof (struct lastlog), SEEK_SET);
34     fread (&ll_entry, sizeof (struct lastlog), 1, fp);
35     fclose (fp);

36     return (&ll_entry);
37 }
```

solutions/lastlog.c

Program E.3   Get a lastlog entry for a given user ID.

Chapter 8

8.1   The uname section of the output from Program 8.1 contains the name of the OS (SunOS), the name of the machine (grover), the release number (5.9), the version number (Generic_112233-07), and the machine type (sun4u). The uname -a command shows all this information, as well as the processor architecture (sparc) and the platform name (SUNW,Sun-Blade-100). The last two pieces of information are probably ascertained by calling the sysinfo function.

In fact, given that this function can also supply all of the information provided by the uname function, it is quite possible that despite its name, the uname command doesn't actually call the uname function. (However, a quick check with the truss utility reveals that this isn't the case. This makes sense because calling uname avoids five calls to sysinfo.)

8.2   No, the new name does not persist across reboots: `sethostname` only sets the hostname of the current system image. When the system boots, one of the boot scripts passes the contents of `/etc/nodename` to `sethostname`, which causes the machine to be given a name. (The foregoing assumes that DHCP is not being used. If a system is a DHCP client, then the DHCP server is usually expected to provide the hostname when the client boots, and the contents of `/etc/nodename` are not looked at.)

8.3   The underlying type of a `clock_t` is a `long`, which in a 32-bit process has a maximum value of 2,147,483,647. 2,147,483,647 clock ticks is 21,474,836 seconds, which is 248 days, 13 hours, 13 minutes, and 56 seconds. (As a matter of interest, a 64-bit process needn't worry about the clock wrapping for more than 33,850 years after the system boots.)

Chapter 9

9.1   An application can take a number of precautions to reduce the effects of DoS attacks on a server.

- Most server applications are written so that incoming requests are handled by different child processes or threads. This is a sensible approach, because otherwise the server process wouldn't be able to accept new connections while it is servicing others. But if the number of child processes or threads is allowed to grow without limit, the resources they require (e.g., virtual memory) could effectively grind the whole machine to a halt. The way to prevent this kind of scenario is to put configurable limits on the resource consumption, by limiting the number of child processes or threads.

- Have each child process (or thread) handle a configurable number of requests and then quit. This prevents the size of the process from growing endlessly (recall that even when we call `free`, the memory isn't actually returned to the OS until the process terminates). Long-running applications, even if they don't have any memory leaks, can grow quite large.

- Use dynamic, rather than static, linking. In addition to the other benefits of dynamic linking, the memory footprint of our application is reduced. This means that we can handle more simultaneous requests, which helps defend against DoS attacks. The memory footprint of dynamically linked applications is reduced because only one copy of the shared libraries is kept in memory.

- Run the application as an unprivileged user, preferably one that is specific to the application. This helps minimize the potential damage that can be caused by an application with exploitable security problems.

We should also minimize the effects of resource depletion by ensuring that the server is generously configured. For example, we should maximize the amount of

RAM in the server and provide a generous amount of swap space. While this is not something an application can do, it *is* a good way to help prevent DoS attacks.

9.2   For this exercise, assume that we have a directory called `chroot`. This directory contains our "Hello World" program, `hello`, and the other necessary files. The actual files required depend on which version of Solaris we're using, as summarized in Figure E.2.

File	Required?					
	2.5	2.5.1	2.6	7	8	9
`/dev/zero`	•	•	•	•		
`/usr/lib/ld.so.1`	•	•	•	•	•	•
`/usr/lib/libc.so.1`	•	•	•	•	•	•
`/usr/lib/libdl.so.1`	•	•	•	•	•	•

Figure E.2   Minimum set of files required in a `chroot` jail.

It is quite likely that programs more sophisticated than `hello` will require more files to be installed into the `chroot`ed environment, particularly shared libraries.

Chapter 10

10.1   If `/etc/passwd` is not readable by all users, and the `passwd` cache of `nscd` (the name service cache daemon) is disabled (either explicitly, or by `nscd` not running), various commands will break, or at least not work as usual. For example, instead of showing user names, the command `ls -l` will just print user IDs. Similarly, the `finger` command will not be able to determine information about users.

Let's look at an example. We'll run the `finger` command twice, before and after changing the permissions on `/etc/passwd`. But first we'll disable and invalidate the `passwd` cache:

```
$ su
Password:
# nscd -e passwd,no          Disable passwd cache
# nscd -i passwd             Invalidate passwd cache
```

In another window, we'll run the `finger` command:

```
$ finger rich
Login name: rich                       In real life: Rich Teer
Directory: /home/rich                  Shell: /bin/ksh
On since Nov 22 11:23:54 on pts/1 from zaphod
No unread mail
Project:
Plan:

Login name: rich                       In real life: Rich Teer
Directory: /home/rich                  Shell: /bin/ksh
On since Nov 22 11:24:14 on pts/2 from zaphod
```

Back in the superuser window, we'll now remove world read access from /etc/passwd:

```
# chmod 440 /etc/passwd
```

and rerun finger:

```
$ finger rich
Login name: rich                         In real life: ???

Login name: rich                         In real life: ???
```

This time, finger doesn't print anything useful.

10.2 The file creation mask determines which permission bits are *cleared* when a file is created. So if we set the file creation mask to 0777, all permission bits will be cleared. The following demonstrates this:

```
$ umask
022
$ rm foo
$ touch foo
$ ls -l foo
-rw-r--r--  1 rich     staff            0 Nov 25 19:23 foo
$ rm foo
$ umask 0777
$ touch foo
$ ls -l foo
----------  1 rich     staff            0 Nov 25 19:24 foo
```

10.3 If we try to create a file that already exists by using either creat or open, the file's permission bits are not changed. We can verify this by running Program 10.4:

```
$ rm foo bar
$ uname -a > foo
$ uname -a > bar
$ chmod 220 foo bar
$ ls -l foo bar
--w--w----  1 rich     staff           66 Nov 25 19:59 bar
--w--w----  1 rich     staff           66 Nov 25 19:59 foo
$ ./umask
$ ls -l foo bar
--w--w----  1 rich     staff            0 Nov 25 20:00 bar
--w--w----  1 rich     staff            0 Nov 25 20:00 foo
```

Note that the although the files are truncated, their permission bits remain unchanged.

10.4 Directories should never have a size of 0 because at a minimum they must always contain entries for *dot* and *dot-dot*. The size of a symbolic link is the number of characters in the pathname to which it points. We can create a symbolic link that has a size of 0 by running the following command:

```
$ rm foo
$ ln -s "" foo
$ ls -l foo
lrwxrwxrwx  1 rich     staff            0 Nov 25 20:08 foo ->
```

10.6 The trick here is to fetch the three file times first by calling stat. We then call utime to set the desired value; the value that we don't want to modify should be set to the corresponding value from stat.

Chapter 11

11.1 There are a number of advantages to implementing /etc/mnttab as a read-only file system. These include:

- Data integrity is better, because it is impossible for a regular process, even if it is privileged, to write to the file. Mounting or unmounting a file system is the only way /etc/mnttab can be updated.

- Applications parsing /etc/mnttab no longer need to lock the file to ensure they have exclusive access to it. This is because the file seen by the process is actually a snapshot that represents the situation at the time the snapshot was taken, and the snapshot is taken atomically with respect to updates. (Any read from the beginning of the file causes a new snapshot to be taken.)

11.2 As Program E.4 demonstrates, yes, a process can access a file it has a file descriptor for if a file system is mounted on top of it.

Running Program E.4 gives us the following:

```
$ su
Password:
# umount /space                          Ensure file system is not mounted
umount: warning: /space not in mnttab
umount: /space not mounted
# ls -al /space
total 4
drwxrwxrwx   2 root      root         512 Dec 19 09:36 .
drwxr-xr-x  26 root      root         512 Aug 17 19:50 ..
# ./ghost
# ls -l /space/foo
/space/foo: No such file or directory
# umount /space
# ls -l /space/foo
-rw-r--r--   1 root      other         67 Dec 19 09:37 /space/foo
# cat /space/foo
This was written before the mount
This was written after the mount
```

There are two main ramifications of this, both of which are security related.

1. A malicious or rogue process could fill up the underlying file system, potentially causing a denial of service. In our example we write to a file called /space/foo. If /space is not mounted, then when we write to this file, we are actually consuming space on the / file system. We could use up all of the space on the root file system, so that (for example) logging files in

solutions/ghost.c

```
 1 #include <stdio.h>
 2 #include <unistd.h>
 3 #include <string.h>
 4 #include <sys/types.h>
 5 #include <sys/stat.h>
 6 #include <fcntl.h>
 7 #include <sys/mount.h>
 8 #include <sys/mntent.h>
 9 #include <sys/fs/ufs_mount.h>
10 #include "ssp.h"

11 #define SPEC "/dev/dsk/c0t0d0s7"
12 #define DIR "/space"

13 int main (int argc, char **argv)
14 {
15     int fd;
16     char *buf1 = "This was written before the mount\n";
17     char *buf2 = "This was written after the mount\n";
18     struct ufs_args args;

19     if ((fd = open ("/space/foo", O_WRONLY | O_CREAT, FILE_PERMS)) == -1)
20         err_msg ("Can't creat foo");

21     if (writen (fd, buf1, strlen (buf1)) == -1)
22         err_msg ("writen failed");

23 #ifdef UFSMNT_LARGEFILES
24     args.flags = UFSMNT_LARGEFILES;
25 #else
26     args.flags = 0;
27 #endif

28     if (mount (SPEC, DIR, MS_DATA, MNTTYPE_UFS, &args, sizeof (args),
29         NULL, 0) == -1) {
30         err_msg ("mount failed");
31     }

32     if (writen (fd, buf2, strlen (buf2)) == -1)
33         err_msg ("writen failed");

34     close (fd);

35     return (0);
36 }
```

solutions/ghost.c

Program E.4 Writing to a file that is underneath a mount point.

/var can no longer be appended to. (An intruder might do this to mask their tracks.) Finding the space that has been consumed in this manner can be a difficult task, requiring the unmounting of all file systems whose mount point is in the full one, until we find the rogue file.

2. An intruder or other malicious user could use this technique to store sensitive information away from the prying eyes of the system

administrator. For example, a password grabber could store a list of user names and their corresponding passwords in a file hidden in this manner. If the file doesn't grow so large as to use up a significant amount of space in the underlying file system (thereby alerting the system administrator that something might be afoot), it is possible that it could remain undetected for a considerable period. Other sensitive information, such as company financials or military secrets, could also be hidden using exactly the same method.

11.3 If we forcibly unmount a file system while processes have files in that file system open, subsequent attempts to access those files will fail, as Program E.5 illustrates.

solutions/unref.c

```
 1 #include <stdio.h>
 2 #include <unistd.h>
 3 #include <string.h>
 4 #include <sys/types.h>
 5 #include <sys/stat.h>
 6 #include <fcntl.h>
 7 #include <sys/mount.h>
 8 #include "ssp.h"

 9 #define DIR "/space"

10 int main (int argc, char **argv)
11 {
12     int fd;
13     char *buf1 = "This was written before the unmount\n";
14     char *buf2 = "This was written after the unmount\n";

15     if ((fd = open ("/space/foo", O_WRONLY | O_CREAT, FILE_PERMS)) == -1)
16         err_msg ("Can't creat foo");

17     if (writen (fd, buf1, strlen (buf1)) == -1)
18         err_msg ("writen failed");

19     if (umount (DIR) == -1)
20         err_ret ("umount failed");
21 #ifdef MS_FORCE
22     log_msg ("Attempting to force");
23     if (umount2 (DIR, MS_FORCE) == -1)
24         err_msg ("umount2 failed");
25 #endif

26     if (writen (fd, buf2, strlen (buf2)) == -1)
27         err_msg ("writen failed");

28     close (fd);

29     return (0);
30 }
```

solutions/unref.c

Program E.5 Accessing a file after its file system has been unmounted.

Running Program E.5 gives us the following results:

```
$ su
Password:
# mount /space                          Ensure file system is mounted
# ./unref
umount failed: forcing: Device busy
write failed: I/O error
# ls -l /space/foo
/space/foo: No such file or directory
# mount /space
# ls -l /space/foo
-rw-r--r--   1 root      other         36 Dec 19 11:11 /space/foo
# cat /space/foo
This was written before the unmount
```

Attempts to `write` to the file after its file system has been unmounted fail.

Chapter 12

12.1 The values for MIN and TIME are 1 and 1. This means that `read` will wait for at least one character to be typed, but will wait no longer than 0.1 seconds for subsequent characters. The `vi` command sets the terminal to non-canonical mode, which is why these values appear in the `stty` output. These values are not printed if we run `stty` for a window in canonical mode.

12.2 The characters we type are not echoed, and we must terminate a line with a newline character (NL) rather than a carriage return (in other words, we must type Control-J to terminate a line rather than pressing the Return key). To restore normal operation, we can use the command `stty sane` (although this command doesn't restore user preferences for characters like ERASE, INTR, and KILL; they will be set to their default values instead).

Chapter 13

13.1 The kernel does detect and avoid deadlock between two processes sharing two files. This makes sense because a design that is susceptible to deadlock is no less likely to have problems with two shared files than with one. If anything, the likelihood of a deadlock situation increases as the number of shared files increases, so it is important that the kernel detect and avoid these situations if possible.

13.2 Unfortunately, no. What we would like to do is have the `ssp_tell_wait_init` function create a temporary, 2-byte file. One byte would be used for the parent's lock, and the other would be used for the child's lock. Calling `ssp_wait_child` would make the parent try to acquire a lock on the child's lock, blocking until it succeeds. Similarly, `ssp_wait_parent` would suspend the child until it can acquire a lock on the parent's lock. The appropriate lock would be released by calling `ssp_tell_child` or `ssp_tell_parent`. This is all fine in theory, but breaks down in practice. This is because `fork` releases all locks, so the child can't start executing owning any locks.

13.3 We can accomplish this by defining the manifest constant `FD_SETSIZE` before
including `<sys/types.h>`. For example, to handle 4096 file descriptors, we
would write

```
#define FD_SETSIZE 4096
#include <sys/types.h>
```

which would define the `fd_set` data type as required.

13.4 Program E.6 measures the capacity of a pipe by using the `poll` function (a similar
solution using `select` is also possible).

solutions/pipe_cap.c

```
 1 #include <stdio.h>
 2 #include <unistd.h>
 3 #include <poll.h>
 4 #include "ssp.h"

 5 int main (void)
 6 {
 7     int pipe_fd [2];
 8     int i;
 9     int n;
10     struct pollfd fds;

11     if (pipe (pipe_fd) == -1)
12         err_msg ("pipe failed");

13     fds.fd = pipe_fd [1];
14     fds.events = POLLOUT;
15     fds.revents = 0;

16     for (i = 0;; i++) {
17         if ((n = poll (&fds, 1, 0)) == -1)
18             err_msg ("poll failed");
19         if (n == 0)
20             break;
21         if (writen (pipe_fd [1], "x", 1) == -1)
22             err_msg ("writen failed");
23     }

24     printf ("Pipe capacity = %d bytes\n", i);

25     return (0);
26 }
```

solutions/pipe_cap.c

Program E.6 Measuring the capacity of a pipe by using `poll`.

On the machines the author tried, the capacity of the pipe was 9216 bytes.
Interestingly, this number is exactly 4096 greater than the constant `PIPE_BUF`,
which is 5120. Recall from Section 8.3 that `PIPE_BUF` is the size of the maximum
guaranteed atomic `write` to a pipe, which is not necessarily the same thing as the
maximum capacity of a pipe. Under certain circumstances, it is possible to `write`
more than `PIPE_BUF` bytes to a pipe atomically, up to the pipe's capacity (although
only `write`s of `PIPE_BUF` bytes or less are guaranteed to be atomic).

Chapter 14

14.1 The command line arguments (represented by `argc` and `argv`) are not stored in global variables (in contrast to the environment, which is accessible by the global variable `environ`). Consequently, it is not possible for a function called by `main` to access them.

14.2 The stack and heap of a process are not allocated until the program is executed by calling one of the `exec` functions. That is, the heap and stack do not form a part of the the program's image on disk, which is why the `size` command doesn't (or indeed, *can't*) report their sizes.

14.3 The `size` command prints the total size of the text, data, and BSS segments, but an executable file contains other information. Most of this extra information is the symbol table, which helps in debugging the program. We can use the `strip` command to remove this information, which reduces the file's size to a figure nearer the total displayed by `size` (the rest of the space is taken up by the Executable and Linking Format (ELF) overhead).

14.4 A dynamically linked program contains just enough information about library routines so that the linker can resolve any references at run time. In contrast, a statically linked program has all of the library's routines in its executable, taking up a large amount of space. This is another reason why we should always link our programs dynamically with the standard C library. (From Solaris 10, it is impossible to do otherwise, because no static versions of the system libraries are supplied.)

Chapter 15

15.1 No function is provided that will tell us what the saved set-user-ID is, so what we must do instead is save the effective user ID when the process first starts.

15.2 Let's consider Figure E.3 and Program E.7.

When `vfork` is called from `func_1`, the stack pointer for the parent process points to the stack frame for `func_1` (as shown in Figure E.3).

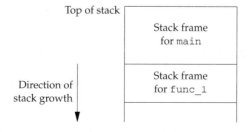

Figure E.3 Stack frame for Program E.7.

solutions/vfork.c

```
 1 #include <unistd.h>
 2 #include "ssp.h"

 3 static void func_1 (void);
 4 static void func_2 (void);

 5 int main (void)
 6 {
 7     func_1 ();
 8     func_2 ();

 9     _exit (0);

10     return (0);
11 }

12 static void func_1 (void)
13 {
14     pid_t pid;

15     if ((pid = vfork ()) == -1)
16         err_msg ("vfork failed");
17 }

18 static void func_2 (void)
19 {
20     char buf [LINE_LEN];
21     int i;

22     for (i = 0; i < LINE_LEN; i++)
23         buf [i] = i % 255;
24 }
```

solutions/vfork.c

Program E.7   Incorrect use of `vfork`.

The `vfork` function causes the child process to execute first. It returns from `func_1` and calls `func_2`, which causes `func_1`'s stack from to be overwritten. The child then initializes `LINE_BUF` bytes of the stack frame. The child then returns from `func_2` and calls `_exit`. The parent process now continues executing, but its stack frame has been changed by the child (recall that after a `vfork`, the child and parent processes share address spaces until the child terminates or calls `exec`). When the parent attempts to return from `func_1`, the return information in the stack frame has been changed by the child and no longer contains valid information.

The usual result of this stack corruption is a `core` dump (this happened on the Solaris 9 UltraSPARC system used by the author), but your system might give different results.

15.3 Program E.8 creates a zombie.

Zombies are shown by the `ps` command as having a status of "Z" and a command string of `<defunct>`:

solutions/zombie.c

```
 1 #include <unistd.h>
 2 #include <stdlib.h>
 3 #include "ssp.h"

 4 int main (void)
 5 {
 6     switch (fork ()) {
 7         case -1:
 8             err_msg ("fork failed");

 9         case 0:
10             _exit (0);

11         default:
12             sleep (2);
13             system ("ps -o s,user,pid,ppid,comm -u rich");
14             break;
15     }

16     return (0);
17 }
```

solutions/zombie.c

Program E.8   Create a zombie and look at it using ps.

```
$ ./zombie
S     USER   PID  PPID COMMAND
S     rich 23367 23365 -ksh
S     rich 24121 24119 -ksh
O     rich  2686  2685 ps
S     rich 23380 23378 -ksh
S     rich  2685  2683 sh
S     rich  4405 23367 vi
Z     rich  2684  2683 <defunct>
S     rich  2683 23380 ./zombie
```

Chapter 16

16.1   Program E.9 prints the foreground process group ID of a given terminal device.
Running Program E.9 gives us the following:

```
$ tty                                    Check which tty we're using
/dev/pts/2
$ ./ttypgid pts/2 &
[1]     9285
/dev/pts/2's process group ID is 23380

[1] +  Done                             ./ttypgid pts/2 &
$ ps -j
  PID  PGID   SID TTY      TIME CMD
23380 23380 23380 pts/2    0:02 ksh
 9282  9282 23380 pts/2    0:00 ps
```

solutions/ttypgid.c

```
 1 #include <stdio.h>
 2 #include <sys/types.h>
 3 #include <sys/stat.h>
 4 #include <fcntl.h>
 5 #include <unistd.h>
 6 #include "ssp.h"

 7 int main (int argc, char **argv)
 8 {
 9     int fd;
10     pid_t pgid;
11     char dev [LINE_LEN];

12     if (argc != 2)
13         err_quit ("Usage: ttypgid terminal");

14     snprintf (dev, LINE_LEN, "/dev/%s", argv [1]);

15     if ((fd = open (dev, O_RDONLY)) == -1)
16         err_msg ("Can't open %s", dev);

17     if ((pgid = tcgetpgrp (fd)) == -1)
18         err_msg ("tcgetpgrp failed");

19     printf ("%s's process group ID is %ld\n", dev, (long) pgid);

20     return (0);
21 }
```

solutions/ttypgid.c

Program E.9   Print a terminal's foreground process group ID.

Notice that we run Program E.9 in the background. By doing this, we ensure that our login shell remains in the foreground process group. If we run Program E.9 in the foreground, *it* will be in the foreground process group and will not show up in the ps output. This is because by the time we run ps, the ttypgid process will have finished executing.

16.2   Program E.10 forks a child process, which subsequently creates a new session.

We can verify that the child becomes a process group leader with no controlling terminal by running the ps command while Program E.10 runs in the background.

```
$ ./pgleader &
[1]     24294
$ ps -jfu rich
      UID   PID  PPID  PGID   SID  C    STIME TTY        TIME CMD
     rich 23367 23365 23367 23367  0   Nov 22 pts/1     0:00 -ksh
     rich 24121 24119 24121 24121  0   Nov 23 pts/3     0:01 -ksh
     rich 23380 23378 23380 23380  0   Nov 22 pts/2     0:02 -ksh
     rich 24295     1 24295 24295  0 11:27:46 ?         0:00 ./pgleader
     rich 24296 23380 24296 23380  0 11:27:46 pts/2     0:00 ps -jfu rich
```

The "?" in the TTY column of our pgleader process indicates that it has no controlling terminal, and the fact that its process and process group IDs are the same indicate that the child became a process group leader.

solutions/pgleader.c

```
1 #include <sys/types.h>
2 #include <unistd.h>
3 #include "ssp.h"

4 int main (void)
5 {
6     pid_t pid;

7     if ((pid = fork ()) == -1)
8         err_msg ("fork failed");
9     if (pid == 0) {
10         if (setsid () == -1)
11             err_msg ("setsid failed");
12         sleep (5);
13     }

14     return (0);
15 }
```

solutions/pgleader.c

Program E.10 Create a new session.

Chapter 17

17.1 If we remove the infinite loop from Program 17.1, the process will terminate the first time it receives a signal. This happens because the pause function returns whenever a signal is caught.

17.2 Figure E.4 shows the stack frames when Program 17.7 is executing.

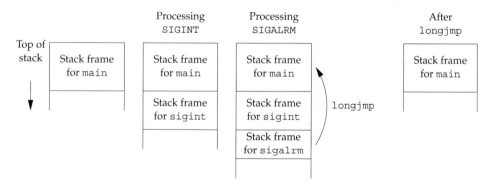

Figure E.4 Stack frames while Program 17.7 is executing.

The longjmp from the SIGALRM handler (sigalrm) back to main effectively aborts the call to the SIGINT handler, sigint.

17.3 An example of this appears in [Libes 1990].

17.4   To send a signal to another process using the `kill` function, our effective user ID must be 0. Including the real user ID of the sender of a signal therefore imparts more information to the signal's recipient than if the effective user ID had been passed.

17.5   If we just call `_exit`, the termination status of the process would not show that the termination resulted from the reception of a `SIGABRT` signal. The termination status would be the argument passed to `_exit` instead.

Chapter 18

18.1   If a process calls `chroot` before calling `openlog` or `syslog`, it will not be able to open `/dev/log` (we are assuming here that the directory into which we `chroot` does not contain a copy of `/dev/log`). The solution to this problem is to have our daemon call `openlog` with `LOG_NDELAY` set in *logopt* before calling `chroot`. Doing this opens the `/dev/log` special file immediately, giving a file descriptor which will still be valid after a successful `chroot`. An FTP daemon is an example of a process likely to use this technique, because it still needs to call `syslog` to log error messages, despite calling `chroot` for security reasons.

18.3   Any command line arguments should be parsed before `daemon_init` is called. Doing so enables us to specify a flag that prevents the process from running as a daemon. We might want to do this to make debugging our program easier, for example. Parsing the command line arguments prior to calling `daemon_init` also allows us to use a flag to specify whether the daemon was started by `inetd`, and pass the appropriate value to `daemon_init`.

18.4   Program E.11 prints the number of the highest open file descriptor.

18.5   No, we can't use a similar technique. This is because a file descriptor is allocated behind the scenes when we call `opendir`. We have no way of knowing the number of this file descriptor, so if we use a loop similar to the one in the `max_fd` function in Program E.11 to close the open descriptors, it is possible that we will close the file descriptor allocated by `opendir` before we are finished with it.

18.6   If we pass the `O_TRUNC` option to `open` and another copy of the daemon is already running, we will delete the process ID stored in the file by the first copy of the daemon. Hence, we can't truncate the file until we know that we are the only copy running.

18.7   We call `one_copy` after becoming a daemon because one of the tasks performed by `daemon_init` is to close all files. If we call `one_copy` first, `daemon_init` would close the file in which we store the process ID, releasing the lock.

Chapter 19

19.1   The `close_other_pipes` function is only called from the child process created by `ssp_popen`. The child process either terminates quickly (in the event of an error),

———————————————————————————————— *solutions/max_fd.c*

```
 1 #include <stdio.h>
 2 #include <stdlib.h>
 3 #include <dirent.h>
 4 #include "ssp.h"

 5 static int max_fd (void);

 6 int main (void)
 7 {
 8     int max;

 9     if ((max = max_fd ()) == -1)
10         err_msg ("max_fd failed");
11
12     printf ("Highest open file descriptor = %d\n", max);

13     return (0);
14 }

15 static int max_fd (void)
16 {
17     DIR *dirp;
18     struct dirent *dir;
19     int fd;
20     int max;

21     max = 0;

22     if ((dirp = opendir ("/proc/self/fd")) == NULL)
23         return (-1);

24     if ((readdir (dirp) == NULL) || (readdir (dirp) == NULL)) {
25         closedir (dirp);
26         return (-1);
27     }

28     while ((dir = readdir (dirp)) != NULL) {
29         fd = atoi (dir -> d_name);
30         if (fd > max)
31             max = fd;
32     }

33     closedir (dirp);

34     return (max);
35 }
```

———————————————————————————————— *solutions/max_fd.c*

Program E.11   Print the number of the highest open file descriptor.

which automatically frees all of its memory, or it calls exec. as a result of the exec, the child process' memory is freed, so as a performance optimization we don't bother to free the entries in the linked list when we close each descriptor.

19.2 If we remove the SIGPIPE signal handler, the parent process will terminate as before (but the message will probably be different). We can tell that the parent was terminated because it received a SIGPIPE signal by checking its termination status from the shell. In the Korn shell (or one of its relatives), the command to print the most recent termination status is echo $?. The number printed is 128 plus the number of the signal (on Solaris, SIGPIPE is signal number 13).

19.3 For the sake of this discussion, let's assume that after we open the pipe, we call system, which runs sleep(1). The wait function waits for the first child process related to the caller to terminate. The first child to terminate is the one created by popen. This is not the child created by system, so it calls wait again, blocking until the sleep is finished. When the sleep process terminates, system returns, having first reaped the status of the sleep process. When we later call pclose, its call to wait will fail, because there are no more child processes to wait for. Hence, pclose will return an error.

19.4 The reader of a pipe or FIFO doesn't need to be sent a SIGPIPE signal when the writer has terminated, because the read will return an end of file notification.

19.5 Program E.12 shows how we can portably open a FIFO for reading and writing. We never use the file descriptor that is open for writing, but leaving it open prevents an end of file being generated when the number of clients drops to 0. Notice that we must be careful when we open the FIFO. We first perform a nonblocking read-only open, followed by a blocking write-only open. (We'd get an error if we tried performing a nonblocking write-only open first.)

Having opened the FIFO for reading and writing, we turn off the O_NONBLOCK flag for the read-only file descriptor. A real program would probably set up an exit handler to remove the FIFO when the program terminates, just after the call to mkfifo (like we did in Program 19.13).

Chapter 20

20.1 If we change Program 20.2 to accept an argument of IPC_PRIVATE, the other programs must be modified to accept an integer message queue identifier instead of a pathname. We could either introduce a new command line option, or assume that a pathname that only consists of digits is the message queue identifier. Most pathnames passed to ftok are absolute, so this is probably a safe assumption. If a message queue identifier is passed to the other programs, they don't need to call ftok.

20.4 Only four lines (15 to 18 inclusive) of code need to change. This:

```
if ((key = ftok (argv [1], 0x42)) == -1)
    err_msg ("ftok failed");
if ((shmid = shmget (key, 0, 0)) == -1)
    err_msg ("shmget failed");
```

becomes this:

```
key = atol (argv [1]);
```

solutions/open_fifo.c

```
1 #include <stdio.h>
2 #include <unistd.h>
3 #include <sys/types.h>
4 #include <sys/stat.h>
5 #include <fcntl.h>
6 #include <errno.h>
7 #include "ssp.h"

8 #define WELL_KNOWN_FIFO "/tmp/ssp_fifo"

9 static int open_fifo (const char *path);

10 int main (void)
11 {
12     int fd;

13     if ((fd = open_fifo (WELL_KNOWN_FIFO)) == -1)
14         err_msg ("Can't open FIFO");

15     return (0);
16 }

17 static int open_fifo (const char *path)
18 {
19     int read_fd;
20     int write_fd;

21     if (unlink (path) == -1) {
22         if (errno != ENOENT)
23             return (-1);
24     }

25     if (mkfifo (path, FIFO_PERMS) == -1)
26         return (-1);

27     if ((read_fd = open (path, O_RDONLY | O_NONBLOCK)) == -1)
28         return (-1);
29     if ((write_fd = open (path, O_WRONLY)) == -1)
30         return (-1);

31     return (clear_fsflag (read_fd, O_NONBLOCK));
32 }
```

solutions/open_fifo.c

Program E.12 Portably opening a FIFO for reading and writing.

Chapter 21

21.1 The parent and child should print the same file offsets. This is because the offset of a file is part of the information associated with its file descriptor, and the two processes are sharing the same descriptor.

21.2 On success, the `poll` function returns the number of file descriptors that have been selected (that is, the number of file descriptors for which the value of `revents` is not 0). The loop that iterates through the array of client file descriptors could terminate when the appropriate number of descriptors have been processed.

Chapter 22

22.1 If we attempt to invoke a server procedure from a client after we've cleared the door's `FD_CLOEXEC` flag and `execed` a new program, a core dump is the most likely result. This is because the address associated with the door's service procedure is likely to be meaningless in the newly `execed` process; random code in the new process will be called as the service procedure.

22.2 The error message we get is:

```
$ ./door_srv3 /tmp/ssp_door
ssp_create: Created server thread 4
door_bind failed: Bad file number
```

Because of the multithreaded nature of the door server, the appearance of this error on a uniprocessor system is nondeterministic (the author had to run this program 17 times before the error manifested itself). On systems with multiple processors, the error is *much* more likely to appear.

22.3 To verify that a `door_call` in progress is allowed to finish when we call `door_revoke`, we call `door_revoke` from our service procedure just before calling `door_return`. (We must also make the door descriptor a global variable, because we must pass it to `door_revoke`.) Running a client twice against this new version of our server gives the following:

```
$ ./door_cli1 /tmp/ssp_door 42
Result = 1764
$ ./door_cli1 /tmp/ssp_door 42
door_call failed: Bad file number
```

The first invocation of the client runs successfully, proving our assertion that in-progress `door_calls` are not affected. The second time we run the client, the `door_call` fails, returning `EBADF`.

22.4 We can pass a pointer to the door descriptor in the cookie to avoid making `door_fd` a global variable. The cookie pointer that we pass to `door_create` is passed to the server procedure every time it is called. Program E.13 shows the code for the modified version of our server.

We can use a similar tactic in Programs 22.11, 22.12, and 22.13. The cookie pointer is available in `ssp_create` (via the `door_info` pointer), so we could pass it to `ssp_thread`, which needs the door descriptor in order to pass it to `door_bind`.

solutions/door_srv.c

```
 1 #include <unistd.h>
 2 #include <sys/types.h>
 3 #include <sys/stat.h>
 4 #include <fcntl.h>
 5 #include <door.h>
 6 #include "ssp.h"

 7 static void server_proc (void *cookie, char *argp, size_t arg_size,
 8     door_desc_t *dp, uint_t n_desc);

 9 int main (int argc, char **argv)
10 {
11     int door_fd;
12     int tmp_fd;

13     if (argc != 2)
14         err_quit ("Usage: door_srv path");

15     if ((door_fd = door_create (server_proc, &door_fd, 0)) == -1)
16         err_msg ("door_create failed");

17     unlink (argv [1]);
18     if ((tmp_fd = creat (argv [1], FILE_PERMS)) == -1)
19         err_msg ("creat failed");
20     close (tmp_fd);
21     if (fattach (door_fd, argv [1]) == -1)
22         err_msg ("fattach failed");

23     for (;;)
24         pause ();
25 }

26 static void server_proc (void *cookie, char *argp, size_t arg_size,
27     door_desc_t *dp, uint_t n_desc)
28 {
29     long arg;
30     long res;

31     arg = *((long *) argp);
32     res = arg * arg;

33     if (door_revoke (*((int *) cookie)) == -1)
34         err_msg ("door_revoke failed");

35     if (door_return ((char *) &res, sizeof (long), NULL, 0) == -1)
36         err_msg ("door_return failed");
37 }
```

solutions/door_srv.c

Program E.13   Passing a door descriptor in a cookie to avoid making it global.

Chapter 23

23.2 If it *was* possible to change an open file's mode, we would use the `SETFL` command of the `fcntl` function. However, `SETFL` does not allow these flags to be set, so it is impossible to change an open file's access mode.

23.3 There are three process groups to consider:

1. The login shell
2. The `pty` process
3. The `cat` process

The first two process groups make up a session, the leader of which is the login shell. The third process group is in its own session. The login shell's process group is a background process group, and the other two are foreground process groups.

23.4 We can add a start header and finish footer to our version of `script` by using the `echo` and `date` commands in a subshell. Program E.14 shows this.

solutions/ssp_script

```
1 #!/bin/sh

2 ( echo "Script started on" `date`;
3 ../pseudo_terms/pty "${SHELL:-/bin/sh}";
4 echo "Script done on" `date` ) | tee typescript
```

solutions/ssp_script

Program E.14 Adding start and stop timestamps to our version of `script`.

23.5 As we can see from this output from `truss`, when the controlling process terminates, the pty slave is sent a hangup signal (`SIGHUP`), thus terminating it:

```
26742:  write(1, " S I G W I N C H   r e c".., 18)     = 18
26742:  ioctl(0, TIOCGWINSZ, 0xFFBFF900)               = 0
26742:  write(1, " 4 0   c o l u m n s   b".., 45)     = 45
26739:  ioctl(3, TIOCSWINSZ, 0xFFBFF954)               = 0
26739:  read(3, " S I G W I N C H   r e c".., 256)     = 65
From pty_child: SIGWINCH received
40 columns by 20 rows (0 pixels by 5 pixels)
26739:  write(1, " F r o m   p t y _ c h i".., 81)     = 81
26739:  _exit(0)
26742:     Received signal #1, SIGHUP, in pause() [default]
26742:  pause()                                        Err#4 EINTR
```

In this output, the process ID of the controlling process is 26739, and that of the pty slave is 26742.

Bibliography

Whenever an electronic copy of a paper referenced in this bibliography was found, its URL is included. Unfortunately, these URLs can change over time, so readers are encouraged to check the errata for this text on the author's home page for any changes: `http://www.rite-group.com/rich`.

Aho, Alfred V., Kernighan, Brian W., and Weinberger, Peter J. 1988. *The AWK Programming Language.* Addison-Wesley, Reading, MA.

> This is a complete book on the AWK programming language. The version described in the book is sometimes called nawk, for "new awk".

ANSI. 1989. *American National Standard for Information Systems—Programming Language C, X3.159–1989.* American National Standards Institute, New York, NY.

> This describes the 1989 version of the ANSI C programming language, and includes a rationale.

AT&T. 1989. *System V Interface Definition, Third Edition.* Addison-Wesley, Reading, MA.

> This is a five-volume set that specifies the application programmer interface (API) and run-time behaviour of SVR4. The topics covered by the various volumes include: Base System and Kernel Extension (Volume 1); Basic and Advanced Utilities Extension, Administered Systems Extension (Volume 2); Programming Language Specification, Software Development Extension (Volume 3); and Window System Extension (Volume 4). Volume 5 consists of updates to the commands and system calls found in Volumes 1 through 4.

Butenhof, David R. 1997. *Programming with POSIX Threads*. Addison-Wesley, Reading, MA.

> A detailed look at multithreaded programming using POSIX threads (Pthreads).

Christiansen, Tom. 1995. *Csh Programming Considered Harmful*. Usenet, comp.unix.shell newsgroup, Message-ID: <538e76$8uq$1@csnews.cs.colorado.edu>.

> An article on why writing shell scripts in the C Shell should be avoided. It can be found at the following URL: http://www.faqs.org/faqs/unix-faq/shell/csh-whynot.

Cockcroft, Adrian, and Pettit, Richard. 1998. *Sun Performance and Tuning: Java and the Internet, Second Edition*. Prentice Hall, Upper Saddle River, NJ.

> This book describes the art and science of performance monitoring and tuning, focusing on Sun hardware and Solaris releases up to and including Solaris 2.6.

Garfinkel, Simson, and Spafford, Gene. 2003. *Practical UNIX and Internet Security, Third Edition*. O'Reilly & Associates, Sebastopol, CA.

> This is a very detailed book on UNIX and Internet security.

Goodheart, Berny. 1991. *UNIX Curses Explained*. Prentice Hall, Upper Saddle River, NJ.

IEEE. 1985. *IEEE Standard for Binary Floating Point Arithmetic*. Also known as *IEEE Std. 754-1985*. Institute of Electrical and Electronics Engineers, Piscataway, NJ.

> This document specifies floating point number formats, basic operations, conversions, and exception conditions. Further information is available from http://www.ieee.org.

IEEE. 1996. *Information Technology—Portable Operating System Interface (POSIX)—Part 1: System Application Program Interface (API) [C Language]*. Also known as *IEEE Std. 1003.1, 1996 Edition*. Institute of Electrical and Electronics Engineers, Piscataway, NJ.

> This version of POSIX incorporates the base API from 1990, the 1003.1b realtime extensions from 1993, the 1003.1c POSIX threads from 1995, and the 1003.1i technical corrections from 1995. It is also International Standard ISO/IEC 9945–1:1996 (E). Further information is available from http://www.ieee.org.

ISO/IEC. 1990. *Programming Languages—C*. American National Standards Institute, New York, NY.

> This book describes the 1990 version of the ISO C programming language. The versions of Solaris we cover in this text are compliant with this version of C.

ISO/IEC. 1999. *Programming Languages—C*. American National Standards Institute, New York, NY.

> This book describes the 1999 version of the ISO C programming language.

Kernighan, Brian W., and Pike, Rob. 1984. *The UNIX Programming Environment*. Prentice Hall, Upper Saddle River, NJ.

> A good, if somewhat dated, reference for additional details of UNIX programming. It covers many standard UNIX tools, including grep, sed, and awk, as well as the Bourne shell.

Kernighan, Brian W., and Ritchie, Dennis M. 1978. *The C Programming Language*. Prentice Hall, Upper Saddle River, NJ.

> A book describing the original version of the C programming language.

Kernighan, Brian W., and Ritchie, Dennis M. 1988. *The C Programming Language, Second Edition*. Prentice Hall, Upper Saddle River, NJ.

> This book describes the original ANSI version of the C programming language.

Knuth, Donald E. 1998. *The Art of Computer Programming, Volume 3: Sorting and Searching, Second Edition*. Addison-Wesley, Reading, MA.

> This multivolume work is widely recognized as the definitive description of classical computer science. Volume 1 discusses Fundamental Algorithms, Volume 2 describes Seminumerical Algorithms, and Volume 3 talks about Sorting and Searching.

Leffler, Samuel J., McKusick, Marshall Kirk, Karels, Michael J., and Quarterman, John S. 1989. *The Design and Implementation of the 4.3BSD UNIX Operating System*. Addison-Wesley, Reading, MA.

> A book describing the data structures and algorithms used in the 4.3BSD UNIX kernel.

Libes, Don. 1990. "Implementing Software Timers", *C Users Journal*, volume 8, number 11.

Libes, Don. 1994. *Exploring Expect*. O'Reilly & Associates, Sebastopol, CA.

> This book describes the expect utility and its scripting language, TCL (Tool Command Language).

Lions, John. 1977. *Lions' Commentary on UNIX 6th Edition with Source Code*. Peer-to-Peer Communications, San Jose, CA.

> A somewhat notorious book that contains the entire source listing of the UNIX 6th Edition kernel and a commentary on the source discussing the algorithms. It is also known as "the Lions book".

Mauro, Jim, and McDougall, Richard. 2001. *Solaris Internals: Core Kernel Architecture*. Prentice Hall, Upper Saddle River, NJ.

> This book describes the design of the Solaris kernel, covering from Solaris 2.5.1 to Solaris 7.

Plauger, P. J. 1992. *The Standard C Library*. Prentice Hall, Upper Saddle River, NJ.

> A complete book on the ISO C library, including a complete implementation of the library in C.

Rago, Stephen A. 1993. *UNIX System V Network Programming*. Addison-Wesley, Reading, MA.

> A book on the transport layer interface (TLI) and STREAMS programming.

Salus, Peter H. 1994. *A Quarter Century of UNIX*. Addison-Wesley, Reading, MA.

SCO. 1996. *System V Application Binary Interface SPARC Processor Supplement, Third Edition*. Santa Cruz Operation, Santa Cruz, CA.

> This is a supplement to the System V Application Binary Interface (ABI), containing ABI implementation details specific to the SPARC processor. It can be found at the following URL: `http://www.sparc.com/standards/psABI3rd.pdf`.

SPARC International. 1999. *SPARC Compliance Definition 2.4.1*. SPARC International, San Jose, CA.

> This book provides information for binary level compatibility on SPARC processors, encompassing the System V Application Binary Interface SPARC Processor Supplement, and extensions and options defined by SPARC International.
>
> The latest version of this document covers the 64-bit SPARC-V9 ABI. It can be found at the following URL: `http://www.sparc.org/standards.html`.

Srinivasan, Raj. 1995. *XDR: External Data Representation Standard*. RFC 1832.

> This document describes Sun's XDR standard. It can be downloaded from the following URL: `http://ftp.rfc-editor.org/in-notes/rfc1832.txt`.

Stevens, W. Richard. 1990. *UNIX Network Programming*. Prentice Hall, Upper Saddle River, NJ.

> This book provides a detailed look at network programming on the UNIX platform. Despite being superseded by the third edition, this book is still useful because of its network applications coverage.

Stevens, W. Richard. 1999. *UNIX Network Programming, Volume 2, Second Edition, Interprocess Communications*. Prentice Hall, Upper Saddle River, NJ.

> This book provides a detailed look at interprocess communications on the UNIX platform.

Stevens, W. Richard, Fenner, Bill, and Rudoff, Andrew M. 2004. *UNIX Network Programming, Volume 1, Third Edition, The Sockets Networking API*. Addison-Wesley, Reading, MA.

> This book provides a detailed look at the sockets network programming API.

Strang, John. 1986. *Programming with Curses*. O'Reilly & Associates, Sebastopol, CA.

Strang, John, Mui, Linda, and O'Reilly, Tim. 1991. *termcap and terminfo, Third Edition*. O'Reilly & Associates, Sebastopol, CA.

Sun Microsystems. 1996. *UltraSPARC I & II User's Manual*. Sun Microsystems, Santa Clara, CA.

> This is a complete technical description of the UltraSPARC I & II processors. Downloadable PDF versions of this, and other UltraSPARC technology manuals, can be found on Sun's web site: `http://www.sun.com/processors/manuals`.

Sun Microsystems. 2002a. *System Administration: Resource Management and Network Services*. Sun Microsystems, Santa Clara, CA.

Sun Microsystems. 2002b. *STREAMS Programming Guide*. Sun Microsystems, Santa Clara, CA.

Sun Microsystems. 2002c. *International Language Environments Guide*. Sun Microsystems, Santa Clara, CA.

Tanenbaum, Andrew S. 1981. *Computer Networks*. Prentice Hall, Upper Saddle River, NJ.

Tuthill, Bill, and Smallberg, David. 1997. *Creating Worldwide Software: Solaris International Developer's Guide, Second Edition*. Prentice Hall, Upper Saddle River, NJ.

Weaver, David L., and Germond, Tom (Editors). 1994. *The SPARC Architecture Manual, Version 9*. Prentice Hall, Upper Saddle River, NJ.

> This book is the specification for Version 9 of the SPARC architecture. It includes definitions of the SPARC-V9 instruction set, registers, and data formats. It can be downloaded from `http://www.sparc.org/standards.html`.

X/Open. 1992. *X/Open Portability Guide, Issue 3*. Prentice Hall, Upper Saddle River, NJ.

> A seven-volume document set covering XPG3. It comprises: Commands and Utilities (Volume 1), System Interfaces and Headers (Volume 2), Supplementary Definitions (Volume 3), Programming Languages (Volume 4), Data Management (Volume 5), Window Management (Volume 6), and Networking Services (Volume 7).

X/Open. 1995. *X/Open Portability Guide, Issue 4*. Prentice Hall, Upper Saddle River, NJ.

> A five-volume document set covering XPG4 and its Base Profile. It comprises: How to Brand—What to Buy (Volume 1), System Interfaces and Headers (Volume 2), Commands and Utilities (Volume 3), System Interface Definitions (Volume 4), and the XPG3–XPG4 Base Migration Guide (Volume 5). XPG4 was the predecessor to the Single UNIX Specification.

Index

Rather than provide a separate glossary (with the majority of the entries being acronyms and abbreviations), this index also serves as a glossary for all the acronyms and abbreviations used in the text. The primary entry for the abbreviation appears under the abbreviation. For example, all references to Interprocess Communication appear under IPC. The entry for the compound term "Interprocess Communication" refers to the main entry under IPC.

The notation "definition of" appearing with a C function refers to the boxed function prototype for that function. The "definition of" notation for a structure refers to its primary definition. Some functions also contain the notation "source code" if a source code implementation for that function appears in the text.

Many functions defined in the text that are used in later examples, e.g., the `set_fsflag` function in Program 4.6, are included in this index. Also included are most functions and constants (such as `ioctl`, `poll`, and `malloc`) that appear in the example programs; trivial functions that appear in most examples, like `open` and `exit`, are not referenced when they appear in example programs.